W9-BHX-816

FINANCIAL MANAGEMENT
Text and Cases

SECOND EDITION

GEORGE C. PHILIPPATOS
University of Tennessee

WILLIAM W. SIHLER
The Darden School
University of Virginia

ALLYN AND BACON
Boston London Toronto Sydney Tokyo Singapore

To our families

Library of Congress Cataloging-in-Publication Data

Philippatos, George C.
Financial management : text and cases / George C. Philippatos, William W. Sihler. — 2nd ed.
p. cm.
Includes bibliographical references and index.
ISBN 0-205-12439-9
1. Corporations—Finance. 2. Corporations—Finance—Case studies.
I. Sihler, William W., 1937– . II. Title.
HG4026.P485 1991
658.15—dc20 90-1120
CIP

Series Editor: Rich Wohl
Series Editorial Assistant: Cheryl Ten Eick
Cover Administrator: Linda Dickinson
Composition Buyer: Linda Cox
Manufacturing Buyer: Louise Richardson
Editorial-Production Service: Editorial Inc.
Editorial-Production Administrator: Mary Beth Finch

Printed in the United States of America.

10 9 8 7 6 5 4 3 2 1 95 94 93 92 91 90

Contents

PART II. BASIC STATEMENTS AND FINANCIAL FORECASTING

PART III: WORKING CAPITAL MANAGEMENT

PART VII: CASE STUDIES

LIST OF CASES

The following 31 case studies are designed to enrich the reader's understanding through real-life applications of varying complexity. The list of cases has been annotated in order to indicate the main subjects covered by each case and to suggest the chapters of this text that address those subjects.

Preface

AUDIENCE FOR THIS BOOK

We appreciate the enthusiastic reception that the initial edition of *Financial Management: Text and Cases* has received, a reception that encouraged us to prepare this second edition. The text is designed for use in a cases in finance course at either the undergraduate or MBA level. One of the key features of our book, which distinguishes it from other case books, is that we include a text portion with our thirty-one cases. Thus, the book can also be used in a two-course sequence of financial management followed by case studies.

Instructors and students have found this unique structure appealing because it helps to bridge the gap between the theory and technique of the traditional financial management course and the application of those materials in the case course. The text portion of our book provides a review or introduction to finance principles without requiring students to purchase a separate theory text.

CHANGES IN THE SECOND EDITION

In preparing this revision, we tried to maintain the blend of theory and application achieved in the first edition. We focused on updating and expanding both our cases and our text, while also integrating the two sections more closely. Thus, the chapters provide the necessary background for the cases and the cases reinforce concepts covered in the text. In particular, we

- added chapters on Time Value of Money (Chapter 1), Cash Flow Expectations and Project Risk (Chapter 2), and Economic and Institutional Environments of the Firm (Chapter 3).
- thoroughly updated and expanded all chapters.
- moved much of the mathematical and advanced theoretical material into chapter appendixes for greater flexibility.
- added questions and problems to the end of the each chapter.
- combined into one chapter (fourteen) the two chapters on Valuations and Portfolio Management.
- added tables in the appendix for the time value of money.

- added nine new cases in international finance, capital cost determination, capital structure management, cash flow analysis, initial offering price/valuation, and capital expenditure.
- thoroughly updated ten of the retained cases.
- greatly expanded the section on how to analyze a case in Technical Note 2 and included an example of a specific case analysis.

SUPPLEMENTS

Financial Management: Text and Cases, Second Edition is accompanied by a strong set of supplements.

- *Instructor's Manual with Lotus 1-2-3 Templates and Files.* This comprehensive manual includes teaching suggestions as well as solutions to all questions, problems, and cases. In addition, all relevant case exhibits are available to instructors on disk as either Lotus 1-2-3 templates or files. If they choose to do so, adopters are free to make copies of the templates for student use.
- *TWIN™ Advanced Educational Version.* A student version of the popular spreadsheet package is available at a special reduced price when packaged with *Financial Management: Text and Cases, Second Edition. TWIN™ Advanced* includes more features than Lotus 1-2-3 Release 2 and can read and write Lotus 1-2-3 files, including macros.

ACKNOWLEDGMENTS

The assistance of many colleagues in the preparation of the various drafts of the sixteen chapters of text is gratefully acknowledged. Some, like D. Choi, SUNY Buffalo; A. Malliaris, Loyola University of Chicago; R. Brown and A. Christofi, The Pennsylvania State University; N. Gressis and Bruce E. Smith, Wright State University; Y. Kim, University of Cincinnati; Mary Pashley, Tennessee Technological University; and K. G. Viswanathan, Hofstra University contributed on an ongoing basis and helped clarify several important points. Others, like H. Grammatikos, University of Wisconsin; S. Rathinasamy, Ball State University; P. Wall, University of Alabama, Huntsville; R. DeFusco, University of Nebraska; P. Koveos, Syracuse University; D. Nawrocki, Villanova University; and G. Tsetsekos, Drexel University, provided extensive reviews on specific parts of the material. And, then, there are those among our colleagues who took the time to review the entire material and provided constructive comments for the revised version. Among these colleagues, we wish to thank D. Ketcham, University of Tennessee, Knoxville; F. Lee Sarver, University of Alabama, Huntsville; T. Puri, University of Scranton; W. Dowling, Austin Peay State University; V. Bhaskar, Duquesne University; Dennis Coffey, Xavier University; M. Muhtaseb, California Polytechnic University, Pomona; R. D. Mennaro, Michigan State University; D. Bigbee, Texas A&I University; D. Hexter and R. Severeins, Kent State University; A. Jackson, Miami University; and D. Fewings, Western Washington University. Additionally, Phillip L. Baird, University of Tennessee, must be singled out for his tireless efforts to improve the quality of the material in the second edition and provide pedagogical applications at the end of each chapter. Finally, Reva Lepore and A. L. Philippatos typed several versions of the revised material cheerfully and efficiently.

Colleagues at The Colgate Darden Graduate School of Business Administration, University of Virginia, who contributed to the development of case material include E. Richard Brownlee, John L. Colley, James C. Dunstan, Mark R. Eaker, Diana R. Harrington, and C. F. Sargent. Mr. Paul H. Hunn, Senior Vice President, Manufacturers Hanover Trust Company, has been most generous with his time over the years in helping with the case and course development. The work of individual research assistants and students is acknowledged in the identification of the respective cases.

Typing of the case material was done over many years by members of The Darden School secretarial staff. Kathleen Collier and Coleen Rock handled the major portion of the final typing effort for the first edition. The new material for the second edition has been prepared primarily by Susan Carter.

The inevitable errors are the responsibility of the authors. We welcome having them brought to our attention so that we can work toward eliminating them in subsequent editions.

1

THE TIME VALUE OF MONEY

I. INTRODUCTION

Two of the most basic factors that characterize investment decisions are *time preference* and *uncertainty*. These two significant factors, along with *market opportunities* and *investor preferences*, form the rectangular foundation that supports both the input requirements and the output considerations of financial decisions. In this chapter we discuss time preference and the time value of money. In Chapter 2 we review the salient aspects of uncertainty and risk. Extensions to financial decision making under risk are provided throughout the volume, and detailed discussions of market opportunities and investor preferences are offered in Parts III and IV.

A. Some Perspectives

"A dollar received today is worth more than a dollar to be received tomorrow." Why? One answer might be that the existence of positive interest rates in the economic system means that money invested today for withdrawal the next day can earn income. That is, a dollar deposited today in a savings account at any bank can begin to earn interest today, whereas a dollar received tomorrow can not. Hence, the dollar received today will be worth more than the dollar to be received tomorrow. Because interest rates exist only in capital markets where surplus economic units (*savers* who lend) transact with deficit economic units (*nonsavers* who borrow), an understanding of the role of savings in a market economy provides the conceptual foundation for the discussion of the time value of money.

Individuals earn income from various sources over time, and in any given period they either spend all or some part of it. The portion of current income that is not expended for consumption remains as savings. Why do people save? The answer to this question is provided by three basic and more or less universal motivations that are related to personal preferences, market anticipations, and uncertainty. They are as follows:

1. Future patterns of consumption are preferred to present ones. Because current patterns of consumption are based on the current distribution of income that provides the wealth for consumption, people save in order to redistribute future income more to their liking and achieve their preferred future patterns of consumption. We shall call this motive for saving the *income or wealth redistribution or transaction motive*.
2. Future preferred patterns of consumption are uncertain and may be left unfulfilled due to unexpected events that will cause a disparity between the preferred levels of consumption and the income available to realize such levels. Hence, the behavior of saving for the future is explained by the *precautionary motive*.
3. Future available market opportunities are unknown at present but many are likely to exist. In order to take advantage of such opportunities, people save some of their present income. This behavior is explained by the *investment* or *speculative motive*.

II. FUTURE VALUE AND COMPOUND GROWTH

A. Annual Compounding

Because a dollar received today is more valuable than a dollar to be received in the future, given the existence of positive interest rates, we must examine the relationship between the two. To illustrate the determinants of the intertemporal relationship among cash flows, consider Tammy Paisley, a twenty-two-year-old recent college graduate. She wants to buy a new car in one year and plans to use the money in her existing savings account as a down payment. The account pays 7 percent annually and the current balance is \$5,000. Tammy wants to know how much will be available for a down payment in one year. The future value of the account will be equal to the sum of the current balance, \$5,000, plus the interest earned on the account over the coming year (\$350 = \$5,000 × 7%), for a total future value of \$5,350.

Symbolically, the formula for computing the future value of a current sum is as follows:

$$FV_1 = PV_0 + I_1, \tag{1.1}$$

where FV_1 = the value of the savings account in one year;
PV_0 = the value of the account at time 0;
I_1 = amount of interest earned over one year;
r = annual rate of interest.

Because $I_1 = PV_0(r)$, equation (1.1) can be rewritten as

$$FV_1 = PV_0 + PV_0(r), \text{ or}$$

$$FV_1 = PV_0(1 + r). \tag{1.2}$$

Substituting the values from the previous example we have

$$\$5{,}350 = \$5{,}000(1 + .07).$$

Now, suppose Tammy wants to buy her car in two years; how much will she have in her account for a down payment? At the end of one year she will have \$5,350 which will earn interest for the second year at an annual rate of 7 percent. If she takes nothing out of the account, the interest received in the first year, \$350, will earn interest in the second year. Hence, the future value of the account will equal the sum of the initial amount plus interest earned in each of the next two years:

$$\$5{,}000 + \$5{,}000(.07) + \$5{,}350(.07) = \$5{,}724.50.$$

Symbolically, the formula for two-period compounding can be expressed as follows:

$$FV_2 = PV_0 + I_1 + I_2$$

Because

$$FV_1 = PV_0(1 + r)$$

and

$$I_2 = FV_1(r),$$

we can perform substitution of values to obtain

$$FV_2 = PV_0(1 + r)(1 + r)$$

Or, in terms of the new scenario, we have

$$\$5{,}724.50 = \$5{,}000(1.07)(1.07) = \$5{,}000(1.07)^2$$

Generally, the future value of an original amount, PV_0, compounded annually at an interest rate, r, for n-number of years is as follows:

$$FV_n = PV_0(1 + r)^n \tag{1.3}$$

The above expression is referred to as the *time value of money equation* and has been formalized into tables of the "Future Value of \$1" received at the end of period n (see Appendix 1). Suppose we want to compute the future value of \$10,000 deposited today in an interest-bearing account and compounded annually at 9 percent for 15 years. We turn to the "Future Value of \$1" Table and locate the *future value interest factor (FVIF)* corresponding to the row for 15 years and column for 9 percent. Notationally,

$$FVIF_{r,n} = FVIF_{9,15} = (1 + .09)^{15} = 3.642,$$

where $FVIF_{r,n}$ is the future value interest factor for r percent and n-years. In terms of our example, we have

$$\text{FVIF}_{r,n} = (1 + r)^n$$

$$\text{FV}_n = \text{PV}_0(\text{FVIF}_{r,n})$$

$$\text{FV}_n = \text{PV}_0(1 + r)^n$$

$$\text{FV}_{15} = \$10{,}000(1.09)^{15} = \$36{,}424.82$$

That is, the original sum of $10,000 will be compounded to $36,424.82 at the end of 15 years.

An interesting question that arises in compounding is how long it would take for an initial sum, or present value, growing at a given annual interest rate, compounded annually, to double in size. If the annual rate of interest or growth is 8 percent, we can locate in the "Future Value of $1" Table in the 8 percent column the FVIF closest to the value of 2. We find that the FVIF in the 8 percent column and the 9-year row is 1.999 and conclude that a sum growing at an 8 percent annual rate will double in about 9 years. The "quick-and-dirty" method would be to resort to the "Rule of 72." By dividing the interest or growth rate into 72, we obtain an approximation of the time required to double an original amount. For example, a bank deposit growing at the rate of 8 percent per year will double in amount in about 9 years because $72/8 = 9$. Similarly, prime commercial real estate expected to appreciate at an annual rate of 24 percent will double in value in about 3 years.

The above examples illustrate the power of compounding and highlight the importance of the *time value of money*. The higher the growth or interest rate, the smaller the time required for an initial amount to double, triple, quadruple, *et cetera*. Figure 1.1 illustrates the impact of different growth rates on future values across time. Here, we see that an initial amount of $100 grows over a period of 20 years to about $260 at 5 percent per year, $460 at 8 percent per year, and $670 at 10 percent per year.

B. Intraperiod Compounding

The previous examples assume that interest is compounded annually, or once per year, but this need not always be the case. Suppose George Oliver, proprietor of George's Lounge and Bar, decides to expand his business by adding a new room with electronic games. He estimates the total cost of the expansion to be $20,000, and calls his banker, Murray Gideon, with whom he has a long-standing business relationship. Murray is willing to advance the loan with the stipulation that principal and interest of 12 percent, compounded quarterly, be repaid in one year. George reckons that 12 percent compounded annually (once per year) is equivalent to 3 percent compounded quarterly (four times per year) with a minor exception. If he borrows $20,000 at 12 percent annual compounding for one year, he will give back $22,400 to repay the original loan. However, if interest is compounded quarterly, he will pay back $22,510 [$= \$20{,}000(1.03)^4$] a difference of $110.

The time value of money equation for the FVIF for an annual interest rate of r percent compounded m times per year is

$$\text{FVIF}^m_{r,n} = [1 + (r/m)]^{(m)(n)} \tag{1.4}$$

and the equivalent annual, or *effective,* rate of interest is

$$r_e = (1 + r/m)^m - 1 \tag{1.5}$$

In George's situation, the effective annual rate of interest is 12.55 percent per year:

$$r_e = (1 + .12/4)^4 - 1 = (1.03)^4 - 1 = .1255$$

If Murray extends the term of the loan to two years, George will owe

$$\text{FV}_{mn} = \text{PV}_0(1 + r/m)^{mn}, \tag{1.6}$$

where $m = 4$ and $n = 2$. In monetary terms,

$$\$20{,}000[1 + (.12/4)]^{(4)(2)}$$
$$= \$20{,}000(1.03)^8 = \$25{,}335$$

Consider the case of daily compounding. A Texas S&L is paying an 11 percent annual rate, compounded daily, 365 days per year. For a holding period of 6 months, what is the FVIF? The general formula for the FVIF associated with an r percent annual interest rate, compounded m times per year for n years is given by equation (1.4):

FIGURE 1.1 Future Values at Various Growth Rates

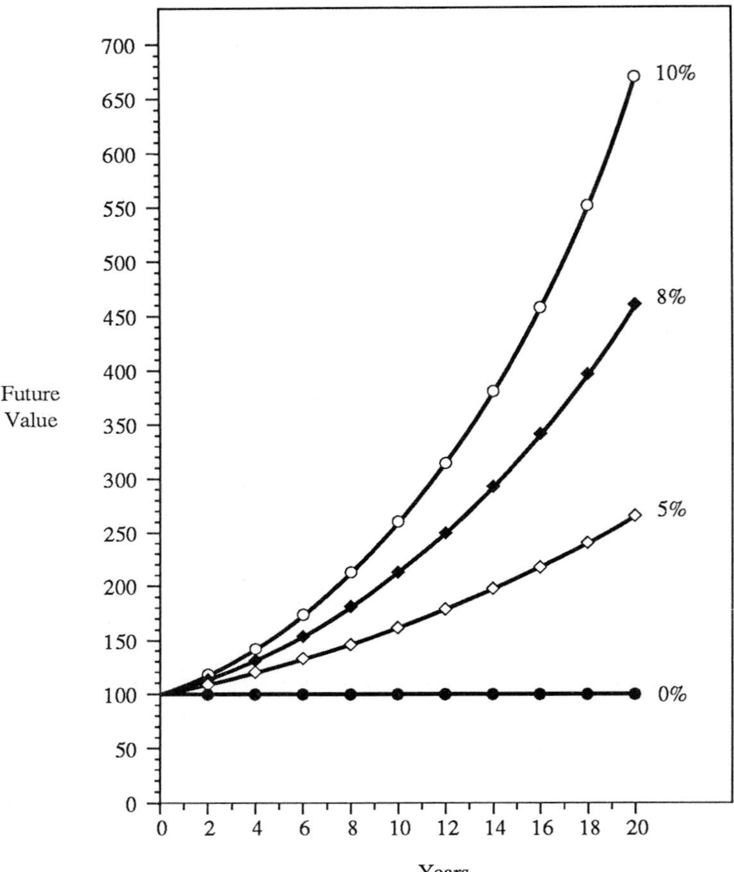

$$\text{FVIF}^{m}_{r,n} = (1 + r/m)^{mn}, \text{ or}$$

$$\text{FVIF}^{365}_{.11,.5} = (1 + .11/365)^{(365)(.5)} = 1.0565$$

Thus, a deposit of \$25,000 in this account for 6 months will have a value of \$26,413 = \$25,000 × 1.0565. Figure 1.2 shows the impact of various compounding intervals on the future value of \$1.00 at 30 percent per year for 1 (one) year.

C. Continuous Compounding

Where the compounding interval is infinitely small, we have the case of continuous compounding. That is, interest payments are spread evenly and continuously throughout the year and reinvested at the same rate as the other funds. Here the FVIF, originally given by equation (1.4), becomes

$$\lim_{m\to\infty} (1 + r/m)^{mn} = e^{rn}, \qquad (1.7)$$

where e = 2.71828. . . , the base for natural logarithms.

Thus, \$1 compounded continuously for *n*-years at *r* percent interest will grow to

$$\$1(e^{rn}) = \$1(2.718)^{rn}$$

The time value equation for continuous compounding, then, is

FIGURE 1.2 Effects of Compounding Intervals on Future Values

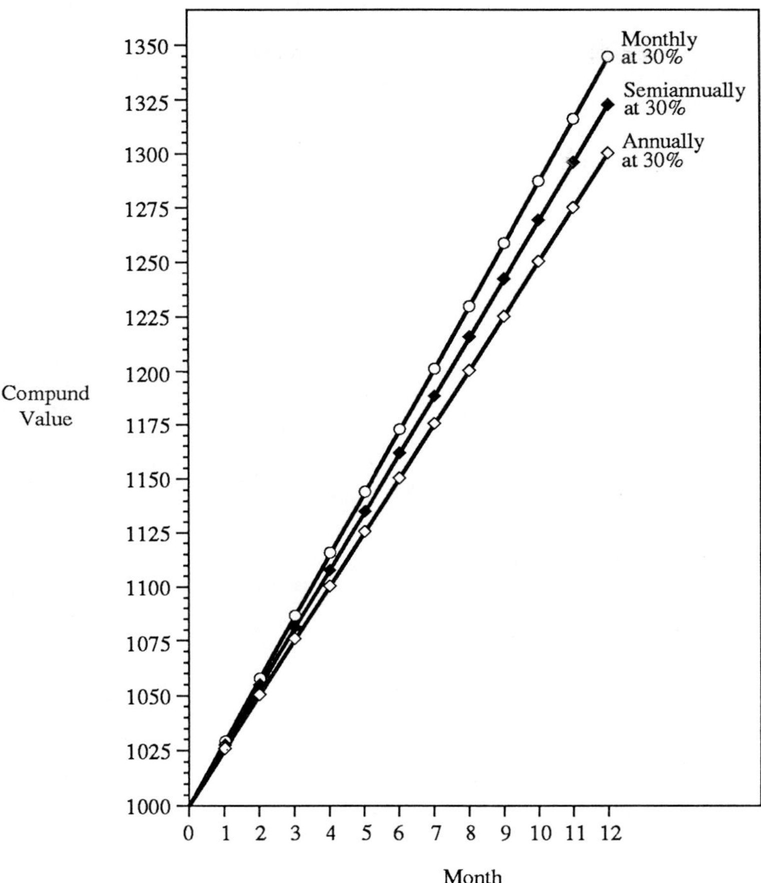

$$FV_n = PV_0(e^{rn}) \quad (1.8)$$

Consider a numerical example that will illustrate the effects of compounding intervals on the growth of capital invested. Suppose an initial sum of $100,000 is invested for two years at 16 percent per year. What would be the accumulated value at the end of two years if interest is compounded (*a*) annually, (*b*) semiannually, (*c*) monthly, (*d*) weekly, (*e*) daily for 360 days, (*f*) daily for 365 days, and (*g*) continuously? The answers are shown in Table 1.1.

TABLE 1.1 Compounding at Variable Time Intervals

(*a*)	$FV_{mn} = PV_0(1 + r/m)^{mn}$	$= \$100{,}000\ (1 + .16/1)^{(1)(2)}$	= $134,560.00
(*b*)	$FV_{mn} = PV_0(1 + r/m)^{mn}$	$= \$100{,}000\ (1 + .16/2)^{(2)(2)}$	= $136,048.90
(*c*)	$FV_{mn} = PV_0(1 + r/m)^{mn}$	$= \$100{,}000\ (1 + .16/12)^{(12)(2)}$	= $137,421.88
(*d*)	$FV_{mn} = PV_0(1 + r/m)^{mn}$	$= \$100{,}000\ (1 + .16/52)^{(52)(2)}$	= $137,645.13
(*e*)	$FV_{mn} = PV_0(1 + r/m)^{mn}$	$= \$100{,}000\ (1 + .16/360)^{(360)(2)}$	= $137,702.94
(*f*)	$FV_{mn} = PV_0(1 + r/m)^{mn}$	$= \$100{,}000\ (1 + .16/365)^{(365)(2)}$	= $137,703.10
(*g*)	$FV_{mn} = PV_0(e^{rn})$	$= \$100{,}000[e^{(.16)(2)}]$	= $137,712.78

D. Implicit Assumptions About Reinvestment Rates

Implicit in the computation of compound future values is the assumption that the intermediate cash flows from the interest payments are reinvested at the same rate as the funds invested originally. Technically speaking, the intermediate cash flows do not have to be reinvested in the same savings instrument, so long as they are reinvested at the same rate and bring in the same quality of earnings for certain. It is precisely this reinvestment rate assumption that makes for a significant difference between simple interest computations where the amount of interest is not reinvested, and compound interest growth where the interest earned is reinvested at the same rate as the base capital.

Suppose $1,000 is invested at 20 percent per year for 10 years. If the investor were to take out the interest payments and use them for consumption, he would collect $200 a year for 10 years, and a total amount of earnings equal to $2,000. However, if the investor were to reinvest the intermediate cash flows from the interest payments at the same rate of 20 percent compounded annually, the total earnings after 10 years would be equal to the compound value less the original capital, $6,192 − $1,000 = $5,192, an amount much larger than the noncompounded earnings of $2,000 over the same time horizon. The situation can be truly magnified over a period of 30 years, where the compounded earnings would rise to $237,376 compared to $6,000 of noncompounded interest. Needless to say, when we have intraperiod compounding, perhaps monthly or daily, the total accumulation will be even greater than that computed through annual compounding.

Now, let us ask the question of reinvestment rates from a different perspective. Suppose that an investor, Simon Pringley, buys a $1,000 bond of the Meltdown Power & Light Company that pays 10 percent per annum at the end of each year and matures in 15 years. The investor has three clear-cut options with the interest payments received: (1) he can consume the proceeds to enhance his standard of living; (2) he can reinvest the proceeds at the same rate of 10 percent; and (3) he can reinvest the proceeds at a higher rate, such as 14 percent per year. We wish to compute the annual compound interest rate received by the investor from the original capital over the entire investment horizon (15 years). This type of compound interest is known as the *annual realized rate of return*.

If the investor does not reinvest the interest earnings (that is, the reinvestment rate equals zero), he will receive $100 per year for 15 years, totaling $1,500, corresponding to an annual realized rate of return that is less than 10 percent. If the funds are reinvested at 14 percent, then the total income from the original investment will be $4,384, which corresponds to an annual realized rate of return of more than 10 percent. Only when the funds are reinvested immediately at 10 percent do we have an annual realized rate of return equal to 10 percent and accumulated interest earnings of $3,177.

E. Annuities and Perpetuities

How did we get the values given in the previous section? The answer requires an understanding of the concept of an annuity. An *annuity* is an asset that pays a fixed equal sum every year for a number of years. For example, the savings and loan association or the mortgage bank that has financed one's home owns an annuity (an asset) that entitles it to receive from the homeowner a fixed mortgage payment every year (or month) for, say 20 years. In fact, every time we promise to make a series of payments (for an automobile, a refrigerator, a television), we have issued the equivalent of an annuity to our creditors. Additional examples are witnessed in lease payments, interest payments for bonds, and all kinds of installment payments for goods bought on credit. As we shall also see later, some investment projects yield uniform cash flows, and in this respect such cash flows are annuities.

Annuities are categorized as to their length (term), the dates of payment, the length of payment intervals, and periods of interest conversion. When such periodic payments are made at the beginning of specified periods, they are referred to as *true annuities*. When the periodic payments and interest payments correspond and are made at the end of each payment interval, we call them *ordinary annuities*. And, when the periodic payments have a definite beginning period but never end, we call them *perpetuities*. We can compute the future value of an ordinary annuity by using the following formula:

$$FV_a = P_p\left[\frac{(1 + r)^n - 1}{r}\right] \quad (1.9)$$

where P_p = periodic payment of equal amount.

Now, let us return to the case of Simon Pringley who bought bonds of the Meltdown P&L Company. By using equation (1.9), we find the accumulated amounts for reinvestment rates of less than 10 percent, equal to 10 percent, or more than 10 percent. The same information can be gathered from the table in Appendix 2 entitled "Future Value of an Annuity of $1." What we must do now is formalize the way of computing the annual realized rates of return for our investor under various reinvestment rate assumptions. This can be achieved by employing equation (1.10):

$$\frac{FV_a + P}{P} = (1 + r_a)^n \quad (1.10)$$

where P = par value of the bond ($1,000), and
r_a = annual realized rate of return

Suppose the periodic payments are reinvested at 9 percent per year, then from equation (1.9) we have

$$\begin{aligned} FV_a &= \$100\left[\frac{(1.09)^{15} - 1}{.09}\right] \\ &= \$100(29.3609) \\ &= \$2{,}936.09 \end{aligned}$$

We can compute the annual realized rate of return r_a by manipulating equation (1.10) to yield

$$\begin{aligned} r_a &= \left(\frac{FV_a + P}{P}\right)^{(1/n)} - 1 \\ &= \left(\frac{2{,}936.09 + 1{,}000}{1{,}000}\right)^{(1/15)} - 1 \quad (1.10') \\ &= .0956 = 9.56\% \end{aligned}$$

III. PRESENT VALUE AND DISCOUNTING

A. Annual Discounting

In the previous section we computed the future value of an amount invested today given an interest or growth rate. The flip side of the problem is to find the value today (or present value) of an amount to be received in the future. Fortunately, the time value equation (1.6) can be manipulated algebraically to yield

$$PV_0 = FV_{mn}(1 + r/m)^{-mn}$$

where all terms are as defined earlier. To illustrate, suppose we want to know the value today of $10,000 to be received in exactly one year if current interest rates are 13 percent per year. To find the present value, we plug the numbers into the time value equation where FV_m = $10,000, $n = 1$, $r = .13$, and $m = 1$.

$$PV_0 = (\$10{,}000)(1.13)^{-(1)(1)} = \$8{,}849.56$$

This procedure is referred to as *discounting* (the opposite of *compounding*). Now suppose we will receive $10,000 in exactly two years. What is the present value of $10,000 received in two years discounted at a 13 percent annual rate of interest? Here, $n = 2$.

$$PV_0 = (\$10{,}000)(1.13)^{-(1)(2)} = \$7{,}831.47$$

In general, the present value of $1 to be received after n periods, discounted at r percent interest rate is

$$PV_0 = \$1(1 + r/m)^{-mn}$$

The discount rate is also referred to as the *rate of return* or *capitalization rate*. It is also generally assumed that this discount rate reflects the minimum rate of return required by investors before they forego present consumption or part with their liquidity, depending on their motivation. Furthermore, we employ the term *discounted cash flows* to indicate the placement of a present value or worth to some future anticipated series of cash flows.

Similar to the "Future Value of $1" Table, the expression for present value has been formalized into tables of the "Present Value of $1" to be received at the end of period n in Appendix 3. In the above example, to find the *present value interest factor* (PVIF) we find the entry in the row corresponding to 2 years and the column for 13 percent. Notationally,

$$PVIF^{m}_{r,n} = (1 + r/m)^{-mn} \tag{1.11}$$

$$PVIF^{1}_{13,2} = (1.13)^{-(1)(2)} = .7831$$

Notice that the $PVIF^{m}_{r,n}$ is merely the reciprocal of $FVIF^{m}_{r,n}$.

B. Interpolation

Suppose the interest rate in the above example is 13.5 percent per year, and we find there is no entry for 13.5 percent in the table. We can still use the information in the table to estimate the $PVIF^{1}_{13.5,2}$. We interpolate from the factors on either side of what would be the 13.5 percent column if it existed. In the row for 2 years, we find the $PVIF_{13,2}$ = .7831 and $PVIF_{14,2}$ = .7695. The $PVIF_{13.5,2}$ should be less than .7831 and greater than .7695, and as 13.5 percent is halfway between 13 percent and 14 percent, we can take the simple average of the two:

$$(.7831 + .7695)/2 = .776307$$

Thus, the present value of $10,000 to be received in 2 years discounted at a 13.5 percent annual rate equals

$$PV_0 = \$10{,}000(.776307) = \$7{,}763.07$$

Interpolation, however, only provides an estimate. If we use our calculators to find $PVIF_{13.5,2}$ = .776262, we do not obtain the same result, although the difference here is small. As the discounting period, n, increases, though, the error increases. This can be seen in Figure 1.3 which shows PVIF plotted graphically against time for various discount rates. We can see that for a given time horizon, the $PVIF_{10,20}$ is not halfway between $PVIF_{5,20}$ and $PVIF_{15,20}$ and the difference increases as n increases. However, the problem with interpolation is irrelevant if we

FIGURE 1.3 Present Value Interest Factors

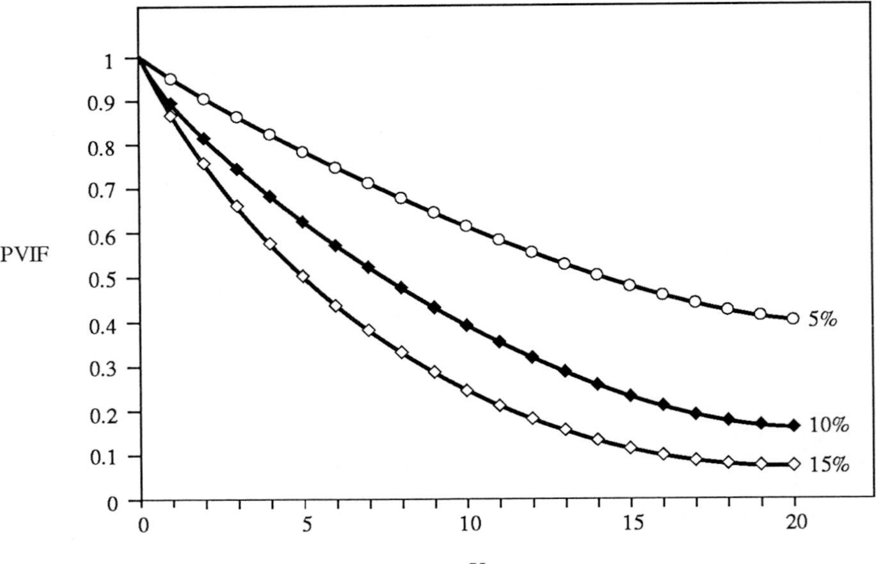

know how to use the time value equations and have a calculator.

C. Intraperiod Discounting

Recall Tammy Paisley, our twenty-two-year-old recent college graduate. She wants to buy her car now instead of waiting, but has little free cash for a down payment. She does, however, have a U.S. government savings bond given to her as a child that matures in exactly one year and will pay \$5,000. What can she do? One option available to Tammy would be to obtain a one-year loan in the amount of the down payment to be repaid with the proceeds from her maturing bond. If current market terms on loans of this type are 12 percent annual interest compounded monthly, how much can she borrow today so that the value of her bond at maturity will be just enough to repay the loan? In other words, what is the present value of \$5,000 to be received in 1 year discounted monthly at a 12 percent annual rate?

Recalling the formula for intraperiod compounding, given by equation (1.6), we have

$$FV_{mn} = PV_0(1 + r/m)^{mn}$$

With the proper algebraic manipulation, we find the formula for the *present value of a future sum* discounted *m* times per year, over *n* years, at *r* percent annual rate, as shown by equation (1.12):

$$PV_0 = FV_{mn}(1 + r/m)^{-mn} \tag{1.12}$$

where $FV_{mn} = \$5{,}000$, $r = 12\%$, $m = 12$, and $n = 1$

$$PV_0 = \$5{,}000(1 + .12/12)^{-(12)(1)} = \$4{,}437.25$$

Hence, Tammy Paisley can borrow \$4,437.25 for her down payment. To extend the example, suppose the bond matures in 15 months and she can obtain a 15-month loan with terms of 12 percent annual interest and monthly discounting. How much can she borrow for a down payment? Here, $n = (15 \text{ months}/12 \text{ months}) = 1.25$ years.

$$PV_0 = \$5{,}000(1 + .12/12)^{-(12)(1.25)} = \$4{,}306.75$$

Figure 1.4 shows graphically the impact of intraperiod discounting at an annual rate of 30 percent. Consider a numerical example that will illustrate the effects of discounting intervals on the value of capital required for an investment. You are asked to find the present value of \$10,000 to be received in 10 years discounted at a 10 percent annual rate (*a*) annually, (*b*) semiannually, (*c*) monthly, (*d*) weekly, (*e*) daily, 360 days, (*f*) daily, 365 days, and (*g*) continuously. The answers are shown in Table 1.2. The formula for continuous discounting in case (*g*) of Table 1.2 was obtained via manipulation of the time value equation (1.8) for continuous compounding:

$$FV_n = PV_0(e^{rn}); \text{ thus}$$

$$PV_0 = FV_n(e^{-rn}) \tag{1.13}$$

D. Relation Between Present and Future Values

There exists a simple relationship between present values and future values computed over the same investment horizon with the same rate of interest. This is shown schematically in Figure 1.5, where we see that \$1,000 compounded annually for 3 years at 15 percent per year grows to a future amount of \$1,520.87. Likewise, the present value of \$1,520.87 discounted annually for 3 years at 15 percent per year equals \$1,000.

E. Present Value of Annuities and Perpetuities

Remember the ordinary annuities whose future values we computed earlier? It is now time to work on the reversal of the basic procedure and obtain the present value of the uniform periodic payments. The present value of an ordinary annuity can be computed from the table in Appendix 4 entitled "Present Value of an Annuity of \$1." It can also be obtained from the basic equation employed to construct that table, which is as follows:

FIGURE 1.4 Effects of Discounting Intervals on Present Values

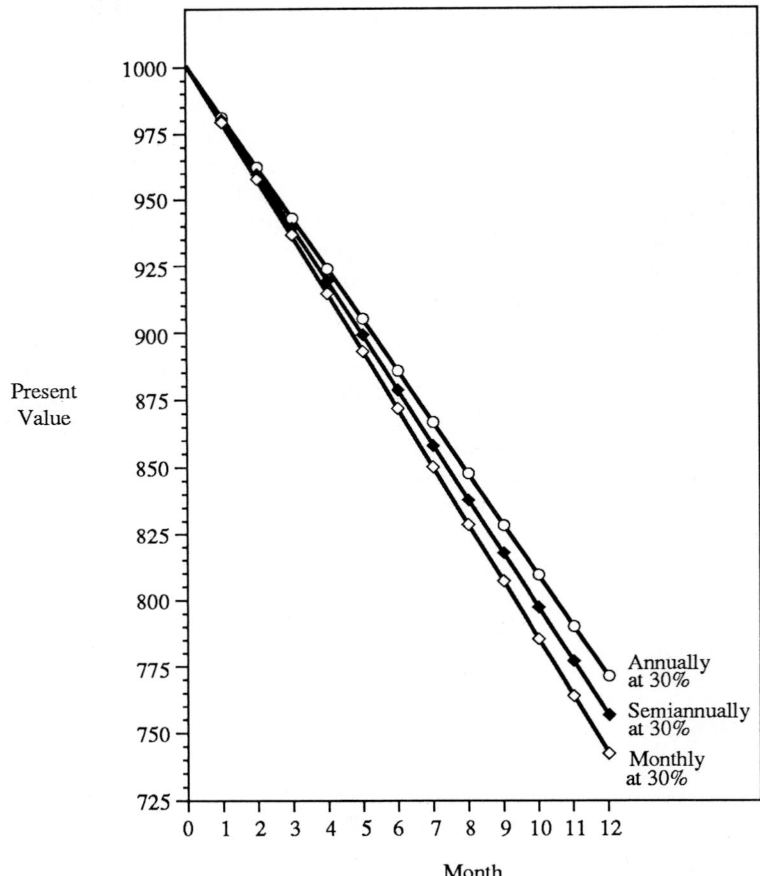

TABLE 1.2 Discounting at Variable Time Intervals

$$(a)\quad PV_0 = FV_{mn}(1 + r/m)^{-mn} = \$10{,}000\left(1 + \frac{.10}{1}\right)^{-(1)(10)} = \$3{,}855.43$$

$$(b)\quad PV_0 = FV_{mn}(1 + r/m)^{-mn} = \$10{,}000\left(1 + \frac{.10}{2}\right)^{-(2)(10)} = \$3{,}768.89$$

$$(c)\quad PV_0 = FV_{mn}(1 + r/m)^{-mn} = \$10{,}000\left(1 + \frac{.10}{12}\right)^{-(12)(10)} = \$3{,}694.07$$

$$(d)\quad PV_0 = FV_{mn}(1 + r/m)^{-mn} = \$10{,}000\left(1 + \frac{.10}{52}\right)^{-(52)(10)} = \$3{,}682.33$$

$$(e)\quad PV_0 = FV_{mn}(1 + r/m)^{-mn} = \$10{,}000\left(1 + \frac{.10}{360}\right)^{-(360)(10)} = \$3{,}679.30$$

$$(f)\quad PV_0 = FV_{mn}(1 + r/m)^{-mn} = \$10{,}000\left(1 + \frac{.10}{365}\right)^{-(365)(10)} = \$3{,}679.29$$

$$(g)\quad PV_0 = FV_n(e^{-rn}) = \$10{,}000[e^{-(.1)(10)}] = \$3{,}678.79$$

FIGURE 1.5 The Relationship Between Present Value and Future Value

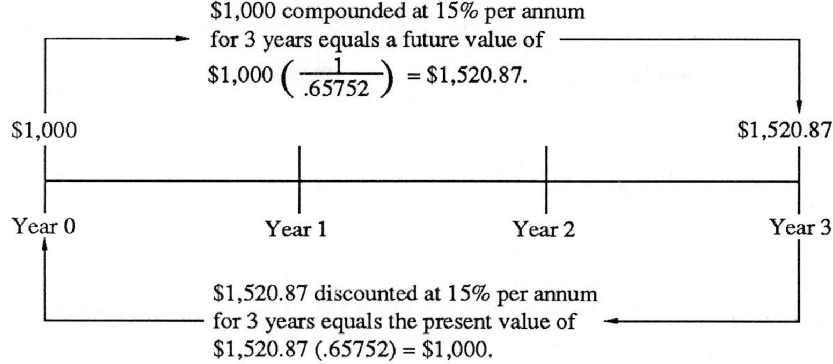

$$PV_a = P_p\left[\frac{1 - (1 + r)^{-n}}{r}\right] \qquad (1.14)$$

where PV_a = present value of an ordinary annuity.

To illustrate the present value computation for ordinary annuities, suppose we wish to find the PV_a for a series of periodic payments of $540 at the end of each month for 24 months, at interest rates of (1) 10.5 percent and (2) 8.3 percent, both discounted monthly. The answers are given below:

1. $$PV_a = \$540\left[\frac{1 - \left(1 + \frac{.105}{12}\right)^{-(12)(2)}}{\left(\frac{.105}{12}\right)}\right]$$

$$= \$540(21.562858)$$

$$= \$11{,}643.94$$

2. $$PV_a = \$540\left[\frac{1 - \left(1 + \frac{.083}{12}\right)^{-(12)(2)}}{\left(\frac{.083}{12}\right)}\right]$$

$$= \$540(22.04379)$$

$$= \$11{,}903.65$$

Now, suppose an auto dealer offers to sell you your dream car for a down payment of $2,000 plus monthly installments of $120.75 for the next 4 years. What is the present worth of this car (or the stream of payments) if the interest rate on the auto loan is 16 percent, compounded monthly? The answer is given below.

$$PV_a = \$2{,}000 + \$120.75\,\frac{1 - \left(1 + \frac{.16}{12}\right)^{-(12)(4)}}{\left(\frac{.16}{12}\right)}$$

$$= \$2{,}000 + \$120.75(35.2855)$$

$$= \$6{,}260.72$$

There is a simple variation to the above formula that allows the computation of present value for growing perpetuities. This is given by

$$PV_p = P_p/(r - g) \qquad (1.15)$$

where g = growth rate in periodic payments.

We can use equation (1.15) to recompute the answer to (1), above, for a growth rate of 4 percent. The answer is as follows:

$$PV_p = \$540/(.105 - .04) = \$8{,}307.69$$

F. Discount Rate

It should be apparent by now that the different formulas employed for present value, future value, annuities, and perpetuities are variations of the basic equation for determining compound interest. For example, we can see all the necessary elements in equation (1.6), and the accompanying schematic in Figure 1.6.

We can determine any of the factors (variables) in Figure 1.6 if the others are given, and the equation can be adapted to solve for the expected rate of return on a bond, stock, or any type of investment involving a series of cash flows; hence the term *discounted cash flow*. For example, we want to calculate the expected rate of return from the purchase of a newly issued U.S. government Treasury bill (T-bill) with exactly one year to maturity. T-bills are short-term obligations of the U.S. Treasury with maturities up to one year. They are sold at discount from face value and pay no explicit interest, but are redeemed at face value at maturity. A \$100,000 face value T-bill with exactly one year to maturity can be purchased today for \$93,023. What is the expected annual rate of return? Referring to equation (1.6) we have

$$FV_1 = \$100{,}000,$$

$$FV_{mn} = PV_0(1 + r/m)^{mn}$$

Solving equation (1.6), above, for r, we obtain

$$r = m[(FV/PV)^{(1/mn)} - 1] \tag{1.16}$$

$$r = 1[(\$100{,}000/\$93{,}023)^{(1/1)} - 1]$$

$$= 1.075 - 1 = .075 = 7.5\%$$

$$= 1\left[\left(\frac{\$100{,}000}{\$93{,}023}\right)^{(1/1)} - 1\right]$$

Now, suppose the T-bill is discounted daily, 360 days per year (m = 360), what is the return? Using equation (1.16), we have

$$r = m[(FV/PV)^{(1/mn)} - 1]$$

$$= 360[(100{,}000/93{,}023)^{(1/360)} - 1]$$

$$= .0723 = 7.23\%$$

Finally, suppose we purchase a 180-day T-bill for \$96,561. What is the annual rate of return? By the same process as above, we obtain

$$r = (360)[(100{,}000/96{,}561)^{(1/180)} - 1]$$

$$= .070 = 7.0\%$$

G. Discounting a Series of Future Cash Flows

Consider a 9.5 percent coupon bond paying interest semiannually. On July 1, 1988, it was selling for \$94,735 and at maturity, December 31, 1990, it will pay a face value of \$100,000. What is the rate of return (or yield to maturity) on this bond if it is held to maturity? The following diagram in Figure 1.7 will help us see the problem.

Each of the five payments received is discounted to its present value at the discount rate, r, which equates the sum of their present values with the current price of the bond. In other words, the value of r in the following equation is the rate of return, or yield-to-maturity, of the bond.

Without the aid of a financial calculator, the yield must be found iteratively, or by trial-and-error. Conceptually, the bond can be thought of as consisting of two different sets of cash flows: (1) a 2.5-year ordinary annuity with five semiannual payments of \$4,750 each, and (2) a lump-sum payment of \$100,000 received in 2.5 years. The problem is to find r such that the sum of the present values of the annuity and the lump sum equals the price of the bond. Utilizing the equations for the present value of an annuity, equation (1.14), and the present value of a future sum, equation (1.12), we have

FIGURE 1.6 Basic Relationships in Time Value of Money

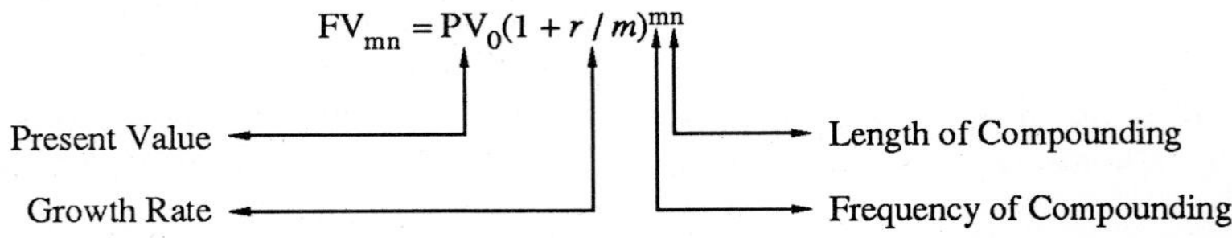

FIGURE 1.7 Discounting a Series of Cash Flows

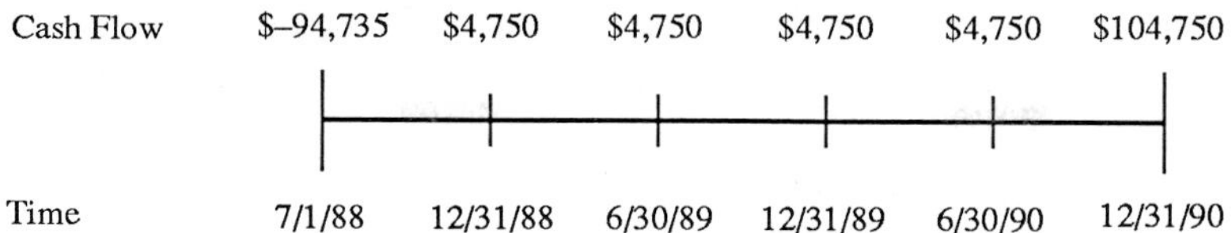

$$\$94{,}735 = \$4{,}750\left[\frac{1-(1+r/2)^{-(2)(2.5)}}{(r/2)}\right] + \$100{,}000(1+r/2)^{-(2)(2.5)}$$

$$\$94{,}735 = \$4{,}750(1+r/2) + \$4{,}750(1+r/2)^2 + \$4{,}750(1+r/2)^3 + \$4{,}750(1+r/2)^4 + \$104{,}750(1+r/2)^5$$

Suppose we choose $r = 11$ percent and solve for the present value of the cash flows from the bond, P_b.

$$P_b = \$4{,}750\left[\frac{1-(1.055)^{-5}}{.055}\right] + \$100{,}000(1.055)^{-5} = \$96{,}797$$

Because P_b is greater than the market price of the bond, we have chosen r too low. Let's try $r = 12$ percent.

$$P_b = \$4{,}750\left[\frac{1-(1.06)^{-5}}{.06}\right] + \$100{,}000(1.06)^{-5} = \$94{,}735$$

The bond's yield is 12 percent because the present value of the cash flows discounted at 12 percent equals the price of the bond. We were lucky to guess the bond's yield on the second attempt, but this iterative procedure can be quite time-consuming without a financial calculator that solves rate-of-return problems.

IV. SUMMARY AND REVIEW

Time value of money refers to the differential valuation of cash flows that are promised sequentially in the future. Given the existence of positive interest rates, a dollar received today is worth more than a dollar to be received tomorrow. People save in order to redistribute future income in desirable ways, in order to accommodate unexpected contingencies that may affect their future consumption patterns, and in order to take advantage of future investment opportunities.

The existence of positive interest rates can be explained by either of the following two hypotheses: (1) *Liquidity preference* which states that since people prefer more liquid assets to less liquid assets, they must be paid a premium to part with their liquidity; (2) *Time preference* which states that lenders sacrifice present consumption for greater future consumption. Hence, lenders require a premium to forego present consumption.

Time preference leads to the time value of money, which is measured through a number of compounding and discounting techniques discussed in this chapter. Compounding and discounting can be performed at intervals that range from yearly to daily and can be extended to continuous form.

QUESTIONS

1. Why does saving occur? Be sure to discuss the motives for saving in the context of certainty and uncertainty.
2. Explain the difference between nominal and real rates of return.
3. Explain the concepts of "surplus" and "deficit" economic units and the roles they play in financial markets.
4. Discuss the following statement: "Present value and future value are opposite sides of the same coin."

PROBLEMS

1. Find the future value interest factor (FVIF) for an ordinary annuity with equal monthly payments for 5 years at a 9 percent annual rate.
2. Suppose you expect to retire in 20 years. You have a retirement account with a current balance of $10,000 earning 7.5 percent annual interest. If you deposit $500 per month for the next 20 years, what will be the value of your account at retirement?
3. Compute the annual realized rate of return for an investor who purchases bonds of the Meltdown Power & Light Company (discussed in this chapter) if reinvestment rates are: (*a*) 8 percent (*b*) 12 percent.
4. The stock of PLS Corporation is currently selling for $13 per share. Some analysts think the company's true value is $17 per share and that the stock price could reach that level in the next 3 months. If the company's next quarterly dividend is expected to be $0.10 per share, compute the expected annualized rate of return if the holding period is 3 months and analysts' expectations are correct. Assume the dividend will be received in 3 months.
5. You have just won your state's lottery and may choose one of the following prizes. (*a*) $15,000,000 today. (*b*) $2,000,000 per year forever increasing at 2 percent per year. (*c*) $25,000,000 in three years. If U.S. Treasury notes are yielding 15 percent per year, which prize would you choose?
6. Generous George's Auto Sales will "tote the note" on a $7,500 car at no interest for $500 down and $116.67 for 60 months. Down the street, Honest Harriet is offering the same car for $1,000 less than George but will not extend credit. If your bank is making used-car loans at an annual interest rate of 11.5 percent, who is offering the better deal?

ANNOTATED BIBLIOGRAPHY

Clayton, Garry E., and Christopher B. Spivey. *Time Value of Money*. Philadelphia, Pa.: W. B. Saunders Company, 1978.

An excellent short volume on the mathematics and concepts underlying the time value of money.

Copeland, Thomas F., and J. Fred Weston. *Financial Theory and Corporate Policy*. 3d ed. Lexington, Mass.: Addison-Wesley Publishing Company, 1988, Chapter 2 and Appendix A.

An excellent source for the concepts and techniques for analyzing the time value of money.

Shao, Stephen P., and L. Shao. *Mathematics for Management and Finance*. 5th ed. Cincinnati: Southwestern Publishing Company, 1986.

A good modern textbook on the mathematics of financial analysis.

2

CASH FLOW EXPECTATIONS AND PROJECT RISK

I. INTRODUCTION

A. Perspectives

In our discussions of the time value of money, we made some implicit assumptions about the outcomes associated with the savings decisions of individuals and business units. Specifically, we assumed that both the streams of earnings and the discount (compound) rates were known in advance with certainty. Hence, when an individual decided to forego part of his or her present consumption for the sake of future larger consumption, there was no doubt about the growth in the income saved or the total income available for consumption in the following consumption period. In the typical illustration, the individual consumer had an income of $1,000.00 available for consumption C_1 in period one and $1,000.00 for consumption C_2 in period two. If the consumer decided to forego $500.00 of consumption in period one and lend (invest) it at 5 percent until period two, there was no uncertainty about the final outcome; that is, in period two, the individual's income available for consumption would be equal to the income earned on the savings. In terms of our example, income available for consumption in period two would equal

$$\$1,000.00 + 500.00 + 25.00 = \$1,525.00$$

In order to ensure that the outcomes were known with certainty, we couched the investment (saving) scenario in terms of bank deposits where both the amount invested (the cost to the investor, so to speak) and the rate of interest (return) were known with certainty. Hence, both the expected cash flows and the rates of growth in the original investment were secure from all contingencies including the possibility of bankruptcy. Investments in the marketplace, however, are not always riskless, and we are faced with the possibility that the true outcomes of investment decisions will differ from our expected outcomes. In this chapter, we review the basics of risk and its impact on the expected returns and future streams of earnings associated with investments.

B. Sources of Uncertainty and Risk

Certainty is characterized by complete information about each course of action, and the advance knowledge that each alternative has a unique outcome. *Uncertainty* and *risk* are characterized by imperfect knowledge about each alternative, and the expectation that each alternative has two or more possible outcomes. How do we distinguish risk from uncertainty? The answer to this depends on the decision maker's knowledge of the possible outcomes and the associated probabilities. That is, if the investor knows the frequency distribution (probabilities) of possible outcomes, he or she is faced with a risky situation that lends itself to prediction.

In order for an event to qualify as a *risky* situation, it must be repetitive in nature and be described by a *frequency distribution*. We can use this frequency distribution to draw observations and make inferences on the basis of objective, statistical techniques. Hence, we can classify most of the contingencies that are commercially insurable as risky situations. In contrast, *uncertainty* exists when the event is not replicable, thus making the situation unique. In this type of situation we cannot draw observations from frequency distributions and derive inferences.

Risk associated with financial decisions derives from the environment in which market participants operate. That is, the earnings streams of firms and individuals are affected by the macroeconomic factors of fluctuations in economic activity, by long-term technological trends in specific industries, by the more predictable seasonal fluctuations that affect most industries, as well as by the changes in the overall level of prices which determines the degree of inflation prevailing in an economy. In addition, for the firm that participates directly or indirectly in international commerce, risk is enhanced by the contingencies associated with the rest of the world.[1]

There are two types of risk associated with financial decisions, *business risk* and *financial risk*. The risk that derives from the product and labor markets in which the firm operates is known as *business* or *operating risk,* and it is attributed to such factors as prices for the firm's products and services, changes in consumer preferences, prices of factor inputs, labor strikes, and a host of related factors. This is the type of risk inherent in a business and it refers to the variability in the earnings of the firm which may range in impact from minor operating difficulties to inability to meet operating expenditures. When measured in terms of the interaction of the earnings streams associated with several investments, this type of risk is typically referred to as *portfolio risk* and is classified into reducible or *diversifiable risk* and *nondiversifiable risk*.

The risk that derives from the money and capital markets in which the firm operates is known as *financial risk* and is attributed to such factors as the cost and availability of funds, as well as the perceptions of the capital market regarding the firm's relative composition of debt and equity. It refers to the possibility that the firm will be unable to meet its financial obligations as they come due, with consequences ranging from temporary insolvency to reorganization and possible bankruptcy. Business risk and financial risk make up the total risk of the enterprise.[2]

C. Flows Impacted by Risk

Operating and financial risk affect the inflows and outflows of company funds that are associated with the company's principal line of business—the *operating flows,* so to speak. There are three types of flows of interest in financial decision making. The first type of flow—*income flow*—is derived after all types of expenses, including income taxes, have been subtracted from operating earnings. It is commonly known as *profits,* or *earnings after taxes* (EAT), or *net income after taxes* (NIAT), and it fluctuates in response to changes that affect revenues or costs. Thus, the income flow corresponds to the standard accounting definition of profit, but it does not mean that this amount of income corresponds to cash available for meeting the firm's obligations or funding needs.

The second type of flow—*funds flow*—refers to the amount of *net working capital* generated by the operations of the firm. The funds flow information tells the decision maker whether enough funds are generated through operations to support present activities and future, planned growth in business.

The third type of flow—*cash flow*—refers to the amount of cash generated from operations and measures the ability of the firm to meet its ongoing obligations. It is this type of flow that is of critical significance in financial management, as we measure the success or failure of financial decisions by the size and quality of the after-tax cash flows generated from an investment outlay. In effect, cash flow consists of earnings after taxes augmented by depreciation and other noncash expenses such as deferred taxes.

Financial decisions focus on both cash inflows and cash outflows when they are paid rather than when they are incurred. Hence, we must mention briefly the various categories of cash outflows associated with a particular investment, as they are incurred. Cash outflows refer to (1) all original cash outlays associated with an investment, which involve the cost of investment plus incidental expenses for freight and installation; (2) the additional short-term investments that accompany the original investment, which involve cash, accounts receivable, and inventory; and (3) other expenses, such as purchase of spare parts. From the sum of these three types of cash outlays, we must subtract the value of the asset at the end of its economic life (i.e., the salvage value) or the value of the asset being replaced by the investment under consideration.

It is apparent by now that fluctuations in the cash outlays for an investment project induce corresponding variability in the after-tax cash flows of the firm. Similarly, fluctuations in the revenues of the firm induce variability in its profits and after-tax cash flows. It is this type of variability that affects the quality of a firm's after-tax cash flows.

II. IMPROVING ESTIMATES OF FUTURE CASH FLOWS

A. Some Perspectives

The firm that operates within a dynamic and changing environment must be especially concerned with financial management. Factors such as institutional adjustments, legal changes, life-cycle considerations, and business-cycle conditions are at the basis of business dynamics. All these factors combine to make the tasks of the financial managers ever more complex as they attempt to forecast future cash flows for individual projects and groups of projects, as well as the entire income-generating asset base of the firm. In effect, financial managers attempt to estimate cash flows by making certain assumptions about the future conditions of the critical factors outlined above, particularly the general economic conditions described by the business cycle. Indeed, all of the types of risk mentioned earlier seem to ride together with the conditions of the business cycle. One of the ways to reduce the risk of projections is to create and maintain a framework that forecasts cash flows. This will not reduce the risk inherent in a specific project, but rather it will enable the manager to assess the degree of risk.[3]

When we talk about *expected cash flow,* we refer to the average value of future cash flows. Unlike the expression *projected cash flow* that refers to a managerial estimate under different circumstances, expected cash flow is a statistical concept. Let us illustrate the concepts by means of a typical illustration. Oregon Mills, Inc., a company whose output and sales are closely linked with commercial and residential construction, is presently evaluating the economic feasibility of putting up an additional manufacturing facility in another nearby location. The treasurer of the firm, ever mindful of the sensitivity of the construction industry to market conditions, has made his cash flow projections for next year along these lines. However, in order to refine his forecast, the treasurer has devised his own classification as shown in Table 2.1, where you will also see the projected cash flows from another competing investment. Notice that the two projects are defined by five possible cash flows each for the next year, and that each cash flow has attached to it a fractional number that indicates the probability of its occurrence. These probabilities reflect the information that management has and are constructed through a combination of objective and subjective information. Also, notice that the probabilities must by definition always sum up to unity (100 percent). What we must do now in order to help the treasurer of Oregon Mills, Inc. is to compute some measure of central tendency and an equivalent measure of dispersion for these projected cash flows. Thus, we shall adhere to tradition and employ the *expected value* or *mean* as a measure of central tendency and the *variance* or *standard deviation* as a measure of dispersion about the mean that serves as a proxy for risk.

The measure of central tendency known technically as the *mean* of a frequency distribution is basically a weighted average of all the observations—the weights being derived from the frequencies or probabilities of occurrence. When

TABLE 2.1 Oregon Mills, Inc.: Cash Flow Projections and Economic Conditions

Economic Conditions	Project A		Project B	
	Probability	*Cash Flow*	*Probability*	*Cash Flow*
Deep Recession	.10	$4,500	.10	$3,000
Mild Recession	.20	5,250	.25	4,500
Normal Conditions	.40	6,000	.30	6,000
Minor Boom	.20	6,750	.25	7,500
Major Boom	.10	7,500	.10	9,000

Project Costs: Project A = $3,000; Project B = $5,000
Project Duration: One year

the mean is used with an historical set of observations (time series), it is often called the *average value;* and when employed with random variables, it is known as the *expected value*. The measure of dispersion about the mean known as the *variance* of a distribution is given by the weighted sum of the squared deviations about the expected value. The *standard deviation* is obtained by taking the square root of the variance.

B. Computation of Expected Cash Flow and Its Standard Deviation

The computation of the expected cash flow is made by weighing each cash flow projection by its probability of occurrence. This is accomplished by means of the following formula:

$$\text{E(CF)} = \overline{\text{CF}} = \sum_{i=1}^{n} \text{CF}_i P_i \tag{2.1}$$

where E(CF) = Expected value of cash flows
$\overline{\text{CF}}$ = Mean or average cash flow
CF_i = Possible value of cash flow, i
P_i = Probability associated with cash flow, i
n = Number of possible cash flows

Using the above formula in (2.1) we can now compute the expected cash flows for Projects A and B that are under review by the management of Oregon Mills, Inc.

$$\begin{aligned}\text{E(CF}_\text{A}) = \overline{\text{CF}}_\text{A} &= \$4{,}500(.10) + \$5{,}250(.20)\\ &\quad + \$6{,}000(.40) + \$6{,}750(.20)\\ &\quad + \$7{,}500(.10)\\ &= \$450 + 1{,}050 + 2{,}400\\ &\quad + 1{,}350 + 750\\ &= \$6{,}000\end{aligned}$$

$$\begin{aligned}\text{E(CF}_\text{B}) = \overline{\text{CF}}_\text{B} &= \$3{,}000(.10) + \$4{,}500(.25)\\ &\quad + \$6{,}000(.30) + \$7{,}500(.25)\\ &\quad + \$9{,}000(.10)\\ &= \$300 + 1{,}125 + 1{,}800\\ &\quad + 1{,}875 + 900\\ &= \$6{,}000\end{aligned}$$

Thus, we see that both Project A and Project B have the same weighted average cash flow—making them equally desirable, other things being equal.

The computation of the standard deviation will proceed as follows:

1. Take the differences of each projected cash flow from the mean value computed above for each project.
2. Raise these differences to the second power.
3. Multiply these squared differences by the probabilities associated with each cash flow.
4. Take the sum of the values above. We call this sum the *variance*.
5. Take the square root of the variance to arrive at the standard deviation of the projected cash flows.

The above operation is accomplished by the

following formula:

$$\text{Var(CF)} = \sigma^2 = \sum_{i=1}^{n} (\text{CF}_i - \overline{\text{CF}})^2 P_i \quad (2.2)$$

where σ^2 = Variance of cash flows, and
σ = Standard deviation of cash flows

Using the above formula in (2.2) we can now compute the variance and standard deviation of each project considered by the management of Oregon Mills, Inc.

$$\begin{aligned}\text{Var}(\text{CF}_A) = \sigma_A^2 &= (\$4{,}500 - 6{,}000)^2(.10) \\ &+ (5{,}250 - 6{,}000)^2(.20) \\ &+ (6{,}000 - 6{,}000)^2(.40) \\ &+ (6{,}750 - 6{,}000)^2(.20) \\ &+ (7{,}500 - 6{,}000)^2(.10) \\ &= \$225{,}000 + 112{,}500 + 0 \\ &+ 112{,}500 + 225{,}000 \\ &= \$675{,}000.\end{aligned}$$

$$\sigma_A = \sqrt{\sigma_A^2} = \sqrt{675{,}000}$$

$$\sigma_A \approx \$822$$

$$\begin{aligned}\text{Var}(\text{CF}_B) = \sigma_B^2 &= (\$3{,}000 - 6{,}000)^2(.10) \\ &+ (4{,}500 - 6{,}000)^2(.25) \\ &+ (6{,}000 - 6{,}000)^2(.30) \\ &+ (7{,}500 - 6{,}000)^2(.25) \\ &+ (9{,}000 - 6{,}000)^2(.10) \\ &= \$900{,}000 + 562{,}500 + 0 \\ &+ 562{,}500 + 900{,}000 \\ &= \$2{,}925{,}000\end{aligned}$$

$$\sigma_B = \sqrt{\sigma_B^2} = \sqrt{2{,}925{,}000}$$

$$\sigma_B \approx \$1{,}710$$

C. Probability Distributions

The cash flows projected by the management of Oregon Mills, Inc. for Projects A and B are shown along with their associated probabilities in Figures 2.1 and 2.2. Several things are worth noting here. *First,* the vertical shaded bars form what is known as a *discrete probability distribution,* because of the finite number of possible outcomes shown. *Second,* the smooth continuous line that goes through the midpoints of the vertical bars forms what is known as the *continuous probability distribution,* indicating an infinite number of possible outcomes. *Third,* in both cases the distributions appear to be symmetric or bell-shaped indicating also that they are *normal distributions.*

Fourth, the two distributions differ considerably in their peakedness or what the statisticians call *kurtosis*. That is, the distribution of cash flows projected for Project A is more peaked (has greater kurtosis) than that for Project B. *Fifth,* although both probability distributions have the same mean, of \$6,000, their standard deviations differ significantly. That is, σ_A = \$822 and σ_B = \$1,710. Now, we know from basic statistics that for a normal distribution the following relationship exists:

$\pm 1\sigma$ from the mean includes about 68% of the area under normal curve
$\pm 2\sigma$ from the mean includes about 95% of the area under the normal curve
$\pm 3\sigma$ from the mean includes 99.7% of the area under the normal curve

Translated in terms of Projects A and B, the above information tells us the following:[4] (1) The cash flows for Project A are likely to range from \$6,000 − (3 × \$822) minimum to \$6,000 + (3 × \$822) maximum. That is, between \$3,534 and \$8,466. (2) There is a 99.7 percent chance that the actual cash flows from Project A will be no less than \$3,534 and no more than \$8,466. (3) Similar computations for Project B indicate that there is a 99.7 percent chance that the actual cash flows will be no less than \$870 and no more than \$11,130.

Thus, on the basis of the above, we can say that although both projects are equally desirable in terms of their expected cash flows, they are not equally desirable in terms of their standard deviations which measure the risk associated with each project. Because the standard devia-

FIGURE 2.1 Project A's Probability Distribution

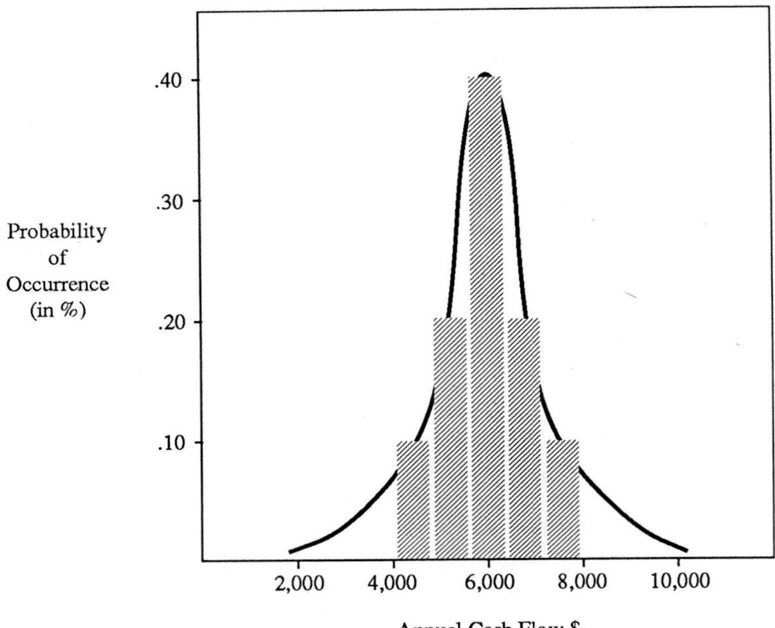

tion is a measure of fluctuation from an expected value, that is a measure of risk, then we can say the following: For any two projects with the same expected values but different standard deviations, the project with the smaller deviation (risk) is the more desirable of the two. In terms of what we have said up to now, Project A is the more desirable of the two projects.

D. Computation of Area Under the Normal Curve

Sometimes the question arises as to the probability that an actual cash flow will be greater (or less) than some established benchmark value. For this we may employ a slightly different measure of dispersion known as the *standard normal deviate, Z*. The formula for Z is

$$Z = \frac{CF - \overline{CF}}{\sigma} \qquad (2.3)$$

where Z = The standardized statistic Z, for which the area under the normal curve is measured in terms of standard deviations from the expected value

$\overline{CF}$ = Mean (average) of cash flows

CF = Possible cash flow of interest

σ = Standard deviation of cash flows

In order to illustrate the meaning of Z, let us take Project A, with an expected value of \$6,000 and standard deviation of \$822. Suppose the treasurer of Oregon Mills, Inc., wants to know the probability of a cash flow of \$7,000 occurring. We can find this through the value of Z.

$$Z = \frac{\$7{,}000 - \$6{,}000}{\$822}$$

$$Z \approx 1.2$$

Looking at the value of $Z \approx 1.2$ in the table entitled "Areas under the Normal Curve" in Appendix 7, we find that it corresponds to 38.49 percent of the area under the curve on the right

FIGURE 2.2 Project B's Probability Distribution

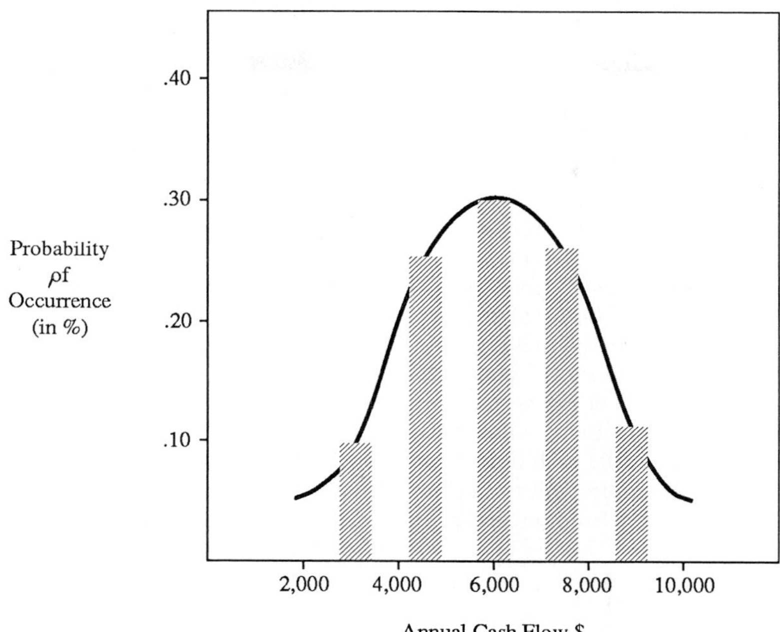

(higher values) side of the expected value of cash flows. This means that there is a 38.49 percent probability that the actual cash flow will be greater than \$6,000 and smaller than \$7,000. Because .5000 − .3849 = .1151, we also see that the area outside Z on the same side of the expected value is 11.51 percent, which means that there is an 11.51 percent probability that the actual cash flow will be greater than \$7,000.

E. Computation of the Coefficient of Variation

When comparing projects of substantially different size, the standard deviation can be a misleading measure of risks. Because significant size differences can distort the relative importance of the standard deviations, we can standardize or *normalize* these measures of risk by dividing them by the expected value of the distribution to obtain the *coefficient of variation* (CV). This is given by

$$CV = \text{Coefficient of Variation} = \frac{\sigma}{\overline{\overline{CF}}} \qquad (2.4)$$

This coefficient of variation provides a measure of risk per unit of return, so to speak. In terms of our two earlier projects we have

$$CV_A = \frac{\sigma_A}{\overline{\overline{CF}}_A} = \frac{\$822}{\$6,000} = .137$$

$$CV_B = \frac{\sigma_B}{\overline{\overline{CF}}_B} = \frac{\$1,710}{\$6,000} = .285$$

The larger the coefficient of variation the riskier the project. In our case we see that Project B is more than twice as risky as Project A—something that was also indicated by the sizes of the standard deviations of the two projects. It should be noted here that because Projects A and B have the same mean values, they are similar in size. Thus, the computation of the coefficient of variation does not add any new information to that offered by the comparison of the standard deviations of the projects.

III. IMPROVING ESTIMATES OF DISCOUNT RATES

The previous discussion in this section dealt with the adjustment of cash flows for risk. In this part we shall discuss two methods of adjusting the discount rate. The first method is subjective and rather practical, while the second method is accepted as being objective and theoretical. Both methods either explicitly or implicitly classify projects into risk classes with graduated discount rates. Both methods are also based on some simple, well-established premises as follows: (1) There is a direct relationship between risk and return. Both managers and individual investors expect higher returns from more risky projects than from less risky ones. (2) Some projects are inherently more risky than others. Obviously, then, investors will discount the cash flows from the riskier projects at higher discount rates (hurdle rates) than the cash flows from the less risky projects.

B. Subjective Adjustment of the Discount Rate

According to the first method, the management of a corporation combines *objective risk* estimates with *subjective risk* estimates to construct a *combined risk* class for a given project.[5] The objective risk estimates are extrapolations from market data that are based on historical objective information. However, the subjective estimates are themselves a challenge to develop. Depending on the company's evaluation procedures, a *relative risk profile* is constructed along the classification of *low, medium,* and *high risk class* with ample gradations within each class. In addition to the risk class groupings, there are several *risk elements*, whose risk content is evaluated in terms of these risk classes. Thus each risk element is evaluated as being in the low, medium, or high risk class. Then the scores from each risk-class gradation are summed and divided by the number of risk elements. This yields the subjective quotient.

This quotient is now used to adjust the company's cost of capital for the risk premiums that must be attached to a specific investment. It is done as follows:

1. The subjective quotient and the objective quotient are added to form a risk class.
2. This combined number is matched with the appropriate *risk index,* as developed by management.
3. The risk-index value is multiplied by the company's cost of capital to form a *subjectively risk-adjusted discount rate.*

For example, suppose the risk-index value for a given project is 1.30 and the required discount rate for the company is 15 percent. The product of the two values yields an adjusted discount rate of 19.5 percent, as shown in Figure 2.3. On the basis of this new, subjectively risk-adjusted discount rate, financial managers can now go back to the expected values of the various cash flows and discount them at the new rate. After deduction of investment costs, this technique computes a *risk-adjusted net present value.*[6]

C. Objective Adjustment of the Discount Rate

The second method of establishing a risk-adjusted discount or hurdle rate is based on the objective and impersonal workings of the capital market. The actual computation is performed by using a simple, equilibrium, capital asset pricing model (CAPM). This simple but analytically powerful framework states that in equilibrium, the investors in the equity of a firm will require a rate of return (hurdle rate), K_e, that is equal to the risk-free rate of return plus a risk premium.[7] Symbolically,

$$K_e = R_f + \text{Risk Premium}$$
$$K_e = R_f + \beta(K_m - R_f) \qquad (2.5)$$

where R_f = Risk-free rate of return from a short-term government security

β = The sensitivity of equity returns to overall market returns, also known as *beta,* or just b.

K_m = The actual rate of return on the market portfolio that can be proxied by an index of economic activity or stock market index

FIGURE 2.3 Subjective Risk Adjustment of Discount Rates

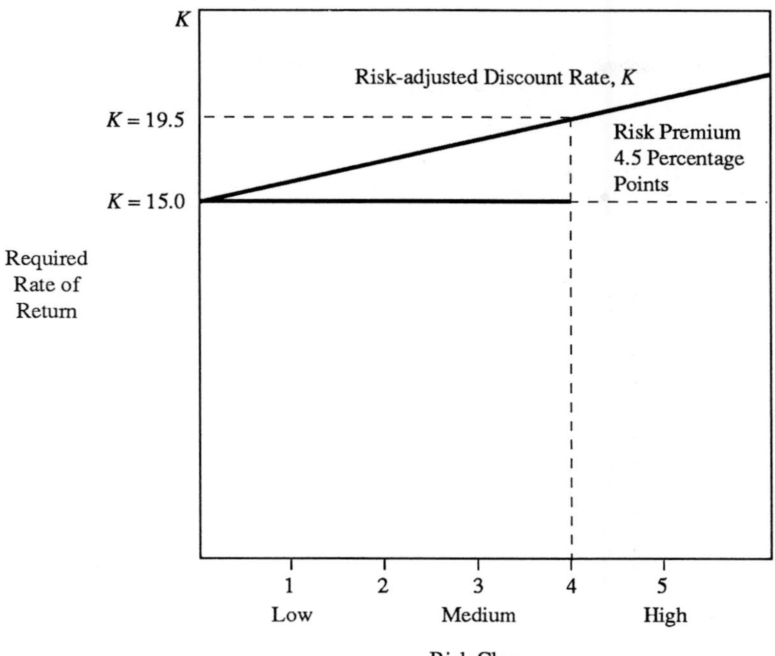

Let us discuss some of the variables in this simple model. *First* of all, the risk-free rate, R_f, serves as a benchmark for safe investments. It is the rate expected to be obtained from a short-term government security held to maturity. Because it is held to maturity, it does not suffer from any risk of returns due to price fluctuations. Moreover, because the government will not, by definition, declare its own securities in default, this type of investment does not have default risk, either.[8] That is why we use it as the benchmark of safe investments with positive, riskless returns. One may think of this rate as being approximated (but not equal to) by the rate of interest earned by money deposited at a bank whose deposits are insured and can be converted to cash on demand.

Second, the rate of return from the market portfolio, K_m, refers to the return associated with a well-balanced portfolio of assets. In countries with highly developed capital markets, the K_m will be observed directly from the market as the return on an established stock market index. In other countries, some well-balanced portfolio returns can serve as proxies for K_m. Notice that we are interested in the difference $(K_m - R_f)$, that is, the true risky return of the market in excess of the risk-free return. The coefficient b serves as the slope of the linear equation, just as the R_f serves as the y-intercept value. Being a slope coefficient, b measures the reaction of the dependent variable, K_e, to a unit change in the independent variable, $(K_m - R_f)$. For example, $b = 1.5$ indicates that as the variable $(K_m - R_f)$ changes by one unit, K_e will change by 1.5 units. The product $b\,(K_m - R_f)$ constitutes the risk premium.

Note that the hurdle or discount rate, K_e, is adjusted not by our subjective estimates but by the objective workings of the marketplace. As K_m changes so does K_e, multiplied by a factor b. The relationship of equation (2.5) is depicted in Figure 2.4a. The straight line that relates expected returns on an individual investment with the re-

FIGURE 2.4 Capital Asset Pricing Model (CAPM), Capital Market Line (CML), and Security Market Line (SML)

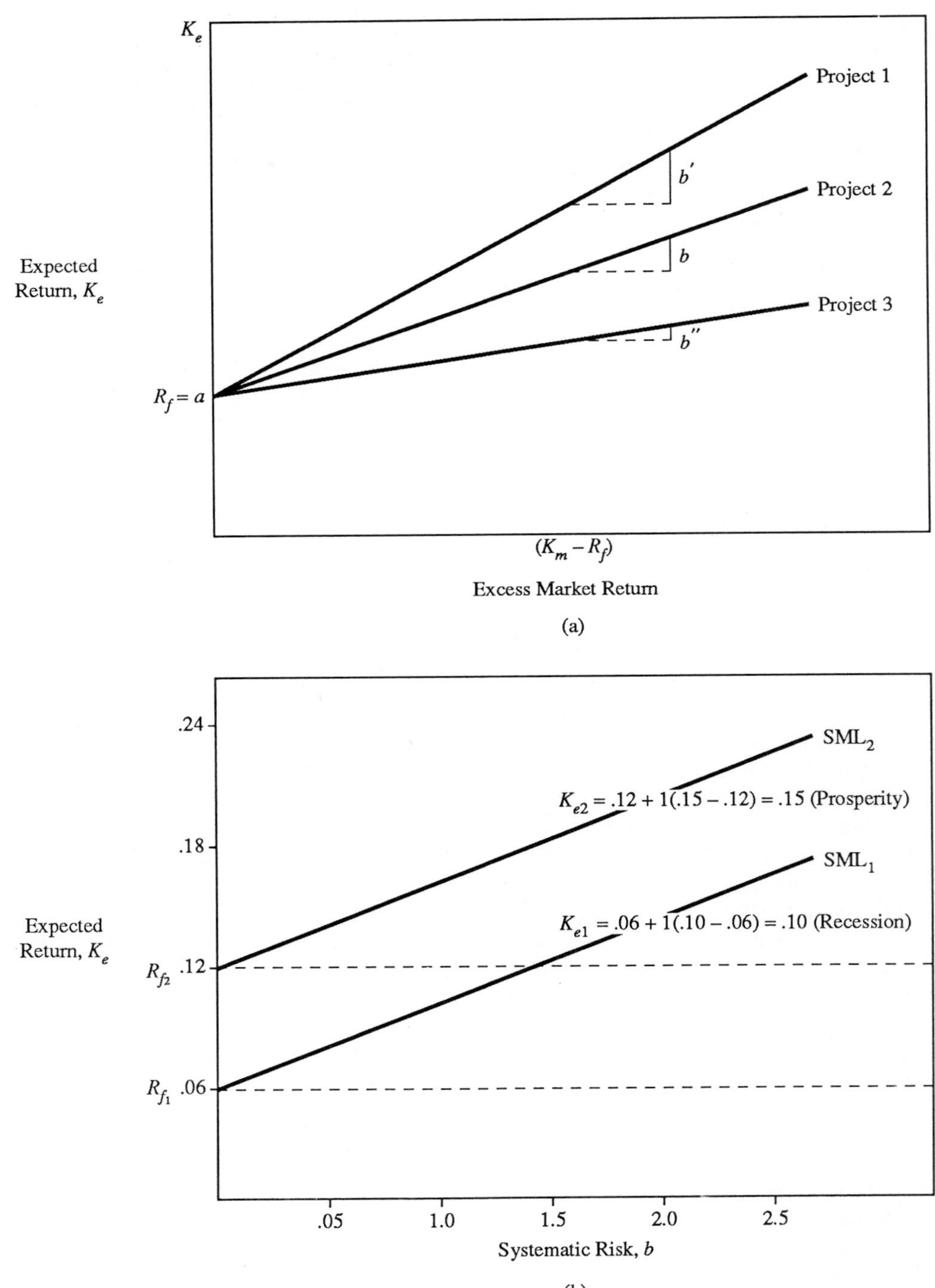

turns of the market portfolio is drawn for three different investments with three different sensitivities (betas) to market returns and, hence, three different risk premia.

The relationship can be rewritten in terms of expected returns, K_e, and b, which due to its systematic comovement with the market return is also called *systematic risk*.[9] This is shown in Figure 2.4*b*, where the linear relationship between K_e and b, also known as the Security (asset) Market Line (SML) is drawn for two states of economic conditions—namely, prosperity and recession. It is also interesting to point out here how simple the actual risk adjustments appear in this example. Note that we have assumed here $b = 1$ in order to show the effects of different economic expectations upon the discount factor.

A more complete picture is shown in Figure 2.5, where the total risk from a project or a firm is decomposed into the risk-free component and the risk premium associated with that project.[10] It should be stressed here that, *when the risk-adjusted discount rate, K_e, has been computed through the CAPM, we then take this rate as the discount factor to use in the time value equation. This is the purpose of the entire procedure: to compute a risk-adjusted discount rate.*

IV. CERTAINTY EQUIVALENTS AND MEAN-VARIANCE METHODS

A. Perspectives on Certainty Equivalents

The basic premise of all certainty-equivalent approaches is the assumption that expected return is to be preferred and risk is to be avoided. Consequently, a rational investor will accept higher risk only if it is accompanied by a higher return. Hence, the expected return from an investment project is discounted by some measure of its riskiness. The additional advantage of this technique is that it proceeds from uncertainty to risk before the discounting operation.[11]

The procedure of reducing an uncertain event

FIGURE 2.5 Security Market Line

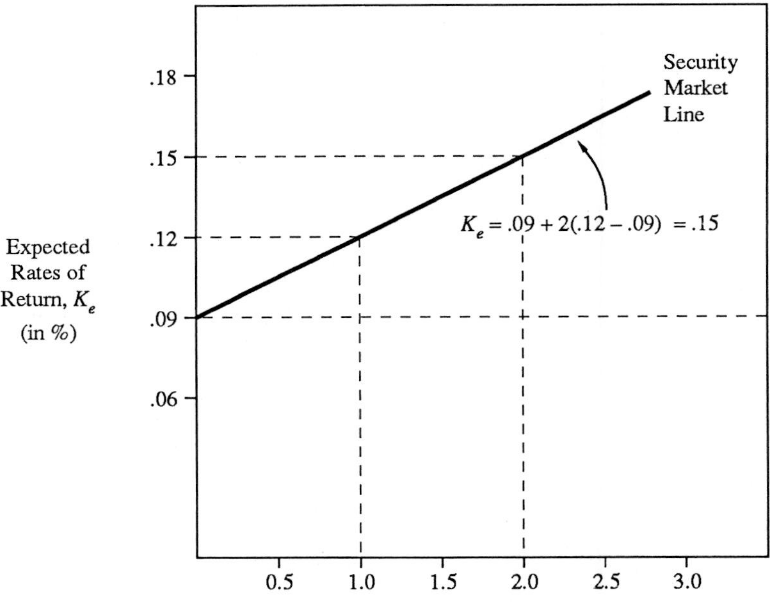

into a risk situation, through some measure of equivalence, involves a straightforward attempt at substitution. We first decide on some measure of central tendency, such as the mean, and some measure of dispersion, such as the standard deviation or variance. Next we proceed, through the construction of some artificial variable, to establish a value that the decision maker will be willing to accept in lieu of some future uncertain value. This new, artificial variable is called a *certainty equivalent,* and it implies that the decision maker will choose among alternative decisions in such a way as to maximize the value of this variable. If such a value is found, we can safely assume that it is as attractive to the decision maker as the uncertain future value.

We shall pursue the construction of certainty equivalents by way of a simple example. Assume that the treasurer of Oregon Mills, Inc., is considering three alternative investment opportunities, as follows:

Project A: Invest some of the cash balances in riskless government bonds which will be held to maturity in 10 years. The return from such investment is .05 and the risk (as measured by the variance) is .00.

Project B: Invest the same amount of funds, for the same time period, in a project with a return of .11 (as measured by the mean) and a risk of .08 (as measured by the variance).

Project C: Invest the same amount of funds, for the same time period, in a project with a return of .18 (as measured by the mean) and a risk of .15 (as measured by the variance).

If the treasurer of Oregon Mills, Inc., decides that he is indifferent in terms of the risk-return characteristics of the three investment opportunities, then the line that connects all three points forms his *certainty-equivalent indifference curve.* This situation is shown in Figure 2.6.

Figure 2.6 indicates that .11 (point B) is the certainty equivalent of .18 (point C). Moreover, it shows that .05 (point A) is the certainty equivalent of either of the two alternatives, because it has a 0 variance. The certainty-equivalent re-

FIGURE 2.6 Certainty-Equivalent Function

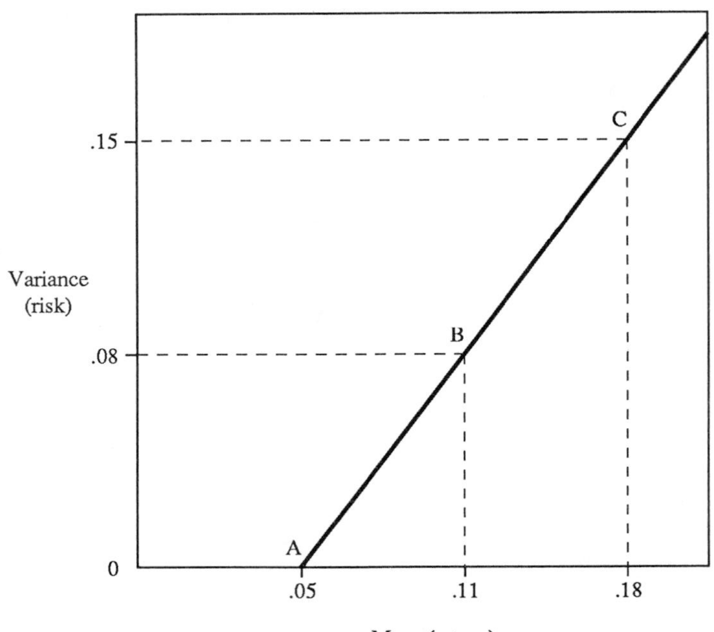

turn function, which relates choices A, B, and C, indicates that the decision maker values certain incremental dollars more than he values risky incremental returns. Hence, he will consider a riskier project only if the expected return is high enough to compensate for the additional risk. Thus, by his own admission, the treasurer has suggested the risk-return combinations that will make him value all three points equally.

Needless to say, the certainty equivalents can be established directly in terms of absolute values of cash flows rather than rates of return. In such cases we establish a procedure for computing present values by using a *constant risk-adjusted discount rate,* also known as RADR.[12]

B. Elements of Mean-Variance Diversification

All of the previous methods discussed ways to incorporate functionally the risk of an asset into its profile of desirability. We shall now review briefly the mean-variance framework which looks at the desirability and risk of a group of investments. The mean-variance approach, which was developed by H. Markowitz,[13] modifies the certainty-equivalence method along the following lines:

1. The mean-variance technique incorporates the notion of boundary conditions or constraints of the $\gtreqless$ type by the use of mathematical programming.
2. The technique incorporates the notion of the interactive effects of the expected returns from a group of investments by the use of covariance of these returns.
3. The technique incorporates the notion of diversification and the selection of investment combinations (portfolios) that will minimize risk (variance) for specified levels of expected return.

Markowitz proved that the rationale that underlies the certainty-equivalence method—namely, a preference for expected returns and an aversion toward risk—can lead to the construction of balanced or diversified portfolios.

We should also note here that the contribution of Markowitz relies primarily in his modification of the certainty-equivalence method to explain the widely practiced economic phenomenon of *diversification*. In this vein, he reoriented the manner in which investors are believed to evaluate potential investment opportunities. Investors no longer look at each asset in isolation. They no longer compare the individual means and variances of Projects A and B; instead they compare the means and variances of the portfolios to which the projects belong. Thus, it is portfolios, and not individual assets, that define the real set of available investment opportunities.

In its simplest form, the portfolio approach suggests that financial managers should select a group of assets that will minimize risk relative to the expected return acceptable to the firm. This way, as the risk decreases so does the discount rate applied to the cash flows of the projects. That is, the mean-variance approach is another—albeit more sophisticated and group-oriented—approach to adjusting the discount rate for risk.

Let us take the total business risk or operating risk associated with any given investment and separate it into two broad components as follows: (1) *systematic risk,* and (2) *nonsystematic risk*.

Systematic risk is attributable to the common economic factor, say overall economic conditions, that affects all assets in the economy in a similar manner. This type of risk, measured by the sensitivity coefficient, β (beta), cannot be diversified away through asset combinations, because it is the risk that remains after all possible diversification has taken place. That is why we call it systematic, due to its one-to-one relationship with the proxy used for economic conditions. However, the average systematic risk, b, from all the assets in a company can be altered by the selling and buying of individual high-beta or low-beta assets to obtain a lower or higher average systematic risk for the company.

Nonsystematic risk is unique or idiosyncratic to the individual asset under consideration by management. This type of risk can be almost completely eliminated through judicious combinations that achieve diversification of assets. A simple representation of this effect is shown in Figure 2.7, where we see that the introduction of a properly selected second asset reduces total

FIGURE 2.7 Risk Reduction and Number of Assets

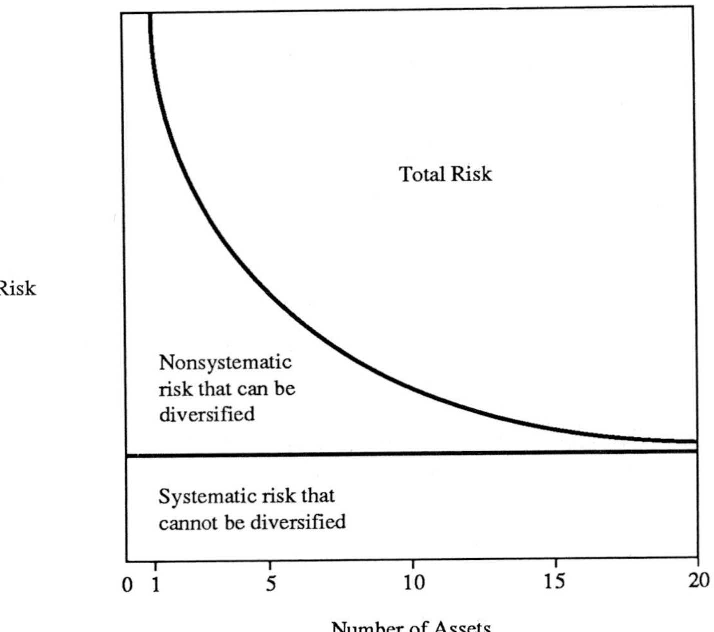

risk significantly, and so on until about 20 assets. At this point, all risk-reduction benefits from diversification are nearly exhausted, on average. Hence, any additional expansion of the firm to new projects will yield almost no benefits but will yield costs for search, selection, monitoring, and revision of the portfolio.

The basic premise of risk reduction through the combination of assets derives from the statistical comovement or correlation of the cash flows of various assets over time. There are three benchmarks to be studied here. If the cash flows from any two assets move together over time in the same direction and by the same amount, we say that the two cash flows are *perfectly positively correlated* and indicate it by $\rho_{ij} = 1$, where i and j refer to the two cash flows, respectively. At the other extreme, if the cash flows from any two assets move together over time but in opposite directions and by the same amount, we say that the two cash flows are *perfectly negatively correlated* and indicate it by $\rho_{ij} = -1$. In between the two extremes of systematic comovement we have the case where the cash flows from any two assets do not have a predominant systematic pattern of comovement but resemble the behavior of two *independent random variables*. We say that in this case there exists *zero correlation* and indicate it by $\rho_{ij} = 0$. Obviously, the extremes of $\rho_{ij} = \pm 1$ and the midpoint of $\rho_{ij} = 0$ do not constitute real-life patterns of behavior for asset cash flows. Rather, the comovement between any pair of asset cash flows ranges between something less-than-perfect positive correlation and something less-than-perfect negative correlation.

Now, with the exception of assets with cash flows that are perfectly positively correlated, the combination of assets with any other patterns of comovement will result in risk reduction through diversification. The extremes are as follows:

1. Two assets with *perfectly positively correlated* cash flows cannot ordinarily be combined and reduce risk.
2. Two assets with *perfectly negatively correlated* cash flows can, under the proper combination, reduce diversifiable risk to zero.
3. Two assets with *zero-correlated* cash flows can reduce diversifiable risk to a minimum

by the equiproportional allocation of the firm's budget between the two projects on a 50%–50% basis.

Naturally, real-life diversification obtains for all other cases with commensurate risk reduction.

V. TIME PREFERENCE AND RISK REVISITED

A. Consumption and Investment Opportunities

At the beginning of this chapter, we introduced the saving decision of the representative individual who is faced with the problem of allocating her income between consumption and savings. In this section, we explore in more detail the behavior of many individuals and business firms whose time preferences are realized in the buying and selling of claims to present and future consumption. The markets where these various claims are traded are known as capital markets; and in a world of certainty, the price attached to these claims is the *market rate* or *risk-free rate of interest*. With no risk, the market rate reflects the interaction of time preferences of many economic agents whose consumption-saving decisions determine the supply and demand for claims and thus their prices. If capital markets are perfectly competitive, the actions of individual traders do not affect the market rate. That is, any saver (lender) can buy as many claims as desired at the market price, and similarly, any borrower may sell claims as desired at the market price.

In what follows the functioning of the capital market is integrated with the opportunity for investment in real (or productive) assets to arrive at one of the most important ideas underlying modern finance, the *Fisher separation principle*. We then consider the individual's saving decision in the face of uncertainty and conclude with some comments on nominal and real interest rates.

Now consider a simple two-period model for an individual who has current income equal to \$10,000 and next-period income equal to \$25,000. With a constant market rate of interest, the individual's borrowing and lending opportunities lie along the straight line BEF shown in Figure 2.8. This line indicates the individual's *consumption opportunity set,* which is expanded in a capital market because of one's ability to trade claims. In the figure, point E represents a situation in which the individual neither borrows nor lends, point F represents the maximum allowable consumption today and zero consumption in the next period, and point B represents the converse—no consumption today, the maximum allowable in the next period. Because point F represents borrowing against all of next year's income, F is the sum of the current income and the present value of next period's income. The slope of line BEF is the interest rate—the gain in value received next period by foregoing consumption in the present one.

Assuming an interest rate of 10 percent, the horizontal distance represented by $0F$ is

$$C_0 + \frac{C_1}{1 + r} = 10{,}000 + \frac{25{,}000}{1.10} = \$32{,}727$$

Because the interest rate is fixed, consumption can occur along any point on line BEF. That is to say, the capital market allows for smooth consumption patterns, because borrowing and lending can occur anywhere along line BEF. The particular point chosen on the line depends on the individual's tastes and preferences for future versus current consumption. Some people may prefer to be above point E and lend, while others may prefer to be below E and borrow. What the capital market does is remove the constraint of consumption being tied directly to income.

If we give individuals the opportunity to invest in productive real assets, the graphical approach taken in Figure 2.8 is altered. Figure 2.9 represents an investment opportunity set that shows how a dollar investment in the current period yields a corresponding dollar cash flow in the next period. Note that the figure assumes that investment opportunities have decreasing marginal returns; that is, as we invest equal amounts in projects, the incremental dollar return decreases. Thus, the first OA dollars invested yield a large cash flow next period, while the investment of AB dollars yields a slightly

FIGURE 2.8 Two-Period Consumption Diagram

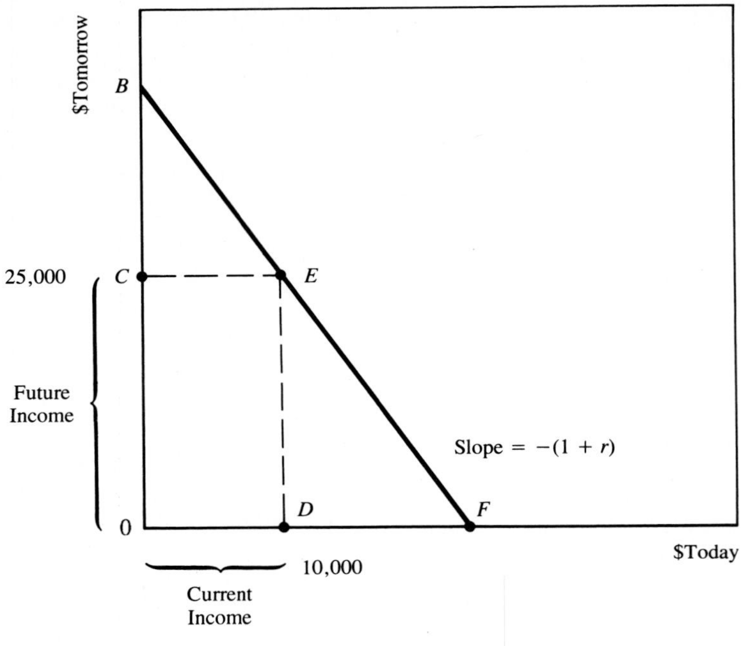

FIGURE 2.9 Two-Period Investment Diagram

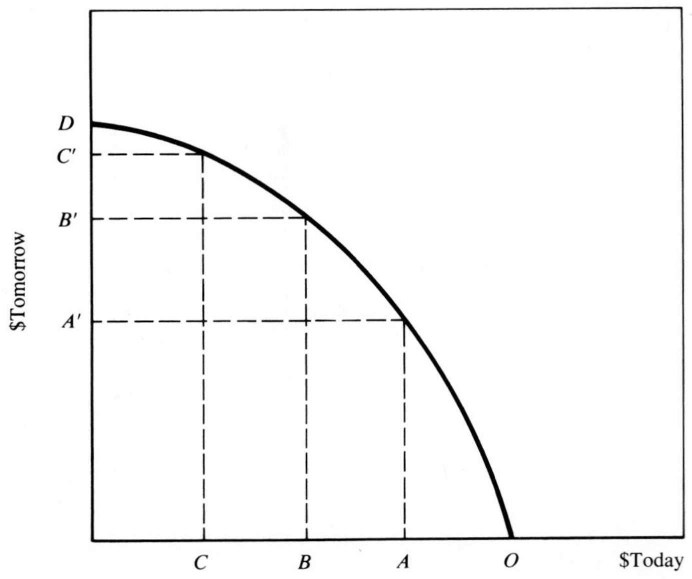

smaller dollar return, and so forth. The shape of the curve plotted in Figure 2.9 is an accurate description of the productive opportunities that all firms face.

The situations depicted in Figures 2.8 and 2.9 can be used to construct Figure 2.10, in which lending and borrowing opportunities are combined with productive opportunities. The investor can now trade along either the curve *MF* or the line *BF*; the only question is whether or not it would be wise to consume a given portion of total wealth (represented by distance 0*F*) and invest the rest in productive opportunities along *MF*. Notice that the investment or production opportunity set represented by the curve (*MF*) dominates the opportunities available in the consumption opportunity set represented by the line (*BF*). Because, like the consumption opportunity set, the production opportunity set provides claims to present and future consumption, the investor can trade these claims in the capital market. Accordingly, consider an investment *LF* in real assets. From Figure 2.10, this investment would return 0*P* dollars next period. Productive opportunities, therefore, yield the consumption pair of $*L* and $*P* next period. However, if this pair is not the desired apportionment of the income, the claims can be traded in the capital market along line *JK*. Thus, regardless of how productive income is apportioned between the periods, investment in real assets yields higher consumption in both periods, as shown by the relative positions of lines *JK* and *BF*.

Let us review and summarize the situation shown in Figure 2.10. Initial wealth is represented by 0*F*, as in Figure 2.8. Investment *LF* in real assets loosens the budget constraint, so that the initial wealth is increased to an amount given by line segment 0*K*. Because the value of the investment is *LK* and costs only *LF*, line segment *FK* represents the asset's net present value (NPV). Note that an investment equal to *LF* is optimal, because any investment beyond

FIGURE 2.10 Two-Period Consumption–Investment Diagram

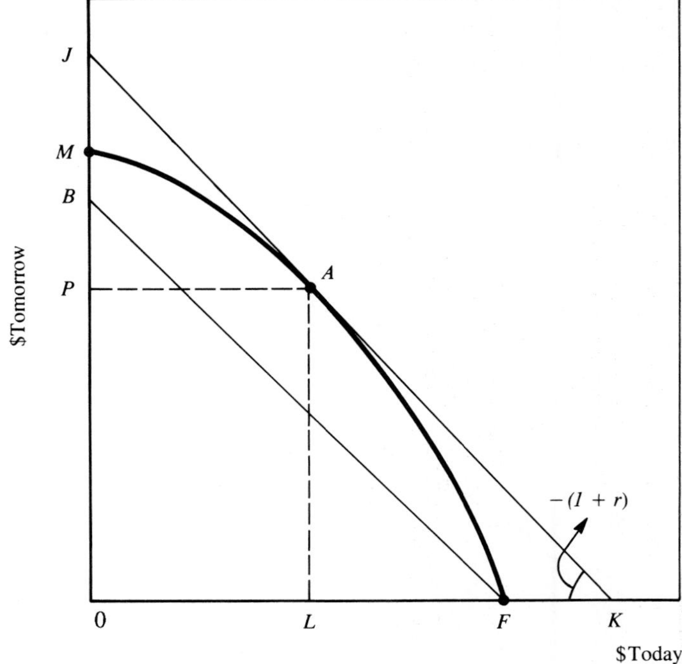

point A will yield rates of return less than the market rate r (indicated by the slope of either line BF or JK). Also, with a fixed market lending rate, all individuals will select the same investment—that represented by point A. Then, depending on one's preferences in regard to future and current consumption, a person could trade along the market line JAK to arrive at the preferred consumption point. This scenario constitutes the well-known *Fisher separation principle* stating that individual preferences do not enter into the production decision. Financial managers need only maximize the firm's net present value; investors may then transact in the capital market to arrive at their desired levels of present and future consumption.

While the separation principle was arrived at by an analysis of a two-period consumption and investment cycle, it can be extended to more periods. As we will see in Chapter 13, the NPV rule is based on the results obtained from a two-period analysis. For the multiperiod case, as long as there are markets for trading all dated claims, the Fisher separation principle and the net present value rule obtain. Chapter 13 outlines the steps that are necessary to calculate project cash flows, as well as the various criteria for evaluation. Although the results obtained there seem limited (because of a variety of restrictive assumptions), the model provides some powerful insights regarding the separation of ownership and control.

C. Utility Considerations

In the face of uncertainty, we need to specify the investor's objectives. The usual specification is that investors act so as to maximize their expected utility of wealth. In a world of certainty, this boils down to their choosing appropriate levels of present and future consumption. In a world of uncertainty, this choice no longer exists. Instead, investors must choose among the various combinations of risk and return offered by alternative investments. If they make both rational and consistent choices, investors can arrive at an index that describes their individual preferences for risk outcomes. In financial analysis we assume that investors are averse to risk, which translates into a utility function of the shape shown in Figure 2.11. (As wealth increases, the relative value of a marginal increase in wealth is smaller.)

The utility approach that is used in the general theory of choice was originally developed by John Von Neumann and Oskar Morgenstern and is referred to as the *maximization of expected utility*. Briefly, it goes as follows: Suppose

FIGURE 2.11 Risk Averter's Utility Function

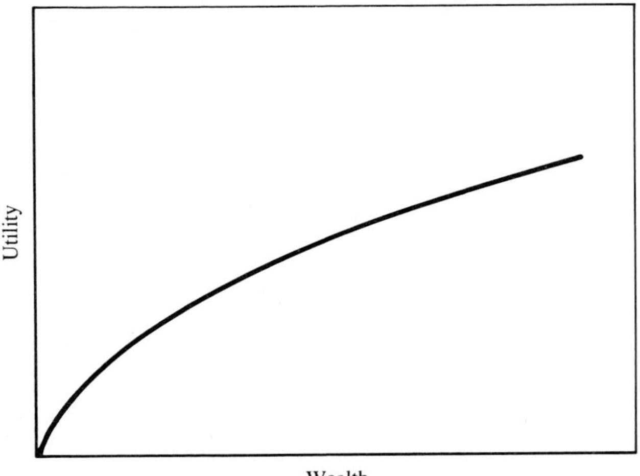

we have determined that an investor's utility-of-wealth function is of the form $u(W) = \ln(W)$. Then, using the information given in the following table, we can compute the expected utility of investments A and B.

Investment A

Outcome	*Probability*
\$ 1	0.30
\$ 5,000	0.50
\$10,000	0.20

Investment B

Outcome	*Probability*
\$ 200	0.40
\$6,000	0.60

The expected utility of each investment is

$$U_A = .30 \ln(1) + .50 \ln(5{,}000) + .20 \ln(10{,}000) = 6.1$$

$$U_B = .40 \ln(200) + .60 \ln(6{,}000) = 7.34$$

Investment B thus yields a higher expected utility than investment A, even though A's expected value is higher than B's (i.e. \$4,500.30 versus \$3,680). Consequently, investment B is preferred to investment A. Note that this is so even though investment B has a 40 percent chance of a very low income. The important point here is that since investor utility is a function of mean and variance, the required return for a particular investment depends on the characteristics of the cash flow distribution.

D. Nominal Interest Rates and Real Returns

At this point we should briefly digress to distinguish between *nominal* and *real* rates of return. Because nominal rates are calculated from nominal cash flows, they do not account for the effect of changing prices on purchasing power. A more meaningful measure of return should thus capture these effects.

To calculate the real return from holding a financial asset, the nominal interest rate must be adjusted for changes in prices over the holding period. Fortunately, the U.S. government compiles and maintains price data that are published periodically. Various indices exist that measure different types of prices. For example, the Consumer Price Index (CPI) measures the level of prices for a basket of goods and services purchased by the typical household relative to some base year. In the same vein, the Producer Price Index (PPI) measures levels of prices paid to the factors of production—raw materials, wages, *et cetera*. The GNP Deflator measures the levels of prices of the various components of current aggregate output. Consequently, period-to-period price changes that have already occurred can be measured by calculating the present change in the level of a given index.

The general formula for computing the real rate of return over a holding period, given the nominal interest rate and the levels of the chosen inflation index at the beginning and end of the holding period, is

$$1 + i_r = \left(\frac{I_0}{I_1}\right)(1 + i_N) \tag{2.6}$$

where I_0 = level of inflation index at the beginning of period;
I_1 = level of inflation index at the end of period;
i_r = real rate of return; and
i_N = nominal rate of return.

To illustrate the use of equation (2.6), suppose that the CPI is our chosen price level index. It has a level of 235 on January 1, 1988 when we purchase a financial asset and an expected level of 255 on January 1, 1989 when the asset matures. If the financial asset offers a nominal interest rate of 15 percent annually, what is the real return on our investment? By substituting the given values, we obtain $1 + i_r = [235(1.15)]/255 = 1.06$. The real return then is about 6 percent, rather than the 15 percent nominally promised by the asset. An alternative means of adjustment is to state the change in prices in percentage terms, as follows:

$$\frac{I_1 - I_0}{I_0} = \% \text{ change in } I = \mathrm{d}I$$

and

$$1 + \mathrm{d}I = I_1/I_0$$

Substituting the above expression into equation (2.6), we have,

$$1 + i_r = \frac{(1 + i_N)}{(1 + \mathrm{d}I)}$$

Ultimately, we can utilize the approximation in expression (2.7) to estimate the real interest rate.

$$i_r \approx i_N - \mathrm{d}I, \qquad (2.7)$$

where ≈ means "is approximately equal to."

VI. SUMMARY AND REVIEW

Cash flow estimates for financial decisions are made under conditions of uncertainty. When uncertainty can be measured, we are faced with situations involving risk. Risk, in turn, derives from the environment in which market participants operate. That is, the earnings streams of individuals and firms are affected by the macroeconomic factors of fluctuations in economic activity, by long-term technological trends in specific industries, by seasonal variations, and by changes in the overall level of prices worldwide.

There are two types of risk associated with financial decisions: operating risk and financial risk. Operating risk is inherent in a business, and it refers to the variability in the earnings of the firm that may result in inability to cover its operating expenditures. When measured in terms of the interactions and interdependence of earnings streams from a group of investments this risk is also referred to as portfolio risk and becomes the benchmark for financial decisions. Financial risk is inherent in the use of debt by the firm, and it refers to the inability of the firm to meet its financial obligations.

Financial managers attempt to measure risk by adjusting either the expected cash flows or the discount rates through probabilistic methods. The measures discussed involve the expected value, the standard deviation, the standard normal deviate, and the coefficient of variation. In addition to computing risk return measures for individual projects, financial managers also compute the respective measures for combinations of assets in order to achieve risk reduction through diversification.

NOTES

1. An additional source of risk exists in relation to the decision maker's perception of the environment and its constraints, but we will not elaborate on this type of risk here.
2. In addition to operating risk and financial risk, managers are concerned with default risk or risk of bankruptcy. This is not a separate category of risk but rather the extreme outcome of either or both of the two basic types of risk discussed earlier.
3. Forecasting of funds needs is discussed in Chapter 5 as a separate topic.
4. At this stage we adjust only the cash flows for risk. In fact, we assume that the discount rate is known and constant.
5. For details on the subjective adjustment of the discount rate, the reader is referred to Gup and Norwood.
6. Although we present this practical approach for its informational value, we do not endorse it necessarily. Ideally, either the cash flows or the discount rate should be adjusted for risk. When both are adjusted, as in the method outlined above, there is good reason to believe that double-discounting has occurred. In such cases, the resulting lower expected net present values will likely lead to the rejection of some potentially profitable projects.
7. We shall cover only the rudiments of the capital asset pricing model here. For a more detailed exposition, the reader is referred to

Chapters 13 and 14 on capital budgeting and valuation in Part V.

8. We exclude the risk of inflation from consideration here.
9. As we discuss later in Chapter 14 on valuation and portfolio selection, systematic risk cannot be reduced through diversification.
10. Please note that by construction the beta value of the market portfolio or index is always $b = 1$.
11. In the techniques outlined earlier, we proceeded on the assumption that uncertainty had already been reduced to risk. Hence, all we had to do was quantify this risk through an appropriately chosen discount rate.
12. The technique for computing present values by using RADR is discussed in some detail in Chapter 13 on capital budgeting.
13. The functional details of the mean-variance approach are discussed in Chapter 14 in this volume.

QUESTIONS

1. Define certainty, risk, and uncertainty. What are the sources of uncertainty in business situations?
2. Define the following terms: business risk, portfolio risk, diversifiable risk, nondiversifiable risk, and financial risk.
3. Define income flow, funds flow, and cash flow.
4. What are the typical measures employed for expectation and risk in financial decisions?
5. What is the rationale for using the coefficient of variation in analyzing investment projects?
6. How do managers account for risk in investment proposals?
7. Briefly outline the methods used by managers to improve estimates of discount rates.

PROBLEMS

1. The L.A.W. Corporation is evaluating two mutually exclusive investment alternatives, A and B. A member of the firm's finance department estimates the betas of the two projects to be .95 and 1.26 for A and B, respectively. In addition, she has compiled the following relevant information:

Rate of return on 90-day T-bills (annualized)	8.5%
Expected rate of return on a market portfolio (annualized)	14%

Compute the discount rates to be applied to the expected cash flows of projects A and B.

2. Continuing with the projects under consideration by the L.A.W. Corporation in problem 1, you have the following cash-flow and state-of-the-economy probabilities:

Economic Condition	*(Probability)*	*Projected Cash Flows (millions)* *A*	*B*
Boom	(.2)	10	25
Moderate Growth	(.4)	6	12
Recession	(.4)	5	3

Required cash outlays for projects A and B are \$3 million and \$9 million, respectively. Given the required rates of return calculated in problem 1, compute for each project: (*a*) expected NPV, (*b*) standard deviation of NPV, and (*c*) coefficient of variation.

3. Consider an individual with a net worth of \$50,000 and the following utility of wealth function:

$$U(W) = 10 + 200(W) - .001(W)^2$$

Furthermore, she is faced with a gamble involving one flip of a fair coin. If the coin comes up heads, she loses \$10,000 and if tails, she wins \$10,000. Find the certain level of wealth providing the same level of utility as the expected utility of wealth if the gamble is accepted.

ANNOTATED BIBLIOGRAPHY

Babcock, G. C. "The Roots of Risk and Return." *Financial Analysts Journal*, January–February 1980, 56–63.

A simple but informative exposition on the risk-return relationship.

Gup, Benton, and Samuel W. Norwood, III. "Divisional Cost of Capital: A Practical Approach." *Financial Management,* Spring 1982, 20–24.

An excellent application of the subjective method of risk adjustment.

Robichek, A. A., and S. Myers. "Conceptual Problems in the Use of Risk-Adjusted Discount Rates." *Journal of Finance,* December 1966, 720–27.

A sound discussion of the relationship between the certainty-equivalent and risk-adjusted approaches to valuation.

Schall, L. D., and G. L. Sundem, "Capital Budgeting Methods and Risk: A Further Analysis." *Financial Management,* Spring 1980, 7–11.

An informative survey on the role of risk in practical capital budgeting decisions.

3

THE ECONOMIC AND INSTITUTIONAL ENVIRONMENTS OF THE FIRM

I. INTRODUCTION

The business firm, small or large, family-owned or publicly traded, like all other organizations, operates within the dynamics of the external environment and the fluidity of its internal organization. Moreover, its decisions and financial outcomes are constrained by the fiscal laws, the labor regulations, and the overall governmental decrees of the country within which it operates. For the national firm, the institutional picture is mostly confined within the home country environment, while for the multinational firm, the institutional environment is expanded to many different host countries.

It is the purpose of this chapter to discuss and review the economic and institutional environments within which the modern firm (particularly the publicly held corporation) operates and to focus on some salient features that can be generalized. Because we deal with universally accepted topics intended for use in many national environments in *Financial Management: Text and Cases* (2d ed., Boston: Allyn and Bacon, 1991), we will abstain from specific institutional and legal details, and stress the aspects that possess sufficient universality to make them globally applicable. For example, products and services of all firms throughout the world are subject to a market-determined life cycle and an economywide or worldwide business cycle. Hence, we can discuss these freely without many qualifications about the national market where a specific firm operates. Another universal environment phenomenon is inflation—the pervasive rise in the overall level of prices—that affects most countries in different degrees. Hence, it can also be viewed from a global perspective.[1]

In this chapter we briefly discuss the dynamics of the economic environment in general, in terms of such aspects as the product life cycle for the firm, the business cycle in the overall economy, the phenomena of inflation and exchange rate restrictions, and the role of national governments in the supervision of business. We then focus on the institutional aspects of business, both internal, such as the structure and organization of firms, and external, such as corporate and individual income taxes. Finally, we review the salient characteristics of financial markets in general, and provide an overview of the U.S. financial markets.

II. THE ECONOMIC ENVIRONMENT OF THE FIRM

The business condition within which firms operate changes constantly, making it both more difficult and more challenging for financial managers to gather information, implement decisions, monitor their impact, and revise decisions in accord with new expectations. Partly, the changing economic conditions are generated internally by the firm and its products as they go through phases of development that resemble a biological life cycle—here called the product life cycle, or the firm life cycle, or the industry life cycle. Other changes are generated by the ebbs and flows of economic activity, represented by the more standard stages of recovery, prosperity, recession, and depression.

Expansions and contractions in economic activity are inherent in economic systems—more so in the Western-type, free-enterprise-based, market systems—and affect different economies and their sectors at different rates. Such cycles are caused by chronic imbalances in aggregate demand and supply that originate internally or externally to the economy and can derive from sources that are economic or noneconomic. Sometimes, these noneconomic origins can be traced to shifts in government fiscal policies or in central bank monetary policies. Sometimes, the imbalances between demand and supply manifest themselves in the form of severe inflation, the chronic presence and systematic pervasiveness of which have wrought havoc on western economies in the 1970s, and have brought the economies of the less-developed and developing nations to their knees.

A. Product Life Cycle and Firm Life Cycle[2]

Products and services evolve through phases that are generally called life cycles. That is, products and services begin with an infancy or pioneering phase, then, if successful, move on to an expansion phase, continue to a maturity phase, and end up at a stagnation or decay phase. Because each product is associated with revenues and costs, the flow of revenues more or less reflects the phases of the product or service life cycle. For example, at the early pioneering phase, revenues flow into the firm at an increasing rate and continue at this rate until about one-third into the expansion phase, when the rate of flow now increases at a decreasing rate. This rate of revenue flow continues until the product or service cycle reaches the middle of the maturity phase, when the flow of revenues starts decreasing in absolute terms and continues to do so throughout the stagnation stage, as shown in Figure 3.1.

FIGURE 3.1 Firm Life Cycle

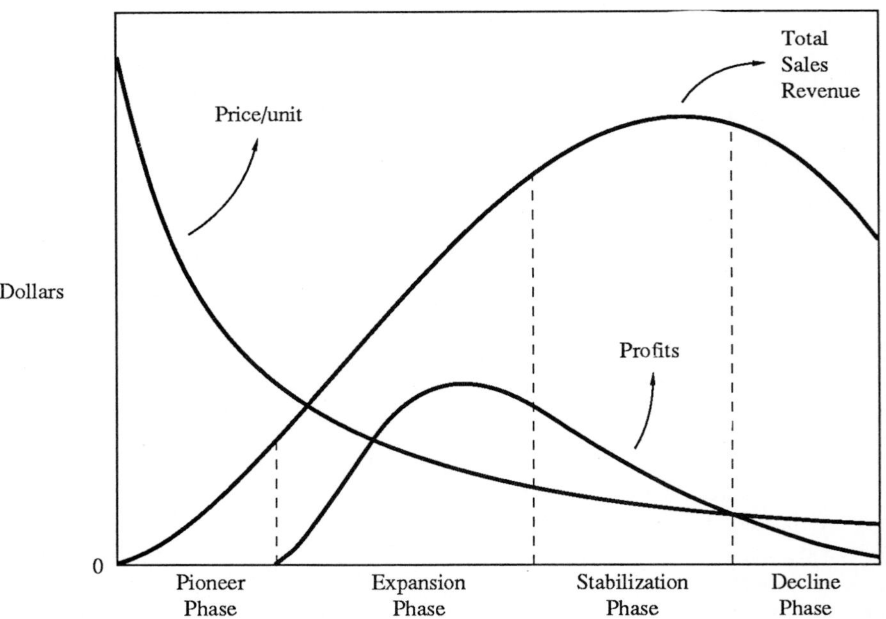

As is expected, total costs (both fixed and variable) at the early phases of a product or service are higher than total revenues. However, near the end of the pioneering phase, total revenues and total costs reach the break-even stage, marking the beginning of profits for the firm. Profits continue to increase until about two-thirds into the expansion phase, when they begin to decline and eventually become negative in the early phases of the stagnation phase.

What is really of importance to us at this point is that the production of commodities and services requires the purchase of plant, equipment, raw materials, labor, and other inputs. Purchases of productive facilities fall under the overall heading of *capital budgeting,* while the decisions to seek specific sources of financing fall under the broad heading of *capital financing*. Now, from the point of view of financial decision making and management, the firm is a collection of revenues and costs or cash flows, so to speak. Hence, if these cash flows move in accordance with the life cycles of their underlying products or services, the job of the financial managers becomes both difficult and challenging. That is, they must continually match cash flows from products and services at the pioneering phase with the respective cash flows of products at the expansion, maturity, and stagnation phases. And, given the dynamic nature of business developments, financial managers must also match the cash flows with the sources of financing and their repayment schedules.

Hence, the concept of product life cycle becomes a significant input in the decision-making process of financial managers. Needless to say, some products have very short life cycles, while others have very long life cycles, and the totality of them makes for the sum of the firm's cash flows. Moreover, the aggregation of life cycles of products at the level of the firm depicts the *firm life cycle,* while a higher level aggregation generates *industry life cycles*.

B. The Business Cycle

The business cycle refers to the external economic conditions and pressures that affect the firm's revenues and costs. These pressures can originate with weather conditions, such as the effects of a drought on agricultural production, or with changes in monetary or fiscal policies intended to curtail or enhance domestic aggregate demand. For smaller developing countries with export-oriented economies based on few exportable resources, business cycles are typically transmitted from the outside world. For example, a recession in the industrialized world will limit their imports of both raw materials (such as copper) and other products from the developing countries. Sometimes, these business cycles may also be imposed by unusual conditions much like those emanating from the world debt crisis.

It is customary to classify the business cycle in terms of four stages—recovery, prosperity, recession, and depression, as shown in Figure 3.2. Each of these phases has significant implications for financial decision making and forces financial managers to adjust their capital budgeting and financing decisions both in terms of timing and in terms of magnitude. More importantly, the presence of the business cycle encourages financial managers to attempt to forecast future economic conditions so that they can prepare financial scenaria in advance.

C. Inflationary Conditions

Inflation refers to the erosion of purchasing power of the local currency in the country where the firm operates. It is an old economic phenomenon the destructive effects of which have played havoc in the economies of the world, with particularly unpleasant consequences in the countries of the developing world. Inflation affects all of the factors of production—land, labor, plant, machinery, raw materials—and of course it distorts the cost and availability of funds in the financial markets. Inflation considerations play a very important role in financial decisions. Indeed, it is not only the magnitude of inflation that is significant in financial management, but also the uncertainty about the future changes in a currency's purchasing power.

FIGURE 3.2 Phases of the Business Cycle

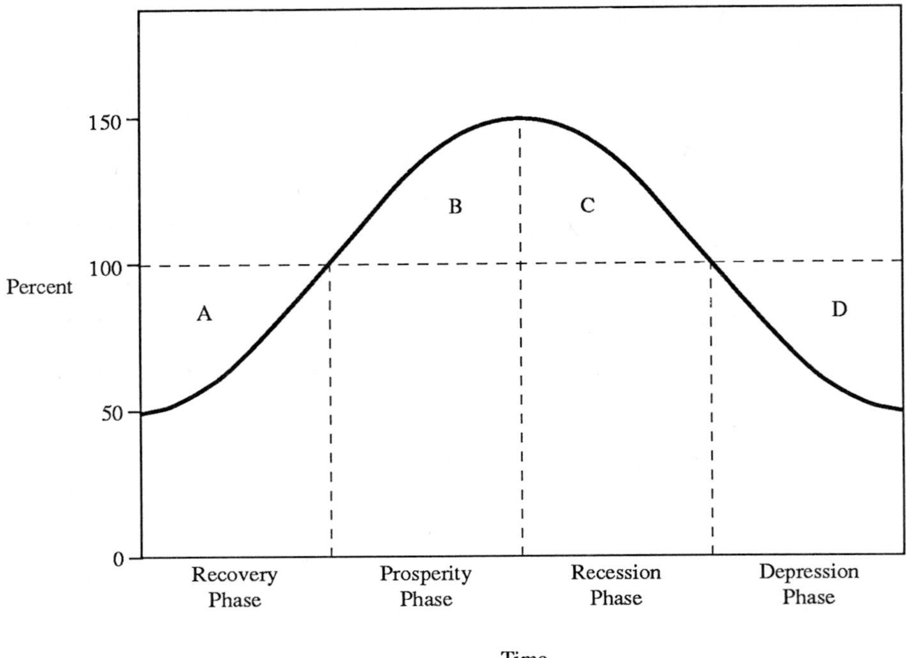

D. Currency Fluctuations

Prices of goods and services of all types are defined in units of a given currency. Because similar commodities or services are traded more or less on an international scale, we find it convenient to convert one currency to another. This can be done either directly, say from Chilean pesos to Japanese yen, or indirectly where both the Chilean pesos and the Japanese yen are expressed in terms of a common denominator, say the U.S. dollar. Thus, we establish an exchange rate that defines the value of one currency in relation to another currency; and, hence, we obtain the value of a commodity in the home market in relation to its value in the currency of another country's market.

Because exchange rates are relative prices, they, like other prices, fluctuate through the actions of buyers and sellers, who take positions to reflect changing expectations about economic conditions in various countries. Because financial managers purchase raw materials and other factors of production from other countries and export many of their firms' products and services to other countries, they are subjected to considerable amounts of exchange rate risk. Thus, exchange rate risk becomes another significant factor in the financial decision-making process, as witnessed by the debates in the U.S. over our trade policies with strong-currency countries like Japan and West Germany.

E. Government Policies

The economic environment of the firm also contains another factor—a nonmarket factor in this case—that plays a significant role in financial decision making. Here we refer to government and its policies vis-à-vis business enterprises and their operations. The government of every country is a major consumer of goods and services, thus affecting conditions of demand, supply, and, of course, relative prices. Governmental policies about corporate and individual taxes affect the net incomes of firms, while monetary policies affect the availability and cost of funds in both local and in foreign currencies. Hence, governmental policies must enter into financial decision making as another significant input.

III. THE OPERATING ENVIRONMENT OF THE FIRM

We have already discussed briefly the economic, or external dynamic environment that surrounds the firm. It is now time to look at the internal dynamics that define the nature and scope of the business enterprise, such as the structure of the business organization. In addition to this, we will spend some time in this section outlining the institutional constraints imposed by corporate and individual tax structures.

A. The Structure of the Business Organization

Generally speaking, there are three broad forms of business organization, namely, the individual proprietorship, the partnership, and the corporate structure.

The *individual proprietorship,* which represents the majority of firms throughout the world, consists of a simple organization with one owner. It is representative of small entities like hardware stores or professional businesses, such as business consultants. Given the small size of the organization and its sole ownership, there are certain advantages and disadvantages associated with this type of business structure. To begin with, the owner of this firm can establish it rather easily and enjoy a large degree of managerial control over both the long-range plans and the operational aspects of the enterprise. As such, the owner-manager can make direct and immediate decisions regarding such things as desired rates of growth, locational changes, marketing strategies, and, of course, amounts of earnings that should be retained and plowed back into the firm for future operations.

Along with the above advantages come several disadvantages. First, the individual ownership form of business places an unlimited liability on the owner-manager for all the losses of the firm. It also limits the sources and scale of financing opportunities available, while it forces all business borrowing to be collateralized by the business and private assets of the owner. Other disadvantages are the lack of continuity in the event the owner dies, and the limited amount of time available for planning due to the strains of daily operational responsibilities. Finally, there is one aspect that can be a disadvantage under some circumstances. It refers to the tax aspects of the private, individual ownership. Owners of individual proprietorship generally pay taxes at the individual income tax rates that may be in some cases higher than those paid by other types of business subject to direct business earnings taxes.

The *partnership* refers to the business organization that has two or more owners or partners. It can be a standard or general partnership, where each partner has unlimited liability, or a limited partnership, where at least one partner has unlimited liability while the other "silent" partners have limited liability. The latter group of partners do not participate in the management of the firm and act more or less like passive investors in the enterprise. In addition to the partnership arrangements of individuals, firms form partnerships for specific purposes. Such partnerships take the form of joint ventures or syndicates among business firms. Among the advantages of partnerships are the ease with which they can be established, the joint control, and the greater ease of obtaining capital compared to a sole proprietorship. The disadvantages are primarily the unlimited liability and the lack of managerial continuity in the event of catastrophic circumstances.

The *corporate form of organization* is by far the most efficient and market-oriented type of business structure. It allows for the separation of ownership and management control, provides for continuity of management responsibility and control, encourages managerial specialization, expands the opportunities for financial sourcing, and affords limited liability to its shareholders or investors. Corporations are the fewest units in every national economy, but their economic strength is such that they represent a substantial part of national wealth.

There are several types of corporate forms. Some are *nonprofit* corporations like foundations, while others are *for-profit* corporations, for example, the well-known economic giants that exist in every country. Both types of corporations can be private or public—the latter being the type of firm with shares traded in a country's stock exchange. Corporations, particularly for-profit ones, issue two types of shares of stock to their investors. The first one is known as *preferred stock,* which typically entitles the owner to a contractual dividend payment and may be voting or nonvoting. The second one is known as *common stock* and entitles the owner to the net profits of the corporation, some of which may be distributed while the remaining are retained for reinvestment. Common stock is typically voting, although there are examples of nonvoting common stock. Corporations also raise debt or borrow long-term capital by issuing debt obligations, known as bonds, that can also be traded in stock or bond markets.[3]

Technically, the voting shareholders of the firm control the long-term activities of the corporation through their ballots during the annual meetings. However, given the realities of separation in ownership and control, true control for operating and strategic purposes lies with the management and the boards of directors that are legally responsible for the corporations.

It is evident that the corporate form of organization has the advantages of limited liability, continuity, liquidity of investment, and management pooling of human resources. However, this form also has it disadvantages, in the sense that large corporations may not be sensitive to the wishes of individual shareholders or sometimes to society at large. Moreover, tax rates on the income of small corporations may be larger in some countries than average tax rates on personal income.

B. Corporate and Personal Income Taxes

Corporate tax rates are the province of national governments, and, hence, differ from country to country. For example, some countries tax a small amount of corporate earnings at a low flat rate and the remaining earnings at a higher flat rate or perhaps a progressive corporate income-tax rate. Other countries tax all corporate earnings at the same rate structure that may be fixed or variable. Some countries, like the U.S., tax corporate income earned at the corporate rate and then the earnings distributed as dividends to shareholders at the individual tax rates. This multiple form of taxation can be particularly vexing for multinational corporations, whose tax payments in host countries may or may not be counted toward taxes owed in the home country.

Still another aspect of corporate taxation arises with respect to the effects of inflation upon the asset values of the firm. For example, most countries allow for some form of adjustment on the prices of inventory items, thus allowing for reductions in corporate income and taxes. Similarly, some countries allow for inflation adjustments or indexation of the values of most corporate assets except land, with corresponding reductions in taxable income.[4]

Other aspects of taxation focus on the individual tax rates in various national jurisdictions. In some countries, personal income-tax rates are progressive and vary directly with a person's income up to some maximum rate. In other countries, these tax rates are fixed and flat, while in some nations there exists an *ad valorem* tax system based on a value added system.[5] We cannot go into details about these tax issues in this volume, as we are interested primarily in the effects of corporate and personal taxes upon the financial decisions of the firm. Remember that the objective of financial decision making is the maximization of shareholder wealth, and this is achieved by maximizing the after-tax cash flows from the asset base of the firm. Hence, corporate and personal income taxes are significant factors in financial decisions.

C. The Tax Reform Act of 1986 (TRA)

The rules and regulations by which individuals and corporations pay taxes in the U.S. were significantly altered with the passage of the TRA. The changes generally involved a reduction in the level of both corporate and personal income tax rates and in the number of different tax brackets as well. For example, prior to 1987 there were 15 different individual tax brackets with rates ranging from 11% to 50%. Under the new law, there are only two brackets with rates of 15% and 28%. The maximum corporate rate was reduced from 46% to 34%. The TRA also reduced the number and amounts of deductions that may be claimed. For example, the investment tax credit for corporations was eliminated, and allowable depreciation deductions were reduced. Also, the 85% exclusion of dividend income to corporations was lowered to 80%; that is, corporations now pay tax on 20% of dividend income received from other firms. Another significant change was the elimination of the distinction between ordinary income and capital gains income. Prior to 1987, they were taxed at different rates. Now, all income is taxed at the ordinary income rates.

1. Corporate Taxes

The TRA provides for the following tax rates on ordinary income of corporations:

15% on the first $50,000
25% on the next $25,000
34% on the amount in excess of $75,000

Furthermore, those firms with taxable income over $100,000 must pay an additional amount over that calculated from the above schedule of rates. The additional amount is the lesser of $11,750 or 5% of taxable income over $100,000. For example, suppose the ABC Company had taxable income of $300,000 in 1988. Its tax bill for the year would be

15% × $ 50,000	=	$ 7,500
25% × $ 25,000	=	6,250
34% × $225,000	=	76,500
		90,250
5% × $200,000	=	10,000
Total Taxes		$100,250

ABC's average tax rate, then, is 33.4% (= $100,250/$300,000).

The *marginal tax rate,* in contrast to the average tax rate, is that rate applied to additional taxable income. Marginal rates are 15% for income less than or equal to $50,000, 25% for income between $50,000 and $75,000, 34% between $75,000 and $100,000, 39% between $100,000 and $335,000, and 34% over $335,000.

Two other significant features of the TRA are the elimination of the investment tax credit and the calculation of an alternative minimum tax (AMT). Firms typically maintain two types of records: one set for the I.R.S. and one for reporting to shareholders. The income calculations will differ to the extent that, for example, accelerated depreciation methods are used for tax purposes while straight-line depreciation is used for reporting. The AMT requires that firms pay a tax equal to 20% of one-half the difference between the two income figures, and the AMT must be paid if its total is more than the regular tax of 34%. For example, suppose the DIP Corporation reports taxable income to the I.R.S. of $2 million and to its shareholders an income of $4 million (see Panel A on top of next page). Under the regular method, its tax bill would be $680,000. The AMT would be equal to 20% of $1,000,000, or $200,000, and thus would not take effect. But if DIP reports income of, say, $10 million to its shareholders (see Panel B on top of next page), the AMT would be $800,000 and this amount would be payable instead of the $680,000. A more complete treatment of corporate taxes is deferred to Chapter 12.

2. Personal Taxes

The TRA provides for the following tax rates on the ordinary income of single individuals as of 1988:

15% on the first $17,850
28% on income of $17,851 to $43,150
33% on income of $43,150 to $100,480, and
28% on income in excess of $100,480.

For years subsequent to 1988, the cutoff points for the 28% income tax rate will be indexed for inflation, so that the brackets will be different from those reported above.

DIP Corporation

Panel A.	*Annual Report*	*Tax Return*
Taxable Income[1]	$ 4,000,000	$2,000,000
Taxes[2]		680,000
AMT[3]	$ 200,000	
Taxes Payable		$ 680,000

Panel B.	*Annual Report*	*Tax Return*
Taxable Income	$10,000,000	$2,000,000
Taxes		680,000
AMT	$ 800,000	
Taxes Payable	$ 800,000	

[1]DIP Corporation uses accelerated depreciation for purposes of calculating its tax bill and straight-line depreciation for reporting to stockholders.

[2]Taxes = (.15)(50,000) + (.25)(25,000) + .34(2,000,000 − 75,000) + 11,750 = $680,000.

[3]AMT = .20(4,000,000 − 2,000,000)(.5) = $200,000.

IV. FINANCIAL MARKETS

A. Wealth and Capital Formation

The economic wealth of a firm can be measured by the market value of its accumulated wealth, and by the rate at which this wealth grows through the reinvestment of retained earnings and other external sources of funds. In the same vein, the economic wealth of a nation can be measured by the value of its accumulated wealth and by its rate of growth through the reinvestment of its aggregate savings. As with the case of a firm, a nation's wealth includes its net assets—both domestic and international. These consist of productive capital or capital goods that include land, buildings, equipment, and inventories, and, in many countries, residential housing because it is thought to produce a service. Claims to assets—such as stocks, bonds, and other financial assets are not considered economic capital, because their inclusion will induce double counting of both the underlying assets and their financial claims. Also excluded from national wealth are consumer durable goods.

In primitive societies, the savers and users of capital were basically the same individuals, with the exception of some minor barter exchanges of capital goods for consumer goods. In this type of environment, there was no need for financing and financial markets. However, in modern economies, the barter system of exchange has given way to instruments representing money and claims to money that accommodate specialization of functions, the division of labor, as well as the transfer of savings from the surplus units (savers) to the deficit units (borrowers). In this type of environment, the formation of capital is achieved through a complicated structure of financial institutions. Granted, some surplus units make direct investments, as in the case of a family using its savings to purchase a home or of a business using its productive capacity. However, the majority of family, business, and government savings is transferred through financial institutions, such as commercial and savings banks, insurance companies, mutual funds, and other such entities in modern financial markets. Indeed, the existence of financial markets and their respective institutional frameworks make the formation of capital possible. Diagrammatic representations of the above framework are given in Figures 3.3 and 3.4.

Technically speaking, when we speak of capital markets, we do not refer to the markets where the physical or economic assets them-

FIGURE 3.3 Direct and Intermediated Transfers of Funds Within a National Financial System

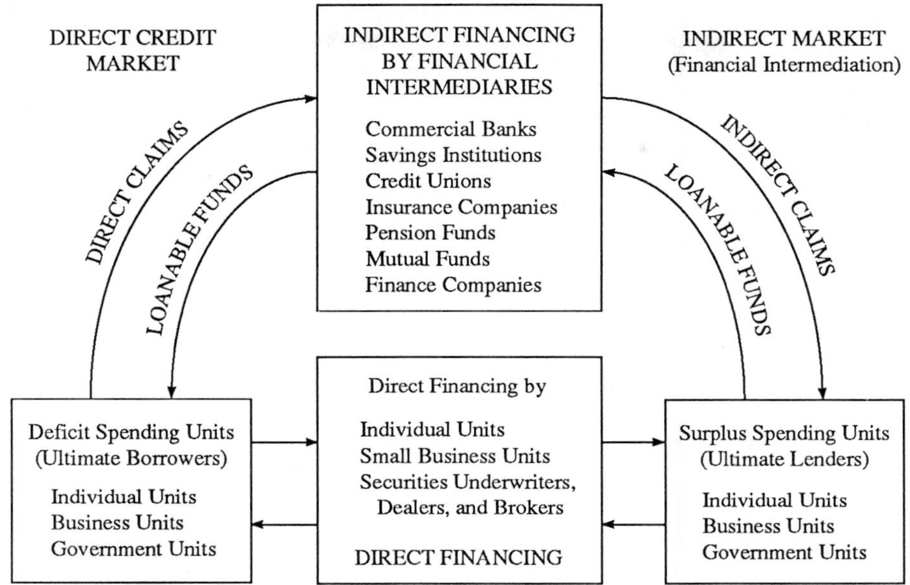

selves are bought and sold. Rather, we refer to the agglomeration of markets for the dollar, yen, peso, or other national currency instruments that represent either a title or a claim to economic capital (or physical assets) and to other resources owned by individuals, firms, and governments. In effect, we can differentiate the terms of economic capital, financial capital, and

FIGURE 3.4 Simplified Framework of National and International Financial Markets

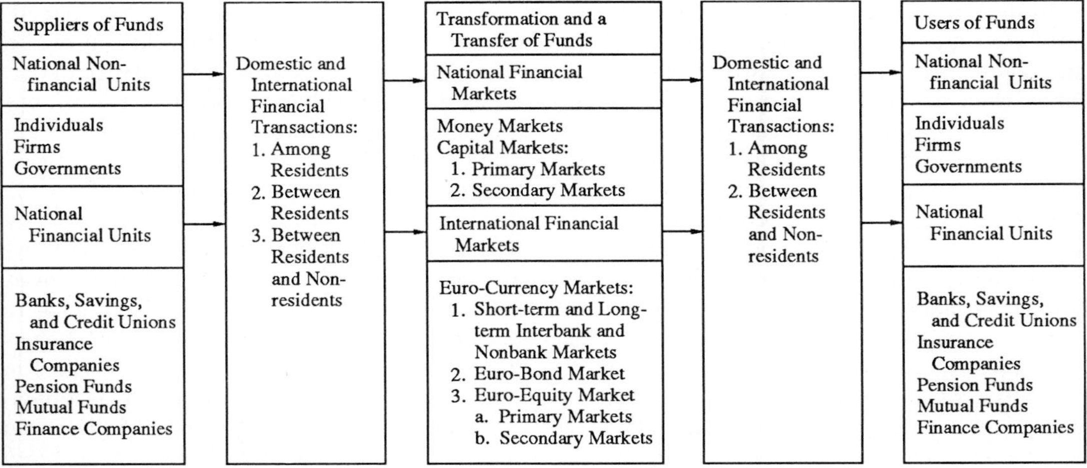

capital markets as follows:

Economic capital represents assets of a more or less permanent nature.

Financial capital, or capital, refers to the money value of the various instruments of ownership and long-term claims to assets.

Capital markets are the markets where these instruments are first issued and then traded. Because some instruments are of short-term nature (one year or less) and others are of longer duration, we refer to the markets where the short-term instruments are transferred as *money markets* and to those where long-term instruments are transferred as *capital markets*.

B. Money and Capital Markets

Money markets facilitate the fast and reliable transfer of short-term financial instruments used in financing the needs of consumers, businesses, and governments. Technically speaking, there are two types of money markets. The first type is found where local banks and other financial institutions provide direct, negotiated financing to their customers who are typically located within the radius of business of such institutions. This type of direct money market includes the cases where local banks funnel funds to their corresponding banks in the big money center banks of a country or perhaps the world.

The second type of money market is a rather open and impersonal network found in the larger money centers of New York, London, Tokyo, and other major cities of the world, where idle funds from a country or many countries are transferred through financial intermediaries such as a nation's central bank, big commercial banks, and dealers of government securities. The suppliers of funds for this open money market are central banks, commercial banks, corporations with idle short-term funds, insurance companies, foreign banks, finance companies, and individuals, whose sole purpose is to invest funds on a safe, liquid, gainful, short-term basis.

Unlike the money markets that specialize in financing investments with a duration of one year or less, the capital markets facilitate the financing of investments of intermediate maturity (up to 10 years) and of long-term maturity (up to 30 years). Capital markets consist of the complex of institutions, mechanisms, and regulations where intermediate and long-term funds are pooled and supplied to various deficit units, and where financial instruments already outstanding are transferred. Also, like their money market counterparts, capital markets can be local, regional, national, or international.

C. The Functions of Capital Markets

Capital markets in private property economies fulfill two fundamental economic functions. The first function is the allocation of the flow of current savings in an economy among users and projects. This is a critical function because saving is, to a large extent, separated from real investment due to the existing differences in preferences and opportunities among market participants. Generally speaking, because households are surplus spending units, they provide a large percentage of net savings, while businesses, being deficit spending units, provide a significant proportion of net real investment through deficit financing.

The second function served by capital markets is the facilitation of transfers in the ownership and control of the stock of existing assets among the various wealthholding units in the economy. The transferring function is further supported by the asset transformation function for both tangible and financial assets. Indeed, the very existence of capital markets provides the financial manager with the challenge of acting as the intermediary between the firm's operations and the market where its securities are either traded directly or evaluated indirectly.

A simple schematic of the intermediary role played by the financial manager is portrayed by Figure 3.5. This diagram follows the cash flows that originate with the investors in the firm as well as the return route from the firm back to its investors. Notice that the flow of cash begins at the time the corporation issues securities in the market in order to raise funds. This dimension is shown by line (*a*) in Figure 3.5. The cash funds are then utilized through the intermediary

FIGURE 3.5 The Role of the Financial Manager as an Intermediary between the Corporation and the Capital Market

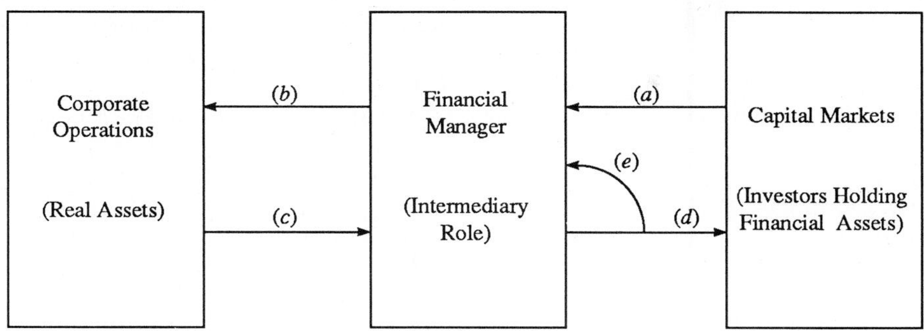

role of the financial manager and are transformed into the real assets that fuel the operations of the business concern, as shown by line (*b*). These real assets eventually generate cash inflows that are set aside for repayment of the original investment, as per line (*c*). Finally, the cash that has been delineated in (*c*) must be reinvested [line (*e*)] or returned to the original investors [line (*d*)].

Thus, the financing decision requires an understanding of capital markets, and, as we have already discussed, so does the investment decision. Hence, capital markets are basic to both the investment decision and the financing decision and provide the framework for valuing financial assets. Now, because financial assets facilitate the operations of the firm, the value of these assets reflects in some indirect way the value of the business enterprise. Finally, as all operations are embedded in time and their outcomes depend on the uncertainty associated with each course of action, we can see how the capital markets provide an institutional exchange framework for resolving business uncertainty over time.

V. U.S. FINANCIAL MARKETS AND INSTITUTIONS

A. Financial Markets and Economic Performance

In the broadest sense, financial markets are any "place" where securities are bought and sold. In fact, many financial markets operate by a network of telephone lines and computers connecting the various participants. The Over-the-Counter (OTC) market for unlisted securities is a good example of this. Others, like the New York Stock Exchange (NYSE) and the American Stock Exchange (AMEX), actually have a physical location and trading floor on which to execute trades.

There are several common ways to classify financial markets. One is according to the *type of securities traded* in the market. New securities being offered for the first time are traded in the *primary market*. Underwriters or investment bankers act as wholesalers that bring sellers and buyers together thereby creating a market. Investment bankers normally buy the new issue from the originator with the intention of reselling it to the public at a higher price. The spread between what they pay for the issue and sell it for is the compensation for their services.

Once securities are purchased by the investing public, they can be further traded in the *secondary market*. This market consists of two segments: the organized exchanges and the OTC market. Organized exchanges have physical locations in buildings where stocks listed on the exchange can be traded using an auction process. There are several organized security exchanges in the United States, and the two largest are the NYSE and the AMEX. These two exchanges dominate the industry by accounting for over 90 percent of the total trading volume. The remaining exchanges are small regional exchanges like the Philadelphia-Baltimore-Washington Exchange with low volume that concentrates on local issues. Each exchange has its own listing requirement with the NYSE being the most stringent.

In strict contrast to the organized exchanges is the OTC market. As we noted in the beginning of this section, the OTC market conducts business through a vast network of telephone lines and computer terminals. Bid and ask prices are matched with the help of a central computer in Connecticut. Unlike the exchanges, the OTC market specializes in stocks not listed on any exchange. With the exception of the NYSE, more securities are traded in the OTC market than on other organized exchanges.

Another way to classify financial markets is according to *how the securities are traded*. Over the last twenty years, two other markets have emerged. In the *third market* institutions trade large blocks of securities with each other through the intermediation of broker-dealers. In the *fourth market,* institutions trade with each other without the services of broker-dealers. Both of these markets allow institutions to trade listed stocks off the exchange floor at reduced transaction costs.[6]

Yet another way to classify financial markets is by the *maturity of securities traded*. Short-term securities with maturities of one year or less are traded in the *money market*. Characteristics of securities traded in this market are summarized in Table 3.1, which presents such instruments as Treasury bills, banker's acceptances, repurchase agreements, negotiable Certificates of Deposit (CDs), and commercial paper. *Treasury bills* are short-term government obligations that serve as a benchmark for liquidity and safety. *Banker's acceptances* are a special security used to facilitate international trade. The role of the international banks in these transactions is to guarantee payment or receive payment for their

TABLE 3.1 Characteristics of Short-Term Money Market Instruments

Instrument	*Denominations($)*	*Maturities*	*Basis*	*Liquidity*
1) U.S. Treasury Bills	10,000 15,000 50,000 100,000 500,000 1,000,000	91 days 182 days 365 days	Discount	Excellent secondary market
2) Federal Agency Securities	From 1,000 to 1,000,000	5 days to 10 years	Discount or coupon	Good for major agencies
3) Banker's Acceptances	25,000 to 1,000,000	30 to 180 days	Discount	Good for large banks
4) Negotiable Certificates of Deposit	25,000 to 10,000,000	1 to 18 months	Accrued interest	Fair to good
5) Commercial Paper	25,000 to 5,000,000	3 to 270 days	Discount	Poor—no active secondary market
6) Repurchase Agreements	500,000 or more	Fixed under contract	N/A	Fixed under contract
7) Money Market Mutual Funds	1,000 or more	May be sold at any time	Net asset value	Excellent—funds will buy shares

clients. Banker's acceptances, then, are used to finance transactions in the money market. *Repurchase agreements* are a means of collecting money on certain securities (usually U.S. Treasury obligations) by "selling" the securities to a bank for a specified sum. In this type of transaction, the original seller signs a repurchase agreement with the bank to buy back the securities within a short period of time for a certain sum. Thus, in many respects, the transaction is similar to a loan with the securities as collateral. For its services, the bank will receive a fee by selling the securities back at a slightly lower fee than it paid for them. *Negotiable CDs* are large, time deposits issued by financial institutions that can be traded in the secondary market. They are negotiable and can be sold to other investors who redeem them at maturity without penalty. Finally, *commercial paper* is issued by corporations as a source of short-term funding. Like the other money market instruments, they can be traded in the marketplace.

In addition to money markets, there are also *capital markets* for securities with maturities greater than one year. This market and its securities will be discussed in detail in appendix 9A.

Regardless of the particular classification of financial markets, the question often arises as to how we should measure the economic performance of any given market. The criterion employed for this purpose requires that we test the *allocational efficiency* of the market. That is, we attempt to determine how closely the market comes to optimally allocating resources (funds) at any given point in time between lenders and borrowers. In perfectly competitive markets, the yield on different financial assets should differ only with respect to risk and maturity. Thus, the presence of *yield differentials* among homogeneous assets would indicate inefficiencies or imperfections in the market.

B. Financial Institutions

Financial institutions provide an important service by bringing the suppliers and demanders of funds together. The process of financial intermediation is accomplished through the issuance of financial securities by a host of complex institutions. This activity improves the efficiency of the financial markets through the optimal employment of scarce resources. This section will introduce the various types of financial institutions and the role each plays in the economy.

1. Depository Institutions

Depository institutions share a common characteristic of accepting deposit funds from savers. Because they have a fiduciary responsibility to depositors, these institutions are closely regulated by government agencies at the federal and state level.[7] These agencies impose restrictions over many of the institutional activities of depository institutions. Regulations restrict the types of investments depository institutions may hold in their portfolios. For example, these institutions are generally prohibited from investing in common or preferred stocks.

The largest group of depository institutions is *commercial banks* (CBs), which may be chartered as national or state banks. Most banks are insured up to $100,000 per account by the Federal Deposit Insurance Corporation, a government agency. The traditional role of commercial banks was to supply short-term funds to individuals, businesses, and government. However, in recent years, they have become department stores for many financial services including long-term lending, credit cards, mortgages, and other related operations.

Savings and Loan Associations (S&Ls) are the second largest group of depository institutions. In today's deregulated environment, S&Ls perform under conditions that bear many similarities with their sister institutions in the commercial banking sector. They may also be chartered at the federal or state level and their deposits are insured by the Federal Savings and Loan Insurance Corporation (FSLIC). Most regulatory control rests with the Federal Home Loan Bank Board (a Federal Reserve counterpart), the FSLIC, and state agencies.[8]

Mutual savings banks (MSBs) are the third group of depository institutions. Although they often have "bank" in their names, they are more closely related to S&Ls than banks. Almost all

MSBs are found in the northeastern portion of the United States where they originated in the 1850s. Charters are provided only at the state level so that each state has sole regulatory control over MSBs within its boundaries. As mutual associations, they are unique in that they may become members of either the Federal Reserve System (FRS) or the Federal Home Loan Bank System for S&Ls. In addition, many are insured by the FDIC, FSLIC, or state insurance systems.

The last group of depository institutions is *credit unions*. They were created as mutual organizations designed to serve the short-term consumer credit needs of members, who are generally required to belong to some specified group with some common relationship. For example, most credit unions are organized to serve the employees of a particular company or industry.

2. Nondepository Institutions

In addition to financial institutions that accept deposits from customers, there are other intermediaries that also channel savings into investment markets. Some of these institutions will be discussed in this section.

The oldest group of nondepository financial intermediaries is *life insurance companies*. Although there are many types of insurance policies (e.g., life, accident, fire), all represent conditional claims against the insurer to be paid if a certain condition occurs. Thus, insurance policies are a form of secondary financial asset. Policyholders pay premiums to insure against a particular risk of financial loss. In essence, the insured is exchanging a large uncertain loss for a smaller certain loss (premium) payable every year. The potential financial loss tends to be large relative to the asset base of the policyholder.

By diversifying, insurance companies reduce their exposure to future losses. Certain insurance policies have a "savings" element attached to them. For example, whole-life insurance policies and annuities have cash surrender values that may be withdrawn or borrowed against by the insured. They generally earn dividends if these amounts remain with the insurance company. In its role as a financial intermediary, the insurer will invest its reserves in a portfolio of bonds and equities.

Investment companies (also known as mutual funds) form another group of nondepository institutions. They offer investors a wide range of programs and objectives. Some mutual funds deal exclusively in common stocks (growth funds) while others specialize in bonds (income funds). Balanced funds flourish for investors desiring the potential growth of common stocks plus the income from bonds. Regardless of the particular program or objective, these funds serve as financial intermediaries through the issuance of their own shares (secondary financial assets). Funds are then reinvested by these institutions into the money and capital markets.

There is one other type of nondepository institution that deserves special mention due to its immense impact on the economy. Almost every American worker has some savings in the form of *pension* or *retirement funds*. Most retirement plans receive contributions from employers who continue "funding" the plan during its existence. Employees acquire vested rights to the funds credited to their accounts over a period of working years. After a given period of time (often five years), an employee becomes "fully vested." This means the employee has nonforfeitable rights to all of the money in his or her account plus income thereon upon retirement or death.

In this way, pension plans serve as forced savings for retirement. During working years, employees' funds are managed for their benefit by a trustee who invests the funds in a multitude of investments. To encourage retirement plans, Congress passed a number of favorable tax laws. Employers are allowed to deduct contributions to the plans while employees are not taxed on them until the money is withdrawn. This allows the retirement funds to accumulate at a faster tax-free rate. Thus, retirement plans are an important financial intermediary between savers and the financial markets.

C. Primary Financial Assets

Unlike real or tangible assets, financial assets represent claims against future income or wealth. They are easily distinguished from real assets because they do not provide the holder with physical services, but offer a store of value and a possible return in the future.

Financial assets exist in the economy because individuals and businesses desire to adjust their patterns of intertemporal consumption. Some people may wish to save portions of their current incomes in order to consume more goods in later years. Others may desire to consume more goods and services than their current incomes would allow. The obvious solution is for the savers to loan the money to those who wish to consume more at the present time. Such transactions between lenders and borrowers typically involve the use of financial assets.

For every financial asset, there is also a financial liability. The lender of the funds receives the financial asset as evidence of a claim against the borrower's future income or wealth. Through the issuance of a primary security, borrowers acknowledge a financial liability in the amount borrowed plus interest to induce lenders to make the loan and compensate them for any risk of default.

Although the above discussion is a simplification of the real world, it is useful because it demonstrates the concept of a primary financial asset or primary security. A *primary financial asset* is created by a direct flow of funds between lenders and borrowers whose major economic activity is the buying and selling of various factors of production or output. This differs from *secondary financial assets* which involve the indirect flow of funds between lenders and borrowers. In the latter case, financial institutions specializing in trading financial assets act as intermediaries between buyers and sellers.

There are a wide variety of financial assets available in the financial markets. They may be classified into two major groups—debt (bonds & notes) and equity (stocks). A *debt* instrument represents a promissory note to repay the principal sum plus any stated interest over some specified period of time. Generally, the principal is returned at the end of the period and the interest is paid periodically over the life of the asset.

Equity represents an ownership claim that is quite different from debt. One important distinction is that equity-holders have a lower priority claim to the assets of the firm during liquidation. This means that debtholders will always be paid first during liquidations and must receive their principal and accrued interest prior to the stockholders' receiving a distribution. The debtholders' preferred status for the distribution of funds is often called the "me-first" rule.

The classification of a security as a primary financial asset is not always clear. Any classification is somewhat ambiguous and borderline cases sometimes occur. Some entities conduct both financial and nonfinancial activities. For example, securities of certain government agencies are particularly hard to classify in that the funds may be used to purchase both goods and financial assets.

D. Financial Intermediation and Secondary Financial Assets

As we indicated in the previous section, it is also possible to have an indirect transfer of funds between the lender and borrower. Under this arrangement, financial intermediaries play a significant role. By specializing in the buying and selling of financial assets, financial institutions act as intermediaries between the ultimate lenders and borrowers.

To accomplish an indirect transfer of funds, financial intermediaries issue their own financial claims. These financial claims are called *secondary financial assets* (or liabilities). Intermediation differs from the process described under primary securities in that nonfinancial borrowers do not issue securities directly to the ultimate lender. Instead, the borrower's financial claims are purchased by a financial intermediary which then issues another financial claim in its own name. Thus, the lender of the funds receives a financial asset against the financial institution rather than the borrower.

The existence of a nexus of financial institutions in an economy has several important implications. *First,* financial institutions have the ability to transform primary financial assets of uncertain value and poor liquidity into secondary financial assets with certain values and high liquidity. This benefits the lender through risk reduction and greater convenience. *Second,* the cost of raising funds for borrowers is significantly reduced through large block purchases of primary securities by financial institutions. There is a fixed cost element to the trading of financial assets that implies an inverse relationship between exchange costs and the value of the transaction. With large asset bases and a high volume of transactions, financial intermediaries have a trading advantage over individual traders. They can spread their fixed costs over a large number of transactions for greater economies of scale.

Third, due to exchange costs, primary securities are imperfectly divisible. This implies that lenders may not be able to achieve optimal diversification without large funds. Thus, risk reduction through diversification may be limited for individual lenders. This same restriction would generally not be applicable for financial institutions which possess greater resources. *Fourth,* there is no reason to believe that the primary security most attractive to lenders would be the same one preferred by the borrowers. With the large variety of securities in existence, it is possible that both parties would find another security more beneficial. This could lead to suboptimal operations if financial institutions did not enter the market to "repackage" the securities into the one desired by both groups. *Finally,* in any economy, there are always small lenders who have neither sufficient funds nor the technical expertise to purchase primary assets on their own accord. However, they can easily afford the smaller denominations of most secondary securities with little risk of loss. This will greatly benefit the whole economy by maximum employment of scarce resources (capital).

VI. SUMMARY AND REVIEW

Chapter 3 has dealt with the economic and financial environments in which the firm operates. Beginning with some universal perspectives in Section I, we then focused our attention in Section II on the economic environment of the firm and discussed such aspects as product life cycle, the business cycle, inflation, currency fluctuations and government policies. In Section III, we discussed the operating environment of the firm in terms of the structure of business organizations and corporate and personal income taxes.

Section IV focused on the financial markets and institutions and discussed such topics as wealth and capital formation, money and capital markets, and attributes and functions of capital markets. Section V concentrated on the U.S. financial markets and institutions with particular emphasis given to such topics as financial markets and economic performance, depository and nondepository financial institutions, primary financial assets, and the role of financial intermediation through secondary financial assets.

NOTES

1. The purpose of Chapter 3 is to construct an overall picture of the environment within which the firm operates. The specific details dealing with U.S. economic and institutional attributes are discussed in the relevant chapters in the book. For example, short-term financial markets are discussed in Appendix 8A, while capital markets are reviewed in Appendix 9A.
2. The reader is referred to Gup (Chap. 2) for an excellent discussion of the life-cycle concept as it applies to financial decisions.
3. The functional details of the various financial instruments used by corporations to tap external sources of funds are discussed in greater detail in Appendices 8A and 9A, respectively.
4. Inflation adjustments and asset indexation are common procedures in most developing countries that suffer from inflationary conditions. In the United States, we do not allow for such provisions.
5. The *value added tax* is common in Europe and has occasionally been discussed as a possible alternative tax system for the United States.
6. The investing public is not involved in these two markets.

7. Some of these agencies include the Federal Reserve Board, the U.S. Comptroller of the Currency, the Federal Deposit Insurance Corporation, the Federal Home Loan Board, and various state banking commissions.
8. The recent plight of S&Ls has resulted in some changes in the regulation of these institutions. Beginning in March 1989, S&Ls are regulated by the Federal Deposit Insurance Corporation (FDIC), which performs similar functions for commercial banks.

QUESTIONS

1. What are some of the national and international environmental factors that both augment and constrain the operations of a firm?
2. What are the meaning and significance of (*a*) the corporate life cycle and (*b*) the business cycle? How do we aggregate the product life-cycle effects to arrive at the firm life cycle and the industry life cycle?
3. Discuss the different types of business organizations and outline their advantages and disadvantages.
4. Draw two schematics that outline the framework for national and international financial markets.
5. Discuss briefly the functions of money and capital markets. How are the two markets interrelated?

ANNOTATED BIBLIOGRAPHY

Altman, Edward I., ed. *Handbook of Financial Markets and Institutions*. New York: John Wiley and Sons, 1987.

A very good source of information on domestic and international financial markets, institutions, and instruments.

Gup, Benton E. *Principles of Financial Management*. New York: John Wiley and Sons, 1983.

A very good source of information on the applications of firm life cycle and business cycle to financial management.

Rose, Peter S., and Donald R. Frazer. *Financial Institutions*. 3d ed. Plano, Tex.: Business Publications, Inc., 1988.

A very good source of information on domestic financial markets, institutions and instruments.

Van Horne, James C. *The Function and Analysis of Capital Market Rates*. 3d ed. Englewood Cliffs, N.J.: Prentice-Hall, Inc., 1985.

A comprehensive source of functional information on capital markets.

4

FINANCIAL STATEMENTS AND RATIO ANALYSIS

I. INTRODUCTION

Financial statements of corporations are constructed for a variety of potential applications. Some of the diverse uses of financial statements are (1) to report on business performance over some relevant accounting period, (2) to provide information that can help predict future earnings and dividends to investors and creditors, and (3) to provide a detailed account of internal business conditions to regulatory agencies such as the Securities and Exchange Commission. Depending on the audience, financial statements can be constructed with differing amounts of detail. For example, management's needs for assessing performance are likely to result in the preparation of highly detailed statements for internal uses. Conversely, statements released to the general public are less detailed and usually represent a highly aggregated account of business conditions. Outsiders may require more detailed data in conducting certain analyses. However releasing such data publicly would also allow competitors to inspect highly proprietary information. We should not be surprised, then, that we as outside analysts see only the highly condensed version of a firm's financial statements.

Analysis of financial statements is focused on the actual past and expected future performance of several critical financial variables, such as:

1. Earnings
2. Reinvestment/payout rate
3. Rate of return
4. Cost of capital
5. Competitive position
6. Risk rate assigned to the company's earnings by investors and lenders

These variables are derived from statements provided by the firm in quarterly or annual reports including the following:

1. *Balance sheet.* This statement reports the financial position of a firm's assets and liabilities, together with the owners' equity, at the end of each accounting period. It is also called the *statement of financial position*.
2. *Income statement*. This statement reports the firm's earnings performance during an accounting period. It summarizes the effects of transactions such as sales and expenses. In this respect, we say that the income statement represents changes (flows), while the balance sheet represents levels (stocks).
3. *Statement of changes in financial position*. This statement details the changes that occurred in balance sheet items during the accounting period. It is also called the *funds flow statement.*

Used collectively, the above financial statements provide a fairly accurate picture of the firm's financial condition. However, there are limitations associated with the use of these statements that should be stressed. Because firms may use different accounting conventions in the preparation of financial statements, we need to be aware of how such differences affect their compatibility and comparability. One of the most troublesome problems is the effect of price-level changes. Price-level changes can have a serious effect on a firm's financial condition. However, the appropriate way to adjust for this "inflation effect" is still a subject of debate and will be discussed later in section IV. In addition to this problem we must also realize that financial statements are affected by both accounting techniques and changes in economic conditions. The latter effect raises the issue of whether there are systematic economic or perhaps even industry influences present in accounting numbers. However, before addressing these issues we shall first discuss the construction and analysis of the various financial statements as well as the ratios derived from them.

II. FINANCIAL STATEMENTS

Because firms use different accounting conventions in the preparation of financial statements, we should be aware of the possible lack of comparability and compatibility. Nevertheless, the considerable consistency that exists makes them fruitful objects of analysis. In this section we shall discuss the four basic financial statements that are of special importance to financial analysts: (1) the statement of profits and losses, also known as the income statement; (2) the balance sheet; (3) the statement of retained earnings; and (4) the statement of sources and uses of funds. This last statement falls under the broad category of changes in a firm's financial position and is occasionally complemented by an additional statement known as "analysis of changes in working capital." Let us present and discuss each of these statements in some functional detail before we articulate the measures and methods employed in their analysis.

A. The Profit and Loss Statement

The *profit and loss statement,* also known as the *income statement* or the *statement of earnings,* describes in considerable detail the major classifications associated with the sales revenue, operating costs, and administrative expenses that are associated with the generation of the company's sales revenue during a specific period of time, typically a quarter or a year. Along with the major groups of revenue and expenses, the profit and loss statement also contains individual subgroupings of various accounts involved in the inflows and outflows through the firm during the fiscal period under study. The difference between the total revenues and total expenditures during the fiscal period constitutes the accounting profits of the firm that are subject to taxes. Please remember at this stage that we will be distinguishing constantly between accounting profits and economic profits, as is proper to do in finance. The latter distinction is meaningful because in financial management economic profits constitute the cash flow available to management for reinvestment and the growth of the firm. These distinctions will be discussed in detail later on in this chapter, but at this stage we shall discuss the income statement by way of the example in Table 4.1, which presents the revenues and expenses of the fictitious Abet Manufacturing Corporation for the year ending December 31, 1988.

Perusal of the figures in Table 4.1 indicates the following. Abet's total revenue consists of \$845,880 in gross sales from its main line of business, the sale of throwout bearings, and \$11,160 in other revenues from its bank deposits, its short-term investments in marketable securities, and from some rental property, for a total revenue from all sources equal to \$857,040. Note that gross sales of throwout bearings is subject to various downward adjustments as follows: Some products that had been sold and shipped to customers were returned for various reasons, making for a reduction of gross sales by \$19,260. Also, because some clients bought the bearings for cash, there was a special price reduction—known in the trade as a "cash discount"—in the amount of \$6,890. Finally, as is customary, the firm made a tentative estimate of the amount of uncollectible accounts receivable at the extrapolated historical proportion of about .021. In this case, the amount is \$17,900. The amounts of the three downward adjustments to gross sales are summed and subtracted from the original figure to yield the account of net sales equal to \$801,830.

The account net sales becomes a meaningful figure from which to subtract the three basic

TABLE 4.1 Abet Manufacturing Corporation: Income Statement for the Year Ended December 31, 1988

Gross sales			$845,880
Less: Returns and allowances		$ 19,260	
Cash discounts		6,890	
Estimated loss on uncollectible accounts		17,900	44,050
Net sales			$801,830
Cost of goods sold:			
Inventory of finished goods, January 1, 1988		67,430	
Cost of goods produced		385,820	
Cost of finished goods available		453,250	
Less: Inventory of finished goods, December 31, 1988		63,910	
Cost of goods sold			389,340
Gross profit			$412,490
Selling expenses:			
Sales salaries	$74,200		
Advertising	32,000		
Travel and entertainment	9,550		
Freight and delivery	4,460	120,210	
General and administrative expenses:			
Officers' salaries	57,300		
Office salaries	27,000		
Taxes	8,120		
Insurance	2,920		
Utilities	8,530		
Depreciation	12,270	116,140	
Total operating expenses			236,350
Total operating income			$176,140
Other revenue and expenses:			
Interest and dividends on investments		3,860	
Rent revenue		7,300	
Total other revenue		11,160	
Less: Interest expense		4,170	
Excess of other revenue over other expense			6,990
Net income before income taxes			$183,130
Estimated income taxes at 34%			62,264
Net income after income taxes			$120,866

classifications of costs associated with the production, sale, and shipment of the throwout bearings and reach the total operating income of the company under study. The first grouping of expenses, the truly variable costs of the firm, known as *cost of goods sold,* goes to the heart of production by taking the inventory of finished goods on January 1, 1988, that amounts to $67,430, plus the cost of goods produced that comes to $385,820, to arrive at the cost of finished goods available which equals $453,250. The next step in this grouping involves the netting of the cost of goods sold by subtracting the balance of the inventory of finished goods brought forward on December 31, 1988, from the previous fiscal period. This set of account adjustment yields the true cost of goods sold, which is subtracted from net sales to yield a second meaningful figure of $412,490 under the heading *gross profit.*

The second grouping of expenses under the heading *selling expenses* consists of some variable costs like freight and delivery at $4,460, and some semivariable operating costs like sales salaries, which combines fixed stipends plus commission at $74,200. When the above expenses are combined with the two other expense entries of advertising and travel and entertainment, we arrive at total selling expenses. The third subdivision of costs, the genuine fixed or overhead costs of the firm, known as *general and administrative expenses,* comprises such overhead cost items as officers' and office salaries, taxes, insurance, utilities, as well as depreciation, which is not a cash-expense entry but is set aside for future replacement of the original investment.

At this stage, the subtotals for selling expenses and general and administrative expenses are subtracted from gross profit to find the figure for *total operating income,* set at $176,140. This amount reflects the net income derived solely from the manufacture and sale of throwout bearings and must be adjusted for the expenses incurred and revenues raised from the peripheral activities of the company. When this is accomplished, we arrive at what is known as *net income before taxes* at $183,130. What remains now is to subtract income taxes. Let us set the tax rate at an artificially high average rate of 34.0 percent which brings the estimated income taxes to $62,264. This allows us to complete the construction of the profit and loss statement with the computation of *net income after taxes*—an entry that captures the activities of a full year of operations into a simple number set at $120,866. This figure will be utilized many times in the construction of such financial statements as the balance sheet, the statement of retained earnings, and the statement of sources and uses of funds. Most importantly, this amount of net income after taxes, properly augmented by the noncash expense of depreciation charges and after some other minor adjustments becomes the true measure of *economic profits,* known as the incremental after-tax cash flow associated with an investment.[1] Thus, whether we analyze an investment from the viewpoint of the firm's management or whether we assume the role of the outside analyst who attempts to evaluate the firm as a potential investment, we will always seek to pinpoint and measure its incremental after-tax cash flow, or economic profits.

B. The Balance Sheet

While the income statement describes the major *flows* of revenues and costs within a given period, we also need a "still picture" of the enterprise at a moment in time, say the closing date of the company's fiscal year.

The type of information that "freezes" the condition of the firm at a moment in time is contained in the second financial statement to be discussed here—namely, the *balance sheet.* In effect, what we are saying is that the income statement of a firm deals with such things as the outflow of finished goods and the inflow of revenues, as well as the inflows of factors of production and the outflows of expenditures. It represents the summation of changes in the various categories of accounts. However, the balance sheet deals with the *stock* of values in the company's possession at a moment in time, typically the end of the fiscal year. It encompasses three basic classifications: assets (A), liabilities (L), and net worth (E), in the well-known identity:

$$\text{Assets} \equiv \text{Liabilities} + \text{Net Worth}$$

The balance sheet at the end of the fiscal year December 31, 1988, shown in Table 4.2, is related to the balance sheet at the beginning of the fiscal year by the income statement for the intervening period presented in Table 4.1. The amount shown for owners' equity (net assets) for the fiscal year ended December 31, 1988, represents the summation of net incomes reported in each of the previous fiscal years, which were not distributed as dividends to the stockholders. Obviously the various asset and liability balances have changed from the beginning of the year, and the net assets during that period have increased by an amount equal to the net income that was not distributed in dividends.[2]

Casual perusal of the balance sheet for the Abet Corporation as of December 31, 1988, reveals some interesting characteristics. They will

TABLE 4.2 Abet Manufacturing Corporation: Balance Sheet, December 31, 1988

Assets			
Current assets:			
Cash		$ 29,940	
Marketable securities at cost (market value $51,250)		56,920	
Notes receivable		3,000	
Accounts receivable	$ 96,950		
Less: Allowance for discounts, adjustments, and doubtful accounts	19,830	77,120	
Inventories:			
Finished goods	44,000		
Work in progress	24,000		
Raw materials	49,660	117,660	
Prepaid insurance		2,520	$287,160
Plant assets:			
Land		11,200	
Building	103,900		
Less: Accumulated depreciation	52,200	51,700	
Equipment	200,300		
Less: Accumulated depreciation	62,800	137,500	200,400
Intangible assets:			
Organization expense		5,600	
Goodwill		18,700	24,300
Investment in stock of PLB Trading Corporation			49,580
Total assets			$561,440
Liabilities			
Current liabilities:			
Bank loans		$ 10,800	
Accounts payable		36,650	
Accrued payroll and other expenses		24,880	
Estimated income taxes payable		42,200	$114,530
Long-term notes, due October, 1996			60,000
Deferred rental revenues			1,800
Owners' equity:			
Capital stock, $10 par value, 5,000 shares issued and outstanding		50,000	
Premium on stock		31,200	
Retained earnings		303,910	385,110
Total liabilities and equity			$561,440

be just highlighted at this stage, as they also will be discussed later in comparative detail in the section that deals with financial ratios. For example, Abet's cash position is slightly higher than 5 percent of total assets and slightly over 10 percent of total current assets. It is also approximately 53 percent of marketable securities. This is unusual for a well-managed firm in the throwout bearing industry, in a year of tight and costly money. Based on conventional rules of thumb, we would expect to find the relationship of a cash to total assets at about 1–3 percent, cash to total current assets at about 2–4 percent, and cash to marketable securities at 3–5 percent.

Of course, the analyst cannot go very far along this line of inquiry, because what is needed must come from comparative data for the firm over time and in relation to its competitors in the industry. These juxtapositions will be drawn later in the section on financial ratios. Nevertheless, we can still make some absolute judgments about the inordinate magnitude of the cash account. We can also infer that the firm is either badly managed by foregoing profitable investment opportunities available for its idle cash or that the firm is accumulating cash for some specific strategic market thrust that requires quick and precise action. Perhaps the firm's investment in the stock of PLB Trading Corporation gives us a clue. It is possible that Abet Manufacturing Corporation is accumulating the cash in order to buy more stock in PLB Trading Corporation and thus gain control over this firm. As we shall discuss later, similar types of analyses can be made with respect to every individual account in the balance sheet and for the income statement, both at a point in time and over a specific horizon that will also involve data from the industry.

C. The Statement of Retained Earnings

The financial information contained in the income statement of a firm must be further augmented to indicate all the changes in the *owner's equity*. This informational improvement is needed in order to account for such events as additions or withdrawals for personal use, adjustments for previous taxes or depreciation charges, or perhaps for unusual windfalls that have been adjusted directly to the firm's equity. Such a complete account of changes in *net worth* values is generally given in the statement of retained earnings, also known as the *statement of earned surplus*. This statement provides the direct linkage between the balance sheets of a company at the beginning and the end of the fiscal period through the account owner's equity, or net worth. Moreover, this type of statement is frequently constructed as a *statement of stockholders' investment* and it contains detailed information on such distributions as *cash dividends* and *stock dividends,* as well as *treasury stock, additional paid-in capital, retained earnings,* and *reserves* for various losses. The statement of retained earnings for the Abet Manufacturing Corporation is given in Table 4.3, below.

Notice that the statement begins with the balance of retained earnings carried forward from the previous fiscal year. To this amount we add the net income for 1988 (see Table 4.1). Note that when the amount of net income after taxes for 1988, that is, $120,866, is subtracted from the retained earnings entry in the balance sheet of Table 4.2, it yields the balance of retained earnings on December 31, 1987. It is in this sense that the statement of retained earnings provides a linkage between balance sheets of successive fiscal periods. Now to return to our computations, the net income for 1988 is increased by a correction for excessive depreciation charges in past years to yield $121,000, which is added to the balance of retained earnings for a total amount of $304,044. Out of this amount Abet pays out dividends totaling $50,000 and makes a payment for additional income tax assessment equal to $6,000. After making these adjustments we obtain the balance of retained earnings for

TABLE 4.3 Abet Manufacturing Corporation: Statement of Retained Earnings for the Year Ended December 31, 1988

Balance of retained earnings, December 31, 1987		$183,044
Add:		
Net income—1988	$120,866	
Correction of excessive depreciation charges in past years	134	121,000
		$304,044
Less:		
Dividends to stockholders	50,000	
Additional income tax assessment	6,000	56,000
Balance of retained earnings, December 31, 1988		$248,044

December 31, 1988, $248,044, to be carried forward for the following fiscal year.

D. The Statement of Sources and Uses of Funds

In the course of business operations, changing economic conditions are reflected in the values of such major accounts as assets, liabilities, and net worth, as well as in the values of the various subaccounts. These changes that affect the values of individual or group accounts over a period of time can be identified, measured, aggregated, and presented in tabular form through the *flow statement*. In effect, a flow statement can be prepared to show the increases or decreases in several account categories that are crucial in financial analysis and planning. For our purposes we can identify three basic flow statements that can be constructed from historical accounting data, as follows: (1) the profit and loss statement; (2) the statement of sources and uses of net working capital; and (3) the statement of cash receipts and disbursements.

As discussed earlier in the chapter, the profit and loss statement measures the inflows and outflows of net assets resulting from the firm's business operations. It does not measure the changes of specific accounts; rather, it presents the total net flows from a particular activity. The other two statements measure the flow of net working capital and the flow of cash, respectively. In financial management we use these last two statements in a combined grouping of *sources and uses of funds. By sources of funds we mean the transactions that increase liabilities or net worth values or reduce asset values. By uses of funds we mean the transactions that reduce liabilities or net worth values or increase asset values.* A simple listing of some of the changes that constitute sources and uses of funds is given in Table 4.4.

TABLE 4.4 Some Sources and Uses of Funds for a Typical Company

Sources of Funds	*Uses of Funds*
Increase in tax accruals	Increase in security holdings
Increase in stock issue	Repayment of debt
Increase in other debt	Increase in accounts receivable
Increase in bank credit	Increase in inventories
Increase in accounts payable	Purchase of plant and equipment
Increase in earned surplus	
Increase in depreciation reserves	

Because the flow of funds through a firm is continual, financial managers must always attempt to match sources and applications (uses) of funds so as to maximize firm value. The simplest way to construct a statement of sources and uses of funds is to compare the balance sheets of the enterprise for two consecutive fiscal periods—for example, two quarters or two years—and compute the changes in each of the accounts. Remember that when these changes are given in terms of rates of change we also construct the *flow of funds* statement. Let us now provide a step-by-step description of the construction of the sources and uses of funds statement for PLB Trading Corporation. As the reader may recall from Table 4.2, this is the company in whose stock the Abet Manufacturing Corporation had invested an amount equal to $49,580.

The first step requires the comparative data from two successive balance sheets, as shown in Table 4.5. The second step involves the computation of the net changes in each of the accounts represented in the balance sheets, as shown in the third column under the heading *absolute change*. The third step distinguishes between sources and uses of funds, in accordance with our guidelines: *that is, transactions that increase liabilities or net worth values or that reduce asset values are sources of funds; conversely, transactions that reduce liabilities or net worth values or that increase asset values are uses of funds*. The fourth step requires the rearrangement of the changes in the successive balance sheets into a sources and uses of funds statement as presented in Table 4.6.

Once the transactions have been rearranged in the form given by Table 4.6 we can observe some of the major activities of PLB Trading Corporation for the fiscal year beginning January 1, 1988, and ending December 31, 1988. For example, we see that the decisions of the financial managers regarding existing market opportuni-

TABLE 4.5 PLB Trading Corporation: Consolidated Balance Sheets and Changes, December 31, 1987 and 1988

	1988	*1987*	*Absolute Change*	*Percentage Change*
Assets	(In Millions of Dollars)			
Cash	$ 58.5	$ 55.0	+$ 3.5	+ .064
Marketable securities	57.0	49.5	+7.5	+ .151
Accounts receivable (net)	112.0	52.5	+59.5	+1.133
Inventories	396.4	465.1	−68.7	− .148
Total current assets	$ 623.9	$ 622.1	+$ 1.8	+ .003
Investment in government securities reserved for long-term expansion	295.0	330.0	−35.0	− .106
Gross plant and equipment	5,692.0	5,400.0	+292.0	+ .054
Accumulated depreciation	3,180.0	2,950.0	+230.0	+ .078
Net plant and equipment	$2,512.0	$2,450.0	+$ 62.0	+ .025
Miscellaneous investments	11.5	16.3	−4.8	− .294
Prepaid expenses	57.0	62.5	−5.5	− .088
Total assets	$3,499.4	$3,480.9	+$ 18.5	+ .005
Liabilities				
Accounts payable	$ 253.0	$ 177.5	+$ 75.5	+ .425
Accrued taxes (net)	75.0	72.1	+2.9	+ .040
Dividends payable	16.0	15.9	+.1	+ .006
Long-term debt due in 1989	12.5	14.3	−1.8	− .126
Total current liabilities	$ 356.5	$ 279.8	+$ 76.7	+ .274
Long-term debt	254.0	317.3	−63.3	− .199
Reserves for insurance, etc.	72.5	68.1	+4.4	+ .065
6% preferred stock	160.0	160.0	0	0
Common stock	1,200.4	1,200.1	+.3	0*
Earned surplus	1,456.0	1,455.6	+.4	0*
Total liabilities and net worth	$3,499.4	$3,480.9	+$ 18.5	+ .005

*Values of rates of change become significant at four digits to the right of the decimal point.

ties during the 1987–1988 period resulted in three major sources of funds.

1. A decrease in inventories of 14.8 percent, from $465.1 million to $396.4 million, freed funds in the amount of $68.7 million. This decrease could have been the result of a number of factors, some of which are as follows:
   a. A justifiable reduction of inventories held at a level in excess of the required minimum.
   b. An unexpected increase in sales due to such factors as market conditions, changes in the firm's terms of trade, or price reductions, without a commensurate increase in production.
   c. An actual or expected strike by any of the labor unions involved in the production or distribution of the company's product.
   d. Several other factors that can be identified only by a knowledge of the actual conditions within the company and its environment, during the fiscal year 1988.
2. An increase in accounts payable of 42.5 percent, from $177.5 million to $253.0 million, that resulted from an additional $75.5 million worth of credit provided by the firm's suppliers of raw materials.
3. A decrease in the amount of investment in government securities reserved for long-term expansion of 10.6 percent, from $330.0 mil-

TABLE 4.6 PLB Trading Corporation: Statement of Sources and Uses of Funds, 1987–1988 (In Millions of Dollars)

Sources of Funds	
Decrease in inventories	$ 68.7
Decrease in government securities	35.0
Decrease in miscellaneous investments	4.8
Decrease in prepaid expenses	5.5
Increase in accounts payable	75.5
Increase in accrued taxes	2.9
Increase in dividends payable	0.1
Increase in reserves for insurance, etc.	4.4
Increase in common stock	0.3
Increase in retained earnings	0.4
Total sources of funds	$197.6
Uses of Funds	
Increase in cash	$ 3.5
Increase in marketable securities	7.5
Increase in accounts receivable (net)	59.5
Increase in net plant and equipment	62.0
Decrease in long-term debt*	65.1
Total uses of funds	$197.6

*Net of long-term debt and long-term debt due in 1989

lion to $295.0 million, resulting from the sale of $35.0 million of these securities.

Against these sources, the management of PLB Trading Corporation applied the funds to the following three major uses of funds:

1. A decrease in the company's long-term debt, including that part due in 1989 of 19.6 percent, from $331.6 million to $266.5 million. This transaction involved a $1.8 million decrease in the long-term debt due in 1989 and a $63.3 million reduction in the amount of the remaining long-term debt.
2. An increase in net plant and equipment of 2.5 percent, from $2,450 million to $2,512.0 million. It is worth noting here that the $62.0 million increase in net plant and equipment is the result of a $292.0 million increase in gross plant and equipment, part of which was financed by the increase in accumulated depreciation (a source of funds) by $230.0 million.
3. An increase in accounts receivable (net of bad-debt allowances) of 113.3 percent, from $52.5 million to $112.0 million. This net use of $59.5 million could have resulted from the extension of better terms of trade to customers and might explain part of the reduction in inventories (a source of funds).

It should be evident by now that the analysis of changes in balance sheet accounts can be continued with more detailed explanations. However, the point here is that the differences in the individual accounts identify the net flows of funds through the firm. These flows have resulted from the decisions of the company's management within the constraints of the overall economic conditions during the period under analysis. Needless to say, additional analysis and interpretation of the meaning of the changes will reveal whether the management of the company has employed the necessary balanced group of sources of funds and the recommended diversified set of applications of funds. This type of augmented analysis will enable the investigator to measure such economic attributes as operational efficiency, liquidity, coverage, and profitability, as will be discussed shortly.

III. COMPARATIVE FINANCIAL STATEMENTS

In this section we shall discuss the nature and mechanics of comparative financial statements in an attempt to extract additional information from these financial records. There are two types of additional information that can be derived from the juxtaposition of data for the same company over time, for many companies at a point in time, and for many companies over time:

1. We can derive information that enables us to construct new forms of financial statements, as was demonstrated in the simple case of PLB Trading Corporation presented in Tables 4.5 and 4.6. Here we utilized balance sheets from two successive periods to develop the information necessary for the statement of sources and uses of funds.
2. We can derive information that enables us to place the financial condition of the firm in per-

spective vis-à-vis its previous performance or the conditions of other related firms in the industry.

The first type of information will be discussed in this section and was also detailed in Chapter 2, when we focused on the distinctions between *income flows, cash flows,* and *funds flows* that go through the firm. The second type of information will be elaborated upon later in this chapter when financial ratios are discussed.

A. Comparison of Financial Statements over Time

Let us first present the simplest case of comparative financial information in terms of Tables 4.7 and 4.8 that show the data for Southeastern Sheet Metal, Inc. (SSM), at the end of the fiscal years 1986, 1987, and 1988. Table 4.7 shows the condensed forms of the comparative income statements that present some interesting patterns of financial flows. For example, in the 3-year period from 1986 through 1988, the net sales revenue of SSM increased by an average annual rate of 2.9 percent, and its cost of goods sold increased by an average annual rate of 2.8 percent. This resulted in an annual increase in gross profit from operations of 3.1 percent on average. Yet, the company's income before taxes and net income after taxes declined steadily over the 3-year period at an average annual rate of 11.1 percent. Why would such performance be manifested? The answer is rather simple, if we take advantage of the comparative information presented in Table 4.7. The company's selling expenses increased by an average annual rate of 9.7 percent and the general and administrative expenses increased by 6.8 percent, yielding an annual average decrease in income before interest and taxes of 4.5 percent. This decrease was aggravated by an immense increase in the interest expense by 40.0 percent annually on average, that was only partially covered by the decrease in income taxes at an average annual rate of 11.0 percent.

In lieu of detailed analysis, we can at this point draw some preliminary inferences from a quick review of the information provided in the comparative balance sheets for 1986 through 1988, as presented in Table 4.8. For example, notes payable (a source of funds) increased by an annual average rate of 134.7 percent, supporting the above increase in interest expense (a use of funds). By similar reasoning, we see that the decrease in the short-term asset cash, as well as the increases in retained earnings, accounts payable, and accrued and other liabili-

TABLE 4.7 Southeastern Sheet Metal, Inc.: Comparative Income Statements for Years Ended December 31, 1986, 1987, and 1988

	1988	*1987*	*1986*	*3-Year Average*	*Average Change (%)*
	(In Thousands of Dollars)				
Sales (net)	$6,665	$6,426	$6,300	$6,464	+ 2.9
Cost of goods sold	5,035	4,876	4,767	4,893	+ 2.8
Gross profit	$1,630	$1,550	$1,533	$1,571	+ 3.1
Selling expenses	505	460	420	461	+ 9.7
General and administrative expenses	551	504	483	513	+ 6.8
Income before interest and taxes	$ 574	$ 586	$ 630	$ 597	− 4.5
Interest expense	127	88	65	93	+40.0
Income before taxes	$ 447	$ 498	$ 565	$ 503	−11.0
Income taxes at 40 percent*	179	199	226	201	−11.0
Net income after taxes	$ 268	$ 299	$ 339	$ 302	−11.1

*For simplicity of computations, we assume a 40.0-percent tax rate for the years 1986–88.

TABLE 4.8 Southeastern Sheet Metal, Inc.: Comparative Balance Sheets, December 31, 1986, 1987, and 1988

	1988	*1987*	*1986*	*3-Year Average*	*Average Change (%)*
Assets	(In Thousands of Dollars)				
Current assets:					
Cash	$ 103	$ 144	$ 310	$ 186	− 41.0
Accounts receivable	1,612	1,150	1,012	1,258	+ 26.9
Inventory	1,285	794	487	855	+ 62.4
Other current assets	44	39	40	41	+ 5.0
Total current assets	$3,044	$2,127	$1,849	$2,340	+ 29.1
Plant assets:					
Land and building	710	725	275	570	+ 80.8
Machinery	590	610	775	658	− 12.3
Other fixed assets	33	51	68	51	− 30.1
Total assets	$4,377	$3,513	$2,967	$3,619	+ 23.8

	1988	*1987*	*1986*	*3-Year Average*	*Average Change (%)*
Liabilities and Net Worth					
Current liabilities:					
Notes payable, bank	$ 399	$ 170	$ 0	$ 190	+ 134.7
Accounts payable	486	254	184	308	+ 64.7
Accrued and other liabilities	285	260	248	264	+ 7.2
Total current liabilities	$1,170	$ 684	$ 432	$ 762	+ 64.7
Long-term liabilities and net worth:					
Long-term debt	924	929	940	931	− 0.8
Common stock	1,100	1,100	1,100	1,100	0
Retained earnings	1,183	800	495	826	+ 54.7
Total liabilities and net worth	$4,377	$3,513	$2,967	$3,619	+ 21.5

ties, provided the sources of funds that were used for such applications (uses) of funds as increases in accounts receivable, inventory, and land and buildings as well as decreases in long-term debt.

B. Common-Size Financial Statements over Time

Another way of analyzing financial statements is to reconstruct them in terms of percentages of sales revenue or total assets, and then delineate the interactions of the various accounts as proportions of the totals. Here again, in order to make some meaningful comparisons, we must compare the behavior of an account either over time or as part of a larger industrial group. Let us first take the case of comparison over time by means of what are known as *common-size financial statements,* where all accounts are presented as percentages, and allow relative judgments about performance. Table 4.9 presents the common-size income statements of SSM for the years 1986 through 1988.

Notice that the net sales figures for each of the three years under study are set equal at 100 percent. This allows us to compare the behavior of each account over time as a percent of the same grand total, that is 100 percent. In this spirit, we can observe that gross profit from op-

TABLE 4.9 Southeastern Sheet Metal, Inc.: Common-Size Income Statements for Years Ended December 31, 1986, 1987, and 1988 (in percentages)

	1988	*1987*	*1986*
Sales (net)	100.0	100.0	100.0
Cost of goods sold	75.5	75.9	75.7
Gross profit	24.5	24.1	24.3
Selling expenses	7.6	7.2	6.7
General and administrative expenses	8.3	7.8	7.6
Income before interest and taxes	8.6	9.1	10.0
Interest expense	1.9	1.4	1.0
Income before taxes	6.7	7.7	9.0
Income taxes at 40 percent	2.7	3.1	3.6
Net income after taxes	4.0	4.6	5.4

erations as a percent of net sales has remained more or less stable over the 3-year period. However, income before interest and taxes as a percentage of net sales decreased from 10 percent in 1986 to 8.6 percent in 1988. Similarly, income before taxes during the 3-year period decreased from 9 percent to 6.7 percent, while net income after taxes also suffered a decrease from 5.4 percent to 4 percent. Table 4.10 shows the common-size balance sheets of SSM for the 3-year period of 1986 through 1988. Here again, similar analysis can be performed to delineate the performance of each asset, liability, and net worth account over time against the same grand totals of 100 percent. In this manner, we can derive inferences about the relative performance of each account over time.

C. Common-Size Financial Statements across Firms

To continue the investigation, we need to make comparisons with other closely related firms in the same industry. This type of analysis compares the firm's performance with that of a few direct, close competitors and perhaps with the average performance for the entire industry in which the firm is classified. Thus, an analyst can evaluate the important variables, like revenues, costs, assets, liabilities, net worth, and their subvariables for a given company vis-à-vis its competitors.

TABLE 4.10 Southeastern Sheet Metal, Inc.: Common-Size Balance Sheets, December 31, 1986, 1987, and 1988 (in percentages)

	1988	*1987*	*1986*
Assets			
Current assets:			
Cash	2.4	4.1	10.4
Accounts receivable	36.7	32.7	34.2
Inventory	29.3	22.6	16.4
Other current assets	1.0	1.1	1.3
Total current assets	69.4	60.5	62.3
Plant assets:			
Land and building	16.2	20.6	9.3
Machinery	13.4	17.4	26.1
Other fixed assets	1.0	1.5	2.3
Total assets	100.0	100.0	100.0
	1988	*1987*	*1986*
Liabilities and Net Worth			
Current liabilities:			
Notes payable, bank	9.1	4.8	0
Accounts payable	11.1	7.2	6.2
Accrued and other liabilities	6.5	7.4	8.4
Total current liabilities	26.7	19.4	14.6
Long-term liabilities and net worth:			
Long-term debt	21.1	26.4	31.7
Common stock	25.2	31.4	37.0
Retained earnings	27.0	22.8	16.7
Total liabilities and net worth	100.0	100.0	100.0

Tables 4.11 and 4.12 provide a picture of the competitive market structure in which SSM operates, for the year 1988. Review of the information in Table 4.11 reveals that SSM has the lowest figures for cost of goods sold as a percentage of net sales at 75.5 percent against 79.4 percent for Competitor A, 76.3 percent for Competitor B, and 78.2 percent for the industry average. Similar inferences can be drawn about general and administrative expenses. However,

TABLE 4.11 Southeastern Sheet Metal, Inc.: Comparative Common-Size Income Statements for the Year Ended December 31, 1988 (in percentages)

	SSM	*Competitor A*	*Competitor B*	*Industry Average*
Revenues	100.0	100.0	100.0	100.0
Expenses				
Cost of goods sold	75.5	79.4	76.3	78.2
Selling expenses	7.6	4.2	3.8	4.2
General and administrative expenses	8.3	10.2	12.5	11.0
Interest expenses	1.9	1.5	3.4	1.2
Income taxes	2.7	1.2	1.7	2.0
Income after taxes	4.0	3.5	2.3	3.4
	100.0	100.0	100.0	100.0

SSM has by far the highest selling expenses, pays the highest percentage of revenues in income taxes, and has the highest proportion of income after taxes at 4 percent. Table 4.12 presents the common-size balance sheets of SSM, its two close competitors, A and B, and the averages for the industry. Here again comparative analysis can be performed and managerial action be

TABLE 4.12 Southeastern Sheet Metal, Inc.: Comparative Common-Size Balance Sheets, December 31, 1988 (in percentages)

	SSM	*Competitor A*	*Competitor B*	*Industry Average*
Assets				
Cash	2.4	5.1	1.7	5.4
Accounts receivable	36.7	30.5	28.6	24.8
Inventory	29.3	25.4	31.4	34.1
Other current assets	1.0	6.2	3.2	3.6
Land and building	16.2	10.9	19.5	12.6
Machinery	13.4	10.6	15.2	17.5
Other fixed assets	1.0	11.3	.4	2.0
	100.0	100.0	100.0	100.0

	SSM	*Competitor A*	*Competitor B*	*Industry Average*
Liabilities and Net Worth				
Notes payable, bank	9.1	8.7	9.5	7.2
Accounts payable	11.1	11.0	10.2	10.9
Accrued and other liabilities	6.5	15.0	14.4	12.0
Long-term debt	21.1	16.2	22.9	18.4
Common stock	25.1	27.6	23.2	25.0
Retained earnings	27.0	21.5	19.8	26.5
	100.0	100.0	100.0	100.0

implemented to improve specific aspects of operations.

IV. FINANCIAL RATIO ANALYSIS

One of the most common methods used to analyze a firm's financial statements is *ratio analysis*. Ratios can be extremely useful tools in evaluating a firm's financial condition, even in the absence of truly detailed operational information. However, ratios are not intended to be the sole instruments used in financial analysis, as they can highlight only strong or weak areas within the enterprise examined. For example, they cannot show the actual cause-and-effect relationships within a firm, although they can serve as indicators of present patterns and potential trends.

Financial ratios are typically classified into the following (nonexhaustive) groupings of a firm's operations:

1. *Liquidity ratios*—measuring the firm's ability to meet maturing short-term obligations.
2. *Activity ratios*—measuring how effectively the firm's assets are being employed.
3. *Leverage ratios*—measuring the relative proportions of debt and equity used to finance assets.
4. *Profitability ratios*—measuring performance relative to some key variable, usually assets or sales.

With these categories in mind, we now proceed with a ratio analysis of P&B Imports financial statements presented in Tables 4.13 and 4.14. The computed values for the ratios are shown in Table 4.15.

A. Liquidity Ratios

As indicated earlier, liquidity is a measure of a firm's ability to meet current financial obligations. Not surprisingly, then, most measures of liquidity involve information on the firm's current account portion of the balance sheet. In theory, most of the firm's current assets can be considered fairly liquid, although the realities of each situation point to different degrees of liquidity for various assets. In view of their liquidity, these current assets can be used as a source of funds to pay for short-term obligations (i.e., current liabilities). One popular way to measuring liquidity is the *current ratio,* defined as

$$\text{Current Ratio (CR)} = \frac{\text{Current Assets}}{\text{Current Liabilities}}$$

TABLE 4.13 P&B Imports: Comparative Balance Sheets (in thousands of dollars)

	1985	*1986*	*1987*	*1988*
Assets				
Cash and securities	$ 61,921	$ 38,480	$ 33,620	$ 16,094
Accounts receivable	15,929	20,012	18,445	20,987
Inventories	54,945	60,337	74,607	79,867
Other current assets	3,799	5,416	12,760	6,648
Intangible assets	—	—	—	3,096
Plant and equipment	224,133	271,987	285,418	283,480
Total	$360,727	$396,232	$424,850	$410,172
Liabilities and Equity				
Accounts payable	$ 24,113	$ 31,824	$ 46,188	$ 35,347
Other current liabilities	45,638	44,336	45,902	43,382
Long-term liabilities	6,674	19,982	25,740	20,284
Deferred tax	26,108	29,750	35,850	39,100
Owners' equity and retained earnings	258,194	270,340	271,170	272,059
Total	$360,727	$396,232	$424,850	$410,172

TABLE 4.14 P&B Imports: Comparative Income Statements (in thousands of dollars)

	1985	*1986*	*1987*	*1988*
Sales	$ 752,654	$ 725,728	$ 735,770	$ 785,043
Cost of goods sold	(491,517)	(486,126)	(508,544)	(549,447)
Federal excise tax	(152,177)	(142,850)	(136,819)	(133,643)
General and Administrative expenses	(51,910)	(59,069)	(74,895)	(82,213)
	$ 57,050	$ 37,683	$ 15,512	$ 19,740
Other income (expense)	22,454	1,372	632	(1,331)
Interest expense	(1,114)	(1,509)	(1,908)	(2,431)
Earnings before tax	$ 78,390	$ 37,546	$ 14,236	$ 15,978
Income tax	(26,188)	(15,775)	(3,150)	(6,500)
Earnings after tax	$ 52,202	$ 21,771	$ 11,086	$ 9,478
Earnings per share	$3.76	$2.54	$1.29	$1.12
Market price per share (Dec. 31)	$29.37	$30.86	$14.71	$11.16
Average consumer price index (1967 = 100)	170.5	181.5	195.4	217.4

All the ratios for P&B Imports are illustrated in Table 4.15. P&B's CR equals 1.57, which indicates that current assets exceed current liabilities by a factor of over 1.5 to 1. However, the CR measure may be somewhat crude, because not all current assets have the same degree of liquidity. In the event of a credit squeeze, it is highly unlikely that some current assets can be easily converted into usable funds.

Accordingly, in order to account for the above bias, we can recompute the CR excluding inventories that are generally less liquid than other assets. This new ratio is referred to as the *quick ratio* or *acid-test ratio* and is computed as

$$\text{Quick Ratio (QR)} = \frac{\text{Current Assets} - \text{Inventory}}{\text{Current Liabilities (CL)}}$$

TABLE 4.15 Comparative Ratios, 1988

	P&B	*Firm 2*	*Firm 3*	*Average*
Current ratio (times)	1.57	1.93	1.32	1.61
Acid test (times)	0.47	1.34	0.59	0.80
Average collection period (days)	9.76	9.01	11.14	9.77
Inventory turnover (times)	6.88	13.34	9.58	9.93
Accounts receivable turnover (times)	37.41	41.68	27.42	35.50
Fixed-asset turnover (times)	2.77	3.05	2.23	2.68
Total-asset turnover (times)	1.91	1.71	1.69	1.77
Debt ratio	0.34	0.51	0.53	0.46
Long-term debt to owners' equity	0.07	0.44	0.56	0.36
Times interest earned (times)	7.57	*a*	6.47	—
Return on total assets (%)	2.31	*a*	7.49	—
Return on sales (%)	1.21	*a*	4.42	—
Return on equity (%)	3.48	*a*	15.84	—

Note: a = net loss for 1988.

or

$$\text{Quick Ratio} = \frac{\text{Cash} + \text{Marketable Securities} + \text{Accounts Receivable}}{\text{Current Liabilities (CL)}}$$

For P&B, the QR equals 0.47, showing that a rather large portion of the current account is composed of nonliquid assets such as inventories. The interpretation of both the QR and the CR follows no known rule of thumb. This is because there are trade-offs to be made with respect to liquidity (holding cash, etc.) and profitability (the opportunity cost associated with holding cash). While other ratios for measuring liquidity can obviously be constructed, the CR and QR are probably the best known and most widely used.

B. Activity Ratios

To measure how effectively a firm uses its assets, we look to a group of ratios that show activity. The most commonly analyzed assets in this group include accounts receivable, inventory, fixed assets, and total assets. However, we are not precluded from looking at other assets. These asset categories were chosen because a large portion of a firm's investment is in inventory, accounts receivable, and fixed assets. To gauge activity, we usually measure how effectively an asset category generates sales or use some related criterion. The first asset activity ratio is the *accounts receivable (AR) turnover,* computed as

$$\begin{array}{l}\text{Accounts Receivable} \\ \text{(AR) Turnover}\end{array} = \frac{\begin{array}{c}\text{Credit Sales} \\ \text{(or Total Sales)}\end{array}}{\text{AR}}$$

This ratio will give an indication of how quickly accounts receivable are collected. For P&B, the AR turnover is 37.41 times per year. Another way to express this concept is the average time taken to collect the accounts receivable, referred to as the *average collection period*. For P&B, this period is equal to 9.76 days (365/AR turnover). This figure can be compared with the company's credit policy to show whether actual collection is in line with expected collection time.

Another major investment in total assets is represented by inventory; here the corresponding effectiveness measure is the *inventory turnover ratio,* given by

$$\begin{array}{l}\text{Inventory (INV)} \\ \text{Turnover}\end{array} = \frac{\begin{array}{c}\text{Cost of Goods} \\ \text{Sold (CGS)}\end{array}}{\begin{array}{c}\text{Ending or} \\ \text{Average Inventory}\end{array}}$$

As with accounts receivable, this ratio indicates how many times inventory turned over during the past period. For P&B, INV turnover equals 6.88 times per year, which is somewhat slower than the industry norm. As an alternative, average inventory can be used rather than ending inventory, especially if inventory displays some seasonal pattern. This approach allows us to compute a better measure of inventory activity, because an abnormally large or small ending inventory figure distorts the inventory turnover ratio.

In addition to ratios that measure current activity, we are also concerned with ratios that measure fixed-asset and total-asset activities. These may be defined as the following two ratios:

$$\text{Total Assets (TA) Turnover} = \frac{\text{Sales}}{\text{Total Assets}}$$

$$\text{Fixed Assets (FA) Turnover} = \frac{\text{Sales}}{\text{Fixed Assets}}$$

Both of these measures give an indication of how effectively management is using total and fixed assets per dollar of sales. For P&B, these are 1.91 and 2.77 times, respectively. The value of the TA turnover ratio means that for $1.00 invested in total assets the firm generates $1.91 in total sales. Note that care should be taken when interpreting this type of ratio for firms with assets that are heavily depreciated. Large accumulated depreciation balances can lead to an overestimate of the firm's total effectiveness.

C. Leverage Ratios

Leverage measures the relative amount of debt used to finance assets. Two common measures of leverage are the *debt ratio* and the *long-term debt to owners' equity ratio:*

$$\text{Debt Ratio} = \frac{\text{Total Liabilities (TL)}}{\text{Total Assets}}$$

$$\begin{array}{c}\text{Long-Term Debt}\\ \text{to Owners'}\\ \text{Equity Ratio}\end{array} = \frac{\begin{array}{c}\text{Long-Term}\\ \text{Debt (LTD)}\end{array}}{\begin{array}{c}\text{Total Owners'}\\ \text{Equity (OE)}\end{array}}$$

For P&B, the values of these ratios are 0.34 and 0.07, respectively, showing that 34 percent of the total assets were financed with debt and that long-term debt represents only 7 percent of the amount of funds contributed by owners.

In addition to these measures, there is a related criterion that measures the firm's ability to meet or cover its interest charges. This criterion is referred to as the *coverage ratio* or *times interest earned (TIE),* and is given by

$$\begin{array}{c}\text{Times Interest}\\ \text{Earned (TIE)}\end{array} = \frac{\begin{array}{c}\text{Earnings before Interest}\\ \text{and Taxes (EBIT)}\end{array}}{\text{Interest Expense}}$$

For P&B, TIE equals 7.57 times, which indicates that operating earnings can clearly cover the fixed-charge obligations owed to creditors.

D. Profitability Ratios

Profitability can be measured in three dimensions—sales, total assets, and owners' equity—and generally can be defined in a number of ways, although for the purposes on hand we will use earnings after taxes (net income). Profitability ratios can now be defined for sales, total assets, and owners' equity as follows:

$$\begin{array}{c}\text{Return on Sales}\\ \text{(Net Profit Margin)}\end{array} = \frac{\text{Net Income}}{\text{Total Sales}}$$

$$\begin{array}{c}\text{Return on Total}\\ \text{Assets (ROA)}\end{array} = \frac{\text{Net Income (NI)}}{\text{TA}}$$

$$\begin{array}{c}\text{Return on Equity}\\ \text{(ROE)}\end{array} = \frac{\text{Net Income}}{\text{Owners' Equity}}$$

For P&B, these measures equal 1.21 percent, 2.31 percent, and 3.48 percent, respectively. The figures measure the amount of profit relative to each dollar in sales, assets, and equity. For example, P&B's profit margin equals 1.21 percent, which indicates that for each dollar in sales \$.0121 is net profit. The other figures can be interpreted similarly.

Based on the formulas presented here and in the section on activity, we can show that the following relationship holds:

$$\frac{\text{NI}}{\text{TA}} = \left[\frac{\text{NI}}{\text{Sales}}\right]\left[\frac{\text{Sales}}{\text{TA}}\right]$$

This formula is actually ROA = Net Profit Margin × Asset Turnover. The relationship highlights two important aspects of return on (total) investment: the profitability of sales and the efficiency of asset management. Combined, the two figures establish the total profitability on assets. Obviously, there can be different combinations of these two factors which result in the same value for ROA. Therefore, if there are any deficiencies in ROA, they may be due to either low profitability or low turnover, or both.

In addition to the preceding relationship, we can also show that the following formula holds:

$$\text{ROE} = \frac{\text{ROA}}{1 - \text{Debt Ratio}}$$

Here we see that if leverage does not affect profitability, then the larger the debt ratio, the larger the corresponding ROE. Therefore, differences in profitability or leverage can cause deviations from the industry norm for the return-on-equity measure. Appendix 4A discusses further the interrelationships present in ratios such as those described above.

E. Framework for Financial Analysis

How do we now collectively analyze a firm's financial condition? One approach might be to compute ratios for a number of years, say five, and use this information in an analysis that makes use of economic and industry conditions. This is a preferred approach, because a ratio in and of itself really conveys very little information (unless the ratio value is at an extreme—either high or low). Therefore, numbers such as these should be evaluated relative to both the firm's past performance and its external environment. A sound approach might be to follow a standard industry convention like the following:

1. Delineate overall economic conditions and how they influence the industry and the firm under study.
2. Study the specific industry conditions and how the firm operates within the competitive structure of its industry.
3. Perform ratio analysis and relate the findings to (1) and (2), above.

This background information collected in parts (1) and (2) can provide valuable support for the conclusions reached from analyzing the firm's financial statements.

Basically, we recognize explicitly that the firm operates in a system of interdependent economic markets, each with its own feedback mechanism. The success of one firm in a relatively small industry may be the exact reason for some other firm's poor performance. Because the firm does not operate in a vacuum, we must recognize that the financial statements are partially the result of the workings of the system of interdependent markets. Therefore, economic and industry analyses help minimize errors in determining the firm's true financial condition.

V. OTHER ISSUES CONCERNING FINANCIAL RATIOS

We have discussed the computation of ratios and their use within a framework for financial analysis. However, as this framework is by no means exhaustive, there are some other important issues that need to be mentioned. They range from comparing ratios against the industry norm to using ratios as predictors of financial distress and accounting for the effects of price-level changes. We also should note that the first two issues discussed in this section represent those factors that are cross-sectional in nature—that is, having to do with differences that may exist among groups of firms at a specific point in time.

A. Industry "Ideal" Benchmarks

As alluded to earlier, proper financial analysis must extend to a comparison of the firm's ratios with industry norms. Clearly, such an analysis involves the definition of an industry and how the firm being analyzed is classified into various categories. Currently there are many published sources of industry averages. For instance, both the Robert Morris Associates *Annual Statement Studies* and the Dun and Bradstreet *Key Business Ratios* report information on many manufacturing, wholesale, and retail industries. Interpreting the ideal benchmark computed by these agencies involves an awareness of the definition of the industry, as well as the estimation procedure used to construct this ideal value or norm.

Economist J. Bain defined an industry as a group of close substitute products each of which is sold entirely to a common group of buyers. Another common definition, the classification technique referred to as SIC (Standard Industrial Classification), specifies an industry with respect to end-product lines. Here, industries are grouped into 2, 3, or 4-digit categories. The 4-digit classification is the narrowest in product-line scope, the 2-digit one the broadest. Clearly, those firms with similar 4-digit SIC codes are those with more homogeneous end products. As we move up to the 2-digit classification, it is very likely that such firms will have quite heterogeneous products. With this in mind, we should note that the usefulness of these classifications may be less than expected.

B. Corporate Diversification

The issue of industrial classification becomes even more complicated by the conglomerate nature of many large firms. For example, consider the various lines of business in which a company like Textron Corporation operates. Textron's sales are derived from such diverse activities as helicopters (Bell Helicopter), watches (Speidel Co.), and chainsaws (Homelite), just to mention a few. As a result, financial analysis of such a company against an industry norm is very difficult; no specific benchmark would be representative of Textron. Because most large firms distribute only consolidated statements, it is impossible to assess the performance of any one line of its business against that of some well-defined industry. This clearly presents a problem, as most agencies report industry norms according to SIC code numbers. Unfortunately, there is little guidance to be offered for analyzing companies with many diverse product lines. However, even if the issue of industrial classification is well defined, problems also arise in the estimation of the industry norm.

C. Estimation of Industry Norm

Very seldom do the reporting agencies indicate the methodology used in collecting data and computing the norm. Ideally, a census should be conducted of all firms within an SIC code industry. From this information a frequency distribution of the ratios, probably by quartiles, can be computed for the reporting of firms overall, as well as by asset size. This is the practice employed by Robert Morris, and Dun and Bradstreet—however, with a *sample* of firms chosen rather than a census taken. For industries with a small number of firms, unknown biases may arise, perhaps excluding one or more of the leading firms in that industry. In addition, unknown biases may arise due to differences in the accounting techniques used to compute such important entries as depreciation, inventory values, and the like. Finally, many agencies use ad hoc criteria for deleting firms that may be considered outliers. Caution must therefore be exercised when interpreting an industry norm.

D. Distribution of Ratios

Earlier, it was noted that P&B's inventory-turnover ratio of 6.88 was slightly lower than the industry average of 9.93 (see table 4.15). In order for this comparison to be valid, significant differences must exist between the financial ratios of firms. To assess this condition, we need to consider the distributions of these ratios within the industry. Standard statistical tests for significant differences involve assumptions about normality in the underlying distribution. In order to evaluate the appropriateness of such assumptions, we may look at various aspects of the distribution. Looking at the frequency distribution at various fractiles can be extremely useful. Or we can apply specialized statistical techniques like the Kolmogorov-Smirnov (KS) one-sample test of normality. Both Robert Morris Associates and Dun and Bradstreet report the quartiles of all ratio distributions. Positive skewness (evidence of nonnormality) usually is present if the difference between the 75th percentile and the 50th percentile is greater than the difference between the 50th percentile and the 25th percentile. (See Foster, 1978, p. 177, for evidence of positive skewness in certain ratios.) Clearly, rejection of the normality assumption would cast doubt on the use of standard statistical tests for significant differences from the industry average. Hence, caution must be exercised when testing for these differences.

E. Other Categories

The classification of financial ratios into the four groups discussed earlier, although conventional, is also largely ad hoc in nature. A different grouping was derived empirically in a study by Pinches et al. (See Foster, 1978, p. 184.) Sampling 221 COMPUSTAT industrial firms, Pinches tested 40 financial ratios and found the following seven factors that appeared to show some homogeneity within a given industry:

1. Return on investment
2. Financial leverage
3. Capital intensiveness
4. Inventory intensiveness
5. Receivables intensiveness
6. Short-term liquidity
7. Cash position

These factors are clearly related to the four categories used earlier. Activity (intensiveness) appears in its component parts, while liquidity is represented by measures of short-term assets and immediate cash. However, the earlier classification scheme was not intended to be exhaustive, and the Pinches study just highlights this problem. As it stands, the perfect classification system (if one exists) has yet to be devised.

F. Industry and Economy Influences

Because a firm's financial ratios change over time, it would be of interest to see whether there are industry- and economy-wide influences that can cause these changes. One approach to studying this phenomenon involves the use of *index models*. An index model posits a relationship between the firm's ratios and the industry averages, as well as economy-wide averages. For the firm's debt ratio (DR), such a relationship may take the form:

$$DR_{it} = a + bDR_{mt} + cDR_{It} + U_{it} \quad (4.1)$$

where DR_{it} = Debt ratio of firm i at time t
DR_{mt} = Debt ratio of all firms in the market at time t
DR_{It} = Debt ratio of all other firms in the ith firm's industry at time t
U_{it} = a random error term for the ith firm in period t

This type of model is referred to as a *multi-index model* because it posits two factors exerting a systematic influence on the debt ratio of the firm under consideration. The use of the model, however, requires the construction of two indices, which have not yet been specified. Clearly, the indices can be value-weighted or equally weighted. Foster (p. 141) finds a high correlation ($R^2 = 0.922$) between equally- and value-weighted indices in most financial ratios, thereby lessening the importance of this issue. As for the appropriateness of these types of indices, a study conducted by King (1966) supports the existence of industry and market influences in stock market returns. Subsequently, Ball and Brown (1967), examining the importance of similar factors in financial ratios, found that approximately 35–40 percent of the variability of a firm's annual earnings can be accounted for by the variability of the earnings of all firms. In addition, about 10–15 percent can be explained by industry factors.

By contrast, Foster (p. 148) finds that the importance of the industry- and economy-wide influences varies across ratios. These influences were strongest for profitability and turnover, and least powerful for liquidity and debt ratios. Overall, these studies suggest that significant industry- and economy-wide influences do exist. Therefore, the analyst can better assess trends that are present in a firm's financial ratios by taking these two systematic factors into account. A study by Bowen and Huber also shows that significant industry differences in ratios exist (see Foster 1978, p. 60). Foster speculates that these may be due to differences in underlying economic conditions. Clearly, the case could be analyzed along the lines of the multifactor index model. However, as there is no well-defined theoretical model to explain differences or changes in financial ratios, the analyst is forced to examine all possible avenues.

G. Ratios as Predictors of Financial Distress

Several interesting studies have been conducted in the area of financial distress. One of them, by Beaver (1966), compared the mean ratios for 79 failed and nonfailed firms and found extreme differences present in the ratios between these two classifications. In addition, Altman (1968), using discriminant analysis on financial ratios, correctly classified 95 percent of the 66 bankrupt and nonbankrupt firms. He used five categories that basically reflected those discussed earlier in the chapter. Although there is no integrated theory to predict financial distress, the Beaver and Altman studies highlight a potential application for utilizing all ratios collectively.

To illustrate the results of the Altman study, let us consider the case of P&B Import Corporation for year-end 1988. Altman constructed an index of bankruptcy based on a weighted score of the following five financial ratios:

X_1 = Working capital to total assets

X_2 = Retained earnings to total assets

X_3 = EBIT to total assets

X_4 = Market value of equity to book value of debt

X_5 = Sales to total assets

For Altman's study, the values of X should be expressed in absolute percentage terms; i.e., the ratio value of 10 percent is expressed as 10.0, and so on for all other ratios. Using the statistical technique of discriminant analysis, Altman constructed an index:

$$Z = .012X_1 + .014X_2 + .033X_3 + .006X_4 + .010X_5 \quad (4.2)$$

to discriminate bankrupt from nonbankrupt firms.

Equation (4.2) represents a weighted sum of financial characteristics, and firms with a score of less than 2.675 are classified as bankrupt or failing, while those with a score greater than 2.675 are classified as healthy or not bankrupt. Based on the information given in Tables 4.13 and 4.14 we can compute the Z-score for P&B for year-end 1988 as follows:

$$Z = .012(10.93) + .014(66.32) + .033(4.48) + .006(450) + .010(191) = 5.817$$

Because P&B has a Z-score greater than 2.675, we can conclude that its financial characteristics are similar to those of firms classified as nonbankrupt. While this example illustrates one way to arrive at a single index of a firm's financial condition, it does not imply that the other methods discussed earlier should be discarded. Only when we combine the results of many different analyses can we accurately assess a firm's financial condition.

VI. SUMMARY AND REVIEW

The data contained in financial statements can greatly enhance our understanding of how a firm operates. Techniques for performing financial analysis range from simple ratios to cross-sectional studies that relate certain key variables to economy- and industry-wide indices. Clearly, the choice of model rests with the desired goal and the degree of sophistication deemed appropriate by the analyst. While these approaches may seem unduly complicated, they highlight the importance of analyzing trends and the external effects on the firm generated by the industry and the economy.

NOTES

1. The after-tax cash flow will typically also include other noncash expenses such as deferred taxes and other deferred obligations. Because these funds are available to the corporation until their actual payment, they become temporary components of the firm's cash flow.
2. We shall discuss later in the chapter the ways of converting the stock values of balance sheets into flow values and compare the percentage changes in the balance sheets for two successive fiscal periods.

QUESTIONS

1. What is the balance sheet and the utility of the information contained therein?
2. What does the income statement represent?
3. Discuss the difference between stocks and flows and how these concepts relate to the balance sheet and income statement.
4. Discuss the various dimensions along which comparative financial analysis can take place.
5. On the occasion of bankruptcy declaration by a major corporation in the transportation industry, an astute external analyst is reputed to have stated the following: "In years of economic prosperity, the income statement is the undisputed king of financial evaluation and performance. But, when the economy is in straits and monetary conditions become restrictive, the balance sheet becomes the informational benchmark in the mind of external analysts." Discuss the meaning and significance of this statement.

PROBLEM

From the information for P&B Imports in tables 4.13 and 4.14, construct common-size balance sheets and income statements for the years 1985–1988. Based on this information, construct a statement of changes in financial condition for the years 1986–1988.

APPENDIX 4A THE DUPONT SYSTEM OF FINANCIAL RATIO ANALYSIS

As noted in Chapter 4, certain ratios can be derived as the products of other ratios. The example presented in this appendix demonstrates the relationships that exist between two ratios: *return on assets* and *return on equity*. It is one of the many instances illustrating how ratios can be used in combination to produce important analytical insights. This type of analysis is usually referred to as a *DuPont analysis* because that company developed the general approach. Exhibit 4A.1 presents partially expanded sets of the various relationships used in the DuPont method.

The first set is the basic relationship that exists for return on investment (ROI). As shown earlier, return on investment can be computed as the product of the net profit margin and asset turnover ratios. Another way to view this relationship is shown in equation (4A.1). In essence,

EXHIBIT 4A.1 Interrelationships Among Ratios

Basic "Dupont Ratios"

Marketing Efficiency × *Production Efficiency* = *Funds Efficiency*

$$\frac{\text{Profit}}{\text{Sales}} \times \frac{\text{Sales}}{\text{Assets}} = \frac{\text{Profit}}{\text{Assets}} \qquad (4A.1)$$

Capital Leverage

Funds Efficiency × *Leverage on Capital* = *Return on Capital (Capital Efficiency)*

$$\frac{\text{Profit}}{\text{Assets}} \times \frac{\text{Assets}}{\text{Capital (LTD + OE)}} = \frac{\text{Profit}}{\text{Capital}} \qquad (4A.2)$$

Leverage on Equity

Return on Capital × *Leverage on Equity* = *Return on Equity (Equity Efficiency)*

$$\frac{\text{Profit}}{\text{Capital}} \times \frac{\text{Capital}}{\text{Equity}} = \frac{\text{Profit}}{\text{Equity}} \qquad (4A.3)$$

Growth in Equity ("Sustainable Rate of Growth")

Return on Equity × *Retention Rate* = *Growth in Equity*

$$\frac{\text{Profit}}{\text{Equity}} \times \frac{\text{Profit} - \text{Dividends}}{\text{Profit}} = \frac{\text{Increase in Retained Earnings}}{\text{Equity}} \qquad (4A.4)$$

total funds efficiency as measured by ROI is the product of the firm's marketing and production efficiencies. Equations (4A.2) and (4A.3) introduce the effect of a company's capital structure. The ratios in those equations reflect decisions that are the primary responsibility of financial executives, whereas the ratios in the first set are under the control of the marketing and production functions.

Equation (4A.2) illustrates how return on capital (long-term debt plus owners' equity) can be enhanced by the use of current liabilities such as trade accounts payable, commercial paper, and bank notes. A company that can acquire relatively more total assets per dollar of capital (by implication, increasing the level of current liabilities) uses its capital more efficiently than a company that does not have this ability. More assets bring more sales and profits. Hence, as shown in equation (4A.2), a higher return on capital results. (The use of such funds, of course, can bring a higher level of financial risk, but this is an argument that will not be followed at this point.) In addition, the earnings on the business must be higher than the cost of the debt in order for a positive benefit to be obtained from using that form of financing.

Just as a company that can obtain additional current liabilities in proportion to its capital may under favorable operating conditions enhance its return on capital, a company that can obtain additional long-term debt (in one of its many forms) in proportion to its equity may enhance its return on equity. This relationship is shown in equation (4A.3). Again, in order for the effect of the leverage to be favorable, the company must earn enough to pay the interest on the debt.

The relationship spelled out in equations (4A.2) and (4A.3) can be compressed into one function by using the ratio of assets to equity as the second component of equation (4A.2). The product of the calculation is the return on equity, as in equation (4A.3).

Equation (4A.4) shows the interactions that exist in the computation of return on equity. A critical variable in this equation is the proportion of earnings paid out as dividends to the various classes of equity owners. For example, if a company earns 10 percent of its equity and pays no dividends, the earnings retained increase equity by the full 10 percent. If the company pays out any portion as dividends, the equity increase by some factor less than 10 percent.

The rate of increase in the equity account is an especially important ratio because it is the rate at which the company can comfortably increase its sales without having to alter its other financial policies. If a company is unwilling to raise new equity, then there is only one growth rate in sales that is consistent with the company's other established operating and financial policies. This rate has been termed the *sustainable rate of growth*. As given in equation (4A.4), the sustainable rate of growth can prove extremely useful in most financial analyses.

While the demonstration that the growth in equity is the sustainable rate of growth is most commonly done in mathematical terms, a graphic illustration may be as efficient and more memorable. First, consider the very simple diagrammatic example in Exhibit 4A.2. The relevant summary ratios that describe the company's operating and financial characteristics are as follows:

Production efficiency:	Sales/Assets = 2 ($1 of assets will generate $2 of sales; $1 of extra sales requires $0.50 of assets.)
Marketing efficiency:	Profit/Sales = 5% (An extra $1 of sales generates an extra $0.05 of profits.)
Leverage on equity:	Assets/Equity = 2 (This is the product of the leverage on capital and the leverage on equity, simplifying the two components into one; note that the implied ratio of total debt to equity is 1/1 = 1.)

As can be seen from the exhibit, these relationships produce a sales volume that is twice

EXHIBIT 4A.2 The Relationship of Profits, Sales, and Assets

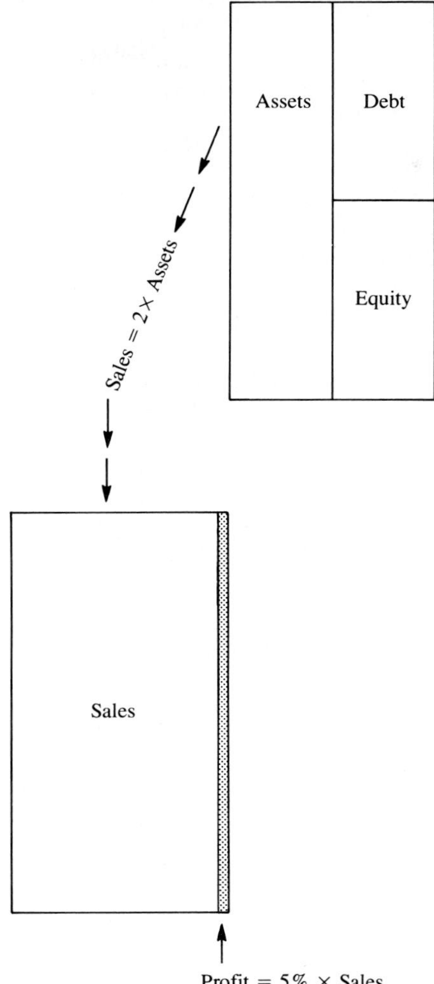

the amount of the total assets. The profits are the sliver of total sales that is left after all costs of operations and taxes are deducted. The balance in the equity account equals the total debt.

The return on equity is the product of the efficiency of funds and the leverage on equity:

Marketing Efficiency		*Production Efficiency*		*Leverage on Equity*		*Return on Equity*
$\frac{\text{Profit}}{\text{Sales}}$	×	$\frac{\text{Sales}}{\text{Assets}}$	×	$\frac{\text{Assets}}{\text{Equity}}$	=	$\frac{\text{Profit}}{\text{Equity}}$
5%	×	2	×	2	=	20%

Exhibit 4A.3 shows the effect of the dividend decision:

Dividend payout ratio: 50%

(By subtraction, the retention

rate is also 50%.)

Funds (usually cash) amounting to half of the profits are removed from the company and paid to the equity owners. The remaining half is added to the equity account. Consequently, the retained earnings amount to a 10-percent increase in the equity account. In terms of the formulas, this may be represented as

EXHIBIT 4A.3 Effects of the Dividend Decision

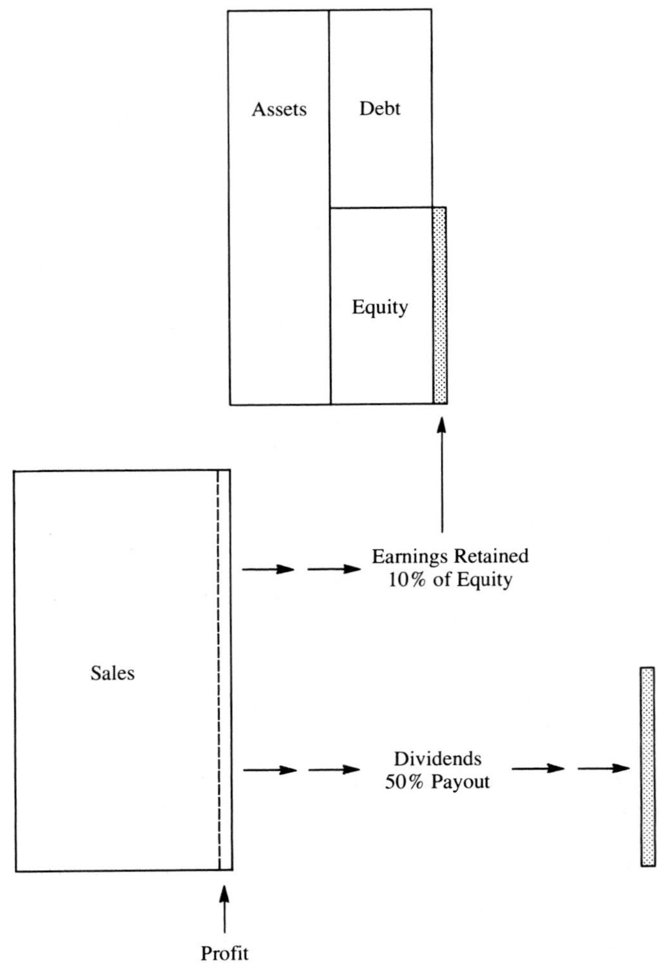

Return on Equity		*Retention Rate*		*Growth in Equity*
$\frac{\text{Profit}}{\text{Equity}}$	×	(1 − Dividend Rate)	=	$\frac{\text{Increase in Retained Earnings}}{\text{Equity}}$
20%	×	50%	=	10%

As shown in Exhibit 4A.4, this 10-percent increase in equity will allow an additional 10 percent debt, given a debt-to-equity relationship of 1/1. In effect, the increase in the equity foundation of a soundly managed company allows a proportionate increase in debt. Because sources and uses must be equal, the 10-percent increase in the liabilities-owners' equity (source) side al-

EXHIBIT 4A.4 The Relationship of Debt and Equity

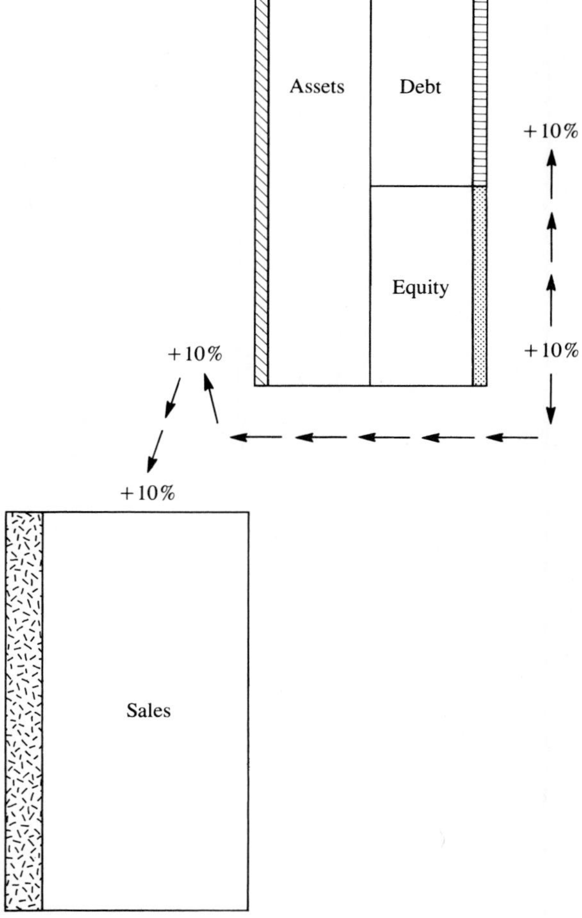

lows management to increase the firm's assets by 10 percent. Furthermore, for each $1 of new assets, the company can generate an additional $2 of sales. Because the sales are twice the assets, however, a $2 increase in sales is the same proportionate increase as a $1 increase in assets. Hence, the 10-percent relationship carried all the way from the equity account to sales.

What happens if sales increase faster than the equity account can grow? This can occur in the common situation in which management is attempting to maintain the company's market share in a rapidly growing market or to enhance it in a more stable one. The demands of the market are large, and rather than constrain the company's sales growth to a level proportionate to that of the equity account, sales are allowed to increase according to market demand.

Exhibit 4A.5 illustrates such a situation, using the interrelationships already established for the 10-percent-growth example. Sales, the initiating variable in this case, have been allowed to grow by 40 percent, requiring a proportionate increase of 40 percent in assets. In absolute terms, the increase in the dollar amount of assets will be half the increase in the dollar amount of sales because the sales-to-asset ratio is 2/1. Accordingly, a 40-percent increase in assets (uses) requires a 40-percent increase in sources, the two of which are of course of equal dollar amounts.

EXHIBIT 4A.5 The Relationship of Sales, Debt, and Equity

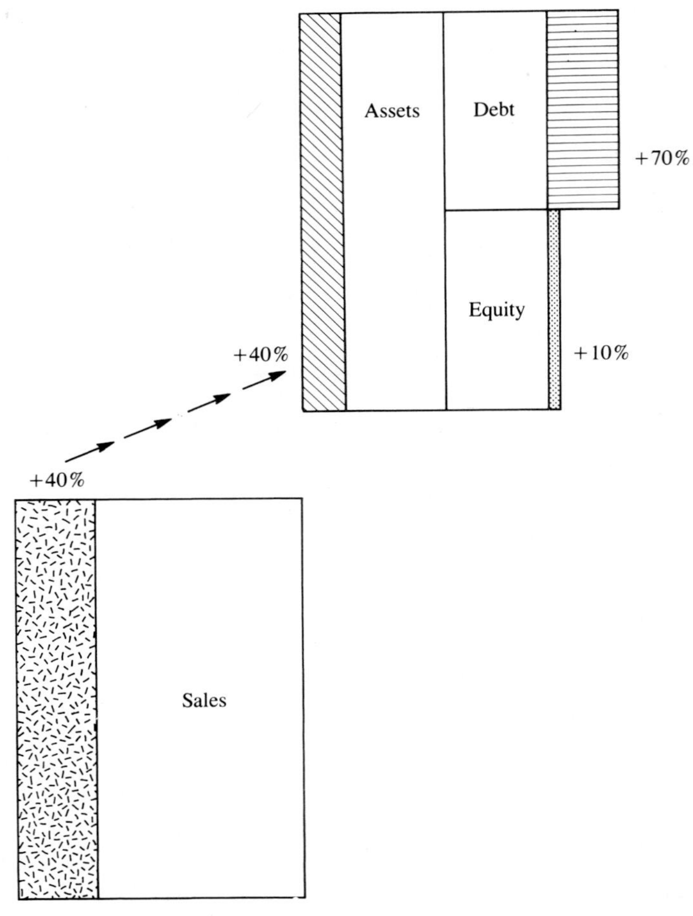

Unfortunately, the increase in equity is only 10 percent. Thus, as Exhibit 4A.5 shows, in order to finance the difference, the debt balance must be increased significantly, by 70 percent. Assuming initial assets of $100, both sides of the balance sheet must rise by $40 to reflect the 40-percent increase. Thus, if retained earnings only increase by $5 (10 percent), the other $35 must come from additional debt. Debt will then increase from $50 to $85 and, whereas the traditional relationship between debt and equity had been 1/1, it is now $35/$5 = 7/1 on the margin for the new funds raised and 85/55 = 1.55/1 on average. Consequently, the asset-to-equity ratio has gone from 2/1 to 2.55/1.

Even allowing for the additional profits and retentions from the new 40-percent sales does not cure the imbalance in the short run. The new leverage on the equity augments the increase in retained earnings growth to 12.75 percent in the future:

1/1 as a source of funds. The missing $13.62 would be provided by the additional debt. Given the additional $1.38 in earnings produced annually by the higher growth in sales, it would take almost 10 additional years with growth of no more than 10 percent to return the proportions to their initial balance.

By making the convenient assumption that the company's initial financial position was optimal, the preceding discussion has avoided many complications of the real world. To cite one example, if the company had been using less than optimal debt, (say the asset-to-capital ratio had been 1/1, with no debt at all for the firm), it could have initially financed the high rate of growth with relatively more proportionate debt than the ultimate target (of 1/1 debt-to-equity in this case). Drawing more than proportionately on one source of funds, however, may quickly use up any spare funds that exist in that category. Even if no initial debt had existed in this example, the addition of debt at the rate of 7/1 for equity would quickly bring the total debt up to the target of 1/1 with total equity.

Marketing Efficiency		*Production Efficiency*		*Leverage on Equity*		*Return on Equity*
$\frac{\text{Profit}}{\text{Sales}}$	×	$\frac{\text{Sales}}{\text{Assets}}$	×	$\frac{\text{Assets}}{\text{Equity}}$	=	$\frac{\text{Profit}}{\text{Equity}}$
5%	×	2	×	2.55	=	25.5%

Return on Equity		*Retention Rate*		*Growth in Equity*
$\frac{\text{Profit}}{\text{Equity}}$	×	(1 − Dividend Rate)	=	$\frac{\text{Increase in Retained Earnings}}{\text{Equity}}$
25.5%	×	50%	=	12.75%

It will take considerable time even at the 12.75-percent rate of growth in the equity account (a 27.5-percent increase) to catch up with the initial shortfall caused by the high rate of sales growth. In absolute dollar terms and allowing for full, immediate profits, the company's assets would increase from $100 to $140, and equity would grow from $50 to $56.38 rather than to the $55.00 under a 10-percent growth alternative. The equity balance should have grown to $70 to retain its basic proportion of

Reliance on such a temporary imbalance must be of relatively limited duration, as the discipline necessary for achieving a sustainable rate of growth must again be recognized. For many rapidly growing companies, this discipline means a difficult choice between raising additional equity funds, slowing growth, or incurring potentially serious financial difficulty and possible financial collapse when the creditors decline to provide further funds or demand repayment of funds already advanced.

As we have seen, when sales increase at a rate different from the sustainable growth rate, one or the other must change. As presented in this analysis, the company would increase its amount of leverage and hence its financial risk. However, the analysis presents the issue of sustainable growth purely in nominal terms; we must recognize that in the face of inflation, the issue may not be so easy to analyze. Moreover, we must also decide on whether to target our capital structure in terms of book or market values if the firm wishes to maintain a stable capital structure. While these issues are clearly beyond the material typically discussed in financial statement analysis, we should be aware that the financial ratios computed in this chapter are clearly the results of both operating and financial decisions.

ANNOTATED BIBLIOGRAPHY

Altman, E. I. "Predicting Railroad Bankruptcies in America." *Bell Journal of Economics and Management Science,* Spring 1973, 184–211.

An early and pioneering work on the use of financial ratios as predictors of corporate bankruptcy.

Ball, R., and R. Watts. "Some Time Series Properties of Accounting Numbers." *Journal of Finance,* June 1972, 663–682.

A fine presentation of the use of time-series techniques with accounting information.

Chen, K. H., and A. Shimerda. "An Empirical Analysis of Useful Financial Ratios." *Financial Management,* Spring 1981, 51–60.

A good study of financial ratios and their relative usefulness.

Foster, G. *Financial Statement Analysis.* Englewood Cliffs, N.J.: Prentice-Hall, 1978.

A sound overall discussion of the techniques employed in modern analysis of financial statements.

Higgins, R. C. "Sustainable Growth Under Inflation." *Financial Management,* Autumn 1981, 36–40.

An outline of the issue of sustainable growth in the presence of inflation.

Lev, B. *Financial Statement Analysis: A New Approach.* Englewood Cliffs, N.J.: Prentice-Hall, 1978.

A very good book on the analysis of financial statements and the use of ratios for diagnostic as well as forecasting purposes.

Lev, B. "Industry Averages as Targets for Financial Ratios." *Journal of Accounting Research,* Autumn 1969, 290–299.

A good paper on the use of financial ratios in the formulation of financial goals.

Nelson, R. *Applied Time-Series Analysis for Managerial Forecasting.* San Francisco: Holden-Day, 1973.

An outstanding introduction to the methodology of time-series analysis.

Pinches, G., K. Mingo, and J. Caruthers. "The Stability of Financial Patterns in Industrial Organization." *Journal of Finance,* May 1973, 389–396.

A fine paper on the breakdown of financial ratios along various dimensions.

Robert Morris Associates, *Annual Statement Studies.* Philadelphia: Robert Morris Associates.

A series that presents information on industry and common-size financial statements.

5

FORECASTING FINANCIAL REQUIREMENTS

I. INTRODUCTION

In the previous chapter, we discussed the construction of the four basic financial statements and several methods of analyzing their contents. While analysis of historical data underlies the assessment of past performance, it is now time to discuss the use of accounting data for projecting both future performance and funding needs. Specifically, we shall examine pro forma financial statements (income statements and balance sheets) as well as cash budgets. Then we shall proceed to the methods employed in the cost-volume-profit analysis typically performed with the production of any commodity or service. This approach is known as break-even analysis and is extended to include forecasting of future sales and revenues. Finally, the chapter will close with a discussion of some operational details on time-series analysis of accounting data with specific reference to such applications as moving averages, seasonal adjustments, exponential smoothing, and regression analysis.

II. FORECASTING FINANCIAL NEEDS

Section I listed some methods that can be used to arrive at forecasts of a firm's earnings or sales. Given a forecast of sales, the analyst may now proceed in a variety of directions to project the firm's anticipated financial needs. We have already discussed the funds flow as a means of estimating the extent to which the present operations of the firm can support future growth. In effect, the funds-flow statement can be employed as a means of forecasting future financial needs. More direct methods involve forecasting the firm's income statements and balance sheets as well as its expected cash inflows and outflows, via cash budgets.

Pro forma statements reflect the expected future performance of the firm over some specified time period (income statement) as well as the firm's likely financial position at various points in the future (balance sheet). However, cash budgets are constructed to identify cash needs and typically are more of a short-range planning tool. Cash budgets may be constructed on a daily, weekly, or monthly basis, while pro forma statements are typically constructed monthly, quarterly, or annually.

Before discussing the topic of funds forecasting, an adequate definition of funds must be established. The *funds* available to an entity are the sum of the short-term credit it can obtain, the long-term debt available, and the equity capital contributed by the owners and left in the business in the form of retained earnings. Funds flow in and out of a business as it changes its scale of operations. For example, a firm's sales may be characterized by a long-term (or secular) increase and this new higher level of sales activity may generate spontaneously the need for more funds. This need can be met in a number of ways, perhaps by long-term borrowing from a commercial bank or an insurance company. In addition to long-term needs for funds, the normal production cycle may also have an impact on the funds required. This cycle can be seen in

Figure 5.1, which is designed to give an overall representation of the flow of funds within the firm, dividing the sources and uses of funds into their longer and shorter term categories.

A well-known method for projecting financial statements is known as the percent-of-sales or *ratio method*. It is based on the assumption that there is a more or less constant relationship between the items in the balance sheet and income statement on the one hand and sales revenue on the other. Because these relationships are captured by the firm's financial ratios, they can provide a rough guide to the magnitude of a company's need for funds in the absence of more precise information. As long as the historical relationships are expected to hold and remain stable during the forecast period, the ratio approach can be very useful. However, we should note that because this approach uses imprecise estimates, it becomes necessary on occasion to combine certain accounts and to round off the figures within reasonable limits. Therefore, this approach is appropriate for forecasting statements with accounts similar to those used in Chapter 4. In addition to the estimates computed with ratios, we could materially improve the statement forecast if we knew the company's capital expenditure plans and maturity schedule of long-term debt. Fortunately, both of these figures are readily available for many companies, and they are frequently given in the annual report or form 10–K. If such information is not available, we should use the past year's level as the estimate for future expenditures.

While the ratio method is typically the only means available to outside analysts, projected financial statements that are for internal use only can be constructed based on in-house information. These statements will be much more precise than those constructed by outside analysts, because they are based on explicit assumptions about operating policies and procedures set by management, which is information unavailable to outsiders. We shall discuss both means of constructing projected financial statements.

A. A Simple Illustration

To illustrate the use of ratios as tools for projecting financial statements, we will draw upon the financial information for Parc Corporation that appears in Tables 5.1 and 5.2. Considering the recent economic optimism, Parc forecasts a 10-percent increase in sales for the coming year. In addition, if the current economic upturn continues, Parc may even be able to achieve a 15-percent increase in sales. These two estimates are reflected in the Low and High columns of Table 5.1.

Reviewing the company's income statements presented in Tables 5.2, we can develop a projected income statement for Parc. Cost of sales has risen somewhat in 1990 to 63.3 percent compared with the low of 62.2 percent in 1989. A continuation of this trend could bring this figure to 64 percent in 1991. If the higher sales figure materialized, the cost-of-sales percentages would probably be a little lower as a result of scale economies. Cost-of-sales percentages of 64 percent for the 10-percent sales increase and 63.5 percent for the 15-percent sales increase were used. Examining the trend in expenses, we arrive at a rough estimate of 26.5 percent of sales for 1991. As seen in Table 5.1, the net income figure developed from this analysis for the 10-percent sales increase was $13 million, slightly lower than the $13.3 million for 1990.

In order to arrive at a forecast for the balance sheet, there are two basic approaches. The first approach is to estimate all accounts with the exception of cash and marketable securities, and then see what funds would be left for investment in these items, that is, cash and marketable securities are used as "plug" or balancing figures. While this is a valid approach, the analyst should also be aware that firms must maintain at all times a minimum level of operating cash balances. However, the use of cash as the plug figure tends to obscure the importance of minimum operating cash requirements. Consequently, the second approach to forecasting the balance sheet requires that the analyst estimate all accounts, including cash and marketable securities, and then use notes payable as the plug figure. With this approach, cash requirements are explicitly accounted for and the analyst can see the level of short-term borrowing required to support a given level of activity. In our illustration, we shall use the second approach.

The asset accounts are analyzed first. From

FIGURE 5.1 Funds Flow Cycle

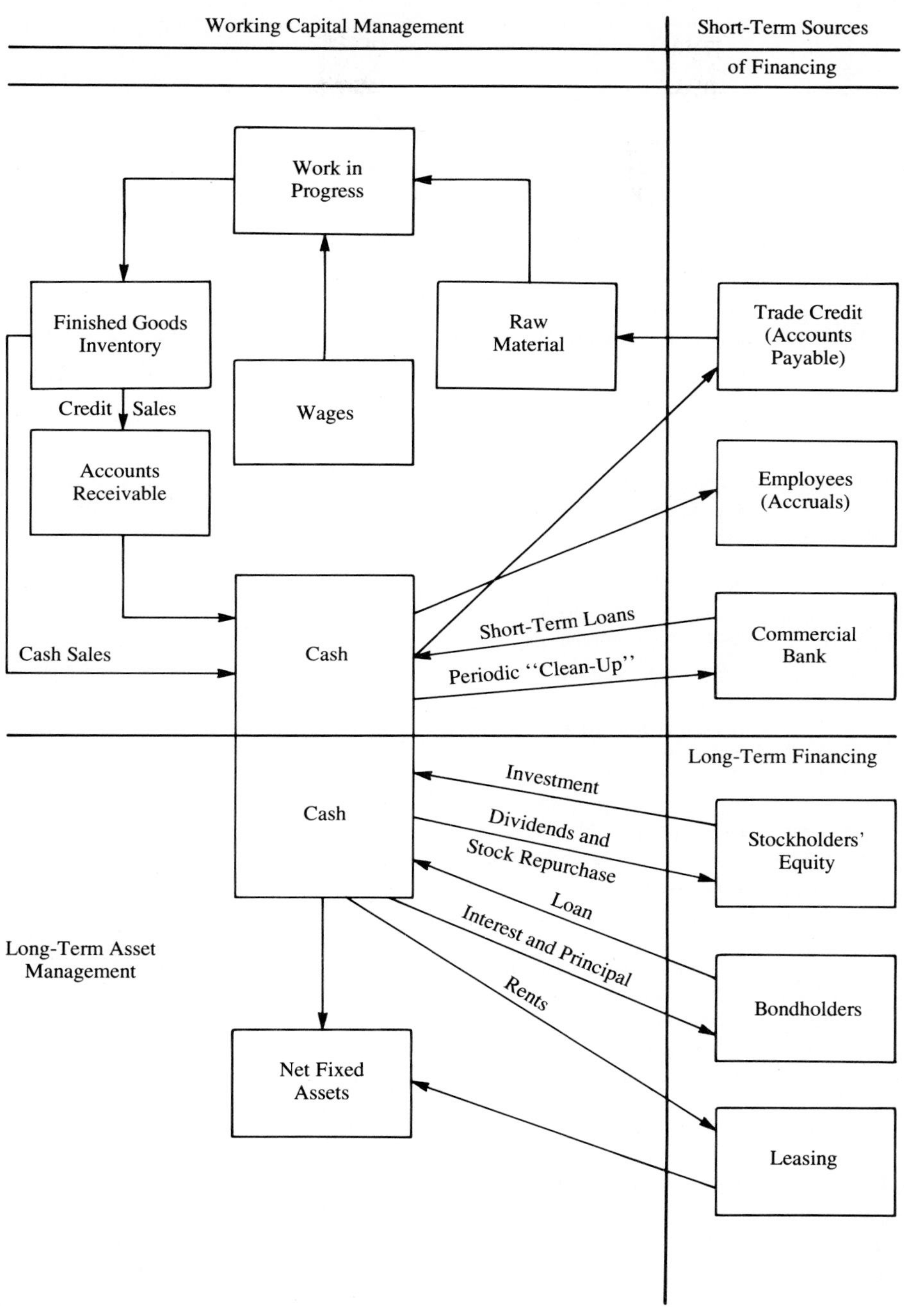

TABLE 5.1 Parc Corporation—Projected Financial Statements for the Year Ended December 31, 1991 (in millions of dollars)

Actual 1990		*Projected 1991*	
		Low	*High*
	Income Statement		
$256.2	Net sales: increase 10%–15%	$282.0	$295.0
162.3	Cost of sales: 64%–63.5%	180.0	187.0
$ 93.9	Gross margin	$102.0	$108.0
66.3	Total expenses: 26.5%	75.0	78.0
$ 27.6	Net operating income	$ 27.0	$ 30.0
0.9	Other expense net of other income	1.0	1.0
$ 26.7	Income before tax	$ 26.0	$ 29.0
13.4	Federal income taxes: 50%	13.0	14.5
$ 13.3	Net income	$ 13.0	$ 14.5
	Balance Sheet		
	Assets		
$ 12.3	Cash and marketable securities (5% sales):	$ 14.1	$ 14.8
24.6	Receivables: 35–37 days' sales	27.1	29.6
44.1	Inventories: 96–94 days' cost of sales	47.4	48.2
12.3	Long-term investments: up $1	13.3	13.3
105.4	Property, plant, and equipment (net): no net change at $282 sales; up $3 at $295 sales	105.4	108.4
2.7	Other assets: no change	2.7	2.7
$201.4	Total assets	$210.0	$217.0
	Liabilities and Equity		
$ 1.2	Notes payable (plug):	$ 3.7	$ 7.2
29.7	Accounts payable: 18% cost of sales	32.4	33.7
5.4	Accrued liabilities: up $1	6.4	6.4
7.5	Federal income tax: 50% liability	6.5	7.2
25.5	Long-term debt: $3 annual retirement	22.5	22.5
$ 69.3	Total liabilities	$ 71.5	$ 77.0
12.0	Preferred stock: no change	12.0	12.0
42.0	Paid-in equity: no change	42.0	42.0
78.1	Retained earnings: add net income and deduct dividends on preferred (0.6) and common (6.0) stock	84.5	86.0
$132.1	Total equity	$138.5	$140.0
$201.4	Total liabilities and equity	$210.0	$217.0

Tables 5.3 and 5.4, we see that year-end cash and marketable securities have been about 5% of annual sales. We furthermore note that receivables and inventories have both been rising in proportion to the volume of business Parc Corporation was doing. (The computations discussed here are derived from the data in Tables 5.1 through 5.4.) The collection period was 35 days' sales on accounts receivable in 1990, down from the 1989 peak of 39.2 days, but up from 32.1 days in 1986. Inventory figures showed a similar pattern, with 95.5 days' cost of sales for 1990. Based on the sales estimates, increased sales would likely cut the days' cost of sales held in inventory by the company. Therefore, 96 days and 94 days are used as the estimates associated

TABLE 5.2 Parc Corporation—Comparative Income Statements for the Years Ended December 31, 1986–1990

	1986	*1987*	*1988*	*1989*	*1990*
			(component percentages)		
Net sales	100.0%	100.0%	100.0%	100.0%	100.0%
Cost of sales*	63.9	66.8	66.5	62.2	63.3
Gross margin	36.1	33.2	33.5	37.8	36.7
Expenses					
Selling	5.8	5.9	6.0	6.5	6.4
Delivery	4.0	4.0	4.1	4.4	3.9
Advertising	5.0	5.0	4.9	4.2	3.8
Research and Development	2.6	2.2	2.2	1.8	2.3
Administrative and general	9.9	10.5	11.4	10.1	9.5
Total expenses	27.3	27.6	28.6	27.0	25.9
Net operating income	8.8	5.6	4.9	10.8	10.8
Interest income	0.1	0.3	0.3	0.2	0.2
Total income	8.9	5.9	5.2	11.0	11.0
Interest expense	0.7	0.7	0.6	0.5	0.6
Income before tax	8.2	5.2	4.6	10.5	10.4
Federal income taxes	4.1	2.6	2.3	5.3	5.2
Net income	4.1%	2.6%	2.3%	5.2%	5.2%

*Includes depreciation.

with the 10-percent and 15-percent increases, respectively. In addition, if the extra sales materialized, accounts receivable turnover might be forced down to a lower value to reflect greater numbers of slow-paying customers. Therefore, 35 and 37 days are used for the lower and higher sales estimates, respectively. As for plant and equipment, that account would probably change by $3 million if the higher sales level were realized. No change was forecast in the other asset accounts, but it appears that Parc Corporation has been adding nearly $1 million a year to its long-term investments. Hence, an allowance for a $1 million investment in 1991 was made.

On the liability side, the ratio of accounts payable to cost of sales increased from 13.3 percent in 1986 to 18.3 percent in 1990. This increase, however, represents a decline from a peak of 20 percent in 1989. Because 18 percent was still 66 days payable, assuming all costs of sales were purchased, realistically speaking, it was unlikely that the ratio would get any higher. Accounts payable, therefore, were estimated at 18 percent of cost of sales for both sales levels.

Other liability accounts are estimated roughly according to the trends of the past record. Accruals seem to be rising about $1 million per year. Because we did not have the debt repayment schedule, we estimated 1991 repayment to be approximately 10 percent of the total debt outstanding.

Most of the equity accounts could be projected easily. No changes were anticipated either in the preferred stock balance or in the paid-in equity accounts. The only change would be in retained earnings, which would be increased by the net earnings figure of $13 or $14.5 million and decreased by the preferred and common dividends of $0.6 and $6.0, respectively, that Parc would pay.

Adding up the totals, we find that the projected uses were $3.7 million larger than the proj-

TABLE 5.3 Parc Corporation—Consolidated Statements of Financial Position, December 31, 1986–1990

	1986	*1987*	*1988*	*1989*	*1990*
			(in millions)		
Assets					
Current assets:					
Cash	$ 9.6	$ 10.2	$ 8.7	$ 7.8	$ 9.3
Marketable securities	1.5	1.8	3.6	3.6	3.0
Receivables	18.6	19.5	20.1	25.2	24.6
Inventories	33.6	40.2	38.1	40.8	44.1
Total current assets	$ 63.3	$ 71.7	$ 70.5	$ 77.4	$ 81.0
Long-term investments	9.9	10.5	10.8	11.7	12.3
Property, plant, and equipment (net)	90.3	97.2	96.6	97.8	105.4
Other assets	3.3	2.7	2.4	2.1	2.7
Total assets	$166.8	$182.1	$180.3	$189.0	$201.4
Liabilities					
Current liabilities:					
Notes payable	$ 1.5	$ 3.9	$ 8.7	$ 2.1	$ 1.2
Accounts payable	18.0	27.6	27.0	28.2	29.7
Accrued liabilities	3.0	4.2	3.9	4.5	5.4
Federal income tax	—	—	—	6.3	7.5
Total current liabilities	$ 22.5	$ 35.7	$ 39.6	$ 41.1	$ 43.8
Long-term debt	30.6	30.3	24.0	22.5	25.5
Total liabilities	$ 53.1	$ 66.0	$ 63.6	$ 63.6	$ 69.3
Equity					
Preferred stock (100 par value)	$ 18.0	$ 18.0	$ 18.0	$ 12.0	$ 12.0
Common stock (1,000,000 shares 1968–70, 1,250,000 shares 1971–73)	30.0	30.0	30.0	37.5	37.5
Paid-in capital	3.0	3.0	3.0	4.5	4.5
Retained earnings	62.7	65.1	65.7	71.4	78.1
Total equity	$113.7	$116.1	$116.7	$125.4	$132.1
Total liabilities and equity	$166.8	$182.1	$180.3	$189.0	$201.4

ected sources at the $282 million sales volume, and this plug figure is used to project the notes payable account. A figure of $7.2 million was used for the $295 million sales volume. The higher volume now presents a problem. Even with the extra $1.5 million in retained earnings, the company's required borrowings would be about $6 million higher than in the most recent year. Accordingly, in order to reduce the need for additional funds, Parc Corporation might attempt to cut back receivables, curtail capital expenditures, or reduce its minimum cash requirement.

As this simple illustration has shown, useful financial statements can be prepared using only approximate information. In the case of the illustration, the estimates could be materially improved if we knew the company's capital expenditure plans and the maturity schedule of its long-term debt. Furthermore, once the income statement and balance sheet are estimated, statements of changes in financial position or of cash receipts and disbursements may be prepared, if desired. The statement of changes in financial position was discussed in Chapter 4. (*Note:* While these statements are

TABLE 5.4 Parc Corporation—Consolidated Income Statements for the Years Ended December 31, 1986–1990

	1986	1987	1988	1989	1990
			(in millions)		
Net sales	$211.2	$217.5	$203.4	$234.3	$256.2
Cost of sales*	135.0	145.2	135.3	145.8	162.3
Gross margin	$ 76.2	$ 72.3	$ 68.1	$ 88.5	$ 93.9
Expenses:					
Selling	$ 12.3	$ 12.9	$ 12.3	$ 15.3	$ 16.5
Delivery	8.4	8.7	8.4	10.2	9.9
Advertising	10.5	10.8	9.9	9.9	9.6
Research and development	5.4	4.8	4.5	4.2	6.0
Administrative and general	21.0	22.8	23.1	23.7	24.3
Total expenses	$ 57.6	$ 60.0	$ 58.2	$ 63.3	$ 66.3
Net operating income	$ 18.6	$ 12.3	$ 9.9	$ 25.2	$ 27.6
Interest income	0.3	0.6	0.6	0.6	0.6
Total income	$ 18.9	$ 12.9	$ 10.5	$ 25.8	$ 28.2
Interest expense	1.5	1.5	1.2	1.2	1.5
Income before tax	$ 17.4	$ 11.4	$ 9.3	$ 24.6	$ 26.7
Federal income taxes	8.7	5.7	4.7	12.3	13.4
Net income	$ 8.7	$ 5.7	$ 4.6	$ 12.3	$ 13.3
Dividends:					
Preferred	$ 0.9	$ 0.9	$ 0.9	$ 0.6	$ 0.6
Common	2.4	2.4	3.1	6.0	6.0
*Includes depreciation	7.0	7.6	8.5	8.9	10.2

useful means of analyzing past funds flows, they are very cumbersome methods of forecasting. Therefore, rather than forecasting them directly, it is easier to derive such statements from one income statement and a balance sheet.)

B. Difficulties in Forecasting with Ratios

The relative ease with which forecasts based on historical ratios can be prepared must not blind the analyst to the dangers the method can have. In the first place, as already noted, relationships in the future may not be the same as those of the past. Second, certain mechanical problems arise in using ratios when the underlying physical activities of the firm change because of seasonal, cyclical, or secular factors.

For example, if a firm's accounts receivable balance is always equal to its most recent 30 days' sales, the ratio of the year-end receivables balance to sales will be constant only as long as sales in the last period are a constant proportion of sales for the year. Should this relationship change, not only would the forecast made be in error, but also the analyst might be lured into believing that management favorably controlled this current asset account while in fact no improvement had occurred at all. This sort of discrepancy can occur as a result of the last month having a different relationship to the total year than that previously established.

Similar analytical problems are encountered in other major current asset and liability accounts. They arise more often in businesses that have a highly seasonal pattern in sales activity. If relationships are not the same with respect to the average, or if they are not constant with respect to each other, different forecasting methods must be used. Obviously, one approach is to use a more detailed set of ratios if such data are available. However, the data are not always available to the outside analyst. Therefore, these examples are more appropriately constructed for an analyst who is employed by the company. In essence, what we need are estimates of how individual transactions will take place and knowledge of what financial accounts they will affect. This means starting with the beginning balance in each account on the financial statements and adding or subtracting an amount that reflects the real physical activity of the firm during the time period under investigation. This method is basically a T-account technique.

An item-by-item forecast will be illustrated using the example of the Toledo Manufacturing Company. Table 5.5 presents the actual balance sheets for December 31 for both 1990 and 1989. In addition, it shows a projected balance sheet for December 31, 1991, which was derived using the procedures detailed in the preceding section. Table 5.6 presents the forecasted income statement for year-end 1991. Note that the information in Table 5.7, which details the activities for most of the accounts, is used in arriving at the forecasted 1991 statements. The monthly details given in Tables 5.7 and 5.8 are not necessary for the projection of year-end statements and will be used only in the development of a schedule of receipts and disbursements.

C. Projecting Cash Receipts and Disbursements

Projected balance sheets and income statements are useful tools for medium- or long-term planning. For shorter projections, many firms use a daily, weekly, or monthly projected statement of receipts and disbursements. A projected statement can be prepared for 1991 from Table 5.7. This statement is shown in Table 5.8; receipts, in this example, consist of collections on

TABLE 5.5 Toledo Manufacturing Company, Inc.—Actual 12/31/89 and 12/31/90 and Projected 12/31/91 (in thousands of dollars)

		Actual 12/31/89	*Actual 12/31/90*	*Projected 12/31/91*
Assets				
Cash in bank (2,7,11,12,13)*		$ 44.1	$ 53.4	$ 44.4
Trade receivables (net) (1,2)		73.2	84.7	101.7
Raw materials (4,5)		26.0	17.1	14.1
Work in progress (5,6,8,9)		56.0	32.3	43.3
Finished goods (9,10)		130.8	86.0	110.0
Manufacturing supplies (4,5)		12.5	9.5	11.5
Property, plant, and equipment (net) (7,8)		450.0	472.5	517.5
		$792.6	$745.5	$842.5
Liabilities and Owners' Equity				
Notes payable (13,15)		$ 73.0	$ 75.0	$150.0
Payables and accruals (4,6,11,12)		62.6	38.6	45.6
Federal income tax liability (13,14)		22.2	11.0	30.0
Long-term debt (13)		210.0	180.0	150.0
Capital stock		300.0	300.0	300.0
Retained earnings (Table 5.6)		124.8	140.9	166.9
Total		$792.6	$745.5	$842.5
			1988	*1989*
Memo:	Net income		$ 31.1	$ 44.0
	Dividends		15.0	18.0
	Depreciation		34.1	45.0

*Numbers in parentheses refer to activities in Table 5.7.

TABLE 5.6 Toledo Manufacturing Company, Inc.—Statement of Income and Retained Earnings Actual for the Year 1990; Projected for the Year 1991 (in thousands of dollars)

		Actual 1990		*Projected 1991*
Net sales (1,2)*		$510.2		$570.0
Less: Cost of goods sold (10)		341.7		346.0
Gross profit		$168.5		$224.0
Less: Selling, general and administrative expenses (3,8,11)	$111.4		$130.0	
Interest expense (13)	15.0	126.4	20.0	150.0
Profit before income tax		$ 42.1		$ 74.0
Less: Federal income taxes (14)		11.0		30.0
Net profit for year		$ 31.1		$ 44.0
Add: Retained earnings at beginning of year		124.8		140.9
		$155.9		$184.9
Less: Dividends (13)		15.0		18.0
Retained earnings at end of year		$140.9		$166.9

*Numbers in parentheses refer to activities in Table 5.7.

accounts as described in activity 2 in Table 5.7. As expected, the largest recurring receipts are cash sales or collections on account.

Table 5.8 shows the difference in receipts and disbursements for each month. When added or subtracted from the beginning cash balance, their difference can be used to show the amount and timing of bank loans needed. The management of Toledo has determined that the firm's cash balance should not fall below $15 thousand, but in March there is $90 thousand more paid out than collected. With an initial cash balance of $71.4 thousand, Toledo Manufacturing would have a negative cash position of $18.6 thousand without an additional loan. Recognizing this cash requirement, the company will plan to borrow an additional $50 thousand in March, $75 thousand in June and $25 thousand in December.

III. BREAK-EVEN ANALYSIS AND REVENUE FORECASTING

A. Perspectives

Financial planners who must eventually decide the type of investment and financing courses of action that will maximize the market value of the firm must rely on some basic information about the forecasted demand for the company's products (or services), the projected input-output relationships in the production phase, and the cost-volume relationships associated with the various levels of projected sales revenues and production costs. This last set of relationships begins with *break-even analysis,* a form of investigation that establishes the number of units or alternatively the level of sales revenue at which the firm's total costs and total revenues will be equal. In other words, management wants to know the level of production and sales revenue at which true profitability begins for a specific product or service under review.

Thus, break-even analysis serves as a "screening" technique to establish the economic feasibility of investment proposals, as well as the sensitivity of the break-even amount to changes in sales prices and costs. In this respect, break-even analysis is one of many techniques that is utilized to measure the impact of investments upon the earnings of the firm. Other more sophisticated techniques like the net present value, the internal rate of return, the benefit-cost ratio, and their counterparts for cases involving uncertainty and risk will be discussed in Chapters

TABLE 5.7 Toledo Manufacturing Company, Inc.—Projected Operating and Financial Activities for the Year Ending December 31, 1991 (in thousands of dollars)

Activity No.	*Description*
1	Sales to be made on account, $580.0. Monthly sales expected to be $46.0, 47.0, 47.0, 48.0, 48.0, 49.0, 50.0, 50.0, 50.0, 50.0, 48.0, 47.0.
2	Cash to be collected from customers, $550.0 representing payment on $560.0 gross receivables net of $3.0 cash discounts and $7.0 sales allowances. Monthly collection expected to be $44.0, 44.0, 44.0, 45.0, 45.0, 46.0, 46.0, 46.0, 47.0, 48.0, 48.0, 47.0.
3	1991 provision for estimated uncollectability of customer accounts, $3.0.
4	Raw materials, $60.0, and manufacturing supplies, $25.0, to be purchased on account.
5	Raw materials, $63.0, and manufacturing supplies, $23.0, to be issued to the factory.
6	Costs in the factory to be incurred on account: Direct Labor $120.0 Indirect Labor 50.0 Maintenance, Utilities, etc. 86.0 $256.0
	Property, plant, and equipment to be purchased for cash, $100.0. Payments made, $20.0 in April, $25.0 in June, and $55.0 in September.
8	Annual depreciation on property, plant, and equipment charged to: Factory $39.0 Selling, general and administrative 6.0 $45.0
9	Transfer of finished goods from factory to finished goods warehouse, $370.0.
10	Cost of finished goods to be shipped from warehouse, $346.0.
11	Selling, general and administrative expenses to be incurred: For cash $ 25.0 — $2.0 January–November; $3.0 in December On account $ 96.0 $121.0
12	Cash to be paid on payables and accruals, $431.0. Monthly payments as follows: $32.0, 34.0, 40.0, 36.0, 36.0, 30.0, 36.0, 48.0, 35.0, 35.0, 34.0, 35.0.
13	Cash to be paid, $154.0 as follows: To meet notes payable due in March, $75.0. To reduce long-term debt, $30.0, to be repaid $15.0 in June and $15.0 in December. For interest on debt, $20.0, to be paid $2.0 in March, $10.0 in June, and $8.0 in December. On federal income tax liability, $11.0 in March. For dividends to stockholders, $18.0, to be paid $4.0 in March, June, and September and $6.0 in December.
14	Federal income tax accrual on 1991 income, $30.0
15	Borrow $150 from bank to provide for necessary financial resources.

TABLE 5.8 Toledo Manufacturing Company, Inc.—Projected Monthly Cash Receipts and Disbursements for the Year 1991 (in thousands of dollars)

	Jan.	*Feb.*	*Mar.*	*April*	*May*	*June*	*July*	*Aug.*	*Sept.*	*Oct.*	*Nov.*	*Dec.*	*Annual Summary*
Projected Receipts													
Collection on account (2)*	$44.0	$44.0	$44.0	$45.0	$45.0	$46.0	$46.0	$46.0	$47.0	$48.0	$48.0	$47.0	$550.0
Projected Disbursements													
Projected, plant and equipment (7)				20.0		25.0			55.0				100.0
Selling, general and administrative (11)	2.0	2.0	2.0	2.0	2.0	2.0	2.0	2.0	2.0	2.0	2.0	3.0	25.0
Payables and accruals (12)	32.0	34.0	40.0	36.0	36.0	30.0	36.0	48.0	35.0	35.0	34.0	35.0	431.0
Notes payable (13)			75.0										75.0
Long-term debt (13)						15.0						15.0	30.0
Interest (13)			2.0			10.0						8.0	20.0
Federal taxes (13)			11.0										11.0
Dividends (13)			4.0			4.0			4.0			6.0	18.0
Total Disbursements	$34.0	$36.0	$134.0	$58.0	$38.0	$86.0	$38.0	$50.0	$96.0	$37.0	$36.0	$67.0	$710.0
Net inflow (or outflow)	10.0	8.0	(90.0)	(13.0)	7.0	(40.0)	8.0	(4.0)	(49.0)	11.0	12.0	(20.0)	(160.0)
Beginning cash balance	53.4	63.4	71.4	31.4	18.4	25.4	60.4	68.4	64.4	15.4	26.4	38.4	53.4
Minimum cash required	15.0	15.0	15.0	15.0	15.0	15.0	15.0	15.0	15.0	15.0	15.0	15.0	15.0
Bank loan needed (15)	—	—	50.0	—	—	75.0	—	—	—	—	—	25.0	150.0
Ending cash balance	$63.4	$71.4	$31.4	$18.4	$25.4	$60.4	$68.4	$64.4	$15.4	$26.4	$38.4	$43.4	$43.4

*Numbers in parentheses refer to activities in Table 5.7.

13 and 14. There are two types of break-even analysis—*linear break-even* and *nonlinear break-even*—and they can be approached through the following three frameworks: (1) the trial-and-error method; (2) the graphic analysis method; and (3) the algebraic analysis method. We shall discuss the two types and three frameworks below, although most of our discussion and all of our examples will focus on linear break-even analysis through the algebraic method.

In order to analyze the functional interactions among volume, operating costs, and product prices, we generally make some simplifying assumptions that are applicable to the case of linear break-even analysis. They are as follows:

1. The selling price per unit of product sold is known and fixed. This type of assumption allows the total revenue to increase in constant proportion to increases in sales. Thus, in effect, we assume that the total revenue curve is a straight line.
2. The firm produces and sells a homogeneous product. This is also an important assumption, although it can easily be bypassed by assuming that the firm produces and sells many products with sales that also fluctuate proportionately. Thus, we can formulate the problem in terms of dollar break-even sales and bypass the assumption of *homogeneity* by substituting the assumption of *proportionality*.
3. The firm has *fixed costs* that are independent of the number of units sold. Such costs that do not increase with volume are represented by (*a*) depreciation expense, (*b*) rent, (*c*) insurance expenses, (*d*) administrative expenses, and (*e*) loan repayments, among others.
4. The firm has *variable costs* that move in direct proportion to the number of units produced and sold. Examples of such costs are (*a*) raw materials for inventories, (*b*) manufacturing supplies, (*c*) sales commissions, (*d*) maintenance, (*e*) utilities like electricity, water, *et cetera,* and, of course, (*f*) direct labor costs.
5. The firm has some costs that are a hybrid between fixed and variable, which are called *semivariable costs*. Examples of such costs are some sales commissions that are fixed up to a certain volume and variable afterward.
6. The firm maintains *constant* quantities of *inventories*.

In Figure 5.2 the different types of costs are illustrated. The fixed costs are shown by the horizontal line, the variable costs by the straight upward sloping line, and the semivariable costs by the upward sloping, stepwise function. For the purposes of computational simplicity we shall assume away the semivariable costs and present the total cost function as follows:

$$\text{Total Operating Costs} = \text{Variable Operating Costs} + \text{Fixed Operating Costs}$$

$$TC = Vc + Fc$$

B. Methods for Determining Break-Even Quantity

As mentioned earlier, there are basically three methods for determining the break-even number of units for a company. By far the most time consuming is the *trial-and-error method,* where the sought-after number of units is obtained by trying several combinations of sales, fixed, and variable costs at given market prices. A simple example of this cumbersome method is given in Table 5.9 in which we are given the following information:

Price per unit, P = \$100;

Variable Cost per Unit, V = \$50; and

Fixed Operating Costs, Fc = \$110,000

Given the above information, we simulate the production process at various levels of sales and find out that in the first 2,200 units produced and sold, the company suffers operating losses that decrease until, at Q = 2,200 the firm reaches the break-even quantity. At levels of production and sales higher than 2,200, the company enjoys operating profits. The reader should note the underlying linearity of the functions which ensure that as quantity sold increases (de-

FIGURE 5.2 Types of Operating Costs

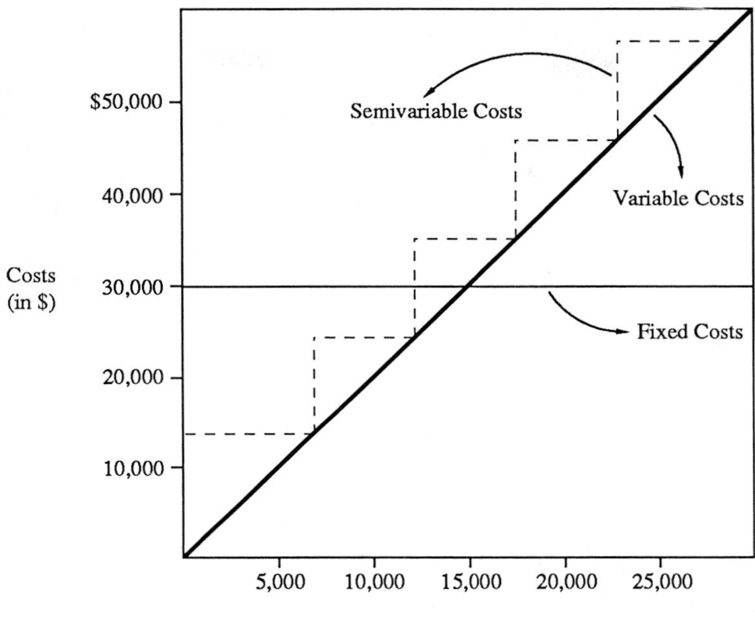

creases) the values for *TR*, *Vc*, *TC*, and EBIT increase (decrease) proportionately. Another thing to be noted here is that after the break-even point, profits increase at a constant rate without a ceiling.

A much easier but less precise method for calculating the break-even quantity is the *graphic analysis method* where the numbers for total operating revenues and total operating costs are plotted on graph paper to establish the point of intersection. This point then becomes the break-even quantity, as shown in Figure 5.3,

TABLE 5.9 Trial-and-Error Method of Computing Break-Even Quantity

(1) *Price Per Unit* *P*	(2) *Quantity Sold* *Q*	(3) = (1) × (2) *Total Operating Revenue* *TR* = *P* × *Q*	(4) *Variable Operating Costs* *Vc* = *V** × *Q*	(5) *Fixed Operating Costs* *Fc**	(6) = (4) + (5) *Total Operating Costs* *TC* = *Vc* + *Fc*	(7) = (3) − (6) *Earnings Before Interest and Taxes* EBIT = *TR* − *TC*	
$100	600	$ 60,000	$ 30,000	$110,000	$140,000	$(80,000)*	Operating Losses
100	1,000	100,000	50,000	110,000	160,000	(60,000)*	
100	1,400	140,000	70,000	110,000	180,000	(40,000)*	
100	1,800	180,000	90,000	110,000	200,000	(20,000)*	
100	2,200	220,000	110,000	110,000	220,000	0 =	Break-Even Quantity
100	2,600	260,000	130,000	110,000	240,000	20,000	Operating Profits
100	3,000	300,000	150,000	110,000	260,000	40,000	
100	3,400	340,000	170,000	110,000	280,000	60,000	
100	3,800	380,000	190,000	110,000	300,000	80,000	

*Variable Costs per Unit, *V* = $50; Fixed Operating Costs, *Fc* = $110,000

FIGURE 5.3 Linear Break-Even Chart

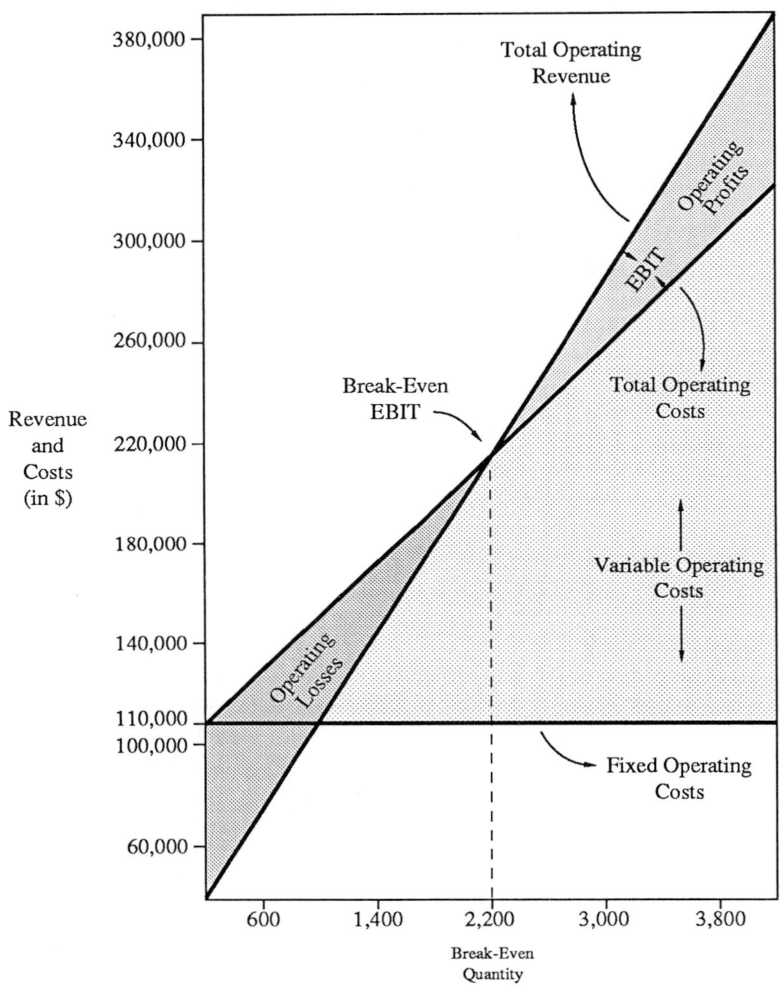

where we have plotted the data from columns (3) and (6) of Table 5.9. Obviously, the solution found by the trial-and-error and the graphic analysis methods should be the same.

The *algebraic method* of determining the break-even quantity provides the simplest and most accurate technique. It is based on the simple equilibrium proposition that at the *break-even quantity* (BEQ), total operating revenues (TR) equal total operating costs (TC). Thus,

$$P \times Q = Fc + (V \times Q) \tag{5.1}$$

$$(P \times Q) - (V \times Q) = Fc$$

$$Q(P - V) = Fc$$

$$Q = \text{BEQ}$$

$$= \frac{Fc}{P - V} \tag{5.1'}$$

The value in the denominator, $(P - V)$, is also known as *contribution margin per unit*. We can rearrange the formula for BEQ to yield the answer for *break-even revenue* (BER), as follows:

$$\text{BER} = \frac{Fc}{1 - \frac{V}{P}} \quad (5.2)$$

Let us now see how all these methods work through a series of applications.

Assume that two professors from a reknowned state university in the southwestern United States have approached Quality Publishers, Inc., with the idea of publishing a new textbook in financial management. On the basis of information from many sources, Quality's finance department has put together the following values:

Fixed Operating Costs, *Fc*:	
Copy Editing	$ 3,200
Promotion Work	4,000
Typesetting	28,000
Art Work	800
	$36,000

Variable Cost per Copy, *V*:	
Bookstore Trade Discounts	$ 2.25
Printing and Binding	1.35
Authors' Royalties	1.00
Salesmen's Commissions	.35
General and Administrative Expenses	.75
	$ 5.70
Selling Price per Copy	$12.00

We are asked to provide numerical solutions for the following items:

1. *a*. Break-Even Quantity (BEQ)
   b. Break-Even Revenue (BER)
2. The number of copies that must be sold to obtain $20,000 in Operating Profits.
3. The profits associated with the following sales levels:
   a. 2,000 copies
   b. 5,714 copies
   c. 10,000 copies

The answers to the above requests are given below:

1*a*. $\text{BEQ} = \frac{Fc}{P - V} = \frac{\$36{,}000}{\$12.00 - \$5.70}$
$= 5{,}714$ copies

1*b*. $\text{BER} = \frac{Fc}{1 - \frac{5.70}{12.00}} = \frac{\$36{,}000}{1 - .475}$
$= \$68{,}571$

2. Number of copies that must be sold to yield profit of $20,000. Contribution Margin per Unit $= P - V = \$6.30$

$$\text{Projected Volume} = \frac{\text{Fixed Costs + Projected Profit}}{\text{Contribution Margin per Unit}}$$

$$= \frac{\$36{,}000 + \$20{,}000}{\$6.30}$$

$$= 8{,}889 \text{ copies}$$

3. Profits with projected sales.
   Profit = (Contribution Margin per Unit × Quantity) Less *Fc*

a. Profit $= (6.30 \times 2{,}000) - \$36{,}000$
$= \$(23{,}400)$

b. Profit $= (\$6.30 \times 5{,}714) - \$36{,}000$
$= \$0$

c. Profit $= (\$6.30 \times 10{,}000) - \$36{,}000$
$= \$27{,}000$

We can also use the algebraic analysis method to draw some inferences about the effects of changes of such variables as prices per unit, fixed costs, and variable costs upon break-even quantity and earnings before interest and taxes. Take, for example, the case of Rowena's Pottery, which makes and sells ornamental plates for tourism. Rowena believes that by lowering the price per plate from \$3.50 to \$3.00 she could increase the volume of sales by 25 percent. The data for this case are given below:

	Current	*Proposed*
Volume of Sales	300,000	375,000
Price per Plate, *P*	\$3.50	\$3.00
Fixed Operating Costs, *Fc*	\$220,000	\$220,000
Variable Operating Costs, *Vc*	\$450,000	\$562,500
EBIT	380,000	?
BEQ	110,000	?

The answers to Rowena's proposals are as follows:

$$\text{Proposed BEQ} = \frac{\$220{,}000}{\$3.00 - \$1.50} = \$146{,}667$$

$$\begin{aligned}\text{Proposed EBIT} &= \$1{,}125{,}000\\ &\quad - (220{,}000 + 562{,}000)\\ &= \$342{,}500\end{aligned}$$

We can generalize this sensitivity of BEQ and EBIT to the three critical variables involved by means of the information in Table 5.10.

C. Some Extensions

The concepts and measures of break-even can be extended along two additional dimensions. The first dimension involves the computation of BEQ for fixed operating costs that entail only cash outlay—that is, BEQ without the depreciation and other noncash expenses. The formula is the same as in equation (5.1′) except that the numerator contains only cash *Fc*.

$$\text{Cash BEQ} = \frac{\text{Cash } Fc}{P - V} \tag{5.3}$$

An example of computing cash BEQ for different configurations of production facilities is provided in the case of ALZ Tectronics, Inc.

ALZ wishes to update its manufacturing process, and it is considering purchasing either Machine 1 or Machine 2. Information concerning the present machinery configuration and the two alternatives is given on the next page. Current sales volume is approximately 75,000 units at a price of \$40 per unit.

Another extension of BEQ, and the type of extension that brings reality into the analysis, is to relax the assumptions of constant prices, constant inventories, and constant costs for any level of production. Such cases bring forth *nonlinear break-even analysis,* which will not be pursued here. However, the nonlinearity of the total cost and total revenue functions brings about at least two break-even solutions, as shown in Figure 5.4. Moreover, as we allow for the realistic situation where fixed operating costs also increase at high levels of production (for additional warehouses, machinery, trucks, *et cetera*), we have the discontinuities of the total cost function shown in Figure 5.5.

TABLE 5.10 BEQ Sensitivity to Changes in Prices and Costs

	Price per Unit		*Fixed Operating Costs*		*Variable Operating Costs*	
	Increase	*Decrease*	*Decrease*	*Increase*	*Decrease*	*Increase*
BEQ	Decrease	Increase	Decrease	Increase	Decrease	Increase
EBIT	Increase	Decrease	Increase	Decrease	Increase	Decrease

Projected Costs	*Present*	*Machine 1*	*Machine 2*
Direct materials	\$ 465,000	\$ 409,000	\$ 315,000
Depreciation on equipment	512,000	627,000	777,000
Direct labor	660,000	485,000	315,000
Salary expense (managerial)	625,000	675,000	715,000
Variable selling expenses	75,000	75,000	75,000
Fixed factory overhead	290,000	365,000	470,000
Other fixed expenses	58,000	78,000	98,000

Compute BEQ and cash BEQ points:

Fixed operating costs	\$1,485,000	\$1,745,000	\$2,060,000
Variable operating costs	1,200,000	969,000	705,000
Variable unit cost	\$16	\$12.92	\$9.4
a. BEQ:	$\frac{1{,}485{,}000}{40 - 16}$;	$\frac{1{,}745{,}000}{40 - 12.92}$;	$\frac{2{,}060{,}000}{40 - 9.4}$
	= 61,875 units;	= 64,439 units;	= 67, 320 units
b. Cash BEQ:	$\frac{\$1{,}485{,}000 - \$512{,}000}{24}$;	$\frac{\$1{,}745{,}000 - \$627{,}000}{27.08}$;	$\frac{\$2{,}060{,}000 - \$777{,}000}{30.6}$
	= 40,542 units;	= 41,285 units;	= 41,928 units

IV. TIME-SERIES ANALYSIS OF ACCOUNTING DATA

A. Perspectives on Time-Series Data

In this section and in Appendix 5A, we will provide some operational details on the time-series analysis and forecasting of critical variables, that is, *revenues* and *costs* with specific reference to such applications as *moving averages, seasonal adjustments, exponential smoothing,* and *regression analysis*.

A simple means of extrapolation is to break the time series into various components. By extrapolating these components into the future, a forecast of the overall time series can be calculated. The most commonly used components of a time series are

1. secular, or long-term trends,
2. seasonal variations,
3. cyclical variations, and
4. irregular variations—also known as the *error term component*.

Irregular variation measures the effects of economic events such as strikes, bankruptcies, natural disasters, political changes, and abrupt changes in energy prices. These effects are thought of as disturbances that affect the smoothness of the time series. Because they are irregular, they are rarely forecast and are typi-

FIGURE 5.4 Nonlinear Break-Even Chart with Unchanging Fixed Costs

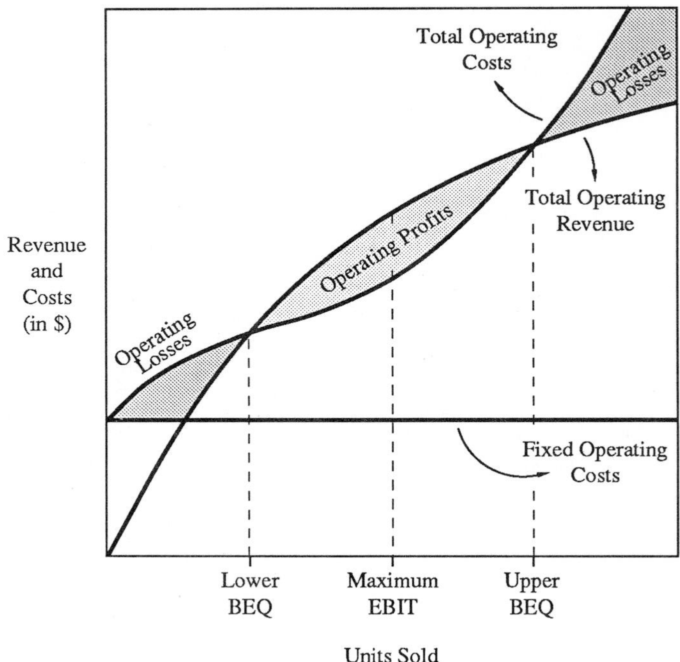

cally thought of as the cause of the forecast error of the model.

The first three components are repetitive in nature with the difference between the three due to the duration of a component. *Seasonal variation* is a cycle that repeats itself over a twelve-month period. *Cyclical variation* is a phenomenon that repeats itself over a 3–5 year period while a *long-term trend* would be evident over periods greater than 5–10 years.

Once the long-term trend has been calculated, then the other components can be considered multiplicative factors that will raise or lower the values of the time series based on the cyclical or seasonal trend.

Examples of the various components are given in Figure 5.6. The long-term trend is the long-term growth in the general economy for a country or industry. The cyclical trend would follow the boom periods and recession periods of the economy. The seasonal variation results from seasonal economic activity such as department store sales. The seasonal variation in figure 5.6 shows a large increase in sales during the later part of the year—such as Christmas shopping—and large drops in sales during the first few months of the year. There are several statistical techniques employed in estimating the various components of time series, such as moving averages, seasonal adjustments, exponential smoothing, and regression analysis.[3]

V. SUMMARY AND REVIEW

Financial forecasting is a follow-up to the analysis of the firm's basic financial statements. Whereas statement analysis concentrates on past performance, forecasting focuses on the future expected performance of the corporation. Toward this goal, we have discussed the use of accounting and economic data for projecting both future performance and funding needs for the firm. Specifically, we utilized pro forma in-

FIGURE 5.5 Nonlinear Break-Even Charts with Changing Fixed Costs

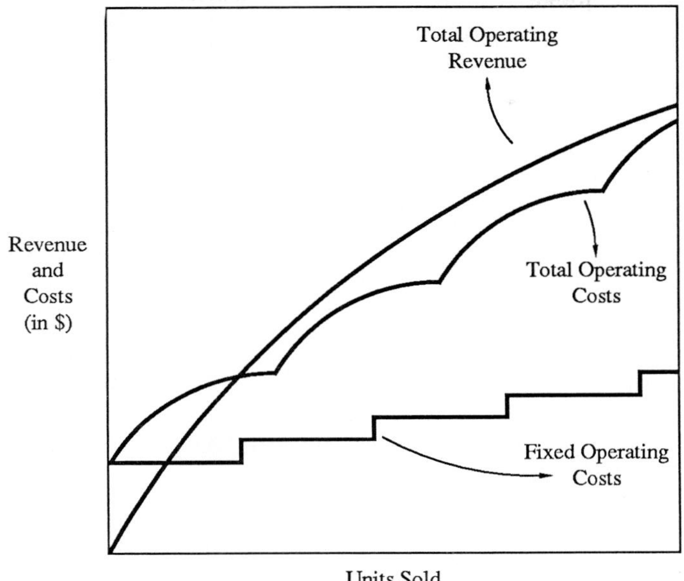

come statements and pro forma balance sheets, as well as cash budgets.

There are several ways to project future performance and financial requirements, and we discussed two well-known methods in this chapter. The first method, known as the percent-of-sales or ratio method is a straightforward extension of the ratio analysis for assessing past performance, discussed in chapter 4. On the assumption of stable and constant relationships between sales revenue and the various entries in the firm's financial statements, financial managers outline several scenaria about future sales revenue. Then, utilizing the established ratio relationships from the most recent periods, financial managers convert the future sales estimates into investment and financing requirements for both the short- and long-term horizons. This

FIGURE 5.6 Components of Time-Series Data

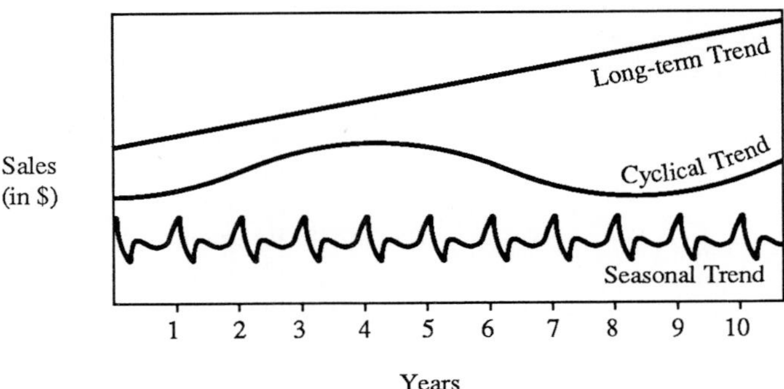

method provides a rough guide to future funding needs and is typically used by outside analysts who must rely on publicly available information.

The second method of forecasting funding needs is typically used by corporate managers and is constructed from in-house corporate data for internal corporate projections. The projections made by this method are more precise than those made by external analysts because they incorporate explicit assumptions about operating policies and procedures set by management. This type of in-house information is generally not available to outside evaluators.

Break-even analysis is employed by financial managers as a "screening" technique to establish the economic feasibility of investment proposals, as well as the sensitivity of the break-even quantity of goods (or sales revenue) to changes in sales prices and costs. In effect, break-even analysis is used to measure the impact of proposed investments on the earnings of a firm. There are two types of such analysis—linear break-even and nonlinear break-even, and they can be performed by any of the following methods: (1) the trial-and-error method, (2) the graphic analysis method, and (3) the algebraic analysis method. In this chapter, we concentrated on the linear break-even analysis and provided illustrations of all three methods of performing it.

In addition to break-even analysis, we also discussed the use of time-series analysis on accounting and economic data for the purpose of projecting funding needs. Time-series data are generally decomposed into secular, seasonal, cyclical, and irregular components. These components, in turn, can be estimated by using the following techniques: (1) moving averages, (2) seasonal adjustments, (3) exponential smoothing, and (4) regression analysis.

NOTES

1. A more detailed discussion of these relationships is given in Chapter 6.
2. Determination of the appropriate level of minimum cash balances is deferred until Chapter 6.
3. See Nelson (1973) for estimation methods in time-series analysis, and Appendix 5A.

QUESTIONS

1. What are the basic differences between current and pro forma financial statements prepared by financial managers?
2. What is the difference between pro forma statements and cash budgets?
3. Discuss the following statement: "The percent-of-sales or ratio method of forecasting is a rough guide to the future performance of the firm."
4. Briefly discuss break-even analysis and the various types and approaches employed.
5. What are the components of a time series of data and how are they estimated for forecasting?

PROBLEMS

1. On the next page, you are given the balance sheets and income statements for the PX Company for the years 1989 and 1990. Use the technique of forecasting with ratios in conjunction with the following assumptions to construct pro forma statements for 1991.

   Assumptions:
   a. Sales are expected to grow by 8 percent.
   b. Depreciation expenses are expected to increase 1 percent.
   c. PX is required to make an additional $500,000 interest payment.
   d. The corporate tax rate should fall to 33 percent of taxable income.
   e. The company will pay out 50 percent of its earnings as dividends to shareholders.
   f. No common stock will be issued.
   g. Accrued taxes are expected to be 75 percent of the annual tax bill.
   h. Accrued wages will be approximately 9 percent of cost of sales.
   i. Ten percent of long-term debt outstanding as of 12/31/90 will be retired.
   j. An investment of $12 million (gross) will be made in fixed assets.
   k. Other assets will be amortized by 50 percent.
   l. Minimum cash required is $8 million.

   What amount of borrowing in the form of short-term notes payable will be required?

PX Company Balance Sheets
(In Millions)

	1989	*1990*
Cash	$ 8.75	$ 5.25
Accounts Receivable	26.25	38.50
Inventories	21.00	26.25
Fixed Assets, Net	87.50	96.25
Others	14.00	8.75
Total Assets	$157.50	$175.00
Notes Payable	$ 35.00	$ .00
Accounts Payable	8.75	14.00
Accrued Wages	3.50	3.50
Accrued Taxes	5.25	8.75
Long-Term Debt	.00	26.25
Common Stock	35.00	45.50
Retained Earnings	70.00	77.00
Total Liabilities and Net Worth	$157.50	$175.00

PX Company Income Statement
(In Millions)

		1989		*1990*
Net Sales		$74.38		$87.50
Operating Expenses				
Cost of Goods Sold	$37.19		$46.75	
Selling, General and Administrative Expenses	7.44		8.31	
Depreciation	7.44		9.21	
Interest	1.49	53.56	1.49	65.76
Net Income before Taxes		20.82		21.74
Tax (35%)		7.29		7.61
Net Income		$13.53		$14.13

2. Due to the fantastic success of an aggressive marketing campaign, the Weaver Underwear Company has received sizable orders from several of the nation's largest department store chains. Consequently, management anticipates the need for an increase in the firm's line of credit. On the basis of the following information, prepare a cash budget for Weaver for the months of June, July, and August; and, in the process, determine the firm's increased borrowing needs (if any) in order to maintain a cash balance of $200,000 at all times.
   a. Purchases of fabric are made two months prior to the month of sale and make up 45 percent of sales. Purchases are paid for in the month prior to sale.
   b. Selling, general, and administrative ex-

penses are expected to be $170,000, $180,000 and $198,000 in June, July, and August, respectively.

c. Total labor costs are expected to be $310,000 in June, and $300,000 in July and August.

d. Actual sales for April and May and projected sales for June through September are presented below:

April	$ 899,000
May	1,079,000
June	1,500,000
July	2,500,000
August	2,750,000
September	3,000,000

e. All of Weaver's sales are on credit with 90 percent collected in the month after sale and 10 percent collected in the subsequent month.

Weaver Underwear Company Balance Sheet May 31 (In Millions)

Cash	$ 89.9
Accounts Receivable	953.6
Inventories	980.6
Fixed Assets, Net	2,808.0
Intangible Assets	495.5
Total Assets	$5,327.6
Accounts Payable	$ 647.8
Notes Payable	719.7
Accruals	381.5
Long-term Debt	809.7
Common Stock	179.9
Retained Earnings	2,589.0
Total Liabilities and Net Worth	$5,327.6

3. Potted Meat Food Products, Inc. earns an annual after-tax income of $5 million on sales of $15.7 million. The firm's average corporate tax rate is 37 percent. Potted Meat manufactures only one product, potted meat food, which sells for 98 cents per can, and variable costs are 43 cents per can.

   a. Calculate the firm's break-even point in cans and dollars and its annual fixed costs.
   b. Compute the effect of a 3-cents-per-can increase in the sales price on the firm's break-even point if unit volume is expected to remain constant.

*4. The PSY Corporation has reported the following sales figures for the years 1988–1990 in millions of dollars:

	1988	*1989*	*1990*
Q_1	—	73.0	79.4
Q_2	88.4	87.4	95.8
Q_3	80.7	81.6	88.9
Q_4	83.2	88.9	97.7

   a. Using the ratio-to-moving-average method, compute seasonal adjustment factors. Employ a 4-quarter moving average and the following weights:

   1989 = .4, 1988 = .6

   b. Using the seasonally adjusted data, compute an exponential smoothing model employing a 4-quarter moving average and $\alpha = 0.1$.
   c. Recompute part *b* with $\alpha = 0.2$.
   d. Using the better of the two models, generate a nonseasonally adjusted forecast for 1991.

APPENDIX 5A LINEAR TIME-SERIES MODELS

Time-series tools, such as Box-Jenkins methods, can be applied to build a linear model to explain the behavior of accounting numbers. Intuitively, we assume that the time-series process is generated by some probability law. For instance, we may posit that earnings Z_t at time t can be represented by the expression:

*This problem can be assigned only in conjunction with Appendix 5A.

$$Z_t = U + U_t + Y_i U_{t-1} + \cdots + Y_q U_{t-q} \quad (5A.1)$$

where U and Y_i are fixed parameters in the process, and the U_t terms represent disturbances with mean zero and variance U^2. In addition, the U_t terms are presumed to be identically and independently distributed. The model depicted by equation (5A.1) is referred to as a *moving average process of length q*, MA(q). (The discussion of time-series models in this appendix parallels the material presented in Foster, Chapter 4.)

A. Random Walk

One model that is often applied in the market efficiency literature is the *random-walk model.* This model suggests that the current observation on some variable is related to its immediately preceding observation, that is,

$$Z_t = Z_{t-1} + U_t \quad (5A.2)$$

where U_t satisfies the assumptions of equation (5A.1). Equation (5A.2) indicates that our best prediction of Z_t is Z_{t-1} if earnings do in fact follow a random walk. To test this equation for adequacy, we need to compute the model's theoretical autocorrelation function and compare it with the sample autocorrelation function for the observed series. An autocorrelation function gives the correlations between Z_t and Z_{t+j}, for some prespecified lag j.

Theoretically, equation (5A.2) stipulates that the autocorrelation coefficients for all lags are zero. Therefore, if our sample autocorrelation coefficients are not statistically different from zero, we can conclude that the random walk model adequately describes our data. For forecasting purposes, the random walk model implies that the most efficient forecast for earnings in 1991 would be the earnings figure in 1990. If statistically significant positive or negative autocorrelations were found, this information could be exploited when arriving at a forecast for 1991 earnings. This notion brings us to the next model, known as the *autoregressive model*.

B. Autoregressive Model

Another common time-series model is the autoregressive process of order p. Here, it is assumed that the current observation X_t is generated by a weighted sum of the past observations and can be expressed as

$$X_t = \phi_j X_{t-1} + \phi_2 X_{t-2} + \cdots + \phi_p X_{t-p} + U_t \quad (5A.3)$$

Let us assume that we have already computed autocorrelations for a firm's earnings and found that there were significant positive autocorrelations at lags of 1, 2, and 3 periods ($r_1 = .90$, $r_2 = .80$, $r_3 = .70$). Then there exists information in the past sequence of observations that will allow us to arrive at a better forecast than that given by the random walk. A model that implies such a pattern as the preceding one is

$$X_t - X_{t-1} = .90(X_{t-1} - X_{t-2}) + U_t \quad (5A.4)$$

The model represented by equation (5A.4) is autoregressive of order 1, that is, AR(1). A theoretical property of such a model is that the autocorrelation at lag k is $(\phi_1)^k$. For instance, ϕ_1 represents an estimate of the autocorrelation for a lag equal to 1 (i.e., ϕ_1 here is .90). Rearranging equation (5A.4) and taking expectations, we obtain

$$E(X_t) = X_{t-1} + .90(X_{t-1} - X_{t-2}) \quad (5A.5)$$

If sales for 1990 and 1989 were \$10 million and \$9 million, respectively, then our forecast for 1991 sales would be

$$\begin{aligned} E(X_{1991}) &= X_{1990} + .90(X_{1990} - X_{1989}) \\ &= 10{,}000{,}000 + .90(1{,}000{,}000) \\ &= \$10{,}900{,}000 \end{aligned}$$

The logical combination of equations (5A.1) and (5A.2) is the mixed autoregressive-moving-average process of order p and q commonly known as ARMA (p, q):

$$X_t = \phi_1 X_{t-1} \cdots + \phi_p X_{t-p} + \delta + Y_1 U_{t-1} + \cdots + Y_q U_{t-q} + U_t \quad (5A.6)$$

Identifying the optimal values for p and q, as well as estimating the values of ϕ_i and Y_i, is somewhat beyond the scope of this appendix. We will, however, broadly outline five steps involved in the Box-Jenkins methodology that are used to arrive at satisfactory values for p, q, ϕ_i and Y_i.

C. Box-Jenkins Methodology

Box-Jenkins (BJ) methods can be used quite successfully in forecasting accounting numbers. The technique basically involves five steps:

1. *Plotting the Data Series*. This step can search for outliers as well as check whether the series is stationary. BJ analysis requires that the series be stationary (i.e., that both the mean and the variance of the series should not vary with time).
2. *Model Identification*. This step involves finding a theoretical BJ model that is consistent with the data. Possible models that can be used here are autoregressive (AR), moving average (MA), and autoregressive-moving-average (ARMA). In each case we need to specify the degree, or length of lag, for both the autoregressive and the moving-average components. These components are referred to as AR(p), MA(q), and ARMA (p, q), where p and q refer to the length of the autoregressive and moving-average processes, respectively. In most cases, the BJ approach is largely heuristic.
3. *Model Estimation*. This step involves estimating the AR and MA processes specified in step 2.
4. *Diagnostic Checking*. This step involves testing the significance of the estimated coefficients as well as the randomness in the resultant error or residuals terms. Nonrandomness in the estimated residuals indicates that the model specified in step 2 is not adequate. In that event, we need to specify a new model and perform steps 2–4 until the model is deemed adequate.
5. *Forecasting*. As we did for equation (5A.3), we can now forecast estimated values for the economic series in question.

Readers who wish a more in-depth discussion of the Box-Jenkins methodology are referred to Nelson (1973) or Box and Jenkins (1976).

ANNOTATED BIBLIOGRAPHY

Box, G. E. P., and G. M. Jenkins. *Time-Series Analysis: Forecasting and Control*. San Francisco, Calif.: Holden-Day, 1976.

A standard reference for the techniques of time-series analysis.

Foster, G. *Financial Statement Analysis*. Englewood Cliffs, N.J.: Prentice-Hall, 1978.

An excellent source on the uses of accounting data for evaluating performance and making projections.

Migliaro, A., and C. L. Jain. *An Executive's Guide to Econometric Forecasting*. New York: Graceway, 1983.

———. *Understanding Business Forecasting*. New York: Graceway, 1985.

Two simple but correct sources on the mechanics and interpretation of business forecasting.

Nelson, C. R. *Applied Time-Series Analysis for Managerial Forecasting*. San Francisco, Calif.: Holden-Day, 1973.

Another standard reference for the techniques of time-series analysis.

Stone, B. K., and W. T. Miller. "Daily Cash Forecasting: A Structuring Framework." *Journal of Cash Management,* October 1981, 35–50.

An important conceptual paper that focuses on the need for problem structuring, approach selection, and measurement modeling before resorting to standard statistical forecasting techniques.

6

THE WORKING CAPITAL CYCLE AND CASH MANAGEMENT

I. INTRODUCTION

In this chapter we discuss working capital management as a managerial function encompassing the decisions that determine the level and composition of both the current asset and the current liability accounts. The *working capital cycle* refers to the ebb and flow of funds through a firm in response to changes in the level or rate of activity in the manufacturing process, the service function, or the marketplace. The changes may be seasonal, and there may be one or more seasons a year. Christmas tree ornaments and lawn furniture fall into the single-season category, while sportswear illustrates the case of a multiple-season business. Other cyclical changes may also be present, as in the machine tool or steel industries. In the very long run, changes can be secular, with the increase and decrease phases stretching over a substantial period of time. Nevertheless, for the purposes on hand, we will concentrate on the seasonal aspects of working capital management. This approach is partly a matter of convenience, because the shorter the cycle, the easier it is to trace the flow of funds. Furthermore, the seasonal pattern of funds is the most common pattern and one which nearly all firms experience at least mildly.

Let us first provide some important definitions of the concepts and measures that are typically encountered in the study of working capital management, such as working capital, net working capital, and working capital management.

Working capital refers to the monetary book values (dollar amounts) of a firm's current assets, such as cash, short-term investments in marketable securities, accounts receivable, and various types of inventories. The main characteristic of the assets in the working capital category is that they are *liquid;* that is, they can be converted ordinarily to cash within the period of a fiscal year or less. The working capital held by the firm at any moment in time is not constant. The dollar amounts of these assets vary to reflect seasonal fluctuations, cyclical business conditions, and funds that are associated with the economy, the industry, and the firm itself.

Typically, working capital is classified into permanent working capital and temporary working capital. *Permanent working capital* refers to the amount of short-term assets that remains more or less stable over long periods of time despite the fluctuations in the firm's sales. That is, permanent working capital constitutes the core amounts of cash, marketable securities, accounts receivable, and inventories that are necessary for the firm to satisfy its normal flow of business. This normal flow of business is increased in special seasons, such as Christmas, Easter, or other significant or festive sales periods, thus giving rise to additional amounts of inventory, accounts receivable, or cash. Such additional amounts delineate the category of *temporary working capital* that is necessary to meet the fluctuations in sales above what is considered by the management as the standard or permanent level.

Net working capital refers to the difference between the short-term assets and the short-term liabilities of the firm. In and of itself, net working capital is a quick reference to the liquidity position of the firm. When used in conjunction with other financial ratios focused on liquidity, the net working capital figure can paint a good picture of a firm in distress.

When net working capital is utilized by itself as a measure of a firm's liquidity it suffers from the same shortcomings as those attributed to the current ratio. This is so because the various elements that comprise current assets possess various degrees of liquidity and certainty. For example, cash is both liquid and certain (absent inflation), while high-quality marketable securities, notes receivable, and accounts receivable are quickly convertible into cash (perhaps at some discount), with minor uncertainty about the conversion price. Inventories, however, at various stages of production, are slower to convert into cash and exhibit major uncertainty about the conversion price. Of course, similar qualifications should be made about current liabilities, as they reflect upon such factors as urgency of repayment, probability and cost of refinancing, *et cetera*. Given the above limitations, the measure of net working capital can be augmented to reflect liquidity of a more homogeneous group of current assets. This can be done by excluding the figure for inventories (or some of the not-so-liquid inventories), much as we do when we augment the current ratio by computing the *acid-test* or *quick ratio*.

Before beginning our discussion of working capital, we need to define the term "funds." *Funds* refer to all resources at the disposal of the company in the form of credit and equity. Thus, when a supplier firm ships goods to a company but does not insist on cash payments, it is basically supplying funds to the other business, just as certainly as if it had given the shareholders a cash loan and then accepted cash from the firm in payment for the goods. Most transactions such as this involve no increase in cash. However, the funds in the business have increased in the sense that the funds will eventually be converted to cash as the account is collected. The cash will then probably be disbursed quickly to purchase more inventory or pay bills, or it may be distributed as dividends to the shareholders. We will employ this concept of funds in our discussion of working capital management.

II. THE BASIC WORKING CAPITAL CYCLE

At the most elementary level, the *working capital cycle* reflects an effort to maintain production at a constant level while sales demand varies with the particular season. It is inefficient and obviously expensive to try to produce as orders are received. Doing so would lead to an undesirable variability in the utilization of all productive inputs and result in lost orders as well as serious delays in delivery of merchandise. To avoid such problems, many manufacturers set their production at a constant level throughout the year and make upward adjustments during peak periods to accommodate the increase in demand.

Initially, inventory will be built up with very little sales activity. It may then grow to a peak level and drop when sales demand begins to outstrip production. However, during this inventory buildup period very little cash has flowed into the business, because most manufacturers sell on credit. During this period sales are strong, and inventory levels may be falling while receivables are on the rise. Funds to finance these assets are provided by suppliers, by bank loans, by taxes recognized on sales but not yet paid, by profits, and probably by drawing down the company's cash balance to its lowest level. As the cycle proceeds, shipments reach their greatest rate, rapidly depleting inventory. Receivables will increase, but cash now begins to flow rapidly into the firm as initial customers begin to pay their bills. At this stage, management begins to pay suppliers, reduce bank loans, and accumulate cash for paying taxes and making whatever distributions are planned for shareholders. By the end of the season, the inventory should have been reduced to its lowest level, the receivables collected, and the company's bills all paid with any remaining funds held in the form of cash ready to start the next annual cycle.

The working capital cycle process appears, and indeed is, very complex. However, it can be simplified by visualizing it as follows. Think of the liability-plus-equity side of the balance sheet as representing sources of funds, with liabilities being fairly passive commitments, relatively unchanged in proportion and kind from one cycle to the next. The equity account, on the other hand, is more active, because it changes according to the company's success in using its assets to generate profits. The assets, representing uses of funds, are the essence of the corporation. They are normally employed in such a way that the company's products can be sold for more than they cost to produce or acquire, thus yielding a return to the suppliers of equity capital. Note that the firm is part of an economic system through which raw materials, labor, and machinery flow. These factors are then combined into salable goods that are sold and converted into funds. The funds move from inventory to accounts receivable and finally into cash. At this final stage, the company returns the funds to creditors and owners and retains a portion for reinvestment to support higher sales volume in the future.

A. Levels of Working Capital: Industry, Business-Cycle and Life-Cycle Effects

The size of a firm's working capital varies according to the type of *business environment* within which it operates. The requirements are typically measured by the ratio of current assets to total assets, and it is expected that production processes that are complicated or highly time-consuming require high levels of inventories. Such demand for high levels of inventories obviously affects the overall level of working capital. Thus, for such complicated processes as aircraft manufacturing, shipbuilding, and heavy industrial construction, the ratio of current assets to total assets is anticipated to be higher than the national average for all industries. By the same token, the wholesale and retail industries generally have high ratios of current assets to total assets due to the uncertainty of market demand and the high penalty costs for shortages. On the other hand, the ratios of current assets to total assets are typically rather low for the food industry, particularly for fresh and perishable staples. Similarly low ratios are observed in the mining industry which, under ordinary circumstances and normal business-cycle conditions, maintains low stockpiles of inventory.

The level of working capital is also influenced significantly by changing business conditions, generally referred to as the *business cycle*. Typically, the current assets of the firm increase during the recovery and prosperity phases of the business cycle to accommodate increased demand and sales of the firm's products during this period. Conversely, when economic conditions turn sour during the recession and depression phases, inventories decline drastically to reflect the new conditions. Thus, the current assets to total assets ratio rises during the upswing and falls during the downswing of the cycle.

Finally, the level of working capital of the firm is also influenced by the stage of the *life cycle* in which both the industry and firm are located. It is known that firms at the pioneering and early expansion stages keep inordinately high percentages of their total assets in cash due to inexperience and the relatively higher degree of uncertainty characterizing such companies. Similar observations can be made about the receivables levels for such firms. But as they survive and move along the life cycle to acquire more experience, their receivables and cash are reduced drastically and stabilized at low, efficient levels.

From a purely accounting standpoint, at any given stage sources and uses must balance. Likewise, over any period the changes in sources and uses must balance. By definition, an increase in an asset or a reduction in a liability is a *use of funds*. Similarly, a reduction in an asset or an increase in a liability is a *source of funds*. With these definitions of sources and uses of funds, we can now consider a representative balance sheet like the one that appears in Table 6.1. For convenience, we can group balance sheet items into the following categories: current assets, fixed assets, current debt, long-term debt, and equity. Viewed in this way, working capital management is concerned with managing current assets and current liabilities, as well as with the interrelationships that may exist among the current accounts and the remaining entries on our

TABLE 6.1 Representative Balance Sheet

Assets	*Liabilities and Equity*
Current Assets	Current Liabilities
Cash	Accounts Payable
Accounts Receivable	Bank Loans
Inventory	Accruals
Long-Term Assets	Long-Term Liabilities
Plant and Equipment	Long-Term Debt
Land	Preferred Stock
Goodwill	Owner's Equity
	Paid-in Capital
	Retained Earnings
TOTAL ASSETS	TOTAL FINANCIAL CLAIMS

representative balance sheet. Within this balance sheet, we may be tempted to identify broad classes of sources and uses of funds. However, it is not very accurate to state that a bank loan was "used" to buy inventory or machinery. It would be more accurate to observe that a bank loan was among the several additional sources of funds that were used to buy inventory. This latter approach will prove useful when discussing capital structure management, capital costs, and capital investment decisions.

B. Funds Flow, Cash Flow, and Income Flow

Funds flow refers to the amount of net working capital generated by the operations of the firm. As we recall, net working capital is the difference between current assets and current liabilities. The funds flow information shows whether internally generated funds can support present operations and future planned growth in business. For example, suppose that management decides to embark on an intensive marketing campaign to increase sales. If the firm has operated efficiently up to this point, it will now require additional fixed assets to generate the additional inventories and these new inventories, along with increases in accounts receivable and cash, will also constitute additional working capital. Now, the funds flows of the firm tell us whether and to what extent internally generated sources of funds (current liabilities) can provide the sources for the two new uses above (increase in fixed assets and increase in working capital). That is, to what extent can increases in short-term liabilities such as accruals and accounts payable offset the increases in current assets required by an increased level of activity?

Cash flow refers to the amount of cash generated from operations and measures the ability of the firm to meet its ongoing obligations. It is the cash flow that is of critical importance in investment decisions where success or failure will be determined by the *size and quality of the after-tax cash flows generated from an investment outlay*. However, before we proceed any further, we should clarify some points about the funds flow, cash flow, and income flow. To begin with, we had stated in earlier chapters that cash flow generally consists of earnings after taxes (EAT) plus depreciation. We had also suggested that although depreciation is a real expense, it does not reduce net working capital. Thus, in order to compute the net working capital provided by operations, we must add depreciation back to the net income after taxes. In similar fashion, we must also add other expenses that do not reduce net working capital. Thus, although depreciation and such other noncash expenses as deferred taxes are added back to the EAT figure, they are not true sources of funds. They must be added back to the EAT to calculate the total funds provided by continuing operations.

Sometimes, the definition of cash flow as EAT plus depreciation and other noncash expenses can be misleading. For example, a firm can show accounting profit (*income flow*) but, due to the convention of accrual accounting, these profits after taxes are not cash, or are partly cash. In this case, when all sales are for credit, we may find that income flow or EAT is a positive number, funds flow (EAT + depreciation) is also a positive number, but cash flow may be a negative number. This type of situation where funds flow and cash flow differ can lead to significant distortions when the sales of the company change appreciably or when the terms of sales (time given to clients to pay) also change drastically. These differences are important to keep in mind as we continue our study of finance, particularly as we highlight the importance of after tax cash flows as benchmarks for investment decisions. The points to remember as we continue are the following: Investment decisions or capital budgeting focus on cash outflows and cash inflows because accounting convention recognizes expenses when they are incurred rather than when they are paid; similarly, accounting convention recognizes revenues when sales are made and not when cash is collected for the sales. As the timing of the cash inflows and outflows differs from the timing of sales and expenses, we must emphasize the importance of the actual cash flows and when they occur. These are the critical figures that are employed in the various discounting techniques of capital budgeting. A simple representation of the timing differences between credit transactions and cash realizations is given in Table 6.2, where one can observe the lead-lag relationships between income, expenses, cash flows, and cash outflows.

C. Investment Outlays

The discussion on cash and funds flows must now be tempered by a brief recognition of the types of outlays that correspond to those flows. For our purposes we shall lump them together under the heading *investment outlays* and discuss them first for new investments and then for replacement investments.

Consider, for example, the Olympus Corporation, a manufacturer of industrial refrigerating equipment. Further assume that the company plans to expand its sales and must purchase additional land, build more manufacturing and warehousing space, and bring in additional machinery. The question that arises at this stage is the following: *What are the types of costs associated with the incremental investment that is needed to facilitate increased sales?* Well, to begin with, we must consider the costs associated with the purchase of land adjacent to the present plant site. To this cost, we must add the costs associated with the construction of the buildings and the cost of purchasing the new machinery. Is this all? No! We must also include such costs as freight, site preparation, and installation of the machinery. Let us classify all of the above costs as *cash outlays for investment,* and symbolize them by C. What other costs might also be involved? Well, increased sales cannot be supported without increased cash balances. And, of course, increased sales will generate higher accounts receivable, which can only be realized through higher levels of inventories. Let us call these outlays *working capital expenses* and symbolize them by W. Finally, let us also admit that the new productive equipment will need some additional investment in "spare parts," which we shall put in the category of *other expenses* and indicate by O.

All of the expenses are shown in Table 6.3, and from now on, when we refer to investment outlays for a new investment, we shall lump together all these costs under one heading, symbolized by I. Notice that we introduced an offsetting cash inflow for the value of an asset at the end of its economic horizon, indicated by D, to mean the disposition of the asset. When we deal with new investments, this disposition refers to the salvage value of an investment. However, when we deal with a replacement investment, particularly an investment that cuts short the life of previous equipment, the salvage value is no longer what had been estimated at the onset of the investment decision. That is, the

TABLE 6.2 Lead-Lag Relationships Between Credit Transactions and Cash Realizations

Cash Receipts	*Cash Disbursements*
Cash Receipts *Lag* Realized Revenues	Cash Disbursements *Lag* Realized Expenses
Cash Receipts *Coincide* with Realized Revenues	Cash Disbursements *Coincide* with Realized Expenses
Cash Receipts *Lead* Realized Revenues	Cash Disbursements *Lead* Realized Expenses

TABLE 6.3 Types of Investment Outlays

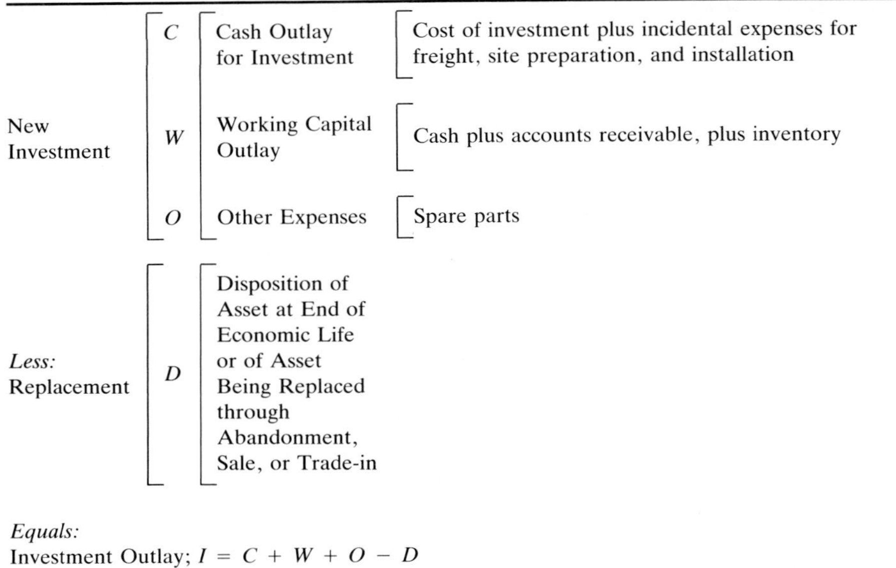

New Investment	*C*	Cash Outlay for Investment	Cost of investment plus incidental expenses for freight, site preparation, and installation
	W	Working Capital Outlay	Cash plus accounts receivable, plus inventory
	O	Other Expenses	Spare parts
Less: Replacement	*D*	Disposition of Asset at End of Economic Life or of Asset Being Replaced through Abandonment, Sale, or Trade-in	

Equals:
Investment Outlay; $I = C + W + O - D$

market value of the old equipment may be greater or smaller than the value carried in the books of the company, where the method of depreciation is reflected. In such cases, the disposition price of the asset must be adjusted for the tax on capital gains or losses from the difference between market value and book value.

D. The Importance of Depreciation

At this point, we should clarify the concepts of depreciation and its importance as a factor in investment decisions. Depreciation can be classified into three types: physical depreciation, accounting depreciation, and economic depreciation or market obsolescence.

Physical Depreciation refers to the normal wear and tear that is expected to reduce the productive capacity of an asset through continuous utilization over its expected useful life. It also refers to the rate of increase in the production costs from the use of a specific asset. This type of depreciation, however, has only conceptual meanings for the modern corporation competing in technologically advanced markets, because assets are usually abandoned before their complete physical deterioration, due to market obsolescence.

Accounting Depreciation refers to the reported charges as per the bookkeeping practices of the corporation. Accounting depreciation may coincide with physical depreciation but the rate of accounting depreciation is usually much higher than that of actual physical deterioration. The discrepancy in the rates depends on the type of asset and the firm's policies, but the flow of accounting charges is bound on the one hand by accounting conventions and on the other by the physical deterioration of the asset. Because depreciation allowances are added to the pool of funds, fast-growing corporations have gone to the legal limits and used depreciation along with retained earnings as steady pools of internally generated funds.

Economic Depreciation refers to the rate of decrease in the revenues generated from the use of a specific asset. Because revenues are determined by the market, economic depreciation refers to the gradual obsolescence of an asset, as the demand for the product or service that it produces diminishes due to changes in market tastes and preferences. Rates of economic depreciation, as determined by the market, may be equal to or greater than the rates of physical and accounting depreciation. It is the liquidating (market) value of an asset that is important rather than its book value. Typically, economic depreciation is higher than the physical or accounting types, because both shifting market preferences and technological progress combine to reduce the liquidating value of an asset.

III. WORKING CAPITAL MANAGEMENT

A. Perspectives

Funds flow can be examined with the aid of Figure 6.1, where the flow is separated into several components. Clearly, the breakdown roughly follows the representative balance sheet. In the figure, we observe that there are many sources of funds that the firm may use. While most sources provide cash, others, such as suppliers, employees, and leasing companies, provide non-cash assets. The upper half of the figure represents the heart of working capital management and is commonly referred to as the *operating cycle*. However, as shown by the cash component, there exists an interdependency between long-term and short-term financial management. Using Figure 6.1, we now may attempt to clarify our earlier definition of funds. Because cash has both long-term and short-term uses, our working definition may be given relative to these particular uses. Thus, cash flows may be examined as the flow of funds that occurs either in the upper half or in the lower half (or in both halves) of Figure 6.1. However we choose to define it, the concept of net working capital is closely related to (and in some cases may be synonymous with) our definitions of funds.

B. A Simple Implementation

Let us now consider the effects of various working capital policies on the financial position of GPT Associates, a hypothetical company. Tables 6.4 and 6.5 present the condensed balance sheet and income statement for year-end 1990.

Some brief comments concerning Table 6.4 are in order. First, net working capital is equal to the difference between current assets and current liabilities. (See Table 6.1 for which items in Table 6.4 fall into these categories.) This difference is $1,720,000 − 560,000 = $1,160,000. From this, we can note that the firm's current ratio is 3.07. The firm's cash flow, defined as earnings available to common plus depreciation, is computed from Table 6.5 to be $281,056. One issue that we may investigate for GPT Associates is the trade-off between the profitability and the liquidity of the firm. Liquidity here refers to the firm's ability to meet maturing short-term liabilities. Defined in this way, it is closely related to working capital management. On the other hand, profitability is concerned with the overall position of the firm as it relates to its shareholders. Because liquidity entails holding low-yielding assets, there is some trade-off between profitability and risk.

For GPT Associates, the current ratio is 3.07, while the rate of return on equity is 13.5 percent. Are there any trade-offs that can be made along these two dimensions? To illustrate the conflicts associated with them, we can look at the information in Tables 6.6 and 6.7, which present two alternative working capital policies.

Alternative I is concerned with liquidity, Alternative II with profitability. While these alternatives are extreme, they do highlight the importance of the trade-offs involved. To examine the effects of the two policies, we can look at three measures: *return on equity* (ROE), the *current ratio* (CR), and *net working capital*.

For Alternative I, a substantial investment is made in current assets. Most notable is the increase in AR (increased by $400,000 from Table 6.4). This increase probably reflects an effort to ease credit terms. Also, reliance on short-term debt is reduced to zero, while long-term sources have been allowed to expand. For convenience, a 7 percent rate of interest is assumed for both short-term and long-term debt. The relaxed credit terms and increased investment in inventory clearly result in a larger enterprise in terms of total assets. If we examine the effects of this policy, we note that liquidity measures (i.e., CR and net working capital) are high, while ROE

FIGURE 6.1 Funds Flow Cycle

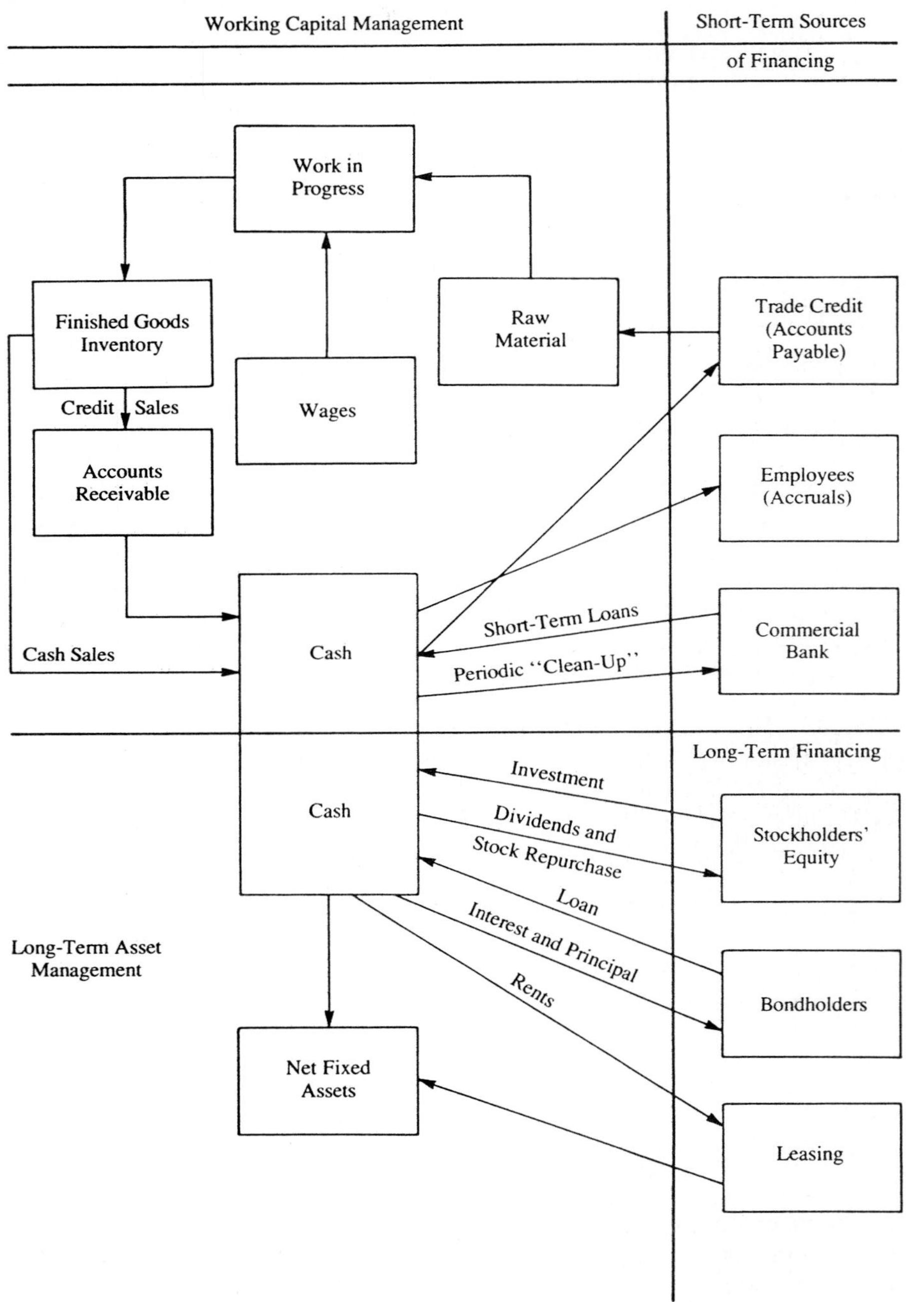

TABLE 6.4 GPT Associates, Inc.—Condensed Balance Sheet, December 31, 1990 (in thousands)

Assets		*Liabilities and Equity*	
Cash	$ 160,000	Accounts Payable	$ 240,000
Accounts Receivable (AR)	800,000	Bank Loan (BL)	200,000
Inventory (INV)	760,000	Other Current Liabilities	120,000
Net Fixed Assets (NFA)	1,680,000	Long-Term Debt (LTD)	800,000
		Preferred Stock (PFD. STK)	400,000
		Owners' Equity (OE)	1,640,000
Total Assets	$3,400,000	Total Liabilities and Equity	$3,400,000

TABLE 6.5 GPT Associates, Inc.—Condensed Income Statement as of December 31, 1990 (in thousands)

Net Sales		$3,520,000
Cost of Goods Sold (CGS)		2,680,000
Gross Income		$ 840,000
Expenses:		
Rent	$ 74,800	
Advertising	60,800	
Depreciation	60,000	
Interest (7%)	70,000	
Salaries	128,000	393,600
Earnings Before Income and Taxes (EBIT)		$ 446,400
Taxes (46%)		205,344
Earnings After Taxes (EAT)		$ 241,056
Preferred Dividend (5%)		20,000
Earnings Available to Common		$ 221,056

TABLE 6.6 GPT Associates, Inc.—Comparative Balance Sheets Under Two Working Capital Alternatives

	Alternative I	*Alternative II*
Cash	$ 240,000	$ 80,000
Accounts Receivable (AR)	1,200,000	400,000
Inventory (INV)	960,000	320,000
Net Fixed Assets (NFA)	1,680,000	1,680,000
Total Assets	$4,080,000	$2,480,000
Accounts Payable	$ 240,000	$ 240,000
Bank Loan (BL)	0	640,000
Other Current Liabilities	120,000	120,000
Long-Term Debt (LTD)	1,200,000	224,000
Preferred Stock (PFD. STK)	400,000	400,000
Owners' Equity (OE)	2,120,000	856,000
Total Liabilities	$4,080,000	$2,480,000

TABLE 6.7 GPT Associates, Inc.—Comparative Income Statements Under Two Working Capital Alternatives

	Alternative I	*Alternative II*
Net Sales	$3,520,000	$3,520,000
Cost of Goods Sold (CGS)	2,680,000	2,680.000
Gross Income	$ 840,000	$ 840,000
Expenses	323,800	323,800
Interest Expense (7%)	84,000	60,480
Earnings Before Income and Taxes (EBIT)	$ 432,200	$ 455,720
Taxes	198,812	209,631
Earnings After Taxes (EAT)	$ 233,388	$ 246,089
Preferred Dividends	20,000	20,000
Earnings Available to Common Shareholders	$ 213,388	$ 226,089
Return on Equity (ROE)	10.07%	26.41%
Current Ratio (CR)	6.7	0.80
Net Working Capital	2,040,000	(200,000)

is low relative to that of Alternative II. Liquidity objectives have been achieved at the expense of profitability.

In contrast to this, Alternative II presents a scenario in which there is a smaller investment in working capital, resulting in a smaller firm in terms of total assets. Also, the firm now relies more heavily on bank loans as a source of funds. Under this policy, net working capital is negative (CR $<$ 1.0). However, return on equity has risen, due to the increased usage of leverage. This alternative clearly illustrates that profitability can be increased at the expense of liquidity. Certainly, we are not implying that such extreme trade-offs are optimal in any sense: what the example has illustrated is merely that trade-offs are possible. (In effect, we are allowing two types of trade-off for the seasonal elemént of the business cycle: a change in the level of asset and risk or a change in the type of asset and risk.) The particular policy adopted by management depends on management's definition of, and aversion to, risk. In addition, it may depend on the business cycle as well as on competitive conditions. However, using the techniques outlined, we can assess the chosen policy's sensitivity to a variety of business conditions. Such an analysis is clearly warranted, especially in turbulent economic times.

IV. CASH MANAGEMENT

A. Introduction

The demand for liquid assets, or *cash,* by individuals and firms is normally attributed to three behavioral motivations: transactions, precautionary, and speculative demands. The *transactions demand* derives from the normal periodicity of payments for the purchase of goods and services. For example, the firm needs liquid funds to pay for raw materials, finished goods, labor inputs, federal and local taxes, and so on. The *precautionary demand* for liquid assets derives from the uncertainty in the origin and timing of cash outflows and inflows. A minimum reservoir of cash, or other highly liquid assets, must always be kept on hand to meet unexpected payments and other contingencies that arise in the course of business operations. Finally, the *speculative demand* for cash balances derives from the desire to take advantage of expected changes in asset prices, typically financial assets. For example, anticipation of lower prices will be translated into increased cash balances that may enable the firm to purchase financial assets at their lowest possible price, and vice versa.

By and large, nonfinancial corporations are

not affected seriously by the speculative motive. Consequently, we shall place the primary emphasis on the transactions and precautionary demands for liquid assets. Usually the transactions needs are met out of cash and demand deposits, while the precautionary balances may be kept in highly marketable securities whose quick conversion into cash makes them liquid enough for the purposes on hand. This is why these two short-term uses are discussed together.

The task of the financial manager in planning the short-term uses of funds involves, among other things, the attainment of an optimum distribution between cash and marketable securities. This task requires an evaluation of the corporate utility function to establish the marginal rates of substitution between the risk of becoming technically insolvent and the return expected from the investment of the liquid funds in noncash uses. Thus the financial manager can, conceivably, strike an optimal balance through the analysis and evaluation of cash flows—both normal (transactions) and precautionary—that directly affect the size of the cash balances.

However, in the typical corporation, most of these cash flows are determined by other functions *within* the organization, for example, production, marketing, and so on, over which the financial manager has little control; or by *outsiders,* for example, customers, suppliers, and creditors, over which the manager has no control. Furthermore, even in cases where the financial manager has some control over the flows of funds, there are still the fluctuations originating with seasonality and product life cycles to cope with, as well as those variations associated with the industry and the overall economy. Hence the analyses of the financial manager must distinguish those flows that are reasonably certain and also attempt to attach probabilities of occurrence to the uncertain flows.

B. The Optimal Level of Cash

Any analysis of the optimal level for cash balances must compare the marginal benefits and costs associated with changes in the original cash balances. For example, cash is required to take advantage of trade and quantity discounts in purchasing, or to achieve and maintain a credit standing that will facilitate financing through banks and other creditors. It is also advantageous to have sufficient liquidity to take advantage of favorable business opportunities or to meet unexpected contingencies. However, as we know, the maintenance of cash balances entails at least three types of costs:

1. There is an *opportunity cost* of foregoing other lucrative investment opportunities; for example, cash can always be used to purchase securities or to expand accounts receivable, inventories, or even plant.
2. There is a cost involved in holding cash, which could otherwise be used to offset both the cost and the financial risk that derive from the firm's short-term debt.
3. There is a cost that excessive reliance on internally generated liquidity can isolate the firm from the short-term financial market.

Once the cash flows have been estimated and the relevant opportunity costs and benefits have been established, the financial manager must construct a model, however simple, that will determine the optimal cash and securities portfolio for the corporation. The first step in the development of a cash-balances model involves the specification of a *cash floor* (constraint) below which the firm will incur definite and measurable costs. This constraint is usually called the *critical minimum balance,* and its existence is justified by such institutional requirements as credit ratings, checking accounts, lines of credit, and risk aversion. The minimum balance may be violated by letting the actual balance fall below it, in which case the shortage costs are determined by the actions of the creditors, banks, and so on; or by postponing the timely payment of accounts payable, in which case the shortage costs are determined by the foregone cash discounts. At any rate, the shortage costs will always be weighted against the opportunity costs of investment in other uses of funds, particularly marketable securities which possess high liquidity. For example, given the cash-flow planning period of the corporation, we can estimate the shortage-cost function rather accurately by assuming that all cash outflows can be deferred until the end of the planning period. In this vein, we must also augment the shortage costs by the transaction costs for the sale or purchase of securities, which, in this case, are used as the alternative uses of funds.

C. A Simple Illustration

Let us illustrate the cash-budgeting problem by way of an example. Assume that a corporate treasurer must allocate \$8,000 between cash and marketable securities, over a planning period of a month. Further assume that all cash outflows can be deferred to the end of the month, and that only one transaction of securities is made thus reducing transactions costs to fixed costs. The treasurer has established the firm's critical minimum balance at \$3,000 and has also estimated that for every dollar that his actual balance is below the critical minimum at the end of the month, the corporation will incur a shortage cost of \$.01 in foregone cash discounts. He has also estimated that the deterioration of his credit rating and other opportunity costs will be worth \$.20 for each dollar that the actual balances are below the critical minimum.

We can formulate the total shortage costs as follows:

$$TC_s = .01X + .2X \tag{6.1}$$

where TC_s is the total shortage costs and X is the dollar amount by which the firm's actual balances are below the critical minimum. The treasurer expects to earn 6 percent per year by investing in marketable securities, or .5 percent per month, which we denote by R; each transaction also involves a constant transaction cost, TC, of \$5, and all transactions are restricted to \$1,000 denominations. If all disbursements can be deferred until the end of the month, and the treasurer does not violate the critical minimum, there are six alternative cash balances to be considered at the beginning of the month—one for each \$1,000 interval from the minimum of \$3,000 to the \$8,000 on hand. The alternative cash balances will be modified by the following estimated probability distribution of the firm's net cash flows at the end of the month:

Probability	.1	.2	.6	.1
Cash Flow	−\$6,000	−\$3,000	−\$1,000	\$2,000

On the basis of the previous information, the treasurer can compute the expected net cost of each of the six alternative cash balances by

$$E(C_n) = E(TC_s) + TC - r \tag{6.2}$$

where $E(C_n)$ = expected net costs
$E(TC_s)$ = expected total shortage cost
TC = transaction cost
r = known and certain return from the investment in securities

Because we have already assigned values to the relevant variables, equation (6.2) becomes

$$E(C_n) = E(.01X + .2X) + 5 - .005M \tag{6.2'}$$

where X is again the actual shortage and M is the amount invested in securities. In the present example, the \$5 transaction cost disappears in the alternative where no securities are purchased. It is also assumed that no securities may be liquidated until the end of the period.

The six alternatives are shown, with the expected net cost of each beginning cash balance C in Table 6.8. As can be seen from the table, the expected net costs of each alternative indicate that placing the entire cash balance in the cash pool and buying *no* marketable securities is the least expensive opportunity. However, the outcome of the example depends on the posited values of at least three basic variables, the variation of which will also significantly alter the final decision: (1) the probability distribution of the expected cash drain, (2) the magnitude of the shortage costs, and (3) the return on the alternative uses of funds (securities).

The example might be made more realistic and elaborate by including other benefits to offset the costs of violating the critical minimum cash balance, beside the alternative investment in securities. These benefits would include all of

TABLE 6.8 Alternative Scenaria for Mixing Cash and Marketable Securities

C	X	TC_s	*Probability*	$E(TC_s)$	M	R	T	$E(C_s)$
3,000	6,000	1,260	.1	126	5,000			
	3,000	630	.2	126				
	1,000	210	.6	126				
				378		25	5	358
4,000	5,000	1,050	.1	105	4,000			
	2,000	420	.2	84				
				189		20	5	174
5,000	4,000	840	.1	84	3,000			
	1,000	210	.2	42				
				126		15	5	116
6,000	3,000	630	.1	63	2,000	10	5	58
7,000	2,000	420	.1	42	1,000	5	5	42
8,000	1,000	210	.1	21	0	0	0	21

the opportunity costs associated with alternative uses of funds, most of which might have substantially higher returns than the earnings on the marketable securities. However, realism implies additional complexity because the inclusion of all possible benefits requires that they be known and precisely quantifiable. The method might also be augmented to encompass two or more planning periods, using similar reasoning. However, once we extend the method to multiperiod decisions, we must also cope with the problem of interdependence among periodic flows. For example, the transaction costs alone warrant interperiod dependence. In this case we must resort to an analytic framework that accounts for the interperiod flow dependencies or to a simulation model. Moreover, even in the single-period case, we must account for the correlation of the flows among the various alternatives and adopt a portfolio-selection approach to the cash-budgeting problem.

D. Collection, Mobilization, and Disbursement of Cash

Because most companies' sales at both the wholesale and the retail levels are made on credit rather than cash, we shall concentrate on the ways that may be utilized to collect payments due from customers as quickly as possible. Of significance here is the concept of *float,* which refers to the time delay between the disbursement of funds by the buyer of the firm's goods or services and the moment of receipt of these funds by the seller. When this float refers to the firm's accounts receivable, we call it *negative float* as it indicates opportunity costs for our firm. When the float refers to accounts payable, we call it *positive float* or just *float,* as it indicates opportunity costs for the supplier companies. The purpose of cash collecting is to reduce float without adversely affecting the company's future revenues and profits.

Improvement of cash collection can be achieved by three different operating procedures. The *first* procedure is to improve the paying habits of the clients through a combination of qualitative efforts (public relations) and quantitative attempts (changing the terms of trade). As this is a specialized and complicated procedure, we shall discuss it in Chapter 7, which deals with accounts receivable. The *second* procedure is to attempt to bypass the collection process by selling (factoring) the company's accounts receivable to another specialized firm that will do the job for a specific amount. As this is also a form of short-term financing, we will handle it in Appendix 8A, which deals with several such techniques. The *third* procedure is to attempt to improve the delivery system for customer payments, so as to reduce as much as possible the delay from the time the customer mails a check to the time the firm can utilize the cash for operating purposes.

Firms that engage in the third procedure for reducing negative float attempt to establish *cash collection accounts* at a number of strategically located banks around the country. This way, the customers of the firm pay their bills locally at banks in their region and the funds are transferred electronically to the central accounts of the firm. Another method utilized extensively is known as a *lockbox system*. A lockbox is a post-office box rented by the firm in a certain location and monitored for a fee by a local commercial bank on a 24-hour day basis. As soon as checks from credit customers arrive in the box, the local bank microfilms and deposits the checks in the account of the receiving firm. This procedure minimizes the delays from both steps (*a*) receipt and deposit of cash payments, and (*b*) accounting for such payments by the receiving company. When companies utilize a series of strategically located lockboxes, we have a lockbox collection system, as shown in the simplified diagram of Figure 6.2 for an imaginary multinational company.

When the cash collection phase is completed, the *cash mobilization* stage begins. This consists of a cash information system and means of transferring cash from one unit of the company to another. This phase, of course, is important for large multidivisional firms that operate in many locations at home and abroad. The intent of cash mobilization is to balance demand and supply and reduce the various costs associated with the holding of cash balances.

Finally, we should say a few things about the *disbursement of funds* for the company's accounts payable. Here the problem consists of centralizing as much of the payments network as possible in order to increase positive float by maximizing delays in payments. Needless to say, when we increase our company's positive float, we also increase another company's negative float—a situation that cannot continue unchecked and without unpleasant consequences. In effect, what we are saying is that lockbox collection is the opposite of remote point disbursement, and the functions of cash collection and cash disbursement are mirror images.

V. CASH MANAGEMENT MODELS

The cash management problem was formalized first in 1952 by W. J. Baumol, who perceived the similarities in the objectives between inventory management and cash management. That is, both types of assets are important to the production cycle of the firm and a minimum amount (stock) of each must always be present in order to avoid costly occasions of illiquidity in cash or stockouts in inventory. However, the presence of both assets also introduces acquisition costs and opportunity costs, as well as delays in replenishment. Hence, the need for optimal ways to ensure the presence of minimum levels of these assets in order to ensure the smooth functioning of the firm's operations within the constraints of various costs. Since the early work by Baumol, several sophisticated models have been developed to deal with the cash management problem.[1]

There are three broad methodological approaches to the modeling of the cash management problem: (1) the deterministic formulation best exemplified by the work of Baumol; (2) the discrete stochastic formulation represented by the work of Miller and Orr; and (3) the generalized stochastic calculus formulation, developed by Frenkel and Jovanovic and articulated by Malliaris (1988). Because the last approach requires significant exposure to stochastic calculus and the Ito equation, we shall concentrate our efforts on the first two methods that are also well known and widely applied. At any rate, the basic tenets of each of these models are the same. That is, because the firm's receipts and disbursements are not synchronous, the financial manager must decide on a minimum amount of cash to be held for the purpose of meeting operating payments. The manager must also decide on a safety level of cash below the specified minimum. When this safety level is reached, the financial manager must replenish the cash held back to its original minimum level. The need for specifying minimum amounts of cash balances derives from the acquisition costs (interest) of

FIGURE 6.2 Interrelationship of Corporate Cash Accounts for a Typical Multinational Firm

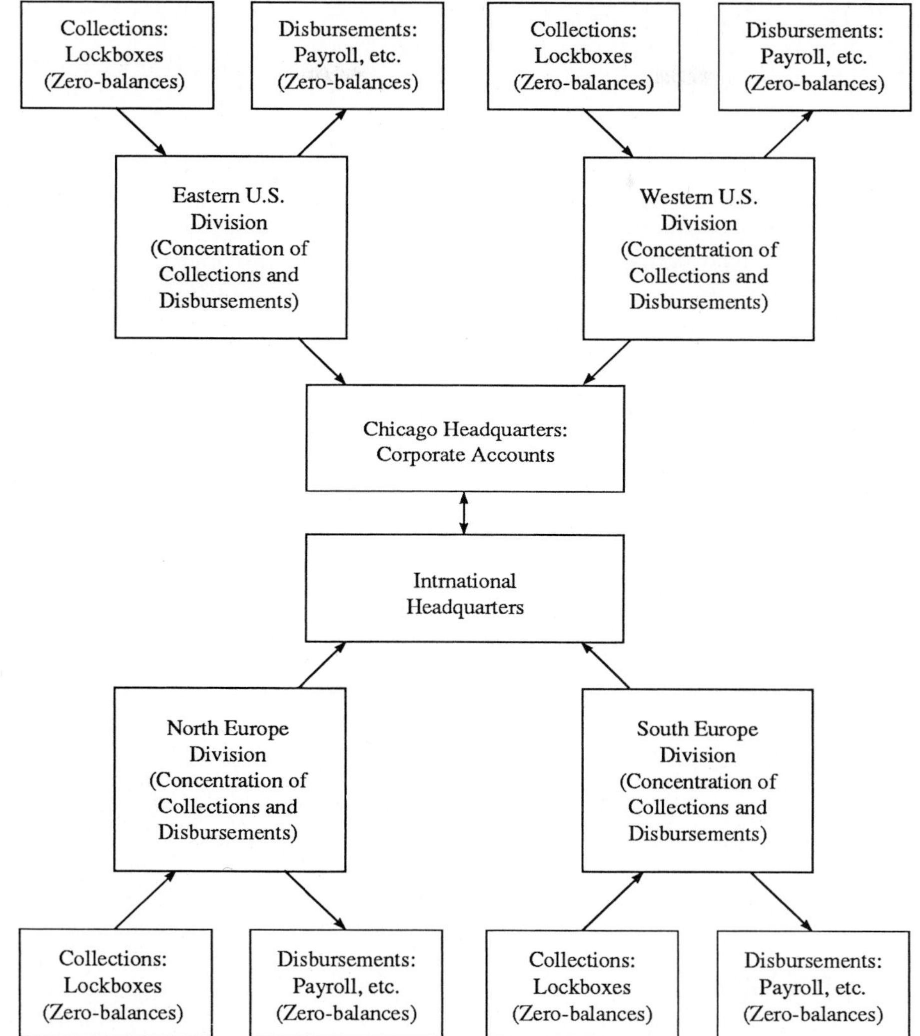

cash and the opportunity costs associated with investment of the cash in the firm's operation or in the market.

The cash management forecasting method deals with two models that bear a close resemblance to the classic economic order quantity models to be discussed in Chapter 8. The following two approaches are more general formulations than the methods described so far for forecasting cash needs in the Parc and Toledo Company cases (Chapter 5), and are useful in attempting to determine the minimum cash balance a company should plan to maintain.

A. Deterministic Approach: The Baumol Model

The Baumol model assumes that cash is drawn from many sources and is used evenly throughout the period under consideration in lots of C dollars. As in the case of Toledo Manufacturing, borrowing during each month will entail a fixed cost of b dollars, and it is further assumed that the cash payout of the corporation is a steady stream totaling T dollars over the period. Baumol's model determines an optimal level of cash balances, so that the sum of transactions costs plus opportunity costs (from holding idle cash) is at a minimum. In certain respects, this approach is a more formalized case of the way in which we arrived at cash balances for Toledo Manufacturing in Table 5.8, and it assumes that transactions occur in a steady stream that is perfectly known in advance.

On the basis of the information given, the total cost TC of maintaining a certain level of cash balances is given by

$$TC = \frac{bT}{C} + \frac{iC}{2} \tag{6.3}$$

where $\frac{bT}{C}$ = the total fixed cost for the period

i = the composite interest rate

$\frac{iC}{2}$ = the opportunity cost of maintaining an average cash balance of $C/2$ during the period

If we wish to minimize the total cost, we can differentiate equation (6.3) with respect to C and set the result equal to zero. Solving then yields the following expression for the optimal cash balance C^*:

$$C^* = \sqrt{\frac{2bT}{i}} \tag{6.4}$$

Equation (6.4) is directly related to the formula for the economic order quantity (EOQ) developed later in Chapter 8. While this approach to cash management seems simple, there are some drawbacks. First, equation (6.4) assumes that disbursements over time are continuous and that there are no unanticipated receipts throughout the period. In addition, the model supposes that the cost of funds is constant and the only motive for cash holdings derives from the transactions demand for these balances.

To illustrate the use of the EOQ model, let us suppose that a firm has estimated cash payments of \$10 million for one month. Suppose also that the fixed cost associated with borrowing is \$200 and the opportunity cost associated with holding cash balances is 10 percent per year. Therefore,

$$C^* = \sqrt{\frac{2(200)(10{,}000{,}000)}{.00833}} = \$692{,}959$$

That is, the optimal transaction size is \$692,959, which results in average cash balances C/2 of \$346,479. This also means that the firm will make approximately 10,000,000/692,959 = 14.4 transactions (conversions) of marketable securities to cash. Using this approach, the total cost will be

$$TC = \frac{200(10{,}000{,}000)}{692{,}959} + \frac{.00833(692{,}959)}{2}$$
$$= \$5{,}772$$

B. Discrete Stochastic Approach: The Miller-Orr Model

If the uncertainty associated with cash payments is large, the simple Baumol model just developed may not be appropriate. With the assumption of (randomly) fluctuating cash balances, however, control theory can be applied to the problem of cash balances. If cash demand fluctuates randomly, we can set upper and lower limits to trigger a transfer to or from marketable securities. Setting these limits requires knowledge of the fixed costs associated with the transaction and the opportunity cost of holding cash, as in the Baumol model. The Miller-Orr Model specifies two control limits: h dollars for an upper bound and L dollars for a lower bound. Figure 6.3 illustrates this concept. When the cash balance reaches the upper bound h, $h - z$ dollars are transferred to marketable securities. If balances reach the lower bound, then $z - l$ dollars are transferred from marketable securities to cash. Note that zero is chosen as a lower limit purely for illustrative purposes; any limit for a lower bound can be set.

The solution for the optimal values of h and z, which depends on b and i as well as the random behavior of cash balances, is

FIGURE 6.3 Cash Balance Behavior in the Miller-Orr Model

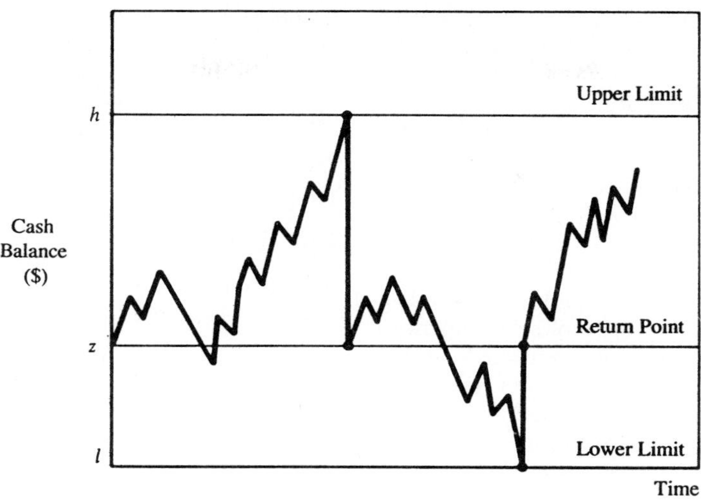

$$z = \sqrt[3]{\frac{3b\sigma^2}{4i}} + l \qquad (6.5)$$

where b = the fixed cost of the transaction
σ^2 = the variance of daily net cash flows
i = the interest rate per day on marketable securities
l = lower control limit

The upper limit is determined by

$$h = 3z - l. \qquad (6.6)$$

As an illustration, suppose that Tandem Bicycle Company's cash flows are very difficult to predict. However, the company's financial managers do know that the standard deviation of daily changes in its cash balance over the past three years is $50,000.

The daily yield on the firm's marketable securities is .0002192 (8 percent per year). Tandem pays a fixed cost of $250,000 each time it transfers funds between cash and marketable securities. Management is willing to accept a cash balance as low as $10,000,000, but no lower. If we apply the Miller and Orr Model to Tandem, we will find that the target cash balance z will be

$$z = \sqrt[3]{\frac{3(250{,}000)(50{,}000)^2}{4(.0002192)}} + 10{,}000{,}000$$

$$= \$11{,}288{,}349$$

and the upper control limit h will be

$$h = 3(11{,}288{,}349) - (10{,}000{,}000)$$

$$= \$23{,}865{,}047$$

VI. CHAPMAN COMPANY: AN INTEGRATED CASH MANAGEMENT CASE

Chapman Manufacturing Company, a New York corporation, had no full-time cash manager before 1990. Only after the company's overextended controller had experienced a series of near disastrous cash shortages in early 1990, was it decided that a full-time cash manager was needed. The person hired for the task, Jack Roland, was a recent MBA graduate from a prestigious Eastern university with extensive internship experience in cash management for a manufacturing firm. Jack Roland was given the following background by president and son of the founder, Mr. Joseph Chapman.

We are a small manufacturing firm. We do not have a separate finance department as such, but our controller and his small staff have been effective until recently at keeping our cash flow under control. However, we experienced critical cash shortages during our seasonal peak months of April and May last year and subsequently we incurred transaction costs of over $6,000,000 for the year. I believe that the bulk of these costs were incurred needlessly as a result of our lack of expertise in this area. What the company needs from you then, Jack, is threefold. *First,* in order to prevent further damage to our business reputation, it is imperative that the fiasco of 1990 not be repeated. *Second,* I would like to see our transaction costs of last year be cut by two-thirds. *Finally,* within the bounds of sound business practice, we need to continue to maximize the earning power of our short-term investments. It's a tall order, but based on your previous experience, I am confident that you can get the job done.

The first model Mr. Roland examined was the classic inventory model developed by Baumol. As we shall see, this model is not well suited to Chapman's policies as it ignores the variability that management is projecting for the cash balance over time.

He arbitrarily selected an amount between the most likely and worst case and applied the model. The problem here is twofold. The opportunity cost associated with holding large cash balances is high, but because we are limited to a fixed number of evenly spaced transactions per year, so is our risk. The calculations follow:

$$Q = \sqrt{\frac{2(200{,}000)(39{,}025{,}000)}{.0825}}$$

$$= \$13{,}755{,}440$$

Beginning balance would be ≈$26,985,000.

Jack Roland estimated two scheduled transactions: one in January, one in June.

(thousands)		*(thousands)*		*(units)*
(69,245 + 26,985)/2	=	48,115 × .0825/3	=	$ 1,323,200
(23,375 + 69,245)/2	=	46,310 × .0825/3	=	1,273,500
(85,275 + 37,130)/2	=	61,202 × .0825/3	=	1,683,100
(54,068 + 85,275)/2	=	69,672 × .0825/3	=	1,916,000
		Opportunity Cost	=	$ 6,195,800
		Transaction Cost	=	400,000
		Total Cost	=	$ 6,595,800
$Q = \sqrt{\frac{2(.05)(39{,}025{,}000)}{.0825}}$			=	$47,303,030 (Not Feasible)
$Q = \sqrt{\frac{2(.015)(39{,}025{,}000)}{.0825}}$			=	$14,190,090 (Feasible)
$Q = \sqrt{\frac{2(.005)(39{,}025{,}000)}{.0825}}$			=	$ 4,730,303 (Not Feasible)

In attempting to determine the best cash-management policy for Chapman Company, Jack Roland examined the two widely utilized alternatives and his own version of a probabilistic method. The assumptions employed to evaluate these alternatives are provided in Table 6.9. Jack Roland also computed cash projections for three possible scenaria (1) best case, (2) worst case, and (3) most likely case. These are shown in Table 6.10, and are graphed in Figure 6.4.

Notice that because Chapman Company will have to transfer $20,000,000 each time, it can get a favorable rate by going the variable route; that is, transaction cost = 20,000,000 × .005 = $100,000, which cuts the transaction cost in half. Thus, total cost = 6,195,800 + 200,000 = $6,395,800.

Another possibility involved the use of a probabilistic method which he recalled from one of his courses in the university but for which he could not identify the contributor. Such an ap-

TABLE 6.9 Assumptions and Parameters for Chapman Company

Brokers' Fee: 2 alternatives—

1. \$200,000 Fixed Cost/Transaction

or

2. Transaction Amount / %

Transaction Amount	%
\$ 0–\$ 9,999,999	5.0
10,000,000– 19,999,999	1.5
20,000,000–Over	0.5

Current Cash and Marketable Securities Position:

Cash Account Balance	\$ 13,230,000
Marketable Securities	(In Currency)
Government Bonds	\$100,000,000
Interest Rate (90-Day) @ 8.25%	

Trading allowed in blocks of \$10,000,000.

Interest/Excess may be placed in a Money Market Account earning 8.25% (60 days or less).

Withdrawals may be made from the Money Market Account at any time without cost.

proach would find the optimal beginning cash balance by equating the probability of a year-end cash surplus with some optimal amount; in Chapman's case:

$$P\,[\text{cash surplus}] = \frac{.005}{.005 + .0825} \approx 5.7\%$$

This assures one transaction at the beginning of the year, at the lowest possible percentage transaction cost.

For simplicity's sake, Mr. Roland assumed that the possible outcomes are *approximately* normally distributed. Using the student-t distribution, he finds that this value lies approximately 1.6 standard deviations from the near value in Chapman's case:

$$\begin{aligned} C &= -258{,}000 + 1.6\ (28{,}850{,}000) \\ &= 45{,}902{,}000 \end{aligned}$$

There would be one transaction at the begin-

TABLE 6.10 Chapman Company Cash Projections: Inflows (Outflows)

	Best Case	*Most Likely*	*Worst Case*
January	\$ 24,570,000	\$ 19,550,000	\$ 16,200,000
February	35,960,000	28,760,000	17,110,000
March	1,000,000	(6,050,000)	(12,050,000)
April	(28,400,000)	(33,900,000)	(41,400,000)
May	(15,930,000)	(21,270,000)	(25,000,000)
June	14,080,000	9,300,000	3,440,000
July	23,600,000	16,750,000	11,200,000
August	56,850,000	49,350,000	33,500,000
September	(19,820,000)	(24,200,000)	(27,680,000)
October	(47,700,000)	(56,650,000)	(62,990,000)
November	10,330,000	7,120,000	5,050,000
December	22,000,000	16,640,000	9,970,000
Net Cash Inflow (Outflow)	\$ 76,540,000	\$ 5,400,000	\$(72,650,000)

Mean = $\overline{X}$ = \$258,056

Standard Deviation = σ = \$28,850,296

FIGURE 6.4 Chapman Company: Projected Trends

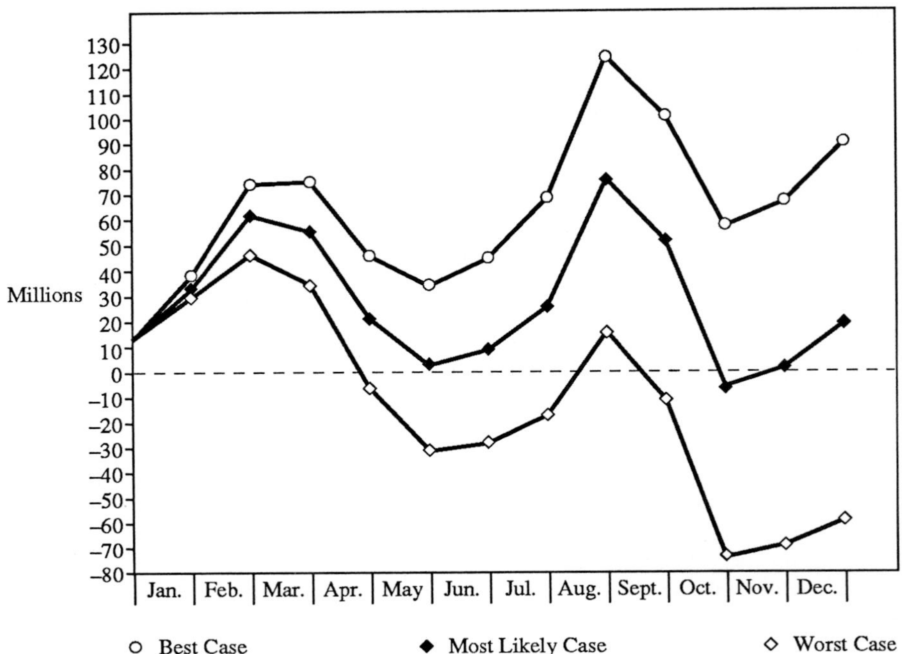

ning of the year, which would amount to: \$45,902,000 − 13,230,000 = \$32,672,000. The Transaction Cost would be: \$32,672,000 × .005 = \$163,360.

Under the most likely scenario, opportunity costs would be

(thousands)		(thousands)		(units)
(45,902 + 88,162)/2	=	$67{,}032 \times \frac{.0825}{3}$	=	\$1,843,400
(88,162 + 42,292)/2	=	$65{,}227 \times \frac{.0825}{3}$	=	1,793,700
(42,292 + 84,192)/2	=	$63{,}242 \times \frac{.0825}{3}$	=	1,739,200
(84,192 + 51,302)/2	=	$67{,}747 \times \frac{.0825}{3}$	=	1,863,000
				\$7,239,300
		Plus Transaction Cost	=	163,360
				\$7,402,660

Notice that while this approach is more costly, it is also less risky (only 5.7 percent chance that one cash withdrawal will exceed our cash on hand at any given time).

Both the scenaria outlined above are based on the assumption that Chapman Company has some definite idea of what their cash needs will be. A third approach which does not require this assumption is based on a model developed by Miller and Orr. Under this system, Chapman's managers would establish a target cash balance and upper and lower control limits and allow the cash balance to fluctuate randomly within these limits. When one of the limits is reached, an appropriate transaction is executed to bring the balance back to target.

According to Mr. Roland's calculations, one target balance z should be

$$z = \sqrt[3]{\frac{3(200{,}000)(2.2803 \times 10^{12})}{4(.000226)}} + 13{,}230{,}000$$

$$= 11{,}481{,}374 + 13{,}230{,}000$$

$$= \$24{,}711{,}374$$

where .000226 is the daily yield on our government bonds (.0825/365), and (2.2803×10^{12}) is the average daily variance on our cash balance ($28{,}850{,}000^2/365$). The upper limit would be

$$h = 3(24{,}711{,}374) - 13{,}230{,}000$$

$$= \$60{,}904{,}122$$

Daily cash projections indicate that the following transactions would occur:

February	1
April	2
May	2
July	1
August	2
September	1
October	6
	15

so that Chapman's transaction cost would be $3,000,000.

However, the opportunity cost would be reduced accordingly:

(21,693 + 13,230)/2	=	$17{,}462 \times \frac{.0825}{3}$	=	$ 480,200
(32,686 + 21,693)/2	=	$27{,}190 \times \frac{.0825}{3}$	=	747,700
(17,179 + 32,686)/2	=	$24{,}932 \times \frac{.0825}{3}$	=	685,600
(46,857 + 17,179)/2	=	$32{,}018 \times \frac{.0825}{3}$	=	880,500
		Total		$2,794,000
		Total cost would be:		3,000,000
				2,794,000
				$5,794,000

The resultant cost constitutes a substantial reduction over the other methods. This is the course of action that Mr. Jack Roland intends to recommend to the company's president, Mr. Joseph Chapman.

VII. SUMMARY AND REVIEW

The foregoing dicussion of working capital produces a fairly complex picture. As we have seen, working capital management must take all possible interdependencies into account, optimizing a single current asset account results in a very myopic approach to the problem. The important point raised here is that working capital management involves trade-offs that may involve liquidity and profitability, as well as other trade-offs. Moreover, some explicit account of risk must be made. This may be accomplished via some of the methods discussed earlier. Regardless of the method chosen, taking account of risk is an important element in working capital. However, the issue becomes extremely complex due to the relationship that exists between the working capital policy and the overall financial policy of a firm.

Cash management refers to the decision-making framework that determines the appropriate levels of cash and marketable securities that must be held on hand to meet the firm's payment requirements. The need for cash management derives from the lack of synchronization between cash receipts and cash disbursements. Because the holding of idle cash has opportunity costs, the financial manager ensures that only a minimum amount is held and the remaining liquidity is assured through the holding of marketable securities that earn a positive return. There are several ways to formulate the cash management problem and obtain meaningful solutions. Two of these methods—the Baumol model and the Miller-Orr model—were discussed in Chapter 6.

NOTES

1. This section is indebted to Malliaris (1988).

QUESTIONS

1. In the context of working capital management, what is the difference between "optimizing" and "satisficing?"
2. Discuss the implications of the accrual method of accounting for the various flows of funds (i.e., income, funds, and cash flows).
3. Can the difference between *accounting* depreciation on the one hand and *physical* and *economic* depreciation on the other diminish the usefulness of book values as a measure of a firm's financial condition?
4. What is meant by the "risk-return trade-off" in the management of working capital?
5. Why should changes in working capital associated with alternative investment proposals be explicitly considered as investment outlays?

ANNOTATED BIBLIOGRAPHY

Knight, W. "Working Capital Management: Satisficing Versus Optimizing." *Financial Management,* Spring 1972, 33–40.

A good paper on the issues of satisficing and optimizing in working capital management.

Malliaris, A. G. "Approaches to the Cash Management Problem." In *Advances in Financial Planning and Forecasting,* edited by C. F. Lee, vol. 3, 231–43. Boston: JAI Press, Inc., 1988.

An excellent exposition of the deterministic, discrete stochastic, and continuous stochastic approaches to cash management.

Sartoris, W. L., and N. C. Hill. "A Generalized Cash Flow Approach to Short-Term Financial Decisions." *Journal of Finance,* June 1983, 349–60.

A treatment of working capital management within a DCF framework.

Sartoris, W., and M. Spruill. "Goal Programming and Working Capital Management." *Financial Management,* Spring 1974, 64–67.

A good application of the Goal Programming approach to working capital decisions.

Smith, K. V. *Guide to Working Capital Management.* New York: McGraw-Hill, 1979.

A good book on overall working capital management with a good treatment of the planning cycle for working capital.

———. "On Working Capital as an Investment by the Firm." In *Readings on the Management of Working Capital,* 2d ed., edited by K. V. Smith, 609–623. St. Paul, Minn.: West Publishing, 1980.

A good paper on working capital as part of the overall capital budgeting framework.

———. *Readings on the Management of Working Capital.* 2d ed. St. Paul, Minn.: West Publishing, 1980.

An excellent book of readings in working capital management.

Van Horne, J. "A Risk-Return Analysis of a Firm's Working Capital Position." *Engineering Economist,* Winter 1969, 71–88.

A good discussion on the incorporation of risk in working capital decisions.

7

MANAGEMENT OF ACCOUNTS RECEIVABLE

I. INTRODUCTION

In modern corporations, accounts receivable (AR) constitute a very important use of short-term funds. As in the case of cash and marketable securities, the management of accounts receivable involves a trade-off between costs and benefits—the costs being the incremental expenditures on collection, bad debts, and any opportunity costs.

Since World War II the volume of outstanding trade and consumer credit has increased significantly. Part of this growth is obviously attributed to the overall increase in economic activity. However, the remainder of the increase is linked to other causes, such as the aggressive use of credit by those firms with adequate financial resources to increase sales.

Various measures of outstanding credit are shown in Table 7.1. Part A, which displays the Sales and Accounts Receivable (AR) balances for all manufacturing corporations, shows that dollar sales from 1950 through 1985 grew at a slower rate than did receivables. Receivables as a percent of sales have gradually increased over the years. Part B indicates the percentage of current assets of all U.S. nonfinancial companies represented by ARs over the years. Part C shows an increase in consumer credit that more than doubled each period, while Part D gives some details of the late eighties. The dollar figures are in billions. Clearly, the huge sums involved highlight the importance of efficiently managing the substantial investment firms undertake in the form of accounts receivable.

II. CORPORATE CREDIT POLICY

The credit policy of a firm consists of a set of operating procedures that are designed to facilitate the effective administration of the firm's credit transactions, and is generally dictated by its socioeconomic and legal environment, its organizational and market limitations, and its established priorities. One factor should be stressed at all times—namely, that the company's trade credit policy should support its sales, rather than *vice versa*. Furthermore, the proper design, implementation, and control of credit policy are essential ingredients for its overall success. Indeed, lack of proper controls in trade credit policy leads inevitably to a preponderance of bad (uncollectible) debts and eventually to a liquidity crunch, as the company's sales produce insufficient cash flows to cover its current liabilities.

It should be stressed here that the overall philosophy of a company's trade policy, that is, whether it will be conservative or liberal, will depend on such factors as the degree of competition, the size of the profit margins, the volume of sales, the overall demand for the product, the size of the company's inventories, its cash position, and the state of the national economy. The various factors and some of the possible interactions of these factors are shown in Table 7.2.

An operationally effective trade credit policy should be concerned with three sets of issues, namely, credit extension, credit collection, and credit control. The first set of issues, *credit ex-*

TABLE 7.1 Measures of Trade Credit Significance (dollar figures in billions)

A. All Manufacturing Corporations

Year	*Sales*	*Accounts and Notes Receivable*	*Receivables as a Percentage of Sales*
1950	$ 181.8	$ 17.0	9.4%
1960	345.8	37.0	10.7
1970	708.8	96.2	13.6
1980	1,894.3	225.7	11.9
1985	2,331.4	293.1	12.6

Source: Federal Trade Commission, *Quarterly Financial Report for Manufacturing Corporations*, various issues.

B. All Nonfinancial Corporations

Year	*Current Assets*	*Accounts and Notes Receivable*	*Receivables as a Percentage of Current Assets*
1950	$ 161.5	$ 55.7	34.5%
1960	289.0	126.1	43.6
1970	572.1	268.0	46.8
1980	1,281.6	491.2	38.3
1985	1,778.5	671.2	37.7

Source: Bureau of the Census, U.S. Dept. of Commerce, *Statistical Abstract of the United States*, 1971, 1981, and 1988 eds.

C. Consumer Credit

Year	*Volume Outstanding*	*Outstanding Credit as a Percentage of Disposable Personal Income*
1950	$ 21.5	10.4%
1960	65.1	18.5
1970	143.1	20.4
1980	385.2	21.1
1986	723.6	23.6

Source: Statistical Abstract of the United States, 1971, 1981, and 1988 eds.

D. Volume of Installment Credit (Consumer)

Date	*Volume Outstanding*
12/76	$193.0
12/77	230.5
12/78	273.6
12/79	312.0
12/80	313.4
12/86	571.8
12/87	613.0
11/88	661.7

Source: Federal Reserve Bulletin, March 1981 and March 1989.

TABLE 7.2 Some Factors Influencing Corporate Credit Policies

Factors	*Conservative Credit Policy*	*Liberal Credit Policy*
Competition	Low Competition	High Competition
Profit Margin	Narrow Profit Margin	Wide Profit Margin
Volume of Sales	Light Volume	Heavy Volume
Customer Demand	High Demand	Low (or Falling) Demand
Inventory Amounts	Low Inventories	High (or Excess) Inventories
Company's Cash Position	Weak Cash Position	Strong Cash Position
National Economic Conditions	Weak (or Uncertain) Economy	Strong (or Expanding) Economy
Type of Product	Customized Products (or Time-Consuming Products)	New or Standardized Products

tension, is best answered by focusing on the following set of questions: (1) To what firms will trade credit be extended? (2) How much credit should be extended to approved companies? and (3) Under what terms and conditions should such credit be extended? The second set of issues, *credit collection* policy, is concerned with the answers to the following questions: (1) What amount of total resources (both human and financial) should be expended in the collection of outstanding credit accounts? (2) At what point in the life of trade credit should such collection-bound resources be expended? and (3) At what point in the life of a specific trade credit should the company abandon collection efforts and simply classify the relevant account as uncollectible? Finally, the third set of issues addresses specifically the ways of *monitoring trade-credit policies* and, to the extent possible, improving their overall effectiveness.

In the next three sections, we will consider each of the three sets of issues in turn, beginning with credit extension policy.

III. CREDIT EXTENSION POLICY

Credit extension policy focuses on the types of firms to which trade credit should be extended, the amounts to be given as credit, and the specific terms under which such trade credit will be allowed. The questions that deal with the approved firms and the amounts of credit can be restated as "How will the company evaluate the worthiness of potential credit customers?" In effect, what we are saying is that the firm must establish some viable system of measurements, which we shall call credit standards and discuss under a separate heading. Customers that meet or exceed the established standards will be granted credit up to a limit based on the interrelated conditions of need and ability to repay the debt. The customer's outstanding credit at any given time may not exceed the established limit; however, the firm may use its discretion to raise limits on a case-by-case method.

A. Credit Terms

When companies offer trade credit to other firms, they prepare a document of terms that includes the following information:

1. The maximum number of days that payment may be deferred by the client-firm. This condition is known as the *credit period.*
2. The time at which the credit period will commence, if it is going to be different from the *invoice date.*
3. The amount of cash discount (if offered) as a percentage of sales price and the maximum number of days that the customer may delay payment and still be entitled to the cash discount. These two terms are referred to as the *cash discount* and the *discount period,* respectively.

As a matter of universal convention, credit terms are typically expressed in the following convenient form:

$d\%/C$ net P days,

where $d\%$ represents the cash discount
C stands for the discount period
P indicates the length of the credit period

Unless otherwise stated in the terms of credit, the credit and discount periods are assumed to commence on the date of invoice. However, many firms choose for convenience the end-of-month as the invoice date. In such cases the terms of credit would be restated as follows:

$d\%/C$ net P days E.O.M.

where E.O.M. stands for End-of-Month.

Thus if a company sells goods or services to another firm and mails an invoice dated January 10, with credit terms 2%/10 net 30, this means that the client firm can pay cash and take advantage of the discount by January 20; if not, the net amount stated in the invoice (without any discount) is due on February 9. If, however, the credit terms are 2%/10 net 30 E.O.M., with an invoice date of January 10, then the client-firm can take the 2% discount by paying cash as late as February 10, while the net amount is not due until March 2. Naturally, individual firms can use many combinations of credit terms to suit their needs and facilitate commercial transactions. Firms may also change credit terms and make them either easier or stricter, something that will be discussed later on as part of the company's credit control policy.

It should be noted at this juncture that, much like the philosophy of a company's credit policy, the length of its credit terms will also be affected by specific factors such as the type of products sold, the price of the product, the size of product inventories, the location of the company vis-à-vis the production plant, and whether the company is a manufacturer, a wholeseller, or a retailer. Some of these configurations are shown in Table 7.3.

TABLE 7.3 Some Factors Affecting Length of Credit Terms

Shorter Terms Offered	*Longer Terms Offered*
For Raw Materials	For Finished Goods
For Brand Name Products	For New Products
For Perishable Goods	For Durable Goods
For Seasonal Products	For Nonseasonal Products
For Inexpensive Goods	For Expensive Goods
For Small Orders	For Large Orders
For Wholesale or Retail Buyers	For Manufacturing Buyers
When Buying Firm is Near	When Buying Firm is Far

Let us illustrate the above points by way of an example. Suppose that Tandem Bicycle Company offers its customers terms of 2%/C.O.D. net 45. This means that the only customers entitled to the 2% cash discount are those who pay "cash on delivery" (C.O.D.) of goods. Such customers pay only \$73.50 per bicycle. Customers who pay for the goods after delivery but within the 45-day credit period will be charged \$75.00 per bicycle.

B. Credit Standards

Companies that wish to evaluate the credit worthiness of present and potential customers must develop some system of *credit standards*. Such a system will enable them to accept the desirable clients and reject the undesirable ones. Of course, the existence and implementation of credit criteria does not always guarantee that poor credit risks will be eliminated altogether from consideration or that all desirable firms will be accepted. However, a system of credit standards definitely enhances the probability that the firm's credit personnel will make the correct decision, if used fairly and consistently. Let us visualize a situation where a potential credit customer under screening for evaluation wishes to establish a long-term credit account with a vendor of goods. Under such circumstances, the vendor's credit manager will typically evaluate the potential customer on the basis of three factors: (1) past credit history, (2) current financial status, and (3) some assessment of the customer's long-term financial soundness. Once the analysis has been made and verified, it must be updated regularly, perhaps annually or semiannually, to reflect any new conditions of the client that may impact on credit worthiness.

There are several approaches employed in the credit evaluation process and we shall discuss here two of the most common and frequently implemented. The first evaluation approach involves the use of sequential-event flow charts or some other procedural method to model the multidecision or "multihurdle" process. In order for the potential customer to be granted credit, the outcome of each decision must be favorable or, at the very least, neutral. A simple variation of this approach requires the decision maker to answer a series of objective and subjective questions. The credit worthiness of the client is determined by a prespecified "correct" combination of answers to both types of questions.

1. The Four C's of Credit

For example, suppose that Tandem Bicycle Company in its formative years employed a simple method of trade credit evaluation based on what is known as the "four C's of credit." These are specifically: *character* (or past credit history); *collateral* (an assessment of whether the customer's finances are sufficient to support borrowing); *capital* (assets and their earning capacity); and *conditions* (factors that are exogenous and outside the control of Tandem and its customers). This type of analysis, portrayed in Figure 7.1, requires that each potential customer must pass through each level in order for credit to be granted. When a customer is approved, a credit limit will be set, at some level assigned by the credit manager, based on a subjective assessment or some arbitrary parameter such as a percentage of the customer's sales.

It should be noted here that the large, complex picture presented in Figure 7.1 may not be fully imposed upon a potential credit client. For example, if the credit manager discovered that a customer's credit history (character) is weak and the record is spotty, the analysis may be terminated at this stage and the credit application rejected. Similar terminations are likely to occur where unusually negative values show up in any of the other three components, as this type of system involves a lot of subjective judgments on the part of the credit staff. The generalized framework for this procedure is shown in Figure 7.2.

2. Credit-Scoring System

The second approach to the evaluation of credit worthiness requires the assignment of specific numerical weights to the four factors (the *C*'s) discussed earlier. Then, the potential credit customer is evaluated on the basis of some overall, typically weighted score. This type of approach is also known as a *credit-scoring system*. A variation of this approach requires that the decision maker answer a series of objective and subjective questions, where the answers are no longer designated as *yes* or *no,* but rather they are graded with a point score. The primary advantage of this flow chart variation is that it allows the credit manager to make an overall decision based on some quantitative factors, rather than going through a series of several partial qualitative decisions. In addition, a scoring system such as the above also allows for easier tracking of customer strengths and weaknesses over time.

3. An Illustration

Let us apply the above scoring system to an example from the files of Tandem Bicycle Company. Assume that since 1980 Tandem has developed a credit-scoring system based on assigning point values to certain questions. A portion of the sample evaluation form that contains a total of twenty questions is reproduced on page 136.

Possible scores for the above questionnaire range from +80 to −40. Tandem's credit manager has set a minimum score of +40 for approval of a customer's credit. Once approved, a customer's credit will be revoked only if the score falls below +40 for two consecutive 6-month periods. As an example of Tandem's credit scoring and monitoring system, we present the case of National Sporting Retail Company, which was approved for credit by Tandem in 1983. Figure 7.3 shows the scores for National Sporting reevaluated at six-month intervals, with evidence that National Sporting's values have fallen below +40 only once during the 1979–1986 period.

FIGURE 7.1 Traditional Credit Analysis Performed by Tandem Bicycle Company

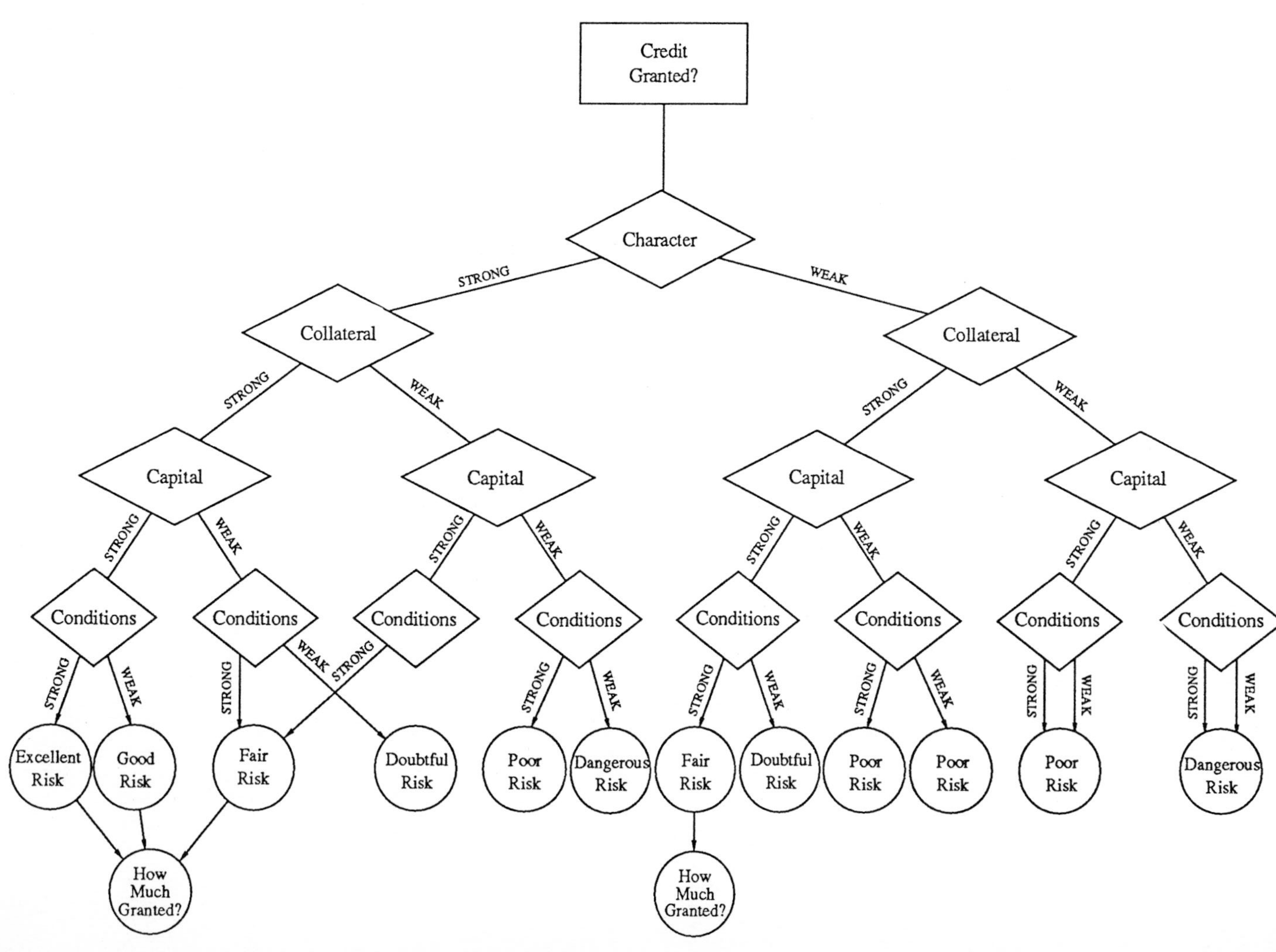

FIGURE 7.2 Sequential Credit Analysis of Customer's Past Record of Payments

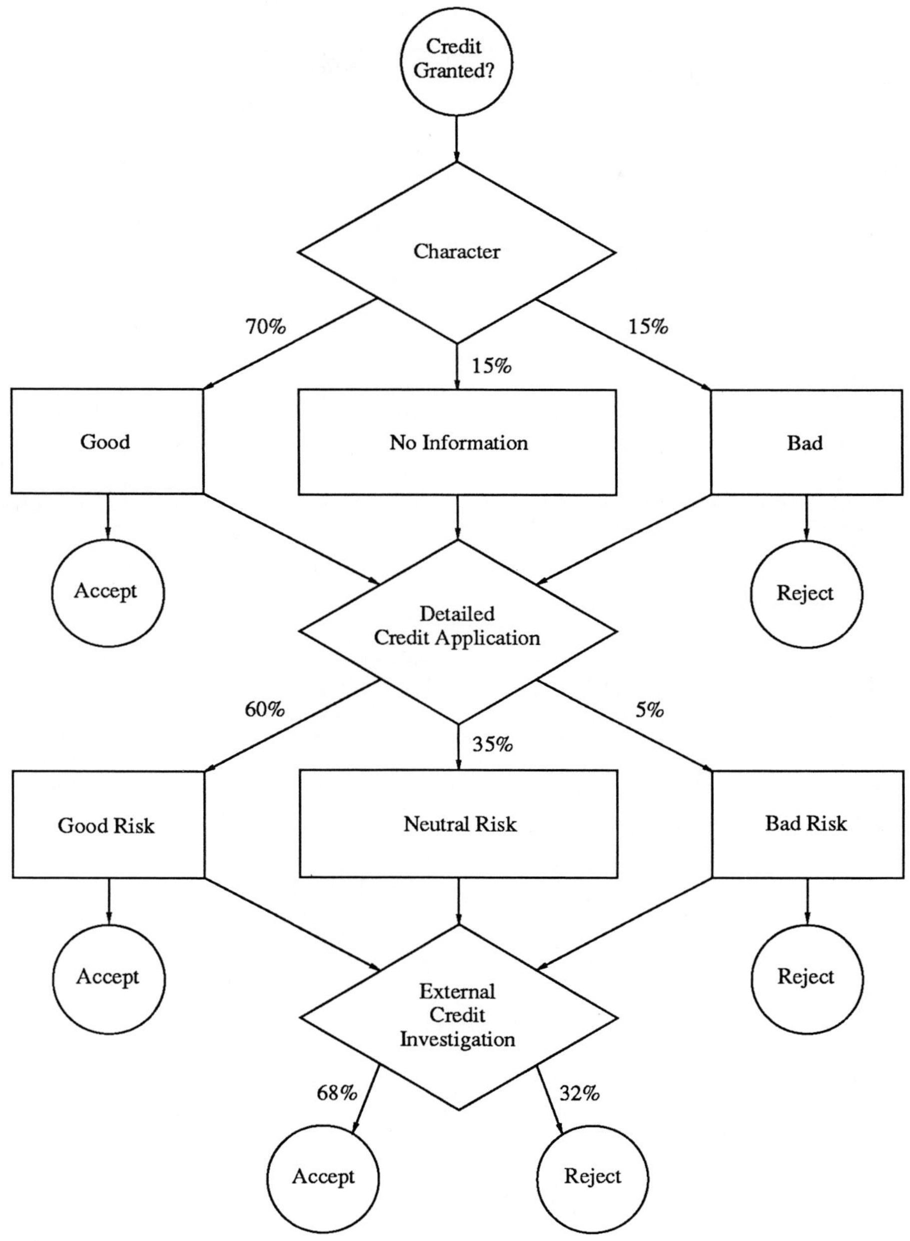

Tandem Bicycle Company
Credit-Scoring System Questionnaire

1. How many times has applicant defaulted on credit/loans in the past 18 months?
   a. 0 (10 points)
   b. 1 (0 points)
   c. 2 or more (−10 points)
2. In how many of the past five years have applicant's earnings per share (EPS) increased? (1 point value for each year of increase)
3. Is applicant's ratio of net working capital to sales:
   a. Greater than the industry average by 10% or more? (4 points)
   b. Within ±10% of the industry average? (2 points)
   c. Less than the industry average by 10% or more? (−2 points).

   ⋮

19. Does applicant have a full-time cash manager or an equivalent professional position?
   a. Yes (3 points)
   b. No (0 points)
20. Assess the economic environment on a scale of −15 = depression to +15 = prosperity.

FIGURE 7.3 Time Series of Credit Scores

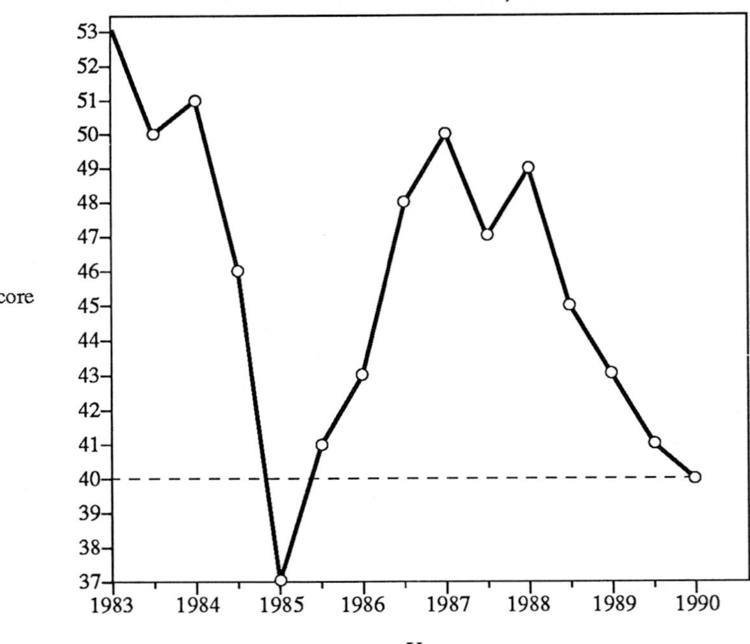

C. Sources of Information

Information that may be used by the credit manager for the company's credit extension decision is available from several internal and external sources. For example, the customer may be asked to supply information regarding the candidate firm's past credit history and current financial status. Such information can be extracted from a well-constructed credit application. Additionally, credit candidates may be asked to provide the names of credit references who have provided trade credit to the applicant on other occasions. Such references will, of course, have to be contacted to verify the information provided in the application.

Other sources of information that are typically supplied through the credit application are the financial statements of the potential client-firm. Certain key ratios that may be obtained from the applicant's comparative balance sheets can provide interesting clues about the firm's financial health. Some of these comparative indicators are: the current ratio; the quick or acid-test ratio; the average age of receivables; and the inventory turnover ratio which indicates how well the applicant firm converts receivables and inventory into cash. The importance of these ratios can be highlighted by way of an example.

Suppose that Tandem Bicycle Company, concerned about its current supply of bicycle tires, has applied for trade credit with the P.B.R. Rubber Company. P.B.R.'s credit manager and her staff have computed several ratios from Tandem's data (in thousands of dollars) as follows:

Net Working Capital

$$= \text{Current Assets} - \text{Current Liabilities}$$

$$= 1{,}108{,}957 - 449{,}400 = 659{,}557$$

Current Ratio

$$= \text{Current Assets/Current Liabilities}$$

$$= 1{,}108{,}957/449{,}400 = 2.47$$

Quick Ratio

$$= \text{Current Assets} - \text{Inventory/Current Liabilities}$$

$$= (1{,}108{,}957 - 363{,}557)/449{,}400 = 1.66$$

In addition, P.B.R.'s staff, concerned about Tandem's ability to convert inventories into cash, have computed the turnover ratios for Accounts Receivable and for Inventories. They are as follows:

$$\text{Accounts Receivable Turnover} = \frac{\text{Credit Sales (or Total Sales)}}{\text{Accounts Receivable}}$$

$$= 2{,}726{,}100/484{,}200$$

$$= 5.63 \text{ Times}$$

$$\text{Inventory Turnover} = \frac{\text{Cost of Goods Sold}}{\text{Ending or Average Inventory}}$$

$$= 2{,}177{,}300/363{,}557$$

$$= 5.99 \text{ Times}$$

As a further point for comparison, the staff at P.B.R. has also computed the relevant industry averages for Tandem's industrial group and have juxtaposed them with the company's figures below.

	Tandem Bicycle Company	*Industry Averages*
Net Working Capital	$659,557,000	$213,720,000
Current Ratio	2.47	2.38
Quick (Acid-Test) Ratio	1.66	1.73
Accounts Receivable Turnover	5.63 Times	6.46 Times
Inventory Turnover	5.99 Times	6.08 Times

In comparing the two sets of data, three points should be stressed: (1) The industry averages may contain companies that employ slightly different accounting conventions, hence the averages may be biased; (2) Because there are at least two methods of computing turnover ratios, it is possible to have inconsistencies; (3) Direct comparisons of some absolute amounts like net working capital may be misleading due to the differences in firm sizes in the industry. As we know, firms of different sizes and in different stages of their life cycle will normally exhibit different working capital and long-term capital structures. Hence, comparisons must be made only after the data have been processed to achieve some homogeneity.

IV. CREDIT COLLECTION POLICY

Credit collection policy deals with the important question of how much of the company's resources should be committed to the collection of overdue invoices by customers. It is also concerned with the proper timing of such resource expenditures. Of course, the cost of collecting money owed to the firm by its customers is but one of many costs that begin with the cost of processing an application, the opportunity costs for carrying the accounts receivable, the routine collection costs, and the past-due collection costs. We shall handle collection costs here under a general umbrella and discuss gains and costs from accounts receivable in Section VI.

Depending upon the particular situation, the range of options available to the firm for collecting its accounts receivable begins with a simple phone call or a form letter and ends with the drastic case of legal action and repossession of assets (merchandise). In such an event, two questions must be answered before taking action on overdue accounts. (1) How large is the account? And, (2) How long overdue is the account? In order to reduce unnecessary collection expenses, companies typically establish some "minimum" procedure that is followed for all debtors. Such procedure generally consists of informing the customer by mail and personalized letter several times within a period of 60–180 days following the invoice due date. Of course, there always comes a time when the costs of pursuing collection outweigh the size of the account. Such time comes earlier for small accounts and later for large ones; and, when it does come, the account must be written off as a bad-debt loss. A simple procedure for credit collections has been established by Tandem Bicycle Company and is shown in Table 7.4.

If all factors are held constant, a firm should pursue the collection of an outstanding debt only if the amount of money it can reasonably expect to recover is likely to exceed the associated collection costs. Let us illustrate this proposition by way of a simple example from the history of Tandem Bicycle Company. Tandem's largest business account since 1986 has been the well-established retailing firm of Sampson Outdoors Company. However, by early 1990 rumors abounded in the market and the popular press that Sampson Outdoors, once a leading retailer, was failing. Tandem's credit collection manager sent Sampson a final notice on April 4, 1990 and followed up with a phone call on April 9. The outstanding balance on the account was $22,500 at that time. Tandem sent a letter on May 4, 1990 revoking Sampson's credit standing and threatening legal action. No response was received, and Sampson Outdoors Company declared bankruptcy on May 20, 1990.

The credit manager of Tandem met with the company's legal advisors who estimated that Tandem could reasonably expect to collect $10,000 in the liquidation of Sampson's assets. They further estimated that the total legal expense for pursuing the case would amount to $5,000. Tandem has already spent $1,000 in its own efforts to collect the amount. However, these are "sunk" costs and should not figure into the decision. Nevertheless, the firm would be better off by $5,000 (= $10,000 − $5,000) if legal action were taken and turned out successful. While Tandem's management was contemplating its options, it was learned on June 1, 1990 that the financial crisis at Sampson Outdoors Company was precipitated by the actions of a highly placed employee who had embezzled over $100,000. A review of the situation by Tandem's attorneys in light of the new information revealed that Tandem could now expect to recover

TABLE 7.4 Tandem Bicycle Company: Summary of Credit Collection Procedures

Time	*Action Required*
15 Days after invoice due date (First notice)	Contact customer by mail. Give invoice number, due date, and amount due. Request prompt payment.
45 Days after invoice due date (Second notice)	Contact customer by mail. Give invoice information. Inform customer that failure to make prompt payment will jeopardize credit standing.
75 Days after invoice due date (Final notice)	Contact customer by mail. Give invoice information. Inform customer that credit standing will be revoked if payment in full is not received in 30 days.
80 Days after invoice due date	Contact customer by phone. Confirm receipt of final notice.
105 Days after invoice due date	Contact customer by mail. Notify customer that credit standing is revoked, and cannot be reinstated unless invoice is paid in full. *IF* account balance exceeds $25,000, inform customer that legal action will be instigated if arrangements for repayment of debt are not made promptly.
135 Days after invoice due date	Debit allowance for doubtful receivables. Credit bad-debt expense. Instigate legal action on accounts exceeding $25,000.

only $2,000 before legal costs, and the additional litigation resulting from this turn of events could continue for several years. It was therefore decided to stop "sinking" additional costs into the collection effort and take the bad-debt write-off of $22,500.

What if, in addition to Tandem, there were several other creditors who were willing to pressure the management of Sampson Outdoors Company into some *voluntary settlement procedure* that would ensure a schedule of future payments when the company's finances improved? In such a case, all the creditors could get together and follow the steps outlined in the schematic of Figure 7.4. Notice that the procedure presented in Figure 7.4 allows for either negotiations with the debtor or court proceedings, depending on the reports given to the creditors by the appointed legal, accounting, and financial experts.

V. EVALUATING RECEIVABLES MANAGEMENT

A. Review of the Credit Division

Evaluating the performance of the credit department is a rather difficult task. One of the poorest ways to evaluate the credit department is to look solely at the total level of bad debts. In the extreme case, this criterion assumes that bad debts should be avoided and that no credit should be extended to the marginal account. But this may result in lost sales and subsequent strengthening of the company's competitors.

In general, evaluation of credit plans is difficult. One approach is to compare the actual bad-debt experience of those credit applicants with a given, specific point score from estimates based on past studies. If the percentage of defaulting accounts is higher than expected, the minimum number of points to obtain credit may be raised (and vice versa).

B. Appraising Collection Practices

The external analyst, to whom detailed information is not usually available, often evaluates the credit extension activity by comparing the volume of receivables outstanding with the sales level. If the size of the AR balance changes proportionately with a change in sales, the analyst tends to conclude that the company's credit policies have not deteriorated. If the volume swells more than proportionately, an external observer may begin to worry about the quality of the accounts.

FIGURE 7.4 A Procedure for Multicreditor Action after Final Collection Notice

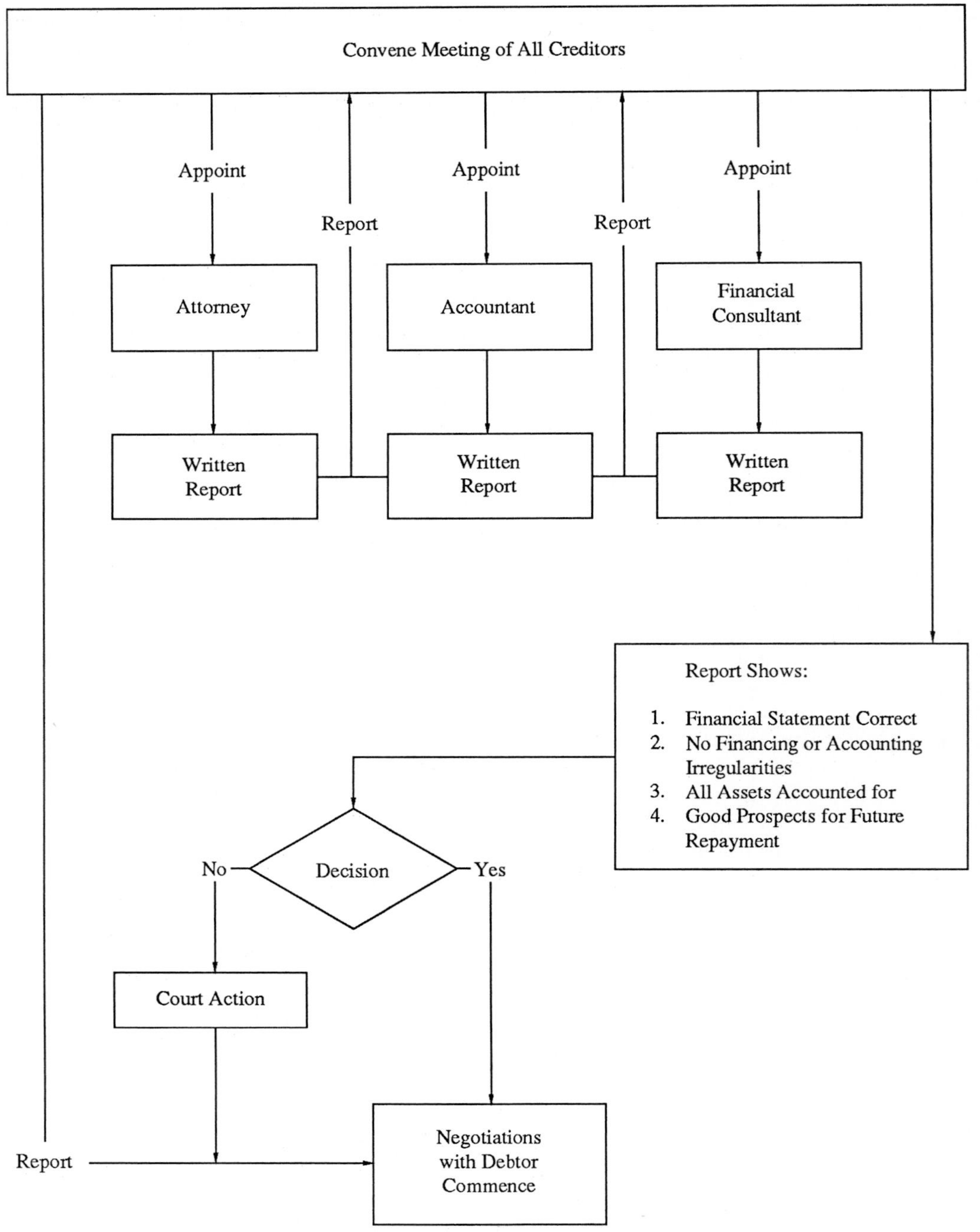

Similarly, the internal analyst is concerned with whether the receivables are being collected as rapidly as possible. For example, if sales increase from $1 million to $2 million and the AR balance remains at 10 percent of sales, its dollar value should double from $100,000 to $200,000. However, if a reduction in collection speed also occurs, the actual balance might rise to $300,000, or 15 percent of sales. That is, while the first $100,000 increase is expected, the second $100,000 increase is not and thus becomes a cause for concern.

Figure 7.5 illustrates the impact of volume and collection changes by arraying the preceding factors against time. Sales of $1 million a year and $2 million a year represent sales per day of $2,740 and $5,480, respectively, and are shown on the horizontal axis as points A and D. To facilitate comparison, the collection period in terms of sales per day is calculated by dividing sales per day into the balance of outstanding receivables as follows:

$100,000/2740 = 36.5 days

$200,000/5480 = 36.5 days

$300,000/5480 = 54.7 days

The first two collection periods are indicated by point B and the third by point F. As the total volume of receivables is the sales per day times the collection period, the areas of the rectangles are an accurate graphical representation of this balance and its components. In the figure, a doubling of sales defines an area ODEB, which is twice the size of the original area OACB.

If there were a slowing in the collection period, it would be represented by an increase to $300,000 in the AR balance, arising from an increase in sales of another $1 million. This

FIGURE 7.5 Impact on Balance in Accounts Receivable of Changes in Volume and Collection Experience

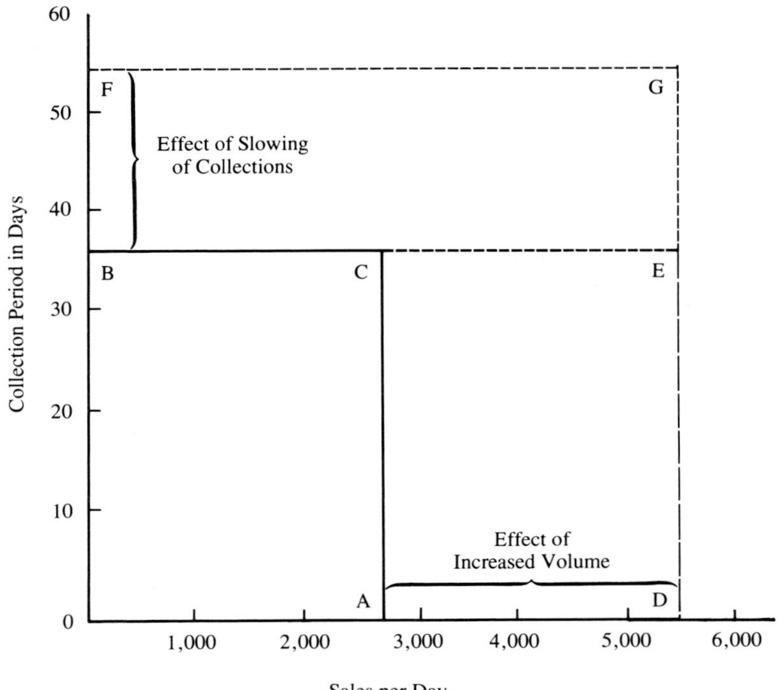

would have the effect of increasing the balance more than proportionately. A simultaneous change of this sort creates a major increase in receivables, adding the area BEGF to the area ADEC created by volume increase alone. If the extra sales have been stimulated in part by a more generous credit policy, management must be careful to anticipate the extra funds required. Managers must then evaluate carefully whether the extra investment in receivables is justified in terms of the extra profit that will be earned.

One other point of concern is the difficulty one encounters in comparing economic activity during different months for those companies that are subject to pronounced seasonal sales patterns. A similar problem is present in the evaluation of companies that operate in longer cyclical patterns. The end of one year may be near the peak of a cycle, and the end of the next year may be approaching a trough. Total sales in both circumstances may be the same, but the working capital position may be strikingly different. Evaluating accounts receivable policy in such an environment may be extremely difficult.

In the remainder of the chapter we will look at receivables management in a seasonal setting—an extremely common setting and one that presents particular difficulties for those attempting to forecast intrayear trade requirements.

C. Constant Collection Period: An Illustration

Tables 7.5 and 7.6 show the collection experience of the Chamberlain Company, a manufacturer of lawn and casual furniture. Table 7.5 lists the monthly sales, which are at a low, level rate of $50,000 a month from September through January. Sales then begin to rise, slowly at first and then quite steeply to a peak of $300,000 in June. Sales decline more rapidly after June than they rose, reaching the $50,000 off-season level again in September.

Chamberlain's collection experience, however, is very stable. As shown in the table, no sales are collected during the first 30 days of the month in which the sales were made. Fifty percent of the sales are collected between 30 and 60 days after sale, and during the 60- to 90-day period an additional 40 percent are collected. The final 10 percent are paid for during the 90- to 120-day period, the third month after sale. The weighted average of day's sales outstanding in the accounts receivable balance is therefore

50% take 30 days to collect	=	15
40% take 60 days to collect	=	24
10% take 90 days to collect	=	9
Average outstanding		48 days' sales

TABLE 7.5 Chamberlain Company—Collection Experience with Collection Period Constant but Fluctuating Sales (in thousands of dollars)*

Sales made in	*PY***	*Jan*	*Feb*	*Mar*	*Apr*	*May*	*Jun*	*Jul*	*Aug*	*Sep*	*Oct*	*Nov*	*Dec*	*TOTAL*
		$50	$80	$100	$150	$250	$300	$100	$70	$50	$50	$50	$50	$1300
Will be collected in:														
Jan	$50													50
Feb	25	25												50
Mar	5	20	40											65
Apr		5	32	50										87
May			8	40	75									123
Jun				10	60	125								195
Jul					15	100	150							265
Aug						25	120	50						195
Sep							30	40	35					105
Oct								10	28	25				63
Nov									7	20	25			52
Dec										5	20	25		50
														$1300

*Collection Schedule: 0 percent current month, 50 percent prior month, 40 percent next prior, 10 percent third prior.

**Column includes collections this year on sales made in the previous year.

TABLE 7.6 Chamberlain Company—Accounts Receivable Balance (in thousands of dollars)

	Jan	Feb	Mar	Apr	May	Jun	Jul	Aug	Sep	Oct	Nov	Dec
A. Accounts outstanding from:												
2nd prior month (10%)	$ 5	$ 5	$ 5	$ 8	$ 10	$ 15	$ 25	$ 30	$ 10	$ 7	$ 5	$ 5
1st prior month (50%)	25	25	40	50	75	125	150	50	35	25	25	25
Current month (100%)	50	80	100	150	250	300	100	70	50	50	50	50
TOTAL	$80	$110	$145	$208	$335	$440	$275	$150	$95	$82	$80	$80
B. Balance, beginning of month	$80	$ 80	$110	$145	$208	$335	$440	$275	$150	$95	$82	$80
Less: collection	50	50	65	87	123	195	265	195	105	63	52	50
Plus: sales	50	80	100	150	250	300	100	70	50	50	50	50
Balance, end of month	$80	$110	$145	$208	$335	$440	$275	$150	$ 95	$82	$80	$80

Alternatively stated, during any given month collections consist of 50 percent of the prior, 40 percent of the second prior, and 10 percent of the third prior month's sales.

Note, incidentally, that the number of days' sales outstanding is calculated on a 30-, 60-, and 90-day base rather than a 45-, 75-, and 105-day base. The reason for this is that the sales made during the month are assumed to be made evenly, so that at the end of the month the average number of days outstanding on that month's sales is only 15 and not 30, even though no collections have been made on any of that month's sales. It is also assumed that payment on each day's sales will be made according to this pattern. That is, if 10 percent of the sales are collected on the 60th day, it is assumed that 10 percent of each day's sales will be paid on the 60th day after sale.

Table 7.6 develops the balance of accounts receivable based on the information sales and collections provided in Table 7.5. The balance is calculated in two ways. The first, presented in Part A of the table, applies constant percentages to the appropriate months:

Proportion Outstanding	*As of May*	*As of September*
100 percent of month just ended	250 (May)	50 (Sep.)
50 percent of prior month	75 (Apr.)	35 (Aug.)
10 percent of second prior month	10 (Mar.)	10 (Jul.)
Total	335	95

A calculation that displays this information and relates the outstanding balances to the sales in those periods in which the balances were created is known as an *aging of accounts receivable*. In the case of Chamberlain Company, the aging would show a constant pattern of 100 percent, 50 percent, and 10 percent relating balances to the periods in which the sales had been made.

The second way of calculating the balance is the customary one used for accounts receivable: beginning balance less collection plus sales. Part B of Table 7.6 yields results identical to those of Part A.

Table 7.7 shows the types of errors and distortions that result when an attempt is made to use various common measures of receivables management in a situation characterized by a fluctuating sales level. It is important to reemphasize that these distortions are caused solely by the fluctuations in sales and not by changes in the collection pattern, which, for Chamberlain, are constant, as noted earlier.

1. Days' Sales Methods

A common way of measuring a company's collection experience is to calculate the number of days' sales, which is shown in the receivables balance. As indicated earlier, this figure is found in two steps as follows:

TABLE 7.7 Chamberlain Company—Alternative Measures of Accounts Receivable Management (in thousands of dollars)

	Jan	*Feb*	*Mar*	*Apr*	*May*	*Jun*	*Jul*	*Aug*	*Sep*	*Oct*	*Nov*	*Dec*
Sales	*$50*	*$ 80*	*$100*	*$150*	*$250*	*$300*	*$100*	*$ 70*	*$50*	*$50*	*$50*	*$50*
Accounts receivable balance	*80*	*110*	*145*	*208*	*335*	*440*	*275*	*150*	*95*	*82*	*80*	*80*
A. Days' Sales Methods:												
1. Average days' sales (1,300 ÷ 365 = 3.56 sales per day)	22	31	41	58	94	124	77	42	27	23	22	22
2. Most recent month's days' sales	48	41	44	42	40	44	82	64	57	49	48	48
3. Most recent 3-month's days' sales	48	55	57	57	60	56	38	29	39	43	48	48
B. Percentage Approaches:												
4. Percentage of assets (assuming assets constant at 2,000)	4	6	7	10	17	22	14	8	5	4	4	4
5. Percent of receivables more than 30 days old	38	27	31	28	25	32	63	53	47	39	38	38

1. Sales per Day = (Total Sales) ÷ (Number of Days in the Period) (When using one year's sales, divide by 365; for one month's, divide by 30.)
2. Days' Receivables = (Balance in Accounts Receivable) ÷ (Sales per Day).

Alternatively, a calculator may be used to find the number of days' sales in the receivables account as

$$\text{Days' Receivables} = \frac{\text{Accounts Receivable Balance}}{\text{Sales}} \times \text{Days in Period}$$

Again, it is important to remember that the number of days used must be consistent with the period for which the sales figure is calculated. For a full year's sales, 365 or 360 is the appropriate number of days. For six months' sales, a figure of 180 days is required.

Rows 1, 2, and 3 of Table 7.7 show three alternative ways of computing the number of days in the accounts receivable balance. Row 1 uses a figure for sales per day based on the average for the entire year: $1,300,000/365 = $3,560. The reason the number of days' sales in receivables fluctuates wildly is that the average daily sales based on the entire year's sales volume is quite different from the average daily sales experienced in any one month. The average daily sales for those months with a volume of $50,000 is only $1,667, less than half the annual average. On the other hand, of course, the average sales per day in June is $10,000, which is over twice the average. Since in the case of Chamberlain the amount of receivables depends to a great extent on the sales of the current month, use of the annual average sales per day as the denominator in the collection calculation produces considerable distortion, except where the current sales level is at approximately the monthly average of $100,000. Thus, in March and August, the days' sales in receivables is approximately correct. Even in those months, however, the figure is distorted because of the rapidly increasing and decreasing sales levels from one month to the next overall.

One way of attempting to evaluate the receivables balance more accurately is to compare it to the most recent 30-days' sales, i.e., to the most recent 30-days' level of sales per day. The results of this calculation are shown in Row 2. The variation here, ranging between 40 days and 82 days, is somewhat less extreme than if the annual average sales are used as the divisor. In fact, given Chamberlain's pattern of collection, when sales stabilize for three months, the correct figure will be shown by this calculation.

This method shows variations because the balance in accounts receivable includes not only sales of the most recent month (of which 100 percent are still outstanding), but also a significant proportion of the prior month's sales (40 percent). Moreover, 10 percent of the second prior month's sales are also included, which could constitute a significant amount of the current sales level if there has been a significant decline in sales recently. August illustrates this very situation, with $30,000 of the accounts receivable balance being outstanding from July's sales and representing over 40 percent of the current sales level of $70,000.

The impact of changing sales rates can be seen in the period from January to May, when sales rise rapidly so that the carryover from previous months is more than offset by the higher current sales level. This brings the calculation down to 40 days in May. By June, however, the rate of change has slowed, so the number of days goes up to 44. During the seasonal sales contraction, which begins in July, the level of sales drops far more rapidly than receivables are run off from the high-volume months. Thus, the days' sales in receivables based on the current month's sales quickly rises, falling back only when the heavy receivables generated during May and June are collected.

Use of an average over more than one month is another way of attempting to develop a smoother measure that reflects more accurately the true state of collections. Because the Chamberlain Company's customers take up to three months to pay, a three-month average might seem sensible. Row 3 shows the results of this calculation, with the days' sales in receivables varying from 29 to 60 days, about the same percentage difference as shown in Row 2. Like the calculation based on the most recent month only, this calculation stabilizes at the correct figure when sales have been level for three months. But it tends to read high when the monthly figure is low, and low when the monthly figure is high.

The reason for this shift between Rows 2 and 3 is that the three-month average puts equal weight on all three months. When sales are rising, this bias tends to hold down the average day's sales for the period compared to the current month. While some of the outstanding accounts are from the earlier months, the major proportion is almost always from the most recent period. Thus, the impact of the most recent period is dampened more than it should be on the way up. As sales decrease, the reverse distortion takes place. The heavy sales volume of the previous month gets equal weight with the light volume of the current month. Some receivables are outstanding from the prior month (50 percent), but 100 percent are outstanding from the current month. Treating all months' sales as though an equal proportion were outstanding makes it appear that collections are coming in faster than before.

2. *Percentage Approaches*

Two other methods, based on percentage calculations, are often used by outside analysts, but they are also subject to the same type of distortions described for the days' receivables methods. Row 4 of Table 7.7 shows the percentage of Chamberlain's assets that would be represented by receivables as the year progressed, assuming that total assets were constant at $2 million. (While this assumption is not absolutely realistic, it is not entirely removed from reality. The total funds in the business over the period may remain relatively constant as they are turned from cash into inventory, the inventory is sold, and the receivables are ultimately collected to restore the cash balance.) The percentage of receivables to total assets is only 4 percent at the low point, but rises to 22 percent at the peak. While this might tempt an analyst to become concerned about the collection experience, the result is entirely due to the calculation method, not to any real change in collection experience. Following the peak selling month, it is natural that a higher proportion of the assets is held in the form of receivables. If it were not, it would be a sign that the inventory had not been reduced as anticipated.

A second common percentage method relates receivables outstanding for more than a specified time, say, 30, 60, or 90 days, to the total receivables balance. A shift in this percentage is sometimes thought to signify a deterioration of collection and perhaps of credit. As shown in Row 5 of the table, the percentage of receivables more than 30 days old varies radically compared to the total balance in the account. Again, the reason is the fluctuation in sales. When current sales are high relative to prior sales, the percentage due from over 30 days is low, as in February through June. In the latter part of the year, when current sales are low compared to prior sales, the percentage due from over 30 days is high. The effect is most misleading, as the actual collection experience of Chamberlain is constant.

If comparisons are made between comparable periods, say June of one year to June of the next, then if the company's sales levels are proportionate in corresponding periods and if its collection experience holds constant, the results of any of these five calculations should be comparable. These are a number of "ifs," but for many companies they hold sufficiently true that the analyst can compare one year-end statement with another without distortion. For example, if Chamberlain ended its fiscal year in July, an outside analyst using average sales for the year would calculate that 77 days' sales were outstanding. As long as about 77 days had been outstanding the year before, the analyst would conclude that the company was not losing control of its credit.

For companies that suffer serious cyclical patterns of more than one year in duration, even such year-end comparisons are difficult. Suppose Chamberlain ended one year's operations in a cyclical position typical of the July figures, with 124 days' (average annual) sales outstanding. If it had happened to end the previous year with a cycle in a December stage, showing only 22 days' sales, the analyst might become needlessly concerned about the company's credit position.

3. A True Aging Method

At this point, the reader is entitled to ask whether there is any accurate way of evaluating receivables. The discussion so far has concentrated on common erroneous methods. Is there a correct method?

The answer is yes, but it is often impossible for the outside analyst to apply it because the figures are not available. Internal management has no such excuse, however, for it should establish its information system so that the proper data are available.

The most accurate method is that shown in Table 7.5 and Part A of Table 7.6, where a true aging of accounts is displayed. On the basis of this information, the analyst who did not know how the example had been constructed could either calculate the collection pattern (when sales made in a given month are collected) or relate the outstanding balances at the end of each month to the sales of the month in which they were made. If the analyst calculated collections, as in Table 7.5, he or she would find that the 50 percent, 40 percent, and 10 percent pattern recurs consistently. In a realistic situation where collection experience is good, some

	Jan	*Feb*	*Mar*	*Apr*	*May*	*(etc.)*
Percent outstanding from						
Sales made in:						
2nd prior month	10	10	10	10	10	10
1st prior month	50	50	50	50	50	50
Current month	100	100	100	100	100	100

minor variation would naturally be expected—but no slipping over time (e.g., 50 percent collected in the second month, then only 45 percent, and finally only 30 percent should be evident).

Relating outstanding balances to month of origin (from Table 7.6), the analyst's tabulation would be as shown on bottom of page 146.

With such a consistent pattern, or even one with modest variation, the analyst would again be able to conclude that the management of working capital had not suffered.

A ratio can be devised to confirm this fact once the base pattern has been found. In the Chamberlain Company's case, the appropriate denominator for each month would be calculated as shown in the following example for June:

	June
10% 2nd prior month's sales	15
50% 1st prior month's sales	125
100% current month's sales	300
Total	440

As calculated earlier, this pattern of collections represents a collection period of 48 days.

By dividing the actual balance by this estimate of what the balance should be, it is possible to determine whether receivables are being collected faster (an index of less than 1) or more slowly (an index of more than 1) than anticipated. The use of this index, however, is not a substitute in a difficult financial situation for careful analysis of the monthly aging of receivables. Early warning signals may be discovered by looking at each month's experience, signals that might not be detected as soon by using the index.

4. *The Iterative Method*

An alternative method is available to the outside analyst who does not always have the information to allow the use of the true aging method. This method is an iterative technique that backs the most recent month's sales out of the accounts receivable balance and then compares the residual in the accounts receivable balance to sales from the next prior month. While the approach is not as accurate as a true aging, it avoids some of the most unreliable aspects of the other methods because it goes part way in relating the outstanding balance to the sales of the periods in which the balance was put on the books.

As shown in Table 7.8, all that is needed to make the calculation is the information on monthly sales and the monthly ending receivables balance. The sales of the most recent month, accounting for the 30 most recent days, are first deducted from the ending receivables balance. The residual represents uncollected amounts of sales made longer than 30 days ago. It may, therefore, be compared with the sales of the next prior 30-day period. The percentage relationship of the balance to the sales in the period 31 to 60 days earlier is calculated and multiplied by the 30 days in the period. As Table 7.8 shows, approximately 57 percent of sales of the prior month remain outstanding, which rounds to 17 days. This figure, plus the initial 30, adds to 47 days, only slightly less than the 48 days provided by the true method. The data in Table 7.8 show that the measurement would work well both as sales are rising and as they are falling.

In the event that more than 60 days of sales are outstanding, the iterative method can be used by making as many more subtractions (at 30-day increments) as are necessary to produce a residual that is smaller than the sales of the corresponding period. For instance, if in the illustration given in Table 7.8 April sales had been only 50, then a balance of 35 would have been left to compare with March sales (not shown here). The days' sales outstanding would then be 60 days plus whatever proportion of the next 30 days back that the 35 residual balance bore to sales of that period, 60 to 90 days earlier.

The defect in the iterative method is that the results may be in error if there is a payment pattern in which there is relatively fast payment for part of the credit sales but very slow payment for the rest. In that case use of the iterative method might result in days' sales outstanding of less than 30 days whereas one-third of the balance might be 60 to 90 days old.

In general, the rule that applies to most current asset and current liability accounts is that particular care is required in interpreting the sales volume and account balance relationships to ensure that they are analyzed in the light of most current business conditions. Comparisons

TABLE 7.8 The Iterative Method of Estimating Days' Sales Outstanding (DSO)

Chamberlain data, end of month:	*May*	*June*	*July*
Accounts Receivable Balance	335	440	275
Deduct sales made in most recent 30 days (e.g., May in May)	250	300	100
Residual balance, originating in prior months	85	140	175
Sales, most recent 31–60 days (e.g., April in May)	150	250	300
Proportion, residual balance to prior sales	57%	56%	58%
Days of prior sales outstanding	17	17	17
Total DSO, including initial 30 days	47	47	47

of unlike periods for highly seasonal companies are especially fraught with danger.

VI. COSTS AND BENEFITS ASSOCIATED WITH ACCOUNTS RECEIVABLE

The extension of trade credit entails three types of cost for the firm granting it. These are (1) carrying costs, (2) routine collection costs, and (3) past-due collection costs. Carrying and routine collection costs can be analyzed under conditions of certainty, while the past-due collection cost enters only when we introduce uncertainty into the analysis.

A. Carrying Costs

Carrying costs refer to the tying up of some of the firm's funds as it lends out to another firm through accounts receivable. In effect, the firm granting the credit cannot invest the equivalent amount of funds into some alternative opportunities that might increase its earnings. It should be noted here that this carrying or opportunity cost is born both during the initial discount period and during the remaining horizon of the credit period. Hence, even when the customer takes the discount and pays for the goods, in say 10 days, the seller must still find some way to recoup the cost of this "free" credit for 10 days.

B. Collection Costs

Routine *collection costs* refer to the operating expenses associated with credit extension as well as within-period collection. For example, the seller, depending on size, may have an entire credit department or just a few staff people accepting, reviewing, and evaluating credit applications. Similarly, the seller needs staffing for the purpose of collecting accounts receivable, where they would keep track of shipment dates, invoice dates, discount period dates, and due dates, as well as send out reminders. Due to standardization of these tasks, the length of the net period does not affect the routine collection costs that are viewed typically as a lump sum. However, as we move from routine collection costs to the costs associated with past due debts, the situation changes drastically. As serious efforts begin to recoup the funds, costs rise sharply. For example, turning over the account to some collection agency will cost a good percentage of the account outstanding. Failing this, it becomes necessary to retain an attorney whose costs will also erode the base amount by some good percentage. Finally, in the event of failure by the debtor company, the trade creditor may well be at the bottom of the priority list for monetary recovery.

C. Costs versus Profits

The behavior of the three types of costs associated with extending trade credit, along with their interaction with the firm's gross profits are depicted in Figures 7.6 through 7.8. Note that Figure 7.7 presents gross profits in the absence of any discounts associated with accounts receivable, while Figure 7.8 allows for the standard 10-day discount period. Also note that the gross profit line drops after the end of the credit period (30th day) to indicate the seriousness of the situation.

Accounts receivable constitute a very important use of short-term funds. As in the case of cash and securities, their management involves a trade-off between benefits and costs—the benefits being the incremental profits from the higher sales that the credit-selling policy produces and the costs representing the incremental expenditures on collection, bad debts, and the opportunity costs. On an intuitive basis, the appeal of investment in accounts receivable rests with the tendency of such a policy to increase unit sales, even though it reduces the net unit profit.

The benefits and costs of investing in accounts receivable can be illustrated analytically as follows: Let the average unit price be denoted by P, the average unit cost by C, and the sales volume by S. Further assume, for the sake of simplicity, that the firm possesses linear revenue and cost functions.

Now, as we recall from earlier material, the profit of the firm, π, is defined as the difference between total revenue (TR) and total cost (TC). Symbolically,

$$\pi = TR - TC \tag{7.1}$$

Figure 7.9 shows the effects of increased investment in accounts receivable. For example, for the firm operating on a cash-and-carry policy, the profit is determined by

$$\pi_1 = TR_1 - TC_1$$

For the firm that institutes a credit policy and

FIGURE 7.6 Behavior of Trade-Credit Costs

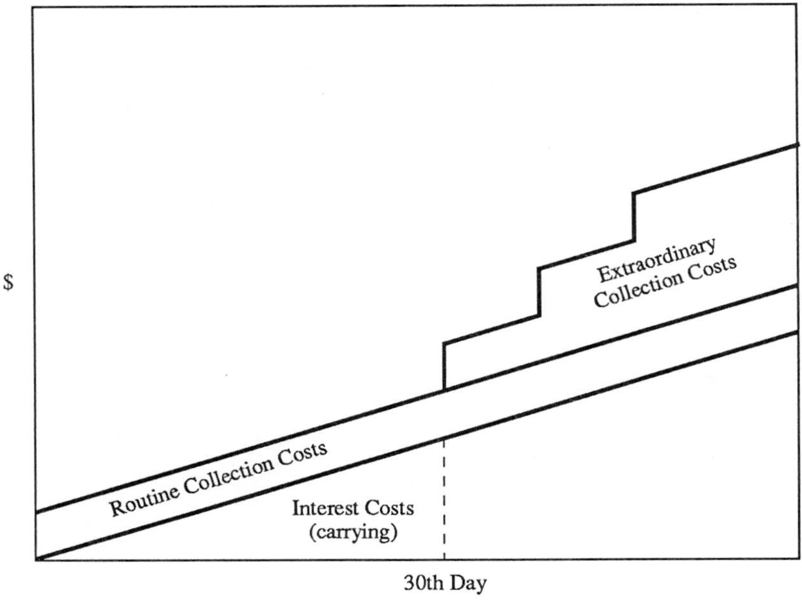

FIGURE 7.7 Benefits and Costs of Trade Credit without Discounts

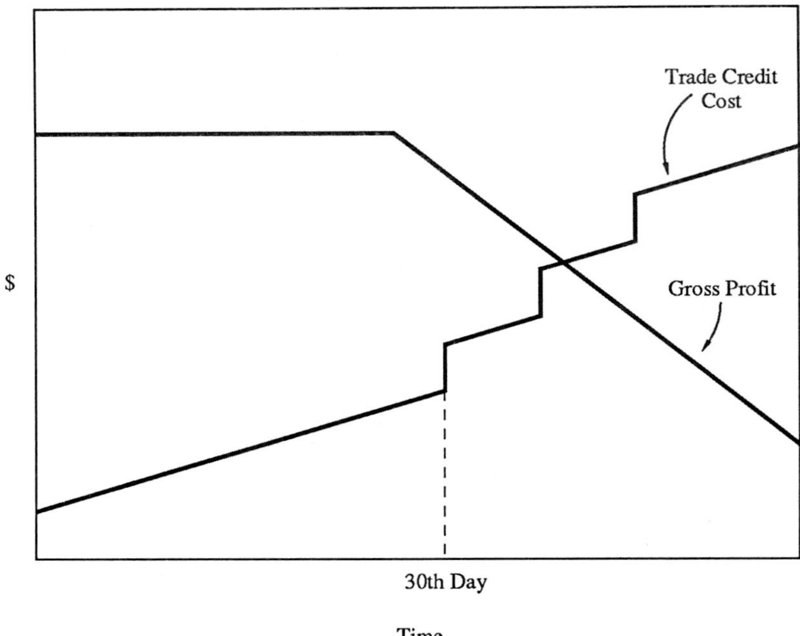

FIGURE 7.8 Benefits and Costs of Trade Credit with Discounts

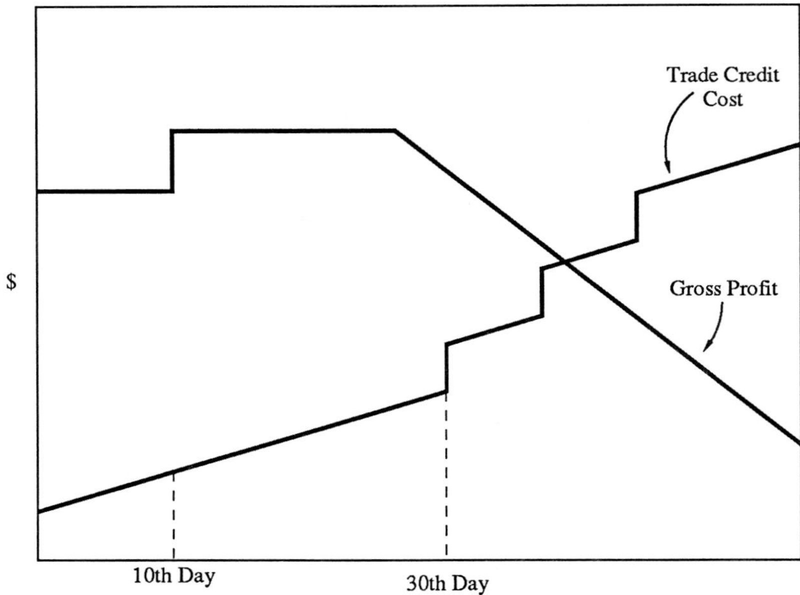

FIGURE 7.9 Effects of Changes in Trade-Credit-Induced Sales upon Revenues, Costs, and Profits

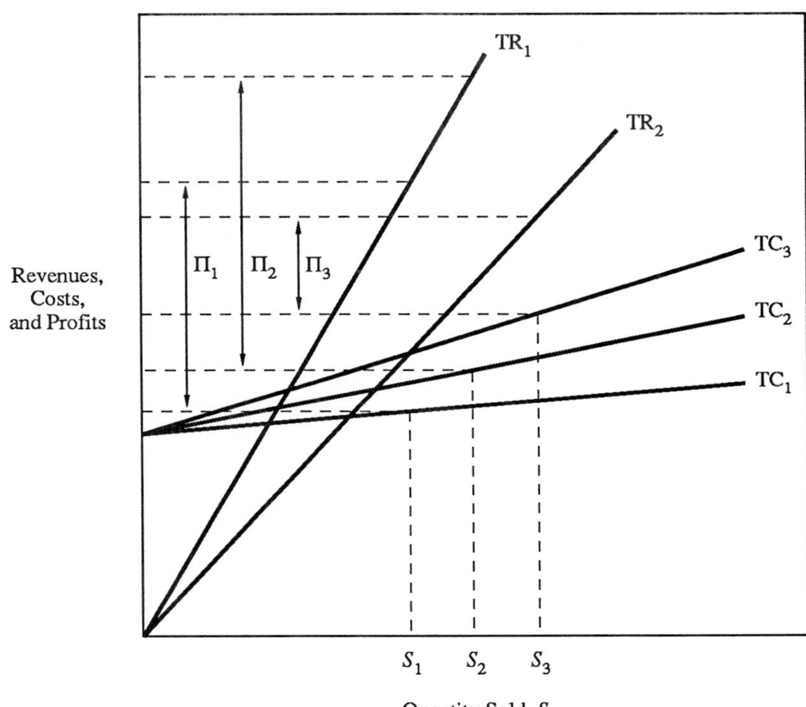

expects *no* delinquency in accounts receivable, the total-cost curve TC_1 is likely to shift slightly upward to TC_2, to account for the increase in the collection expenditures necessary to handle the additional accounts at sales level S_2. Thus the profit is now determined by

$$\pi_2 = TR_1 - TC_2$$

However, at some point in time, reality must enter in terms of delinquent collections and bad debts. The effects of these developments are likely to be manifested by a downward shift of the total revenue and an upward shift of the total cost functions. Hence the new profit, at sales level S_3, is determined by

$$\pi_3 = TR_2 - TC_3$$

It is obvious that the optimal credit policy is the one that maximizes the objectives of the corporation, but it is important to notice here that there is a twofold effect in receivables investment. *First,* there is an increased sales effect that, given the same accounts receivable turnover, will necessarily bring additional *receivables. Second,* there is a slower, average collection period that also increases the funds required to maintain the current receivables policy. Thus the double-edged impact on the increased investment in receivables must be weighed in terms of the opportunity costs of the funds invested, and compared to the profitability of the increased sales.

D. Return on Investment in Accounts Receivable: An Illustration

An example will illustrate the determination of the return on an investment in accounts receivable. Assume that a firm's product sells at $20 per unit, of which $15 represents variable costs (including credit costs). Current annual sales are all on a cash-and-carry basis and total \$2 million. Fixed costs amount to an average of \$2 per unit. The company anticipates that an extension of credit will increase sales to \$2.5 million, if a 30-day collection period is granted. For the sake of simplicity, let us also assume that the introduction of the new policy will not affect the marginal cost, and that all customers will take advantage of the 30-day credit option.

Based on this information, we can compute the return on receivables investment as follows. We first compute the total average cost:

$$\text{Total fixed costs} = \$200{,}000$$

$$\text{Total variable costs} = (125{,}000)(15)$$
$$= \$1{,}875{,}000$$

$$\text{Total costs} = 200{,}000 + 1{,}875{,}000$$
$$= \$2{,}075{,}000$$

$$\text{Total average cost} = \frac{2{,}075{,}000}{125{,}000}$$
$$= \$16.60$$

When we multiply the ratio of this cost to unit price by the average accounts receivable (annual sales divided by turnover), we determine the additional investment required to implement the new credit policy:

$$\left(\frac{16.60}{20.00}\right)\left(\frac{2{,}500{,}000}{12}\right) = \$172{,}917$$

Now, we know that the profitability of the incremental investment is given by 25,000 units times \$5 per unit = \$125,000. Hence the rate of return r on the new credit policy is

$$r = \frac{125{,}000}{172{,}917} = 72\%$$

It is important to remember here that the investment by the firm does not require the entire new balance in the average accounts receivable, but rather only that portion that represents the *cost of the goods on account*. Furthermore, the computed rate of return is an *ex post magnitude* for a specific project, within a specific policy.

In addition to the investment in receivables, the granting of discounts is also an important variable in controlling the flow of funds through accounts receivable. Such discounts may have considerable effect on product demand and the level of losses through bad debts. In the case of discounts, we are primarily interested in whether such policy will speed collections at a high enough rate to offset the costs of this policy. For example, assume that a corporation has credit sales of \$10 million and an average collection period of 90 days. The firm does not extend discounts but a preliminary investigation has indicated that the introduction of the standard terms, that is, 2/10, net/30, will induce 60 percent of its customers (in dollar volume) to participate, and that the firm's average collection period will be reduced to 30 days. What are the expected benefits and costs of such policy?

The answer to the above can be simply outlined, as follows:

1. There will be a revenue loss from the proportion of customers that participate in the trade-terms policy, equal to (.6)(.02)(\$10 million) = \$120,000 (*gross, undiscounted*).
2. The increased turnover from 4 to 12 will reduce the average accounts receivable from \$2.5 million to \$833,333.
3. Assuming that the cost of goods sold is 0.90 per dollar of sales, the average investment in receivables will be reduced by (\$2,500,000 – \$833,333)(.9) = \$1,500,000.
4. Assuming that the opportunity cost of the funds invested in receivables is 10 percent, there is a *gross undiscounted* benefit of \$150,000.

Hence the gross undiscounted benefits exceed the gross undiscounted costs. However, once we introduce futurity and uncertainty into the computations, the values will change and the final decision may not support the above rule-of-thumb approach.

Another serious consideration in managing accounts receivable involves the assignment of correct probability estimates for expected bad-debt losses. As we know, the relaxation of credit standards encourages marginal customers with higher likelihood for default. For example, assume that a corporation anticipates that an extension of its *net* period will increase sales from \$1 million to \$1.4 million. The firm expects that this new policy will increase the average collection period from one to two months, the bad-debts account will increase from 1 to 10 percent of sales, and the collection costs, which are part of variable costs will be raised by \$1 per unit of sales. Under the existing policy, the firm sells 100,000 units with fixed costs of \$100,000 and variable costs of \$7 per unit. Hence, with the introduction of the new policy, the average cost per unit will be the fixed costs plus the new variable costs of \$8 per unit divided by the number of units sold under the new policy:

$$\frac{100{,}000 + 1{,}120{,}000}{140{,}000} = \$8.714$$

Furthermore, the expected bad-debt losses will be

$$(1{,}400{,}000)(.10)(8.714/10) = \$122{,}000$$

while the current costs of bad-debt losses are

$$(1{,}000{,}000)(.01)(8/10) = \$8{,}000$$

Hence the expected incremental losses from the bad-debt account are \$114,000. These must be balanced against increased operating profits of (400,000)(.2) = \$80,000. It is obvious that the extension of the net period will result in gross undiscounted losses of \$34,000. Furthermore, the average investment required by the new policy is 1,400,000/6 or \$233,333, against the present average investment in receivables of 1,000,000/12 or \$83,333. This difference is explained by the fact that the average collection period under the new policy will increase from one to two months, as well as by the increased average investment.

In the previous examples it was assumed, among other things, that the demand function was independent of the collection policies of the corporation. However, intensive collection policies are likely to affect sales efforts adversely. Also, managers attempting to measure the effects of credit policy on the other current fund considerations should be aware of the increased inventories and cash required to support the higher levels of sales that invariably result from a more liberal credit policy. Thus the estimation of such things as increased demand, the average collection period, the quality of accounts receivable, the credit rating of the firm, and other variables associated with credit policy is at best a very difficult task. Nevertheless, the financial manager must take these relationships into account because they also affect the ability of the firm to secure its own short-term financing.

VII. EVALUATING CHANGES IN CREDIT POLICY

When a firm's credit policy must be changed to accommodate changing market conditions, such a change must be based on benefit/cost analyses of the present and proposed cases. In this section we shall address changes in credit terms and in collection policies. The overall procedure followed by corporations for evaluating proposed changes in credit policy is as follows:

1. Estimate the expected changes in such critical variables as sales volume, sales revenue (net of discounts), bad-debt expense, and profits.
2. Compute cash flows with the changes and subtract current cash flows to obtain incremental values.
3. If incremental cash flows from changes are positive, institute new policies; otherwise, make no changes.
4. In the event that the proposed change affects the firm's riskiness (and therefore its cost of capital), then the proposed alternative's cost of capital must be estimated and the cash flows for each alternative must be evaluated as a perpetuity at the appropriate cost of capital.

Let us illustrate the above with a simple example. Suppose that the Vernon Computer Company is entertaining a proposal to establish a 2 percent cash discount for payment received within 10 days. It is estimated that sales volume will increase by 10 percent; that 25 percent of the customers will take the discount, and that no change in bad-debt expense will occur. Vernon's ratio of after-tax profit to sales is 8 percent. Current sales volume is 500,000 units at $1,000 unit. Then,

	Current Policy	Proposed Policy	
Sales	500 × 1,000 = 500,000	412.5 × 1,000 = 412,500	Cash
		137.5 × 980 = 134,750	Discount
Profit	@ 8% = 40,000	Total Sales 547,250	
		Profit @ 8% 43,780	

Hence, incremental profit = $3,780. Notice that we assume that all incremental profits contribute directly to cash flows. Such an assumption simplifies our solution here, but does not take into account such a key variable as production capacity.

Another alternative is for Vernon Computer to extend its credit terms (now net 30 days) to net 45 days. This move would also increase sales volume by 10%, but with no loss in revenue from the discount. However, bad-debt expense would increase by $300.

Assume the firm's marginal tax rate to be 40%. Then,

	Current Policy	Proposed Policy
Sales	500 × 1,000 = 500,000	550 × 1,000 = 550,000
Profit	@ 8% = 40,000	44,000
Increased Bad-Debt Expense (300 × (1 − .4)) after taxes		180
		43,820
Incremental Profit		3,820

If the decision is an "either-or" choice, the second option would be preferred. However, what if extending its credit period would make Vernon appear riskier in the eyes of its own creditors? Suppose that as a result, Vernon's cost of capital[1] increases to 10 percent, where in the other cases it is 9 percent. Then, the real incremental value of the second strategy would be

$$\frac{3{,}820}{.10} < \frac{3{,}780}{.09}$$

Hence, the discount strategy should prevail.

VIII. SUMMARY AND REVIEW

Chapter 7 discusses the second major entry in the management of short-term assets, namely, accounts receivable, which constitute the lifeline of the firm in the process of converting inventories to cash. In modern times, rather than requiring immediate payment of cash for commercial transactions, firms defer collection of the monetary value for goods and services sold to other firms for some specified period of time, typically 30 to 60 days.

Like the cash-marketable-securities decision, the receivables policy of the firm involves trade-offs between the benefits of increased sales and higher profits and the additional costs that arise from the collection expenses, bad-debt expenses, and the time value of money. Hence an attempt must be made to measure the return of a particular investment policy. This estimate requires projections of the additional revenues and expenses that will be generated and the effect that the policy will have on the average collection period of the firm.

Several important factors are discussed as dimensions of receivables policy: the discount percentage and period, the credit period, and the collection policy. As we might expect, relaxing the credit policy (lengthening the credit or the discount period, increasing the percentage of the discount, and so on) will generate increased sales. However, unless caution is exercised as to the customers to whom credit is granted, any benefits gained might be more than offset by increases in both the collection expense and the bad-debt losses that are incurred by the firm. Admittedly these relationships are difficult to estimate, but they must be considered when the credit policy of the firm is reviewed.

NOTES

1. The concept of the cost of capital and ways to measure it are discussed in Part V. For the purposes of this illustration, the cost of capital refers to the required rate of return (RRR) or hurdle rate discussed in Chapter 1.

QUESTIONS

1. What do we mean by a firm's *credit policy* and what are the main issues of concern in developing an effective trade policy?
2. Identify the critical factors affecting corporate credit policy and discuss their specific effects.
3. In general terms, discuss the costs and benefits associated with the extension of credit.

PROBLEMS

1. Philipps Novelties, Inc. is giving serious thought to changing their cash-only sales policy to a credit policy with terms "net 30." They estimate that their annual sales will increase from \$20,500,000 to \$30,000,000, based on sales prices of \$250 per unit, and assuming that all customers of the firm will take advantage of the 30-day credit period. At the company's current level of sales, fixed costs are \$70 and variable costs are \$160 per unit, respectively. If the proposed policy were adapted, what would be the rate of return on investment in accounts receivable versus the present cash sales?
2. An aggressive credit manager has taken the helm of Clear Head Pharmaceuticals, S.A., a small producer of cold and sinus medicines. Currently, sales are about \$15 million a year with an average collection period of three months. The credit manager believes that by establishing terms of 2/10 net/30, the collection period can be reduced to 20 days, on the average. Given that the costs of the goods sold represent 80 percent of the selling price, assume that 50 percent of the current sales will take advantage of the discount and that all of the funds recovered from the receivables can be invested at 6 percent. Should the new credit policy be adopted?
3. In its desire to increase its market share and reduce its heavy losses, the Ready Bike Company is considering a boldly liberal credit policy. Currently sales are 1 million bikes per year and the gross is \$75 million. Variable costs of production and distribution are \$75 per unit, and fixed costs are \$10 million. The average collection period is one month, and bad-debt expenses average 2 percent of gross sales. The new credit policy would accept all accounts regardless of the risk, extend the credit period to increase the average collection period to two months, and probably increase bad-debt expenses to 5 percent of gross sales. Ready realizes that this policy will not improve the income statement much, but he believes that most of the losses and increased expenses will be offset by increased sales of 20 percent. If even Ready Bike will not accept losses of more than \$1,000,000 on the policy, should it be adopted?

ANNOTATED BIBLIOGRAPHY

Boggess, W. "Screen-Test Your Credit Risks." *Harvard Business Review,* November–December 1967, 113–122.

A good review of screen testing and consumer credit techniques.

Copeland, T., and N. Khoury. "Analysis of Credit Extension in a World with Uncertainty." *Readings on the Management of Working Capital. 2nd ed.* Edited by K. Smith, 323–30. St. Paul, Minn.: West Publishing, 1980.

An application of the CAPM to the investment in accounts receivable.

Hill, N., and K. Riener. "Determining the Cash Discount in the Firm's Credit Policy." *Financial Management,* Spring 1979, 68–73.

A good discussion of cash discounts and their effects on the management of accounts receivable.

Hill, N. C., R. A. Wood and D. R. Sorenson. "Factors Influencing Corporate Credit Policy: A Survey." *Journal of Cash Management,* December 1981, 38–49.

A good review of managerial attitudes toward credit policies.

Johnson, T. O. "Credit Terms Policy and Corporate Payments Practices." *Journal of Cash Management,* September 1982, 14–22.

A good paper on the dynamics of change and how they will affect corporate credit policies in the future.

Lewellen, W., and R. Johnson. "Better Ways to Monitor Accounts Receivable." *Harvard Business Review,* May–June 1972, 101–109.

An early study that outlines the biases encountered in evaluating the performance of accounts receivable.

Sachdeva, K. S., and L. J. Gitman. "Accounts Receivable Decisions in a Capital Budgeting Framework." *Financial Management,* Winter 1981, 45–49.

A treatment of credit policy as an integral part of capital budgeting.

Sartoris, W. L., and N. C. Hill. "Evaluating Credit Policy Alternatives: A Present Value Framework." *Journal of Financial Research,* Spring 1981, 81–89.

A treatment of the credit decision within a DCF framework.

Smith, K. V. *Guide to Working Capital Management.* New York: McGraw-Hill, 1979.

A good book on overall working capital management with a good treatment of accounts receivable.

Stone, B. "The Payments-Pattern Approach to the Forecasting and Control of Accounts Receivable." *Financial Management,* Autumn 1976, 65–82.

A discussion of the monitoring of accounts receivable through a payments-pattern approach.

8

MANAGEMENT OF INVENTORIES

I. INTRODUCTION

Inventories constitute the third major entry in a firm's clustering of short-term assets, following cash and accounts receivable. On average, they also make up a significant amount of investment. Indeed, if we exclude firms from the service sector of the economy, that keep small, if any, inventories, the importance of inventories for the remaining sectors becomes strikingly critical. Thus, inventories are significant current assets whose levels, composition, and fluctuations must be managed and controlled carefully. Additionally, given the vast variety of parts, materials, and commodities that must be inventoried for the production and distribution process, it is obvious that the management of inventories is a rather complex function.[1]

A. Rationale for Inventories

The need for and existence of inventories can be explained by the fact that the movement of economic goods through complex manufacturing and distribution processes requires time. This fact gives rise to carrying costs that are necessary to maintain stocks of raw materials or finished goods. Once a firm has decided to accumulate stocks of raw materials or finished goods in order to facilitate production or distribution, it must also commit funds for the purchase and maintenance of these stocks. These funds take the form of investment in warehouse and storage facilities, insurance coverage, obsolescence, spoilage, as well as the implicit cost associated with the holding of inventory. This, of course, represents the opportunity cost or the yield that could be earned by investing the funds in another short-term asset of approximately similar risk.

In order to investigate the effects of inventory, we must first and foremost recognize that the type of inventory a company will carry depends significantly on the nature of its business. For instance, service companies, such as most utilities, advertising agencies, transportation companies, and accounting firms carry very little inventory, if any at all. Moreover, some service companies by the nature of their business have a heavy proportion of their investment in fixed assets, which implicitly sets the limit on the amount of service the company can provide. For such firms, inventory takes the form of operating supplies, fuel, parts, and similar items which are quite small in proportion to total sales revenue. At the other end of the spectrum, the inventory requirements of retail and wholesale firms are quite different from those of service-oriented companies. The major purpose of retail-wholesale businesses is to carry inventory of a type, quantity, and style so that the consumer can obtain it quickly; that is, these firms provide the service of immediacy.

Clearly then, the nature of inventory management depends on the type of firm. In a service type of business, inventory management is not critically important, while in manufacturing and retail businesses (where inventory represents a rather large investment), careful attention needs to be paid to it. Before delving into the management of inventory, let us first look at some of the common production processes encountered in business.

B. Production Processes and Inventory Needs

The inventory requirements of manufacturing firms are extremely complex. Not only do these firms usually maintain some stocks of finished goods, but manufacturing firms must also maintain stocks of raw material and goods in process. The nature of the inventory held by a manufacturing company depends both on the nature of its production process and on management decisions about whether to produce to order or produce for market demand. The three types of production systems commonly encountered are continuous process, assembly, and job shop. Many companies use more than one form of production in their manufacturing operations, and the three types typically overlap. However, some knowledge of the characteristics of each is useful in thinking about the financial implications of an inventory system.

A *continuous-process* production system is one in which the goods being produced are converted from raw material into a finished product with very little dead time between each intermediate stage. Continuous production processes are highly capital intensive and require very small amounts of labor inputs. Oil refineries are good examples of firms with continuous production systems. A general characteristic of continuous production processes is that they need very small amounts of inventories of the work-in-process category. In most cases, inventory takes the form of raw materials that are stockpiled in advance. In addition, small quantities of finished goods will also be held at the end of the production process. While these processes seem quite long, the elapsed time from the raw material stage to the finished good stage may be as short as a few days. For example, in most large paper mills a tree can be converted into a roll of paper in a matter of days.

At the other extreme is the *job-shop* production system in which individual orders are unique, and each one must be processed separately. Goods produced by this method are generally of high value and typically large. For instance, ships, special machine tools, and satellites are examples of goods produced this way. However, job-shop-produced goods may also be small, such as small specialty tools or jewelry. Work here is performed by artisans, highly skilled in some portion of the production process. In most job-shop manufacturing operations, production is started only when an order is received. Hence, a job shop's major inventory commitment is to work in process. Finished goods are usually delivered immediately to the customer. Raw materials are ordered only as they are required for production. In a sense, most job shops display inventory characteristics that are precisely the opposite of the continuous-process manufacturing operation, and, as we would expect, these operations have different financial needs as well.

The *assembly* method of production fits between the pure continuous system and the discrete job-shop system. It is by nature more labor intensive than the continuous system. Work is brought to the worker, but it does not remain long at each station. This particular system is suitable when large numbers of relatively standardized products are manufactured. Automobile production lines are generally recognized as the first large-scale assembly methods, although Eli Whitney pioneered this approach in the manufacturing of rifles. The assembly method requires more work-in-process inventories than most continuous systems but generally less than job-shop operations.

C. Types of Inventories and Costs

Inventories are typically classified into three main categories: (1) raw materials inventories; (2) work-in-process inventories; and (3) finished goods inventories. *Raw materials* are inputs that are employed for manufacturing but have not yet been committed to the production process. These may include such items as lumber, metals, fabrics, paints, screws, small parts, and so on. *Work-in-process* inventories refer to items that have gone through some stages of production and are also partially or fully assembled, but need a few more operations before they can be ready for shipment to customers. *Finished goods* inventories are items that are ready for sale to clients of the firm.

The relative amounts of the various types of inventories kept by firms depend also on the seasonality of the firm's business, as well as the factors mentioned earlier in this section. For example, Tandem Bicycle Company must keep a large inventory of finished goods during the Christmas holiday buying season, but needs relatively small amounts of inventories in raw materials during the same period of time. However, in February the inventories of finished goods will be low and raw materials orders will be sent out in order for the firm to produce for the high-sales seasons of spring and summer. Of course, the relative classes of inventory differ among firms. What may be a finished good for a chemical company becomes a raw material for a pharmaceutical firm, and so on down the production process.

Another way of classifying inventories is in terms of their value as part of the firm's investment. In other words, inventory is viewed as part of the overall composite known as *working capital,* the values of which are found in the firm's balance sheet. Such values will depend upon the accounting conventions employed by the firm.

Generally, there are three accepted techniques for valuing inventory, known as FIFO, LIFO, and average cost.[2] FIFO stands for *first-in-first-out* and assumes that sales of inventory are based on the original costs of the items rather than the current costs. This type of inventory valuation in times of inflation penalizes the economic profits of the firm, while its swells falsely its accounting profits. LIFO stands for *last-in-first-out* and means that the cost of goods sold is based on current inventory replacement prices. This type of inventory pricing is good for periods of rising inflation in that it adjusts accounting profits to reflect as closely as possible economic profits. *Average costing* of inventories stands for the typical compromise between true, replacement costs and historic inventory costs. Obviously, FIFO and LIFO yield extreme results and should be used when the appropriate conditions exist for the costs of purchasing and production. Also, when these costs are stable all three methods will give the same values.

Costs for the purchase and maintenance of inventories are typically classified into four categories: (1) ordering costs; (2) storage or carrying costs; (3) shortage costs; and (4) system or system-maintenance costs. *Ordering costs* are the expenses associated with placing an order to purchase or replenish inventory stocks. These ordering costs reflect the supplier's costs of filling out order forms, invoices, and other forms, as well as the costs of locating, preparing, and shipping the requested materials. *Carrying* or *storage costs* are the expenses associated with warehousing the inventory until it is used in the production cycle (or is sold in the case of non-manufacturing firms). Carrying costs generally include costs of renting warehouse space, or in-house storage costs that are provided directly by the manufacturing or wholesale firm.

The concept of *shortage or stockout costs* is more difficult to quantify than the simpler, more direct ordering and carrying costs. *Shortage costs* are the equivalent amounts of profits foregone in the event that the firm runs out of goods and must place such goods on backorder. Additionally, they include the extra costs of ordering as well as the potential costs of losing a good customer to another competitor forever, because of the shortage. Of course, the severity of shortage costs will depend on economic conditions as well as on company behavior. For example, a stock-out that occurs during a period of unexpectedly high demand is less likely to result in permanent losses of customers or even temporary losses of sales than during a period of normal business operations. In the latter case, your clients expect you to fulfill predictable inventory orders. A related concept here is known as *surplus costs of inventory* and refers to the expenses incurred by firms that overstock systematically without apparent economic justification. Such costs involve both the excess storage expenses as well as the opportunity costs associated with other potential investments.

Finally, the system-maintenance costs refer to the overhead costs associated with the overall management of the inventory process.

II. INVENTORY AND PRODUCTION CONTROL SYSTEMS

A. An Overview

Because the nature and scope of inventory are so complex and permeating, its management is the responsibility of several departments. At the same time, the costs of inventories have become the bone of contention in many competitive industries, where the proper integration of inventory management into production and overall planning has produced significant economies of scale. Indeed, for the automobile production industries of Europe, Japan, and the United States, the competitive edge may very well be determined by what is now euphemistically called "materials handling" and is better known as *inventory management*.

Managers of manufacturing companies have been confronted with an array of production control systems that go by such names as Materials Requirements Planning (MRP), Kanban or Just-in-Time Inventories (JIT), Optimized Production Technology (OPT), and Flexible Manufacturing Systems (FMS). These are all well-integrated systems of production planning where the roles of other functions such as marketing, purchasing, and finance are subsumed under the overall production plan of the firm. We shall discuss each of the above systems in some detail and try to put their characteristics in perspective.

The recent advances in production planning technology, outlined briefly above, have allowed managers the opportunity to integrate production operations and planning to an unprecedented degree. Several such integrated systems have emerged in the past few years. Some of these systems are limited in scope to facilitating more effective inventory control. Others are more ambitious and attempt to integrate inventory, planning, and purchasing into a large production environment. In such an environment inventory is planned primarily to accommodate smooth and expeditious production patterns. The role of the financial manager is diminished under such systems, as is the role of the marketing manager. Let us proceed with a brief review of the various systems, bearing in mind that we only hope to provide some background information that will make the reader more conversant about the issues and the variables that enter into the choice of such a system.

B. Computerized Inventory Systems

Within the past ten years or so, computer access has become a reality for firms of all sizes. One of the most popular uses of the computer for managers has been in the area of inventory control. The extent of such managerial use of computers varies from simple listings of item number, quantity on hand, and other cursory information to complete programs such as the IBM developed IMPACT system.

Software developments like IMPACT are complete inventory control systems, that can perform virtually all tasks related to inventory control, such as forecasting of product demand, analysis of probabilities for stockouts, computations of economic order quantities, and reorder points. More advanced systems can, of course, take into account quantity discounts, multiple products from the same supplier, and other such functional details.

Computer inventory systems, just like all systems, have their advantages and disadvantages. On the positive side, there are savings in inventory costs, and the consequent improvement in crucial liquidity ratios, for example, current ratio, quick ratio, and inventory turnover. Additionally, there are considerable savings in personnel, including the opportunity to reassign creative individuals to other critical, noncomputerized tasks where they can help in the decision-making process of the firm. On the negative side, the cost of a complex, in-house computerized system can be significant and is justified economically only where size and complexity of operations meet some critical parameters. In effect, as for everything else, there are cost and benefits to be studied.

C. Materials Requirements Planning (MRP)

Materials Requirements Planning views inventory management as subsidiary to the firm's production schedule. As such, it constitutes a radical departure from the classic Economic

Order Quantity (EOQ) models that strive to establish cost-minimizing order quantities or reorder points for each item under control. Thus, fabrication and purchases under the MRP system are planned and implemented such that an item will be supplied to the system just shortly before it is needed in the next phase of production.

Materials Requirements Planning draws a distinction between independent demand for the firm's products, which is external to the firm and must be estimated, and dependent demand, which is the result of internal decisions and can be known with certainty. High priority is given to avoiding stockouts, an effort supported by very detailed information that necessitates the monitoring of every part and subassembly on a weekly basis.

Materials Requirements Planning is best suited for large-scale, mass-production environments like manufacturers of automobiles, consumer appliances, and electronics. As such, it has been of significant help to firms with the appropriate mode of production by reducing stockouts, lowering carrying and ordering costs, smoothing production, and even improving customer services. Of course, the nature of MRP is such that it makes it a highly complex, detailed, and formalized system of operations. All employees are trained to work within the system, and informal approaches to task accomplishments cannot be tolerated.[3] Hence, the discipline and attention to details required by MRP make it quite costly and rather time-consuming to implement.

D. Kanban or Just-in-Time Inventories

The *Kanban* system, also called *Just-in-Time Inventories,* was developed in Japan. It is basically similar to MRP in that its primary goal is the facilitation of the production process. By its very nature, Kanban seeks to deliver a high-quality product at low cost and on schedule. Hence, work-in-process inventories are minimized, as are all other stocks between successive production tasks. Indeed, some Japanese firms have managed to time the ordering of parts so that they arrive only just before they are needed, and are delivered directly to the production line. This type of system, dubbed "just-in-time inventories," basically eliminates carrying costs. In effect, Kanban integrates the firm's suppliers into the production process through emphasis on vendor quality control.

Practitioners of the Kanban system have reported significant benefits through the decrease in inventories, shorter lead times, higher productivity, better quality, and, of course, reduction in needed plant space. The users of the system have also reported several weaknesses and outright disadvantages in the Kanban system. For example, the basic philosophy of the system is predicated on the proposition that workers perform their best when trusted with responsibility and authority. Hence, for firms where this attitude is not the norm, Kanban will have difficulties. Additionally, the Kanban system is sensitive to sudden fluctuations in demand and can break down in extreme conditions. Finally, large items that are not produced regularly cannot be incorporated into the system and must be scheduled separately.[4]

E. Emerging Systems of Inventory Control

New systems are being tested and evaluated presently that treat inventory costs as one component of the broader production scheme in the company. One of these systems, known as *Optimized Production Technology* (OPT), is a proprietary system that is completely integrated and designed to maximize production and minimize work-in-process inventory, subject to management priorities and plant capacity. The nature of Optimized Production Technology requires that management make wholesale changes in its philosophy and in its cost accounting procedures.

Another new system, known as *Flexible Manufacturing Systems* (FMS) takes the traditional automation to its ultimate conclusion by automating the entire factory. It is claimed by the proponents of FMS that the system is capable of increasing the firm's productivity and variety of products dramatically. Such results will, in turn, place a greater burden on the marketing function and force top-level managers to take a more integrative approach to decision making.

III. BASIC TECHNIQUES FOR INVENTORY CONTROL

The complexity of inventory management and its multiple interdependent variables can be greatly reduced through the development of some conceptual framework that will enhance our understanding and will also improve our decision-making ability. The cornerstones of such a conceptual framework for inventory management and control are the *ABC Method* and the *Economic Order Quantity (EOQ) Model.* The ABC method is a general approach to management in terms of a set of priorities, while the EOQ is a classic example of specific inventory problem-solving methodology based on a set of beginning assumptions. Some foundations of these basic concepts are already factored into the more complex systems discussed in the previous section.

A. The ABC Method

As we have already discussed, any inventory system entails a set of interactive costs. Forms must be filled out, personnel must be hired to monitor stocks, and inventory levels must be assessed at regular intervals. The easiest way to control such costs involves the utilization of a technique known as the *ABC Method.* This method requires that management classify its various types of inventory into a small but meaningful number of broad categories based on cost per unit. This way, managers can focus most of their attention on the higher cost items in stock. The top priority is accorded to A-type items that also have the highest unit costs. Lower priorities are given to B-type items, C-type items, *et cetera,* that have commensurably lower unit costs.

Of course, the name of the method, that is, *ABC,* does not imply that there will exist only three categories of inventories. This type of decision will always depend on the firm's particular operating environment. However, it should be stressed at the very outset that the utilization of a large number of categories may very well produce adverse effects and eventually defeat the very reason for employing the ABC Method, which is to focus greater attention on the most critical items of inventory in terms of their unit costs. Nevertheless the concern for high-cost inventory items must always be balanced for critical levels of low-per-unit-cost items whose shortage may halt the production process of the firm.

Let us illustrate the above consideration by way of a simple example from our familiar bicycle manufacturer. Assume that Tandem Bicycle Company utilizes an AB inventory system for its work-in-process stock. Tandem's inventory-management committee classifies as *A* all items with a high unit cost and which are also particularly sensitive to periodic design changes or modifications. This category includes the bicycle seat, the handlebar, and most of the gearshift mechanism. The committee classifies as *B* such lower cost items as nuts, bolts, and washers, as well as the remaining parts of the bicycle assembly (for example the body, wheels, *et cetera*) that are relatively insensitive to design changes. Notice that the body of the bicycle, as well as the tires that are purchased from an outside vendor, can be much more expensive than the handlebars. However, a significant modification or outright change in design can leave Tandem with thousands of obsolete handlebars if these items are not controlled adequately. Also, because Tandem markets its bicycles primarily to families (who, in the opinion of management do not demand state-of-the-art tires), and utilizes standard sizes, the importance of tires as control items within the AB inventory system is reduced.

B. The Basic Economic Order Quantity (EOQ) Model

The Economic Order Quantity (EOQ) model was developed around the turn of the century and has been employed as a "classic" cost balancing technique. Its versatility was encountered first in this book with reference to cash management through the Baumol model.[5] While the EOQ model in practice is not as easily workable as its simple mathematical formulation makes it appear, the technique provides strong insight into the functions of a good inventory system.

At this stage, we shall present the basic tenets of the EOQ model through a set of eight underlying assumptions. They are as follows:

1. Demand for each inventory item under consideration is given and known in advance.
2. The rate of demand for each item is constant (described by a linear function).
3. Inventory supplies can be replenished instantly.
4. Replenishment of inventories occurs when stocks reach zero items.
5. The quantity ordered, Q, is a continuous variable that does not change from one order to the next.
6. The unit cost per item ordered is constant.
7. The planning horizon of the firm is infinite.
8. All variables are fixed over time.

Figure 8.1 presents a pictorial view of the above assumptions. Notice that as time goes by, periodic replenishments of inventory take place. Based on the above eight assumptions, a simple equation is developed and solved for the value of the order quantity variable, Q^*, which minimizes the sum of carrying and ordering costs for the item.

The solution of the basic EOQ equation is as follows:

$$Q^* = \sqrt{\frac{2 \times \text{Demand} \times \text{Ordering Costs}}{\text{Carrying Costs}}} \tag{8.1}$$

where Q^* is known as the *economic order quantity*. Notice that the average inventory for the item under consideration will be given by $Q^*/2$, while the number of orders that must be placed during the period is given by Demand/Q^*.

Let us illustrate the simple EOQ model by way of an example. Assume that Tandem Bicycle Company employs a special lubricant in its production machinery. Although production is seasonal, the machinery must be lubricated daily, making the rate of consumption for the

FIGURE 8.1 Graphic Depiction of a Simple EOQ Model

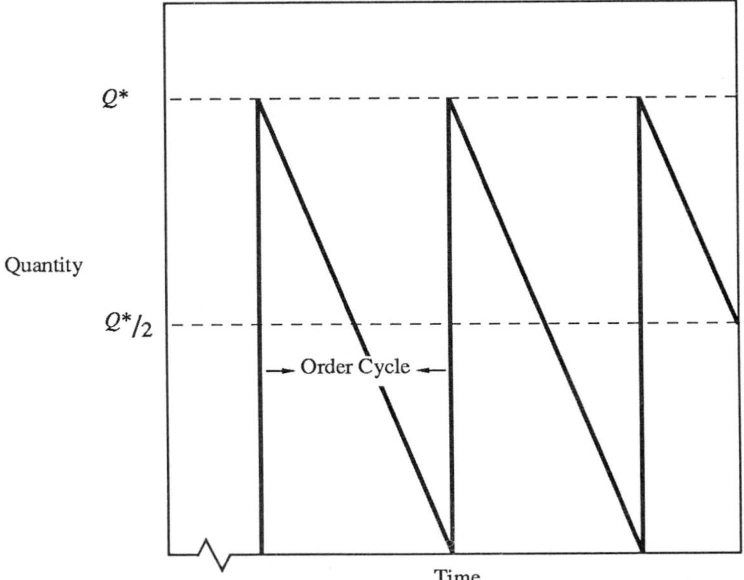

lubricant (almost) constant. Tandem's production manager knows with certainty that 24,000 liters of lubricant will be needed for the current period. Ordering costs for the lubricant are \$50.00 per order made, while the carrying costs are estimated at \$0.15 per liter per period. Using the basic EOQ model, the optimal solution is given as

$$Q^* = \sqrt{\frac{2 \times 24{,}000 \times \$50}{\$0.15}}$$

$$= 4{,}000 \text{ liters per order;}$$

and

$$\frac{24{,}000}{4{,}000} = \text{6 orders should be placed during the period.}$$

C. Extensions of the Basic EOQ Model

The basic EOQ model has been extended and several dimensions have been added to it in order to make it more functional and realistic. We shall discuss some of these extensions briefly here and illustrate each by way of a simple example.

1. EOQ with Lead Time for Orders

In real world situations the simplistic assumption that inventories can be replenished instantly must be modified. Time is needed for requisition forms to be completed, submitted, and processed by the firm's personnel. More time is needed for the requested inventory item to be located in stock and eventually transferred to where it is needed. If the item must be ordered from an outside vendor, still more time must be consumed. All of these time intervals are examples of what is known as *lead time*. The inclusion of lead time in the EOQ model does not alter the value of Q^*. Rather it necessitates ordering before inventory supplies are depleted. Figure 8.2 depicts the EOQ system with lead-time intervals. Notice that t_c^* is the optimal time between replenishment of inventory supplies,

FIGURE 8.2 EOQ with Lead Times

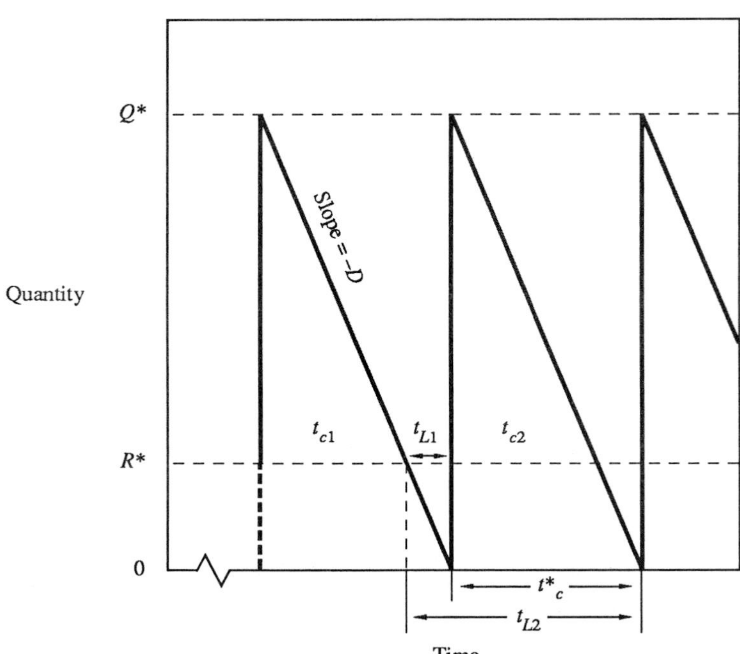

while t_{c1} and t_{c2} are lead times satisfying the conditions $t_{L1} < t_c^*$ and $t_{L2} > t_c^*$. In order to prevent a stockout, it is necessary for the firm to order before inventory supplies reach zero level. What we must do is establish a reorder point R^* such that the ordered inventory must arrive exactly at the end of one cycle and the beginning of another. That is, we must have the goods in place at exactly the length of the optimal cycle, t_c^*.

For the case where $t_{L1} < t_c^*$ the reorder point should be established at

$$R^* = t_{L1} \times D \tag{8.2}$$

where D = demand

The case where $t_{L2} > t_c^*$ implies that stockout can be avoided only if the lead times from several shipments overlap. This situation, in turn, implies that the firm must begin with Q^* and R^* values that are nonoptimal. Otherwise, a shortage will occur early in the inventory cycle. We can illustrate this point rather easily by extending the conditions in the previous example. Assume that the length of the time period for Tandem Bicycle is 360 days, and that 9 days are needed between the time the order for lubricant is placed and the shipment is received. In this case the order should be placed at

$$R^* = t_L \times D$$

$$\textit{where } t_L = \frac{\text{lead time in days}}{\text{length of period in days}}$$

Then $R^* = 9/360 \times 24{,}000 = 600$ liters. In other words, the lubricant should be reordered when the supply level reaches 600 liters.

2. *EOQ With Shortage Costs*

As we have already discussed, the shortage of any critical inventory component can cause factory shutdowns and lost sales, which are typically identified as *shortage costs*. Such shortage costs are not treated explicitly in the basic EOQ model. Nevertheless, managers find it necessary to plan for the event of shortages. The basic EOQ model with shortages is shown in Figure 8.3. The shortage cost per ordering cycle is presented by each triangle below the x-axis in the figure. When the shortage cost is incorporated

FIGURE 8.3 EOQ with Shortages

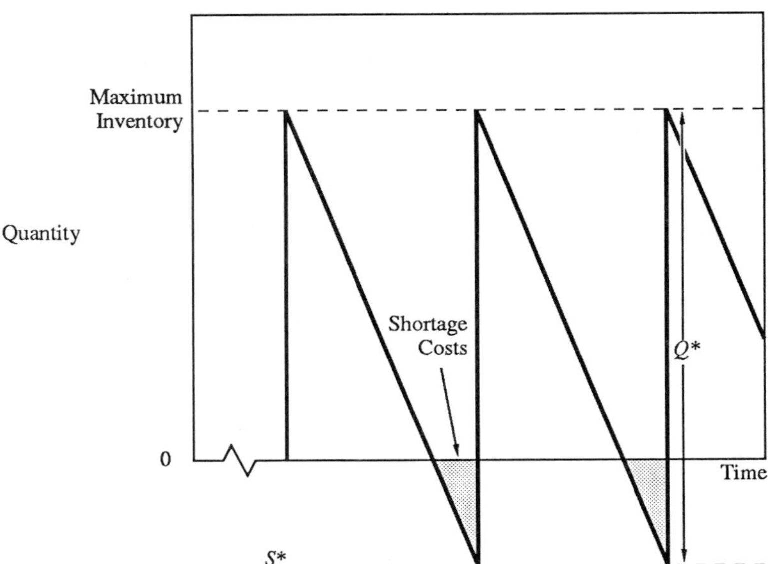

into the EOQ model, the optimal order quantity must be resolved to minimize the total of carrying, ordering, and shortage costs. The solution is then given as

$$Q_s^* = Q^*\sqrt{\frac{\text{Carrying Cost} + \text{Shortage Cost}}{\text{Shortage Cost}}} \qquad (8.3)$$

where Q_s^* and Q^* stand for the optimal order quantities with and without shortage costs, respectively. Here, the maximum shortage quantity, S^* will be given by

$$S^* = Q^*\left(\sqrt{\frac{\text{Carrying Cost} + \text{Shortage Cost}}{\text{Shortage Cost}}} - \sqrt{\frac{\text{Shortage Cost}}{\text{Carrying Cost} + \text{Shortage Cost}}}\right) \qquad (8.4)$$

Let us illustrate the above point by way of another example from the Tandem Bicycle Company. Suppose that the supply of lubricant is disrupted for some reason, creating shortages. The production manager realizes that without this lubricant and even with some available substitute there will be significant losses in efficiency, which are estimated at \$3.00 per liter per period. Under the circumstances, the optimal order quantity is

$$\begin{aligned} Q_s^* &= 4{,}000 \times \sqrt{\frac{\$0.15 + \$3.00}{\$3.00}} \\ &= 4{,}000 \times 1.0247 \\ &= 4{,}098 \text{ liters} \end{aligned}$$

And, the maximum shortage quantity is

$$\begin{aligned} S^* &= 4{,}000\left(\sqrt{\frac{.15 + 3.00}{3.00}} - \sqrt{\frac{3.00}{0.15 + 3.00}}\right) \\ &= 4{,}000(\sqrt{1.05} - \sqrt{.952}) \\ &= 196 \text{ liters} \end{aligned}$$

3. EOQ with Quantity Discounts

As EOQ models have developed and been used by practitioners, there have been several new extensions that have enriched the applicability of this simple technique. We have already discussed extensions that involve lead time and shortage costs. What we propose to do at this stage is introduce one additional but significant extension that accounts for the price breaks offered by many vendors to select customers on the basis of quantities purchased. By being able to prepackage their materials into a small number of lot sizes, the vendors can save in processing costs, and can afford to pass on some of these cost savings to their large-quantity buyers. For the customer (buyer) firm, the solution entails the purchase of the lot size that minimizes the total of carrying, holding, and purchasing costs.

Inventory models with price breaks have appeared in many varieties that include one price break, two price breaks, and three or more price breaks—all depending on the quantities bought from the vendor. The case of two price breaks is shown pictorially in Figure 8.4. Here quantities ranging from zero to Q_1 are sold at prices P_1. For quantities between Q_1 and Q_3, a different price, P_2, is paid, while for quantities larger than Q_3, price P_3 is paid. Notice that the original cost function, without price breaks is the highest in Figure 8.4, defined by TC(Q, P_1). The function with the one price break is defined by TC(Q, P_2), and the function with two price breaks is defined by TC(Q, P_3).

We shall illustrate the complications that enter into the EOQ decision-making framework when quantity discounts are allowed, by reference to Tandem Bicycle Company. Suppose that Tandem's lubricant vendor offers a quantity discount to customers based on the following schedule:

Quantity Ordered (in Liters)	*Discount Offered (in Percent)*
500–1,999	1%
2,000–4,999	2%
5,000–9,999	3%
10,000–over	4.5%

The regular charge for the lubricant has been \$1.50 per liter, and we determined earlier that $Q^* = 4{,}000$ liters. Hence, the total cost of in-

FIGURE 8.4 Total Costs of Inventory with Two Quantity Discounts

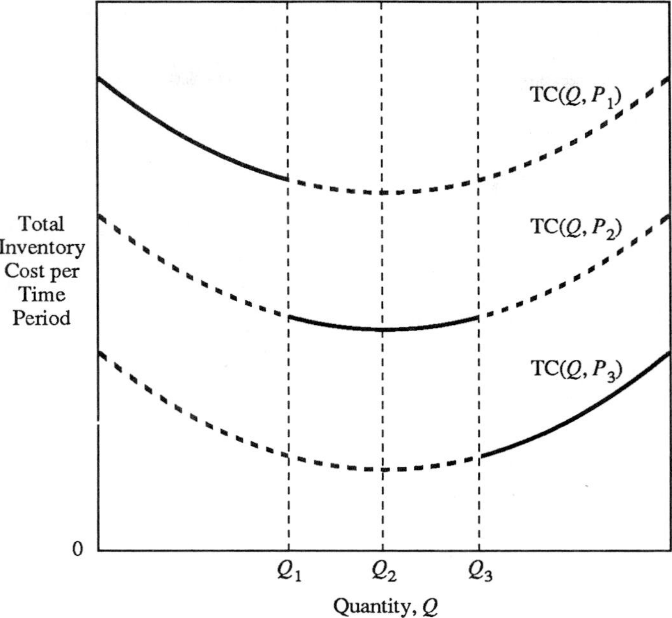

ventory, including the cost of the purchased item at this level, would be as follows:

$$TC = \left(\frac{\text{Demand}}{\text{Order Quantity}} \times \text{Order Cost}\right) + \left(\text{Average Inventory} \times \text{Carrying Cost}\right) + (\text{Demand} \times \text{Purchase Price}) \quad (8.5)$$

As we recall from the earlier illustrations, demand is 24,000 liters, ordering cost is $50, and carrying cost is $0.15 per unit. Note also that, under our assumption of constant demand, average inventory will be $Q^*/2$. Hence, we can solve for the optimal order quantity at 4,000 liters and have

$$\begin{aligned} TC &= \frac{24{,}000}{4{,}000}(\$50) + \frac{4{,}000}{2}(\$0.15) \\ &\quad + (24{,}000)(\$1.50)(.98) \\ &= \$300 + \$300 + \$35{,}280 \\ &= \$35{,}880 \end{aligned}$$

The only possibilities for lower cost would occur at the minimum quantities following each price break; that is, at 5,000 and 10,000 liters. In order to complete the logical cycle, we must now compute TC for these two quantities, above. For the quantity of 5,000 liters we have

$$\begin{aligned} TC &= \frac{24{,}000}{5{,}000}(\$50) + \frac{5{,}000}{2}(\$0.15) \\ &\quad + (24{,}000)(\$1.50)(.97) \\ &= \$240 + \$375 + \$34{,}920 \\ &= \$35{,}535 \end{aligned}$$

And for the quantity of 10,000 liters we have

$$\begin{aligned} TC &= \frac{24{,}000}{10{,}000}(\$50) + \frac{10{,}000}{2}(\$0.15) \\ &\quad + (24{,}000)(\$1.50)(.955) \\ &= \$120 + \$750 + \$34{,}380 \\ &= \$35{,}250 \end{aligned}$$

Hence, in this case, it is best to order in lots of 10,000 liters.

D. Stochastic Inventory Models

The inventory models discussed so far have assumed that materials demand and lead times are known and constant (a *deterministic* model). Naturally, the realities of the market place are anything but deterministic. Thus, although deterministic inventory models provide useful approximations to situations, it is best to factor uncertainty into the model, particularly if the variances are large. This uncertainty can be incorporated by treating either demands or lead times or both as random variables. A pictorial representation of inventory behavior with *stochastic* (random) demand but constant lead time is given in Figure 8.5.

The variation developed here allows for demand during the lead time between ordering and receipt of inventory to be expressed as a random variable, d_L. It is, of course, necessary to assume some type of probability distribution for the lead-time variable. This can be done either by extrapolating information from historical data or in some more-or-less arbitrary fashion. We will define the *probability density function* for lead-time demand as $f(d_L)$, and the *cumulative density function* as $F(d_L)$. Let us also denote expected demand as $\overline{D}$, ordering costs per unit per time period as C_o, and holding costs per unit per time period as C_h. Finally, we shall denote shortage costs by C_s, and state that they are assessed on a per unit basis.

In order to minimize the sum of all costs above, given the probability distribution function, we must solve the following equation simultaneously for order quantity, Q, and for reorder point, R.

FIGURE 8.5 EOQ Model with Stochastic Demand and Constant Lead Time

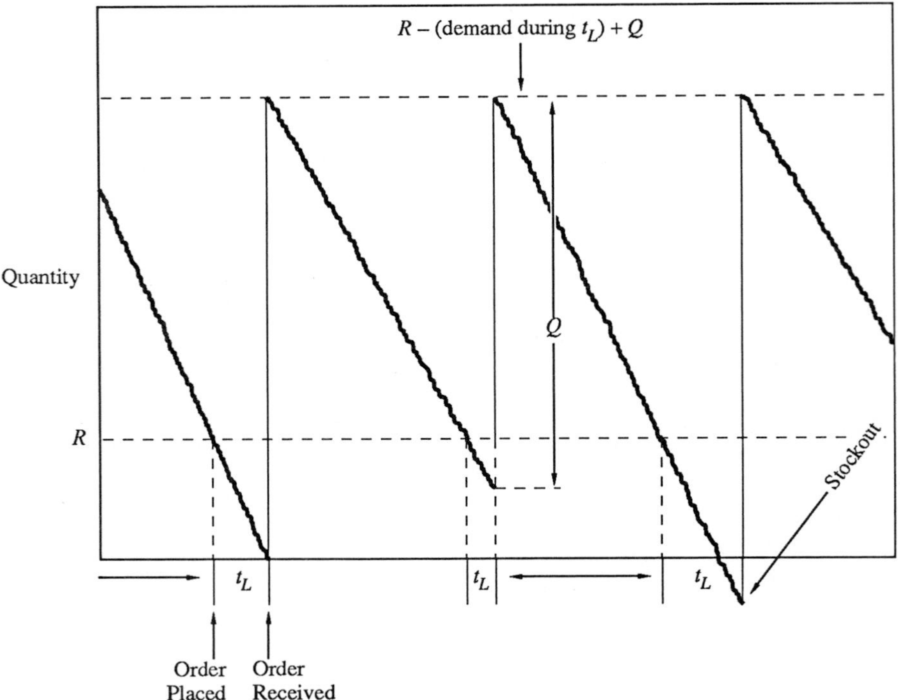

$$Q^*_{\text{Stochastic}} = \sqrt{\frac{2\overline{D}[C_o + C_s \sum_{dL>R} (d_L - R)f(d_L)]}{C_h}} \quad (8.6)$$

and

$$F(R) \geq 1 - \frac{QC_h}{C_s\overline{D}} \quad (8.7)$$

Expressions (8.6) and (8.7) constitute a system that can be solved through an iterative procedure that consists of the following steps:

1. Find a beginning, trial value for Q, using the basic formula for the EOQ model,

$$Q = \sqrt{2DC_o/C_h}$$

2. Substitute the above value into equation (8.7) and solve for R.
3. Substitute the R-value from step (*b*) into equation (8.6) and solve for Q.
4. Substitute the Q-value from step (*c*) into equation (8.7) and solve for R.
5. Repeat steps (*b*) and (*c*), above, until Q and R converge.

Let us illustrate stochastic EOQ models by way of an example which builds on the earlier case of Tandem Bicycle Company where we computed the EOQ with shortage costs. Suppose that Tandem's management cannot say with certainty what level of demand will obtain during the lead time between placing an order and receiving the goods. They can, however, form a crude probability distribution (shown in Table 8.1).

Suppose that we treat the demand for the lubricant as a random variable with an expected value of 24,000 liters. Drawing data from the previous illustrations, we recall that ordering costs were $50 per order and carrying costs were $0.15 per liter. Let us further assume that the penalty cost is $0.20 per liter. With all this information we can follow the iterative procedure outlined above in a stepwise fashion:

TABLE 8.1 Tandem Bicycle Company: Stochastic Inventory Model

Lead-Time Demand (R)	*Probability $f(d_L)$*	*Cumulative Probability $F(d_L)$*
560	.05	.05
570	.10	.15
580	.125	.275
590	.15	.425
600	.20	.625
610	.15	.775
620	.10	.875
630	.075	.95
640	.05	1.00

1. The trial Q is obtained from the solution of the basic EOQ, where $Q^* = 4{,}000$ liters.
2. Substituting $Q^* = 4{,}000$ liters into equation (8.7) we obtain

$$F(R) \geq 1 - \frac{4{,}000\ (\$0.15)}{\$0.20\ (24{,}000)}$$

$$\geq .875,$$

which implies that $R^* = 620$

3. Substituting $R^* = 620$ into equation (8.6) we obtain

$$Q^* = \sqrt{\frac{2(24{,}000)[\$50 + \$0.20[(630 - 620)(.075) + (640 - 620)(.05)]]}{0.15}}$$

$$= 4{,}013.98 \text{ liters.}$$

4. Repeating the procedure we obtain $R^* = 620$ once again.

It should be noted here that while Q^* does not change significantly, the presence of uncertainty causes managers to order earlier than under conditions of certainty.

IV. SUMMARY AND REVIEW

In Chapter 8 we completed our discussion of the current asset accounts with the management of inventories. The management of inventories, unlike the management of every other asset discussed in this volume, overlaps significantly with the production, distribution, and marketing functions of the firm. This became amply clear in Section II where we discussed the most commonly employed and best-known inventory and production systems. Under these systems, inventories are not individual assets with actual and opportunity costs; rather, they are input materials to be delivered at the appropriate work station in time for the production cycle.

Under the above circumstances, we are justified in stating that there are only financial overtones to the management of inventories. At any rate, we believe that although inventory management may seem somewhat removed from financial management, its administration is governed by the same principles that govern other short-term uses of funds. Inventories are an essential investment for every enterprise if it is to maintain continuity in its operations. There are several distinct groups of costs associated with maintaining inventories: (1) *carrying costs,* which arise from the need to store and insure the inventory, (2) *procurement costs,* which are incurred in the handling of inventory shipments, (3) *stock costs,* which are the consequence of shortages and surpluses in the inventory level, and (4) *system costs,* which are the overhead expenses of inventory management. As with cash management, two simple models have been outlined for inventory management: a probabilistic model and the economic order quantity model. In turn, these are subject to the same sorts of criticism and praise as were the models for cash management.

NOTES

1. As will soon be apparent by reading the chapter, the topic of inventory management is still rather production oriented with some financial overtones. Despite the efforts being made to highlight the financial consequences of this important investment, the tide is moving in the opposite direction stressing integrated production-distribution systems planning and control. Hence, this chapter will, by virtue of the above constraints, be kept short and to the point, in order to remain true to the financial orientation of the volume. We shall return to inventories again in Appendix 8A, when we discuss sources of short-term financing.
2. There is another method that is invoked in situations of extreme and unpredictable inflation, known as NIFO—*next-in-first-out.*
3. One of the basic tenets of MRP is that all work centers or plants in the system have limited capacity. Hence, the system's effectiveness is greatly reduced where there exist discrepancies in the capacities of the work centers.
4. As the Kanban system is presently evolving rather steadily, one would expect many of the above weaknesses to be worked out over the next five to ten years of implementation.
5. The Baumol cash-balancing model discussed in Chapter 6 is, in fact, a simple extension and application of the basic inventory EOQ model.

QUESTIONS

1. How does the responsibility for the management of inventories differ from that of the other current asset accounts?
2. What is the rationale for holding inventories? Would there be a need for inventories under certainty?
3. Discuss the types of production processes that exist and how inventory management differs from one process to the next.
4. Define and discuss the various types of inventory costs.

PROBLEMS

1. Suppose that in a world of certainty, market demand for the products of Skateboards, Inc. rises to 3,500 skateborads per month from the previous level of 2,000 per month. The cost per skateboard is still $30, while ordering costs are $50 per order. Carrying costs remain at 12% per annum. Compute the optimal

order quantity for (*a*) the old demand and (*b*) the new demand.

2. a. Suppose that the increase in demand for skateboards, described in (1) above, was also accompanied by an overall increase in costs, symmetrically by 15%. What would be the optimal order quantity under these conditions?
   b. Compute the average inventories and frequency of order placement for Skateboards, Inc.
   c. What are the total monthly inventory costs?
3. The Juarez Chemical Co. anticipates the following demand schedule for its sodium chloride:

Quantity Demanded (barrels)	100	110	120	130
Probability	.2	.4	.3	.1

The company's shortage costs per barrel are \$75, while its carrying costs have been estimated at \$45 per barrel. Juarez's gross profit per barrel has been computed at \$330. Determine the optimum level of sodium chloride inventory for the company.

APPENDIX 8A MANAGEMENT OF SHORT-TERM LIABILITIES

A. Perspectives

Chapters 6 through 8 concentrated on the short-term uses of funds for the firm and focused on such interrelated accounts as cash, marketable securities, accounts receivable, and inventories. It is now time to direct our attention to the management of short-term sources of funds and focus on such entries as accounts payable, accruals, and the short-term borrowing that is undertaken through financial institutions, primarily banks.

The Appendix is presented in three sections as follows. Section B discusses the management of accounts payable under the heading "Trade Credit." Section C deals with the standard source of short-term borrowing—unsecured bank loans—and the issuance of commercial paper by large corporations. Finally, Section D deals with financing through the pledging of accounts receivable and inventories.

B. Trade Credit Financing

Trade credit refers to the sale of goods on *non-cash* terms. It is the other side of the accounting ledger that records the transactions between any two firms. Generally speaking, the amount recorded as *accounts receivable* by the *seller* of commodities is seen as *trade credit* by the *buyer*. This source of financing short-term uses—typically inventories—is by far the most common, easy to obtain, and sizable in monetary value. There are basically three categories of trade credit: *open accounts, notes payable,* and *trade acceptances*.

1. *Open accounts*. This form of credit is better known as *accounts payable* and is the most prevalent form of trade credits. The availability of open accounts is almost automatically dictated by the terms of sale; there is no formal agreement, and, most often, no decision on the part of the lender.
2. *Notes payable*. This form of credit occurs when formal acknowledgment of the debt is called for. Such notes, better known as *promissory notes,* imply a greater enforcement power than the accounts receivable because of their formality.
3. *Trade acceptances*. This form of credit also involves a formal recognition of the debt. Under this method of short-term financing, delivery of the goods is not completed until the seller accepts a draft drawn by the buyer. It requires that the buyer designate a bank at which debt repayment will be arranged, thus conferring on the trade acceptance some degree of marketability.

As the use of open-end credit is very large in monetary value and also rather universal, we shall concentrate on this form of short-term financing. By doing so, we will be able to focus on the functional aspects of the activity, without being unduly constrained by the legal and institutional factors that offset notes payable and trade acceptances.

The availability of open-end trade credit is generally determined by four important factors: (1) the nature of the product; (2) the seller's financial position; (3) the buyer's financial position; and (4) the terms of sale, that is, the cash discounts.

1. Benefits and Costs of Trade Credit

Financial managers must find ways to balance the advantages of trade credit against its costs as this will determine the amount of credit utilized. The most apparent advantage of trade credit derives from the ready availability of this short-term source of funds. Of course, advantages rarely come unaccompanied from costs, and we will detail some of these costs and their implications below.

Let us first review the standard terms of trade credit. To begin with, frequently trade credit is extended on the basis of a grace period following delivery of the merchandise. In such cases, the purchasing firm is not required to pay cash in advance or on delivery of the goods, but it is expected to settle up with the seller within 15–30 days. Here, the costs associated with trade credit can be found in any of the following: (1) It may be hidden within the prices of the goods sold. (2) It may be absorbed by the seller, who wishes to liquidate excess inventories. (3) It may be spread between (1) and (2) above.

In general, however, the credit terms available to the trade are more specific, thus making the calculation of the borrower's cost an easy task. In such cases, the cost of trade credit is a function of three variables: (1) the rate of discount or subsidy to the purchaser for early payment of the goods; (2) the discount period within which the subsidy to the purchaser is valid; and, (3) the so-called net period within which the merchandise must be paid at the full unsubsidised price. For example, in the typical case the terms will be 1 percent or 2 percent discount for payment within 10 days, and full-price payment afterwards but still within the typical 30-day credit limit. This will be shown as

1/10, net 30
or 2/10, net 30

Hence, when a cash discount is offered and the buyer decides to forego the cost-reduction opportunity, the cost of credit is clear and easily computable. For example, if merchandise worth 1,000 dollars is sold on terms of 1/10, net 30, the firm that takes the full net period has the use of the 1,000 dollars credit for a definite period of 20 days at a prespecified cost. In other words, if payment is made within 10 days of the receipt of merchandise (or invoice data), a 1 percent discount is allowed. But, if the discount is not taken, payment is due 30 days after the date of the invoice. In this example, the firm will have the use of the funds for 20 days at a cost of 10 dollars or at an annual interest cost of $(1/99)(360/20) = 18.12$ percent. Hence the cost of trade credit is clear when terms are granted on an individual-order basis.

It is also customary for sellers to lump all purchases together and bill buyers at one time during the month; thus credit terms for all sales are initiated on a certain date. For example, suppose that, instead of a discount, a credit charge of 1 percent is made for all unpaid acounts within the net period. If 1,000 dollars worth of merchandise is bought, and the net period is 30 days after billing at the end of the month, the credit cost depends on the time of the purchase. For the firm that purchases merchandise at the beginning of the month and chooses to bypass the net period by one month, there are, in effect, 60 days of credit at the effective annual interest cost of $(1/100)(360/60) = 6$ percent. On the other hand, if the purchase is made on the thirtieth day of the month, the buyer reduces the credit period to 31 days, and his effective annual interest cost becomes $(1/100)(360/31) = 11.6$ percent. In this case, the 30-day net period in between is not reflected in the credit cost because it is granted automatically by the seller.

Another credit cost that must be considered is the opportunity cost involved in stretching payments past the net period. This case is illustrated in Figure 8A.1. As can be seen, if the discount is taken, there is no explicit credit cost. Its existence is likely to be reflected either in the price or the availability of the merchandise, and probably cannot be avoided. Once this period is violated, however, a definite explicit cost is

FIGURE 8A.1 Costs of Trade Credit

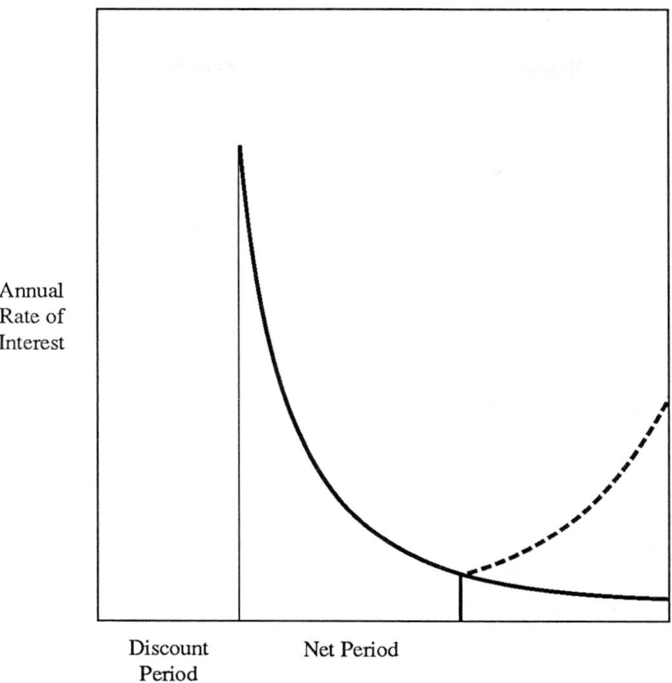

incurred, which declines steadily until the end of the net period. Ostensibly, if the net period is violated, this cost continues to decline and approaches the time axis asymptotically. However, repeated failure to meet the normal credit terms raises serious questions about the firm's credit rating. Such occurrences may well hinder the firm's future efforts to obtain credit from other sources. This opportunity cost is hard to pinpoint, but is shown by the increasing (dashed) portion of the cost curve in Figure 8A.1.

The trade-credit policy of the firm can have important implications for the management of the short-term uses of funds. For example, taking advantage of cash discounts requires an added cash outflow that must be reckoned with by the cash or financial manager. Moreover, the availability and size of trade credit obtained will affect the level of average cash balances. In the same vein, the availability and size of trade credit will make possible a more liberal collections policy with respect to the firm's own accounts receivable. The terms that the firm can secure through its trade-credit policy will also influence the carrying costs of inventories, and may well have a significant influence on the size of inventories. Hence it is difficult to divorce the analysis of trade credit from the short-term uses of funds—the optimal policy must be determined jointly.

In the final analysis, the question of trade-credit costs vis-à-vis other forms of financing may be trivial, largely because these costs are often unavoidable and are relatively inexpensive. More important, however, is the management of the *marginal* portions of credit that must be analyzed on the basis of their benefits and costs. These are usually the decisions that must be made in taking advantage of a discount or avoiding a penalty. Careful analysis of these marginal factors and alternative sources of financing will lead to an acceptable trade-off between all the costs and benefits involved in the trade-credit policy of the firm.

2. Implications of Trade Credit

Let us put some of the earlier arguments in perspective and then extend the discussion to some important implications. To begin with, once trade credit terms are offered, the purchaser will likely be paying for the credit by accepting higher priced goods. For the small businessman with limited or no access to the money markets, the existence of trade credit is a blessing, even at rather high costs. Simply put, if the trade credit were not available many small enterprises would not last long. However, for the successful firm with access to the money markets and the banking systems, trade credit may be prohibitively expensive. In this case, the established firm that is forced to accept the terms of credit may be paying a fee for staying in business. Second, it should be pointed out that even small discounts of 1 percent to 2 percent on the price of the goods may be too costly to be passed up in that they would reflect approximately 18 percent and 36 percent annual costs of borrowing.

Third, if managers decide against taking the discount, then the best policy would be to hold back on the payment until the last day of the net period. Because the dollar amount that the buyer must surrender for the credit is fixed, the longer that the buyer can put off the final payment the cheaper the credit the firm gets. More to the point, credit costs will diminish as the time increases between the end of the discount period and the end of the net period, as shown clearly in Figure 8A.1. Suppose, for example, terms of 1/10, net/90. Then, for a manager who took advantage of the full line of credit extended, the cost would be 1 dollar in interest for $99 borrowed for 80 days. Now, because the business year includes only four periods of 90-day lengths, the annualized interest cost would be 4/99. In this case, even the terms 2/10, net/90 would cost no more than 8/98 per annum. Finally, the point can be made that, for firms with very high inventory turnover, some terms of trade may provide financing periods longer than the inventories stay in the warehouse. In such cases, the seller finances some of the buyer's other expenses in addition to the goods sold.

3. Some Illustrations

As we have seen from Figure 8A.1, the cost of trade credit decreases at the beginning as the number of days from invoice rises. The cost curve continues to fall as the net period increases and it reaches its low point at the standard calendar intervals for "net periods," for example, 30 days, 60 days, and 90 days. Let us now investigate the behavior of trade-credit costs over a period of time, in sequential monthly intervals from January to September.

Assume, as shown in Table 8A.1, that an imaginary retailer buys inventories each month valued at $1,000 in the official invoices. The seller of the goods provides the following terms, 1/10, net/30 days. Further assume that our imaginary retailer is not well versed in the terms of credit and does not exploit the opportunity offered by the seller. In effect, the retailer acts as if he borrows $990 and pays another $10 in interest at the time of final settlement. Because it is customary to put out the invoices at the end of the month of purchase, we can see that for a net period of 30 days, supplies bought in January must be fully paid by the end of February. Similarly for goods bought in February, the final settlement will be the end of March. Thus, at the end of February the $1,000 in accounts payable from January purchases are paid and go off the book. Similar logic applies to purchases in February.

Now, following Table 8A.1, notice that for purchases of goods made in March and April the net period changes from 30 days to 60 days. Hence, the accounts payable for these purchases are carried on the books for two months for payment at the end of April and at the end of May. Again assume that, for some reason, the net period for purchases made in the months of May through August is increased to 90 days. The accounts payable corresponding to these purchases are carried on the books for three months. The changes in the net period from 30 to 60 to 90 days have obviously affected the total accounts payable. Thus, without any change in the actual deliveries of supplies, the total ac-

TABLE 8A.1 Accounts Payable Outstanding at End of Month (in thousands of dollars)

Net Period	*Purchases by End of Month*	*February*	*March*	*April*	*May*	*June*	*July*	*August*	*September*
30 Days	January	1,000							
	February		1,000						
60 Days	March			1,000	1,000				
	April				1,000	1,000			
90 Days	May					1,000	1,000	1,000	
	June						1,000	1,000	1,000
	July							1,000	1,000
	August								1,000
Total A/P outs		1,000	1,000	1,000	2,000	2,000	2,000	3,000	3,000
"Principal" repaid		990	990	0	990	990	0	990	990
"Interest" paid on $990 borrowed:									
for 20 days		10	10	0					
for 50 days					10	10	0		
for 80 days								10	10
Annual Rate of Interest									
Paid 10/990 multiplied		18							
by: 360/2 = 18.18		180/990	180/990	0					
360/50 = 7.27					72/990	72/990	0		
360/80 = 4.24								42/990	42/990

counts payable increases from $1,000 in April to $2,000 in May through July, when it increases again to $3,000 in August and September.

Another interesting point is the pattern of payments on the so-called principal of 990 dollars and the 10 dollars of the so-called interest. Because our retailer does not take advantage of the discount offered for goods purchased in January and February, we can compute the interest paid implicitly as follows. Because the interest is paid for the use of credit for 20 days, and there are 18 such 20-day periods in a year of 360 days, the annualized rate of interest paid implicitly will be (10/990 × 18) = 180/990 = 18.18 percent. As the net period increases to 60 days, the annual interest is computed at (10/990 × 7.2) = 72/990 = 7.27 percent. Similarly, for a net period of 90 days, the annual interest is computed at (10/990 × 4.2) = 42/990 = 4.24 percent.

Moving along the information in Table 8A.1, we notice that for the months of April and July, the retailer pays neither "capital" nor "interest." This is so, because these two months begin the transition in the net period from 30 to 60 days and from 60 to 90 days respectively. It should be noted here that if the change in the net period were reversed and the original terms were 90 days with subsequent compression to 60 days and 30 days, the effects on payments would have been to pile up two months' payments into one.

C. Bank Loan Financing

1. Overall Considerations

In addition to the more-or-less automatic source of financing known as trade credit, businesspeople have recourse to other sources of funds. One of the largest and most frequently sought after is the type of financing available through such financial institutions as banks of various types, insurance companies, and other such institutions with business flows that are more predictable than the average manufacturing or commercial establishment.

There are two types of bank loans—*secured bank loans* and *unsecured bank loans*. Secured bank loans are made on the basis of collateral pledged by the firm. For long-term loans, the firm usually pledges such long term assets as fixtures, equipment, and land. For short-term loans the company collateralizes such short-term assets as inventories and accounts receivable, as we shall discuss more thoroughly in Section D.

2. Unsecured Bank Loans

As we stated earlier, short-term bank loans are payable within one year or less. Such loans are generally offered in the following three arrangements with banks.

1. *Line of credit:* This is an informal arrangement between the bank and its customer. The specified amount constitutes a ceiling of the credit availability at any time, and it is typically based on the bank's assessment of the credit worthiness of the borrower. It is subject to adjustment or renewal, if the conditions warrant. Many banks also require that the borrowing firm be without bank debt at some time during the fiscal period, but this requirement varies and is subject to negotiation between the two parties. An additional feature of the line of credit is that there is no legal obligation on the part of the bank to extend the promised credit, if the borrower's credit standing changes.
2. *Revolving credit agreement:* This type of loan constitutes a legal commitment for the bank. It differs from the line of credit in this respect, and also in that a fee is usually required on the unused portion of the total credit. Moreover, a revolving credit agreement frequently extends beyond a year, and thus ceases to be a short-term source of funds.
3. *Transaction loan:* This type of loan is undertaken when a firm needs funds for a specific purpose. For example, a custom-made bicycle manufacturer may need to borrow for inventories necessary for the completion of an order. The prime determinant of the loan and its terms is the bank's evaluation of the project-generated cash flows.

The cost of bank loans is determined largely by the interest rate, which is usually a matter of negotiation between the bank and the firm's management. The interest rate charged usually depends on the credit worthiness of the firm and is based on some type of *prime rate*—a uniform rate being charged to the large companies with the highest credit ratings. Prime customers notwithstanding, the typical bank loan is made at some premium over the prime rate, and the size of the premium depends on the bargaining position of each party, the previous relations between bank and firm, personal considerations, and, above all, the credit worthiness of the firm.

The interest rate charged is not, of course, the only cost involved in bank loans. For example, banks usually require the maintenance of demand-deposit balances, which are normally a percentage of the total loan commitment. The maintenance of compensating balances usually raises the effective cost of bank loans, but only to the extent that the required balances are larger than the ones normally deposited by the firm with the bank. For example, if a \$10,000 bank loan is made at 6 percent and the bank requires that 15 percent of the loan be kept in compensating balances, the borrowing firm would have access only to \$8,500, instead of the original \$10,000 loan. As a result, the effective annual interest cost is no longer 6 percent, but $600/8{,}500 = 7.06$ percent.

The true cost of a bank loan also depends on the methods of assessing charges and repayment. The loan may be *discounted,* in which case the interest charge is deducted in advance, thus slightly increasing the effective cost. For example, if \$10,000 at 5 percent are discounted for one year, other things being equal, the effective annual cost becomes $500/(10{,}000 - 500) = 5.26$ percent. In the same vein, if the loan is repayable on an *installment* basis, beginning immediately, the effective annual cost is *doubled* because the average balance outstanding is halved. If the loan used in the above example were to be repaid on an installment plan, its effective cost would become $500/4{,}750 = 10.5$ percent.

3. Commercial Paper

Large and successful companies have also found a rather attractive source of financing through transactions in the so-called *commercial-paper market. Commercial paper* consists of the unsecured promissory notes of large firms, sold primarily to other large firms and financial institutions. However, because the notes are unsecured and sold in the market, only the most credit-worthy firms are able to take advantage of this source of funds. Commercial paper is available through *dealers,* who function primarily as brokers, and through *direct placement* to the lender. The dealer market is composed of several major dealers who earn a commission by buying the commercial paper from borrowers and selling it to investors. The market for commercial paper is highly organized and sophisticated. However, the direct-placement market is composed of large-sales finance companies who tailor both the maturity and the amount of the notes to the needs of the investors. Thus the maturities and amounts of directly placed paper cover a wide range of combinations.

Commercial paper is usually cheaper than unsecured bank loans—and this cost differential increases in periods of easy money. Moreover, commercial paper is a larger source of funds for corporations that undertake heavy financing, and it eliminates the inconvenience of maintaining compensating balances with several participating banks. Finally, the sale of commercial paper keeps the firm in touch with the money market and paves the way for future tapping. However, the impersonal nature of the commercial-paper market affords little opportunity for negotiation to the firm, and excessive concentration in it will isolate the firm from the bank sources.

D. Financing Through the Pledging of Accounts Receivable and Inventories

In order to minimize the risks of accommodating short-term borrowing, many lenders require that, in addition to demonstrating credit worthiness, borrowers pledge some of their short-term assets, typically accounts receivable or inventories. *Accounts receivable* represent one of the firm's most liquid assets and have become a very desirable object of secured loans. Most accounts receivable financing is undertaken either by banks or finance companies, and can be facilitated by the *assignment* or pledging of the accounts, or by the *factoring* of the receivables. The lending institution is interested in the quality of the receivables and carefully inspects the accounts in order to determine their credit rating. It is also concerned with the average size of the accounts, given the high cost of processing. Hence, on the basis of the average quality and size of the accounts, the lender determines the percentage of their face value that will be lent to the borrowing firm.

Short-term financing through accounts receivable can be obtained in two ways:

1. *Assignment* of accounts receivable can be arranged either on a notification or a nonnotification basis. In both cases the borrower signs a promissory note and a security agreement. Under the *notification* basis, the buyer of the merchandise is duly notified of the assignment of the account and makes direct payment to the lender. This gives the lender an added security in that the borrower cannot withhold payments. On the other hand, under the *nonnotification* basis, the buyer of the merchandise is not informed of the new arrangement and continues making payments to the borrower who, in turn forwards the funds to the lender. The lender can check the payments against the records that are furnished, but the lender does not have as much control as with the notification agreement. However, in both cases, the borrower retains title to the receivables.
2. In the *factoring* of accounts receivable, title is transferred to the *factor* (i.e., lending institution) which manages and collects the accounts. Consequently, the lending institution shoulders both the collection costs and the bad-debt losses; for this reason, the factor usually refuses to accept very risky accounts. Needless to say, the borrowing firm that factors its own receivables avoids the costs of processing and the risk of default. However, the factor may be employed to perform *only* the credit-risk and collection functions, without the lending responsibilities, for a flat fee of perhaps 2 percent of the receivables.

Under this arrangement, if the firm needs some cash before the accounts are collected, it can obtain the cash from the factor at some prespecified interest cost.

For example, suppose that receivables, $100,000 worth, are factored at a 2 percent collection fee, that is, at an immediate cost of $2,000. Further assume that the firm needs the funds and must borrow from the factor at 8 percent. If the terms of all receivables are net/30, the firm will incur the following charges: $(\$98{,}000)(.08)^{30}/_{360} = \$653.33$. Hence the total cost of factoring (and borrowing) will be $2,000 + $653.33 = $2,653.33. It should also be added that the factoring firm has no recourse to the seller in the event of bad-debt losses.

There are several advantages to short-term financing through receivables, not the least of which is the flexibility it affords the borrowing firm. The seller firm may continue to finance its receivables on a more or less automatic basis; if its sales expand or contract, it can vary the financing proportionately. Another advantage consists of relieving the borrowing firm of substantial credit and collections costs and, to a degree, from a considerable part of its cash management. Finally, this source of short-term financing is ideally suited—and often the only alternative—to small, relatively unknown, and financially weak firms.

Nevertheless, accounts receivable financing is very costly—the cost of borrowing alone being several points higher than the prime interest rate. In addition, by financing its own receivables, the firm is using a highly liquid asset as security and thus weakens its credit worthiness to banks and other creditors. Hence in evaluating the costs and benefits of accounts receivable financing, all the advantages and disadvantages must enter into the decision framework.

In addition to accounts receivable, *inventories* also serve as a highly acceptable form of collateral for short-term financing due to their relatively high degree of liquidity. Lenders typically determine the actual value of inventories by such market-oriented concepts as marketability, price stability, and so on, but the final loan decision is based on the credit worthiness of the borrower. Inventory financing arrangements vary in accordance with the type of inventories secured, the custodian involved, and of course, the legal and institutional characteristics of the country. In this spirit, three types of inventory financing arrangements can be highlighted, as follows:

1. An arrangement is provided by the *floating lien* on *all* the inventories of the borrowing firm. The floating lien can be extended to any length of time to include future as well as present inventories; it can also be extended to cover accounts receivable. Yet, the floating-lien arrangement does not provide a generally viable form of short-term financing, primarily because it is vague and yields little control to the lender.
2. Another method of inventory financing, known as *trust receipt,* transfers title of the merchandise to the lender and allows the borrower to hold the merchandise in trust for the lending institution. Typically, the secured merchandise is physically separated in the warehouse of the borrower and specifically identified in the security agreement. This arrangement provides a better control for the lender than the floating lien, in that it provides a definite means of access to the collateral; however, effective control over the care and disposition of the collateral is still difficult.
3. To offset these inconveniences, another method—*warehousing*—has been increasingly favored for securing inventory loans. Under this arrangement, the borrower stores the inventories in a public warehouse, which issues a receipt to the lender, known as a *terminal warehouse receipt.* The warehouse will release inventories to the borrower only on the explicit authorization of the lender—who thereby gains strict control over the collateral. However, the means of control provided by the method also makes it inflexible and excessively costly.

Some of the problems of terminal warehousing are alleviated by *field warehousing,* which allows for loans to be made against inventory that remains on the premises of the borrower. Under this method, the lender exercises some supervision by contracting the services of a third party—the field-warehousing company—to act as the control agent. Field warehousing is distinguished by two features: public notification of the arrangement and supervision of the inventories by a third party. Moreover, field warehousing provides considerable flexibility for the borrower with respect to the amount of funds available. It is tied to the growth of the inventories and related directly to the financing needs of the borrower. In addition, improved warehousing practices reduce both losses and labor costs. But, like the previous methods, field warehousing is still a high-cost source of short-term funds.

8A QUESTIONS

8A1. What are the three main categories of trade credit? Define each of the categories and give specific examples.

8A2. Discuss in some detail the benefits and costs of trade credit.

8A3. Discuss the various types of loans extended by banks for short-term borrowing, and define their specific characteristics regarding interest, early discounting, and compensating balances.

8A4. Define and discuss commercial paper as an instrument of short-term financing.

8A5. Discuss the assignment and factoring arrangements for financing through accounts receivable.

8A6. Discuss the three main methods of inventory financing and provide supporting examples.

8A PROBLEMS

8A1. Determine the effective annual interest rate of not taking the cash discount, given the following terms:

2/10, net 30	4/10, net 30
2/10, net 60	net 60
1/10, net 60	5/10, net 60

8A2. The Philipps Engine Company is planning to borrow $1,500,000 from their local bank in Atlanta, Georgia. The bank charges 12.5 percent interest and discounts the loans. (*a*) Determine the funds that will be available to Philipps Engine Company for its business use. (*b*) Determine the effective interest rate. (*c*) Suppose that the local bank in Atlanta also decides to require 10 percent compensating balances; what would be the effective annual rate of interest under this scenario?

ANNOTATED BIBLIOGRAPHY

Buffa, E. S., and W. H. Taubert. *Production-Inventory Systems: Planning and Control.* Homewood, Ill.: Richard D. Irwin, 1972.

A comprehensive volume covering inventory systems and rather detailed cost balancing approaches to inventory management.

Gurnani, C. "Economic Analysis of Inventory Systems." *International Journal of Production Research,* March–April 1983, 261–77.

Discusses investment in inventory in terms of a wealth-maximizing framework.

Kim, Y. H., and K. H. Chung. "Economic Analysis of Inventory Systems: A Clarifying Analysis." *International Journal of Production Research,* 23(4): 761–67 (1985).

Sequel to the preceding Gurnani article.

MacPhee, William A. *Short-Term Business Borrowing: Sources, Terms and Techniques.* Homewood, Ill.: Dow Jones-Irwin, 1984.

A comprehensive source of information on short-term borrowing practices and techniques.

Magee, J. F. "Guides to Inventory Policy: Problems of Uncertainty." *Harvard Business Review,* March–April 1956, 103–16.

A good discussion of approaches to managing inventory under conditions of uncertainty.

Shapiro, A. "Optimal Inventory and Credit-Granting Strategies under Inflation and Devaluation." *Journal of Financial and Quantitative Analysis,* January 1973, 37–46.

A review of some of the important issues in inventory management in the face of inflation and exchange rate devaluation.

Smith, K. V. *Guide to Working Capital Management.* New York: McGraw-Hill, 1979.

A comprehensive source on working capital

management that contains a solid treatment of inventories.

Smith, K. V. *Readings on the Management of Working Capital*. 2d ed. St. Paul, Minn: West Publishing, 1980.
A fine selection of survey articles covering many aspects of inventory management and providing the background for this chapter.

9

THE DEBT-EQUITY FRAMEWORK: THEORY OF CAPITAL STRUCTURE

I. INTRODUCTION

This chapter sets out a conceptual framework regarding the main choices and trade-offs that must be made in capital structure and investment decisions. Subsequent chapters develop this framework more fully and lay out the analytical approaches to the decisions.

An elementary rule of scientific research is to vary only one component at a time. The effects of changes in that component are then not blurred by a multitude of other changes whose precise impact cannot be identified. The same rule applies to the analysis of decisions about long-term capital. If management is considering an increase in the company's assets, for example, it should first determine the effect of this decision on earnings and risk while holding the debt percentage constant. Likewise, a change in the debt position of the company need not be considered only in the context of a major capital expenditure program: repurchase of shares is a direct way of altering the capital structure without the confusion of additional operating earnings. If each idea, independently considered, proves analytically sound, then the two combined are also likely to be attractive. The danger of beginning with a combined analysis is that a good idea may be sufficiently good to carry along a far less attractive one that is coupled with it.

A review of the basic financial and accounting identities will illustrate options provided by careful, step-by-step analysis. The basic accounting principles require that any net increase in assets (a use of funds) must come from only two sources: an increase in debt or an increase in equity (or both). The increase in equity can be the result of an increase in preferred stock or of an increase in the common shareholders' equity. (Because preferred stock is such a special financial instrument, it will be ignored for the rest of this discussion.) Common equity, in turn, can increase as the result of the issue of new common shares or from earnings retained in the company (or from both sources combined). Retention, of course, comes from profits less dividends.

The preceding interrelationships between sources and uses, as well as the interactions among the various sources, are shown in diagrammatic form in Figure 9.1. The two main capital structure decisions are in regard to the appropriate proportions of debt and equity, and the appropriate proportions of retained earnings and dividends, that a company should have.

The owners of an enterprise must make four fundamental financial decisions, summarized in the following three accounting relationships. Note that the first and third equations are linked because the assets generate the profit.

$$\text{Assets} = \text{Debt} + \text{Equity} \tag{9.1}$$

$$\text{Equity} = \text{Paid-in Capital} + \text{Retained Earnings} \tag{9.2}$$

$$\text{Retained Earnings} = \text{Profit after Tax} - \text{Dividends.} \tag{9.3}$$

Based on these relationships, the four deci-

FIGURE 9.1 Sources and Uses of Funds

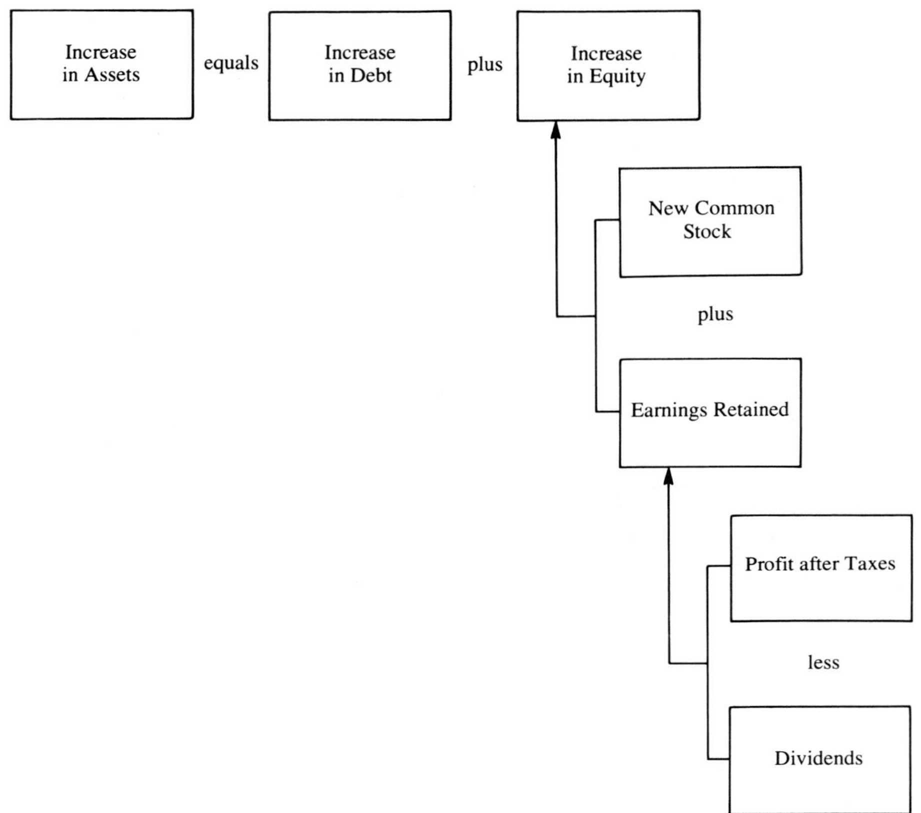

sions relative to the creation of financial value are

1. Which assets should be accepted for investment and how much should be invested in each (equation [9.1], left-hand side)? This decision determines the profits and value available to the investors.
2. How should the investment funds be raised? Specifically, what proportion of the assets should be financed with debt and what proportion with equity (equation [9.1], right-hand side)? This decision determines who gets the earnings and in what order.
3. How should the equity claim on the value be structured? Are the owners willing to admit new investors to ownership by offering new equity for sale (equation [9.2])? This decision potentially gives others a portion of the existing value in order to create potentially greater value from the new investments.
4. What earnings should be retained and what dividends should be paid out (equation [9.3])? This decision allocates the investors' funds to the existing entity through an involuntary subscription of new equity or frees cash for the investor to use in other activities.

The order in which these decisions are listed above is usually the order followed in actual economic life. An entrepreneur has an insight that appears likely to create value. On the basis of the attractiveness of the idea, the entrepreneur raises capital to acquire the necessary assets. Once the venture becomes profitable, the owner has to decide how to allocate the profits between opportunities within the business and external opportunities.

Once a decision is made regarding assets, there are limited degrees of freedom in the decisional network on the source side. For example, if a given debt proportion is established, and a company decides not to issue new common stock, then a maximum dividend payout is established by default. Where only three variables sum to a required total, establishing two of the variables automatically determines the value of the third. Thus, if a company sets a dividend policy and a debt policy, the amount of new common stock it must issue to finance its asset requirements is thereby determined. If the dividend policy does not permit the company to retain sufficient funds to provide the proportion of new equity funds generated internally, there is no choice but to raise new equity capital externally through the issue of stock. Each dollar of dividends paid out above the level required to generate the equity funds internally will require an extra dollar of new external equity to be raised.

We can represent these relationships with the following equation:

$$TA_t \equiv B_t + W_t$$

where TA_t = total assets of the firm at time t
B_t = total borrowing (debt) by the firm at time t
W_t = the firm's net worth at t

The equation corresponds to the familiar accounting identity that total assets at any point in time equal the sum of the firm's liabilities B_t and net worth W_t.

Suppose management has determined that it requires a given net investment in total assets over the coming year. Then total assets at the end of the year, TA_{t+1}, will equal the beginning balance plus investment I_t: $TA_{t+1} = TA_t + I_t$. Thus, the change in total assets, $\Delta TA = TA_{t+1} - TA_t$ equals net investment: $\Delta TA = I_t$, which must be financed with either additional borrowing, an increase in net worth or some combination. We now have

$$\Delta TA = \Delta(B_t + W_t) = B_{t+1} - B_t + W_{t+1} - W_t$$

$$\Delta TA = \Delta B_t + \Delta W_t \tag{9.4}$$

Furthermore, we know that the change in net worth equals net income NI less dividends D plus (minus) the issue (repurchase) of shares of stock S:

$$\Delta W_{t,t+1} = NI_{t,t+1} - D_{t,t+1} + S_{t,t+1}$$

Substituting into equation (9.4), we have

$$\Delta TA = \Delta B + NI - D + S$$

or alternatively,

$$\Delta TA - NI = \Delta B - D + S \tag{9.5}$$

Taking the left-hand side as given, we can see that the firm's debt and dividend policies automatically determine the amount of new equity to be raised. In general, if any two of the three policy variables on the right-hand side of equation (9.5) are set, the third is necessarily specified.

For instance, consider a company that requires \$1 million net additions to its assets. Suppose the firm's debt-to-capital policy is 40 percent, and debt is currently at that proportion of the capital structure. The company can then raise only \$400,000 of the required \$1 million from debt; the other \$600,000 must come from additions to the equity account. If the firm's profits are \$1.2 million, and if its policy is to pay out 60 percent of its profits as dividends, it will retain only \$480,000. The remaining \$120,000 it requires will have to be raised through the issue of new common stock, or one of the other basic policies will have to be modified. If the debt-to-capitalization ratio is retained, then the firm must decide whether it is more important to maintain the 60 percent payout ratio (and go to the equity market) or to avoid raising new equity (and cut the payout back to 50 percent). Any payout of more than 50 percent requires that some other policy be altered.

Some companies have the luxury of slack financial resources. That is, they have extra cash or debt capacity available, or their payout is lower than their target. This was the case for many companies at the beginning of the 1960s; they were highly liquid, and their debt ratios were well below safe limits. The failure to appreciate that the consumption of these resources is a one-shot opportunity, that spare cash and debt capacity are generally available only once and do not regenerate themselves as fast as the firm's asset needs grow, may have led management in these companies into unwise expansion programs initially financed by debt. It was not until several years later, when the impact of these decisions on dividends and new equity requirements became more obvious, that the marketplace reacted fully to the adverse situation. By then, however, the damage had been done: financial flexibility had been lost.

In what follows in this chapter, as well as throughout the text, the major capital structure and asset investment decisions will be discussed in an iterative manner. That is, all variables but one are held constant, and the impact of variations in that one variable is explored. Then another variable is analyzed in the same fashion, and so on, until all the variables have been investigated. Finally, because of the actual complexity of the interrelations among the variables, it will be wise to stand back and ask whether the entire picture makes sense.

It is possible to start anywhere in the process—with the asset decision, the capital structure decision, or the dividend decision, as long as the entire decision circle is completed. It often seems easiest, for purposes of exposition as well as decision, to begin by making some tentative decisions on the net increase in assets to be financed and the earnings that will be available for retention. The debt and equity options available should be explored and the best one selected. Then, with a reasonable debt-equity policy having been selected, the analysis turns to the dividend policy question. Finally, with the capital structure settled, and perhaps a reasonable estimate of capital costs available, the assets that were tentatively selected to get the analytical process started are reevaluated.

This order of decisions (i.e., capital expenditure policy, capitalization policy, dividend policy) will be much utilized in the chapters that follow. In the next section we will review some of the recent theories on capital structure as they address the issues of its relevance for minimizing the cost of capital and maximizing the value of common stock. This theoretical review will provide the necessary foundations for the evaluation of major financial decisions by the firm.

II. THEORIES OF CAPITAL STRUCTURE

Some of the early results pertaining to the relevance of capital structure are discussed in some detail in Chapters 10 and 12. There, the original 1958 Modigliani and Miller (MM) arguments are presented for capital structure irrelevance in a world without taxes, and for capital structure relevance in a world with corporate taxes. Since the original contributions by Modigliani and Miller, the controversy surrounding the theoretical relevance of the capital structure decision has taken a variety of new directions. The most notable of these discussions introduces differential personal taxes. In addition, arguments concerning bankruptcy costs and a variety of other imperfections have led to the conclusion that capital structure is relevant in maximizing the value of a firm's common stock.

To discuss the question of capital structure relevance here, we will examine a firm whose investment and dividend decisions are known and constant. Within this framework, we will examine only the effects of a change in the capital structure. Because we are holding the investment and dividend decisions constant, we can conclude that any such effects are due entirely to a change in capital structure. After discussing the various theories of firm valuation, we will turn to the various ways in which a firm can actually determine its capital structure.

In order to present the various theories of capital structure and examine the effects of a changing capital structure, we make the following assumptions:

1. No corporate or personal income taxes exist.

2. Changes in capital structure are effected by issuing debt to repurchase stock. Doing this keeps the firm's capitalization constant in terms of dollars.
3. The firm pays out all of its earnings as dividends.
4. Investors have homogeneous expectations concerning the probability distribution of future cash flows.
5. Operating earnings remain constant in perpetuity.

In addition, we use the following definitions:

r_d = rate of return on debt
r_e = rate of return on equity
r_A = average rate of return on total assets of the firm
NOI = net operating earnings (income)
V = market value of the firm
B = market value of debt
S = market value of equity
I = annual interest charges
D = earnings available to common stockholders

Because all cash flows evolve in perpetuity, we can state the following about the various rates of return:

$$r_e = \frac{D}{S}$$

$$r_d = \frac{I}{B}$$

$$r_A = \frac{\text{NOI}}{V}$$

$$r_A = r_e\left(\frac{S}{V}\right) + r_d\left(\frac{B}{V}\right) \tag{9.6}$$

For example, because the cash flows to stockholders evolve as a perpetuity, we may use the simple present-value formula:

$$S = \frac{D}{r_e}$$

to solve for the value of the firm's common stock. Thus, the rate on equity is simply $r_e = D/S$. The same reasoning applies to the other rates of return in the preceding definitions.

Our concern now is the behavior of r_e, r_d, and r_A as the ratio B/S (debt to equity) changes. Some of these questions are addressed in greater detail in Chapter 12. Here, we state only the basic conclusion of each of three approaches regarding the effects of a changing capital structure upon the market value of the firm.

A. The Net Income Approach

The net income (NI) approach, originally advanced by David Durand (1959), assumes that the costs of both equity and debt remain unchanged as the ratio of debt to equity B/S becomes larger. Thus, if more debt is used in the firm's capital structure, we expect the overall cost of capital to decline as long as $r_e > r_d$. This case is illustrated in Figure 9.2, where the firm's overall cost of capital, r_A, declines as the ratio B/S increases. The relationship obtains because managers employ a greater proportion of the less expensive source of funds (debt) and a smaller proportion of the costlier source of funds (equity). Note, however, the heuristic assumption of constant values for r_e and r_d at much higher levels of debt. In addition, the approach suggests that the firm should use as much debt as possible, because as r_A approaches r_d, the total firm value V will be at a maximum. The logical question is, of course, "How will the firm be able to maintain a low cost of funds in the extreme case of 100 percent debt, because on that occasion debtholders are effectively the new owners?"

B. The Net Operating Income Approach

The net operating income (NOI) approach assumes that r_A is unaffected by the amount of debt used in the capital structure. Support for the NOI position derives from the well-known MM Proposition I, which is discussed in Chapter 12. Essentially, MM conclude that in a perfect capital market, value is determined by the firm's real productive assets, not by how management goes about repackaging claims against those assets. That is, only the left-hand side of the bal-

FIGURE 9.2 Cost of Capital: Net Income (NI) Approach

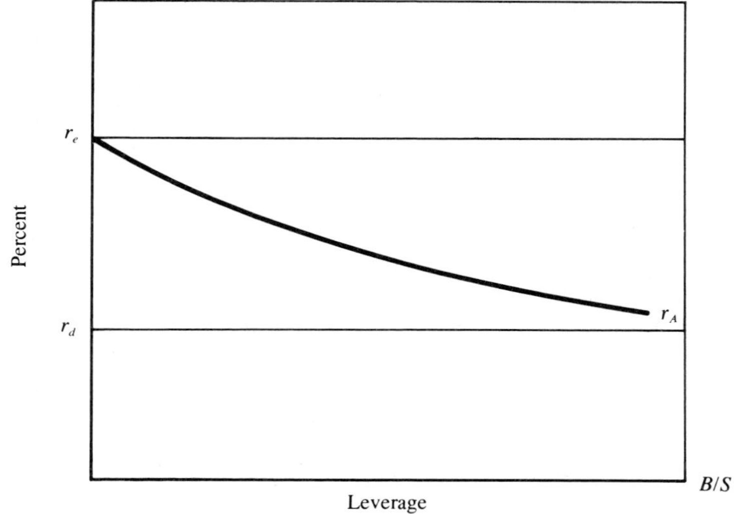

ance sheet matters; capital structure decisions are of no consequence to the market value of the firm. This relationship is depicted in Figure 9.3, where, as with the NI approach, the firm's cost of debt is assumed to be constant for all values of B/S. In the NOI approach, however, the cost of equity, r_e, increases directly with the higher values of B/S in order to compensate stockholders for the additional debt in the firm's capital structure. Because the increase in r_e is

FIGURE 9.3 Cost of Capital: Net Operating Income (NOI) Approach

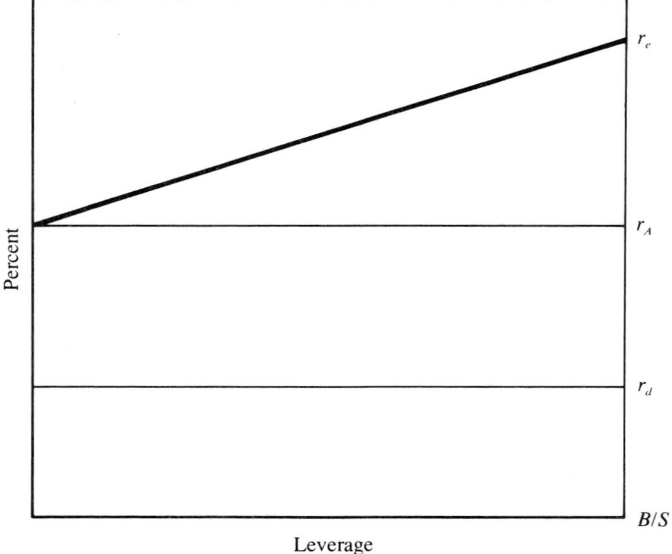

just sufficient to offset the use of more borrowed funds, the overall cost of capital remains constant.

To illustrate the NOI approach, consider two firms U and L. Firm U has no debt in its capital structure (it is unlevered), while firm L has $4 million of debt financing. The following table presents the relevant characteristics for each firm. These firms have equal NOI and are assumed to be of equal risk. Furthermore, the rate of return on total assets is 10 percent for firm U and 11.11 percent for firm L. The goal here is to show the transactions by which an investor who owns, for instance, 1 percent of the shares of firm U can obtain a higher rate of return by purchasing securities of firm L.

	Firm U	*Firm L*
NOI	$ 1,000,000	$1,000,000
B	0	$4,000,000
r_d	N/A	.04
I	0	$ 160,000
D	$ 1,000,000	$ 840,000
r_e	.10	.168
S	$10,000,000	$5,000,000
V	$10,000,000	$9,000,000
r_A	.10	.1111

Our investor, Wanda, currently holds $100,000 of Firm U stock ($10,000,000 × 1 percent). Because both firms are assumed to pay out 100 percent of earnings as dividends, Wanda's rate of return on her investment is currently 10 percent (= $10,000/$100,000). Now, suppose she sells her stock in firm U and invests $40,000 in the bonds and $60,000 in the stock of firm L. What is her expected rate of return? Because she holds 1 percent of the bonds, she will receive $1,600 in interest, and from her investment in 1.2 percent of the shares of stock (60,000/5,000,000) she will receive dividends of $10,080. So the rate of return on her investment of $100,000 is now equal to:

$$(1{,}600 + 10{,}080)/100{,}000 = 11.68\%$$

But what happens if other stockholders in firm U undertake the same transactions as Wanda? By selling firm U stock and buying the bonds and stock of firm L, investors will drive down the value of firm U stock and bid up the shares of firm L. The process will continue until the rates of return on total assets of both firms are equal. This is the basic thrust of the NOI approach, that identical commodities (in this case, claims on NOI) cannot sell at different prices in equilibrium.

C. The Traditional Approach

The position of the traditionalists is that an optimal capital structure exists and that the firm can achieve a maximum valuation by using the appropriate amount of financial leverage. Thus, the traditionalists minimize a firm's cost of capital. Below the optimal capital structure that they posit, too little debt deprives the shareholders of the value of leverage. Above the optimal point, the rise of the debt costs offsets the benefits of leverage. The position of the traditional approach to capital structure is illustrated in Figure 9.4 where, in contrast to the other two approaches, the rates r_A, r_e, and r_d vary with B/S. It should be noted here, however, that the firm's overall cost of capital, r_A, attains a minimum at point M. According to the traditional position, the value of B/S that minimizes the cost of capital also maximizes the market value of the firm's stock. Thus, the combination of debt and equity instruments is highly relevant to market valuation. There are also many variations of the traditional approach, all of which lie somewhere between the NI and NOI approaches.

III. CAPITAL STRUCTURE AND MARKET IMPERFECTIONS

We now turn our attention to a discussion of the various imperfections present in capital markets and how they affect the capital structure decision. Arguments for the irrelevance of capital structure have been attacked on various grounds, but they can all generally be classified as related to market imperfections. Essentially, there are five general categories of such imperfections that might make the capital structure decision relevant:

FIGURE 9.4 Cost of Capital: Traditional Approach

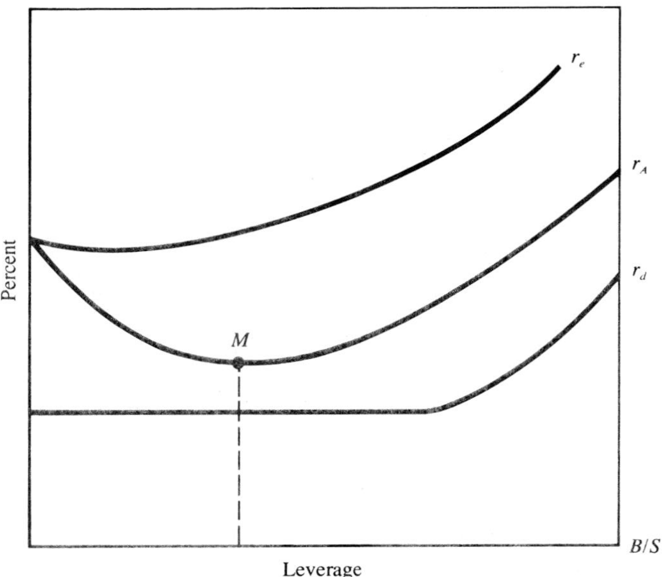

1. Bankruptcy costs
2. Problems with personal leverage
3. Different borrowing costs
4. Corporate and personal income taxes
5. Agency costs

A. Bankruptcy Costs

Bankruptcy costs refer to the possible leakages to third parties, such as attorneys, in the event that the firm must be reorganized or liquidated. At very high levels of leverage and with adverse economic conditions, the possibility of bankruptcy may be a serious consideration. Therefore, for high values of B/S, the firm may be unattractive to investors: stockholders and bondholders will receive less if bankruptcy costs are present, and in perfect capital markets lenders will pass these costs on to the stockholders in the form of higher interest rates on debt. *Ex ante,* the owners of the firm bear the cost of bankruptcy. The upshot is that there exists a unique value of B/S that maximizes the value of the firm. We will discuss this result further in the section on corporate and personal taxes.

While some scholars have concluded that bankruptcy costs are important, Haugen and Senbet (1978) have presented an argument for their irrelevance. In essence, they conclude that if all economic agents are rational, bankruptcy costs can be avoided. Certainly, this is so, because the company can simply reorganize by selling stock to repurchase the outstanding debt, and presumably this "informal" reorganization has lower costs than a formal one. But given the realities of the marketplace, in which not all economic agents are rational, it is an empirical matter just how important bankruptcy costs are.

B. Effects of Personal Leverage

The MM proposition of irrelevance is based partly on the ability of investors to issue debt on their own account as a substitute for corporate leverage. The assumption is that corporate leverage and personal leverage are perfect substitutes. However, if investors do issue personal debt, their liability will not be limited, as would be the case with corporate leverage. For this reason, personal leverage may not substitute fully for corporate leverage.

In reply to this objection, we may note that

while the MM argument is presented only for individuals and firms, it does not preclude financial intermediaries from performing the arbitrage function. In this sense, the MM proposition relies not really on individuals per se, but on a market in which arbitrage opportunities are bid away. Financial intermediaries can perform these duties, with the debt they issue being a perfect substitute for corporate leverage. Therefore, the objection does not refute the MM proposition.

To illustrate the ability of investors to "undo" corporate leverage, consider a levered firm that chooses to retire all of its outstanding debt by issuing stock. The firm has the following characteristics before and after the restructuring.

	Before	*After*
NOI	\$ 1,000,000	\$ 1,000,000
B	\$ 4,000,000	0
r_d	.04	N/A
I	\$ 160,000	0
D	\$ 840,000	\$ 1,000,000
r_e	.14	.10
S	\$ 6,000,000	\$10,000,000
$V = S + B$	\$10,000,000	\$10,000,000
r_A	.10	.10

The Wanda Investment Company (WIC) held 1 percent of the shares in the levered firm prior to restructuring and thus earned a rate of return of 14 percent on that investment:

$$.01(840{,}000) \div .01(6{,}000{,}000) = .14$$

Assuming that WIC did not purchase any of the newly issued shares, the proportion of ownership is now 0.6 percent after restructuring. So the rate of return on the investment of \$60,000 is now 10 percent:

$$.006(\$1{,}000{,}000) \div 60{,}000 = .10$$

The problem now is that WIC was completely satisfied with its rate of return on investment of 14 percent before the restructuring and wishes to maintain that return without investing additional funds.

Suppose that WIC can borrow at a 4% annual rate of interest (again, we are in a no-tax world) to buy more shares of the restructured firm. Specifically, WIC borrows \$40,000 and buys more stock. The return in dollar terms, then, will consist of dividend income less interest expense, which in this case equals \$10,000 − \$1,600 = \$8,400. Consequently, the rate of return on invested funds of \$60,000 equals 14 percent, the same as prior to the restructuring.

C. Borrowing Rate Differentials

If there are capital market imperfections, individuals can borrow only at rates that are effectively higher than the rates available to corporations. Nonetheless, from the previous section, the MM proposition still holds, because financial intermediaries can replace individuals in the arbitraging process.

D. Corporate and Personal Income Taxes

The existence of corporate and personal income taxes alters the original MM proposition of capital structure irrelevance. In a world that has corporate taxes, there may in fact be an advantage to using debt. To examine this statement, consider two identical firms, U and L. Firm U does not use leverage, while firm L does. Table 9.1 presents the relevant information for both firms. Because firm L employs leverage, the cost of which is tax deductible, there are more earnings available for the common stockholders. Therefore, firm L is more highly valued than firm U. As residual claimants to all cash flows, the stockholders receive the entire benefit of the value of the tax shield. A simple way to express the present value of the tax shield is given by equation (9.7), where T_c stands for the corporate tax rate.

$$\text{PV Tax Shield} = \frac{T_c r_d B}{r_d} = T_c B \qquad (9.7)$$

Essentially, the value of the tax shield is the present discounted value of all future shielded income. Because all cash flows in our model evolve in perpetuity, the simple present-value

TABLE 9.1 Effects of Corporate Taxes—A Two Firm Comparison

	Firm U	*Firm L*
1. NOI	$ 5,000	$ 5,000
2. Taxes (34%)	1,700	1,700
3. Profit before interest, but after taxes	$ 3,300	$ 3,300
4. r_A for debt-free company	.10	.10
5. Value of (3)	$33,000	$33,000
6. Interest on debt*	0	1,200
7. After-tax cost of interest	0	792
8. Tax savings on interest	0	$ 408
9. Value of tax shield**	$ 0	$ 3,400
10. Total Value (5) + (10)	$33,000	$36,400

**Note:* Here we assume that the firm has $10,000 in 12% bonds outstanding in perpetuity. The tax savings (1,200(1 − tax rate)), therefore, are also a perpetuity.
**The value of the tax shield is $T_cB(.34 \times \$10,000)$ or the present value of the tax shield in perpetuity at 12% is ($408/.12).

formula is used to arrive at the value of the tax shield.

Because the firm has $10,000 in bonds outstanding, with a tax rate of 34 percent we arrive at $3,400 for the value of the tax shield. From MM's Proposition I, adjusted for taxes, we know that the value of the firm equals the value of an otherwise identical unlevered firm plus the value of the tax shield generated by the use of debt. Formally,

$$V^L = \frac{NOI(1 - T_c)}{\rho} + T_cB \tag{9.8}$$

where ρ = capitalization rate for an all-equity firm

V^L = value of the levered firm

V^U = NOI $(1 - T_c)/\rho$ is the value of an unlevered firm

We can observe the relationship described by equation (9.8) with the aid of Figure 9.5, which shows that the value of the firm increases as the firm gets into more debt. Figure 9.5 also depicts the position of those who argue that bankruptcy costs matter. With bankruptcy costs, the value for the firm follows the path $V^{L'}$ and reaches a maximum value at point A.

As argued earlier, the importance of bankruptcy costs is an empirical issue. Is it possible for bankruptcy costs to offset the large tax advantages associated with the use of debt? A

FIGURE 9.5 Comparison of MM Propositions with and without Taxes

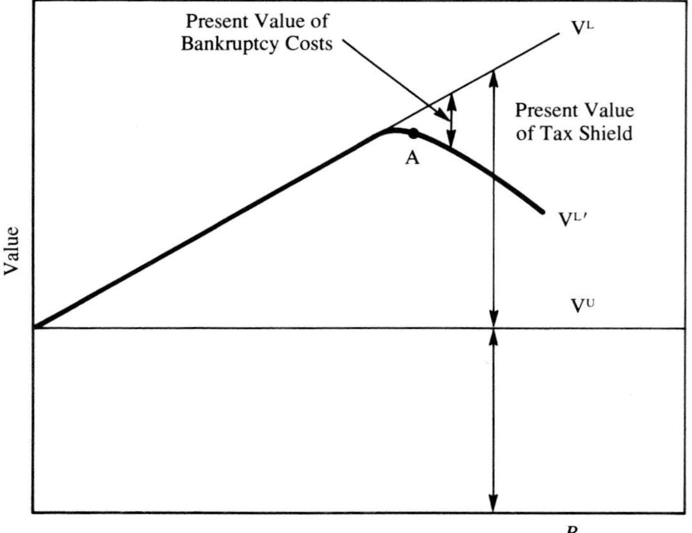

study by Jerold Warner (1976) examined the costs of bankruptcy and reorganization for a sample of eleven railroads between 1930 and 1955. The findings show that direct bankruptcy costs averaged 5.3 percent of the market value of the firms' securities over the 10-year period that these firms were in bankruptcy. These are the actual *ex post* costs, not the *ex ante* costs presented in Figure 9.5. The findings, then, seem to suggest that the effects of bankruptcy costs are not very important.

If we now allow progressive personal taxes to enter the picture, the MM proposition with taxes is changed. Suppose that an investor pays a higher marginal tax on income earned from owning the bonds of a corporation than from the firm's common stock. Any advantage that the firm derives from issuing debt results in a disadvantage to owners of the bonds. Therefore, the advantage to using debt may be less than what is suggested by equation (9.8). Miller (1977) shows that the value of the levered firm under the assumptions of personal taxes is

$$V^{\mathrm{L}} = V^{\mathrm{U}} + G_{\mathrm{L}} \tag{9.9}$$

$$\text{where } G_{\mathrm{L}} = \left[1 - \frac{(1 - T_c)(1 - T_{ps})}{(1 - T_{pd})}\right] B \tag{9.9$'$}$$

is the tax advantage, in which

T_{pd} = personal tax rate on income from owning bonds

T_{ps} = personal tax rate on income from owning stock

T_c = corporate tax rate

Notice that the original MM formulation assumed no personal taxes (or no differential). Given this assumption, the gain from leverage, G_{L}, simply becomes $T_c B$, which is the present value of the tax shield due to leverage.

If T_{pd} is greater than T_{ps}, the tax advantage G_{L} associated with debt is less than $T_c B$. Miller's model can thus be seen as an important step forward in the analysis of a firm's capital structure, as it incorporates both corporate and personal taxes. From this vantage point, Miller examines the equilibrium conditions that exist in the economy. If corporations adjust their supply of debt to satisfy clienteles of investors in different marginal tax brackets, then in equilibrium $(1 - T_c)(1 - T_{ps}) = 1 - T_{pd}$. The advantages of debt will have been completely eliminated, and we again have the MM irrelevance proposition. Clearly, Miller's equilibrium model has added more fuel to the controversy about the existence of an optimal capital structure.

Building on Miller's equilibrium model, however, De Angelo and Masulis show that with the existence of nondebt tax shields (i.e., depreciation, investment tax credits, *et cetera*), the corporate tax benefits of leverage disappear after some point. Their argument is that increasing use of debt increases the probability that the firm will have no taxable income. In such a case, the firm will realize no benefits from its nondebt tax shields, so any increase in debt beyond some point (the point being determined by the availability of alternative tax shields) provides no tax advantage. Consequently, there will be an optimal capital structure for each firm at debt ratios less than 100 percent.

E. Agency Costs

Agency costs arise in many situations in which a principal contracts with an individual (the agent) to perform some service. In the context of the theory of the firm, we can think of the principals as the owners of the firm and the agents as the managers. Michael Jensen and William Meckling (1976) have presented a theory of how these principal–agent relationships lead to what are known as *agency costs*. With debt in the capital structure, these costs can take any or all of the following forms:

1. The existence of debt in the capital structure may cause the firm to forego profitable investment opportunities. These deadweight losses are considered part of the agency cost associated with using debt.
2. The bondholders of the firm may expend funds to monitor the behavior of the firm's

managers. In addition, firm managers may bond themselves so that their performance does not erode the bondholders' claim on the firm. Both monitoring and bonding costs are considered part of the cost of the principal–agent relationship.

3. The costs may be associated with bankruptcy and reorganization, as discussed earlier.

All of the above agency costs contribute to a decline in the value of the firm. It is the responsibility of owners of the firm to decide how much leverage to use in order to balance the tax advantages and the agency costs associated with debt. The analysis of agency costs presents one more dimension in the controversy concerning the existence of an optimal capital structure.

IV. SUMMARY AND REVIEW

The various theories of capital structure that have been presented illustrate that there is no easy answer to the question of what the effects of capital structure are on the market value of the firm. The MM proposition of irrelevance has recently been revitalized in the form of *Miller's equilibrium*. That analysis and the many variations it has generated place the issue in a much richer economic environment. However, at the present time there is still no consensus on the issue, although a consideration of bankruptcy costs, agency costs, and a variety of other market imperfections may aid in a better understanding of the effects of capital structure.

QUESTIONS

1. Compare and contrast the net income and net operating income theories of capital structure.
2. Describe the interrelationships between sources and uses of funds.
3. Describe the foundation underlying the irrelevance-of-capital-structure argument.
4. What does it mean to say that investors can "undo" corporate leverage?
5. How does the existence of nondebt tax shields impact the irrelevance-of-capital-structure argument?

APPENDIX 9A LONG-TERM FINANCING: MARKETS AND INSTRUMENTS

For their long-term financing needs, corporations resort to the capital market where securities of more-than-one-year maturities are issued and traded. Such securities include corporate debt and equities, U.S. government notes and bonds, U.S. government agency issues, and state and local government issues. In this appendix, we shall briefly discuss the debt and equity instruments utilized by publicly traded corporations for long-term financing and the primary and secondary markets in which these financial instruments are originally issued and subsequently traded by the investing public.

A. Corporate Debt Instruments

Although it is customary to refer to fixed income securities with maturities ranging from 1–10 years as *notes* and those with maturities exceeding 10 years as *bonds,* we shall refer to both types of instruments as bonds because in most respects they are similar instruments. Both notes and bonds provide for intermediate interest payments (or coupon payments) and a final payment at maturity consisting of the face value of the financial instrument plus the final coupon payment. Coupon payments are usually made on a semiannual basis, although there are exceptions. For example, *zero coupon bonds* pay only the face value at maturity without intermediate payments. In this respect, zero coupon bonds are a form of *pure discount bonds*. Bearer bonds are issued and traded with the coupons attached which the holder presents for payment when due. For registered bonds, ownership is recorded and the payments are made to the registered owner. Both corporate and U.S. government debt securities are typically issued in $1,000 denominations, while bonds of state and local governments have a minimum denomination of $5,000. Corporate bonds may be secured by specific real assets of the issuing firm (*mortgage bonds*) or by the creditworthiness of the borrower (*debenture bonds*). Furthermore, debenture bonds may be categorized in terms of the priority of claims on the assets of the corporation in the event of default. That is, the *senior* claims known as unsubordinated debentures, have priority over the *junior* securities, known as subordinated debentures. Also, the majority of corporate debt issues are placed through underwriters, while those of various governments are sold to dealers on the basis of competitive bids.

The holders of corporate bonds are typically protected through a set of restrictions placed on the activities of the issuing firm. These restrictions are set forth in an *indenture* which, in addition to detailing the obligations of the issuing corporation, also designates a *trustee* charged with protecting the interests of the bondholders. The indenture requires, among other things, the following: (1) payments associated with the issue to be made in a timely manner; (2) limits to be placed on the amount of dividends that can be paid to equity shareholders and on the amount of additional debt the corporation may issue; (3) maintenance of specific values for various financial ratios; and (4) payability of the entire principal in the event of default.

In addition to protecting the interests of bondholders, the indenture may include *call provisions,* which give the issuing corporation the right to pay off all or part of the bonds during some specified time period prior to maturity. Call provisions are particularly valuable to firms that are forced to issue fixed income securities during periods of high interest rates. Should interest rates fall, such firms may retire high coupon issues through refinancing at more favorable cost terms. Finally, the indenture may also include a sinking fund provision which obligates the issuing firm to reduce the principal amount of a specific debt issue each year. Sinking funds may require direct action of the firm through the purchase of debt annually or indirect action through the appointed trustee. Either action effects the gradual retirement of the debt issue.

B. Corporate Equity Instruments

The value of the shareholders' interest carried on the firm's balance sheet (book value) is the sum of the common stock at par value, paid in capital and total retained earnings. Firms may issue two or more classes of *common stock*—for example, *Class A* that have priority to dividends but no voting rights and *Class B* that have voting rights but their claims to dividends are subordinated to those of Class A. In this respect, Class A shares are similar to *preferred stock,* which is an equity instrument with some attributes similar to debt securities. That is, the owners of preferred stock receive periodic payments stated as a percentage of the stock's par value which can be either fixed or floating. Preferred dividends take precedence over the dividends of common stock, in that such dividends must be paid before any amounts are distributed to common shareholders. However, unlike the case of bondholders, preferred shareholders cannot initiate bankruptcy proceeding if the firm pays no dividends. Also, unlike coupon payments, preferred dividends are not deductible for corporate income tax purposes.

Preferred shares are often issued with a call provision either at par or at some preestablished premium over par. *Participating* preferred stock entitles the holder to receive extra dividends if the earnings allow, and *convertible* preferred may be exchanged for another security, typically the firm's common stock, under prespecified conditions.

C. Primary Markets for Corporate Equities

New securities are sold (or placed) in the primary capital market. Such placements can be *private placements* or *public offerings*. In the former case, the issuing corporation may place a new issue with one or several institutional investors, who may or may not release it into the secondary market. Such private placements reduce costs and the time required for the issuing corporation to place the new issue. In the latter case, a new issue of securities may be placed through an investment banker. The investment banker may underwrite the entire issue or form a consortium of underwriters to perform the task. Such underwritings may consist of a *firm commitment* to purchase the shares from the issuing corporation at a specified discount and assume the risk of distributing (reselling) the issue in the secondary market. Alternatively, the investment banker may undertake a public offering on a *best efforts* agreement and not assume the risk of distribution into the secondary market. Still, a third way of placing new stock issues is the so-called *rights offering* which enables existing shareholders to maintain their proportionate share of ownership in the corporation. The firm can insure itself against the problems of undersubscription from present shareholders through a *standby agreement* with an investment banker. This arrangement ensures the purchase of the unsubscribed shares by the investment banker at an agreed-upon price.

Prior to an issue of securities, firms are required by law to submit specific documentation to the Securities and Exchange Commission (SEC). Because this registration procedure is both costly and time consuming for frequent issuers of securities, the SEC, beginning in 1982, offered corporations the option of registering securities for up to two years prior to their sale. This arrangement, known as *shelf registration,* has provided frequent issuers of securities with additional flexibility both in the timing of issues and in negotiations with investment bankers.

D. Secondary Markets for Corporate Equities

The major stock markets are organized exchanges where trading is conducted at a central location. There are two national stock exchanges in the United States, the New York Stock Exchange (NYSE) and the American Stock Exchange (AMEX)—with the NYSE being larger by far both in capitalization and in trade volume. Firms listed in these exchanges must meet certain criteria for acceptance. In addition, there are several regional stock exchanges, such as the Boston, Cincinnati, Midwest, Pacific, and Philadelphia Stock Exchanges. Member firms in the various stock exchanges specialize in various types of trading activity and are known as (1) *commission brokers,* who execute public orders for a fee, (2) *floor traders,* who trade strictly on their own account, and (3) *specialists,* who maintain limit orders on certain securities. A *limit order* is an order to buy or sell at or better than a given price if and when the security should reach that price. In contrast to limit orders, *market orders* are orders to buy or sell at the best currently available price.

In addition to the national and regional exchanges, there is the Over-the-Counter Market (OTC) which is not an organized exchange with a central location. Rather, it is a nationwide network of securities brokers and dealers, each of whom makes a market in a group of stocks. The network, known as the National Association of Securities Dealers Automated Quotations System (NASDAQ), provides information to subscribers instantaneously on all securities traded in the system.

ANNOTATED BIBLIOGRAPHY

Altman, E. I. "A Further Empirical Investigation of the Bankruptcy Cost Question." *Journal of Finance,* September 1984.

A good empirical study on borrowing and bankruptcy costs.

Durand, D. "Cost of Debt and Equity Funds for Business." In *The Management of Corporate Capital.* Ed. Ezra Solomon, 91–116. New York: Free Press, 1959.

The original exposition on the net income approach to capital structure.

Ferri, M. G., and W. H. Jones. "Determinants of Financial Structure: A New Methodological Approach." *Journal of Finance,* June 1979, 631–644.

An interesting approach to the debt–equity framework.

Haugen, R. A., and L. W. Senbet. "The Irrelevance of Bankruptcy Costs to the Theory of Optimal Capital Structure." *Journal of Finance,* June 1978, 383–394.

A new irrelevance argument for bankruptcy costs.

Jensen, M., and W. H. Meckling. "Theory of the Firm: Managerial Behavior, Agency Costs and Ownership Structure." *Journal of Financial Economics,* October 1976, 305–360.

A good paper on the agency framework for the analysis of capital structure.

Miller, M. H. "Debt and Taxes." *Journal of Finance,* May 1977, 261–275.

A very clear presentation of capital structure in the presence of corporate and personal income taxes.

Modigliani, F., and M. H. Miller. "The Cost of Capital, Corporation Finance and the Theory of Investment." *American Economic Review,* June 1958, 261–297.

The seminal paper on the topic of capital structure.

Warner, J. "Bankruptcy Costs, Absolute Priority and the Pricing of Risky Debt Claims." University of Chicago Working Paper, July 1976.

Am empirical study of the actual costs associated with reorganization and bankruptcy.

10

BASIC DEBT–EQUITY DECISIONS

I. INTRODUCTION

The firm has available to it a variety of sources for financing. Debt, preferred stock, and common stock are three external sources that the firm can use to raise money and finance its capital investment projects. Retained earnings is an internal source of funds. Why do firms choose one source over another? This debt–equity question will be examined using an approach known as EBIT (earnings before interest and taxes)–EPS (earnings per share) analysis. This approach is just one way to analyze the capital structure decision, which, again, involves tradeoffs between risk and return, the two concepts at the basis of financial decision making.

II. TYPES OF RISK

Risk, as it appears to the corporation, can be defined along various dimensions. The two kinds of risk that the firm faces are (1) *business risk,* which is the risk associated with the firm's operations, and (2) *financial risk,* which is the risk associated with incurring the fixed charges of debt or preferred stock.

For present purposes, we will define business risk as the uncertainty associated with a firm's future operating income or earnings before interest and taxes (EBIT). As mentioned in Chapter 2, variability in a firm's sales or income can be caused by changes in the general level of economic activity, by increased competition from other firms in the industry, or by just plain bad decisions by the management of the firm. Because there generally is no foreknowledge of these kinds of things, there will always be some uncertainty associated with the firm's level of EBIT. These factors and others contribute to the firm's basic business risk. As such, both stockholders and bondholders of the firm are subject to business risk, and it is the job of the financial manager to find the optimal capital structure that balances all risks. Business risk can be conveniently summarized by looking at the following kinds of variability:

1. *Demand variability.* Stable demand for a firm's product will, *ceteris paribus,* usually result in lower business risk.
2. *Sales price variability.* Lower variability in sales prices usually results in lower business risk.
3. *Input price variability.* High uncertainty in input prices can cause high business risk.
4. *Operating revenues variability.* Ability to adjust sales prices as input prices change can smooth fluctuations in operating revenues.
5. *Fixed costs.* Firms that have a high level of fixed costs (operating leverage) are subject to high business risk because a reduction in demand does not alter the payment of these costs.

This last point, the degree of operating leverage (DOL), is a convenient way to summarize one aspect of a firm's business risk. In fact, the degree of operating leverage used by a firm may be dictated by the industry in which it operates. For example, firms that are highly capital intensive, as well as those that employ highly skilled workers, usually have high fixed costs. If they are high, such costs may be the overriding reason for a firm's chosen degree of operating leverage.

III. CHARACTERISTICS OF FINANCING

A. Debt Financing[1]

A firm can borrow money by issuing a variety of debt instruments. For large corporations, the instrument usually issued is a *debenture,* which is an unsecured bond. The bond contract, or *indenture,* specifies the amount of money to be borrowed plus the interest payments the firm must make. In addition, the indenture usually includes some restrictive covenants. These may be restrictions on dividends, or on the issue of debt that is more senior to the current debt. As creditors of the firm, debtholders have priority over all other classes of security holders. That is, they are legally entitled to payment prior to preferred stockholders or common stockholders. While this may seem like a drawback to issuing debt, an important advantage is the fixed-claim nature of the bond contract; that is, bondholders receive only the amount stipulated in the indenture. Common stockholders, as residual claimants, share in all the benefits of any extraordinary earnings. In addition to this, the cost of debt is tax deductible, which lessens the eventual cost to the firm. Thus, the three important characteristics of debt are

1. it has priority over earnings,
2. it is a fixed claim, and
3. its cost is tax deductible.

B. Preferred Stock

Preferred stock has characteristics that lie somewhere between debt and common stock. The payment to preferred stockholders comes in the form of a preferred dividend that is a fixed dollar amount per share. However, some preferred shares can be *participating*—that is, if earnings are unusually high, preferred dividends may be increased. Preferred stockholders are paid before common stockholders, but after bondholders. However, unlike debt payments, preferred dividends can be postponed. In such instances, the firm is not exposed to the penalties of failing to make an interest payment. Also, unlike debt payments, preferred dividends are *not* tax deductible.

As with debt contracts, preferred stockholders are protected by a cumulative sharing agreement. In the event that preferred dividends are in arrears, no common dividends can be paid until all preferred dividends are paid. Preferred stock has no specified maturity (although it may be callable) and no voting rights. The characteristics of preferred stock can be summarized as follows:

1. Preferred stock has firm ownership with a fixed claim.
2. Postponement of preferred dividends is possible.
3. It has no specified maturity.
4. Preferred stockholders have no voting rights.
5. Its dividends are not tax deductible.

C. Common Stock

Firms can also raise money by selling common shares. The shares represent residual claims, and owners of these shares are owners of the firm. As owners, common shareholders have voting rights. That is, they have the opportunity to vote for members to be elected to the board of directors. As residual claimants on the firm's earnings, common stockholders are not guaranteed to receive cash payments. In terms of priority, they stand behind preferred stockholders and bondholders. However, in return for this, they are given limited liability. That is, as owners of a firm, common stockholders have their liability restricted to the amount of the original investment. If the firm fails, creditors have no recourse against the common stockholders of the firm. The distinguishing characteristics of common shares can be summarized as follows:

1. Common shares represent ownership claims.
2. Dividends are neither guaranteed nor even required.
3. Shareholders generally have voting rights.
4. Dividends are not tax deductible.

D. Retained Earnings

The earnings that remain after meeting all required payments are retained earnings. Retained earnings therefore differ from the three preceding forms of financing in that they represent an internal source of funds. In this respect, they do not involve the creation of new owners or creditors. However, because they are closely related to the firm's dividend policy, retained earnings may be highly variable. The distinguishing characteristics of retained earnings follow:

1. A high retained earnings policy may result in lower current dividends, but may increase future dividends.
2. Retained earnings do not result in dilution of ownership, as is the case with the sale of new shares.
3. Funds for retained earnings come from internal sources.
4. Issue costs associated with the sale of new stocks or bonds are avoided.

E. The "FRICTO" Framework

The packaging devices with which management can try to increase the company's value involve changing the prospective gains and risks associated with security issues and issuing them in the proportions that create the biggest total value. At one extreme, the common shareholders have the least security, the least protection from unfavorable events, but the most to gain if all goes well. Whatever is left over after prior commitments are satisfied is available to them. As total earnings expand, they generally get the entire increase once all other claims have been met. The least risky capital structure is one with all equity; but its disadvantage is that any gain must be shared widely.

The senior secured debtholders are at the other extreme. Their contract with the company contains a variety of protective devices that restrict the ability of the company to commit its resources contrary to their interests. They have the ability to go after the payments due them, seizing (after the appropriate legal skirmishes) the company's property, if necessary, to obtain their due. In exchange for this protection and security, however, the senior debtholders must normally give up the chance to share in the company's earnings over a certain specified amount—their interest payment. Thus, no matter how big the pie gets, the size of their piece is fixed in absolute terms; but it is well protected. The increase (or decrease) in the size of the pie goes to the account of less well-protected owners—who must wait for their share until the senior securities have been served. A capital structure containing debt is thus more risky, but the benefits do not need to be as widely shared.

The analysis of the position of the various parties is yet another variation on the risk-versus-return question. As one of the Rothchilds is alleged to have asked when he was approached for investment advice, "Young man, do you want to eat well or sleep well?" The more junior the security, the more it appeals to an eat-well investor. The more senior, the more it is a sleep-well security.

The factors that must be considered in appraising the risk and the return involved in the capital structure decision can be grouped into six headings—five major ones and a sixth, all-inclusive category that allows for the special aspects of situations. These factors, the first letters of whose names form the "FRICTO" acronym, are as follows:

*F*lexibility
*R*isk
*I*ncome
*C*ontrol
*T*iming
*O*ther

The listing is strictly mnemonic, not in order of relative importance.

The *income* component of "FRICTO" generally favors the senior security. *Risk* and *flexibility* almost always point toward common stock. The remaining elements can tip the scale in either direction depending on a company's circumstances and the present and prospective financial markets. Balancing these conflicting factors requires great skill and judgment.

IV. THE TARGET CAPITAL STRUCTURE

A. Operating Leverage

As mentioned earlier, a firm with a large amount of fixed costs is said to have a high degree of operating leverage (DOL). To illustrate this concept, let us consider the case of Minimax Company. Minimax is considering an expansion that will raise expected EBIT from $3,570,000 to $4,870,000 in the next three years. This will be accomplished by increased efficiency in production, resulting in a lower variable cost per unit produced. While the expansion might seem desirable, the new higher expected level of EBIT is also accompanied by a greater degree of risk. In addition, management feels that fixed costs will probably double with the proposed expansion. One way to examine the new risk is to compute the firm's new break-even point (i.e., the number of units sold such that total revenue equals total cost), as well as its degree of operating leverage. Table 10.1 provides the required information.

Under the current situation, the firm has fixed costs amounting to $2 million with a corresponding break-even point of 40,000 units. If the firm accepts the expansion, the break-even point becomes 60,000 units. Note also that the variability in EBIT is much larger with the proposed expansion; that is, the firm will face more business risk due to the greater variability in operating income. Let us suppose that the firm expects demand to be 100,000 units, with or without the proposed expansion. The situation may be summarized by means of the DOL, which is computed as

$$\text{DOL} = \frac{\text{Percentage change in EBIT}}{\text{Percentage change in output Q}}$$

Let us compute the current DOL and the DOL after expansion for an arbitrary change in demand of 20,000 units (i.e., from 100,000 to 120,000 units):

$$\text{DOL}_{\text{Current}} = \frac{\dfrac{\$4\text{M} - \$3\text{M}}{\$3\text{M}}}{\dfrac{120{,}000 - 100{,}000}{100{,}000}} = \frac{33\%}{20\%} = 1.65$$

$$\text{DOL}_{\text{Expansion}} = \frac{\dfrac{\$6\text{M} - \$4\text{M}}{\$4\text{M}}}{\dfrac{120{,}000 - 100{,}000}{100{,}000}} = \frac{50\%}{20\%} = 2.50$$

Note: M = millions of dollars

TABLE 10.1 Operating Information for Minimax Company

Current Situation: Selling price = $200.00; Variable costs = $150.00; Fixed costs = $2 million

Units Sold, Q	*Sales*	*Operating costs*	*EBIT*
20,000	$4 million	$5 million	−$1 million
40,000	$8 million	$8 million	0
60,000	$12 million	$11 million	$1 million
100,000	$20 million	$17 million	$3 million
120,000	$24 million	$20 million	$4 million

With Proposed Expansion: Selling price = $200.00; Variable costs = $100.00; Fixed costs = $6 million

Units Sold, Q	*Sales*	*Operating costs*	*EBIT*
20,000	$4 million	$8 million	−$4 million
40,000	$8 million	$10 million	−$2 million
60,000	$12 million	$12 million	$0
100,000	$20 million	$16 million	$4 million
120,000	$24 million	$18 million	$6 million

Thus, under the present conditions, for every 1-percent change in sales volume, there will be a 1.65-percent change in EBIT. However, if the firm decides to expand, a 1-percent change in sales volume will produce a 2.50-percent change in EBIT. This magnification effect (leverage) comes from the reduction in variable costs, as well as from the increase in fixed costs. Note that as long as we are above the break-even point, this magnification effect produces desirable results. However, it does not come without a cost, namely, the risk associated with having a higher break-even point. Even without considering the fixed costs associated with financing (i.e., debt), which we have left out of our analysis, we can clearly see that the particular DOL chosen will have an impact on a firm's capital structure decision. In the context of the FRICTO framework, once DOL is chosen, it must be weighed against and balanced with the amount of debt and equity to issue so as to maintain some degree of flexibility in other aspects of the firm's operations.

B. EBIT–EPS Analysis

To further elaborate the preceding balancing aspect of capital structure, let us consider the financing of Minimax's expansion using EBIT–EPS analysis, discussed earlier. Table 10.2 presents the relevant information for Minimax's capital structure decision. Note that the firm is earning $3 million before interest and taxes, and that its total capital structure of $15 million is entirely equity, represented by 500,000 shares of common stock and retained earnings. After allowing for taxes of 34 percent, earnings per share are $3.96, as shown in Part A of the table.

TABLE 10.2 The Minimax Company: An Example of a Capital Structure Decision

A. Present Situation: 1990

Earnings before interest and taxes (EBIT)	$3,000,000
Taxes (at rate of 34%)	1,020,000
Profit after taxes	$1,980,000
Earnings per share	$3.96
Dividend per share	$1.62
Capital structure	
Debt	$ –0–
Preferred stock	–0–
Common stock, par $10.00 (500,000 shares)	5,000,000
Earnings reinvested in the business	10,000,000
Total	$15,000,000

B. Problems: $5,000,000 are needed to take advantage of major new product.

	Anticipated EBIT w/o Expansion	*Additional EBIT from Expansion*	*Total Potential EBIT*
1994	$3,570,000	$1,300,000	$4,870,000

C. Financing Alternatives

1. $5,000,000 12% Debentures due in 20 years. Interest = $600,000 per year.
2. $5,000,000 50,000 shares of $100 10% cumulative preferred stock. Dividends = $500,000.
3. $5,000,000 91,000 shares of common stock, netting $55, an 8.3% discount (including all costs) from the present market price of $60 (15.2 P/E on 1990 EPS of $3.96). Dividends = $147,420.

Part B outlines the company's problem: it wishes to expand its assets to increase expected future growth. The expansion, which will cost $5 million, will increase anticipated earnings before interest and taxes (EBIT) from $3,570,000 to $4,870,000 in three years. Because the company does not have sufficient cash to finance the expansion from its present resources, it must raise $5 million in new funds. In late 1990 management was considering the following three alternatives outlined in Part C of the table.

Debenture Option. A debenture is an unsecured bond (as opposed to a mortgage, which is the term for a bond that has been granted security against real estate) that must be repaid in 20 years. The debenture option is the most demanding on the company's cash resources at the present time. Interest payments each year will amount to $600,000.

Preferred Stock Option. Another alternative the company has is to issue 50,000 shares of cumulative preferred stock. Investors who are interested in buying this security require only an annual dividend of 10 percent, which is payable at the discretion of the company's directors. The annual cash cost will be $500,000 for dividends. Unlike holders of a debenture, the preferred shareholders cannot go to court to enforce payment of their annual capital service because their contract does not allow them to. Instead, their main protection is the requirement that any preferred dividend that is skipped will have to be paid before the company can make any dividend payment at all to the common shareholders. In other words, the preferred dividends will cumulate if they are not paid. Finally, any time the company fails to pay four consecutive preferred dividends, the preferred shareholders will be entitled to elect two directors to the board in addition to the ten directors the common shareholders normally elect.

Common Stock Option. The third alternative being considered by management is the sale of 91,000 shares of common stock to the public. Management estimates that the company would actually receive only $55 a share, $5 less than the current market price of $60. Issuing costs and the need to offer the stock at a slight discount below market to attract new shareholders account for this 8.3-percent discount. The $60 current market price is 15.2 times the price–earnings ratio on the per-share current earnings. The dividend yield (dividends per share divided by market price) is 2.7 percent, given the present dividend of $1.62. Dividends on the new shares will be $147,420.

From the existing shareholders' point of view, the income considerations generally favor a company's issuing senior securities such as debt or preferred stock rather than more equity. The new funds will generally be invested to increase the company's operating earnings, its earnings after all costs except the servicing costs required for capital and taxes. New equity will share proportionately in all the earnings, both present and future. New senior securities will share only to a limited amount. If the new earnings are greater than the costs of the senior securities, the entire difference will accrue to the present equity shareholders.

V. COMPUTATIONAL PROCEDURES

A. Basic Mechanics

The calculations in Table 10.3 illustrate the impact on earnings per share (EPS) of the three options Minimax Company management is considering. The debenture option restates the results as though the new financing had been outstanding for the entire time. Beginning with the earnings before interest and taxes (EBIT), interest is deducted from the earnings stream. In the other two alternatives no tax deductions are allowed for capital charges, so the amount of the tax is calculated on the EBIT itself. Because of the interest expense, the profit after tax for the debt alternative is the lowest in absolute dollars.

Once interest has been subtracted, there are no further charges to be eliminated from the debt alternative before the earnings available for common stock are reached. Profits after taxes are also the same as earnings available for the common shareholders in the common-stock al-

TABLE 10.3 Impact on EPS, 1990

	Bonds	*Preferred*	*Common*
Number of shares	500,000	500,000	591,000
1990 pro forma EBIT	$3,000,000	$3,000,000	$3,000,000
Interest	600,000	0	0
Profit before taxes	$2,400,000	$3,000,000	$3,000,000
Taxes (34%)	816,000	1,020,000	1,020,000
Profit after taxes	$1,584,000	$1,980,000	$1,980,000
Preferred dividends	0	500,000	0
Available for common	$1,584,000	$1,480,000	$1,980,000
EPS	$3.17	$2.96	$3.35
Decline from $3.96	$0.79 = 20%	$1.00 = 25%	$0.61 = 15%
Payout on dividend of $1.62	51%	55%	48%
1994 projected EBIT	$4,870,000	$4,870,000	$4,870,000
Interest*	600,000	0	0
Profit before taxes	$4,270,000	$4,870,000	$4,870,000
Taxes (34%)	1,451,800	1,655,800	1,655,800
Profit after taxes	$2,818,200	$3,214,200	$3,214,200
Preferred dividend	0	500,000	0
Available for common	$2,818,200	$2,714,200	$3,214,200
EPS	$5.64	$5.43	$5.44
Decline from $6.43 "AzWuz" EPS	$0.79 = 12%	$1.00 = 16%	$0.99 = 15%
Payout on dividend of $1.62	29%	30%	30%
Minimum EBIT for zero EPS			
Available for common	$ 0	$ 0	$ 0
Preferred dividend	—	500,000	0
Profit after taxes	0	500,000	0
Taxes (34%)	0	257,576	0
Profit before taxes	0	757,576	0
Interest	600,000	0	0
Required EBIT	$ 600,000	$ 757,576	$ 0

*Because the purpose of this analysis is to show the effect of the different EBIT levels on alternative financing plans, it is *essential* to hold constant the financial charges for a given plan. Thus, even if changes in financing were anticipated by 1994 (such as by retirement of some of the debt or a new issue of stock), for the purpose of this analysis the financing charges used should be those of the *first full year*. An additional calculation would be required to allow for further changes in financial structure.

ternative. For the preferred-stock alternative, however, the amount available for the equity holders must be split between the preferred and the common equity. This is accomplished by subtracting the $500,000 required for preferred dividends from the profit-after-tax figure, leaving only $1.48 million available for the common equity. This is the smallest absolute amount of earnings for common shareholders.

For all three options, earnings available for the common shareholder must now be divided among the various claimants. Because in the common-stock alternative 91,000 additional shares will have to be issued, the total number of outstanding shares will be 591,000. It turns out that the common stock has the highest earnings per share at the $3 million EBIT level, a figure of $3.35. The debt alternative comes in next with $3.17, and the preferred-stock option is last with $2.96. In all the options, of course, there is a decline from the reported earnings, reflecting the claim on earnings of the new financing but including none of the new earnings expected from the investment.

Table 10.3 also shows what can be expected when the expansion project is completed in 1994. The extra earnings from the new investments are more than adequate to offset the cost of even the preferred dividends. With no additional equity shares issued, the preferred-stock alternative still does not outperform the common stock alternative, which, in turn, is less profitable than the debenture alternative.

B. EBIT–EPS Charts

While the calculations in Table 10.3 are useful, it is often helpful to be able to see the impact of the alternatives on income at a variety of EBIT levels. To show this, a chart relating EBIT to EPS can be prepared in the manner of Figure 10.1. That chart was developed using the figures from Table 10.3, but any two EBIT levels may be arbitrarily selected for the purpose of establishing two points on each curve plotted.

Note in the figure that the lines cross the horizontal axis at the points calculated for the zero EPS in Table 10.3. The common-stock line runs through the intersection of the axes at the zero point, the debenture line is offset to the right by $600,000 (the interest cost), and the preferred-stock line crosses at $757,576 (the preferred dividend adjusted to a before-tax figure). For each million dollars of EBIT, the common-stock line increases by $1.12 EPS. The other two lines rise faster, at $1.32 per million dollars of EBIT. The debt and preferred-stock lines are parallel because they have the same number of shares outstanding.

Because of their higher slopes ($1.32 versus $1.12) and intercepts to the right, the lines charting the effect on income of the senior financing alternatives intersect the line that describes the common-stock financing. This feature is a graphic display of the point made previously that senior financing can result in a lower starting point for the common shareholder but, once earnings begin to move upward, EPS move upward more rapidly. That is what is meant by the term *leverage:* the higher the slope of one line relative to another, the greater the relative change and, therefore, the greater the leverage. In the United Kingdom, this phenomenon is known as *gearing,* by analogy to a similar mechanical principle.

When EBIT reaches a level above $3,900,600 in the debt-issue alternative, and a level of $4,925,000 in the preferred-stock alternative, the earnings per share under the senior security alternatives are higher than under the common-stock route. That is, above these points, leverage is "attractive" or "favorable" as compared with its value in the common-stock plan. Table 10.4 shows how the EBIT equivalence points between alternatives can be calculated precisely.

It is interesting to note the nature of the dilution in EPS that is expected to occur as a result of the various alternative schemes. For example, from Table 10.3 the expected dilution of earnings per share associated with the issuance of debt is $0.79 compared to what the EPS would have been with no new financing (the so-called "AzWuz" EPS). This, of course, is expected to happen regardless of the level of the earnings before interest and taxes. The $0.79 in earnings dilution represents the interest cost after taxes [$600,000(1 − .34)] divided by the old number of shares. It should also be stressed here that this dilution is more significant at low levels of EBIT than at high levels, as Table 10.3 clearly demonstrates. Moreover, due to the contractual nature of the dividend payment on the preferred stock, the dilution effect of the preferred-stock alternative is similar to that associated with the issue of debentures.

When it comes to the dilution of earnings per share associated with the common-stock alternatives, however, we notice a different behavior. Because the new common shareholders are entitled to their share of 15 percent (91,000/591,000) of the company's profits, the earnings of Minimax are diluted at all levels of earnings

FIGURE 10.1 EBIT–EPS Chart

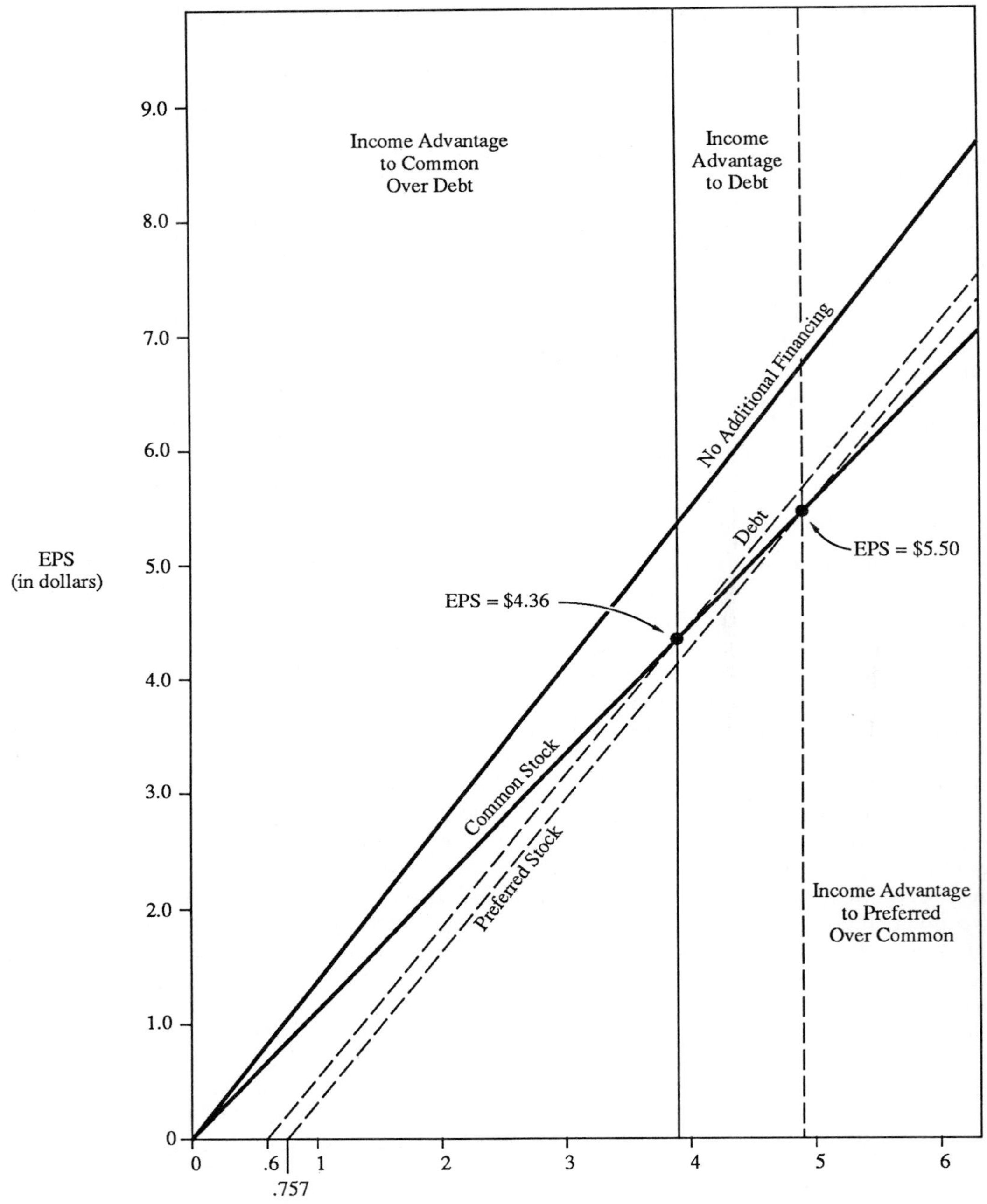

TABLE 10.4 Calculation of EPS Equivalence Points, 1994

Formula

$$\text{EPS} = \frac{(\text{EBIT} - \text{Interest})\ (1 - \text{Tax Rate}) - \text{Preferred Dividends}}{\text{Common Shares Outstanding}}$$

Debt vs. Equity

$$\frac{(\text{EBIT} - 600)\ (.66)}{500} = \frac{(\text{EBIT} - 0)\ (.66)}{591}$$

which yields

$$\text{EBIT} = \$3{,}900{,}600$$

Substitution of this value into the EPS formula yields

$$\text{EPS} = \$4.36$$

Preferred Equity

$$\frac{(\text{EBIT} - 0)\ (.66) - 500}{500} = \frac{(\text{EBIT} - 0)\ (.66)}{591}$$

which yields

$$\text{EBIT} = \$4{,}925{,}000$$

Substitution of this value into the EPS formula yields

$$\text{EPS} = \$5.50$$

before interest and taxes. Hence, the actual dollar effect of the dilution associated with the issue of new common equity varies as the EBIT changes, becoming larger at higher levels of EBIT. In other words, whereas the senior-claim securities create *constant dollar* dilution, the common-stock alternative creates *constant proportionate* dilution.

The equivalence points noted in Figure 10.1 may be interpreted as the points where the constant dollar dilution created by the issuance of debentures or the issuance of preferred stocks equals the constant proportionate dilution from the additional common stock.

The same methodology is used when a company has existing debt or other senior securities outstanding. In preparing a chart or in calculating an equivalence, it is necessary to include the appropriate allowances for the existing securities as well as for new ones. Thus, if Minimax already had interest charges of $120,000, all of the lines of Figure 10.1 would be shifted to the right by $120,000, and this amount would have to be included appropriately in all the calculations shown in Tables 10.3 and 10.4.

By itself, the EBIT–EPS chart is not a magic device that will tell the decision maker which financing alternative to choose. It does, however, aid in the analysis by indicating relative rates of change, positions, and points of relative attractiveness. For example, after the new capital is raised, earnings under the debt alternative will immediately be higher at EBIT equal to $4.87 million (the projected level of EBIT for 1994 when debt is compared to common stock). For the case of preferred versus common stock, the latter option shows a higher EPS figure at the estimated EBIT of $4.87 million in 1994.

Under this scenario, issuance of debt is the best alternative, issuance of additional common stock is the second best, and the preferred-stock alternative is the least attractive. However, in the near term the EPS will be highest with common-stock issuance. Thus, we are reminded once again that all potential benefits of leverage must be weighed against the potential costs in making decisions about the capital structure of the firm.

C. Financial Leverage

The concept illustrated by Figure 10.1 is known as financial leverage. *Financial leverage* refers to the responsiveness of shareholder income for a given change in EBIT and is created by the use of financial instruments that have fixed charges. Firms that are financed entirely by equity will have a degree of financial leverage equal to one. That is, for every 1-percent change in EBIT, there will be a 1-percent change in EPS. Debt or preferred stock will move this factor away from unity. The degree of financial leverage is given by

$$\text{DFL} = \frac{\text{Percentage change in EPS}}{\text{Percentage change in EBIT}}$$

To illustrate, consider a 10-percent change in EBIT from an original level of \$3,900,600. At this point both common stock and debt yield an EPS equal to \$4.36. Thus, because for both of these,

$$\text{EPS} = \frac{(\text{EBIT} - \text{Interest})(1 - \text{Tax Rate})}{\text{Common shares outstanding}}$$

it follows that

$$\text{DFL}_{\text{stock}} = \frac{(4.79 - 4.36)/4.36}{10\%}$$

$$= 1.0 \textit{ (under stock financing)}$$

and

$$\text{DFL}_{\text{debt}} = \frac{(4.87 - 4.36)/4.36}{10\%}$$

$$= 1.17 \textit{ (under debt financing)}$$

Therefore, if the firm uses debt, a 1-percent change in EBIT will produce a 1.17-percent change in earnings per share, better than financing by issuance of stock. Note, however, that financial leverage works in both directions: if EBIT were to fall by one percent, then the percentage decline in EPS would be larger for the debt-financing alternative. This is just one of the risks associated with the use of financial instruments such as debt or preferred stock.

The logical extension of these leverage concepts is known as the *degree of total leverage,* which is defined as

$$\text{DTL} = \frac{\text{Percentage change in EPS}}{\text{Percentage change in output (Q)}}$$

or

$$\text{DTL} = \text{DOL} \times \text{DFL}$$

Let us consider the current (1990) situation of Minimax Company, with an expected sales demand of 100,000 units (i.e., EBIT equal to \$3 million) and bonds used to finance the expansion. From Table 10.3 the interest expense will be \$600,000. The two basic formulas we will require are

$$\text{DOL} = \frac{\text{Sales} - \text{Variable Cost}}{\text{Sales} - \text{Variable Cost} - \text{Fixed Cost}}$$

and

$$\text{DFL} = \frac{\text{EBIT}}{\text{EBIT} - \text{I}}$$

Therefore, for Minimax, at an EBIT level of \$3 million (using figures from Table 10.1),

$$\text{DOL} = \frac{\$20 - 15}{\$20 - 15 - 2} = 1.67$$

$$\text{DFL} = \frac{\$3{,}000{,}000}{\$3{,}000{,}000 - 600{,}000} = 1.25$$

Hence, if Minimax were operating at an EBIT level of \$3,000,000 with bonds financing the expansion, the percentage change in EPS for a given percentage change in output would be

$$DTL = 1.67 \times 1.25 = 2.09$$

Under these assumptions, if output were to rise by 1 percent, then EPS would rise by 2.09 percent. As is evident, financial leverage magnifies the already present degree of operating leverage. Unfortunately, financial theory has yet to develop an accepted way of simultaneously determining the optimal DOL and DFL, although in its pure form it suggests that financing does not alter value regardless of the DOL.

D. Cash Flow and Debt Service

An important consideration in determining the target capital structure is the ability of the firm to meet its fixed obligations. Such obligations include servicing outstanding debt (principal and interest), preferred stock dividends, and lease payments. Leases are discussed in Appendix 10A, but for now it is sufficient to recognize that lease payments are contractual obligations (as are interest and principal payments on debt) and thus should be included in this analysis. Because fixed obligations must be paid in cash, we thus look to the size and variability of the firm's cash flows in order to determine its ability to meet those obligations as they come due. In general, the greater the level and stability of the firm's cash flows, the greater the firm's debt capacity.

A particularly useful tool for measuring debt capacity is the coverage ratio which may be constructed in several ways. The *Times Interest Earned* (TIE) ratio is obtained by dividing EBIT by annual interest. Returning to Minimax, given an expected 1994 EBIT of $4,870,000 and interest of $600,000 under the debt option, the firm's TIE ratio would be 8.1 × (= $4.87m ÷ $0.6m). Realized EBIT can be as much as 88 percent below projections before Minimax is unable to meet its interest payments from operating earnings. Furthermore, to the extent that cost of goods sold contains an allowance for depreciation, the TIE ratio understates the ability of the firm to meet its fixed charges. That is, cash flow is the primary variable of interest in determining debt capacity, thus deductions for depreciation that enter the calculation of EBIT must be added back. For example, if Minimax's 1994 projected EBIT includes depreciation of $1 million, the ratio of operating cash flow to interest charges would be 9.8 × (= $5.87m ÷ $.6m).

The TIE ratio can be easily modified to measure the firm's ability to meet all of its fixed obligations from operating cash flow. To do so, the denominator is augmented by including required sinking fund payments, lease payments, or preferred dividends.

VI. OTHER CONSIDERATIONS

A. Explicit Costs

Up to now, it has been argued that above the equivalence point senior securities have a less unfavorable impact on income and more favorable impact on growth of earnings per share than common stock does. The latter part of this statement is true without qualification; the former needs a minor elaboration. By way of illustration, it has already been pointed out that Minimax's 1990 pro forma earnings per share under the preferred-stock alternative are less than under the common-stock option.

It is easy to determine whether a senior issue will cause more immediate dilution of earnings than a common issue will by comparing the immediate, or explicit, costs of the two securities. The *explicit* cost in absolute dollars is that amount which must be earned immediately on the net proceeds of the issue in order to avoid dilution of the existing earnings per share. It is more usual, however, to express the cost in percentage terms rather than absolute dollar ones. The rate is the absolute dollar cost divided by the proceeds of the issue.

Explicit costs are not difficult to determine. In fact, except for some minor issuing costs, they are generally the after-tax cost of interest for a debt alternative, the dividend cost of a preferred stock, and the "earnings yield" (which is the reciprocal of the price–earnings ratio) for a common-stock issue.

The exposition suggests the following general rule: *in considering a choice of securities, the immediate adverse impact on income will be lowest for the security with the lowest explicit cost.*

Thus, if The Minimax Company had enjoyed a price–earnings ratio of, say, 50 times, the explicit cost of equity (earnings–price ratio) would have been 1/50, or 2 percent. This would have been less than the 7.92 percent for the debt, and the immediate impact of the equity issue would have been less severe than the impact of the debt. Consequently, the equity line in Figure 10.1 would have been more sloped upward than shown—that is, the EPS equivalence between the debt and common-stock alternatives would have been much farther to the right. It is a high price–earnings ratio that has permitted high-flying companies to issue equity with less immediate dilution than debt would have caused them to have.

On the other hand, if a company is really a high-growth company, its EBIT will increase rapidly, pushing quickly to the right in Figure 10.1. Because the slope of the equity line is always less than that of the debt due to the greater number of shares outstanding, it will not be long before the EBIT moves to the right of the EPS equivalence point. After this, a higher EPS will be shown if the debt alternative has been taken.

Properly evaluating the short- and long-term requirements for good earnings in these instances is a very difficult task. The EPS advantage may be only a short one. But even a short advantage may be necessary to get the company through a difficult stage of its growth. It may well be worth taking, even at some possible cost in the long run.

B. Hidden Costs

Using only explicit costs as a guide in the cost of financing ignores costs that the shareholder may experience, but which are not recorded on the income statement of the company. These costs, which are sometimes referred to as *hidden,* or *joint,* costs, are those changes of value that appear in the shareholder's portfolio as a result of the financing decision. While the explicit cost of additional debt is almost always less than the explicit cost of additional equity in any normal circumstances where a profit is being shown, the total costs, including the hidden costs, for the two methods can be equal. Occasionally, the hidden cost of debt might even be greater than the cost of equity. Hidden costs are thus very important to consider, but they are equally difficult to identify.

If a company's price–earnings ratio or multiple remains constant after a financing, then the impact on the market value of the shareholder's portfolio will reflect only the explicit costs of the financing. Whichever alternative has the lowest explicit cost will produce the smallest loss in the portfolio value. Over time, regardless of the immediate impact, the alternative with the smallest increase in the number of shares outstanding will have the greatest favorable impact on the current shareholder's asset position if the company is growing.

The assumption that the price–earnings multiple will remain constant is the critical one. Suppose it drops under one or more of the alternatives? Then it will not be possible to use simple rules about immediate explicit cost or longer term dilution to decide which solution will be the best one. If the price–earnings ratio drops because the shareholders are worried about the risk of the additional debt, it is possible that the alternative that produces the highest earnings per share will also be the one that generates the lowest market price when the change in the price–earnings ratio is taken into account. At least, the relative attractiveness of the option will be less than indicated solely by the earnings-per-share differences.

Because it is the common shareholders whose point of view we are taking, it is important that the ultimate effect on them be considered. Looking only at the intermediate effect on EPS is not enough. Accordingly, both the earnings and the price–earnings ratio must be evaluated. In other words, the manner in which the capital structure of a company is organized may have an impact on the market value of a share of the common stock—on the cost of equity—reducing the price–earnings ratio more than proportionately to an increase in earnings. Thus, equity costs are affected not only when new equity is issued: an issue of senior securities may have an impact on equity costs, which is why this type of cost is called a *joint* cost by some authors. If the negative effect is greater than the advantages offered by less dilution, the total result is to raise the cost of financing to the company; but if the increase in capital cost for the equity is less than the increase in earnings offered, the overall cost has been reduced.

What might cause changes in the price–earnings ratio? Why might it be lower when the company is financed one way than when it is financed another? The answers to these questions involve considerations of risk and flexibility in capital structure financing.

C. Risk

Risk events are defined, somewhat arbitrarily, to be those potentially adverse, irregularly recurring events whose impact can be evaluated with some degree of accuracy and which might interfere with the orderly servicing of financial obligations. Management may not know when the next risk event will occur, but it has had experience in dealing with risk events in the past, knows what actions are likely to be required to combat them, knows some of their danger signals, and can often minimize their impact. To use an organic analogy, risky events are like colds rather than serious lung problems. In the aerospace jargon, these would be "known unknowns."

The most common types of risk situations are business cycles, both on the downswing and the upswing. These cyclical expansions and contractions begin creating strains as a company strives to meet demands of customers who, in good times, want delivery yesterday. Then demand dries up, and the company must scramble to trim back its operations, conserve its resources, and prepare for the increase in demand which usually will follow. Management has little control over when a change in the cycle will occur, although from accumulated information and experience in dealing with such situations, it can estimate the magnitude of the impact that type of development will have on earnings and cash. Hence, at least the ability of the company to service its senior securities and maintain its dividend can be estimated.

Risk problems do not usually call for additional capital; the challenge they present is the orderly management of existing obligations.

D. Flexibility

Flexibility aspects of the capital structure decision are very similar to risk problems and are analyzed in much the same way. A firm's financial *flexibility* may be defined as its ability to quickly restructure its internal uses of funds and to raise new funds in order to meet a major need for additional funds created by a crisis. Flexibility is thus involved with both sides of the balance sheet.

In contrast to a risk problem, a flexibility crisis involves one of the large number of improbable but possible events that would threaten the basic structure of the business. These are events with which the firm has had little historic experience and hence has no real knowledge of its ability to respond. It is "a thing which goes bump in the night," in the words of the Scottish Book of Common Prayer.

The differences between risk and flexibility problems are solely of degree, the risk event usually being resolved by conversion of earning assets to cash whereas the flexibility crisis requires the conversion of cash to earning assets. Thus, one firm's crisis may be a normally recurring risk problem for another. At the extremes risk and flexibility questions can be clearly distinguished, but toward the middle of the spectrum they blend together. A normal business cycle can usually be analyzed as a risk; a major depression is more likely to present a flexibility crisis. Typical of flexibility problems that have occurred in recent years was the bankruptcy of Rolls Royce, which created a flexibility crisis for Lockheed. Similarly, a number of firms depending on the commercial paper markets experienced flexibility problems when Penn Central Railroad failed. Others have been severely threatened by the sudden introduction of government controls or by devaluations. Restrictions on the availability of petroleum products presented many companies with unexpected and difficult problems. Failures of banks such as

Penn Square or of major customers have shaken financial institutions. In the pharmaceutical industry, the firm of Johnson and Johnson experienced a flexibility crisis leading to its failure when one of its products allegedly contained cyanide and killed several consumers. These are all sudden, obviously unforeseen events.

E. Analyzing the Flexibility Position

Because of the unique nature of each firm's potential flexibility crises, it is difficult to be precise in proposing universal rules for analyzing them. First, management must try to identify as specifically as possible the nature of such risks. Are they product-life problems, such as might be found in high-technology business? Are they price-erosion threats? Are they difficulties with receivables collection or inventory? Prolonged labor unrest? Are they transfer-of-payment problems or international monetary disorders of the type that might confront an international company? Might the company be subject to pollution regulations that will require substantial compliance funds? Once the more likely flexibility problems have been identified (and management must be continually alert to changes in prospective flexibility problems), management must do its best to estimate their effect on the financial circumstances of the company. Clearly, the more difficult it is for the company to rearrange its internal financial operations to generate the funds necessary to meet a flexibility crisis, the more important it is for the company to maintain easy access to outside funds—through debt, equity, or use of cash balances set aside for emergencies and other kinds of extraordinary events.

An example may help illustrate the point. The management of a major producer of automotive parts identified a number of events that it thought constituted the major flexibility problems the company faced. These included the obsolescence of a major product line, substantial price cuts by competitors attempting to buy market share, major additional requirements for research and development, major additional requirements for capital investment to attain the level of sales and profits expected, and failure of the company's foreign subsidiaries to perform effectively. Close examination showed that in all probability the most serious financial problems would be caused by product obsolescence, price problems, and cash drains of the foreign operations. The other problems, in the judgment of management, would not cause a flexibility crisis.

The serious problems were explored in great detail. Using the best information available about what might happen (but never had happened), management tried to judge the company's ability to marshal its internal resources to provide the funds necessary to survive these crises. Funds not available internally would have to be raised from the outside. Management found that $30 million in outside funds would likely be required to combat either the obsolescence of a major product or a degenerating price situation. Foreign problems would require $20 million more.

A sufficient reserve of debt to combat all these problems, plus a small reserve for odds and ends, would absorb all debt that management believed the company could acquire from its financial sources. In fact, the small proportion of debt presently on the books might have to be refinanced with equity. Moreover, plans to borrow additional debt to support prospective growth would certainly have to be abandoned. But both of these actions were unattractive because issuing additional stock would not only dilute earnings but also threaten the control enjoyed by the major shareholders.

Management concluded that the likelihood of one of the flexibility crises being realized was fairly strong, strong enough to justify keeping some insurance in the form of debt capacity. However, the probability of two major simultaneous crises occurring was so much less that full insurance was not required. The probability of more than two occurring simultaneously was so small that in management's judgment it did not justify any further sacrifice of current benefits. Thus, in balancing the possible dangers of lack of resources against the immediate sacrifice of income, management decided that the company should retain sufficient flexibility in the form of debt reserves to protect against one $30 million problem and to go some way toward another major problem or a combination of minor problems. Accordingly, the debt reserve was set at $45 million.

F. The Minimax Situation

Although sufficient information has not been presented about the Minimax Company to permit an in-depth analysis of its internal flexibility or of the nature of the flexibility problems that might arise in its environment, a brief, general comment is possible. As was noted in the discussion of risk, servicing of proposed debt requirements is barely sufficient in severe cyclical conditions. In the case of Minimax, the basic nature of the company's growth suggests that it should place a premium on maintaining easy access to outside funds to finance its debt requirements, which will probably exceed any generation of internal funds. Fortunately, the company enjoys a price–earnings multiple of 15.2, which is a healthy one for a small company whose stock is probably traded inactively. A major issue of common stock in a time of poor earnings or in a poor stock market could result in a significant erosion of market price.

It is thus doubtful that Minimax would have much room to maneuver if a flexibility crisis arose. The situation would be even more severe if the flexibility crisis coincided with a risk problem. Management must decide carefully, therefore, whether the gain of $0.20 (= $5.64 − $5.44) in earnings per share by 1994 shown in Table 10.3 is sufficient to justify the commitment of a major portion of the company's flexibility reserves.

G. Timing

Timing decisions include two major capital structure questions. One is in regard to the sequence in which the debt and equity issues should be arranged. The other, which involves only the debt decision, is whether to raise long-term debt immediately or to defer a long-term issue by using one or more short-term arrangements as interim financing in the expectation that a more favorable long-term debt market will appear. In either context, the timing decision does not refer to the speed with which an issue can be made.

Unlike income considerations, which usually favor debt, or risk and flexibility considerations, which usually favor equity, the timing decision does not *ex ante* favor either debt or equity. The usual problem results from the temptation to wait until later to issue all long-term forms of financing. Interest rates will fall; they have never been so high! Earnings will rise, the P/E ratio will certainly rise with it, and the market price will soar! The temptation is frequently to extemporize by issuing short-term debt to defer the problem for a period of months. Appendix 10A discusses in more detail some of the issues pertinent to timing.

VII. ADDITIONAL BASIC DEBT–EQUITY DECISIONS

The decision to issue debt–equity or preferred stock can depend on factors other than those presented in the EBIT–EPS analysis. Some of these factors are (1) the sequencing of issues, (2) the term structure of the firm's debt, and (3) control. Each of these will be briefly discussed in turn.

A. Sequencing of Issues

The tendency to delay equity issues is strong. In Minimax's case, for instance, a strong increase in earnings is expected by 1994, whereas an equity issue in 1990 would not capitalize on the full benefits of the increased earnings of the new project. Therefore, the longer Minimax can wait, the higher the price should be if the price–earnings multiple remains at 15.2. Furthermore, the optimist will argue, as earnings pick up strongly, the price–earnings ratio may increase. By waiting, the company should enjoy a price enhanced by an increase in both earnings and the price–earnings multiple, a "double-whammy," which would significantly reduce dilution.

In 1994, of course, the argument for delay may run along different lines. Then, an issue of stock should be further deferred because its purpose will be merely to "roll over" existing short-term debt. However, the purchaser of new equity issues is not enthusiastic about such a purpose because it does not promise additional earnings. All it promises is stability. Therefore, he or she would argue, debt financing should be continued until the company can go to the market with a good story to tell about prospective earnings from its investment plans.

At this point, the argument outlined in the first paragraph is readvanced—and equity is somehow never attractive. The argument tends to run in circles, with jam yesterday and jam tomorrow but never jam today.

When a company is contemplating a sequence of debt and equity issues, which is often the case if equity is under consideration for a growing company, it is important for the management to realize that it is not considering *whether* to issue equity but rather *when*. The company's risk posture and flexibility position, as evaluated by management, call for equity. That decision has been made. The question is whether a delay is likely to save enough dilution and to enhance the market value of the present shareholders enough to justify the shareholders' being asked to take the risk of a delay. Prices and price-multiples go down as well as up. Market conditions deteriorate as well as improve. Unexpected problems arise in delivering upon earnings promises. The judgment is whether the extra potential benefits in price justify the potential risk and flexibility problems of delaying an equity issue.

B. Term Structure of Debt

Analyzing the term structure of a company's debt, deciding when to go long and when to temporize with a short-term issue in the hope that long-term rates will fall, is somewhat simpler than the debt–equity sequence decision. There are some aspects of risk and flexibility involved, of course. For example, the banks might find themselves in a credit pinch and be reluctant to renew short-term credit. Or the company's financial position might degenerate, making the conversion to long-term debt impossible. But relative to the basic debt or equity question, the problem is primarily one of cost, with only a mild seasoning of exposure to risk.

The cost of a poor term-structure decision is more than it might appear to be because of two factors. First, the differential cost of a mistake in issuing long-term debt is more than the interest differential between the actual issue and the lower cost opportunity that was missed. On a $10 million loan, for example, the difference between 6 percent and 7 percent is $100,000 a year before taxes and $66,000 after taxes, a total of $1.32 million if it is a 20-year loan with no sinking fund. This $1.32 million must also be financed in order to keep the capital available to the company at the equivalent level under both options. Thus, interest (or other costs) on this additional financing must be allowed for, and so on. Second, in order to keep the debt–capital ratio the same, some proportion of these extra costs must be financed with equity.

Great care in considering the future of interest rates is clearly required when making the decision to issue long-term securities in the debt market. It is particularly important, in the current financial situation, to avoid easy generalities such as, "The rates haven't ever been higher, so let's wait. . . ." This is a correct decision at the peak, of course, but on the road up many companies (as well as the federal government) missed opportunities to lengthen their debt maturities at interest rates that in retrospect are bargains.

C. Control

The control aspects of a financial decision generally favor issuing debt. Even in those situations when the immediate explicit cost of debt, and hence the immediate dilution of earnings, is less with debt than with equity, an equity issue always dilutes the voting control of the existing shareholders. The importance of voting control varies widely, however. It is particularly important in a few relatively easy-to-identify circumstances.

Control is not apt to be important in a company whose shareholder group is widely spread and does not contain significant voting blocks. For example, the largest holders of American Telephone and Telegraph are thought to control no more than a percent or two of the shares outstanding. A company's largest holders are often "nominees," brokerage firms whose customers do not elect to have their shares registered in their own individual names but who would certainly vote their shares individually if a proxy contest for control of management should break out.

Control is much more important when management itself or its supporters hold significant blocks of stock. In that case, a control problem will arise if management detects that a potentially hostile investor is accumulating a significant position.

In the more common case, where a significant proportion of ownership is in the hands of an individual, a family, or a business group, control conflicts are apt to arise with particular virulence at three points:

1. When the company is completely owned by the group, and a stock would admit outsiders for the first time.
2. When the financing decision would lower the controlling group's ownership to less than 50 percent.
3. When the proportion held would be reduced to some vulnerable level, often believed to be 20–25 percent of the ownership.

VIII. SUMMARY AND REVIEW

A company's capital structure affects its shareholders' income. Other things being equal, the higher earnings per share the shareholder enjoys, the better off the shareholder will be. However, "other things" are not always equal. The company's ability to survive in risk circumstances and its flexibility to fend off major crises play an important role in its shareholders' well-being. Because the higher-income debt route often increases a firm's exposure to risk and decreases its flexibility, the impact of the attendant dangers on the price–earnings ratio must be evaluated in order to assess whether higher but riskier earnings on the market price and hence on the shareholder's value are desirable.

Timing decisions are an important aspect of a capital structure policy. Although neutral with respect to the long-term debt and equity policy of a company, they may dictate temporary departures from the policy in order to take advantage of the market structure for security issues. Control of timing is essential to a company.

Most companies are faced with a host of other factors relevant to the capital structure decision, any one of which may be important enough to tip the balance if the scales are otherwise relatively evenly weighted. It is not possible to enumerate all of these, but a few of the most common ones deserve mention.

The speed and certainty with which proceeds are required may incline a firm to issue private debt rather than equity or even public debt at a given time. An unsettled market may incline management toward taking the private route if things can be negotiated rapidly and with a minimum of documentation. The question is more properly one of timing: the company would probably be better off utilizing short-term financing until markets stabilize, but circumstances do not always permit such luxuries. For example, in a period of rapidly rising rates management may think that the slightly higher rate paid immediately for a private placement may be lower than the public one would ultimately be by the time underwriting has been effected.

Another consideration is the desire of the owners of a private company to create a market for its stock. Even though the firm's financial needs might be adequately fulfilled by debt issues, it is generally thought that a company will have a more favorable reception for its common stock if the proceeds are to be used for the company's benefit. Thus, an initial issue of stock by the company to finance internal requirements may help the price of the issue. Later on, or maybe even simultaneously, the owners may issue part of their personal holdings in the company. Or, it may merely be important to have the stock traded for estate valuation and perhaps diversification purposes at a later time.

Similarly, owners usually desire to broaden the market for the stock, so that there will be sufficient investor interest to form a reasonably sized pool of willing buyers and sellers. If the number of publicly traded shares is too low—as a rule of thumb, below 200,000 to 400,000 shares—brokerage houses will not have sufficient motivation to create a market for the security or to call it to the attention of their clients.

Then the stock will probably trade at a lower price than it would with a more active market.

The remedy may be to issue additional stock to the public, which will create the opportunity for more trading and perhaps a higher price. When such opportunity is foreseen as likely, management will be strongly tempted to issue stock regardless of the company's debt capacity and the additional earnings-per-share debt would bring. Indeed, if stock is issued, the market price may well increase as a result of the enhancement of the price–earnings ratio.

A sound analytical approach is a necessary ingredient for a wise capital structure plan. It is not sufficient, however. Neither is the necessary careful assessment of a company's past record and future prospects. The final necessary element, which together with the other items is sufficient, is the judgment as to whether the rewards justify the risks. Two managerial staffs might be in total agreement on the first two considerations. Because one staff was more sensitive to risk than the other, however, the final decision of the two might be entirely different. One would tend to eat well and the other would sleep well.

NOTES

1. See also Appendix 9A for additional details on the sources of long-term financing.

QUESTIONS

1. Compare and contrast internal and external sources of funds.
2. Distinguish between business and financial risk.
3. Discuss the factors that must be considered in appraising the risk (return trade-offs) involved in the capital structure decision.
4. What are the differences between explicit and hidden costs?

PROBLEM

1. A newly established manufacturing firm is considering three mutually exclusive alternatives for financing the acquisition of its productive facilities.
   1. Issue 1,000,000 shares of common stock at $20 per share.
   2. Issue 750,000 shares of common stock at $20 per share and $5,000,000 of bonds with a 10-percent coupon.
   3. Issue 500,000 shares of common stock at $20 per share and $10,000,000 of bonds with a 10-percent coupon.

   The management expects earnings before interest and taxes (EBIT) to be $2.5 million. Given this information, you are to:

   a. conduct an EBIT/EPS analysis of the three alternatives assuming a corporate tax rate at 35 percent;
   b. compute interest coverage ratios for each alternative.

APPENDIX 10A LEASING*

A. Introduction

Leasing has become a very popular alternative to the outright purchase of capital equipment. Indeed, we can state with some confidence that almost all types of assets can be leased today. For example, GATX is the largest lessor of railcars, while IBM is the largest lessor of computers. Banks and independent leasing companies are also quite active in this market. These firms usually purchase equipment and lease it to users at costs slightly below those of the firm they purchased the equipment from. Hence, leasing provides another outlet for firms to acquire assets that are usually purchased via the sale of stock or debt.

Leases come in a variety of forms, in all of which the lessee (user) promises to make a series

*The tax advantages of leasing changed significantly with the Tax Reform Act of 1986. Hence, the present appendix is included to add perspective to alternative sources of financing.

of payments to the lessor (owner). As with most bond contracts, a lease contract specifies both the amount and timing of the payments. In some cases the lease contract is designed to meet the user's needs for a given period of time, at the end of which the leased equipment reverts to the owner. In other cases the lessee includes an "option to purchase" at the end of the contract period. Either of these varieties of lease may be of two general types: operating and financial. An *operating,* or service, lease is a short-term lease that is cancellable during the contract period. A *capital,* or financial, lease is a lease that extends over the useful life of the asset without a cancellation option. A capital lease is very much like issuing debt in that it entails a long-term obligation in the form of a series of regular payments (much like interest). Therefore, in some respects leasing and borrowing have similar cash-flow consequences. However, there are some subtle differences between the two. If the lease is a *full-service type,* the lessor will maintain and insure the equipment, as well as pay any property taxes due. In a *net lease,* the lessee assumes responsibility for these costs. As we might guess, most capital leases are of the latter variety.

In the case of capital leases, new assets are usually involved. The new asset is purchased by the leasing company, and the lessee contracts for the use of the asset. Arrangements such as this are called *direct* leases. On the other hand, we commonly see arrangements known as *sale-and-leaseback,* in which a company sells an asset it owns to a leasing company and then immediately contracts to lease it back from the buyer. More complicated arrangements are seen in the form of *leveraged* leases, in which the lessor borrows part of the cost of the asset to be leased, with the lease contract serving as collateral for the loan.

B. Accounting for Leases

Leasing raises a variety of issues that are not usually considered when a firm buys an asset outright. The legal owner of the leased asset is the lessor, who is allowed to deduct any depreciation from taxable income. However, from an economic (rather than legal) point of view, the lessee with a capital lease really receives the true benefits of the asset, because, although the lessee bears all the risk, he or she receives all cash flows in excess of the lease payment. Nevertheless, in case of bankruptcy or reorganization, legal ownership does make a difference: if the lessee fails to make a payment, the asset can be immediately claimed by the lessor. In this way, a lease contract is somewhat different from a secured or unsecured loan, because the lessor is the actual owner of the asset.

The relative positions of a *secured lender* and a *lessor* depend on the nature of the items being financed and the conditions of the borrower/lessee. As is discussed in Appendix 15B the legal position of a lessor with respect to a bankrupt company is not good. The lessor is limited to recovering the property plus a maximum of three years' rentals in compensation for proven damages (such as renovations needed to re-lease the property). With respect to damage claims, the lessor is in the general creditor category. By contrast, the secured lender is entitled to the proceeds from the sale of the secured asset, up to the amount of the debt. If, as is often the case, the proceeds do not entirely satisfy the debt, the secured lender becomes a general creditor for the entire balance of the unpaid amount.

Given the better position the secured lender has, one might wonder why any source of funds would be willing to write a lease. The reason lies in the matter of ownership. A lessor owns the property and thus can repossess it with a minimum of legal complication if the rental payments are missed. The secured lender, by contrast, has to undertake a major legal effort to force sale of the collateral, which may include forcing the borrower into bankruptcy. The lessor's weak legal position is thus enhanced by the threat that the property can be removed if payments are not met. Also, the more valuable or critical the leased items are to the success of the operation, the more likely other creditors are to defer (or even contribute) payments so that the lease commitments can be met. Thus, when the lessor of the elevator meets the holder of the mortgage in the lobby of the apartment building that is in financial difficulty, it is apt to be the lessor of the elevator who receives full payment.

This institutional factor is the reason many businesses, such as printers, grocery stores, and even power companies, find that they can get more funding or cheaper funding by using leases rather than by secured borrowings. Another institutional aspect of leases is the impermissibility of the lessee to prepay in the event that interest rates drop. Unlike loans, which may be subject to prepayment under a variety of conditions, capital leases generally grant the lessor a security that cannot be bought out except at negotiated terms satisfactory to the lessor. For this reason, at times of high interest rates, lessors may quote terms that are apparently below market in order to entice borrowers into contracts that will protect the lessor's position if rates fall.

Because the lessor is the legal owner of the asset, a natural question arises regarding how we treat the asset for tax as well as accounting purposes. Lease payments are treated as rent, and the lessor must include these payments as part of taxable income. Because the leased asset is not owned by the lessee, the user is not entitled to any of the depreciation charged against the asset. The lessee may deduct the lease payment for tax purposes, but the IRS must agree that the contract is a genuine lease and not a secured loan agreement in disguise before it will allow the lessee to do so. In this respect, lease provisions that are viewed suspiciously by the IRS include:

1. stipulating that part of the payment is interest,
2. an option giving the lessee the opportunity to purchase the asset for a nominal value at expiration,
3. limitations on the lessee's right to issue debt or pay cash dividends.

While the preceding list is by no means exhaustive, provisions such as these point to the contract's being a secured loan in disguise. In such instances, the IRS may rule that no lease exists, and the typical tax and accounting standards for loans would then be enforced. This last observation brings us to the accounting treatment of leases.

Prior to 1976, lease financing was called *off-balance-sheet financing*. By this is meant that a firm may lease an asset and show neither the asset nor the corresponding liability on its balance sheet; notation of such a contract was relegated to a brief footnote. All capital leases contracted after December 31, 1976, however, must have been capitalized and placed on the firm's balance sheet. In order to do this, the present value of the lease payments must be calculated and entered alongside debt on the liability side of the balance sheet. In addition, this amount must be shown as an asset on the left-hand side of the balance sheet. The asset then will be amortized over the lease's life. This amortization is deducted from book income in a manner similar to depreciation. Likewise, interest ascribed to the "debt equivalent" will be charged against income.

To distinguish between purely operating and capital leases, the Financial Accounting Standards Board (FASB) in 1976 issued Statement No. 13, "Accounting for Leases." This statement provides criteria by which leases may be classified as either capital or operating. From the standpoint of the lessee, *capital leases* must meet any one of the following provisions:

1. The lease agreement gives ownership to the lessee prior to expiration of the lease.
2. The lessee can purchase the asset at a bargain price when the lease expires.
3. The lease lasts for at least 75 percent of the asset's economic life.
4. The lease payment's present value is at least 90 percent of the asset's value.

Any lease that does not meet any of these requirements is considered to be an *operating lease*. In essence, the rules force us to recognize that the financial effects of leasing are somewhat closely aligned with those of debt financing, and, therefore, the lease should be considered to be a major form of debt.

C. Rationale for Leasing

Why should a company consider leasing an asset rather than borrowing and buying the asset outright? Briefly, some of the reasons for leasing are as follows:

1. Short-term leases give a certain degree of flexibility and convenience. For example, we may prefer to enter into a short-term lease agreement with IBM so that we may change systems as technology improves. Short-term leases are always operating leases.
2. The option to cancel a short-term lease can be quite valuable. Computers are often leased on a short-term basis, reducing the risk the lessee is forced to accept due to the potential obsolescence of the leased asset.
3. Some full-service leases include maintenance. The services are probably reflected in the lease payment, however.
4. Leasing may provide an opportunity for transfer of a valuable tax shield. Firms in low tax brackets (due to losses) may engage in a sale–leaseback arrangement that allows the leasing company to use the depreciation tax shield. In return for this, the lessor may receive lower lease payments.
5. Leasing may have certain tax advantages over ownership. Although the Tax Reform Act of 1986 was expected to hurt the leasing business because it reduced depreciation benefits and eliminated investment tax credits, tax reform has actually energized the industry. Under the 1986 law, corporations are required to pay an alternative minimum tax (AMT) equal to 20 percent of half the difference between income reported to shareholders and that reported to the IRS as taxable income. The AMT must be paid if it is greater than the regular tax of 34 percent.

   When a company purchases equipment, it typically uses straight-line depreciation for financial reporting and accelerated depreciation for computing taxable income. Thus, a gap is created in income reported to the IRS and that reported to shareholders, and the firm is subjected to the AMT. However, if the equipment is leased, the same deduction for lease payments is taken on both sets of books, and no gap is created.

The preceding list is, of course, not exhaustive: in many instances the decision to lease depends on the particular situation. However, in addition to the valid reasons, there are poor reasons for leasing, as follows:

1. Some leases are in fact off-balance-sheet financing and will affect the book income and assets reported by the firm. Invoking this reason for leasing is somewhat dubious, because the effect of the lease is probably truly reflected in the firm's stock value—whether it does or does not appear on the books.
2. The leasing decision may bypass the controls usually placed on regular capital expenditures.
3. Sometimes it is claimed that leasing preserves capital, because the leasing company provides 100 percent financing. Note, however, that we could just as easily borrow and purchase the asset without affecting cash balances. Leasing is not a panacea.

Again, the list is by no means exhaustive. And despite that, it is important to be aware of the advantages leasing provides as a viable alternative to borrowing and purchasing an asset.

The next question is how to value a financial lease and compare it with other alternatives. Among the factors that must be considered are the respective cash flows from the financial terms themselves, the discount rates to be used in the flows, the value of the property at the end of the lease, and whether there will be any additional debt capacity under one or the other financial arrangement.

D. The Value of a Capital Lease

To examine the issue of how to value a financial lease, let us look at the possible acquisition of a new fleet of cars for a hypothetical firm, DEF Corporation. The proposal to acquire a new fleet lists the cost of the fleet at approximately $200,000. The cars will last for only 4 years and are expected to be of little value after this time. Table 10A.1 gives the direct cash flow consequences of entering into a leasing agreement with GPT Leasing Company. The table is constructed assuming an annual lease payment of $45,000 and a corporate tax rate of 34 percent.

To begin, we value the direct cash flows, shown in the "Total" line of the table. Because these are assumed to be relatively safe, we discount them at the same rate used by secured bondholders (i.e., 10 percent). The net present

TABLE 10A.1 Cash Flow Information for Leasing Project, DEF Corporation*

	0	*1*	*2*	*3*	*4*
1. Cost of cars	+200				
2. Lease Payment	−45	−45	−45	−45	
3. Tax Shield of Lease Payment		+15.3	+15.3	+15.3	+15.3
4. Lost Depreciation Tax Shield†		−17	−17	−17	−17
Total	+155	(46.7)	(46.7)	(46.7)	(1.7)

*All figures are in thousands.
†Assume that depreciation is computed using the straight-line method.

value (NPV) of these direct cash flows is

$$\text{NPV} = +155 - \frac{46.7}{(1.1)} - \frac{46.7}{(1.1)^2} - \frac{46.7}{(1.1)^3} - \frac{1.7}{(1.1)^4}$$

$$= 37.70 \text{ or } \$37{,}700.00 \qquad (10\text{A}.1)$$

At this point, the direct cash flows result in a positive NPV. However, we must not stop here in our analysis. Rather, we should recognize that leasing is similar to borrowing, and, therefore, it displaces debt. To see why this is so, suppose that DEF Corporation usually maintains a debt ratio of 40 percent. If the company were to buy the fleet of cars outright, $80,000 would be raised in the form of debt, the remainder coming from retained earnings. However, if DEF were to lease the fleet of cars, it would acquire an asset worth $200,000 and also would assume the lease liability (debt) of $200,000 (assuming that the present value of the lease payment is $200,000). In that case, the firm's debt ratio would become higher than 40 percent.

If DEF Corporation wishes to maintain its debt ratio, it must increase equity and decrease borrowing. Therefore, because leasing has in effect displaced the company's borrowing while leaving the equity decision unaffected, the question of lease versus buy is really a decision between leasing and borrowing. In other words, DEF Corporation promises to pay in years 1 through 4 the amounts indicated in the "Total" line of Table 10A.1. By making the promise to a lessor, DEF as a result is precluded from making the same promise to a lender. Thus, the lease displaces borrowing, and the issue of lease versus buy in effect requires a choice between leasing and borrowing.

To compare these two alternatives unambiguously, we must determine the equivalent loan, i.e., a loan that matches the lease liability at each point in time. For our purposes, this means that we calculate the cash-equivalent loan that could be obtained in exchange for the cash flows in years 1 through 4 under the lease. These calculations are shown in Table 10A.2, where line 5 replicates the relevant columns 1–4 of the "Total" line in Table 10A.1.

A number of methods can now be used to evaluate the proposed leasing decision. Three of these give essentially the same results, as follows:

1. Compare the financing provided by the lease with that provided by the loan by comparing the cash flows from both alternatives. Because the equivalent loan and the lease have the same cash flows in periods 1–4, we need only look at period 0. There, the difference between the financing provided by the lease and that provided by the equivalent loan is $30,230 ($155,000 − 124,770). The lease therefore provides a higher immediate cash inflow and should be accepted.

2. Calculate the adjusted present value (APV) of the lease, as discussed in Chapter 13.

$$\text{APV} = \text{Base-case NPV} + \text{Present value of side effects of the project}$$

or

$$\text{APV} = \text{Base-case NPV} - \text{NPV of equivalent loan}$$

The base-case NPV is the project's value if it were an all-equity-financed project. The side effect in that case is the displaced debt that arises from use of the capital lease. From equation 10A.1, the base-case NPV = \$37,700. The NPV of the equivalent loan can be computed from line 5 of Table 10A.2 as follows:

$$\text{NPV} = 124.77 - \frac{46.7}{(1.1)} - \frac{46.7}{(1.1)^2} - \frac{46.7}{(1.1)^3} - \frac{1.7}{(1.1)^4} = \$7{,}470 \quad (10\text{A}.2)$$

Therefore, the APV of the lease is

$$\text{APV} = \$37{,}700 - \$7{,}470 = \$30{,}230$$

which is exactly the same as that given by method 1. (The fact that the equivalent loan has a positive NPV of \$7,470 is due to the tax shield generated by the loan. In fact, if we were to discount the tax shield (line 2–line 3 in Table 10A.1) by the firm's opportunity cost of capital, we would get \$7,470.)

3. Calculate the project's NPV with an adjusted discount rate. One of the variety of ways to do this is to use the formula

$$r_j^* = r_j(1 - T_c L_j) \quad (10\text{A}.3)$$

suggested by Modigliani and Miller (MM), in which

r_j^* = adjusted discount rate

r_j = opportunity cost of capital

T_c = corporate tax rate

L_j = project's proportional contribution to borrowing power

Because leasing displaces borrowing on a dollar-for-dollar basis, set $L_j = 1$ and solve for r_j^*:

$$r_j^* = .10(1 - .34) = .066 \quad (10\text{A}.4)$$

Therefore, from Table 10A.1, the project's NPV with the adjusted rate is

$$\text{NPV} = 155 - \frac{46.7}{(1.066)} - \frac{46.7}{(1.066)^2} - \frac{46.7}{(1.066)^3} - \frac{1.7}{(1.066)^4} = \$30{,}230 \quad (10\text{A}.5)$$

The value arrived at in equation 10A.5 is the same as that given by methods 1 and 2. The

TABLE 10A.2 Equivalent Loan for Lease versus Buy Decision, DEF Corporation*

	0	*1*	*2*	*3*	*4*
1. Amount Borrowed at Year's End	124.77	86.31	45.31	1.59	0
2. Interest Paid at 10%		12.48	8.63	4.53	.159
3. Interest Paid after Taxes (34%)		8.24	5.70	2.99	.105
4. Principal Repaid		38.46	41.00	43.71	1.59
5. Net Cash Flow	124.77	(46.7)	(46.7)	(46.7)	(1.7)

*The simplest way to find the equivalent loan is to compute the present value of the cash flows in years 1 through 4 discounted at the after-tax borrowing rate (6.6%).

approach is correct as long as all cash flows are discounted at the same rate.

From the preceding analysis, we begin to see that DEF Corporation will be better off if it leases the fleet of cars—i.e., the lease decision results in a positive NPV. However, if the car manufacturer is in the same tax bracket as DEF Corporation, then, from the viewpoint of the lessor, the problem is exactly the reverse of the one viewed by DEF, and the project would have an NPV that is negative. Thus, one party benefits only at the expense of the other. Why, then, do businesses ever engage in leases?

The answer is that if both parties have very *different tax rates,* it is possible for both of them to gain. For example, if DEF's tax rate were zero, there would be no lost depreciation tax shields, and the lease would be a positive NPV arrangement for both parties.

To see this, note that in Table 10A.1 lines 3 and 4 would have only zeros so that the NPV at the resulting cash flows would be

$$\begin{aligned} \text{NPV} &= 155 - \frac{45}{1.1} - \frac{45}{1.1^2} \\ &\quad - \frac{45}{1.1^3} = 43.09 \\ &= \$43{,}090 \end{aligned}$$

which is larger than the NPV of $37,700 calculated in (10A.1), above. Furthermore, the amount of debt displaced would fall to 111.91 = $45/1.1 - 45/1.1^2 - 45/1.1^3$ or $111,910. The lease payments are discounted at a 10 percent rate here because the before-tax and after-tax borrowing rates are equal. The APV of the lease then becomes

$$\begin{aligned} \text{APV} &= \text{Base-case NPV} \\ &\quad - \text{NPV of equivalent loan} \\ &= 43{,}090 - 0 = \$43{,}090 \end{aligned}$$

The NPV of the equivalent loan is zero because DEF's marginal tax rate equals zero. The lease payments, then, can be structured so as to create positive NPV for both DEF and the lessor. In general, if the lessor and lessee have either different tax rates, costs of capital, or investment opportunities for funds, a lease can be devised that will generate positive NPV for both. Leasing, then, is a popular alternative in such cases.

In essence, leasing allows firms to transfer unused tax shields to those firms that can use these shields to their advantage. It is also possible for borrowers to use leases to adjust their cash flows in ways which may allow them to use funds for high-return investments.

In the case of DEF Corporation, it was assumed that the property would have relatively little value at the expiration of the lease. Sometimes this expectation fails to be realized, resulting in a rude disappointment to the lessee, as, for example, those airline companies that leased many of their early jet aircraft in order to take advantage of the lessors paying the investment tax credits by way of reduced lease rates. When the leases ran out, the lessees found to their disappointment that an expected new generation of aircraft had not materialized, and their existing equipment had market prices close to their original costs (although well below the cost of new equipment of the same model, thanks to inflation). As a result, the lessors were able to realize substantial capital gains through sale of the aircraft or by re-leasing them at terms close to those of the original lease.

The airline example delineates a situation of unanticipated gains to the lessor and costs to the lessee. In other instances, both the lessor and the lessee come to an agreement that allows the lessor to recover some *terminal value*. The lessor takes a lower return than a straight lease might bring in anticipation of an offsetting gain at the end. The lessee, of course, is making the opposite bet, or at least is wagering that the equipment will be of no value to the lessee's operations at that time. This use of a lease makes it akin to a participating security such as convertible debt or preferred stock. The analysis of this complication utilizes the framework outlined above with the addition of an estimate for the cost of purchasing the asset at the time the lease runs out. That is, in the context of Table 10A.1, a fifth line would include an estimate of the cost to DEF of buying the fleet of cars from the lessor at fair market value at the end of the lease. Different estimates of the asset value or different discount rates may make a lease arrangement more attractive to both parties than a straight secured loan.

The final complication in the analysis is whether additional funds are available under a lease or a loan arrangement. Theoretically, it should make no difference to a company's debt capacity whether it resorts to the use of secured debt or a lease. In reality, however, legal, institutional, and other considerations exist that may nullify one or more of the assumptions upon which the theoretical equivalence rests. If so, the availability of funds and the cost of funds may not be the same for both options. For instance, as noted earlier, the lessor may offer below-market rates because of a different estimate of the behavior of future rates. Or, because of the legal bargaining advantage enjoyed by a lessor, the lease may provide more against the property than the secured credit will. In this type of situation, the analysis must be modified to allow for the value of the extra funds provided by one of the alternatives. One way this can be accomplished is by discounting the earnings generated by the additional funds net of interest costs.

Finally, just as leasing may sometimes generate funds that are not available with a loan, a secured loan may occasionally generate funds that are not available with a capital lease. Because the borrower has title to the property, the borrower can refinance it should additional value be created (either real or nominal) or as the original loan is retired. This alternative, too, can be analyzed by proper adjustment of the cash flows to allow for the earnings on the new funds available.

E. Summary and Review

The following general principle derives from a mathematical analysis of the lease-versus-buy decision that a firm is sometimes compelled to make: lease if the financing generated by a lease exceeds that which is generated by an equivalent loan; or if the lease's APV is positive; or if the lease's net present value is positive using the MM cutoff rate. Under some circumstances all those conditions are equivalent. In general, the gains from leasing are related to the differences in the lessor's and lessee's marginal tax bracket. The higher the tax rate of the lessor relative to the lessee, the more the potential gain for both. Leasing, therefore, offers a viable alternative to the borrow-and-buy decision and should be examined within a capital budgeting framework.

10A QUESTIONS

10A1. List and discuss several good reasons why a firm would consider leasing an asset versus borrowing and buying it outright.

10A2. How would you respond to the following statement made by the chief financial officer of the DMIS Corporation?

> We should lease that machinery because buying it would expand our asset base and make our return on total assets look worse than if we lease.

10A3. How is it that leases can have positive net present values for both lessor and lessee?

10A PROBLEM

10A1. Suppose that the Meat Packing Company (MP) is considering leasing new refrigeration equipment that would cost MP $500,000 to purchase. Given the following information, evaluate the proposed leasing decision from the perspective of MP and the lessor, Midwest Leasing.

1. *Lease Terms:* $55,000 per year for seven years plus $55,000 upon execution of the contract.
2.

	Meat Packing	*Midwest*
Tax Rate	15%	34%
Borrowing Cost	12%	10%

3. Midwest can purchase the equipment for $450,000 and will depreciate it on a straight-line basis over five years.

It may be assumed that Meat Packing

will adopt the same depreciation schedule if the equipment is purchased. At the expiration of the lease, the equipment will have a value of $200,000 to Midwest but is expected to be worth nothing to MP. For Midwest, capital gains are taxed at the same rate as ordinary income (34%).

In evaluating the lease, be sure to calculate its adjusted present value; also, find the NPV of the lease for Midwest.

ANNOTATED BIBLIOGRAPHY

Abdel-Khalik, A. R. *The Economic Effect on Lessees of FASB Statement No. 13, Accounting for Leases*. Stanford, Connecticut: FASB of Financial Accounting Association, 1981.

A good study on the economic effects of FASB 13 upon lessees.

Beranek, W. "Research Directions in Finance." *Quarterly Review of Economics and Business,* Spring 1981, 6–24.

An extensive review, together with a bibliography, of the literature on capital structure.

Copeland, T. E., and J. F. Weston. "A Note on the Evaluation of Cancellable Operating Leases." *Financial Management,* Summer 1982, 60–65.

How to evaluate leases that have cancellable options.

Crawford, P., C. P. Harper, and J. J. McConnell. "Further Evidence on the Terms of Financial Leases." *Financial Management,* Autumn 1981, 7–14.

An analysis of financial leases made by commercial banks in Houston, Texas from 1973–1980.

Donaldson, G. "Strategy for Financial Emergencies." *Harvard Business Review,* November–December 1969, 67–79.

An interesting discussion of financial planning.

Gritta, R. D. "The Effect of Financial Leverage on Air Carrier Earnings: A Break-Even Analysis." *Financial Management,* Summer 1979, 53–60.

A discussion of the effects of financial leverage on the earnings of a specific industry.

Handorf, W. C. "Flexible Debt Financing." *Financial Management,* Summer 1974, 17–23.

A further discussion on flexibility.

Hung, H., and A. Rappaport. "Debt Capacity, Optimal Capital Structure and Capital Budgeting." *Financial Management,* Autumn 1978, 7–11.

A presentation of additional insights on debt capacity and capital structure.

Ingberman, Man., J. Ronen, and G. Sorter. "How Lease Capitalization Under FASB Statement No. 13 will Affect Financial Ratios." *Financial Analysts' Journal,* January–February 1979, 28–40.

A solid analysis of the specific effects of FASB 13 upon financial ratios.

Kaplan, R. S. "Purchasing Power Gains on Debt: The Effect of Expected and Unexpected Inflation." *Accounting Review,* April 1977, 369–78.

A good discussion of the effect of value on expectations regarding inflation.

Levy, H., and M. Sarnat. "Leasing, Borrowing, and Financial Risk." *Financial Management,* Winter 1979, 47–54.

A good discussion of computing appropriate cash flows in evaluating the lease-versus-buy decision.

Miller, M. H., and C. W. Upton. "Leasing, Buying, and the Cost of Capital Services." *Journal of Finance,* June 1976, 761–86.

A slightly more rigorous approach to the lease-versus-buy decision than that given in the previous entry.

Myers, S. C., D. A. Dill, and A. J. Bautista. "Valuation of Financial Lease Contract." *Journal of Finance,* June 1976, 799–819.

Discusses the approach to valuing leases considered in this chapter.

Scott, D. F., and D. J. Johnson. "Financing Policies and Practices in Large Corporations." *Financial Management,* Summer 1982, 51–59.

A discussion of the results of a survey on corporate financing practices.

11

DIVIDEND POLICIES

I. INTRODUCTION

The dividend policy of the firm is generally viewed as a complicated, as well as controversial, issue. Two important concerns are the procedures followed by firms that pay dividends and whether or not dividend policy affects the market value of the firm. While the former issue deals mainly with the institutional aspects of the dividend decision, the latter is largely concerned with whether shareholders, on average, are concerned enough with the particular dividend policy adopted by management so as to affect market values by their reactions. A variety of opinions exists on this question, ranging from the claim that dividends are important, to the claim that they are irrelevant in market valuation.

Before discussing the question of relevance, the interdependence of dividend policy and financing through retained earnings should be noted. Four interdependent financial decisions were identified in the discussion of the framework for financial decisions in Chapter 9: (1) the level of assets, (2) the mix of debt and equity in the capital structure, (3) the decision whether to go to the public market to raise common stock, and (4) the portion of earnings to be paid out in dividends. One approach to the dividend decision is illustrated in Figure 11.1: make the other three decisions first and pay out any residual amount in dividends. If the amount to be paid is greater than that obtained in this manner, the funds have to be obtained by altering one of the other decisions. As financial managers, we need to be concerned with how our long-term decisions affect the value of common stock. The dividend decision is clearly an integral part of that concern, and it is important in considering the effect of dividends to be aware of which trade-offs are explicitly or implicitly being made. Needless to say, this complicates the analysis of relevance.

To examine the relevance of dividend policy, we must first analyze the policy in isolation by asking the question, "What effect does dividend policy have, given the firm's investment and financing decisions?" By phrasing the question this way, we present the dividend decision as involving a sequence of trade-offs between retaining earnings, paying dividends, and issuing new shares, as shown in Figure 11.1. With this in mind, let us first discuss how firms pay dividends.

II. THE MECHANICS OF DIVIDEND PAYMENTS

Dividends represent a distribution of earnings to the shareholders of the firm that are usually declared on a quarterly basis by the board of directors and paid to stockholders of record. For example, the board of directors of American Express Company announced on March 24, 1986 that dividends of $0.34 per share would be payable on April 10 to all shareholders of record as of April 4, 1986. A shareholder of record is an individual whose name is recorded on the company's books as an owner of shares on a specific date. Therefore, if your name first appeared on American Express' books at the close of business on March 31, you would be considered a shareholder of record.

FIGURE 11.1 Interactions Between Investment, Financing, and Dividend Decisions

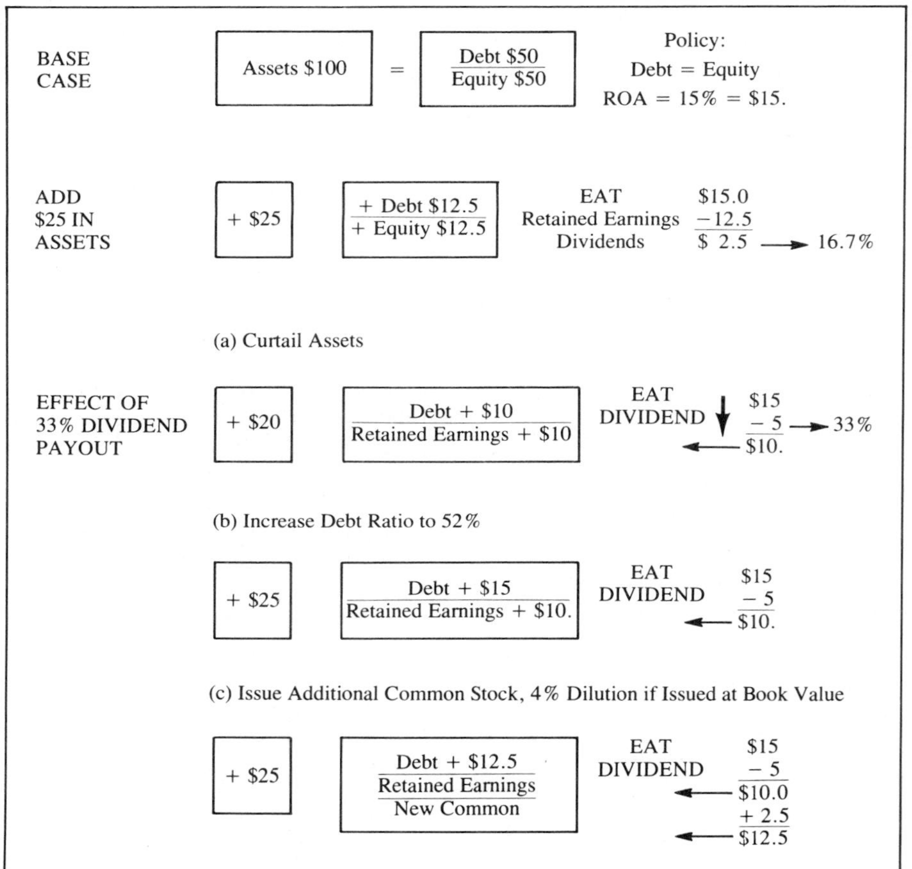

Buying and selling of shares takes place continually throughout the year, with lags of up to several days between the date of sale and the time the firm is informed of the transaction. Thus, it is possible for an owner of American Express shares to sell them on April 3 and still be considered the shareholder of record on that date and for several days thereafter. Consequently, the brokerage industry has a practice that the right to the dividend goes with the stock up to, but not including, four business days before the record date. Four days before the record date, the stock will trade *ex dividend* (without the dividend). Going *ex dividend,* therefore, usually causes the stock price to drop approximately by the amount of the dividend.

The *cash dividend* is one way to declare dividends. Another way is to declare them in the form of noncash assets, such as shares owned by the corporation in another company, or *stock dividends* in a company's own stock. Other methods of distribution include share-repurchases which are similar in effect to cash dividends.

A stock dividend is really very much like a stock split. For example, if a firm declares a 10 percent stock dividend, all shareholders will receive 10 extra shares for each 100 currently owned. Because the existing earnings must now support a larger number of shares outstanding (i.e., 110, as compared to the earlier 100), share prices must obviously decrease proportionately.

Hence, shareholder total wealth is unaffected by the stock dividend. In theory, what is gained in shares should be exactly offset by a reduction in the market price of the security. However, if a company's stock is trading higher than the "popular" range of $40 to $60 per share, a stock dividend may serve to lower the value per share into the popular range and thereby increase the demand for it, especially by individuals. Although individuals are not as prominent a force in the market as they once were, their influence is still felt. An individual holding a diverse portfolio of $200,000, for example, and wishing to hold "round lots" of 100 shares or multiples of round lots, could invest in approximately 2 lots each of 20 securities at an average price per share of $50. Thus, a share with a price of $200 may not have the broad appeal it would have if split into four shares worth $50 each. Moreover, if splitting the stock puts its price in the popular range and increases its relative demand, the price–earnings ratio and total value may also rise. For shares traded on the New York Stock Exchange, share distributions of less than 25 percent are treated as stock dividends, while anything larger is a stock split. Financial accounting for splits is slightly different than for dividends. In the case of a stock dividend, a transfer is made from retained earnings to equity capital, while a split results in a reduction of the par value of the security. In both cases, the number of shares will increase on the balance sheet.

One other popular method of distributing cash to shareholders is through the repurchase of shares. While not quite the same as issuing a dividend, share repurchasing also provides a way for firms to return cash to their shareholders, and it may even yield some tax benefits. When wage and price controls were in effect during 1973 and 1974, government restrictions on dividend payments prompted firms to repurchase shares as a means of returning cash to their shareholders. A good example of such a firm is IBM. Finding itself with excess cash balances, IBM repurchased shares in 1974 totalling approximately $1.4 billion. For those shareholders who sold back shares pro rata to IBM, the sale represented an opportunity to participate in a cash distribution and pay capital gains rather than ordinary income tax, while still maintaining their proportionate ownership. While this may seem like an attractive way to reduce payment of income taxes, regular stock repurchases are sometimes viewed by the Internal Revenue Service as dividends in disguise and treated accordingly, particularly in the case of small, closely held companies.

III. FACTORS INFLUENCING THE DIVIDEND DECISION

Before discussing some of the theoretical models that have been advanced to answer the question "How do companies decide on a particular dividend policy?" let us examine some of the factors that financial managers need to consider when planning a long-term dividend policy. We can break these down into five fairly distinct categories:

1. Profitability of investment opportunities
2. Tax considerations
3. Legal requirements
4. Liquidity needs
5. Cost considerations

Let us consider each of these in turn.

A. Profitability of Investment Opportunities

The profitability of investments may have some bearing on the dividend policy chosen by the firm. Young companies with high growth opportunities may find that all of their earnings must be allocated to potentially profitable investments, leaving no cash for dividends. Implementing a policy of allocating all earnings to investment may then be preferable to paying dividends and subsequently selling new shares to raise necessary cash in that it saves on the transaction costs associated with the issuance of new shares. (Obviously, such a policy also defers income taxes for the shareholders.) Indeed, during the pioneering and expansion stages of a firm's development, cash requirements may be extremely high. However, during the stabilization and maturity phases, which are characterized by reduced investment opportunities, cash requirements decline. Firms are then in a better cash position to pay stable streams of dividends.

From this analysis, we see that, besides short-run operating decisions, long-run strategic decisions may influence a firm's dividend behavior. Thus, the strategic aspects of financial management should not be overlooked when evaluating a firm's dividend policy. Indeed, the life-cycle concept of the firm, which views the enterprise in terms of the four phases of development discussed earlier, may be a useful tool in determining future cash needs and then setting the appropriate dividend policy.

B. Tax Considerations

Shareholder taxes may also affect the dividend decision if dividends are taxed at a higher rate than capital gains. Firms may thus retain earnings rather than pay dividends, and thereby raise the value of their productive assets and the firm's shares. Shareholders could then sell their shares and pay lower taxes on the capital gains. The point is that the effective tax rates of the firm's shareholders may provide an incentive for a low dividend payout policy in order to lessen their tax payments. We will return to this point in a later section, because the 1986 Tax Act taxes capital gains at ordinary income rates.

C. Legal Requirements

Legal requirements can take a variety of forms, including the following:

Tax on Excessive Retained Earnings. If the firm accumulates cash in excess of some limit deemed reasonable by the IRS, the IRS can impose a surtax on the unreasonable accumulation.

Contractual Restrictions. Firms may be required by contractual relationships with their bondholders to restrict the number or amount of dividends to the common shareholders. Protective covenants like this are rather routine and are usually written into the indenture of the bond agreements.

Statutory Constraints. States may impose laws that prevent firms from paying dividends in excess of retained earnings plus paid-in surplus. Such a constraint acts much like a contractual restriction in that it provides some cushion of safety for creditors.

D. Liquidity Needs

Firms may hold cash balances to meet unexpected liquidity requirements. Thus a policy to maintain an adequate level of liquidity can obviously affect the cash dividend policy of the corporation.

E. Cost Considerations

Cost considerations can enter into the dividend picture in the form of expenditures incurred by the firm because of external financing or costs incurred by shareholders in the liquidation of their shares. As indicated earlier, by financing investments with retained earnings, firms do not incur the costs associated with the sale of stock or bonds. Conversely, firms that adopt a residual dividend policy that is subordinated to their investment requirements may exhibit a highly erratic dividend stream. In that case, individual and institutional investors who desire a steady income stream may be forced to sell shares when investment is high and dividends are low. From the standpoint of transaction costs, investors may prefer a level or steady dividend policy. Firms may then attract a "clientele" for their shares based on costs as well as tax considerations.

With the exception of legal considerations, the factors that influence dividends are often conflicting. Consequently, how do we, as financial managers, evaluate the trade-off of tax and cost considerations when attempting to arrive at a long-term dividend policy? This question moves us logically to a discussion of the theoretical models that attempt to analyze the dividend decision and its corresponding impact on shareholder welfare.

IV. EFFECTS OF DIVIDEND POLICIES ON CORPORATE MARKET VALUES

In what is perhaps the earliest recognition of the functional link between dividends and the per share market price of a security, John Burr Williams (1938) defined the market value of a financial asset as the present value of all the estimated future dividends, properly discounted for futurity and the alternative opportunities available to the investor. However, as the work of Williams was primarily based on the goal of maximizing the profits of the firm, a number of modifications have been made to his positive framework.

Since the time of Williams a significant number of authors have attempted to functionally link the dividend policies of the firm with market valuation. These efforts can be classified in terms of three broad hypotheses regarding the active or residual role of dividends, as follows:

1. *The passive-residual hypothesis,* primarily associated with the work of James E. Walter (1956, 1963) who formulated the problem in terms of the magnitudes of the marginal rate of return from a proposed investment and the market–capitalization rate. So long as the former is larger than the latter the firm must retain and reinvest 100 percent of its earnings. If the converse holds, the firm must distribute 100 percent of its earnings in dividends; while equality of the two rates implies indifference between retention and payout. In a later and more rigorous framework, Eugene M. Lerner and Willard T. Carleton (1964) integrated the capital-budgeting and financing decisions of the firm within the context of market valuation and, again, relegated the dividend decision to a residual status.
2. *The irrelevance-of-dividends hypothesis,* first proposed by Merton Miller and Franco Modigliani (1961), is based on the proposition that the investment decisions of the firm are independent of its dividend policy; hence, the present and future dividends of the firm are irrelevant to the valuation of its earnings in the marketplace. This conclusion is reached on the basis of the following three assumptions:

   a. There are many investors in the capital market with free and uniform access to relevant information, absence of transaction costs, and uniform taxation of dividends and capital gains. However, even when this assumption of perfect markets is relaxed, the authors have shown that the basic conclusion holds.
   b. The investors are indifferent about capital gains and dividends. This assumption derives directly from assumption (*a*) above, in terms of perfect markets and uniform taxation of capital gains and dividends.
   c. There exists complete certainty about the future investment program and profits of each corporation. However, the authors have shown that, even when some uncertainty is introduced, the current market price of the firm's securities remains unaffected by future dividend payments.

3. *The dividend-effect hypothesis,* typically associated with the work of Myron J. Gordon (1962, 1968), posits a direct relationship between the dividend policies of the firm and the market valuation of its earnings. Gordon's conclusions are based on the assumption that investors generally exhibit risk-averse behavior, and they associate future dividends (returns) with a higher risk factor than present dividends (returns).

As we near the conclusion of this section, we must state that the effects of dividends upon the market valuation of the firm remain as controversial as the effects of capital structure upon valuation. To wit, Modigliani and Miller have insisted that Gordon has confounded the dividend policies of the firm with its investment policies, while Gordon has consistently defended his original formulation. On the other hand Modigliani and Miller have also admitted to situations where changes in the dividend rate might affect security prices, as follows:

1. For firms with long-established and generally appreciated policies of stable adjustments to target payout ratios, it is possible that investors will interpret a change in the dividend rate as an announcement that the management has revised its expectations about future profits. Thus, changes in dividends under this situation might possess an *informational content*.
2. Such firms also are likely to attract investors whose preferred time pattern and stability coincide with the dividend policies of these firms, thus reflecting a *clientele effect.*

3. Finally, it is possible that some firms might exploit the informational content of dividends to affect market share prices in the short run. However, this deliberate distortion cannot prevail in the long run.

In addition to the above, there are some hypotheses that focus on dividend levels and adjustments of such levels to reflect changes in the patterns of earnings and investment opportunities. A well-known hypothesis in this category has been proposed by Lintner (1956) and will be presented in some detail in Section V.

V. MODELS OF DIVIDEND POLICY

One of the earliest investigations into the behavior of corporate dividend policy was conducted by John Lintner in the mid-1950s. Lintner interviewed corporate managers and found them convinced that shareholders were entitled to a fair share of earnings. In addition, managers expressed the belief that some long-run target payout ratio should be established and targeted. Because a fixed payout ratio of dividends as a proportion of earnings would result in changing dividends, managers were reluctant to adopt a strict policy based on a dividend payout ratio. Stability, therefore, seemed to play an important role in the dividend decision. Dividends would be increased only when management concluded that earnings increases were permanent and could support the new higher levels of dividends. In such instances managers would move part way to some desired long-run goal, the amount of movement obviously dictated by managerial conservatism.

On the basis of the above observations, Lintner developed a simple model to explain dividend behavior. According to this model, changes in dividends are described by the expression:

$$\text{DIV}_t - \text{DIV}_{t-1} = \lambda(\text{DPR} \times \text{EPS}_t - \text{DIV}_{t-1}) \quad (11.1)$$

where DIV_t = dividend at time t
λ = adjustment rate
DPR = target dividend payout ratio
EPS_t = earnings per share at time t

From Lintner's model, the current dividend is calculable as an average of past earnings. The more conservative the company's management, the lower the value of λ is in equation (11.1), and the more slowly the company moves towards its target goal.

A 1968 study by Fama and Babiak supported the findings of Lintner. It showed that, on average, firms set a target dividend payout ratio (DPR) of approximately 50 percent, and in any one year the adjustment factor λ is about one-third. From the Fama–Babiak results, we can see how Lintner's model can be used to predict dividends in period t based on, say, DIV_{t-1} = \$1.00, DPR = 0.50, EPS_t = \$3.00, and λ = 0.33. Solving equation (11.1) for DIV_t, we have

$$\text{DIV}_t = \$1.00 + .33(.50 \times \$3.00 - \$1.00) = \$1.17$$

Therefore, the predicted dividend in period t is \$1.17.

From Lintner's analysis, it is plain that managers believe that dividends are a relevant financial decision. For those analysts who also believe that dividends are important, the shares of the firm may be valued using dividend valuation models developed by Gordon and Shapiro (1956) or Lerner and Carleton (1964).

The Gordon–Shapiro model is based on the assumption that investors purchase shares for the stream of dividends they expect them to provide. In this framework, share prices are determined by capitalizing the future dividend stream at a particular rate. In the discrete-case model, Gordon and Shapiro assume an infinite horizon and a firm without debt, which implies that all corporate growth is derived from retained earnings. If the firm's dividends are expected to grow at a rate proportional to their current level, then the expression for the current share price P_0 is

$$P_0 = \frac{D_1}{k - g} \quad (11.2)$$

where D_1 = next period's dividend
k = capitalization rate
g = constant growth rate

If we further assume that the firm anticipates a

constant rate of return r and a constant dividend payout rate b, we can rewrite equation (11.2) as

$$P_0 = \frac{(1 - b)Y_1}{k - rb} \qquad (11.3)$$

where Y_1 = income of the firm in period one
rb = g
$1 - b$ = retention rate

Let us apply the Gordon and Shapiro model to examine the valuation of the shares of the hypothetical Matrix Computer Company. One data point and two estimates are needed to solve equation (11.2). Suppose that $D_1 = \$1.00$ and the needed estimates are $k = 0.10$ and $g = 0.05$. The market price for the company's shares will then be

$$P_0 = \frac{D_1}{k - g} = \frac{\$1.00}{.10 - .05}$$
$$= \$20.00$$

While the Gordon and Shapiro model may have some overly restrictive assumptions, it gives us a benchmark against which to assess the desirability of investment in the hypothetical Matrix Computer Company, as well as a methodology for arriving at discount rates for inputs into other models.

A more integrated approach to valuation in the spirit of the Gordon and Shapiro model was subsequently developed by Lerner and Carleton (1964). The Lerner and Carleton model, which integrates the investment and financing decisions of the firm into a stock valuation equation, requires specification of the interactions between conditions in the product and factor markets, capital structure, and investor expectations. This formulation represents a substantial extension of the Gordon and Shapiro framework in that it takes into account a variety of factors and provides more detail than any previous single-equation model.

While Lintner's model sheds some light on the dividend decision, equation (11.1) clearly cannot tell the whole story. As mentioned earlier, many factors need to be considered by the financial manager. To complicate matters, dividends may have an information effect. For example, if General Motors were to raise its current dividend by 10 percent, and its share prices subsequently rose, can we conclude that dividend policy directly affects share values? Not necessarily, for while it may be true that investors like higher payout ratios, the resultant increase in share prices may be entirely caused by an "information effect," i.e., the "information" perceived about the company's future that the dividend increase conveys. Lintner's interviews indicated that companies usually raise their dividends only if future earnings are expected to be high enough to support the new dividend. Because shareholders and managers have different sets of information regarding the future profitability of the firm, dividend policy may be perceived by investors as a "signal" of future prosperity, adding to the already existing problems in trying to assess whether dividend policy affects firm value.

In general, two hypotheses have been advanced that attempt to explain dividend behavior. One school of thought argues that institutional and other imperfections, such as taxes, transactions costs, and the like, are so important that they make dividend policy highly relevant to the value of the shares. The alternative view is the "perfect markets" school of thought. Adherents of this view argue that the dividend policy chosen by the firm is irrelevant and that the welfare of shareholders is largely unaffected by either high or low dividend payouts. Let us examine these two theories as they relate to the firm's long-run dividend policy.

VI. DIVIDENDS IN A PERFECT CAPITAL MARKET

The controversial question regarding the effects of dividend policy on the firm's market value was examined rigorously by Miller and Modigliani (MM) in 1961, assuming no difference in the tax rate paid by investors on capital gains or dividends, investor rationality, and perfect capital markets. A *perfect capital market* is one in which prices fully reflect all available information. In such a market the opportunity for abnormal profits does not exist; that is, owners of shares are compensated with a normal market return adjusted for risk.

In order to analyze the effect of dividend policy on market value in the MM theory, we will assume that the firm has selected an investment program as well as the necessary financing program. Within this framework, any residual funds will be paid out in the form of dividends. (See alternative (a) in Figure 11.1: note that these assumptions allow us to isolate the effects of a change in dividends only.) Suppose now that the firm decides to change its dividend policy, given the fixed investment and financing policies: if there is a dividend increase, the added funds must be financed through the sale of more shares. Because the investments chosen by the firm are fixed, total firm value also remains fixed, and consequently the sale of new shares will result in a dilution of the current share price—a reduction that will exactly match the dividend increase.

Plainly, in a perfect capital market, what the old shareholder gains in added dividends is lost via the decline in share price. In such a situation, value has been transferred from old shareholders to new shareholders—a value transfer equal to the amount of the dividend increase. Hence, from the old shareholders' point of view, cash can easily be generated by selling shares, thus making a dividend gain–capital loss versus a capital gain–dividend loss a matter of indifference. In an efficient capital market prices reflect the true value of assets traded, thereby ensuring that shareholders will get a fair price for shares sold. Thus, in the world of MM, the dividend decision will be a residual outcome of the firm's investment and financing decisions and will fluctuate year by year.

As is evident from the preceding discussion, the MM perfect-market theory ignores taxes, the cost of issuing new shares, the cost to shareholders from selling shares, and the possible information effect generated from irregular dividend streams. These imperfections, however, do not undermine the foundations of the original irrelevance argument by MM. Given the perfect-capital-market assumption, MM's conclusion that dividends are irrelevant to the value of shares is correct, because in this kind of market investors can alter the income stream generated by the firm through arbitrage by buying or selling shares. The appendix to this chapter presents a more formal proof of the MM irrelevance proposition.

A. Objections to Modigliani and Miller

Many of the immediate objections to the MM irrelevance argument rest with the market imperfections discussed earlier. To begin with, we may view internal financing as superior to external financing because (1) internal financing does not require the sale of new shares and the accompanying flotation costs; and (2) old shareholders will earn income as capital gains (with the then lower taxes) rather than as dividends. Given these institutional realities, then, why would firms ever pay dividends? The biases involved seem to point to low or even zero dividend payouts. As a case in point, a study by Lewellen, Stanley, Lease, and Schlarbaum (1978) demonstrated that investors in high marginal tax brackets principally own shares with low dividend yields and vice versa. While this is of course not direct evidence in support of low payouts, the study does highlight the importance of taxes in the dividend policy controversy.

Analysis of other market imperfections points us to the opposite conclusion—that high payout is a superior dividend policy. For example, many individuals rely heavily on the income generated from dividends on their stock portfolios to support their established standard of living. While it is true that these shareholders can generate cash from selling shares, it is much simpler to invest in a company, such as General Motors, which mails a regular quarterly dividend. Furthermore, such an investment may prove cheaper for the shareholders, as they do not incur the the transaction costs associated with selling a small number of shares. Then, besides this shareholder clientele, there are financial institutions that are legally restricted from owning shares in firms that do not have a proven dividend record. For these institutions, firms with a high dividend payout are the only recourse they have for share ownership, and often the firms will be highly sought after, thereby experiencing share price increases.

High payouts can also be rationalized on other grounds, such as the "information content of dividends." Long, unbroken strings of dividend payments may be an indication of a firm with a stable earnings pattern. Dividends may then provide information about a firm's financial well-being. However, it has been argued by MM that investors are eventually able to see for themselves whether a firm's earnings stream is stable; hence, there is no need for a high dividend payout to signal earnings stability. Management should be concerned not with the level of the dividend payout, but only with changes in dividends that are ultimately based on the assessment of higher future earnings.

B. Dividend Irrelevance Again

The market imperfections arguments, with their attendant "clientele effects," may lead us to believe that either a high or a low dividend payout is optimal. In either case, the argument is for the relevance of dividends to the market valuation of company shares. Two recent studies, by Black and Scholes (1974) and Miller and Scholes (1978), return to the irrelevance proposition of MM. Black and Scholes argue that the supply of dividends can be assumed to be fixed. If so, they propose, we may then assume that the observed (equilibrium) dividend policies chosen by firms reflect each firm's belief that it could not increase its value by altering its dividend policy. All "clienteles" will then be satisfied because in equilibrium it is a matter of indifference which "clientele" a firm caters to. Therefore, there will be no relationship between dividend payout and the value of the firm. The empirical work conducted by Black and Scholes tends to support this theory.

Miller and Scholes suggest a tax-based reason why there should be no relationship between firm value and dividend policy. Their argument rests on the ability of investors to "launder" away their tax liability on dividends via a mechanism known as tax arbitrage. The series of transactions suggested by Miller and Scholes to obtain tax arbitrage is as follows: Suppose an investor expects to receive $300 in dividends and $300 in capital gains income during the upcoming year, representing a 6-percent yield on a $10,000 investment in common stock. Suppose further that interest payments on borrowing can be deducted against investment income. Then if the investor borrows $15,000 at 5 percent and invests $25,000 ($10,000 plus the $15,000 borrowed) in the common stock, the investor's year-end return will appear as follows:

Ordinary Income

Dividends = 0.03 × $25,000 = $750
Less Interest = 0.05 × $15,000 = $750
Net Ordinary Income × $0

Capital Gains

Gain = 0.03 × $25,000 = $750

Thus, the investor has reduced ordinary income to zero and pays tax only on the capital gain of $750. Miller and Scholes argue that the captial gains rate is effectively zero, so in their analysis, taxes can be completely eliminated. However, the increased leverage subjects the investor to greater risk. Consequently, the situations before and after the transactions are not directly comparable. But given the current tax environment (e.g., dividends and capital gains both taxed at the ordinary income rate), the tax arbitrage model becomes unnecessary even though Miller and Scholes's basic conclusion is strengthened.

An alternative suggested by Miller and Scholes deals with the existence of insurance as a vehicle for tax-free, risk-free accumulation. Rather than borrow $15,000, the investor can borrow an amount such that the before-tax interest cost exactly equals the amount of the dividend. Our investor could borrow $6,000 (= $300/.05) and buy $6,000 of insurance in order to maintain the original risk position. Thus, if the interest on the loan is $300, it can be deducted from dividend income, leaving no tax liability. In effect, because no taxes are currently paid on the interest earnings accumulated in the insurance policy, the investor has postponed the taxes on this transaction. The upshot is that because individuals can effectively undo any chosen dividend policy, they would not be willing to pay a premium for the shares of those firms with liberal payout policies.

In closing, it should be noted that while the studies by Black and Scholes and Miller and Scholes have shed new light on the analysis of the dividend decision, the empirical evidence to date has not resolved the controversy.

VII. THE EMPIRICAL EVIDENCE

In this section, we shall review some of the important empirical studies on dividend policies and their effects. Such studies have spanned a horizon of nearly thirty years, and are in general still inconclusive regarding the central theme of dividend policy—namely, its effect on market valuation.

The material will be presented along the following format. *First,* we shall examine tests of the hypothesis that corporations behave as if they had a target dividend payout, toward which they moved steadily, cautiously, and with a time lag. *Second,* we shall review the neoclassical view of Miller and Modigliani that dividends do not really matter, except for an attraction of investors to the corporation with their preferred payout ratios—the so-called dividend clientele effect. *Third,* we shall discuss briefly the hypothesis that changes in the dividend payouts of corporations with a steady history of constant payouts have announcement effects upon the market—the so-called signaling or informational content hypothesis. *Finally,* we shall end the review of empirical studies with a series of empirical tests regarding the relationship between dividends and market value of the firm.

A. Dividend Policy and Managerial Behavior

One of the earliest studies on managerial attitudes toward dividend policies and payout rates was conducted by Lintner. First published in 1956, the research was performed on annual data from 1941 through 1951 for a sample of U.S. corporations. The basis for Lintner's hypothesis was derived from interviews with the executives of twenty-eight select U.S. companies, through which the following observations were made: (1) neither the present nor the future dividend payout mattered as much as the change in the existing rate of dividend payout; (2) managers were interested only in changes of payout rates that could be sustained and would not be reversed; (3) dividend decisions were based primarily on drastic but sustainable changes in the firm's earnings; (4) the pattern of dividend behavior was not affected significantly, if at all, by the investment financing requirements of the firm.

On the basis of the interview-derived observations, Lintner formulated a simple model of changes in dividends per share as a function of the target dividend payout rate and the previous year's payout, where the target payout is always a fraction of the current period's earnings. Lintner found that his simple lag-variable equation explained 85 percent of the changes in dividend payout rates. He also computed the average target payout at 50 percent of firm earnings, and found that the average speed of adjustment toward new, higher target payouts was about 30 percent per annum. Lintner's results were strengthened by a later study performed by Fama and Babiak, who tested data from 201 firms for the period 1947–1964. Fama and Babiak found that a slightly modified version of Lintner's original model yielded results that were slightly better than those found by Lintner.

However, the results of Lintner and Fama and Babiak notwithstanding, the record on dividend behavior is not entirely clear. For example, Bicksler (1967) attempted to find out whether the target payout ratio, as estimated by Lintner's model, is consistent with the dividend policy that is expected to increase the market price of stock, as estimated by a descriptive share-price model. Bicksler estimated the target payout ratio for 14 industries and fitted two stock valuation models (for lagged earnings and market prices) to cross-sectional data, in order to estimate the preferences of the investors for dividends. On the basis of his results, Bicksler concluded that there was no statistically significant relationship between the target payout ratios, derived from Lintner's model, and the share prices yielded by the two stock valuation models.

In another study Ezzell (1970) attempted to examine explicitly the existence of possible systematic effects of a managerial policy of dividend stabilization on the market price of the firm's securities. Ezzell concluded that there is a direct empirical relationship between dividend-rate instability and market share prices, indicating an implicit preference of investors for firms with variable dividend rates.

The stability-of-dividend hypothesis was also examined by Mantripragada (1971) who attempted to find out whether reaction to instability differed during bull and bear markets, as well as reactions to instability in capital gains. On the basis of his results, Mantripragada concluded as follows: (1) when instability refers to nonportfolio type of investments, there exists no consistent support for Lintner's hypothesis; (2) when instability refers to portfolio type of investments, there exists a systematic inverse relationship between stock prices and the nondiversifiable instability in dividends; (3) there was no consistent support of the hypothesis that investors prefer a stable rate of growth in dividends; and (4) there existed, in most cases, a statistically significant direct relationship between share prices and capital-gain instability.

Our review of corporate behavior about dividend policies will close with two older but related empirical studies. In the first study, Darling (1957) attempted to measure the effects of such factors as current and past earnings, depreciation, changes in sales volume, and liquidity on the dividend policies of corporations. Darling concluded that companies will adjust their dividends to new earnings gradually and in line with a stabilization policy. In the second study, Brittain (1966) attempted to delineate the major determinants of corporate dividend policy and the effects of public policy upon trends in dividend payments. Brittain modified the basic Lintner model by incorporating "more relevant income measures" as well as long-run fluctuations in the payout ratio. He concluded that the actual dividend is gradually adjusted in line with the target payout ratio.

B. Clientele and Announcement Effects

As the studies in the previous section indicate, the majority of the empirical evidence supports the hypothesis that managers prefer stable dividend payouts, and adjust them toward new targets slowly. Nevertheless, the basic question, as to why managers prefer such stability, has not been answered yet. One of the early attempts to provide such an answer was made by Miller and Modigliani (1961), who suggested that managers were reluctant to change existing long-established payout ratios, because the change would entail undesired transaction costs for the stockholders of a firm. That is, existing stockholders would sell their shares in the open market. This type of hypothesis can be tested indirectly by searching for the profiles of shareholders and their preferences. In effect, they hypothesized that investors in high-income-tax brackets would prefer to receive most of their investment returns in the form of the then low-taxed capital gains. Such investors would gravitate toward companies with low dividend yields, while investors in low-income-tax brackets would prefer the shares of companies with high dividend yields.

Several empirical studies were conducted to test for *clientele effects*. In one of the earliest, Elton and Gruber (1970) attempted to measure such effects by measuring the average price decline in a company's stock, immediately after the payment of dividend (*ex dividend*). Elton and Gruber found that the average price decline, as a percent of dividend paid, was nearly 78 percent, with an implied marginal tax bracket for U.S. investors on average at about 36 percent. The authors concluded that there appeared, indeed, to exist a clientele effect, as posited by Miller and Modigliani. The presence of clientele effects was studied more recently by Pettit (1977) who hypothesized that companies with low dividend yields will find clienteles among investors with (1) high income, (2) younger people, (3) people whose portfolios have high systematic risk (*beta*), and (4) investors whose tax brackets for ordinary income and capital gains differed substantially. Pettit drew his client profiles from the portfolios of more than 900 investors of a large brokerage firm between the years 1964 and 1970. On the basis of the evidence he concluded in favor of the existence of clientele effects. The research by Pettit was followed a year later by another extended study that utilized the same data base Pettit had used. This study was conducted by Lewellen, Stanley, Lease, and Schlarbaum (1978), who researched investor profiles and found only a very weak and insubstantial clientele effect.

Hence, the picture on the existence of clientele effects that are strong enough to justify managerial dividend decisions is not really clear. Indeed, the old tax rate differential between ordinary income and capital gains created a tax-type of arbitrage for people in very high and very low income brackets, but the empirical evidence has not shown this clientele effect to be a strong factor.

The clientele effect studies were based on the premise that investors preferred specific levels of dividend yields because of the tax rate differentials and, therefore, gravitated toward specific companies with the appropriate dividend policies and payouts. An additional premise was that the yields were stable over time and were changed only reluctantly and slowly in order to minimize transaction costs for stockholders who were disenchanted and sold their shares. This last behavioral characteristic about managerial decision making and behavior also implies that the stockholders themselves liked stability and interpreted any increases in dividend payouts as messages about new and permanently higher levels of earnings. As higher expected earnings at a constant capitalization rate imply higher expected net present values, the share prices of the firm also rise accordingly.

Hence, public announcements of dividend increases may have a *signaling* effect upon the market and result in the share prices of the respective corporation being bid to higher levels. Of course, for announcements of dividend increases to be meaningful in terms of market values, they must convey information about future cash flows that cannot be conveyed unambiguously through other factors. Thus, one can study the impact of announcements regarding changes in cash dividends or cash splits upon market value in order to determine the empirical content of such information.

One of the early studies on the *signaling hypothesis* about dividend changes was performed by Fama, Fisher, Jensen, and Roll (1969), who concluded that when stock splits were accompanied by cash dividend announcements there were price increases or decreases in the market prices of the respective stocks depending on the direction of the dividend change. These price reactions persisted even after the share prices were adjusted for the stock-split effect. The above research was followed by several other studies. In one of these, Watts (1973) found that, indeed, there was *information content* associated with announcements of dividend payout changes, but it was of no economic significance. In other words, its monetary value was not large enough to cover transaction costs for someone with monopolistic access to this information. The results of Watts are at odds with previous and past empirical studies on dividend announcements. For example, Pettit (1972, 1976) found that announcement of dividend changes contains significant economic information. This conclusion was substantiated by Kwan (1981) who improved upon Pettit's methodology, as well as by Aharony and Swary (1980), who separated the information contents of quarterly earnings reports from the information content of unexpected dividend changes.

Hence, we must conclude that the majority of empirical evidence supports the signaling hypothesis about dividend changes.

C. Dividend Policy and Market Value

As the reader will recall, one of the early contributors of share-price valuation was Myron J. Gordon. He sought to find out which financial variable is actually capitalized by investors in the market, that is, only earnings, earnings reinvested plus dividends, *et cetera*. Gordon tested several versions of the model and concluded that, with the exception of individual cases, the evidence pointed to the importance of dividends in the determination of market values of common stock. In a follow-up study, Friend and Puckett (1964) revised Gordon's equations and retested with a different set of data and significant respecification of accounting and economic variables. They concluded that the retained earnings variable is more significant than dividends in determining market values.

All of the previous studies were performed

without real statistical and economic control for the risk variable, primarily because a proper model had not been widely accepted at the time. Since 1974, however, several empirical studies have been conducted with models that control for risk, primarily CAPM-type equations. We shall briefly review two studies which basically tested the proposition that if the effective tax rate on capital gains is lower than effective tax rates on dividend income, investors will demand higher rates of returns from companies with higher dividend payouts in order to compensate for the higher amount of taxes paid. The first empirical study along these lines was conducted by Black and Scholes (1974) who concluded that the expected returns on high-dividend-yield securities do not differ significantly from those of low-dividend-yield securities. The follow up study was conducted by Litzenberger and Ramaswamy (1979), who improved on the work of Black and Scholes by utilizing individual securities rather than portfolios and monthly observations rather than annual data. Litzenberger and Ramaswamy found that the risk-adjusted returns are higher for higher dividend-yield securities than for low-dividend-yield financial assets. That is, higher dividend payouts are undesirable and hence, higher returns must be promised to attract investors to such stocks.

Therefore, the evidence from empirical studies generally supports the Miller–Modigliani proposition that dividends are irrelevant from the point of view of the individual firm. Yet, nagging doubts still persist, particularly when the opinions of professional financial managers are canvassed. For example, an issue of *Financial Management* (Autumn 1985) published a "Survey of Management Views on Dividend Policy," by H. Kurt Baker, Gail E. Farrelly, and Richard B. Edelman. The authors surveyed the opinions of the Chief Financial Officers from 562 firms listed in the New York Stock Exchange. Of these, 150 were utilities, 309 were manufacturing, and 103 were wholesale/retail firms. The results of the survey can be summed up as follows: (1) The major determinants of dividend payments today are similar to those found by Lintner in the mid-1950s. Of particular importance was continuity of dividend payments. (2) The Chief Financial Officers surveyed believed that dividend policy affects market values of corporate shares. Indeed, the respondents were aware of both the *clientele* and the *signaling effects* associated with dividend policy.

VIII. SUMMARY AND REVIEW

Dividends can take a variety of forms, from regular cash dividends to the share repurchases conducted by companies like IBM and Teledyne. In addition, dividends can be influenced by such factors as state law and the firm's life cycle. Lintner's interviews indicate that managers believe that shareholders are entitled to a fair share of earnings and that a stable or level stream is probably desirable. While this may not be entirely true for young, growth-oriented firms, it does apply to older, more established firms. Lintner's interviews also suggest that dividend increases and decreases can have an "information effect," a topic that is currently receiving much attention in the literature on finance.

While early work suggested that dividends affect firm value, the pioneering work by Miller and Modigliani demonstrated that under perfect capital markets the dividend decision is just another detail of the cash budget and is therefore irrelevant. Many objections were raised to the Miller–Modigliani work on the grounds that various market imperfections militated against the relevance of dividends for market valuation. The most compelling argument for such relevance rests on the then different tax treatment of dividends as against capital gains. However, although this argument is supported by some indirect evidence, it does not fully explain why companies continue to pay out such a large portion of their earnings in the form of dividends. Miller and Scholes demonstrated that in a world of taxes, dividends may be irrelevant if investment opportunities exist which allow investors to "launder" their dividend income.

The relevance and irrelevance hypotheses discussed in this chapter are somewhat incomplete and also extremely sensitive to the assumptions made in the underlying models. Nevertheless, as financial managers, we need to be aware that our views concerning dividend policy may have an impact on the discount rate chosen in the evaluation of capital investment projects. If we feel that the sale of new equity entails substantial flotation costs and thereby raises the discount rate, our attitude also implies that dividends are relevant to the firm. If so, the dividend decision may be a critically important management prerogative.

QUESTIONS

1. Why would states enact legislation barring firms from paying dividends in excess of retained earnings plus paid-in surplus?
2. Lintner's investigations into corporate dividend policies revealed that the managers interviewed believed stability of dividends to be a significant factor in dividend decisions. What does this imply about the relevance of dividend policy on the value of the firm? (Hint: Consider the interaction between investment and dividend policies.)
3. In general, how do you think the dividend policies of firms with significant growth opportunities would compare with those of firms operating in fairly mature, stable industries?
4. How would you expect the dividend policies of firms subject to significant cash flow uncertainty to compare to those of firms in general?
5. List and discuss the three major hypotheses regarding the role of dividends.

PROBLEMS

1. Suppose that ABC stock is currently selling for $50 per share and management announces a 15 percent stock dividend. What would you expect the price of the stock to be after the distribution?
2. In the Miller and Scholes tax arbitrage model, consider an investor who currently holds $100,000 of PLB Corporation stock which pays no dividend. Because the PLB shares represent a long-term investment, the tax rate on capital gains is effectively zero. In contrast, our investor must pay a 34 percent tax rate on ordinary income; however, interest expense may be deducted from ordinary income in computing taxes due. Interest on borrowings is 10 percent, and there are insurance policies that yield a risk-free, tax-free rate of return of 7 percent per year. PLB stock is currently selling for $50 per share and is expected to appreciate at an annual rate of 13 percent. Now, suppose the company announces it will pay a dividend of $2.00 per share. Describe the transactions by which our investor can maintain her original after-tax rate of return on invested wealth.
3. Consider a firm whose stock currently trades at $25 per share and pays an annual dividend of $1.00 per share. The company has grown at an average annual rate of 12 percent over the last few years, and this trend is expected to continue. Using the Gordon–Shapiro model, calculate the required rate of return on the firm's shares.

APPENDIX 11A PROOF OF THE DIVIDEND-IRRELEVANCE PROPOSITION BY MILLER AND MODIGLIANI

Formally, the irrelevance proposition of Miller and Modigliani can be derived from the firm's cash budget constraint. Consider a firm that will pay d_1 in dividends per share (D_1 dividends in total) and issue new shares at a price v_1. (Here and in what follows, subscripts 1 and 0 refer to time periods 1 and 0, respectively.) If the firm is an all-equity enterprise and has n shares outstanding (*ex dividend*), then the aggregate value of the old common shares is $V_1^{\text{old}} = nv_1$. If the firm now issues m new shares, the aggregate value of these new shares will be $V_1^{\text{new}} = mv_1$. Letting R_1 be operating revenue, W_1 operating costs, and I_1 gross investment (depreciation plus net new investment), we can express the firm's cash budget as

$$R_1 + V_1^{\text{new}} = W_1 + D_1 + I_1 \quad (11A.1)$$

or

$$D_1 - V_1^{new} = (R_1 - W_1) - I_1 \quad (11A.2)$$

After the issuance of new shares, the value of the firm will be $V_1 = V_1^{old} + V_1^{new}$ (or $V_1^{old} = V_1 - V_1^{new}$). Valuing the old shares in a one-period model will reflect the present value of future dividends and the share value one period hence. That is,

$$V_0 = \frac{n(d_1 + v_1)}{(1 + r)} = \frac{D_1 + V_1^{old}}{(1 + r)} \quad (11A.3)$$

Because $V_1^{old} = V_1 - V_1^{new}$, upon substitution into equation (11A.3), we have

$$V_0 = \frac{D_1 + V_1 - V_1^{new}}{(1 + r)} \quad (11A.4)$$

Solving equation (11A.2) for D_1 and substituting the result into equation (11A.4) yields the following expression for the value of the firm:

$$V_0 = \frac{V_1 + (R_1 - W_1) - I_1}{(1 + r)} \quad (11A.5)$$

As equation (11A.5) shows, dividends play no role in determining the value established at time zero—that is, they are irrelevant. Thus, in a perfect capital market, dividends are merely a detail of the cash budget constraint.

ANNOTATED BIBLIOGRAPHY

Black, F. "The Dividend Puzzle." *Journal of Portfolio Management,* Winter 1976, 5–8.

A good, informative discussion of the uncertainty regarding dividend policy.

Black, F., and M. Scholes. "The Effects of Dividend Yield and Dividend Policy on Common Stock Prices and Returns." *Journal of Financial Economics,* May 1974, 1–22.

An empirical paper that provides support for the hypothesis of dividend irrelevance within the capital asset pricing model (CAPM) framework.

Brittain, J. A. *Corporate Dividend Policy.* Washington, D.C.: The Brookings Institution, 1966.

An early empirical test of the Lintner dividend model.

Fama, E. F., and H. Babiak. "Dividend Policy: An Empirical Analysis." *Journal of the American Statistical Association,* December 1968, 1132–61.

Another empirical test, involving fairly sophisticated statistical techniques, of the Lintner model for dividend behavior.

Gordon, M. J., and E. Shapiro. "Capital Investment Analysis: The Required Rate of Profit." *Management Science,* October 1956, 102–10.

A development of the commonly employed Gordon growth model for valuing corporate shares. Served for a number of years as the cornerstone of dividend valuation models.

Lerner, E. L., and W. T. Carleton. "The Integration of Capital Budgeting and Stock Valuation." *American Economic Review,* September 1964, 683–703.

The first attempt at integrating the investment and valuation processes.

Lewellen, W. G., K. L. Stanley, R. C. Lease, and G. G. Schlarbaum. "Some Direct Evidence on the Dividend Clientele Phenomenon." *Journal of Finance,* December 1978, 1385–99.

A good paper on the relationship between an investor's tax status and dividend preference.

Lintner, J. "Distribution of Incomes of Corporations among Dividends, Retained Earnings and Taxes." *American Economic Review,* May 1956, 97–113.

A classic paper that provides an analysis of how companies set dividend policy. Based on information Lintner gathered by interviewing companies in the 1950s.

Miller, M. H., and F. Modigliani. "Dividend Policy, Growth and the Valuation of Shares." *Journal of Business,* October 1961, 411–33.

The pioneering work showing dividend irrelevance in a perfect capital market. The first major study to question the dividend relevance argument, and still leading the way in the continuing controversy over dividends.

Miller, M. H., and M. S. Scholes. "Dividends and Taxes." *Journal of Financial Economics,* December 1978, 333–64.

A good discussion of the dividend irrelevance

argument in the presence of taxes and U.S. tax laws.

Poterba, J. M., and L. H. Summers. "The Economic Effects of Dividend Taxation." In *Recent Advances in Corporate Finance,* Ed. E. I. Altman and M. G. Subrahmanyam, 227–84. Homewood, Ill.: R. D. Irwin, 1985.

An excellent empirical study on the economic distortions produced by the double taxation of corporate income.

Rappaport, A. "Inflation Accounting and Corporate Dividends." *Financial Executive,* February 1981, 20–22.

An interesting approach to the determination of the maximum affordable dividends based on the interplay of planned growth, investment, and financing.

12

COST OF CAPITAL

I. INTRODUCTION

Funds provided for investment come from a variety of sources, both internal and external to the corporation. Stockholders hold claims against the firm's residual income and, in sales or liquidation, against assets, while bondholders have a fixed, prior claim on both the income and the assets of the firm. In addition, investors in the firm obtain some degree of control. Shareholders participate in the decision making process via the annual stockholders' meetings, while debtholders' rights are outlined in the indentures of the various bond agreements. Because each class of investors is faced with different degrees of risk, they also demand a different rate of return. For investors, this required rate of return is thought of as the opportunity cost of allocating their funds in other projects of equal risk.

In order for firms to evaluate the desirability of investment projects, managers must know the minimum required rate of return demanded by investors. This risk-adjusted rate is referred to as the *cost of capital*. Knowledge of the cost of capital allows us to use the capital-budgeting techniques to be presented in Chapter 13, where it is demonstrated that investments that yield a rate of return greater than the cost of capital are deemed acceptable, because they yield a positive net present value and increase the wealth of shareholders. While the cost of capital, in itself, seems to be a simple concept, in a world of uncertainty it becomes a very complex issue. Calculation of the required rate on various categories of debt instruments (if the rate is not already stated) is easy enough; but convertible securities present an analytical challenge, and the equity cost is very difficult to estimate.

Ironically, the cost of equity capital for the closely held firm is easy to determine: the analyst merely has to ask the owners the earnings rate at which they would prefer to have their funds in the firm rather than withdraw them as salaries or dividends. But this information cannot be directly elicited from the large body of stockholders who own the typical large, contemporary corporation. Hence, the estimates must be made indirectly. Before turning to that effort, however, it is necessary to consider the effect of the mix of debt in the capital structure on the cost of capital.

II. THE COST OF CAPITAL IN A MODIGLIANI–MILLER WORLD

The validity of certain computational formulas in capital-cost estimation relies rather heavily on the theory of capital structure and the models developed by Modigliani and Miller (MM). In a series of seminal papers that began in 1958, these authors showed that in a perfect capital market both the cost of capital and the company's market value are independent of the capital structure chosen by the firm. This proposition thus allows for complete separation of a firm's financing and investment decisions. Indeed, from the viewpoint of a decentralized capital budgeting system, the proposition has a great impact, implying that a firm can evaluate investment projects without being concerned about the specific sources of funds. MM's argument is really the financial counterpart of the law of conservation of value in the field of economics. Briefly, this law states that if we have two income streams X and Y, with values $V(X)$ and $V(Y)$, then the value of the combined income stream $V(X + Y)$ will be equal to the sum of the two original, individual values. More formally, $V(X + Y) = V(X) + V(Y)$. Thus, regardless of how a firm packages the claims against its assets, the values of those assets are unaffected. A firm's value is dictated by the productive capacity of its real assets and not by the manner in which these assets are financed. This notion of capital structure irrelevance constitutes what is known as *MM's Proposition I*. Its thesis applies even if the firm has more than two classes of claims against its assets.

In a world without taxes, MM's Proposition I can be written as

$$V^{L} = D + E = V^{U} \tag{12.1}$$

where V^{L} = value of levered firm
V^{U} = value of all-equity (unlevered) firm
D = value of outstanding debt
E = value of outstanding equity

To derive the implications of (12.1) or the cost of capital, suppose that the firm generates a constant expected operating stream of earnings in perpetuity. Then we can derive the following expression for the return r_A on the firm's assets:

$$r_A = \frac{\text{expected net operating income (NOI)}}{\text{market value of the firm } (V^{L})} \tag{12.2}$$

Equation (12.2) is the present value of a perpetuity.

Under the MM assumptions, NOI and V^{L} are unaffected by the firm's capital structure so r_A will likewise be unaffected. Our concern from this point on will be to examine the relationship between r_A and the required rates of return for all claimants (in this case, debt and equity holders).

Let r_D and r_E be the required rates of return on debt and equity, respectively. If we assume that NOI is distributed to all security holders, then

$$\text{NOI} = r_D D + r_E E \tag{12.3}$$

where D and E represent the market value of debt and equity, respectively. Consequently equation (12.2) may be rewritten as

$$r_A = \frac{r_D D + r_E E}{V^{L}} = r_D \frac{D}{V^{L}} + r_E \frac{E}{V^{L}} \tag{12.4}$$

or, equivalently,

$$r_E = r_A + \frac{D}{E}(r_A - r_D) \tag{12.5}$$

which constitutes the basis for *MM's Proposition II*. Equation (12.5) shows that, as the firm employs more leverage, the required return on equity, r_E, increases to compensate shareholders for the higher level of risk borne. As mentioned in Chapter 9, this relationship depicts the hidden costs associated with debt financing. While it is usually true that $r_D < r_E$, using more of the cheaper source of funds causes a corresponding increase in the rate required by shareholders. In essence, shareholders want to be compensated for the added financial risk. MM's Proposition II (or equation [12.5]) simply expresses the functional relationship between r_E and the leverage ratio. We will soon see how r_E, r_A, and r_D behave graphically.

III. THE WEIGHTED AVERAGE COST OF CAPITAL (WACC)

Equation (12.4) represents an overall rate of return on a company's assets that is known as the *weighted average cost of capital* (WACC). The WACC can be used to evaluate investment projects that have risk characteristics similar to the risk associated with the firm's existing assets. Two assumptions are necessary in using the WACC as a measure of the cost of capital:

1. New investments must have the same risk content as the existing assets of the firm. In other words, the projects under considera-

tion must be average-type projects and have similar risk characteristics to past projects accepted by the firm.

2. MM's Proposition I must hold.

Note especially the inclusion of Proposition I for a decentralized capital budgeting decision framework. We can now evaluate a project by computing its cash flows as if it were financed entirely by equity and then use the WACC in the computation of the project's NPV. Let us graphically compare the behavior of r_A, r_D, and r_E, using the MM hypothesis and what has been referred to as the traditional (WACC) hypothesis. (See Chapter 9 for a review of these variables and their respective definitions.) Figures 12.1 and 12.2 present the behavior of these three rates according to the MM model and a variant of the Net Income viewpoint, respectively. In Figure 12.1, the overall cost of capital, r_A, is unaffected by the ratio D/E, while in Figure 12.2, r_A declines as the firm uses more debt. Note in Figure 12.2 that, as expected, $r_E > r_D$, because equity is usually considered more risky than debt. Note also, however, that the net income approach implies that if the firm were financed 100 percent by debt ($D/V = 1.0$), debtholders would become the new owners and demand a required rate r_D that is considerably less than that required by the old shareholders. Clearly, such a situation is problematic. Accordingly, the traditional position recognizes that both r_E and r_D will rise as D/E increases. This situation is shown in Figure 12.3.

Observe in Figure 12.3 that as long as the financing policy leaves NOI unaffected, the point r_A^* which minimizes the WACC also maximizes the value of the firm. Observe also that the traditionalist position results in a lower value of r_E than that predicted under MM. Clearly, in the most idealized world of MM, we get the r_A represented by the dashed line. If the position of the traditional school is correct, levered shares must provide some benefits, because investors pay a premium and this consequently yields a lower value for r_E. However, this so-called clientele effect cannot be long-lived. We expect financial managers to switch to the capital structure that is most attractive to investors. If the "clientele" were satisfied, there would be no further benefit to switching; only those firms that initially found the unsatisfied "clientele" would

FIGURE 12.1 Cost of Capital: MM's Proposition II

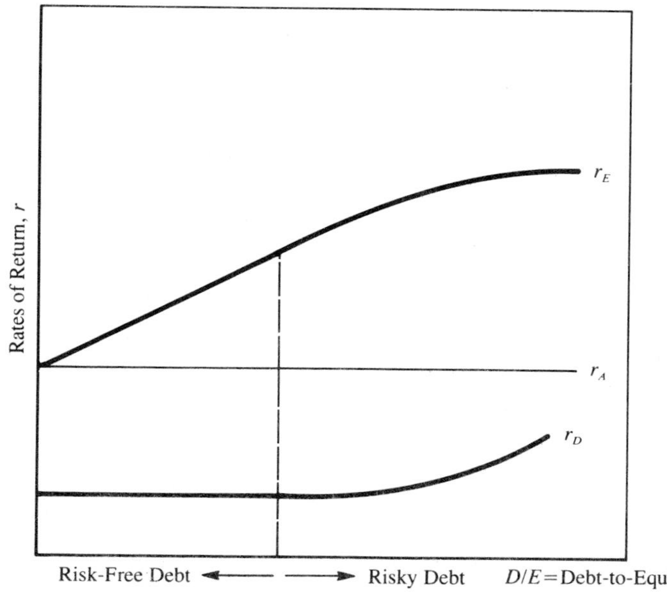

FIGURE 12.2 Traditional (WACC) Position

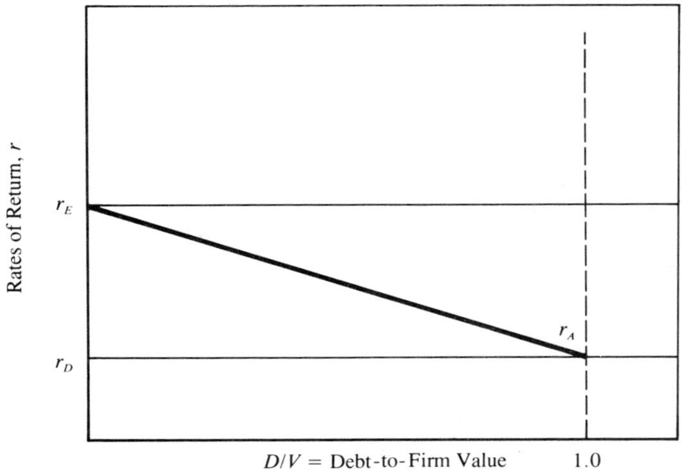

FIGURE 12.3 Relationship Between MM and Traditional Views on Cost of Capital

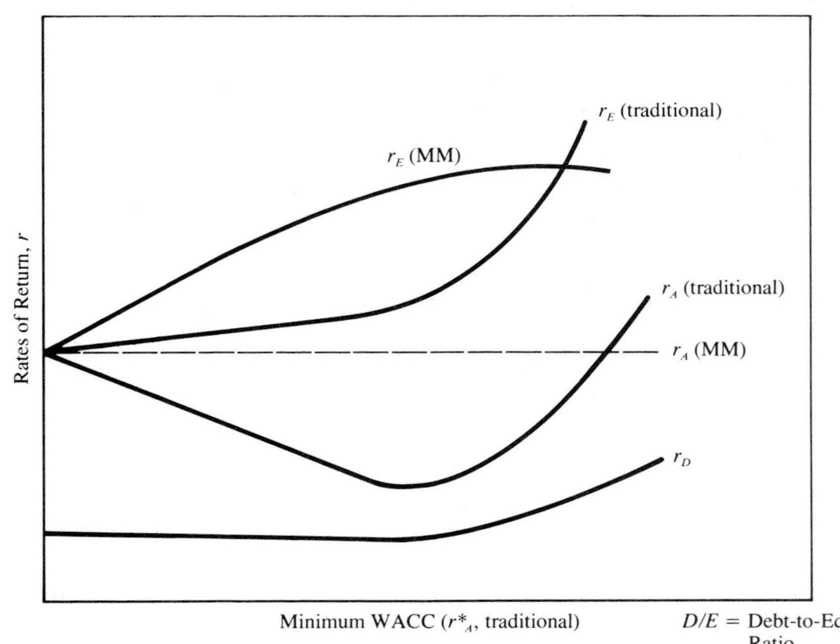

be able to affect their market value. From this point forward, one "clientele" would be just as good as any other, leaving the firm's overall cost of capital unaffected by its capital structure decisions. This and other points will be discussed further in the next section.

IV. TAXES AND THE COST OF CAPITAL

The idealized world of MM ignores the effects of taxes on both market valuation and the cost of capital. Because corporate and personal income taxes are a reality, however, it is necessary to see how their presence affects the MM propositions. Clearly, corporate income taxes play a role in a consideration of the differences between debt and equity financing. For although the payment of dividends is not deductible for corporate income tax purposes, the payment of interest, which is incurred after debt is issued, is a valid deductible expense for tax purposes. To see this, consider two firms, L and U, which have identical operating earnings of $1,000, except that L has borrowed $1,000 at a 10 percent rate of interest. The following simplified income statements illustrate the differences between firms L and U.

	Firm U	*Firm L*
NOI	$1,000	$1,000
Interest	0	100
Income before Taxes	$1,000	$ 900
Taxes (34 percent)	340	306
Net Income Available to Stockholders	660	594
Total to Stockholders and Bondholders	660	694
Interest Tax Shield (0.34 × $ interest)	$ 0	$ 34

The increased total payment to all security holders of firm L is exactly $34, an amount equal to the tax shield provided by the deductibility of interest charges. This comes about because the $100 deductible expense lowers pretax income by $100 and also lowers the tax liability by $34. The net cash outflow for the $100 interest expense after taxes is then only $66 = $100 (1 − Tax Rate). As mentioned earlier, if the hypothetical situation persisted in perpetuity, the firm could look forward to a value higher than that attained through all-equity financing. However, the existence of a tax shield raises the issue of the relevant discount rate to be used in evaluating its monetary significance to the firm. The usual approach is to discount the tax shield at the cost of debt used to generate the interest shield, i.e., r_D. Thus, for the levered firm in our example, the value of the perpetual tax shield would be $34/.10 = $340. However, we can also compute the PV of the tax shield by making use of the relationships:

$$\text{Interest} = r_D D$$

$$\text{PV (Tax Shield)} = \frac{T_c(r_D)D}{r_D} = T_c D \quad (12.6)$$

where T_c represents the corporate tax rate. As long as we operate in an efficient market, all the benefits of the tax shield will accrue to the stockholders.

The foregoing example illustrates the effect taxes have on the MM world. A restatement of MM's Proposition I that includes the present value of the tax shield is

$$V^L = V^U + \text{PV(Tax Shield)}$$

or

$$V^L = V^U + T_c D \quad (12.1')$$

Similarly, MM Proposition II may be restated so as to take account of the cost of equity:

$$r_E = r_A + (1 - T_c)(r_A - r_D)(D/E) \quad (12.5')$$

In the adjusted version of MM represented by equations (12.1′) and (12.5′), we must now admit that leverage will affect the cost of capital, or cutoff rate. (This statement is known as *MM Proposition III*.) Note that in a world without taxes the cutoff rate for investments by the firm is equal to the rate of capitalization for an all-equity income stream because $V^L = V^U$. However, in a world with corporate taxes, V^L does not necessarily equal V^U, and the cutoff rate applicable to the evaluation of new investments will generally depend on the firm's leverage ratio.

An expression for the applicable cutoff rate in a world with corporate taxes is derived in the appendix to this chapter. From that derivation, the appropriate cutoff rate or cost of capital is

$$r^* = r_E(1 - T_c L) \tag{12A.5}$$

where L represents the firm's target debt ratio. Using equation (12A.5) for the calculation of a project's NPV will result in the correct valuation under the assumptions set forth by MM. Simply stated, if we discount the unlevered cash flows generated by the project by an amount r^*, we will arrive at the true "levered" value. That is, r^* will take into account the present value of the tax shield generated through the use of debt.

V. THE WEIGHTED AVERAGE COST OF CAPITAL AND TAXES

As an alternative to MM's Proposition III, the WACC may be used to compute or evaluate present values of investment projects. However, as presented in equation (12.4), the WACC cannot take taxes into account. Accordingly, it must be restated as either

$$r^* = r_D(1 - T_c)\frac{D}{V} + r_E\frac{E}{V} \tag{12.4'}$$

or

$$r^* = r_D(1 - T_c)L + r_E(1 - L) \tag{12.4''}$$

Note that the term $r_D(1 - T_c)$ simply gives us the after-tax cost of the debt used by the firm.

Expressed this way, the WACC is appropriate for those projects that are similar to the firm in all aspects (i.e., average projects). In other words, the WACC is good for projects whose acceptance cannot affect the firm's debt ratio L or its risk position. We should note that equation (12.4″) is not necessarily inconsistent with MM's Proposition III, as given in equation (12A.5). In fact, it can be shown that under a long list of restrictive assumptions, equation (12.4″) will give the same cutoff value as equation (12A.5). The interested reader is referred to the article on adjusted present value by Myers (1977). Also, Miles and Ezzell (1980) discuss the effect of uneven cash flows and project life on the MM proposition.

The intuitive idea behind the WACC concept is that when an investment project yields enough to cover the promised debt payment and provide an adequate return for shareholders, the project is inherently desirable. To see how equation (12.4″) is derived, assume the firm is currently operating at its target debt ratio (i.e., $L = D/V$). Then the amount of debt needed to finance the investment will be

$$\text{Amount of Debt} = L \times \$ \text{ Investment}$$

For equity, a similar equation holds:

$$\text{Amount of equity} = (1 - L) \times \$ \text{ Investment}$$

In order for a project to be profitable, the investment must yield an income stream that exceeds the after-tax payoff to both stockholders and bondholders. This payoff is

$$r_D(1 - T_c)L \times \$ \text{ Investment} + r_E(1 - L) \times \$ \text{ Investment} \tag{12.7}$$

If the project's income exceeds the value of equation (12.7), the project should be accepted. On a percentage basis, we have

$$\frac{\text{Income}}{\text{Investment}} > r_D(1 - T_c)L + r_E(1 - L) \tag{12.7'}$$

which is just the weighted average cost of capital (equation [12.4″]).

According to Myers (1977), the appropriateness of the WACC (i.e., its giving the correct hurdle rate) usually involves the following qualifying assumptions:

1. The project offers a constant, perpetual

stream of cash flows and is expected to make a permanent contribution to debt capacity.
2. The project leaves the firm's risk characteristics unaffected.
3. The firm is already at its target debt ratio and will remain there after the adoption of the project.
4. The firm's currently held assets are expected to generate a constant after-tax cash flow per annum in perpetuity.

Some of these assumptions have been relaxed by later researchers.

As of now, we have two relative criteria for the computation of the firm's cost of capital, both of which allow for only one side effect—the tax shield generated by the debt used in the capital structure. Clearly, if other side effects are important, the firm cannot use either of these criteria. In that case, it is more appropriate to use the adjusted present value (APV) concept proposed by Myers, which will be discussed in Chapter 13.

VI. CALCULATING THE AVERAGE COST OF CAPITAL

Equation (12.4″) is commonly extended to encompass not only debt and common stock, but also preferred stock. In that form it is given as

$$r_A = P_1 r_D(1 - T_c) + P_2 r_E + P_3 r_p \qquad (12.8)$$

where P_1, P_2, and P_3 represent the proportions of debt, equity, and preferred stock, respectively, in the capital structure, and r_p represents the rate of return required by preferred stockholders. The issue now is how to determine the various rates of return and relative proportions of each means of financing.

The most commonly used procedure for calculating the various rates of return is to use the current market rates observed on debt, common stock, and preferred stock. As we shall soon see, the rates on debt and preferred stock are easier to calculate than the rate for common stock. And while the approaches to be suggested seem fairly straightforward, we should recognize that the methods used for calculating these various rates are, at best, approximations. Moreover, the use of equation (12.8) requires that the firm's capital structure be at certain specified proportions and that project acceptance not alter either these proportions or the firm's risk characteristics. As long as these two criteria are met, both equation (12.4″) and equation (12.8) will give the correct hurdle rate for capital investment projects.

A. Rate on Debt

To calculate the rate of debt, we look to the current market-determined rates. These can be best calculated simply by looking at the yield to maturity for the company's bonds. The yield to maturity is a more accurate reflection of the opportunity cost of debt than coupon rates specified in prior bond issues because business conditions may have changed. Furthermore, we are attempting to estimate capital costs for future investment. Existing debt has presumably been invested in previous projects and is thus unavailable for new investment. The yield to maturity can at least account for some of these changes better than an extrapolation of past coupon rates. Therefore, the rate usually used for r_D in equation (12.4″) is the current yield to maturity. If the firm happens to have more than one bond issue outstanding, as is usually the case, we can apply the same method to all issues and compute a market-weighted average rate of return. This rate is then used as the relevant cost of debt in equation (12.4″) or equation (12.8).

B. Rate on Preferred Stock

Preferred stock usually represents a claim against earnings that is positioned between creditors and shareholders. However, as the name implies, preferred stock is a type of ownership claim and is usually perpetual in nature. (For example, a firm may have an issue of preferred stock outstanding which pays a fixed $6.00 dividend per year.) We can therefore use the formula:

$$P = \frac{D}{r_p} \qquad (12.9)$$

for the present value of a perpetual stream to value the preferred stock. P and D represent the price of the preferred stock and the dividend, respectively.

Solving equation (12.9) for r_p yields

$$r_p = \frac{D}{P} \tag{12.9'}$$

If $P = \$60$, then, for a fixed \$6.00 dividend per year, the computed rate for $r_p = 10$ percent. As in the case of debt, we can use a market-weighted average for the firm that has more than one issue of preferred stock outstanding.

C. Rate of Common Stock

The rate of common stock, r_E, is the most difficult to compute, because unlike the payments to preferred stockholders and bondholders, the cash payments to common stockholders are not fixed. One method for estimating r_E is based on the dividend valuation models for common stock. Two such models, one for a level perpetual dividend stream and the other for a growing perpetual stream, are respectively given by

$$P_0 = \frac{D_1}{r_E} \tag{12.10}$$

and

$$P_0 = \frac{D_1}{r_E - g} \tag{12.11}$$

where P_0 represents today's stock price, g represents the growth expected in dividends, and D_1 represents next period's dividend. (That is, if D_0 is today's dividend, $D_1 = D_0(1 + g)$.) Using either of equations (12.10) or (12.11), we can arrive at an estimate of the cost of equity. Moreover, solving equation (12.11) for r_E yields

$$r_E = \frac{D_1}{P_0} + g \tag{12.11'}$$

which states that the required return on common stock equals the dividend yield (D_1/P_0) plus the expected growth in dividends (the capital gain yield g).

Although dividend valuation models specify constancy of many factors such as growth, profitability, payout and price–earnings ratio, most of which do not apply for extended periods of time, the models nevertheless had wide acceptance in prior years. They are still in use today primarily as supplements to other approaches which will be discussed shortly. Finally, dividend models are very easy to work with.

D. Estimating the Proportions of Debt and Equity

Several choices are available for estimating the proportions to be used in the calculation of the WACC. One is to use the proportions represented on the firm's balance sheet. Another is to use target weights. Still another involves proportions computed from market-value weights.

The questions regarding book versus market value appear to have been put to rest as the financial academic industry has settled upon the target weight's proportions of capital structure as the appropriate weights to use. These weights represent the proportions in which funds are currently being raised. Furthermore, book ratios will ultimately approach target ratios through the addition of new capital at target ratios. Market values are subject to severe distortion, particularly if the debt carries a low coupon and has thus been significantly discounted. That discounted figure may not reflect management's expectation of the way funds will be obtained in the future.

The following example will help clarify the methodology of computing the WACC. Suppose that a firm is currently operating at its target capital structure of 45 percent debt, 5 percent preferred and 50 percent common equity. The current yield-to-maturity on the firm's outstanding bonds is 8 percent; the yield on its preferred stock is 6 percent, the dividend yield on the common stock is 10 percent, and dividends are expected to grow in the future at a rate of 3 percent. We can thus compute $r_E = .10 + .03 = .13$. Moreover, assuming a 34 percent tax rate, the firm's overall cost of capital from equation (12.8) is

$$r_A = .45(.08)(1 - .34) + .5(.13) + .05(.06)$$
$$= .092$$

Therefore, the firm's WACC is 9.2 percent. This figure can be used as a hurdle rate for evaluating capital investment projects, or as the discount rate used to compute a project's net present value.

VII. COST OF CAPITAL FOR PROJECTS WITH DIFFERENT RISK

Up to this point, very little has been said about risk. In the preceding analysis risk was held constant, because we assumed that new projects had the same risk characteristics as past projects adopted by the firm. But this assumption need not be, and usually is not, the case. Accordingly, what effect will risk have and how do we account for it? The Capital Asset Pricing Model (CAPM) developed by Sharpe (1964) and subsequently synthesized by Rubinstein (1973) has been proposed as the appropriate framework to use in valuing risk for cost-of-capital decisions. According to this model,

$$E(R_j) = R_F + \beta_j[E(R_m) - R_F] \quad (12.12)$$

where $E(R_j)$ = the expected rate of return on asset j
R_F = the risk-free rate of return
$E(R_m)$ = the expected rate of return on the market portfolio
β_j = a measure of relative risk defined as $\text{Cov}(R_j, R_m)/\text{Var}(R_m)$ and commonly known as *beta*.

The differences between the MM cost of capital, the CAPM, and the WACC are illustrated in Figure 12.4. Notice that, if the project under consideration has the same risk as the firm (i.e., $\beta_A = \beta_{\text{Firm}}$), then the appropriate cutoff rate is the WACC. If the project has a different risk than the firm (i.e., $\beta_A \neq \beta_{\text{Firm}}$), a cutoff rate different from the WACC should be used. Consider project A, with an actual return of $\hat{R}_A$. This return is lower than the firm's WACC, because the project has lower risk (i.e., $\beta_A < \beta_{\text{Firm}}$). Consequently, $\hat{R}_A$ should be compared with the av-

FIGURE 12.4 The Relationship Between CAPM and WACC

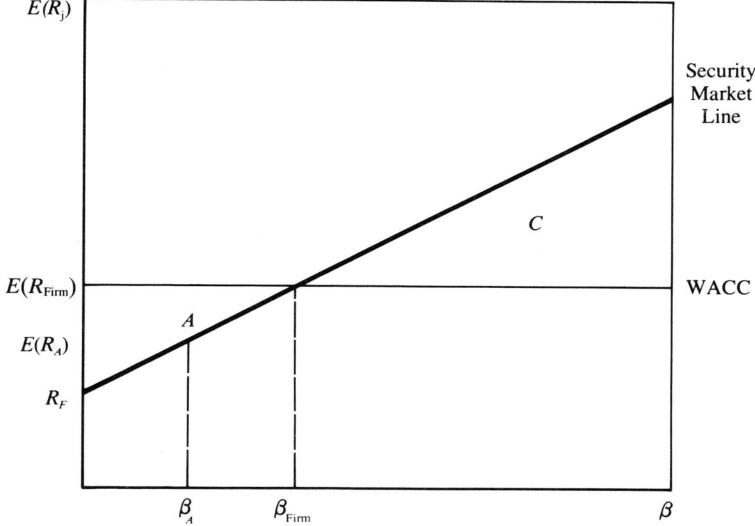

erage rate of return for projects in A's risk class as measured by beta. The figure shows that for a project with A's risk, the expected rate of return is $E(R_A)$. Thus, because $\hat{R}_A > E(R_A)$, project A is acceptable and, if undertaken, would increase shareholders' wealth. Project C, however, is another matter because its actual return falls below that expected for its risk class. The firm should reject it. (See Chapter 13 for a discussion of the computation of asset betas.)

To pursue the matter a little further, let us consider how the CAPM can be applied to the traded securities of the firm. The CAPM is an equilibrium model that relates risk and return for all assets. Therefore, equation (12.12) holds for the expected return on equity, r_E, i.e.,

$$r_E = R_F + [E(R_m) - {}_F]\beta_E^L \qquad (12.13)$$

where β_E^L represents the systematic risk of the equity in a levered firm. If we assume that there are corporate taxes and that the corporation issues risk-free debt ($r_D = R_F$), then the after-tax WACC becomes

$$\text{WACC} = (1 - T_c)r_D \frac{D}{V} + r_E \frac{E}{V} \qquad (12.14)$$

This is strikingly similar to equation (12.4′).

A. An Application

The theoretical results developed so far can be used to compute the cost of capital for a hypothetical company, MM Inc. Suppose the company currently has a capital structure of 30 percent debt to total assets (at market values) and can continue to borrow at the prevailing risk-free rate of 13 percent up to a debt-to-value ratio of 40 percent. Let the current corporate tax rate be 34 percent and the expected rate of return in the market be 18 percent. Suppose β for MM Inc. has been estimated to be .80. Let us consider three important questions regarding a new investment project:

1. What are the company's WACC and cost of equity?
2. How will the WACC change if the target debt ratio is employed rather than the current 30 percent?
3. If a potential project has an expected yield of 12 percent and risk characteristics similar to the firm, should it be accepted?

First, we make use of the CAPM to compute the cost of (levered) equity capital:

$$\begin{aligned} r_E &= R_F + [E(R_m) - R_F]\beta_E^L \\ &= .13 + [.18 - .13].80 = .17 \end{aligned}$$

Then, using the value of r_E, we compute the WACC

$$\begin{aligned} \text{WACC} &= (1 - T_c)R_F \frac{D}{V} + r_E \frac{E}{V} \\ &= (1 - .34)(.13)(.30) + .17(.70) \\ &= .145 \end{aligned}$$

If the firm increases its use of debt up to the target level of 40 percent, the resultant cost of equity will also change. Therefore, we can use the MM definition of the weighted average cost of capital to compute the new WACC. Recall that the MM definition of a hurdle rate is computed by adjusting an unlevered equity capitalization rate by a factor that takes the side effect of debt financing into account. As long as the firm's overall business risk is not changed, the value of the unlevered capitalization rate will not change. Thus, given a WACC of 14.5 percent, we can solve for the implied value of ρ (the unlevered equity capitalization rate) at a debt level of 30 percent. We have

$$\begin{aligned} \text{WACC} &= \rho\left(1 - T_c \frac{D}{V}\right) \\ \rho &= \frac{\text{WACC}}{1 - T_c(D/V)} \\ &= \frac{14.5}{1 - .34(.30)} = 16.15\% \end{aligned}$$

Now suppose ρ is unchanged even at a debt ratio of 40 percent. Then if the firm moves to its 40-

percent target debt ratio, by the MM formula, we have

$$\text{WACC} = .1615(1 - .34(.40)) = .1395$$

Hence, the project should be rejected because the rate of return of 12 percent is less than the cost of capital regardless of the capital structure chosen (i.e., the project's NPV < 0). In cases such as this the cost of equity will necessarily rise if the firm employs more debt to compensate owners for the higher level of risk borne.

What if the project's systematic risk is different from that of the firm? How will this affect the WACC figures computed at the two different debt levels? To answer these questions, suppose that, for the project's operating (unlevered) cash flows, $\beta = 1.1$. Then the resulting $E(R)$ computed from the CAPM equation will represent the required rate of return of an equity income stream. Thus, we can use the MM version in addition to the CAPM to compute the WACC for the project. From the CAPM, the required rate of return on the project is

$$E(R) = .13 + [.18 - .13]1.1 = 18.5\%$$

This number represents the required rate of return for an equivalent all-equity-financed income stream. Therefore, the required rate of return under each capital structure will be

$$\text{WACC}_{30} = .185(1 - .34(.30)) = 16.61\%$$

$$\text{WACC}_{40} = .185(1 - .34(.40)) = 15.98\%$$

Using these two numbers, we may assess the project's profitability in the manner discussed earlier. As is evident from Figure 12.4, projects must be evaluated with a cost of capital that reflects systematic risk. To compute a correct cost, therefore, we must be familiar with the MM concept of cost of capital as well as the CAPM model.

B. Other Practical Considerations

The CAPM requires estimation of three critical variables: The riskless rate of return, the market rate of return, and the relationship of the individual security to market return (the "beta" of the security). In recent years, a critical aspect of these estimates has been addressing the inflationary expectations that observed rates incorporate. In particular, when inflationary expectations are high, it may be inappropriate to use, for example, the rate of return on long-term Treasury bonds as an estimate of the risk-free rate. This is because it incorporates a premium for both inflation and maturity risk. Because maturity risk has already been included in the market's required rate of return on equities, using the long-term government rate would cancel out the maturity premium when calculating the required *excess* return on equities.

Since the late 1970s, U.S. financial markets have experienced both significant volatility and inflationary expectations (by historical standards), which complicate the computation of required rates of return. Consequently, many analysts have turned to the studies of Ibbotson and Sinquefield which suggest (1) that the rate of return on short-term government securities (T-bills) has been close to 0 percent (net of inflation), (2) that the maturity risk between short- and long-term Treasuries has been about 1 percent, and (3) that the excess return on the market over short-term Treasuries has been about 9.2 percent. So, what does this mean? During inflationary periods, it may be appropriate to use the Ibbotson–Sinquefield estimates as a starting point (i.e., the short-term real riskless rate of return is about 0 percent and the spread of short-term Treasuries and common stock is 9.2 percent) in combination with current inflationary expectations. In the context of our previous example with MM, Inc., we might estimate its required return on equity as $r_E = 0\% + (.092)(.8) + .10 = 17.4\%$ where inflation is expected to be 10 percent.

We should also point out that any single point-estimate of required rates of return should be viewed with a healthy degree of skepticism because estimating the variables in the CAPM equation can be fraught with error. In addition to the difficulties just described in estimating the risk-free rate, firms change over time and as a result their betas will also change. Consequently, using beta estimates derived from historical data can be dangerous. The point here is that the apparent simplicity of the CAPM does not imply that it may be used as a substitute for subjective judgment based on sound and thorough analysis.

VIII. RELATED ISSUES IN THE COST-OF-CAPITAL CONTROVERSY

A. Capital Structure, Cash Flows, and the WACC

Financial Management (Summer 1979) highlighted an interesting discussion of some practical concerns regarding the WACC. We conclude the chapter by outlining some of these issues.

As mentioned previously, the definition of a cutoff rate (or weighted average cost of capital) implies that a rate exists (the WACC) at which capitalizing the unlevered cash flows yields the firm's or the project's levered value. Arditti and Levy (1977) raised serious questions regarding this standard "textbook" approach to the cost of capital. The controversy centered on the use of total cash flows as proposed by the authors and was reconciled by Shapiro (1979), who showed that the use of operating cash flows yielded results similar to those obtained from total cash flows. This result is particularly important because we do not need to take the interest tax subsidy into account when calculating operating cash flows. Comparatively speaking, then, the operating cash flow (textbook) approach proves much simpler than the total cash flow method suggested by Arditti and Levy.

Other problems that have arisen in connection with the appropriateness of the cost of capital relate to the behavior of the market value weights used in computing the WACC. Recall that one of the basic assumptions underlying computation of the WACC is that (1) the firm is at its target D/V ratio, and (2) project acceptance will not change the relative amount of debt and equity in the capital structure. To see what this assumption implies and the possible confusion it may cause, assume that a firm invests $\$I$ in an investment that has NPV ≥ 0. Should the firm finance this investment of $\$I$ by raising the product $(D/V)(\$I)$? If the project's NPV $= 0$, then the market value of the firm will remain unchanged, and $(D/V)(\$I)$ is the correct amount of debt issued. However, what if NPV > 0? Under these circumstances, the value of the firm will rise by the NPV and it must raise $(\$I + \text{NPV})(D/V)$ in debt to maintain a constant leverage. Any other amount will change the market-value-to-debt ratio. Thus, adherence to the assumption of constant market value proportions is a necessary condition for the use of WACC to be correct. Rather than debate the correctness of the WACC, however, we should (and need to) investigate whether the issuance and retirement of debt yields a constant or varying debt ratio. The interested reader is referred to the Summer 1979 and Spring 1974 issues of *Financial Management* to browse through a collection of papers addressing the issues concerned.

B. Divisional Cost of Capital

The preceding discussion was concerned with the computation of a single cost of capital used in evaluating all investment projects. This single cost of capital is correct as long as all the divisions of a firm have similar risk and financial characteristics as the firm as a whole. If they do not, then we need to compute a cost of capital for each division.

One approach to the divisional cost of capital is to treat the division as a separate company and use the CAPM to derive an expression for the division WACC. If no data are available for the division, proxy data from a traded company with similar characteristics can be used. One investigation in this area was conducted by Gup and Norwood (1982), who examined the practices of Fuqua Industries, a firm with twenty-two divisions. Fuqua's approach to the divisional cost of capital is as follows:

1. Assess the risk class of the division via subjective and objective risk assessments.
2. Assign each risk class an index number.
3. Compute the divisional cost of capital, which

is equal to the product of the risk index from step 2 and the company's overall cost of capital (i.e., the standard textbook or CAPM cost of capital).

Although this approach is somewhat ad hoc in nature, Fuqua Industries explicitly recognizes that a divisional cost of capital is needed due to its diverse business interests. Even though the risk assignment might seem arbitrary, company managers obviously know a lot about their divisions. This knowledge is put directly into the adjustment of the corporate cost of capital for divisional differences in risk and financial structure.

C. Irrelevance of Capital Structure Revisited

The fundamental conclusions which follow from the MM analysis are somewhat disturbing, because they imply that either capital structure has no effect on firm value (in a no-tax world) or that firms should employ 100 percent debt financing (in a world with corporate taxes). But, why do we observe the predominance of firms using combinations of debt and equity, and how can we explain regularities in leverage across firms in different industries? In other words, have we overlooked factors implying that capital structure does indeed affect firm value? We will discuss here three potential reasons for the existence of an optimal capital structure that contains both debt and equity: bankruptcy costs, signaling theories, and agency costs.

If *bankruptcy* costs are significant (and there is some disagreement on this point), then we may have an optimal capital structure determined by the tax benefits of debt relative to the increasing probability of bankruptcy and associated costs. In bankruptcy, a significant portion of the firm's resources is diverted to third parties which reduces firm value. Third party payments include primarily legal and trustee fees required in the settling of claims against the firm. Thus, the optimal capital structure would be determined at the point where the marginal tax benefit from an additional dollar of debt is exactly offset by expected marginal bankruptcy costs.

Signaling theories are based on the existence of information asymmetries between the firm's management and outside investors. Ross (1977) points out that in an MM context, the market's perception of the value of the firm may be incorrect. Assuming that management knows the true value of the firm, it can send signals to the market in a variety of ways including capital structure changes. Thus, if changes in capital structure cause the firm's securities to be revalued by the market, then the use of debt will impact firm value.

Although we touched upon *agency costs* in an earlier chapter, it will be helpful to elaborate a bit here. Jensen and Meckling (1976) assert that due to the existence of agency costs in both the debtor–creditor and manager–shareholder relationships, the cash flows earned by the firm are not independent of capital structure. The agency costs of debt can best be illustrated with an example. Suppose the firm is considering two alternative investments with the same expected return but different variances. Project 1 will pay off either \$50,000 or \$10,000 with equal probability at the end of the period, while project 2 will pay off either \$35,000 or \$25,000 with equal probability. Suppose the firm shows only project 2 to a lender and asks to borrow \$20,000. The lender will advance the funds because in either case, the payoff will be enough to cover the debt. If the required investment in each project is \$25,000, the firm will opt for project 1 because the owners will capture most of the gain on the upside while the lender will suffer the loss on the downside. The point here is that the existence of debt creates an incentive for the owners to invest in risky projects (perhaps with negative net present value). By so doing, a transfer of wealth from lenders to borrowers results. Consequently, lenders typically insist on a variety of restrictions and monitoring devices to protect their interests. These mechanisms are not costless, and lenders will discount the price of the firm's debt securities as a result.

Conflicts in the manager–shareholder relationship create agency costs of equity. For example, consider a firm 100 percent owned by the manager. Should the manager choose to purchase teak trash cans for the corporate office, she will bear the full cost of diverting the firm's resources from more productive uses. If an equity interest in the firm is sold to outside investors, however, the owner-manager will bear only a fraction of the cost of her consumption of perquisites (perks). Consequently, the outside owners will share monitoring costs to protect their interests, and these costs will rise as their percentage ownership increases.

The result here is that with agency costs of both debt and outside equity, there will be some optimal combination of the two that will minimize total agency costs.

IX. SUMMARY AND REVIEW

The cost of capital is a topic that is central to financial analysis. Recent developments in the analysis of the cost of capital have their origins in the valuation relationships developed by Miller and Modigliani (MM). While it may initially appear that the WACC and MM definitions of a hurdle rate differ, the two are in fact similar under certain assumptions. An extension to the MM concept of the WACC incorporates the idea of risk, a difficult item to account for in any model of the cost of capital. An attractive alternative to the extended MM theory is the single-period CAPM, which, though not without shortcomings, also brings risk into the analysis of the cost of capital. If there is more than one side effect associated with project acceptance, Myer's APV may be a more appropriate method to use.

QUESTIONS

1. Would it be appropriate to estimate the firm's cost of debt capital by looking at the coupon rate on prior debt issues? Why or why not?
2. What are the limitations associated with dividend valuation models applied to the firm's cost of equity capital?
3. Describe the choices available for estimating the proportions of debt and equity in the capital structure.
4. How does the "law of conservation of value" underlie the MM proposition of the irrelevance of capital structure on firm value?
5. What happens to the MM proposition if outsiders do not have the same information as the firm's management, that is, if informational asymmetries exist?

PROBLEMS

1. Consider a firm with a marginal tax rate of 34 percent, a debt-to-total-capitalization ratio of .25, and a beta on its stock of 1.2. The before-tax cost of debt for this firm is 12 percent; the risk-free rate of return is 6 percent, and the expected return on the market portfolio is 19 percent. Calculate the firm's WACC.
2. Assuming that the WACC calculated in problem 1 is the required return for an unlevered firm, what is the implied beta for an unlevered firm?
3. Referring to problem 1, suppose the firm is considering a project with an estimated beta (unlevered) of 1.4. What is the appropriate hurdle rate for the project under consideration?

APPENDIX 12A COST OF CAPITAL ADJUSTED FOR TAX SHIELD

To derive an expression for the cost of capital adjusted to take account of the tax shield benefits, we begin with MM's Proposition I, adjusted to include the effects of taxes:

$$V^L = V^U + T_c D \qquad (12A.1)$$

Let $V^U = \overline{X}/r$, where $\overline{X}$ is the perpetual average unlevered cash flow and r is the appropriate capitalization rate for an all-equity stream. Then equation (12A.1) can be rewritten as

$$V^L = \frac{\overline{X}(1 - T_c)}{r} + T_c D \qquad (12A.2)$$

Equation (12A.2) allows us to arrive at the appropriate rate for the cost of capital. Consider a firm contemplating an investment in the amount ΔI that generates a corresponding increase in $\overline{X}$, D, and V^L of $\Delta\overline{X}$, ΔD, and ΔV^L, respectively. Stockholders will clearly be willing to undertake this investment if the change ΔV^L in the value for the firm is greater than the incremental investment (i.e., if their wealth will increase). We can therefore restate equation (12A.2) in the form of an acceptance criterion. Accordingly, for convenience, let the value of D be zero originally. Then,

$$\frac{\Delta V^L}{\Delta I} = \frac{\Delta\overline{X}(1 - T_c)}{(\Delta I)(r)} + T_c\frac{\Delta D}{\Delta I} > 1 \qquad (12A.3)$$

In other words, we accept the project if $\Delta V^L > \Delta I$.

Rearranging equation (12A.3) into an expression that highlights the after-tax change in net operating earnings and the appropriate opportunity cost of capital, we have

$$\frac{(1 - T_c)\Delta\overline{X}}{\Delta I} > r\left(1 - T_c\frac{\Delta D}{\Delta I}\right) \qquad (12A.4)$$

where the left-hand side represents the after-tax change in earnings and the right-hand side represents the appropriate opportunity cost of capital. The issue of contention in equation (12A.4) is the term $\Delta D/\Delta I$. For example, Modigliani and Miller state that

> If D^*/V^* denotes the firm's long-run "target" debt ratio . . . then the firm can assume, to a first approximation at least that for any particular investment $dB/dI = D^*/V^*$. (Modigliani and Miller, 1963, p. 441)

In other words, we can interpret the change in debt brought about by the new investment as the firm's target debt ratio (percent debt in the firm). Therefore, letting L represent the long-run target debt ratio, r^* the project cutoff rate, and letting $\Delta D/\Delta I = L$, we obtain

$$r^* = r_E(1 - T_c \times L) \qquad (12A.5)$$

which constitutes MM's Proposition III with the addition of corporate taxes. This adjusted formula for the cost of capital takes into account one side effect brought about by the use of debt: the tax shield. The MM adjusted cost of capital therefore applies only in those cases in which a tax shield attributable to debt financing is the only side effect. The introduction of other factors clearly complicates the calculation of an adjusted cost of capital and is much more easily handled by the adjusted present value concept developed by Myers. (See Chapter 13.)

ANNOTATED BIBLIOGRAPHY

Arditti, F., and H. Levy. "The Weighted Average Cost of Capital as a Cutoff Rate: A Critical Analysis of the Classic Textbook Weighted Average." *Financial Management,* Fall 1977, 24–34.

A critical examination of the use of the WACC as a hurdle rate.

Gup, B., and S. Norwood, III. "Divisional Cost of Capital: A Practical Approach." *Financial Management,* Spring 1982, 20–24.

An interesting, practical approach to the divisional cost of capital.

Jensen, Michael C., and William H. Meckling. "Theory of the Firm: Managerial Behavior, Agency Costs and Ownership Structure." *Journal of Financial Economics* 3(1976): 305–60.

A must reading in modern finance.

Miles, J., and R. Ezzell. "The Weighted Average Cost of Capital, Perfect Markets and Project Life: A Clarification." *Journal of Financial and Quantitative Analysis,* September 1980, 719–30.

A good presentation of the effects of project life on the equivalence between the WACC and the MM hurdle rate.

Modigliani, F., and M. H. Miller. "Corporate Income Taxes and the Cost of Capital." *American Economic Review,* June 1963, 433–43.

A restatement of the MM propositions relating to firm value and the hurdle rate in the presence of taxes.

Myers, S. C. "Interactions of Corporate Financing and Investment Decisions—Implications for Capital Budgeting." *Journal of Finance,* March 1977, 211–17.

A good discussion of the adjusted present

value concept and how it relates to the conventional and MM hypotheses.

Ross, S. A. "The Determination of Financial Structure: The Incentive Signalling Approach," *Bell Journal of Economics,* Spring 1977, 23–40.

Another must reading in modern finance.

Rubinstein, M. "A Mean-Variance Synthesis of Corporate Financial Theory." *Journal of Finance,* March 1973, 167–81.

A pioneering article in the application of CAPM to corporate financial policies.

Shapiro, A. "In Defense of the Traditional Weighted Average Cost of Capital as a Cutoff Rate." *Financial Management,* Summer 1979, 22–23.

One paper in a collection that is devoted to the controversy surrounding the WACC.

Van Horne, J. C. "An Application of the Capital Asset Pricing Model to Divisional Required Returns." *Financial Management,* Spring 1980, 14–19.

A real-life case study centered on the application of CAPM to the determination of the divisional cost of capital.

13

CAPITAL BUDGETING

I. INTRODUCTION

Capital budgeting is the overall process of evaluating potential investment opportunities through a series of steps that enable decision makers to screen various projects and compute their respective cash flows. Given the magnitude and significance of this task, it is easy to see that the evaluation of new capital investments is in an area that takes a large amount of the financial manager's time and effort. After all, the financial manager must arrive at an accurate estimate of cash flows, as well as establish an overall criterion against which to measure profitability. Here, we will need to review the concept of present value, as well as learn how to compute the appropriate cash flows to be discounted. These tasks require that great attention be paid to details involving the treatment of taxes, depreciation, and the like. Once we establish a list of inflows and outflows, the procedures for valuing these flows can be discussed.

II. COMPUTATION OF CASH FLOWS

Because capital budgeting is concerned with the allocation of the firm's scarce resources, it is important first to highlight again the relevant earnings and expenditure streams associated with a given project. A cash inflow or outflow is the actual receipt or payment of an amount of money. As defined here, the term *cash flow* will denote the difference between the dollar inflows and outflows within the firm. However, accounting statements are not constructed on a cash basis; therefore, we will need to pay attention to how the accounting convention affects the computation of cash flows. For instance, a large investment in plant and equipment is not usually expensed totally in the purchase period. Instead, such large outlays are capitalized and the cost is depreciated over the useful life of the asset. As a result, the profits stated on the firm's income statement are not an accurate reflection of the firm's cash flow. Furthermore, to complicate matters, revenues and expenses are recorded when incurred rather than at the time of receipt or payment. Such peculiarities of accounting convention must be recognized in computing cash flows.

To take the analysis one step further, the appropriate cash figure to discount is the sum of the inflows net of all cash outflows. Moreover, because taxes represent an outflow, the relevant cash flows to be discounted should be the net of all taxes. In addition, we need to be aware of how the project's acceptance affects all aspects of the firm. Of course, from the capital budgeting standpoint, the only cash flows we should be concerned with are the incremental cash flows associated with the project. However, if we neglect all else, we may be unaware of incidental effects on the overall well-being of the firm. For example, acceptance of a new manufacturing procedure may require a much larger investment in accounts receivable and inventory. Should this investment be considered in our evaluation of the project? The answer is clearly a resounding yes: because the firm must expend added dollars in working capital, these dollars are directly related to the project in question. Another common example is when accountants decide to allocate existing overhead to a new project line.

Clearly, the overhead that already exists is not an incremental cost. Thus, whether the firm accepts or rejects the project has no bearing on the total overhead expenses of the firm. However, if the project generates new overhead expenses, these should be considered in the computation of the project's cash flows.

Two other important issues that pertain to a discussion of cash flow are sunk costs and opportunity costs. To illustrate the possible confusion, suppose that a project is currently under way for which $1 million has already been spent. Suppose also that a reevaluation is suggested and undertaken. Should the past $1 million have any bearing on the continued progress of the project? Not at all, for the $1 million already spent is a *sunk cost* and cannot be recovered. That is, regardless of whether we continue or stop the project, the $1 million is gone. On the other hand, the bearing of *opportunity costs* on the project must be considered, for these costs are, economically, very much real. For example, a firm that currently owns property upon which a new plant will be built must implicitly recognize that such property can in fact have alternative uses and must consequently evaluate the opportunity cost of the property.

To see how a project's cash flows are actually computed, suppose that a hypothetical firm, CAPM Inc., is considering an investment of a new minicomputer service that costs $100,000 and will generate cash flows over the next five years. Table 13.1 presents a worksheet of the relevant items used in the calculation of after-tax cash flows. Line 1 gives a forecast of the project's sales over the next five years. Operating costs and other costs are given on lines 2 and 3, respectively. For purposes of allocating depreciation expense, the firm estimates a salvage value of $10,000 on the new computers and uses the straight-line method of depreciation. (The particular method of depreciation employed has an impact upon the complexity of the methodology used to compute the firm's cash flows; however, it does not change the general approach presented here.) Because the depreciable cost is $90,000 (asset cost − salvage value), depreciation each year comes to $18,000 and is included in the operating costs as indicated on line 2. Therefore, to compute taxable income, the firm subtracts the operating expenses, including depreciation, and other costs from the sales revenue. Taxes are equal to the tax rate (.34) multiplied by taxable income. We will assume that, in years when taxable income is negative, the firm carries back the current

TABLE 13.1 Cash Flow Calculations, CAPM Inc.

Period	*0*	*1*	*2*	*3*	*4*	*5*	*6*
1. Sales	$ 0	$ 5,000	$120,000	$300,000	$500,000	$450,000	
2. Operating Costs (Including Depreciation)	0	21,000	98,000	168,000	318,000	298,000	
3. Other Costs	33,333	10,000	0	0	0	0	
4. Tax on Operations	−11,333	−8,840	7,480	44,880	61,880	51,680	
5. Earnings after Tax (1 − 2 − 3 − 4)	−22,000	−17,160	14,520	87,120	120,120	100,320	
6. Cash Flow from Operations (5 + Depreciation)	−22,000	840	32,520	105,120	138,120	118,320	
7. Change in Working Capital	0	5,000	10,000	15,000	30,000	25,000	$−30,000
8. Capital Investment and Salvage	−100,000	0	0	0	0	0	10,000
9. Net Cash Flow (6 − 7 + 8)	−122,000	−4,160	22,520	90,120	108,120	93,320	40,000
10. Present Value at 15%	−122,000	−3,617	17,028	59,254	61,818	46,396	17,293

NPV = $76,172

year's loss and receives a refund on the amount of taxes paid in the previous year. Cash flow from operations is indicated on line 6. Note that depreciation is added back because it is a non-cash expense. Added investment in working capital is indicated on line 7, where the figures represent the firm's outlay for those items necessary for the operation of the new computer service. Note that in year 6 CAPM is able to recapture some of its investment in working capital. From this point on, the after-tax cash flow computation is carried out easily. In essence, line 9 is just cash flow from operations minus the added investment in working capital. Line 9 therefore represents the cash flows to be used in judging the desirability or profitability of the project.

III. CAPITAL BUDGETING METHODS

Several methods are available for evaluating the acceptability of the project whose cash flow is calculated in Table 13.1, including:

1. Payback (PBK)
2. Net present value (NPV)
3. Profitability index (PI)
4. Internal rate of return (IRR)

A. Payback Period (PBK)

Payback represents the number of time periods (usually years) necessary for the project to recoup the initial investment and is computed as

$$\text{Payback} = \frac{\text{Initial Investment}}{\text{Annual Cash Flow}} \tag{13.1}$$

Thus, suppose we consider a project that costs \$100,000 and generates cash flows of \$20,000 per year for 10 years. The project's payback period is, then, \$100,000/20,000 = 5 years.

While equation (13.1) applies only to those projects having uniform cash flows, the payback concept can be readily extended to cases of nonuniform cash flows, like that of the CAPM, Inc. Project in Table 13.1. Adding the cash flows of the first three years gives \$108,480. Payback time is therefore approximately 3 ½ years for this project (i.e., \$122,000/(108,480/3)). This computed payback can now be compared with some minimum cost recovery period established by management. If the firm has established a payback time of three years for similar projects, then, based on the payback criterion, the project would not be acceptable.

Another example of the payback method is given in Table 13.2, where we compare two projects with different cash flow patterns and two different ways of computing the payback period. The decision criterion for the company is a payback period of 4 years or less, and the computational details are given below. Note that when the payback period is computed to recover initial investments, both projects are acceptable. However, when the criterion requires the recovery of 150 percent of initial investment, neither of the projects is acceptable.

The *decision criterion* is as follows:

Accept if Payback is less than maximum acceptable payback period of company.
Reject if Payback is more than maximum acceptable payback period of company.

In terms of our example in Table 13.2, for Project A, we have the following:

a. $\text{Payback Period (A)} = \dfrac{\$19{,}800}{\$6{,}160} = 3.21 \text{ years}$

b. $\text{Payback Period (A)} = \dfrac{\$19{,}800 + .50(\$19{,}800)}{\$6{,}160}$

$= 4.82 \text{ years}$

For Project B, we have the following:

a. $\text{Payback Period (B)} = \dfrac{\$20{,}677}{\$6{,}600} = 3.13 \text{ years}$

b. $\text{Payback Period (B)} = \dfrac{\$20{,}677 + .50(\$20{,}677)}{\$6{,}600}$

$= 4.70 \text{ years}$

While payback is a simple criterion, it is limited by the fact that it does not consider any cash flows that are generated after the payback period. Therefore, bias may arise if the majority,

TABLE 13.2 Investment Selection through the Payback Period Criterion

	Project A		*Project B*	
Year	*Initial Cost*	*After-Tax Cash Flow*	*Initial Cost*	*After-Tax Cash Flow*
	$19,800		$20,677	
1		$6,160		$4,400
2		6,160		5,500
3		6,160		6,600
4		6,160		7,700
5		6,160		8,800
5-Year Average*		$6,160		$6,600
a. Payback Period (Initial Outlay):	3.21 years		3.13 years	
b. Payback Period (Initial Outlay + 50%)	4.82 years		4.70 years	

*For uneven cash flows, one may use the annual after-tax cash flows, as we do here, or the incremental method from the actual cash flows.

or even a significant portion, of the project's return occurs after the payback period. In addition to this, payback does not recognize the fact that current dollars are more valuable than future dollars—it ignores the time value of money, so to speak. Accordingly, while payback may be a good rule of thumb, we should consider only those investment criteria that take into account the time value of money. The remaining three methods do just that.

B. Net Present Value (NPV)

1. Some Perspectives

The net present value method, commonly known as NPV, incorporates the time value of money into a simple accept-or-reject criterion. The basis for the NPV method is the concept of present value discussed in most elementary finance and accounting textbooks. According to this concept, the value of an asset is computed by summing the present discounted value of each component cash flow. The rate of discount is represented by the investor's required rate of return or opportunity cost of funds. In most situations, the NPV method nets the current period costs of an asset from the value of the asset. A project's NPV is computed as follows:

$$\text{NPV} = \sum_{n=1}^{t}\left[\frac{R_n}{(1+K)^n}\right] - \sum_{n=1}^{t}\left[\frac{C_n}{(1+K)^n}\right] \quad (13.2)$$

where R_n = the annual (or intraperiod) inflows for each year from 1 to t

C_n = the annual (or intraperiod) outflows for each year from 1 to t, including tax payments;

K = the cost of capital, or the required rate of return for the project

It must be noticed here that equation (13.2) presents a situation where both the benefits and the costs are extended over a period of time, something that may be called *continuous input–continuous output* patterns of flows. However, the typical investment situation discussed in the financial literature is the *point input–continuous output,* where the project outflows are made in the beginning of the investment horizon and the benefits extend over time. Let us be conventional and proceed with the standardized example, which will give us a slightly different formula for the NPV.

$$\text{NPV} = \sum_{n=1}^{t} \left[\frac{\text{CF}_n}{(1 + K)^n} \right] - I_0, \qquad (13.3)$$

where CF_n = the *after-tax* cash inflow for each year (or intraperiod)
I_0 = the investment outlay made in year zero

Let us review equation (13.3) in some detail. The rule for acceptance or rejection is that the rational investor should view all projects that yield a positive NPV as tentatively acceptable. Why? Because the NPV gives the size of the firm's profits from the specific projects, properly discounted by the required rate of return. Therefore, a positive NPV denotes positive profits, properly adjusted for time preference. What about projects with NPV = 0? These are break-even types of investments that earn just exactly the required rate of return and should also be acceptable on the margin. And projects with NPV < 0? These do not indicate money-losing investments that should always be rejected. They only indicate investments whose returns are not as high as the firm's required rate of return.

What we wish to stress here is that NPV > 0 will place the project in the acceptable category for further screening and comparative decision making. Similarly, a project with NPV = 0 or NPV < 0 should not be rejected outright on the basis of arithmetic results alone. If the firm engages in a strategic investment that will create or transfer value some years later than the horizon measured by the NPV equation, it is natural to expect low or even negative NPVs, because this type of investment is motivated by survival or higher order priorities. For example, the takeover of a competitor may be so costly that the NPV from the next 10 years of cash flows will be negative. However, after the firm's survival, the cash flows will be positive and large.

It is important to view all the criteria discussed in this chapter for what they are. That is, they are decision schemes couched under ideal conditions that always allow the decision maker to reach a "yes" or "no" answer. They are also better—because they are discounted—than the techniques discussed under the payback criterion. But, real decisions are not made under ideal conditions, and most investment decisions are not of the routine replacement type. Thus, when strategy comes into the picture for, say survival, value transformation, life cycle or sometimes even business cycle, the NPV and other criteria discussed here must be viewed as the first phase of analysis for a decision to be made when other critical factors are also fully accounted. Let us classify projects as *mandatory* or *voluntary,* where the former are imposed on the firm by society at large. Such mandatory investments are accepted on grounds other than their value contribution. On the other hand, voluntary projects of nonstrategic significance to the firm must follow the simple rule of

Accept if NPV > 0;
Reject if NPV < 0.

That is, the acceptance of projects with NPV > 0 will result in value creation, while the acceptance of investments with NPV < 0 will result in value reduction. Finally, the acceptance of projects with NPV = 0 will maintain the value of the firm at its present level.

Projects that can be accepted (or rejected) independently present no problems to the decision maker. However, life is a bit more complicated among financial decision makers, for they have to choose the investment project (or projects) that add the greatest value to the firm. For these choices they must handle what we call in finance *mutually exclusive projects,* that is, projects that are *substitutes* or *competitive*. In such cases, the net present value rule also requires that not only should NPV > 0 but also that we accept that project with the highest positive NPV value. It should also be noted here that rational economic decision making requires that one of the following be observed:

1. The firm begins with the highest NPV project and continues accepting projects until the last dollar invested yields NPV = 0, thus ensuring that the marginal rate of return from the last dollar invested will be equal to the cost of capital. This is the case where there is no budget constraint or where available profit-

able opportunities can be covered by the existing budget.
2. The firm begins with the highest NPV project and continues accepting projects until its investment budget is completely allocated. This is the case where the size of the existing budget restricts the number of projects to be accepted.

Finally, there are projects whose acceptance is contingent upon the acceptance of other related projects, such as machinery and the plant to house it. These types of projects indicate *complementary* relationships and are formulated in terms of *contingent* or *dependent* proposals. Thus, the project under study and the investment upon which its implementation is contingent must be part of the same proposal and reviewed as an inseparable bundle of cash flows.

2. Computational Aspects of Net Present Value

We shall begin our presentation of the computational details involved in the NPV criterion by reviewing an earlier example from Table 13.2. The information is reproduced in augmented form in Table 13.3. Let us now take the information for each of the two projects and compute their net present values. Beginning with Project A, and assuming a cost of capital, $K = 8\%$, we have

$$NPV_A = \frac{\$6{,}160}{(1+.08)^1} + \frac{\$6{,}160}{(1+.08)^2} + \frac{\$6{,}160}{(1+.08)^3} + \frac{\$6{,}160}{(1+.08)^4} + \frac{\$6{,}160}{(1+.08)^5} - \$19{,}800$$

$$= \$5{,}704 + \$5{,}281 + \$4{,}890 + \$4{,}528 + \$4{,}192 - \$19{,}800$$

$$= \$24{,}596 - \$19{,}800$$

$$= \$4{,}796$$

Because the after-tax cash flows are uniform, of specified size, timing, and duration, we can view this problem as being equivalent to an annuity formulation. Thus, we can use the table entitled "Present Value of an Annuity ($1)" in Appendix 4, where at the intersection of the interest rate column for $i = 8\%$, and the years row for $n = 5$, we find the value, $PV_a = 3.9927 \approx 3.993$. Then, we can find the net present value of Project A, as follows:

$$NPV_A = (\$6{,}160 \times 3.993) - \$19{,}800 = \$4{,}796$$

Let us go on with the NPV computation of

TABLE 13.3 Investment Selection Through Various Criteria

	Project A			*Project B*		
Year	*Initial Cost*	*After-Tax Cash Flow*	*Project Ranking*	*Initial Cost*	*After-Tax Cash Flow*	*Project Ranking*
	$19,800			$20,677		
1		$6,160			$4,400	
2		6,160			5,500	
3		6,160			6,600	
4		6,160			7,700	
5		6,160			8,800	
Payback Period (Initial Outlay)		3.21 years	2		3.13 years	1
Payback Period (Initial Outlay + 50%)		4.82 years	2		4.70 years	1
Net Present Value		$4,796	2		$5,000	1
Profitability Index		1.2422	1		1.2418	2
Internal Rate of Return		16.8%	1		15.8%	2

Project B also discounted at $K = 8\%$. We shall perform the operations this time by finding the corresponding values for $(1 + K)$ for each year through the "Present Value of $1" table in Appendix 3. Thus we shall look for the present value factor at the column for 8% and in the rows for year 1 at .92593, year 2 at .85734, year 3 at .79383, year 4 at .73503, and year 5 at .68058. Then,

$$\begin{aligned} NPV_B &= (\$4{,}400)(.92593) + (\$5{,}500)(.85734) \\ &\quad + (\$6{,}600)(.79383) + (\$7{,}700)(.73503) \\ &\quad + (\$8{,}800)(.68058) \\ &= \$4{,}074 + \$4{,}715 + \$5{,}239 + \$5{,}660 \\ &\quad + \$5{,}989 - \$20{,}677 \\ &= \$25{,}677 - \$20{,}677 \\ &= \$5{,}000 \end{aligned}$$

As an additional illustration we also present the computations in Table 13.4, where 2 projects of 3-year duration are discounted to their net present values at a cost of capital $K = 15\%$. These two projects are mutually exclusive and require no explicit ranking. Thus, on the basis of the NPV rule, only Project 1 is acceptable as it has the largest NPV value at NPV = $3,840, versus NPV = $864 for Project 2.

Finally, returning to the cash flows CF_n for the hypothetical firm, CAPM, Inc., we see them computed in Table 13.1. If we assume a cost of capital of 15 percent, then the project's NPV will be $76,172. In that case we should accept the project, because it has a positive NPV. To see the reasoning behind this, consider valuing a financial asset with cash flows similar to those represented by the CAPM, Inc. project in Table 13.1. In a world of certainty, with a discount rate of 15 percent, the asset would be valued at $198,172 (the PV of the cash flows). However, CAPM, Inc. apparently has monopoly access to the project at a cost substantially less than its value. Consequently, the difference of benefit over cost (NPV) must represent an addition to the overall value of the firm. Alternatively, the amount $76,172 represents the present-value premium the project would earn above what would be earned by an investment returning 15 percent. Therefore, CAPM, Inc. should accept the project. If the NPV were negative, the firm would reject the project.

Note that the use of NPV in the example disregarded the side benefits associated with the financing of the project (i.e., the tax shield generated through the use of debt financing). However, the cash flows computed in Table 13.1 are relevant cash flows for all-equity-financed firms. The implicit assumption in the example was that

TABLE 13.4 Net Present Values of Projects 1 and 2

		Project 1		*Project 2*	
1	*2*	*3*	*4*	*5*	*6*
Year	*Present Value of $1 Discounted at 15%*	*After-Tax Cash Flows*	*Present Value of Cash Flow Discounted at 15% (col. 2 × col. 3)*	*After-Tax Cash Flows*	*Present Value of Cash Flow Discounted at 15% (col. 2 × col. 5)*
1	$ .870	$50,000	$ 43,500	$60,000	$ 52,200
2	.756	45,000	34,020	40,000	30,240
3	.658	40,000	$ 26,320	28,000	18,424
Total discounted cash flows			$103,840		$100,864
$\sum_{n=1}^{3} R_n(1+r)^{-n} - \sum_{n=1}^{3} C_n(1+r)^{-n} =$			$ 3,840		$ 864

Cost of projects: Project 1 = $100,000; Project 2 = $100,000
Salvage value at end of third year: zero for both projects
Method of depreciation: straight line for both projects

the financing and investment decisions can be made separately. Nonetheless, we must still *require that the NPV method arrive at a value that reflects the tax shield generated by the inclusion of debt in the capital structure.*

As shown in Chapter 12, *discounting the firm's cash flows with an after-tax weighted average cost of capital (WACC) results in the correct computation of a project's value.* Used in the same fashion, NPV allows us to have a decentralized capital-budgeting system. Moreover, because discounting at the WACC incorporates the effects of debt financing, we need not be concerned with the sources of financing. To account for other side effects generated by project acceptance, however, the adjusted present value (APV) method, described later in the chapter, may be the appropriate model.

Let us now focus on the Net Present Value criterion in terms of its advantages and disadvantages both as an analytical technique and a practical decision rule. The *advantages* of the NPV criterion are as follows:

1. Unlike the payback period criterion, the NPV criterion accounts for the time value of money.
2. The NPV criterion discounts the cash flows from a project at the cost of capital, thus recognizing explicitly both the financing costs and the returns required by the company's shareholders.
3. The NPV criterion yields answers in monetary units, thus making it easier for managers to match them with the monetary inputs from the investment budget.
4. The NPV criterion can be easily modified to account for investment risk.

The *disadvantages* are the following:

1. The NPV criterion assumes that the intermediate cash flows are reinvested at the cost of capital, thus creating confusion when this does not occur.
2. The NPV criterion assumes that the cost of capital remains constant for the duration of the project's life, thus underestimating NPV when K is reduced and overestimating NPV when K is increased.
3. The NPV criterion can be confusing, particularly at NPV $= 0$, where this is confounded with a zero return for a project.
4. The NPV criterion, being measured in monetary units, makes it difficult to decide on the desirability of investments with different NPVs and different outlays. For example, it is easy to decide between Projects 1 and 2 in Table 13.4, because both projects have equal outlays. However, for Projects A and B in Table 13.3 the situation can be confusing because they have different outlays, and we have not ranked them in terms of relative profitability.

Before we end this section, we should recapitulate the main points of the net present value criterion. They are as follows:

1. The net present value criterion utilizes the cost of capital as the discount rate. Here we assume that management knows the true rate of return required by the market, also known as the *external rate of return*.
2. The net present value criterion is computed on the assumption that all the intermediate cash flows are reinvested at the same rate as the original cash flows, that is, at the cost of capital.

In addition to the above, the net present value criterion can be meaningfully applied as follows:

1. Use the criterion to maximize the net present value from a sequence of future after-tax cash flows associated with a single, specific project. Here the criterion requires that we take every single feasible proposal that will maximize the wealth of the firm.
2. Use the criterion to maximize the net present value of a combination of complementary or independent proposals. Here the rule concentrates on the maximization of the firm's wealth through the combination of projects rather than through a project with the higher NPV.
3. Use the criterion to accept an incremental proposal whose NPV > 0. Here the rule is meaningful only if the incremental project is independent of all other proposals in the company's capital budget.

We must state one more time that the acid test of an investment criterion is its ability to rank projects on the basis of their relative profitability, correctly and consistently.

C. Profitability Index (PI)

1. Some Perspectives

The net present value criterion netted out the present value of the costs from the present value of the benefits to arrive at an absolute monetary value of profitability. However, if instead of taking the difference between the discounted benefits and costs, we took the ratio of these discounted values, we would have a relative measure of profitability commonly known as the discounted *benefit–cost ratio* (BCR). This is shown in equation (13.4), where it should be noted that the same discount rate is used for both benefits and costs.

$$\text{BCR} = \sum_{n=1}^{t} \left[\frac{R_n}{(1+K)^n} \right] \Big/ \sum_{n=1}^{t} \left[\frac{C_n}{(1+K)^n} \right] \tag{13.4}$$

A simpler version of the BCR is given for the point input–continuous output pattern of cash flows, where the outlay for the investment is made fully in the beginning. Under this case we have

$$\text{BCR} = \sum_{n=1}^{t} \left[\frac{R_n}{(1+K)^n} \right] \Big/ I_0 \tag{13.5}$$

This version of BCR is also known as the *profitability index* (PI) and it separates the original investment from subsequent outlays associated with the project. The reason for it is that for the original investment cost the management had some discretion in accepting or rejecting the proposal, whereas subsequent costs must be made to maintain the value of the investment. The criteria for acceptance here are equivalent to those for the NPV, except that the benchmark is not zero but unity. Specifically, projects with BCR > 1 are profitable and should be placed in the "acceptable" category. Projects with BCR $= 1$ return just enough to cover the required rate of return. Projects with BCR < 1 return less than the required rate of return. In practice, much like the case of NPV, the projects or combinations of projects eventually accepted and implemented may very well include values of BCR $\gtreqless 1$, depending on their urgency, strategic value, risk-reduction potential, and many other practical and important reasons.

2. Computational Aspects of the Profitability Index

Let us compute the PI values for investment projects A and B shown in Table 13.3.

$$\text{BCR}_\text{A} = \frac{\$24{,}596}{\$19{,}800} = 1.2422$$

$$\text{BCR}_\text{B} = \frac{\$25{,}677}{\$20{,}677} = 1.2418$$

The value of BCR_A is slightly greater than the value of BCR_B. Note that the value to the left of the decimal point indicates recovery of the original investment, while the value to the right of the decimal point indicates the relative rate of return. We can always subtract unity from the BCR to net out the original investment and obtain the relative rate of return directly. We shall perform this additional simplification for Projects 1 and 2 that were introduced in Table 13.4.

$$\text{BCR}_1 = \frac{\$103{,}840}{\$100{,}000} = 1.0384 - 1$$
$$= .0384$$

$$\text{BCR}_2 = \frac{\$100{,}864}{\$100{,}000} = 1.0086 - 1$$
$$= .0086$$

It should be noted here that both the NPV and the BCR criteria rank Project 1 higher than Project 2. Moreover, because the initial outlay for both projects is the same \$100,000, the comparison and the subsequent ranking are meaningful. However, for Projects A and B the situation is reversed, although by a slight factor. That is, although $\text{NPV}_\text{A} < \text{NPV}_\text{B}$, we have $\text{BCR}_\text{A} > \text{BCR}_\text{B}$. This reversal is not unusual among projects that are mutually exclusive, although in our case Projects A and B are not presented as mutually exclusive. Moreover, the reversals in rankings create problems for the decision maker.

The case for the benefit cost ratio or profitability index can be summarized in terms of the advantages and disadvantages claimed. The *advantages* are as follows:

1. Like the NPV, the Profitability Index criterion accounts for the time value of money.
2. Like the NPV, the PI criterion discounts the after-tax cash flows from a project at the cost of capital.
3. Unlike the NPV, the PI criterion computes the desirability of investment on a "per-dollar-invested" basis. Thus, it highlights the relative desirability of an investment by abstracting from the question of scale (size).
4. Like the NPV, the PI can be adjusted to account for investment risk.

The *disadvantages* are the following:

1. Like the NPV, the PI criterion assumes that the intermediate cash flows are reinvested at the cost of capital.
2. Like the NPV, the PI criterion assumes that the cost of capital remains constant throughout the useful economic life of the project.
3. Like the NPV, the PI criterion can be confusing, particularly when PI = 1.
4. Unlike the NPV, the PI criterion does not express in absolute terms the expected economic contribution of the project.

D. The Internal Rate of Return

1. Some Perspectives

The NPV and PI criteria were based on the explicit assumption that the correct discount rate to use with any investment was the cost of capital or required rate of return. Additionally, it was assumed implicitly that this cost of capital remained constant for the duration of the project and also served as the reinvestment rate for intermediate cash flows. An alternative criterion, that is also used rather commonly by business executives, does not impose a discount rate on a given investment. Known as the *internal rate of return* or the *internal rate of discount,* this criterion computes the discount rate directly from the cash inflows and cash outflows associated with an investment.

The *internal rate of return* (IRR) (or rate of return on investment) criterion expresses the estimated value of a project as a single overall rate of return per annum. The rate of return in this case is equal to the discount rate at which the present values of expected outlays and cash earnings are exactly equal. Other names for this criterion are the internal rate of profit, the internal rate of discount, the marginal efficiency of capital (MEC), and the discounted cash flow technique (DCF). The internal rate of return can be computed by equation (13.6).

$$\sum_{n=1}^{t} \frac{R_n}{(1+\rho)^n} = \sum_{n=1}^{t} \frac{C_n}{(1+\rho)^n} \tag{13.6}$$

where ρ is the internal rate of return. It should be said here that equation (13.6) can be derived from equation (13.2) by setting NPV = 0. However, the discount factor used for the internal rate of return is not the same as the one used for the net present value method. In fact, in equation (13.6) we solve for ρ by trial and error, while in (13.2) we assume K as the cost of capital.

As was the case with the other criteria, we can rewrite equation (13.6) above, for the simpler case of point input–continuous output flows, as follows:

$$\sum_{n=1}^{t} \frac{R_n}{(1+\rho)^n} = I_0 \tag{13.7}$$

Another equivalent way of expressing the IRR criterion is

$$\sum_{n=1}^{t} \frac{R_n}{(1+\rho)^n} - I_0 = \text{NPV} = 0 \tag{13.8}$$

The procedure for computing the internal rate of discount is tedious but not overly complicated. We must solve a polynomial in ρ by trial and error. As a first approximation we choose an estimated starting rate, say the payback reciprocal, and compute the present values for the left-hand side (cash earnings) term of equation (13.7). Then we subtract from it the investment outlays and, according to the result, proceed as follows:

1. If the difference between the present value of expected cash earnings and the project outlays is positive, we try again with a higher starting discount rate.
2. If the difference between the present value of the cash earnings and the investment outlays is negative, we try again with a lower starting rate.
3. If the difference between the two values of benefits and costs is exactly equal to 0, we have arrived at the rate of discount that equalizes the present value of the stream of cash earnings with the investment outlay. That is, we have computed the IRR for the project under review.

The internal rate of return is a rate that represents the compound rate of return on an investment. This compound rate can be compared to the firm's required rate of return or some other opportunity cost. In terms of utilization, the IRR can be employed with independent projects as follows:

If IRR $\geq$ cost of capital, the proposal is placed in the acceptable category.

If IRR $<$ cost of capital, the proposal may be considered acceptable only if there are other reasons, such as urgency, risk reduction, and other circumstances as discussed with the NPV and the PI criteria.

2. Computational Aspects of the Internal Rate of Return

Returning to our previous examples of Projects A and B in Table 13.3 and Projects 1 and 2 in Table 13.4, we can compute the IRR values and consider them along with the NPV and PI. For Project A we have the following:

$$\$19{,}800 = \frac{\$6{,}160}{(1+K)^1} + \frac{\$6{,}160}{(1+K)^2} + \frac{\$6{,}160}{(1+K)^3} + \frac{\$6{,}160}{(1+K)^4} + \frac{\$6{,}160}{(1+K)^5}$$

$$\$19{,}800 = \$6{,}160 \sum_{n=1}^{5} \left[\frac{1}{(1+K)^n}\right]$$

$$\$19{,}800 = \$6{,}160 \times \text{(Value from "Present Value of Annuity" Table)}$$

$$\frac{\$19{,}800}{\$6{,}160} = 3.214$$

This value is found by locating the nearest approximation at $n = 5$ years. It corresponds to the values between $K = 16\%$ (3.2743) and $K = 17\%$ (3.1993), and by interpolation we have

$$K = \rho = 16.8\% \text{ for IRR}_A$$

For Project B the computations will be somewhat more cumbersome due to the fact that the cash flows over the 5-year period are not uniform and the case cannot be treated as an annuity. We shall begin with a discount rate, say $K = 15\%$.

Step 1. Try $K = 15\%$.

$$\text{NPV} = 0 = \frac{\$4{,}400}{(1+.15)^1} + \frac{\$5{,}500}{(1+.15)^2} + \frac{\$6{,}600}{(1+.15)^3} + \frac{\$7{,}700}{(1+.15)^4} + \frac{\$8{,}800}{(1+.15)^5} - \$20{,}677$$

$$= \$3{,}826 + \$4{,}159 + \$4{,}340 + \$4{,}403 + \$4{,}375 - \$20{,}677$$

$$= \$21{,}103 - \$20{,}677$$

NPV $= \$426 > 0$. Therefore, we must try another value of $K > 15\%$.

Step 2. Try $K = 16\%$.

$$\text{NPV} = 0 = \frac{\$4{,}400}{(1+.16)^1} + \frac{\$5{,}500}{(1+.16)^2} + \frac{\$6{,}600}{(1+.16)^3} + \frac{\$7{,}700}{(1+.16)^4} + \frac{\$8{,}800}{(1+.16)^5} - \$20{,}677$$

$$= \$3{,}793 + \$4{,}087 + \$4{,}228$$

$$+ \$4{,}253 + \$4{,}190 - \$20{,}677$$

$$= \$20{,}551 - \$20{,}677$$

NPV $= -126 < 0$. Therefore, $.16 > \rho > .15$.

Step 3. Find ρ where $NPV_B = 0$. One simple way to get the exact value for IRR_B is to proceed by interpolation as follows:

$$IRR_B \approx 15 + \left[\left(\frac{426}{126 + 426}\right)(1)\right] = 15 + \frac{426}{552}$$

$$IRR_B \approx 15 + .8$$

$$IRR_B \approx 15.8\%$$

Alternatively we can interpolate as follows:

$$IRR_B \approx 16 - \left[\left(\frac{126}{126 + 426}\right)(1)\right] = 16 - \frac{126}{552}$$

$$IRR_B \approx 16 - .2 = 15.8\%$$

Notice that the denominator in step 3 is always the sum of the absolute values of the two net present values obtained through two different K rates. Also, if we begin with the lower rate that yielded a positive NPV, we add to it the ratio of its NPV divided by the sum of the absolute values of the NPVs. If we begin with the higher rate that yielded a negative NPV, we subtract from it the ratio of its NPV divided by the sum of the absolute values of the NPVs. Finally, the number (1) also has a specific meaning. It denotes the difference between the two rates that yielded the last positive NPV and first negative NPV, that is $16\% - 15\% = 1\%$. If the numbers were different, say $15\% - 12\% = 3\%$, then the number in the parentheses would be equal to 3.

Following the three steps outlined above, we can now compute the IRR values for Projects 1 and 2 in rather quick strokes, without much detail. Remember from Table 13.4 that the cash flows from the two projects have already been discounted at 15%. That is, step 1 has already been completed. Let us proceed with Project 1 as follows:

$$\text{At } K = 15\%,\ NPV_1 = \$3{,}840$$

$$\text{At } K = 18\%,\ NPV_1 = \$-964$$

$$IRR_1 \approx 15 + \left[\left(\frac{3{,}840}{3{,}840 + 964}\right)(3)\right]$$

$$= 15 + 2.40$$

$$IRR_1 \approx 17.4\%$$

Similarly, for Project 2, we have

$$\text{At } K = 15\%,\ NPV_2 = \$864$$

$$\text{At } K = 16\%,\ NPV_2 = \$-611$$

$$IRR_2 \approx 15 + \left[\left(\frac{864}{864 + 611}\right)(1)\right] = 15 + .58$$

$$IRR_2 \approx 15.6\%$$

Let us now focus on the IRR criterion in terms of the advantages and disadvantages attributed to it by scholars and practitioners. The *advantages* of the IRR criterion follow:

1. Like the NPV and PI, the internal rate of return accounts for the time value of money.
2. Unlike the NPV and the PI, the IRR does not discount the cash flows at the cost of capital, but rather it searches for the true rate of return associated with a particular project. This project-sensitive rate of return can then be compared with the firm's cost of capital and decisions can be made.
3. The IRR provides a compound rate of return on investment that does not take financing costs explicitly into account. This can be an advantage over NPV when financing costs are increasing.
4. Like the NPV and the PI, the IRR can be adjusted to reflect the presence of risk in a project.

The *disadvantages* of the IRR criterion are as follows:

1. The Internal Rate of Return assumes that the intermediate cash flows are reinvested at the compound rate ρ.
2. The trial-and-error method of obtaining the IRR is cumbersome.
3. The IRR criterion, being a relative rate, over-

looks the monetary size of the investment—much like the case of the PI criterion.
4. Under some circumstances, the IRR equation, being a t-degree polynomial with t-roots, can produce many solutions (rates).

3. Other Attributes of the Internal Rate of Return

Now, let us pursue the internal rate of return criterion in greater detail. To begin with, there is no direct correspondence between the net present value criterion and the internal rate of return criterion. For example, if the cost elements involve only an initial outlay and no subsequent payments, while all the benefit elements are returned at the end of the useful life of the assets, then the rate of return ρ can be viewed as the rate of growth, compounded annually, that transforms an initial input (outlay) into the final output (yield).

E. Other Discounted Cash Flow Criteria

In addition to the three DCF criteria of NPV, PI, and IRR, there are some other decision criteria that are both analytically sound and practically popular. These are (1) the net costs criterion, (2) the annual benefit–cost ratio, (3) the net terminal value criterion, and (4) the uniform annuity series or equivalent annual charge. We shall discuss them briefly below.

1. The Net Costs Criterion

The net costs criterion involves the minimization of average cost (cost per unit of output), reduced to present values, of the entire productive activity of the firm, present and future. It is popular among businesspeople, production engineers, and accountants, and is both all-inclusive and discounted. However, this technique becomes complicated by the problem of cost imputations in joint-product manufacturing and by the problem of depreciation. We shall not pursue this criterion further, other than to mention that it relates directly the cycle of product demand to production and investment demand.

2. The Annual Benefit–Cost Ratio

The annual benefit–cost ratio converts discounted annual costs into equivalent average annual outlays that are, in turn, compared to the average annual returns. The comparison of the average discounted inflows and outlays determines the desirability of the investment proposal. The rule for accept or reject is that a project should be accepted if the gross ratio of the annual benefits over the annual costs is greater than 1. In the same vein, we can get the net ratio by taking the difference: gross ratio -1 = net ratio. The annual benefit–cost ratio, popular among engineers, gives exactly identical answers with the discounted benefit–cost ratio when salvage value is included. However, the latter is preferred in view of the simplicity and ease of computation.

3. The Net Terminal Value

The net terminal value is used to compound the cash inflows and outlays forward to some future terminal date. It is the converse of discounting the same flows to their present value. The rule for accept-or-reject decisions is that a project should be accepted if its net terminal value (the difference between the compounded benefits and costs) is greater than 0. It should be obvious that there is a complete parallel between the compounded net terminal value and the discounted net present value. However, human nature being what it is, we prefer the former technique because it focuses on present magnitudes.

4. The Uniform Annuity Series or Equivalent Annual Charge

The uniform annuity series is a method that we employ when dealing with mutually exclusive projects of unequal duration. Rather than repeating the project with the shorter duration until the two projects have equal duration or repeating both projects to infinity, we have the opportunity of finding the uniform annuity series (UAS) for each project. Then, we choose the project with the higher uniform annuity series. The UAS is defined as the annuity whose present value equals the net present value of the project under consideration. Thus we have

$$\text{Equivalent Annual Charge} = \text{UAS} = \frac{\text{NPV of Project}}{\text{PV of Annuity Factor}}$$

IV. MULTIPLE RATES OF RETURN AND OTHER CASH-FLOW ISSUES

As Figure 13.1 indicates, the typical NPV profile is negatively sloped with respect to the discount rate and ordinarily has a single point of intersection with the horizontal axis. However, there are cases of multiple intersections or rates. The existence of multiple rates of discount was first addressed by Lorie and Savage. To see how they can occur, let us consider what types of projects have the typical NPV profile shown in Figure 13.1. If we confine ourselves to projects that are point input (i.e., that have a single outlay) and continuous output (i.e., generate continuous cash flows), as is the case in Table 13.1, we will arrive at the typical NPV profile. In these projects, we see a negative outflow at first, followed by positive inflows. However, if any of the intermediate cash flows CF_t are negative and large, then we can no longer state with certainty that the NPV profile declines monotonically with the discount rate r. As is evident from equation (13.8), we then have a polynomial function with r roots; consequently, the uniqueness of r cannot be guaranteed. (For more details on multiple rates of return, see Bierman and Smidt 1980, 58–63.)

Before concluding the discussion of methods, one additional comment is in order. The CAPM, Inc. example we have been considering assumed that the firm used straight-line depreciation over the project's life. Because depreciation is a non-cash expense, it provides a tax shield in the form of reduced taxes. As taxable income is reduced by the amount of the depreciation, the shield generated yearly is equal to the tax rate multiplied by the yearly depreciation (i.e., .34 × 18,000 = \$6,120). Notice, however, that the earlier a dollar is received for any one project, the larger the present value. Therefore, other things being equal, it would be better to spread the \$90,000 in depreciation for CAPM, Inc.'s hypothetical investment over a five-year period, so that earlier years are allocated larger depreciation sums.

Two popular methods of accelerated depreciation are the sum of the year's digits (SYD)

FIGURE 13.1 Net Present Value Profile

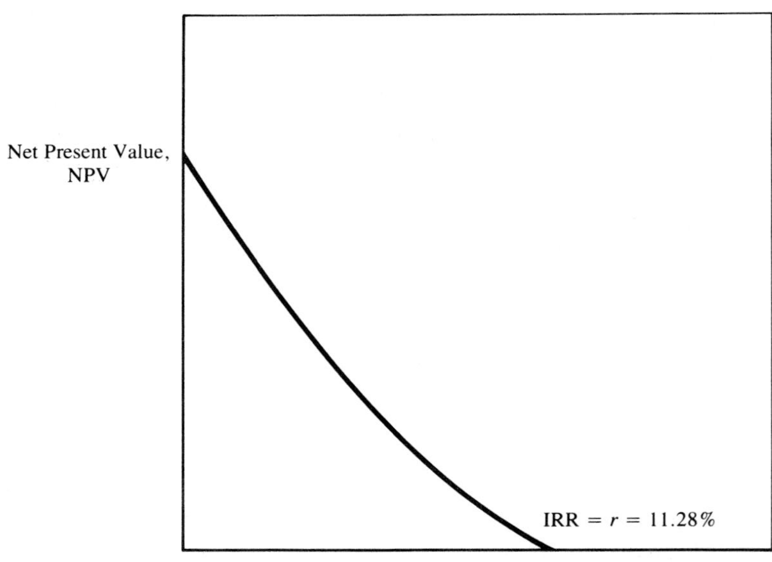

and the double declining balance. Both of these methods compute depreciation in such a way that the first year receives the highest depreciation, the second the next highest, and so forth. The obvious impact of such schemes in considering investment proposals is that we will arrive at a higher NPV because the value of the tax shield will increase through the use of accelerated depreciation. Moreover, the accelerated cost recovery system (ACRS) specifies that a firm may take depreciation at an accelerated rate. Basically, under this system, all assets are classified as having 3-, 5-, 10-, or 15-year depreciable lives with no salvage value. Depending on the classification of an investment proposal, the allowable accelerated depreciation must be computed in accordance with ACRS.

V. INVESTMENT UNDER CAPITAL RATIONING

The foregoing discussion of project evaluation assumed that ample funds were available for all investment projects under consideration. That is, in order to accept all projects with a positive NPV, we must have sufficient financial resources. When sufficient financial resources are not available, and the firm is unable to accept all projects with positive NPV, *capital rationing* is said to exist. (A similar problem exists when only one of several competing projects can be accepted.) One way to look at the problem of capital rationing is through the use of the PI. As mentioned earlier, the PI is a benefit–cost ratio in which the numerator is the present value of the project's net cash flows (i.e., PI represents the monetary present value per dollar invested). Accordingly, consider the following projects and their corresponding cash flows, net present values, and profitability indexes:

Suppose that the firm is considering only projects A, B, and C, and has a rationing program in effect that sets a maximum of only $15 million in expenditures. Clearly, the firm may select either project A alone or both projects B and C. One simple way to overcome the selection problem is to rank investments by their PI and select the project with the highest PI, the second highest PI, and so forth, until the limit on spending is met. In this way, we are assured of getting the most in present value for our spending limit. According to this criterion, we would take project C first and then B.

This simple procedure, however, will break down when we consider all four projects as a group, with constrained resources of $15 million in each period. The failure is due to the fact that project D does not require any outlay in the current period. In addition, if any of the four projects A through D are dependent or mutually exclusive, the PI ranking method will no longer yield correct and consistent decisions. In such instances, there are more appropriate methods for finding the "best" package of investments to undertake. These methods use techniques of mathematical programming, such as linear programming (LP), to solve for the optimal package or grouping of investment projects. (See Chapter 14 for mathematical techniques that deal with such activities as valuation, portfolio selection, and portfolio management.)

Simply stated, the objective of a linear programming model is to find the set of projects that gives the maximum present value subject to a variety of constraints. For capital rationing, the constraints require that the rationing limit is met in each period and that negative percentage values for the project accepted are not allowed.

Projects	CF_0	CF_1	CF_2	*NPV(@15%)*	*PI*
A	−15	35	10	23	2.5
B	−7.5	10	15	12.5	2.6
C	−7.5	6	20	12.8	2.7
D	0	−30	50	11.7	1.4

VI. CAPITAL BUDGETING AND THE CAPITAL ASSET PRICING MODEL (CAPM)

Up to now very little has been said about project risk and the rate of discount to be used in the evaluation of capital investments. Obviously, projects that are considered risky should be discounted at higher rates, as investors wish to be compensated for the added risk. In what follows, we will consider the capital asset pricing model (CAPM), which is the standard modern technique employed in pricing risk. Further details on the CAPM and the security market line (SML) are given in Chapter 14.

The CAPM states that a security's expected rate of return in equilibrium is linearly related to risk. Mathematically,

$$E(R_j) = R_F + [E(R_M) - R_F]\beta_j \quad (13.9)$$

where $E(R_j)$ = expected return on security j
R_F = risk-free rate
$E(R_M)$ = expected return on market
β_j = a measure of sensitivity, relating how the security's expected return reacts to the market (the measure is referred to as "beta")

Equation (13.9) proves very useful once the various inputs necessary to estimate $E(R_j)$ are computed. Unfortunately, however, the estimation of beta for physical assets is rather difficult. Consequently, the CAPM does not give us a simple way in which to estimate the discount rate for a project. The problem is that the CAPM is a single-period valuation expression, while most real-life capital budgeting problems clearly extend beyond the one-year horizon. Nevertheless, although the theory does not have all the answers, it can point us in the right direction as we attempt to evaluate risk. The approach we will follow here is related to the discussion of risk in Chapter 12.

We begin with the estimation β_j. First, note that the easiest beta to estimate is the beta associated with a firm's common stock. Because historical rates of return on most securities are available from such services as COMPUSTAT or the Center for Research on Security Prices (CRSP) at the University of Chicago, the computation of stock betas is simplified. Moreover, because beta measures how a stock's rate of return responds, on average, to market movements, the well-known technique of linear regression can be used to estimate its value. Thus, by regressing the security's return against the market return, we can compute beta as

$$\beta_j = \frac{\text{Cov}(R_j, R_M)}{\text{Var}(R_M)} \quad (13.10)$$

where $\text{Cov}(R_j, R_M)$ represents the covariance of returns between security j and the market, and $\text{Var}(R_M)$ represents the variance of the market returns. Let us suppose that a company's stock beta is $\beta = 1.1$, with a risk-free rate of $R_F = .09$ and a market return of $R_M = .15$. Then, according to the CAPM, the company's required rate of return, given by equation (13.9) is

$$E(R_j) = .09 + (.15 - .09)1.1 = 15.6\%$$

However, the value 15.6 percent is not the company's overall cost of capital, as $E(R_j)$ represents only the company's cost of equity capital. The discount rate k used in capital budgeting is the hurdle rate that reflects both the firm's business risk as well as its financial risk. That is, the computed beta is the reaction coefficient for the firm's common stock, not for the entire asset base of the firm. Nevertheless, we can express the beta of an asset as a function of the betas on debt and equity. Mathematically, the equation is

$$\beta_{\text{asset}} = \beta_{\text{debt}} \frac{\text{debt}}{\text{debt} + \text{equity}} + \beta_{\text{equity}} \frac{\text{equity}}{\text{debt} + \text{equity}} \quad (13.11)$$

Essentially, equation (13.11) states that the beta for the asset base is simply a weighted average of the stock and bond betas. This should be obvious, as the asset base is financed with debt and equity. Hence, given the beta of an asset, we could use the CAPM equation (13.9) to compute the required rate of return on the asset under consideration. This rate would then be the relevant discount rate to be used in the capital budgeting NPV equation (13.2).

To illustrate the computation, let us assume that the firm's $\beta_{debt} = .60$, and that its debt-to-total-capitalization ratio is .40. Then, if acceptance of the project will not alter the existing capital structure of the firm (not always a valid assumption—see Chapter 12), the overall asset-base beta is

$$\beta_{asset} = .60(.40) + 1.1(.60) = .90$$

Using this result, we can compute the asset's required rate of return, that is,

$$E(R_{asset}) = .09 + (.15 - .09).90 = 14.4\%$$

Therefore, we should discount the project's cash flows shown in Table 13.1 at the rate of 14.4 percent.

While it may be difficult to compute asset betas due to lack of available hard data in the capital budgeting process, the CAPM approach forces the financial manager to consider project risk in the evaluation of investments. One approach the manager might take is to assume that project risk is affected by the cyclical nature of a firm's business operations and rely on existing evidence showing that those firms with cyclical earnings do in fact have high betas. This is a simple example of how high asset risk might be translated into a higher rate of return. The certainty-equivalent method, discussed in the appendix to this chapter, represents another way to adjust for risk.

VII. ADJUSTED PRESENT VALUE (APV)

Myers (1974) has recast the original MM proposition into a normative framework for asset valuation. His approach considers how investment and financing may interact and is known as the *adjusted present value* (APV) method. Earlier, we stated that a project should be valued without considering the sources of financing (i.e., the investment decision is separated from the financing decision). On the other hand, as mentioned in Chapter 12 the side effects associated with debt financing can be incorporated into the discount rate. Moreover, if still other side effects exist, the use of a single risk-adjusted discount rate becomes complex. That is when the APV method by Myers comes into the decision process.

The APV criterion starts with assumptions similar to those of the NPV. In particular, cash flows are computed as if the firm were all-equity financed, a situation known as the *NPV base case*. Consider a (point-input-and-continuous-output) project with an initial outlay of $5 million that is expected to generate level cash flows of $1 million per year for 10 years. The investor's required rate of return is 10 percent. The NPV base case is

$$\begin{aligned} \text{NPV} &= -5.0 + \sum_{t=1}^{10} \frac{1.00}{(1.10)^t} \\ &= \$1.1446 \text{ million} \end{aligned}$$

However, there may be side effects associated with the project, for example, flotation costs associated with the sale of securities, or an increase in the firm's debt capacity. Now, suppose the firm issued $5 million of common stock to finance the project. Then, because investment bankers charge a fee for issuing securities, the firm will have to raise more than the necessary $5 million. If the fees amount to, say, 4 percent of the proceeds, the firm will have to issue $5.20 million of common stock. (The $.20 million in fees counts as flotation costs.) The APV of this project would then be

$$\begin{aligned} \text{APV} &= \text{NPV Base Case} - \text{Flotation Costs} \\ &= 1.1446 - .20 = .9446 \end{aligned}$$

Thus, even in the presence of issue costs, the project has a positive present value of $944,600. Clearly, then, the APV approach can easily handle such side effects.

As mentioned in Chapter 12 there may be positive side effects associated with the use of debt financing—namely, the deductibility of interest for tax purposes. Restating MM's proposition to take account of corporate taxes, we have

$$\text{Firm Value} = V^{U} + \text{PV(Tax Shield)}$$

where V^{U} is the value of our otherwise identical all-equity firm. The APV criterion also incorporates the side effect of debt, as follows:

$$\text{APV} = \text{NPV Base Case} + \text{PV (Tax Shield)}$$

To see how this formulation works, suppose that the project's acceptance prompts the firm to borrow an additional $2 million with a coupon rate of 9 percent and interest paid at the end of each year. Then, assuming a tax rate of .34 the tax shield provided by the interest expense is .34 ($2 million × .09) = $61,200 per year for 10 years. Now, because the tax shield is just as risky as the interest payments that generate it, the PV can be computed as follows:

$$\begin{aligned}\text{PV(Tax Shield)} &= \sum_{t=1}^{10} \frac{61{,}200}{(1.09)^t} \\ &= \$392{,}761\end{aligned}$$

Under these circumstances, the project's APV is

$$\begin{aligned}\text{APV} &= 1.1446 - .20 + .393 \\ &= \$1.3376 \text{ million}\end{aligned}$$

A. APV and Discount Rates

There is an obvious preference for the use of a single discount rate that embodies the side effects of debt financing in the evaluation of capital investments. Discount rates can of course be adjusted in the APV framework: if the only side effect is the tax shield provided by the use of debt, then the adjusted discount rate is the same as the one used for the cost-of-capital computation. But if there are many other side effects, the use of a single discount rate becomes extremely complex. Recall that the use of an adjusted discount rate (for example, the WACC) requires that the project be a carbon copy of the firm. When this is not the case, use of the APV is more appropriate and, as we have seen, is easier than trying to come up with a single discount rate.

B. Some Recent Developments in Asset Pricing

Ross (1978) has developed an arbitrage approach to valuation that can be applied to capital budgeting for risky streams. In an efficient capital market in which prices reflect true value, arbitrage is said to exist if two assets that are perfect substitutes sell at different prices. However, arbitrage is inconsistent with equilibrium in the market, so that the two assets must sell at the same price. Ross develops his example as follows: Suppose that we have an investment that generates cash flows over time. If we could find a portfolio of traded assets the exactly replicates our project's cash flows, we could then compute a value for this asset. Because the portfolio of traded assets exactly replicates the cash flow of the investment, the two, by definition, are perfect substitutes.

Ross goes on to show that the two assets—the portfolio of traded assets and the investment project—must have the same value. Moreover, because the capital market has already valued the portfolio of traded assets, in order to avoid arbitrage the value of the investment is necessarily equal to the value of the portfolio. Notice that we do not need either certainty equivalents (see Appendix 13A) or risk-adjusted discount rates to arrive at the project value. As long as capital markets are efficient, the portfolio of traded assets reflects the investment's true value. But then, with this information, it becomes a simple matter to apply the NPV criterion:

$$\begin{aligned}\text{NPV} &= \text{value of arbitrage portfolio} \\ &\quad - \text{investment cost}\end{aligned}$$

We would then accept the project if NPV is greater than zero.

Ross's approach to valuing risk streams has been examined empirically by Gehr (1981) and is discussed in more detail in Chapter 14.

VIII. SUMMARY AND REVIEW

Among the methods of evaluating project profitability are those that take into account the time value of money, as well as project risk. While the latter is clearly a difficult concept to quantify, at least three approaches—CAPM, CE, and RADR (see Appendix 13A)—do incorporate risk. At this time, it is difficult to say which of the three is the best to use; a comparison of results from all of them may be the most interesting, and even appropriate, way to see how risk (measured so differently) affects project value.

Computation of project cash flows is the chief ingredient in calculating project profitability. Although such computation may be performed under the assumption of straight-line depreciation, current tax laws (ACRS) allow for different results in the computation and hence in the measure of project profitability. Tax issues will probably always be extremely important, given the ever-changing tax environment.

APPENDIX 13A REEXAMINING RISK IN CAPITAL BUDGETING

An examination of the CAPM equation (13.9) indicates that the required rate of return on an asset is related to two factors: the risk-free rate, which is the compensation for the time preference or futurity of returns, and the term $(E(R_M) - R_F)\beta_j$, which represents the compensation for bearing risk. The end result, $E(R_j)$, is the sum of these two components, i.e., futurity and risk. While adding time and risk together in a single-period context presents few problems, the multiperiod application of *risk-adjusted discount rates* (RADRs) implies something about the manner in which risk is being resolved over time. Nonetheless, over a horizon of more than one period it may be inappropriate to discount cash flows using the RADR method. One way to examine the issue is to approach the problem through a concept known as *certainty equivalence*.

In order to apply the RADR method to equation (13.3) for NPV, we must know that all cash flows are to be discounted at a risk-adjusted rate. If so, then equation (13.3) may be restated as

$$NPV = -I_0 + \sum_{t=1}^{n} \frac{CF_t}{(1 + \text{RADR})^t} \quad (13A.1)$$

where RADR is the appropriate (constant) risk-adjusted discount rate computed from the CAPM. An alternative way of adjusting for risk is to restate the cash flows CF_t on a risk-adjusted basis. In other words, we can ask the following basic question: What is the minimum certain return that could be exchanged for the risky return in cash flow CF_t? This minimum certain return is known as the *certainty equivalent* and will be referred to as CEQ_t. Because it is possible to restate all CF_t in terms of their risk-adjusted CEQ_t, risk adjustment is no longer necessary for the discount rate. Rather, the CEQ incorporates risk into the cash flow. Moreover, CEQ_t is risk free by construction (i.e., CEQ_t is certain), then the appropriate discount rate to be used is the risk-free rate R_F. The certainty-equivalent approach to computing NPV is then

$$NPV = -I_0 + \sum_{t=1}^{n} \frac{CEQ_M}{(1 + R_F)^t} \quad (13A.2)$$

Suppose we now apply a constant RADR, as in equation (13A.1). What will that suggest about the way in which risk is being resolved? Because equations (13A.1) and (13A.2) should give the same asset NPV, an investigation of the behavior of risk can be performed by combining the two equations. Also, note that we can always express CEQ_t as α_t CF_t, where α_t is just the certainty-equivalent adjustment factor. That is, suppose CF_t = \$100 and its corresponding CEQ_t = \$90. Then α_t simply becomes .90.

With the preceding in mind, from equations (13A.1) and (13A.2) we get

$$\sum_{t=1}^{n} \frac{CF_t}{(1 + r)^t} = \sum_{t=1}^{n} \frac{\alpha_t CF_t}{(1 + R_F)^t} \quad (13A.3)$$

Now consider a project with two cash flows represented by CF_1 and CF_2. From equation (13A.3),

$$\frac{CF_1}{1 + r} = \frac{\alpha_1 CF_1}{1 + R_F}$$

and

$$\frac{CF_2}{(1 + r)^2} = \frac{\alpha_2 CF_2}{(1 + R_F)^2}$$

If the RADR, r, is assumed constant, we can examine the behavior of the risk adjustment coefficients α_t. Accordingly, solving equation (13A.3) for α_t, we find that

$$\alpha_t = \left(\frac{1 + R_F}{1 + r}\right)^t \qquad (13A.4)$$

Because r is usually greater than R_F, the term in parentheses is less than 1.0, as we would expect from the definition of α_t. Notice now that a constant value of r implies that the certainty-equivalent adjustment factor α_t declines at a constant rate through time. Therefore, as long as we believe this to be the case, we are justified in using the RADR method.

Let us give an example of how the method works. Suppose that the two future cash flows $CF_1(100)$ and $CF_2(200)$ are equally risky. Suppose also that $r = 15\%$ (a constant), while $R_F = 9\%$. Because CF_1 and CF_2 are equally risky, α_1 must equal α_2. If, furthermore, the adjustment factor is .80, then we can value the two cash flows according to the CEQ approach and the RADR approach, respectively, as follows:

$$\text{CEQ: PV} = .80(100)/(1.09) + .80(200)/(1.09)^2$$
$$= \$208$$

$$\text{RADR: PV} = 100/(1.15) + 200/(1.15)^2$$
$$= \$238$$

In this instance, the RADR method gives a higher PV. The reason, however, is because of the way in which the RADR treats the evolution of risk through time via the α_t coefficients. From equation (13A.4) the RADR implies that $\alpha_1 = .947$ and $\alpha_2 = .90$. Thus, not only does the RADR method view the cash flows as being of different risk, but also it underestimates the actual risk (i.e., $\alpha = .80$) of the cash flows as estimated by the financial manager. Hence, whenever we cannot assume that risk increases at a constant rate over time, use of the RADR method is inappropriate for capital budgeting decisions.

13A QUESTIONS

13A1. What is meant by the term "sunk costs"? "Opportunity costs"? How do they pertain to the process of capital budgeting?

13A2. Discuss the advantages and disadvantages of the NPV, PI, PBK, IRR, and CEQ approaches to evaluation of investment alternatives.

13A3. How does the reinvestment rate assumption impact the techniques for analysis of investment alternatives that account for the time value of money?

13A PROBLEMS

13A1. A project proposal has the following expected cash flows:

Year	*0*	*1*	*2*	*3*	*4*
Inflow		\$355,000	\$425,000	\$510,000	\$590,000
Outflow	\$150,000	\$158,000	\$265,000		

The company's cost of capital is estimated to be 12 percent. Calculate the following:

a. net present value
b. profitability index
c. interval rate of return
d. payback period

13A2. You are given the following after-tax cash flows from three projects.

Year	*Project 1*	*Project 2*	*Project 3*
0	−$140,000	−$100,000	−$80,000
1	60,000	57,600	22,200
2	59,720	56,200	25,720
3	44,760	41,400	26,160
4	42,960	39,600	26,960
5	41,760	38,400	23,800
6			23,760
7			23,120
8			22,480
9			21,880
10			−12,000

The operating (unlevered) betas for each project are estimated to be .5, 1.6, and 1.1 for projects 1, 2, and 3, respectively. The firm's target debt-to-total-capitalization ratio is 35 percent, and the before tax cost of debt is 12 percent. The current rate of return on T-bills is 9 percent and the expected return on the market portfolio is 15 percent. The firm's tax rate is 34 percent.

Compute the hurdle rate, net present value, and profitability index for each project.

13A3. A firm is considering a project with the following projected before-tax cash flows.

Year	*Before-Tax Cash Flows*
0	−$2,000,000
1	10,000
2	10,000
3	10,000
4	500,000
5	700,000
6	900,000
7	1,200,000
8	1,300,000
9	1,500,000
10	25,000

The asset under consideration would be depreciated on a straight-line basis over 5 years for tax purposes. The corporate tax rate is 34 percent, and the hurdle rate for this project is 11 percent. The final cash flow represents the resale value of the asset and thus the capital gain from its disposition (as it will have been fully depreciated). The initial cash flow represents the cost of the asset. In addition, working capital of $20,000 will be required over the project's life if the project is accepted. Tax savings may be used to offset tax liabilities from the firm's ongoing operations.

Calculate the NPV and PI for this project.

ANNOTATED BIBLIOGRAPHY

Babcock, G. C. "The Roots of Risk and Return." *Financial Analysts Journal,* January–February 1980, 56–63.

An interesting presentation of delineating the return and risk of a firm by analyzing earnings trends and volatility from financial statements.

Bierman, H., and S. Smidt. *The Capital Budgeting Decision.* 5th ed. New York: Macmillan, 1980.

A good general text on capital budgeting.

Gehr, A. K. "Risk-Adjusted Capital Budgeting Using Arbitrage." *Financial Management,* Winter 1981, 14–19.

A discussion of a numerical example using the arbitrage approach developed by Ross.

Harrington, R. *Modern Portfolio Theory and the Capital Asset Pricing Model.* Englewood Cliffs, N.J.: Prentice-Hall, 1983.

A small and concise user's guide to CAPM,

providing a good discussion of the advantages and limitations of that model.

Lewellen, W. G., H. P. Lanser, and J. J. McConnell. "Payback Substitutes for Discounted Cash Flow." *Financial Management,* Summer 1973, 17–23.

An early work on ways to reconcile DCF techniques with management's penchant for using payback-period methods.

Myers, S. "Interactions of Corporate Financing and Investment Decisions—Implications for Capital Budgeting." *Journal of Finance,* March 1974, 1–25.

A discussion of the concept of adjusted present value.

Myers, S. C., and S. W. Turnbull. "Capital Budgeting and the Capital Asset Pricing Model: Good News and Bad News." *Journal of Finance,* May 1977, 321–32.

A good paper on the limitations of CAPM for capital-budgeting decisions. The authors spell out the conditions that must be met in order to employ CAPM validly in capital budgeting.

Rendleman, R. J., Jr. "Ranking Errors in CAPM Capital Budgeting Applications." *Financial Management,* Winter 1978, 40–44.

An extension of the preceding Myers and Turnbull paper. The author shows that, even under some strict qualifications, CAPM application to capital-budgeting decisions may yield erroneous rankings of projects.

Robichek, A. A., and S. Myers. "Conceptual Problems in the Use of Risk-Adjusted Discount Rates." *Journal of Finance,* December 1966, 720–27.

A discussion of the relationship between the certainty-equivalent and risk-adjusted approaches to valuation.

Ross, S. A. "A Simple Approach to the Valuation of Risky Streams." *Journal of Business,* July 1978, 453–75.

A presentation of the concept of arbitrage as it applies to valuing risky streams for capital budgeting.

Rubinstein, M. E. "A Mean-Variance Synthesis of Corporate Financial Policy." *Journal of Finance,* March 1973, 167–82.

A discussion of the application of the CAPM to capital-investment decisions.

Schall, L. D., and G. L. Sundem. "Capital Budgeting Methods and Risk: A Further Analysis." *Financial Management,* Spring 1980, 7–11.

An interesting survey of capital budgeting practices that finds, among other things, that in times of uncertainty firms tend to use less sophisticated capital-budgeting methods.

Weingartner, H. M. "Capital Rationing: Authors in Search of a Plot." *Journal of Finance,* December 1977, 1403–32.

A survey of the controversy on whether capital constraints invalidate the NPV rule.

Weston, J. F. "Investment Decisions Using the Capital Asset Pricing Model." *Financial Management,* Spring 1973, 25–33.

A simple and concise exposition on the use of CAPM in making investment decisions.

14

ASSET VALUATION AND PORTFOLIO MANAGEMENT

I. INTRODUCTION

Underlying the general process of asset valuation in the market place are several important concepts that were discussed in Chapters 1 and 2. Specifically, time value of money, return and risk, and market exchange opportunities are central to the process of valuation.[1] In this chapter we shall discuss valuation of "risky streams" from asset combinations (portfolios) employing the capital asset pricing model (CAPM). This material is augmented by extensions of the basic valuation framework to the option pricing model (OPM) and the arbitrage pricing theory in Appendices 14A and 14B, respectively. We will see how these models can be used to answer questions regarding the valuation of stocks, bonds, and warrants, to name a few of the possible applications.

II. VALUING RISKY ASSETS

A. Measuring Portfolio Risk

In describing how investors select a portfolio of risky assets, we use the earlier definition of risk as the standard deviation of returns offered by an investment.[2] However, the formula for the calculation of risk needs to be extended. Accordingly, suppose we are considering an investment in two assets, *A* and *B*, with the following characteristics:

State	*Probability*	*Return on A*	*Return on B*
Boom	0.25	18%	5%
Normal	0.50	10%	8%
Recession	0.25	−5%	5%
Expected Return	—	8.25%	6.5%
Standard Deviation	—	8.32%	1.5%

Suppose now that we invest equal amounts of money in both *A* and *B*. The characteristics of this portfolio are given in the following table:

State	*Probability*	*Return on Portfolio*
Boom	0.25	11.5%
Normal	0.50	9%
Recession	0.25	0%

The expected return on the portfolio is 11.5(.25) + 9.0(.50) + 0.0(.25) = 7.375%, which is the average of the expected returns on securities *A* and *B*. However, the standard deviation of the portfolio, 4.38 percent, is not equal to the weighted average of the standard deviations of the individual securities. The reason is that securities *A* and *B* are correlated with each other (i.e., their returns covary).

From statistical theory, the standard deviation σ_p of a sum of random variables is

$$\sigma_p = \sqrt{\sum_{j=1}^{n}\sum_{i=1}^{n} X_i X_j \sigma_{ij}} \quad (14.1)$$

where X_i, X_j = percentage amount invested in securities i and j
σ_{ij} = covariance of securities i and j
n = number of securities in portfolio p

The formula for the covariance σ_{ij} is similar to that for the variance and can be stated as

$$\sigma_{ij} = \sum_{s=1}^{m} (R_{is} - \overline{R}_i)(R_{js} - \overline{R}_j) P_s \quad (14.2)$$

where R_{is} = return on security i in state s
P_s = probability of state s occurring
m = number of states

For the example of the security portfolio of A and B, equation (14.1) can be expanded, and the variance expressed as

$$\sigma_p^2 = X_A^2\sigma_A^2 + X_B^2\sigma_B^2 + 2X_A X_B \sigma_{AB} \quad (14.3)$$

Using the statistical information presented earlier in the table, we can compute the covariance between securities A and B. From equation (14.2), the covariance is equal to .0002625. Substituting this value, along with the relevant individual standard deviations, into equation (14.3), we can compute the portfolio standard deviation as

$$\sigma_p^2 = X_A^2\sigma_A^2 + X_B^2\sigma_B^2 + 2X_A X_B \rho_{AB}\sigma_A\sigma_B \quad (14.3')$$

If $\rho_{AB} = 1$, then equation (14.3′) becomes

$$\sigma_p^2 = X_A^2\sigma_A^2 + X_B^2\sigma_B^2 + 2X_A X_B \sigma_A\sigma_B$$
$$= (X_A\sigma_A + X_B\sigma_B)^2$$

Taking the square root of both sides results in a solution for the standard deviation. In the presence of perfect positive correlation, σ_p becomes

$$\sigma_p = X_A\sigma_A + X_B\sigma_B$$

Therefore, only when security returns are perfectly positively correlated is the portfolio standard deviation a weighted average of the individual security standard deviations. If there is less than perfect positive correlation, then the portfolio standard deviation will be less than a weighted average of the two individual standard deviations. Thus, the simple two-security example suggests that if we diversify and include securities with less than perfect positive correlation, we can reduce the dispersion of the probability distribution of returns for the portfolio.

B. Portfolio Selection

From the discussion of investor utility considerations in Chapter 2, expected utility can be

$$\sigma_p = \sqrt{(.50)^2(.0832)^2 + (.50)^2(.015)^2 + (2)(.50)(.50)(.0002625)}$$
$$= 4.38\%$$

As expected, this value is the same as that found in the example. An interesting observation about equation (14.3) can be made by noting that equation (14.2) can be expressed as

$$\sigma_{ij} = \rho_{ij}\sigma_i\sigma_j$$

where ρ_{ij} = correlation between i and j

Substituting the right side of this new expression into equation (14.3) yields

expressed as some function of mean variance; that is,

$$E(U) = f(\overline{R}, \sigma_R^2)$$

where $\overline{R}$ and σ_R^2 are as before, and f represents the given function. Also, from the discussion of risk aversion, we know that investors will prefer more return to less return and less risk to more risk. With these pieces of information, we can derive indifference curves with shapes similar to those shown in Figure 14.1. All points along an

FIGURE 14.1 Indifference Curves in the Risk–Return Space

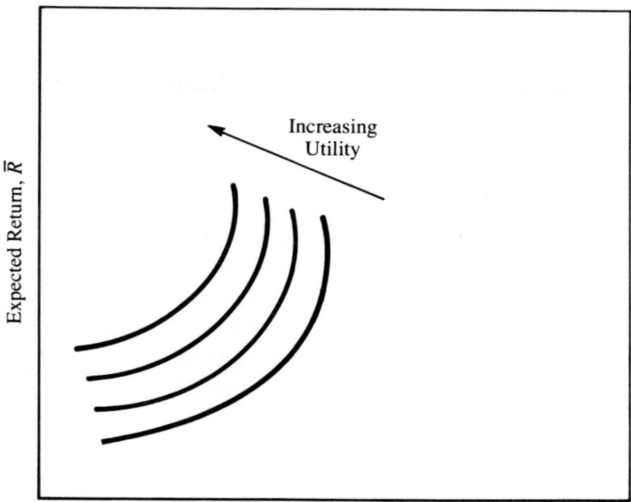

indifference curve give the various combinations or risk and return that yield the same level of expected utility. Because we assume that returns are jointly normal or that investors have quadratic utility, the investment opportunities available to investors can be summarized by expected return and standard deviation. The opportunity set generated by using means and variances is depicted in Figure 14.2.

All points in the shaded area of Figure 14.2

FIGURE 14.2 Investment Opportunity Set

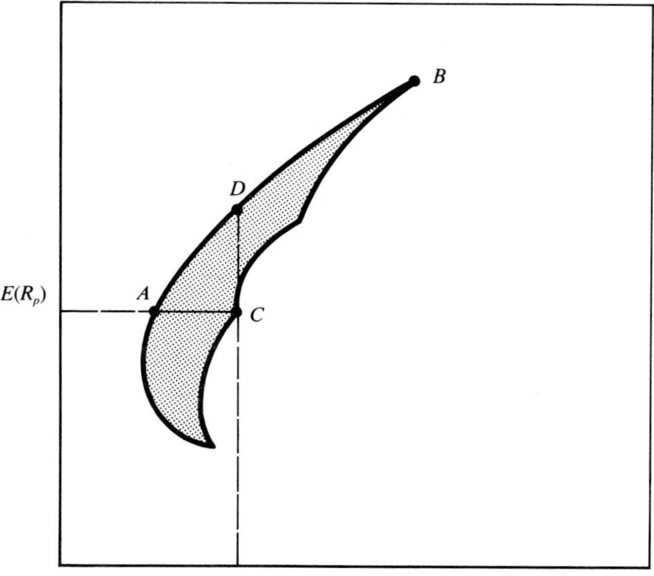

represent possible portfolios with particular risk–return levels. However, only a proper subset of these are efficient. In fact, we need be concerned only with those portfolios that have the highest expected return for a given level of risk. Accordingly, consider the two portfolios D and C in the figure. Both offer the same level of risk, but D offers a higher expected return. We therefore say that *D dominates C*. Portfolios that lie on the curve between points A and B are also said to be efficient and the entire set is called the *efficient set* or *efficient frontier*. Notice that if investors' indifference curves have the same characteristics as those shown in Figure 14.1, then, in order to maximize expected utility, investors will hold only mean–variance (EV) efficient portfolios. That is, they will select a portfolio for which the indifference curve is tangent to the efficient set. Figure 14.3 shows how one representative investor selects a portfolio. Here the highest indifference curve is tangent at point A.

If a risk-free security exists, the portfolio-selection problem is slightly modified. (*Risk-free securities* are those that will pay a known and certain future return; U.S. Treasury bills are good examples of securities that are approximately risk free.) Investors can hold risky asset portfolios (as given by the efficient set) in combination with the risk-free security. If they can lend and borrow at the rate of interest r, then the efficient set becomes the straight line rMZ shown in Figure 14.4. Points on this line represent portfolios that are combinations of the portfolio M and the risk-free asset. Points below M (e.g., A) are lending portfolios; that is, a proportion of the investor's funds is invested (lent) in the risk-free asset and the remainder is invested in M. Points above M are borrowing portfolios; that is, they are leveraged in the sense that the investor borrows at the risk-free rate and invests the borrowed funds together with his own wealth in M. Because line $rAMZ$ is the new efficient set, investors will choose a portfolio along this line at the point at which their indifference curve is tangent to the line.

C. The Capital Asset Pricing Model (CAPM)

If all investors choose portfolios in accordance with the precept that they always act so as to maximize expected utility, then we can develop a theory for pricing risk. Suppose all investors

FIGURE 14.3 Optimal Portfolio Selection: Risky Assets Only

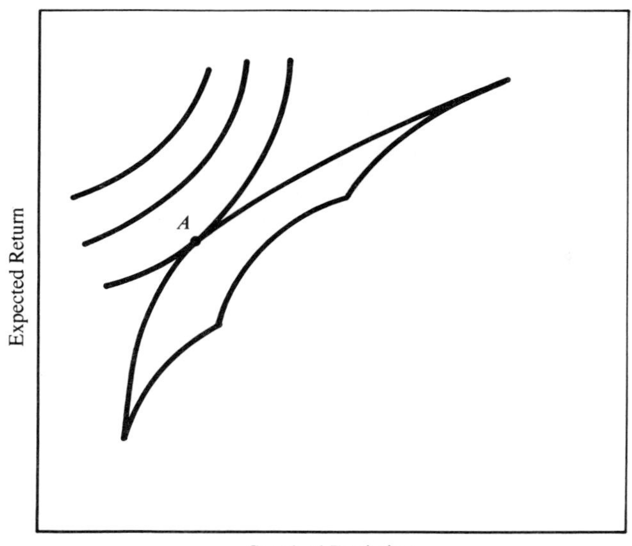

FIGURE 14.4 Portfolio Selection with a Risk-Free Asset

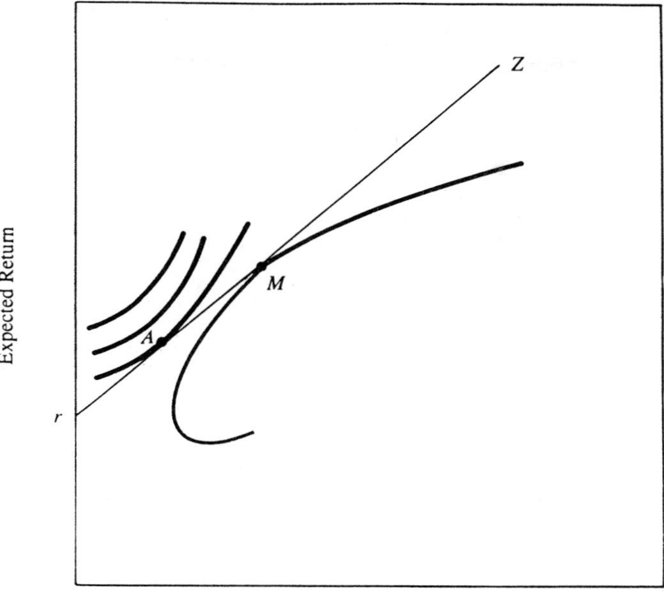

share the same expectations concerning the efficient set depicted in Figure 14.4. Then they will hold portfolio M in some combination with the risk-free asset. Under these circumstances portfolio M becomes the market portfolio representing the totality of all assets held at risk by society. Because all investors hold some combination of M and the risk-free asset, line $rAMZ$ describes the risk–return trade-off offered in the market. Line $rAMZ$ is referred to as the *capital market line* (CML) and is given by equation:

$$E(R_p) = r + \left[\frac{E(R_m) - r}{\sigma_m}\right]\sigma_p \qquad (14.4)$$

where $E(R_p)$ = expected return on portfolio p
σ_p = standard deviation of portfolio p
$E(R_m)$ = expected return on the market portfolio M
σ_m = standard deviation of portfolio M

Equation (14.4) is the equation of a straight line with intercept r and slope λ' equal to $(E(R_m) - r)/\sigma_m$. Essentially, the equation shows the combinations of return and risk required by investors. The slope of the CML, λ', represents the market price of risk; that is, it shows the amount of additional expected return required per unit of risk.

From Figure 14.4, we can derive a separation theorem for risk, first developed by Tobin (1958), that is analogous to the Fisher separation principle for production. Essentially, this theorem states that the optimal portfolio of risky assets held by an investor is independent of the investor's individual preferences. Thus, the individual's portfolio problem now takes place in two steps: first the investor determines the optimal portfolio M of risky assets (an objective process); then he or she decides what proportion of funds to invest in M, with the remainder invested in the risk-free asset (a subjective process, depending purely on personal preferences).

Equation (14.4) implies that there is an equilibrium, which satisfies all preferences, between expected return and unavoidable risk for each security in M. This relationship is none other than the CAPM, developed by Sharpe and Lintner, which was examined in the context of capital budgeting in Chapter 13. Here, the CAPM states that the expected return on a security is determined by its unavoidable risk, because in portfolio M all the unique (security-specific) risk has been diversified away. Thus, according to the CAPM, the only important (priced) risk is the covariation of the security's return with the return of the market. Formally, we have

$$E(R_j) = r + \left[\frac{E(R_m) - r}{\sigma_m^2}\right] \mathrm{Cov}(R_j R_m), \quad (14.5)$$

where $E(R_j)$ = expected return on security j
$\mathrm{Cov}(R_j R_m)$ = covariance of security j with the market
σ_m^2 = variance of the market

Alternatively, equation (14.5) may be expressed as

$$E(R_j) = r + [E(R_m) - r]\beta_j \quad (14.6)$$

$$\text{where } \beta_j = \frac{\mathrm{Cov}(R_j, R_m)}{\sigma_m^2} = \frac{\rho_{jm}\sigma_j\sigma_m}{\sigma_m^2}$$

The relationship given by equation (14.6) is known as the *security market line* (SML) and states that the expected return on a security is comprised of two parts: the price of time preference, represented by the pure rate of interest r; and the risk premium, represented by the product of the market's return above the risk-free rate, $E(R_m) - r$, and the security's systematic risk β. Equation (14.6) is depicted graphically in Figure 14.5.

The upshot of the preceding CAPM analysis is that we need to be concerned with a project's systematic risk in addition to its return. Unsystematic risk is not important because it can be diversified away. The CAPM is thus seen as relevant not only to capital budgeting, but also to asset valuation.

FIGURE 14.5 Security Market Line

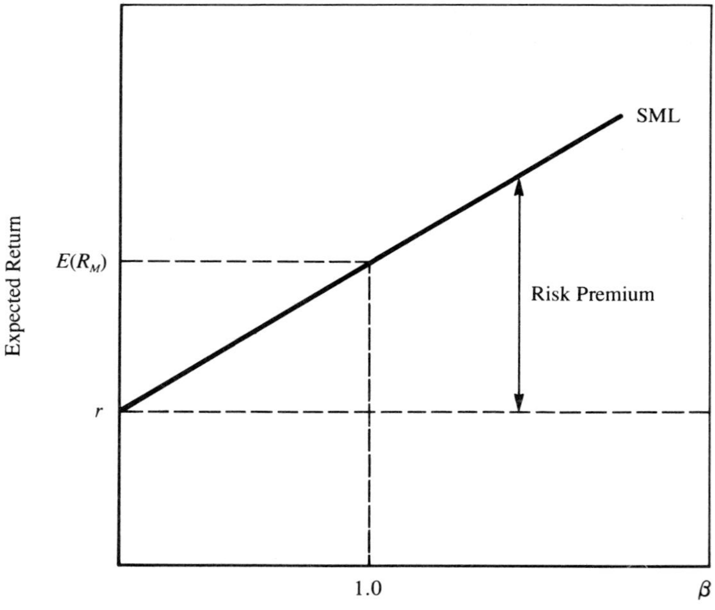

III. PORTFOLIO MANAGEMENT

We have discussed the concepts of risk and return, as well as ways in which investors might choose portfolios based on these two parameters. A key concept developed in relation to return was mean–variance (EV) efficiency. That is, among all the possible combinations of securities, we need only be concerned with those that have the highest expected return for a given level of variance (or, alternatively, lowest variance for a given level of expected return). The set of all such portfolios is referred to as the *efficient set*. The portfolio selection problem has therefore been simplified in that only those portfolios that are EV efficient need be examined.

The selection of EV-efficient portfolios is usually presented in terms of financial assets, typically shares of common stock. This convention, however, should not distract from the overall strategic significance of portfolio policies that are directed toward asset diversification and risk reduction by the firm's management. That is, as has been stressed virtually throughout this text, investment management is an ongoing process that begins with the inception of the firm and continues throughout its market life. As such, the creation of new divisions, the search for new profitable opportunities, the acquisition of other divisions or firms, the divestiture of some projects or firms, and the extension of similar activities to international markets constitute integral phases of the overall process of portfolio management. The firm is a collection of cash-flow-generating assets that must be initially allocated to some profitable activity, monitored continually, evaluated regularly, and redeployed periodically in order to reduce the firm's exposure to risk at acceptable levels of return.

We will follow tradition in this chapter and illustrate portfolio management in terms of financial securities, because this approach is easy to follow and pedagogically well received. However, we will take pains to view portfolio management in its totality as an ongoing process and focus on the various phases of the investment management process of which portfolio selection is only a part. In other words, we will discuss portfolio management within a conceptual framework that decomposes the decision-making process of the financial manager into separate but interrelated phases. A simple presentation of this process is shown in Figure 14.6, where both the interrelationships and the feedback loops are depicted. We will briefly discuss each of the component parts of the process and then concentrate in more detail on some of the more critical ones.

The first phase of portfolio management is *portfolio planning,* which involves the interaction of three important elements: (1) specification of the investor's (client's) profile, (2) specification of the manager's profile, and (3) the setting of the decision criteria for various investments. Among the elements of interest in the investor's profile are the investment horizon, the objectives of the investor in terms of return and risk, and, of course, the investor's financial needs during the time that funds are committed. Similarly, for the manager's profile, we are interested in his or her objectives, record of past performance, and efficiency in putting together client portfolios. Finally, the client's and manager's profiles are linked together through the establishment of investment criteria that will be used as benchmarks during the evaluation phase. Needless to say, communication procedures between the client and the manager, follow-throughs for evaluation, and the frequency of reviews must also be established in this phase of portfolio management.

The second phase of portfolio management—*investment analysis*—focuses on the various individual assets that might enter into the portfolio and involves the following interrelated functions: (1) economic analysis, (2) industry analysis, (3) asset analysis, and (4) future projections. *Economic analysis* refers to the study of the various factors that affect the investor, such as the stage of the business cycle, the present and future expected levels of inflation, monetary and fiscal policies, and international economic and political developments. Being outside the control of the decision maker, these factors effectively constitute the overall boundaries of achievable performance. *Industry analysis* moves the decision a bit closer to target selection because it concentrates on specific segments of

FIGURE 14.6 The Portfolio Management Process

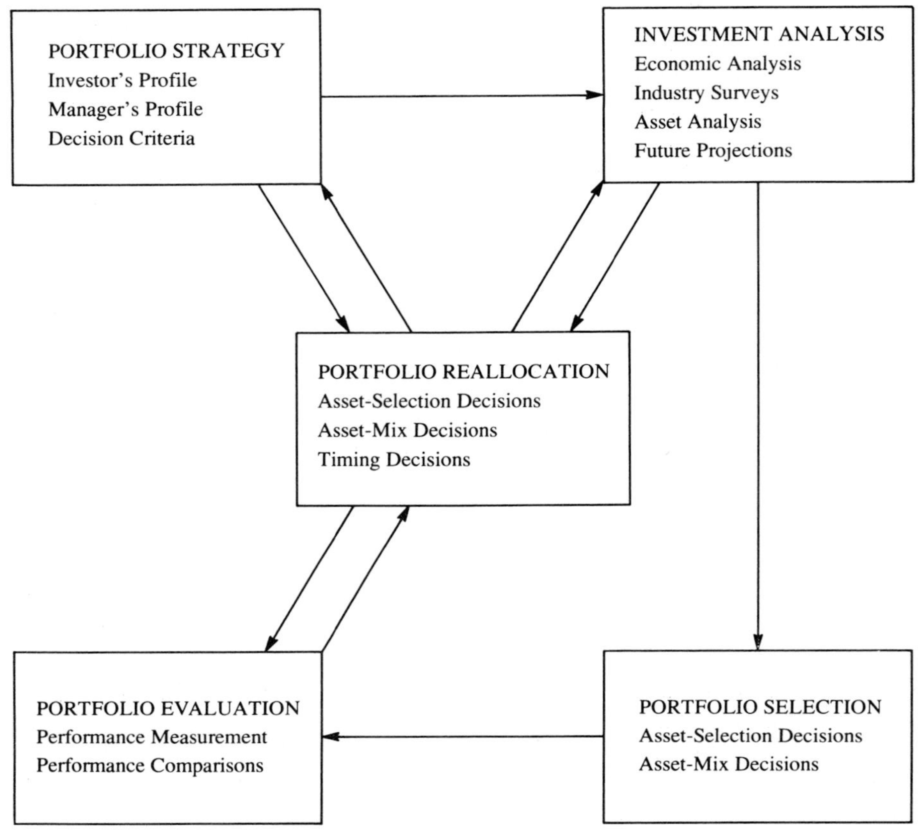

Note: Similar schematics with minor variations are used in the literature to portray the flow of investment decisions.

the economy that have more or less homogeneous performance. Industry analysis includes the study of the present and future prospects of various industrial groups and the effects of the various overall economic factors upon these industries. *Asset analysis* involves the screening steps that reduce the potential opportunities to manageable size for follow-up scrutiny and final selection of the portfolio. Finally, *future projections* or forecasts are made that reflect the expectations of the analyst about the values of various important variables.

The third phase in portfolio management concentrates on the *selection* of that combination of assets from which the financial manager will choose the final portfolio that is compatible with the investor's objectives. This phase involves (1) major-mix decisions and (2) asset-mix decisions. *Major-mix decisions* involve the allocation of investment funds to various categories of assets, such as stocks, bonds, real estate, cash, cash equivalents like Treasury bills, and the like. Once the major-mix decision has been made, the *individual assets* from the various categories are selected to form the portfolio.

The fourth phase in portfolio management deals with the *evaluation of performance*. An ongoing phase, it monitors the market value of the portfolio over time from the date of its original constitution to the end of the specific horizon. The performance evaluation phase requires the construction of two elements, measurement and comparison. *Measurement* requires the construction of performance criteria for individual assets or portfolios of assets. *Comparison* requires the construction of an external benchmark against which to compare the performance of the financial managers.

The last phase in portfolio management involves the *revision* of the portfolio and its *reconstitution* with different assets. Revision is achieved through the sale of some individual assets from some of the existing categories of assets and the purchase of new assets. As such, it involves (1) major-mix decisions, (2) asset-selection decisions, and (3) timing decisions. *Timing decisions* are those that deal with the time intervals, the frequency of revisions, and the time of reconstitution of the portfolio. Needless to say, portfolio revision involves a decision on the proportional allocation of funds among the various assets in the reconstituted portfolio. Because of its importance, let us examine the concept in some detail.

IV. PORTFOLIO REVISION

The objective of portfolio management is to maximize the return of a combination of assets within a given risk class. Within this objective, portfolio revision policies can be classified into four courses of action:

1. Undertake a complete revision
2. Perform a controlled revision
3. Maintain the initial proportions
4. Do nothing

A. Complete Portfolio Revision

Undertaking a complete portfolio revision dictates that the efficient set should be recomputed each time expectations indicate that the chosen portfolio is no longer optimal. In a complete revision, the purchased portfolio will be liquidated and the proceeds reinvested. It is likely that such a policy will entail rather large revision costs and brokerage commissions, as well as capital gains and losses. Portfolio revision requires that we estimate how far the portfolio is from being optimal. Then, based on this estimate, we can weigh the potential benefits against the expected revision costs in our decision to revise.

B. Controlled Portfolio Revision

The controlled portfolio revision policy tolerates portfolios that are considered suboptimal. As the name implies, only minor revisions are performed. One way to proceed might be as follows. We examine the marginal impact on the portfolio's expected return $E(R_p)$ and variance $\sigma^2(R_p)$ due to a contemplated change in the proportional weights of all securities (i.e., included and excluded securities). Then, if the calculated marginal return from the change does not affect the currently desired risk class, and if it exceeds the revision costs, we make the change. Figure 14.7 illustrates the concept of revision for three suboptimal portfolios X, Y, and Z. The preferred risk class is represented by σ_D, with D^* the optimal portfolio for that risk class. Portfolio revisions (i.e., changes in proportionate weights) that yield the largest change in expected return without changing the desired risk class should be selected. Therefore, we iteratively revise until

$$\Delta E(R_p) - \frac{\text{Dollar Revision Cost}}{\text{Dollar Investment}} = \text{Net Marginal Return}$$

is at a maximum.

C. Maintaining Initial Proportions

Maintaining the initial proportions of the portfolio implies that these proportions remain optimal. Therefore, any portfolio revision that is consistent with such a policy will maintain the weights W_i of the assets in the portfolio, and any cash distributions made must be invested in such a way that all securities maintain their original proportional participation. Unfortunately, the policy may generate rather large transactions costs and thus become unprofitable. It also suffers from the changing $E(R_p)$ and $\sigma^2(R_p)$ of the portfolio over time, because the expected returns, variances, and covariances of the initial securities are bound to change.

FIGURE 14.7 Portfolio Revision

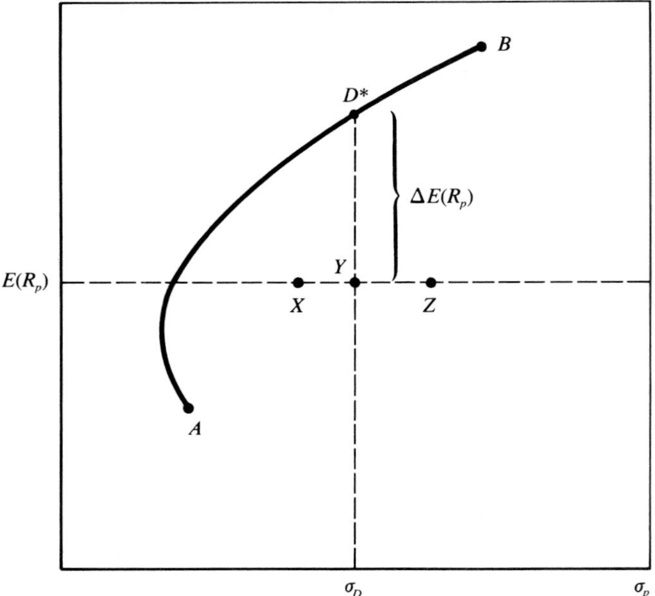

D. Doing Nothing

Doing nothing is simple and incurs no revision costs. As market values change, the proportional participation of each security in the optimal portfolio will also change. Doing nothing can be combined with controlled revision so that the original investment is not revised at all, but dividend income is controlled. The "do-nothing" policy offers simplicity and the ability to keep the portfolio near the efficient set.

To summarize, portfolio revision allows us to alter our initial portfolio so that we move closer to the desired portfolio within a given risk class (i.e., portfolio D^* in Figure 14.7). However, market imperfections result in substantial costs each time we wish to revise. Such costs include the following:

1. Commissions for buying securities
2. Commissions for selling securities
3. Transfer taxes
4. Capital gains and dividend income taxes
5. Revision costs, i.e.,
   a. Costs of collecting new information
   b. Computer costs for estimating the efficient set
   c. Costs associated with the broker–client relationship

All these costs must be balanced against the potential gains to be gotten from periodically or continually revising the investment portfolio.

V. PORTFOLIO EVALUATION

The evaluation of portfolios is concerned with comparing the return achieved on a particular portfolio with that of some benchmark portfolio. For such a comparison to be valid, the benchmark portfolio must be in the same risk class as the portfolio under evaluation. This requires that we clearly define what is meant by risk and unambiguously decide which method to use to compute return and risk.

Because portfolios are subject to a variety of inflows and outflows (i.e., there is a different amount of money available to be invested in each period), the computed return should be a time-weighted rate. Accordingly, consider the following scenario of inflows and outflows over a period of three months:

	Month			
	0	*1*	*2*	*3*
Portfolio value before transactions	500	520	650	460
Inflow (outflow)	0	100	(200)	
Amount invested	500	620	450	
Ending value	520	650	460	
Percent return	4	4.8	2.2	

We cannot simply look at the ending value relative to the beginning value; rather, we must take into account the amount of money available in each period. To do so, we compute the time-weighted return:

$$R = (1 + R_0)(1 + R_1)(1 + R_2) - 1$$

For the three-month period, we get

$$R = (1.04)(1.048)(1.022) - 1 = 11.4\%$$

In essence, we have traced the performance of one monetary unit through time by compounding period by period.

Now let us consider risk. Two measures of risk are employed in portfolio performance evaluation. *Total risk* is usually measured by the standard deviation of return; *nondiversifiable risk* is measured by the beta coefficient. The performance evaluation itself may be carried out using a number of measures, not the least of which is the one-parameter technique. We next discuss four different measures that use this technique.

A. Excess Returns to Variability

Figure 14.8 shows how we combine a risk-free asset with an optimal risky asset portfolio. As

FIGURE 14.8 Portfolio Selection with a Risk-Free Asset

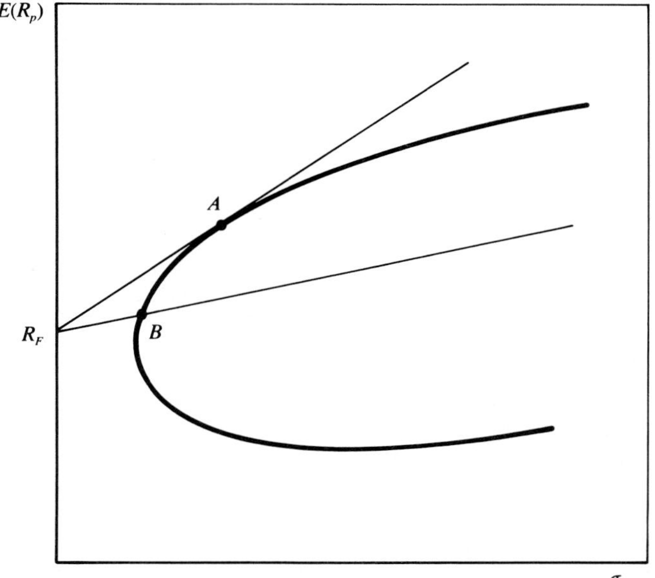

mentioned earlier, all investors will attempt to hold a mix of the risk-free asset (with return R_F) and portfolio A. Portfolio A is chosen because combining it with the risk-free portfolio yields combinations of risk and return that dominate all other portfolios (portfolio B, for instance). Combining the risk-free asset with portfolio A yields a line with a maximum slope in the $E(R_p)$, $\sigma(R_p)$ space. From elementary geometry this slope is $[E(R_p) - R_F]/\sigma(R_p)$. This ratio is referred to as the *Sharpe measure of performance* and is expressed formally as

$$S_p = \frac{E(R_p) - R_F}{\sigma(R_p)} = \frac{\text{excess return}}{\text{total risk}} \qquad (14.7)$$

Equation (14.7) is also called an *excess-return-to-variability ratio*.

Next, consider Figure 14.9. Suppose that point M represents the risk–return characteristics of the Standard and Poor's top 500 stocks (S&P500). Other points represent the risk–return characteristics of a variety of mutual funds. Because a ray from the risk-free return to any point in the figure represents the excess-return-to-variability ratio, we can assess performance relative to the performance of the S&P500. Points that lie above line R_FMZ have outperformed the S&P500, while those that are below have inferior performance. For investors concerned with total risk, the Sharpe measure allows the evaluation of performance with respect to that parameter. Investors who wish to have a different risk from that offered by the S&P500 Index could achieve that by borrowing and lending.

B. Differential Returns to Total Risk

Another way to evaluate performance is to examine the differential return earned on a portfolio. The differential is computed relative to the naive strategy of investing in both the market portfolio and the risk-free asset for a desired level of risk. Because the equation of a line from R_F to the market portfolio M is

$$E(R_p) = R_F + \left[\frac{E(R_M) - R_F}{\sigma_M}\right]\sigma(R_p) \qquad (14.8)$$

the measure is the difference between the return on our portfolio or mutual fund and the return

FIGURE 14.9 Evaluation of Investment Performance: Excess Returns to Total Risk

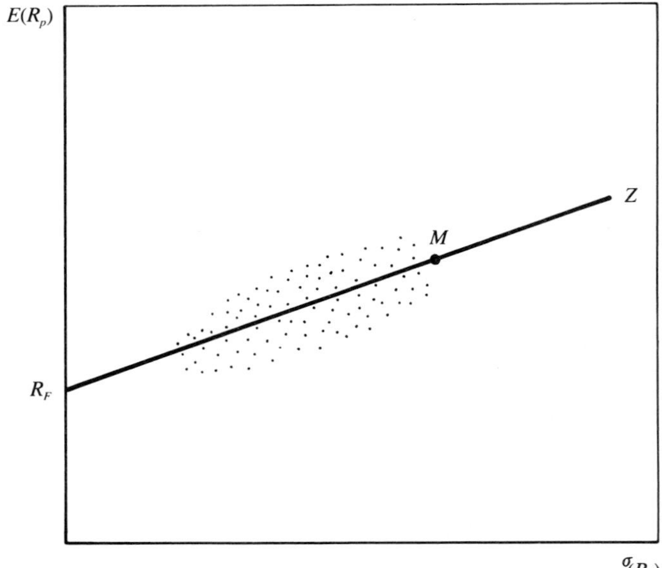

predicted by the capital market line given by equation (14.8). Given a benchmark portfolio, both the Sharpe and the differential return measures will rank a test portfolio's performance identically relative to the benchmark.

C. Excess Returns to Nondiversifiable Risk

According to the CAPM, in a state of market equilibrium an asset's return is linearly related to its beta coefficient. Thus, all assets, as well as portfolios, will lie along a straight line as shown in Figure 14.10. Now the CAPM states that

$$E(R_j) = R_F + [E(R_M) - R_F]\beta_j \quad (14.9)$$

If all we are concerned with its nondiversifiable risk, then we can evaluate performance relative to beta risk. A measure that does so is known as *Treynor's measure* T_p and is computed as

$$T_p = \frac{E(R_p) - R_F}{\beta_p} = \frac{\text{excess return}}{\text{systematic risk}} \quad (14.10)$$

where β_p is the beta coefficient for the portfolio. Of course, investors will prefer those portfolios with the highest T_p.

D. Differential Returns to Nondiversifiable Risk

As in the case of total risk, differential returns can be measured in the context of beta risk. Toward that end, Jensen (1969) developed a differential performance measure that is based on the asset-pricing implications of equation (14.9). Jensen measures a portfolio's performance by restating that equation as

$$E(R_j) = R_F + J_j + [E(R_M) - R_F]\beta_j \quad (14.11)$$

where J_j is Jensen's measure of abnormal performance.

J_j measures the vertical distance between an asset's return and that predicted by the security market line (SML). Figure 14.11 illustrates this measure for two portfolios, A and B. Because portfolio A lies above the SML, its Jensen measure, J_A, is greater than zero. Conversely, because B lies below the SML, its Jensen measure, J_B, is less than zero. The figure suggests that

FIGURE 14.10 Evaluation of Investment Performance: Excess Returns to Nondiversifiable Risk

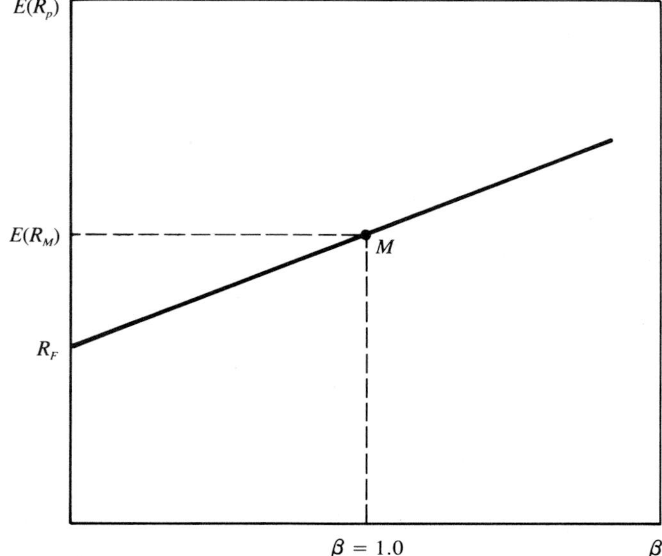

FIGURE 14.11 Jensen's Measure of Differential Performance

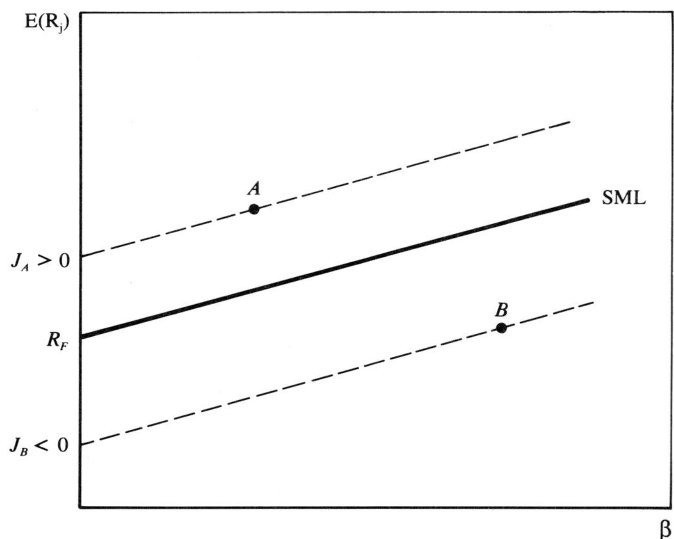

security B is overpriced and hence offers a lower expected return, while A is underpriced, thus offering a higher expected return.

VI. SPECIFIC ASPECTS OF PERFORMANCE

We now examine some specific aspects of portfolio performance using a technique developed by Fama (1972). In Figure 14.12, the straight line $R_FA'MA''$ represents the standard SML. If we choose a portfolio with beta risk β_A, then the vertical distance AA' is the Jensen measure of performance. According to Fama, this measure is the return associated with selectivity. Observe that although portfolios A and A' have the same systematic risk, A is not a market portfolio because it is not located on $R_FA'MA''$. Therefore, in order to earn excess returns, A must incur some diversifiable risk. Is the extra risk incurred worth it? Put another way, if portfolio A represents all of our net worth, should we be concerned with whether the extra return is worth the extra risk? The question is really one of determining whether it is systematic risk or total risk that is important. If we are concerned with total risk only, we can still evaluate performance in the $E(R)$, β space. All we need do is compare A with a portfolio that has the same total risk. A'' is such a portfolio.

In Figure 14.12, the distance $E(R_A) - E(R_{A''})$ is the measure of the extra return earned on portfolio A relative to a portfolio with the same total risk. This distance is referred to as *net selectivity,* because it represents the extra return earned on a portfolio even after we take into account the systematic risk of a portfolio with equivalent total risk. Now because portfolios A and A'' have the same total risk, the difference $E(R_{A''}) - E(R_{A'})$ is the portion of selectivity due to *diversification*. Accordingly, we have decomposed total selectivity into net selectivity and diversification. This decomposition can be represented as follows:

$$\left.\begin{array}{l} E(R_A) \\ E(R_{A''}) \\ E(R_{A'}) \end{array}\right] \begin{array}{l} \mapsto \text{Net Selectivity} \\ \mapsto \text{Diversification} \end{array} \quad \text{because } \sigma(R_A) = \sigma(R_{A''})$$

We can continue the decomposition with respect to the return we earn for bearing risk, i.e., $E(R_{A'}) - R_F$. Suppose we have invested in a

FIGURE 14.12 Decomposing Performance

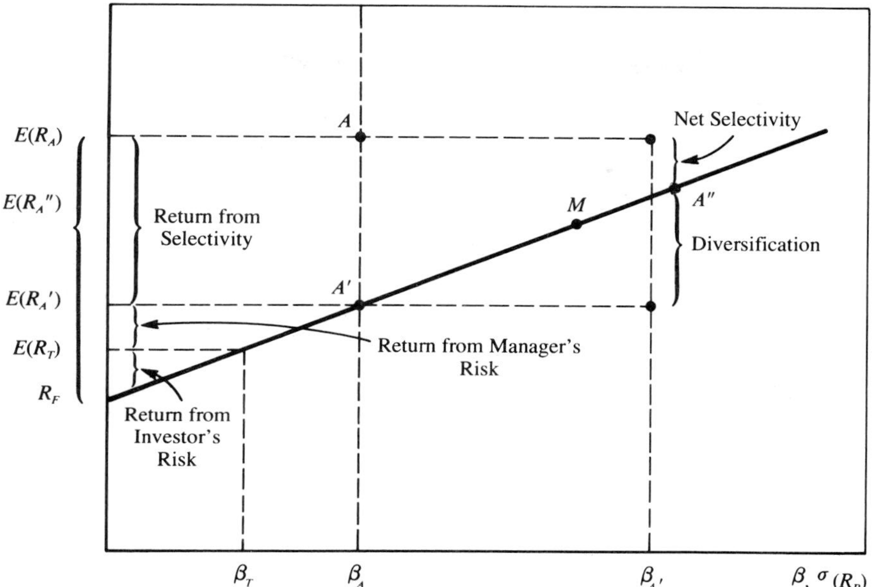

mutual fund with a target level beta of β_T, as indicated in Figure 14.12. (Keep in mind that we are still concerned with the actual performance of A.) Then we have the following two components: $E(R_T) - R_F$ referred to by Fama as the return associated with the investor's *a priori* risk of the fund; and $E(R_{A'}) - E(R_T)$, the return associated with the manager's risk position. Therefore, we have the following new breakdown for portfolio performance:

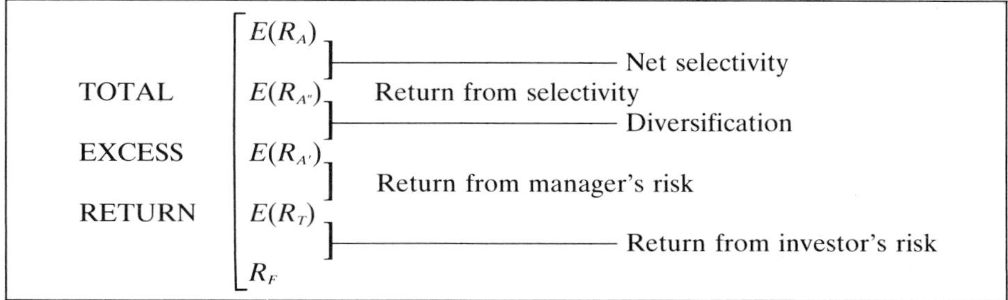

present purposes, let the S&P500 represent the market portfolio (portfolio M in Figure 14.12). Then, if market movements do not entirely capture the movement of the returns on our portfolio, we may be bearing some diversifiable risk. Suppose we now correlate the returns on our portfolio with the returns on the S&P500. Then, if the correlation indicates that only a moderate amount of variation is accounted for by general market movements, we may be bearing substantial nondiversifiable risk as well. If a substantial amount of our money is invested in this portfolio, the preceding information on net selectivity becomes extremely important.

Let us now, as individual investors, consider the diversification aspect of performance evaluation. To do so, we need to specify some surrogate measure for the market portfolio. For

VII. SUMMARY AND REVIEW

Modern theory of asset valuation views each project as an integral part of the existing asset base of the firm. As such, it examines the interaction between the cash flows of each new asset under consideration and the cash flows of the existing assets of the firm within a portfolio framework. The portfolio management process involves five interrelated phases—strategy, analysis, selection, revision, and evaluation. In this chapter, we focused on the last three phases of portfolio management.

Continuous revision and evaluation are important elements of portfolio management. The decision to revise the initial portfolio involves an analysis of both the costs and the potential benefits of doing so. Because capital markets are somewhat imperfect, continuous revision will generate rather large brokerage and information-search costs. Therefore, we must consider the decision to revise the portfolio relative to investment goals.

The analysis of the performance of a portfolio plays a large role in determining whether the portfolio should be revised. Portfolio performance can be divided into two parts: the return from selection and the return associated with risk bearing. Each of these aspects must be evaluated if the investor is to make a sound decision regarding revision of the portfolio. In particular, the definition of risk is relevant: two evaluations of the same portfolio will differ depending on whether one is employing a concept of total risk or a concept of market risk alone.

NOTES

1. In addition to the material in Chapters 1 and 2, the reader may review the discussion of dividend valuation models in Chapter 11.
2. A quick review of the concepts of time preference, risk, and utility is provided in Chapter 2.

PROBLEMS

1. Consider two assets, A and B, with the following characteristics:

$$R_A = 20\% \qquad R_B = 12\%$$

$$\sigma_A = 13\% \qquad \sigma_B = 4\%$$

If the returns on assets A and B are uncorrelated (i.e., $\rho_{AB} = 0$), what combination of the two will have the least risk? (The solution is obtained by minimizing the portfolio standard deviation with respect to the proportions invested in each asset subject to the constraint that 100 percent of total funds are invested, i.e., $X_A + X_B = 1$.)

2. What is the return and standard deviation of the portfolio above?
3. Now assume that $\rho_{AB} = -1$. What are the proportions invested in A and B in the minimum risk portfolio? What are the return and standard deviation of this portfolio?
4. Consider two assets, X and Y, with the following characteristics:

State of Economy	*Probability*	*Return on X*	*Return on Y*
Boom	.30	25%	.09%
Moderate Growth	.40	15%	.12%
Recession	.30	−10%	.13%

a. Calculate the expected return and standard deviation for each asset. The standard deviation for an asset i is

$$\sigma_i = \left[\sum_{s=1}^{M} P_s(R_{is} - \overline{R}_i)^2\right]^{1/2}$$

where M = the number of possible outcomes
P_s = the probability of a particular outcome
R_{is} = the return on asset i in state s
$\overline{R}_i$ = the expected return on asset i.

b. Calculate the covariance of returns between X and Y.

$$\sigma_{XY} = \sum_{s=1}^{M} (R_{XS} - \overline{R}_X)(R_{YS} - \overline{R}_Y))P_S$$

c. Calculate the minimum variance portfolio of assets X and Y.
d. What is the expected return and standard deviation of this portfolio?

5. (Appendix 14A)* Consider a hypothetical firm with only stock and pure discount bonds outstanding. The bonds will mature in exactly 2 years with a face value of \$1 million. The current value of the firm is \$1.5 million and its variance of rate of return equals .5. If the risk-free rate of return is 10 percent, calculate the value of the bonds and stock.

APPENDIX 14A THE OPTION PRICING MODEL (OPM)

A. Basic Concepts

This appendix will present another extremely useful valuation model. This valuation approach also discusses the value of an asset relative to another asset. To introduce this model, we will consider a class of financial instruments known as *options,* and in particular, a species known as the *call option*. By definition, a call option gives the holder the right to purchase a share of stock at a specified price, the *exercise price E*, up to a specified date, the *expiration date*. We now proceed to develop a theory for valuing a call option and see how such a valuation can be applied to financial theory.

We begin by defining a subclass of call options known as *European options*. European options can be exercised *only* at the expiration date, while their American counterparts can be exercised at any time prior to expiration. Suppose that the stock on which the option is written pays no dividends. Then the value of the European call c is given by

*Problem 5 must be solved in conjunction with the material in Appendix 14A.

$$c = \text{Max}[S - E, 0] \qquad (14\text{A}.1)$$

where S = stock price
E = exercise price

To illustrate the concept contained in equation (14A.1), suppose that an IBM call option is written with an exercise price of \$130. Then, if at the expiration date IBM stock is selling for \$125, the associated call option is worth

$$c = \text{Max}[\$125 - 130, 0]$$

The value of the European call at expiration is plotted in Figure 14A.1. As long as the stock price is below E, the option value is zero. If S were above E, the option's value would be $S - E$, which is indicated by the 45° line in the figure. Obviously, the person who sold the option contract loses a dollar for every dollar the option buyer gains—this is a zero-sum game.

To examine further how the value of an option is arrived at, consider an option with one period to expiration (referred to as t). At expiration the call value is simply given by equation (14A.1). However, given a period t to expiration, it is possible that the option's market value is greater than its theoretical value. For example, suppose the call option written on IBM (E = \$130) expires in three months. Then even if IBM is currently trading at \$125, it is still possible for the option to have a value greater than zero, as long as there is some chance that IBM's stock will rise above \$130. For this opportunity, we are willing to pay a premium. Figure 14A.2 shows the possible relationships between an option's value and various expiration dates $t_3 > t_2 > t_1$. Options with a longer time to expiration, written on the same stock with an exercise price of E, will be worth more, because the longer lived option allows us all the opportunities afforded the option with a shorter life plus something more. Note that there is an upper boundary on the value of the option indicated by line $0U$, which is a 45° line, representing a call value equal to the stock value. That is, the highest possible option value is the stock value

FIGURE 14A.1 Option Value at Expiration

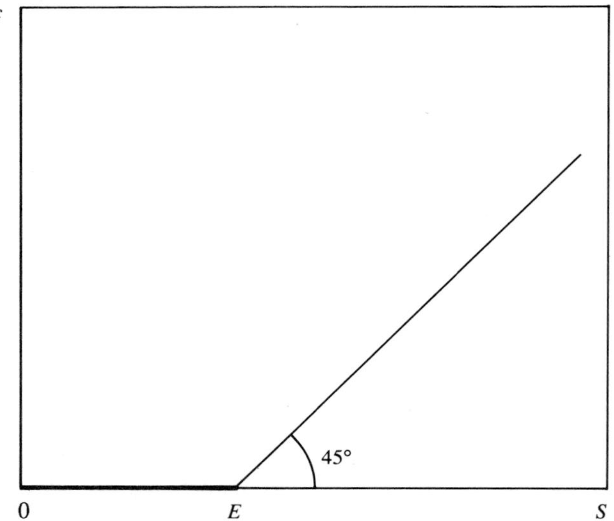

itself. As mentioned earlier, line EL represents a lower boundary on the option's value. As is evident from the diagram, a call option's price is dependent on the price of the underlying security. This is why option pricing is a relative-pricing model. The strength of such a model lies in the fact that most investments can be seen as some type of option. The next section illustrates how one can arrive at an exact option price.

B. Equilibrium Value of an Option: The Black–Scholes Model

To illustrate the exact formula for an option price, we must first discuss how to construct a

FIGURE 14A.2 Option Value for Various Expiration Dates

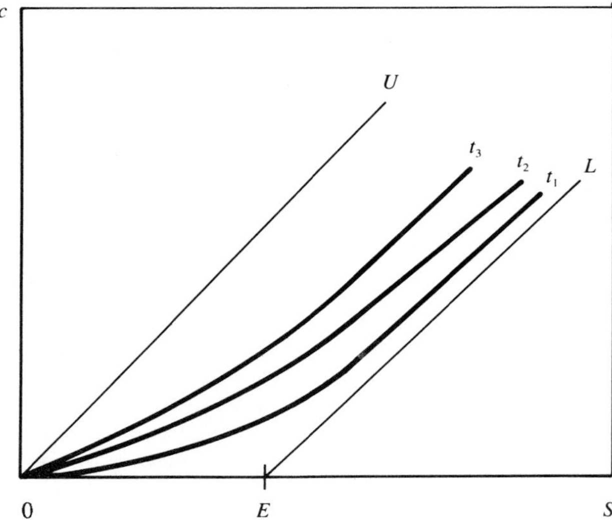

hedged position. Suppose we decide to make an investment that involves a long position in the stock (own the stock) and a short position in the stock's call option (sell the call). Consider a simplified situation in which the stock price can take only one of two values next period—uS or dS, where uS is higher than the current value and dS is lower. (Therefore, u represents "1 + the percentage price increase on the stock" and d represents "1 − the percentage decline.") If the probability of uS occurring is q, (then the probability of dS occurring is $1 - q$), and we can depict the outcome at expiration as follows:

Currently	*Probability*	*End of Period*
	3/4	$1.10(100) = \$110 \equiv uS$
$S = 100$	1/4	$.80(100) = \$80 \equiv dS$

Suppose now that the stock has a call written with an exercise price equal to \$100. Then the possible option values at expiration are the following:

Stock Price	*Probability*	*Option Value*
110	3/4	$\text{Max}[110 - 100, 0] = \$10 \equiv uC$
80	1/4	$\text{Max}[80 - 100, 0] = \$0 \equiv dC$

Hence, the expected value of the option is \$7.50.

It has been shown by Cox, Ross, and Rubinstein (1979) that the ratio of stock share to options that is appropriate for maintaining a riskless position is given by

$$h = \frac{uC - dC}{uS - dS} = \frac{\$10 - 0}{110 - 80} = \frac{1}{3}$$

Therefore, we should purchase 1 share of stock and write 3 call options. With such a distribution, the end-of-period value of this portfolio of stock and options will be

Stock Price	*Value of Position in Stock*	*Value of Position in Option*	*Value of Portfolio*
\$110	$1(110) = \$110$	$-3(10) = -\$30$	\$80
80	$1(80) = 80$	$-3(0) = 0$	\$80

Thus, regardless of the stock price outcome, the portfolio's ending value will always be \$80. This simple example illustrates a very important concept in option pricing: it is possible to establish a risk-free hedge. With this conclusion in mind, let us consider the *option pricing model* (OPM) developed by Black and Scholes (1973).

In the OPM, an exact expression is developed for the equilibrium value of an option on a stock that makes no dividend payments. Black and Scholes (B–S) use the concept of a riskless hedge in addition to six specific assumptions to arrive at the desired expression for option value. We can illustrate how to form the B–S hedge portfolio with the aid of Figure 14A.3.

Consider the option discussed in the preceding example with an exercise price of \$100. Suppose the stock price is currently \$105, with a corresponding option price of \$10. At a price of \$105, the slope of the option value line is approximately equal to 3/4. Therefore, for every 3 shares of stock held long, we should short 4 options. If this ratio is continuously maintained, then our portfolio will have a return that is certain. The situation is similar to the risk-free hedge established earlier: because the portfolio's outcome is certain, we should earn approximately the risk-free rate of interest.

From this point B–S go on to solve for the option pricing formula:

$$c = SN(d_1) - Ee^{-rt}N(d_2) \qquad (14A.2)$$

where S = stock price
E = exercise price
e = 2.1728 (base for natural logarithms)
r = short-term interest rate
t = length of time in years to expiration of option
$N(d)$ = value of cumulative normal density function

FIGURE 14A.3 Establishing the Hedge Ratio

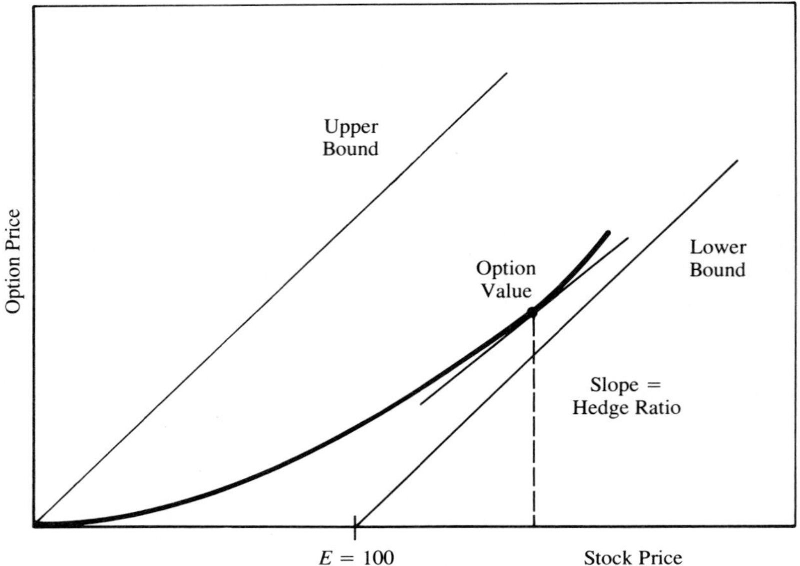

$$d_1 = \frac{\ln(S/E) + \left(r + \frac{1}{2}\sigma^2\right)t}{\sigma\sqrt{t}}$$

$$d_2 = \frac{\ln(S/E) + \left(r - \frac{1}{2}\sigma^2\right)t}{\sigma\sqrt{t}}$$

where ln = the natural logarithm
σ^2 = variance of the continuously compounded return on the stick

From equation (14A.2), the option price is a function of observable variables. Accordingly, let us work out an example of a real-world option using this equation. In December 1982, IBM stock was selling at \$92.875. Associated with this stock was a call option with E = \$95, expiring in April 1983. The risk-free rate at the time was estimated at 8 percent, and the instantaneous variance of the stock return was estimated at .365. Time to expiration was 126 days, for our purposes 126/365 = .345. Solving for d_1 and d_2, we substitute the relevant values into equation (14A.2) and get

$$c = \$92.875N(.191) - \$95e^{-.08(.345)}N(-.163)$$
$$= \$92.875(.57) - \$95(0.973)(.44) = \$12.28$$

This estimated value of \$12.28 is very close to the actual price observed on the Chicago Board Options Exchange (CBOE). However, we should note that equation (14A.2) is extremely sensitive to the estimate of standard deviation. Consequently, because σ^2 is estimated using past data, we should exercise caution in employing the B–S model, as the estimated relationship may not hold in future periods. In addition, empirical evidence shows that the B–S model misprices options that are deep-in-the-money (S much larger than E) or deep-out-of-the-money (S much less than E). One explanation for this phenomenon may be that the process governing the stock price is drastically different when the option is deep-in or deep-out-of-the-money. In any event, we must be extremely cautious as well in using the B–S model to find underpriced or overpriced options.

C. Extensions and Applications of the OPM

One of the advantages of the OPM is the ease with which it can be applied to many complex situations. For example, because all financial claims can be considered to be options to some income stream, we may apply the Black–Scholes OPM to the valuation of risky investments. The following two applications are presented in this spirit.

1. Valuation of Warrants

Warrants are liabilities that function very much like options. Corporations (rather than exchanges) issue the warrants, which give the holder the right to purchase the corporation's common stock at a specified price for a specified period of time (usually a period of years). Some of the ways in which warrants differ from the simple option discussed earlier are as follows:

1. The rate of variance may not be constant because of the long expiration date.
2. The exercise price of the warrant may change.
3. Firms involved in mergers may have their warrants modified.

While these and other technical reasons complicate matters, the Black and Scholes formula can be used as an approximation for valuing the warrants of a corporation.

2. Valuation of Common Stock and Bonds

Consider a hypothetical firm with only stock and pure discount bonds (i.e., bonds that are similar to 90-day Treasury bills) outstanding, with a maturity date indicated by T. At T, the firm will pay the bondholders the promised payment B and distribute any remainder of the firm's value V to its shareholders. However, if at expiration the value of the firm is less than B, the shareholders receive nothing. Using the concept developed in equation (14B.1), we may then view the shareholder's value at expiration as

$$S = \text{Max}[V - B, 0]$$

In this view, the shareholders actually hold an option on the firm's assets (because, in effect, the bondholders own the assets). Therefore, using equation (14A.2) we can solve for S to obtain

$$S = VN(d_1) - Be^{-rt}N(d_2) \qquad (14\text{A}.3)$$

Next, let D be the market value of the debt. Then, because $V = S + D$, it follows that

$$\begin{aligned} D &= V - S \\ &= V - VN(d_1) + Be^{-rt}N(d_2) \qquad (14\text{A}.4) \\ &= V[1 - N(d_1)] + Be^{-rt}N(d_2) \end{aligned}$$

While this example may seem unrealistic, it does give us a reasonable approximation of both bond and stock values. The OPM is very powerful because almost all corporate liabilities can be viewed as options. Viewing financial assets and liabilities in this light gives us another approach to valuing risky streams.

APPENDIX 14B AN ARBITRAGE APPROACH TO VALUING RISKY STREAMS

In Chapter 13, *arbitrage* was defined as that property which is said to exist when two assets that are perfect substitutes for each other (in all respects) sell for different prices. In such a situation, we could buy the lower priced asset and simultaneously sell the higher priced asset to earn (an arbitrage) profit. But doing so is inconsistent with equilibrium in both financial and commodity markets. Arbitraging will therefore force the prices of the perfect substitutes into equality.

Given this notion of arbitrage, Ross (1979) has developed an approach to project valuation, called the arbitrage pricing theory (APT), in which he argues that a project's cash flows can be exactly replicated by an "arbitrage" portfolio of traded assets. If so, we can view the arbitrage portfolio and the project as perfect substitutes. Then, in order to prevent arbitrage, the portfolio and the project must have the same value. Because the portfolio is comprised of traded assets, its value is simply the sum of the individual asset values. Accordingly, if the portfolio's value is represented by P and the cost of the asset by C, we can posit the following acceptance criterion: *Accept the project if* $P - C > 0$, *or, equivalently, if the project's NPV* > 0.

While the existence of a linear valuation (i.e., simply summing traded asset values) is somewhat difficult to prove, Ross's result gives us another alternative to use in capital budgeting. Let us briefly look at an application of Ross's ideas presented by Gehr in *Financial Management* (1981).

The difficulty with Ross's approach lies in trying to find the portfolio of traded assets that replicates the project's cash flow. Gehr uses a binomial analysis, much like that used in the discussion of the Black and Scholes model in Appendix 14A. To see how it works suppose we have the opportunity to invest \$100 in some project. Suppose also that one of two possible states of nature can occur next period, either a boom or a recession. The various outcomes for the project and a publicly traded asset (stock X) are as follows:

State	*Stock X*	*Project*
Boom	\$13	\$140
Recession	9	100

Letting S denote the stock price and f the project cash flow, we can formulate the valuation problem schematically for a current stock price of \$12 and a risk-free rate of 10 percent:

$$S = \$12 \quad r = 10\% \quad \begin{cases} S = \$13 \quad f = \$140 \\ S = \$9 \quad f = \$100 \end{cases}$$

Now if a and b represent the number of shares of stock to buy and the number of dollars invested in the risk-free asset, respectively, the value of the cash-equivalent portfolio can be determined by means of a system of simultaneous equations. Essentially, we need to guarantee that the cash portfolio yields \$140 if the boom occurs. This is represented algebraically by

$$13a + 1.10b = \$140$$

The first term represents the dollar return from the stock position; the second stands for the dollar return from investing in the risk-free asset. For the two-state case, we have

$$13a + 1.10b = \$140$$
$$9a + 1.10b = \$100$$

Solving for a and b gives 10 shares of stock and \$9.09 invested in the risk-free asset, so that the value of the portfolio is 10(\$12) + \$9.09 = \$129.09, replicating the value of the project in question. We can now compute the project's NPV:

$$\text{NPV} = P - C = 129.09 - 100 = \$29.09$$

Because the project's value exceeds its costs, we should accept the project. Note that the calculated NPV is risk adjusted, as the asset values used to calculate P have already taken risk into account. Therefore, this approach allows us to sidestep the problems associated with risk-adjusted discount rates. The approach, of course, can easily be extended to problems of more than one period.

ANNOTATED BIBLIOGRAPHY

Black, F., and M. Scholes. "The Pricing of Options and Corporate Liabilities." *Journal of Political Economy,* May–June 1973, 637–754.

The seminal work that establishes an exact option-pricing formula.

Cox, J. C., S. A. Ross, and M. Rubinstein. "Option Pricing, A Simplified Approach." *Journal of Financial Economics* 7(1979):229–63.

A good presentation of the binomial approach to option pricing.

Gehr, A. "Risk-Adjusted Capital Budgeting

Using Arbitrage." *Financial Management*, Winter 1981, 14–19.

By far the simplest exposition of the use of APT in risk-adjusted capital investment analysis. The basis of the discussion in this text.

Markowitz, H. *Portfolio Selection: Efficient Diversification of Investments*. Cowles Foundation Monograph 16. New Haven: Yale University Press, 1959.

The original work on mean–variance diversification, based on an earlier publication by the author.

Riley, W. B., Jr., and A. H. Montgomery. *Guide to Computer-Assisted Investment Analysis*. New York: McGraw-Hill, 1982.

A good, practical source of computational techniques and programs for investments and portfolio selection.

Ross, S. A. "A Simple Approach to the Valuation of Risky Streams." *Journal of Business*, July 1979, 254–86.

A very clear exposition of the arbitrage-pricing approach to the valuation of risky streams.

Rubinstein, M. "A Mean–Variance Synthesis of Corporate Financial Theory." *Journal of Finance*, March 1973, 167–82.

A good synthesis of the uses of CAPM in corporate financial policy.

Sharpe, W. F. "Capital Asset Prices: A Theory of Market Equilibrium under Conditions of Risk." *Journal of Finance*, September 1964, 425–42.

The original presentation of the CAPM by one of its developers.

15

MERGERS AND ACQUISITIONS

I. INTRODUCTION

Merger activity in the United States during the last 15 years was at an all-time high. This wave of mergers has involved many firms of considerable size and has entailed some fairly large costs. For example, it is reported that the number of mergers costing at least $100 million rose from 14 in 1975 to 113 in 1981. (Appendix 15A presents a listing of the top 20 merger transactions in terms of dollar value for the second and third quarters of 1988.) Thus, some firms spent a significant amount of money in the search for and actual acquisition of other firms. Those firms that did the spending were making rather substantial capital outlays for investments that are rather difficult to evaluate. The reason for the difficulty is because the benefits and costs associated with mergers and acquisitions are not easy to define: buying another company involves special tax, legal, and accounting complications that must be incorporated into the analysis of costs and benefits.

If markets are perfect, of course, then, where market prices exist for actively traded securities, the price paid in an acquisition should be the price in the marketplace. In *acquisitions,* however, management of the acquiring firm is usually attempting to identify and acquire an undervalued entity and translate the additional potential value into profits for the shareholders of their firm. Some of this unrecognized value may remain with the sellers, provided their representatives are skillful enough to identify and bargain successfully for it. In *mergers,* the joint parties are attempting to create greater value from the combination, which will be shared between them. Hence, market prices may not be the appropriate indices for calculating the value of a deal.

The sources of value in both acquisitions and mergers are many, but they can be broken down chiefly into two categories: (1) earnings, including current earnings, prospective earnings, i.e., the net of investment, and synergistic earnings; and (2) assets, including hidden assets and redundant assets.

Current earnings are earnings on the current asset base and are usually the foundation of typical present-value calculations. *Prospective earnings* represent new sources of value which are thought to be available to the company that is being acquired and which may offer opportunities that are as yet unrecognized by the market to those individuals in the acquiring firm who are alert to them. In paying for these (potential) earnings, the purchaser must remember to deduct the additional funds required to obtain them. Finally, *synergistic earnings* are those profits that can be obtained only by the efficient combination of the two enterprises, as, for example, when one entity possesses excellent marketing skills while the other half of the partnership has efficient production.

Asset values are generally thought to be comprehended by the valuation of the earnings, which they of course produce. In most cases, therefore, neither net asset value nor book value per share is given much consideration in pricing a merger. A possible exception is in the case of financial institutions. When a bank trades below book value, it is an implicit statement that the marketplace does not believe that the assets are worth what they were when they were put on the books. Consequently, the management of financial institutions is generally very reluctant to confirm that impression by selling stock below book or by accepting less than book value in a merger.

In some undervalued situations, however, the purchaser believes that it has identified assets whose value is not fully capitalized by the marketplace. These *hidden assets,* which may include such intangibles as tax carryforwards or debt capacity, may not have been analyzed and yet are available to create extra value for the proper purchaser. (It is worth noting that sometimes these intangibles can have a negative influence on value, as, for example, when there is a potential adverse tax judgment or unfunded pension liability threatening a firm.)

Redundant assets are assets that are not essential to the main business of the enterprise. Often they are not generating their full potential earnings and in that respect, then, are identical to hidden assets. Real estate can be a redundant asset, as can the film libraries of motion picture companies. Indeed, in the early days of television, film libraries were a redundant asset, not being used very much at all.

The attempt to realize values through mergers and acquisitions must often be done with one eye on what the market *might think* and the other on what it *should do*. Thus, management may feel constrained by a concern for the effects of the transaction on the company's earnings per share and dividends per share. Will the potential future growth be perceived favorably enough to offset the effect of an immediate drop in earnings per share? Conversely, if the merger enhances immediate earnings per share, will it dilute it in the longer run? Can the new combination maintain the dividends required by the post-merger shares if equity has to be given away as part of the acquisition or issued to finance cash costs? What are the short- and intermediate-term balance sheet effects? These questions all address market realities which may hinder management in its efforts to create longer run values through mergers and acquisitions.

II. MERGERS, ACQUISITIONS, AND DIVESTITURES: SOME RECENT ACTIVITY

Mergers have become a significant phenomenon in the U.S. capital markets over the last decade or so. It appears that external growth through acquisition of other firms is now a popular mode of capital spending by U.S. corporations. In fact, during the last few years, a significant percentage of the largest American firms has been involved in one or more mergers, divestitures or leveraged buyouts (LBOs). For example, American Stores acquired Lucky Stores in the second quarter of 1988 for $2.5 billion. In the same quarter, West Point-Pepperell completed the acquisition of J. P. Stevens & Company for $1.2 billion, and in the third quarter, General Electric purchased the chemical operations of Borg-Warner Corporation for $2.3 billion. In what follows, we will review some of the trends in mergers during the second and third quarters in 1988.

In the second quarter of 1988, 775 merger transactions were completed for a total value of $55 billion. However, the twenty-five largest transactions accounted for more than 55 percent of the total ($31.4 billion). During the third quarter, 791 transactions were consummated for a dollar value of $44 billion. A number of large dollar deals occurred during both quarters. For example, 29 transactions valued between $100 million and $1 billion and 21 worth more than $1 billion were consummated during the two quarters. Purely domestic deals involving U.S. corporations on both sides of the merger transaction predominated, although takeovers of U.S. firms by foreign corporations also totaled $23 billion during the same period. The interested reader is referred to the Jan–Feb 1989 issue of *Mergers and Acquisitions,* 23(4).

In terms of specific industries, it appears that the retailing industry set the record with 88 mergers during the two-quarter period worth $21.1 billion. In addition to the Campeau Corporation–Federated Department Store merger for $6.5 billion, other large deals included the takeover of Firestone Tire and Rubber by

Bridgestone of Japan for $2.6 billion, the leveraged buyout of American Standard for $2.4 billion, and Amoco's purchase of Dome Petroleum for $3.7 billion. Other industries in which larger merger deals materialized include the electrical and electronic machinery industry, with 81 transactions worth $6.3 billion, and the chemical industry with over 29 mergers valued at $5.5 billion. Total value of mergers notwithstanding, it appears that the banking industry was the most active sector of the economy, with 101 merger deals worth over $1.7 billion consummated. Here, the most important transaction involved the purchase of First Kentucky National by National City Corporation for $628 million.

Investment in other firms by means of integral acquisition has been a popular method of drastic portfolio reconstitution by U.S. corporations. However, portfolio management requires that, in addition to major investment decisions, managers engage in continual fine tuning of a firm's portfolio of assets. Such fine adjustments are typically manifested in divestitures of divisions or functional units that enable companies to redeploy their productive assets for improvements in efficiency and adjustments in the risk–return configuration of the firm. Divestiture activity in the second and third quarters of 1988 encompassed 518 transactions worth $38.5 billion, an amount that actually understates the true value of total divestitures, since about one-half of the sell-off events did not reveal price data. (See *Mergers and Acquisitions,* Jan–Feb 1989, 66.)

Notable events included the sale by Staley Continental of its food service business to SYSCO Corporation for $700 million, the divestitures of a total of five department store chains by Federated for $2.6 billion, and Kohlberg Kravis Roberts' leveraged buyout of Duracell for $1.8 billion. Other divestitures involved the LBO of Montgomery Ward which resulted in the sale of its credit card operations to General Electric for $1 billion. Table 15.1 summarizes some of the aggregate activity in mergers, acquisitions, and sell-offs.

As the tempo of merger activity has picked up throughout the eighties, so have the efforts by managers of U.S. corporations to develop defense strategies and build antitakeover protection into their charters and bylaws. Antitakeover amendments include super majority voting systems, requiring a certain proportion, say 75 percent, of shareholders to approve a merger; staggered elections for directors, which tend to lengthen the time necessary to effect change of control; "golden parachutes," which are very generous severance packages awarded to existing management if they are fired due to takeover; and "poison pills," which, among other options, give existing shareholders the option to

TABLE 15.1 Profile of Mergers and Acquisitions*

	1st Quarter 1988		*2nd Quarter 1988*		*3rd Quarter 1988*	
Classification	*Number*	*Value*	*Number*	*Value*	*Number*	*Value*
1. Domestic Transactions	762	$28,957.3	648	$42,756.1	653	$27,901.1
2. Foreign Acquiring American	119	8,935.4	95	11,856.4	91	11,961.5
3. American Acquiring Foreign	37	332.7	32	796.5	47	4,165.6
4. Total Acquisitions	918	$38,225.4	775	$55,409.0	791	$44,028.2
5. Number Reporting Prices	392		431		402	
6. Percent Reporting Prices	43		56		51	
7. Divestitures	277	10,067.1	270	20,538.9	248	18,059.8
8. Number Reporting Prices	100		132		130	
9. Percent Reporting Prices	36		49		52	
10. LBOs	77	5,487.1	61	15,657.1	65	7,590.2
11. Number Reporting Prices	31		40		37	
12. Percent Reporting Prices	40		66		57	

*Adapted from *Mergers and Acquisitions*, Jan–Feb 1989, 66. All values are in millions of dollars.

buy at a large discount the shares of a successor company formed by a stock takeover. All of these measures are intended to slow down, or even deter, an unwanted absorption by another firm. The desired end result is, of course, the attainment of better terms on the proposed merger deal.

III. MOTIVES FOR MERGER AND SOURCES OF VALUE

Merging of two firms can be categorized as either vertical, horizontal, or conglomerate. A *vertical merger* is said to exist when two firms achieve a successive functional relationship—that is, when the output of one firm is a production input for or is marketed by the other firm. Many of the mergers in the 1920s were vertical. A *horizontal merger* occurs between firms whose products are substitutes. Finally, a *conglomerate merger* occurs between companies whose products are unrelated. Most mergers over the last 20 years have been of the conglomerate variety.

The most common reasons why firms merge or acquire are related to

1. Bargains
2. Economies of scale
3. Economies of scope
4. Economies of vertical integration
5. Elimination of inefficiencies
6. Utilization of unused tax shields
7. Utilization of surplus funds (including unused debt capacity)
8. Combination of complementary resources

While this list is not exhaustive, it does represent some of the sensible motives for merging. Keeping in mind the sources of value mentioned earlier, let us consider each of the items on the list in turn.

1. First, firms may merge because one company's management identifies an undervalued situation on the basis of the other company's existing earnings—that is, the company sees a *bargain* before it. Even in cases where nearly full value is paid, mergers may occur because one firm lacks the management depth necessary to continue operations in the event of the retirement of its general manager. Second, future opportunities of one of the firms may be undervalued in the market, creating a net present value for the purchaser, even if there is no joint value created and after allowing for the necessary investment to capitalize on the opportunities. Third, a company may have assets it is not using efficiently in its present business because they are, at best, only indirectly related to the production of its earnings stream. These assets may not be fully reflected in the company's value because of the uncertainties associated with when they might be converted to more productive uses.

The next four rationales for merger fall in the category of *synergistic* reasons—the creation of greater value through the combination than would be attained by the sum of the separate entities. In practice, synergies are often more speculative and ephemeral than anticipated, to the disappointment of many parties to the transaction. Nevertheless, the types of value generation expected from the merger fall into the following categories.

2. The merger of two firms may result in *economies of scale* due to the increased size of the new firm. Economies of scale refer to the reduction in the average unit cost of output as production activity increases. Economies of scale are usually the goal of horizontal mergers. The economies come about because of the efficiency gained in such areas as production, accounting, financial control, and central management.
3. The merger of two firms may result in economies due to the new firm's increased size relative to the number of products produced. These *economies of scope* refer to a reduction in the average unit cost to produce two or more products that usually share a common input.
4. Vertical mergers, in which a company merges with a supplier or customer, usually seek *economies of vertical integration*. These types of mergers give the acquiring company as much control as possible in both input and output markets. In addition, coordination

and administration can be made much easier. Because the product lines involved are usually complements of each other, the vertical merger may allow the integrated firm to take advantage of the special knowledge that arises in various stages of the production process.

5. Firms with poor earnings due to inefficient operation or financial management may be natural candidates for takeover bids. The acquiring company may then use its management expertise to salvage the failing firm. In this sense, a merger may *eliminate inefficiencies*.

Although sources of value are generally derived from ongoing or new streams of cash (or earnings), occasionally assets have a value independent of the stream which is presently or prospectively being generated. The following two instances illustrate this condition.

6. Firms with substantial losses may be unable to use the potentially valuable tax shields generated by capital investment or, in some cases, even the tax shields generated by the losses. Merging with a firm that is generating taxable profits allows that firm to use the valuable *tax-loss carryover*. Buying a company for this reason and liquidating its assets, however, may motivate the Internal Revenue Service to challenge the transaction and the use of the tax reduction. Consequently, it is sometimes preferable to buy the stock of the firm that has the carryover and use the firm as the vehicle to acquire other, cash-rich, profitable firms, paying their owners more than they could obtain from companies that do not have the tax advantage.
7. Firms that are in the maturity stage of their life cycle may find themselves with a great deal of cash and debt capacity and few profitable investments. As discussed in Chapter 11, these firms may pay high dividends, subjecting their owners to large potential income taxes. As a remedy, they may acquire cash-poor companies as a way of *employing their capital*. Alternatively, they may themselves be targets of firms seeking to absorb them or by cash-poor firms who see the acquisition as a less expensive way of generating funds for growth than raising debt and equity directly.

Finally, there is a form of synergistic catch-all.

8. In some instances, small firms may be acquired by large firms that seek a *missing ingredient* for their production or marketing operations. For example, small firms that need a sophisticated marketing operation may find it cheaper to merge with a firm that has an established sales operation. Indeed, even large firms with deficiencies in certain areas may use this rationale to justify a merger.

IV. MERGER THEORIES

Several theories have been offered to analyze both the motivations and the effects of mergers. In this section, we shall present some of these theories pertaining to conventional mergers, that is nonconglomerate mergers.

There are five theories related to conventional mergers, as follows:

A. Differential Efficiency among Firms

The differential efficiency theory focuses on the effect of mergers. That is, it views merger performance in terms of the resulting efficiency of the combined firm. Suppose there are two firms: X with high efficiency and Y with low efficiency. If the merger results in Y's efficiency raised to the level of X, then the merger is desirable in that it yields both a private gain to firm Y and a public gain to society at large. The differential efficiency theory of mergers is rather general and in its extreme form it would justify the presence of only one firm worldwide.

B. Tax Advantages in Mergers

The tax advantage theory focuses on such fiscal realities as the tax treatment of ordinary gains and capital gains, the double taxation of corporate earnings at the firm level and at the shareholder level (dividends), the sheltering of accumulated gains, and inheritance taxes. Hence, its universality is limited to certain countries and periods of time where these institutional distortions prevail. Briefly stated, the theory explains how mature firms acquire growth firms on their way to success. This way, they reduce income taxes through the purchase cost and substitute them with expected future capital gains taxes that may be lower. When the acquired firm has reached maturity, the acquiring firm can capitalize future earnings by reselling the acquisition. Similar scenaria can be made for the purchase of firms with accumulated losses or the selling of closely held firms by owners approaching retirement. Needless to say, as the tax codes are modified regularly, the theory that concentrates on tax considerations loses its appeal.

C. Agency Problems

Agency problems arise in modern large corporations with widely dispersed ownership. In such corporations, the managers own only a small share of the equity and have little incentive to work toward the full benefit of all shareholders. In addition, they engage in excessive consumption of perquisites. Because the widely spread shareholders cannot monitor the behavior of managers, specifically designed compensation packages and market discipline ensure managerial behavior. For our purposes, market discipline enters into consideration through the threat of takeovers of laggard firms and the replacement of their managers. Thus, the threat of a takeover resolves the agency problem and improves managerial performance. An earlier variant of the agency explanation—known as the managerial theory of mergers—suggests that managers strive to increase the size of their firms in order to increase their own compensation commensurately.

D. Market Valuation

While the market is in general a fair assessor of a firm's value, there exist individual cases where the market has undervalued a firm's economic wealth. One of the reasons for this may be that the management of the firm or another potential acquirer may possess better information about the firm's true value. This situation—known as *informational asymmetry*—leads to acquisitions at prices higher than the market values but less than the true value. Another variant of market value distortions focuses on the market value of a firm's assets in relation to their replacement cost. This relationship, better known as *Tobin's q-ratio,* shows that on average U.S. firms in recent years have been undervalued vis-à-vis their replacement costs. Hence, it is cheaper to acquire an existing undervalued firm than to invest in new additional capacity.

Distortions in market valuation may also explain mergers in terms of *synergy*. This is the case where the value of the combined firm post-merger is greater than the sum of the values of the individual firms involved in the merger. As we know from the previous section, synergy can obtain through economies of scale, economies of scope, or economies in specific functions such as finance, marketing, or planning. Synergy can also obtain through economies or efficiency in overall coordination as in the case of vertical integration. An extension of this concept focuses on the market power that can result from mergers through increased market share. This behavior, however, can run into antitrust reactions when market concentration by any firm exceeds prescribed levels.

E. Strategic Redeployment of Resources

Firms that reach a critical stage in their life cycle may engage in restructuring of their assets, that is, in strategic redeployment of their resources through long-range planning. Some firms may move toward greater diversification and proceed by acquiring existing firms that are undervalued. Others may refocus their products and services toward a few related areas, and proceed first by divesting unrelated units and then by acquiring existing companies in their chosen areas of activity.

V. FINANCIAL COSTS OF EXCHANGE

A. Cash Financing

In the analytical discussion of the gains and costs associated with mergers, we will deal with two firms, X and Y. We postulate that firm X is considering the possible purchase of firm Y, and we are concerned with whether a gain would result from the purchase. To analyze this potential investment in another company, we will employ the valuation concepts used in Chapter 12. In economic terms, a gain exists if

$$V(X + Y) > V(X) + V(Y) \qquad (15.1)$$

or

$$\text{Gain} = V(X + Y) - [V(X) + (V(Y)] > 0$$

where $V(X + Y)$ = value of the merged firms
$V(X)$ = value of the firm X
$V(Y)$ = value of firm Y

If equation (15.1) holds, then there is an economic rationale for the merger based on the profits from the transaction. However, as we will see, this condition may depend on the way the merger is financed.

To begin, suppose that cash is used to finance the merger. Then the cost to firm X of acquiring firm Y is

$$\text{Cost} = \text{Cash} - V(Y) \qquad (15.2)$$

For firm X, the net present value (NPV) of the merger is

$$\text{NPV} = V(X + Y) - [V(X) + V(Y)] - [\text{Cash} - V(Y)] \qquad (15.3)$$

If NPV is positive, then firm X should go ahead with the merger.

Equation (15.3) highlights the gains and costs associated with the merger. The first two terms isolate the overall economic gains from the merger. From this gain, the cost of acquiring firm Y is subtracted. The significance of equation (15.3) is that it illustrates how much of the gain resulting from the merger the owners of firm X get to keep. By contrast, equation (15.2) indicates the amount of the gain that goes to the former owners of firm Y. In essence, equation (15.3) is just one way of examining the difference between the wealth position of the owners of firm X with the merger as against their wealth without the merger.

Note that one way of estimating the values involved in a merger is to discount the respective earnings streams at the appropriate risk-adjusted discount rates for the companies separately and together. If the discount rates used are those of the cost of equity, then the costs should include an allowance for the risks of leverage; the stream to be discounted would be the cash flow after interest, taxes, and debt repayments that cannot be refinanced. If the discount rates are the weighted after-tax capital costs, then the stream should be the earnings before interest but after taxes.

From equations (15.1), (15.2), and (15.3), we can examine the costs associated with the merger transaction. These equations also imply that determining the cost of a merger is easy. However, the situation becomes complicated if investors expect firm X to acquire firm Y, especially if such expectations are already reflected in firm Y's stock price. To examine this possibility, we can rewrite equation (15.2) as

$$\text{Cost} = (\text{Cash} - V'(Y)) + (V'(Y) - V(Y)) \qquad (15.4)$$

where $V'(Y)$ = market value for firm Y, and
$V(Y)$ = true or "intrinsic" value of Y as a separate entity

Equation (15.4) distinguishes between the true value $V(Y)$ and the market value $V'(Y)$ of the firm. This distinction makes economic sense but becomes necessary only in the event that $V'(Y)$ already reflects the possible gains from the merger. To see why this is so, consider that in order to estimate the cost of the merger, the owners of Y's shares are concerned with $V(Y)$.

As owners, they see two possible outcomes: (1) $V(Y)$, the value of the shares without the merger; and (2) $V'(Y)$, the value of the shares with the merger. But if $V'(Y)$ already reflects the potential gains to be derived from the merger, then, in determining the costs associated with the merger, the second outcome will overstate the value of $V(Y)$. This is in fact why it becomes difficult to evaluate the cost of the merger.

An example may help to illustrate the point. Consider the following table.

Prior to Merger Announcement

	Firm X	*Firm Y*
Market Price/Share	\$50	\$30
Number of Shares	1,000,000	400,000
Market Value	\$50 million	\$12 million

Suppose that firm X intends to pay \$13 million for firm Y, and that $V'(Y) = V(Y) = \$12$ million. Then, according to equation (15.4),

$$\begin{aligned} \text{Cost} &= (\$13{,}000{,}000 - \$12{,}000{,}000) \\ &\quad + (\$12{,}000{,}000 - \$12{,}000{,}000) \\ &= \$1{,}000{,}000. \end{aligned}$$

However, if Y's present price reflects the possible gains from the merger, matters are complicated. For suppose the price per share of Y rises to \$31, so that $V'(Y) = \$12{,}400{,}000$. Then,

$$\text{Cost} = \$1{,}000{,}000 + \$400{,}000 = \$1{,}400{,}000$$

because firm X must still pay a \$1 million premium over the market value of firm Y.

It is even possible for the market to underestimate the true value for firm Y. In that case, the eventual cost to firm X will be less than \$1 million. In either case, firm X must compare the actual and potential costs with the respective benefits from the merger.

B. Stock Financing

When firms X and Y exchange shares, the task of estimating costs becomes more complicated than it is in the case of cash financing. Suppose firm X offers 260,000 shares of its stock rather than \$13 million in cash. Then the cost of the stock (Cost_s) may be calculated as

$$\begin{aligned} \text{Cost}_s &= 260{,}000 \times \$50 - \$12{,}000{,}000 \\ &= \$1{,}000{,}000 \end{aligned}$$

Is the computed value the true cost? There are three reasons why this cost may not be the correct figure:

1. Y's value may not be \$12 million
2. X's value may not be \$50 million
3. Y's shareholders receive some part of the merger gain because they are now shareholders in the combined firm.

To see what is meant by the preceding, consider case 3. Here, firm Y's shareholder will have an interest in the merged firm, represented by the proposition:

$$p = \frac{260{,}000}{1{,}000{,}000 + 260{,}000} = .2063$$

Therefore, the shareholders of firm Y will own approximately 21 percent of the merged firm. The cost of this merger is really the difference between what firm Y's shareholders receive and what they give up in exchange; i.e.,

$$\text{Cost}'_s = pV(XY) - V(Y) \qquad (15.5)$$

where $V(XY)$ = value of the combined firm ($X + Y$)

Now suppose that prior to the merger announcement $V(X) = V'(X)$, $V(Y) = V'(Y)$, and the estimated economic gain given by equation (15.1) is \$2 million. Then $V(XY) = V(X) + V(Y) + \text{Gain} = \$50$ million + \$12 million + \$2 million. Therefore, the true cost is

$$\begin{aligned} \text{Cost}'_s &= pV(XY) - V(Y) \\ &= .2063(\$64{,}000{,}000) - \$12{,}000{,}000 \\ &= \$1.20 \text{ million} \end{aligned}$$

Here Cost'_s exceeds Cost_s, because stock prices observed prior to the merger do not reflect the economic gains associated with the event. Indeed, Cost$'_s$ reflects both the gains from the merger and how these gains are divided between the shareholder groups of firms *X* and *Y*. With an exchange of stock, the cost depends on the eventual gain, and the effects of any undervaluation or overvaluation will be shared with the acquired firm's shareholders. In this sense, a merger transaction financed by the exchange of stock lessens these effects as compared to a cash exchange.

VI. ASSESSING THE OUTCOME OF A MERGER

A. Effects on EPS

As the previous section has made clear, the theoretical framework within which a merger should be evaluated is quite precise and not overly complex. In contrast, the practical considerations involved in making the estimates necessary to judge whether a merger or acquisition will be a success, i.e., whether it will create a positive NPV for at least one of the parties, are imprecise and quite complex. A relatively simple example will serve to illustrate the nature of some common complexities that can occur in merger analysis.

Consider Table 15.2, which lays out five years of some past financial information for Companies *X* and *Y*, along with a five-year projection. Company *X*, the larger, shows much more sluggish growth and seems vulnerable to downturns such as occurred in 1985 and which are again forecast for 1991. It pays a steady dividend, maintaining the payment per share in poor years and lagging increases as earnings per share increase. Company *Y*, on the other hand, is growing rapidly. It showed little effect of the economic problems of 1985, although in 1991 its management forecasts that its earnings will only hold steady (or at least not decline) in the anticipated recession. The company pays no dividends, requiring that all its internally generated funds be marked for investment in the highly profitable projects it has available to it.

Now consider Table 15.3, which shows the effect of Company *X*'s purchasing Company *Y* at the end of 1988 for 15 times earnings, \$3,750,000, in cash. Let us assume that Company *X* trades at 10 times earnings, reflecting its relatively lower growth rate.

If the companies are properly priced in the market, Company *X*'s equity value should not change as a result of the merger. This is because the value added by Company *Y* should be offset by the increased debt (or reduced cash) on Company *X*'s balance sheet and a corresponding reduction in the price–earnings ratio. It is clear, however, that the merger will enhance the growth in Company *X*'s earnings per share from the levels anticipated in Table 15.2 before the merger. Note, however, that even though 100 percent of the purchase price was assumed to be borrowed and hence would add to Company *X*'s interest payments, there was no allowance for the likely requirement that goodwill would be created by the transaction and would have to be amortized. This charge against earnings would decrease the net positive effect on the earnings per share.

Now, might not the higher growth in earnings per share result in an increase in Company *X*'s price–earnings ratio? Furthermore, if the dividend payout expected from Table 15.2 is maintained under the cash-purchase conditions, assuming that the cash is available for this increase (which may be a doubtful assumption if Company *Y* needs the resources to grow), then won't the additional dividends reinforce the possibility of an increased price–earnings ratio? This is the type of difficult judgment that must be made even if the cash price for Company *Y* shows a break-even NPV. In fact, it should be considered even if the NPV is positive.

The judgment becomes still more difficult if the purchase is made by an exchange of stock, as illustrated in Table 15.4. Assuming that the merger took place through a "pooling of interest," in which goodwill would not be created but for which past earnings would be restated as though the firms had been merged throughout the period, the results are quite different than in the case of the cash purchase. Now, despite Company *Y*'s high growth rate, the combined

TABLE 15.2 Basic Data for Merger Analysis (thousands of dollars except per-share figures)

	Actual					Forecast				
	1984	*1985*	*1986*	*1987*	*1988*	*1989*	*1990*	*1991*	*1992*	*1993*
COMPANY X										
Shares outstanding	500 all years									
Profit after taxes	$1,000	$900	$1,000	$1,100	$1,210	$1,330	$1,470	$1,200	$1,500	$1,600
Earnings per share	$2.00	$1.80	$2.00	$2.20	$2.42	$2.66	$2.94	$2.40	$3.00	$3.20
Dividends	$400	$400	$400	$400	$440	$480	$530	$530	$530	$600
Dividends per share	$0.80	$0.80	$0.80	$0.80	$0.88	$0.96	$1.06	$1.06	$1.06	$1.20
Payout	40%	44%	40%	36%	36%	36%	36%	44%	35%	38%
COMPANY Y										
Shares outstanding	100 all years									
Profit after taxes	$100	$125	$160	$200	$250	$300	$375	$375	$430	$515
Earnings per share	$1.00	$1.25	$1.60	$2.00	$2.50	$3.00	$3.75	$3.75	$4.30	$5.15

TABLE 15.3 Cash Purchase (thousands of dollars except per-share figures)

Company *X* purchases Company *Y* for 15 × *p/e* in cash: $3,750

	Actual					*Forecast*				
	1984	*1985*	*1986*	*1987*	*1988*	*1989*	*1990*	*1991*	*1992*	*1993*
Shares outstanding	500 all years									
Company *X* profits	$1,000	$900	$1,000	$1,100	$1,210	$1,330	$1,470	$1,200	$1,500	$1,600
Company *Y* profits						300	375	375	430	515
Interest on price (AT)						188	188	188	188	188
Profit after taxes	1,000	900	1,000	1,100	1,210	1,442	1,657	1,387	1,742	1,927
Earnings per share	$2.00	$1.80	$2.00	$2.20	$2.42	$2.88	$3.31	$2.77	$3.48	$3.85
Change in Co. *X* EPS	0.0%	0.0%	0.0%	0.0%	0.0%	8.3%	12.6%	15.4%	16.0%	20.3%
Payout as before	40%	44%	40%	36%	36%	36%	36%	44%	35%	38%
Dividends	$400	$400	$400	$400	$440	$519	$597	$610	$610	$732
Dividends per share	$0.80	$0.80	$0.80	$0.80	$0.88	$1.04	$1.19	$1.22	$1.22	$1.46
Change in Co. *X* DPS	0.00%	0.00%	0.00%	0.00%	0.00%	8.33%	12.26%	15.09%	15.09%	21.67%

TABLE 15.4 Merger by Exchange of Common Stock (thousands of dollars except per-share figures)

Company *X* merges with Company *Y*										
Issues stock at 10 *p/e*:				$24.20						
Cost of Company *Y* at 15 *p/e*:				$3,750						
New shares:				155						
For each Company *Y* share, Company *Y* shareholders receive				1.55 shares						
			Actual					*Forecast*		
	1984	*1985*	*1986*	*1987*	*1988*	*1989*	*1990*	*1991*	*1992*	*1993*
Shares outstanding	655									
Co. *X* P.A.T.	$1,000	$900	$1,000	$1,100	$1,210	$1,330	$1,470	$1,200	$1,500	$1,600
Co. *Y* P.A.T.	100	125	160	200	250	300	375	375	430	515
Total P.A.T.	1,100	1,025	1,160	1,300	1,460	1,630	1,845	1,575	1,930	2,115
Effect on Company *X* shareholders (Same as will be reported on a pooling-of-interest basis)										
Earnings per share	$1.68	$1.56	$1.77	$1.98	$2.23	$2.49	$2.82	$2.40	$2.95	$3.23
Change in Co. *X* EPS	−16.00%	−13.33%	−11.50%	−10.00%	−7.85%	−6.39%	−4.08%	0.00%	−1.67%	0.94%
Payout as before						36%	36%	44%	35%	38%
Dividends per share			No change, 1984–1988			$0.90	$1.02	$1.06	$1.03	$1.23
Change in Co. *X* DPS						−6.25%	−3.77%	0.00%	−1.90%	2.50%
Effect on Company *Y* shareholders per old Company *Y* share										
Earnings per share						$3.86	$4.37	$3.72	$4.57	$5.01
Change in Co. *Y* EPS						28.67%	16.53%	−0.80%	6.28%	−2.72%
Dividends per share						$1.39	$1.57	$1.64	$1.60	$1.90

earnings per share, as restated, are much lower than the earnings Company *X* had formerly. Even future earnings will be lower through 1993, except for the recession year of 1991, when they will be unchanged. Dividends will also decline from the initial levels forecast.

Company *Y* shareholders, however, appear to be considerably better off, once their situation has been adjusted for the fact that they hold 1.55 shares of Company *X* for each share they used to own in Company *Y*. Their earnings per share are increased substantially in the short term, declining significantly only in 1991. In the meantime, they are enjoying a very attractive dividend compared to their former situation. What will the market think? That is the big question.

Obviously, if Company *Y*'s price were lower, Company *X* would show better results sooner. But then, if Company *Y*'s shareholders plan to hold onto the shares in Company *X*, would they be better off with fewer shares but a better market price? Of course, if Company *Y* were growing faster (or Company *X* more slowly), the positive effect on Company *X* would occur earlier than 1993. And what about the synergistic effects of the merger? What would they be in terms of the price–earnings ratio and the market price of the combination? Eventually, the reaction on all these matters will be known, but major judgments are required *before* such knowledge is available.

There are many other questions regarding the evaluation of mergers that are beyond the scope of this text to examine, but some of them can at least be mentioned. For example, what is the effect on value of the resulting capital structure and the way the transaction is financed? How might redeployment of redundant assets enhance value? And what, if any, sophisticated alternative securities are there that might be used to effect the purchase? The touchstone in all cases is whether value will be created, and this is often measured by an appraisal of the earnings per share (a relatively straightforward computation) and the price–earnings ratio (a judgment about the market's demands and seldom straightforward) to see whether the market price will be increased.

One final consideration that is worthy of note is that because of the particularly difficult judgmental nature of a merger analysis, and because in most instances there may be an overlap between the seller's minimum price and the buyer's maximum, the skill of the negotiating team is critical to the creation of a satisfactory deal. This is particularly true if the parties to the merger expect to work together after the transaction is completed.

B. Analysis of Value

While the previous section was concerned primarily with the impact of merger on EPS, it is now time to focus on likely valuation effects. In fact, some authors assert that the correct way to evaluate a merger is not the effect on EPS, but rather the impact on market value. In other words, will the merger create value for the acquiring firm's shareholders (i.e., is it a positive NPV investment)? Consequently, we shall discuss a general framework for estimating NPV that is directly analogous to the evaluation of investment projects discussed in Chapter 13 on capital budgeting. We should reiterate, however, that given the complex nature of the merger transaction, there is no single, simple rule for determining NPV. Rather, the analyst must put together the pieces of a complex puzzle using not one, but as many relevant tools as are available. The following discussion will rely on the concepts and techniques developed in earlier chapters in order to accomplish our objective of placing a value on the target firm.

Although our analysis is focused on the future, a good place to begin is with an examination of historical data. Such data include book value, earnings, dividends, and stock prices, as well as growth and reinvestment rates. With the exception of stock prices, each of these variables is reflected in some way in the target firm's balance sheets. However, because there is rarely a close connection between historical costs and current value, the reported book value of assets must be adjusted to reflect both current market values and replacement values. The *market values* of the firm's assets refer to the prices they would bring in an orderly liquidation. *Replace-*

ment value, in contrast, is the cost required to replicate the firm's operations. Market values can be estimated by obtaining independent appraisals of the firm's land, plant, and equipment (or fixed assets). Given the short-term nature of cash, receivables, and inventories, however, their book values are probably a reasonably good estimate of their market values. Receivables and inventories may need some adjustment for bad debts, obsolescence and inflation, while the cash account obviously requires no adjustment whatsoever. Replacement value will be determined by the current costs of reconstructing manufacturing and distribution facilities, and purchasing land and equipment of similar quality. With restated book values, it is then a simple matter to calculate the target firm's book value per share which provides a reference point in further analysis of value.

The next step involves a straightforward calculation of the relationships between EPS, dividends per share (DPS), and stock prices of the acquiring and target firms. These relationships may be captured in the computation of ratios. Furthermore, the procedure may be extended to encompass future earnings, and in this case, ratios should be calculated based on various assumptions as to growth rates. The objective of this ratio analysis (not to be confused with ratio analysis of financial statements discussed earlier in the text) is to estimate an appropriate exchange ratio of the acquiring firm's shares for those of the target. Given an exchange ratio and the price per share of the acquiring firm's stock, the value of the target firm's shares can then be calculated. For example, if the stock price of the acquiring firm is \$10 per share and an analysis of past and projected EPS indicates an exchange rate of 1.2 shares for each of the target shares, the value of the target stock is then \$12 (= \$10 × 1.2).

Perhaps the most crucial aspect of the analysis is to determine whether the target is likely to be a generator of excess cash, or *free* cash. *Free cash flow* is defined to be cash flow from operations net of required investment in fixed assets, working capital, research and development, advertising, and so forth. Historical relationships between sales and fixed assets, working capital (net of excess cash), and advertising expenditures may be helpful in estimating free cash flow. In contrast, the past relationship between sales and R&D expenditures may or may not be helpful depending on the characteristics of the industry in which the target firm operates. Again, these estimates should be calculated under various growth rate assumptions. For a more detailed discussion of cash flow forecasting, the reader is referred to Chapter 5.

Having calculated expected cash flows, the next step is to develop the appropriate rate for discounting those cash flows to obtain their present value. As discussed in Chapter 13, "Capital Budgeting," the WACC (or hurdle rate) may be estimated by use of the capital asset pricing model (CAPM) and the dividend discount model. The Gordon–Shapiro dividend valuation model defines the cost of equity capital as the sum of dividend yield plus growth: $K_e = D_1/P_0 + g$. In the case of merger, however, the current price (value) is not observable; it is the object of our analysis. Hence, we will concentrate on the CAPM approach to determine the appropriate hurdle rate.

Since the late 1970s, both the debt and equity markets have been fairly volatile making estimation of the CAPM parameters (R_f, R_m, and β) somewhat difficult. Consequently, the analyst should not place too much faith in single point estimates of R_f and R_m computed from current financial market data. As a reference, however, the returns estimated by Ibbotson and Sinquefield on stocks and bonds over the 1926–1976 period may be used. On average over the 50-year period, the excess return on stocks ($R_m - R_f$) has been about 9.2 percent. In addition, the return on short-term Treasuries (T-bills), adjusted for inflation, has been 0 percent, and the differential return between T-bills and T-bonds has been about 1 percent. Thus, current T-bill rates may be taken as an estimate of short-term inflationary expectations and current T-bond yields minus 1 percent as an estimate of long-run inflationary expectations. In general, then, the required return on asset j would be calculated as follows:

$$R_j = R_f + (R_m - R_f)\beta_j + i$$

where R_f = the real return on T-bills (0%)
$(R_m - R_f)$ = 9.2%
i = expected inflation

Returns derived in this manner may be compared with those using current nominal rates to estimate a likely range of required returns for the asset. Another complication arises if the target is a closely held or private company making estimates of beta unavailable. In this event, subjective assumptions based on the target's business risk will be required. The overall hurdle rate then is the all-equity-capitalization rate adjusted for leverage and taxes: $R^* = R_E[1 - (T_c)(D/V)]$ (see Chapter 12, "Cost of Capital").

To place a final value (or range of values) on the target firm, we take the present value of both the cash flows and an estimate of terminal value. We should note here that if the target is expected to be a net *user* of funds over the prescribed holding period, the intermediate cash flows will be negative. Hence, the positive return on investment will consist entirely of the terminal value of the target firm. The final figure will also include adjustments for excess cash on hand and side effects such as unused tax shields.

VII. LEGAL, TAX, AND ACCOUNTING CONSIDERATIONS IN MERGERS

A. Legal Considerations

Mergers raise many legal questions, most of which are governed by the Sherman Act of 1890, the Federal Trade Commission (FTC) Act of 1914, and the Clayton Act of 1914. The Sherman Act declares that

> Every contract, combination . . . or conspiracy, in restraint of trade is illegal and that every person who shall . . . attempt to monopolize . . . any part of . . . commerce is in violation of the law.

The FTC Act states that it is illegal to engage in actions which use "unfair methods of competition" and "unfair or deceptive acts or practices." In the same spirit, the Clayton Act indicates that the acquisition of another firm's assets or stock "in any line of commerce" or "in any section of the country" whose effect "may be substantially to lessen competition or tend to create monopoly" is illegal. This passage is from Section 7 of the Clayton Act, and it is now the main rule of law used in most antitrust cases.

While the foregoing excerpts seem to suggest that the tendency is to prohibit mergers, only a small number have actually been challenged by either the Justice Department or the FTC. Usually, those mergers that draw the attention of these government branches are mergers involving rather large firms. Consequently, horizontal and vertical mergers among such firms are very difficult to consummate. On the other hand, given the numerous mergers that actually take place, it is illuminating to consider the various ways in which firms that are planning to merge facilitate acquisitions.

Essentially, there are three ways to gain control over another firm: merger, acquisition of stock, and acquisition of assets. Up to now, the term *merger* has been used to mean any general combination of two firms. However, under state law, a merger involves the total transfer of the assets and liabilities of the selling firm to the purchasing firm. Thus, after the merger is completed, the selling firm will no longer be considered a separate entity. Most states require that at least two-thirds of the shareholders in both firms approve the merger. Dissenting shareholders can have their shares bought at an impartially determined fair value. If, instead of an outright sale of the assets and liabilities of one firm to another, the two firms combine to form an entirely new firm, the process is called a *consolidation*. Here neither firm is identified as buyer or seller, but the rules for merger must still be satisfied.

In the acquisition of a company's stock by another company, the buying firm must deal only with the selling firm's shareholders. However, if the buying firm acquires less than 80 percent of the selling firm's shares, the buyer must pay tax on 15 percent of any subsequent dividend received from the selling firm.

In buying the assets of the selling company outright, the acquiring firm purchases title to specific assets and need not be concerned with minority shareholders in the selling firm. As one might guess, the purchase of individual assets requires no consent from the buying firm's shareholders and only a 50-percent majority vote from the selling firm's shareholders.

B. Tax Implications

Mergers may result in either a taxable or a tax-free acquisition. In a taxable transfer, the selling shareholders are treated as if they actually sold their shares. They must therefore report any capital gains or losses. In a tax-free transfer, the selling shareholders are viewed as if they were simply exchanging their old shares for new shares. No gains or losses need be reported. In addition to the effects on shareholders, the merged firm also merits different attention. In a taxable transfer, the merged firm must submit the assets of the selling firm for revaluation and recomputation of depreciation charges for tax purposes. In a nontaxable transfer, the merged firm is treated simply as the sum of the two individual firms.

What, then, determines a merger's tax status? In order to have tax-free status, three conditions must be satisfied:

1. The acquisition cannot be solely for tax purposes; i.e., some business purpose must be served.
2. The selling firm must continue to exist; i.e., the merged entity should not sell off the assets of the acquired firm.
3. The shareholders of the selling firm must get a significant interest in the buying firm—according to the IRS, at least 80 percent of the exchange offer, in the form of voting stock.

How do these requirements match up with the three forms of acquisition? As long as the merger transaction satisfies the requirements, it will be considered a tax-free acquisition. On the other hand, for a stock acquisition to be considered tax free, the entire payment must be in the form of voting stock and the buyer must purchase almost all the property of the selling firm with at least 80 percent of the assets paid for with voting stock. A simple example will suffice to examine the effects of tax status on both buying and selling firms.

Suppose RAD Associates owns a laundromat that was purchased in 1986 for $500,000. The laundromat's equipment is depreciated on a straight-line basis over its expected useful life of 10 years. Annual depreciation is $50,000, and in 1989 the laundromat had a net book value of $350,000. Due to the unusual growth of the local economy, the laundromat's economic value is currently estimated at $450,000. Also, RAD Associates currently has $60,000 in a money market fund. Now suppose RAD Associates were to sell its business holdings to GPT Inc. for $510,000. How can we go about examining the possible tax consequences? The following table shows some simple effects of the sale:

	Taxable	*Tax Free*
1. Effect on RAD Associates	RAD recognizes $100,000 capital gain.	Capital gain realized when GPT, Inc., shares are sold.
2. Effect on GPT, Inc.	Laundromat revalued to $450,000. Depreciation rises to $64,285 over the next 7 years.	Laundromat's value stays at $350,000 with depreciation of $50,000 per year.

From the table, RAD Associates is clearly better off with a tax-free transfer, whereas GPT, Inc., will probably prefer a taxable transfer because the depreciation for the next 7 years is higher. Thus, there will very likely be a difference of opinion regarding the desired tax status of the merger. Because RAD will recognize a profit on the original $500,000 investment, Richard A. DeFusco, its founder, will prefer the nontaxable transfer. However, because the market value of the laundromat is substantially larger than its book value, GPT, Inc., will prefer the taxable transfer, in order to take advantage of the larger depreciation shield.

C. Merger Accounting

A merger can be accounted for either as a purchase of assets or as a pooling of interests. The *pooling-of-interests* method simply adds together the balance sheets of each firm to arrive at the "new" balance sheet for the merged firm. Under *purchase accounting,* the outcome is more complicated and somewhat different. Suppose firm X acquires firm Y and pays a premium which amounts to $500,000 over the value reported on Y's books. Then, since firm X has acquired an asset represented by firm Y, the additional $500,000 must appear on the combined balance sheet. To make the combined balance sheet balance, the $500,000 is recorded on the asset side as goodwill. As one might guess, all this seems quite arbitrary, as there is no effect on the ultimate cash flow of the combined firm because goodwill is not allowed as a deduction from taxable income.

D. Tender Offers

The mergers discussed so far have generally involved the active participation of the management and boards of the buying and selling firm. However, this participation need not always be the case: firms that wish to acquire other businesses may do so by buying shares directly from the stockholders of the firm in question. Such action is referred to as a *tender offer,* which stipulates that the acquiring company is willing to purchase shares at a fixed price from any shareholder. This method of merger can obviously be used if the management of the target firm attempts to hold out for too high a price. Tender offers were an extremely attractive method of acquisition during the sixties, but their use waned during the seventies. During the last five years, however, they have again become a popular device in takeover bids.

VIII. EMPIRICAL EVIDENCE ON MERGER RETURNS

Empirical studies on merger returns have focused primarily on whether these unique events produce temporary abnormal returns for the acquired or the acquiring firm. The overall evidence suggests that the shareholders of the acquired firms obtain significant gains in the short period just before the date the merger is announced. The evidence also suggests that the acquired firms had not been good market performers before the acquisition. The shareholders of the acquiring firms on average had neither gains nor losses in the period just before the merger announcement date. In earlier periods, the evidence shows that the acquiring firms were good market performers. Moving now to specifics, we shall review some of the merger studies briefly.

The earliest study on merger profitability was performed by Kelly (1967). He chose a sample of 21 mergers that yielded increases in sales of at least 20 percent and matched them with a control sample of 21 nonmerging firms, for the period 1946 to 1960. Kelly utilized five measures of profitability, including market measures, for the five years prior and the five years after the merger. The overall results suggest little or no synergy associated with the merging firms vis-à-vis the nonmerging firms.

Another early study on merger synergy was performed by Hogarty (1970) who developed market-based investment performance indexes for 43 acquiring corporations. Comparison of these market performance values with the respective industrial indexes showed a 5 percent negative synergy for the acquiring firms. Still another early study on merger returns was performed by Lev and Mandelker (1972), who employed for the first time a specific experimental design involving paired comparisons of comparable merging and nonmerging firms. Using a sample of 69 pairs of firms and a period of five years before and after the merger, Lev and Mandelker found that the shareholders of the acquired firms gained about 5.6 percent from the merger event.

In perspective, the evidence from the early studies on merger returns is at best conflicting and beset with methodological problems. Hence, we shall now proceed with a brief review of some more recent empirical studies that also employed modern asset pricing models. These studies also establish empirically verifiable periods of investigation by observing the behavior of the *average residuals* (ARs) and the *cumulative average residuals* (CARs) before and after the merger. Specifically, the CARs are scanned for patterns prior to the event, thus establishing the merger-related activity in market returns. Then another period adjacent to this is established where the patterns of CARs are random, thus establishing the estimation period.

The first of the studies to employ modern asset pricing methodology was performed by Halpern (1973). Halpern focused on the merger premiums for acquiring and acquired firms involved in 75 acquisitions. He found that information about the merger exists in the market in the seven-month period prior to the announcement. Prior to the seventh month and back to the twenty-third month, the CARs behave randomly. The end-result of Halpern's study is that smaller acquired firms obtain a premium from the merger but larger acquired firms show no such evidence of gains. In another study, Mandelker (1974) utilized more sophisticated methodology and found that the acquiring firms obtain positive average residuals, which are not statistically significant. However, the CARs of the acquired firms were also positive, indicating abnormal gains from the mergers. Similar results were obtained by Elbert (1975, 1976) who employed methodology comparable to Mandelker. The overall results of Mandelker were also confirmed in a study of 149 mergers by Langetieg (1978).

In a more recent study, Dodd (1980) employed the market model to test merger-related abnormal returns in a sample of 151 merger announcements rather than merger consummations. After elimination of the cancelled mergers, Dodd found that the two-day announcement CARs for acquiring firms indicated negative abnormal returns of 1 percent, while the equivalent returns for the acquired firms were positive and large (about 13 percent). Similar results were obtained by Asquith (1980) and Malatesta (1982).

IX. SUMMARY AND REVIEW

Mergers have become increasingly popular during the last decade. Accordingly, it is imperative that financial managers realize the legal implications of such combinations. Furthermore, complications also arise in computing the costs and benefits of mergers. This computation is not only difficult, but it may also depend on the method of financing used.

While there is no general theory that serves as a guide in the decision to merge, capital-budgeting concepts can be used to evaluate the profitability of a merger. In general, all other things being equal, a firm should merge if the NPV of the combination is positive. Complications to this *ceteris paribus* clause involve issues concerning the legality of the merger, its tax status, and the computation of costs, as well as anti-takeover tactics employed by some corporate managers.

APPENDIX 15A
TOP 20 MERGERS, LEVERAGED BUYOUTS, AND DIVESTITURES BY DOLLAR VALUE 4/1/88 TO 9/30/88[1]

Acquiring Company	*Acquired Company*	*Value in $ Million*
Second Quarter 1988		
Bridgestone Corp. of Japan	Firestone Tire & Rubber Co.	2,661.5
American Stores Co.	Lucky Stores, Inc.	2,508.6
Kelso & Co.	American Standard, Inc.[2]	2,431.2
Kohlberg Kravis Roberts	Duracell, Inc.[2]	1,800.0
Dun & Bradstreet Corp.	I.M.S. International, Inc.	1,588.8
BFB Acquisition Corp.	Montgomery Ward & Co., Inc.[2]	1,500.0
May Department Stores Co.	Federated D.S. (Filene's and Foley's)[3]	1,500.0
Tate & Lyle PLC	Staley Continental, Inc.	1,452.1
Occidental Petroleum Corp.	Cain Chemical, Inc.	1,250.0
Kohlberg Kravis Roberts	Stop & Shop Cos., Inc.[2]	1,227.6
Third Quarter 1988		
Campeau Corp.	Federated Department Stores, Inc.	6,506.2
Amoco Corp.	Dome Petroleum, Ltd.	3,766.1
General Electric Co.	Borg-Warner Corp. (chemical unit)[3]	2,310.0
PA Holdings Corp.	Pneumo-Abex Corp.[2,3]	1,230.0
Riklis Family Corp.	E-II Holdings, Inc.[3]	1,200.0
Itel Corp.	Henley Group, Inc. (units)[3]	1,194.0
CJI Industries, Inc.	Triangle Industries	825.6
WAF Acquisition Corp.	Charter Medical Corp.[2]	819.1
PepsiCo, Inc.	Grand Metropolitan, Inc. (units)[3]	705.0
SYSCO Corp.	Staley Continental, Inc.[3] (food service business)	700.0

1. Adapted from *Mergers & Acquisitions,* Jan–Feb 1989, 65 and Sep–Oct 1988, 69.
2. Leveraged buyout
3. Divestiture

QUESTIONS

1. What are some of the reasons firms engage in takeover activity?
2. What do agency problems have to do with mergers and acquisitions?
3. Describe the connection between synergy and market value.
4. What difficulties arise in estimating the parameters of the CAPM?
5. What adjustments should be made to book values so that they more accurately reflect firm value?
6. In the context of adjusted present value discussed in Chapter 13, what might be considered as "side effects" of mergers?
7. If the expected operating cash flows of a target firm (i.e., its cash flows before interest is deducted) are discounted at a rate which includes the effects of leverage and taxes, is it necessary to account explicitly for unused debt capacity? Why or why not?
8. In general, what three ways exist for obtaining control of a firm? What are the tax implications of each alternative?

PROBLEMS

1. Firm X is considering the acquisition of firm Y financed by an exchange of stock. The management of X believes the current market price of Y accurately reflects its intrinsic value. Given the following information, calculate the cost to firm X of acquiring firm Y if it must pay a $1 million premium over market value with an exchange of stock.

	X	Y
Market Price/Share	\$50	\$30
Number of shares	1,000,000	400,000
Market Value	\$50,000,000	\$12,000,000

(*Hint:* Refer to equations (15.1) through (15.5).)

2. If the price of X rises to \$51/share, what is the cost of the acquisition?
3. If the price of X is \$50/share and that of Y is \$31/share, what will be the cost of the acquisition?
4. If the price of X is \$51/share and that of Y is \$29/share, and the total gain from the acquisition ($V(XY) - V(X) - V(Y)$) is \$2 million, what will be the effect on the wealth of the shareholders of firm X? of firm Y?

ANNOTATED BIBLIOGRAPHY

"Corporate Takeovers—The Unfriendly Tender Offer and the Minority Stockholder Freezeout." Special issue of *Business Lawyer,* May 1977.
A good discussion of takeovers and their possible negative effects.

Duhaime, I. M., and H. Thomas. "Financial Analysis and Strategic Management." *Journal of Economics and Business,* 35(1983): 413–40.
An interesting survey of various financial approaches to strategic management.

Halpern, P. "Corporate Acquisitions: A Theory of Special Cases? A Review of Event Studies Applied to Acquisitions." *Journal of Finance,* May 1983, 297–317.
A good review of the empirical work on merger benefits as well as merger theories.

Howell, R. A. "Plan to Integrate Your Acquisitions." *Harvard Business Review,* November–December 1970, 66–70.
A presentation of a framework for different classifications of mergers, as well as a methodology for analyzing possible merger candidates.

Mergers and Acquisitions 19 (Fall 1984).
A presentation of much of the background for data on mergers during 1984.

Myers, S. C. "A Framework for Evaluating Mergers." In *Modern Developments in Financial Management,* edited by S. C. Myers, 633–45. New York: F. A. Praeger, 1976.
A presentation of the framework used in this chapter to analyze mergers.

Rappaport, A. "Financial Analysis for Mergers and Acquisitions." *Mergers and Acquisitions,* Winter 1976, 18–36.
An early but interesting paper that approaches the valuation of the firm from the point of view of managerial rather than market expectations about future performance.

Steiner, P. O. *Mergers: Motives, Effect, Policies.* Ann Arbor: University of Michigan Press, 1975.
A good analysis of merger motives in addition to their effects on the U.S. economy.

Von Bauer, E. E. "Meaningful Risk and Return Criteria for Strategic Investment Decisions." *Mergers and Acquisitions,* Winter 1981, 5–17.
An interesting approach to the evaluation of risk and return requirements for strategic investments like mergers, acquisitions, and divestitures.

APPENDIX 15B REORGANIZATION AND BANKRUPTCY*

A. Introduction

Mergers, acquisitions, takeovers, and other types of business combinations bring temporary dislocations to the portfolio of assets known as the firm and eventually lead to portfolio revisions in the form of divestitures, spin-offs, and other such acts of investment fine tuning. The life cycle of a firm, however, does not always bring external growth and success. In many

*The material in this appendix was adapted from drafts originally prepared by Mr. David A. Harrison. The suggestions made by Mr. Paul H. Hunn, Vice-President, Manufacturers Hanover Trust Company; Andrew DeNatale, Esq., Stroock & Stroock & Lavan; and Professor J. C. McCoid, II, University of Virginia Law School, are acknowledged with appreciation. These individuals bear no responsibility, of course, for any errors. The discussion in this appendix is not intended to be a substitute for legal counsel, nor does it purport to be a comprehensive treatment of the subject. It is an introduction and review to aid in clear discussion of financially troubled situations.

cases, firms find themselves strapped financially and surrounded by shrinking markets. Often, firms in such financial difficulties will look seriously for a merger partner. (See, for example, the Memorex–Burroughs merger researched by Dosoung Choi and Michael P. Bates and abstracted in *Mergers and Acquisitions,* Fall 1984, 72–75.) Sometimes, however, the firm may go into bankruptcy. Bankruptcy is a state of affairs that may eventually be followed by total liquidation and disappearance of the firm as a business entity. Alternatively, bankruptcy may result in partial liquidation, recapitalization, reorganization, and the eventual reappearance of the firm as a smaller, leaner, and more efficient unit that will attempt to succeed once again in the competitive marketplace.

Let us look at some of the more commonly discussed causes of business failure. There are many ways in which a business can fail, some of which are as follows:

1. *Economic failure* occurs when a firm's revenues do not cover its costs.
2. *Technical insolvency* occurs when a firm cannot meet its maturing current obligations. Such difficulty may be only a temporary situation, however.
3. *Bankruptcy* has a specific legal meaning. In order for a firm to be bankrupt, it must meet the criteria established by the Federal Bankruptcy Act.

Business failures are generally attributed to a variety of causes. For example, Dun and Bradstreet's specialized publication, *The Business Failure Record,* lists many reasons for business failure, all of which can be subsumed under the following four categories: (1) lack of specialized experience in a specific type of business; (2) lack of managerial experience; (3) uneven experience in specific but important functional areas, such as marketing, production, or finance; and (4) managerial incompetence. Two of the most notable business failures of the 1970s involved Penn Central and W. T. Grant, with a combined total asset value in excess of $8 billion. Such dramatic business failures will leave significant marks on both stockholders and creditors alike. Thus, business reorganizations attempt to protect creditors while simultaneously salvaging enough equity in the firm through recapitalization to help make the business a productive, tax-paying entity once again. Recently, a comprehensive new bankruptcy law known as the *Bankruptcy Code of 1978* was enacted by Congress. The Code represents an effort to simplify the legal technicalities and routines associated with filing for bankruptcy, reduce costs of the process to all parties, and correct what were considered abuses or inequalities that had developed under the old legislation. Almost immediately, further revisions were required, so that bankruptcy practices remain slow in settling into new routines.

B. The Bankruptcy Code of 1978

In contrast to previous bankruptcy law, which required that one of five specific acts (such as granting of a security interest when insolvent) had to occur before a debtor could be forced involuntarily by a creditor to submit to the court's jurisdiction, the new Code promulgates the criterion that the inability of the debtor to pay debts as they become due is sufficient cause for involuntary submission to the court. Thus, a company with relatively illiquid assets, such as land, might be more readily forced into bankruptcy proceedings even though in the long run it would have sufficient assets to pay its debts in full. Another condition which allows for the filing of an involuntary petition is the appointment of a custodian or a custodian's taking possession of substantially all of a debtor's property within 120 days before the petition was filed.

Under the code, eight chapters govern proceedings for individuals and businesses. The following table lists the chapters and the aspect of bankruptcy they deal with:

Chapter	*Subject*
1	General Provisions, Definitions and Rules of Construction
3	Case Administration
5	Creditors, Debtors and the Estate
7	Liquidation
9	Adjustment of the Debt of a Municipality
11	Reorganization
13	Adjustment of the Debts of Individuals with Regular Income
15	United States Trustees

The chapters that are most applicable to businesses are Chapters 7 and 11. Chapter 7 specifies that during a liquidation proceeding a trustee is appointed to collect all nonexempt property, sell the property, and distribute the proceeds. Filing under this chapter may be voluntary by the debtor or forced by the creditor.

Chapter 11, which covers reorganization proceedings rather than the details of liquidation, does provide for liquidation plans. The intent of this chapter is to specify the ground rules of consensual plans, which are often encouraged by circumstances in which the creditors' claims will be more completely paid if the debtor continues to operate and generate future earnings. Nevertheless, a liquidating plan is spelled out for circumstances in which the parties agree it is preferable to a Chapter 7 procedure. Chapter 11 is available to most debtors on either a voluntary or an involuntary basis. It provides for a creditors' committee and specifies the rules for creditor acceptance of a plan.

C. Voluntary Settlements

When a debtor is not able to meet its financial obligations, the debtor will often first attempt to gain a voluntary arrangement for new terms. This arrangement might include rescheduling payments to stretch them out (an extension), reducing the interest rates, or compromising creditor positions or amounts (composition). The primary advantages to the creditor of a voluntary settlement are that it limits adverse publicity, allows for continued business relationships, permits flexibility in contractual agreements, and requires much lower administrative costs than a court-supervised bankruptcy. For these reasons, and because the creditor realizes that there is little to gain by forcing the borrower into the courts, most restructurings are done on a voluntary basis.

If, however, the company declares bankruptcy within 90 days of the voluntary agreements, the court may conclude that the compromise was a preference and void it. Another potential problem is that if a group of creditors accepts a voluntary plan but the company later files a bankruptcy petition anyway, the court may consider the voluntary plan as binding. The critical weakness of voluntary settlement efforts is that during the bargaining process all parties are subject to the threats of truculent creditors, who may use their obstinancy as a way of extricating themselves from the situation. Furthermore, without oversight by the bankruptcy courts and public examination of the records, creditors may become suspicious of one another and suspect the company is playing favorites.

The voluntary settlements available to debtors in distress share several common characteristics, some of which are as follows:

1. Insolvency occurs when the firm is unable to meet its maturing current obligations. In these circumstances, there may be a restructuring of the firm's debt obligations.
2. In most cases, new funds must be raised in order to improve and maintain working capital.
3. The basic cause of the business failure, whether it is manufacturing inefficiencies, uneven management experience, or management incompetence, must be identified and the problem solved.

Further discussion of business reorganization requires a brief review of some of the mechanics of formal bankruptcy proceedings—in particular, as they relate to the Bankruptcy Code of 1978 as it applies to business.

D. Bankruptcy Proceedings

As stated in the Bankruptcy Code, in order to petition for involuntary bankruptcy, if there are twelve or more creditors, at least three creditors with unsecured claims totaling at least $5,000 must file a petition. When there are fewer than twelve creditors, a single creditor with unsecured claims greater than $5,000 is sufficient for a petition. The only other requirement is that either the debtor is in "equitable insolvency," meaning that bills are not being paid as they come due, or that within 90 days before the petition, a receiver, assignee, or custodian took possession of substantially all the business property. If, in the opinion of the court, the required circumstances do not pertain, a judgment may be granted for costs, attorney fees, and damages against the petitioning creditors. Hence, the penalties for an error in filing an involuntary petition can be severe.

Upon filing a petition, an "automatic stay" takes effect. A stay halts the efforts of creditors to collect funds due them, to obtain a lien or seize assets, or otherwise to gain any unfair advantage. It restricts secured creditors from taking further actions to collect claims or to enforce liens. Also, creditors are prohibited from sending dunning letters, using setoffs, or enforcing prepetition judgments against the debtor. A secured creditor can gain relief from a stay only if the creditor can prove that the debtor has no equity interest in the secured property and that the property is not necessary for an effective reorganization or that there is insufficient protection of the property value. The court has broad latitude in providing "adequate protection" for the creditor's security in the property during the period of the stay, until the creditor can obtain the proceeds of its sale.

After the filing under Chapter 11, the court ordinarily appoints the seven largest unsecured creditors to serve as a committee representing that group. The judge has the power to appoint similar committees to represent secured creditors and equity holders, if requested, as well as the broad latitude to modify committee size and composition to ensure adequate representation yet maintain a manageable group. The committee, which normally retains counsel and accounting support, can consult with the trustee or debtor on the plans for reorganization and can investigate a debtor's actions and financial condition. The debtor's existing management usually runs the company during the reorganization, unless fraud or dishonest actions are exposed or the court decides that it is in the interest of the creditors to appoint a trustee.

We next consider some of the specific aspects involved in the reorganization proceedings under Chapter 11.

1. Reorganization Plans

In a Chapter 11 proceeding, only the debtor may file a Plan for Reorganization during the first 120 days, unless a trustee has been appointed. When the debtor does file within 120 days, no outside plans may be submitted until after 180 days. These dates can be changed at the discretion of the court in which the bankruptcy petition was filed. If a trustee has been appointed, however, any party may file a plan immediately.

The terms of a Plan may alter the rights of any class of creditors, but all members within a class must be treated equally. The terms are free from security registration requirements and from compliance with state law, which makes the process much more expeditious. The court reviews the information in the Plan to ensure that it meets the specific and complex requirements relating to content and disclosure.

A class of creditors accepts a Plan if more than one-half the class in number and two-thirds in dollar amount approve it. Rights of individuals who do not approve the Plan are protected by the requirement that the Plan be in their "best interests" by not "impairing" their position. A Plan meets this test by providing at least as much value as a claimant would receive in liquidation.

If the Plan is not approved by all classes, and if the position of any class is impaired, then the courts may "cram down" a Plan, provided at least one class has accepted it and that the non-approving, impaired classes are treated "fairly and equitably." A "fair and equitable" Plan will leave secured creditors (1) in possession of the collateral with residual claims against other assets up to the value of the debt, or (2) with the proceeds of the collateral plus residual claims, or (3) with the "indubitable equivalent" of the claims. A "fair and equitable" Plan will either pay unsecured creditors in full or deny junior claimants any value as long as a more senior claim is not completely satisfied, provided also that no senior class may receive more than 100 percent of its claims. Interesting problems can arise when a senior creditor attempts to pass value down the ladder in order to obtain cooperation from a creditor on a lower rung. Creditors in intervening positions may be able to block the plan.

Covenants or clauses that place a debtor in automatic default are nullified by the automatic stay that arises when a debtor files for bankruptcy. Also, a trustee may assume, reject, or assign executory contracts and unexpired leases even if prohibited by the contract or lease. Creditors may file claims for proven damages, subject to certain limitations. For example, claims for damages arising from the termination of real estate leases are limited to the *greater* of one year's rental payments or 15 percent of the remaining portion of the lease, subject to a maximum of three years' rental payment. Limitations are also placed on claims under employment contracts.

In essence, a reorganization requires that claims be recognized on the basis of legal and contractual priorities. This basic doctrine of a fair and equitable plan requires sound financial decisions during a reorganization. As with the valuation of any firm or asset, the following steps must be carried out:

1. Future sales must be estimated.
2. Operating conditions must be analyzed so that an estimate of the cash flow can be calculated.
3. An accurate estimate of the discount rate must be determined.
4. The present value based on steps 2 and 3 must then be computed.
5. The priority classification for the distribution of earnings must be calculated.

The feasibility of the fair and equitable plan should be judged by the adequacy of the earnings of the firm to cover the fixed charges owed to the various classes of creditors. Another criterion may involve whether there is a willing buyer for the firm at the price found in step 4 of the list.

2. *Creditor Classes in Liquidation*

The law establishes a priority of classes of creditors in the event of liquidation: secured creditors, priority claims, general creditors, and equity holders. The law, which is quite technical in this area, also creates subgroups in these major classifications which are relevant in allocating distributions and hence in related negotiations.

Subject to certain exemptions, secured creditors are supposed to be entitled to the quiet enjoyment of their collateral in their own part of the "enchanted forest." Property that has been pledged as security is not supposed to be taken for the benefit of any other party until the secured debts have been satisfied. Usually the security will be converted to cash under supervision of the court, but occasionally secured creditors will receive their security in kind. Any proceeds or value of the collateral not needed for this purpose remain in the "estate" for distribution to the other creditors. If the value of the collateral is less than the secured claim, the unsatisfied amount, or deficiency, becomes an unsecured claim.

The priority claims classification includes administrative expenses of the bankruptcy proceeding itself, including all post-filing costs of operating the business, such as maintenance, repairs, storage, and selling costs, as well as taxes on property liquidated. Also included are expenses of the trustee and any legal fees incurred. In the event that a Chapter 11 event is subsequently converted into a Chapter 7 liquidation, administrative and other expenses of the liquidation will be senior to claims and expenses of the Chapter 11 proceeding.

Within the priority group, the first subclass includes creditors whose claims stem from activities that occurred following the court's having determined that it has jurisdiction. The second subclass includes creditors whose claims arose between the date of filing and the date of the court's determination or the appointment of a trustee. This breakdown into subclasses helps debtors obtain credit to continue the operation of a business during the reorganization. If any creditor believes that its interests are weakened by the business' continuing, it can plead to the court to move the proceedings into Chapter 7.

In third priority are wages, including vacation and severance pay. This priority includes only those accruals extending from 90 days before the petition was filed to the present time, or from 90 days prior to the business' ceasing operations. There is a limit on claims per individual employee of $2,000.

The fourth priority includes those liabilities to benefit plans incurred within 180 days of filing of the petition, up to an aggregate amount of $2,000 times the number of employees, less any payments made during this 180-day period and during the period of court oversight, and less wages paid under the third priority.

The fifth group is money deposits by certain customers, primarily individual consumers. Claims are limited to $900 per customer. (Behind the primary creditors comprising the first four priority groups come the unsecured creditors, including any unsecured claims of secured creditors and claims for damages for disavowed contracts.)

Finally, the claims of preferred and common stockholders are settled if any money remains. This last position on the priority ladder is reserved for preferred and common stockholders because of their position as residual claimants on whatever value the company may have.

3. Tax Effects

The tax implications of a reorganization in bankruptcy or a liquidation are both complex and potentially critical. A tax carryforward may be one of the major assets of a bankrupt company, although taking advantage of this carryforward has become increasingly difficult as the laws and regulations have been tightened. For example, under the tax laws prevailing before the new Code was adopted, a company in bankruptcy did not have to count forgiven debt as income. Tax provisions adopted subsequent to the new Code require that debt forgiveness be treated as income up to the limit of any tax carryforward. This adjustment restores symmetry to the tax law (the creditor's expense is the bankrupt's income), but it was bitterly opposed by those who believed that the reduction of the carryforward would greatly reduce the number of companies that could successfully be restored to financial health. Highly specialized tax counsel is often required to ensure that recoveries and benefits are maximized in a bankruptcy.

E. Summary and Review

Business failure and the resulting possibility of reorganization are fairly complex issues that are governed by various laws. Even in such circumstances, however, it is necessary to arrive at a value for the firm, whether for reorganization or liquidation. Thus, most of the concepts pertaining to valuing assets are applicable to estimating a fair value of the failing firm. This value may be used as input in a liquidation or reorganization plan through Chapter 7 or 11 of the Bankruptcy Code of 1978.

ANNOTATED BIBLIOGRAPHY

All of the following references contain legal discussions.

Bankruptcy Reform Act of 1978. Chicago: Commerce Clearing House, 1978.

"Bankruptcy: A New Ball Game." *Dun's Review,* April 1978, 98.

Cocheo, S. "New Bankruptcy Law: How It May Affect Banks." *ABA Banking Journal,* October, 1979, 49.

Epstein, D. *Debtor–Creditor Law*. Minneapolis, Minn.: West Publishing Company, 1980.

Koufman, R. "NACM's Position on the New Bankruptcy Act." *Credit and Financial Management,* September 1977, 14.

Rome, D. "The New Bankruptcy Act and the Commercial Lender." *Banking Law Journal,* May 1979, 389.

Rosenbert, S. L., and R. U. Sattin. "The New Bankruptcy Code: More Clout for Unsecured Creditors." *Credit and Financial Management,* September 1979, 12.

Teitelbaum, J. "Preferences Old and New." *Credit and Financial Management,* September 1979, 15.

16

INTERNATIONAL FINANCIAL MANAGEMENT

I. INTRODUCTION

In the life cycle of a firm, which begins with its pioneering phase and continues through expansion and eventual maturity, there generally comes a time when it must consider the challenges and opportunities of expanding its production, investment, and financing activities outside its own national boundaries. Such decisions are usually preceded by the firm's having had considerable experience as exporters of goods and services, eventually leading to the establishment of production facilities in several foreign countries which are strategically located to serve the firm's many foreign markets. Once the corporation becomes multinational, it must also deal with the new dimensions of decision making in an international environment.

Truly multinational enterprises (MNEs) derive a considerable proportion of their income from production, sales, and distribution facilities located in many countries whose units of currency are different from the currency of the home country. Naturally, the assets, liabilities, and net worth that generate foreign income for the multinational corporation (MNC) are also expressed in units of various national currencies which differ from the currency of the home country. These differences require that the entries in the balance sheets and income statements of subsidiaries be translated back into the home currency for inclusion and integration into the firm's domestic statements, in order to produce the consolidated financial statements.

To facilitate the translation of financial stocks from the balance sheets and financial flows from the income statements of the firm and its subsidiaries from one currency to another, we employ the simple device of exchange rates. An exchange rate is always defined in terms of the number of units of a given national currency that are needed to obtain a unit of another currency. In the United States, exchange rates are generally quoted in terms of the number of U.S. dollars ($ U.S.) needed to buy a unit of another currency. From the viewpoint of dollar holders (dollar sellers), this constitutes a direct quotation. In other countries, exchange rates are generally quoted in terms of the number of local currency units required to purchase one U.S. dollar. From the point of view of foreign currency holders (dollar buyers), this is also a direct quotation. However, what constitutes a direct quotation for foreign currency holders becomes an indirect quotation for U.S. dollar holders, and vice versa. For example, consider some quotations from the *Wall Street Journal,* which publishes quotations daily. On Wednesday, March 29, 1989, the direct quotation of the exchange rate between the U.S. dollar and the Canadian dollar was $0.8356, meaning that one Canadian dollar could be bought on that day for $0.8356. Or, to put it differently, the holder of a U.S. dollar could get 1/0.8356 = 1.1967 Canadian dollars, in terms of the indirect quotation. In the same vein, we find that the direct quotation for exchanging U.S. dollars into British pounds is $1.6865, while the indirect quotation was 0.5929 for Wednesday, March 29, 1989.

Exchange rates are set during working days in the foreign exchange market, which, unlike its relatives that deal in stocks and bonds, is not a centralized marketplace. Rather, it is a loosely connected but highly informed network of national central banks and rather large commercial banks. These banks maintain correspondent accounts with their counterparts in other countries and buy and sell various currencies on behalf of their depositors who transact international business. Currency may be purchased by clients for immediate delivery (usually one to two business days later), in which case their exchange rate quotations are given at the so-called spot rate of exchange. For example, the direct quotation for the spot rate of exchange between U.S. dollars and Japanese yen for Wednesday, March 29, 1989, was $0.007512, and the indirect spot rate was 133.12. Alternatively, clients can transact in foreign currencies for delivery some time in the future, say 180 days later, in which case their exchange rate quotations are given at the so-called forward rate for a specific number of days. For example, the direct quotation for future delivery of Japanese yen, for Wednesday, March 29, 1989, was $0.007544 for 30 days forward, $0.007620 for 90 days forward, and $0.007749 for 180 days forward.

II. BUSINESS RISKS IN TRANSNATIONAL OPERATIONS

Firms that produce, distribute, and sell goods and services internationally increase the prospects of their business or operating risks due to the additional environmental complications involved in transnational operations. That is, whereas domestic firms are affected primarily by factors such as changes in inflation, productivity, interest rates, expectations, the phase of the business cycle, industry factors, and the phase of their life cycle within their own national boundaries, international firms are subjected to the uncertainties and influences of these factors from many countries. Moreover, in addition to these, transnational enterprises that engage in investment-financing activities in foreign countries are subjected to political risks that range from restrictions on the repatriation of profits to the extreme case of outright expropriation of their assets. In what follows, we discuss some of these risks, particularly the exchange rate risk, which constitutes the most important type of additional business risk for transnational corporations operating in the Western hemisphere.

A. Exchange Rate Risk

Because exchange rates, like all other market prices, fluctuate continually to reflect the changing expectations of the market participants about the economic prospects in the respective countries, financial managers of transnational corporations can be exposed to a considerable degree of exchange rate risk. Their exposure to such risk takes three basic forms.

1. *Translation exposure,* which affects the values of assets and liabilities as they are translated from the domestic currency to the home-country currency. This type of exposure is larger when the translation is made from the weak currencies of less developed countries (LDCs) to the strong currencies of highly industrialized countries like the United States.
2. *Economic exposure,* which affects the value of future expected income denominated in a foreign currency, as this income will eventually be converted into domestic currency.
3. *Transaction exposure,* which affects the value of fixed contracts signed by a corporation in a foreign currency for consummation at some future specified date. Sometimes, transaction exposure is also realized when the assets of a foreign subsidiary are liquidated.

Because the requirement by a subsidiary to translate foreign asset and liability values into domestic currency entails translation risk for the corporation, it will be useful to briefly review standard accounting practices as they relate to the balance sheet. We shall proceed by way of a rather simplified example. Suppose that W.W.S., Inc. does business both in the U.S. and in Germany, where its subsidiary, W.W.S. Germany, N.V., utilizes Deutsche Marks (DM) as its functional currency. At the beginning of period t, the W.W.S. subsidiary has the following balance sheet values:

W.W.S. Germany, N.V., Balance Sheet in DM

Current Assets	100 DM	Current Liabilities	50 DM
		Equity	50 DM
			100 DM

In order to simplify things, we assume that the exchange rate at the beginning of period t is 1 DM = \$0.50 U.S., or \$1 U.S. = 2 DM. On the basis of this exchange rate, the German subsidiary's balance sheet can be translated into U.S. dollars as follows:

W.W.S. Germany, N.V., Balance Sheet in $ U.S.

Current Assets	$50.00	Current Liabilities	$25.00
		Equity	25.00
			$50.00

Now suppose that at the end of period t no commercial transactions have taken place at the German subsidiary. However, the value of the U.S. dollar has fallen relative to the German Mark such that 1 DM = \$0.55 U.S., or \$1 U.S. = 1.82 DM. Now the balance sheet of W.W.S. Germany, N.V., when translated from DM to $ U.S., appears as follows:

W.W.S. Germany, N.V., Balance Sheet in $ U.S.

Current Assets	$55.00	Current Liabilities	$27.50
		Equity	27.50
			$55.00

Because no commercial transactions have taken place, there should be no changes in the equity account of W.W.S. Germany, N.V. However, a change has occurred through currency translation, and we must account for it. In 1982, the Financial Accounting Standards Board issued FASB No. 52, which sets rules for foreign currency translation. According to the rules set out in this document translation gains and losses are accumulated in a separate account and disclosed with shareholder equity. Furthermore, all balance sheet values are translated at the current exchange rate. Thus, from the preceding balance sheet, the equity account at the end of the period t is decomposed as follows:

Equity	$25.00
Translation Gain (Loss)	2.50
Net Equity	$27.50

To conclude the example, suppose that, due to the lack of business, all of the assets of W.W.S. Germany, N.V., are liquidated in period $t + 1$. Then the balance sheet of the German subsidiary, denominated in DM, will appear as follows:

W.W.S. Germany, N.V., Balance Sheet in DM

Cash	100 DM	Current Liabilities	50 DM
		Equity	50 DM
			100 DM

Assuming no further changes in the exchange rate, W.W.S., Inc. now realizes a \$2.50 U.S. transaction gain from the liquidation of the assets of its German subsidiary. Under the rules of FASB No. 52, this transaction gain is reported in the income statement of the parent company, resulting in a balance sheet that, when translated into $ U.S., would appear as follows:

W.W.S. Germany, N.V.,
Liquidation Balance Sheet in $ U.S.

Cash	$55.00	Current Liabilities	$27.50
		Equity	27.50
			$55.00

The \$2.50 U.S. transaction gain has been added to retained earnings.

B. Other Types of Risk

When firms go abroad, they carry with them the political, social, legal, and cultural behavior of the home country, as well as the basic goals of the parent corporation. However, such attitudes and aspirations, even after significant adjustment to the local environment, often conspire to bring about conflicts with the legal, political, social, or cultural attributes of the host country. For a foreign firm operating in a host country, success can be achieved only by significant contributions to the national aspirations of that country. Failure to do so spells out problems that may eventually range from excessive restrictions on the repatriation of profits to the nationalization or even outright expropriation of the company's assets. These actions by the host government, of course, make the difference between continued operations and forced liquidation.

In addition to these political risks, which are more pronounced in smaller nations, multinational corporations also face the following significant risks that derive partly from the fact that they deal with several different sovereign countries:

1. *Risk of noncompletion of a contract or transaction due to unforeseen circumstances.* This risk is manifested in large, government-backed construction projects that are cancelled when the country's economy declines seriously.
2. *Sovereign risk.* This kind of risk applies mostly to financial lenders who have extended loans to smaller nations directly, or indirectly via government-owned enterprises. Again, as the local economic environment worsens, the risk of delays or even nonpayment of interest and principal increases significantly.

Both of the preceding risks have become dreadful realities during the late 1970s and 1980s.

III. BASIC EXCHANGE RATE RELATIONSHIPS

In the preceding discussion of exchange rate risk, it was necessary to simplify matters and treat changes in exchange rates as given. Here, we turn our attention to the underlying factors that influence exchange rates and the fundamental relationships that may be used to determine and perhaps forecast exchange rates.

The forward price of a currency typically differs from the spot price of the same currency, as was shown in the example with Japanese yen. If a given forward currency price exceeds its spot price, we say that the currency is trading at a *forward premium*. Conversely, if the spot price exceeds the forward price, we say that the currency is trading at a *forward discount*. Whether currencies trade at forward premium or forward discount depends on three interactive economic factors: interest rates, inflation, and expectations. Firms operating in foreign countries typically pursue any of three alternative financial strategies in their efforts to hedge or cover their exchange rate risk. *First,* the firms may buy or sell currencies in the forward market. *Second,* the firms may engage in transactions in the international money market. *Third,* the firms may attempt to estimate the spot rate of exchange in order to reduce uncertainty about future exchange rates. In general, firms and other economic agents will select the strategy that, through arbitrage, will minimize their transaction costs or maximize their advantages. The actions of these economic agents define a set of equilibria that govern the fluctuations of exchange rates. These fundamental relationships will be discussed in the remainder of the section under the subheadings of Interest Rate Parity, International Fisher Effect, and Purchasing Power Parity.

A. Interest Rate Parity

Investors need not feel constrained to make investments denominated exclusively in one currency. For example, an individual could choose to invest a given amount of money in U.S. government securities that would earn a rate of interest $r_\$$. Alternatively, the same person could invest the equivalent value in U.K. government securities that would earn an interest rate $r_£$. At the end of a 1-year holding period, the basic amount invested in U.S. dollars and pounds sterling would be multiplied by $(1 + r_\$)$ and $(1 + r_£)$, respectively. The difference, if any, could then be expressed as $(1 + r_\$)/(1 + r_£)$. Of course, investors have several other investment options available. For example, they could take the same amount of money, buy pounds sterling (or sell them short) on the spot foreign exchange market, and sell (or buy) these pounds forward. This action would lock in an interest rate equal to

$$r_{\$,£} = \frac{F(\$, £) - S(\$, £)}{S(\$, £)} \tag{16.1}$$

where $F(\$, £)$ and $S(\$, £)$ are the respective forward and spot rates for the U.K. sterling pound relative to the U.S. dollar.

Which of the various investment options is the "best"? If the U.S. government securities yield a higher rate of interest than those of the U.K., they will be preferred by both U.S. and U.K. investors, who will sell and buy U.S. dollars in order to facilitate their investment plans. The selling of sterling pounds would cause the spot price of pounds sterling to fall until U.S. investors could obtain an equal rate of return by investing solely in the foreign exchange market. This would also make the dollar-denominated investment less attractive to U.K. investors. The opposite would, of course, be true if the U.K. investment provided a higher return. Then, both the U.S. and the U.K. investors would prefer investment in U.K. government securities, selling dollars and buying pounds sterling until equilibrium is again reached.

In general, the difference in interest rates between any two countries will be reflected in the spot and forward exchange rates for the two countries. Specifically, given any two countries, the percentage difference in interest rates will be equal to the forward premium or discount for the currencies of these countries, as shown in equation (16.2).

$$\frac{1 + r_D}{1 + r_F} = \frac{F_{(D,F)} - S_{(D,F)}}{S_{(D,F)}} + 1 \tag{16.2}$$

The simple principle defined by this equation is more formally known as the *Interest Rate Parity Theorem* (IRPT).

In practice, interest rate parity does not hold precisely. Several market imperfections typically combine to distort the relationship between interest rates and spot and forward prices. These imperfections include transaction costs; political risks in the form of asset expropriation, nationalization, or freezing; taxes; liquidity differences between securities of different countries; as well as outright government intervention. Nevertheless, such market imperfections are not sufficient to guarantee inordinate profits to investors through arbitrage.

B. International Fisher Effect

The noted economist, Irving Fisher, some years ago suggested that the nominal rate of interest (or return) promised by a security cannot serve as the measure of changes in an individual's wealth. The premise was based on the distortion of the nominal rate by the rate of inflation in the economy. Fisher defined the real rate of return as being equal to the nominal rate less the expected inflation and argued that this real rate truly reflected the expected changes in wealth. Symbolically,

$$1 + r_n = (1 + r)(1 + \tilde{P}) \tag{16.3}$$

where r = real rate of return
r_n = nominal rate of return
$\tilde{P}$ = expected inflation

The basic premise of equation (16.3) is known as the *Fisher Effect,* and, when applied on an international scale, it produces an interesting result. For example, if we assume that individuals and firms are wealth maximizers, it is logical to conclude that capital will flow into countries whose assets offer the greatest real rate of return. Thus, for equilibrium to exist in the international financial markets, the real rate of interest offered in all countries must be the same. That is,

$$1 + r_D = 1 + r_F \tag{16.4}$$

where r_D = domestic rate of interest
r_F = foreign rate of interest
r = real rate of return

This idea is, of course, an extension of the IRPT.

Rearranging equation (16.4) and substituting from equation (16.3) yields

$$\frac{1 + r_{nD}}{1 + \tilde{P}_D} = \frac{1 + r_{nF}}{1 + \tilde{P}_F} \tag{16.5}$$

and

$$\frac{1 + r_{nD}}{1 + r_{nF}} = \frac{1 + \tilde{P}_D}{1 + \tilde{P}_F} \tag{16.6}$$

Thus, the *International Fisher Effect* states that the differences in nominal interest rates between any two countries must be equal to the differences in expected inflation rates for the two countries.

C. Purchasing Power Parity

Suppose that an arbitrageur in London bought 1,000 ounces of silver when the price of the metal in both the London and New York markets was \$5.00 per ounce ($P_L = P_{NY} =$ \$5.00). Suppose that the price in New York now rises to $P_{NY} =$ \$5.25 per ounce, presenting the arbitrageur with the following opportunity: by selling the silver inventory in New York, the arbitrageur makes a profit of

$$1{,}000(\$5.25 - \$5.00) = \$250.00 \text{ before taxes,}$$

assuming that other things remain the same. Were this scenario real, we would expect other arbitrageurs also to buy silver in the London market and sell it in the New York market, as long as arbitrage profits could be made. The resultant upward pressure on silver prices in London and downward pressure in New York would eventually bring about an equilibrium position where $P_L = P_{NY}$. This scenario illustrates the basic premise of what is known as the *Purchasing Power Parity Theorem* (PPPT).

In its simplest form, the PPPT states that under conditions of free, competitive markets the price of a good will be the same everywhere in the world. Symbolically,

$$P_D = E_{(D|F)} P_F \tag{16.7}$$

or

$$E_{(D|F)} = \frac{P_D}{P_F} \tag{16.7$'$}$$

where P_D and P_F are prices in domestic and foreign currencies, respectively, and $E_{(D/F)}$ is the exchange rate between these currencies.

While the analytical nature of the PPPT is plain, there exist several market imperfections that distort the predictive power of the theorem. Chief among these are: (1) differences in the standard of living among various countries; (2) changes in government policies in the sovereign nations involved (e.g., tariffs, and import and domestic content restrictions); (3) transportation costs; (4) information lags between markets; (5) differences in the price ratios of international goods to domestic or "local" goods; and (6) differences in risk premia of different countries. The IRPT and PPPT are often referred to as the "Law of One Price" to encompass both the price of money and the price of goods or services. At any rate, regardless of market imperfections, the PPPT appears to describe a strong equilibrium force in the international financial markets.

Notice that, for a price change on one side of equation (16.7) or (16.7′) to take place, a balancing change is required on the other side. Thus, if we add an inflation term $(1 + \tilde{P})$ to (16.7), it becomes

$$(1 + \tilde{P}_D) = E_{(D/F)}(1 + \tilde{P}_F) \tag{16.8}$$

and, after substitution and simplification, becomes

$$\tilde{P}_D = \tilde{P}_F \tag{16.8$'$}$$

In effect, in order for the exchange rate between any two countries to remain constant, the respective inflation rates must be equal. Otherwise, the change in the expected spot rates will equal the expected change in inflation. That is,

$$\frac{1 + \tilde{P}_D}{1 + \tilde{P}_F} = \tilde{E}(D/F) \tag{16.9}$$

D. Summary of Basic Relationships

The Interest Rate Parity Theorem states that the percentage difference in interest rates between two or more countries should be reflected in the forward premium, or discount, of their currencies. That is,

$$\frac{1 + r_D}{1 + r_F} = \frac{F_{(D,F)} - S_{(D,F)}}{S_{(D,F)}} + 1 \qquad (16.2)$$

In other words, an investor should not be able to make any more or any less money by investing in international money markets than by investing in the forward exchange market. The returns on such investments, r_D and r_F respectively, may be nominal or real (the Fisher case).

The Fisher Effect, when applied to the IRPT, implies that differences in nominal rates from country to country must reflect inflation expectations for each country—that is,

$$\frac{1 + r_D}{1 + r_F} = \frac{1 + \tilde{P}_D}{1 + \tilde{P}_F} \qquad (16.6')$$

The Purchasing Power Parity Theorem implies that changes in spot rates must be tied to changes in the expected levels of prices, as shown by combining equations (16.2) and (16.6):

$$\frac{1 + \tilde{P}_D}{1 + \tilde{P}_F} = \frac{F_{(D,F)} - S_{(D,F)}}{S_{(D,F)}}$$

Hence, interest rates, inflation expectations, and exchange rates are all interrelated by the equations:

$$\frac{1 + r_D}{1 + r_F} = \frac{1 + \tilde{P}_D}{1 + \tilde{P}_F} = \frac{F_{(D,F)} - S_{(D,F)}}{S_{(D,F)}} + 1 \qquad (16.2'')$$

where the *r*'s denote nominal interest rates.

To recapitulate, occasional opportunities for arbitrage do appear, as they must in dynamic markets. However, the arbitraging actions of investors have an equilibrating influence on the international and domestic financial markets. That is, when adjusted for market imperfections, distortions in the basic relationships are seen as temporary phenomena.

IV. MULTINATIONAL CAPITAL BUDGETING AND THE COST OF CAPITAL

The risks and rewards from international investments must be considered within the overall framework of financial decision making for the firm. However, there are sufficient differences between domestic and transnational investment environments for the latter to warrant special attention. Some of these differences stem from the fact that we cannot agree about what differentiates one host country from another. Is it their different currencies? It is perhaps their different rules, regulations, tax laws, and institutions? Or is it their different languages and cultures that may shape different tastes and preferences? The answer to these questions will condition the overall response about domestic versus international investments. For example, if we assume that differences between any two host countries are well defined by their different currencies, we can establish scenarios of international exchange and devise simple rules for trade-off between domestic and international investments.

The rule to remember is that investments, whether domestic or transnational, cannot be studied separately from the existing portfolio of assets held by investors. We can illustrate this principle by two extreme environments of international competition and financial market structure. Suppose on the one hand that the various national capital markets have become fully integrated into single world capital markets populated by international investors who hold well-diversified international portfolios. In such an environment, a U.S. company with a British subsidiary would be subjected to the same degree of risk both at home and in the U.K. Hence, it would demand the same expected rates of return for projects undertaken in either country. On the other hand, we can assume a noncompetitive market environment where capital markets in the U.S., U.K., and the rest of the world are fully segmented. That is, the investors in each country hold portfolios that specialize solely in stocks of their own national markets. In this type of economic environment the U.S. parent and its U.K. subsidiary would not be subjected to the same risk (except by chance). Consequently, the firm would demand different expected rates of return from the home and foreign operations. However, in such a case, the potential risk-reduction benefits of diversification will ensure mixed-asset portfolios and spell the beginning of at least some form of capital market integration. Indeed, the true scenario lies between the two extremes presented, and actual market integration is significant, particularly among the large, industrialized countries of the Western world.

The basic principles of financial decision making must be further augmented when making overseas investments to account for at least three significant complications: (1) The estimation of cash flows from transnational investments is generally far more complex and demanding than the estimation of those for domestic investments. The reasons for such complexity stem from the different social, economic, legal, and institutional factors that affect the demand for the firm's products or services in the host country. To the extent that the nature, scope, and effects of such factors cannot be easily forecast and properly accounted for, forecasts of cash flows from host-country subsidiaries will be less reliable than their counterparts from the home country. (2) The estimation of cash flows from foreign subsidiaries is further complicated by the fact that such cash flows are denominated in several currencies that must be converted (translated) into U.S. dollars. This phenomenon is part of the foreign exchange or currency risk that was discussed earlier. (3) Cash flows from foreign subsidiaries can be reduced, diverted, delayed, or completely blocked by indirect policies or deliberate actions of the governments in the host countries where the company has subsidiaries. This is a significant phenomenon that, in the extreme, may take the form of loss of foreign assets in addition to the loss of income. At any rate, for the purposes of the parent company, the only cash flows that are relevant for forecasting, discounting, and eventual decision making are those that the foreign subsidiary can repatriate legally and freely.

The possibility that host-country government activities will limit the parent firm's flexibility to redeploy its resources and take advantage of other investment opportunities has encouraged the development of several devices for shifting cash flows among several components of the international business network. Prominent among these are the following: (1) *Transfer pricing* refers to the pricing policies used by companies on sales between the parent and its subsidiaries or among subsidiaries. The way this device works, if it is permitted or goes undetected, is simple. The firm or one of its subsidiaries may overprice components or semiassembled products that are shipped to host countries that have severe restrictions on the repatriation of profits. In this manner, the firm ensures part of its cash flows by overpricing the inputs in a worldwide production system. Transfer pricing that is not "arm's length" is also employed to minimize taxable profits in host countries that have high corporate taxes. Here, the firm may attempt to overprice factor inputs that are shipped to high-tax host countries and underprice these same inputs for low-tax host countries. (2) *Royalty payments* are made by the various foreign subsidiaries to the parent company for such services as patents, technical know-how, and production processes. Here again, excessive royalty fees allow the firm to repatriate profits above the limits set by the host country. (3) *Management fees* are another form of royalties, specifically earmarked for management services offered by the parent company to the foreign subsidiary. This form of indirect profit repatriation is used rather infrequently, as it is not approved in many countries.

V. INTERNATIONAL FINANCING

Firms that contemplate the establishment of foreign subsidiaries have three alternatives for financing the new operations: (1) They can import funds from the home country; (2) they can raise the necessary financing from local sources in the host country; and (3) they can raise the funds by resorting to the international money and capital markets. Because the international financial markets operate under fewer regulatory restrictions than their counterparts in the U.S., American corporations have availed themselves of a number of flexible and creative financial instruments that have been developed in these international markets. For example, short-term and medium-term funds are available in the Eurodollar and Eurocurrency markets, and long-term funds are available in the Eurobond and Euroequity markets.

Eurodollars refer to any U.S.-dollar-denominated bank deposits that are held outside the United States. A more general term for currencies that are deposited and held outside their respective countries is *Eurocurrencies,* which refers to the convertible national currencies, of the major industrial nations, that are available for borrowing. Whether a loan is made in Eurodollars or some other freely convertible currency, the distinguishing characteristic of Eurocurrency financing is that all loans are extended on floating interest rates. The floating rate is based on the London interbank offer rate (LIBOR) and is set as a fixed margin above this benchmark. The margin above LIBOR remains fixed for as long as the borrower's risk remains the same. However, the interest rates are fixed for a period of time, typically 6 months, and then are adjusted to reflect the LIBOR at that time. Thus, although the margin or spread may remain the same for the duration of a loan contract, the changing LIBOR base changes the actual interest rate charged every 6 months or so. Note that the margin varies directly with the risk of the borrower, while loan maturities range from 3 to 10 years.

For long-term borrowing, firms can resort to international debt or equity financing in the Eurocapital markets or other important national markets. Four types of long-term bonds that are popular are (1) foreign bonds, (2) Eurobonds, (3) multicurrency bonds, and (4) unit-of-account bonds. Let us briefly consider each in turn.

Foreign bonds are long-term debt instruments issued by a corporation in a country other than its home base and denominated in the currency of that country. Hence, the borrowing corporation assumes the entire exchange rate risk associated with the issue. *Eurobonds* are bonds issued outside the home country but denominated in the currency of the firm's home country. Because the lenders actually make the loan and agree to take payments of both interest and principal in a foreign currency, they assume the entire exchange rate risk associated with the bond.

In contrast to foreign bonds and Eurobonds, *multicurrency bonds* facilitate the sharing of currency risk between borrowers and lenders. In effect, lenders are allowed to choose two or more currencies in which they are to be repaid interest and principal. This arrangement effectively reduces the exposure of lenders to currency risk and increases the equivalent risk of borrowers commensurably. Finally, *unit-of-account bonds* are issued on some composite index or basket of currencies, where the unit may be expressed as either a sum of units of several currencies or a percentage mix of several currencies. Such units or currency "cocktails" have included Special Drawing Rights (SDRs), the European Composite Unit (EURCO), and the European Unit of Account (EUA) utilized among the countries of the European Economic Community (EEC). Generally speaking, unit-of-account bonds have not taken their share of the international bond market, despite their obvious diversification advantages.

VI. INTERNATIONAL MERGERS AND ACQUISITIONS

A. Some Perspectives

Corporations invest abroad in two basic forms: (1) portfolio investment and (2) direct investment. *Portfolio investment* is motivated primarily by the quest for risk reduction through the process of diversification that originally begins in the home country and eventually takes the form of a worldwide portfolio. Because the reason for portfolio investments is risk reduction, the proportions of ownership in each foreign asset is likely to be small and noncontrolling. However, foreign *direct investment* is motivated by the desire to control foreign operations in host countries, and thus involves large proportions of ownership in foreign firms. Foreign direct investment, much like domestic investment can be channeled in two forms: (1) the establishment of completely new facilities abroad, and (2) the acquisition of an existing facility through merger or some other form of transaction.

International direct investment has grown rapidly since World War II and has increased from about $66 billion in 1960 to about $600 billion in 1985. For U.S. corporations, direct investment abroad reached $260 billion in 1986 and $309 billion in 1987 while foreign direct investment in the U.S. reached $209 billion and $262 billion, respectively. In effect, U.S. corporations accounted for about 40 percent of the total worldwide foreign direct investment, while the U.S. hosted about 34 percent of total international investment. In addition, direct trade between U.S. parent companies and their foreign affiliates and between U.S. affiliates and their foreign parents accounted for about 40 percent of total U.S. exports and total U.S. imports in 1986. (See *International Direct Investment: Global Trends and the U.S. Role,* U.S. Department of Commerce, 1988 Edition.)

International mergers and acquisitions have become a conventional means of foreign direct investment both by U.S. corporations and by non-U.S. firms. For example, between 1979 and 1985 U.S. corporations engaged in about 916 acquisitions abroad worth about $9.5 billion. During the same period, foreign corporations acquired 1,309 firms worth about $61.81 billion.

B. Recent Trends in International Mergers and Acquisitions

Table 16.1 presents a comprehensive picture of merger and acquisition activity for the period 1979–85. The information is presented both by the number of transactions and dollar value for each of the seven years involved. The table is segmented into three panels, as follows: (1) The top panel shows the mergers and acquisitions made by U.S. corporations in foreign countries. As can be seen from the table, the largest number of transactions took place in 1983, with the largest dollar value realized in 1984. (2) The middle panel shows the mergers and acquisitions made by foreign corporations in the U.S. Here it appears that 1985 was the benchmark year for both transactions and dollar value. (3) Finally, the bottom panel presents the ratio of FDI in the U.S. to U.S. FDI abroad. It is interesting to note here that when the averages are computed there were about 1.5 foreign acquisitions in the U.S. for every acquisition by U.S. corporations abroad. Also, on average, about $7.6 were invested by foreign corporations in the U.S. through mergers for every $1 invested through mergers abroad by U.S. corporations. This picture of larger dollar acquisitions in the U.S. compared to dollar acquisition abroad is evident for every year except for 1983.

TABLE 16.1 International Profile of Mergers and Acquisitions Completed, 1979–1985

		1979	*1980*	*1981*	*1982*	*1983*	*1984*	*1985*
U.S. Investment Abroad	Number of Transactions	120	113	83	139	148	139	174
	Dollar Value (billions)	1.45	1.68	0.87	1.02	1.36	2.01	1.11
Foreign Investment in U.S.	Number of Transactions	146	170	267	222	116	182	206
	Dollar Value (billions)	4.3	7.7	16.3	5.5	2.17	8.04	17.8
Ratio of Foreign Investment in the U.S. to U.S. Investment Abroad	Number of Transactions	1.22	1.50	3.22	1.6	0.78	1.31	1.18
	Dollar Value (billions)	2.97	4.58	18.7	5.4	1.60	4.00	16.04

Source: Adapted with modifications from *Mergers and Acquisitions*, March–April 1986, 78.

When the foreign mergers and acquisitions—both in the United States and abroad—are placed into perspective, it appears that such activity, although growing, is minuscule by comparison with the total mergers involving U.S. corporations. This is shown in Table 16.2 for the period 1983–85. Note that domestic U.S. mergers, although declining for the period, still constitute the largest percentage of the total. Nevertheless, international mergers involving U.S. corporations either as acquirers or as targets have increased over the period from 6.8 percent to 13.6 percent of the total merger dollar value. It should also be noted here that the industry areas in which international mergers and acquisitions take place represent rather well the domestic U.S. merger scene.

Nevertheless, some industry trends appear to emerge. For example, during the 1983–85 period, the majority of foreign acquisitions by U.S. firms was made by five types of industries, i.e., engineering and other services, machinery (except electrical), distribution and wholesale trade, chemicals and allied products, and food and allied products. By the same token, the majority of foreign acquisitions in the U.S. during the same three-year period was made by seven types of industries, i.e., business services, oil and gas extraction, printing and publishing, machinery (except electrical), holding and investment companies, distribution and wholesale trade, and chemicals and allied products. Finally, it appears that most of the foreign acquiring corporations are from the United Kingdom and Canada followed by Japan, the Netherlands, France, and Sweden.

Finally, Tables 16.3 and 16.4 present detailed information on the two-way merger activity involving U.S. corporations during the fourth quarter of 1985. Table 16.3 shows the merger activities of ten U.S. acquiring corporations from nine different industries that bought into existing firms in seven countries. Table 16.4 presents the merger transactions of ten foreign acquiring corporations from six different industries that bought partially or fully into ten U.S. corporations.

Let us try to put all of the above information on international mergers in some perspective. International acquisitions are only a small part

TABLE 16.2 International Profile of Mergers and Acquisitions Completed, 1983–1985

All Activity	*Number of Transactions*	*% of Total*	*Value $ Million*	*% of Total*	*Average Transaction Size*
			1983		
US Acquiring US	2,075	88.7	48,335.5	93.2	23.3
Non-US Acquiring US	116	5.0	2,175.4	4.2	18.8
US Acquiring Non-US	148	6.3	1,360.1	2.6	9.2
TOTAL	2,339	100.0	51,871.0	100.0	17.1
			1984		
US Acquiring US	2,625	89.1	113,982.6	91.9	43.4
Non-US Acquiring US	182	6.2	8,040.7	6.5	44.1
US Acquiring Non-US	139	4.7	2,004.2	1.6	14.4
TOTAL	2,946	100.0	124,027.5	100.0	34.0
			1985		
US Acquiring US	2,773	87.9	120,269.1	86.4	43.4
Non-US Acquiring US	206	6.5	17,827.7	12.8	86.5
US Acquiring Non-US	174	5.6	1,115.2	0.8	6.4
TOTAL	3,153	100.0	139,212.0	100.0	45.4

Source: Adapted with modifications from *Mergers and Acquisitions*, March–April 1986, and the "1984 Profile."

TABLE 16.3 American Acquisitions Abroad Ranked by Sales of Acquiring Firm, 4th Quarter, 1985

U.S. Acquirer	*Revenues in $ Million*	*Net Income of Acquirer in $ Million*	*Industry of Acquiring Firm*	*Target*	*Country of Target*
Aetna Life & Casualty Company	15,411.0	128.0	Insurance	La Estrella, SA	Spain
Dart & Kraft, Inc.	9,758.7	455.8	Food & Allied Products	Everest Group	Australia
Amerada Hess Corporation	8,277.2	170.5	Oil	Monsanto Oil Company	United Kingdom
FMC Corporation	3,337.8	38.0	Transportation Equipment	Equisa	Spain
Sterling Drug, Inc.	1,827.3	143.4	Chemicals & Allied Products	Maggioni Farmaeutici, SPA	Italy
Armstrong World Industries	1,569.2	92.2	Rubber & Plastic Products	Karl Klein Enterprise	W. Germany
Norton Company	1,209.6	60.4	Stone, Clay, Glass	Carborundum Abrasives, Inc.	Canada
John Blair	844.0	10.5	Business Services	Selkirk Communications, Ltd	Canada
McCormick & Company, Inc.	788.4	54.6	Food & Allied Products	Industria e Commercio Jimmi, Ltd	Brazil
Figgie International Holdings, Inc.	720.7	17.4	Machinery except Electrical	J. H. Fenner	United Kingdom

Source: Adapted with modifications from *Mergers and Acquisitions*, March–April 1986, 181–86.

of the domestic acquisitions in the various countries of the world. For example, in the two-year period 1986–87, there were 15,146 domestic mergers and acquisitions in the nine key national markets of the world, indicating the magnitude of industrial restructuring worldwide. Of these combinations, the United States accounted for 7,421, followed by the United Kingdom with 2,260 and Canada with 2,240 mergers and acquisitions. (See *Mergers and Acquisitions,* July–August 1987, 58.) Indeed, we can say that corporations attempt to ensure survival, growth, and risk-dispersion through both national and international diversification of productive assets. In addition, conditions in various national markets, currency realignments, and worldwide deregulation of many industries have made it more economical and meaningful to buy into existing businesses than begin operations *de novo*.

VII. SUMMARY AND REVIEW

There are numerous opportunities, benefits, and risks associated with the strategic thrust of a corporation into the international arena through the establishment of foreign subsidiaries. These elements must all enter into the decision-making situation; in particular, the new risks add to the business risks that already exist in domestic operations. The new risks are two in number: currency or exchange rate risk and political risk, the latter of which is a risk associated with the sovereignty decisions of the host country.

Currency exchange risk is closely tied to the fundamental exchange rate relationships on which currencies are priced and transacted internationally. The three kinds of equilibria that govern fluctuations in the exchange rate are interest rate parity (IRP), purchasing power parity (PPP), and Fisher effects. All three must be

TABLE 16.4 Foreign Acquisitions in the U.S.A. Ranked by Sales Revenue of Acquiring Firm, 4th Quarter, 1985

Foreign Acquirer	*Revenues in $ Million*	*Net Income in $ Million*	*Industry of Acquirer*	*Country of Acquirer*	*U.S. Target (Acquired)*
British Petroleum	$51,096.8	$1,280.6	Oil	United Kingdom	General Ionex Corporation[c]
Hoechst, AG	13,662.4	439.0	Chemicals	Germany	Penick Corporation[a]
Imperial Chemical Industries	11,296.3	666.9	Chemicals	United Kingdom	West Chemical Product[a]
General Electric Company, PLC	6,456.9	512.7	Insurance	United Kingdom	Financial Security Assurance, Inc.[c]
Broken Hill Proprietary Company	4,710.0	441.3	Oil & Gas Extraction	Australia	Monsanto Oil Company
Beecham Group, PLC	2,829.3	214.6	Chemicals	United Kingdom	Revlon, Inc.[a]
Burmah Oil, PLC	1,992.4	48.4	Chemicals	United Kingdom	Yates Manufacturing Company
News Corporation, Ltd.[b]	1,751.8	105.3	Motion Pictures	Australia	TCF Holdings
Blue Circles Industries, PLC	1,053.0	87.6	Stone, Clay, Glass	United Kingdom	Williams Brothers, Inc.
Ivaco, Inc.	911.3	25.8	Primary Metals	Canada	President's Island Steel & Wire

Source: Adapted with modifications from *Mergers and Acquisitions*, March–April, 1986, 174–80.
[a]Indicates that a unit rather than the entire company was acquired.
[b]Indicates that the acquirer was the company itself. All other acquirers were themselves units or subsidiaries of larger companies.
[c]Indicates the acquisition of partial ownership interest in the company.

taken into account in international capital budgeting, determining costs of capital, and international financing, along with some of the complications that arise when a domestic corporation becomes a multinational enterprise.

QUESTIONS

1. What are the types of foreign exchange exposure to which multinational corporations are subject?
2. Describe the theoretical constraints on exchange rate relationships.
3. What market imperfections exist that distort the predictive ability of the Purchasing Power Parity Theorem?
4. Describe the mechanisms for avoiding the effect of host-government activities which limit the parent firm's flexibility to redeploy resources.
5. Compare and contrast portfolio investment versus direct investment.

PROBLEMS

1. If the direct exchange rate between the U.S. dollar ($U.S.) and Canadian dollar ($C) is 0.8356 and that between $U.S. and Japanese Yen (JY) is 0.007512, what is the direct exchange rate between the $C and JY?
2. What is the annualized rate of return from the following transactions?

a. Buy \$1 million of JY spot at .007512 (direct quote).
b. Invest the proceeds [i.e., (1,000,000/.007512)JY] in a 30-day Japanese government security (JGS) yielding 3 percent annualized.
c. Sell forward 30 days $\frac{1,000,000}{.007512}(1.03)^{30/360}$ JY at an exchange rate of .007544.

(*Hint:* Think of this problem in terms of its cash flows.)

3. Assume that the JY/\$U.S. direct spot rate is .007512, the 180-day forward rate is .007749, and the current yield on 180-day Japanese government securities (JGS) is 3 percent annualized. What will the rate of return on the following transactions be? (Again, calculate the cash flows first).
   a. Borrow \$1 million at a cost of 8 percent for 180 days.
   b. Buy \$1 million of JY spot.
   c. Invest the proceeds in a 180-day JGS.
   d. Sell JY forward 180 days an amount equal to the maturity value of the JGS.

ANNOTATED BIBLIOGRAPHY

Dufey, G., and I. H. Giddy. *The International Money Market.* Englewood Cliffs, N.J.: Prentice-Hall, 1978.

A standard reference on the subject of money markets of the world.

Eiteman, D. K., and A. I. Stonehill. *Multinational Business Finance*. 3d ed. Reading, Mass.: Addison-Wesley Publishing Company, 1982.

A standard textbook on multinational financial management, with good sections on capital budgeting and working capital management.

Feiger, G., and B. Jacquillat. *International Finance: Text and Cases.* Boston: Allyn and Bacon, 1982.

A solid source of information on the international monetary system and on markets and institutions for offshore financing.

Journal of Cash Management, February–March 1983.

An issue devoted primarily to the international aspects of cash management and foreign exchange exposure.

Levi, M. *International Finance.* New York: McGraw-Hill, 1983.

A good source of information on the overall aspects of international finance.

Riehl, H., and R. M. Rodriguez. *Foreign Exchange Markets.* New York: McGraw-Hill, 1977.

A comprehensive, practical guide to the mechanics and operations of the currency markets of the world.

Rodriguez, R. M. "Measuring and Controlling Multinationals' Exchange Risk." *Financial Analysts Journal,* November—December, 1979, 49–55.

A good, practical paper on currency risk.

Rodriguez, R. M., and E. Carter. *International Financial Management.* Englewood Cliffs, N.J.: Prentice-Hall, 1984.

Another standard textbook on the overall aspects of international financial management.

Shapiro, A. C. *Multinational Financial Management.* 2d ed. Boston: Allyn and Bacon, 1986.

A standard textbook with special strengths in the area of international working capital management.

Weston, J. E., and B. Sorge. *Guide to International Financial Management.* New York: McGraw-Hill, 1977.

A very informative guide on the mechanics and operations of international financial management.

CASE STUDIES

Technical Note 1

THE UNITED STATES' ECONOMY IN REVIEW (1965–1989)

I. INTRODUCTION

All business decisions are made within an economic context whether or not the manager is consciously aware of that context. For many routine decisions, the degree of the manager's consciousness is not important: a distant awareness of the phase of the business cycle is enough. Other decisions, however, such as those directly affecting the financial condition of the company, are best made with the state of the economy consciously in mind. Naturally, these decisions vary with economic conditions; we would not expect management to reach the same conclusion regarding, say, the way in which a project is to be financed in a period of economic stability as it would in a period of hyperinflation.

The case studies in this book are largely based on events that occurred between the mid-1960s and the late 1980s. Thus, the financial decisions discussed were made under widely disparate economic conditions—from periods of strong growth and low inflation to periods of economic stagnation with double-digit inflation and double-digit interest rates. If these cases are not considered in light of the then-current economy, an important element of the decision-making process will be lost. Accordingly, this introductory note provides a brief overview of the economy from the mid-1960s to the late 1980s to remind the reader of the conditions under which the decisions presented in the cases took place.

II. THE PERIOD 1965 TO 1972

Although the roots of the economic problems of the 1980s can be traced to the Roosevelt administration of the Depression era, the buds first flowered in the mid-1960s, the years of the Johnson presidency. Under his Great Society program, Johnson wanted to achieve and maintain, supported as necessary by government spending, an unemployment rate of no more than 4 percent. American involvement in the Vietnam War was at its height in 1965 and 1966 and, fearing that Congress would cut his Great Society program if it knew the truth about the cost of the Vietnam buildup, Johnson hid the facts. This concatenation of events led to what is now referred to as the "guns and butter" policy. The private sector was booming, and demand for output—butter—(and the money to pay for that output) was high; in addition, the public sector was competing with the private sector for goods in the form of war materials—guns—and the funds with which to purchase them.

In this period, both government and private spending rose by $22 billion. (Exhibit 1 charts the rise in Gross National Product during the period and beyond.) At first, William McChesney Martin, then chairman of the Federal Reserve, fought administration pressure to hold interest rates down, but he gave up his efforts in 1966 and allowed the money supply to increase, creating the first of many waves of inflation. Then, having reconsidered, and fearing the effects of an excessive rate of monetary growth, Martin halted the expansion. The result was the small recession of 1966–1967.

The pendulum then returned, and a high rate of monetary growth was reestablished. In addition, in early 1967, Johnson finally asked Congress for a tax surcharge to help finance the war. Congress skirted the issue until the middle of the following year, but then it did enact a 10-percent surcharge. The fear, however, that this would cause tremendous damage to the economy caused Martin to ease the restraints on the growth of the money supply once again.

Some analysts believe this to be the worst mistake that government economists had made since World War II. As a result of the Federal Reserve's monetary policy and Johnson's Great Society program, in conjunction with the Vietnam War, the growth in the consumer price index rose steadily from 2 percent in 1965 to 6 percent in 1970. (Exhibit 2 shows inflation from 1966 to 1988, as indicated by some major indices.) President Nixon then came along and battled the rising inflation rate in the classic manner—by calling a halt to the growth in government spending. When this policy failed to show any signs of success within its first two years, Nixon, in his impatience, imposed a 90-day price freeze in August 1971.

The government budget swung in and out of deficit throughout the late 1960s. It was in surplus for the last time in 1969, for, as illustrated in Exhibit 3, although spending increased steadily, receipts declined in 1971 as a result of the 1969–1970 recession. Due to the rising rate of inflation, nominal GNP was rising at an even greater rate than public spending in spite of the recession, although the economy (as measured by real GNP) actually lost ground in 1970 for the first time since 1947.

The volume of trading in the stock market had been relatively steady for decades, but it began to rise rapidly throughout the 1960s. As Exhibit 4 shows, the Dow Jones industrial average increased 300 points in that decade, lost 150 points in the 1969–1970 recession, but then regained 200 points by 1972. Exhibit 5 shows the Standard & Poor's 500 earnings/price ratio.

Throughout the period of rising inflation rates in the late 1960s, the producer price index (PPI) failed to keep pace with the consumer price index (CPI) and the GNP deflator. The PPI made up for lost ground, in 1973, catching and surpassing the other two due to rising energy costs. The rate of inflation also affected nominal interest rates, which rose throughout the latter half of the 1960s. Nominal rates peaked in 1969 and 1970 (the prime lending rate reached 8 percent), but the rate of inflation actually caused real rates to decline throughout most of the period. (Exhibit 6 graphs interest rates from 1966 to 1987.)

The recession that ushered in the next decade also caused corporate profits to decline, but by 1972 the recovery yielded profits higher than the previous 1968 peak. By the early 1970s, the United States was also importing more than it was selling abroad. In 1971 and 1972, the weakening current account, shown in Exhibit 7, went into a record deficit position. Also, the unemployment rate of 4 percent, which Johnson had sacrificed so much to achieve, disappeared with the onset of the recession and reached 6 percent by the end of 1970. (Exhibit 8 depicts the trade-weighted value of the dollar, 1967–1988.)

III. THE 1973-TO-1980 HORIZON

The year 1973 ushered in an entirely new way of doing business. The Organization of Petroleum Exporting Countries (OPEC) became the nemesis of every other free-world country when it recognized the powerful money-making tool that its members possessed. The price of crude oil rose from less than $4.50 per barrel in January 1973 to $15.00 by the beginning of the next year. The economy was still struggling to overcome the effects of the 1969–1970 recession when the oil embargo was imposed. Suddenly, PPI caught up to and surpassed the CPI, changing the nature of inflation from demand–pull to cost–push. As a result, growth in industrial production ground to a halt: in both 1974 and 1975, real GNP shrank and unemployment rose as inflation approached double-digit levels. Returns on both assets and equity, which had not yet recovered from the 1969–1970 recession, plummeted again, utilization of industrial capacity was down to 70 percent, and expenditures on research and development, which had been declining for over ten years, bottomed out. By 1973, the stock market had dropped 250 points, and stock prices in constant dollars were down to the levels of the 1930s.

But the oil embargo was not the only shock to the American way of life in the mid-1970s: the Watergate investigations were in progress, Vice President Agnew resigned, the U.S. retreated from Vietnam, and, thanks in part to OPEC, the previously unknown phenomenon of "stagflation"—inflation in the midst of a recession—was strangling the economy.

By 1974, the Standard & Poor's 500 returns had declined 21 percent from their 1972 levels, bond returns had lost 1 percent and, due to inflation and the Federal Reserve's policy of controlling interest rates rather than the money supply, companies were often borrowing at negative real interest rates. As a result, most new corporate financing was debt, often in the form of publicly placed bonds. In their efforts to stave off long-term borrowings under these economic conditions, corporations increased their short-term debt even as cash holdings declined, causing liquid assets as a percentage of short-term liabilities to decrease. In addition, the federal debt as a percentage of GNP, which had been falling steadily since the end of World War II, began to rise due to the sharp increase in the federal deficit in the mid-1970s, as illustrated in Exhibit 9.

All these events increased the uncertainty surrounding future foreign exchange rates, making international trade transactions that much more complicated and potentially less profitable. The trade balance flirted with a surplus in 1975, but it plunged into deficit in 1976, reaching a temporary trough in 1978. Similarly, the current account balance went into deficit, but not as severely, due to the moderating effects of the strong service balance; between 1972 and 1979, exports of services had climbed from $28 billion to $102 billion.

When Carter was elected President in 1976, it was due in part to his promise to reduce the "misery index"—an inflation rate of 6 percent and 7.5 percent unemployment. The economy did begin to rebound in 1976, led by a short-lived decline in inflation and interest rates. However, in spite of the Federal Reserve's policy of controlling interest rates as a matter of first importance, the prime lending rate rose in 1978 from 7.75 percent to 11.75 percent. In 1979, corporate profits peaked as the recovery slowed. And, as a result of the Federal Reserve's policy (in conjunction with another increase in petroleum prices), inflation crossed the double-digit threshold, reaching 11.2 percent in 1979 as measured by the CPI.

In late 1979, Paul Volcker, the new chairman of the Federal Reserve, responded to economic pressures to lift interest rate controls. As a consequence, by December 1980, the prime rate peaked at 21.5 percent. This upsurge did not halt the skyrocketing inflation rate, however, which slowed only after it reached 13.5 percent in 1980.

IV. THE 1980S

If the United States had been suffering in 1976, it was in even worse condition in 1980. Not only was the country grappling with the Iranian hostage crisis, the implications of the Three Mile Island nuclear power disaster (which caused problems for virtually all other nuclear power stations under construction), and renewed fuel shortages that led to lines at the gas pumps, but the economy was in dismal condition. Unemployment was 7.5 percent and falling in 1976; but in 1980 it was 7.5 percent and rising, and the rate of inflation had increased from 6 percent to 13.5 percent. In addition, whereas real GNP had risen 5.4 percent in 1976, it declined 0.3 percent in 1980. The prime lending rate rose from an annual average of 6.83 percent in 1977 to 15.27 percent in 1980, ending the year at an all-time high of 21.5 percent.

President Reagan's policy of supply-side, trickle-down economics was implemented with the Economic Recovery Act of 1981. This policy was designed in part ultimately to increase federal tax receipts to defray the then-record-high 1981 deficit of $73 billion. The size of the deficit continued to rise, hitting well over $200 billion in 1986 before declining to a level of about $150 billion.

The economic recovery of the early 1980s was surprisingly strong and developed into one of the longest periods of growth the U.S. had ever experienced. First, the clamp on the money supply put into effect by the Federal Reserve System in 1979 started to have effect by the end of 1981, and inflation slowed to a range of 2.6 to 3.9 percent for most of the 1980s. An over-valued dollar aided this, until the last few years of the decade, by making imports inexpensive and contributing to a massive foreign trade imbalance that quickly turned the United States into history's largest debtor nation. Corporate equity securities prices rose sharply in the 1980s, until a peak was hit in 1987 followed by an extremely sharp decline in the stock market. Even this proved only a temporary pause, with the strength of the underlying economy carrying growth on and promoting a recovery of the market to its former levels in about 18 months. Unemployment, which peaked at almost 10 percent at the end of 1982, fell to levels that threatened increased inflationary wage pressure by 1989.

The economic strength was not evenly spread through all sectors, however. The economy continued to suffer international trade problems for most of the decade because of the high level of the dollar. On another front, the hundreds of billions of dollars that U.S. banks had lent to less-developed countries around the world, and particularly in Latin America to Mexico, Brazil, and Argentina, were not being repaid. Despite repeated and lengthy negotiations, the problem of the debt repayment and the underlying causes of the payment suspensions had not been resolved by 1989. Its potential magnitude had been reduced, however, as the capital of many U.S. banks had grown sufficiently in the interim to permit management to write off the loans.

The effect of these losses on international trade, which had become relatively anemic, remained unclear. Also unclear was the magnitude and potential effect of a worldwide resurgence in protectionist sentiment. Those countries with adverse trade imbalances seemed to be relying more on excluding imports. Those countries with positive trade imbalances were reluctant to make their home markets more accessible.

A second major problem area in the U.S. economy during the decade was caused by the dramatic drop in the price of oil. It fell from $35 or more a barrel at its high to $12 or less on the spot market, before a recovery to about $20. This price decline caused great dislocations among oil-exporting counties but some relief to oil-importing countries. In the United States, energy-consuming areas such as New England and the mid-Atlantic states prospered in a low-cost energy environment, with New England's growth picking up to become among the highest in the country.

On the other hand, however, the effect of the price decline of oil was devastating to the southwestern part of the United States. This area depended on a high price for oil to justify operating its more expensive production, to support the oil exploration industry, and to repay debts incurred in getting new oil capacity on line. The drop in oil prices caused drastic retrenchment in the oil and energy sector which slowly spread to real estate and banking. By the end of the decade, virtually all the major Texas commercial banks had undergone one or more massive reorganizations, often resulting in a heavy or complete loss to their shareholders. Many prominent wealthy figures were forced into personal bankruptcy as their ventures failed.

A third major financial development was the continuing crisis in the thrift industry. Savings and Loans and Mutual Savings Banks had traditionally raised money through passbook savings accounts and invested in long-term real estate mortgages. This strategy worked very effectively as long as the yield curve increased with maturities so that long-term money earned more than short-term. It also required that the yield curve not rise significantly so that the cost of existing deposits did not increase above the level at which the funds had been invested. Unfortunately, neither of these conditions held during the 1970s and 1980s.

The initial response to the problem during the 1970s, when the thrift institutions were rapidly consuming their accumulated capital because they had to pay greater interest on their deposits than they were earning on their assets, was to allow the institutions greater powers to invest in new types of assets. In effect, they were granted similar powers to commercial banks but were not as constrained by the laws prohibiting branch banking or even interstate banking.

Some thrifts (including thrifts acquired by large commercial banks) had the management skill to take effective advantage of these opportunities and to build very solid, large, and profitable financial institutions. Others, unfortunately, did not have the managerial skills to accomplish this. Still others, it appears in retrospect, took advantage of the ability to offer insured deposits to raise money for investment in high-risk or even fraudulent schemes to "get rich quick" for their owners. In addition, many thrifts in the Southwest were hard hit by the problems in the oil industry. When the failures caused by these problems began to roll in, the

Federal Savings and Loan Insurance Corporation was left with obligations totaling over $100 billion and well in excess of its ability to pay. The final determination of how the bill would be met was still being explored by the administration and the Congress in early 1989.

Finally, one major event of the decade turned out to be far less of an event than was initially feared. On October 19, 1987, the stock market in the United States (and other markets around the world) underwent a dramatic one-day decline, followed by several more days in which the market dropped significantly. From its peak in August 1987 to the end of the year, the Standard & Poor's average declined 28 percent.

The stock market had risen rapidly during 1986 and early 1987. By summer, it was increasing but at a slower rate. In October, the prospect of an interest-rate war between the United States and West Germany triggered selling on the stock market, which escalated into a major retreat. The use of computerized trading and of hedging techniques was widely thought at the time to have accelerated the decline, although subsequent studies have called this conclusion into question.

Regardless of the cause of the decline, however, astute management by the monetary authorities around the world ameliorated the effect of the drop and headed off the expected severe recession. Even the forecasted end to the acquisition and leveraged-buyout boom, hit hard also by the new tax legislation effective in 1987, did not materialize. The 1980s thus approached its end recording one of the longest periods of growth and prosperity in the history of the United States.

Technical Note 1

EXHIBIT 1 GROSS NATIONAL PRODUCT—NOMINAL AND REAL

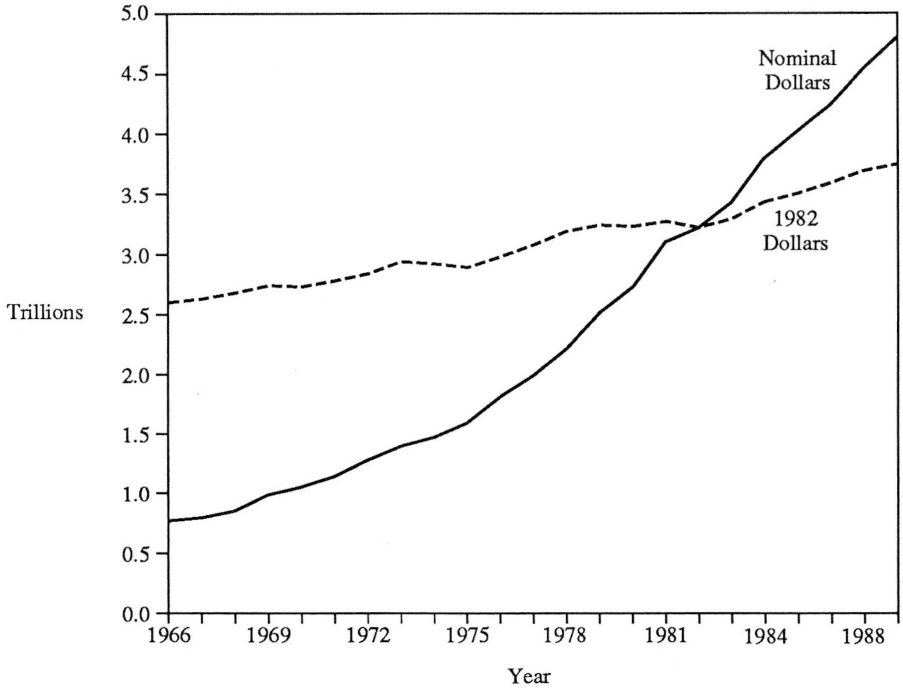

Sources: Economic Report of the President, February 1988. *Survey of Current Business Statistics,* U.S. Bureau of Economic Analysis.

Technical Note 1

EXHIBIT 2 INFLATION—CPI, PPI, GNP DEFLATOR

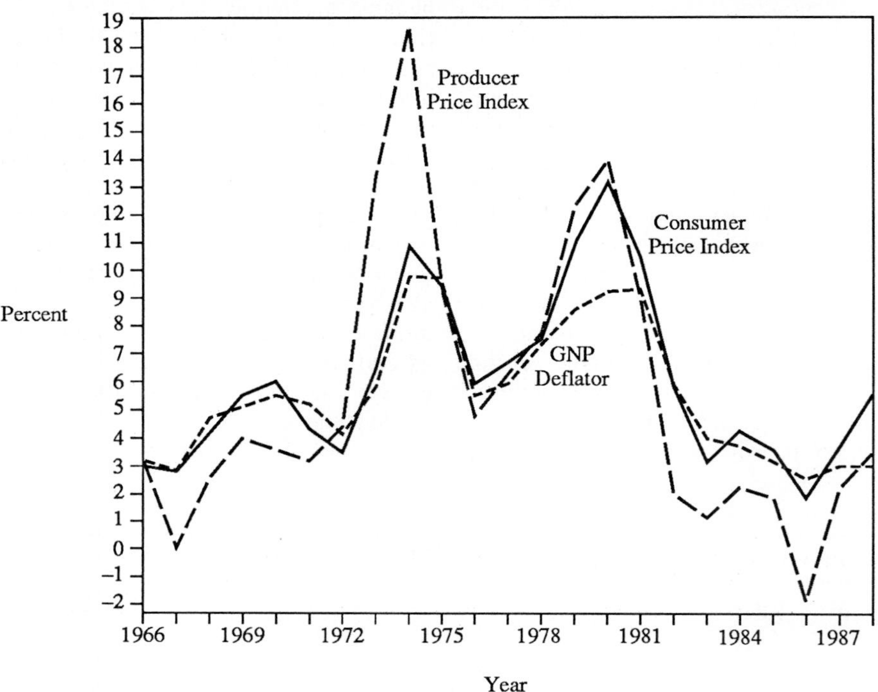

Sources: Economic Report of the President; Survey of Current Business Statistics, U.S. Bureau of Economic Analysis.

Technical Note 1

EXHIBIT 3 FEDERAL DEFICIT AND DEBT

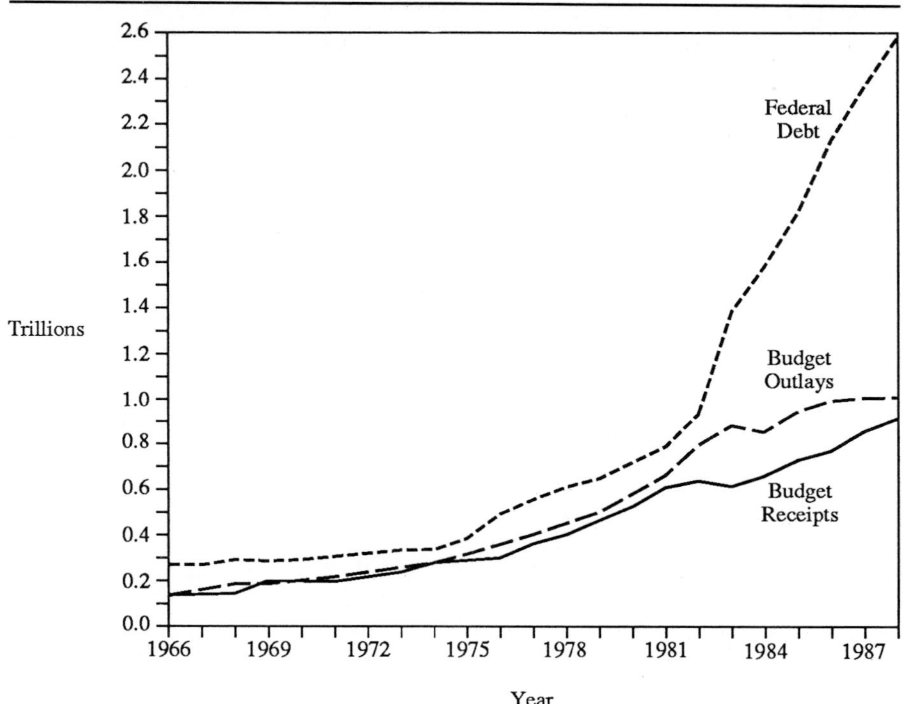

Sources: Economic Report of the President; Survey of Current Business Statistics, U.S. Bureau of Economic Analysis. (1988 figures are estimates)

Technical Note 1

EXHIBIT 4 DOW JONES INDUSTRIALS AVERAGE

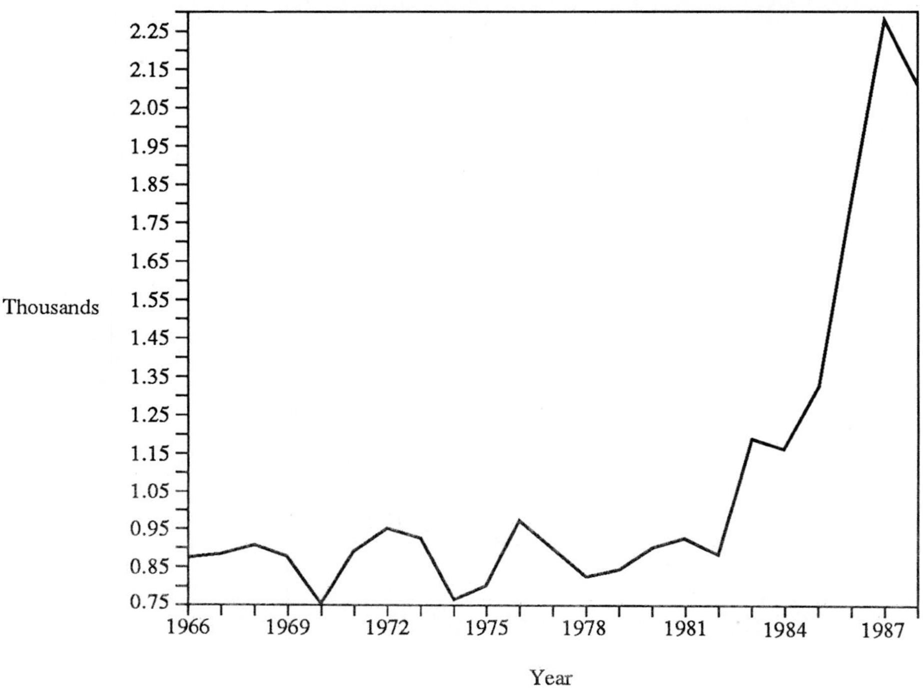

Sources: Economic Report of the President; New York Stock Exchange. *Note:* These averages can conceal major intrayear fluctuations such as that of 1987, when the stock market ended the year 28 percent below its August peak.

Technical Note 1

EXHIBIT 5 STANDARD & POOR'S 500 AVERAGE COMMON STOCK YIELDS—EARNINGS/PRICE RATIOS

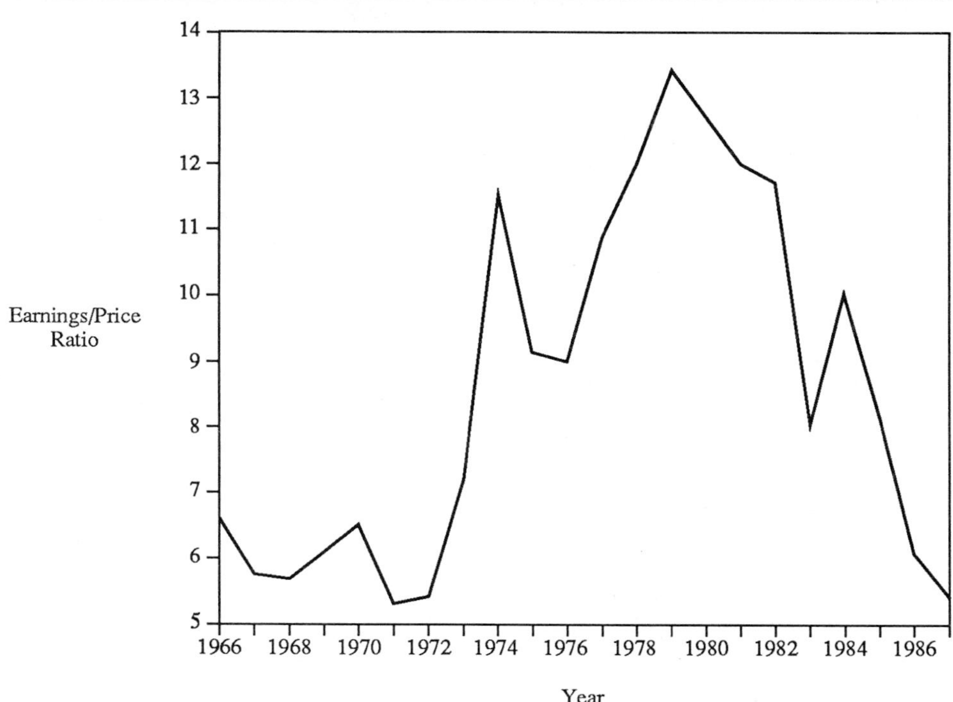

Sources: Economic Report of the President; Standard & Poor's Statistical Service. *Note:* These averages can disguise significant intrayear changes, such as occurred in 1987, when the stock market dropped 28 percent from its peak in August to the end of the year.

Technical Note 1

EXHIBIT 6 INTEREST RATES—BONDS AND PRIME LENDING RATE

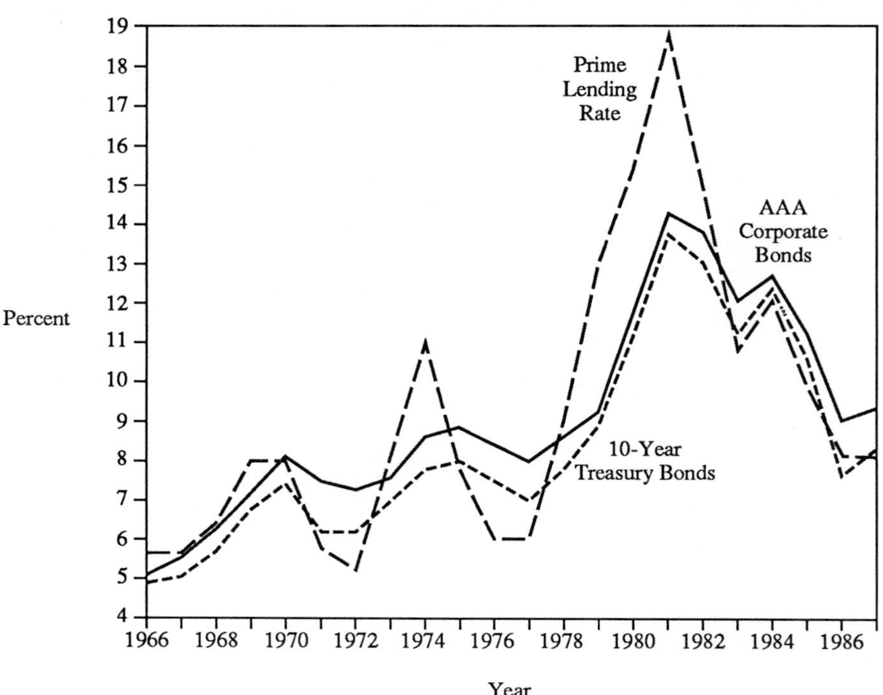

Sources: Economic Report of the President; Survey of Current Business Statistics, U.S. Bureau of Economic Analysis.

Technical Note 1

EXHIBIT 7 U.S. CURRENT ACCOUNT

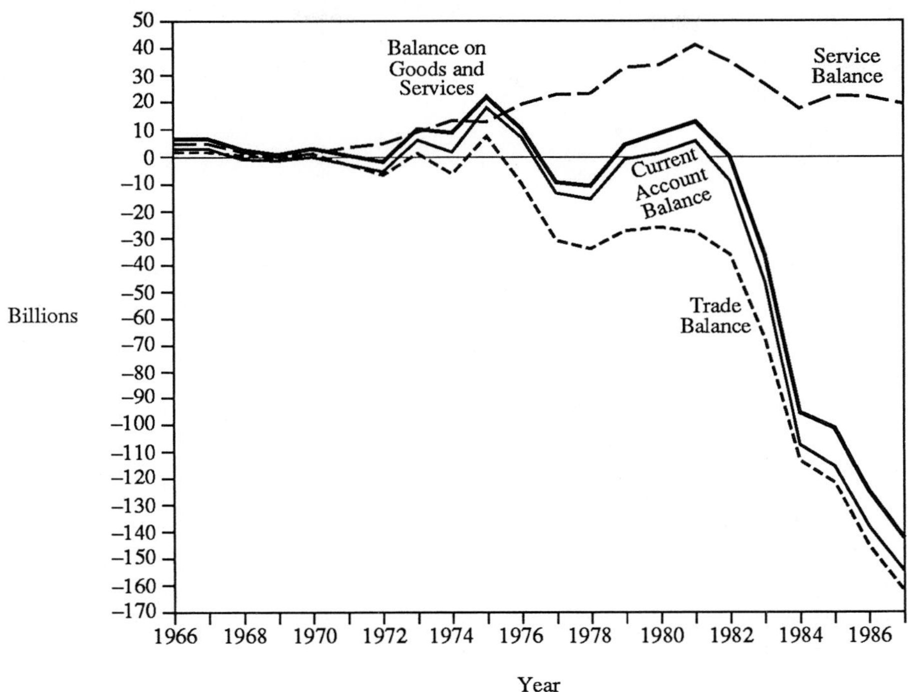

Source: International Financial Statistics, International Monetary Fund.

Technical Note 1

EXHIBIT 8 TRADE-WEIGHTED VALUE OF THE U.S. DOLLAR (March 1973 = 100)

Year	*Value*
1967	120
1968	122
1969	122
1970	121
1971	118
1972	109
1973	99
1974	101
1975	98
1976	106
1977	103
1978	92
1979	88
1980	87
1981	103
1982	110
1983	125
1984	139
1985	143
1986	112
1987	97
1988	93

Source: Board of Governors, Federal Reserve System.

Technical Note 1

EXHIBIT 9 FEDERAL DEBT/GNP

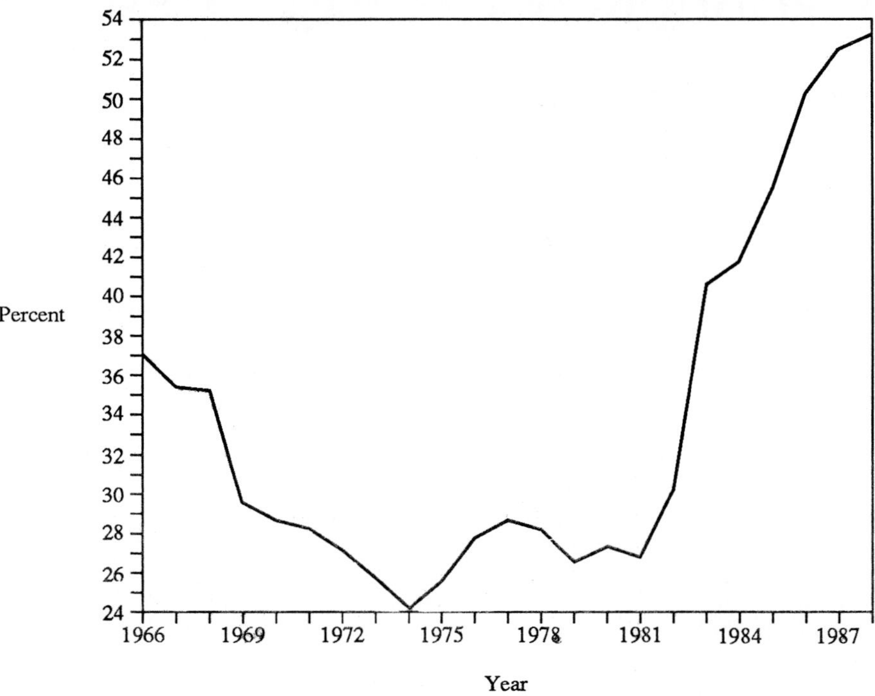

Sources: Economic Report of the President, February 1988.

Technical Note 2

AN INTRODUCTION TO CASE ANALYSIS

I. A PERSPECTIVE ON THE EFFICIENT USE OF CASES

There are perhaps as many approaches to case analysis as there are teachers using cases in the classroom. Nevertheless, there are some common pedagogical practices which tend to contribute to effective results with the methodology. For example, programs that rely heavily on case content are generally designed and paced so that students gradually, and often unconsciously, develop the skills needed for efficient case analysis and effective case discussion. Other programs do not afford this leisurely learning process. Thus, students who are suddenly confronted with substantive cases (as distinguished from end-of-chapter problems about Company ABC) may find useful a few hints about how to get the maximum learning from the time spent on preparation. These observations and suggestions are provided with a sense of modesty, however, because, as was once observed about a cookbook, they may offer little comprehendible to the novice and nothing worthy of the expert. With luck, they might be of use to those at an intermediate level of experience.

It is helpful to begin by noting a few purposes which cases are not equipped to accomplish well and some ways in which cases cannot be used efficiently. Negative though this tack may appear, it will help define safe channels within which the craft of case use is effective.

First, the purpose of case analysis is not to catch the errors and glitches which, embarrassingly but inevitably, creep into the text despite the vigorous effort of all concerned to catch them. (The authors, of course, welcome these problems being brought to their attention so that corrections can be made.) Good cases seldom rely on tricks—on Easter eggs hidden from the student but revealed to and by the instructor—as part of the learning structure.

Nevertheless, the student does not always have to agree with management's (or the case's) statement of the problem or of the set of solutions. Often a critical part of the analysis is the determination that the stated problem is incorrect or incomplete in its specifications. The case should have the characteristics of a good mystery story: all the information needed for the identification of the problem and its solution should be available to the reader. The challenge should be to interpret the data creatively and effectively and to bring imagination to developing a solution to the issue at hand.

Second, cases are generally not efficient in conveying substantive information. Readings supplemented with lectures are a better combination. Indeed, in order to protect the confidences and proprietary information of the individuals and companies that cooperate in case development by providing the information from which a case is constructed, the facts may have to be altered: details are distorted, and names, times, and even industry settings may have to be changed. The objective is to maintain the dimensions and content of the managerial decisions, but the disguise may require straying from the strict facts of the situation. It is thus dangerous to cite a case "fact" as indicative of the true state of the world at the time and place indicated other than for use in that particular case. (*Principles* developed and learned, on the other hand, should be portable.)

The cases in this book are therefore designed as self-contained units, standing alone and not requiring the student to do research outside the case in order to complete a reasoned analysis and decide on a course of action. Imagination and creativity are welcome, provided that flights of fancy are supported by a solid analytical structure.

Third, cases are usually not intended to be neat, compact presentations, gently guiding the reader from a set of prescribed assumptions to a predetermined conclusion. Unlike textbook problems, which specify the difficult decisional variables and leave the reader with little more to do than filling in the blanks, an effective case will provide the evidence from which the *analyst* has to make judgments regarding the critical assumptions and then work out the implications of these assumptions.

This unsettling aspect of cases is compounded by the fact that finance is a forward-looking function. Accounting, for instance, is concerned with accurately recording and reporting what has happened or is happening. Financial problems are not of the past in this sense; finance is much more concerned with what will happen to future value (to the market price of a company, for example) if certain actions are taken (such as a change in the dividend policy).

Although the future is unknown, estimates of the future are essential if today's decisions are to attempt to allow for and even influence future conditions and results. Often, however, these estimates are highly uncertain, causing many students to be uncomfortable with analyzing finance cases. This is especially true for those who have been immersed in studies such as accounting, economic history, or statistical methods, where there is usually an answer, and often only one answer. After a few sessions of being exposed to financial case analysis, however, most students contend easily with rounding to the nearest million rather than carrying the analysis to the dollar.

Many cases in this book contain mechanical aspects which provide drill in the basics of financial disciplines. The time and effort spent on these parts of the cases vary depending on the requirements of the instructor, which should be based on considerations such as the sophistication of the students. In some situations, most of the class discussion will be devoted to covering the fundamental mechanics. In others, the same case can be used in a discussion of policy issues. A truly rich case has many dimensions and can even be used in different functional areas, reflecting a challenging original situation.

In summary, the cases in this text have not been planned primarily to educate the student in the details of the industry or company in which the case is placed. They are intended to stand alone for analytical purposes. The student is expected to root around in the data to identify the important information, to use this information to project appropriate aspects of the future, and to settle on a course of action to resolve whatever problems the analysis determines exist.

II. AN OVERALL FRAMEWORK FOR CASE ANALYSIS

Despite the disadvantages of cases just mentioned, the methodology does have a number of strengths. First, cases are designed to help the student develop skills in the analysis and resolution of unstructured problems. Such skills include the following:

1. Problem identification and verification
2. Development of alternative ways of resolving the problem
3. Evaluation of the alternatives
4. Selection and implementation of the most effective alternative

It is important to emphasize that, as with actual events, there is usually no single "right" answer that is clearly superior to all others in the analysis of cases. There may indeed be an infinite number of ineffective solutions, but there is usually also more than one that will work well, and others that will work well in the presence of certain conditions. Thus, one advantage of case analysis is the opportunity to identify more than one alternative and the circumstances in which alternatives will be most effective.

Closely allied with this functional framework are the analytical skills peculiar to the discipline of finance. The cases are designed to develop and enhance these skills, including the interpretation of financial data and the use of basic financial techniques in the areas of forecasting, working capital analysis, and capital structure design. Early development of skills in financial analysis is important because the numbers on the balance sheets and income statements are cognate to the shadows of reality on the wall of Plato's cave. Like the shadows, the numbers must be quickly transformed from flickering, two-dimensional images to sharp, multidimensional pictures in color and with stereophonic sound in order for the analysis to be fully and effectively completed.

III. TECHNIQUE FOR CASE ANALYSIS

Six steps embody the technique by which cases are most effectively analyzed.

STEP 1: Develop an understanding of the circumstances in which the events of the case take place and the problem is situated.
STEP 2: Identify the perspectives involved, including that from which the decision will be made.
STEP 3: Validate the problem as stated by individuals in the case and identify unstated, hidden problems.
STEP 4: Develop alternative solutions to the problems validated and identified.
STEP 5: Evaluate the alternatives to determine their attractiveness and select the alternative that appears most attractive or least unattractive.
STEP 6: Determine whether the best alternative can be implemented.

Let us consider each step in turn.

STEP 1: Develop an understanding of the circumstances in which the events of the case take place and the problem is situated.

Developing this understanding requires thinking about and, if at all possible, developing answers to questions such as, What are the current and projected economic situations the decision maker faces? How will these situations affect the company's circumstances? Will management have to cut price? Cut volume? Cut costs? and What will the effect of growth be on the firm? Similar questions can be asked about the competitive situation, e.g., Is the firm a new one, fighting to get into an established market with a new product? Or is it an old one, struggling to hold on to market share in the face of new, aggressive firms?

Yet another question is, What does the company have to do well to compete, grow, and become or remain healthy? Because control over expenditures and resource allocation is the essence of finance (not just of capital expenditure management), it is important to consider a company's need to commit funds to the following:

1. Research and development (Yes, if new products are key)
2. Plant and equipment (Probably, if low-cost production is key)
3. Inventory and accounts receivables (Undoubtedly, if support of a distribution system is required)

The more basic cases in this book do not offer much opportunity to flesh out these issues in detail because the situations are often abbreviated and compact, but even in an early case such as that of Dynapump a great deal is to be gained by reflecting on why the management allocated funds the way they did. Learning to put oneself in the shoes of management, to try to see the problem as management does and interpret the context of the case as management interprets the environment, is a skill to be encouraged. Thus, what is going on in Stuart Furniture's environment (Case 11) that seems to be impelling management to press ahead with plans for a major new factory?

In accomplishing step 1, there is much value to be derived from the use of a strong but realistic imagination and from drawing on experiences in similar circumstances. The student can only benefit from trying to imagine what the company might look like once one gets beyond its receptionist. Will one see smoke, fire, and bits of hot metal flying around? Will the company have a clean-room assembly atmosphere? What will the inventory look like? How much of it is where? What about the overhead? Is it engineering? marketing? How quickly can overhead expenditures be changed? What level of sophistication is required in supervision of the employees? What might go wrong in the company? Who are the typical customers, and what are their problems? Do they need financing? Can they put orders in well in advance? What do the company's suppliers want? How can the company help the suppliers and thereby perhaps obtain the benefits of more regular supplies at lower cost? These and similar questions go a long way toward developing the skills required by step 1 of the case-analysis technique.

STEP 2: Identify the perspectives involved, including that from which the decision will be made.

The basic objective of financial decisions is the creation of value for the residual owners or beneficiaries of the enterprise. Hence, the appropriate point of view for the analysis of most of the cases is that of the owner of the equity. Furthermore, there is usually a high degree of identity between the equity owners and management. For instance, in many of the cases presented, management has a significant ownership position in the company. In most of the other cases, senior management undoubtedly has a significant portion of its own personal wealth invested in the firm. The student should thus be cautious about separating what is good for "the company" from what is good for the "shareholder." Sometimes these may differ, but normally the effort to make a distinction suggests that the analyst's perspective has begun to blur.

There are, of course, other points of view that must be considered in coming to a decision, including the perspectives of other suppliers of funds (e.g., banks, insurance companies, and suppliers) and of those who provide other goods and services, such as the employees (and even management, which may have special needs for security or compensation if asked to take personally risky decisions). But it remains helpful to have one "bottom-line" position when attempting to work out a solution that will be at least satisfactory to the rest of the parties. This single economic perspective can simplify matters considerably and is of course in direct contrast to the complexities of decisions involving public policy, where there is no easily identified residual beneficiary.

STEP 3: Validate the problem as stated by individuals in the case and identify unstated, hidden problems.

For the most part, the cases contain in their first few paragraphs a statement of the problem as seen by the major players in the situation. The pedagogic purpose of this statement is to help the student more efficiently interpret subsequent information as it might be viewed by those involved. Occasionally the situation does not have a stated problem, but the existence of a problem is suggested by assorted symptoms that all is not working well.

When no problem is stated, the first task is to use the evidence provided, and any additional evidence that can be discovered, to determine the nature of the problem. The same techniques are used in this task as are used to determine whether the problems mentioned in the case are the real problems or whether they are also symptoms of some larger issues that need to be resolved.

It is at this stage that the techniques of financial analysis become especially important: First the student can quickly "eyeball" the financial situation and the changes in financial relationships to pick out any major variations. For example, if sales have doubled over five years' time, have assets doubled as well? Has debt? Has equity? Have profits? After these changes in relationships have been located, the subcomponents can be checked in greater detail. (For instance, perhaps accounts receivable days outstanding have stretched, helping explain an increase in the asset-to-sales ratio.)

Cutting into the "melon" of financial analysis can be accomplished by answering the following kinds of questions:

What is the sales trend? Is the general movement over recent years up, down, or sideways? Do sales fluctuate wildly from year to year, or are they stable?

What has the relation been of profit to sales? Is the company getting more profitable, less profitable, or holding its own? What accounts for these changes? (This analysis may require looking at the company's environment as well as checking out the various components of the income statement, such as cost of sales and selling, and general and administrative expenses.) How responsive is profitability to increases or decreases in sales? How sensitive is it to competition?

What has been the relationship of assets to sales (or sales to assets) over the period in question? Are assets being used more (less assets to sales) or less (more assets to sales) efficiently? In this analysis, care must be taken to allow for the effects of inflation or deflation and of accounting conventions such as LIFO inventory, which may dramatically alter the financial relationships.

What trends in financial structure are evident? Is debt increasing in relationship to assets or equity? If so, which part of debt: trade payables, accruals, bank debt, long-term debt, or leases? What are the special characteristics of this debt that might cause difficulties for management?

Given the probability, the asset relationships, and the financial structure, what has the status been of the return on assets ($P/S \times S/A = P/A$) and the return on equity ($P/A \times A/E = P/E$)?

Are the projected future financial results, position, and needs based on expectations provided in the case consistent with those same projected quantities based on historic trends modified by anticipated changes?

Other techniques, such as analysis of the sources and uses of funds, supplement the foregoing ratio tools.

STEP 4: Develop alternative solutions to the problems validated and identified.

A case will frequently contain one or more suggested ways of resolving the problems that are specified. For example, if the company needs funds (a common situation for an interesting financial discussion), an alternative such as entering into long-term debt or issuing common stock may be stated. After first analyzing the proposed ideas, the student should not feel inhibited about considering other alternatives, which creative use of the student's imagination can help develop. For instance, in addition to raising funds, could the company reduce the need for financing by increasing its profitability? By reducing the dividend? By curtailing capital investments or using other assets more efficiently? Or, instead of debt financing, might lease financing be appropriate?

The creativity used to develop the alternatives is put to the test in the following step.

STEP 5: Evaluate the alternatives to determine their attractiveness and select the alternative that appears most attractive or least unattractive.

The evaluation step is a difficult one. Its objectives are not stated in an entirely positive way because problem solving does not always create new value or better circumstances compared with the former situation. Sometimes, the problem is to keep a bad situation from getting worse.

If financial markets were perfect, there would be no differences in risk-adjusted values among the various alternatives, at least as far as the owner of the residual value is concerned. However, perfect markets do not make for attractive profits; it is only through the search for and discovery of imperfections that extraordinary profits are made. Therefore, when considering the alternative solutions, it is important to analyze the effects the solutions have on the various parties. For example, is it possible to give one group greater security without a proportionate increase in perceived risk by others? What are the boundaries of marginal satisfaction? How far should they be crossed in an effort to ensure acceptance and participation by the various interested parties?

In contrast to the relative precision allowed by the techniques used in step 3, the analysis in this step is highly subjective. In fact, it is largely a marketing analysis: What do the various suppliers of funds (i.e., consumers of promises to pay in the future) require to be willing to part with their assets? What rates, terms, and conditions must be offered? What is the resulting risk and return to the residual owner? Will the equity owner eat sufficiently better to justify giving up some sleep? Will this be true of the other suppliers of funds? Though subjective, an analysis of and response to these questions is necessary to come up with the most viable alternative. And, it is particularly important that the options proposed by management or stated in the case be thoroughly evaluated. This is a reflection of the real world in which a supervisor expects to have the supervisor's requests and suggestions given careful consideration before other alternatives are proposed.

STEP 6: Determine whether the best alternative can be implemented.

Although stated last, it could effectively be argued that this step should come after step 4 in order to ensure that unrealistic alternatives are discarded before soaking up the time required by step 5, the comparative analysis. On the other hand, it is hard to determine the feasibility of an alternative in the abstract, without consideration of the interests involved. This principle has been adopted here: in order to reduce the chance of missing a good idea, the chance of wasting time considering an impractical one is accepted.

There are several reasons why the apparent best alternative might not be feasible. For example, legal objections may suddenly be discovered. Or timing may not be propitious; that is, the solution of the problem may not be able to wait for the ideal moment but might have to be accomplished quickly and consequently less valuably.

If circumstances defeat the best alternative at this point, the analyst has to back up to step 5, step 4, or even step 3 to reevaluate the situation and the alternatives. Reevaluation is an easy process if a number of attractive options seem to be available: if the best will not work, there are others almost as satisfactory. If only one solution can be found, however, and if that cannot be implemented, then either the problem will have to remain unsolved or all the analyst's creative powers will have to be called on to reshape the alternative(s) to fit the circumstances.

IV. SUMMARY AND REVIEW

The framework of problem identification, idea generation, idea evaluation, and problem resolution is not unique to the analysis and solution of financial cases or problems. The skeleton holds together problem-solving activities of all types and in all areas of endeavor. It can be applied from as simple an activity as ordering a meal in a restaurant to a complex financial structuring question. It is fascinating to listen to a skilled executive talk through a problem, first building up a rich network of alternatives and options and then discarding those which, on a comparative basis, are less attractive. Ultimately, the executive comes to a decision which by then seems obvious, given the criteria applied in the comparative analysis.

Of course, the specific interest here is the application of this intellectual framework to the solution of financial problems. The basic tools of financial analysis are essential to the process. Nevertheless, once the issues rise above the mechanical level, judgments come into play—judgments concerning marketing, controllership, operations and manufacture of goods, and all sorts of behavioral considerations. The cases for analysis in this book attempt to rise above the mechanical precisely by not providing easy assumptions, but by giving the student the opportunity to determine the appropriate assumptions, and by incorporating the nonfinancial considerations into the decision whenever possible. We hope that the student and the instructor will have as much fun using these cases as we and our classes have had with them.

V. AN EXAMPLE

To illustrate how this analytical process works, we shall consider the case of the Rivers Company. After a brief description of the situation, the six analytical steps described above will be applied to resolving the problem.

A. The Rivers Company

Rivers Company was a manufacturer of lawn and garden chemicals and supplies. One of its distributors, Timbers Company, was a rapidly growing firm with the potential for becoming an important outlet for Rivers in New England. Although the credit relationship had been satisfactory, Mr. Rains, Rivers' credit manager, was concerned that Timbers' weak financial position boded ill for the safe receipt of payment for future shipments. In particular, he thought that extended credit terms, especially if granted during the slow winter months, often ultimately caused problems because the distributor proved to be unable to pay in the spring and thus was unable to stock new merchandise.

Cultivation of new distributorships was important to Rivers because as many as 10 percent of Rivers' customers disappeared each year as a result of sale, merger, or discontinuation of the business. The proportion of failures was as high as 20 percent for new distributorships. It was easy to enter the distribution business, which required an investment of only $30,000 to $60,000.

Rivers' products were primarily standardized, with competition coming in the form of service rather than price or product differentiation. It was considered very important to have adequate stocks in the distributors' warehouses and for the distributors to support the brand in order to reinforce a positive brand image in the consumer's mind.

Rivers' average gross profit was 25 percent of sales, and the net margin was 10 percent. The company's target return on net worth was 20 percent after taxes.

Goods were customarily shipped on open account with terms of 2/10, n/30 (a 2 percent discount was offered for payment within ten days; otherwise the full amount was due within 30 days). About half of Rivers' customers took the 2 percent discount; most of the remainder paid after 30 days. In a few instances, Rivers extended longer terms of up to 90 days but insisted on having a formal note executed in these cases. Shipments were normally made only in an amount up to an established credit limit and then only after receipt of payment on any overdue bills. The sales department often complained, however, that this practice made it difficult for the distributors to maintain adequate inventories to service peak seasonal demand.

Although Rivers did not ship on consignment, it had experimented with providing field warehousing arrangements for some of its promising new distributorships. Under a field warehousing arrangement, a portion of the distributor's warehouse would be partitioned off and leased for a nominal fee to a field warehousing company. One of the distributor's employees would be bonded, put on the payroll of the field warehouse company, and placed in charge of the warehouse. When not engaged in field warehouse responsibilities, this individual could be assigned to work for the distributor.

The field warehouse would be posted with signs indicating that the field warehouse premises and its contents were not the distributor's property so that other creditors would not be misled about the ownership of the merchandise if they visited the distributorship. Furthermore, if the distributor encountered financial problems, there would be little difficulty in identifying Rivers' merchandise. Title had never transferred, and the merchandise had been physically separated from the distributor's inventory. Rivers could usually recover its merchandise from a field warehouse for a cost of 5 percent. Its loss on accounts receivable in a similar circumstance averaged 50 percent of the face value of the receivables.

Rivers would ship goods to the field warehouse's address in care of the field warehouse company, whose employee would receive them and then release them to the distributor under the terms Rivers specified. Usually, the arrangement provided that the warehouse employee could advance a certain dollar amount of merchandise to the distributor. Once that amount had been reached, the distributor would have to deposit cash or a check to the warehouse company account at a local bank and present the deposit slip to the warehouse employee before any further merchandise was released. The total amount of merchandise released to the customer in advance of payment would not exceed the dollar limit Mr. Rains specified.

The incremental cost of field warehousing to the distributor was modest. The field warehouse firm charged a fee of 0.1 percent of the value of the goods handled plus reimbursement for all out-of-pocket expenses such as the wages of the warehouse employee.

The Timbers Company, Rivers' customer, was in its third year of operation. It had been founded by Mr. Woods, who had formerly worked for a similar company in an adjacent area. After operating briefly in a partnership, Mr. Woods bought out his partner and converted the business to a sole proprietorship. As a result, Timbers itself did not pay corporate income tax. Its earnings were consolidated into Mr. Wood's personal income tax statement and taxed at his appropriate marginal tax rate.

During its second year of operations, Timbers' sales were $1,020,000. Cost of goods sold was generally 80 percent of sales price for a distributor. The company reported a profit of $91,000 before Mr. Woods' withdrawals for tax payments ($16,520) and personal compensation ($32,000).

Timbers' balance sheet as of September 30 of the fiscal year just ended, in thousands of dollars, was as follows:

TIMBERS COMPANY
Balance Sheet as of September 30

Current Assets		Current Liabilities	
Cash	$ 5.4	Accounts payable	$186.9
Accounts receivable	156.9	Notes payable	40.5
Inventory at cost	106.8	Accruals	9.3
Other	4.5	Due owner for taxes	32.7
Total current assets	$273.6	Total current liabs.	$269.4
Equipment, net depn.	34.8		
Goodwill	11.7	Capital	50.7
	$320.1		$320.1

Rivers' sales manager, Ms. Waters, was very impressed with Timbers' rapid growth and the vigorous selling efforts Mr. Woods had undertaken. She believed that Timbers would become a major customer of Rivers. She endorsed the idea of offering Timbers a field warehouse facility.

Ms. Waters and Mr. Rains estimated that a distributorship such as Timbers would stock on average 1,750 items provided by over 80 suppliers. Approximately one-third of the total sales and inventory would be items that Rivers could supply. The remainder of the line would be of noncompetitive products. In the previous year, however, Timbers bought only $39,000 from Rivers.

Despite Ms. Waters' enthusiasm, Mr. Rains thought that Timbers' balance sheet was weak. Timbers' payments tended to be late, although prompt payment had been received for the initial purchases. All payments were then brought current after the end of Timbers' first fiscal year. Payments were again delayed during the peak season of the year just completed. A delayed payment in three monthly installments for a $12,000 shipment was arranged to accomodate peak-season needs. Its terms were adhered to by Timbers. Currently, payments were on schedule. The maximum amount of credit outstanding to Timbers was $18,000, granted during the slow payment period in Timbers' first year. More recently, the outstanding balance due from Timbers had averaged about $9,000.

Ms. Waters reported that Mr. Woods was favorably disposed to a field warehouse arrangement. Among other advantages he saw was the possibility of drawing out less than a full case of merchandise at a time. While Rivers could not legally require that Timbers buy all its merchandise in the Rivers' line from Rivers in exchange for the field warehouse accomodation, Mr. Woods indicated he knew that the field warehouse only made sense if the volume were significant. He had therefore indicated that if the field warehouse were established, he would probably buy from Rivers to the exclusion of its competitors.

Mr. Rains' plan was to ship $100,000 (at Rivers' sales price, Timbers' cost) of faster-moving merchandise to the field warehouse. Mr. Woods had told Ms. Waters that he thought he could make payment in time to take the discounts within the 2/10, n/30 terms on a draw of $7,500 against the inventory. (Once the $7,500 figure for the draw against the warehouse had been reached, Mr. Woods would in effect be expected to pay cash for any subsequent merchandise drawn out.) In addition, Timbers would be asked to purchase $1,000 of very slowly moving items on standard terms.

If the Timbers' experiment worked, Mr. Rains thought field warehousing could be offered to other promising new distributors. Eventually, 10 to 20 field warehouses could be in operation. Presumably, as a distributor developed a stronger financial position, its field warehouse arrangement would no longer be necessary and could be eliminated.

B. The Analysis

Step 1. Ensuring a satisfactory understanding of the circumstances is relatively uncomplex in this very summary, abbreviated situation. Distributors, such as Timbers, are very important to the manufacturers like Rivers because the distributors hold inventory close to the retailer, able to supply it much more quickly than the manufacturer could. In addition, the distributors can manage the credit demands of their local customers more accurately and efficiently than the manufacturer can. Having a good network of distributors is thus very important to Rivers.

As the description indicates, however, it is relatively easy to enter the distribution business, and many entrants subsequently fail. The margins are so narrow that there is not much room to make errors with respect to pricing, inventory, or credit. Therefore, Rivers is exposed to a significant risk that any new distributor will go broke, leaving Rivers unable to collect its accounts receivable. Rivers thus must help promising new entrants without exposing itself to excessive risk. The question is whether the field warehouse arrangement offers a means for balancing the rewards and the risks in resolving this dilemma.

There is little doubt that Timbers qualifies as a potential financial problem as well as a potentially significant customer. With respect to the latter, Mr. Woods has developed his business from nothing to a sales level of slightly over $1 million in two years. He is turning his assets rapidly, with a sales/asset ratio of 3.19:1. A distributor displaying this type of rapid growth would be very attractive to Rivers and very useful in increasing Rivers' market share.

Interpreting Timbers' profitability is difficult because of its status as a sole proprietorship, inextricably intertwined with Mr. Woods' personal affairs. The profit on sales of 8.9 percent appears attractive, but allowance has to be made for Mr. Woods' compensation and for taxes. If $48,520 is a fair estimate of this sum, the profit on sales falls to 4.2 percent (still respectable for a distributor). The 13.3 percent profit on assets is also attractive, but the 83.8 percent profit on equity is distorted because there is so little equity in the business.

Mr. Woods, himself, is supplying only 15.8 percent of the firm's resources in the form of equity capital. Suppliers are providing 58.4 percent, with notes (probably from suppliers but possibly from banks) amounting to another 12.6 percent. Suppliers are thus providing at least 83 days cost of sales ($816,000 at 80 percent of sales) in the form of payables, plus possibly another 17 to 18 days in the form of notes, to bring the total precariously close to 100 days of purchases. Because accounts payable are larger than inventories, the merchandise in effect had been sold long before it was paid for.

At 15.4 percent of sales, Timbers' receivables represent 56 days sales outstanding. It is possible that this ratio overstates the collection period because of the fall selling season taking place just before the close of the company's fiscal year. If sales in August and September were higher than average, the days-sales-outstanding calculation would indicate more days sales were outstanding than would be the case in fact. On the other hand, inventories are 13.1 percent (48 days) of cost of goods sold. This appears high for a company entering its very slow seasonal sales period.

Accounts receivable will be reduced as sales drop off for the winter. It is unlikely, however, that during the slow months there will be a significant reduction in the inventory level. It seems very unlikely that enough current assets will be converted to cash to enable Mr. Woods to cut his trade payables to 30 days, a cut of two-thirds (over $150,000) of the existing amounts due.

Step 2. Identification of the perspective from which the decision will be made reveals a more complex problem than might initially appear to the analyst. First, Mr. Rains wants to minimize the chance of loss. If he is evaluated only on the quantity of losses Rivers incurs, he will not be enthusiastic about considering the profits from the relationship. If his performance is measured in a manner that allows for the profits on marginal accounts as an offset to credit losses, then his perspective will be somewhat broader.

Ms. Waters orientation is toward sales, and thus her interest is primarily in maintaining a growing and dynamic distribution network.

Finally, it is important to consider Mr. Woods' position. An unwise arrangement with Rivers could severely damage his promising business. If that were to happen, and it were determined that Rivers' officers had been exercising undue influence over Timbers in order to promote Rivers' interests, Rivers could be liable to Timbers, to Mr. Woods, and to Timbers' other creditors for the damage.

Step 3. Part of the problem has already been validated in the process of accomplishing the first analytical step, in which Timbers' financial situation was reviewed and was found weak. The other aspect of problem validation in this situation is to confirm that Rivers *should* be interested in the Timbers account.

During the past fiscal year, Rivers sold $39,000 to Timbers. Rivers' cost of goods sold was $29,250 at a 75-percent cost of sales, and Rivers should have earned $3,900 after taxes on these transactions. Timbers' payments have not always been prompt, however, so assuming only 30 days sales outstanding would be too generous. Timbers' payment period appears to be at least 83 days, although there is some indication that Rivers has been able to enforce more prompt payment, perhaps averaging 45 days. An 83-day payment period on Rivers' total annual cost of sales to Timbers of $29,250 would amount to an average investment at cost of $6,651 in accounts receivable from Timbers.

A profit of $3,900 on an investment of $6,651 is clearly in excess of the 20 percent target return on investment. It is an indication of how attractive even marginal distributors can be (provided they are not cannibalizing the sales Rivers is making through other distributors). Even if Rivers allowed Timbers extended 90-day terms during the spring and summer, the average balance at cost of sales would only be one-quarter ($7,312) of the $29,250, on which a profit of $3,900 would still be very attractive. Under these circumstances, however, the exposure to loss might be greater because of the very high balance for three months rather than a smaller balance year-round.

In the Rivers–Timbers situation, an unstated problem lurks to trip the unwary analyst. Will the proposed field warehouse arrangement work? Probably not, with the result that new alternatives must be developed if the parties are to achieve their objectives.

The proposal will not work because Timbers needs resources to support accounts receivable as well as inventory. Placing inventory in the field warehouse helps solve Timbers' need for a broad selection of merchandise, conveniently located. But this form of financial resource will not help Timbers carry its relatively long accounts receivable.

There are a number of ways this problem can be demonstrated. For example, if one-third of Timbers' line could be supplied by Rivers, then the field warehouse would substitute for one-third of Timbers' inventory, $35,600 as of September 30. Clearly, the $100,000 of inventory in the field warehouse would be a significant increase in the amount of inventory to which Timbers could have access.

In order to clean up the payables due to other suppliers of these products, Timbers would return their unsold merchandise for credit. If merchandise of this type represented one-third of sales and cost of sales ($272,000 out of cost of sales of $816,000 at 80 percent of sales) and Rivers had sold $39,000 to Timbers, then Rivers represented 14.3 percent of Timbers' business in the Rivers' line. That proportion of the inventory would be returned to Rivers (probably just moved to the field warehouse); the balance ($30,496) of the $35,600 would go to the competitors.

The other suppliers are owed much more than $30,496, however. It was already noted that the inventory on hand was less than the amount due suppliers. Hence, a mere return of the inventory will not offset the sums due. If the Rivers line of products accounts for one-third of Timbers' business, suppliers of these products should account for one-third of Timbers' payables. Including the notes payable, this amount is $75,800, of which Rivers' proportionate share

(14.3 percent) is $10,839. Thus, return of $30,496 in merchandise will repay less than half of the amount ($64,961) due to Rivers' competitors. Even the $7,500 proposed draw from the field warehouse is far from enough to square these accounts. It would be very unrealistic to assume these firms would allow Timbers to defer payment after Timbers had stopped doing business with them.

An alternative way of illustrating the problem is to assume that Timbers was just starting its business. Rivers ships $100,000 of merchandise to the field warehouse. Timbers expects annual sales of $272,00 (at cost of goods sold) of this merchandise, approximately $745 per calendar day. The draw of $7,500 allows Mr. Woods to remove merchandise for the first ten days before he has to start paying cash for it.

In addition, Mr. Woods has the capital resources he has contributed to the business, totaling $83,400 including the sums due him. He will also have use of the funds provided by the accruals, services received for which he has not yet paid, bringing the total to $92,700. Unfortunately, $34,800 was spent on equipment, and apparently he spent $11,700 buying out his partner. These two expenditures leave a total of $46,200 for use to support current assets. Only one-third ($15,400) of this sum would be available for the Rivers' line because the rest would be needed to support sales of other products. The $15,400 would allow another 21 days of cost of sales to be purchased from the inventory in the field warehouse, a total of 31 days in all.

Unfortunately, the customers appear to take 56 days to pay. On the 31st day, therefore, Mr. Woods would be unable to fill further orders for the types of products Rivers supplies, and he would be unable to fill any further orders until the 56th day, when he receives payment from the sales he made on the first day.

Rather than selling $745 every day of the year, Mr. Woods would only sell on 31 out of 56 days, 55.4 percent of the time. The volume of Rivers' products sold would therefore drop from $272,000 to $151,000.

Step 4. Increasing its volume from $39,000 to $151,000 might be acceptable to Rivers. The $100,000 inventory provided plus the $7,500 draw would amount to $80,625 at Rivers' cost (75 percent). The profit on Rivers' sales would be $15,100 after taxes, a return of 18.7 percent but having much less risk exposure than Rivers had under the existing arrangement.

It is unlikely that Mr. Woods would be satisfied at the reduction in volume once he discovered what had happened. He therefore would back out of the deal, which would result in needless expense to one or both of the parties to have set up and then dismantled the field warehouse. Or, he might just quietly resume buying from his other sources. This would be unsatisfactory to Rivers because even at $151,000 in sales, the business is far from providing sufficient profit to return 20 percent on the field warehouse investment.

What Timbers appears to need is a sufficient draw from the field warehouse to support its receivables. In rough terms, if one-third of sales is of Rivers' products, one-third of the receivables ($52,300) represents those sales. Mr. Woods has his own and miscellaneous sources of $15,400 to apply to these needs, leaving $36,900 required from the company's suppliers. Deducting the gross margin of 20 percent indicates that Timbers' cost of goods sold to generate sales of $36,900 would be $29,520. It is this amount that Mr. Woods must be allowed to draw from the field warehouse, rather than $7,500, if he is to meet the sales target he and the Rivers' executives have been discussing.

Another alternative would be for Rivers to abandon the field warehouse arrangement and allow Timbers to buy on open account its needs for inventory ($35,600 at one-third of existing inventory) and for receivables ($29,520, as derived in the last paragraph). The total committed by Rivers to this arrangement would be $65,120 compared with $129,520 under the field warehouse scheme.

A virtually infinite number of combinations and permutations of these alternatives exist.

Step 5. The net profit to Rivers from either form of satisfactory support to Timbers would be the same, 10% on sales of $272,000. As calculated in the previous section, using the field warehouse, Rivers would have a total investment of $129,520 (of which $29,520 would be the draw). Using the open account shipment method, the investment would be $65,120. The 21 percent return on the gross investment in the first instance would barely make the 20 percent hurdle rate; the return of 41.8 percent in the second instance would exceed it by a comfortable margin.

Mr. Woods would probably prefer the field warehouse arrangement, as modified to make it work, because he would have a larger stock of inventory on which to draw. The question thus is whether Mr. Rains would find sufficient comfort from the collateral to justify investing an incremental $64,000 for no incremental monetary return. In effect, Mr. Rains could support on open account virtually two credits of the Timbers type whereas he could support only one using the field warehouse.

Approximately 20 percent of Rivers' distributors of the Timbers type fold up each year. If 50 percent of the receivables from a failed account are lost, then the *expected* loss after taxes (of 34 percent) from the receivables of an account such as Timbers would be 6.6 percent ($.2 \times .5 \times .66$). Similar calculations show an expected loss of 0.66 percent ($.2 \times .05 \times .66$) on a field warehouse inventory that must be recovered.

The expected benefits and costs of committing the same capital to the two different financing methods can be estimated as follows:

A. Use field warehouse for one distributor	
Investment in field warehouse inventory	$100,000
Investment in accounts receivable at Rivers' cost	29,520
Total investment	$129,520
Profit per year on $272,000 sales	$ 27,200
Less after-tax loss allowances:	
Field warehouse inventory (0.66%)	660
Receivables (6.6%)	1,948
Net profit	$ 24,592
Net return on investment	19.0%

B. Finance two distributors through open account	
Investment in accounts receivable at Rivers' cost	$130,240
Profit per year on $544,000 sales	$ 54,400
Less after-tax loss allowance:	
Receivables (6.6%)	8,596
Net profit	$ 45,804
Net return on investment	35.2%

Even though the losses from the second approach are higher than they are for the first one, the profits will be larger even after allowing for the greater chance of loss.

In the event information was not available to help Mr. Rains assess these probabilities, a spread-sheet sensitivity model could be used to determine at what critical percentages (for example, the percentage of accounts failing) the relative attractiveness of the alternatives would reverse. Judgment could then be focused on whether the probable percentages would be more or less than the critical levels.

Step 6. From Rivers' perspective, given the assumptions made, it appears that the best arrangement would be simply to increase Timbers' line of credit and to make similar arrangements in other cases where the prospects were as good. Whether this solution can be implemented depends on how Mr. Rains' performance is evaluated.

If he is evaluated on the contribution made by marginal risk accounts, the open-account alternative would be very attractive to him. If he is evaluated on the credit losses of the company, he will be impelled to use the field warehouse system. In that case, however, he might suggest to his superiors that an alternative incentive and evaluation program could increase the company's profits.

In summation, we have applied the six-step case analysis template to the situation Mr. Rains of the Rivers Company confronted. First, we identified the aspects of the situation that were important to the various parties. Second, we found that we had to deal with the interests of parties that had not been clearly identified initially. Third, we found that the problem was not quite as simple as the players thought it was. Fourth, we worked out several alternatives for resolving the situation. Fifth, we identified the most attractive alternative. Finally, we tried to determine the circumstances under which the best alternative might be acceptable and those which would force acceptance of a less satisfactory solution.

In applying the six steps, it was often necessary to interpret the data provided and to push the qualitative and quantitative information to discover insights not made explicit in the exposition. Assumptions were not always provided. The resolution was not simply a matter of entering data into a calculator or computer template. Case analysis has an element of the detective story to it; new perspectives can open up as the result of asking what the importance of a given item of information might be.

Even with this element of uncertainty, however, very few cases reflect the full unstructured environment in which managers must function. A case usually has been pruned of most inessential facts and focused carefully on a limited number of decisions. In the real world of administration, the pruning and focusing is often the most important function of the manager's job.

Nevertheless, the case analysis rubric discussed in this section applies not only to financial issues or even just to classroom cases. It applies to all types of general problem analysis and resolution.

Case 1

FIGURES ARE REVEALING (1987–88)

The investment, financial, and profitability characteristics of different industries vary, often significantly. For example, some industries require substantial investments in property, plant, and equipment, while others may have a larger proportion invested in liquid assets, such as cash and accounts receivable. Differences frequently exist in the means of financing assets. A particular industry may rely extensively on long-term debt in contrast to one in which trade credit is readily available. Also, certain measures of profitability and asset utilization will reveal significantly different results in industry comparisons. Financial statements and the ratios computed from them reflect these and other differences among industries.

Exhibit 1 presents balance sheet percentages and selected ratios and market information for a company selected from each of the 14 industries listed below. The company's fiscal year is also indicated. Study this information and associate each set of figures with a particular industry. Be prepared to explain the basis of your selections.

	Industry	Fiscal year
1.	Commercial bank (regional)	12/87
2.	Life insurance company	12/87
3.	Electric utility	12/87
4.	Domestic airline	6/88
5.	Provider of information-based services	12/87
6.	Provider of temporary office, health care, and other help	12/87
7.	Paper and forest products	12/87
8.	Automobile manufacturer	12/87
9.	Textile manufacturer	9/87
10.	Meat packer	10/87
11.	Grocery store chain	2/88
12.	Drug store chain	8/87
13.	Jewelry store chain	12/87
14.	Department store group	1/88

In preparing the summary financial statements, current maturities of long-term debt were included with notes payable, leased property with owned property, and capitalized leases with long-term debt. Accruals and taxes currently payable were included as other current liabilities, and deferred taxes were included as other liabilities. Goodwill was counted as other assets, along with investments.

EXHIBIT 1 BALANCE SHEET PERCENTAGES AND SELECTED RATIOS (1987–1988)

Company	*A*	*B*	*C*	*D*	*E*	*F*	*G*	*H*	*I*	*J*	*K*	*L*	*M*	*N*
Balance Sheet Percentages														
Cash & equivalents	20.7%	14.3%	3.1%	22.5%	16.7%	9.2%	0.4%	2.8%	22.3%	4.4%	1.4%	0.1%	3.0%	2.7%
Accounts receivable	43.0	11.2	40.4	9.8	2.9	21.7	46.3	27.0	60.4	7.0	12.0	3.0	4.8	25.3
Inventories	0.0	0.9	0.0	14.1	20.7	19.6	34.2	24.0	0.0	7.6	0.0	3.6	51.0	21.8
Other current assets	0.0	2.3	2.3	2.6	0.9	1.9	0.9	0.9	0.6	2.3	2.3	1.5	1.7	9.8
Prop., plant, & eq., net	2.6	62.0	29.2	31.2	57.4	37.8	12.3	42.6	7.6	57.6	0.6	82.5	39.5	26.4
Other assets	33.7	9.2	25.0	19.9	1.4	9.8	5.9	2.7	9.1	21.1	83.8	9.2	0.0	13.9
Total assets	100.0%	100.0%	100.0%	100.0%	100.0%	100.0%	100.0%	100.0%	100.0%	100.0%	100.0%	100.0%	100.0%	100.0%
Notes pay. & cur. mat.	14.9%	0.6%	0.0%	4.2%	0.9%	7.3%	25.0%	0.7%	0.0%	0.0%	3.9%	2.8%	1.8%	7.3%
Accounts payable	62.8	9.7	3.4	20.4	18.5	10.8	16.6	14.7	2.8	3.2	3.6	1.7	17.9	9.1
Other current liabilities	0.0	13.9	20.5	15.0	7.7	13.1	10.6	9.9	36.0	7.0	4.0	2.9	14.5	5.6
Long-term debt & leases	1.7	12.7	11.0	3.9	26.5	7.0	28.8	19.3	0.0	27.9	6.5	39.8	12.2	19.8
Other liabilities	14.4	24.7	19.1	15.1	6.2	8.3	4.9	11.4	0.0	13.1	58.8	14.3	7.9	8.0
Preferred stock	0.6	0.0	0.0	0.0	0.0	0.0	0.0	0.0	0.0	3.8	0.3	7.5	0.0	0.0
Common stock & surplus	1.7	11.4	21.7	2.8	3.7	1.7	8.0	3.1	11.7	8.0	3.6	22.5	5.6	20.3
Retained earnings	3.8	27.1	24.3	38.7	36.5	51.7	6.0	41.0	49.5	37.0	19.4	8.6	40.1	30.0
Total liabilities & equity	100.0%	100.0%	100.0%	100.0%	100.0%	100.0%	100.0%	100.0%	100.0%	100.0%	100.0%	100.0%	100.0%	100.0%

EXHIBIT 1 ***(continued)***

Company	*A*	*B*	*C*	*D*	*E*	*F*	*G*	*H*	*I*	*J*	*K*	*L*	*M*	*N*
Selected Ratios														
Revenues/Assets	0.10	1.20	2.45	1.59	3.07	3.32	1.07	1.71	4.10	0.76	0.31	0.33	3.15	1.09
Profit/Revenues	6.0%	4.4%	4.6%	6.5%	2.8%	2.0%	2.9%	4.2%	3.2%	8.8%	6.7%	14.8%	2.4%	4.2%
Profit/Assets	0.6%	5.3%	11.2%	10.3%	8.5%	6.6%	3.1%	7.2%	13.0%	6.7%	2.1%	4.9%	7.6%	4.6%
Assets/Equity	16.3	2.6	2.2	2.4	2.5	1.9	7.1	2.3	1.6	2.0	4.3	2.6	2.2	2.0
Profit/Equity	9.5%	13.9%	24.2%	24.8%	21.3%	12.3%	21.8%	16.3%	21.2%	13.7%	8.8%	12.8%	16.6%	9.1%
A/R Days revenue out.	1606.9	33.6	59.4	22.1	3.4	23.6	155.8	56.8	53.1	33.4	140.5	32.3	5.5	83.6
Inventory turnover (COGS/Inv.)	n.a.	122.5x	n.a.	9.3x	10.6x	14.2x	1.4x	5.2x	n.a.	7.1x	n.a.	7.0x	4.3x	3.6x
Current ratio	0.82	1.19	1.91	1.24	1.52	1.68	1.57	2.17	2.14	2.10	1.36	1.11	1.77	2.72
Dep'n/Cost of sales	4.9%	5.5%	5.6%	5.4%	2.6%	1.7%	5.5%	3.3%	0.7%	9.2%	0.8%	12.5%	1.8%	4.6%
Total debt/Assets	93.9%	61.6%	54.0%	58.6%	59.8%	46.5%	86.0%	55.9%	38.8%	51.2%	76.6%	61.5%	54.3%	49.7%
Long-term debt/Equity	28.1	33.0	23.9	9.4	66.0	13.1	205.8	43.7	0.0	57.2	27.7	103.2	26.8	39.3
Total equity/Assets	6.1	38.4	46.0	41.4	40.2	53.5	14.0	44.1	61.2	48.8	23.4	38.5	45.7	50.3
Price-earnings ratio	15.0x	8.5x	17.2x	4.9x	13.6x	17.2x	14.1x	14.1x	20.1x	10.5x	9.7x	9.6x	21.5x	13.4x
Beta	0.85	1.05	1	1.2	0.95	1	1.25	1.25	1.25	1.3	1	0.7	1.15	1.1
Sales growth, 5-yr. compound	11.0%	6.0%	8.0%	7.0%	7.5%	9.0%	20.9%	11.0%	21.0%	6.0%	9.0%	1.0%	15.0%	1.5%

Case 2

EVERETT INDUSTRIES, INCORPORATED

Upon completion of her M.B.A. program in June 1973, Ms. Lynn Revere took a job as assistant to Mr. Kenneth Bedford, treasurer of Everett Industries, Incorporated. Everett Industries, located in Pittsburgh, Pennsylvania, was a diverse company with a number of manufacturing and service divisions. Its products included basic metals, specialty metal parts and products of a variety of types, hand tools, and consulting and engineering services.

Total corporate sales had grown rapidly, from about $80 million in 1968 to almost $135 million in 1972. Total earnings after taxes had risen from $3.6 million in 1968 to $4.7 million in 1972, although a significant decline in earnings had been reported during the recessionary year of 1970. Earnings per share, between 1968 and 1972, rose from $1.24 to $1.60.

When Ms. Revere reported to work on the first day, Mr. Bedford said, "I know you're aware of the overall financial results of the company. I think you'll find it useful to get better acquainted with its various parts. A quick way will be for you to look over the subsidiary statements. Why don't you look at these, and after lunch I'd like you to tell me what you think of them.

"By the way," Mr. Bedford added, "you'll find there are some statements of our competitors in these files. Why don't you give some thought to how well we are doing by comparison."

Ms. Revere decided to concentrate first on the major divisions of Everett. Three of these divisions are described briefly in Exhibit 1, which also includes a brief statement about a major competitor in each area. Financial statements for this group of companies appear in Exhibits 2 through 7.

Ms. Revere quickly noted that Everett's subsidiaries differed in a number of ways from the outside competition. Everett paid corporate taxes, for example, on a consolidated basis. Each of the subsidiaries and divisions transferred to the parent company the amount of funds it would have had to pay as an independent unit. If this amount was transferred just before year end, the divisional balance sheet would show a relatively small potential tax liability. On the other hand, if the account was not cleared out by year end, the subsidiary would show much higher liabilities for tax than would an independent company which paid its estimated tax on an installment basis.

Similarly, because there were no problems of income taxes on the intercompany transfer of funds, Everett's subsidiaries did not pay regular dividends to the parent company. Funds were loaned back and forth between the parent and subsidiary companies until it was decided to make a formal dividend payment. For her analysis, Ms. Revere restored intercompany loans to the cash balances of cash-rich divisions but left intercompany borrowing on the books of the cash-short companies as short-term loans.

Case 2 Everett Industries, Incorporated

EXHIBIT 1 EVERETT INDUSTRIES, INCORPORATED

Everett Division

SOMERVILLE ENGINEERING SERVICES COMPANY
(Exhibit 2)

Active in a wide variety of management services, concentrated in the engineering and architectural areas. The company took on private and public projects such as bridges, waterfronts, airports, highway systems, manufacturing plants, and office buildings. While Somerville prepared the design and managed the construction, it did not actually serve as contractor. Projects frequently took a number of years to complete. Revenues were recorded on a percent-of-completion basis. Projects were both fixed price and cost-plus-fixed-fee.

CAMBRIDGE QUALITY PRODUCTS, INC.
(Exhibit 4)

The products of this division were recognized as having the highest quality available in the popular to upper-price range of the hand tool market. Most of the production, however, was marketed under a private label by a leading retail chain. The production process involved shaping and finishing of raw materials in forging and machining operations. Highly skilled labor was required. A new plant had recently been opened. Its lease of $6 million was not capitalized on Cambridge's books.

WINCHESTER METALS CORPORATION
(Exhibit 6)

Operated eight plants producing a large variety of manufactured and extruded aluminum shapes as well as casting ingots which were sold to other fabricating and finishing firms. Its products were used in a wide variety of industrial and consumer durable items ranging from truck trailers to outdoor furniture. Marketing activities were confined largely to the Midwest and the East Coast.

Competition

JACOBS ENGINEERING COMPANY
(Exhibit 3)

Performed a broad range of professional services in the engineering and manufacturing areas, primarily for manufacturing companies. These included feasibility studies of all types, planning and location studies, and services for the design, construction, and start-up of plants. On some projects Jacobs provided materials, equipment, and labor. Because the profit on such sales was much smaller than on professional services, the ratio of profits to sales changed as a result of changes in the business mix.

SNAP-ON TOOLS CORPORATION
(Exhibit 5)

Distributed more than 8,000 items of mechanics' tools and similar equipment, which accounted for more than 80% of sales. The remaining sales included tool chests and automotive testing equipment. The company manufactured about 70% of its products sold. Products which were branded were sold primarily through a large network of independent distributors to whom inventory was provided on consignment. Snap-on also financed the receivables created for the ultimate customers, which were primarily mechanics and automotive repair shops.

KELLER INDUSTRIES
(Exhibit 7)

A leading producer of aluminum products and components for the housing and consumer markets, which accounted for 68% and 32% of sales, respectively. The product line included aluminum windows (of which Keller was the largest manufacturer), patio doors, outdoor furniture, ladders, and fans. Sales of building products were made primarily through a chain of warehouses but also directly to builders. Consumer products were sold directly to retailers.

EXHIBIT 2 SOMERVILLE ENGINEERING SERVICES COMPANY, SUMMARY FINANCIAL STATEMENTS (dollar figures in thousands)

	1968	*1969*	*1970*	*1971*	*1972*
INCOME STATEMENT					
Net revenues	$6,950	$7,541	$8,823	$9,860	$9,686
Cost of sales	2,563	2,951	3,813	4,129	4,097
Gross operating profit	4,387	4,590	5,010	5,731	5,589
Selling, gen. and admin. exp.	2,248	2,714	3,126	3,670	3,982
Operating profit	2,139	1,876	1,884	2,061	1,607
Other income (deductions)	—	18	8	(36)	(4)
Income taxes	1,153	1,007	959	1,018	817
Net income	$ 986	$ 887	$ 933	$1,007	$ 786
BALANCE SHEET					
Assets					
Cash, marketable securities	$ 811	$ 598	$ 463	$ 548	$1,824
Accounts receivable	2,239	2,610	2,854	3,897	4,000
Inventory	92	154	159	124	150
Other current assets	18	4	37	38	40
Total current assets	3,160	3,366	3,513	4,607	6,014
Property, plant & equipt., net	475	553	594	628	650
Other assets	54	62	428	245	350
Total assets	$3,689	$3,981	$4,535	$5,480	$7,014
Liabilities and net worth					
Bank notes, etc.	$ —	$ —	$ 620	$ —	$ —
Accounts payable	841	270	339	362	300
Long-term debt, current	—	—	54	54	48
Current income taxes	326	(94)	28	—	967
Other current liabilities	419	445	142	259	300
Total current liabilities	1,586	621	1,183	675	1,615
Deferred taxes	778	1,148	1,201	1,720	1,570
Long-term debt	—	—	257	191	149
Other	—	—	—	—	—
Total liabilities	2,364	1,769	2,641	2,586	3,334
Equity accounts	1,325	2,212	1,894	2,894	3,680
Total liabilities & net worth	$3,689	$3,981	$4,535	$5,480	$7,014
RATIO ANALYSIS					
Gross profit ÷ sales	63.1%	60.9%	56.8%	58.1%	57.7%
Net income ÷ sales	14.2	11.8	10.6	10.2	8.1
Receivables ÷ sales	32.2	34.6	32.3	39.5	41.3
Inventory ÷ sales	1.3	2.0	1.8	1.2	1.5
Current ratio	2.0×	5.4×	3.0×	6.9×	3.7×
Sales ÷ total assets	1.9	1.9	1.9	1.8	1.4
Net income ÷ total assets	26.7%	22.3%	20.6%	18.4%	11.2%
Net income ÷ capitalization	74.4	40.1	43.4	32.6	20.5
Net income ÷ equity	74.4	40.1	49.3	34.8	21.4
Total debt ÷ total assets	64.1	44.4	58.2	47.2	47.5

Case 2 Everett Industries, Incorporated

EXHIBIT 3 JACOBS ENGINEERING COMPANY, SUMMARY FINANCIAL DATA (dollar figures in millions)

	1968	*1969*	*1970*	*1971*	*1972*
INCOME STATEMENT					
Net revenues	$6.79	$12.20	$21.00	$23.90	$14.22
Cost of sales	5.23	9.66	16.38	19.10	11.07
Gross operating profit	1.56	2.54	4.62	4.80	3.15
Selling, gen. and admin. exp.	1.05	1.69	2.80	3.00	2.90
Operating profit	0.51	0.85	1.82	1.80	0.25
Other income (deductions)	0.11	0.10	0.04	0.14	(0.01)
Income taxes	0.31	0.47	0.98	0.92	0.10
Net income	$0.31	$0.48	$0.88	$1.02	$0.14
BALANCE SHEET					
Assets					
Cash, marketable securities			$1.47	$2.50	$1.95
Accounts receivable	1968–1969 Balance		2.09	2.88	2.62
Inventory	Sheet information		—	—	—
Other current assets	not available		0.08	0.09	0.21
Total current assets			3.64	5.47	4.78
Property, plant & equipt., net			0.91	2.54	2.46
Other assets			0.36	0.33	0.28
Total assets			$4.91	$8.34	$7.52
Liabilities and net worth					
Bank notes, etc.			$0.20	$0.20	$0.02
Accounts payable			1.00	1.68	1.27
Long-term debt, current			—	—	—
Current income taxes			1.04	1.18	0.80
Other current liabilities			—	—	—
Total current liabilities			2.24	3.06	2.09
Deferred taxes			—	—	—
Long-term debt			—	—	—
Other			—	—	—
Total liabilities			—	—	—
Equity accounts			2.67	5.28	5.43
Total liabilities & net worth			$4.91	$8.34	$7.52
RATIO ANALYSIS					
Gross profit ÷ sales	23.0%	20.8%	22.0%	20.1%	22.2%
Net income ÷ sales	4.6	3.9	4.2	4.3	1.0
Receivables ÷ sales	—	—	9.9	12.0	18.4
Inventory ÷ sales	—	—	—	—	—
Current ratio	—	—	1.6×	1.8×	2.3×
Sales ÷ total assets	—	—	4.3	2.9	1.9
Net income ÷ total assets	—	—	17.9%	12.2%	1.9%
Net income ÷ capitalization	—	—	33.0	19.3	2.6
Net income ÷ equity	—	—	33.0	19.3	2.6
Total debt ÷ total assets	—	—	45.6	36.7	27.8

EXHIBIT 4 CAMBRIDGE QUALITY PRODUCTS, INC. SUMMARY FINANCIAL STATEMENTS (dollar figures in millions)

	1968	*1969*	*1970*	*1971*	*1972*
INCOME STATEMENT					
Net revenues	$37.4	$42.2	$40.2	$45.0	$53.7
Cost of sales	31.9	36.2	34.7	38.0	45.9
Gross operating profit	5.5	6.2	5.5	7.0	7.8
Selling, gen. and admin. exp.	1.6	1.9	2.0	2.2	2.2
Operating profit	3.9	4.3	3.5	4.8	5.6
Other income (deductions)	(0.1)	—	—	—	—
Income taxes	2.1	2.3	1.7	2.2	2.9
Net income	$ 1.7	$ 2.0	$ 1.8	$ 2.6	$ 2.7
BALANCE SHEET					
Assets					
Cash, marketable securities	$ 2.5	$ 2.5	$ 2.8	$ 4.6	$ 6.8
Accounts receivable	3.2	4.1	3.4	4.2	4.5
Inventory	8.0	9.4	12.2	10.9	11.9
Other current assets	—	—	—	—	—
Total current assets	13.7	16.0	18.4	19.7	23.2
Property, plant & equipt., net	6.5	6.7	6.4	6.2	6.2
Other assets	0.2	—	—	—	—
Total assets	$20.4	$22.7	$24.8	$25.9	$29.4
Liabilities and net worth					
Bank notes, etc.	$ —	$ —	$ —	$ —	$ —
Accounts payable	1.1	1.5	3.0	2.0	2.3
Long-term debt, current	—	—	—	—	—
Current income taxes	1.3	0.6	0.8	2.1	2.4
Other current liabilities	1.2	1.9	1.7	1.8	2.3
Total current liabilities	3.6	4.0	5.5	5.9	7.0
Deferred taxes					
Long-term debt	0.6	0.5	0.5	0.4	0.4
Other	—	—	—	—	—
Total liabilities	4.2	4.5	6.0	6.3	7.4
Equity accounts	16.2	18.2	18.8	19.6	22.0
Total liabilities & net worth	$20.4	$22.7	$24.8	$25.9	$29.4
RATIO ANALYSIS					
Gross profit ÷ sales	14.7%	14.6%	13.7%	15.6%	14.5%
Net income ÷ sales	4.5	4.7	4.5	5.8	5.0
Receivables ÷ sales	8.6	9.7	8.5	9.3	8.4
Inventory ÷ sales	21.4	22.2	30.3	24.2	22.2
Current ratio	3.8×	4.0×	3.3×	3.3×	3.3×
Sales ÷ total assets	1.8	1.9	1.6	1.7	1.8
Net income ÷ total assets	8.3%	8.8%	7.2%	10.0%	9.2%
Net income ÷ capitalization	10.1	10.7	9.3	13.0	12.0
Net income ÷ equity	10.5	11.0	9.6	13.3	12.3
Total debt ÷ total assets	20.6	19.8	24.2	24.3	25.2

Case 2 Everett Industries, Incorporated

EXHIBIT 5 SNAP-ON TOOLS CORPORATION, SUMMARY FINANCIAL DATA (dollar figures in millions)

	1968	*1969*	*1970*	*1971*	*1972*
INCOME STATEMENT					
Net revenues	$58.5	$66.3	$76.5	$88.4	$105.1
Cost of sales	26.2	30.2	34.6	39.9	48.5
Gross operating profit	32.3	36.1	41.9	48.5	56.6
Selling, gen. and admin. exp.	20.7	23.5	27.0	31.3	36.2
Operating profit	11.6	12.6	14.9	17.2	20.4
Other income (deductions)	—	0.1	—	—	0.3
Income taxes	6.1	6.7	7.4	8.5	9.7
Net income	$ 5.5	$ 6.0	$ 7.5	$ 8.7	$ 11.0
BALANCE SHEET					
Assets					
Cash, marketable securities	$ 5.1	$ 1.4	$ 1.9	$ 1.3	$ 4.3
Accounts receivable	13.0	15.3	15.4	17.7	21.7
Inventory	19.0	23.2	26.9	30.3	33.3
Other current assets	0.7	0.9	1.4	1.7	1.6
Total current assets	37.8	40.8	45.6	51.0	60.9
Property, plant & equipt., net	7.7	8.8	11.1	11.9	13.8
Other assets	0.1	0.1	0.1	0.1	0.1
Total assets	$45.6	$49.7	$56.8	$63.0	$ 74.8
Liabilities and net worth					
Bank notes, etc.	$ —	$ 0.5	$ 2.2	$ —	$ —
Accounts payable	2.0	2.5	2.9	3.7	4.8
Long-term debt, current	0.6	0.6	0.6	0.6	0.6
Current income taxes	2.5	1.4	1.3	1.9	1.6
Other current liabilities	5.6	6.8	7.3	8.8	11.9
Total current liabilities	10.7	11.8	14.3	15.0	18.9
Deferred taxes	—	—	—	—	—
Long-term debt	3.2	2.7	2.1	1.6	1.0
Other	—	—	—	—	—
Total liabilities	13.9	14.5	16.4	16.6	19.9
Equity accounts	31.7	35.2	40.4	46.4	54.9
Total liabilities & net worth	$45.6	$49.7	$56.8	$63.0	$ 74.8
RATIO ANALYSIS					
Gross profit ÷ sales	55.2%	54.4%	54.8%	54.9%	53.9%
Net income ÷ sales	9.4	9.1	9.8	9.8	10.5
Receivables ÷ sales	22.2	23.1	20.1	20.0	20.6
Inventory ÷ sales	32.5	35.0	35.2	34.3	31.7
Current ratio	3.5×	3.5×	3.2×	3.4×	3.2×
Sales ÷ total assets	1.3	1.3	1.3	1.4	1.4
Net income ÷ total assets	12.1%	12.1%	13.2%	13.8%	14.7%
Net income ÷ capitalization	15.8	15.8	17.6	18.1	19.7
Net income ÷ equity	17.4	17.0	18.6	18.8	20.0
Total debt ÷ total assets	30.5	29.2	28.9	26.3	26.6

EXHIBIT 6 WINCHESTER METALS CORPORATION, SUMMARY FINANCIAL STATEMENTS (dollar figures in millions)

	1968	1969	1970	1971	1972
INCOME STATEMENT					
Net revenues	$15.0	$14.5	$16.0	$22.2	$26.4
Cost of sales	13.7	13.2	14.6	19.8	23.1
Gross operating profit	1.3	1.3	1.4	2.4	3.3
Selling, gen. and admin. exp.	0.6	0.7	0.7	1.2	1.5
Operating profit	0.7	0.6	0.7	1.2	1.8
Other income (deductions)	(0.1)	—	(0.1)	(0.1)	—
Income taxes	0.3	0.3	0.3	0.5	0.9
Net income	$ 0.3	$ 0.3	$ 0.3	$ 0.6	$ 0.9
BALANCE SHEET					
Assets					
Cash, marketable securities	$ 0.3	$ 0.2	$ 0.3	$ 0.3	$ 0.1
Accounts receivable	1.2	1.4	2.9	3.5	4.6
Inventory	1.1	2.1	1.5	3.4	3.7
Other current assets	—	—	—	0.2	0.3
Total current assets	2.6	3.7	4.7	7.4	8.7
Property, plant & equipt., net	1.4	1.6	1.8	3.4	3.4
Other assets	0.3	0.2	0.2	0.2	0.2
Total assets	$ 4.3	$ 5.5	$ 6.7	$11.0	$12.3
Liabilities and net worth					
Bank notes, etc.	$ 0.3	$ 1.2	$ 1.1	$ 1.2	$ 1.1
Accounts payable	0.8	1.1	1.7	3.9	4.2
Long-term debt, current	0.2	0.2	0.2	0.4	0.3
Current income taxes	0.2	0.1	0.3	0.3	0.8
Other current liabilities	0.2	0.1	0.1	0.3	0.3
Total current liabilities	1.7	2.7	3.4	6.1	6.7
Deferred taxes	—	—	0.1	0.1	0.2
Long-term debt	0.4	0.3	0.4	1.4	1.1
Other	—	—	—	—	—
Total liabilities	2.1	3.0	3.9	7.6	8.0
Equity accounts	2.2	2.5	2.8	3.4	4.3
Total liabilities & net worth	$ 4.3	$ 5.5	$ 6.7	$11.0	$12.3
RATIO ANALYSIS					
Gross profit ÷ sales	8.7%	9.0%	8.8%	10.8%	12.5%
Net income ÷ sales	2.0	2.1	1.9	2.7	3.4
Receivables ÷ sales	8.0	9.6	18.1	15.8	17.4
Inventory ÷ sales	7.3	14.5	9.4	15.3	14.0
Current ratio	1.5×	1.4×	1.4×	1.2×	1.3×
Sales ÷ total assets	3.4	2.6	2.4	2.0	2.1
Net income ÷ total assets	7.0%	5.4%	4.5%	5.4%	7.3%
Net income ÷ capitalization	11.5	10.7	9.4	12.5	16.7
Net income ÷ equity	13.6	12.0	10.7	17.6	20.9
Total debt ÷ total assets	48.8	54.5	58.2	69.1	65.0

Case 2 Everett Industries, Incorporated

EXHIBIT 7 KELLER INDUSTRIES, INC., SUMMARY FINANCIAL DATA (dollar figures in millions)

	1968	*1969*	*1970*	*1971*	*1972*
INCOME STATEMENT					
Net revenues	$90.3	$95.9	$91.3	$100.4	$130.1
Cost of sales	66.4	71.3	66.8	70.8	90.9
Gross operating profit	23.9	24.6	24.5	29.6	39.2
Selling, gen. and admin. exp.	15.7	18.7	18.6	20.2	25.0
Operating profit	8.2	5.9	5.9	9.4	14.2
Other income (deductions)	(0.9)	(1.1)	(1.3)	(1.4)	(1.7)
Income taxes	3.0	2.2	2.2	3.8	6.0
Net income	$ 4.3	$ 2.6	$ 2.4	$ 4.2	$ 6.5
BALANCE SHEET					
Assets					
Cash, marketable securities	$ 2.7	$ 2.2	$ 4.4	$ 4.6	$ 2.1
Accounts receivable	14.7	15.8	14.6	17.8	22.9
Inventory	23.2	24.1	19.8	22.6	27.5
Other current assets	0.7	1.9	2.2	1.8	2.3
Total current assets	41.3	44.0	41.0	46.8	54.8
Property, plant & equipt., net	12.1	16.3	15.6	14.9	18.0
Other assets	0.6	0.7	1.3	2.3	3.8
Total assets	$54.0	$61.0	$57.9	$ 64.0	$ 76.6
Liabilities and net worth					
Bank notes, etc.	$ 4.7	$ 3.0	$ —	$ 0.7	$ 8.0
Accounts payable	13.9	7.5	7.8	10.5	10.9
Long-term debt, current	0.8	1.0	1.0	1.0	0.9
Current income taxes	2.8	1.7	1.8	3.2	3.6
Other current liabilities	1.8	2.9	1.6	0.3	0.3
Total current liabilities	24.0	16.1	12.2	15.7	23.7
Deferred taxes	—	0.3	0.6	0.9	1.0
Long-term debt	9.5	23.3	22.2	22.0	20.9
Other	—	—	—	—	—
Total liabilities	33.5	39.6	35.0	38.6	45.6
Equity accounts	20.5	21.4	22.9	25.4	31.0
Total liabilities & net worth	$54.0	$61.0	$57.9	$ 64.0	$ 76.6
RATIO ANALYSIS					
Gross profit ÷ sales	26.5%	25.6%	26.8%	29.5%	30.1%
Net income ÷ sales	4.8	2.7	2.6	4.2	5.0
Receivables ÷ sales	16.3	16.5	16.0	17.7	17.6
Inventory ÷ sales	25.7	25.1	21.7	22.5	21.1
Current ratio	1.7×	2.7×	3.4×	3.0×	2.2×
Sales ÷ total assets	1.7	1.6	1.6	1.6	1.7
Net income ÷ total assets	8.0%	4.3%	4.1%	6.6%	8.5%
Net income ÷ capitalization	14.3	5.8	5.3	8.9	12.5
Net income ÷ equity	21.0	12.1	10.5	16.5	21.0
Total debt ÷ total assets	62.0	64.9	60.4	60.3	59.5

Case **3**

DYNAPUMP CORPORATION

In January 1982, Ms. Karen Thompson, an account officer at Midwestern Security Bank, was reviewing the financial activities of the Dynapump Corporation. The company president, Mr. Allen Smith, had recently requested an increase in Dynapump's $4 million line in anticipation of continued rapid sales growth. Dynapump had issued common stock in 1980, but the proceeds proved insufficient to meet its growing financial requirements. By the end of 1981, therefore, the company had nearly exhausted its $4 million revolving credit facility with Midwestern Security. In addition, slow payments to trade creditors had prompted calls to the bank concerning the financial soundness of Dynapump. (Exhibits 1 and 2 present Dynapump's recent financial statements.)

Mr. Smith also asked about a "cash cap" on interest payments at the present level of 16 percent. If rates increased, the amount due would be accrued but not paid until the rates dropped back below 16 percent.

COMPANY BACKGROUND

The Dynapump Corporation was founded in 1974 to produce pumps and related equipment. An excellent marketing effort contributed to the company's good reputation in the industry and to an impressive 31 percent compound sales growth rate since 1978. Its midwestern location afforded good access to regional markets, and the growing number of company-operated sales offices was largely responsible for penetrating more distant domestic and international markets. The company also utilized a large network of independent distributors. Its products were well established in the portable and stationary segments of the pump market. The company was noted for its engineering and technical expertise, which was giving it entry to special markets.

Product innovation, an important factor in the company's rapid growth, had resulted in a diversified product line and in the introduction of more reliable and economical pumps. In 1979, for example, Dynapump had acquired a license to incorporate a new technology into its product design. These innovations considerably reduced downtime and maintenance costs. Installation costs associated with the new generation of pumps were lower because of size and weight reductions made possible by the new technology. Also, Dynapump had recently developed a superior, patentable internal lubricant which in tests had noticeably improved the operational characteristics of its pumps.

Although the licenses were readily obtainable, the larger companies in the industry continued to concentrate on producing less-advanced designs, despite the acknowledged benefits of the new technology. Their existing production facilities, representing a large capital investment, were not capable of producing the new design. Dynapump was thus able to achieve increasing market penetration with its products.

To a large extent, Dynapump's production process involved assembling of basic components, castings, and other parts supplied by several major manufacturers. These purchased components, most of which were available from multiple sources, typically amounted to 80 percent of the product cost. Dynapump manufactured those components which were not readily available externally, including advanced designs developed through the company's research activities.

The labor force of 200 people was not unionized. Employees enjoyed generous fringe benefits including profit sharing, free lunches and

Case prepared by Kevin Ramundo with the cooperation of individuals and institutions that wish to remain anonymous. Certain of the company's characteristics and financial information have been changed to protect confidential information without altering the nature of the managerial decision.

uniforms, flexible working hours, subsidized grocery shopping and gasoline purchases, and the use of excellent sports facilities. Despite being paid wages lower than the surrounding area, the labor force was stable with minimal turnover.

Mr. Smith and the other executives of the company had had substantial experience in the industry, especially in marketing and engineering, before establishing Dynapump. Company executives collectively owned 23 percent of the outstanding common stock.

INDUSTRY

The pump industry was quite competitive, with the largest of four major manufacturers having a 40 percent share of the portable and stationary market. Successful penetration of a market depended on providing a broad product line. No one company dominated any geographical region of the United States. An industry growth rate of 15 percent was predicted based upon expected growth among the principal users of pumps, the construction and mining industries. Currently, Dynapump had approximately 10 percent of the portable and stationary pump market.

The largest manufacturers, in contrast to Dynapump, were vertically and horizontally integrated; consequently, they were relatively low-cost producers. Despite this advantage, Mr. Smith thought price-cutting by the largest manufacturer was unlikely because it could encourage antitrust investigation.

Within the industry, there was strong speculation that the Environmental Protection Agency (EPA) would impose additional noise reduction standards on pumps. Mr. Smith had assured the bank that Dynapump had the required technology for compliance, but he was unable to elaborate on the costs involved and the effect on profit margins.

FINANCIAL CONDITION

In recent discussions with Mr. Smith, Ms. Thompson learned that sales forecasts indicated annual growth during 1982 and 1983 in the range of 20 to 30 percent. While sharing in the overall industry growth, Dynapump expected to increase its market share through aggressive marketing, service delivery, and product innovation.

The decline in cost of goods as a percentage of sales from 63.4 percent in 1979 to 61.2 percent in 1981 reflected the increased proportion of direct sales being made through Dynapump's sales offices. This trend was expected to continue, but costs would return to approximately 63 percent because of the increasing proportion of overseas sales on which smaller margins were realized. Growth in the number of sales offices explained higher selling, general, and administrative expenses.

Rental equipment revenue was predicted to increase 10 percent annually, requiring similar net expansion in that asset group. Capital expenditures on plant and equipment were estimated at $3 million during the next two years. Utilization of investment tax credits would keep income taxes at the rate recently experienced.

Increasing pressure from trade creditors had convinced Mr. Smith to accelerate payments in the future. He did not, however, expect to be able to meet the industry standard of sixty days.

During their conversation, Ms. Thompson inquired about the possibility of a stock issue as an alternative to additional debt financing. The company's investment banker believed that an issue would be feasible but undesirable so soon after the 1980 issue. Mr. Smith thought that the stock was undervalued at the current price–earnings ratio of 11 and was not seriously considering this alternative. Ms. Thompson thought that his reluctance reflected his desire to avoid diluting his 10 percent equity interest.

In Ms. Thompson's opinion, Dynapump was not giving the proper attention to financial planning. External financing had been required in each of the last three years, past financial forecasts had been inaccurate, and unexpected requests for line increases had occurred regularly. If she did decide to lend additional funds, Ms. Thompson would have to recommend an appropriate loan structure, interest rate, and, perhaps, security arrangements.

In completing her review of Dynapump, Ms. Thompson noted that the current unsecured bank line at prime plus 1 percent had been approved in 1979 when the bank was aggressively seeking new customers. Conditions had changed, loan demand was strong, and the prime interest rate was at 16 percent. In early 1982, the bank was interested in reducing its loan portfolio risk.

Case 3 Dynapump Corporation

EXHIBIT 1 INCOME STATEMENTS FOR YEARS ENDING DECEMBER 31, 1979–1981 (in thousands except per-share figure)

	1979	*1980*	*1981*
Net sales	$12,641	$18,131	$28,758
Cost of goods sold	8,016	11,145	17,589
Gross profit	$ 4,625	$ 6,986	$11,169
Selling, general, and administrative expenses	3,025	4,512	7,091
Depreciation expense*	185	289	517
Interest expense	188	161	461
Profit before tax	$ 1,227	$ 2,024	$ 3,100
Taxes	582	900	1,391
Profit after tax	$ 645	$ 1,124	$ 1,709
Common shares outstanding	1,049	1,313	1,313
Earnings per share	$0.61	$0.86	$1.30

*Approximately half the depreciation expense was incurred for the rental equipment.

Case 3 Dynapump Corporation

EXHIBIT 2 BALANCE SHEETS AS OF DECEMBER 31, 1979–1981 (in thousands)

	1979	*1980*	*1981*
ASSETS			
Cash	$ 703	$ 951	$ 1,352
Accounts receivable	2,720	4,232	5,721
Inventory	3,225	5,485	8,149
Prepaid expenses	49	25	123
Current assets	$6,697	$10,693	$15,345
Gross fixed assets	$1,319	$ 1,883	$ 2,710
Accumulated depreciation	319	325	523
Net fixed assets	$1,000	$ 1,558	$ 2,187
Rental equipment	514	960	1,311
Other assets	300	334	414
Total assets	$8,511	$13,545	$19,257
LIABILITIES AND NET WORTH			
Trade accounts payable	$1,757	$ 2,955	$ 5,011
Income taxes payable	211	244	472
Accruals	419	534	945
Other current liabilities	94	149	—
Current liabilities	$2,481	$ 3,882	$ 6,428
Deferred taxes	$ 68	$ 121	$ 217
Long-term debt due banks	2,126	2,199	3,560
Common stock	1,814	4,197	4,197
Earned surplus	2,022	3,146	4,855
Total liabilities and net worth	$8,511	$13,545	$19,257

Case 4

PIEDMONT PAPER PRODUCTS COMPANY

On March 15, 1989, Ms. Marilyn Meade, loan officer at Fidelity State Bank and Trust Company of Charlotte, North Carolina, was reviewing the credit file of Piedmont Paper Products Company. Mr. S. Ormand Stephens, president of Piedmont, had just called requesting a 90-day waiver of a covenant in Piedmont's $2.7 million term loan agreement with Fidelity and with National City Bank of Atlanta, Georgia. Mr. Stephens informed Ms. Meade that preliminary financial statements just completed for the 1989 fiscal year, which ended February 28, showed Piedmont would be in violation of a covenant which specified that Piedmont maintain a current ratio of at least 1.5 times. Mr. Stephens attributed the problem to temporary industry conditions which had resulted in Piedmont's accumulating an excess of inventory. Paper prices had been rising, and Mr. Stephens had wanted to lay in a supply at lower prices. Recent increases in bank interest rates had made this an expensive strategy. The company had also stretched its accounts payable somewhat to finance these requirements.

As part of an inventory reduction effort, Mr. Stephens was cancelling a contract with Universal Paper, Inc., calling for Piedmont to purchase 1,500 tons a month from Universal. This action would require Piedmont to clear up its $900,000 account with Universal by April 1. He also wished to bring down Piedmont's payables balance to a more reasonable level of 50 days as soon as possible, with a target of 45 days as a corporate objective.

Case prepared with the cooperation of individuals and institutions that wish to remain anonymous. Certain of the company's characteristics and financial information have been changed to protect confidential information without altering the nature of the managerial decision.

Piedmont had an offer of a six-month loan of $1 million from Imperial Valley Paper Corporation, Piedmont's most important and oldest supplier, to help support Piedmont's financial needs until its inventory level could be reduced. The loan would require the approval of Imperial Valley's directors, which was expected to be granted at the board's next meeting in June. Piedmont was currently buying 6,000 tons a month from Imperial Valley and 1,900 from several smaller suppliers. It was planned to maintain these purchase levels.

PIEDMONT PAPER PRODUCTS COMPANY

Piedmont, located in Winston-Salem, produced brown paper shopping bags. The conversion of Kraft paper into shopping bags was not a complicated procedure. Little investment in plant and equipment was required. The market was fragmented and localized, with key success variables being quality of service and proximity to the end user. Piedmont was well established in the area within a 500-to-600-mile radius of Winston-Salem.

Piedmont's business was subject to some cyclical variation, although management had shown considerable ability to increase unit volume as prices fell. The following table provides summary operating results for 1982–1985, and Exhibits 1 and 2 present complete financial statements for 1986–1989. Net profits for 1983, 1984 and 1986 were adversely affected by extraordinary losses from a fire.

	(thousands of dollars)			
	1982	*1983*	*1984*	*1985*
Sales	15,630	16,123	16,323	19,632
Net Profit (FIFO basis)	377	74	(20)	539

Sales in the fiscal year ended February 28, 1989 were $38.9 million. Two-thirds of this total was produced speculatively, with the other third being made-to-order specialty bags for large New York department stores such as Saks Fifth Avenue and Tiffany's.

Periodic shortages of raw paper had been a serious problem in the past. Management had decided in the last two years to build raw material inventory in order to hedge against supply shortages and price inflation. Raw material inventory currently composed 77 percent of inventories' total dollar value. Its value on a first-in, first-out cost was approximately 40 percent greater than the last-in, first-out basis (averaging $176 a ton) on which the statements in Exhibits 1 and 2 were prepared. The LIFO accounting method increased the cost of goods sold in 1986 by about $400,000 and the cost had been averaging about $700,000 more in subsequent years from what it would have been under FIFO accounting.

Purchases had been running at 9,400 tons per month with sales of 9,000 tons per month. Raw paper costs had recently been about $250 per ton. The supply of paper had become much more plentiful in the last three months due mainly to the decline in paper consumption and the excess capacity in the paper industry as a whole. Mr. Stephens could foresee no raw paper shortages during the next few years. He therefore planned to reduce Piedmont's current raw material inventory of 36,000 tons to 21,000 tons by the end of December, 1989. There were no plans to try to reduce the dollar level of either the work-in-process or finished goods inventories. The average LIFO cost of the 15,000 tons was $200 a ton.

Mr. Stephens projected sales in the fiscal years 1990 and 1991 to be $39.9 million and $41.7 million, respectively. Despite the apparent cooling off of the economy, he had not yet detected any softening in demand for Piedmont's products or in its cost of materials. (The shipment schedule for fiscal year 1990, presented in Exhibit 3, was prepared on this assumption, with cost of sales other than raw materials expected to be approximately 11 percent of sales.) He estimated that sales could grow to $46.7 million before it would be necessary to increase plant capacity. Capital expenditures of $290,000 were planned in fiscal year 1990 for plant modernization, to be installed in the latter half of the year. Depreciation of $45,000 a month was expected in 1990. Selling, general, and administrative costs would be at least $400,000 a month and perhaps as high as $420,000.

With respect to other changes in the balance sheet, the accounts receivable balance was currently 40 days' most recent sales outstanding based on sales of $2,880,000 in February and about the same in January. Mr. Stephens thought this figure would increase to 45 days' most recent sales outstanding in March and April, with a return to 40 days' most recent in May. He expected the 40 days' most recent sales outstanding to be the collection period also in February 1990. The income taxes due on February 28, 1989 had already been paid earlier in March. Payments of one-fourth of total annual estimated tax liabilities (at the tax rate of 34 percent) would be due 15 days after the end of each fiscal quarter. Accruals were not expected to change significantly at the level of operation forecast.

THE LOAN AGREEMENT

During a recent visit to Piedmont, Ms. Meade had been impressed by its facilities as well as by its management. Mr. Stephens and Mr. Robert S. Phillips, the vice president of Piedmont, owned about 80 percent of the company's stock. The remainder of the stock was owned by their relatives and associates.

All of Piedmont's long-term debt was held by Fidelity and National City Bank, with the exception of a small loan of $43,000 from a stockholder which was not being amortized. The $2.7-million bank term loan was taken down on February 28, 1987 and was being amortized in quarterly installments of $97,500 plus interest, which began June 30, 1988. Final maturity of National City's 62 percent participation was June 30, 1992, when amortization of Fidelity's portion would begin.

The terms of the loan required Piedmont to maintain a current ratio of not less than 1.5 times and net current assets of at least $2.5 million. Compliance with the covenants was to be determined by reference to the certified financial statements, which were prepared on a LIFO basis. Short-term debt was restricted to $1.5 million above the $1.0 million advanced to Piedmont by Mr. Stephens himself in 1986 and was being provided by Fidelity at prime. The short-term debt was subordinated to the long-term bank debt, but none of the company's debt was secured. Net worth was to be maintained at not less than $2.53 million. Dividends were prohibited. The interest for the long-term debt was 2 percent above prime, the prime rate currently being 10 percent.

Piedmont's debt service had been satisfactory. Until now, there had been no problem with the loan covenants.

FIDELITY'S SITUATION

Piedmont was a major customer of Fidelity. Mr. Stephens and Mr. Phillips also were involved as investors in a number of other local businesses which had present or potential banking relationships with Fidelity. In late 1988 and early 1989, the credit crisis had restricted Fidelity's ability to increase credit facilities to any except their best customers. Fidelity, however, was a conservatively managed institution and therefore had not experienced the severe liquidity and profit problems of some other banks in the region. The bank's emphasis in March 1989 remained on cautious increases of lines to only the best customers.

National City Bank of Atlanta was an important correspondent of Fidelity's. A portion of Piedmont's term loan had been offered to them because Fidelity was becoming concerned at the size of its exposure to Piedmont even though Fidelity could have managed the entire line within its legal limit. Mr. Stephens had welcomed the addition of a second bank. He, too, had become uneasy with the size of the line and had indicated his intention to involve other banks if Fidelity did not take the initiative.

Fidelity was the agent for the loan, with National City participating as a last-in, first-out lender.

Ms. Meade had told Mr. Stephens she would provide a reply to his request within a week, but before she had completed her analysis, Mr. Stephens had called again.

"For a variety of family reasons," he said, "we have been asked to buy out the 20 percent interest in Piedmont which Bob Phillips and I don't own. We think they will settle on a price of $1 million or perhaps $1.2 million at the outside." He explained that the purchase would have to be effected by Piedmont's buying the stock for its treasury sometime during the last half of the fiscal year. "We're going to have our annual shareholders' meeting in a couple of weeks," Mr. Stephens continued, "when we'll be talking this over further. I know the question will come up about what the banks think, so I thought I'd ask plenty of time in advance."

Case 4 Piedmont Paper Products Company

EXHIBIT 1 INCOME STATEMENT FOR THE FISCAL YEARS ENDING FEBRUARY 28, 1986–1989 (dollar figures in thousands)

	1986	*1987*	*1988*	*1989**
Net sales	$21,290	$24,750	$32,070	$38,890
Cost of goods sold	16,240	19,860	25,300	31,050
Gross profit	$ 5,050	$ 4,890	$ 6,770	$ 7,840
Selling and administrative expenses	3,260	3,550	4,360	4,860
Depreciation	390	440	500	520
Interest expense	270	420	420	470
Other expense (income)	(80)	(60)	(80)	(160)
Profit before tax	$ 1,210	$ 540	$ 1,570	$ 2,150
Tax	590	250	540	730
Extraordinary charges	210	-0-	-0-	-0-
Net Profit	$ 410	$ 290	$ 1,030	$ 1,420

*Preliminary and unaudited.

Case 4 Piedmont Paper Products Company

EXHIBIT 2 BALANCE SHEETS FOR THE FISCAL YEARS ENDING FEBRUARY 28, 1986–1989 (dollar figures in thousands)

	1986	*1987*	*1988*	*1989**
ASSETS				
Cash	$ 90	$ 130	$ 240	$ 250
Accounts receivable	2,220	3,050	2,900	3,840
Inventory (LIFO)	4,570	4,560	5,190	8,220
Prepaid expenses	120	160	150	270
Current assets	$7,000	$ 7,900	$ 8,480	$12,580
Net fixed assets	1,970	2,050	2,250	3,030
Other assets	280	300	430	810
Total assets	$9,250	$10,250	$11,160	$16,420
LIABILITIES AND OWNERS' EQUITY				
Notes payable	$2,940	$ 1,000	$ 1,000	$ 2,440
Accounts payable—trade	2,900	2,900	2,480	5,540
Income taxes payable	90	40	640	270
Current maturity long-term debt	130	100	340	390
Accruals	460	460	250	320
Current liabilities	$6,520	$ 4,500	$ 4,710	$ 8,960
Deferred taxes	100	100	120	120
Long-term debt	90	2,820	2,470	2,060
Total liabilities	$6,710	$ 7,420	$ 7,300	$11,140
Common stock and capital surplus	80	80	80	80
Earned surplus	2,460	2,750	3,780	5,200
Total owners' equity	$2,540	$ 2,830	$ 3,860	5,280
Total liabilities and owners' equity	$9,250	$10,250	$11,160	$16,420

*Preliminary and unaudited.

Case 4 Piedmont Paper Products Company

EXHIBIT 3 FISCAL YEAR 1990 SHIPPING SCHEDULE

Period	*Tons Shipped*
March 1989	8,500
April	10,000
May	9,000
June	8,000
July	8,000
August	9,500
Sept.–Nov.	33,000
Dec. 1989–Feb. 1990	24,000
TOTAL	110,000

Case 5

JOYCE CHEMICAL COMPANY

As Edward Cummings walked past his boss's door, Mr. Browning hailed him. "Ed, come on in," he called. "Here's a situation that needs a fast review. Why don't you see what you can do with it."

Mr. Cummings, who had come to work with Joyce Chemical Company as a senior credit representative in October, 1971, was a recent graduate of a managerially oriented MBA Program. He had worked with a bank for a year after graduation, until he joined Joyce. He was responsible for evaluating credit customers and supervising credit and collection arrangements for higher risk accounts in the Chicago area under the immediate supervision of Mr. Browning, the regional credit manager. Although Joyce had organized its manufacturing and sales along product lines, credit management was centralized for all product groups through regional credit offices. Joyce was a medium-sized chemical company, with headquarters in the Midwest.

On Mr. Browning's desk was a thick pile of papers, bulging out of one of the red folders used to file difficult accounts. "The local sales rep in plastic resins called this morning to say he heard one of our more interesting clients [here Mr. Browning raised his eyebrows] is in the hospital. Rumor has it that he had another bleeding ulcer attack a couple of days ago. I'll bet he was overindulging while celebrating New Year's Eve even though he's had this problem for a couple of years and it has been getting more severe. Anyway, the account is not strong. Call the hospitals to see if you can track him down. Look over the account to see what we need to do. You're supposed to be trained in this sort of decision making. Let me know what you recommend by midafternoon." With those words and a smile, Mr. Browning pushed the folder across the desk to Mr. Cummings.

Mr. Cummings first called several hospitals, and finally found that a Mr. Pound, of the proper address, had indeed suffered a severe ulcer attack, was in intensive care, and could not be disturbed. Before calling Mr. Pound's company, Eliot Manufacturing Corporation, Mr. Cummings reviewed the information available in the credit file.

ELIOT MANUFACTURING COMPANY

Mr. Pound had worked for some years as a salesman for a company producing plastic garment hangers and miscellaneous fastenings and clips for the garment industry. In the early 1960s, Mr. Pound decided to go into business for himself, founding Eliot Manufacturing Company. Joyce Chemical agreed to supply him with his raw materials.

The credit file noted that Mr. Pound was the sole owner of the company. He also appeared to be the only member of management with drive and experience in general business and sales. Two other officers of the firm had left during the difficult 1971 fiscal year, partly as an economy move and partly as a result of differences about how the business should be operated. A credit investigation noted that little confidence should be placed in Mr. Pound's new management team.

The plastic hanger business was characterized by intensive competition. Plastic hangers of certain specifications were essentially a commodity, with no product or brand differentiation. Entry into the business was relatively easy, with second-hand injection molding machines being comparatively inexpensive. The dies were somewhat more expensive, but once obtained could be used virtually indefinitely.

Competition among plastic fabricating firms was on a price, service, and delivery basis. Competition among the suppliers of resin seldom took the form of price concessions, however.

Credit accommodations were a more normal form. Thus, the essential characteristic for success in the garment hanger business was high volume and low unit cost, attained by maximum utilization of machines (often on a three-shift basis), aggressive personal selling efforts, and careful control of overhead. Fast-cycle machines were an advantage. Eliot's equipment was relatively inefficient by current standards.

Although Mr. Pound had attempted to diversify his product line, his efforts had been unsuccessful. Eliot's business thus continued to be heavily dependent on the garment business, whose cyclical nature caused periodic problems for its suppliers.

HISTORY OF THE RELATIONSHIP BETWEEN JOYCE AND ELIOT

Joyce's original terms in 1963 included a $5,000 line of credit to Eliot on a net 30-day basis. By 1967, these terms had been changed to $50,000 on a 60-day basis. This credit arrangement was maintained until 1968 even though, on several occasions, Joyce's exposure temporarily exceeded the credit limit. In November 1968, however, Eliot Manufacturing was unable to meet its payment schedule. At the suggestion of Mr. Pound, Joyce raised its credit limit to $100,000 and in addition accepted a delayed payment note for the $31,000 representing September 1968 purchases. (Recent financial statements are included in Exhibits 1, 2, and 3.)

After reviewing Eliot's performance in the fiscal year ending March 31, 1969, Joyce's marketing department urged higher credit limits so that Joyce would remain Eliot's prime supplier of resin. A total of 4.5 million pounds of the resin had been sold to Eliot in fiscal 1969. Joyce's credit line was in excess of $140,000, all of which was utilized. During 1969, Eliot had doubled its plant capacity, financed by a three-year mortgage loan at a 12 percent interest rate from its factor.

By December 1970, Joyce's exposure had widened to a $150,000 credit line at 75 days plus a 12-month note arrangement for $50,000 of Eliot's outstanding payables, beginning in March 1971. To compensate for this expanded risk, two provisions were made. First, Joyce took a secondary secured position on Eliot's equipment, receivables, and inventory, which were worth an estimated $300,000 in liquidation. The equipment alone was worth perhaps $50,000. In addition, Joyce was granted the security of a $100,000 life insurance policy on Mr. Pound and assumed the annual premium of about $600.

During fiscal 1971, Eliot attempted to counter slackening demand resulting from fashion changes and uncertainties in the garment industry. This aggressive sales program resulted in a sizable charge to income for doubtful collection of outstanding accounts receivable during that year.

The financial deterioration, however, continued. To reduce costs, the sales manager, the controller, and several other employees were released. In March 1971, after unsuccessfully attempting to get Joyce's release of its security so that further capital could be raised, Mr. Pound suffered a major ulcer attack. Eliot Manufacturing also defaulted on its first note payment to Joyce on March 15th.

By this time, Joyce's marketing department favored terminating the relationship with Eliot, which would probably force the company into bankruptcy. Mr. Cummings gathered that Eliot had been cutting its prices so low that its competition was accusing Joyce of giving price breaks. The marketing department was embarrassed by the unjustified allegations. Yet, during the remainder of calendar 1971, Eliot remained in business even though terms were cash payment on delivery of raw material. Deliveries were made three to four times a week. Each delivery required a cash payment of $3,000 to $4,000.

As the summary income statement in Exhibit 2 points out, sales remained at a depressed level throughout most of fiscal 1972. Resin sales to Eliot had declined to 4.2 million pounds. Mr. Pound was optimistic about a turnaround in fiscal 1973. He confidently expected to purchase 5.0 million pounds of resin during calendar 1972.

In late calendar 1971, Joyce agreed to a $150,000 demand note and an installment note to cover the defaulted $50,000. Payment on the former was suspended until late 1972 while $2,000 monthly installments were to be applied against the defaulted $50,000 note until March 1972, when further payments would be renegotiated upon the close of Eliot's fiscal year.

Throughout this period, Mr. Pound had primarily utilized funds provided by Joyce as trade credit and the proceeds realized from accounts receivable loans from a factor to keep his business going. As best Mr. Cummings could determine from the credit file, Joyce was the only trade payable account of any significance. The factor would loan up to 80 percent of approved accounts at an interest rate of approximately 13.5 percent a year.

According to the most recent balance sheet of September 30, 1971 (provided in Exhibit 3), the factor was also due $37,500 on the machinery mortgage, currently being retired at about $4,000 per month. Mr. Cummings thought this equipment might bring $50,000 if liquidated in an orderly manner in the open market. Other assets included accounts receivable that appeared to be generally collectible, although they were pledged to cover the factor's receivable loan, which had totaled $141,000 on September 30, 1971. Miscellaneous assets of about $50,000 would have little value above liquidation costs.

From the record, Mr. Cummings gathered that Mr. Pound had been a difficult person to negotiate with. His mercurial disposition and behavior made it hard to obtain firm understandings which, when agreed to, seemed quickly to become cloudy. He seemed to find it hard to distinguish between his personal life and the corporation. During the period of financial strain, for example, Eliot Manufacturing had at least temporarily been the owner of a vacation home and power boat in a fashionable resort area north of Chicago. Thus, Mr. Pound's personal guarantee of the payables was of little financial value.

PROFITABILITY OF THE ACCOUNT

The plastic resin sales were part of Joyce's industrial plastics division. While it was more profitable than some other molding materials, other division products that required the same equipment, such as high-density polyethylene, were more lucrative. The estimated financial characteristics of the plastic resin were as follows:

Sales price per pound	10.00¢
Manufacturing costs	4.95
Freight and handling	1.07
Assigned overhead (mostly R & D)	0.40
Allocated overhead	0.87
Depreciation	0.64

While Joyce had no established minimum rate of return for accounts receivable, in recent years the company had been earning approximately 5 percent after tax on total assets.

A FINAL CALL

With his study of the credit file complete, Mr. Cummings called Eliot Manufacturing to ask Mr. Pound's second-in-command, the controller, how the company was getting on.

"How's the boss?" asked Mr. Cummings when the controller came on the line.

"Oh, he's away on a selling trip," said the controller.

After only a momentary pause, Mr. Cummings thanked the controller for this information, said he would call later, and hung up the phone.

Case 5 Joyce Chemical Company

EXHIBIT 1 ELIOT MANUFACTURING COMPANY, INCOME STATEMENT FOR FISCAL YEARS ENDING MARCH 31 (dollar figures in thousands)

	1967	*1968*	*1969*	*1970*	*1971*
Net Sales	$972	$1194	$1330	$1741	$1788
Cost of goods sold	812	977	991	1350	1497
Gross margin	$160	$ 217	$ 339	$ 391	$ 291
Provision for doubtful accounts	—	—	—	5	53
Selling and administrative expenses	138	188	275	309	314
Interest	—	—	—	55	61
Employee profit sharing	—	15	15	—	—
Net income before tax*	$ 22	$ 14	$ 49	$ 22	($137)
Depreciation charged to operations	$ 22	$ 28	$ 37	$ 40	$ 51

*The Eliot Manufacturing Company had elected in 1960 to file as a "Subchapter S" corporation, whereby its profits or losses were transferred for tax purposes to the stockholders individually. Taxable net income is not taxable to the company under these conditions but is taxable to the shareholders even though no dividends have been paid.

6 months ending September 1971	
Sales	$679
Cost of goods sold	532
Net income	22*
9 months ending December 31, 1971**	
Sales	$1,060
Cost of goods sold	833
Net income	24*

*Includes $2,000 from sale of land, house, and improvements for approximately $32,000 from which the mortgage was satisfied. Depreciation of $24,000 charged to operations.

**Estimated as of December 15, 1971.

EXHIBIT 3 ELIOT MANUFACTURING COMPANY, BALANCE SHEET AS OF MARCH 31, 1967–71, AND SEPTEMBER 30, 1971 (dollar figures in thousands)

	March 31,					*Sept. 30,*
	1967	*1968*	*1969*	*1970*	*1971*	*1971*
ASSETS						
Cash	$ 9	$ 12	$ 6	$ 10	—	$ 15
Accounts receivable	141	151	204	376	326	235
Inventory	35	25	53	85	76	67
Loan receivable	15	22	23	17	35	25
Other	4	3	14	10	23	14
Total current assets	$204	$213	$300	$498	$460	$356
Fixed assets (net)*	135	161	238	291	225	173
Other	4	4	3	10	8	7
Total Assets	$343	$378	$541	$799	$693	$536
LIABILITIES						
Overdraft	—	—	—	—	$ 6	—
Accounts payable	$151	$153	$190	$236	$288	$ 86
Due finance company	108	78	165	231	220	178
Notes payable—trade	3	2	6	34	50	185
Other loans payable	10	12	7	36	33	26
Payroll taxes and accrued expenses	13	30	46	27	51	27
Total current liabilities	$285	$275	$414	$564	$648	$502
Long-term debt**	39	70	45	131	81	48
Total liabilities	$324	$345	$459	$695	$729	$550
Common stock and surplus	32	32	32	33	33	33
Retained earnings	(13)	1	50	72	(65)	(43)
Treasury stock	—	—	—	(1)	(4)	(4)
Total liabilities and net worth	$343	$378	$541	$799	$693	$536

*On March 31, 1969, 1970, and 1971, a house was carried in the gross fixed-asset account at approximately $24,000. The associated mortgage of $18,000 was shown as long-term debt. The house was sold and the mortgage repaid before September 30, 1971.

**Includes current portion of:	$25	$46	$24	$ 50	$52	$24
Long-term debt due finance co.	—	—	—	$112	$62	—

Case 6

CHISTE COMPONENTS CORPORATION

In October 1988, Mr. George Murphy, loan officer at Empire National Bank of New York, was reviewing the file of Chiste Components Corporation (CCC). CCC's management, expressing concern with the slow sales growth in their Electronic Parts Division, had requested $1.0 million of additional bank debt to finance the opening of two new franchised distributors. This was to be a prelude to raising more equity to finance more distributors. Empire was the agent for a five-bank lending group which had already extended an $8.5 million 30-day line of credit to CCC. CCC also had $7.9 million of long-term debt owed to insurance companies. Exhibits 1 and 2 present consolidated financial statements for the fiscal years ended September 30, 1986 through 1988.

CCC, founded in 1951, had developed into a manufacturer and distributor of peripheral computer equipment, such as keyboards and inexpensive video display units, and hardware. The computer equipment and electronic parts were organized into two separate divisions, each with its own plant. Interdivisional sales were negligible, in part because both divisions purchased many components and subcomponents from contractors. Significant discounts were available for prompt payment to suppliers. The need to take these discounts limited CCC's ability to stretch its accounts payable. Both plants and the corporate offices were located in Wilmington, North Carolina. The company enjoyed an excellent reputation for its top-quality products within its price ranges.

The present management took control of the company in 1981 with the goal of expansion through the introduction of new products and broader distribution. CCC began selling terminals in 1982 and by 1988 offered six different models ranging in price from $250 to $450. A selection of keyboards was also offered in the computer equipment line. The rest of the computer equipment line had also been expanded. Three new modems were introduced in fiscal year 1988 with prices ranging from $90 to $200. These products were marketed nationwide through specialty stores, catalog sales,. and major chains. Financial statements for the Computer Equipment Division are shown in Exhibits 3 and 4.

The Electronics Parts Division currently packaged, assembled, or manufactured and distributed over 2,500 different condensers, resistors, transistors, fuses, integrated circuits, jacks, switches, connectors, cables, and other hardware items. These parts did not require high technology to manufacture and generally retailed for less than $1 per item although some assemblies could sell for $100 or more. The division had no problem meeting production targets, as subcontracting levels (currently about 30 percent of the division's production) could be changed easily. The Parts Division's total fixed costs were approximately $3.7 million per year excluding interest. CCC's management did not plan to expand its manufacturing capacity for electronic parts but rather planned to concentrate on their marketing. Management was most concerned that the parts' sales performance had not matched that of the computer equipment. Exhibits 5 and 6 provide financial statements for the Parts Division.

The Parts division sold directly to national chains and since 1986 had also used franchised distributors to sell to small specialty electronics outlets. Sales to these franchised distributors in 1986, 1987, and 1988 were $5.0 million, $5.7 million, and $4.6 million respectively. The marketing strategy of using franchised distributors, which CCC's management intended to emphasize, was credited with boosting the Parts Division's sales from $18.0 to $22.1 million in fiscal 1986. Ten franchises were opened that year, but no new ones had been added since.

The agreement between CCC and the franchised dealers specified that the latter were to purchase 75 percent of their goods from CCC. They were prohibited from carrying competing lines of electronic parts and were expected to push CCC's products devotedly. The agreement further specified that CCC would accept one-year notes as payment for inventory purchased by the franchises and would buy back any obsolete inventory. These small specialty distributors were often in a weak working-capital position, and such financial support was necessary for them to be able to carry a broad selection of CCC's parts. CCC was also to render marketing and management advice.

The franchised distributors reported sales of \$6.4 million in 1986, \$5.9 million in 1987, and \$6.5 million in 1988. The distributors' markup on selling price was 25 percent. Approximately one-third of their purchases and sales represented other companies' products. These were said to be noncompeting items. CCC did not object to the distributors' failure to maintain a product mix of 75 percent CCC merchandise because management thought these outlets were an integral part of CCC's overall distribution network and represented the best management available. No inventory had been repurchased from the franchises. Management thought, though, that "obsolete" inventory could be sold to the public at 35 percent of its retail selling price.

CCC's management estimated the electronic parts market at over \$500 million annually. They anticipated a growth rate of 8 percent per year. The industry had been characterized by rapid technological advances such as the widespread adoption of transistors beginning in the middle 1960s, the appearance of inexpensive integrated circuits in the 1970s, and the development of personal computers in the 1980s. The electronic parts industry was very competitive, with no one company believed to have greater than a 10 percent share of the market. Management believed that further expansion of the franchised distribution system was necessary to achieve their sales growth target of 10 percent a year. They had therefore requested a renegotiation of their present loan to permit \$1.0 million of additional bank debt.

The bank loan agreement prohibited CCC's incurring additional long-term debt. It also required a current ratio of at least 200 percent at the end of each fiscal year and minimum net working capital of \$10.0 million at all times. The interest rates were 8 percent for the line and 9.5 percent for the long-term insurance company debt. The principal repayment for the insurance company debt was \$790,000 per year, due September 30, 1989 through 1998.

There were 800,000 shares of CCC's common stock outstanding with a market price of \$9.50 per share. The price–earnings ratio had ranged between 13 and 27 in 1986, and 13 and 24 in 1987. In 1988, the range had been 4 to 16. The company did not pay dividends in 1986 or 1987 and had no plans to do so in the future.

Empire National Bank had been lending to CCC since 1981 and was committed to providing 20 percent of CCC's borrowing. The banking relationship had been satisfactory, although CCC's management occasionally had not been prompt in supplying requested information. The lending officers thought these delays were the result of disorganization on the part of CCC's management rather than indicating a desire to conceal. Interest rates were rising in October 1988 although money could not be termed tight. Empire's posture was still to actively solicit new business.

Mr. Murphy, as loan officer of the lead bank, contemplated the recommendation he must make to the lending group. CCC's management requested a reply within seven days.

Case 6 Chiste Components Corporation

EXHIBIT 1 CONSOLIDATED INCOME STATEMENT FOR THE FISCAL YEARS ENDING SEPTEMBER 30, 1986–88 (dollar amounts in millions)

	1986	*1987*	*1988*
Net sales	$27.1	$27.1	$30.9
Cost of goods sold*	21.1	20.6	23.3
Gross profit	$ 6.0	$ 6.5	$ 7.6
Selling and administrative expenses	3.7	3.7	4.4
Interest expense	1.0	1.1	1.3
Profit before tax	$ 1.3	$ 1.7	$ 1.9
Federal and state income taxes	0.6	0.8	0.8
Net income	$ 0.7	$ 0.9	$ 1.1
*Includes depreciation of:	0.5	0.4	0.4

Case 6 Chiste Components Corporation

EXHIBIT 2 CONSOLIDATED BALANCE SHEETS AS OF SEPTEMBER 30, 1986–88 (dollar amounts in millions)

	1986	*1987*	*1988*
ASSETS			
Cash	$ 0.5	$ 0.6	$ 0.7
Accounts receivable	8.2	9.6	10.4
Inventories	8.1	9.8	11.5
Total current assets	$16.8	$20.0	$22.6
Property, plant and equipment (net)	3.0	3.0	3.6
Other assets	1.6	1.7	2.2
Total assets	$21.4	$24.7	$28.4
LIABILITIES AND OWNERS' EQUITY			
Accounts payable	$ 0.5	$ 0.8	$ 1.0
Notes payable—banks	6.1	6.7	7.9
Other current liabilities	0.8	1.6	1.6
Total current liabilities	$ 7.4	$ 9.1	$10.5
Long-term debt	6.0	6.7	7.9
Total liabilities	$13.4	$15.8	$18.4
Preferred stock	0.2	0.2	0.2
Common stock	1.6	1.6	1.6
Retained earnings	6.2	7.1	8.2
Total owners' equity	$ 8.0	$ 8.9	$10.0
Total liabilities and owners' equity	$21.4	$24.7	$28.4

Case 6 Chiste Components Corporation

EXHIBIT 3 COMPUTER EQUIPMENT DIVISION, INCOME STATEMENTS FOR THE FISCAL YEARS ENDING SEPTEMBER 30, 1986–88 (dollar amounts in millions)

	1986	*1987*	*1988*
Net sales	$ 5.0	$ 6.4	$ 8.4
Cost of goods sold*	3.4	4.4	5.8
Gross profit	$ 1.6	$ 2.0	$ 2.6
Selling and administrative expenses	0.8	1.0	1.3
Interest expense	0.2	-0-	0.1
Profit before tax	$ 0.6	$ 1.0	$ 1.2
Federal and state income taxes	0.3	0.5	0.5
Net income	$ 0.3	$ 0.5	$ 0.7
*Includes depreciation of:	0.1	0.1	0.1

Case 6 Chiste Components Corporation

EXHIBIT 4 COMPUTER EQUIPMENT DIVISION, BALANCE SHEETS AS OF SEPTEMBER 30, 1986–88 (dollar amounts in millions)

	1986	*1987*	*1988*
ASSETS			
Cash	$ 0.2	$ 0.3	$ 0.5
Accounts receivable	0.8	1.0	1.7
Inventories	0.8	2.0	2.6
Total current assets	$ 1.8	$ 3.3	$ 4.8
Property, plant and equipment (net)	0.8	0.7	0.9
Other assets	1.1	1.0	1.5
Total assets	$ 3.7	$ 5.0	$ 7.2
LIABILITIES AND OWNERS' EQUITY			
Accounts payable	$ 0.1	$ 0.2	$ 0.4
Intercompany borrowing	0.1	(0.1)*	0.8
Other current liabilities	0.3	1.0	1.1
Total current liabilities	$ 0.5	$ 1.1	$ 2.3
Long-term debt	0.4	0.6	0.9
Total liabilities	$ 0.9	$ 1.7	$ 3.2
Common stock	0.5	0.5	0.5
Retained earnings	2.3	2.8	3.4
Total owners' equity	$ 2.8	$ 3.3	$ 4.0
Total liabilities and owners' equity	$ 3.7	$ 5.0	$ 7.2

*A $100,000 loan from the Computer Equipment Division to the parent.

Case 6 Chiste Components Corporation

EXHIBIT 5 ELECTRONIC PARTS DIVISION, INCOME STATEMENT FOR THE FISCAL YEARS ENDING SEPTEMBER 30, 1986–88 (dollar amounts in millions)

	1986	*1987*	*1988*
Net sales	$22.1	$20.7	$22.5
Cost of goods sold*	17.7	16.2	17.5
Gross profit	$ 4.4	$ 4.5	$ 5.0
Selling and administrative expenses	2.8	2.6	3.1
Interest expense	0.8	1.1	1.1
Profit before tax	$ 0.8	$ 0.8	$ 0.8
Federal and state income taxes	0.4	0.4	0.3
Net income	$ 0.4	$ 0.4	$ 0.5
*Includes depreciation of:	0.2	0.2	0.2

Case 6 Chiste Components Corporation

EXHIBIT 6 ELECTRONIC PARTS DIVISION, BALANCE SHEETS AS OF SEPTEMBER 30, 1986–88 (dollar amounts in millions)

	1986	*1987*	*1988*
ASSETS			
Cash	$ -0-	$ -0-	$ -0-
Accounts receivable	7.4	8.6	8.7
Inventories	7.3	7.8	8.9
Total current assets	$14.7	$16.4	$17.6
Property, plant and equipment (net)	1.4	1.6	1.7
Other assets	0.3	0.4	0.5
Total assets	$16.4	$18.4	$19.8
LIABILITIES AND OWNERS' EQUITY			
Accounts payable	$ 0.3	$ 0.5	$ 0.5
Intercompany borrowing	10.1	11.6	12.5
Other current liabilities	0.4	0.4	0.3
Total current liabilities	$10.8	$12.5	$13.3
Long-term debt	0.4	0.3	0.4
Total liabilities	$11.2	$12.8	$13.7
Common stock	1.3	1.3	1.3
Retained earnings	3.9	4.3	4.8
Total owners' equity	$ 5.2	$ 5.6	$ 6.1
Total liabilities and owners' equity	$16.4	$18.4	$19.8

Case 7

ILLINOIS MANUFACTURING COMPANY

On February 28, 1975, Mr. E. Miller Garfield, loan officer at Boothe National Bank of Chicago, was reviewing the credit file of Illinois Manufacturing Company (IMC). He had just received a telephone call from Mr. Hatcher H. Oates, treasurer of IMC, requesting a third increase in IMC's seasonal loan, from $5.0 million to $7.0 million. The management of IMC had asked for a decision by March 10.

Illinois Manufacturing Company, with sales of $22.9 million in the fiscal year ending September 30, 1974, manufactured garden, farm, and light industrial fencing. The plant and corporate offices were located in Chicago. Steel rod was purchased from domestic and foreign sources, cleaned in acid, coated with lime, and mechanically drawn into wire. The wire was then woven into screen, twisted into netting, or welded into mesh and fence. Afterwards, the wire was regalvanized or coated with polyvinyl chloride. IMC employed 300 unionized workers at its plant.

Nonindustrial lines accounted for 95 percent of sales, with 75 percent going to the lawn and gardening fence market. IMC's share of total industry sales in its major product lines ranged from 20 percent to 50 percent. Competition ranged from fully integrated major steel companies to small local companies. The wire fence, netting, and screen business was primarily regional in nature.

IMC had difficulty attracting large customers because of capacity constraints. A $5.0 million expansion program was therefore undertaken and had been completed in September 1974. Of the total, $4.5 million had been supplied by long-term debt with the other $.5 million to be generated from operations. Plant capacity was increased from 15,000 tons to 39,000 tons per year, and more warehouse space was provided. The current level of production was 24,000 tons per year.

The Adams Company, a large hardware chain, was IMC's largest customer, usually accounting for 15 percent of total sales. Adams purchased on "dating" basis, whereby invoices were due on May 10 for all shipments made between May 1 of the previous year and the current April 30. Terms for general sales were ½ percent/10 net 30 days.

IMC had been a customer of Boothe National since 1915. The relationship had been satisfactory, and Boothe currently provided all of IMC's seasonal working capital. The current line was for $5.0 million at 10 percent. IMC was expected to liquidate the loan by June of each year and be out of the bank for at least 120 days. Although the Lake Forest Bank had expressed interest in doing business with IMC, the latter's management preferred restricting IMC's seasonal borrowing to Boothe if Boothe would provide for its working capital needs.

The Hayes Mutual Life Insurance Company was the only other lender to IMC. In May 1973, Hayes entered into a note purchase agreement which provided for borrowings by IMC at 8.75 percent of not less than $3.5 million nor more than $4.5 million. These funds were used for the plant expansion project. Principal payments of $350,000 were due annually January 1, 1976 through 1986, with a $650,000 balloon due January 1, 1987. Interest payments were due monthly.

The note purchase agreement specified that the company must maintain working capital equal to $3.0 million or 50 percent of its consolidated current liabilities, whichever was greater. The incurrence of further long-term

Case prepared by David N. Webb with the cooperation of individuals and institutions that wish to remain anonymous. Certain of the company's characteristics and financial information have been changed to protect confidential information without altering the nature of the managerial decision.

debt, the disposal of a substantial portion of assets and mergers, unless the acquiring company was in the continuing corporation, were prohibited. In addition, IMC could not declare dividends nor redeem or acquire any of its capital stock unless the aggregate of these dividends, redemptions, and acquisitions did not exceed 50 percent of net income made after September 30, 1972 plus $1.0 million.

IMC was a very closely held company. The two major stockholders were president and vice president of the company. Dividend payments were a significant part of their income.

IMC's management had originally estimated IMC's fiscal year 1975 seasonal loan needs at $1.6 million. (Projected monthly financial statements prepared in July 1974 are presented in Exhibits 1 through 4.) Mr. Garfield had approved the line almost as a matter of routine.

Mr. Oates came to Mr. Garfield in September 1974 to request a $2.4 million increase in IMC's seasonal loan to a new level of $4.0 million. Mr. Oates predicted a shortage of steel rod by February 1975 and proposed that IMC purchase 18,000 tons of steel during the first four months of the fiscal year. The other 6,000 tons required would be purchased in approximately equal amounts over the subsequent eight months, as shown in Exhibit 7. Mr. Oates submitted the statements included as Exhibits 5, 6, and 7 in support of the request. Mr. Garfield contacted representatives of two large domestic steel companies. They agreed with Mr. Oates' prediction of continuing difficulty in obtaining steel. Mr. Garfield therefore increased IMC's line to $4.0 million.

In early January 1975, Mr. Oates requested an additional $1.0 million increase in IMC's line. Mr. Oates cited increased steel rod costs as the cause of this need for additional working capital. IMC had purchased 9,000 tons of foreign steel through the first quarter of fiscal 1975 at $.08 per pound more than anticipated. The scarcity of domestic steel rod necessitated this purchase. At the end of December, inventories were $1.76 million higher than estimated in the revised projections made in September 1974. (Actual financial statements for October 1974 through February 1975, the first five months of the 1975 fiscal year, are presented in Exhibits 8 through 11.)

IMC's management predicted a strong February–April "summer" reorder cycle of at least the forecasted sales levels. Mr. Oates thought this another justification for the requested $1.0 million increase in IMC's line of credit.

Boothe's past experience with IMC had been that the sales forecasts were often inaccurate. Mr. Garfield called the purchasing vice president of Adams Company to determine his outlook for the lawn and garden fence market. Mr. Garfield was told that demand was very strong. Purchasing executives for two other large hardware chains expressed the same opinion. Boothe therefore extended IMC's line to $5.0 million.

By the end of February, sales had not materialized as forecasted. Mr. Oates requested an additional $2.0 million on February 28. (His letter to Mr. Garfield is reproduced in Exhibit 12.) IMC's need was critical because its cash balance had dropped to less than 50 percent of the minimum IMC's management thought was needed to carry on operations.

In considering IMC's request for an additional $2.0 million, Mr. Garfield remained aware of the Lake Forest Bank's interest in IMC. Money was currently tight, with interest rates for short-term debt over 12 percent. Mr. Garfield had been informed that his bank wished to maintain a cautious lending policy. IMC's management requested a decision by March 10.

EXHIBIT 1 PROJECTED MONTHLY STATEMENTS OF INCOME AND RETAINED EARNINGS FOR THE FISCAL YEAR ENDING SEPTEMBER 30, 1975 (dollar amounts in thousands)

		Fiscal Year 1975 Projections												
	Fiscal Year 1974 Actual	*1974 October*	*November*	*December*	*1975 January*	*February*	*March*	*April*	*May*	*June*	*July*	*August*	*September*	*Fiscal Year 1975 Total*
General sales	$19,500	$1,670	$1,410	$1,300	$2,300	$2,200	$2,100	$2,290	$2,300	$2,300	$2,070	$1,490	$1,280	$22,710
Sales to Adams Company	3,440	100	100	200	500	600	600	800	400	400	100	100	100	4,000
Total sales	$22,840	$1,770	$1,510	$1,500	$2,800	$2,800	$2,700	$3,090	$2,700	$2,700	$2,170	$1,590	$1,380	$26,710
Cost of sales[1]	17,160	1,340	1,150	1,140	2,130	2,130	2,060	2,350	2,040	2,040	1,650	1,210	1,040	20,280
Gross profit	$ 5,780	$ 430	$ 360	$ 360	$ 670	$ 670	$ 640	$ 740	$ 660	$ 660	$ 520	$ 380	$ 340	$ 6,430
Selling & admin. exp.	3,590	310	320	330	340	340	350	350	360	360	360	360	360	4,140
Interest expense	370	30	30	30	40	40	40	40	30	30	30	30	30	400
Profit before tax	$ 1,820	$ 90	$ 10	$ –0–	$ 290	$ 290	$ 250	$ 350	$ 270	$ 270	$ 130	$ (10)	$ (50)	$ 1,890
Tax	870	40	–0–	–0–	140	140	120	170	130	130	60	–0–	(30)	900
Profit after tax	$ 950	$ 50	$ 10	$ –0–	$ 150	$ 150	$ 130	$ 180	$ 140	$ 140	$ 70	$ (10)	$ (20)	$ 990
Beg. retained earnings	3,300	3,930	3,980	3,990	3,910	4,060	4,210	4,260	4,440	4,580	4,640	4,710	4,700	3,930
	$ 4,250	$3,980	$3,990	$3,990	$4,060	$4,210	$4,340	$4,440	$4,580	$4,720	$4,710	$4,700	$4,680	$4,920
Less dividends	320	–0–	–0–	80	–0–	–0–	80	–0–	–0–	80	–0–	–0–	80	320
End. retained earnings	$ 3,930	$3,980	$3,990	$3,910	$4,060	$4,210	$4,260	$4,440	$4,580	$4,640	$4,710	$4,700	$4,600	$4,600

Forecast prepared July 1974. Actual results for fiscal year 1974 added later for analytical convenience.

[1]Depreciation is charged out of inventory at $30 per ton.

EXHIBIT 2 PROJECTED MONTHLY BALANCE SHARE FOR THE FISCAL YEAR ENDING SEPTEMBER 30, 1975 (dollar amounts in thousands)

	Fiscal Year 1974 Actual	*Fiscal Year 1975 Projections*											
		1974			*1975*								
	September	*October*	*November*	*December*	*January*	*February*	*March*	*April*	*May*	*June*	*July*	*August*	*September*
ASSETS													
Cash and marketable sec.	$ 1,370	$ 1,620	$ 1,200	$ 500	$ 500	$ 500	$ 500	$ 500	$ 2,910	$ 2,840	$ 3,050	$ 3,060	$ 2,260
Accounts receivable[1]	2,540	2,910	2,790	2,840	4,320	4,990	5,470	6,440	3,080	3,480	3,350	2,840	2,630
Inventories[2]	3,240	3,590	4,130	4,680	4,240	3,800	3,430	2,770	2,420	2,070	2,110	2,590	3,240
Total current assets	$ 7,150	$ 8,120	$ 8,120	$ 8,020	$ 9,060	$ 9,290	$ 9,400	$ 9,710	$ 8,410	$ 8,390	$ 8,510	$ 8,490	$ 8,130
PP&E (net)	8,570	8,580	8,590	8,600	8,600	8,610	8,600	8,610	8,600	8,590	8,600	8,600	8,610
Other assets	320	320	330	330	340	350	350	360	360	360	360	370	370
Total Assets	$16,040	$17,020	$17,040	$16,950	$18,000	$18,250	$18,350	$18,680	$17,370	$17,340	$17,470	$17,460	$17,110
LIAB. AND OWNER'S EQUITY													
Accounts payable[3]	$ 720	$ 1,170	$ 1,170	$ 1,170	$ 1,170	$ 1,170	$ 1,170	$ 1,170	$ 1,170	$ 1,170	$ 1,170	$ 1,170	$ 1,170
Accrued expenses[4]	610	550	560	570	590	590	600	600	600	600	600	600	600
Accrued taxes[5]	540	580	580	80	220	360	210	150	280	190	250	250	–0–
Notes payable	–0–	–0–	–0–	480	1,220	1,180	1,370	1,580	–0–	–0–	–0–	–0–	–0–
Cur. por. of long-term debt	–0–	–0–	–0–	–0–	350	350	350	350	350	350	350	350	350
Total current liabilities	$ 1,870	$ 2,300	$ 2,310	$ 2,300	$ 3,550	$ 3,650	$ 3,700	$ 3,850	$ 3,400	$ 3,310	$ 2,370	$ 2,370	$ 2,120
Long-term debt	4,000	4,500	4,500	4,500	4,150	4,150	4,150	4,150	4,150	4,150	4,150	4,150	4,150
Total liabilities	$ 5,870	$ 6,800	$ 6,810	$ 6,800	$ 7,700	$ 7,800	$ 7,850	$ 8,000	$ 6,550	$ 6,460	$ 6,520	$ 6,520	$ 6,270
Capital stock	6,240	6,240	6,240	6,240	6,240	6,240	6,240	6,240	6,240	6,240	6,240	6,240	6,240
Retained earnings	3,930	3,980	3,990	3,910	4,060	4,210	4,260	4,440	4,580	4,640	4,710	4,700	4,600
Total owners' equity	$10,170	$10,220	$10,230	$10,150	$10,300	$10,450	$10,500	$10,680	$10,820	$10,880	$10,950	$10,940	$10,840
Tot. Liab. & owners' equity	$16,040	$17,020	$17,040	$16,950	$18,000	$18,250	$18,350	$18,680	$17,370	$17,340	$17,470	$17,460	$17,110

[1]See Exhibit 3.

[2]See Exhibit 4.

[3]Includes 30 days' raw material purchases.

[4]Includes 30 days' selling and administrative expenses, 30 days' interest expense, and 15 days' direct labor ($210).

[5]One-fourth of estimated yearly tax is paid December 15, April 15, June 15, and September 15. Taxes due from previous year will be paid in equal installments on December 15 and March 15.

NOTE: Forecast prepared July 1974. Actual balance sheet for September 30, 1974 added later for analytical convenience.

EXHIBIT 3 PROJECTED MONTHLY ACCOUNTS RECEIVABLES BALANCES FOR THE FISCAL YEAR ENDING SEPTEMBER 30, 1975 (dollar amounts in thousands)

	October	*November*	*December*	*January*	*February*	*March*	*April*	*May*	*June*	*July*	*August*	*September*	*Total*
General sales	$1,670	$1,410	$1,300	$2,300	$2,200	$2,100	$2,290	$2,300	$2,300	$2,070	$1,490	$1,280	$22,710
Sales to Adams Company	100	100	200	500	600	600	800	400	400	100	100	100	4,000
Total sales	$1,770	$1,510	$1,500	$2,800	$2,800	$2,700	$3,090	$2,700	$2,700	$2,170	$1,590	$1,380	$26,710
Plus begin. A/R	2,540[1]	2,910	2,790	2,840	4,320	4,990	5,470	6,440	3,080	3,480	3,350	2,840	2,540
Less collections[2]	1,400	1,630	1,450	1,320	2,130	2,220	2,120	6,060	2,300	2,300	2,100	1,590	26,620
Ending A/R	$2,910	$2,790	$2,840	$4,320	$4,990	$5,470	$6,440	$3,080	$3,480	$3,350	$2,840	$2,630	$2,630

[1]$900 of which is owed by Adams on sales to them since May 1974.

[2]35 days' sales outstanding.

NOTE: Forecast prepared July 1974.

EXHIBIT 4 PROJECTED MONTHLY INVENTORY BALANCES FOR THE FISCAL YEAR ENDING SEPTEMBER 30, 1975 (dollar amounts in thousands)

	1974			*1975*								
	October	*November*	*December*	*January*	*February*	*March*	*April*	*May*	*June*	*July*	*August*	*September*
Raw Materials and Supplies:												
Opening balance	$1,230[1]	$1,230	$1,230	$1,230	$1,230	$1,230	$1,230	$1,230	$1,230	$1,230	$1,230	$1,230
Plus purchases[2]	1,170	1,170	1,170	1,170	1,170	1,170	1,170	1,170	1,170	1,170	1,170	1,170
Less transfers to work in process	1,170	1,170	1,170	1,170	1,170	1,170	1,170	1,170	1,170	1,170	1,170	1,170
Closing balance	$1,230	$1,230	$1,230	$1,230	$1,230	$1,230	$1,230	$1,230	$1,230	$1,230	$1,230	$1,230
Work in Process:												
Opening balance	610[3]	610	610	610	610	610	610	610	610	610	610	610
Plus raw material additions	1,170	1,170	1,170	1,170	1,170	1,170	1,170	1,170	1,170	1,170	1,170	1,170
Plus cost of production[4]	520	520	520	520	520	520	520	520	520	520	520	520
Less transfers to finished goods	1,690	1,690	1,690	1,690	1,690	1,690	1,690	1,690	1,690	1,690	1,690	1,690
Closing balance	$ 610	$ 610	$ 610	$ 610	$ 610	$ 610	$ 610	$ 610	$ 610	$ 610	$ 610	$ 610
Finished Goods:												
Opening balance	$1,400[5]	$1,750	$2,290	$2,840	$2,400	$1,960	$1,590	$ 930	$ 580	$ 230	$ 270	$ 750
Plus additions from work in process	1,690	1,690	1,690	1,690	1,690	1,690	1,690	1,690	1,690	1,690	1,690	1,690
Less cost of sales	1,340	1,150	1,140	2,130	2,130	2,060	2,350	2,040	2,040	1,650	1,210	1,040
Closing balance	$1,750	$2,290	$2,840	$2,400	$1,960	$1,590	$ 930	$ 580	$ 230	$ 270	$ 750	$1,400
TOTAL CLOSING INVENTORY	$3,590	$4,130	$4,680	$4,240	$3,800	$3,430	$2,770	$2,420	$2,070	$2,110	$2,590	$3,240

[1]Includes 2,100 tons of steel and $684 of non-steel raw materials.

[2]Monthly purchases include $520 of steel and $650 of non-steel raw materials.

[3]Includes 700 tons of steel.

[4]Includes $60 depreciation charged each month to production costs ($30 per ton).

[5]Includes 1,700 tons of steel.

NOTE: Forecast prepared July, 1974.

EXHIBIT 5 REVISED PROJECTED MONTHLY STATEMENTS OF INCOME AND RETAINED EARNINGS FOR THE FISCAL YEAR ENDING SEPTEMBER 30, 1975 (dollar amounts in thousands)

		Fiscal Year 1975 Projections												
	Fiscal Year 1974 Actual	1974 October	November	December	1975 January	February	March	April	May	June	July	August	September	Fiscal Year 1975 Total
General sales	$19,500	$1,670	$1,410	$1,300	$2,300	$2,200	$2,100	$2,290	$2,300	$2,300	$2,070	$1,490	$1,280	$22,710
Sales to Adams Company	3,440	100	100	200	500	600	600	800	400	400	100	100	100	4,000
Total sales	$22,940	$1,770	$1,510	$1,500	$2,800	$2,800	$2,700	$3,090	$2,700	$2,700	$2,170	$1,590	$1,380	$26,710
Cost of sales[1]	17,160	1,340	1,150	1,140	2,130	2,130	2,060	2,350	2,040	2,040	1,650	1,210	1,040	20,280
Gross profit	$ 5,780	$ 430	$ 360	$ 360	$ 670	$ 670	$ 640	$ 740	$ 660	$ 660	$ 520	$ 380	$ 340	$ 6,430
Selling & admin. exp.	3,590	310	320	330	340	340	350	350	360	360	360	360	360	4,140
Interest expense	370	30	30	40	50	60	60	60	30	30	30	30	30	480
Profit before tax	$ 1,820	$ 90	$ 10	$ (10)	$ 280	$ 270	$ 230	$ 330	$ 270	$ 270	$ 130	$ (10)	$ (50)	$ 1,810
Tax	870	40	–0–	–0–	130	130	110	160	130	130	60	–0–	(30)	860
Profit after tax	$ 950	$ 50	$ 10	$ (10)	$ 150	$ 140	$ 120	$ 170	$ 140	$ 140	$ 70	$ (10)	$ (50)	$ 950
Beg. retained earnings	3,300	3,930	3,980	3,990	3,900	4,050	4,190	4,230	4,400	4,540	4,600	4,670	4,660	3,930
	$ 4,250	$3,980	$3,990	$3,980	$4,050	$4,190	$4,310	$4,440	$4.540	$4,680	$4,670	$4,660	$4,640	$4,880
Less dividends	320	–0–	–0–	80	–0–	–0–	80	–0–	–0–	80	–0–	–0–	80	320
End. retained earnings	$ 3,930	$3,980	$3,990	$3,900	$4,050	$4,190	$4,230	$4,400	$4,540	$4,600	$4,670	$4,660	$4,560	$ 4,560

[1]Includes depreciation of $30 per ton sold.

NOTE: Prepared September, 1974.

EXHIBIT 6 REVISED PROJECTED MONTHLY BALANCE SHEETS FOR THE FISCAL YEAR ENDING SEPTEMBER 30, 1975 (dollar amounts in thousands)

	Fiscal Year 1974 Actual	Fiscal Year 1975 Revised Projections											
		1974			1975								
	September	October	November	December	January	February	March	April	May	June	July	August	September
ASSETS													
Cash and marketable sec.	$ 1,370	$ 1,620	$ 740	$ 500	$ 500	$ 500	$ 500	$ 500	$ 1,170	$ 1,140	$ 1,920	$ 2,230	$ 1,750
Accounts receivable[1]	2,540	2,910	2,790	2,840	4,320	4,990	5,470	6,440	3,080	3,480	3,350	2,840	2,630
Inventories[2]	3,240	4,060	5,320	6,720	6,820	6,080	5,410	4,450	3,800	3,150	2,890	3,060	3,240
Total current assets	$ 7,150	$ 8,590	$ 8,850	$10,060	$11,640	$11,570	$11,380	$11,390	$ 8,050	$ 8,040	$ 8,160	$ 8,130	$ 7,620
PP&E (net)	8,570	8,580	8,590	8,600	8,600	8,610	8,600	8,610	8,600	8,590	8,600	8,600	8,610
Other assets	320	320	320	330	340	350	350	360	360	360	360	370	370
Total assets	$16,040	$17,490	$17,760	$18,990	$20,580	$20,530	$20,330	$20,360	$17,010	$16,990	$17,120	$17,100	$16,600
LIABILITIES AND OWNERS' EQUITY													
Accounts payable[3]	$ 720	$ 1,640	$ 1,890	$ 2,020	$ 1,170	$ 870	$ 870	$ 870	$ 870	$ 870	$ 870	$ 860	$ 700
Accrued expenses[4]	610	550	560	580	600	610	620	600	600	600	600	600	600
Accrued taxes[5]	540	580	580	90	220	350	190	130	260	180	240	240	–0–
Notes payable	–0–	–0–	–0–	1,660	3,260	3,770	3,680	3,670	–0–	–0–	–0–	–0–	–0–
Cur. por. of long-term debt	–0–	–0–	–0–	–0–	350	350	350	350	350	350	350	350	350
Total current liabilities	$ 1,870	$ 2,770	$ 3,030	$ 4,350	$ 6,140	$ 5,950	$ 5,710	$ 5,570	$ 2,080	$ 2,000	$ 2,060	$ 2,050	$ 1,650
Long-term debt	4,000	4,500	4,500	4,500	4,150	4,150	4,150	4,150	4,150	4,150	4,150	4,150	4,150
Total liabilities	$ 5,870	$ 7,270	$ 7,530	$ 8,850	$10,290	$10,100	$ 9,860	$ 9,720	$ 6,230	$ 6,150	$ 6,210	$ 6,200	$ 5,800
Capital stock	6,240	6,240	6,240	6,240	6,240	6,240	6,240	6,240	6,240	6,240	6,240	6,240	6,240
Retained earnings	3,930	3,980	3,990	3,990	4,050	4,190	4,230	4,440	4,540	4,600	4,670	4,660	4,560
Total owners' equity	$10,170	$10,220	$10,230	$10,140	$10,290	$10,430	$10,470	$10,640	$10,780	$10,840	$10,910	$10,900	$10,800
Total Liabilities & owners' equity	$16,040	$17,490	$17,760	$18,990	$20,580	$20,530	$20,330	$20,360	$17,010	$16,990	$17,120	$17,100	$16,600

[1]See Exhibit 3.

[2]See Exhibit 7.

[3]Includes 30 days' raw material purchases.

[4]Includes 30 days' selling and administrative expenses, 30 days' interest expense, and 15 days' direct labor ($210).

[5]One-fourth of estimated yearly tax is paid December 15, April 15, June 15, and September 15. Taxes due from previous year will be paid in equal installments on December 15 and March 15.

NOTE: Forecast prepared September 1974.

EXHIBIT 7 REVISED PROJECTED MONTHLY INVENTORY BALANCES FOR THE FISCAL YEAR ENDING SEPTEMBER 30, 1975 (dollar amounts in thousands)

	1974			*1975*								
	October	*November*	*December*	*January*	*February*	*March*	*April*	*May*	*June*	*July*	*August*	*September*
Raw Materials and Supplies:												
Opening balance	$1,230[1]	$1,700	$2,420	$3,270	$3,810	$3,510	$3,210	$2,910	$2,610	$2,310	$2,010	$1,700
Plus purchases[2]	1,640	1,890	2,020	1,710	870	870	870	870	870	870	860	700
Less transfers to work in process	1,170	1,170	1,170	1,170	1,170	1,170	1,170	1,170	1,170	1,170	1,170	1,170
Closing balance	$1,700	$2,420	$3,270	$3,810	$3,510	$3,210	$2,910	$2,610	$2,310	$2,010	$1,700	$1,230
Work in Process:												
Opening balance	610[3]	610	610	610	610	610	610	610	610	610	610	610
Plus raw material additions	1,170	1,170	1,170	1,170	1,170	1,170	1,170	1,170	1,170	1,170	1,170	1,170
Plus cost of production[4]	520	520	520	520	520	520	520	520	520	520	520	520
Less transfers to finished goods	1,690	1,690	1,690	1,690	1,690	1,690	1,690	1,690	1,690	1,690	1,690	1,690
Closing balance	$ 610	$ 610	$ 610	$ 610	$ 610	$ 610	$ 610	$ 610	$ 610	$ 610	$ 610	$ 610
Finished Goods:												
Opening balance	$1,400[5]	$1,750	$2,290	$2,840	$2,400	$1,960	$1,590	$ 930	$ 580	$ 230	$ 270	$ 750
Plus additions from work in process	1,690	1,690	1,690	1,690	1,690	1,690	1,690	1,690	1,690	1,690	1,690	1,690
Less cost of sales	1,340	1,150	1,140	2,130	2,130	2,060	2,350	2,040	2,040	1,650	1,210	1,040
Closing balance	$1,750	$2,290	$2,840	$2,400	$1,960	$1,590	$ 930	$ 580	$ 230	$ 270	$ 750	$1,400
TOTAL CLOSING INVENTORY	$4,060	$5,320	$6,720	$6,820	$6,080	$5,410	$4,450	$3,800	$3,150	$2,890	$3,067	$3,240

[1]Includes 2,100 tons of steel and $684 of non-steel raw materials.
[2]Includes steel and $650 of non-steel raw materials.
[3]Includes 700 tons of steel.
[4]Includes $60 depreciation charged each month to production costs ($30 per ton).
[5]Includes 1,700 tons of steel.
NOTE: Revised forecast prepared September, 1974.

EXHIBIT 8 STATEMENT OF INCOME AND RETAINED EARNINGS FOR THE FIVE MONTHS ENDING FEBRUARY 28, 1975 (dollar amounts in thousands)

	1974 *October*	*November*	*December*	*1975* *January*	*February*	*Actual Total Oct.–Feb.*	*Revised Projected Total Oct.–Feb.*
General sales	$1,580	$1,260	$1,290	$1,910	$1,700	$7,740	$ 8,880
Sales to Adams Company	70	70	160	400	480	1,180	1,500
Total sales	$1,650	$1,330	$1,450	$2,310	$2,180	$8,920	$10,380
Cost of sales[1]	1,250	1,010	1,100	1,990	1,870	7,220	7,890
Gross profit	$ 400	$ 320	$ 350	$ 320	$ 310	$1,700	$ 2,490
Selling & administrative expenses	310	320	330	340	340	1,640	1,640
Interest expense	30	30	40	60	70	230	210
Profit before tax	$ 60	$ (30)	$ (20)	$ (80)	$ (100)	$ (170)	$ 640
Tax	30	(15)	(10)	(40)	(50)	(85)	300
Profit after tax	$ 30	$ (15)	$ (15)	$ (40)	$ (50)	$ (85)	$ 340
Beginning retained earnings	3,930	3,960	3,945	3,855	3,815	3,930	3,930
	$3,960	$3,945	$3,935	$3,815	$3,765	$3,845	$ 4,270
Less dividends	-0-	-0-	80	-0-	-0-	80	80
Ending retained earnings	$3,960	$3,945	$3,855	$3,815	$3,765	$3,765	$ 4,190

[1]Includes depreciation of $30 per ton.

Case 7 Illinois Manufacturing Company

EXHIBIT 9 ACTUAL MONTHLY BALANCE SHEETS, SEPTEMBER 1974 TO FEBRUARY 1975 (dollar amounts in thousands)

	Fiscal Year 1974 September	*1974 October*	*November*	*December*	*1975 January*	*February*	*Revised Projection February 1975*
ASSETS							
Cash and marketable securities	$ 1,370	$ 1,630	$ 490	$ 490	$ 470	$ 220	$ 500
Accounts receivable[1]	2,540	2,790	2,550	2,750	3,780	4,060	4,990
Inventories[2]	3,240	4,530	6,460	8,480	9,150	8,670	6,080
Total current assets	$ 7,150	$ 8,950	$ 9,500	$11,720	$13,400	$12,950	$11,570
Property, plant & equipment (net)	8,570	8,570	8,580	8,600	8,600	8,590	8,610
Other assets	320	320	320	330	330	340	350
Total assets	$16,040	$17,840	$18,400	$20,650	$22,330	$21,880	$20,530
LIABILITIES AND OWNER'S EQUITY							
Accounts payable	$ 720	$ 2,020	$ 2,420	$ 2,600	$ 2,790	$ 1,890	$ 870
Accrued expenses	610	550	560	590	610	620	610
Accrued taxes[3]	540	570	555	60	20	(30)	350
Notes payable	-0-	-0-	180	2,805	4,355	4,895	3,770
Current portion of long-term debt	-0-	-0-	-0-	-0-	350	350	350
Total current liabilities	$ 1,870	$ 3,140	$ 3,715	$ 6,055	$ 8,125	$ 7,725	$ 5,950
Long-term debt	4,000	4,500	4,500	4,500	4,150	4,150	4,150
Total liabilities	$ 5,870	$ 7,640	$ 8,215	$10,555	$12,275	$11,875	$10,100
Capital stock	6,240	6,240	6,240	6,240	6,240	6,240	6,240
Retained earnings	3,930	3,960	3,945	3,855	3,815	3,765	4,190
Total owner's equity	$10,170	$10,200	$10,185	$10,095	$10,055	$10,005	$10,430
Total liabilities and owners' equity	$16,040	$17,840	$18,400	$20,650	$22,330	$21,880	$20,530

[1]See Exhibit 10.
[2]See Exhibit 11.
[3]Excess taxes due from previous year are paid in equal installments on December 15 and March 15. The income tax tax credit is carried forward until payment is received on the tax refund claims against prior year's taxes. The initial installment of $215 due on 1975 estimated taxes was paid in December 1974 and was deducted from the Accrued Tax account rather than shown as an asset, Prepaid Taxes.

Case 7 Illinois Manufacturing Company

EXHIBIT 10 ACTUAL ACCOUNTS RECEIVABLE BALANCES FOR THE FIVE MONTHS ENDING FEBRUARY 28, 1975 (dollar amounts in thousands)

	October	*November*	*December*	*January*	*February*	*Total*
General sales	$1,580	$1,260	$1,290	$1,910	$1,700	$7,740
Sales to Adams Co.	70	70	160	400	480	1,180
Total sales	$1,650	$1,330	$1,450	$2,310	$2,180	$8,920
Plus beginning A/R	2,540[1]	2,790	2,550	2,750	3,780	2,540
Less collections	1,400	1,570	1,250	1,280	1,900	7,400
Ending A/R	$2,790	$2,550	$2,750	$3,780	$4,060	$4,060

[1]$900 of which is owed by Adams on sales to them since May 1974.

EXHIBIT 11 INVENTORY BALANCES FOR THE FIVE MONTHS ENDING FEBRUARY 28, 1975 (dollar amounts in thousands)

	1974 October	*November*	*December*	*1975 January*	*February*	*Actual Total Oct.–Feb.*	*Revised Projected Total Oct.–Feb.*
RAW MATERIALS							
Opening balance	$1,230[1]	$2,080	$3,130	$4,340	$5,090	$ 1,230	$ 1,230
Plus purchases[2]	2,020	2,420	2,600	2,140	870	10,050	8,130
Less transfers to work in process	1,170	1,370	1,390	1,390	1,390	6,710	5,850
Closing balance	$2,080	$3,130	$4,340	$5,090	$4,570	$ 4,570	$ 3,510
WORK-IN-PROCESS							
Opening balance	$ 610[3]	$ 610	$ 680	$ 690	$ 690	$ 690	$ 610
Plus raw material additions	1,170	1,370	1,390	1,390	1,390	6,710	5,850
Plus cost of production[4]	520	520	520	520	520	2,600	2,600
Less transfers to finished goods	1,690	1,820	1,900	1,910	1,910	9,230	8,450
Closing balance	$ 610	$ 680	$ 690	$ 690	$ 690	$ 690	$ 610
FINISHED GOODS							
Opening balance	$1,400[5]	$1,840	$2,650	$3,450	$3,370	$ 1,400	$ 1,400
Plus additions from work in process	1,690	1,820	1,900	1,910	1,910	9,230	8,450
Less cost of sales	1,250	1,010	1,100	1,990	1,870	7,220	7,890
Closing balance	$1,840	$2,650	$3,450	$3,370	$3,410	$ 3,410	$ 1,960
Total Closing Inventory	$4,530	$6,460	$8,480	$9,150	$8,670	$ 8,670	$ 6,080

[1]Includes 2,100 tons of steel and $684 of non-steel raw materials.
[2]Includes steel and $650 per month of non-steel raw materials.
[3]Includes 700 tons of steel.
[4]Includes $60 depreciation charged each month to production costs ($30 per ton).
[5]Includes 1,700 tons of steel.

Case 7 Illinois Manufacturing Company

EXHIBIT 12

February 28, 1975

Mr. E. Miller Garfield
Loan Officer, National Banking Group
Boothe National Bank
777 Dauphine Avenue
Chicago, Illinois 35200

Dear Mr. Garfield:

This letter confirms our telephone conversation in which I requested an increase in our company's line of credit from $5.0 million to $7.0 million. This money will be used to finance increased inventories and to raise the cash balance. IMC's cash balance has fallen to $220,000 from the $500,000 which we believe is needed to carry on operations.

According to the revised plan, 18,000 tons of steel rod were purchased during the first four months of fiscal 1975. Unfortunately, we could not locate the entire quantity from our usual sources. The purchase from foreign sources of 12,000 tons of steel rod at $420.00 per ton, as opposed to the anticipated $260.00 per ton, has raised the inventory requirements by $1.92 million. In addition, sales have been only 80% of forecast in January and February.

Considering our firm's current backlog of orders, we anticipate March sales at $2.4 million: $1.88 million general and $.52 million to Adams Company. After March, sales are uncertain, but we hope this upward trend will continue throughout the 1975 fiscal year. Sales of $26.7 million are expected in fiscal 1976. Selling prices for fencing have remained firm, with the average for IMC's several product lines being $1,110 per ton.

Currently, IMC produces 2,000 tons of finished goods per month. The average price of steel rod in raw material inventory is currently $361.00 per ton. The inventory also includes $684,000 of nonsteel raw materials. One ton of raw material is required per ton of finished goods. We use $325.00 of nonsteel raw material per ton of finished goods. These costs vary directly with production.

The cost of production (excluding raw materials) is $260.00 per ton of finished goods. Approximately 60% of this cost is fixed over the short term. The variable portion of the cost of production is directly proportional to the number of tons of finished goods produced.

The high fixed percentage is due mainly to a union agreement which requires salary payments to men laid off at 75% of normal for up to one year. IMC has a good relationship with labor, and we wish to maintain our policy of level production and even employment.

IMC's cost of sales should average 86% until all the foreign steel is sold. We expect this to occur when cumulative sales from October 1, 1974, have reached $25 million. Cost of sales should average 76% afterwards. The FIFO method of inventory valuation is used. The contracts outstanding for the purchase of steel rod at $260.00 per ton, at which price steel is now readily available, are cancellable upon 30 days notice.

Sincerely,

Hatcher H. Oates
Treasurer
Illinois Manufacturing Company

Case 8

PADGETT BLANK BOOK COMPANY

Negotiations with Padgett Blank Book Company had been going on for almost a year, and Mr. Francis Libris hoped the time had come when they could be pushed to a mutually satisfactory conclusion. If not, Padgett might elect to seek another bank as its source of funds. Alternatively, Mr. Libris would be subject to criticism by his superiors for failing to deliver on his commitment to manage and structure the relationship properly. Mr. Libris was vice president of the Windsor Trust Company of New York, one of the largest banks in the United States. He was responsible for the Midtown commercial lending center of the bank, to which Padgett's account was assigned because its small executive offices were on an upper floor of the same building in which the center was located. It was a significant account for the center and an important one to its profitability.

Padgett had borrowed relatively small amounts off and on from Windsor since it had first established an account with the bank in 1939. Even the acquisition of several small companies (for less than $1 million each) in the late 1970s and early 1980s did not require high levels of debt. The acquisition of a long-coveted competitor at an attractive price on short notice in early 1988 brought Padgett suddenly to the bank, asking for an additional $3.6 million loan. Combined with the $3.6 million already outstanding at that time, Windsor's total exposure could rise to $7.2 million, well in excess of the $5 million advised credit line which had been approved for the company. The request was granted nevertheless, under an internal guidance line of $8 million, and the rate was continued at prime. Mr. Libris had been working since then to structure the arrangements on a more orderly basis than 90-day notes with no protective covenants.

It was now January 1989. Mr. Libris hoped to have the new terms worked out so that they could be reflected on the financial statements for the 1989 fiscal year which would end April 30. Although he knew there was some possibility that the results of a negotiation completed before the auditors finished their field work could be shown in the report, he preferred to have the arrangements made without this complication.

Mr. Libris wondered whether he should take a fresh look at the situation. He had originally attempted to persuade Padgett's management to finance part of the company's requirements in the form of long-term debt from a life insurance company. When the financial vice president declined this idea, Mr. Libris decided to see how the loan could be repaid to the bank within the period initially suggested by the credit committee. As time had gone on, he began to think that these constraints might not be appropriate to the situation and that a more creative solution might prove acceptable both to the credit committee and to Padgett's management. Because Mr. Libris knew he would have to get the approval of his superiors before he undertook a different initiative with Padgett's management, time was getting exceedingly short. He had to develop both the implications of the credit committee's original decision and of any alternatives which appeared to be superior.

PADGETT BLANK BOOK COMPANY

The Padgett Blank Book Company, a closely held, publicly traded (over-the-counter) company, manufactured a variety of stationery products including notebooks, loose-leaf binders, forms, and filler paper for students and record-keeping purposes. The company was over 100 years old. Its ownership remained primarily with

 This case was prepared from material written by Paul H. Hunn, Senior Vice President, Manufacturers Hanover Trust Company, whose cooperation is acknowledged with appreciation.

the descendants of the founders, now a large and widely spread group. Few family members were active in the company's management, and the major connection with most of the owners came in the form of the quarterly dividend check. A few members of the family depended on the dividends for the majority of their income. Most of the shareholders considered Padgett just another investment and an illiquid one at that because the market for the company's stock was extremely thin. A significant payout was considered important by management.

Management, which was largely professional, appeared competent, responsible, and reasonably effective. Its expertise was largely in operations, which were carried on at a number of plants in the New England and mid-Atlantic areas, and in marketing, which was controlled out of the executive office in New York. Management was not financially oriented, Mr. Libris had observed.

Padgett's customers were some 5,000 wholesalers and retailers in the United States and Canada. No single customer or small group of customers accounted for a substantial share of Padgett's sales. Terms were 2/10 net 30, but few customers took the discount, and many stretched payment for an additional 30 days. The business had a slight seasonal peak in the late summer when big back-to-school sales took place. Because the company attempted to maintain level production in order to reduce unit cost in the highly competitive market, a seasonal variation of about $2 million occurred in its borrowing pattern. The peak occurred in the summer.

A consolidation had been taking place in the business since the early 1970s, initially caused by the high inflation rate of that period which made it difficult for small firms to finance their current assets. Financial difficulties and inventory problems resulting from the subsequent mid-seventies recession further reduced the level of the competition. Changes in the tax rules effective in 1986 provided new impetus for the smaller companies to sell. Finally, the sharp drop in the stock market in October 1987 combined with a resurgence of paper price increases and shortages of supply had frightened some owners, such as those at Tri-State Tablet, enough that they put their firms on the market. It had not been possible to pass all these the price increases through to the customers because of strong competition from large, integrated paper companies. In Padgett's case, the drop in the corporate tax rate helped compensate for smaller margins.

Many competitors had been acquired by national corporations with strong marketing skills and good financial resources. The response of Padgett's management had been to acquire smaller companies which fit into its product or marketing needs. The acquisition of its competitor, Tri-State Tablet Company, in April 1988 was the culmination of these efforts.

Padgett's financial statements for fiscal year 1988 had been given an unqualified opinion by the national C.P.A. firm that audited them. Straight-line depreciation was used for reporting purposes with accelerated depreciation used for taxes. Inventory had been valued on a lower of cost (FIFO) or market basis. Financial statements for the 1985–1988 fiscal years are presented in Exhibits 1 and 2. Exhibit 3 is a standard computer spread used by Windsor's credit department to organize a company's financial statements for analysis.

PADGETT'S RELATIONSHIP WITH WINDSOR TRUST

Windsor Trust had historically been Padgett's only lending bank and was the only lending bank in early 1989. Among other benefits of this relationship, Padgett used Windsor Trust as the depository for its substantial New York state and Federal tax payments. So far during the 1989 fiscal year, Padgett's average collected balance with Windsor had been $524,000. Affiliated companies and subsidiaries had balances which had averaged $231,000. The loan balances outstanding had ranged from $3.3 to $7.2 million, with an average of $5.05 million. The loan had last been cleaned up for an extended period from March 31, 1985 to January 4, 1986.

Padgett maintained a small deposit relationship with the Phoenix Bank of Manhattan, a major bank which had long been soliciting a more important role in the company's financial arrangements. In addition, several out-of-town banks were used to service the various plant locations.

The speed with which the Tri-State Tablet acquisition had been made had not allowed for careful planning of the financial arrangements. Mr. Libris's superiors had been reluctant to double the loan to Padgett in the absence of a carefully structured financial program as well as appropriate protective covenants. With Mr. Libris's assurance that these questions could be quickly resolved, the divisional senior vice president had authorized the loan and established a new temporary credit limit of $8 million. It had been expected, however, that the loan would be formally structured long before January 1989, which was a source of embarrassment to Mr. Libris. He knew he would also be embarrassed and his profit plan damaged if he should lose the account to Phoenix or if it were taken over completely by an insurance company.

Once the dust created by the acquisition had settled down, Mr. Libris met with John Ruhl, Padgett's financial vice president, to discuss the company's plans. Based on these conversations, Mr. Libris and Windsor's credit department prepared a preliminary financial forecast for Padgett's 1989–1992 fiscal years. Summary figures from this forecast are presented in Exhibit 4.

Mr. Libris was distressed to note that, even under what he thought were assumptions that minimized the need for funds, Padgett would still have $4.4 million in short-term debt on the books at the end of 1992 fiscal year. Assuming the company could generate about $1 million in "undedicated" cash each year thereafter, a total of eight years would be required to retire the debt. This was considerably longer than the typical bank five-year term loan which a company of Padgett's size might expect. Windsor was willing to stretch to six years for important relationships, but a seven-year term loan would be considered a bit long for a company like Padgett which did not enjoy the financial flexibility afforded firms having easy entry to the public capital markets.

Mr. Libris decided that a need of this duration appropriately called for insurance company financing. After he had met with officers of several companies, he wrote Mr. Ruhl to propose a 12- to 15-year loan and to quote terms an insurance company might offer. (Mr. Libris's letter is reproduced as Exhibit 5.) He also pointed out that Windsor might be able to structure an arrangement which would allow the bank to take the seasonal needs while the insurance company would take the long-term core requirements of $5 million.

Mr. Ruhl's response was emphatically negative. While he appreciated the information, he reported that management did not like the high, fixed rates that were currently being charged. Furthermore, management did not like the idea of an elaborate set of covenants. Mr. Ruhl said that he particularly disliked the type of covenant that could throw the company in default without management's explicit action. "Violation of a debt–capital ratio, for instance," explained Mr. Ruhl, "could occur as the result of an adverse year rather than anything we do. I don't mind agreeing not to borrow or pay dividends if certain conditions would result, but I just don't see agreeing to a lot of things that are out of my control. I can't see getting tied up in all these technicalities." Mr. Ruhl indicated that he did not see anything wrong with the present, friendly, informal loan. "After all," he said, "if you don't like what we're doing—anything at all—you can call your entire loan at the end of any 90-day period. Isn't that better protection for you than fancy agreements?"

In the months that followed this disappointing outcome, Mr. Libris met frequently with Mr. Ruhl in order to get a thorough understanding of the business. He planned to prepare a forecast of future needs which would accurately reflect Padgett management's thinking and his own insights into the company. By late in 1988, preliminary estimates for the 1989 fiscal year were becoming available so that Mr. Libris could incorporate them into his forecasts. The forecasts, which were prepared showing the effects of 5 percent, 10 percent, and 15 percent growth in sales over the 1990–1992 fiscal years, are included as Exhibit 6.

Mr. Ruhl thought that this effort was most helpful, although he noted that two last-minute changes should be incorporated in the planning. First, he expected to shift to LIFO inventory valuation for the 1989 fiscal year, which would result in a tax benefit of $500,000. Second, management had decided to dispose of a redundant warehouse which had been part of the Tri-State acquisition. Management expected to receive $700,000 from the cash sale and tax refunds on the book loss.

ALTERNATIVES

Mr. Libris still thought that splitting the loan—maybe with the bank's own real estate department—had promise. For instance, Padgett owned outright a large, general-purpose warehouse. Its appraisal value of $3 million was in excess of the amount at which it was carried on the books. Although Mr. Libris was not an experienced real-estate lending officer, he believed the property would be attractive collateral for a mortgage loan. Another alternative might be to wait until the loan had been partly retired and then invite another bank to share the remainder for the duration of the repayment. Part of the loan could be rotated between banks to allow each one a cleanup period of several months. Finally, he had discovered that Padgett's small Canadian operation was self-contained with a negligible amount of intercompany transfers and charges. With net current assets of $1.8 to $2.0 million to offer as collateral and no direct debt, the Canadian subsidiary could probably raise $1.0 million from Canadian banks. The Canadian banks would require a "floating charge," a form of security agreement, against all current assets.

Although U.S. banking law and practice was not identical with Canadian and British practice with respect to "floating liens," asset-based finance might offer useful alternatives. It would be expensive to take effective security against Padgett's receivables because the company had so many customers and the average account was relatively small. A factoring arrangement might be suitable, in which Padgett could sell its accounts on a nonrecourse basis to a commercial finance company. Windsor Bank itself did not operate a factoring function, however. It would be necessary to find one that had experience in the paper distribution business or the costs of the factoring, which were usually about 2 percent of accounts purchased, would be too high. On the other hand, if Padgett factored its accounts, it could eliminate its credit department and would have no bad debts.

Windsor could always grant credit against the security of the accounts receivable even though not monitoring the accounts as closely as a factor would. The loan would be limited to a percentage of receivables in order to provide some protection against losses. A security interest in the inventory could also be required, although the granting of this security could upset some major paper companies who were Padgett's sources of supply.

MONEY MARKET CONSIDERATION AND PRICING ASPECTS

Funds were readily available in the financial markets in January 1989, although the prime rate had risen rapidly during 1988 and now stood at 10 ½ percent. The prime's low in recent years had been 7 ½ percent from September 1986 to March 1987. By January 1988, prime had risen to 8 ¾ percent. Thirty-day commercial paper was currently yielding 9.30 percent, up from 8.82 percent the first week in December 1988. The Treasury yield curve was relatively flat, with 1-year notes trading at 9.07 percent, 5-year notes at 9.18 percent, 10-year bonds at 9.17 percent, and 30-year bonds at 9.0 percent.

These increases in the interest rates were an issue that Mr. Libris would have to address in preparing a proposal for Mr. Ruhl. First, should the loan (or loans) be priced at a fixed rate or at a floating rate? Fixed-rate loans were generally offered at a premium of ½ to 1 percent above the floating rate.

In adjusting the prime rate to the conditions of the borrower, Windsor bank officers often used what they termed a "risk premium" system. This approach added or subtracted 25 basis points (¼ percent) to the price for such factors as the size of the company's sales (add points for small size and lack of access to public markets), purpose, term, escalating versus level payments, debt profile, liquidity posture, and (subtract points for) relationship benefits (e.g., balances, tax payments, and corporate trust). Of course, the final rate had to be checked against the market, which in Padgett's case was highly competitive as the result of Phoenix's interest.

Second, Mr. Libris was considering whether to offer Padgett a "cash cap" on the loan, if Mr. Ruhl decided to put a significant portion of it on a floating rate. A *cash cap loan* was one that established a maximum rate of interest due currently in cash as well as an index rate by which the total interest due would be determined. If the index rose above the cash cap rate, the difference between total interest and the cash cap amount due would be set up as a separate loan on the respective books. Interest on this loan would also be calculated under the index-cash-cap arrangement. When the index interest rate again declined below the cash cap rate, the borrower would continue to pay at the cash cap rate, with the difference being used to amortize the separate "cash cap" loan. When that loan had been repaid, the interest rate would fall to the index level.

Because of the complications which had already been experienced and which were likely to arise in the course of completing the negotiations, Mr. Libris knew that he had no more time to collect information. He had to work quickly toward a satisfactory resolution of the loan structure with Padgett's management.

Case 8 Padgett Blank Book Company

EXHIBIT 1 INCOME STATEMENTS FOR THE FISCAL YEARS ENDED APRIL 30, 1985–1988 (thousands of dollars)

	1985	*1986*	*1987*	*1988*
Net sales	$26,331	$27,219	$36,897	$41,308
Cost of goods sold	15,728	16,077	21,937	24,555
Depreciation and amortization	*	510	667	739
	$10,603	$10,632	$14,293	$16,014
General and admin. expense	$ 5,814	$ 5,087	$ 7,139	$ 7,821
Selling expense	**	1,878	2,603	3,147
Operating expenses	$ 5,814	$ 6,965	$ 9,742	$10,968
Operating profit	$ 4,789	$ 3,667	$ 4,551	$ 5,046
Interest expense	—	32	220	379
Other expenses (income)	83	(42)	(39)	(71)
Profit before taxes	$ 4,706	$ 3,677	$ 4,370	$ 4,738
Income taxes	2,702	1,893	2,216	2,132
Profit after taxes	$ 2,004	$ 1,784	$ 2,154	$ 2,606
Number of shares (000)	1,000	1,115	1,116	1,118
Earnings per share	$ 2.00	$ 1.60	$ 1.93	$ 2.33
Dividends per share	$ 1.00	$ 1.00	$ 1.00	$ 1.00

*Included in cost of goods sold in 1985.

**Included in general and administrative expenses in 1985.

Case 8 Padgett Blank Book Company

EXHIBIT 2 BALANCE SHEETS AS OF APRIL 30, 1985–1988 (thousands of dollars)

	1985	*1986*	*1987*	*1988*
Assets				
Current Assets				
Cash and securities	$ 1,691	$ 266	$ 658	$ 834
Accounts receivable	4,734	5,542	6,360	7,754
Inventory	7,276	7,743	10,959	14,360
Prepayments and other	233	194	153	563
Total current assets	$13,934	$13,745	$18,120	$23,511
Property, plant, equipt.	—	$ 8,718	$11,265	$12,468
Less: Accumulated depn.	—	3,384	4,912	5,209
Net prop., plant, equip.	$ 4,797	$ 5,334	$ 6,353	$ 7,259
Other assets	59	257	386	224
Total assets	$18,790	$19,336	$24,859	$30,994
Liabilities and Owners' Equity				
Current Liabilities				
Short-term notes	$ —	$ —	$ 3,118	$ 7,221
Accounts payable	1,127	1,619	2,158	1,958
Accruals	395	397	703	1,014
Other current liabilities	271	251	418	824
Current portion, long-term debt	615	117	51	52
Total current liabilities	$ 2,408	$ 2,384	$ 6,448	$11,069
Long-term debt	$ 338	$ 221	$ 507	$ 455
Deferred taxes	538	568	714	756
Other liabilities	136	126	116	151
Total liabilities	$ 3,420	$ 3,299	$ 7,785	$12,431
Owners' equity				
Common stock	$ 5,587	$ 5,587	$ 5,587	$ 5,587
Retained earnings	9,783	10,450	11,487	12,976
Total owners' equity	$15,370	$16,037	$17,074	$18,563
Total liabilities and net worth	$18,790	$19,336	$24,859	$30,994

EXHIBIT 3 CASH FLOW AND RATIO ANALYSIS, FISCAL YEARS ENDED APRIL 30, 1985–1988 (dollar figures in thousands)

	1985	*1986*	*1987*	*1988*
Sources				
Profit after taxes plus depn. and amort.*		$ 2,294	$ 2,821	$ 3,345
Deferred taxes		30	146	42
New long-term debt		—	337	—
New short-term debt		—	3,118	4,103
Accounts payable		492	539	(200)
Accruals		2	306	311
Other current liabilities		(20)	167	406
Other liabilities		(10)	(10)	35
Total Sources		$ 2,788	$ 7,424	$ 8,042
Uses				
Dividends paid in cash		$ 1,117	$ 1,117	$ 1,117
Capital expenditure		979	1,575	1,530
Repayment of long-term debt		615	117	51
Accounts receivable		808	808	1,404
Inventory		467	3,216	3,401
Prepayments and other current assets		(39)	(41)	410
Other assets		198	129	(162)
Intangibles*		68	111	115
Total Uses		$ 4,213	$ 7,032	$ 7,866
Change in cash and securities		$(1,425)	$ 392	$ 176
Working capital	$11,526	$11,361	$11,672	$12,442
Profitability				
Sales growth	n.a.%	3.4%	35.6%	12.0%
Gross profit margin	40.3	39.1	38.7	38.8
Operating expenses/sales	22.1	25.6	26.4	26.5
Pre-tax margin	17.9	13.5	11.8	11.5
After-tax margin	7.6	6.6	5.8	6.3
Return on aver. owners' equity	n.a.	11.4	13.0	14.6
Return on total assets	10.7	9.2	8.7	8.4
EBIT/Total assets	25.0	19.2	18.5	16.5
Dividend payout	50.2	62.6	51.9	42.9
Turnover on Sales				
Receivables	5.6×	4.9×	5.8×	5.3×
Inventory	3.6	3.5	3.4	2.9
Accounts payable	23.4	16.8	17.1	21.1
Working capital	2.3	2.4	3.2	3.3
Fixed assets	5.5	5.1	5.8	5.7
Net worth	1.7	1.7	2.2	2.2

Case 8 Padgett Blank Book Company

EXHIBIT 3 (*continued*)

	1985	*1986*	*1987*	*1988*
Leverage				
Total debt/owners' equity	23.3%	20.6%	45.6%	67.0%
Long-term debt/owners' equity	2.2	1.4	2.9	2.4
Interest coverage	n.a.	115.9×	20.9×	13.5×
Liquidity				
Quick ratio	2.7×	2.4×	1.1×	.8×
Current ratio	5.8	5.8	2.8	2.1

*Intangibles amortized as purchased.

Case 8 Padgett Blank Book Company

EXHIBIT 4 SUMMARY FIGURES FROM PRELIMINARY PROJECTION OF FINANCIAL POSITION, FISCAL YEARS ENDED APRIL 30, 1989–1992 (millions of dollars)

	1989	*1990*	*1991*	*1992*
Net sales	$55.2	$60.7	$66.8	$73.5
Profit after taxes	3.3	3.6	4.2	4.8
Noncash charges	.9	.9	1.0	1.1
Cash generated from operations	$ 4.2	$ 4.5	$ 5.2	$ 5.9
Disposition of assets	.2	—	—	—
Total sources	$ 4.4	$ 4.5	$ 5.2	$ 5.9
Dividends	$ 1.1	$ 1.1	$ 1.1	$ 1.1
Increase in working capital*	2.4	2.4	3.1	3.6
Capital expenditures	1.0	1.0	1.0	1.0
	$ 4.5	$ 4.5	$ 5.2	$ 5.7
*Including retirement of short-term debt:	.7	.2	.8	1.1
Leaving a balance of in short-term debt	6.5	6.3	5.5	4.4

Assumptions:

1. 10% sales growth
2. 6–6 1/2% after-tax margin
3. Accounts receivable turnover 5.7 (17.5% of sales)
4. Inventory turnover 3.6 (27.8% of sales)
5. Accounts payable turnover 21.3 (4.7% of sales)

Case 8 Padgett Blank Book Company

EXHIBIT 5 MR. LIBRIS'S LETTER OUTLINING PROPOSED TERM LOAN ARRANGEMENT

May 15, 1988

Mr. John Ruhl
Vice President—Finance
Padgett Blank Book Company
New York, NY

Dear John:

Thank you for the opportunity last week to review the financial plans you have for Padgett. This letter sets forth our thoughts relating to the need for properly incorporating your bank loan into these plans.

Currently, Padgett has $6,853,000 outstanding in short-term 90-day notes, and we understand that an additional $1.0–$1.5 million is likely to be borrowed to support new receivables of your new acquisition. This is in contrast with the circumstance of May 1986 when we financed your previous acquisition, and our loan outstanding increased from $500,000 to $1,850,000. At that time, an anticipated restructuring of the loan was postponed until a clearer definition of longer term corporate cash need could be ascertained.

In late 1987, we expressed an interest in discussing with you a restructuring of the then loan outstanding so that legitimately long-term funds could be sourced on a proper long-term basis. Our subsequent conversations and cash flow study were complicated by the anticipated major acquisition and its impact.

Enclosed is a copy of our most recent Padgett forecast, the results of which we have jointly reviewed. On balance, our feeling is that the forecast may tend to understate the cash requirement in that it assumes moderate sales growth, the upholding of traditional margins, and tight control over capital expenditures and dividends. The forecast does seem to indicate a long-term need of at least $5 million which cannot be properly funded through the bank on anything resembling a full-payout term loan basis.

Given what appears to be the clear nature of the need, it seems appropriate that financing discussions with an insurance company be initiated. This suggestion is rooted in our firm feeling that it is strategically unwise from the standpoint of the company, as well as that of the bank, to fulfill substantial long-term financial need through the continued use of 90-day notes.

On a confidential basis and without revealing your name, we have talked with three insurance companies within the last week. Discussions included the following generalized parameters for life insurance company lending:

amount:	no problem
term:	12–15 years
rate:	fixed, 9 1/2% minimum
payback:	level payments desired but flexibility offered, e.g., three years of grace
prepayment:	all want protection designed to discourage it; however, there are provisions for prepayment without penalty if they were to turn you down for a requested increase in amount and you were able to obtain a commitment from another source
availability of money:	good

There is the possibility of bank participation in the first five years of an insurance company loan, but (as you can well understand) it is the lender taking the longest maturities who controls the negotiation of loan agreement covenants from the lenders' point of view. Inclusion of the Bank

EXHIBIT 5 (*continued*)

whose interest rates are geared to a floating prime rate offers a partial hedge, without guarantee, against known fixed interest cost. Bank pricing would probably look like the prime rate plus 1/4% for the first three years and prime plus 1/2% for years four and five. While an insurance company loan requires no deposit balances to be maintained, we would expect balances of 5% against the average loan outstanding. A 5% balance increment is roughly equivalent to 1/4% in interest rate.

We all recognize the fact that interest rates have again risen; however, the Economics Department of this Bank does not feel that long-term interest rates will see reduced levels in the foreseeable future. Financing demands on the capital markets are expected to continue strong, inflation psychology seems to be rising, the deficits are not yet under control, and any advantage to be gained in avoiding the long-term market is, at best, marginal. It might, in fact, be dangerous.

For any needs consistent with prudent bank lending, Windsor Trust stands ready to finance your business. Our desire to assist in every way we can is complete and sincere.

Sincerely,

/s/ frank
Francis Libris
Vice President
Windsor Trust Company

EXHIBIT 6 PROJECTED FINANCIAL STATEMENTS FOR 1990–1992 FISCAL YEARS ENDING APRIL 30, ASSUMING 5%, 10%, AND 15% SALES GROWTH (dollar figures in millions except per-share figures)

	1988	1989	*5% Growth*			*10% Growth*			*15% Growth*		
	Actual	*Est.*	*1990*	*1991*	*1992*	*1990*	*1991*	*1992*	*1990*	*1991*	*1992*
A. Income Statements											
Sales, net	$41.32	$57.80	$60.69	$63.72	$66.91	$63.58	$69.94	$76.93	$66.47	$76.44	$87.91
Cost of sales	24.56	36.08	37.27	38.86	40.81	39.05	42.65	46.93	40.82	46.61	53.61
Depn. & amort.	0.74	0.94	0.91	1.00	1.10	0.91	1.00	1.10	0.91	1.00	1.10
General & admin.	7.82	10.23	10.75	11.29	11.87	11.26	12.40	13.65	11.77	13.55	15.59
Selling expense	3.15	4.61	4.84	5.09	5.35	5.08	5.60	6.15	5.30	6.11	7.03
Operating profit	$ 5.05	$ 5.94	$ 6.92	$ 7.48	$ 7.78	$ 7.29	$ 8.29	$ 9.10	$ 7.67	$ 9.17	$10.58
Interest expenses*	0.38	0.95	0.80	0.72	0.61	0.90	0.86	0.81	1.01	1.10	1.18
Other exp. (income)	(.07)	(.71)	0.07	0.07	0.07	0.07	0.07	0.07	0.07	0.07	0.07
Pre-tax earnings	$ 4.74	$ 5.70	$ 6.05	$ 6.69	$ 7.10	$ 6.31	$ 7.36	$ 8.22	$ 6.59	$ 8.00	$ 9.33
After-tax earnings	2.61	3.42	3.63	4.01	4.26	3.79	4.42	4.93	3.95	4.80	5.60
Earnings per share (1,118)	$ 2.33	$ 3.06	$ 3.25	$ 3.59	$ 3.81	$ 3.39	$ 3.95	$ 4.41	$ 3.54	$ 4.29	$ 5.01
Dividends per share	1.00	1.03	1.08	1.19	1.27	1.13	1.31	1.47	1.18	1.43	1.66

Note: Figures may not add because of rounding.
*Includes interest calculated on the cash deficit at 11%.

EXHIBIT 6 (*continued*)

	1988	1989	5% Growth			10% Growth			15% Growth		
	Actual	*Est.*	*1990*	*1991*	*1992*	*1990*	*1991*	*1992*	*1990*	*1991*	*1992*
B. Balance Sheets											
Assets											
Cash (minimum)	$ .83	$ 1.17	$ 1.23	$ 1.29	$ 1.36	$ 1.29	$ 1.42	$ 1.56	$ 1.35	$ 1.55	$ 1.78
Excess cash	—	—	.01	.73	1.24	—	—	—	—	—	—
Acc. receivable	7.75	10.12	10.62	11.15	11.71	11.13	12.24	13.46	11.63	13.38	15.38
Inventory	14.36	16.18	16.99	17.84	18.74	17.80	19.58	21.54	18.61	21.40	24.61
Prepayments, etc.	.56	.23	.24	.26	.27	.26	.28	.31	.27	.31	.36
Total current assets	$23.51	$27.71	$29.10	$31.27	$33.32	$30.48	$33.52	$36.87	$31.86	$36.64	$42.14
Plant & equip.	12.47	13.27	14.27	15.27	16.27	14.27	15.27	16.27	14.27	15.27	16.27
Less: accum. depn.	5.21	6.04	6.95	7.95	9.05	6.95	7.95	9.05	6.95	7.95	9.05
Net plant & equip.	$ 7.26	$ 7.23	$ 7.32	$ 7.32	$ 7.22	$ 7.32	$ 7.32	$ 7.22	$ 7.32	$ 7.32	$ 7.22
Other	.22	.11	.11	.11	.11	.11	.11	.11	.11	.11	.11
Total assets	$30.99	$35.05	$36.54	$38.71	$40.65	$37.91	$40.95	$44.20	$39.29	$44.07	$49.47
Liabilities and Owner's Equity											
Short-term notes	$ 7.22	$ 7.45	$ 6.29	$ 5.50	$ 4.35	$ 6.29	$ 5.50	$ 4.35	$ 6.29	$ 5.50	$ 4.35
Acc. payable	1.96	2.72	2.85	3.00	3.14	2.99	3.29	3.62	3.12	3.59	4.13
Accruals	1.01	1.44	1.52	1.59	1.67	1.59	1.75	1.92	1.66	1.91	2.20
Other	.82	1.15	1.21	1.33	1.40	1.27	1.39	1.53	1.33	1.61	1.85
Current portion, LTD	.05	.05	.05	.05	.05	.05	.05	.05	.05	.05	.05
Total current liabilities	$11.06	$12.82	$11.93	$11.48	$10.61	$12.19	$11.98	$11.47	$12.46	$12.66	$12.58
Long-term debt	.46	.40	.35	.30	.25	.35	.30	.25	.35	.30	.25
Deferred taxes	.76	.80	.80	.80	.80	.80	.80	.80	.80	.80	.80
Other	.15	.20	.20	.20	.20	.20	.20	.20	.20	.20	.20
Cash deficit*	—	—	—	—	—	1.02	1.37	1.89	2.01	3.44	5.23
Total liabilities	$12.43	$14.22	$13.28	$12.78	$11.86	$14.56	$14.65	$14.61	$15.82	$17.40	$19.06
Common stock	5.59	5.59	5.59	5.59	5.59	5.59	5.59	5.59	5.59	5.59	5.59
Retained earnings	12.98	15.24	17.67	20.34	23.18	17.76	20.71	24.00	17.88	21.09	24.82
Total owner's equity	$18.56	$20.83	$23.25	$25.93	$28.77	$23.35	$26.30	$29.59	$23.47	$26.68	$30.41
Total liability & owner's equity	$30.99	$35.05	$36.53	$38.71	$40.63	$37.91	$40.95	$44.20	$39.29	$44.07	$49.47

*Includes interest calculated on the cash deficit at 11%.

EXHIBIT 6 (*continued*)

	1988	1989	5% Growth			10% Growth			15% Growth		
	Actual	*Est.*	*1990*	*1991*	*1992*	*1990*	*1991*	*1992*	*1990*	*1991*	*1992*
C. Cash Flow											
Sources											
After-tax earnings		$ 3.42	$ 3.63	$ 4.01	$ 4.26	$ 3.79	$ 4.42	$ 4.93	$ 3.95	$ 4.80	$ 5.59
Noncash charges		.94	.91	1.00	1.10	.91	1.00	1.10	.91	1.00	1.10
Funds from operations		$ 4.36	$ 4.54	$ 5.01	$ 5.36	$ 4.70	$ 5.42	$ 6.03	$ 4.86	$ 5.80	$ 6.69
Deferred taxes		.04	—	—	—	—	—	—	—	—	—
Accounts payable		.76	.14	.14	.14	.27	.30	.33	.41	.47	.54
Accruals		.43	.07	.07	.08	.14	.16	.17	.22	.25	.29
Other and miscellaneous current liability		.33	.06	.12	.07	.12	.12	.14	.17	.27	.24
Other liabilities		.05	—	—	—	—	—	—	—	—	—
Other assets		.11	—	—	—	—	—	—	—	—	—
Total sources		$ 6.08	$ 4.81	$ 5.34	$ 5.65	$ 5.22	$ 6.00	$ 6.67	$ 5.66	$ 6.79	$ 7.76
Uses											
Dividends		$ 1.16	$ 1.21	$ 1.34	$ 1.42	$ 1.26	$ 1.47	$ 1.64	$ 1.31	$ 1.59	$ 1.86
Capital expenditures		.80	1.00	1.00	1.00	1.00	1.00	1.00	1.00	1.00	1.00
S.T. debt		(.23)	1.16	.79	1.15	1.16	.79	1.15	1.16	.79	1.15
L.T. debt		.05	.05	.05	.05	.05	.05	.05	.05	.05	.05
Minimum cash		.34	.06	.06	.06	.12	.13	.14	.18	.20	.23
Accounts receivable		2.36	.50	.53	.56	1.01	1.11	1.22	1.52	1.74	2.01
Inventory		1.82	.81	.85	.89	1.62	1.78	1.96	2.43	2.79	3.21
Prepay & def. charge		(.33)	.01	.01	.01	.02	.02	.03	.04	.04	.05
Intangibles		.11	—	—	—	—	—	—	—	—	—
Total uses		$ 6.08	$ 4.80	$ 4.63	$ 5.14	$ 6.24	$ 6.35	$ 7.19	$ 7.69	$ 8.20	$ 9.56
Net cash flow		—	.02	.71	.51	(1.01)	(.35)	(.52)	(2.03)	(1.41)	(1.80)
Cumulative		—	.02	.73	1.24	(1.01)	(1.36)	(1.88)	(2.02)	(3.43)	(5.23)

EXHIBIT 6 (*continued*)

	1988	1989	5% Growth			10% Growth			15% Growth		
	Actual	*Est.*	*1990*	*1991*	*1992*	*1990*	*1991*	*1992*	*1990*	*1991*	*1992*
D. Analytical Ratios											
Profitability											
Sales growth	12.0%	39.9%	5.0%	5.0%	5.0%	10.0%	10.0%	10.0%	15.0%	15.0%	15.0%
E.P.S. growth	20.7	31.4	6.2	10.3	6.3	10.8	16.5	11.2	15.5	21.4	16.5
Gross profit margin	38.8	35.9	38.6	39.0	39.0	38.6	39.0	39.0	38.6	39.0	39.0
Operating exp./sales	26.5	25.7	25.7	25.7	25.3	25.7	25.7	25.7	25.7	25.7	25.7
Pre-tax margin	11.5	10.3	10.0	10.5	10.6	9.9	10.5	10.7	9.9	10.5	10.6
After-tax margin	6.3	5.9	6.0	6.3	6.4	6.0	6.3	6.4	5.9	6.3	6.4
Return on average owner's equity	14.6	17.4	16.5	16.3	15.6	17.1	17.8	17.6	17.9	19.1	19.6
Return on total assets	8.4	9.8	9.9	10.4	10.5	10.0	10.8	11.2	10.1	10.9	11.3
EBIT/total assets	16.5	19.0	18.7	19.1	19.0	19.0	20.1	20.4	19.4	20.7	21.2
Dividend payout	42.9	33.8	33.3	33.3	33.3	33.3	33.3	33.3	33.2	33.2	33.2
Turnover											
Receivables	5.3×	5.7×	5.7×	5.7×	5.7×	5.7×	5.7×	5.7×	5.7×	5.7×	5.7×
Inventory	2.9	3.6	3.6	3.6	3.6	3.6	3.6	3.6	3.6	3.6	3.6
Accounts payable	21.1	21.3	21.3	21.3	21.3	21.3	21.3	21.3	21.3	21.3	21.3
Working capital	3.3	3.6	3.5	3.2	2.9	3.5	3.3	3.0	3.4	3.2	3.0
Fixed asset	5.7	8.0	8.3	8.7	9.3	8.7	9.6	10.6	9.1	10.4	12.2
Net worth	2.2	2.8	2.6	2.4	2.3	2.7	2.6	2.6	2.8	2.9	2.9
Leverage											
Total debt/owners' equity	67.0%	68.3%	57.1%	49.3%	41.3%	62.3%	55.7%	49.3%	67.4%	65.2%	62.7%
Long-term debt/owners' equity	2.4	1.9	1.5	1.1	0.9	1.5	1.1	0.8	1.5	1.1	0.8
Interest coverage	13.5	7.0	8.7	10.3	12.6	8.0	9.6	11.1	7.5	8.3	8.9
Liquidity											
Quick ratio	.8×	1.0×	1.0×	1.1×	1.3×	1.0×	1.1×	1.3×	1.1×	1.2×	1.4×
Current ratio	2.1	2.2	2.4	2.7	3.1	2.5	2.8	3.2	2.6	2.9	3.3
Working capital	$12.44	$14.89	$19.40	$29.98	$29.55	$18.29	$21.46	$25.23	$19.40	$23.98	$29.55

Case 9

MISSISSIPPI MILLING COMPANY

In early April 1976, top management of the Mississippi Milling Company was faced with the necessity of obtaining $10 million of outside capital. This, in conjunction with internally generated funds, would be used to expand the wet corn milling capacity of the New Orleans plant from 75,000 to 100,000 bushels per day and to acquire the Myers Company, a regional franchise bottler of nationally advertised soft drinks.

COMPANY

Mississippi Milling was primarily engaged in the milling of corn and soybeans. Corn was first converted into starch, itself an end product, which was generally further refined into high-fructose corn syrup (HFCS). HFCS was sold in concentrations of 42 percent and 55 percent to brewers, soft drink bottlers, confectioners, and other food preparers. In general, it was used to replace sugar. Soybeans were processed to produce animal feeds, edible protein products, and vegetable oil. In recent years, however, soybean products had gained wide acceptance as food for humans. Production of meat extenders and meat substitutes made from soybeans had increased substantially. Growth in this area was projected at 20 percent per year for the next five years.

Mississippi Milling had decided to acquire the Myers Company, a long-standing customer, for several reasons:

1. Mississippi Milling would gain the advantages of vertical integration, because Myers incorporated HFCS in its products.
2. Although relatively small, Myers had a good profitability record; present management intended to remain.
3. This was the first step in a plan to diversify away from exclusive dependence on the milling industry.

Diversification was considered necessary to reduce Mississippi's exposure to the cyclical earnings inherent in the production of agriculturally based commodity items. Two factors led to cyclical earnings:

1. Raw material prices were subject to rapid changes due to factors such as weather, transportation costs, government policies, and world-wide demand. (Mississippi Milling had a wholly-owned subsidiary which engaged in hedging in the commodities markets in an effort to stabilize both the price and the availability of raw materials.)
2. As in the aluminum and steel industries, milling capacity tended to be added in large increments, leading to conditions where demand and supply were frequently in disequilibrium. High utilization of available capacity was essential, and industry overcapacity resulted in severe price competition. Consequently, margins were subject to extreme fluctuations.

COMPANY HISTORY

Mississippi Milling was founded at the turn of the century in New Orleans by Mr. Henry La Font, a French immigrant. Starting with $1500, La Font began by selling starch door to door and to the Navy supply house in New Orleans. The business proved to be profitable, and in 1910 La Font purchased a starch-making plant with a capacity of 500 bushels of corn per day. This was the entry of La Font into the milling business. Mr. La Font died in 1937, leaving the company to his family. Management fell to his daughter, Catherine. Ms. La Font proved to be an ex-

Case prepared by Alton Martin with the cooperation of individuals and institutions that wish to remain anonymous. Certain of the company's characteristics and financial information have been changed to protect confidential information without altering the managerial decision.

tremely capable and energetic manager, noted for her dogmatic and uncompromising insistence on quality and her spicy rejoinders to shippers who attempted to deliver sub-par raw materials to the plant.

To reduce inheritance and estate tax problems, Ms. La Font decided to take the company public in 1950. At the time of the initial offering, the company acquired its present name. The influx of equity, combined with increasing demand for both its corn and soybean products, allowed the company to continue to grow and prosper. By the early 1970s, Mississippi Milling was firmly entrenched as the regional leader in its industry. It was at this time that HFCS was first established as an economically viable substitute for industrial sugar.

Before her retirement from active management in 1965, Ms. La Font brought in new managerial talent, including several MBAs. Their charge was to continue to increase company assets, sales, and profits. Her skill in choosing managers was proven by the rapidly expanded sales of the company. (Exhibits 1 and 2 present income statements for five years from 1971–75 and the balance sheet as of December 31, 1975.)

THE PROBLEM

As previously mentioned, Mississippi Milling needed funds both to diversify and to expand. The critical decision was the selection of the appropriate external vehicle to secure the capital needed to augment internally generated funds. Mississippi's president, Mr. Andrew Ericson, had met with his investment bankers who presented him with the following options:

1. A private placement with an insurance company of $10 million of 15-year debentures. The rate was set at 9.25 percent. Sinking fund requirements were $500,000 a year for 14 years, with a balloon payment of $3 million at the end of year 15. Legal and other costs were $35,000, and the money would be available within 30 days. Although there were restrictive convenants with this loan, both the legal and financial staffs concluded they were neither overly burdensome nor would they prevent the company from adhering to its previously established plans.
2. A public offering of 102,300 shares of preferred stock, at a par value of $100 and a coupon of 8.25 percent. (Exhibit 3 presents currently prevailing rates.) Issue costs would be approximately $2.25 a share, with legal and registration fees of another $50,000. Time to issue date would be 70 days. Redemptions would begin after 5 years at the rate of $500,000 (5,000 shares) per year, selected at random.
3. A public issue of 200,000 shares of common stock to net $50.00 a share. Underwriting fees would be 4 ½ percent of the issue price of $52.35. Legal and other fees would amount to $55,000. The money would be available 10–12 weeks after the decision was made.

Mr. Ericson decided to turn the analysis of the vehicles over to Ms. Margaret Gasque, a recent M.B.A. graduate. Her task was to recommend which financing method was the best for the company. (Capital market data are provided in Exhibit 3 and the terms of the company's existing debt are summarized in Exhibit 4.)

An additional consideration was a projected drop in earnings for the current year. Based on the 800,000 shares currently outstanding, earnings after tax were expected to decrease to about $6.8 million, or $8.50 a share. Higher raw material costs and flat selling prices were expected to squeeze margins. Once the new investments were on stream, they were expected to add before-tax earnings of $2 million to the levels that would otherwise exist. The board expected to maintain the dividend at the recently established rate of $0.25 per quarter.

After due deliberations, Ms. Gasque recommended to Mr. Ericson the use of debt financing. Her most pressing concern was the effect the financing would have on dilution of earnings per share. Debt would reduce earnings by approximately 58¢ a share, preferred by $1.05, and a common stock issue by $1.70. Because earnings were already expected to fall, Ms. Gasque didn't want to accentuate the decline any further. An additional consideration was the low cost of debt: even with the $10,000,000 addition to long-term debt, the weighted average cost of all debt was 8.888 percent before tax, as shown in Exhibit 5. After income taxes of 50 percent, the cost was only 4.44 percent.

Mr. Ericson was in general agreement with Ms. Gasque's recommendation. However, the decision would ultimately be made by the board of directors. The proper choice was important, and Mr. Ericson wished the board members to be briefed before the next meeting so they could familiarize themselves with the issues. Accordingly, he asked Ms. Gasque to visit several of the board members and get their opinions on the matter. Her mission was to identify the members' attitudes about the various options. Notes taken from her meetings follow:

Mr. Richard K. Powell, partner in a Baton Rouge public accounting firm and a grandson of the founder.
Appears that with this move Mississippi Milling will never pay off its debt. No sooner do we pay off present debt than someone wants to borrow again. Advocates discipline that is earned by paying back debt. Need to save cash for the "hard times that are coming!" If a company has to borrow continuously, it is going broke.

Mr. Chris Maher, attorney.
Also hesitant to get into additional debt. Feels "best time to borrow money is when you don't owe any." Would like to pay off existing debt, then consider new borrowings. Favors common stock issue. In his opinion, dilution of earnings not a major factor because stock is "conservative," bought by those in "for the long haul, with year-to-year changes in earnings not a consideration. Anyway, the market price is at a fantastic level—up almost three times since last year." (The company's stock price record is given in Exhibit 6.)

Mr. Allen Shelly, barge company owner.
Says debt too expensive. Combined interest and sinking fund is a before-tax cash drain of $1,925,000, or 19 percent of money borrowed. Suggests issue of common stock. Could pay up to $1.20 dividend per share to present shareholders from after-tax cash flow and cash drain would be the same as on the debt. Additional stock may increase trading and help to increase stock prices.

Ms. Frances Kelly, owner of famous New Orleans restaurant.
Favors the preferred stock for two main reasons. First, it really isn't debt, so it keeps the equity portion of total capitalization high. Second, because redemptions don't start until the fifth year, the company has "breathing room" without risk of default on redemptions. Combines the best of debt and equity from the lender's viewpoint because it locks in a good interest rate and guarantees the return of capital at some point in the future.

Mr. Tim Price, investor.
Strongly favors debt issue. Additional debt has advantage of not diluting earnings nearly as much as other means of financing. Inflation also benefits debtors as they pay off debt in cheaper dollars. Notes that the PE multiple for all stocks is declining. In the long lead time to a stock issue, the market could collapse.

After reviewing these notes with Ms. Gasque, Mr. Ericson knew that if he were to prevent a long, argumentative board meeting, he would have to have a solid action plan to present. His argument would have to be convincing but at the same time not combative. Mr. Ericson didn't want to have to outvote any member; he preferred decisions to be unanimous.

Case 9 Mississippi Milling Company

EXHIBIT 1 STATEMENT OF EARNINGS FOR FIVE YEARS ENDED DECEMBER 31, 1975 (dollar figures in thousands, except per-share data)

	1971	*1972*	*1973*	*1974*	*1975*
Revenue:					
Net sales	$50,092	$50,413	$69,212	$93,208	$116,518
Other—net	329	349	372	532	509
Total revenue	$50,421	$50,762	$69,584	$93,740	$117,027
Costs and expenses:					
Cost of goods sold	42,201	42,575	59,537	79,925	91,710
Selling, general, admin.	6,149	6,144	6,797	7,828	9,305
Interest	545	695	781	919	736*
Less capitalized interest	(188)	(140)	—	—	—
Minority interests	140	109	255	445	188
Total	$48,847	$49,383	$67,370	$89,117	$101,939
Earnings before taxes	1,574	1,379	2,214	4,623	15,088
Income taxes, net of ITC	765	413	1,030	2,364	7,535
Net earnings	$ 809	$ 966	$ 1,184	$ 2,259	$ 7,553
No. of shares outstanding	800,000	800,000	800,000	800,000	800,000
Earnings per share	$1.01	$1.21	$1.48	$2.82	$9.44
Dividends per share	0.70	0.70	0.70	0.70	0.85
Price range: high	$18¼	$16⅜	$15⅝	$22½	$64¼
low	$12⅛	$13¼	$10¼	$11⅞	$19⅞

*In 1976, interest on the existing long-term debt will be about $375,000. The remainder of the interest shown was paid on short-term seasonal borrowings to finance inventory and hedging activities.

Case 9 Mississippi Milling Company

EXHIBIT 2 BALANCE SHEET AS OF DECEMBER 31, 1975 (thousands of dollars)

ASSETS	
Cash and marketable securities	$ 7,029
Receivables, net	10,252
Inventories	11,302
Deferred taxes	413
Prepaid expenses	119
Total current assets	$29,115
Property and equipment, at cost	42,875
Less accumulated depreciation	(19,796)
Property and equipment, net	$23,079
Total assets	$52,194
LIABILITIES AND STOCKHOLDERS' EQUITY	
Notes payable	$ 136
Accounts payable	5,265
Accruals	4,360
Total current liabilities	$ 9,761
Long-term debt	4,626
Deferred items	3,616
Minority interests	1,117
Total liabilities	$19,120
Preferred stock—1,000,000 shares authorized, none outstanding	0
Common stock, no par value, 800,000 shares outstanding	4,500
Retained earnings	28,574
Total stockholders' equity	$33,074
Total liabilities and stockholders' equity	$52,194

Case 9 Mississippi Milling Company

EXHIBIT 3 SELECTED MONEY MARKET RATES, FEBRUARY 1975 TO FEBRUARY 1976[1]

		Common Stocks				
	Preferred Stocks	*Dividend Yield*	*P/E Multiple*	*Bank Prime*	*All Corp. Bonds*	*Industrial Bonds*
1975						
February	8.07%	4.61%		8.96%	9.33%	9.01%
March	8.04	4.42	10.10×	7.93	9.28	9.05
April	8.27	4.34		7.50	9.49	9.30
May	8.51	4.08		7.40	9.55	9.37
June	8.34	4.02	8.28×	7.07	9.45	9.29
July	8.24	4.02		7.15	9.43	9.26
August	8.42	4.36		7.66	9.51	9.29
September	8.56	4.39	9.06×	7.88	9.55	9.35
October	8.58	4.22		7.96	9.51	9.32
November	8.50	4.07		7.53	9.44	9.27
December	8.57	4.14	8.61×	7.26	9.45	9.26
1976						
January	8.16	3.8		7.00	9.33	9.16
February	8.00	3.67		6.75	9.23	9.12

[1]From *Federal Reserve Bulletin*, March 1976.

Case 9 Mississippi Milling Company

EXHIBIT 4 SCHEDULE AND DETAILS OF COVENANTS ON EXISTING LONG-TERM DEBT AS OF DECEMBER 31, 1975 (in thousands)

4⅛% Debentures	458*
8¾% Sinking Fund Debentures	3,570**
Other loans—maturities to 1999	598
Total	$4,626***

*4⅛% Bonds—"A" rated by Moodys, issued 7/1/54, maturity 7/1/79.

1. Sinking fund of $72,000/year.
2. Not secured by any lien.
3. Company will not create any funded debt if, on consolidated basis, net tangible assets are less than 1.75 times funded debt *or* if net earnings before interest and taxes averaged for 3 consecutive fiscal years are less than 5 times the annual interest charges on funded debt.
4. Company will not pay dividends on common stock greater than consolidated net income after 12/31/53 plus $975,000 plus proceeds of any stock sale plus any present debt converted into stock.

**8¾% Bonds—"A" rated by Moodys, issued 6/1/71, and due 6/1/96.

1. Sinking fund of $168,750/year.
2. Not secured by any lien.
3. Company will not create additional senior funded debt unless net tangible assets are greater than or equal to 175% of consolidated senior funded debt.
4. Company will not pay cash dividend on or acquire capital stock in excess of consolidated net earnings after 12/31/70 plus net proceeds of, or fair value of, property acquired through sale or exchange of stock or debt converted into stock after 12/31/70 plus $1.5 million.

***Interest on this debt will be approximately $375,000 in the 1976 fiscal year.

Note: As of 12/31/75, $11 million of retained earnings was not restricted by debt instruments. "Net tangible assets" equals total assets less intangible assets and current liabilities.

Case 9 Mississippi Milling Company

EXHIBIT 5 WEIGHTED AVERAGE COST OF DEBT, AFTER $10 MILLION DEBENTURE ISSUE (dollar amounts in thousands)

Principal		*Interest rate*		*Interest payment*
$10,000	×	0.0925	=	$ 925
3,570	×	0.0875	=	312
458	×	0.0412	=	18
283	×	0.08	=	23
315	×	0.07	=	22
$14,626				$1,300

$$\frac{\$\ 1{,}300}{\$14{,}626} = 8.888\%\text{ before tax}$$

Case 9 Mississippi Milling Company

EXHIBIT 6 STOCK PRICE RANGES, FIRST QUARTER 1976

Week ending	*Volume (00)*	*High*	*Low*	*Close*
1/9	70	\$57 3/8	\$52 1/2	\$52 1/2
1/16	102	46 7/8	46 1/8	46 1/4
1/23	63	46	44 1/4	44 1/4
1/30	206	47 1/4	45 3/8	47
2/6	46	47 1/2	46 1/2	47 1/2
2/13	91	50 1/8	49	49 3/4
2/20	51	52 1/4	51 7/8	52 1/8
2/27	38	47 3/4	46 1/2	46 7/8
3/5	57	50 1/4	48 3/4	48 3/4
3/12	56	52 3/4	48 3/4	51 3/4
3/19	29	51 3/4	51	51 3/4
3/26	106	62 1/4	60 3/8	61 1/2
4/2	17	57 1/4	55 7/8	55 7/8

Case 10

KADOTA SEMANEK CORPORATION

The Kadota Semanek Corporation was formed in February 1988 as the result of the acquisition by Kadota Film, Image, & General Company of Semanek Pharmaceutical Company (SPC). Kadota was one of the world's largest producers of imaging products. Its vibrant packages were evident in retail outlets the world over, and it also had a significant share of the industrial imaging market. Initially a byproduct of its imaging business, Kadota's chemical products had developed into a large, separate business.

Several years earlier, Kadota's management had selected two additional product lines for development: health care and life sciences. Both of these industries enjoyed and were expected to continue to enjoy above average profit margins. Health care, at least, was projected to grow at a rate in excess of the gross national product. To implement this strategy, Kadota was internally developing a world-class research nucleus. In addition, acquisitions were being sought for companies with strong development and marketing capabilities in the pharmaceutical industry.

In late 1987, SPC became the target of a hostile takeover. SPC, which manufactured, marketed, and distributed prescription pharmaceuticals (ethical drugs), over-the-counter medicines (proprietary drugs), and household consumer products, fit Kadota's criteria for an acquisition. Acquiring SPC would be a further important step in diversifying away from Kadota's mature core businesses. SPC also offered substantial cost efficiencies in research, manufacturing, and distribution as well as economies in purchasing. Perhaps as much as $120 million in increased operating earnings before taxes could be expected from the merger.

Kadota therefore entered the bidding as a "white knight," ultimately winning ownership of SPC at a cost of $5.1 billion. The acquisition would be one of the largest ever effected outside the energy industry, and some security analysts were arguing that Kadota had paid too much for SPC. Because of the amount of debt the transaction put on Kadota's balance sheet, the two major bond-rating agencies had downgraded Kadota's debt rating to A2/A.

PROSPECTS

Exhibit 1 lists the sales and operating profits from continuing operations for the two companies. Both firms had experienced significant problems in recent years, inherent in the risky nature of their businesses. SPC had been forced to write off $19 million in 1985, for example, when disposing of a subsidiary that no longer fit the company's strategic plan. Kadota had been forced to withdraw from a major new product line because of an unfavorable court decision. The full extent of the damages had not yet been determined, and a number of analysts had been disturbed by the size of the damages claimed. The example of Texaco was still close at hand. Calmer analysts argued that $500 to $750 million was a reasonable estimate of the costs yet to come rather than the $1 to $2 billion figures that had been mentioned. In addition, product quality problems had forced the withdrawal of a new product from the marketplace for redesign.

Nevertheless, Kadota's management believed that sales of the merged companies would grow at approximately 10 percent a year. Profits in 1988 would increase faster. From a base pro forma level of earnings before interest and taxes in 1987 of $2,475 million, earnings before interest and taxes would increase to $2,855 million (including synergies) in 1988 and to $3,140 mil-

This case was developed with the cooperation of Mr. Mark A. Seigel, Principal, Morgan Stanley and Company Incorporated. Details have been changed to protect confidential information, but the nature of the managerial decision has not been altered.

lion in 1989. Because the amortization of goodwill could not be taken as a deduction from taxable income, Kadota's tax rate would be higher than the statutory rate of 34 percent. Management estimated a 40 percent rate would apply for the next several years. Ironically, the lower the before-tax profit, the higher the effective tax rate would be.

Estimating asset requirements to support this growth was somewhat more difficult. (A preliminary pro forma balance sheet consolidating the companies is provided as Exhibit 2.) The Asset/Sales ratio for both companies had been increasing over the last five to seven years, but it appeared to have stabilized on a consolidated basis of 1/1 excluding the goodwill account. The Asset/Sales ratios appeared to increase somewhat in the first year of an economic downturn but then to decline again as business either recovered or remained at a lower level. Capital expenditures had been averaging 135 percent of depreciation, so that no flows from these noncash charges would be available to finance working capital. Amortization of the goodwill would account for about $100 million a year in additional noncash charges.

Kadota had $2.2 billion in long-term debt outstanding, and SPC had $208 million in long-term debt and $140 million in short-term debt. Interest cost on this outstanding debt was currently $216 million a year. None of the issues had significant current maturities due nor would significant repayments be required for the next three years.

KADOTA'S FINANCIAL POLICIES

The task facing Mr. Robert Rochester, Kadota's chief financial officer, in late February 1988 was developing and executing a plan to finance the acquisition. A $5 billion temporary bridge loan had been arranged with a consortium of international banks at an attractively narrow spread over the bank's cost of funds. Commercial paper in the amount of $500 million had also been sold. These were temporary measures, however, to tide Kadota over until permanent financing could be arranged.

Traditionally, Mr. Rochester had aimed for an average ratio of 35 percent of long-term debt to capitalization but had been willing to let the ratio rise temporarily to 40 percent. In recent years, however, the ratio had fallen below 35 percent despite occasional repurchases of common stock. If possible, the ratio of fixed-rate and floating-rate long-term debt was kept at 50/50. Kadota management also wished to attain an average borrowing rate of no more than 9.5 percent.

Considering the controversy surrounding the SPC acquisition and the recent drop in the rating of Kadota's debt, Mr. Rochester wanted a highly successful issue which held its relative value in the secondary market. This would establish a benchmark for the further issues that would probably follow.

Although it was not possible to calculate accurately the "beta" of the consolidated company because Kadota had no trading record in its newly expanded state, its investment bankers estimated that it would have a beta of 1.00 at its target capitalization. This translated into an "unlevered" beta of .76. The bankers also told Mr. Rochester that they estimated the current short-term risk-free interest rate to be 7 percent (implying a short-term inflation rate of between 6 and 7 percent depending on the estimate of the long-run real short-term interest rate) and an equity market premium over the risk-free rate of 6 percent. Inflation had not been as high as 6 percent for several years. It was currently running at about 4 percent.

Dividends per share were targeted at 50 percent of earnings per share in typical years. In years when reported earnings fell for unusual reasons, the dividends per share would be maintained if possible although the payout percentage would increase as a result. Dividends were currently being paid at the annual rate of $1.80 per share.

THE ALTERNATIVES

Preliminary discussions with the investment bankers had allowed Mr. Rochester to begin to rough out the options available to Kadota. First, it would be possible to raise the entire $5.1 billion (over a reasonable time period) in publicly held 30-year debt at the following rates:

Up to $2.5 billion	10.00%
$2.5 up to $4 billion	10.25%
$4 billion and higher	10.50%

Exhibit 3 provides rate spread information and Exhibit 4 presents the current yield chart for Treasury issues.

Mr. Rochester and the board of directors had been disappointed when the rating agencies had dropped the ratings of Kadota's debt. (Exhibit 5 provides summary details for Standard & Poor's AA- and A-rated companies.) The advantages of a higher rating included a financial image consistent with the business image Kadota Semanek wished to project. A strong balance sheet also permitted the use of debt to finance sudden requirements, such as the SPC acquisition, without rating and cost penalties.

A lower debt rating would have a higher cost of debt, but this might be offset by a lower overall cost of capital. More debt and less equity would increase the return on the equity, provided funds being invested would return more than the interest rate.

Because the acquisition of SPC was a cash purchase, Kadota's equity accounts would not change significantly when the two companies were consolidated. Kadota's current equity totalled $6,013 million out of a total capital figure of:

TABLE 1 Consolidated Capital Structure, December 1987 (millions)

Existing SPC debt	$ 346
Existing Kadota debt	2,420
Bridge Loan	5,100
Equity	$ 6,013
Total capital	$13,881

Assuming a 35 percent ratio of long-term debt to capital, the maximum amount of debt would be $4,785 million. Given the existing $2,558 million in debt, Mr. Rochester could raise $2,227 million in debt and remain within Kadota's capital guidelines.

If he elected this course of action, he would have to raise the balance of $2,873 million in equity. Early 1988 was not the most attractive time to issue equity, however. During the stock market's precipitous drop following the market break of October 1987, Kadota's common stock had declined from a high of $70 1/8 to a low of $42, where it had remained. Its failure to recover modestly along with the rest of the market was attributed to uncertainties about the merger and the litigation. Mr. Rochester believed that when these were cleared up, as he expected they soon would be, the stock price might increase several dollars per share.

Issuing common stock in the volume required to maintain the debt ratio at 35 percent would require a 10 percent discount (including all issuing costs), for a net price of $38 a share. Kadota had 334.7 million shares outstanding in early 1988.

THE FINANCIAL MARKETS

Interest rate forecasts by the economists of major investment banks, as summarized in Exhibit 6, were unanimous in projecting a decline in rates during the first half of 1988 and an increase thereafter. Major differences of opinion existed, however, regarding the extent of the decline. One authority forecast June 1988 rates on 30-year Treasuries as low as 7 percent, whereas another projected trading to remain in an 8 1/2 percent to 9 1/2 percent range. By the end of the year, rates as high as 11 percent were discussed.

The Treasury market had been somewhat volatile recently, as shown in the following table.

TABLE 2 Closing Yields on 10-Year Treasuries (8 1/8s of 1988)

Date	*Yield*
Monday, February 22	8.23%
Tuesday, February 23	8.17
Wednesday, February 24	8.20
Thursday, February 25	8.24
Friday, February 26	8.17
Monday, February 29	8.15

Prices on the market Tuesday morning continued to rise, with yields falling to 8.125 percent by noon.

THE ANALYTICAL ISSUES

Mr. Rochester saw the following analytical issues that needed to be addressed:

1. How much of the acquisition should be financed with debt? (For the preliminary analysis, Mr. Rochester decided to explore the extremes of all debt financing versus maintaining the traditional 35 percent debt policy.)
2. What should the composition be of the debt used: short-term versus long-term, floating versus fixed?
3. How fast should Kadota move to implement the financing plan?

Case 10 Kadota Semanek Corp.

EXHIBIT 1 SALES AND OPERATING EARNINGS, 1980–1987 KADOTA COMPANY AND SEMANEK PHARMACEUTICALS (millions)

	Kadota		*Semanek*	
Year	*Sales*	*Operating Earnings**	*Sales*	*Operating Earnings*#
1987	$13,305	$2,111	$2,301	$328
1986	11,550	724**	1,990	300
1985	10,631	561***	1,754	278
1984	10,600	1,547	1,725	255
1983	10,170	1,027	1,757	245
1982	10,815	1,860	1,646	247
1981	10,337	2,060	1,646	232
1980	9,734	1,896	##	##

* Before deduction of interest.
** After unusual and special charges of $654 million.
*** After unusual and special charges of $563 million.
# After deduction of interest.
Not available on a comparable basis with the subsequent years.

Case 10 Kadota Semanek Corp.

EXHIBIT 2 PRO FORMA CONSOLIDATED BALANCE SHEET AS OF DECEMBER 31, 1987 (in millions)

Assets	
Cash and marketable securities	$ 1,337
Accounts receivable	3,464
Inventories	2,440
Other current assets	552
Total current assets	$ 7,793
Property, plant & equipment	14,477
Less: Accumulated depreciation	7,516
Net property, plant & equipment	$ 6,961
Goodwill	4,127
Other	1,220
Total assets	$20,101
Liabilities and Shareholders' Equity	
Short-term debt	$ 140
Bridge financing	4,900
Accounts payable	3,648
Other current liabilities	763
Total current liabilities	$ 9,451
Long-term debt	2,420
Other long-term liabilities	2,217
Total long-term liabilities	$ 4,637
Total liabilities	$14,088
Common stock and paid-in capital	933
Retained earnings	7,139
Less: treasury stock	(2,059)
Total equity (334.7 million shares)	$ 6,013
Total liabilities & equity	$20,101

Case 10 Kadota Semanek Corporation

EXHIBIT 3 CORPORATE 30-YEAR NEW ISSUE SPREADS REOFFER YIELD OVER TREASURIES (1980–87)

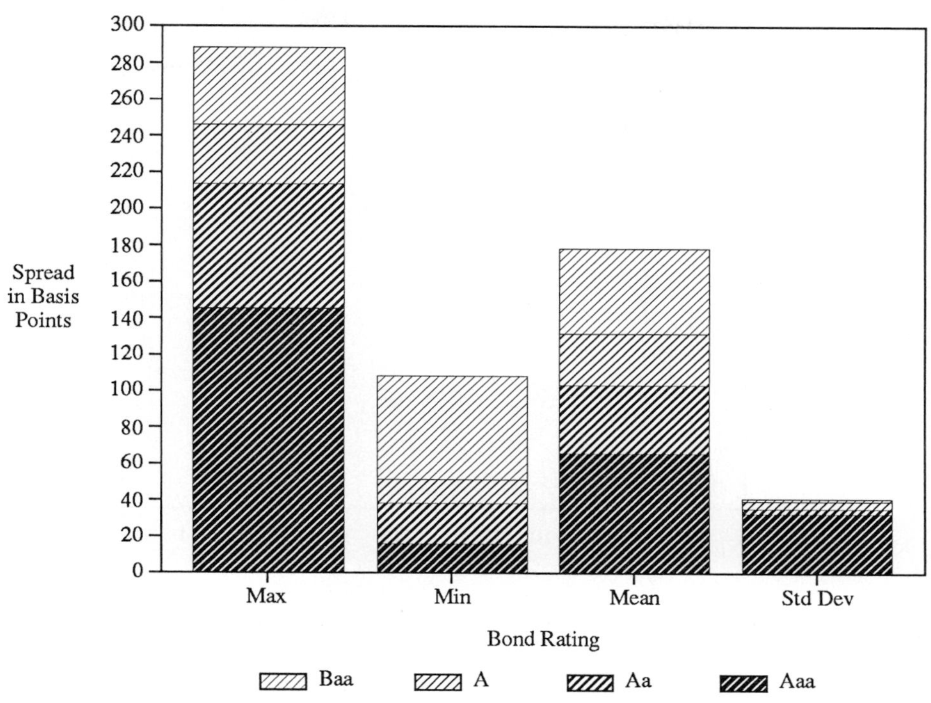

Case 10 Kadota Semanek Corporation

EXHIBIT 4 TREASURY YIELD CURVE, FEBRUARY 22, 1988

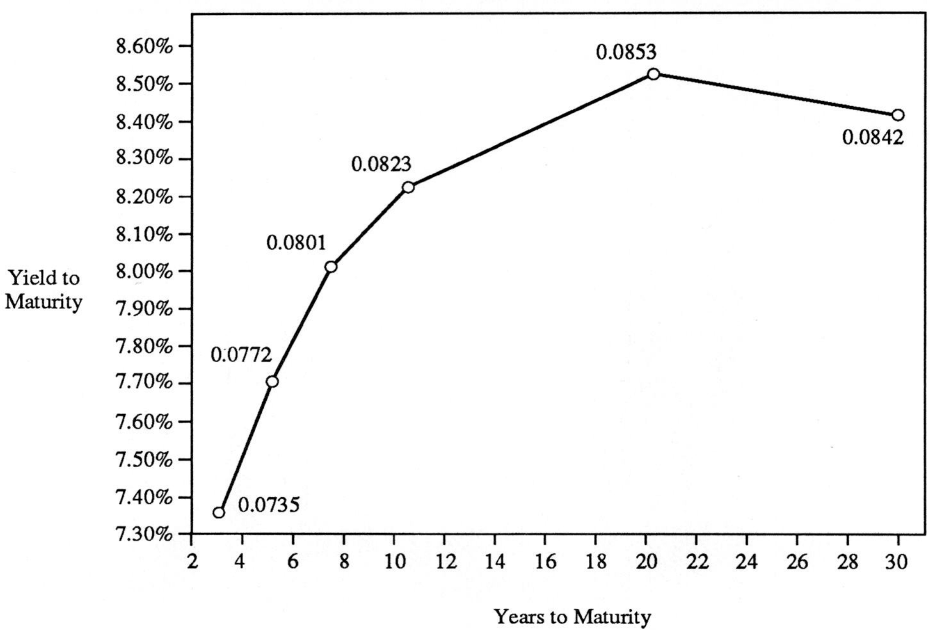

Case 10 Kadota Semanek Corporation

EXHIBIT 5 FINANCIAL CHARACTERISTICS OF COMPANIES WITH DEBT RATED AA AND A BY STANDARD AND POOR'S

Characteristic	*AA*	*A*
Total debt/Adjusted Book Cap.	12.5%–33.4%	23.8%–41.6%
Pre-tax interest coverage	4.8×–13.1×	3.6×–8.1×
Pre-tax fixed charges coverage	2.8×–6.3×	2.2×–4.1×
Cash flow/Total debt	56.9%–177.2%	34.4%–73.1%

Note: These data are for 1986 fiscal years and include only companies in the top three quartiles of each category.

EXHIBIT 6 INTEREST RATE OUTLOOK OF SELECTED INVESTMENT BANKS

Morgan Stanley	Rates on the long bond may fall to 8 1/2% by midyear. But over-consumption in the U.S., a drop in the dollar, and the spectre of higher inflation may push yields as high as 11% by late 1988. If inflationary expectations remains quiescent throughout 1988, despite the falling dollar, the upsurge in interest rates will be postponed until 1989.	Merrill Lynch	Anticipates decline in inventory levels and reduced consumer spending will push rates on 30-year Treasury bonds to as low as 8.6% in early 1988. Increased inflation and a lower dollar late in 1988 will then increase yields on the long bond to approximately 9.4%.
First Boston	Rates on 30-Year Treasury bonds may fall as low as 7% by June because of decreased inventory levels and reduced consumer spending. Expects economy to accelerate in the second half of 1988, testing capacity constraints in various industries and pushing yields on the long bond to 11%.	Salomon Brothers	Slowed economic growth in early 1988 may cause rates on 30-Year Treasury bonds to fall as low as 8% by June. By late 1988, thinks increased consumer spending, greater capital expenditures, and a higher inflation rate will push yields on the long bond to between 9 1/2%–10%.
Goldman Sachs	Thinks improved trade figures, a relatively stable dollar, and slowed economic growth in the first few months of 1988 will cause 30-Year Treasury bonds to maintain a trading range of 8 1/2%–9 1/2%. By late 1988, however, large trade and budget deficits, a weaker dollar, and the possibility of higher inflation rates may force rates on the long bond to over 10%.	Shearson Lehman	Weak consumer spending and the possibility of a recession should cause rates on 30-Year Treasury bonds to fall to 8 1/4% during the first few months of 1988. If a recession is avoided, rates may climb to 9% by year-end. If, however, a recession does occur, yields on the long bond could fall to 7 1/2% late in 1988 or early in 1989.

Case 11

STUART FURNITURE CORPORATION

In late August 1971, Mr. Thomas Sheraton, president of Stuart Furniture Corporation, was studying alternative methods of financing the expansion of the company. The expansion program would require a total investment of $11.5 million through October 1973, but $3.5 million could be generated internally from earnings and more efficient use of existing current assets. Hence, the plan was to raise $8 million in new money. Mr. Sheraton had been discussing a variety of alternatives with Stuart's investment bankers over several months. Because most of the capital would be needed during the next twelve months, it had been agreed that the entire amount should be raised through the immediate sale of a single security. Mr. Sheraton's final recommendation to the board of directors on the form this issue should take was to be presented at the board meeting on September 2, 1971.

Management's initial inclination had been to raise the entire $8 million by means of an equity issue. Stuart's common stock was currently trading at an all-time high price of $33 a share in the over-the-counter market. Mr. Sheraton believed the company could net $31 after discounts and issuing costs. The excellent market price and the belief that an equity issue would better maintain Stuart's reputation as a conservatively financed company were the reasons equity was being strongly considered.

On the other hand, the investment bankers had suggested raising the capital by means of a 7 percent, 10-year note placed with a group of institutional investors. They believed debt would be less expensive for Stuart's stockholders.

Case adapted from a report prepared by Tanya Parker with the cooperation of individuals and institutions that wish to remain anonymous; it was revised by John T. Guertler, Research Assistant. Certain of the company's characteristics and financial information have been changed to protect confidential information without altering the managerial decision.

COMPANY BACKGROUND AND PLANS

Founded in 1955 by a group of investors with extensive experience in the furniture business, the company began operations in an abandoned cabinet plant in Stuart, Virginia, to produce moderately priced furniture. By 1967, sales were $10 million, and the company had acquired a second plant in Martinsville, Virginia.

In 1967, a fire in the Martinsville plant and the death of the company's president temporarily interrupted Stuart's growth. Late that year, Mr. Sheraton was elected president and chief executive officer. A thirty-five-year-old graduate in furniture engineering from North Carolina State University, Mr. Sheraton placed great emphasis on growth. Under his leadership, and with an experienced and professional secondary management team, Stuart prospered. In fiscal year 1970, sales reached $16.2 million and earnings had increased to $740,000. Selected financial statements are presented in Exhibits 1 and 2.

Mr. Sheraton was planning for continued growth. Although 1970 had been a poor year for the furniture industry, Stuart had increased its sales and earnings by 8.7 percent and 27.6 percent, respectively. Sales for the next five years were projected to more than double, with earnings growing at a slower rate. (Financial forecasts for fiscal years 1971–75 are shown in Exhibit 3.) The company's expansion plans were to double production capacity by late 1973 to be able to meet this demand. A 548,000 feet-square factory costing $8 million was to be built near Danville. It would be the largest and most modern factory in the furniture industry. Another $500,000 would be needed to renovate and equip the Stuart plant to accommodate the Plastics Division and to permit expanded production there.

Additional working capital of $3 million would be needed to support the expanded facilities and sales program, bringing the total requirements to $11.5 million through October 1973.

FURNITURE INDUSTRY

The furniture industry was highly fragmented. Of the over 5,000 furniture manufacturers, almost two-thirds had fewer than 20 employees. Fewer than 30 companies in 1969 had sales exceeding $15 million in an industry whose sales reached $5 billion. In the previous five years, the industry had experienced an increase in merger and acquisition activity. Industry leaders acquired smaller furniture manufacturers at the same time major corporations in other fields were diversifying by acquiring some of the larger furniture companies. In the late 1960s Thomasville Furniture, with sales of $65 million, was acquired by Armstrong Cork, and Drexel Enterprises (sales of $78 million) was acquired by U.S. Plywood–Champion Papers.

Cyclical growth also characterized the furniture industry. Although the 1960s saw an average compounded growth in furniture shipments of 5.7 percent, "downturns" had occurred three times in that decade, creating hardships for those companies lacking adequate capital resources. Selected aggregate industry statistics are presented in Exhibit 4.

Intense price competition at the manufacturing levels had historically been a way of life in the furniture industry. As a result, the industry had become more sophisticated, requiring more attention to marketing, technology, and profit-oriented management.

The industry's immediate prospects were encouraging. The economic slowdown of 1970 had passed, and the industry was now on the upswing with the economy in general. The furniture industry was also expected to benefit from demographic changes as the baby boom generation reached the 25-to-35-year-old age bracket—the years in which families made their largest purchases of furniture. Exhibit 5 shows comparative financial information for three major independent furniture companies and Stuart, as well as debt ratios for several additional firms.

STUART'S STRATEGY

According to Mr. Sheraton, Stuart manufactured a very short line of furniture: "We don't take a lot of new products to the market." Stuart's product line in 1971 included eight styles of bedroom furniture, five dining room styles, and over fifteen pieces of occasional furniture such as roll-top desks, hostess carts, and wine cabinets. The styles were mostly of ornate and traditional design, usually made of wood. A few items featured elaborately designed plastic molding and facing that resembled wood.

By concentrating on only two or three new styles for each of the two annual furniture markets, and by closing out an equal number of older and less popular lines, the company was able to avoid extensive proliferation of its lines and resulting manufacturing inefficiencies. Likewise, Stuart was able carefully to research buyers' tastes and their willingness to spend before a new product reached the manufacturing state.

A sales force of about 50 persons sold the company's products nationwide to over 5,000 customers. The sales force, which was allowed to represent noncompetitive furniture products to a limited degree, had been very stable with virtually no turnover in four years. Marketing efforts were concentrated on regional chains and warehouse-showroom discount firms because Stuart's management believed these outlets were most suitable for the mass merchandising the product's price range required. One of Stuart's major discount outlets, Lewitz Furniture, was experiencing phenomenal growth, having 14 new stores opening in 1971 with 18 to 24 more projected for 1972.

In 1971, Stuart was operating at maximum capacity in its four separate manufacturing facilities. A 290,000 feet-square building in Stuart housed the general offices and the principal plant. It mainly produced bedroom and dining room lines. Occasional furniture was produced in the 150,000 feet-square plant in Martinsville. The wood veneer used in the Stuart and Martinsville plants was produced in a small plant in Danville, Virginia. A building in Stuart was leased to produce polymer (plastic) components. This last plant provided half the plastics the company required; the remainder was purchased from outside sources. To avoid cost squeezes due to rising material costs, management had frequently purchased large amounts of lumber and log prior to anticipated price increases.

Stuart provided full-time employment for 950 people. There was no union in the plants, and management considered its labor force to be very productive. Factory production averaged \$25,000 per employee, compared to an industry average of less than \$16,000. A surplus of labor existed in the Stuart area.

FINANCIAL POSITION AND PROPOSED FINANCING

Stuart currently had long-term debt of \$800,000 along with \$100,000 due within one year. The interest rate was 5 1/2 percent, and principal repayments of \$100,000 were required each year in two installments. Covenants required the company to maintain minimum working capital of \$2.25 million.

Stuart had gone public in 1956, issuing 170,000 shares (equivalent to 308,000 shares after subsequent stock dividend and splits) of its \$5 par value common stock. Currently, there were 600,000 shares outstanding, of which officers and directors owned about 20 percent. Dividends at an annual rate of \$0.40 per share were being paid, with no plans under consideration to change this rate.

The two alternative proposals to raise the \$8 million were:

1. Common Stock: 258,000 shares of common stock could be sold to the public to net the company \$8 million, barring any major change in market conditions prior to the issue date. This would be some 90 days after the decision and hence after the close of the 1971 fiscal year. Issue costs and discounts would be approximately \$2 a share. (Exhibit 6 presents the company's recent stock prices.)
2. Debt: The provisions on the 7 percent 10-year note would likely be:
   a. Semiannual principal payments of \$400,000 to begin 30 months after the loan was taken down.
   b. A final payment of 25 percent (\$2,000,000) at the end of the ten-year term.
   c. During the first year, working capital would have to be maintained at 50 percent of the amount borrowed. Thereafter, the percentage would increase 10 percent a year until it reached a maximum of 80 percent of the outstanding loan.
   d. Stockholders' equity would be at least \$6,000,000.
   e. Interest would be paid quarterly.

Mr. Sheraton had to make the decision. He wanted to do what was best for the company and be able to explain his decision to the board of directors on September 3.

Case 11 Stuart Furniture Corporation

EXHIBIT 1 BALANCE SHEETS AS OF NOVEMBER 1 (millions of dollars)

	1968	*1969*	*1970*	*June 13, 1971*
ASSETS				
Current assets:				
Cash	$0.26	$0.23	$0.24	$0.63
Receivables	2.09	2.37	2.73	3.10
Inventories*	2.03	2.27	2.55	2.68
Other	0.08	0.10	0.11	0.14
Total current assets	$4.46	$4.97	$5.63	$6.55
Fixed Assets				
Gross	$3.79	$3.94	$4.09	$4.24
Less: accumulated depreciation	1.35	1.55	1.78	1.89
Total fixed assets	$2.44	$2.39	$2.31	$2.35
Total assets	$6.90	$7.36	$7.94	$8.90
LIABILITIES AND CAPITAL				
Accounts payable and accrued expenses	$0.62	$0.90	$1.02	$1.05
Current maturities of long-term debt	0.10	0.10	0.10	0.10
Dividends	—	—	—	0.05
Taxes	0.36	0.25	0.26	0.50
Total current liabilities	$1.08	$1.25	$1.38	$1.70
Long-term debt (5½%)	$1.05	$0.95	$0.85	$0.80
Stockholders' equity (600,000 shares)	4.77	5.16	5.71	6.40
Total liabilities and capital	$6.90	$7.36	$7.94	$8.90

*Finished goods represent 40% of total inventory.

Case 11 Stuart Furniture Corporation

EXHIBIT 2 STATEMENTS OF INCOME (millions of dollars except per-share figures)

	Fiscal Year Ended November 1					32 Weeks Ended	
	1966	1967	1968	1969	1970	6/14/70	6/13/71
Net sales	$10.62	$10.65	$12.93	$14.91	$16.20	$ 9.26	$12.79
Cost of products sold	8.53	8.80	10.46	12.01	12.74	7.24	9.68
Gross margin	$ 2.09	$ 1.85	$ 2.47	$ 2.90	$ 3.46	$ 2.02	$ 3.11
Selling, general and administrative expenses	1.11	1.22	1.42	1.60	1.84	1.09	1.36
Interest expense	0.08	0.07	0.07	0.06	0.05	0.03	0.03
Profit before taxes	$ .90	$ .56	$ .98	$ 1.24	$ 1.57	$ .90	$ 1.72
Income taxes	0.44	0.27	0.51	0.66	0.83	0.48	0.87
Income before extraordinary items	$ 0.46	$ 0.29	$ 0.47	$ 0.58	$ 0.74	$ 0.42	$ 0.85
Extraordinary item—net of tax	—	.15	—	—	—	—	—
Net income	$ 0.46	$ 0.44	$ 0.47	$ 0.58	$ 0.74	$ 0.42	$ 0.85
Earnings per share*							
Before extraordinary item	$ 0.77	$ 0.48	$ 0.78	$ 0.97	$ 1.23	$ 0.70	$ 1.42
Extraordinary item	—	.25	—	—	—	—	—
Net income	$ 0.77	$ 0.73	$ 0.78	$ 0.97	$ 1.23	$ 0.70	$ 1.42
Cash dividends per share*	$ 0.27	$ 0.27	$ 0.27	$ 0.30	$ 0.30	$ 0.23	$ 0.27
Depreciation included in cost figures above	n.a.	n.a.	0.21	0.22	0.22	n.a.	n.a.

*Based on 600,000 shares outstanding, adjusted for stock dividends and splits.

Case 11 Stuart Furniture Corporation

EXHIBIT 3 PROJECTED EARNINGS BEFORE INTEREST AND TAXES (dollar figures in millions)

	1971	1972	1973	1974	1975
Net sales	$20.80	$25.00	$31.00	$37.00	$42.00
Cost of goods sold	15.74	18.90	23.47	28.00	31.79
Gross margin	5.06	6.10	7.53	9.00	10.21
Selling, administrative and general expenses	2.23	2.70	3.35	4.00	4.54
Earnings before interest and taxes	$ 2.83	$ 3.40	$ 4.18	$ 5.00	$ 5.67
Depreciation included in cost figures above	0.23	0.75	1.00	1.00	1.00

Case 11 Stuart Furniture Corporation

EXHIBIT 4 FURNITURE INDUSTRY STATISTICS: 1960–1970

Year	*Manufacturer's Shipments (millions of dollars)*	*Index of Production (1967 = 100)*	*Wholesale Furniture Price Index (1967 = 100)*	*Profitability Index (1967 = 100)**
1960	2803	65	90.8	n/a
1961	2704	62	91.1	n/a
1962	2976	69	91.9	57
1963	3182	75	92.6	58
1964	3436	82	93.3	82
1965	3678	91	94.1	96
1966	3913	101	96.6	114
1967	3999	100	100.0	100
1968	4442	107	103.9	104
1969	4787	112	108.3	121
1970	4864	108	111.6	84

*Based on an unweighted average of the American Furniture, Bassett, and Henredon companies.

Case 11 Stuart Furniture Corporation

EXHIBIT 5 SELECTED 1969 DATA ON FURNITURE MANUFACTURING COMPANIES (dollar figures in thousands, except per-share figures)

	American Furniture	*Bassett Furniture*	*Lane Company*	*Stuart Furniture*
Capitalization				
Long-term debt	$ 258	$ 1,437	$ 4,767	$ 950
Preferred stock	—	—	1,397	—
Common and surplus	17,754	70,379	38,810	5,002
Total	$18,012	$ 71,816	$45,974	$ 5,952
Sales	$37,132	$139,293	$77,427	$14,908
Earnings	$ 1,884	$ 12,033	$ 4,849	$ 584
Current ratio	3.2	7.2	4.3	4.0
Working capital	$11,607	$ 45,651	$26,778	$ 3,726
Working capital as a percent of common equity	65.4%	64.9%	67.3%	74.5%
Earnings as a percent of sales	5.1%	8.6%	6.3%	3.9%
Earnings as a percent of common equity	10.6%	17.1%	12.2%	11.7%
Earnings per share	$0.70	$2.00	$1.93	$0.97
Dividend per share	$0.28	$0.80	$0.60	$0.30
Price/earnings ratio	16.2×	17.8×	16.2×	7.2×

	Debt/Equity	*Debt— Total Capitalization*	*Price/Earnings (Est. 1970)*
American Furniture	1.5%	1.4%	16.2×
Bassett Furniture	2.0%	2.0%	17.8×
Baumritter Furniture	35.7%	26.3%	11.8×
Cochrane Furniture	21.9%	18.0%	8.0×
Gravely Furniture	13.3%	11.7%	12.0×
Henredon Furniture	33.1%	24.9%	13.0×
Hickory Furniture	17.8%	15.1%	12.7×
Lane Company	11.6%	10.4%	16.2×
Rowe Furniture	21.9%	18.0%	9.5×
Stuart Furniture	19.0%	16.0%	9.2×
Average	17.8%	14.4%	12.6×

Case 11 Stuart Furniture Corporation

EXHIBIT 6 PRICE RANGE OF COMMON STOCK

The following table shows, for the periods indicated, the range of high and low bid and asked price quotations for the company's common stock, as reported by the National Quotation Bureau, Inc., adjusted for all stock dividends and splits.

		Bid		*Asked*	
		High	*Low*	*High*	*Low*
1966		8¾	6¼	10	7¼
1967		6¼	5¼	6¾	5½
1968		10½	5½	10¾	6
1969	first quarter	9¼	7¾	10	8½
	second quarter	9¼	7¾	9¾	8½
	third quarter	8¼	6¾	9	7½
	fourth quarter	9¼	7¼	9¾	7¾
1970	first quarter	8½	7¼	9	7¾
	second quarter	8¾	7¼	9¼	8
	third quarter	9½	7¼	10¼	7¾
	fourth quarter	12¾	9¼	13¼	9¾
1971	first quarter	19¼	12	20	12¾
	second quarter	31¼	19¼	32½	19¼

Case 12

ENTERPRISE MACHINERY CORPORATION

In early 1984, Mr. James Kirk, president of Enterprise Machinery Corporation, was completing his review of the company's past and projected financial activities through 1987. Six million dollars in notes payable matured at the end of the current year, but the projections indicated that after 1985, external financial needs would decline. During 1984, $6.2 million of external financing would be required. Alternative fund sources included a private placement of up to $8 million in senior notes with a group of insurance companies or a common stock issuance of an equal amount.

A board meeting had been scheduled for the next week to discuss the projected deficit and the two financing options. Realizing that the prospect of additional debt financing would precipitate heated discussion of Enterprise's highly leveraged financial condition, Mr. Kirk decided to discuss the alternatives with Mr. Robert McCoy, the company's account officer at the Federation National Bank. (Exhibits 1, 2, 3, and 4 present financial statements for 1979–83 and projections through 1987.)

INDUSTRY

As a producer of hydraulic pumps, Enterprise competed in an industry that was quite concentrated. Its four largest competitors accounted for 67 percent of pump sales and were active in other industrial equipment markets. These companies had dominated the pump industry for many years and had achieved substantial economies of scale. (Exhibit 5 presents comparative information on Enterprise and the industry leaders.) Through vertical integration, additional economies had been realized. Despite production cost advantages enjoyed by the largest producers, price-cutting tactics were unlikely in light of previous government allegations of predatory pricing practices within the industry. Maintaining a competitive position in the industry depended on the ability to produce a reliable and economical pump and to provide a product line and good customer service.

The 1983 market for pumps was estimated at $1.5 billion, an increase of 8 percent since the previous year. Sales forecasts for 1984 indicated a 10 percent growth rate based on anticipated gains in capital expenditures among the principal users of pumps—the mining and construction industries. Industry growth similar to that forecasted for the current year was expected through 1988.

Industry experts suspected that the Occupational Safety and Health Administration would soon impose noise reduction standards on the industry. The proposed regulations could be met with existing technology. The costs of compliance and the effect on profit margins had not yet been determined.

COMPANY BACKGROUND

Enterprise Machinery Corporation was founded in 1972 to produce hydraulic pump systems. The founders, Mr. Kirk and Mr. Scott, Enterprise's vice president of engineering, had held executive positions with Reliance Corporation, a major competitor, until they resigned in 1972. Noticing a weakness in the service organization of the industry leaders, Messrs. Kirk and Scott formulated an innovative marketing strategy emphasizing service delivery and technical assistance to customers. A growing number of company-operated sales offices were established to implement the strategy and to penetrate re-

Case prepared by Kevin Remundo with the cooperation of individuals and institutions that wish to remain anonymous. Certain of the company's characteristics and financial information have been changed to protect confidential information without altering the managerial decision.

gional, national, and international markets. A large network of independent distributors supplemented the company's direct selling efforts. These factors, together with the availability of a broad product line, were primarily responsible for the 37 percent compound sales growth rate Enterprise had experienced since 1979. Enterprise currently had a 5 percent market share.

Enterprise's sales growth was expected to continue to exceed that of the industry. Enterprise management forecasted a 17 percent annual sales growth rate through 1988. Market share gains would result from penetrating the markets of smaller companies which were unable to offer good service and broad product lines and by expanding international sales.

Enterprise had been vigorously expanding its participation in international markets, where its products were being well received. A European sales subsidiary accounted for 35 percent of 1983 sales, up from 10 percent in 1981 when it was organized. In 1982, exclusive marketing rights in Japan and South Korea had been obtained for certain products Enterprise was making under patents licensed from other firms. Also, the company had recently committed substantial resources to its marketing efforts in Africa.

Within the industry, Enterprise's pumps enjoyed wide acceptance, and the company was well known for its technical and engineering expertise. The company's equipment rental program had been successful in increasing awareness of the company and its products among commercial users and potential purchasers. While rental revenues were insignificant, many equipment purchases were the direct result of previous rental arrangements.

Product innovation, another factor in the company's success, had resulted in the development of pumps with unmatched performance specifications and economy. In 1978, for example, a license was acquired to use a new compression technology which significantly reduced downtime and maintenance costs. In addition to being more reliable, the new generation of pumps could be installed at lower cost because of size and weight reductions made possible by the new technology. More recently, the research and development group had introduced a new sealing agent with longer life and superior operating characteristics.

Despite the acknowledged benefits of the new compression design and the general availability of the requisite license, the major producers in the industry continued to concentrate on earlier designs. Altering their existing production facilities to manufacture the new design would require a substantial investment and would restrict their participation in the lucrative replacement parts market.

The production process essentially involved the assembling of purchased components and castings which represented 80 percent of the product cost. Most components were widely available from major manufacturers. Enterprise manufactured those parts which were not readily available from external sources, including advanced designs developed by the company's research and development group.

The company's 250 production workers were not organized. They enjoyed generous fringe benefits including flexible working hours; profit sharing; subsidized grocery shopping, gas purchases, and lunches; and the use of modern recreational facilities. The labor force was content with its work environment as reflected in minimal turnover and the failure of two recent unionization attempts.

The officers of the company were thoroughly familiar with the industry as a result of their previous professional associations and an average of six years' employment with Enterprise. Principal strengths of the management group were in marketing and engineering. Management collectively owned 25 percent of the company's outstanding common stock and would probably receive 8,000 additional shares annually during the foreseeable future under the stock bonus plan.

FINANCIAL CONDITION

As Mr. Kirk reviewed the company's performance over the last four years, he noticed some unfavorable trends which adversely affected profitability. Cost of goods sold as a percentage of sales had increased from 60 percent in 1981 to 62 percent in 1983. This trend coincided with a growing proportion of international sales on which smaller margins were realized. However, higher prices received by the company as a result of its expanded direct selling activities partly compensated for the margin squeeze on international sales. As more sales offices were opened, selling, general, and administrative expenses increased disproportionately to sales. To finance its rapid sales growth, the company was forced to increase its borrowings, which resulted in an increasing percentage of each sales dollar going for interest expense. The net effect of these trends was a decline in net income as a percentage of sales from 6.3 percent in 1979 to 3.6 percent in 1983.

Messrs. Kirk and Scott also suspected that Enterprise's current assets were not being efficiently managed. Recently, accounts receivable balances had grown at a rate exceeding sales growth. The company had been unable to achieve its stated goal of 180 days' cost of goods sold in inventory, except temporarily in 1980 when an internal manufacturing capability was introduced.

Although liquidity ratios were similar to the industry average, accounts payable had been stretched to 122 days' purchases (calculated assuming purchases approximate 80 percent of cost of goods sold) in 1983. Credit reporting services had noted that 75 percent of the suppliers had not been paid promptly, and trade creditors were becoming impatient with the company's inability to make timely payment. Typical trade terms were 60 days.

The degree of financial leverage had increased significantly since 1979. The $14.3 million in long-term debt was comprised of $7 million in notes payable to banks, $6 million in senior notes payable to insurance companies, and approximately $1.3 million in equipment obligations payable to banks. After considering a 20 percent compensating cash balance required by the banks, the effective interest rate on the bank term debt was approximately 8.5 percent, and interest on the insurance company obligations was 11.25 percent. The equipment purchase notes carried a 10 percent interest rate. The most important covenants on the institutional debt required the company to maintain consolidated working capital of $10 million, a total debt–equity ratio of no more than 2.10×, and current assets equal to at least 175 percent of current liabilities. (Scheduled maturities of long-term debt and the components of current notes payable are presented in Exhibits 6 and 7.)

ALTERNATIVE SOURCE OF FUNDS

The insurance company debt alternative consisted of up to $8 million in senior notes due in 1999 with amortization to begin in 1988. The interest rate would probably be 9 1/4 percent. The new senior notes would limit the payment of dividends and the purchase of treasury shares to an amount not to exceed consolidated net income earned after December 31, 1983, plus proceeds from stock sales in excess of $3 million. There were also limitations on increases in executive compensation. The proposed debt placement would involve legal and other fees totaling $25,000.

The company's investment bankers had indicated that between 275,000 and 580,000 shares could be sold at approximately $15 per share. Enterprise would realize $13.75 per share after paying the underwriters' commissions. Related issuance costs would amount to $50,000. The company was closely held, with 52 percent of the outstanding stock owned by 49 individuals including members of management. The last public issue of common stock occurred in 1979. (Quarterly stock prices since 1980 are recorded in Exhibit 8.)

Mr. McCoy had been in charge of the Enterprise account since 1980 and was quite familiar with the company. Federation Bank had been the lead bank since the company's inception. Existing company obligations to the bank included a $3.6 million line of credit due currently and $4 million in long-term notes payable. Although unexpected requests for additional term and line borrowings had occurred regularly as the result of inaccurate financial projections, the banking relationship had been mutually satisfactory.

In preparation for his meeting with the president, Mr. McCoy reviewed the company's financial forecast for 1984 through 1987. He noted that sales were forecast to increase 17 percent annually and that external financial requirements reached a high of $8.6 million in 1985 and declined to $5.5 million in 1987. Also, during 1984–1987, the forecasts indicated existing long-term institutional debt would be reduced by $3.8 million.

In light of declining profitability, Mr. McCoy wondered about the company's ability to finance the forecasted sales growth and to reduce borrowings simultaneously from internally generated funds. Forecasted inventory balances seemed unrealistic, and accounts payable projections suggested an insensitivity to the growing number of dissatisfied trade creditors. During their meeting, he conveyed his doubts concerning the accuracy of the forecast. Mr. Kirk agreed that some questionable assumptions may have been used in its preparation and was planning to prepare another forecast.

The discussions then turned to the financing alternatives. In commenting on debt servicing, Mr. McCoy suggested that Enterprise would have sufficient earnings to cover adequately the burden of existing and proposed debt, but he noted that higher interest expense was a factor in the company's declining profitability. The stock was currently selling at a price–earnings ratio of 9 times as opposed to 17 times in 1980, when it reached an historical high.

Mr. McCoy suggested that the relatively low price–earnings ratio might reflect investor concern over steadily increasing financial leverage and associated risk in the absence of corresponding gains in earnings per share. The investment community realized that Enterprise had been unable to maintain its profit levels during the period of high sales growth and, perhaps, doubted that slower growth as projected would lead to improvements. If this trend did continue, he believed it would be prudent for the company to issue stock to reduce the proportion of debt in its capital structure. This course of action would reduce the risk associated with earnings and could lead to higher price–earnings ratios in the future. Debt capacity would be conserved, enhancing the company's future financial flexibility. In addition, interest rates were expected to fall during 1984 and 1985.

Alternatively, a debt issue now would use up debt capacity and introduce additional risk to existing and potential shareholders. As a consequence, the price–earnings ratio might fall. In Mr. McCoy's opinion, future equity market conditions would be more favorably influenced by a lower level of risk than by higher earnings per share resulting from selecting the debt alternative.

Mr. Kirk did not completely agree with the banker's evaluation of stock price behavior, but he had observed that generally other companies in the industry with less leverage had higher price–earnings ratios.

Mr. Kirk was pleased with the discussions, which had helped him identify and understand certain issues that would be raised at the board meeting next week. His recommendation to the board would depend on his revised financial projections and subsequent analysis.

Case 12 Enterprise Machinery Corporation

EXHIBIT 1 CONSOLIDATED INCOME STATEMENTS FOR YEARS ENDING DECEMBER 31, 1979–1983 (in thousands except earnings-per-share data)

	1979	*1980*	*1981*	*1982*	*1983*
Net sales	$18,131	$28,757	$41,938	$49,064	$64,684
Cost of goods sold	11,145	17,589	25,197	29,804	40,213
Gross profit	$ 6,986	$11,168	$16,741	$19,260	$24,471
Selling, general, and administrative expenses	4,492	7,091	10,798	13,686	17,764
Depreciation*	289	517	723	990	1,400
Earnings before interest and taxes	$ 2,205	$ 3,560	$ 5,220	$ 4,584	$ 5,307
Interest	161	357	727	791	1,486
Profit before taxes	$ 2,044	$ 3,203	$ 4,493	$ 3,793	$ 3,821
Taxes	900	1,438	1,965	1,288	1,510
Profit after taxes	$ 1,144	$ 1,765	$ 2,528	$ 2,505	$ 2,311
Common shares outstanding	1,253.1	1,325.7	1,305.5	1,340.3	1,361.7
Earnings per share	$0.91	$1.33	$1.94	$1.87	$1.70

*Approximately half of the annual depreciation charge was added to the accrued depreciation account, while the remainder was netted out against the rental equipment account.

Case 12 Enterprise Machinery Corporation

EXHIBIT 2 CONSOLIDATED BALANCE SHEETS AS OF DECEMBER 31, 1979–1983 (in thousands of dollars)

	1979	*1980*	*1981*	*1982*	*1983*
ASSETS					
Cash	$ 661	$ 1,425	$ 2,172	$ 2,036	$ 2,401
Accounts receivable	4,232	5,721	8,193	8,607	15,649
Inventory	5,485	8,149	14,279	18,575	22,339
Prepaid expenses	25	123	85	286	355
Current assets	$10,403	$15,418	$24,729	$29,504	$40,744
Gross fixed assets	1,883	2,710	4,007	7,246	9,094
Accumulated depreciation	325	523	778	1,183	1,829
Net fixed assets	1,558	2,187	3,229	6,063	7,265
Rental equipment (net)	960	1,311	1,561	2,186	3,314
Other assets	334	414	698	383	727
Total assets	$13,255	$19,330	$30,217	$38,136	$52,050
LIABILITIES & SHAREHOLDERS' EQUITY					
Notes payable	$ 233	$ 500	$ 1,245	$ 1,366	$ 6,076
Accounts payable	3,405	4,923	8,519	9,178	10,983
Income taxes payable	244	513	501	116	577
Accruals	642	973	1,398	1,562	2,503
Current liabilities	$ 4,524	$ 6,909	$11,663	$12,222	$20,139
Deferred taxes	121	247	351	465	733
Long-term debt	1,667	3,100	6,400	11,000	14,337
Common stock	3,797	4,163	4,364	4,505	4,586
Earned surplus	3,146	4,911	7,439	9,944	12,255
Total shareholders' equity	$ 6,943	$ 9,074	$11,803	$14,449	$16,841
Total liabilities & shareholders' equity	$13,255	$19,330	$30,217	$38,136	$52,050

Case 12 Enterprise Machinery Corporation

EXHIBIT 3 COMMON STOCK PRICES FROM MARCH 31, 1980 TO DECEMBER 31, 1983

	1984	*1985*	*1986*	*1987*
Net Sales[a]	$75,680	$88,546	$103,599	$121,210
Cost of goods sold[b]	46,165	54,013	63,195	73,938
Gross profit	$29,515	$34,533	$ 40,404	$ 47,272
General, selling, & administrative expenses[c]	19,677	23,022	26,936	31,515
Depreciation[d]	1,700	2,000	2,200	2,400
Earnings before interest and taxes	$ 8,138	$ 9,511	$ 11,268	$ 13,357
Interest on existing debt	1,490	1,225	1,138	1,026
Interest on new debt[e]	287	683	750	601
Profit before tax	$ 6,361	$ 7,603	$ 9,380	$ 11,730
Taxes[f]	2,862	3,421	4,221	5,278
Profit after tax	$ 3,499	$ 4,182	$ 5,159	$ 6,452
Common shares outstanding	1,370	1,378	1,386	1,394
Earnings per share	$2.55	$3.03	$3.72	$4.63

*Assumptions used in projections:

[a]17% annual sales growth.

[b]Cost of goods sold at 61% of sales.

[c]General, selling, and administrative expense at 26% of sales.

[d]Depreciation as given, approximately ⅔ being added to accumulated depreciation and ⅓ charged to rental equipment.

[e]Plug figure on Exhibit 4 balance sheet is financed with 9¼% senior notes based on average balance from one year-end to the next (half-year in 1984).

[f]45% tax rate.

Case 12 Enterprise Machinery Corporation

EXHIBIT 4 PROJECTED BALANCE SHEETS* AS OF DECEMBER 31, 1984–1987 (in thousands of dollars)

	1984	*1985*	*1986*	*1987*
ASSETS				
Cash	$ 3,450	$ 3,910	$ 4,692	$ 5,060
Accounts receivable[a]	15,136	17,709	20,719	24,242
Inventory[b]	24,365	27,006	29,484	32,042
Prepaid expenses	300	340	408	440
Current assets	$43,251	$48,695	$55,303	$61,784
Gross fixed assets	$10,400	$14,400	$15,500	$16,700
Accumulated depreciation	2,963	4,297	5,764	7,365
Net fixed assets[c]	$ 7,437	$10,103	$ 9,736	$ 9,335
Rental equipment (net)	3,964	4,414	4,714	4,911
Other assets	1,275	1,445	1,734	1,875
Total assets	$55,927	$64,927	$71,487	$77,905
LIABILITIES & SHAREHOLDERS' EQUITY				
Notes payable (plug)	$ 6,220	$ 8,616	$ 7,743	$ 5,569
Accounts payable[d]	11,352	13,282	15,540	18,181
Income taxes payable	400	600	700	700
Accruals	2,475	2,805	3,366	3,630
Current maturity—long-term debt	280	957	969	1,582
Current liabilities	$20,727	$26,260	$28,318	$29,662
Long-term debt	$14,057	$13,100	$12,131	$10,549
Deferred taxes	600	680	816	880
Common stock[e]	4,789	4,952	5,127	5,267
Earned surplus	15,754	19,936	25,095	31,547
Total shareholders' equity	$20,543	$24,888	$30,222	$36,814
Total liabilities and shareholders' equity	$55,927	$64,927	$71,487	$77,905

*Assumptions used in projections:
[a]Accounts receivable equal 72 days' sales.
[b]Inventory equals 190, 180, 168, and 156 days' cost of goods sold, respectively, through 1987.
[c]As given.
[d]Accounts payables equal 110 days' purchases.
[e]Increases reflect distribution under stock bonus plan.

Case 12 Enterprise Machinery Corporation

EXHIBIT 5 INDUSTRY COMPARISON, FISCAL YEARS ENDING 1982

	Enterprise	*Reliance*	*U.S. Pump*	*McKinney*	*Fluco*
Sales (000,000)	$ 49	$ 280	$423.1	$553.3	$1,708.3
Profit/sales	5.1%	6.4%	7.7%	6.0%	7.0%
Profit/net worth	17.3%	10.3%	13.3%	15.1%	14.7%
Current ratio (×)	2.39	2.94	5.22	3.00	2.30
Quick ratio (×)	.89	1.10	2.08	1.30	.99
Total debt/equity	161%	41%	44%	63%	106%
Long-term debt/capitalization	43%	2%	19%	17%	38%
Times total charges earned (×)	3.16	n.a.	5.95	5.18	3.56
Earnings per share	$ 1.87	$ 2.70	$ 1.71	$ 3.51	$ 6.42
Average common stock market price	$13.50	$27.00	$23.18	$32.20	$ 72.50
Price–earnings ratio (×)	7.2	10	13.5	9.1	11.3
EPS 3-year growth rate	12.0%	n.a.	−.1%	43.8%	9.6%
Dividends per share	—	$ 2.00	$ 0.76	$ 1.62	$ 2.48
Dividends/earnings	—	74%	44%	46%	39%
Dividends/market price	—	7.4%	3.3%	5%	3.4%

Case 12 Enterprise Machinery Corporation

EXHIBIT 6 MATURITY SCHEDULE OF LONG-TERM DEBT AS OF DECEMBER 31, 1983

1985	$ 280,197
1986	957,356
1987	968,947
1988	1,581,749
1989	748,978
Thereafter	9,800,000
	$14,337,227

Case 12 Enterprise Machinery Corporation

EXHIBIT 7 COMPONENTS OF CURRENT NOTES PAYABLE AS OF DECEMBER 31, 1983

Notes payable to banks under line of credit	$3,600,000
Current maturities of long-term equipment purchase obligations	270,700
Miscellaneous notes	139,907
Notes payable to West German branch of domestic bank	2,065,621
	$6,076,228

Case 12 Enterprise Machinery Corporation

EXHIBIT 8 COMMON STOCK PRICES FROM MARCH 31, 1980 TO DECEMBER 31, 1983

	Market Price		*Most Recent 4-Quarter*	
Quarter Ending	Bid	Ask	*Earnings*	*Price–Earnings Ratio (×)**
3/31/80	$13.63	$14.50	$1.35	10.4
6/30/80	11.50	12.50	1.04	11.5
9/30/80	18.25	19.25	1.07	17.5
12/31/80	16.00	16.25	1.33	12.0
3/31/81	14.75	15.75	1.29	11.8
6/30/81	12.25	13.00	1.42	8.9
9/30/81	10.75	11.25	1.57	7.0
12/31/81	9.13	9.25	1.94	4.7
3/31/82	16.00	16.50	1.86	8.7
6/30/82	13.75	14.25	1.85	7.6
9/30/82	12.63	13.13	1.96	6.6
12/31/82	9.75	10.13	1.87	5.3
3/31/83	17.00	17.50	1.80	9.6
6/30/83	12.50	13.00	1.56	8.2
9/30/83	11.75	12.25	1.44	8.3
12/31/83	15.25	15.50	1.70	9.0

*Based on most recent 4-quarter earnings.

Case 13

PYRUS, INCORPORATED

Mr. Edgar Watson, chief financial officer of Pyrus, Incorporated, was considering the various financing alternatives available to the company. Pyrus management had proposed a $1.4 billion capital-expenditure program to be carried out over the next five years, and it was up to Mr. Watson to determine the best means of financing these requirements. This task was particularly challenging in light of the economic and financial conditions that existed in the first quarter of 1982. Senior management's interest in converting Pyrus's outstanding commercial paper into longer term instruments further complicated the analysis. In order to ferret out the better alternatives, Mr. Watson reviewed the company's current financial status, sifted through various capital market forecasts, and had a series of conversations with the account officer at Pyrus's bank.

THE PAPER PRODUCTS INDUSTRY

Pyrus, Incorporated, was a large manufacturer of a broad range of paper products, from fine writing paper to newsprint and grocery bag kraft paper. The company's financial statements are given in Exhibits 1 and 2. The paper products industry was very susceptible to fluctuations in the business cycle and was currently attempting to shake off the effects of the latest, unusually debilitating, recession. Exhibit 3 provides historical financial background for the industry. Operating and net income margins had declined as a result of soft prices and slack demand. They were not expected to improve until well into the second half of 1982. In general, paper company stocks were expected to perform below the stock market average for the entire year.

Two particularly good years for the industry, 1978 and 1979, were marked by capacity expansion, which was now plaguing many companies; the need to run operations at a high percentage of capacity had yielded large inventories and low prices.

Newsprint capacity was expected to increase relatively rapidly over the next several years. While a paperworkers' strike in western Canada was a looming possibility, its potential effect was not deemed to be as great as might otherwise have been expected because publishers, printers, and paper distribution firms had built up sizeable stocks of paper. Higher quality paper production capacity was also expected to grow faster than demand, so in general the outlook was bleak for the industry for the rest of 1982. The long-term outlook was positive, however, because the United States was the world's lowest-cost producer of paper and, therefore, would probably dominate the world export market throughout the rest of the decade.

All of the paper companies had been forced to make large capital expenditures over the previous several years, for two reasons. First, tightened environmental protection and safety laws had necessitated the purchase of more and improved antipollution and safety devices. Pyrus planned to devote $400 million of the $1.4 billion capital expenditure program to meeting the various regulatory requirements. Second, the increased price of energy was squeezing paper companies' margins still more. By 1978, many companies had augmented their use of traditional fuels with heat recovery systems and thermomechanical pulping facilities. The latter allowed the recovery of energy in the form of steam and also provided a better pulp material. Pyrus, however, had waited until late 1979,

Case revised by Casey S. Opitz from original material prepared by Richard S. Swasey, Jr., with the cooperation of individuals and institutions that wish to remain anonymous. Certain of the company's characteristics and financial information have been changed to protect confidential information without altering the managerial decision.

when fuel prices had hardened and had continued to rise, to invest in the necessary equipment. This decision contributed to the company's recent comparatively low profit margins, as shown in Exhibit 3. Pyrus planned to invest the remaining $1 billion from the capital expenditure program in modernization and the development of fuel conversion and conservation projects.

THE FINANCIAL MARKET

The period from late 1981 to early 1982 was viewed as the calm before the storm. The U.S. economy was pulling out of recession and interest rates were falling, but the general opinion among economists and analysts was that the recovery would be relatively weak due to a swelling demand for limited funds by both the public and private sectors. Corporate profits throughout the economy had been small in the recent past, so it was recognized that any growth in 1982 would have to be externally funded. At the same time, the U.S. budget deficit was forecasted to reach $80 billion. The government was expected to compete with the private sector for available funds, driving up interest rates. Exhibits 4 through 15 provide information on historical and projected interest rates and debts of various types, both public and private.

Demand for new credit was projected to rise by $50 billion in 1982 to $468 billion, but the sources of credit supply were not expected to change much. The difference would be made up by purchases of securities by the private sector. In addition to the growing debt burden that was being placed on firms, real growth was expected to be hampered by the continuing monetarist stance of the Fed, lingering high inflation rates, and the lack of success on the part of firms attempting to strengthen their solvency positions. Corporate bond offerings were projected to break record levels and domestic corporate issuers to face increased competition for funds from foreign issuers in the U.S. market. Stock issuances were also foreseen to be rising very rapidly, but they were expected to provide only a small portion of total capital requirements.

The Federal debt held privately was projected to reach a record of $135 billion. All such financing was to be carried out through Treasury bills and marketable coupons. In addition, it was anticipated that state and local governments would increase their total long-term debts by over $5 billion through the issuance of municipal bonds.

The limited economic growth anticipated in 1982 was to begin in the second half of the year and to be concentrated primarily in the residential investment, household consumption, and U.S. defense sectors. Only limited plant expansion and equipment purchases and, as a result, relatively small growth in inventory stocks were foreseen. Most of the private sector growth was to be spurred by rising disposable incomes, which would also increase savings and money-market deposits. This, in turn, would fuel the expansion of credit. The expansion of unused Federal Reserve credit was expected to continue through the first half of 1982, providing banks with additional resources. As a result, long-term interest rates would zigzag upward to 1981 levels by the end of 1982. The rise in short-term rates was projected to be lower because of investors' preferences for lending short-term in light of the growing Federal deficit and the resulting uncertainty over long-term rates.

PYRUS'S FINANCING OPTIONS

The management of Pyrus was interested in converting the company's commercial paper into longer term instruments. Fluctuating interest rates and the consequent uncertainty associated with a large amount of outstanding P-2 paper made management very uneasy. The possibility that the market could close to a commercial-paper rollover acted as an additional stimulus. Exhibit 16 shows the market P-1 rates and the P-1/P-2 spread. (P-1 and P-2 are Prime 1 and Prime 2, the highest and second highest commercial paper ratings, respectively, granted by Moody's Investor Services.) Management was also concerned about the company's amount of short-term debt and feared that the company's bond rating could be downgraded if analysts thought Pyrus was losing too much flexibility.

Exhibit 17 outlines financial projections and, specifically, the fund requirements for Pyrus, which reflect management's recent capital expenditure decisions. The forecast includes provision for the retirement of Pyrus's outstanding commercial paper over the next two years. The projections indicated the cumulative net funds need would peak in the fourth year at $250 million.

Mr. Watson eliminated the possibility of an equity issue because the industry's stock prices were depressed and the company's stock was already selling below book value. He met with the loan officer at Pyrus's bank to discuss the borrowing options open to the company. The banker gave Mr. Watson two alternatives: a $200 million revolving line of credit or a $75 million term loan.

The revolving credit would consist of a $200 million standby line for 2 years, with the balance to be converted to a 5-year term loan at the end of the 2-year period. Of the total, $50 million was to be used as a backstop for Pyrus's commercial paper. For the first 2 years, the interest rate was to float at 1.5 percentage points over the 90-day bank certificate of deposit rate, which was 13.5 percent at the time. The rate of the term portion was to be negotiated at the end of 2 years. The company was to pay a commitment fee of 0.5 percent on the unused portion of the credit, and Pyrus was, by covenant, to maintain a current ratio of 1.25 to 1 as well as a net working capital position of at least $100 million.

The $75 million term-loan option was an 8-year note. Only interest would be paid for the first 4 years. In years 5 through 7, 20 percent of the principal was to be paid each year, with a 40 percent balloon payment at the end of the 8th year. The interest rate was to be fixed at 16.75 percent with no prepayment allowed. Under the agreement, Pyrus was to maintain a net working capital position of $135 million and a long-term debt-to-capital ratio of no more than 44 percent.

With regard to long-term financing, the company's investment banker suggested either a private placement or a public issue of debentures. A private placement could be made immediately, or a forward commitment for a private placement of Pyrus's bonds could be arranged by the investment bank with a major insurance company. A $100 million private placement would entail a 10-year term with a 15 percent sinking fund in years 5 through 9 and a 25 percent balloon payment in the final year. Again, no prepayment was to be permitted. The proposed working capital and long-term debt-to-total-capital covenants were to be similar to those included in the commercial bank's term-loan offer. In addition, Pyrus was to be restricted to selling no more than $50 million in assets without approval of the lender. Dividends were to be limited to earnings less sinking-fund requirements. The investment banker mentioned a rate of 15 1/8 percent as a possibility, but the actual rate could not be set for another 6 months when the loan would be taken down. A bridge loan might be necessary for the first half year.

Pyrus's current bond rating was single A: in light of that, the investment banker recommended a $125 million public-issue mortgage bond or a debenture. The mortgage bond would require security of $100 million of timberland at book value, and the coupon rate was presumed, for discussion purposes, to be 14 3/8 percent for 20 years. The debenture was to have a coupon rate 25 basis points higher than the mortgage rate and could be called after 8 years at 107, declining to 100 at the 15th year. The mortgage bond could be refinanced without penalty once amortization had begun in the 11th year. Both issues would prohibit additional senior debt if long-term debt was to be greater than 50 percent of capitalization. The mandatory sinking-fund requirement for both was to be 10 percent of the original issue, beginning in the 11th year and completely retiring the debt in the 15th year. Underwriting costs were to be 0.85 percent.

Another bond alternative open to Pyrus was an industrial revenue bond with interest which would be nontaxable to the investor. Approximately $40 million of Pyrus's proposed expenditures qualified for this lower cost option; the typical interest rate, due to the tax benefits, averaged about 70 percent of the prime rate. This type of bond was backed by a mortgage and the guarantee of the company, and it usually provided that the interest rate would rise in the event that the IRS disallowed it as tax-exempt.

With these options in mind, as well as the possibility of issuing more commercial paper, Mr. Watson weighed the alternatives. He recognized the need for the company to maintain some reasonable degree of flexibility, and he also recognized that the various prognostications, both his own with regard to the company and those of economists and analysts with regard to the state of the economy and the market, might well be wrong. The future of interest rates was the one projection that bothered him the most. If Pyrus were to take out a long-term loan and rates were to drop, an unnecessarily large expense would be incurred. On the other hand, if Pyrus went the route of short-term borrowings and rates were to rise, the company would have the same problem.

Case 13 Pyrus, Incorporated

EXHIBIT 1 BALANCE SHEETS AS OF DECEMBER 31 (millions of dollars)

	1979	*1980*	*1981*
ASSETS			
Cash and marketable securities	$ 32	$ 29	$ 33
Accounts receivable	198	219	202
Inventories	283	294	318
Other current assets	31	33	23
Total current assets	544	575	576
Property and equipment, net	943	1,079	1,069
Timber, timberlands, and deposits	167	230	236
Investments and other assets	102	127	175
Total assets	$1,756	$2,011	$2,056
LIABILITIES AND SHAREHOLDERS' EQUITY			
Commercial paper	$ 0	$ 100	$ 73
Notes payable	19	1	0
Current portion of long-term debt	22	19	17
Income taxes payable	2	19	15
Accounts payable and accrued liabilities	265	277	292
Total current liabilities	308	416	397
Long-term debt, less current portion	428	504	511
Deferred income taxes	95	78	80
Other long-term liabilities	41	52	60
Shareholders' equity	884	961	1,008
Total liabilities and shareholders' equity	$1,756	$2,011	$2,056
BASIC RATIOS			
Long- and short-term debt total capitalization	36.8%	41.3%	39.6%
Short-term debt total capitalization[a]	2.9	7.3	5.4
Long-term debt total capitalization[a]	33.6	34.0	34.2
Net working capital	$ 236	$ 159	$ 179

[a]Total capitalization includes interest-bearing debt and shareholders' equity.

Note: Material in Exhibits 5 through 16 was selected from *1982 Prospects for Financial Markets*, a publication of Salomon Brothers. Reprinted with permission.

Case 13 Pyrus, Incorporated

EXHIBIT 2 CONSOLIDATED INCOME STATEMENTS AS OF DECEMBER 31 (millions of dollars except per-share figures)

	1979		*1980*		*1981*	
Net Sales	$2,188	100.0%	$2,264	100.0%	$2,331	100.0%
Costs and Expenses	2,014	92.0	2,105	93.0	2,181	93.6
Income from Operations	174	8.0	159	7.0	150	6.4
Other Income, Net	24	1.1	11	0.5	51	2.2
Less:						
Interest Expense	30	1.4	37	1.6	61	2.6
Income Taxes	36	1.6	19	0.8	48	2.1
Net Income	$ 132	6.0	$ 114	5.0	$ 92	4.0
Average Shares Outstanding (thousands)	26,810		26,835		26,850	
Net Earnings per Share	$4.92		$4.25		$3.43	
Dividends per Share	1.25		1.40		1.65	
Ratios						
Times Interest Earned (earnings before interest and taxes, interest charges)	6.6×		4.6×		3.3×	

Case 13 Pyrus, Incorporated

EXHIBIT 3 PAPER INDUSTRY DATA

INCOME/SALES RELATIONSHIPS

Company	*Operating Income/Sales 1979*	*Operating Income/Sales 1980*	*Net Income/Sales 1979*	*Net Income/Sales 1980*
Chesapeake	20.4%	21.4%	8.1%	9.1%
Consolidated	23.8	22.6	12.3	10.3
Crown Zellerbach	12.4	7.8	4.8	3.2
Gr. No. Nekoosa	17.2	16.8	7.8	7.2
Hammermill	8.9	8.8	3.3	3.4
International Paper	13.7	12.0	5.6	11.6
James River	10.0	8.5	4.5	3.8
Pyrus	8.0	7.0	6.0	5.0
St. Regis	13.8	12.7	6.3	6.3
Union Camp	20.5	20.4	10.9	10.5

LONG-TERM DEBT/CAPITAL AND RETURN ON ASSETS

Company	*Long-Term Debt/Capital 1979*	*Long-Term Debt/Capital 1980*	*Return on Assets 1979*	*Return on Assets 1980*
Chesapeake	24.2%	22.0%	9.1%	10.4%
Consolidated	9.5	7.9	16.0	13.6
Crown Zellerbach	34.6	29.0	6.2	4.1
Gr. No. Nekoosa	30.3	26.9	8.2	8.2
Hammermill	38.9	35.3	5.4	5.6
International Paper	27.2	23.0	10.8	6.0
James River	39.4	46.9	10.7	9.8
Pyrus	33.6	34.0	7.5	5.7
St. Regis	29.6	35.0	7.0	6.4
Union Camp	19.7	23.9	10.5	10.0

Case 13 Pyrus, Incorporated

EXHIBIT 4 HISTORIC DATA AND MAJOR BANK'S RECENT FORECAST FOR 1981–86

SHORT-TERM INTEREST RATES

Annual	*90-Day Commercial Paper*	*90-day CDs (Security Market)*	*Fed Funds*	*91-Day Treasury Bill*	*182-Day Treasury Bill*	*90-Day Euro-dollar*
1967	5.10	5.02	4.22	4.33	4.64	5.46
1968	5.92	5.86	5.66	5.35	5.48	6.36
1969	7.85	7.77	8.21	6.69	6.86	9.76
1970	7.70	7.57	7.18	6.44	6.54	8.51
1971	5.02	5.01	4.66	4.34	4.50	6.57
1972	4.83	4.65	4.43	4.07	4.46	5.41
1973	8.20	8.37	8.73	7.02	7.16	9.25
1974	10.01	10.25	10.50	7.87	7.91	10.92
1975	6.25	6.43	5.82	5.82	6.11	6.95
1976	5.24	5.27	5.05	5.00	5.28	5.57
1977	5.54	5.58	5.54	5.27	5.51	6.00
1978	7.94	8.17	7.93	7.22	7.57	8.78
1979	10.97	11.22	11.20	10.04	10.02	11.97
1980	12.66	13.05	13.36	11.62	11.47	14.02
1981	15.38	15.92	16.36	14.01	13.73	16.67
1982	10.63	10.88	10.88	9.63	9.71	11.20
1983	9.19	9.44	9.19	8.81	8.99	9.58
1984	9.50	9.75	9.69	9.08	9.23	9.80
1985	9.75	10.00	10.00	9.19	9.35	10.02
1986	8.31	8.56	8.38	8.06	8.19	8.58

INTERMEDIATE-TERM INTEREST RATES

Annual	*2-Year Treasury Note*	*7-Year Treasury Note*	*Aa Utility Rate (5–7 years)*
1967	—	—	—
1968	—	—	—
1969	—	3.57	4.69
1970	—	7.38	8.04
1971	—	6.18	6.85
1972	—	6.14	6.66
1973	—	6.86	7.38
1974	—	7.71	8.90
1975	—	7.90	8.56
1976	—	7.42	8.02
1977	6.45	7.23	7.70
1978	8.34	8.36	8.71
1979	10.11	9.48	10.08
1980	11.78	11.43	12.80
1981	14.58	14.09	15.12
1982	11.25	11.94	12.31
1983	9.59	10.01	10.39
1984	9.39	9.43	10.34
1985	9.00	9.15	9.71
1986	8.18	8.31	8.71

Note: Annual averages as of December 10, 1981.

Case 13 Pyrus, Incorporated

EXHIBIT 4 *(continued)*

LONG-TERM INTEREST RATES

Annual	*U.S. Treasury Bond (20-year)*	*Aa Utility Bond*	*Baa Utility Bond*	*Municipal Bond (high grade)*	*Mortgage Rate (commitment)*
1967	5.01	5.92	—	3.72	—
1968	5.45	6.65	—	4.21	—
1969	6.33	7.85	—	5.46	—
1970	6.89	8.76	—	6.05	—
1971	6.12	7.69	8.45	5.09	—
1972	6.01	7.42	7.86	4.92	—
1973	7.12	7.83	8.24	4.95	—
1974	8.05	9.41	10.68	5.78	—
1975	8.19	9.45	12.02	6.25	9.10
1976	7.86	8.67	9.86	5.73	9.00
1977	7.67	8.33	8.85	5.17	8.96
1978	8.50	9.10	9.69	5.58	9.70
1979	9.33	10.24	11.05	6.09	11.27
1980	11.39	13.11	14.63	7.98	14.00
1981	13.75	16.25	17.38	10.50	16.48
1982	12.44	14.13	14.94	9.95	14.25
1983	10.36	11.26	12.05	7.76	12.30
1984	9.98	11.09	12.15	7.76	11.56
1985	9.71	11.13	12.41	7.79	11.39
1986	8.43	10.00	10.64	7.01	11.28

Note: Annual averages as of December 10, 1981.

EXHIBIT 5 SUMMARY OF SUPPLY AND DEMAND FOR CREDIT (billions of dollars)

	Annual Net Increases in Amounts Outstanding						
	1976	*1977*	*1978*	*1979*	*1980*	*1981*[a]	*1982*[b]
Net Demand							
Privately Held Mortgages	$ 70.5	$108.0	$116.0	$105.0	$ 70.9	$ 72.2	$ 71.7
Corporate & Foreign Bonds	39.1	39.1	31.8	36.1	37.9	27.4	28.8
Subtotal Long-Term Private	109.6	147.1	147.8	141.1	108.8	99.6	100.5
Short-Term Business Borrowing	14.1	49.0	76.0	91.4	55.0	127.1	142.1
Short-Term Other Borrowing	40.7	50.7	65.5	52.8	20.7	47.0	59.7
Subtotal Short-Term Private	54.8	99.7	141.5	144.2	75.7	174.1	201.8
Privately Held Federal Debt	73.0	74.5	81.7	77.4	118.0	113.5	135.4
Tax-Exempt Notes and Bonds	17.6	28.9	32.5	27.7	33.0	31.0	30.7
Subtotal Government Debt	90.6	103.4	114.2	105.1	151.0	144.5	166.1
Total Net Demand for Credit	$255.0	$350.2	$403.5	$390.4	$335.5	$418.2	$468.4
Net Supply							
Thrift Institutions	$ 70.5	$ 82.0	$ 73.5	$ 55.9	$ 57.9	$ 39.7	$ 41.1
Insurance, Pensions, Endowments	49.0	68.1	73.2	63.6	75.4	70.8	76.7
Investment Companies	2.9	7.0	6.4	25.5	22.5	69.4	64.0
Other Nonbank Finance	12.9	13.4	18.9	26.4	16.6	33.3	41.4
Subtotal Nonbank Finance	135.3	170.6	172.0	171.3	172.3	213.2	223.1
Commercial Banks	60.8	84.1	105.9	103.9	83.3	115.0	126.8
Business Corporations	9.0	2.3	0.9	8.3	3.7	6.8	7.7
State & Local Government	4.0	13.3	11.1	9.5	7.3	11.0	8.2
Foreign	19.6	47.2	58.8	8.9	37.9	17.9	16.0
Subtotal	228.7	312.9	346.9	301.9	304.5	363.9	381.8
Residual (mostly household direct)	26.3	37.3	56.6	88.5	31.0	54.3	86.6
Total Net Supply of Credit	$255.0	$350.2	$403.5	$390.4	$335.5	$418.2	$468.4

[a]Estimated.
[b]Projected.

Case 13 Pyrus, Incorporated

EXHIBIT 6 GROSS ISSUANCE OF MEDIUM-TERM DEBT—U.S. GOVERNMENTS AND STRAIGHT CORPORATES (billions of dollars)

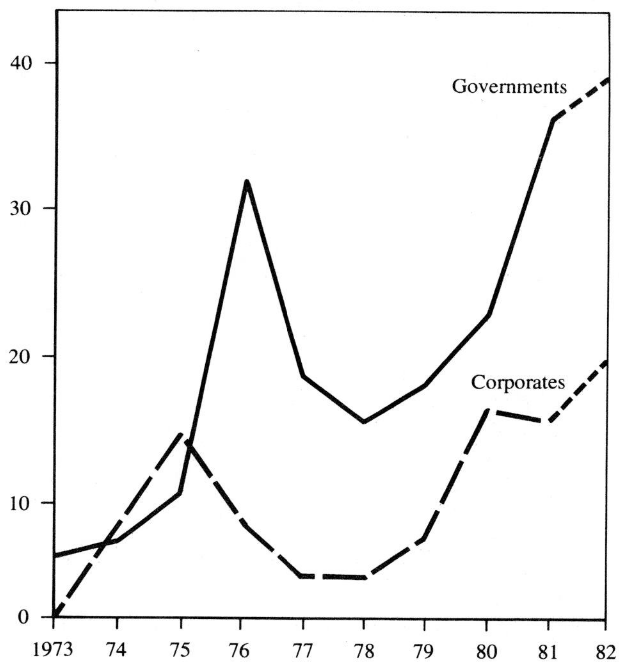

Case 13 Pyrus, Incorporated

EXHIBIT 6 (*continued*) GROSS ISSUANCE OF MEDIUM-TERM DEBT—U.S. GOVERNMENTS AND STRAIGHT CORPORATES (billions of dollars)

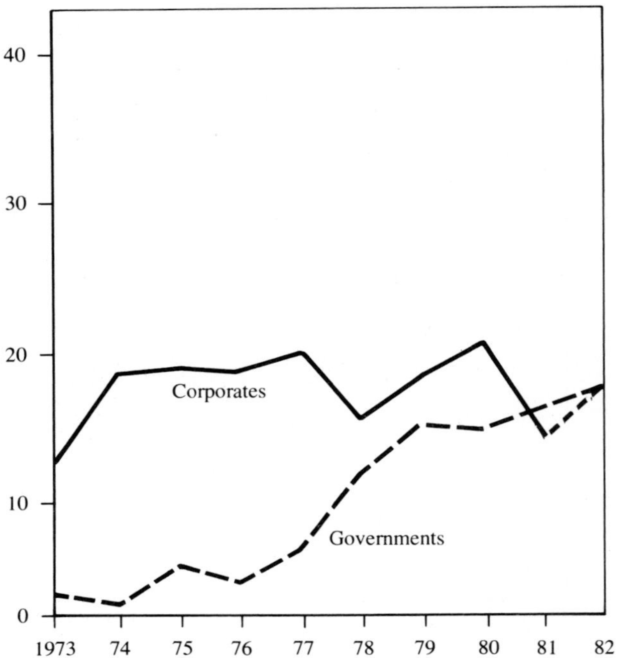

Case 13 Pyrus, Incorporated

EXHIBIT 7 THE COURSE OF INTEREST RATES IN RECENT YEARS (%)

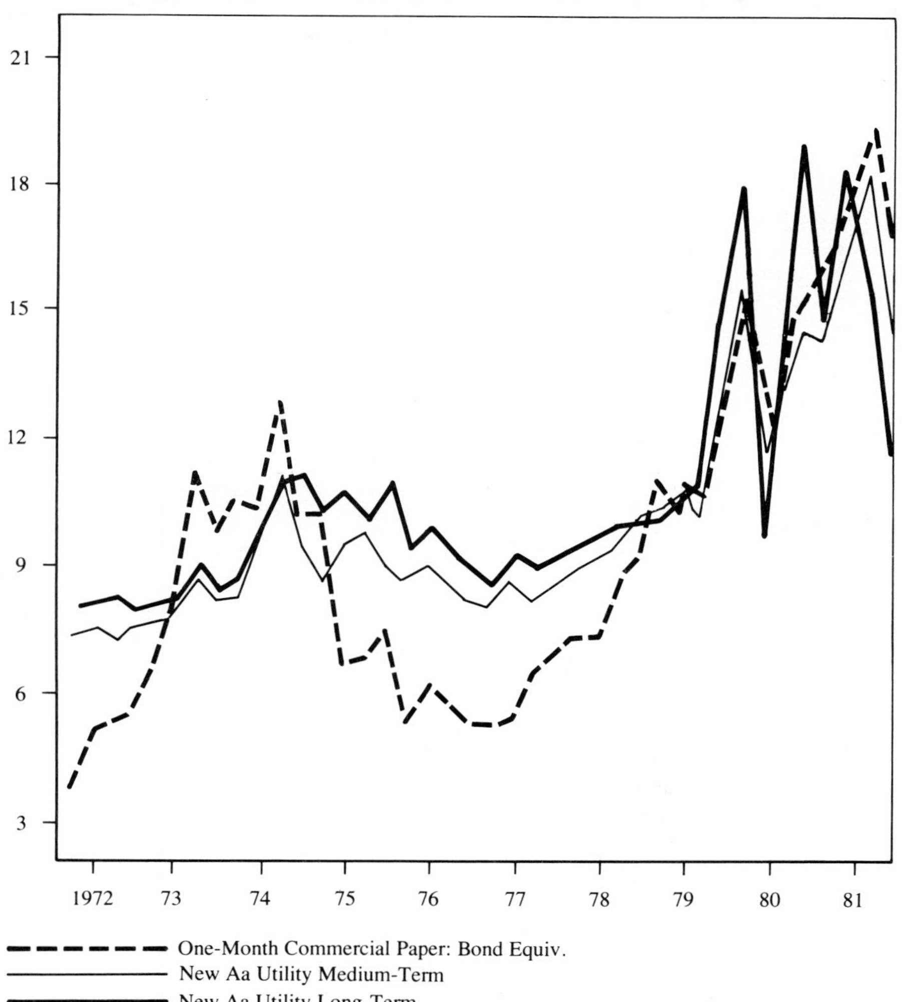

EXHIBIT 8 DOMESTIC CORPORATE AND FOREIGN BONDS SOLD IN U.S. (billions of dollars)

	Annual Issuance, Retirements & Net Increases in Amounts Outstanding							*Amount Outstanding*
	1976	*1977*	*1978*	*1979*	*1980*	*1981*[c]	*1982*[d]	*31 Dec. 81*[c]
Domestic Corporate								
Public Straight Issues								
Long	17.2	18.4	13.9	16.9	19.1	12.5	16.1	
Medium	7.3	3.6	3.6	6.1	14.9	14.3	18.8	
Private Straight Issues[a]	16.0	20.8	19.5	17.9	13.5	10.6	8.4	
Convertible Issues	1.0	0.8	0.3	0.7	4.3	4.1	3.2	
Less Maturities & Retirements	10.5	9.7	9.2	10.4	14.2	17.7	22.3	
Plus Exchanges (net of conversions)	−0.5	−0.3	0.3	2.9	−0.5	−0.3	0.2	
Net Issuance	30.6	33.6	28.4	34.1	37.2	23.5	24.3	*488.0*
Foreign Sold in U.S.								
Canadian Issues	6.1	3.0	3.1	2.2	2.1	4.4	5.5	
Other Countries' Issues	2.3	2.5	2.2	1.2	0.7	1.8	1.4	
International Issues	2.2	1.9	0.5	1.1	0.6	0.6	0.7	
Less Retirements[b]	2.1	1.9	2.4	2.5	2.7	2.9	3.2	
Net Issuance	8.5	5.5	3.4	2.0	0.7	3.9	4.4	*48.9*
Combined Net Issuance	39.1	39.1	31.8	36.1	37.9	27.4	28.8	*536.9*
Ownership								
Mutual Savings Banks	2.8	1.2	0.1	−1.1	0.7	−1.8	−1.2	*19.4*
Life Insurance Companies	16.9	18.8	17.3	11.6	8.7	9.3	8.0	*188.1*
Property Liability Companies	3.9	3.7	1.8	2.0	3.6	4.0	4.2	*31.1*
Private Noninsured Pension Funds	−0.3	6.6	5.9	5.7	4.4	1.9	4.0	*60.0*
State & Local Retirement Funds	5.1	6.0	9.0	3.2	9.7	7.0	10.0	*101.7*
Foundations & Endowments	0.7	0.6	0.2	0.2	0.3	0.2	0.6	*13.7*
Taxable Investment Funds	0.3	1.1	−0.7	0.8	1.3	0.6	0.4	*9.0*
Security Brokers & Dealers	−1.3	0.0	−0.6	0.1	0.1	0.7	1.0	*2.0*
Total Nonbank Institutions	28.2	37.8	33.0	22.5	28.7	21.8	27.0	*425.0*
Commercial Banks	−0.6	−0.3	−0.6	−0.5	0.5	0.2	0.1	*6.6*
Foreign[b]	0.8	4.0	2.1	1.2	5.1	4.0	4.0	*22.0*
Residual: Households Direct	10.7	−2.4	−2.7	12.9	3.6	1.4	−2.3	*83.3*
Total Ownership	39.1	39.1	31.8	36.1	37.9	27.4	28.8	*536.9*

[a]Adjusted to delivery date (as opposed to offering date) basis.

[b]Purchases of new issues by foreigners are included in retirements and thus are not in ownership calculation.

[c]Estimated.

[d]Projected.

EXHIBIT 9 CORPORATE BONDS BY TYPE OF ISSUE (billions of dollars)

	Annual Issuance, Retirements & Net Increases in Amounts Outstanding							*Amount Outstanding*
	1976	*1977*	*1978*	*1979*	*1980*	*1981*[c]	*1982*[d]	*31 Dec. 81*[c]
Straight Public Debt								
Cash Offerings								
Public Utility	6.1	5.7	4.7	5.5	7.3	7.6	9.8	
Communication	2.2	2.6	2.8	3.7	5.8	3.8	6.7	
Transportation	2.8	2.1	0.8	0.8	1.4	1.0	1.0	
Industrial	5.9	3.9	3.2	5.7	10.0	7.1	8.0	
Sales Finance	4.6	3.4	3.7	2.9	4.2	5.0	5.6	
Other Finance and Real Estate	2.3	3.7	1.7	3.8	3.0	1.8	2.4	
Commercial & Miscellaneous	0.6	0.6	0.6	0.6	2.2	0.6	1.4	
Total Cash Offerings	24.6	22.0	17.5	23.0	34.0	26.8	34.9	
Less Cash Retirements[a]	5.8	5.0	4.5	5.6	9.3	12.1	16.0	
Net Issuance Public Straight Debt	18.8	17.0	13.0	17.4	24.7	14.7	18.9	*309.3*
Straight Private Debt[b]								
Cash Offerings								
Public Utility	2.3	1.9	2.4	2.9	2.1	1.7	2.1	
Communication	0.3	0.4	0.5	0.5	0.5	0.5	0.3	
Transportation	2.2	1.7	3.2	2.5	3.0	1.1	0.5	
Industrial	7.3	11.6	8.4	8.1	4.9	3.4	3.0	
Sales Finance	0.5	0.8	0.8	0.5	0.3	0.4	0.2	
Other Finance and Real Estate	2.2	2.2	2.1	1.7	1.1	0.8	0.6	
Commercial & Miscellaneous	1.4	2.1	2.1	1.6	1.7	2.8	1.7	
Total Cash Offerings	16.0	20.8	19.5	17.9	13.5	10.6	8.4	
Less Cash Retirements	4.5	4.6	4.6	4.7	4.8	5.2	5.6	
Net Issuance Private Straight Debt	11.5	16.2	14.9	13.2	8.7	5.4	2.8	*150.7*

[a]Includes sinking fund purchases.
[b]Many private placements have equity features.
[c]Estimated.
[d]Projected.

EXHIBIT 9 *(continued)*

	Annual Issuance, Retirements & Net Increases in Amounts Outstanding							*Amount Outstanding*
	1976	*1977*	*1978*	*1979*	*1980*	*1981*[c]	*1982*[d]	*31 Dec. 81*[c]
Convertible Bonds								
Cash Offerings (mostly public)								
Public Utility	0	0.1	0	0	0	0.1	0.2	
Communication	0	0	0	0	0	0.2	0.3	
Transportation	0.1	0.1	0	0.2	0.2	0.3	0.1	
Industrial	0.8	0.7	0.2	0.2	2.9	2.2	2.0	
Sales Finance	0	0	0	0	0	0.1	0	
Other Finance and Real Estate	0	0	0.1	0.2	0.6	0.4	0.3	
Commercial & Miscellaneous	0	0	0.1	0.1	0.5	0.8	0.4	
Total Cash Offerings	1.0	0.8	0.3	0.7	4.3	4.1	3.2	
Plus Exchanges Net of Conversion	−0.5	−0.3	0.3	2.9	−0.5	−0.5	−0.3	
Less Calls & Other Retirements	0.2	0.1	0.1	0.1	0.1	0.2	0.3	
Net Issuance Convertible Debt	0.3	0.4	0.5	3.5	3.7	3.4	2.6	*28.0*
Net Issuance All Corporate Bonds	30.6	33.6	28.4	34.1	37.2	23.5	24.3	*488.0*
Memo: Sector Analysis								
Nonfinancial Corp.	23.7	23.6	20.6	25.7	28.7	17.5	16.7	*398.0*
Savings & Loan (mortgage backed)	0	0.9	0.5	1.1	0.3	0	0	*2.8*
Nonbank Financial Corporations	5.4	5.6	6.0	4.7	5.6	4.0	5.1	*64.2*
Commercial Banks	1.5	3.5	1.3	2.6	2.6	2.0	2.3	*23.0*
Total Net Change Outstanding	30.6	33.6	28.4	34.1	37.2	23.5	24.3	*488.0*

[a]Includes sinking fund purchases.
[b]Many private placements have equity features.
[c]Estimated.
[d]Projected.

Case 13 Pyrus, Incorporated

EXHIBIT 10 SOURCES AND USES OF CORPORATE FUNDS[a] (billions of dollars)

	Annual Income, Expenditures & Net Increases in Amounts Outstanding							*Amount Outstanding*
	1976	*1977*	*1978*	*1979*	*1980*	*1981[e]*	*1982[f]*	*31 Dec. 81[e]*
Analysis in Brief								
Profits Before Taxes and IVA	134.5	153.1	173.8	192.8	183.8	178.6	173.7	
Plus Inventory Valuation Adjustment	−14.7	−15.8	−24.3	−42.6	−45.7	−32.8	−48.9	
Repatriated Foreign Profits	6.0	5.7	9.4	15.1	12.5	8.3	11.5	
Less Federal Tax Payments	45.2	59.7	65.3	71.0	70.3	71.0	71.1	
Less Dividends	38.2	41.6	46.2	52.3	58.8	66.7	72.9	
Plus Depreciation	90.7	104.1	115.9	131.9	149.7	172.9	199.1	
Internal Cash Generation	133.2	145.8	163.3	173.9	170.8	189.4	191.4	
Physical Investment	170.1	195.9	226.1	257.9	252.5	286.9	323.2	
Plus Net Trade & Consumer Credit	8.6	11.8	14.6	15.4	6.2	8.3	7.5	
Less Internal Cash Generation	133.2	145.8	163.3	173.9	170.8	189.4	191.4	
Equals Operational Requirements	45.5	61.9	77.4	99.4	87.9	105.8	139.3	
Plus Reqs. for Financial Assets	12.1	26.7	12.6	12.3	16.2	13.8	3.1	
Equals External Requirements	57.7	88.6	90.0	111.7	104.1	119.6	142.4	
Uses of Funds								
Plant & Equipment[b]	129.0	149.4	175.0	202.0	212.6	238.6	262.8	
Land[c]	10.2	10.3	11.1	13.4	14.9	17.4	18.4	
Mineral Rights	4.0	2.5	2.0	4.7	6.5	6.3	12.0	
Direct Foreign Investment	11.6	11.5	15.7	23.7	18.2	14.6	18.4	
Residential Construction	2.5	3.7	2.4	0.6	0.1	−0.1	1.6	
Inventories Adjusted for Valuation	12.8	18.5	19.9	13.5	0.3	10.1	9.9	
Total Physical Investment	170.1	195.9	226.1	257.9	252.5	286.9	323.2	
Net Trade & Consumer Credit[c]	8.6	11.8	14.6	15.4	6.2	8.3	7.5	*170.0*
Demand Deposits & Currency	2.4	1.6	4.4	5.3	2.3	−2.5	−1.8	*67.4*
Time Deposits[c]	2.1	4.8	2.0	4.7	1.7	5.6	1.5	*43.2*
U.S. Governments	2.1	−3.7	−4.5	0.9	−2.5	−0.7	−0.2	*3.7*
Federal Agencies	0	−0.4	0.7	−1.3	0.5	0	0	*1.7*
Open Market Paper[c]	5.0	−0.1	0.2	3.9	3.9	3.7	3.0	*36.3*
State & Local Securities	−1.1	0	0.2	0	−0.2	0	−0.2	*3.5*
Repurchase Agreements	2.3	1.2	5.5	2.6	6.6	5.4	4.0	*28.3*
Foreign Deposits	1.7	1.3	2.4	1.5	0.9	5.6	3.0	*19.0*
Other Assets (net)	−2.3	22.0	1.7	−5.3	3.0	−3.3	−6.2	
Total Uses	190.9	234.4	253.3	285.6	274.9	309.0	333.8	

[a]Nonfarm, nonfinancial corporations.

[b]Comparable Commerce Department Survey Data:

(Actual Spending 1976–1980: July–August Survey 1981)							
	171.5	198.1	231.2	270.5	295.6	321.5	NA
Percentage Change							
Survey	8.8	15.5	16.7	17.0	9.3	8.8	NA
NIA	10.4	18.0	17.8	15.6	5.8	10.5	9.4

[c]Our estimates. All else from Federal Reserve Board of Governors, Flow-of-Funds.

[d]At market.

[e]Estimated.

[f]Projected.

Case 13 Pyrus, Incorporated

EXHIBIT 10 (*continued*)

	Income Expenditures & Net Increases in Amounts Outstanding							*Amount Outstanding*
	1976	*1977*	*1978*	*1979*	*1980*	*1981*[e]	*1982*[f]	*31 Dec. 81*[e]
Sources of Funds								
Mortgage Debt	12.1	19.7	22.1	22.8	20.1	21.7	24.0	*270.7*
Bank Term Loans[c]	−2.1	2.2	11.7	19.6	6.8	17.6	21.0	*133.9*
Bank Short-Term Loans[c]	5.9	18.4	18.4	23.6	20.0	27.4	27.5	*207.6*
Finance Company Loans	8.4	13.5	11.5	10.2	3.1	10.7	12.5	*89.2*
U.S. Government Loans	.0.2	0	1.7	1.2	1.5	1.0	1.1	*9.4*
Net Sales of Open Market Paper[c]	2.7	2.4	1.9	9.4	4.4	15.1	17.1	*49.2*
Net New Tax-Exempt Bond Issues	2.5	4.8	3.7	3.6	2.5	3.7	5.0	*27.4*
Net New Taxable Bond Issues[c]	23.7	23.6	20.6	25.7	28.7	17.5	16.7	*398.0*
Net New Stock Issues[c]	4.3	4.0	−1.6	−4.4	17.0	4.9	17.5	*1,220.0*[d]
Total External Sources	57.7	88.6	90.0	111.7	104.1	119.6	142.4	*2,405.4*
Internal Cash Generation	133.2	145.8	163.3	173.9	170.8	189.4	191.4	
Total Sources	190.9	234.4	253.3	285.6	274.9	309.0	333.8	

[a]Nonfarm, nonfinancial corporations.

[b]Comparable Commerce Department Survey Data:

(Actual Spending 1976–1980: July–August Survey 1981)	171.5	198.1	231.2	270.5	295.6	321.5	NA
Percentage Change							
Survey	8.8	15.5	16.7	17.0	9.3	8.8	NA
NIA	10.4	18.0	17.8	15.6	5.8	10.5	9.4

[c]Our estimates. All else from Federal Reserve Board of Governors, Flow-of-Funds.

[d]At market.

[e]Estimated.

[f]Projected.

Case 13 Pyrus, Incorporated

EXHIBIT 11 CORPORATE STOCK ISSUES, COMMON AND PREFERRED (billions of dollars)

	Annual Issuance, Retirements & Net Issuance							*Amount Outstanding[c]*
	1976	*1977*	*1978*	*1979*	*1980*	*1981[e]*	*1982[f]*	*31 Dec. 81[e]*
Gross New Cash Offerings								
Public Utility	6.1	6.1	5.2	5.5	6.3	5.3	6.9	
Communication	0.8	1.4	0.2	0.5	0.6	1.4	2.8	
Transportation	0	0.5	0.3	0.3	0.5	0.7	0.4	
Industrial	3.0	2.5	2.9	3.7	10.3	13.0	11.7	
Sales Finance	0	0	0	0.1	0	0	0	
Other Finance and Real Estate	0.8	1.0	1.6	1.4	3.0	5.2	6.7	
Commercial & Miscellaneous	0.4	0.5	0.5	1.0	1.8	2.3	2.1	
Plus Dividend Reinvestment[d]	0.5	0.7	1.2	1.9	2.5	3.0	4.2	
Plus Stock Options & Foreign Sales[d]	2.7	3.0	2.6	3.0	3.5	4.5	5.6	
Total Cash Offerings[a,b]	14.3	15.7	14.6	17.3	28.6	35.5	40.3	
Less Cash Retirements[d]	9.5	11.0	14.7	17.6	9.8	27.9	18.2	
Plus Conversions (net of exchanges)[d]	0.5	0.3	−0.3	−2.9	0.5	0.3	−0.2	
Net Issuance	5.3	5.0	−0.4	−3.3	19.4	7.8	21.9	*1,661.0*
Ownership								
Mutual Savings Banks	0.1	0.4	0.1	−0.1	−0.5	−0.4	−0.2	*3.8*
Life Insurance Companies	3.0	1.2	−0.1	0.6	1.2	2.4	2.1	*58.5*
Property Liability Companies	0.9	1.2	2.0	3.2	3.1	2.0	1.3	*36.3*
Private Noninsured Pension Funds	7.3	4.5	1.9	6.1	9.6	12.6	12.7	*199.1*
State & Local Retirement Funds	3.1	3.7	2.6	4.1	5.3	5.2	6.7	*52.3*
Foundations & Endowments	2.0	1.0	1.3	7.0	4.0	5.5	5.5	*51.1*
Taxable Investment Funds	−2.4	−3.7	−1.6	−2.8	−1.8	0	0.8	*47.0*
Security Brokers & Dealers	0.5	0.2	−0.3	−0.6	0.8	2.0	1.7	*3.8*
Total Nonbank Finance	14.5	8.3	5.8	17.6	21.7	29.3	30.6	*451.9*
Foreigners	2.8	2.7	2.5	1.7	5.3	8.0	7.4	*128.3*
Residual Households Direct	−12.0	−6.0	−8.7	−22.6	−7.6	−29.5	−16.1	*1,080.8*
Total Ownership	5.3	5.0	−0.4	−3.3	19.4	7.8	21.9	*1,661.0*
[a]Includes annual preferred offerings of:	2.8	3.9	2.8	3.5	3.6	2.2	3.9	

[b]Adjusted to delivery date (as opposed to offering date) basis.
[c]At market.
[d]Our estimate.
[e]Estimated.
[f]Projected.

EXHIBIT 11 (*continued*)

	Annual Issuance, Retirements & Net Issuance							*Amount Outstanding*[c]
	1976	*1977*	*1978*	*1979*	*1980*	*1981*[e]	*1982*[f]	*31 Dec. 81*[e]
Changes in Market Value of Holdings								
Institutions & Foreigners:								
Market Value, Start of Year	279.1	335.6	327.8	353.8	400.9	514.2	580.2	
Plus Gross Purchases	77.9	64.7	88.5	106.0	178.0	204.0		
Less Gross Sales	60.6	53.7	80.2	86.7	151.0	166.7		
Plus Appreciation	39.2	−18.8	17.7	27.8	86.3	28.7		
Equals Market Value, End of Year	335.6	327.8	353.8	400.9	514.2	580.2		
Households:								
Market Value, Start of Year	570.4	670.0	618.0	634.3	776.7	1,059.3	1,080.8	
Plus Gross Purchases	162.4	164.7	216.6	258.3	403.4	426.8		
Less Gross Sales	174.4	170.7	225.3	280.9	411.0	456.3		
Plus Appreciation	111.6	−46.0	25.0	165.0	290.2	51.0		
Equals Market Value, End of Year	670.0	618.0	634.3	776.7	1,059.3	1,080.8		
All Holders:								
Market Value, Start of Year	849.5	1,005.6	945.8	988.1	1,177.6	1,573.5	1,661.0	
Plus Gross Purchases	240.3	229.4	305.1	364.3	581.4	630.8		
Less Gross Sales	235.0	224.4	305.5	367.6	562.0	623.0		
Plus Appreciation	150.8	−64.8	42.7	192.8	376.5	79.7		
Equals Market Value, End of Year	1,005.6	945.8	988.1	1,177.6	1,573.5	1,661.0		
[a]Includes annual preferred offerings of:	2.8	3.9	2.8	3.5	3.6	2.2	3.9	

[b]Adjusted to delivery date (as opposed to offering date) basis.

[c]At market.

[d]Our estimate.

[e]Estimated.

[f]Projected.

Case 13 Pyrus, Incorporated

EXHIBIT 12 OPEN-MARKET PAPER (billions of dollars)

	Annual Net Increases in Amounts Outstanding							*Amount Outstanding*
	1976	*1977*	*1978*	*1979*	*1980*	***1981[b]***	***1982[c]***	***31 Dec. 81[b]***
Outstanding								
Dealer Placed	3.2	4.0	7.1	15.1	8.0	33.7	38.3	*87.5*
Directly Placed[a]	1.1	7.9	11.2	13.1	3.1	17.2	21.7	*85*
Bankers' Acceptances	3.8	2.9	8.3	11.6	9.4	10.0	10.8	*64.7*
Total	8.1	15.0	26.4	39.8	20.6	60.9	70.9	*237.2*
Less Federal Agencies	0	0.2	−1.2	0.1	0	−0.1	0	*0.3*
Less Federal Reserve Banks	−0.1	0	−0.4	0.1	0.1	−0.8	0.3	*0*
Privately Held	8.3	14.8	28.0	39.6	20.5	61.7	70.6	*236.9*
Ownership								
Mutual Savings Banks	0.4	0	0.7	1.9	1.7	1.2	0.3	*5.1*
Savings & Loan Associations	−0.1	−0.3	0.4	0.7	1.5	0.1	0.4	*5.0*
Life Insurance Companies	0.4	−0.3	1.5	1.6	2.2	4.0	5.7	*14.2*
Private Noninsured Pension Funds	0	0.2	0.3	0.6	0.8	1.1	1.5	*3.6*
State & Local Retirement Funds	−0.1	−0.1	0.5	1.0	1.0	1.1	1.3	*4.0*
Foundations & Endowments	−0.1	−0.1	0	0.2	0.2	0.2	0.3	*1.5*
Money Market Funds	0.4	0.1	2.6	15.6	12.3	46.8	35.9	*78.3*
Taxable Investment Funds	−1.1	1.1	1.1	−0.2	0.9	−0.7	0.8	*3.1*
Total Nonbank Finance	−0.2	0.6	5.7	21.5	20.4	53.8	46.2	*114.8*
Commercial Banks	3.2	0.2	−2.3	1.8	1.0	0	−0.3	*12.1*
Business Corporations	5.0	−0.1	0.2	3.9	3.9	3.7	3.0	*36.3*
State & Local Governments	−0.1	2.0	2.5	3.0	−0.5	2.0	1.2	*9.4*
Foreign	3.1	4.4	8.8	7.3	5.2	8.0	7.5	*47.5*
Residual: Households Direct	−2.7	7.7	13.1	2.1	−9.5	−5.8	13.0	*16.8*
Total Ownership	8.3	14.8	28.0	39.6	20.5	61.7	70.6	*236.9*
Memo: Sector Analysis of Liabilities								
Nonfinancial Corporations	2.7	2.4	1.9	9.4	4.4	15.1	17.1	*49.2*
Noncorporate Business	1.3	0.6	−0.8	1.0	0.8	0.3	0.5	*7.2*
Finance Companies	3.3	8.3	7.8	13.5	−0.7	23.5	27.6	*83.7*
Commercial Banks	−0.8	1.3	6.7	4.5	5.6	6.0	9.5	*32.0*
Real Estate Investment Trusts	−0.3	0	0.1	0.1	−0.2	0	0.1	*0.6*
Foreigners	1.9	2.4	10.7	11.3	10.7	16.0	16.1	*64.5*
Total Net Change	8.1	15.0	26.4	39.8	20.6	60.9	70.9	*237.2*

[a]Assumes directly placed paper is issued almost solely by financial coporations.
[b]Estimated.
[c]Projected.

EXHIBIT 13 LOANS* (billions of dollars)

	Annual Net Increases in Amounts Outstanding							*Amount Outstanding*
	1976	*1977*	*1978*	*1979*	*1980*	*1981*[a]	*1982*[b]	*31 Dec. 81*[a]
Loans by Type								
Business	5.8	34.2	48.1	51.9	34.5	65.4	71.5	*505.8*
Consumer Installment	21.5	36.4	41.9	39.2	1.4	22.6	31.3	*335.4*
Consumer Noninstallment	3.9	3.7	5.7	7.1	0.9	4.9	6.5	*77.1*
Other	15.2	10.5	17.9	6.6	18.4	19.5	21.9	*143.4*
Total Loans	46.4	84.8	113.6	104.8	55.2	112.4	131.2	*1,061.7*
Ownership								
Mutual Savings Banks: Consumer	0.3	0.5	0.7	0.1	0.1	0.1	0.4	*4.1*
Savings & Loan Associations: Consumer	1.1	1.5	0.3	3.7	2.7	2.7	2.1	*20.1*
Credit Unions: Consumer	5.5	6.4	6.7	2.2	−2.5	3.6	4.6	*47.7*
Finance Companies:								
Business	8.6	13.5	11.5	10.1	3.4	13.5	15.9	*101.6*
Consumer	3.6	7.7	11.3	15.7	9.6	15.5	19.0	*108.3*
Commercial Banks:								
Business	−4.6	19.4	32.9	28.8	30.4	49.5	50.8	*367.0*
Consumer, Installment	10.8	18.6	23.6	18.2	−8.4	1.8	5.7	*147.6*
Consumer, Noninstallment	1.2	3.6	2.5	1.7	−1.3	0	0.9	*30.9*
Other	13.6	7.1	3.5	6.3	3.6	20.5	20.7	*103.9*
Business Corporations: Consumer	2.9	1.8	2.4	4.7	2.1	3.8	5.2	*53.7*
Foreign								
Business	1.8	1.3	3.7	12.9	0.7	2.3	4.8	*37.2*
Other	1.7	3.5	14.4	0.3	14.8	−0.1	1.2	*39.4*
All Lenders: Total Loans	46.4	84.8	113.6	104.8	55.2	112.4	131.2	*1,061.7*
Summary of Short-Term Borrowing								
Business Loans	5.8	34.2	48.1	51.9	34.5	65.4	71.5	*505.8*
Open-Market Paper	8.3	14.8	28.0	39.6	20.5	61.7	70.6	*236.9*
Total Business Borrowing	14.1	49.0	76.0	91.4	55.0	127.1	142.1	*742.7*
Consumer Installment	21.5	36.4	41.9	39.2	1.4	22.6	31.3	*335.4*
Consumer Noninstallment	3.9	3.7	5.7	7.1	0.9	4.9	6.5	*77.1*
Other	15.2	10.5	17.9	6.6	18.4	19.5	21.9	*143.4*
Total Other Borrowing	40.7	50.7	65.5	52.8	20.7	47.0	59.7	*555.9*

*Excludes loans included elsewhere, such as mortgages and open-market paper.

[a]Estimated.

[b]Projected.

Case 13 Pyrus, Incorporated

EXHIBIT 14 COMMERCIAL BANKS[1] (billions of dollars)

	Annual Net Increases in Amounts Outstanding							*Amount Outstanding*
	1976	*1977*	*1978*	*1979*	*1980*	*1981*[a]	*1982*[b]	*31 Dec. 81*[a]
Loans to (or for):								
Domestic Corporate Business, Term	−2.2	1.8	10.9	14.9	5.3	16.1	20.1	*124.0*
Domestic Corporate Business, Short-Term	4.2	17.5	15.5	15.4	20.8	26.6	23.6	*180.3*
Domestic Noncorporate	−3.6	0.9	0.3	0.5	1.9	3.2	3.3	*14.6*
Foreign	0.5	−0.4	3.4	−1.4	2.8	2.9	2.5	*19.5*
Finance Companies	−1.9	0.6	4.1	−1.2	1.2	0.9	1.3	*21.8*
Other Nonbank Finance	−1.6	−1.0	−1.3	0.6	−1.6	−0.1	0.2	*6.9*
Total Business	−4.6	19.4	32.9	28.8	30.4	49.5	50.8	*367.0*
Agriculture	3.0	2.5	2.5	2.8	0.5	5.7	5.2	*37.3*
Security	6.2	1.8	−3.0	−0.8	1.2	5.6	5.5	*25.5*
Miscellaneous	4.4	2.8	4.0	4.3	1.9	9.2	10.0	*41.1*
Total Other	13.6	7.1	3.5	6.3	3.6	20.5	20.7	*103.9*
Mortgage	15.1	27.6	35.3	31.1	19.4	27.1	30.0	*290.0*
Consumer Installment	10.8	18.6	23.6	18.2	−8.4	1.8	5.7	*147.6*
Consumer Noninstallment	1.2	3.6	2.5	1.7	−1.3	0	0.9	*30.9*
Total Loans	36.1	76.3	97.8	86.1	43.6	99.0	108.1	*939.4*
U.S. Governments	18.1	−2.2	−6.7	−0.4	15.3	8.1	10.0	*116.0*
Federal Agencies	1.5	0.9	6.8	7.4	9.7	6.2	5.0	*66.7*
Open Market Paper	3.2	0.2	−2.3	1.8	1.0	0	−0.3	*12.1*
Corporate & Foreign Bonds	−0.6	−0.3	−0.6	−0.5	0.5	0.2	0.1	*6.6*
State & Local Securities	2.6	9.2	10.9	9.6	13.2	1.6	3.8	*149.0*
Total Credit	60.8	84.1	105.9	103.9	83.3	115.0	126.8	*1,289.9*
Reserves	1.0	3.6	5.9	1.5	−1.0	−3.6	−3.0	*43.6*
Total Financial Assets	59.8	87.7	111.8	105.4	82.3	111.4	123.8	*1,333.5*
Demand Deposits (private nonbank)	11.1	17.2	16.1	25.3	13.1	−12.1	2.0	*304.1*
Demand Deposits (U.S.)	−0.1	4.3	6.8	0.4	−2.6	−1.8	−2.5	*10.2*
Large Time Deposits	−18.0	23.9	44.3	8.3	42.8	28.3	33.1	*282.8*
Other Time Deposits	56.9	28.1	10.9	31.0	41.0	50.7	53.8	*512.7*
Commercial Paper	−0.8	1.3	6.7	4.5	5.6	6.0	9.5	*32.0*
Net Adv. from (to) Foreign Branches	−3.9	−6.5	2.3	16.6	−21.1	16.4	12.3	*1.7*
Repurchase Agreements & Fed Funds	13.6	9.0	20.2	16.3	18.8	9.0	10.2	*113.8*
Net New Bond Issues	1.5	3.5	1.3	2.6	2.6	2.0	2.3	*23.0*
Equity Accounts	7.1	4.9	7.8	7.5	8.0	9.5	8.7	*104.3*
Other Liabilities (net of misc. assets)	−7.6	2.0	−4.6	−7.1	−25.9	3.4	−5.6	*(51.1)*
Total Liabilities (net)	59.8	87.7	111.8	105.4	82.3	111.4	123.8	*1,333.5*

[1]Domestically chartered banks and their domestic affiliates.
[a]Estimated.
[b]Projected.

Case 13 Pyrus, Incorporated

EXHIBIT 15 HOUSEHOLD INCOME, SAVINGS, AND THE RESIDUAL (billions of dollars)

	Annual Income, Expenditures, and Net Increases in Amounts Outstanding							*Amount Outstanding*
	1976	*1977*	*1978*	*1979*	*1980*	*1981*[d]	*1982*[e]	*31 Dec. 81*[d]
Personal Income	1,391.2	1,538.0	1,721.7	1,943.8	2,160.2	2,409.7	2,624.7	
Personal Taxes, Federal Fees, etc.	196.8	226.5	258.8	302.0	338.5	386.8	405.1	
Disposable Personal Income	1,194.4	1,311.5	1,462.9	1,641.7	1,821.7	2,022.9	2,219.6	
Consumption, Finance Charges, etc.[a]	1,111.9	1,237.5	1,386.6	1,556.6	1,720.4	1,196.0	2,170.4	
Personal Savings, NIA	82.5	74.1	76.3	86.2	101.3	106.9	112.2	
Plus Credit from Government Insurance, etc.	17.7	22.5	27.9	24.4	35.3	32.0	35.7	
Plus Durables in Consumption	40.0	50.2	56.3	52.4	33.8	36.9	37.5	
Capital Consumption, Durables	116.9	128.6	143.1	159.9	178.1	198.0	220.5	
Capital Consumption, Other	29.0	33.4	39.0	45.4	52.7	61.2	71.2	
Gross Savings	286.1	308.8	342.6	368.3	401.2	435.0	477.1	
Less Residential Construction Expenditures	60.6	80.7	97.1	106.6	93.8	95.6	92.9	
Less Total Durable Goods	156.8	178.8	199.3	212.3	211.9	235.8	255.0	
Less (nonprofit) Plant & Equipment Expenditures	5.7	5.9	6.5	7.2	7.4	7.6	7.9	
Plus Consumer Credit	25.4	40.2	47.6	2.3	27.5	37.8	412.5	
Plus Mortgage Credit	61.5	93.0	107.6	115.9	83.8	67.0	66.0	*1007.3*
Plus Security Credit	5.1	1.3	1.3	−1.2	5.0	7.6	7.0	*31.3*
Plus Other Loans	2.8	5.1	6.3	7.3	16.9	15.4	22.3	*99.1*
Plus Net Disinvestment in Noncorporate Business	12.1	7.6	13.4	18.3	23.7	25.7		
Plus Proceeds, Sale Real Assets	23	41.3	40.7	55.5	87.0	38.4	60.5	
Net Increase in Financial Assets	193.3	231.9	255.4	279.4	301.4	275.6	340.6	*4,802.6*
Less Contractional Savings[b]	52.4	66.1	73.8	66.9	89.0	85.1	94.8	*1,093.9*
Equals Discretionary Investment	140.9	165.8	181.6	212.5	212.4	190.5	245.8	*3,708.7*

[a]Includes interest expense and transfer payments abroad.
[b]Insurance and pension reserves.
[c]At market.
[d]Estimated.
[e]Projected.

Case 13 Pyrus, Incorporated

EXHIBIT 15 (*continued*)

	Annual Income, Expenditures, and Net Increases in Amounts Outstanding							*Amount Outstanding*
	1976	*1977*	*1978*	*1979*	*1980*	*1981*[d]	*1982*[e]	*31 Dec. 81*[d]
Investment Funds Total	0.5	4.8	8.9	38.7	37.4	115.2	103.7	*286.0*
Foundation & Endowments	2.7	1.6	2.1	7.7	5.0	6.5	7.1	*72.4*
Savings Accounts	107.5	107.6	100.1	77.1	131.2	50.6	66.0	*1,345.0*
Demand Deposits & Currency	15.8	20.5	22.6	23.1	15.4	−6.6	−1.5	*261.4*
Total Intermediate Investment	126.6	134.5	133.7	146.6	189.0	165.7	175.3	*1,964.8*
U.S. Governments	3.4	16.6	26.6	37.5	15.5	23.4	39.7	*251.9*
Federal Agencies	3.0	1.1	4.8	20.4	6.6	2.5	7.2	*62.6*
Open-Market Paper	−2.7	7.7	13.1	2.1	−9.5	−5.8	13.0	*16.8*
Corporate & Foreign Bonds	10.7	−2.4	−2.7	12.9	3.6	1.4	−2.3	83.3
Mortgages	7.7	11.0	11.4	12.5	8.5	9.9	6.2	*133.8*
State & Local Securities	4.3	3.4	3.6	3.3	6.4	22.8	22.8	*114.5*
Total Credit	26.3	37.3	56.6	88.5	31.0	54.3	86.6	*663.1*
Stocks	−12.0	−6.0	−8.7	−22.6	7.6	−29.5	−16.1	*1,080.8*[c]
Total Direct Investment	14.3	31.3	47.9	65.9	23.4	24.8	70.5	*1,743.9*
Total Discretionary Investment	140.9	165.8	181.6	212.5	212.4	190.5	245.8	*3,708.7*

[a]Includes interest expense and transfer payments abroad.
[b]Insurance and pension reserves.
[c]At market.
[d]Estimated.
[e]Projected.

Case 13 Pyrus, Incorporated

EXHIBIT 16 RATES ON A1/P1 COMMERCIAL PAPER

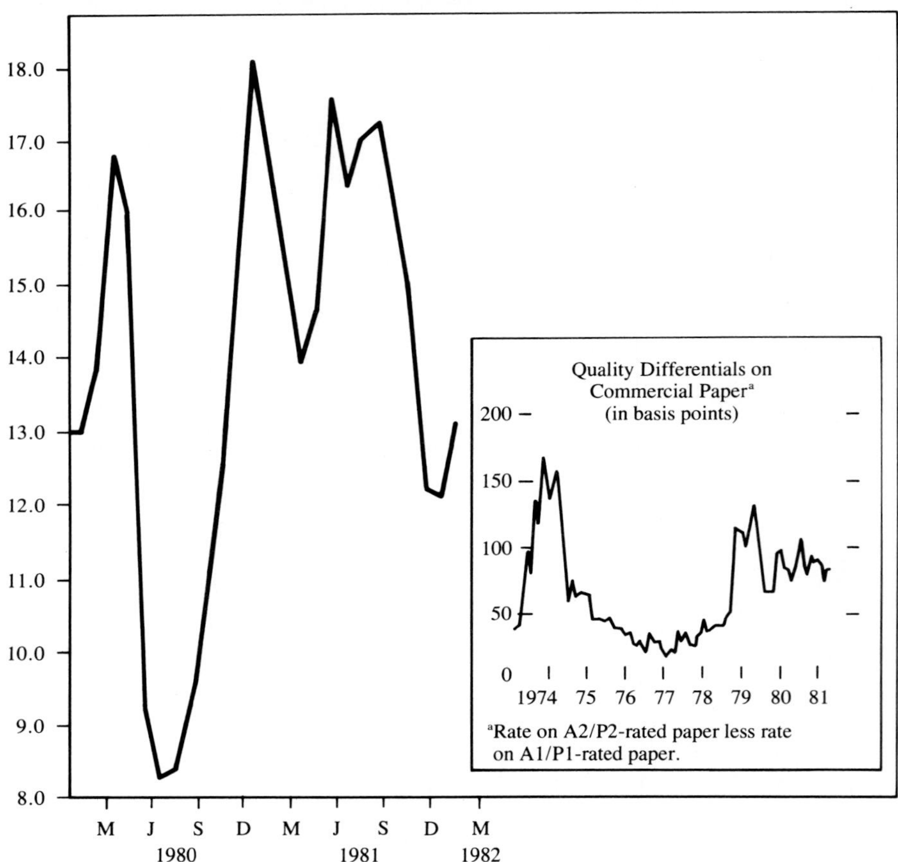

[a]Final data as of November 25, 1981.

Case 13 Pyrus, Incorporated

EXHIBIT 17 FORECAST OF FUND REQUIREMENTS (millions of dollars)

	1982	*1983*	*1984*	*1985*	*1986*
SOURCES					
Net income[a]	$ 121	$ 150	$ 168	$ 187	$ 208
Cash Dividends	(40)	(50)	(56)	(62)	(69)
Retained earnings	81	100	112	125	139
Depreciation/Depletion	123	136	149	162	170
Total sources	$ 204	$ 236	$ 261	$ 287	$ 309
REQUIREMENTS					
Additional Working Capital	$ 1	$ 9	$ 8	$ 9	$ 8
Capital Expenditures	300	260	290	285	260
Retirement of Commercial Paper	40	33	—	—	—
Total needs	341	302	298	294	268
Sources less needs	$(137)	$ (66)	$ (37)	$ (7)	$ 41
Additional Capital Requirements, Cumulative[b]	$ 137	$ 203	$ 240	$ 247	$ 206

[a]Interest has been held at current amounts on long-term debt, which assumes maturing long-term debt is refinanced at the same rate. These rates were somewhat lower than market rates in 1981. Interest on additional debt has not been deducted.

[b]Exclusive of refinancing of maturing long-term debt. During the 1982–1986 period, between $15 and $20 million in long-term debt would mature each year. No balloon maturities would occur during this period.

Case 14

OFFICE COMPUTER SYSTEMS, INC.

It was late December 1980, and James Dunmire, vice president of finance of Office Computer Systems, Inc. (OCS), was facing a unique situation. It had been ten years since his company had needed to finance capital expenditures from sources other than internally generated funds. However, two circumstances had developed that now required OCS to seek financing from other sources:

1. The board has just approved a three-year program to build new headquarters costing \$80 million. The first phase was scheduled to begin in March 1981 and would cost \$30 million during the first year. Phase 1, which would include constructing accommodations for the vital engineering and technical sections of OCS, was considered critical to the company's health and vitality in 1983 and later years.
2. A small international distributorship of office computers had become available for purchase. The acquisition, estimated to cost \$10 million, fit perfectly into OCS's marketing strategy of distributing its product line internationally in order to take advantage of the expanding and profitable foreign markets.

Further complicating OCS's funding problem was the need for the company to continue upgrading existing facilities and equipment to support the introduction of new products and lines planned for 1981 and 1982. Early estimates indicated that 1981 payments for this purpose would reach almost \$12 million. Total expenditures, combining the first two projects with the latter, would total \$52 million, and this figure did not include incremental working capital needed to support the anticipated growth in sales.

Estimated capital needed for 1982–1983 fiscal years, which included the last two phases of the new headquarters construction plus ongoing projects, would result in significant additional outside financing. As Mr. Dunmire sat in his Sacramento office, he considered the ways available to OCS to raise enough cash to meet future requirements.

BACKGROUND

Office Computer Systems, Inc., was incorporated in California in July 1970. The company produced computer-based systems for the fully integrated business office. Since 1970, OCS had developed into a leading supplier of dispersed data-processing systems that could be wired together for small-office use. The systems were designed to include multicomputer networks, telecommunication equipment, switching systems, and, more recently, word processing, all for the electronic office of the future. Supporting the equipment was highly developed software, and each system could be interconnected with the others, allowing users to share capacity. Recent developments had increased the product's reliability, because a single processor could cease functioning without interrupting the work of the other parts of the system. A major marketing effort was planned for those features in 1981, even at the cost of a temporary reduction in profitability, in order to lay the foundation in the marketplace for subsequent rapid growth. It was anticipated that marketing expenses would have to be maintained at a relatively higher level after the initial program was finished.

THE INDUSTRY

The surge in the small-office computer industry occurred during the early 1960s as processing

Case prepared as a basis for class discussion rather than to illustrate either effective or ineffective handling of an administrative situation.

bottlenecks became more frequent when large numbers of users made increasing demands on central mainframes. The market exploded several years later, and by 1980 this segment of the computer data-processing industry comprised 11 percent of the $55 billion in total revenues generated. Exhibit 1 presents anticipated industry growth and other selected industry statistics.

There were several benefits of small-office computer systems. During the 1970s, they had become increasingly sophisticated, they were less expensive, and now they were more convenient than ever to use. As shown in Table 1, by 1975 this segment of the industry had reached 3.5 percent, and in 1980 the percentage had increased to 11 percent. By 1985, the estimated share was expected to be almost 13 percent.

While small-office computers would lead industry growth as increased product innovation and rapid customer acceptance stimulated sales of electronic intra- and interoffice systems, other segments were expected to stagnate. The sluggish 1981 business forecasts and high interest rates would prevent many potential users from purchasing mainframes, and smaller companies servicing the data-processing segments of the market were anticipating or experiencing downturns in new business development.

Industry projections had greatly affected the thinking of many large mainframe manufacturers. In particular, the possible entry of IBM into the higher growth segments of the industry could affect some firms. During the past twelve years, the Justice Department had an antitrust suit pending against IBM, which still controlled about 60 percent of the mainframe market. IBM was thought to have been reluctant to enter the high-growth segments of the computer data-processing industry, fearing that such an entry, usually characterized by product innovation and development of new market strategies, would hinder its chances of obtaining a favorable verdict in the suit with the Justice Department.

Recent technological changes in other segments of the market had greatly expanded the relative size of the industry, and a proliferation of new companies had enhanced competition. This meant that large mainframe manufacturers such as IBM could slowly enter the higher growth areas without instigating too much of a protest. IBM, Sperry, NCR, Burroughs, and Honeywell appeared to be developing strategies to introduce office automation equipment, advanced communications gear, data-processing systems, and customized software and services.

While entry of these large companies into the small-business computer market was a threat, current suppliers of these systems had many more years of expertise. As a consequence, these companies had reaped the profit and large market-share benefits of early entry into the small-office computer field. In addition to OCS, several companies had been serving and selling to this segment for some time, including Xerox, Hewlett-Packard, Digital Equipment Company, Wang Laboratories, and Datapoint. Exhibit 2 presents 1980 financial results and selected statistics on these companies.

During the previous ten years, industry analysis had identified four main areas in which general-purpose computer systems producers had to do well if they expected to be competitive:

1. A broad and flexible product line
2. An effective sales and service force
3. A worldwide distribution system
4. A management commitment to provide for and maintain a leading product line through

TABLE 1 Computer/Data-Processing Industry Product-Market Segmentation

	1975	*1980*	*1985 est.*
Mainframes	83.0%	60%	36%
Minicomputers	9.5	17	21
Small-business computers	3.5	11	13
Office word processors	4.0	6	10
Desktop computers	—	6	20

the funding of an aggressive research and development program.

OCS's primary competition had successfully accomplished these tasks. Although OCS had, since its inception, been able to keep up with its rivals (evidenced by high growth and accelerating profits), management now believed it was imperative to make high dollar commitments to several major projects in order to maintain or enhance its market position. Included in the package were a consolidated headquarters building, the acquisition of an international distributorship, and an intensive marketing effort.

OFFICE COMPUTER SYSTEMS, INC.

From its inception in 1970, OCS had grown rapidly, with sales increasing at 45 percent per year over the past four years and profits expanding at 50 percent. In fiscal 1980, sales were estimated to reach $255 million, and profits after tax of $16.3 million were expected. Proportionate increases were expected to continue for the next three years. Although this growth was dramatic, OCS's gross profit margins were 4 to 6 percent below their competition's. One reason for this was that during the early years of OCS's existence, demands from customers forced management to expand without the benefit of capacity planning. In fact, around the Sacramento area, the company was operating out of 20 different buildings, and supervision and control had become increasingly difficult.

In spite of these logistic problems, OCS had been able to increase earnings and earnings per share every quarter since 1970, a fact management was very proud of. This success was reflected in a steady rise in OCS's stock price, and Wall Street analysts were actively promoting this Cinderella story to stock market investors. The stock was currently selling at an all-time high, as shown in Exhibit 2. Results of financial performance from 1978–1980, including balance sheets and income statements, are shown in Exhibits 3 and 4.

Although OCS had experienced high growth, it had always been able to fund capital expenditures and working capital needs by cash flow generated from internal operations. Because management counted on reinvestment of earnings each year to support new growth, no dividends were paid to stockholders. In its most recent annual report, OCS stated that "the company had never paid cash dividends to date, nor does it plan to pay cash dividends in the future." Returns to stockholders had thus come entirely from the stock's market appreciation.

OCS's capital project spending during fiscal 1981 was projected to be $52 million, and continued requirements for 1982 and 1983 were estimated at $40 million and $44 million, respectively, not including additional working capital needs. OCS's forecasts and financing requirements are given in Exhibit 5. OCS had traditionally followed an extremely conservative position on debt policy with its debt-to-capital ratio averaging less than 5 percent. Management's philosophy was that during the start-up phase of OCS's life cycle, debt capacity should be maintained as a reserve against uncertain economic conditions, as exemplified by weak industry results during the 1973–1974 recession. However, management had now decided that increased competition necessitated the capital investment OCS was about to make, and the main question was how to meet these consequent financing requirements.

The funds needed for 1982 would probably be obtained by a limited recourse sale of a large proportion of the leased equipment OCS had placed with its customers. Major leasing companies were currently negotiating with management, but they had indicated the transaction could not be completed until the effectiveness of the new products had been established, probably not until early 1982. Thus, other sources must be sought.

THE ALTERNATIVES

As a starting point, Mr. Dunmire contacted a leading investment banking house in order to learn what might be available to OCS in the long-term capital markets and what conditions each alternative might carry. He learned that three options were open.

1. *Debt.* The first alternative was either a public or private placement of $55 million in debentures. The public issue would be underwritten by a syndicate of investment banking houses, and the private placement would be negotiated with a small group of insurance companies. Currently, corporate bond yields were at record levels. Complicating OCS's problem was the fact that the company had never used these options before, and Mr. Dunmire was unsure about the costs of the issue. A Baa-rated bond was currently yielding more than 14.50 percent, as shown in Exhibit 6, slightly more than the rate OCS would have to pay. The investment banker outlined the following specifics of each issue:

   a. A *public issue* for $55 million with a coupon rate of 13.875 percent. Legal and accountant fees, payment for registering the securities, and printing and mailing costs were estimated at $100,000. In addition, an underwriting fee of 0.875 percent of the amount of the issue was required. Maturity of the debentures would be 25 years with no sinking-fund payments required for the first 5 years. Thereafter, equal annual payments of $2,750,000 would be scheduled until maturity.
   b. The maturity of a *private placement* would be 20 years with sinking-fund payments beginning at the end of the third year. The coupon rate would be slightly higher at 14.375 percent, although issuing costs, including underwriting fees, would be only 0.4 percent of the package. The bonds would be nonrefundable for the first 10 years except for the $3.06 million annual sinking fund requirements. In addition, the insurance companies would require tighter restrictions, such as limitations on use of further debt leverage, maintenance of the current ratio at 2 to 1, a limit on major capital expenditures not already planned, and dividend restrictions, although no dividends were planned.

2. *Common Stock.* The second option was a public offering of 3,400,000 shares of OCS common stock at a price of $17 a share, about 7 percent below the current market price of $18.25. Underwriting fees plus $105,000 in consulting costs would reduce net proceeds to OCS to approximately $16 a share. Mr. Dunmire was not only concerned about the new stock diluting current shareholder ownership, he was also worried about what might happen to market conditions, and thus the issuing price, during the time before the securities could be issued. The waiting period before the stock was issued could be as long as 90 days.
3. *Convertible Debt.* The vice president was attracted by the prospects of the third option. A public placement of $55 million in convertible debt was possible at a coupon rate of 12.625 percent. Issuing costs and restrictive covenants would be about the same as the public straight debt package. No repayments would be required for the first 7 years. Thereafter, 5 percent would be retired each year, leaving a 40 percent balance in the 20th year. The debt would be convertible at $22 (45.5 shares of common stock per $1,000 bond totaling 2,500,000 shares), about 20 percent above the current stock price of $18.25. The call price would be $24.

The advantages were immediately apparent. By issuing debt now with a convertible feature, the marginal cost would be less than that of the other alternatives. If stock prices, based on anticipated increases in earnings and earnings per share, continued to rise, the conversion would mean less dilution than the common stock issue. In addition, conversion, expected in about 12 months, would immediately reduce the company's debt leverage, thus freeing up debt capacity for additional borrowing 2 to 3 years hence.

Such an alternative, however, ran the risk of the stock price's not appreciating to the point at which conversion could be forced. Forced conversions were usually successful when the market price of the common stock exceeded the conversion price by 20 percent. The amount by which the market price had to exceed the conversion price depended, to a large degree, on the relative size of the convertible and on the amount by which the call price was above the conversion price. The greater the size of the issue, the greater the pressure on the market price when the issue was called. The larger the issue, the more significant could be the drop in the market price during the conversion period.

If the market price did not rise enough, the company could be left with a hung convertible. A hung convertible would reduce the company's flexibility for raising additional funds to meet expansion plans after 1981. Institutional investors might be reluctant to buy the common stock of a company that had frozen them into an unsuccessful convertible. The continued presence of the convertible could also hamper issuing additional debt because of uncertainty about how long the contractual payments required by the convertible would have to be covered.

MARKET CONDITIONS

Mr. Dunmire knew that these alternatives would have to be viewed within the context of current market conditions. Interest rates were at historical highs, and uncertainty about 1981 economic forecasts were reflected in the volatility of short-term interest rates during 1980, shown in Exhibit 7. The following comments illustrate recent conditions:

The Fed has not been able to slow the growth of the money supply. The financial markets, anticipating further credit tightening from Washington, continue to push the cost of short-term monies upward. The corporate borrower, in this type of market, shies away from the bond market because of high rates and acquires the necessary funding through the banks and commercial paper market (provided they are prime credits). The banks, faced with higher costs for funds and increased demand for funds, have to respond with higher rates. However, the financial markets have had some favorable news. Spokesmen for Mr. Reagan let it be known that the President-elect is considering a freeze on federal hiring, a freeze on federal wages, and a freeze on federal borrowing. If these conditions materialize under a new economic game plan, then possible reduction in short- and long-term rates could occur sooner then expected.

Exhibit 8 highlights market interest rates in December 1980.

THE DECISION

As Mr. Dunmire reviewed the alternatives before his final recommendation to senior management and the board of directors, he knew that selection of the right alternative was critical if OCS expected to follow its strategic plan. The decision needed enough flexibility to enable OCS to return to the financial markets no later than 1983, but the timing of any issue had to take current economic conditions and industry projections and characteristics into account. In addition, if the recommended alternative involved a straight debt package, Mr. Dunmire realized that he would have to reverse management's conservative position on debt. He wondered whether the convertible option might serve as the best solution, satisfying both the company's financial requirements and aversion to debt policy. A recommendation had to be made within the next three weeks.

Case 14 Office Computer Systems, Inc.

EXHIBIT 1 COMPUTER/DATA-PROCESSING INDUSTRY COMPOSITE STATISTICS (millions of dollars)

					Forecasts		
	1977	*1978*	*1979*	*1980*	*1981*	*1982*	*1984–1986 est.*
Revenues ($)	34,937	41,328	47,183	55,044	60,700	68,900	110,000
Operating Margin (%)	27.7	27.1	25.0	23.7	23.0	23.5	24.0
Depreciation ($)	2,894	3,010	3,301	3,903	4,450	5,000	7,200
Net Profit ($)	3,780	4,533	4,776	5,375	5,625	7,000	12,200
Income Tax Rate (%)	46.2	46.0	44.8	39.9	42.0	42.5	42.0
Net Profit Margin (%)	10.8	11.0	10.1	9.8	9.3	10.2	11.1
Working Capital ($)	9,462	10,000	10.949	11,821	13,500	15,000	250,000
Long-term Debt ($)	2,477	2,846	4,438	6,021	7,900	9,000	11,500
Net Worth ($)	20,705	23,245	26,601	30,586	34,650	38,900	59,000
Earned on:							
Total Capital (%)	16.7	17.8	16.0	15.4	14.0	16.0	18.0
Net Worth (%)	18.3	19.5	18.0	17.6	16.2	18.0	20.7
Retained to Common Equity (%)	10.4	11.4	9.4	9.9	9.5	9.5	11.0
All Dividends to Net Profit (%)	44.0	42.0	48.0	44.0	47.0	47.0	42.0
Average Annual P/E Ratio (×)	13.2	11.6	12.2	10.7	NA[a]	NA	17.0
Average Annual Earnings Yield (%)	7.6	8.6	8.2	9.4	NA	NA	5.9
Average Annual Dividend Yield (%)	3.3	3.6	3.9	4.1	NA	NA	2.5

Source: Investment survey.
[a]Not available.

EXHIBIT 2 INFORMATION ON SELECTED GENERAL-PURPOSE COMPUTER SYSTEMS PRODUCTS COMPANIES (dollars in millions except per-share figures)

	Xerox				*Hewlett-Packard*				*Digital Equipment Corporation*			
	1977	*1978*	*1979*	*1980*	*1977*	*1978*	*1979*	*1980*	*1977*	*1978*	*1979*	*1980*
Gross Revenues ($)	5,076.9	5,901.9	7,027.0	8,196.5	1,360.0	1,728.0	2,352.0	3,099.0	1,058.6	1,436.6	1,804.1	2,368.0
Operating Profit Margin (%)	31.5	30.6	29.2	26.3	19.6	19.4	20.6	21.0	19.5	20.0	18.9	19.1
Net Income ($)	406.6	464.9	563.7	619.2	121.5	153.0	203.0	269.0	108.5	142.2	178.4	249.9
Net Profit Margin (%)	8.0	7.9	8.0	7.6	8.9	8.9	8.6	8.7	10.3	9.9	9.9	10.6
Return on Equity (%)	20.6	19.0	18.8	17.0	14.7	15.3	16.4	17.4	5.0	6.0	7.0	8.9
Earnings per Share ($)	5.06	5.77	6.69	7.33	1.07	0.32	1.72	2.24	2.78	3.40	4.10	5.45
Dividends per Share ($)	1.49	2.00	2.30	2.70	0.10	0.13	0.18	0.20	—	—	—	—
Dividend Payout (%)	26.0	35.0	34.0	37.0	9.0	9.0	10.0	9.0	—	—	—	—
Common Stock Price Range:												
High ($)	58¾	64	69⅛	71¾	21⅞	23⅛	31⅜	48½	54	54⅞	69½	98¾
Low ($)	43⅛	40½	52⅝	48⅝	17	15⅜	20⅜	25½	35⅝	38½	48⅝	56¾
P/E Ratio (×)	10.0	9.1	9.0	8.2	18.2	14.7	15.1	16.6	16.1	13.7	14.5	14.3
Capitalization (1980):												
Deferred Taxes ($)				123.8				70.0				61.2
Long-Term Debt ($)				893.3				29.0				88.4
Equity ($)				3,624.7				1,547.0				2,829.3
Beta (1980)				1.25				1.15				1.30
Shares Outstanding (thousands)	80,375	80,521	84,137	84,400	113,916	116,040	118,296	120,442	39,259	39,873	40,605	45,568
Moody's Bond Rating (1980)	Investment Grade: Aa				Investment Grade: Aa				Investment Grade: Aa			

continued

EXHIBIT 2 *(continued)*

	Wang				*Datapoint*				*Office Computer Systems, Inc.*			
	1977	*1978*	*1979*	*1980*	*1977*	*1978*	*1979*	*1980*	*1977*	*1978*	*1979*	*1980*
Gross Revenues ($)	134.4	198.1	321.6	543.3	103.0	162.3	232.1	318.8	83.7	129.8	183.7	255.1
Operating Profit Margin (%)	19.3	21.8	22.6	22.8	28.0	28.4	28.8	27.1	**18.5**	**18.8**	**18.8**	**20.2**
Net Income ($)	9.1	15.6	28.6	52.1	8.4	15.3	25.3	30.5	4.8	7.7	11.5	16.3
Net Profit Margin (%)	6.8	7.9	8.9	9.6	8.1	9.4	10.9	10.5	5.7	5.9	6.3	6.4
Return on Equity (%)	14.7	17.7	20.8	24.2	15.0	18.0	22.0	18.0	6.7	10.1	13.1	15.7
Earnings per Share ($)	0.22	0.35	0.59	1.00	0.64	1.03	1.46	1.74	0.44	0.70	1.05	1.49
Dividends per Share ($)	0.02	0.03	0.06	0.10	—	—	—	—	—	—	—	—
Dividend Payout (%)	14.0	9.0	10.0	10.0	—	—	—	—	—	—	—	—
Common Stock Price Range:												
High ($)	4	8	17⅜	45⅝	10¼	19⅛	20¾	35⅛	8½	11⅜	15½	18¼
Low ($)	1⅝	3	8½	10¼	4⅜	8½	12	19⅛	4⅝	5⅜	8	10⅜
P/E Ratio (×)	12.8	16.3	21.9	29.9	10.5	10.1	12.0	13.3	14.9	12.0	11.0	10.0
Capitalization (1980):												
Deferred Taxes ($)				19.5				1.3	—	0.1	0.5	0.9
Long-Term Debt ($)				214.1				3.9	2.8	2.6	2.4	2.2
Equity ($)				191.5				169.1	67.3	79.9	91.4	107.7
Beta (1980)				1.70				1.50				1.65
Shares Outstanding (thousands)	41,136	45,596	48,360	50,908	12,780	15,999	16,410	16,990	10,875	10,901	10,915	10,934
Moody's Bond Rating (1980)	Lower Medium Grade: Ba				Lower Medium Grade: Ba				Not Rated			

Case 14 Office Computer Systems, Inc.

EXHIBIT 3 BALANCE SHEETS 1978–1980 (millions of dollars)

	Period Ending 12/31/78	12/31/79	12/31/80
ASSETS			
Cash	$ 2.8	$ 4.0	$ 1.4
Accounts receivable	27.2	35.6	48.1
Inventory	26.0	33.0	43.2
Total current assets	56.0	72.6	92.7
Real estate, machinery, and equipment	15.6	17.9	19.5
Equipment leased	26.2	31.9	41.9
Prepaid and deferred items	1.4	1.9	2.1
Total assets	$ 99.2	$124.3	$156.2
LIABILITIES AND EQUITY			
Accounts payable	$ 4.7	$ 11.7	$ 19.6
Current maturity, long-term debt	0.2	0.2	0.2
Taxes	5.4	7.1	10.2
Accruals	10.2	14.9	19.3
Total current liabilities	20.5	33.9	49.3
Long-term debt	2.4	2.2	2.0
Deferred taxes	0.1	0.5	0.9
Total liabilities	23.0	36.6	52.2
Common stock	0.8	0.8	0.8
Paid-in surplus	53.1	53.1	53.1
Retained earnings	22.3	33.8	50.1
Total equity	76.2	87.7	$104.0
Total liabilities and equity	$ 99.2	$124.3	$156.2

Case 14 Office Computer Systems, Inc.

EXHIBIT 4 INCOME STATEMENTS 1978–1980 (millions of dollars)

	Period Ending 12/31/78		12/31/79		12/31/80	
Net sales	$129.8	100.0%	$183.7	100.0%	$255.1	100.0%
Costs of goods sold	70.1	54.0	97.6	53.1	132.7	52.0
Gross profit	59.7	46.0	86.1	46.9	122.4	48.0
General administrative expenses	10.1	7.8	14.7	8.0	28.3	11.1
Engineering/product development	9.1	7.0	13.2	7.2	21.4	8.4
Marketing	26.2	20.2	36.9	20.1	42.6	16.7
Total expenses	45.4	35.0	64.8	35.3	92.3	36.2
Operating profit	14.3	11.0	21.3	11.6	30.1	11.8
Income taxes	6.6	5.1	9.8	5.3	13.8	5.4
Net profit after taxes	$ 7.7	5.9%	$ 11.5	6.3%	$ 16.3	6.4%

Case 14 Office Computer Systems, Inc.

EXHIBIT 5 PROJECTED INCOME STATEMENTS AND BALANCE SHEETS 1981–1983 (millions of dollars)

	1981	*1982*	*1983*
Sales	$382.7	$574.1	$861.1
Cost of goods sold	206.7	310.0	465.0
Gross profit	176.0	264.1	396.1
Selling, general, and administrative expenses	41.9	62.9	94.5
Research and development expense	22.0	22.0	22.0
Marketing expenses	91.8	137.8	206.7
Total expenses	155.7	222.7	323.2
Earnings before interest and taxes	20.3	41.4	72.9
Interest expense	0.2	0.2	0.2
Net income before taxes	20.1	41.2	72.7
Taxes (46 percent)	9.2	19.0	33.4
Net income after taxes	$ 10.9	$ 22.2	$ 39.3
ASSETS			
Cash	6.0	6.0	6.0
Accounts receivable & inventory	142.5	213.8	320.7
Net property, plant & equipment, and leased equipment	97.5	91.0	144.0
Other	2.5	2.5	2.5
	$248.5	$313.3	$473.2
LIABILITIES & EQUITY			
Accounts payable	$ 30.4	$ 53.6	$ 86.5
Current maturity, long-term debt	0.2	0.2	0.2
Taxes	18.0	20.1	25.0
Accruals	28.7	43.1	64.6
Total current liabilities	77.3	117.0	176.3
Long-term debt	1.8	1.6	1.4
Deferred taxes	1.3	2.0	3.1
Total liabilities	80.4	120.6	180.8
Common stock	0.8	0.8	0.8
Paid-in surplus	53.1	53.1	53.1
Retained earnings	61.0	83.2	122.5
Total equity	$114.9	$137.1	$176.4
External financing required	53.2	55.6	116.0
	$248.5	$313.3	$473.2

Assumptions

1. Sales growth at 50 percent annually.
2. Cost of goods sold at 54 percent of sales.
3. R&D costs steady at $22 million annually.
4. Interest on any new debt not included.
5. No dividend payments.
6. Normal expenditures, plus all three phases of the construction of the new headquarters building and acquisition, are included in property, plant & equipment account, net of depreciation.
7. Sale of $45 million of leased equipment to leasing companies in 1982.

EXHIBIT 6 CORPORATE BOND YIELDS BY RATINGS—QUARTERLY AVERAGES 1978–1980

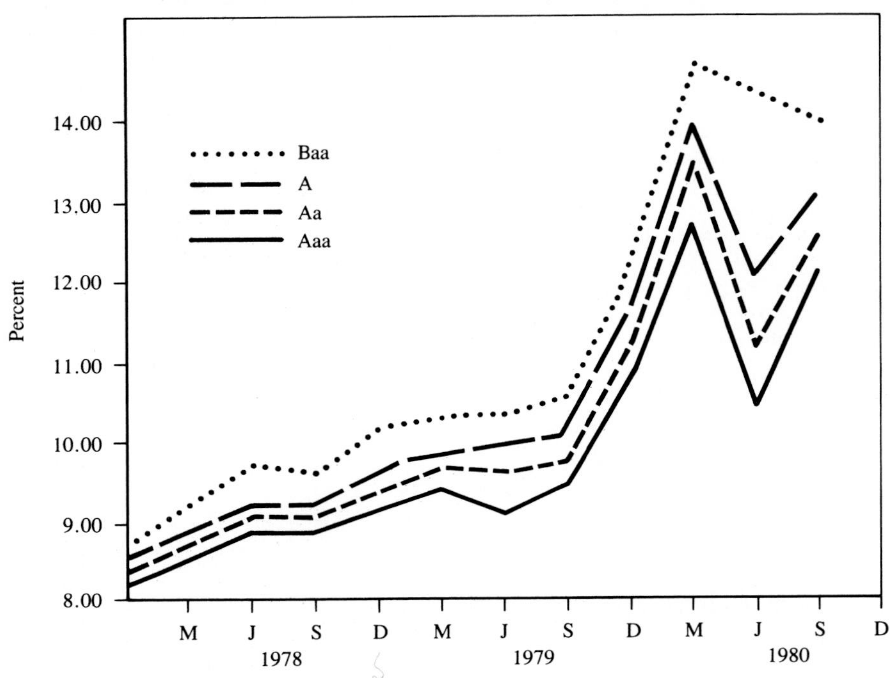

Case 14 Office Computer Systems, Inc.

EXHIBIT 7 MONEY MARKET RATES 1980

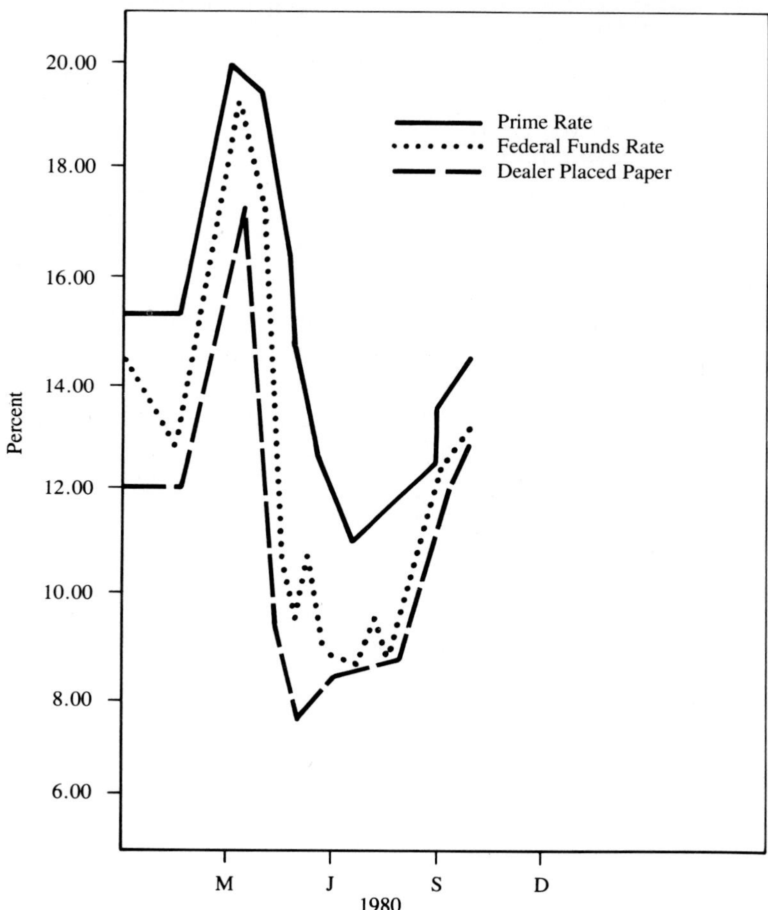

Case 14 Office Computer Systems, Inc.

EXHIBIT 8 MARKET INTEREST RATES DECEMBER 1980

Prime Rates: Boston: 21.50 percent (12/19/80) New York: 21.50 percent (12/19/80)
Federal Funds Rate: 18.00 percent–20.00 percent
Repurchase Agreements: 14.00 percent–16.00 percent

Short-Term Investments

Maturity in Days	*Certificates of Deposit Boston/NYC*	*Commercial Paper*	*Treasury Bills*	*Tax-Exempt Project Notes*
30	18.00%	19.875%	15.01%	NA[a]
30	17.50	17.00	14.97	NA
90	17.00	16.00	14.85	8.25%
180	14.00	15.50	14.11	8.25
270	11.00	15.00	13.68	8.40
360	11.00		12.85	8.40

U.S. Treasury Notes and Bonds

Maturity	*Coupon*	*Offer*	*Yield*
03/31/82	15.00%	100.22%	14.17%
08/15/83	11.875	96.18	13.34
03/31/84	14.25	102.20	13.14
05/15/85	14.375	104.12	12.96
05/15/95	12.625	99.26	12.62

[a]Not available.

Case 15

INTREPID DRILLING CONTRACTORS, INC. (A)

By early April 1980, Mr. David Roberts believed he had gathered enough information to allow him to analyze the choice between financing two oil-drilling rigs with a lease or financing their purchase with a loan. Mr. Roberts was treasurer and chief financial officer of Intrepid Drilling Contractors, Inc. (Indricon), a new firm which specialized in the contract drilling of 5,000-to-25,000-feet-deep oil wells in the midcontinental basin of the United States. This potentially rich source of crude oil had become economically attractive as the price of Middle East oil had risen, and drilling in the area had increased dramatically as the controls on the price of domestic oil were relaxed.

Indricon had been founded in 1978 by Mr. James Scott and Mr. William Turnbull. Mr. Scott was well known for his expertise in managing oil-drilling operations, having worked in the area for his entire career. In his late 50s and having decided he wished to work for himself, he left the major firm with which he had been employed for many years to establish Indricon. Mr. Turnbull, a wealthy individual who had known Mr. Scott for a long time and greatly respected his abilities, personally provided the financial support for the venture.

Messrs. Scott and Turnbull had established Indricon as a Sub-Chapter S Corporation. This arrangement allowed the owners to benefit from the protection of the corporate legal form while also enabling them to report the corporation's earnings as though it were a partnership. This was important to Mr. Turnbull because of his high personal tax bracket and need for tax shelters. It was less important to Mr. Scott, who derived his main income from his salary as president and general manager of Indricon.

Although Mr. Turnbull was wealthy, with a net worth of at least $25 million, much of his wealth was relatively illiquid. It was invested in high-quality real estate he had developed and in proven mineral deposits, most of which he had located himself. Indricon had therefore been financed with minimal cash contribution from the owners. The $21 million of long-term debt raised to purchase the four drilling rigs the company was already operating had been guaranteed personally by Messrs. Scott and Turnbull. Net working capital requirements were relatively small, although considerable skill was required on Mr. Roberts' part to manage the cash flow.

Indricon's net worth, reflecting losses in its first two years, was a negative $600,000. The losses had been incurred in the company's start-up phase, in the building of the company's first four rigs and in setting them up on their first jobs, and in the fabrication costs of the two new rigs under construction. (All of the rigs were built to Mr. Scott's specifications and were considered among the best in the industry.) On the basis of the backlog of orders which had been placed with the company, Mr. Roberts expected Indricon to earn $1.8 million before taxes in its next fiscal year. Earnings would probably increase above that level in later years, significantly so if more rigs were added. By late 1982, earnings might be running at an annual rate of $3 to $4 million. Mr. Roberts anticipated that the tax arrangements would be shifted to straight corporate form as earnings became strongly positive.

Mr. Roberts had negotiated two ways of financing rigs five and six. Both of the methods were structured so that the 10 percent investment tax credit would be utilized for tax purposes by Indricon (and, ultimately, by its owners under the Sub-Chapter S arrangement).

One alternative was a loan of $8.5 million managed by the bank which had arranged Indricon's earlier financing. The interest rate would be fixed at 18 percent for the life of the loan, with annual payments of $1,891,375 for 10 years. Indricon could depreciate 80 percent of the cost of the rigs over 10 years, allowing for a 20 percent salvage value at the end of the tax life. Either accelerated or straight-line depreciation over 10 years could be used, but the depreciation method could not be changed once the initial selection had been made (except for the shift to straight line in the later years under the accelerated depreciation alternative). A period longer than 10 years could be used, as actual life expectancy for drilling rigs was up to 14 years depending on maintenance programs and tax considerations.

The lease alternative would require quarterly payments of $400,000 ($1,600,000 annually) for 10 years. The lease payments were lower than the debt payments in part because the lessor was willing to recapture only 80 percent of the value of the equipment during the life of the lease. The remainder would be recovered when Indricon (or some other drilling company) purchased the rig from the lessor at the end of the lease. While the purchase price would have to be market value at that time in order to have the lease payments fully deductible for tax purposes, Mr. Roberts had negotiated the right of first refusal at the appraised price. This agreement would satisfy the Internal Revenue Service requirement for a fair market value transaction at the conclusion of the lease.

Mr. Roberts expected, based on his experience in the industry, that the rig would be appraised at 30 percent of its initial cost, although it might be possible that it would drop as low as 25 percent, if the demand for drilling equipment was extremely poor in 10 years, or might be as high as 35 percent if the market was very good. Used rigs 10 years old were currently selling for about 50 percent of their original cost.

Mr. Roberts believed that the terms of the lease would not require Indricon to capitalize it on the balance sheet. It would be counted as a tax-oriented, nonfinancial lease for tax purposes.

Indricon's owners were pleased with the rapid progress the company was making. They believed that its growth was limited primarily by its financial requirements. Two of the rigs currently in operation had been financed with leases, and two had been financed by loans and were owned directly by Indricon. Mr. Roberts believed that, in fact, the company's equity interest was 13 percent higher in the owned rigs than shown on the balance sheet. Certain fabrications costs and overruns had been paid for by Indricon and expensed, rather than capitalized, which helped account for the company's net loss. In addition, because of the rights to buy the two leased rigs at appraised value, there was perhaps unrealized equity even in the leased rigs.

Because of the company's apparently higher leveraged condition, the lenders had required Mr. Turnbull to pledge assets to support his guarantee of Indricon's debt. Additional property would probably have to be pledged if the loan were taken, but this had not yet been negotiated. The lessor, however, would be satisfied simply with the guarantee of the owners.

The owners had been approached informally on several occasions about whether Indricon was for sale. One prospective buyer wanted Mr. Scott to concentrate on rig design and construction, but Mr. Scott did not wish to limit his future activities in this manner. Several other major companies, some in the energy business and others wishing to enter it, had indicated that they would welcome being contacted if Indricon should be for sale, provided Mr. Scott would sign a contract to continue to work with the company for a period of years. Mr. Roberts wondered whether the prospect of the company's sale should be factored into his analysis and, if so, how.

A decision was becoming urgent because the new rigs were virtually completed. Indricon was expected to pay for them shortly, and any delay would be embarrassing as well as costly in drilling revenues lost.

Case 16

INTREPID DRILLING CONTRACTORS, INC. (B)

Mr. David Roberts, treasurer and chief financial officer of Intrepid Drilling Contractors, Inc. (Indricon), asked his new assistant, Mr. George Pearson, to prepare an analysis of the lease-or-buy decision which had to be made for two new drilling rigs presently under construction, as described in Intrepid Drilling Contractors, Inc., (A). Mr. Pearson had joined Intrepid six months earlier to assist Mr. Roberts in treasury and controllership functions. He had worked for a commercial bank for two years after he had received his MBA from a prominent midwestern business school, and then he had accepted the position at Indricon. He was eager to become more familiar with Indricon's financial options because he remembered that he had often heard his finance and accounting professors say that leasing was basically the same as debt and could seldom provide the lessee with any significant financial advantage. He wondered if this generality applied in Indricon's case.

After obtaining the loan amortization schedule (shown in Exhibit 1), Mr. Pearson prepared a schedule showing the effect of the two alternatives on reported earnings, assuming a 50 percent tax rate. The effect of the lease payment was easy to calculate. Annual payments were $1.6 million, which would reduce reported earnings by $800,000 a year, if the company were to prepare its reports as though it were a public company. The effects of ownership would be the deductions for interest (which would decline as the loan was repaid) and depreciation. Mr. Pearson assumed that the company would use sum-of-the-years-digits (SOYD) depreciation for both tax and reporting purposes. Nevertheless, he also calculated the effect of using the straight-line method. These calculations are shown in Exhibit 2. On either a straight-line or the SOYD basis, the reported cost of ownership would be greater than the reported cost of leasing for the first six years.

Mr. Pearson then turned to analyze the cash flow effects. He anticipated these would be more important to the present owners, especially considering the tight cash position forecast for the company in the next several years. In preparing a cash flow analysis, Mr. Pearson knew there were complications in selecting a correct tax rate to use. He was not familiar with the personal tax situations of Mr. Scott and Mr. Turnbull, Indricon's owners. He suspected Mr. Turnbull's marginal tax rate was much higher than Mr. Scott's, but it was also possible it could be much lower because of careful tax planning. In any event, if Indricon elected to report as a regular corporation for tax purposes, the rate would change to approximately 50 percent.

Mr. Pearson therefore decided to test the effects of differing tax rates by preparing his analysis at three different tax rates: 30 percent, 50 percent, and 70 percent. He also prepared a schedule showing the effect on cash outflows of using straight-line rather than accelerated depreciation. If the company were to operate at a loss for a few years, it might be desirable to use a less rapid rate of depreciation in order to avoid the possibility of losing a tax-loss carryforward. Exhibit 3 lists the basic cash flows of the two financing alternatives and the assumptions underlying the depreciation calculations. Because accelerated depreciation clearly provided for a lower level of cash outflow for the first few years,

Case prepared with the assistance of Mr. Alton Martin and with the cooperation of individuals and institutions that wish to remain anonymous. Certain of the company's characteristics and financial information have been changed to protect confidential information without altering the nature of the managerial decision.

Mr. Pearson decided to utilize those estimates for further analysis.

As shown in Section A of Exhibit 4, he calculated the differences between the cash required for the debt–own alternative and the lease alternative, allowing for the three different tax rates. Because he was uncertain what Indricon's capital cost was, he discounted the flows at several rates for comparative purposes. The result of Mr. Pearson's calculations are shown in Part B of Exhibit 4. (Because of the complexities he saw, he limited his further calculations to a 50 percent tax rate.)

An estimate of the additional debt capacity which might be available under the lease alternative proved difficult to make. In the first place, there was the question of whether Indricon would actually have any more unused debt capacity if it leased the rigs than if it borrowed to finance their purchase. If not, then no further analysis was needed. If so, however, the questions were how much and how to allow for it in the analysis.

In order to be able to see the implications of possible answers to these questions, Mr. Pearson prepared the figures shown in Exhibit 5. First, he calculated the extra debt which would be available assuming that Indricon could borrow 10 percent, 20 percent, and 30 percent more with the lease than with the debt. As shown in Part A of Exhibit 5, this would increase Indricon's borrowing capacity by $680,000 to $2,040,000.

These funds would presumably be invested in profitable projects, such as additional rigs, equipment, and working capital, which would return more than the cost of the debt. If Indricon could borrow at 13 percent and invest at 15 percent, for example, the before-tax return would be a spread of 2 percent, or approximately 1 percent after taxes. Inflation on the one hand and floating interest rates on the other made it unlikely that the spread would be constant, but Mr. Pearson was uncertain how that should be handled. He did calculate the annual earnings which would result from two higher spreads, 3.5 percent and 6 percent, which are also shown in Exhibit 5, Part A.

The calculations in Part B of Exhibit 5 discount the annual flows from the various borrowing levels and spreads to present-value sums at discount rates selected from those Mr. Pearson had used to analyze the cash flow differentials in Exhibit 4. These figures represented the amount by which the lease costs would be reduced by the profits made from using the extra debt, if the appropriate underlying assumptions were valid ones. For instance, if Indricon could borrow 20 percent more with the lease than it could with the debt alternative ($1,360,000) and earn a spread of 3.5 percent, its annual profit would be $47,600 for the next 10 years, and the present-value inflows of $292,500 represent the amount by which the total cost of the leasing program would be reduced at a discount rate of 10 percent.

Mr. Pearson realized that if Indricon owned the rig and it retained a significant market value, he could probably refinance the debt from time to time. The restructuring would take the form of increasing the amount of debt outstanding against the security and perhaps an amortization schedule which allowed for a significant balloon payment when the loan matured. These adjustments would favorably alter the cash flows of the debt alternative. Mr. Pearson decided to test the effect of refinancing by assuming that in the 5th year he could roll over and increase the debt without changing the interest rate or the annual payment schedule on the original loan. He decided, for simplification, to assume that the increase in the borrowing would become a balloon payment due in the 10th year.

At the end of the 5th year, approximately $2.6 million of the debt would have been repaid. Because he thought some of this amount might be restructured, Mr. Pearson decided to test the effect on the present-value costs of reborrowing $0.8, $1.6, and $2.5 million with a lump-sum maturity in the 10th year. Although the total payment was not changed by this shift in timing, the delay would reduce the net present-value costs of the debt alternative, after allowing for the extra interest on the sum rolled over, as shown in Exhibit 6.

Finally, if Indricon leased the equipment, at the end of 10 years some arrangement would have to be made to secure continued use of the rigs. Perhaps the lease could be renegotiated at this time, but Mr. Pearson had no idea what terms would be mutually acceptable. He decided it would be simpler to calculate the cost of buying the rigs from the lessor at the end of the lease. He calculated the cost of purchase at various appraised values in addition to the 30 percent which was his best guess for its value in 10 years, as provided in Exhibit 7. These figures were then discounted to the present at the several discount rates he had been using in his analysis. This approach assumed that Indricon would have use for the rigs.

Mr. Pearson realized that these figures would allow him to make an appropriate comparison between the lease and ownership of the rigs if the rigs were to be bought in the 10th year and used by the company. The figures would be slightly inaccurate in the event it was not worthwhile to buy the rigs or that they would be bought for resale. In that event, and if Indricon had initially purchased the rigs, they would have been put up for sale. The price at which they were sold would have tax complications because Indricon might realize more or less than their book values.

At this point, a quick calculation showed that Mr. Pearson had already developed enough data to analyze 1,200 different outcomes for the 50 percent tax bracket alone. Rather than prepare further information, Mr. Pearson decided he needed to give some thought to structuring his analysis in an orderly way. He thought a review of his assumptions might be a good way to start. Once he had sorted out a reasonably small number of likely alternatives, he could begin to determine which variables significantly influenced the decision.

Case 16 Intrepid Drilling Contractors, Inc. (B)

EXHIBIT 1 AMORTIZATION SCHEDULE ($8,500,000 principal, 10 years, 18% interest, $1,891,375 annual payment*)

Year	*Interest Payment*	*Principal Payment*
1	$ 1,530,000	$ 361,375
2	1,464,953	426,422
3	1,388,197	503,178
4	1,297,625	593,750
5	1,190,750	700,625
6	1,064,637	826,737
7	915,825	975,550
8	740,226	1,151,149
9	533,019	1,358,356
10	288,515	1,602,860
Total, Years 1–10	$10,413,747	$8,500,002**

*Actual payment = $1,891,374.45.
**Due to rounding.

Case 16 Intrepid Drilling Contractors, Inc. (B)

EXHIBIT 2 REPORTED INCOME EFFECT IF RIG PURCHASED*

Year	*(1) Interest*	*(2) Straight-Line Depreciation*	*(3) Reduction in Reported Income Using St. Line Deprec = (1 + 2) × .5*	*(4) Sum-of-Year's-Digits Depreciation*	*(5) Reduction in Reported Income Using SOYD Deprec = (1 + 4) × .5*
1	$1,530,000	$680,000	$1,105,000	$1,236,365	$1,383,183
2	1,464,953	680,000	1,072,477	1,112,727	1,288,840
3	1,388,197	680,000	1,034,099	989,090	1,188,644
4	1,297,625	680,000	988,813	865,455	1,081,540
5	1,190,750	680,000	935,375	741,818	966,284
6	1,064,637	680,000	872,319	618,182	841,410
7	915,825	680,000	797,913	494,545	705,185
8	740,226	680,000	710,113	370,909	555,568
9	533,019	680,000	605,510	247,273	390,147
10	288,515	680,000	484,258	123,637	206,076

*Yearly interest and principal payments of $1,891,375, 20% salvage value, straight-line and sum-of-years-digits depreciation, 50% tax rate.

Case 16 Intrepid Drilling Contractors, Inc. (B)

EXHIBIT 3 AFTER-TAX CASH OUTFLOWS

A. Purchase Alternative: 20% Salvage Value for Depreciation. $1,891,375 Payment Made Yearly.

1. Straight-Line Depreciation

				After-Tax Cash Outflows (1) − [(tax rate) × (2 + 3)]		
Year	*(1) Payments*	*(2) Interest*	*(3) Depreciation*	*30% Tax*	*50% Tax*	*70% Tax*
1	$1,891,375	$1,530,000	$680,000	$1,228,375	$ 786,375	$ 344,375
2	1,891,375	1,464,953	680,000	1,247,889	818,899	389,908
3	1,891,375	1,388,197	680,000	1,270,916	857,277	443,637
4	1,891,375	1,297,625	680,000	1,298,088	902,563	507,038
5	1,891,375	1,190,750	680,000	1,330,150	956,000	581,850
6	1,891,375	1,064,637	680,000	1,367,984	1,019,057	670,129
7	1,891,375	915,825	680,000	1,412,628	1,093,463	774,298
8	1,891,375	740,226	680,000	1,465,307	1,181,262	897,217
9	1,891,375	533,019	680,000	1,527,469	1,289,866	1,042,262
10	1,891,375	288,515	680,000	1,600,821	1,407,118	1,213,415

2. SOYD Depreciation

Year	*(1) Payments*	*(2) Interest*	*(3) Depreciation*	*30% Tax*	*50% Tax*	*70% Tax*
1	$1,891,375	$1,530,000	$1,236,365	$1,061,466	$ 508,193	($ 45,081)*
2	1,891,375	1,464,953	1,112,727	1,118,071	602,535	86,999
3	1,891,375	1,388,197	989,090	1,178,189	702,732	227,274
4	1,891,375	1,297,625	865,455	1,242,451	809,835	377,219
5	1,891,375	1,190,750	741,818	1,311,605	925,091	538,577
6	1,891,375	1,064,637	618,182	1,386,529	1,049,966	713,402
7	1,891,375	915,825	494,545	1,468,264	1,186,190	904,116
8	1,891,375	740,226	370,909	1,558,035	1,335,808	1,113,581
9	1,891,375	533,019	247,273	1,657,287	1,501,229	1,345,171
10	1,891,375	288,515	123,637	1,767,729	1,685,299	1,602,869

B. Lease Alternative: Yearly payments of $1,600,000 for 10 years.

1–10	$1,600,000	—	—	$1,120,000	$ 800,000	$ 480,000

*Represents net cash inflow from tax loss.

Case 16 Intrepid Drilling Contractors, Inc. (B)

EXHIBIT 4 CASH FLOW COMPARISON OF LEASE FINANCING VERSUS LOAN FINANCING

A. After-Tax SOYD Loan Cash Outflow Less After-Tax Lease Cash Outflow (figures in parentheses indicate cash flow advantages for loan financing)

	Tax Rates		
Year	*30%*	*50%*	
1	$ (58,534)	$ (291,807)	$ (525,081)
2	(1,929)	(197,465)	(393,001)
3	58,189	(97,268)	(252,726)
4	122,451	9,835	(102,781)
5	191,605	125,091	58,577
6	266,529	249,966	233,402
7	348,264	386,190	424,116
8	438,035	535,808	633,581
9	537,287	701,229	865,171
10	647,729	885,299	1,122,869
Total	$2,549,626	$2,306,878	$2,064,127

B. Present Value of Cash Flow Differentials Shown in Part A Discounted at the Rate Specified (figures in parentheses indicate net present-value cash flow advantages for *loan* alternatives) (dollar figures in thousands)

	Tax Rates		
Discount Rate	*30%*	*50%*	*70%*
0%	$2,550	$2,307	$2,064
5	1,730	1,384	1,038
8	1,387	1,009	630
10	1,203	811	419
11	1,121	724	328
12	1,046	646	245
13	977	574	171
14	912	508	103
15	853	447	41
20	617	213	(190)
25	453	61	(331)
30	337	(39)	(415)

Case 16 Intrepid Drilling Contractors, Inc. (B)

EXHIBIT 5 PRESENT VALUE OF AFTER-TAX EARNINGS FOR 10 YEARS RESULTING FROM INVESTING ADDITIONAL DEBT CAPACITY AVAILABLE BY USE OF LEASE FINANCING

A. Annual After-Tax Earnings

Additional Debt Obtained	*As a Percent of Cost of Rig*	*As a Percent of Amount Financed**	*After-Tax Spread (at 50%) Earned Over Cost of Debt*		
			1%	*3.5%*	*6%*
$ 680,000	8%	10%	$ 6,800	$23,800	$ 40,800
1,360,000	16%	20%	13,600	47,600	81,600
2,040,000	24%	30%	20,400	71,400	122,400

*Lease allows 20% residual value; amount financed = .80 × $8,500,000 = $6,800,000.

B. Present Value of Earnings for 10 Years (dollar figures in thousands)

Annual After-Tax Flow	*Discount Rates*						
	0%	*10%*	*11%*	*12%*	*13%*	*14%*	*15%*
$ 6.8	$ 68.0	$ 41.8	$ 40.0	$ 38.4	$ 36.9	$ 35.5	$ 34.1
13.6	136.0	83.6	80.1	76.8	73.8	70.9	68.3
20.4	204.0	125.3	120.1	115.5	110.7	106.4	102.4
23.8	238.0	146.2	140.2	134.5	129.1	124.1	119.4
40.8	408.0	250.7	240.3	230.5	221.4	212.8	204.8
47.6	476.0	292.5	280.3	269.0	258.3	248.3	238.9
71.4	714.0	438.7	420.5	403.4	387.4	372.4	358.3
81.6	816.0	501.4	480.6	461.1	442.8	425.6	409.5
122.4	1,224.0	752.1	720.8	691.6	664.2	638.5	614.3

Case 16 Intrepid Drilling Contractors, Inc. (B)

EXHIBIT 6 NET REDUCTION IN PRESENT VALUE COST (AFTER 50% TAXES) RESULTING FROM REFINANCING IN THE FIFTH YEAR OF PART OF DEBT TO BALLOON MATURITY (thousands of dollars)

	Amount Refinanced		
Discount Rate	*$800*	*$1,600*	*$2,500*
10%	$ 19	$ 38	$ 59
11	35	70	110
12	49	98	153
13	61	122	191
14	71	143	223
15	80	160	250

Case 16 Intrepid Drilling Contractors, Inc. (B)

EXHIBIT 7 COST OF PURCHASING RIG AT END OF LEASE (dollar figures in thousands)

Discount	*Value as a Percent of Original Total Cost*					
Rate	*20%*	*25%*	*30%*	*35%*	*40%*	*50%*
0%	$1,700	$2,125	$2,550	$2,975	$3,400	$4,250
10	655	819	983	1,147	1,311	1,639
11	599	748	898	1,048	1,197	1,497
12	547	684	821	958	1,095	1,368
13	501	626	751	876	1,002	1,252
14	459	573	688	802	917	1,146
15	420	525	630	735	840	1,051

Case 17

S. G. CLEVELAND COMPANY (A) AND (B) (ABRIDGED)

In early November 1964 Mr. John G. Carlisle, newly elected vice president in charge of finance of the S. G. Cleveland Company, was preparing to recommend a dividend policy to the firm's board of directors. Six months earlier the board had made temporizing adjustments in the dividend payment level, pending a more thorough study of what the company's payout target should be, and what factors should be considered in evaluating a proposed dividend change.

BACKGROUND

The S. G. Cleveland Company had been founded in 1934 by Mr. Walker Q. Gresham, shortly after he had purchased the exclusive manufacturing rights for an operating model of a diesel engine superior to existing products in both speed and output for the weight. The company emerged from the consolidation of several manufacturing companies in which Mr. Gresham had acquired controlling interest during the depression years of the early 1930s. Volume from these activities was well below capacity levels at the time, and new products were being actively sought. The diesel engine soon became the firm's key product. By the time the corner was turned in 1937 and profits were earned, the accumulated investment by Mr. Gresham approximated $600,000 for 31.2 percent of the outstanding shares. Profits were earned each year thereafter.

The company grew rapidly throughout the postwar period until sales approximated $194 million in 1963. Both sales and profits after taxes increased at a compound rate of over 14 percent per annum. Return on net worth averaged 18 percent. In this regard, management strove to maintain careful control over its uses of capital. Inventory turnover at Cleveland, for example, was 7.6 in 1963, about the same as turnover in its most efficiently managed competitors and above the 3.4 average for all competitors (turnover figures based on sales). Plant capacity changes were also planned carefully to avoid tying up funds in unutilized space and equipment. The resulting turnover of assets contributed materially to the high return on net worth. The funds to finance the expansion came from retained earnings and debt sources. No additional common stock was sold for this purpose. Nevertheless, only 17 percent of long-term capital on Cleveland's books at the end of 1963 was of a debenture character. Selected income statement and balance sheet information pertaining to these years is presented in Exhibits 1 and 2. A summary of cash flows is included as Exhibit 3.

Several developments facilitated financing growth. Dividend payout approximated only 19 percent of earnings, and retained earnings averaged about 13 percent of net worth. Working capital requirements incidental to growth had proved relatively modest, and only 45¢ worth of net current investments were necessary to finance an increase of $1 in sales. Plant investments tended to be larger. Here, however, the rapid rate of growth worked to the company's advantage. Depreciation throw-off substantially exceeded the capital required for maintenance and modernization of facilities. Under accelerated write-off provisions, depreciation amounted to nearly 7 percent of net worth and helped materially to reduce the firm's dependence upon outside capital.

The company's principal product was a diesel

engine designed for a long operating life in heavy-duty trucks. During the postwar period Cleveland's sales benefited from the growth in total intercity transport of freight, the increasing share of this market garnered by heavy-duty trucks, the increasing use of diesel engines by truckers, and the improving penetration of this diesel market by Cleveland's products. In consequence the number of units sold by Cleveland rose fourfold between 1950 and 1964.

The intercity trucking industry was expected to continue to grow but at a slower rate. The diesel engine's share of new production probably would increase as demand rose for the superior horsepower required to travel more miles per year at higher speeds with larger loads on improved highways. Also, a new line of lightweight diesels appeared capable of competing on a value basis against gasoline engines in that segment of the market where engine weight reduced total "allowed" carrying capacity. Finally, Cleveland strove to make its own products obsolete by significant technological improvements, and its research staff sought continually to force the pace in the industry.

Nevertheless, there were warning signs on the horizon. Detroit Diesel Engine, an operating division of General Motors Corporation, had perfected its own product line and was now considered a serious competitor in the heavy-duty market, and Cleveland's 60 percent share of the market for heavy-duty automotive diesel engines was under increasing pressure. Cleveland's efforts to leapfrog the Detroit Diesel product had led to the somewhat premature introduction of a product that was superior but not wholly free of minor bugs. Technological competition was increasing in intensity.

As the Cleveland product was a subcomponent, albeit a vital one, of trucks made by other firms, it was always possible that these purchasers would decide to make instead of buy, or at least would use this threat to achieve price reductions. These risks had been anticipated, and Cleveland employed a strong sales force to persuade truckers to specify its products to gain the proved tough performance quality and the operating economy of its diesels. The Cleveland management had also built a strong specialized distributor organization to provide competent service to customers at convenient locations.

By means of an intensive cost-reduction program, Cleveland had reduced product costs by over 30 percent in recent years and hence had been able to reduce sales prices for engines despite rising material and labor costs. The company's research outlays were extensive, but competitors with more diverse interests in sources of motive power were able to investigate this area more broadly. There was always the risk that some revolutionary source of power—perhaps the gas turbine—might make the diesel engine obsolete. The exposure to risk was somewhat reduced by the lead time necessary to perfect and test the design of a complex engine that must operate under the taxing strain of highway use.

Efforts were already underway to diversify Cleveland's markets. Management had recently entered the medium-duty truck market with a new lightweight diesel. This market (trucks making in-town and other short-haul deliveries and weighing 8 to 12 tons) currently amounted to 120,000 units annually. Fuel utilization in such vehicles did not justify a price for a diesel engine much higher than the price of a gasoline engine of the durability characteristics required in the American market. A revolutionary new line of engines to be offered to this market by Cleveland in early 1965 appeared promising competitively with respect to both price and performance. Although marketing people hoped these engines would "catch fire" and command a dominant market position within 10 years' time, financial plans were drawn up on a somewhat more conservative basis. Any marked acceleration in the rate of penetration or in the growth in size of markets could put a strain on Cleveland's production facilities and require major unscheduled capital expenditure outlays.

Penetration by Cleveland of the markets for construction equipment engines was rising. New and very powerful diesel engines scheduled for release early in 1966 promised to help strengthen the competitive position in the construction markets, and a recently developed natural gas engine had new characteristics of importance to the stationary power markets. Cleveland also made transmission equipment and subcomponents, such as crank shafts, filters, and castings, for other developing markets.

Opportunities were being developed extremely rapidly overseas as well. Although diesel engines were widely used overseas, most of these energy sources were less powerful than the engines Cleveland specialized in. There had been negligible opportunities to market American diesels until recent years. As new road systems were built, however, heavier loads and higher speeds were becoming more important. In short, the overseas market was moving in the direction of American diesel designs. Management expected to make heavy resource commitments in the overseas markets in the immediate years ahead. Other opportunities overseas were also being pursued aggressively.

As a result of all of these recent changes, Cleveland had progressed from a company with one product primarily made at one location to a multiproduct, multimarket, multiplant, and multinational company. There were now eight plants, including six overseas units as well as two international licensees, and other facilities were being planned and constructed.

CORPORATE GOALS

Continued rapid growth at a 15 percent compounded rate was an extraordinarily important management objective, one that was pushed continuously and vigorously. Much concrete planning went into achieving related growth goals. One such study of long-term developments is summarized below:

The achievement of a 15 percent compounded rate of growth through 1975 will mean that "Cleveland will:

1. be a billion-dollar company in sales volume with $60 million in after-tax profits;
2. be a truly international company with at least one-third of its sales and profits generated in markets outside the United States and Canada and have major manufacturing offices throughout the world; and
3. have at least one-third of its sales and profits coming from products besides diesel engines or other products in the current Cleveland line."

With regard to the last point, the Cleveland management proposed to develop about one-quarter of the new products through internal research on allied product lines. The rest would come through acquisition of products useful in maintaining a strong competitive position in the power market.

Management sought cash acquisitions primarily, and the resulting possible requirements for funds (a recent, small acquisition had required almost $10 million) increased the importance of flexibility to the company. At the same time, any adverse reaction in the market price of Cleveland's common stock might prevent other attractive mergers that could only be completed on the basis of an exchange of stock.

Although the Cleveland stock was now 27.6 percent owned by a tightly knit group of the founder's family, management was directed to run the affairs of the company in the interests of the public shareholders. As an important matter of principle, Mr. Gresham, Jr., the chairman of the board, and other family members actually sought to maximize the growth in the long-term market value of their Cleveland holdings. Selected data concerning stockholders of Cleveland as of December 31, 1963, are shown in Exhibit 4. There had been no significant changes in 1964.

Mr. Gresham's objectives were summarized as follows:

> Quite simply, we aim to be number one in each market in which we serve, world-wide. We plan to be the volume producer in that portion of each market reasonably available to Cleveland; to have the highest quality, most complete, most appropriate, most advanced line of products in our chosen fields, to be the most efficient producer and therefore the leader in value as well as in quality.

Towards these ends, Mr. Gresham absorbed himself in understanding not only the overall picture of company operations, but also the significant details in all important areas of the business. He was continually asking probing and challenging questions to make certain his officers were achieving the high standards he set before them.

Mr. Gresham sought to give responsibility early to unusually promising men, and to challenge them to develop their managerial skills quickly and thoroughly. Mr. Carlisle, who graduated from the Harvard Business School in 1960, was a case in point. In November 1964 he was offered and he accepted the post of vice president in charge of finance at Cleveland, with responsibilities over all financial activities.

DIVIDEND POLICY CONSIDERATIONS

The dividend history of Cleveland is reviewed in Exhibit 5, as background for the dividend discussions commencing in the spring of 1964.

In May 1964 Mr. Ralph Martin, vice president and treasurer of Cleveland, recommended that the following actions be taken:

1. Authorize a 5-for-4 stock split payable June 26, 1964, to shareholders of record at the close of business on June 12, 1964;
2. Announce the intention of declaring a cash dividend of $0.80 a share annually on the increased number of shares.

Discussions surrounding these recommendations touched off a thoroughgoing review of dividend policy—a review that was still unresolved in early November 1964.

The cash dividend change proposed by Mr. Martin would have increased the cash payout for 1964 to 19.2 percent of the estimated earnings of $15.5 million for the year. This payout level would have been only slightly higher than the 18.7 percent average for the last 5 years and the 16.5 percent payout for 1963. The existing cash dividend rate was equivalent to $0.48 a share after the proposed stock split. The proposed increase in the cash dividend, therefore, was 66⅔ percent.

Mr. Martin's reasons for his recommendations were these: recent and prospective increases in sales and earnings justified an increase in dividends. The specific changes recommended fitted the historical pattern of cash dividend increases and stock splits granted under comparable earnings circumstances. Finally, forecasts indicated that funds requirements in the foreseeable future could be financed from retained earnings plus moderate borrowings even after the proposed changes took effect.

Mr. Martin's report noted that a prominent investment banker, a friend of the management, was particularly interested in seeing the dividend increased to $0.80, not $0.60, because the payout resulting from a smaller increase was "not high enough" for a company like Cleveland. Other investment bankers, however, believed that there was no way to pinpoint the exact package of cash dividend and stock split that would achieve maximum results, so that "right" payments were strictly a matter of judgment. Cash dividends were thought by some to be more important for a listed than an unlisted company.

The report also addressed the questions: Should a growth company pay dividends if this necessitates borrowing? And if so, how much borrowing should be tolerated? Mr. Martin noted that total cash dividends paid by Cleveland since 1951 compared closely to the amount borrowed over the period, $13.8 million. This debt was well below the level (generally one-third of capital) regarded as safe by bankers, insurance companies, and investment bankers.

Mr. Martin's proposal stirred a considerable controversy, principally because the change in dividend seemed particularly sharp. Later in May, Mr. Albert Dudley, an outside director and a member of the Finance Committee, submitted a memorandum in support of the action proposed by Mr. Martin. The report said in part:

> Although there is no definitive work in this area, professionals have expressed opinions that to enhance price–earnings multiples a dividend policy should: (1) express management's faith in the company's strong secular [earnings] trend (i.e., making small increases even in years when profits decline or are level; keeping pace with profit growth trends); (2) make payout in the 30-percent-to-50-percent range for companies in the 10-percent-to-20-percent annual growth class; (3) be related to itself, and not be affected by the situation of particular shareholders; (4) avoid the

use of extras; (5) be clearly enunciated so that investors can give it full credence.

We do not know enough about these considerations yet. This proposal is based on our conviction that our payout needlessly dropped below our past practice. In the past we have followed a policy of paying dividends that will not impair expansion and that are sustainable.

Mr. Dudley proposed that the dividend policy of the company should be studied thoroughly and that recommendations should be submitted at the board meeting of November 1964.

On May 25, 1964, Mr. Dudley's ideas were incorporated in an interoffice memorandum from Mr. Martin to the president of Cleveland, Mr. Patrick Parry, and to the chairman, Mr. Gresham. The memorandum added:

The investment bankers all consider that our present payout is too low and some suggest that we work towards a minimum payout of around 30 percent. Should we hold the present 15 cents quarterly dividend rate on the increased shares, the annual payout based on earnings of $16 million would be about 17 percent. With the proposed 20 cent quarterly rate [In the opinion of an investment banker, Cleveland's quarterly dividend rates should be divisible by 5. Payment of pennies was thought to suggest unwarranted accuracy.] on new shares, the annual payout would be 23.5 percent, a meaningful improvement in our payout.

Other key Cleveland officers subsequently raised several questions. For example, Mr. Parry asked: Why increase the payout when people buy Cleveland stock for capital gains, not dividends? Can the dividend be sustained if, as seems quite possible, 1965 proves to be a year of economic downturn, and we are simultaneously increasing our borrowing substantially? What specific benefits can be expected if the dividend increase is granted? Should we wait until December? Will we be in danger of running out of earned surplus if we have a 5-for-4 stock split now?

In response to various questions, Mr. Dudley, on behalf of the Finance Committee, submitted the following appraisal to Messrs. Gresham and Parry:

It seems to me that a great many side issues have cluttered up the basic questions. As I see it, the basic questions are these:

1. Why pay any dividend at all?
2. What can the company pay and ensure long-term growth?
3. What is the optimum relationship between payout and stock price?
4. Why do present shareholders own Cleveland?
5. Do you believe in the figures backing up our ability to pay?

Taking these questions in order:

1. Dividends should be paid because market valuation tends to be improved thereby, except for cases in which growth is clearly so rapid that all earnings are needed to finance it.
2. Cleveland's forecast of cash flow and cash needs show that (*a*) a proposed 80-cent dividend after a 5-for-4 stock split can be paid and sustained under foreseeable conditions; (*b*) from that level annual increases averaging 15 percent per year can be paid through 1972, given 15 percent average annual increase in net profits; (*c*) even with a downturn in business in 1965, it would be possible to pay an additional 10 percent stock dividend in 1964 and a 5 percent dividend in 1965; (*d*) cash budgets provide for capital expenditures and changes in net working capital of $28.9 million in 1964 (vs. capital expenditures of $16.3 million in 1963), rising to $47.2 million in 1972 and working capital rising in proportion to sales; and (*e*) in no case does the unused term credit decline below $19 million, nor does term debt rise above 28½ percent of capitalization. In addition, the company now has a short-term credit line of $5 million that is not used in the forecast.
3. Regarding the optimum relationship between payment and stock price, I have to say that we must rely on opinions and judgment. There is little definite evidence in this field. We do know that:

   a. Other companies with better annual growth rates (18 percent to 35 percent) than Cleveland (15 percent) (IBM, Bristol-Myers, Avon, Texas Instruments, Hertz,

Emerson Electric, and Magnavox) have higher payouts (25 percent–61 percent) than Cleveland at the proposed rate of 25 percent.

b. Professional opinion is: *payout that does not restrict growth* tends to enhance market value.

c. It seems logical that *given a similar and sustainable growth rate,* the stock with the higher payout will sell at a higher multiple.

(A word of caution—the investment community expects action on May 29. Undoubtedly some anticipation is in the current price. Therefore, we should expect some near-term selling on the "good news.")

4. Referring to the question of why people own Cleveland, there are these possibilities:

   a. It could be classified in the mind as a super growth stock on which dividend is not important. This seems less likely because our rate (15%) is not as high as rates of super growth industry companies, which run from 25 percent to 35 percent.
   b. It could be held in anticipation of continued growth and better dividend. This seems more likely because the 12 percent–18 percent "growers" in the manufacturing industry traditionally pay out more and Cleveland has low leverage, which suggests ability to pay.
   c. It could be held by people anticipating no change at all—15 percent growth, low payout.

   There is some risk that, if we are in category (a), higher payout would be interpreted as anticipating slower potential growth.

   We think that Cleveland is more likely considered to be in category (b) because our low leverage suggests ability to pay more. However, some statement of policy to the analysts should be made to clarify our position here. It is important to show that we can both grow and maintain payout, as our figures suggest.

5. Regarding the last question as to whether the figures can be believed, we have combed them carefully and they make sense. Furthermore, they have a strong safety factor in unused credit. If growth speeds up so that cash is needed, a slowdown in dividend *increases* should not be harmful.

To put all this in perspective, these recommendations suggest payout in the 25 percent area. This is still low by most standards and, if we can *prove that better multiples come with higher payout,* we may well recommend another increase in November.

Advantages and disadvantages of 5/4 plus 80 cents now versus 5/4 plus 60 cents now and smaller increases later on are:

Advantages

1. Investment community expects action and should not be disappointed by the combination.
2. Strong dividend action, when financially justified, could well be construed as faith in the future.
3. Market should be stronger near term than if action is done in a series of splits that come later. Sellers, contributors, and givers would benefit. Everyone would benefit if the company had to use stock in a merger near term.
4. Such dividend action should tend to dispel any impression that dividend policy is dominated by family. This becomes more important as we become listed and more of a public company.

Disadvantages

1. By waiting, we will know more about the effect of payout on the multiple before taking additional action.
2. We would run some risk that a series of small stock dividends would run us out of earned surplus if we had a series of low profit years. (Stock dividends in 1964 and 1965 would reduce earned surplus—with stock dividends, transfers from earned to capital surplus must be made at market value of dividend shares issued.)
3. By waiting, we will know more about potential capital needs in November.

After discussing the alternatives, the board of directors decided on a compromise solution pending more intensive study. The board declared a quarterly cash dividend of 15 cents a share on the common stock, payable to shareholders of record at the close of business on June 12, 1964, and authorized a stock split on the common stock amounting to one additional share for each three shares held. The board indicated its intention of continuing the same cash dividend rate on the increased number of common shares outstanding. The action would increase the cash dividends by 33⅓ percent.

In making the announcement, the directors said:

> . . . Continuance of the regular dividend, of course, depends upon future earnings, the financial needs of the company, and other relevant factors.
>
> All shareholders should recognize that [a stock split] of this nature does not increase any shareholder's percentage of ownership in the company, but instead merely has the effect of dividing his existing ownership into a greater number of shares.

In the months immediately after the board meeting, the financial management of Cleveland received reports from various investment bankers concerning the dividend question. These reports raised no points that had not already been considered. The position of one report was subsequently amplified in a letter to Mr. Dudley:

> . . . It is clear that people are not buying Cleveland for yield. We feel that if a yield is less than 4 percent in today's market the yield factor does not govern purchase. As long as Cleveland is able to profitably employ retained earnings and modestly increases the dividend periodically (if possible, annually, as it has over the past ten years), the market should regard the shares favorable. . . . We believe only a very large increase in the dividend, putting it on a yield basis, would of itself increase the price of the stock. . . .

THE DIVIDEND ISSUE

On October 1, 1964, Cleveland common stock was listed on the New York Stock Exchange. Shortly thereafter Mr. John Carlisle was brought in as financial vice president of Cleveland. As dividend policy was to be one of the important subjects of a late November board meeting, Mr. Carlisle was soon involved in preparing his recommendations—recommendations that would have to take into account the estimates of profits and funds requirements shown in Exhibit 6. In addition, he had gathered information on payout and price–earnings ratios for a variety of companies, as shown in Exhibits 7 through 10. Mr. Carlisle intended his analysis to cover the questions raised by Mr. Dudley's memorandum.

To focus his analysis, Mr. Carlisle proposed to compare dividend policies involving extremes of 0 percent and 35 percent as well as the company's traditional rate of 20 percent.

Once he had clarified the issue of payout policy, he intended to refine his conclusions, with the purpose of reaching a set of immediate recommendations.

EXHIBIT 1 CONSOLIDATED INCOME DATA, YEARS ENDED DECEMBER 31, 1948–1963, AND NINE MONTHS ENDED SEPTEMBER 30, 1964 (dollar figures in millions)

	Sales	*Cost of Goods Sold*	*Selling and Adm. Exp.*	*Profit Before Tax*	*Profit After Tax*	*Earnings per Share**
1948	$ 28.6	$ 21.6	$ 3.3	$ 3.7	$ 2.3	$0.46
1949	23.3	18.1	3.5	1.6	1.0	0.20
1950	42.6	31.7	4.8	6.2	2.8	0.57
1951	60.6	44.6	6.5	9.7	2.7	0.56
1952	54.6	43.6	7.3	3.6	1.9	0.38
1953	56.0	43.4	8.8	3.6	1.6	0.33
1954	59.2	43.9	9.2	6.0	2.9	0.59
1955	81.0	57.2	14.3	9.5	4.5	0.94
1956	105.8	75.9	17.9	11.9	5.7	1.19
1957	111.2	79.9	20.3	10.6	5.1	1.06
1958	108.8	79.6	20.0	8.6	3.9	0.80
1959	147.0	100.6	28.2	17.7	8.2	1.68
1960	135.8	95.4	26.0	13.7	6.0	1.23
1961	129.3	89.5	24.3	14.8	6.3	1.28
1962	167.3	111.8	32.6	22.9	10.6	2.15
1963	194.3	126.8	39.4	28.2	13.5	2.72
9/30/1964**	164.1	107.2	35.0	22.1	11.2	2.26

*On the basis of 4,954,082 shares outstanding on June 30, 1964, after the stock split.
**Subject to year-end audit adjustment.
Note: All data have been disguised to protect the proprietary interests of the cooperating firm.

Case 17 S. G. Cleveland Company (A) and (B) (Abridged)

EXHIBIT 2 CONSOLIDATED BALANCE SHEETS AS OF DECEMBER 31, 1953, 1958, 1963, AND SEPTEMBER 30, 1964 (dollar figures in millions)

Assets	*1953*	*1958*	*1963*	*Sept. 30 1964**
Cash	$ 2.7	$ 4.2	$ 4.6	$ 3.9
Marketable securities	—	4.9	3.5	2.1
Accounts receivable, net	6.0	15.4	26.7	25.9
Inventories (FIFO)	9.8	12.4	25.7	33.6
Total current assets	$18.5	$36.9	$ 60.5	$ 65.5
Investments and other assets	0.7	8.4	4.1	5.9
Plant and equipment	14.3	33.1	71.0	81.8
Less: Reserve for depreciation	(4.4)	(10.9)	(23.1)	(26.7)
Net plant and equipment	$ 9.9	$22.2	$ 47.9	$ 55.1
Other assets	0.7	1.2	2.1	2.5
Total assets	$29.8	$68.7	$114.6	$129.0
Liabilities and Stockholders' Equity:				
Notes payable, current portion	$ —	$ —	$ 1.1	$ 1.6
Accounts payable	2.7	5.1	7.8	7.5
Accrued liabilities	1.5	5.2	10.9	14.8
Accrued retirement trust	0.3	0.6	1.1	0.9
Provision for federal tax	0.4	—	0.5**	2.2**
Total current liabilities	$ 4.9	$10.8	$ 21.4	$ 27.1
Notes payable	7.0	20.0***	9.0	7.8
Other notes payable	—	3.6	6.9	6.5
Res. for future fed. inc. tax	—	1.0	7.2	8.1
Total long-term liabilities	$ 7.0	$24.6	$ 23.1	$ 22.4
Preferred stock	1.0	—	—	—
Common stock	3.3	6.3	9.3	12.4
Capital surplus	3.2	8.1	24.4	21.3
Retained earnings	10.4	18.9	36.4	45.8
Stockholders' equity	$17.9	$33.3	$ 70.2	$ 79.5
Total liabilities and stockholders' equity	$29.8	$68.7	$114.6	$129.0

*Subject to year-end audit adjustment.

**Net of marketable securities: $7.4 in 1963 and $6.2 on September 30, 1964.

***$5.0 due 1960–1964; $15.0 due 1960–1972.

Details may not add to totals because of rounding.

Note: All data have been disguised to protect the proprietary interests of the cooperating firm.

EXHIBIT 3 STATEMENT OF SOURCES AND APPLICATIONS OF FUNDS, 1954–1963 (dollar figures in millions)

	1954	1955	1956	1957	1958	1959	1960	1961	1962	1963
Internal Sources of Funds										
Profits after taxes	$ 2.88	$ 4.52	$ 5.70	$ 5.11	$ 3.90	$ 8.23	$ 6.03	$ 6.31	$10.62	$13.51
Less: Dividends	0.70	0.72	0.86	1.08	1.20	1.27	1.47	1.61	1.78	2.23
Retained earnings	$ 2.18	$ 3.80	$ 4.84	$ 4.03	$ 2.70	$ 6.96	$ 4.56	$ 4.70	$ 8.84	$11.28
Depreciation	1.84	2.10	2.55	2.32	2.98	3.63	4.26	4.28	4.68	5.27
Internally generated funds	$ 4.02	$ 5.96	$ 7.39	$ 6.35	$ 5.68	$10.59	$ 8.82	$ 8.98	$13.52	$16.55
Reserve for future federal income taxes	—	—	—	0.59	0.41	0.23	1.28	1.26	1.74	1.67
Net cash from operations	$ 4.02	$ 5.96	$ 7.39	$ 6.94	$ 6.09	$10.82	$10.10	$10.24	$15.26	$18.22
Internal Applications of Funds										
Net changes in working capital, excl. of cash	$(0.25)	$ 2.46	$ 2.05	$ 2.38	$(0.62)	$ 4.74	$(0.69)	$ 1.54	$ 4.05	$ 4.38
Capital assets	1.43	2.63	5.39	9.03	5.65	11.75	8.49	7.27	8.35	11.99
Investments and other assets	0.47	0.59	1.50	3.59	2.13	(4.43)	(0.43)	(0.41)	1.90	(0.92)
Federal income taxes—prior years	1.38	—	—	—	—	—	—	—	—	—
Total internal applications	$ 3.03	$ 5.68	$ 8.94	$15.00	$ 7.16	$12.06	$ 7.37	$ 8.40	$14.30	$16.35
Net excess (deficiency) of cash from internal operations	$ 0.99	$ 0.28	$(1.55)	$(8.06)	$(1.07)	$(1.24)	$ 2.73	$ 1.84	$ 0.96	$ 1.87
Funds Supplied by Changes in Financial Position										
Decrease (increase) in liquid assets	$(2.03)	$ 1.51	$(0.28)	$(0.68)	$(4.97)	$ 3.62	$(1.22)	$(2.94)	$ 1.03	$ 0.59
Increase (decrease) in long-term debt	1.21	(0.98)	1.81	8.65	5.94	(2.51)	(1.62)	0.91	(2.03)	(2.51)
Stock options exercised	—	0.07	0.02	0.09	0.10	0.13	0.11	0.19	0.04	0.05
Preferred stock retired	(0.17)	(0.88)	—	—	—	—	—	—	—	—
Net funds supplied	$(0.99)	$(0.28)	$ 1.55	$ 8.06	$ 1.07	$ 1.24	$(2.73)	$(1.84)	$(0.96)	$(1.87)

Note: All data have been disguised to protect the proprietary interests of the cooperating firm.

Case 17 S. G. Cleveland Company (A) and (B) (Abridged)

EXHIBIT 4 VARIOUS COMPARISONS OF THE STOCKHOLDER GROUP

Summary, December 31, 1963	*Number of Shares*	*Percentage of Outstanding Shares*	*Number of Shareholders*
Officers, directors, and families	185,778	5.0%	62
Officers, directors, and families (retired)	38,271	1.0	16
Family of founder	1,025,495	27.6	9
Investment banking group	81,742	2.2	23
Distributors, employees, and families	36,041	1.0	52
Employees and families	141,191	3.8	425
Outside investors	2,207,043	59.4	3,329
Total	3,715,561	100.0%	3,916

	12/31/60	*12/31/63*
	Number of Shares	
Officers, directors, and families	144,691	185,778
Officers, directors, and families (retired)	—	38,271
Family of founder	742,211	1,025,495
Investment banking group	75,025	85,742
Miscellaneous large holders	878,863	1,289,300
Miscellaneous other holders	838,672	1,094,975
Total	2,679,462	3,715,561

	12/31/60	*12/31/63*
	Percentage of Shares	
Officers, directors, and families	5.4%	5.0%
Officers, directors, and families (retired)	—	1.0
Family of founder	27.7	27.6
Investment banking group	2.8	2.2
Miscellaneous large holders	32.8	34.7
Miscellaneous other holders	31.3	29.5
Total	100.0%	100.0%

Note: "Miscellaneous large holders" shown as of 12/31/60 includes "outside" investors who own or control more than 800 shares; in 12/31/63 it includes all "outside" investors who own or control more than 1,000 shares. Cleveland distributors and Cleveland employees are included in "Miscellaneous other holders" regardless of the size of holdings.

All data have been disguised to protect the proprietary interests of the cooperating firm.

Case 17 S. G. Cleveland Company (A) and (B) (Abridged)

EXHIBIT 4 (*continued*)

SHAREHOLDERS BY TYPE

		Shares	
	Shareholders	*Number*	*Percentage*
Individuals			
Male	1,643	1,108,804	29.8%
Female	1,025	1,430,004	38.5
Joint accounts	890	95,753	2.6
Fiduciaries			
Individual	68	32,606	0.9
Institutions	13	252,699	6.8
Brokers	210	764,296	20.6
Institutions	67	31,399	0.8
Total	3,916	3,715,561	100.0%

Note: All data have been disguised to protect the proprietary interests of the cooperating firm.

EXHIBIT 5 SELECTED DATA ON COMMON STOCK, 1949–1963

		Earnings per share		*Cash dividends per share*		*Percentage of*	*Bid Prices, Over-the-Counter Market*#			*Price–Earnings*	*Cash Dividends*
	Stock Distributions	*As Reported**	*Adjusted***	*As Reported**	*Adjusted***	*Payout****	*High*	*Low*	*Close*	*Ratios*##	*Yield*##
1949	—	$2.32	$0.20	$1.00	$0.09	43.1%	1.25	1.25	1.25	6.3	7.2%
1950	20% stk. div.	7.35	0.57	1.50	0.13	20.4	2.875	1.25	2.50	3.9	5.2
1951	20% stk. div.	6.13	0.56	1.25	0.13	20.4	4.375	2.625	4.25	6.6	3.1
1952	10% stk. div.	3.26	0.38	1.10	0.14	31.8	5.25	3.625	4.125	10.1	3.4
1953	—	2.87	0.33	1.00	0.14	34.8	4.125	2.375	2.50	6.4	5.6
1954	5% stk. div.	4.33	0.59	1.00	0.14	23.1	3.875	2.375	3.875	6.6	3.6
1955	5-for-4 split	6.50	0.94	1.00	0.14	15.3	7.875	4.25	7.25	7.7	1.9
1956	5-for-4 split	6.59	1.19	1.00	0.18	15.2	12.125	6.875	11.125	9.3	1.6
1957	10% stk. div.	4.69	1.06	1.00	0.22	21.3	14.25	8.375	8.75	8.3	2.5
1958	5% stk. div.	3.62	0.80	1.00	0.25	30.7	16.875	8.625	16.375	18.2	1.5
1959	—	6.48	1.68	1.00	0.26	15.4	24.875	16.375	22.50	13.4	1.2
1960	2-for-1 split (April) 5% stk. div.	2.36	1.23	0.58	0.30	24.3	22.625	15.125	22.625	18.4	1.3
1961	10% stk. div.	2.34	1.28	0.60	0.33	25.5	37.25	20.125	35.375	27.6	0.9
1962	5-for-4 split	3.58	2.15	0.60	0.36	16.8	41.00	25.25	37.875	17.6	1.0
1963	—	3.64	2.72	0.60	0.45	16.5	47.625	36.75	36.75	13.5	1.2
1964	4-for-3 split (June)	3.13 (est)	3.13 (est)	0.60###	0.53###	16.8 (est)	54.0†	49.00	49.75†	15.9	1.1

*As reported before stock dividends and splits except for 1960, when the 2-for-1 split took place in April. All other stock distributions were made near the year-end.

**Adjusted to basis of shares outstanding after 4-for-3 split in June 1964.

***Based on total amounts.

#Adjusted to basis of shares outstanding after June 1964, to nearest eighths.

##Based on closing prices.

###Based on payments for first three quarters (annual rate).

†New York Stock Exchange quotations for period from October 1 to November 2.

Note: All data have been disguised to protect the proprietary interests of the cooperating firm.

EXHIBIT 6 REVISED FORECASTS FOR 1964–1970 SHOWING MAXIMUM SUSTAINABLE PAYOUT OF DIVIDENDS TO BE 35% (dollar figures in millions)

	1964	*1965*	*1966*	*1967*	*1968*	*1969*	*1970*	*Total 1964–1970*
Needs exclusive of dividends								
Capital program	$ 33.0	$ 35.0	$ 34.7	$ 32.2	$ 33.7	$ 37.0	$ 42.0	$ 247.6
Working capital	(4.1)	10.7	7.1	9.6	3.5	5.4	5.2	37.4
Total needs	$ 28.9	$ 45.7	$ 41.8	$ 41.8	$ 37.2	$ 42.4	$ 47.2	$ 285.0
Sources								
After-tax profits	$ 14.9	$ 15.7	$ 18.0	$ 19.0	$ 20.2	$ 22.8	$ 26.4	$137.0
Depreciation and goodwill	6.4	8.7	10.9	13.3	15.7	17.6	19.6	92.2
Misc. distributor mortgages	0.4	8.8	1.6	—	—	—	—	10.8
Total sources	$ 21.7	$ 33.2	$ 30.5	$ 32.3	$ 35.9	$ 40.4	$ 46.0	$240.0
Additional borrowing needed	$ 7.2	$ 12.5	$ 11.3	$ 9.5	$ 1.3	$ 2.0	$ 1.2	$ 45.0
Borrowing at beginning of period	12.3	19.5	32.0	43.3	52.8	54.1	56.1	12.3
Cumulative borrowing needed before dividends	$ 19.5	$ 32.0	$ 43.3	$ 52.8	$ 54.1	$ 56.1	$ 57.3	$ 57.3
Borrowing capacity								
Maximum borrowing possible with 40% debt ratio and 35% payout*	$ 53.3	$ 60.1	$ 67.9	$ 76.1	$ 84.8	$ 94.7	$106.1	
Cumulative borrowing before dividends	19.5	32.0	43.3	52.8	54.1	56.1	57.3	
Cumulative borrowing for dividends*	5.2	10.7	17.0	23.7	30.8	38.8	48.0	
Unused borrowing capacity	$ 28.6	$ 17.4	$ 7.6	$ -0.4	$ -0.1	$ -0.2	$ 0.8	
Resulting capitalization								
Equity	$ 79.9	$ 90.1	$101.8	$114.1	$127.2	$142.0	$159.2	
Debt	24.7	42.7	60.3	76.5	84.9	94.9	105.3	
Total capitalization	$104.6	$132.8	$162.1	$190.6	$212.1	$236.9	$264.5	
Percentage of debt capitalization	23.6%	32.2%	37.2%	40.1%	40.0%	40.1%	39.8%	

*Mr. Carlisle had obtained permission to experiment with a debt-to-capitalization ratio of 40%, but there had been no commitment that this ratio would be chosen. With this limitation, a dividend payout of 35% was possible. The work sheet calculations were as follows:

	1964	*1965*	*1966*	*1967*	*1968*	*1969*	*1970*	*Total 1964–1970*
After-tax earnings	$ 14.9	$ 15.7	$ 18.0	$ 19.0	$ 20.2	$ 22.8	$ 26.4	$137.0
Dividends at 35% payout	5.2	5.5	6.3	6.7	7.1	8.0	9.2	48.0
Addition to equity	$ 9.7	$ 10.2	$ 11.7	$ 12.3	$ 13.1	$ 14.8	$ 17.2	$ 89.0
Previous equity	70.2	79.9	90.1	101.8	114.1	127.2	142.0	70.2
Total equity	$ 79.9	$ 90.1	$101.8	114.1	$127.2	$142.0	$159.2	$159.2
Debt capacity (40% of capitalization = ⅔ equity)	$ 53.3	$ 60.1	$ 67.9	$ 76.1	$ 84.8	$ 94.7	$106.1	$106.1

Note: All data have been disguised to protect the proprietary interests of the cooperating firm. Forecast prepared November 1964.

Case 17 S. G. Cleveland Company (A) and (B) (Abridged)

EXHIBIT 7 PRICE–EARNINGS AND DIVIDEND DATA FOR MACHINERY, ELECTRICAL EQUIPMENT, AND SELECTED AUTOMOTIVE FIRMS

No.	*Company*	*Growth Code**	*P/E Ratio 3-Year Average*	*Payout 3-Year Average*	*EPS 1963 Divided by EPS 1953*
1	General Electric	1	28.7	77.4	1.49
2	Westinghouse	1	26.2	88.4	0.56
3	Joy Manufacturing	1	24.3	94.9	1.56
4	Otis Elevator	0	22.6	61.7	2.47
5	Cutler-Hammer	1	21.1	56.3	1.20
6	Black & Decker	0	19.7	58.6	2.67
7	Cincinnati Milling	1	18.7	71.2	0.97
8	Worthington	1	18.5	81.3	0.48
9	Ingersoll-Rand	1	18.4	98.4	1.28
10	Caterpillar	0	17.5	44.4	3.64
11	Link-Belt	1	16.4	75.3	0.92
12	Square D	0	15.9	65.2	2.73
13	McGraw-Edison	1	15.9	65.1	1.39
14	Clark Equipment	0	15.4	51.2	2.69
15	Eltra Corp.	1	15.4	54.2	1.15
16	Cooper-Bessemer	1	15.2	76.2	1.26
17	Blaw-Knox Co.	1	14.9	59.5	0.70
18	LOF Glass	0	14.7	69.6	2.02
19	Gardner-Denver Co.	0	14.3	58.8	2.08
20	Dana Corp.	0	14.1	68.98	2.86
21	Chicago Pneumatic	1	14.1	67.8	1.53
22	Combustion Engineer.	1	14.0	62.1	0.93
23	Ex-Cell-O	1	13.9	55.9	1.51
24	Timken Bearing	0	13.3	60.9	2.59
25	Federal Mogul-Bower	0	13.3	52.0	2.36
26	Babcock & Wilcox	0	13.3	46.9	1.77
27	Grinnell	1	13.0	30.7	1.19
28	Rockwell-Standard	1	12.7	67.7	1.24
29	Torrington Co.	0	11.0	46.4	2.17
30	Foster-Wheeler	0	10.5	18.7	n.a.
31	Warner & Swasey	1	9.2	33.7	1.37
32	S.G. Cleveland	0	15.5	19.0	8.24

*Growth Code: 1 = −9% to 5% growth; 0 = 5% to 14% growth.

Case 17 S. G. Cleveland Company (A) and (B) (Abridged)

EXHIBIT 8 PRICE–EARNINGS VS. PAYOUT—MACHINERY, ELECTRICAL, AND AUTOMOTIVE

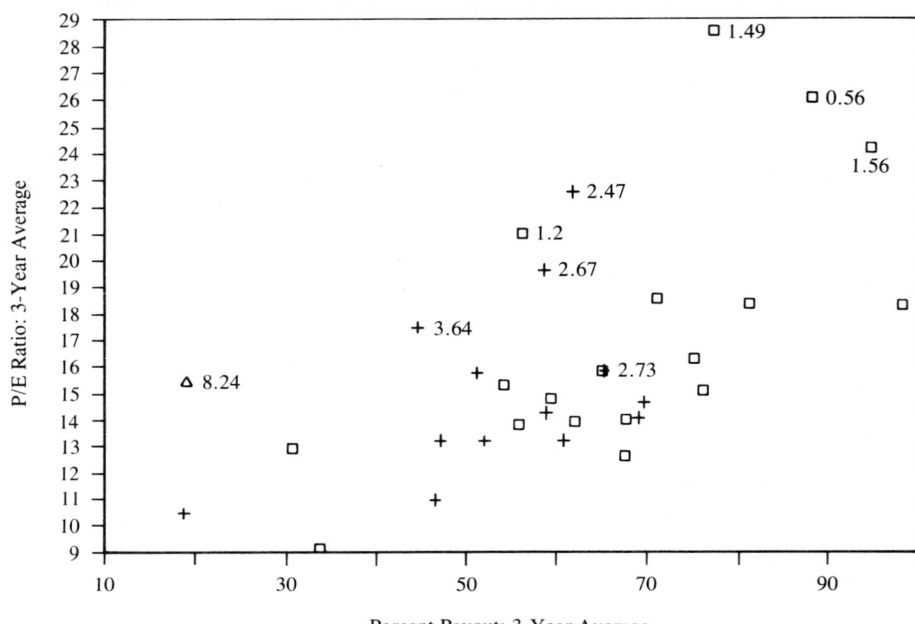

□ −9 to 5% Growth

+ 5 to 14% Growth

Δ SGC

Case 17 S. G. Cleveland Company (A) and (B) (Abridged)

EXHIBIT 9 PRICE–EARNINGS AND DIVIDEND DATA FOR COMPANIES WITH 10-YEAR ANNUAL GROWTH RATES IN EXCESS OF 13%

No.	*Company*	*Cycle Code**	*P/E Ratio 3-Year Average*	*Payout 3-Year Average*	*EPS 1963 Divided by EPS 1953*
1	Xerox Corporation	N	63.50	21.00	28.25
2	IBM Corporation	N	59.80	35.80	7.60
3	Polaroid Corporation	N	56.70	0.80	7.68
4	Varian Associates	N	54.20	0.00	14.50
5	Prentice-Hall, Inc.	N	41.90	45.10	4.18
6	3-M Corporation	C	41.30	49.10	4.94
7	Beckman Instruments	N	40.30	0.00	1.80
8	Avon Products	N	38.30	56.20	12.88
9	Litton Industries	N	36.90	0.00	4.50
10	ARA, Inc.	N	36.70	0.00	4.28
11	American Hospital Supply	N	33.60	35.30	3.57
12	Perkin-Elmer Corporation	N	33.20	0.00	2.26
13	Fairchild Camera	C	33.00	27.20	1.55
14	Thiokol Chemical	C	31.20	0.00	21.60
15	Smith, Kline, French	N	31.00	65.60	6.82
16	Texas Instruments	N	30.60	18.60	7.09
17	Bristol-Myers Co.	N	29.70	49.20	7.54
18	Rohm & Hass Co.	C	29.70	21.10	4.20
19	Ginn & Co.	N	28.00	50.10	N.A.
20	American Home Products	N	27.80	66.60	4.30
21	Norwich Pharmacal	N	27.40	61.60	4.34
22	Zenith Radio Corporation	N	27.20	55.30	3.55
23	Hertz Corporation	C	26.30	59.60	4.02
24	Chesebrough-Pond	N	25.50	49.30	2.45
25	Magnavox Co.	N	23.90	50.00	5.22
26	Howard Johnson Co.	N	23.50	0.00	10.13
27	AMF	C	22.80	66.80	6.48
28	Bobbie Brooks, Inc.	N	22.70	33.20	11.40
29	Harvey Aluminum	C	22.70	106.80	1.64
30	Aerojet General	N	22.40	0.10	5.06
31	Air Products	C	22.40	7.10	4.52
32	E.J. Korvette	N	21.50	0.00	5.25
33	Winn-Dixie Stores	N	21.50	86.60	3.52
34	Heublein, Inc.	N	21.10	40.30	8.06
35	Emerson Electric	N	19.90	47.60	3.67
36	Colonial Corporation	N	19.80	29.20	12.00
37	Ark.-Louis. Gas	N	19.40	55.10	6.86
38	R.J. Reynolds	N	18.00	52.00	4.01
39	Piper Aircraft	C	16.40	63.40	11.08
40	Spiegel, Inc.	C	15.90	67.60	7.77
41	Crown Cork & Seal	C	15.60	0.00	10.06

*Cycle Code: N = non-cyclical; C = cyclical.

EXHIBIT 9 (*continued*)

No.	*Company*	*Cycle Code**	*P/E Ratio 3-Year Average*	*Payout 3-Year Average*	*EPS 1963 Divided by EPS 1953*
	S.G. Cleveland	C	15.50	19.00	8.24
42	Safeway Stores	N	15.30	74.70	2.57
43	Avco Corporation	C	14.40	53.00	5.85
44	Celanese Corporation	C	14.40	49.50	4.02
45	Dominion Stores	C	14.20	33.30	2.88
46	Buyak Cigars	N	14.00	66.40	1.97
47	Dominion Foundries	C	13.50	49.20	3.30
48	Kerr-McGee Oil	C	13.20	29.20	5.15
49	Pittson Co.	C	13.00	28.00	3.17
50	First Charter Fin.	C	12.80	0.00	2.58
51	DBS	N	12.70	41.70	4.44
52	Algoma Steel	C	12.30	35.70	6.57
53	Lorillard	N	11.60	55.60	3.63
54	American Distilling	N	11.50	40.30	6.92
55	McLouth Steel	C	11.30	0.00	2.69
56	Falconbridge Mines	C	11.10	44.30	2.83
57	General Tire	C	10.80	22.20	3.67
58	McDonnell Aircraft	C	9.60	20.70	6.85
59	Massey-Ferguson	C	8.80	31.20	3.99

*Cycle Code: N = noncyclical; C = cyclical.

Case 17 S. G. Cleveland Company (A) and (B) (Abridged)

EXHIBIT 10 PRICE–EARNINGS VS. PAYOUT—GROWTH COMPANIES

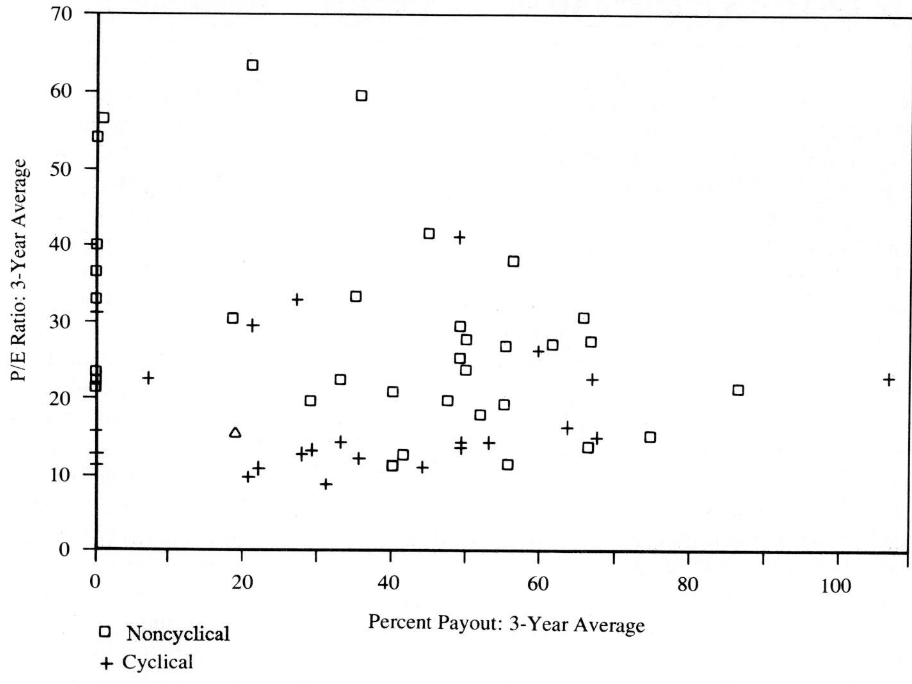

Case 18

SLEEP SURFACE CORPORATION

The year ending December 31, 1987, had been an exhausting one for the management of Sleep Surface Corporation, newly renamed to reflect its broad product line. Founded as the Midwest Mattress Company in the early 1900s, it was one of the initial firms franchised to manufacture and sell the Pacifica mattress. Over the course of many years, Pacifica built itself into a nationally known brand and on a consolidated basis was the largest producer of mattresses in the world. Its brand name was one of the best known of any product in the United States.

Despite this marketing success, however, the franchisees had not found cooperating easy and had increasingly turned to the courts to settle their disputes among one another and with the franchisor. Ultimately, Midwest Mattress, the only publicly held mattress company in the United States, bought out all but one small Pacifica franchise and also bought out the Pacifica franchisor organization. This task had primarily been accomplished during late 1986. Sleep Surface's sales had risen from $267 million in 1985 to $598 million in 1987 primarily because of the acquisition of the rest of the Pacifica group.

Somewhat earlier, Midwest Mattress had also purchased Sleepy Hollow Company, another mattress company with national distribution which sold a high-end product line through upmarket department and furniture stores; New Concept Bedding, one of the original watermattress firms which marketed a quality product; and Fashion Furniture, which produced pine waterbed furniture and accessories. Sleepy Hollow and several of the Pacifica franchisees which Sleep Surface now owned also produced convertible sofas. Given this collection of sleep products, the directors determined that the Midwest Mattress name was no longer properly descriptive. It was decided that Sleep Surface Corporation was a more encompassing name for the company. (Recent financial statements for Sleep Surface are summarized in Exhibits 1 and 2. Exhibit 3 presents a 10-year history of selected financial data.)

Ronald Edwards, president and chief operating officer of Sleep Surface, had had his hands full in 1987 with the problems of meshing the activities of a number of major, formerly independent units now suddenly operating under one umbrella. Not only were there the normal problems of establishing common accounting and reporting systems and procedures, allocating customers among the plants, sorting out marketing structure, and managing diverse computer hardware and software, but this had to be accomplished in an atmosphere complicated by the long years of litigation. Nevertheless, Mr. Edwards was again beginning to think ahead to plan intermediate tactics if not long-term strategy.

One of Mr. Edwards's concerns had always been the efficient allocation of capital. He had been careful in calculating the returns to be received before authorizing investments in plant and equipment. He was not sure that all the other Pacifica franchisees had been as careful. He was also not convinced that Sleep Surface's existing collection of assets represented the proper combination of assets to maximize the company's value in the future. Some of the ancillary operations should probably be sold; other product lines should be expanded or acquired.

Furthermore, $165 million of debt, together with $100 million in new common stock, had been taken on to finance the Pacifica acquisitions. These issues represented a significant increase in the company's 1986 capital of $140 million. During the forthcoming five years, prin-

This case was developed from public information with the help of individuals who wish to remain anonymous. Details may have been altered in some instances for the purpose of facilitating student analysis without changing the nature of the managerial decision.

cipal repayments on the debt would be in the vicinity of $2 million to $2.5 million annually, which was considered modest. Mr. Edwards wondered whether repayment of the debt should be accelerated or even whether stock should be repurchased if funds were available.

It was not possible to prepare a cash forecast with any degree of certainty, but the mattress industry was a relatively somnolent business. Industry statistics suggested that the total number of units sold in the United States had been relatively flat or even declining for over a decade. Pacifica's growth, achieved through aggressive marketing, product development, and intense price competition, had come at the expense of the so-called "no-name" producers. These were local firms making private-label merchandise for their customers or marketing locally under their own name. Even one of the smaller national franchise arrangements had gone bankrupt, unable to compete in the market conditions that developed in the early 1980s. As a result, Mr. Edwards did not anticipate a continuation of the rapid growth the Pacifica brand had enjoyed, let alone the explosive growth resulting from the acquisition program in recent years. He assumed that growth would return to more modest levels.

Based on that assumption, he sketched in the following estimate of funds available after allowing for normal operations and investments:

	Millions
Sources of Funds	
Profits retained in the business	$22.6
Exercise of options	.6
Total sources of funds	$23.2
Use of Funds	
Accounts receivable, inventories, etc.	$ 2.2
Property, etc., net of depreciation	3.5
Reduction of payables	1.0
Total uses of funds	$ 6.7

Even allowing for the $1.6 million debt repayment due in 1988, it appeared that Sleep Surface would generate a considerable amount of cash.

Mr. Edwards, a perceptive and thoughtful student of current management theory and practice, thought it could be helpful to develop an estimate of Sleep Surface's cost of capital as an initial stepping stone in deciding how to allocate the spare cash among the competing alternate uses. He knew that many theoreticians argued that each investment should be analyzed according to its individual risks and that the company's weighted capital costs inadequately reflected the proper return to be obtained from a given investment. "T-bills trade at the same rate for everyone," Mr. Edwards remembered having heard someone say, "regardless of the risk of the purchaser. It's the risk of the investment that counts." Having an estimate for the company, Mr. Edwards thought, would at least give him a benchmark when it came to assessing the other alternatives and comparing them to the possibility of reducing the capital through debt repayment or stock purchase.

There were other substantial obstacles to estimating the company's capital costs. As a result of the acquisition activities, Sleep Surface had experienced quite erratic growth, often temporarily well above the long-term growth rate for the industry. The capital structure had been changed as a result of the Pacifica acquisition. There were no other publicly traded companies whose main product was mattresses, although Bassett Furniture had recently added a small mattress business to its diverse furniture products.

Mr. Edwards nevertheless decided that the exercise was worth the effort but initially not worth a vast amount of time. He therefore asked Mr. Thomas, the company's financial vice president, to gather data quickly on publicly traded companies in the furniture business. (This information is included in Exhibit 4.) Mr. Edwards also asked Mr. Thomas to come up with his own estimate of Sleep Surface's capital costs.

Mr. Edwards would also prepare an estimate, and the two executives would then compare notes. Mr. Thomas reminded Mr. Edwards of the tax complication Sleep Surface faced. Because amortization of the goodwill (and certain other expenses) was not allowed as an expense for tax purposes, Sleep Surface's tax rate appeared higher than the statutory marginal rate of 34 percent. It was ironic, Mr. Thomas noted, that the higher Sleep Surface's earnings, the lower its reported tax rate would be. Conversely, if reported earnings declined far enough, the tax bill could be greater than 100 percent of pretax profits.

THE CAPITAL STRUCTURE

Sleep Surface's long-term obligations were $185.6 million at the end of 1987. There were three components to this sum. First, the company had drawn $95.0 million of its $125.0 million revolving credit line with a group of commercial banks. The rate was a floating one, five-eighths of a percentage point above the composite certificate of deposit rate of the participating banks. The banks' rate had been averaging 7 1/2 percent, creating a borrowing cost for Sleep Surface of 8 1/8 percent.

The second component was $15 million of capitalized industrial development revenue bonds and leases. All but $3 million were at fixed rates which averaged 9.5 percent. The remainder were on a floating rate of 75 percent of prime. In late 1987, the prime rate was 8.75 percent.

The final part of Sleep Surface's long-term obligations was $75 million (at par value) of convertible subordinated debentures, which were currently trading at 86 percent of par. The interest rate on the debentures was 6 percent. A $1,000 debenture was convertible into 43.956 shares of common stock, which implied a conversion price of $22.75. The mandatory sinking fund would not begin until 1998.

Sleep Surface's common stock price had been quite volatile, a situation compounded by the sharp drop in the stock market in October 1987. The range for the year was from a high of $24 3/8 in the third quarter to a low of $11 1/8 in the fourth quarter. By December 31, the price had recovered somewhat and closed at $13.75 per share.

MARKET RETURNS

Mr. Thomas noted that he had just seen a report of the market return calculations prepared annually by the consulting firm Ibbotson Associates. He had jotted down the summary information, shown in Table 1, for average rates of return for the 1926–87 period:

Table 1 Rate of Return

	Nominal		*Excluding Inflation*	
Investment	*Geometric*	*Arithmetic*	*Geometric*	*Arithmetic*
Treasury bills	3.5%	3.5%	0.4%	0.5%
Long-term govt's	4.3	4.6	1.2	1.7
Small company common stock	12.1	17.7	8.8	14.2
Common stock	9.9	12.0	6.6	8.8
Inflation	3.0	3.2		

Mr. Edwards asked what the differences between geometric and arithmetic returns were. Mr. Thomas said that as best he could remember from his statistics course, the geometric rate was a compound rate over time whereas the arithmetic was just the average of the growth rates each year. For instance, if $100 grew by 20 percent a year and then fell by 20 percent, the arithmetic growth rate would be zero. The geometric would be negative because the sum would go from $100 to $120 and then fall back to $96. For short-term investments, in the vicinity of one year, the arithmetic rate might be "more accurate" to use. For longer periods, the compound or geometric would be preferable.

In December 1987, 90-day Treasury bills were yielding 5.77 percent, which was approximately the average rate for the year. U.S. government 10-year bonds were yielding 8.99 percent, above the year's 8.39 percent average. Comparable figures for the 30-year Treasuries were 9.12 percent and 8.58 percent. The average 1987 Consumer Price Index had risen 3.6 percent above the 1986 figure.

Case 18 Sleep Surface Corporation

EXHIBIT 1 INCOME STATEMENTS FOR THE YEARS ENDED DECEMBER 31, 1985–1987 (millions of dollars except per share figures)

	1985	*1986*	*1987*
Net sales	$267,321	$297,405	$598,149
Cost of goods sold	182,247	202,836	381,013
Gross profit	$ 85,074	$ 94,569	$217,136
Selling, general, admin.	65,521	69,383	152,076
Interest	2,458	1,860	15,426
Profit from continuing operations before tax	$ 17,095	$ 23,326	$ 49,634
Income taxes	8,579	11,698	26,263
Discontinued operations	(3,651)	—	—
Profit before extraordinary item	$ 4,865	$ 11,628	$ 23,371
Extraordinary item (pension plan termination)	1,877	—	—
Net profit	$ 6,742	$ 11,628	$ 23,371
Earnings per share			
Primary net	$0.42	$0.72	$1.15
Fully diluted			1.12

EXHIBIT 2 BALANCE SHEETS AS OF DECEMBER 31, 1986 AND 1987

	1986	*1987*
Assets		
Cash and temporary investments	$ 1,591	$ 31,125
Accounts receivable, net	45,115	91,687
Inventories	34,411	74,667
Recoverable taxes and misc.	956	9,527
Total current assets	$ 82,073	$207,006
Property, plant, and equipment	73,435	169,897
Accumulated depreciation	18,264	28,360
Net property, plant, and equipment	$ 55,171	$141,537
Goodwill, net of amortization	15,565	150,615
Patents, trademarks, etc., net	5,747	16,374
Notes receivable and other	8,819	10,153
Total long-term assets	$ 30,131	$177,142
Total assets	$167,375	$525,685
Liabilities & Stockholders' Equity		
Current maturities, long-term debt	$ 1,443	$ 1,614
Accounts payable	8,104	23,945
Accrued expenses	15,211	46,846
Income taxes	2,104	—
Total current liabilities	$ 26,862	$ 72,405
Long-term obligations	15,009	185,605
Deferred income taxes	4,010	29,971
Total long-term liabilities	$ 19,019	$215,576
Total liabilities	$ 45,881	$287,981
Common stock and paid in capital	75,920	176,899
Retained earnings	45,848	60,554
Foreign currency translation		938
Less: Treasury stock at cost	274	687
Total shareholders' equity	$121,494	$237,704
Total liabilities & shareholders' equity	$167,375	$525,685

EXHIBIT 3 SUMMARY FINANCIAL INFORMATION FOR THE YEARS 1978–1987 (dollar figures in millions except per-share figures)

	1978	*1979*	*1980*	*1981*	*1982*	*1983*	*1984*	*1985*	*1986*	*1987*
Net sales	$46.9	$49.0	$52.2	$64.2	$67.4	$98.8	$205.7	$267.3	$297.4	$598.1
Net earnings	3.3	10.8	4.2	5.8	6.0	7.7	13.7	6.7	11.6	23.4
Total assets	28.6	39.2	37.1	45.9	48.2	61.3	157.2	160.2	167.4	525.7
Working capital	10.2	15.2	13.5	16.1	17.9	17.5	52.4	54.0	55.2	134.6
Long-term obligations	1.8	1.8	4.0	8.2	8.2	8.1	17.8	14.6	15.0	185.6
Stockholders' equity	20.6	25.6	25.0	29.0	32.9	37.8	113.9	115.8	121.5	237.7
Per share data										
Earnings per share (net)	$ 0.24	$ 0.80	$ 0.36	$ 0.54	$ 0.55	$ 0.70	$ 0.89	$ 0.42	$ 0.72	$ 1.15
Fully diluted										$ 1.12
Cash dividends per share	$ 0.10	$ 0.13	$ 0.15	$ 0.20	$ 0.24	$ 0.29	$ 0.40	$ 0.40	$ 0.40	$ 0.42
Market price of common stock										
High for the year	$ 2.125	$ 2.500	$ 2.375	$ 4.750	$ 5.875	$15.250	$ 17.250	$ 16.875	$ 16.375	$ 24.375
Low for the year	1.375	1.625	1.625	1.750	2.750	5.500	13.375	10.875	11.250	11.250
Stockholders' equity	1.50	2.12	2.34	2.68	3.00	3.42	7.05	7.15	7.49	10.80
Ratios										
Profit from continuing operations/net sale	7.1%	8.8%	8.2%	9.1%	8.9%	7.8%	5.6%	3.2%	3.9%	3.9%
Net sales/net assets	2.3×	1.9×	2.1×	2.2×	2.0×	2.6×	1.8×	2.3×	2.4×	2.5×
Equity/total liabilities	260.0%	190.0%	210.0%	170.0%	210.0%	160.0%	260.0%	260.0%	260.0%	83.0%
Long-term obligations/capital	8.0	6.6	13.8	22.0	20.0	17.6	13.5	11.2	11.0	43.8
Return on average equity	16	17	17	22	19	22	12	7	10	13
Price-earnings ratio (average of high & low price)	7.3×	6.4×	5.6×	6.0×	7.8×	14.8×	17.2×	33.0×	19.2×	15.5×

EXHIBIT 4 SELECTED STATISTICS OF COMPANIES IN THE FURNITURE INDUSTRY

			Five-Year Growth Rate					Beta	
Company	*Sales (millions)*	*Book Value*	*Earnings*	*Dividends*	*P/E Ratio**	*Yield**	*Debt/Capital Ratio*	*Levered*	*Unlevered*
Armstrong World	$2,365	$19.40	26.5%	6.5%	11.5×	2.4%	17%	1.40	1.28
Bassett Furniture	475	31.28	6.5	2.0	15.8	2.5	0	1.00	1.00
Dresher, Inc.	44	2.92	n.a.	n.a.	19.0	1.2	56	1.20	0.97
Flexsteel	156	8.05	7.5	11.0	12.7	2.7	9	0.80	0.76
Hon Industries	555	18.99	6.5	4.5	15.8	2.1	25	0.65	0.57
Ladd Furniture	387	5.49	n.a.	n.a.	13.7	1.1	29	1.25	1.09
La-Z-Boy Chair	487	8.97	15.0	13.0	13.0	2.2	30	0.80	0.69
Leggett & Platt	649	13.01	16.5	16.0	13.7	2.8	28	1.00	0.87
Miller, Herman	574	8.69	20.5	27.0	16.8	1.9	22	1.00	0.89
Mohasco	807	5.74	n.a.	17.5	11.3	1.2	14	1.25	1.16
Shelby Williams	160	30.68	20.0	48.0	19.1	1.3	26	1.00	0.88
Thomas Industries	322	17.11	8.5	11.0	11.2	1.2	21	1.00	0.90
Average			14.2%	15.7%	14.5×	1.9%	23%	1.03	0.92
Sleep Surface	598	10.8	11.5%	15.5%	16.3×	2.2%	41%	1.05	0.88

*Calculated on the average market price for the year.

Case 19

NATIONAL BANK OF LOS ANGELES

John Schultz, chief financial officer of the National Bank of Los Angeles (NBLA), sat down at his desk, putting in front of him the pile of material he had received that morning. It was August 10, 1988, but even the view over the Hollywood hills from his tenth-floor corner office did not catch his attention. He had just returned from a small seminar, hosted by the bank's CPA firm, covering a hot new topic: risk-based capital requirements.

Before going to the seminar, Mr. Schultz had read a few articles about the new capital requirements which were to be implemented by the regulatory authorities over the next few years. Even after the seminar, he was still not sure what the implications were for NBLA and how he should respond. Many large banks could have trouble meeting the new capital adequacy ratios agreed upon by the Group of Ten countries (Belgium, Canada, France, Germany, Italy, Japan, Netherlands, Sweden, Switzerland, United Kingdom, and the United States) and Luxembourg. NBLA's situation was challenging because it had had many problems in recent years, the most severe having been the write-off of more than $1.4 billion of Latin American debt in 1987. Mr. Schultz, however, felt that the loan portfolio had now been cleared of any significant bad loans. It was time to move forward.

NBLA's chairman of the board wanted a report with recommendations from Mr. Schultz within the week on the subject of capital adequacy, covering everything from geographic strategy, such as further expansion, to product strategy, including pricing and the elimination of any products. Mr. Schultz was also responsible for determining whether NBLA would meet the new capital adequacy ratios through future profit retention or whether outside capital would have to be obtained.

Prepared by Mr. William Epstein with the assistance of Mr. Richard Crawford.

NATIONAL BANK OF LOS ANGELES

Although not headquartered in New York, NBLA was considered a money center bank. As of December 31, 1987, it had total assets of $75.7 billion. (Exhibits 1 and 2 present recent financial statements.) Its size and global presence had made it a significant player in all the financial markets. Founded in 1905, the bank had grown rapidly serving the California market. In particular, the NBLA had a loyal base of diverse, middle-market customers. The service given to these companies was among the best in the industry.

As was common among other money center banks, NBLA's recent growth had come mainly from global expansion, both in terms of operations and international loans. (Exhibits 3 and 4 summarize the portfolio in 1986 and 1987.) Domestic loan demand had been sluggish; the industry thus jumped at the opportunity to finance developing countries at attractive rates of interest. This ultimately proved to be disastrous; NBLA was not the only bank to write off billions of dollars in Latin American debt. NBLA had significantly curtailed its international activity as the result of these problems and was considering expanding its presence in the western retail bank marketplace.

At the end of 1987, the Federal Reserve Bank's existing capital adequacy target was a minimum primary capital ratio of 5.50 percent and a total capital ratio of 6.00 percent. The calculation for NBLA is shown in Exhibit 5.

THE BASLE COMMITTEE

On December 10, 1987, the Basle Committee on Banking Regulations and Supervisory Practices (generally called the Basle Committee), a group composed of the central banks of the Group of Ten countries and Luxembourg, published for comment a framework for assessing the capital adequacy of international banking organizations. The need for a worldwide basis to measure banks' capital had arisen as a result of the uncertain economic conditions and a growing perception of the risk presented by off-balance sheet (OBS) products not previously subject to regulation. Furthermore, the lack of a uniform regulatory environment could give a bank an advantage in some markets but put it at a disadvantage in others.

In the United States, the Federal Reserve Board was especially concerned with the growing risks from member bank's off-balance sheet activities. The ten largest U.S. banks had standby letters of credit, interest rate swaps, and foreign exchange contracts, all off-balance sheet items, which represented almost 132 percent of their total assets. Predictably, because these off-balance sheet items were not included in the calculation of any capital adequacy ratios, the costs to the banks of providing such products were considered much less than traditional services appearing as balance sheet items and requiring the banks to maintain capital in support of those assets. The savings were at least in part passed along to the ultimate consumer, but the thin pricing that had developed for many OBS products was considered too small for the risk involved.

The regulatory bodies were also concerned with measuring the varying degrees of risk associated with a bank's assets. In the United States, all assets (treasury bills or international loans) were weighted equally in calculating capital adequacy ratios. This evaluation system had prompted many banks to reduce their liquidity, moving from investments in cash and government securities to loans and other higher risk investments, presumably with higher returns, in order to increase their return on assets. This possible lack of liquidity was a major concern to federal regulators, especially if a money center bank ran into problems.

A variety of ways of calculating capital adequacy were used elsewhere in the world and, partly as a result, the required level of acceptable capital varied widely. In some systems, banks appeared to operate with virtually no capital. Consequently, even the narrowest of spreads over the cost of funds and doing business could produce an acceptable return on equity. This condition put the banks headquartered in more stringent regulatory systems at a great competitive disadvantage. They could pass up the business, lower their profitability on equity, or upset their regulatory groups. Both the banks affected and their regulators began to press for more uniformity of approval.

The search was not an easy one. Not only did regulatory practices and philosophies differ among the major economic powers, but the purpose and function of the financial institutions differed, as did the nature of the ownership. Should a bank owned by a national government, for example, be required to have any capital at all? Should it be required to make a profit if its purpose was to maintain employment? What should be done with respect to doubtful loans in economic systems that do not permit bankruptcy but instead encourage borrowing from government-owned banks? It took extended and complex negotiations to agree on the framework of an approach. Even then the United States and the United Kingdom forced the issue by announcing the adoption of a joint approach without waiting for the other major players to have agreed in advance. Ultimately, the result was the Basle agreement.

The Basle agreement had three parts. The first, and most critical, was a common definition of capital. Because accounting methods varied from country to country, capital was divided into two tiers. The first tier was considered *core* capital, which was simply reported common shareholders' equity plus cumulative preferred stock up to 25% of core capital. By 1992, core capital had to be calculated net of all goodwill, and any new goodwill incurred subsequent to the adoption of the rules had to be deducted immediately. The second tier, called *supplementary* capital, included everything else in the capital structure, such as undisclosed reserves, general loan loss reserves, preferred stock above the core capital limit, and subordinated debt. This second tier was a compromise which allowed countries some flexibility in regulating their banks. Some rules that applied to supplementary capital were: Tier 2 capital was limited to 50 percent of net capital; subordinated debt could not account for more than half of secondary capital; the amount of loan loss reserves to be included would be limited to 1.25 percent of weighted risk assets by 1992; and, where banks were allowed to include the unrealized gains on equity securities in supplemental capital (such as in Japan), the gain would be discounted by 55 percent to reflect market volatility and tax liability.

The second part of the Basle agreement established a capital ratio standard. To ensure a minimum acceptable standard, the initial standard for first tier capital was set equal to the respective banks' 1987 core ratio. By 1990, core capital had to be at least 3.625 percent of risk-weighted assets (to be discussed below) and 4.00 percent by 1992. Total Tier 1 and Tier 2 had to be double these proportions, and the Federal Reserve indicated these would be minimum levels above which banks would be encouraged to operate.

The final part of the Basle accord established "risk weights" for both on- and off-balance sheet items. These weights ranged between 0 percent and 100 percent, with 100 percent the most risky. Each asset was assigned a weight based on the risk category it fell in. For example, cash was assigned a weight of 0 percent; commercial loans a weight of 100 percent. (The categories and weights to be applied to U.S. banks are outlined in Exhibits 6 and 7.) The sum of the weighted assets was the bank's risk-adjusted assets, to be used in calculating the capital adequacy ratio.

CONCLUSION

The Basle Committee's guidelines for capital adequacy had serious ramifications. NBLA was going to have to develop a new strategy. With continuing bank consolidation likely and with interstate banking being phased in over the next few years, Mr. Schultz wanted to be able to acquire other banks to take advantage of deregulation. The rule eliminating goodwill from the capital adequacy computation would make acquisitions more difficult for NBLA.

Of course, NBLA could always raise additional capital to effect its compliance and allow room for maneuver. NBLA had just issued an additional $500 million in perpetual floating rate preferred stock. This security offered corporate investors a significant tax advantage over debt of comparable quality. The average cost on NBLA's preferred, all of which was floating rate adjusted quarterly, was 9.07%. The lower yield at which these preferreds could be sold was particularly attractive to companies, such as NBLA, that were paying relatively low taxes. The use of preferred stock in such circumstances was considered to reduce the cost of capital to the issuer. The preferred stock could be counted as part of Tier 1 capital to a maximum of 25 percent of Tier 1 capital. Any residual amount could be counted as part of Tier 2 capital.

Common stock was another source of potential capital, although not an attractive one. The price of NBLA stock had dropped to a low of $25.62 in the weeks after the October 19, 1987 stock market crisis, less than half the high for the year of $62.00. The price had recovered somewhat in early 1988, however, and by April was trading in the range of $29.00 to $31.50, about 60 percent of the book value of $51.75 as of December 1987. The yield was approximately 11 percent on the current dividend of $3.40. NBLA's beta was 1.13. Book value had grown at a compound rate of 5 percent to 6 percent over the previous 10 years, but some analysts were forecasting a 19 percent to 29 percent growth over the next 5 years. The loss in 1987 complicated the interpretation of these forecasts, however.

Another alternative would be to reduce the size of the bank's assets through sale of loans and loan participations, especially of those types of assets whose sale would significantly reduce the capital requirements. Not only would this action shrink assets, but NBLA would be able to retain some of the spread. Depending on the type of transaction, the profit could either be recorded at the time of sale or over the remaining term of the loan. Mr. Schultz wondered, however, what the reaction would be of the bank's loyal middle-market customers when they discovered that NBLA had sold off their loans. Competition was intense in the California markets, and NBLA had been promoting itself as a reliable provider of business finance.

Finally, the allocation of assets could be altered or riskier products modified in order to accommodate the capital requirements. Higher pricing would help, but it was possible that some product lines might have to be dropped.

In order to address these two latter alternatives, Mr. Schultz would have to determine how profitable the various product lines were. Although he did not have the time before he was due to meet with the chairman to prepare a detailed study, he thought he could make a rough estimate of the capital costs of the major components of NBLA's capita. This information would allow him to estimate a weighted cost for each product to compare to that line's earnings rate.

The *real* short-term riskless rate had been running relatively high since 1981 compared to its long-run average. In 1981 and 1982, for example, the 30-day T-bill rate had returned almost 8 percent on a real basis. This figure had fallen to 2 percent by late 1987, but it was again rising in 1988. By mid-year, it was back to a real rate of 3 percent and still rising. By comparison, the real rate of return on the 30-day T-bill over the 1926–1987 period had been calculated to be only 0.4 percent.

The historic spread, 1926–1987, between the real short-term riskless rate and the return on common stocks was 6.6 percent (geometric mean) and 8.8 percent (arithmetic mean).

Mr. Schultz had a lot of important work that needed to be completed before he briefed the chairman. In order to project the bank's capital requirements, he first had an assistant prepare a listing (included as Exhibit 8) of all the bank's off-balance sheet instruments, as of December 31, 1987, which would be subject to risk adjustments. His assistant also provided Mr. Schultz with detail on the bank's investment securities as follows (in millions):

TABLE 1 National Bank of Los Angeles Tabulation of Investment Securities

	One Year or Less	*Greater than One Year*
U.S. & Agencies	$ 73	$7,098
State & Agencies	$226	$2,942
Foreign	$315	$1,758

Although the terms of the Basle agreement were not completely firm and the implementation not yet completely agreed by the several U.S. regulatory authorities, Mr. Schultz expected no significant changes following an early August vote of 5–1 by The Federal Reserve Board.

Case 19 National Bank of Los Angeles

EXHIBIT 1 BALANCE SHEET AS OF DECEMBER 31, 1986–1987 (millions of dollars)

	1986	*1987*
Assets		
Required reserves with the Federal Reserve Banks	$ 880	$ 1,400
Cash and due from domestic banks	2,564	4,574
Cash and due from foreign banks	3,717	5,407
Federal funds sold to domestic banks	1,358	2,525

Case 19 National Bank of Los Angeles

EXHIBIT 1 ***(continued)***

	1986	*1987*
U.S. short-term securities under resale agreement	1,192	2,218
Trading account assets (net)		
U.S. and agency issues of one year or less to maturity	1,828	1,095
U.S. and agency issues of greater than one year to maturity	601	455
Investment securities	9,344	12,412
Loans	49,281	62,250
Less: Allowance for loan losses	(836)	(2,585)
Net loans	$48,445	$59,665
Premises and equipment	593	1,321
Due from customers on acceptance	2,315	1,901
Accrued interest receivable	823	1,371
Other assets*	2,046	3,392
Total assets	$75,706	$97,736
Liabilities		
Total deposits	$48,818	$69,386
Short-term debt	16,679	17,089
Acceptances outstanding	2,333	1,906
Accounts payable and accruals	895	1,564
Other liabilities	1,260	1,443
Long-term subordinated debt**	773	1,263
Other long-term debt	1,048	1,334
Total liabilities	$71,806	$93,985
Stockholders' Equity		
Preferred stock	$ 388	$ 880
Common stock	760	875
Capital surplus	476	1,025
Accumulated translation adjustment	(5)	23
Retained earnings	2,299	966
Treasury stock	(18)	(18)
Total stockholders' equity	$ 3,900	$ 3,751
Total liabilities and stockholders' equity	$75,706	$97,736

*Includes $500 of goodwill.
**Qualifies as primary capital.

Case 19 National Bank of Los Angeles

EXHIBIT 2 INCOME STATEMENT FOR THE YEARS ENDING DECEMBER 31, 1985–1987 (millions of dollars except per share figures)

	1985	*1986*	*1987*
Interest Income			
Loans	$5,068	$4,662	$5,221
Investment securities	465	530	879
Trading account assets (net)	161	159	132
Federal funds sold and securities under resale agreements	150	165	323
Deposits in other banks	260	195	336
Total interest income	$6,104	$5,711	$6,891
Interest Expense			
Deposits	$2,638	$2,223	$2,911
Short-term borrowings	1,347	1,198	1,289
Long-term debt	154	142	176
Total interest expense	$4,139	$3,563	$4,376
Net interest income	$1,965	$2,148	$2,515
Provision for loan losses	$ 352	$ 549	$1,865
Net interest income after provision for loan losses	$1,613	$1,599	$ 650
Noninterest Income			
Trust fees and commissions	$ 105	$ 125	$ 197
Fees for other banking services	511	546	768
Trading account profits	29	59	93
Foreign exchange trading profits	127	129	191
Investment securities gains	161	186	71
Settlement of pension obligation	—	—	158
Other income	28	104	75
Total noninterest income	$ 961	$1,149	$1,553
Noninterest Expense			
Salaries	$ 775	$ 870	$1,188
Employee benefits	176	210	230
Occupancy expense	248	249	314
Equipment expense	158	167	222
Other expenses	558	638	1,142
Total noninterest expense	$1,915	$2,134	$3,096
Income (loss) before taxes	$ 659	$ 614	$ (893)
Income taxes	170	111	175
Net income	$ 489	$ 503	$(1,068)

Case 19 National Bank of Los Angeles

EXHIBIT 2 ***(continued)***

	1985	*1986*	*1987*
Earnings per share	$9.16	$9.46	$(20.85)
Dividends per share	$3.10	$3.25	$3.40
Market price range per share	$41.25–58.00	$51.00–70.50	$25.62–62.00
Price–earnings ratio	4–6×	5–7×	n.m.
Book value per share	$57.00	$63.80	$51.75

Case 19 National Bank of Los Angeles

EXHIBIT 3 LOAN PORTFOLIO COMPOSITION AS OF DECEMBER 31 (in millions)

	1986	*1987*
Domestic Loans		
Commercial and financial	$20,633	$23,786
Real estate:		
Construction	2,564	4,936
Commercial mortgages	2,896	4,350
Residential mortgages	2,696	4,264
Consumer loans	5,266	7,121
Other	255	616
Total	$34,310	$45,073
International Loans		
Commercial and financial	$ 6,283	$ 7,613
Banks and other financial institutions	2,783	3,101
Governments and official institutions	3,493	2,980
Residential mortgages	1,101	2,278
Other	1,311	1,205
Total	$14,971	$17,177

Case 19 National Bank of Los Angeles

EXHIBIT 4 GEOGRAPHIC DISTRIBUTION OF EARNINGS (millions of dollars)

	Total Revenue	*Income Before Taxes*	*Net Income*
1985			
International:			
Europe	$ 915	$ 68	$ 50
Latin America	680	104	77
Asia and Pacific	439	(19)	(14)
Middle East and Africa	143	9	7
North America	164	36	27
Total International	$2,341	$ 198	$ 147
United States	$4,724	$ 461	$ 342
Total	$7,065	$ 659	$ 489
1986			
International:			
Europe	$ 859	$ 116	$ 96
Latin America	594	62	51
Asia and Pacific	315	0	0
Middle East and Africa	124	(13)	(11)
North America	123	(5)	(4)
Total International	$2,015	$ 160	$ 132
United States	$4,845	$ 454	$ 371
Total	$6,860	$ 614	$ 503
1987			
International:			
Europe	$ 965	$ 273	$ 214
Latin America	503	(1,505)	(1,490)
Asia and Pacific	318	(107)	(105)
Middle East and Africa	109	(134)	(130)
North America	120	(2)	(2)
Total International	$2,015	$(1,475)	$(1,513)
United States	$6,429	$ 582	$ 445
Total	$8,444	$ (893)	$(1,068)

Case 19 National Bank of Los Angeles

EXHIBIT 5 CAPITAL RATIO CALCULATION, 1987 FEDERAL RESERVE BOARD GUIDELINES

	December 31	
	1986	*1987*
Common stockholders' equity	$3,512	$2,871
Preferred stock	388	880
Mandatory convertible securities	773	1,263
Allowance for loan losses	836	2,585
Primary capital	$5,509	$7,599
Secondary capital*	980	1,254
Total capital	$6,489	$8,853
Primary capital as a percent of gross assets**	7.20%	7.58%
Total capital as a percent of gross assets**	8.48%	8.82%

*Includes long-term debt meeting certain maturity and preference ranking criteria.
**Gross assets are total assets plus the allowance for loan losses.

Note: Cost of Funds

1. Secondary capital currently had an average cost of 9.3%. Approximately 30% was fixed rate; the remainder was floating rate.
2. Mandatory convertible securities had an average current cost of 8.7%. About 30% was fixed rate; the remainder was floating rate.
3. All of the preferred stock was floating rate preferred whose rate was reset quarterly. Its current cost was 9.07%.

EXHIBIT 6 ON-BALANCE SHEET CONVERSION WEIGHTS FOR U.S. BANKS

Risk weight	*Instruments*
0%	—Cash and currency items —All balances with Federal Reserve Banks —Securities (direct obligations) issued by U.S. government or its agencies with maturities of one year or less
10%	—Securities issued by U.S. government or its agencies with maturities of over one year and all other claims on the U.S. government or its agencies —Securities and other claims guaranteed by the U.S. government or its agencies —Portions of loans and other assets collateralized by securities issued by, or guaranteed by, the U.S. government or its agencies or by cash on deposit in the lending institution —Federal Reserve bank stock
20%	—All claims on domestic depository institutions —Claims on foreign banks with an original maturity of one year or less —Claims guaranteed by, or backed by the full faith and credit of, domestic depository institutions —Local currency claims on foreign central governments to the extent the bank has local currency liabilities in the foreign country —Cash items in the process of collection —Securities and other claims on, or guaranteed by U.S. government-sponsored agencies —Portions of loans and other assets collateralized by securities issued by, or guaranteed by, government-sponsored agencies —General obligation claims on, and claims guaranteed by, U.S., state, and local governments that are secured by the full faith and credit of the state or local taxing —Claims on official multilateral lending institutions or regional development institutions in which the U.S. government is a shareholder or a contributing member
50%	—Revenue bonds or similar obligations, including loans and leases, that are obligations of U.S., state, or local governments, but for which the government entity is committed to repay the debt only out of revenues from the facilities financed —Credit equivalent amounts of interest rate and foreign exchange rate related contracts, except for those assigned to a lower risk category —First mortgages on 1–4 family domestic residential property
100%	—All other claims on private obligors —All other assets

Source: Alexander G. Cole. "Risk-based Capital: A Loan and Credit Officer's Primer." *The Journal of Commercial Bank Lending* (August 1988), 4–21. Adjusted for subsequent decisions of the Federal Reserve Board.

Case 19 National Bank of Los Angeles

EXHIBIT 7 OFF-BALANCE SHEET CONVERSION WEIGHTS

Risk Weight	*Instruments*
100%	—Direct credit substitutes and acceptances —Sale and repurchase agreements and asset sales with recourse, where the credit risk remains with the bank —Forward agreements to purchase assets, including financing facilities with certain drawdown —Acquisitions of risk participations in bankers acceptances and participations in direct credit substitutes
50%	—Certain transaction-related contingent items, i.e., performance bonds, warranties and standby letters of credit related to particular transactions —Note issuance facilities and revolving underwriting facilities —Unused commitments with a maturity* exceeding one year, including commercial credit lines.
20%	—Short-term self-liquidating trade-related contingencies, i.e., documentary credits collateralized by the underlying shipments
5%	—Exchange rate contracts with maturities of one year or more
1%	—Exchange rate contracts with maturities of less than one year
0.5%	—Interest rate contracts with maturities of one year or more
0%	—Interest rate contracts with maturities of less than one year —Unused commitments with maturities* of less than one year, or which can be canceled at any time.

*After 1992, the original maturity rather than the remaining maturity will be the determining criterion.

Source: Alexander G. Cole. "Risk-based Capital: A Loan and Credit Officer's Primer." *The Journal of Commercial Bank Lending* (August 1988), 4–21. Adjusted for subsequent decisions of the Federal Reserve Board.

EXHIBIT 8 OFF-BALANCE SHEET ITEMS AS OF DECEMBER 31, 1987 (billions of dollars)

Instrument	*Amount*	*Typical Pricing (annualized)*
Standby letters of credit	$ 12.2	25 to 50 bp; as low as 10 bp for large, 3A companies
Long-term unused commercial lines of credit	41.0	Same as standby letters of credit
Commerical trade letters of credit	1.6	50 to 75 bp
Long-term exchange rate contracts	85.0	A positive margin if possible; a negative if necessary
Short-term exchange rate contracts	152.6	Same as long-term exchange rate contracts
Long-term interest rate contracts*	102.4	20 to 25 bp

*Such as interest rate and currency swaps, future rate agreements, forward interest rate contracts, and interest rate caps and floors.
Note: A basis point (bp) equals 0.01 percent annual interest; 100 bp equals 1 percent.

Case 20

CFS ASSOCIATES, INC.

In January 1988, Mr. Jack Alexander was preparing a presentation to Mr. C. F. Sargent, president of CFS Associates, Inc., regarding a new program on "Japanese Management Techniques" (JMT). Mr. Alexander, the company's vice president in charge of program development, had developed three alternative strategies for producing and promoting the new program. The alternatives did not require the same investment amounts, and they also yielded different profits and cash flows. He wanted to rank them in order of attractiveness and select which to recommend to Mr. Sargent.

Mr. Sargent had founded the company ten years earlier while he was a professor of business policy at a major midwestern university. The company's first products had been the printed manuals and visual aids that Mr. Sargent had used in his highly popular classes at the university and in management training programs he had conducted for corporate clients. He had long been interested in cross-border and cross-cultural management problems, so many of his activities had an international slant to them. In 1980, Mr. Sargent resigned from the university to devote full time to his new company. Mr. Alexander, who had extensive experience in educational publication including the production of audiovisual materials, had been engaged at that time to help develop and produce more elaborate executive training programs.

The business expanded rapidly and was soon producing a series of self-contained courses designed to be administered by the purchasing company's own staff. These complete training packages included video tapes, audio tapes, training manuals for instructors, and workbooks, cases, and other material for participants. In 1987, the company had offered forty-two different training programs of this type. In addition, CFS itself conducted contract in-house and public programs and courses. Sales had reached over $5 million, and the level of profits was attractive.

Although Mr. Sargent had long been an advocate of the importance of studying Japanese management, it was only in late 1987 that he and Mr. Alexander had time to begin the development of a major training activity with a focus on that subject. Initially, JMT would be a proprietary offering by CFS on its premises. Self-contained courses might be spun off later.

The consultants were sure the proposed program would be a big seller. The impressive strength of the Japanese economy, even in the face of the yen's reaching post–World War II highs, ensured continued interest in Japanese techniques. The level of Japanese investment in the United States created new interest in the topic. Books on Japan and Japanese management practices continued to be on best-seller lists.

CFS Associates, planning to capitalize on these developments, had made arrangements for the authors of several of the current best sellers to prepare material and participate in the development of video content for the JMT program. Mr. Alexander had spent $18,000 over the past six months on a feasibility study and in negotiating arrangements with various outside authorities to participate and for the use of their material. CFS clients had been enthusiastic about the proposal, and several had placed firm orders for places in the first JMT offerings.

Although Mr. Alexander was confident of the success of the JMT program, he had not yet decided on the production and marketing strategies to be used to achieve maximum profitability of the program for CFS. After the appropriate consultations with other staff members and outside suppliers, he had compiled estimates of costs and revenues for each of the three most likely strategies. His task now was to recommend which one should be adopted.

CFS Associates used several different methods of evaluating investments in capital equipment and in proposed programs. Mr. Alexander did not have a strong financial background and thus did not feel comfortable calculating elaborate returns. Because they involved nothing more than simple arithmetic, he could calculate the *average rate of return* and *payback*. The measure of payback was simply the number of years it took to recover the initial investment from the cash flows (although some more conservative analysts used profits). The average rate of return was computed as

$$\text{ARR} = \frac{\text{Average Annual Net Income after Taxes}}{\left[\dfrac{\text{Original Cost} + \text{Salvage Value}}{2}\right]}$$

Mr. Alexander's calculations indicated that all three strategies would meet or exceed the firm's required 20 percent average rate of return and 7-year payback. Because finance was not his area of expertise, Mr. Alexander planned to turn further calculations over to the controller. (Exhibit 1 summarizes the estimates of sales, marketing costs, and depreciation expenses for the three JMT strategies.) Nevertheless, he would have to be able to analyze the controller's calculations in order to make a recommendation to Mr. Sargent and be able to defend it.

STRATEGY I

New programs were generally estimated to have a sales life of 10 years. Experienced with similar programs indicated that a moderate marketing effort throughout the 10-year life would result in peak sales occurring during the 4th or 5th year, with sharply declining sales following in later years. Strategy I would therefore involve a strong marketing effort in years 1 to 5 in order to saturate the market during this period. The program would then be harvested in years 6 to 10, with no further expenditures made on marketing. The out-of-pocket cost for the program (including royalties to the authors) would be budgeted at the 50 percent of sales CFS experienced on average for its courses.

This alternative required an initial investment of $225,000 in building modifications and equipment in order to accommodate the special instructional techniques that were part of the JMT course design. Development costs of $235,000 included engineering, writing, and design costs incurred in production of the program. These costs were treated as current expenses by CFS's accountants and could be deducted from taxable income in the year they were incurred. CFS's financial analysis considered the after-tax development costs as being part of the investment in a project.

Working capital, in the form of materials, videos, royalty payments, advertising and promotion, and accounts receivable, would amount to 20 percent of sales. As with the other two strategies, the working capital would be recovered as sales declined, with any residual being recovered at the end of the 10-year period.

STRATEGY II

Mr. Alexander had found that an alternative marketing strategy was to price a program lower in the initial years and, in the 5th or 6th year, to put on an additional marketing effort for a "new and improved" version. This alternative's success depended for its effectiveness on reducing the level of competition by cutting back on the initial profits. Profits from the longer life could compensate for the lower profits initially. This strategy required the same investment in development and facilities that Strategy I did, but it would require a higher level of working capital, 25 percent of sales. Mr. Alexander estimated that total dollar sales would be the same for both programs on the assumption that cutting price would at least be offset by higher unit volume in the earlier years. For Strategy II, Mr. Alexander estimated that the contribution after out-of-pocket costs would be only 40 percent rather than the standard 50 percent.

STRATEGY III

CFS was planning to increase its use of interactive video-computer learning techniques. These were expensive training programs to develop, but Mr. Alexander thought the JMT course would lend itself to these techniques and would be greatly enhanced by them. If successful, a program using these techniques would be an industry leader, attracting strong sales and greatly enhancing the reputation of CFS as an educational innovator. Strong sales could be expected until the very end of the 10-year program life.

Strategy III required $275,000 for physical investment, slightly more than the other strategies because of the capital facilities and equipment needed. Initial developmental costs would be particularly high, amounting to $435,000, which could be expensed in the year incurred. Working capital would be 25 percent of sales.

The investment cost of this strategy did not include an allocation for the part of the required computer capacity that could be obtained by using equipment CFS already owned. The computer, which was 2 years old, had a current book value of $80,000. It was being depreciated over the remaining 5 years of its 7-year life by the double-declining-balance method CFS used for depreciation. At the moment, this computer was only being used at 50 percent of its capacity, so half of its depreciation charges were being assigned to general corporate overhead. The JMT program could utilize the spare capacity, although over the next several years, it was expected that other new programs would use the capacity if the JMT program did not.

OTHER ISSUES

Mr. Alexander guessed that $6,000 of CFS's total administrative overhead of $200,000 would be assigned to the Japanese program. He wondered whether this was an accurate assessment, because it did not vary according to the revenues of the program. CFS had a 34 percent marginal tax rate and used double-declining depreciation (10-year average life for these projects) with no salvage values and with the half-year convention for depreciation in the first year. Mr. Sargent had established a 15 percent target as the company's capital cost, but he was willing to adjust the target depending on the special risk considerations a project might have.

Mr. Alexander had asked the controller to check his calculations of payback and average rate of return as well as work out the internal rate of return, the net present values, and an NPV index for the alternatives.

Case 20 CFS Associates, Inc.

EXHIBIT 1 PROJECTED SALES AND MARKETING AND DEPRECIATION EXPENSES FOR "JAPANESE MANAGEMENT TECHNIQUES" (in thousands of dollars)

Year	*I*	*II*	*III*
Projected Sales			
1	$275	$275	$300
2	450	450	400
3	660	660	600
4	655	660	650
5	475	660	700
6	200	660	750
7	100	660	800
8	100	660	800
9	100	625	650
10	50	375	400
Projected Marketing Expenses			
1	$ 50	$ 50	$ 75
2	50	50	75
3	50	50	50
4	50	50	50
5	50	50	50
6	0	75	75
7	0	75	75
8	0	75	75
9	0	50	40
10	0	35	25
Projected Depreciation Expenses			
1	$ 22.5	$ 22.5	$ 27.5
2	40.5	40.5	49.5
3	32.4	32.4	39.6
4	25.9	25.9	31.7
5	17.3	17.3	21.0
6	17.3	17.3	21.0
7	17.3	17.3	21.0
8	17.3	17.3	21.0
9	17.3	17.3	21.0
10	17.3	17.3	21.0

Case 21

ALUMINUM FABRICATING COMPANY

In September of 1988, Jerry Anderson, assistant comptroller of the Aluminum Fabricating Company (AFC), was preparing a financial analysis of the six capital projects that were to be reviewed by the budget committee during the coming week. Jerry had joined AFC the previous month after completing an MBA program at a small midwestern university. This financial analysis was the first real assignment he had received from AFC's comptroller, David Stiles, and Jerry wanted to make a good impression.

AFC

AFC was founded in 1962 as a fabricator of specialized aluminum hardware and molding parts for the auto industry. In its factory in Flint, Michigan, AFC produced aluminum parts by both the stamping and extrusion processes. Once formed, the parts were usually polished and anodized before shipment to the customers. (Anodization is a process whereby aluminum parts are electrochemically treated to obtain a corrosion-resistant finish.) In the late 1970s, the company began to diversify in an attempt to become less dependent on the cyclical auto industry. By 1988 it was fabricating parts for aluminum windows, ladders, and industrial lighting fixtures, as well as parts for several consumer products. In all, the company produced more than 800 different parts, over half of which were for nonautomotive customers.

As part of the capital budgeting procedure, all departments at AFC were required to submit a capital expenditure proposal for projects costing over $20,000. These proposals included justification and description of the project, as well as details on the projected costs and revenues. The comptroller's office reviewed these proposals and prepared a financial analysis of each project. The budget committee (which consisted of AFC's president, treasurer, director of operations, and director of research and development) relied heavily on these financial analyses in making their capital expenditure decisions.

Three pairs of mutually exclusive capital projects had been submitted for review at the September meeting of the budget committee: two proposals for the production of new parts, two proposals for the purchase of a new extrusion press, and two alternatives for the replacement of a stamping press.

PRODUCTION OF NEW PARTS

The first set of projects required AFC to choose between two orders they had received for the production of extruded parts. Because their extrusion presses were near capacity and new equipment could not be installed in time to meet the contract deadline, only one of these projects could be accepted.

The first order, from the Tade Corporation, called for the production of a special part for a line of chainsaws. Tade was a new customer to AFC and had the potential of becoming a major source of business. Although the Tade project appeared to be quite lucrative in the long run, the contract called for the delivery of the parts to be spread over a 3-year period, with most of the sales being recorded in the final year.

The other order was from one of AFC's largest nonautomotive customers, the Wilson Electric Company. Wilson needed a new component part on an urgent basis. The part could be produced easily and would provide a steady cash flow over the 3-year contract. Although Wilson had been a good customer for the last 12 years, they had recently switched several of their components from aluminum to plastic, and orders from the Wilson Company had declined 15 percent during the last 2 years.

The projected sales for the two projects were as follows:

Year	*1*	*2*	*3*
Tade	$30,000	$40,000	$110,000
Wilson	55,000	55,000	55,000

Both projects were expected to have start-up costs of $13,000 and require a $16,000 investment in new equipment. Costs of materials and labor for extrusion projects were estimated at 65 percent of sales, and administrative costs at 5 percent of sales. The start-up costs would be expensed for tax purposes at the time incurred.

EXTRUSION PRESS

The second pair of projects involved the purchase of a new extrusion press. AFC had been forced to turn down several contracts recently because it lacked sufficient extrusion capacity. The major point of debate was over the size of a new press. A small press would have a relatively low initial cost and would enable AFC to fill most of the orders it currently received. A larger press, although costing considerably more, would allow AFC to meet all its current orders as well as possibly expand its product line by producing the larger parts used in several consumer products. In this way, it was argued, a larger press would help the company further reduce reliance on the beleaguered auto industry, which was experiencing one of its worst years ever.

The small press would handle aluminum billets up to 4 inches in diameter and would cost $650,000, installed. This press was expected to produce sales of $750,000 a year for a 10-year life, at the end of which it would have a salvage value of $20,000. The larger press had an installed cost of $1.0 million and could accept billets up to 8 inches in diameter. This press was expected to produce annual sales of $1,075,000 for the next 10 years and have a salvage value of $45,000 at the end of this period.

AFC's management knew that some of the sales being attributed to the new presses would come from parts that would otherwise have been produced on AFC's current extrusion presses. The resulting reduction in sales for the current presses was expected to be $100,000 per year for the remaining 7 years of their estimated life. As with all extrusion projects, labor and materials for the new presses were estimated at 65 percent of sales and administrative costs at 5 percent of sales.

REPLACEMENT OF STAMPING PRESS

The final project was the selection of one of two options for replacing an old stamping press which had been proposed because of the rapidly rising repair costs for the old machine and the greatly improved efficiency of two new types of presses that had recently come on the market. The old press had been fully depreciated and was estimated to have a salvage value of $1,000.

The two replacement options differed primarily in service life and cost of the presses. The first would cost $65,000, installed, and was expected to last 5 years, to produce annual savings of $28,000, and to have a salvage value of $5,000 at the end of 5 years. The alternative press had an installed cost of $90,000 and an expected life of 10 years. Its annual savings were also estimated to be $28,000 per year and it would have the same $5,000 salvage value at the end of 10 years as the first press.

As Jerry started to prepare his analysis, he recalled that David Stiles had told him that the company typically calculated both payback and net present value in evaluating capital projects. AFC was currently using a 15 percent hurdle rate for all projects and its effective tax rate was 34 percent.

The company calculated depreciation allowances using the 200 percent declining-balance method, as required by the Tax Reform Act of 1986. Salvage proceeds in excess of book value at the time of salvage were taxed at income tax rates. The four presses under consideration were classified as 7-year property, while the equipment needed for the production of new parts was classified as 3-year property. The depreciation schedules for the assets were the following:

Percent of Investment Recovered in Year under 200% Declining-balance Method

Year	*Property Class* 3-year	7-year
1	66.7%	28.6%
2	16.7	20.5
3	16.6	14.5
4	—	9.1
5	—	9.1
6	—	9.1
7	—	9.1

After applying AFC's criteria to the six projects, Jerry began to wonder if calculating payback and net present value were the best methods with which to make the analysis. He thought that perhaps also using internal rate of return and profitability index measures, as had been done in his MBA program, might be useful to help rank these capital projects.

Case 22

THE DIMMESDALE BUILDING

"Well, there are the numbers," Ms. Pearl Prynne said to herself as she put down the sheets of printout she had generated from her computer. "Now all I have to do is to make sense out of them so that I can explain them to Mother."

Mrs. Hester Prynne, Pearl's mother, was a prominent actress of substantial means who personally managed a significant portion of her investments. She had been greatly alarmed by the performance of the stockmarket in the two years following the "crash" of October 1987. Despite the market's having recovered most of the ground it had lost, a high degree of volatility persisted, culminating in another sharp drop in October 1989. Mrs. Prynne was also troubled by the volatile interest rates, which had whipsawed up and down displaying the same type of instability the stockmarket had shown.

In recent months, as a result, Mrs. Prynne had begun to wonder about the investment strategy she had followed for years. It had been her practice to allocate her portfolio one-third to stocks, one-third to United States government (or agency) bonds, and one-third to tax-free municipal bonds. Recently she had been reading articles that suggested real estate was an investment vehicle that had most consistently stayed ahead of, or at least kept pace with, inflation. Other articles, however, cautioned that the demographics were not favorable to real estate investments during the 1990s, arguing that the constant-dollar value of real property was likely to drop during the decade.

The community in which Mrs. Prynne lived between engagements, Charlottesville, Virginia, seemed unlikely to be affected by these adversities. A university community with excellent professional services, reasonable amenities, and satisfactory transportation connections to Washington, D.C., and New York, it was slated to have continued growth during the decade as demand for education rose and its reputation as a retirement location attracted affluent new residents. In recent years, real estate appreciation in the area had averaged five percent but had been much greater on certain properties. Mrs. Prynne therefore decided to look for opportunities to invest in local real estate.

Furthermore, as an individual subject to the Alternative Minimum Tax, "passive losses" of real estate limited partnerships had few benefits for her. She wanted to be an "active manager," within the meaning of the tax law, for any real estate investment. That requirement would dictate a local investment, probably in commercial office buildings or rental apartments. Mrs. Prynne let it be known among the real estate brokers that she was prepared to invest if the proper opportunity presented itself.

In early November, Roger Chillingworth, a real estate dealer specializing in commercial real estate, called Mrs. Prynne to say that he had found an exciting opportunity, the Dimmesdale Building in downtown Charlottesville. Over the phone, Mr. Chillingworth indicated that the building could probably be purchased for somewhat less than the $550,000 asking price. It had an assumable mortgage with an interest rate of 70 percent of prime, which was currently 11.5 percent. Although the rate was floating, Mr. Chillingworth said that the monthly payments were fixed at $5,653.28. If the prime rate changed, the mix of principal and interest would change and the duration of the loan would be adjusted to compensate.

Mrs. Prynne thought the idea was worth investigating, so she visited the building and collected a variety of information from Mr.

This case was prepared by Professor James C. Dunstan with the assistance of individuals who wish to remain anonymous. Data have been changed to protect confidential information without altering the nature of the managerial decision.

Chillingworth. By that time, it was close enough to the Thanksgiving break that she decided to wait until her daughter, who was currently concentrating in finance in the second year of her MBA program at a respectable business school, could help with the analysis.

The Dimmesdale Building, Mrs. Prynne found, had originally been built in the 1920s as an automobile dealership for one of the most luxurious brands, in the days when dealerships tended to look like banks. With the passage of time, the dealers found downtown locations very inconvenient for their customers, and all of them had moved to outlying locations. The building had been underutilized for years.

In 1981, Arthur Dimmesdale, the scion of a prominent local family and a recent graduate of architecture school, persuaded his family that the building could be converted into first-class office space and put the Dimmesdale name on the map, so to speak. The building was well located for this purpose, close to the city and county legal center, adjacent to a parking garage, and near the main offices of the three major banks in the city.

The family bought the building, and Mr. Dimmesdale went to work gutting the building and installing large, spacious office suites. The outside was modernized and refreshed, presenting an appropriately impressive exterior. Because of the urban renewal aspect of the project, $650,000 of the cost was covered by the issuance of a municipal tax-free bond held by a local bank. The $100,000 of equity was provided by Mr. Dimmesdale and his family through a limited partnership of which Mr. Dimmesdale was the general partner.

Unfortunately, the financial results were not as satisfactory as the architectural ones. In each of the three years, the limited partners had been required to invest further cash because the debt service and operating expenses had exceeded the rental revenue. The partners had thus voted to sell the building, and Mr. Dimmesdale had given Mr. Chillingworth a six-month exclusive on marketing it.

Although Mr. Chillingworth indicated the building had a rent roll potential of $70,000, Mrs. Prynne thought that a $65,000 figure looked more likely for 1990, after allowing for a three percent vacancy. Operating expenses, excluding interest and depreciation, were running $19,000. Considering the recent renovations, which had had time to age sufficiently that any major problems should have already shown up, it was unlikely that significant maintenance expenditures should be required other than those allowed for in the budget.

For simplicity's sake, Mrs. Prynne assumed that she would take possession January 1, 1990, with the loan payment schedule as listed in Exhibit 1, for a price of no more than $550,000 (equity cash of $66,000). The land in the transaction would be valued at $68,000; the remainder of the price ($482,000) would be depreciated over 31.5 years at $15,302 a year. Mrs. Prynne presumed she would own the building herself and as an active manager be able to write off any losses against her other income. Her marginal tax rate was 28 percent, although the future tax rates were extremely uncertain. President Bush had been unsuccessful in obtaining a special, lower rate for capital gains, which were taxed the same as income under the existing rules. Likewise, the congressional proposal that the marginal tax rate should be raised to 33 percent had not been passed. It appeared that both positions would again be promoted in 1990.

On the Friday after Thanksgiving, Pearl Prynne reviewed this information with her mother and then sat down to analyze the data. The complexity of the situation was greater than she had initially expected, so she constructed a computer model that would enable her to test different analytic approaches and different assumptions about the future. Exhibit 2 shows the results using Mr. Chillingworth's assumptions plus one of Pearl's own, that the building could be sold five years hence at the same price her mother paid for it.

First, Pearl constructed a statement showing the taxable income from the building. In Case 1, she constructed a simple operating cash flow from the building, which showed a net present value of $22,513 at a discount rate of 20 percent. Pearl thought this was a reasonable rate given the other investment opportunities her mother had and the risk of the project.

The results from other methods were not as attractive. Case 2 was similar to Case 1 but allowed for the cash requirements to service the principal on the debt. Pearl discovered that her mother would have to invest considerable cash to cover the debt service, which would result in a negative present value of almost $40,000. In Case 3, Pearl took a "free cash flow, total value" approach, using a weighted cost of capital (based on a capital value equal to the cost of the property) to calculate a weighted rate appropriate for each year's "unlevered" flows. The results of this analysis looked even worse, a negative figure of $103,000.

The fourth case differed from the third in using actual taxes paid rather than assessing taxes on a pro forma basis on the earnings-before-interest and taxes figure. This case still produced a negative value, however, of $68,000. The final case, based on free cash flow but deducting principal payments each year, was less negative. It showed a present value loss of $22,000.

The variation in present values amazed Pearl because she had been taught that only minor variations should occur even if she used different valuation approaches, provided she kept her assumptions constant. Moreover, rather than confuse her mother, Pearl wanted to select the one most realistic method to discuss with her.

Although many of the results she had developed were negative, they had been based on static assumptions that were conservative. Perhaps they had been too conservative. She wondered how significant the growth in the sales price or the rent roll would be. In particular, she wanted to learn whether there were any directions the negotiations might take that would enhance the project's attractiveness.

Case 22 The Dimmesdale Building

EXHIBIT 1 SCHEDULE OF DEBT PAYMENTS

Year	*Month*	*Interest*	*Princ Pmt*	*Princ BOM*	*Princ EOM*
1	1	$3,246.83	$2,406.45	$484,000.00	$481,593.55
	2	3,230.69	2,422.59	481,593.55	479,170.96
	3	3,214.44	2,438.84	479,170.96	476,732.12
	4	3,198.08	2,455.20	476,732.12	474,276.92
	5	3,181.61	2,471.67	474,276.92	471,805.25
	6	3,165.03	2,488.25	471,805.25	469,316.99
	7	3,148.33	2,504.95	469,316.99	466,812.05
	8	3,131.53	2,521.75	466,812.05	464,290.30
	9	3,114.61	2,538.67	464,290.30	461,751.63
	10	3,097.58	2,555.70	461,751.63	459,195.94
	11	3,080.44	2,572.84	459,195.94	456,623.10
	12	3,063.18	2,590.10	456,623.10	454,033.00
2	1	3,045.80	2,607.48	454,033.00	451,425.52
	2	3,028.31	2,624.97	451,425.52	448,800.56
	3	3,010.70	2,642.58	448,800.56	446,157.98
	4	2,992.98	2,660.30	446,157.98	443,497.68
	5	2,975.13	2,678.15	443,497.68	440,819.53
	6	2,957.16	2,696.12	440,819.53	438,123.41
	7	2,939.08	2,714.20	438,123.41	435,409.21
	8	2,920.87	2,732.41	435,409.21	432,676.80
	9	2,902.54	2,750.74	432,676.80	429,926.06
	10	2,884.09	2,769.19	429,926.06	427,156.87
	11	2,865.51	2,787.77	427,156.87	424,369.10
	12	2,846.81	2,806.47	424,369.10	421,562.63
3	1	2,827.98	2,825.30	421,562.63	418,737.33
	2	2,809.03	2,844.25	418,737.33	415,893.08
	3	2,789.95	2,863.33	415,893.08	413,029.75
	4	2,770.74	2,882.54	413,029.75	410,147.21

Case 22 The Dimmesdale Building

EXHIBIT 1 (*continued*)

Year	*Month*	*Interest*	*Princ Pmt*	*Princ BOM*	*Princ EOM*
	5	2,751.40	2,901.88	410,147.21	407,245.33
	6	2,731.94	2,921.34	407,245.33	404,323.99
	7	2,712.34	2,940.94	404,323.99	401,383.05
	8	2,692.61	2,960.67	401,383.05	398,422.38
	9	2,672.75	2,980.53	398,422.38	395,441.85
	10	2,652.76	3,000.52	395,441.85	392,441.33
	11	2,632.63	3,020.65	392,441.33	389,420.67
	12	2,612.36	3,040.92	389,420.67	386,379.76
4	1	2,591.96	3,061.32	386,379.76	383,318.44
	2	2,571.43	3,081.85	383,318.44	380,236.59
	3	2,550.75	3,102.53	380,236.59	377,134.06
	4	2,529.94	3,123.34	377,134.06	374,010.72
	5	2,508.99	3,144.29	374,010.72	370,866.43
	6	2,487.90	3,165.38	370,866.43	367,701.05
	7	2,466.66	3,186.62	367,701.05	364,514.43
	8	2,445.28	3,208.00	364,514.43	361,306.43
	9	2,423.76	3,229.52	361,306.43	358,076.92
	10	2,402.10	3,251.18	358,076.92	354,825.74
	11	2,380.29	3,272.99	354,825.74	351,552.75
	12	2,358.33	3,294.95	351,552.75	348,257.80
5	1	2,336.23	3,317.05	348,257.80	344,940.75
	2	2,313.98	3,339.30	344,940.75	341,601.45
	3	2,291.58	3,361.70	341,601.45	338,239.74
	4	2,269.02	3,384.26	338,239.74	334,855.49
	5	2,246.32	3,406.96	334,855.49	331,448.53
	6	2,223.47	3,429.81	331,448.53	328,018.72
	7	2,200.46	3,452.82	328,018.72	324,565.90
	8	2,177.30	3,475.98	324,565.90	321,089.91
	9	2,153.98	3,499.30	321,089.91	317,590.61
	10	2,130.50	3,522.78	317,590.61	314,067.83
	11	2,106.87	3,546.41	314,067.83	310,521.43
	12	2,083.08	3,570.20	310,521.43	306,951.23
6	1	2,059.13	3,594.15	306,951.23	303,357.08
	2	2,035.02	3,618.26	303,357.08	299,738.82
	3	2,010.75	3,642.53	299,738.82	296,096.29
	4	1,986.31	3,666.97	296,096.29	292,429.32
	5	1,961.71	3,691.57	292,429.32	288,737.75
	6	1,936.95	3,716.33	288,737.75	285,021.42
	7	1,912.02	3,741.26	285,021.42	281,280.16
	8	1,886.92	3,766.36	281,280.16	277,513.80
	9	1,861.66	3,791.62	277,513.80	273,722.18
	10	1,836.22	3,817.06	273,722.18	269,905.12
	11	1,810.61	3,842.67	269,905.12	266,062.45
	12	1,784.84	3,868.44	266,062.45	262,194.01
7	1	1,758.88	3,894.40	262,194.01	258,299.61
	2	1,732.76	3,920.52	258,299.61	254,379.09
	3	1,706.46	3,946.82	254,379.09	250,432.27
	4	1,679.98	3,973.30	250,432.27	246,458.97
	5	1,653.33	3,999.95	246,458.97	242,459.02
	6	1,626.50	4,026.78	242,459.02	238,432.24
	7	1,599.48	4,053.80	238,432.24	234,378.44
	8	1,572.29	4,080.99	234,378.44	230,297.45

Case 22 The Dimmesdale Building

EXHIBIT 1 (*continued*)

Year	*Month*	*Interest*	*Princ Pmt*	*Princ BOM*	*Princ EOM*
	9	1,544.91	4,108.37	230,297.45	226,189.08
	10	1,517.35	4,135.93	226,189.08	222,053.15
	11	1,489.61	4,163.67	222,053.15	217,889.48
	12	1,461.68	4,191.60	217,889.48	213,697.88
8	1	1,433.56	4,219.72	213,697.88	209,478.15
	2	1,405.25	4,248.03	209,478.15	205,230.12
	3	1,376.75	4,276.53	205,230.12	200,953.59
	4	1,348.06	4,305.22	200,953.59	196,648.38
	5	1,319.18	4,334.10	196,648.38	192,314.28
	6	1,290.11	4,363.17	192,314.28	187,951.11
	7	1,260.84	4,392.44	187,951.11	183,558.67
	8	1,231.37	4,421.91	183,558.67	179,136.76
	9	1,201.71	4,451.57	179,136.76	174,685.19
	10	1,171.85	4,481.43	174,685.19	170,203.76
	11	1,141.78	4,511.50	170,203.76	165,692.26
	12	1,111.52	4,541.76	165,692.26	161,150.50
9	1	1,081.05	4,572.23	161,150.50	156,578.27
	2	1,050.38	4,602.90	156,578.27	151,975.37
	3	1,019.50	4,633.78	151,975.37	147,341.59
	4	988.42	4,664.86	147,341.59	142,676.73
	5	957.12	4,696.16	142,676.73	137,980.57
	6	925.62	4,727.66	137,980.57	133,252.91
	7	893.90	4,759.38	133,252.91	128,493.53
	8	861.98	4,791.30	128,493.53	123,702.23
	9	829.84	4,823.44	123,702.23	118,878.79
	10	797.48	4,855.80	118,878.79	114,022.99
	11	764.90	4,888.38	114,022.99	109,134.61
	12	732.11	4,921.17	109,134.61	104,213.44
10	1	699.10	4,954.18	104,213.44	99,259.26
	2	665.86	4,987.42	99,259.26	94,271.84
	3	632.41	5,020.87	94,271.84	89,250.97
	4	598.73	5,054.55	89,250.97	84,196.42
	5	564.82	5,088.46	84,196.42	79,107.95
	6	530.68	5,122.60	79,107.95	73,985.36
	7	496.32	5,156.96	73,985.36	68,828.39
	8	461.72	5,191.56	68,828.39	63,636.84
	9	426.90	5,226.38	63,636.84	58,410.46
	10	391.84	5,261.44	58,410.46	53,149.01
	11	356.54	5,296.74	53,149.01	47,852.27
	12	321.01	5,332.27	47,852.27	42,520.00
11	1	285.24	5,368.04	42,520.00	37,151.96
	2	249.23	5,404.05	37,151.96	31,747.91
	3	212.98	5,440.30	31,747.91	26,307.60
	4	176.48	5,476.80	26,307.60	20,830.80
	5	139.74	5,513.54	20,830.80	15,317.26
	6	102.75	5,550.53	15,317.26	9,766.74
	7	65.52	5,587.76	9,766.74	4,178.98
	8	28.03	4,178.98	4,178.98	(0.00)

Case 22 The Dimmesdale Building

EXHIBIT 2 PRESENT VALUE CALCULATIONS

Assumptions

Initial principal	$484,000	Maximum price	$550,000
Prime rate	11.50%	Maximum equity	66,000
Percent of prime	70.00%	Land cost	68,000
Interest rate	8.05%	Depreciable amount	482,000
Years	10	Depreciation years	31.5
Months	8	Annual depreciation	$15,302
Monthly payment	$5,653.28	Marg. indvl. tax rate	28.0%
		Net rental income	$65,000
		Operating expense	19,000
Rate of change in rental income		Appreciation rate	0.0%
and operating exp.		Sale price, yr. 5	550,000
	0.0%	Discount rate	20.0%

	Year				
	1	*2*	*3*	*4*	*5*
Net rental income	$ 65,000	$65,000	$65,000	$65,000	$65,000
Operating expense	19,000	19,000	19,000	19,000	19,000
Operating income	$46,000	$46,000	$46,000	$46,000	$46,000
Interest expense	37,872	35,369	32,656	29,717	26,533
Depreciation	15,302	15,302	15,302	15,302	15,302
Profit before tax	($7,174)	($4,671)	($1,958)	$981	$4,166
Income tax	(2,009)	(1,308)	(548)	275	1,166
Profit after tax	($5,165)	($3,363)	($1,410)	$706	$2,999
CASE 1: Taxable Income					
Profit after tax	($5,165)	($3,363)	($1,410)	$706	$2,999
Plus: Depreciation	15,302	15,302	15,302	15,302	15,302
Plus: Equity recovery					66,000
Plus: Profit on sale					76,508
Less: Tax on sale					21,422
Cash flow	$10,136	$11,939	$13,892	$16,008	$139,387
Net present value	$22,513				
CASE 2: Cash Flow Allowing for Total Debt Burden					
Profit after tax	($5,165)	($3,363)	($1,410)	$706	$2,999
Plus: Depreciation	15,302	15,302	15,302	15,302	15,302
Less: Principal payments	29,967	32,470	35,183	38,122	41,307
Plus: Net cash on sale					221,627
Cash flow	($19,831)	($20,532)	($21,291)	($22,114)	$198,621
Net present value	($39,948)				

EXHIBIT 2 (*continued*)

	Year				
	1	*2*	*3*	*4*	*5*
CASE 3: Free Cash Flow, Total Value, Weighted Average Cost of Capital					
Debt/total capital	85.1%	79.4%	73.2%	66.5%	59.3%
Weighted average after-tax cost of capital	7.9%	8.7%	9.6%	10.5%	11.6%
Discount factor	0.927	0.846	0.760	0.670	0.578
Profit before interest and after tax	$22,103	$22,103	$22,103	$22,103	$22,103
Plus: Depreciation	15,302	15,302	15,302	15,302	15,302
Plus: Receipts from sale of property after tax					528,578
Cash flow	$37,404	$37,404	$37,404	$37,404	$565,982
Present value	$34,661	$31,643	$28,412	$25,045	$327,290
Net present value	($102,949)				
CASE 4: Free Cash Flow, Total Value, WACC Using Actual Taxes Paid					
Profit before interest and taxes	$30,698	$30,698	$30,698	$30,698	$30,698
Plus: Depreciation	15,302	15,302	15,302	15,302	15,302
Less: Taxes	(2,009)	(1,308)	(548)	275	1,166
Plus: Receipts from sale of property after tax					528,578
Cash flow	$48,009	$47,308	$46,548	$45,725	$573,411
Present value	$44,488	$40,021	$35,358	$30,616	$331,586
Net present value	($67,923)				
CASE 5: Free Cash Flow, Total Value, WACC, Actual Taxes and Debt Service					
Profit before interest and taxes	$30,698	$30,698	$30,698	$30,698	$30,698
Plus: Depreciation	15,302	15,302	15,302	15,302	15,302
Less: Taxes	(2,009)	(1,308)	(548)	275	1,166
Less: Principal payments	29,967	32,470	35,183	38,122	41,307
Plus: Receipt from sale of property, net taxes					528,578
Cash flow	$18,042	$14,837	$11,365	$7,603	$532,105
Present value	$16,719	$12,552	$8,633	$5,091	$307,700
Sum of present values	$350,694				
Less: Principal balance	306,951				
Less: Initial equity	66,000				
Net present value	($22,257)				

Case 23

SUMTER CORPORATION

From his office overlooking the harbor in Charleston, South Carolina, William J. Gibbs, executive vice president at Sumter Corporation, a shipping and stevedoring company, watched a six-hundred-foot container ship slowly navigate up the channel to the docks. The reports on his desk included machine usage data, maintenance expense reports, and capital investment proposals. The capital expenditure decisions for the next year would be based upon this information. In addition, Mr. Gibbs had just received a letter from two of Sumter's major competitors which proposed merging all three firms' maintenance facilities in both Charleston and Savannah. In light of the intense competition that Sumter faced in July 1987, Mr. Gibbs knew that the decisions he made would have a significant effect on the future of Sumter. As the container ship passed from his view, Mr. Gibbs turned to his desk to begin organizing his analysis.

INDUSTRY BACKGROUND

A full-service shipping and stevedoring company was typically organized according to the two major functions it provided the ship lines: agency (or shipping) and stevedoring.

Agency

The agency side of the business performed several services for the ship lines. Every piece of cargo aboard a vessel had to be documented individually and cleared through customs; a manifest listing every item on board the ship had to be prepared and communicated to the ship's next port of call prior to its docking. To handle the considerable paperwork generated each time a ship docked, ship lines hired the agency department to perform the necessary documentation. Other agency services included reserving berths on the dock and ordering the ship's supply and repair needs so that all work could be completed while the ship was in port. The agency department also sold and booked cargo for ship lines that did not have their own sales offices in the region.

Over the years, the agency part of the business had not altered significantly. The major impacts had been the increase in the volume of documentation and the emergence of affordable computer technology. The agency firms could aggregate and transfer data much more efficiently than in previous years.

Stevedoring

The stevedoring department coordinated all of the details of the actual loading and unloading of a ship. Ship lines compensated the stevedoring firms on the basis of a given rate per ton per container. In addition, the ship lines rented the dock and crane facilities at a set rate. On the East Coast, these facilities were generally constructed and owned by the state port authority in order to encourage trade in the state.

Stevedoring labor was drawn from the International Longshoremen's Association (ILA), a union that provided labor on a daily basis from a large pool of workers. Within the United States, the ILA was one of the most powerful unions. Contracts were negotiated on a national level and specified every detail of the conditions under which the union members worked. Crew (gang) sizes were specified, pay scales were set, and complex work rules were detailed for each type of job. Grievance procedures were long and difficult; thus, only the most severe infractions were taken to grievance.

In summary, the stevedoring firm provided three primary services. First, it ordered the dock

This case was prepared by David Maybank III, MBA'88, and revised by Deborah A. Kelleher, MBA'89, under the supervision of John L. Colley, Jr., Almand R. Coleman Professor of Business Administration.

and crane facilities that were needed to load or unload a ship from the state port authority. Second, it drew the necessary labor from the ILA and provided supervision for that labor as it loaded and unloaded the cargo. Most importantly, the stevedoring firm provided all of the equipment such as fork lifts, tractors, trailers, and other items which were needed to move the cargo from the ship to its resting place in the dock warehouse or parking lot.

THE COMPETITION

The mature nature of the industry and the minimal barriers to entry had fostered intense competition among shipping and stevedoring firms. Potentially, a new firm could enter the business within a few days by simply hiring a foreman to manage the labor and by leasing tractors and fork lifts. In addition, firms located in given ports could bid for a contract in another port with little or no presence there and still win the contract. Because labor was drawn randomly, training and methods improvements were virtually impossible to achieve. Consequently, firms had trouble differentiating themselves by the service they offered or by an area of distinctive competence.

As a result, the ship lines were exceptionally price sensitive and exerted considerable pressure on the stevedoring firms to keep rates low. Ship lines often changed stevedores because of a difference of a few pennies per ton in the quoted rates. In addition, a ship line would split its agency and stevedoring business between different firms in order to maintain a strong presence with many firms.

As a result of the severe price competition, firms with the best-managed overhead and the lowest loading and unloading rates were frequently the most successful. The level of investment in capital equipment, therefore, had a significant impact on the success of the firm. Variability of daily demand complicated all investment analyses. On a given day, the firm might not own enough equipment to meet all its needs; on the next day, half of the equipment might sit idle. The short-term nature of shipping line contracts (12 months) further complicated investment decisions. Investments in fixed expenses, such as tractors or fork lifts, had to be evaluated carefully in light of the possibility that the current volume of business might not be renewed for the next year.

COMPANY HISTORY

After World War II, the volume of shipping in the port of Charleston increased substantially, and the sole stevedoring company in that port experienced conflicts of interest among its competing clients. In 1947, former employees of the original firm founded Sumter Corporation as an alternative full-service stevedoring and agency company. Sumter captured a respectable share of the Charleston market over the next 30 years, operating by procedures established at the company's founding. By the early seventies, however, all of the original owners had passed away and the surviving families brought in professional managers. Under the new leadership, the company fell into a slow decline. Increased competition from new entrants into the Charleston market eroded Sumter's market share, and by 1978, the company was losing money. Increasingly concerned that the firm might collapse, the absentee owners searched to recoup their investment and decided to sell the company.

In a highly leveraged, seller-financed buyout, David Maybank, Jr. purchased the company on December 18, 1978. The resulting high level of debt service costs dictated a strategy of cost control and expansion in order to generate the cash needed to retire the debt. From the time of purchase to 1988, the company grew from four to twelve major accounts and from $3.3 million to $24 million in annual sales. In the process, Sumter expanded major operations to a second port in Savannah, Georgia and also worked ships calling in four other smaller East Coast ports. Mr. Gibbs thought that this high growth rate might have concealed some basic operating inefficiencies at Sumter. Specifically, he wondered if Sumter was using the proper method for analyzing capital expenditures.

THE CAPITAL EXPENDITURE ISSUE

Number of Tractors

The first issue Mr. Gibbs wanted to resolve was the question of the optimum number of tractors to own, which would be supplemented with rental tractors. At the time of Gibbs' analysis, Sumter owned 19 tractors. Exhibit 1 details the hours each piece of equipment was used during the first six months of 1987. Exhibit 2 presents data on the costs of acquiring new tractors. Purchase prices and expenses were expected to escalate at 5 percent a year. For purposes of his analysis, Mr. Gibbs decided to use an approximate useful life of 9 years, with a residual value of 20 percent of the original price. Sumter's estimated tax rate was 30 percent. Tractors were specialized pieces of equipment used to haul containers (on wheels) from the shipyard to the crane where they were loaded onto the ship, or conversely, to pick up containers at the crane and haul them to the shipyard. Up to 1,200 such moves could be made per ship. Normally, seven tractors were used for each gang of workers. A ship could be worked by one to four gangs, depending on the speed at which the ship's owners wanted to unload the ship. Any number of ships could be in port on a given day.

In the event that Sumter needed more tractors than it owned, Terminal Services, an independent rental firm, rented supplementary tractors at $18.00 per hour. This fee included transporting the tractor to and from the dock and all repair and maintenance costs. Terminal Services imposed a four-hour minimum rental. Exhibit 3 shows the hourly usage of rental tractors, by day, for the period April–June 1987.

The Rental Option

Mr. Gibbs also wanted to investigate the option of selling all of the current tractors to Terminal Services and renting 100 percent of Sumter's tractor needs. Under this plan, Terminal Services would purchase the 19 tractors currently owned by Sumter for the negotiated values shown in Exhibit 1. Terminal Services would then cover all of Sumter's tractor needs at a renegotiated rate of $16.50 per hour per tractor. The rental fee would include transporting the tractors to the dock where they were needed, eight hours of fuel, and all maintenance costs. This option would allow Sumter to save the direct costs of ownership of the tractors, to eliminate two of their five mechanics, and to avoid replacing many of the tractors which were approaching the end of their useful lives. The company would not be able to dismantle its maintenance shop, however, because there was no current rental source for the 20 fork lifts used in Sumter's operations. As a result maintenance would have to continue to be done by Sumter. This option concerned Mr. Gibbs because it placed Sumter's long-term tractor costs at the mercy of a single supply source.

THE MAINTENANCE SHOP ISSUE

When the company was purchased in 1978, much of the equipment was quite old, with an average age of over 12 years. Management reasoned that because the company had a large maintenance shop, it would be cheaper to repair old equipment than to purchase new equipment. This policy created both parts expenses and reliability problems for Sumter. In the early eighties, the company sold all of its old equipment and replaced it with new equipment. The immediate result of this change was a substitution of depreciation costs or lease expenses for repair costs. New equipment broke down less and thus had lower repair expenses. Exhibit 4 provides a summary of maintenance shop expenses for the period of January–June, 1987. At that time, the average age of the fleet of tractors was approximately 5 years, and the repair costs, which were the sole responsibility of the company, were once again increasing.

The rapid growth in the company was creating pressure on management to make some long-term decisions about the strategic direction the company was going to take in managing the cost of its maintenance and equipment department. This department was the single most costly expense center in the company. Merging maintenance operations with the two competing firms was therefore an attractive proposition from a financial viewpoint. Recent articles in *The Journal of Commerce* highlighted a trend among competing stevedoring firms to combine their maintenance shops and equipment fleets in order to reduce duplication of resources, to achieve higher utilization, and to reduce costs. This trend had been taking place largely in smaller firms or firms that were in financial distress. Clearly, reducing the cost of the equipment fleet and maintenance operations would enhance Sumter's ability to quote favorable rates. Mr. Gibbs, however, was concerned that combining Sumter's maintenance operations with those of its competitors would be a logistical nightmare. Sumter prided itself on the quality and reliability of its equipment. Whether the cost savings would justify the loss of what was clearly a competitive advantage was an open question. Mr. Gibbs did not want to pass up the opportunity without first getting a clearer idea of the impact that the first two options would have on the maintenance facility costs at Sumter.

THE CHALLENGE

With so many options to analyze, Mr. Gibbs decided to call in his assistant. After outlining the situation, Mr. Gibbs said, "David, here's the data on tractor utilization. If we both work on these issues, maybe we can reach some decisions by tomorrow morning."

EXHIBIT 1 TRACTOR USAGE IN HOURS JANUARY–JUNE 1987

Number of Tractor	Year of Purchase	Hours of Use							Negotiated Value	Book* Value
		Jan	Feb	Mar	Apr	May	Jun	YTD		
#149	1979	75	127	77	123	0	N/A	402	12,000	0
#150	1979	201	167	114	108	93	27	710	12,000	0
#151	1979	0	107	77	114	105	88	491	12,000	0
#154	1981	43	59	41	100	273	85	601	14,000	0
#155	1981	30	3	0	7	30	6	76	14,000	0
#156	1981	0	341	120	101	110	47	719	14,000	0
#157	1981	109	164	154	96	85	115	723	14,000	0
#158	1981	105	81	96	54	96	52	484	14,000	0
#159	1981	1	5	95	101	199	N/A	401	14,000	0
#160	1981	179	88	231	101	61	116	776	14,000	0
#161	1981	151	91	153	134	110	54	693	14,000	0
#162	1981	145	88	159	106	142	85	725	14,000	0
#163	1981	125	100	77	29	114	67	512	14,000	0
#164	1981	140	134	103	92	143	79	691	14,000	0
#165	1981	39	57	119	11	22	49	297	14,000	0
#166	1984	190	183	90	319	104	154	1040	16,000	14,800
#167	1984	67	34	76	65	181	134	557	16,000	14,800
#168	1984	244	68	80	99	274	161	926	16,000	14,800
#169	1984	208	238	91	250	208	224	1219	16,000	14,800
Total Hrs.		2052	2135	1953	2010	2350	1543	12043	268,000	59,200
Average Hrs.		108	112	103	106	124	81			

Note: No (or low) hours indicate tractors with a broken hour meter or in for repairs. This pattern is representative of normal operations.

*The purchase prices of the tractors were $33,000 in 1979, $35,000 in 1981, and $37,000 in 1984. The company used the straight-line method to depreciate the tractors over 5 years and planned to dispose of them after 9 years' use at 20 percent of the purchase price.

Case 23 Sumter Corporation

EXHIBIT 2 1987 NEW TRACTOR COST ESTIMATE

Hurdle rate	15 percent
Purchase price	$39,000
Repairs	$ 2,000 per year
Property tax	$180 per year
Insurance	$320 per year

EXHIBIT 3 RENTAL TRACTOR HOURLY USAGE APRIL–JUNE 1987

	Rental Tractor #																	
April	*1*	*2*	*3*	*4*	*5*	*6*	*7*	*8*	*9*	*10*	*11*	*12*	*13*	*14*	*15*	*16*	*17*	*Total*
	(Number of Hours Use per Day)																	
5	4	4	4	4	4													20
6	9	9	9	9	9	9	9	9	9	9	9	9						108
8	8	8	8	8	8	8	8	8	8	4	4	4	4	4	4			96
10	9	9																18
11	13	13	13	13	13	13	13	8	8	4								111
14	9	9	9	9	9	9	9	9	9	9								90
15	5	4																9
20	8	7	7	7	7	7	7	7										57
21	10	10	4	4	4	4	4	4	4									48
22	4																	4
27	8	8	8	8	8	8	8											56
28	5	5	5	5	5	5	5	5	5	5	5	5	5					65
TOT HRS	92	86	67	67	67	63	63	50	43	31	18	18	9	4	4	—	—	682

	Rental Tractor #																	
May	*1*	*2*	*3*	*4*	*5*	*6*	*7*	*8*	*9*	*10*	*11*	*12*	*13*	*14*	*15*	*16*	*17*	*Total*
	(Number of Hours Use per Day)																	
1	13	13	13	13	13	13	13	13	13	6	6	6	4	4	4	4	4	155
3	7	7																14
5	11	11	11	11	11													55
7	6	6	6															18
9	6	6	6	6	6	6	6	6	6	6	6	6	6	6				84
10	10	10	10	10	10	10	10	8	9	9	9	9	9					123
11	15	15																30
12	7	7	7															21
14	5	5	7*															17
22	10	10	10	10	10	10	10											70
25	12	12	12	12	11	11	11	11	11	11								114
26	13	13																26
30	12	12	12	12														48
TOT HRS	127	127	94	74	61	50	50	38	39	32	21	21	19	10	4	4	4	775

*Note that the third tractor rented on May 14 was used more hours than the first and second tractors rented on the same day.

EXHIBIT 3 ***(continued)***

	Rental Tractor #																									
June	*1*	*2*	*3*	*4*	*5*	*6*	*7*	*8*	*9*	*10*	*11*	*12*	*13*	*14*	*15*	*16*	*17*	*18*	*19*	*20*	*21*	*22*	*23*	*24*	*25*	*Total*
	(Number of Hours Use per Day)																									
3	4																									4
5	12	12	12																							36
12	14	14																								28
16	8	8	8																							24
17	11	11	11	11	11	11	11	11	11	11	11	11	11	11	8	8	8	4	4	4	4	4	4	4		206
18	8	8	8	8	8																					40
19	12	12	12	12	12	12	12	12	12	12	12	12	12	12												168
22	7	7	7	7	7																					35
26	11	11	11	5	5	5	5	5	5	5	5															73
27	8	8																								16
TOT HRS	95	91	69	43	43	28	28	28	28	28	28	23	23	23	8	8	8	4	4	4	4	4	4	4		630

Case 23 Sumter Corporation

EXHIBIT 4 SUMMARY OF MAINTENANCE SHOP EXPENSES JANUARY–JUNE 1987

		1987
Tractor Expenses		
Fuel	$ 15,641	
Parts	16,702	
Lease payments	38,361	
		$ 70,704
Fork Lift Expenses		
Fuel-LP gas	9,050	
Parts	19,621	
Lease payments	49,188	
		$ 77,859
Unallocated Expenses		
Mechanics	107,722	
Shop overhead	54,473	
		$162,195
Total Shop Expenses		$310,758

Case 24

WINSTON FURNITURE COMPANY, INC.

INTRODUCTION

In mid-August 1987, Mr. Michael Easterly, head of the investment banking department at the Thomson McKinnon Securities, Inc. (Thomson) office in Atlanta, was evaluating the details of a proposed $10 million public offering of Winston Furniture Company, Inc. (Winston) common stock. He needed to determine the price at which the stock would be offered to the public. Mr. Brown, the president of Winston who held 35.5 percent of the company's outstanding stock, and a local investment group (which held 51 percent) were naturally interested in receiving the highest price possible. Mr. Brown had borrowed to finance part of his stock ownership under terms that provided for sharing the appreciation of the stock with the lenders. Other officers of the company did not own shares but had a nominal amount under option.

Mr. Easterly was slightly uncomfortable because Thomson had relatively little experience with firms in the furniture industry. Bringing in a co-manager with a good reputation in this industry could help with the offering but would greatly reduce Thomson's management fee.

COMPANY BACKGROUND

Winston designed, manufactured, and sold casual furniture for both outdoor and indoor use. Winston's products were constructed of aluminum, wrought iron, and tubular steel, and were offered in numerous style collections. The products featured durable painted finishes and extensive use of fabric cushions and vinyl strapping in various color patterns. The company had combined a cost-efficient manufacturing process, an effective marketing organization, and responsive shipping and customer service programs to become one of the largest sellers in the United States of upper-medium price, quality metal casual furniture.

Winston began business in 1975 as a division of Marathon Corporation, a privately held company. On March 28, 1986, management of Winston and certain investors acquired the aluminum furniture business of Marathon's division in a leveraged buy-out. On November 29, 1986, Winston acquired the wrought iron and tubular steel furniture business (Lyon-Shaw) of the B. B. Walker Company, which diversified Winston's product lines and expanded its presence in the upper-medium-priced casual furniture segment. Winston's executive offices were located in Birmingham, Alabama, and its manufacturing facilities were in Haleyville, Alabama and Salisbury, North Carolina.

The development and operations of Winston's business were considered to be largely dependent upon the continued active participation of its current management team. This team consisted principally of William Brown, president; Bobby Tesney, general manager; and Steve Hess, vice president of marketing and sales. This team collectively had over 30 years experience in the furniture industry.

Management's goal was to produce a high-quality product of superior design and style at the lowest possible manufacturing cost and deliver it in a timely manner to dealers and their customers. To this end, Winston had extensively refurbished and modernized the Haleyville facility in 1984 and 1985 at a cost of approximately $1.5 million. The most significant improvement was the installation of a state-of-the-art power-coated painting system. As a result of these changes, Winston had reduced the number of plant personnel from 325 to 285, lowering manufacturing costs. These low manufacturing costs, combined with management's philosophy of strict cost controls in other areas, had enabled

This case was adapted from a Supervised Business Study prepared by Mr. Philip E. Haydon.

Winston to increase gross margins without the necessity of substantial price increases.

In August 1987, the company was in the process of modifying the manufacturing systems at the Salisbury plant to implement the policies and procedures used at Haleyville. These changes principally included the addition of another state-of-the-art painting system and would cost approximately $1 million.

The company was marketing its products through independent sales representatives, primarily to specialty patio, department, and furniture stores and to certain commercial customers. Winston had a total of 3,000 active customer accounts, the majority of which were located east of the Rocky Mountains. The opportunity thus existed to expand to the West Coast.

Winston's consolidated income statements, including pro forma data combining Lyon-Shaw for all of 1986 and analysts' projections for 1987, are shown in Exhibit 1. Recent balance sheets are provided in Exhibit 2.

Winston had been saddled with large debt servicing requirements over the past several months, which had significantly impaired earnings. The debt had arisen from both the leveraged buy-out and the Lyon-Shaw acquisition in 1986. Thus, management had approached Mr. Easterly regarding a public equity issuance as a way of reducing the debt service.

INDUSTRY BACKGROUND

The casual furniture industry was highly competitive and included a large number of manufacturers, none of which dominated the market. Nonetheless, some competitors had greater sales volumes and greater financial resources than Winston. Entry into the upper-medium-priced segment of the metal casual furniture market may have been restricted somewhat by the specialized distribution channel used. The significant capital investment required for plant and equipment to achieve sufficient economies of scale also deterred new competitors from entering the market.

Although there was an increasing amount of foreign-produced casual furniture being imported into the United States, Winston's sales had not been adversely affected. The metal furniture produced abroad was generally limited in design styles and colors, of lesser quality than the company's products, and was marketed in the lower-end price range.

Management believed that customers made their purchase decisions based on quality, styling, design, availability, prompt delivery, personal service, and price, as well as on their respective discretionary incomes. While short-term sales would largely depend on domestic economic performance, demographic trends were expected to give the furniture industry a boost into the 1990s as "baby-boomers" hit the prime age to make purchases.

Furniture and home furnishings industry sales were approximately $5.5 billion in 1986 and were projected to grow at a rate of 5 percent to 7 percent a year for the next decade.

THOMSON MCKINNON SECURITIES INC.

Founded in 1885, Thomson McKinnon was the largest privately held retail-oriented investment banking and brokerage firm. It provided a broad array of investment products and services to individuals and institutions and a full range of corporate financial services to middle market companies. The transactions it concentrated on were in the $5 to $150 million range. Since 1983, the firm had managed or co-managed underwritings for seventy-seven clients raising nearly $2 billion.

The investment banking activity, staffed by over eighty professionals, was headquartered in New York City. A major office for the southeastern region was located in Atlanta, where six professionals were on the staff. The firm also had thirty-six other offices in the southeast and was represented in all eleven states in the region. The strategy was to provide southeastern clients with the local marketplace familiarity, local accessibility, and market penetration advantages enjoyed by regional firms, along with the resources of a large, national investment bank.

THE PUBLIC OFFERING

Mr. Easterly knew that the average price–earnings ratio for the industry was about 13. Betas of companies in the industry were 0.75 in an up market and 1.00 in a down market. According to *Value Line,* profit margins averaged about 4.5 percent; ROE, 13 percent; ROA, 7 percent; debt-to-equity ratios, 40 percent; and dividend payout, 25 percent. In order to make comparison with similar firms in the industry, he had an analyst prepare information on nine other firms, presented in Exhibit 3.

A variety of factors usually determined the size and price of an offering. Typically, public offerings took place for no less than $10 million, and between 20 percent and 45 percent of a company was sold. This dollar amount suited Winston's needs well, but management wanted to limit the amount of control given up and to sell the stock for at least $15 a share. This would represent a fivefold increase in price over management's original cost basis of $3 per share.

In addition to the pricing issue, Mr. Easterly was debating whether to share this deal with a co-manager. By bringing in another investment bank with its own distribution network, Thomson would be able to spread its underwriting risk. Thomson had had some recent disappointing experience in placing issues on its own and wanted to avoid such events in the future. Furthermore, the market might receive this issue more favorably from a firm that had recognized expertise in the furniture industry, which Thomson was lacking. Bringing in a qualified furniture co-manager would likely achieve a broader distribution of the stock among investors, especially by ensuring the participation of institutional investors. This broader distribution could generate higher stock prices along with a strong aftermarket.

A co-manager would not cost Winston any additional management fees. Thomson, however, would have to split its $250,000 fee (2 1/2 percent) with the co-manager. It also ran the additional risk of losing Winston as a client as the co-managers jockeyed for position with the firm.

In considering a co-manager, Mr. Easterly wanted a regional firm with a strong reputation in the furniture industry and with some knowledge of Winston. There were two candidates that stood out from the rest of the crowd in meeting these criteria: Robinson Humphrey and Wheat First Securities. Robinson, located in Atlanta, was a well-known name in furniture. Due to its proximity to Winston, it was surely familiar with the company. Wheat, based in Richmond, Virginia, was not in direct competition with Thomson's Atlanta office. Wheat's expertise with furniture companies was widely recognized. It had been invited by Winston a few months earlier to take this issue to market but had turned Winston down.

Underwriting risk was shared proportionally among co-managers, as were fees. Thus, in this transaction, if a co-manager was invited to participate, both risk and fees would be shared 50-50.

UNDERWRITING PROCEDURE

Several days prior to an offering, the underwriter(s) will have contacted potential customers and normally will have taken enough verbal orders or expression of interest (on the basis of a preliminary prospectus) at the yet undetermined offering price to place the entire offering. If possible, the underwriter(s) will have overallotted the offering. Industry practice provided that issuing companies grant the underwriter(s) an option to purchase up to 15 percent additional shares over the originally planned amount to be offered, called the "Green Shoe" after the issue in which this practice was originated. This arrangement permitted the underwriter(s) to take a short position in the offering so as to effect stabilization (as described later) without market risk. The Green Shoe also permitted the underwriter(s) to earn 15 percent more in commissions, as well as to satisfy demand on the part of institutional clients.

Five days before the offering date, the underwriter(s) signed a contract (the Underwriting Agreement) to purchase all of the shares to be offered at a specified price. Should the market take a drastic turn downward in the interim five days, the offering could be cancelled, and the underwriter(s) would incur no loss.

Should the market only soften somewhat, however, the offering would probably proceed as planned. In this case, however, investors would likely attempt to avoid their verbal orders to purchase the stock at the offering price because the stock's value in the open market would be expected to fall after issuance. The underwriter(s) could thus lose orders but would be forced to purchase the stock at the price specified in the Underwriting Agreement. They could therefore be stuck holding a significant number of shares with a market value below the price paid to the company.

During and immediately following the offering, the underwriter(s) bought and sold shares to stabilize the stock price on the market, known as "making a market" in the stock. This activity could last from one hour to one month following the offering. The underwriter(s) would lose on these transactions if the offering price was too high or if the market softened. Of course, the Green Shoe overallotment option helped to mitigate the risk by allowing the underwriters to sell short ahead of the issue and cover with the Green Shoe shares if the regular issue sold out.

If the price was too low, the stock would go to a large premium above the issue price, and the company would not have received the full value of the offering.

Underwriters made a market in recently issued stock to reinforce a reputation for successful offerings and to provide better service to underwriting clients and investors. At the same time, underwriters generally expected the investor in new issues to hold the stock for a reasonable period and certainly not to sell it during the stabilization period. Investors who sold out too quickly might not be offered shares in subsequent issues.

In August 1987, the market appeared quite strong for Winston's initial public offering. (Price indices and over-the-counter volume are provided in Exhibit 4.) There was another reasonably recent furniture company issue on the market, and comparable companies were trading high. Most analysts felt that both underwriters and corporations faced only downside risk by waiting on the market. Mr. Easterly knew he had some decisions to make. Should he bring in a co-manager and, if so, whom? How many shares should Winston issue at what price in order to raise the $10 million?

EXHIBIT 1 CONSOLIDATED STATEMENTS OF INCOME (thousands of dollars)

	FY Ended 12/31/82		FY Ended 12/31/83		FY Ended 12/31/84		FY Ended 12/31/85		Pro Forma* FY Ended 12/31/86		Pro Forma* Trailing 12 months 3/31/87		Projected FY Ended 12/31/87	
Net sales**	$14,399	100.0%	$17,643	100.0%	$19,706	100.0%	$20,876	100.0%	$30,463	100.0%	$31,396	100.0%	$34,897	100.0%
Cost of sales	10,096	70.1	11,688	66.2	13,456	68.3	12,157	58.2	19,091	62.7	19,393	61.8	21,348	61.2
Gross margin	$ 4,303	29.9%	$ 5,955	33.8%	$ 6,250	31.7%	$ 8,719	41.8%	$11,372	37.3%	$12,003	38.2%	$13,549	38.8%
Selling, G&A, R&D expenses	2,526	17.5	3,215	18.2	3,463	17.6	4,000	19.2	5,309	17.4	5,303	16.9	6,092	17.5
Operating income	$ 1,777	12.4%	$ 2,740	15.6%	$ 2,787	14.1%	$ 4,719	22.6%	$ 6,063	19.9%	$ 6,700	21.3%	$ 7,457	21.3%
Amortization	19	0.1	18	0.1	18	0.1	18	0.1	1,185	3.9	1,226	3.9	1,361	3.9
Earnings before interest & taxes	$ 1,758	12.3%	$ 2,722	15.5%	$ 2,769	14.0%	$ 4,701	22.5%	$ 4,878	16.0%	$ 5,474	17.4%	$ 6,096	17.4%
Interest expense	546	3.8	336	1.9	343	1.7	223	1.1	2,816	9.2	2,868	9.1	2,769	7.9
Interest income	0	0.0	0	0.0	(31)	−0.2	(59)	−0.3	(75)	−0.2	(66)	−0.2	(51)	−0.1
Earnings before taxes	$ 1,212	8.5%	$ 2,386	13.6%	$ 2,457	12.5%	$ 4,537	21.7%	$ 2,137	7.0%	$ 2,672	8.5%	$ 3,378	9.6%
Income taxes***	560	3.9	1,091	6.2	1,095	5.6	2,121	10.2	1,061	3.5	1,299	4.1	1,554	4.5
Net income	$ 652	4.6%	$ 1,295	7.4%	$ 1,362	6.9%	$ 2,416	11.5%	$ 1,076	3.5%	$ 1,373	4.4%	$ 1,824	5.1%
Net Income Per Common Share														
As reported Primary#									$ 1.61		$ 2.06		$ 2.73	
Fully diluted##									$ 1.08		$ 1.37		$ 1.81	
Cash flow (net income plus depreciation & amortization)									$ 2,511				$ 3,929	
EBIT/Interest As reported									1.7×		1.9×		2.2×	
Compound Annual Growth Rates (1983–1986)			Revenues**											
			Operating		36.7%									
			income		30.3%									
			EBIT		21.5%									

Note: Percentages may not total due to rounding.

*Pro forma data prepared as if the acquisitions of Winston and of Lyon-Shaw occurred on January 1, 1986.

**Sales for FY'82, FY'83 and FY'84 include gross sales of a previously owned wrought iron division of $6,554,000, $5,963,000, and $3,639,000, respectively. This division was sold in 1984. Compound annual growth rate for revenues excludes wrought iron sales in 1983.

***Because of state income taxes and the amortization for reporting purpose of goodwill not deductible for tax purposes, the company's tax rate will be a few percentage points higher than the federal statutory tax rate.

#Current shares of common stock outstanding total 667,000.

##Includes 359,000 shares of common stock to be issued upon conversion of $500,000 of convertible subordinated notes.

Case 24 Winston Furniture Company, Inc.

EXHIBIT 2 CONSOLIDATED BALANCE SHEETS (thousands of dollars)

	March 28, 1986	December 31, 1986	June 26, 1987
	(division of Marathon)		(unaudited)
Assets			
Cash	$ 4	$ 280	$ 101
Accounts receivable, net	8,533	10,001	5,735
Inventories	1,403	3,079	2,591
Prepaid expenses	156	363	213
Total current assets	$10,096	$13,723	$ 8,640
Property, plant & equip.	3,749	5,916	6,083
Accum. depreciation	1,869	395	795
Net prop., plant & equip.	$ 1,880	$ 5,521	$ 5,288
Other assets, inc. goodwill	41	13,419	12,955
Total Assets	$12,017	$32,663	$26,883
Liabilities & Equity			
Notes payable	$ 2,545	$ 5,268	$ 1,337
Accounts payable-trade	342	1,113	1,200
-intracompany	1,915	0	0
Accrued expenses	473	1,344	1,571
Accrued income taxes	0	288	625
Payable on LS acquisition	0	3,823	0
Total current liabilities	$ 5,275	$11,836	$ 4,733
Long-term debt*	1,737	17,671	18,143
Deferred income taxes	13	37	63
Common stock (666,667 shares outstanding)	0	67	67
Paid-in capital	0	1,933	1,933
Retained earnings	0	1,119	1,944
Corporate investment	4,992	0	0
Total equity	$ 4,992	$ 3,119	$ 3,944
Total Liabilities & Equity	$12,017	$32,663	$26,883

*See note on next page.

EXHIBIT 2 (*continued*) NOTE ON LONG-TERM DEBT (thousands of dollars)

Investment	*Balance June 26, 1987*	*Current Interest*	*Annual Amortization*	*Repayment Term*
7% Industrial Development Bond	$ 435	$ 30.4	$60–$85	1986–1992
14% Subordinated Notes	14,500	2,030.0	1,812	1990–1997
14% Convertible Subordinated Notes*	500	70.0	—	1997
Floating rate term at prime plus 2 1/2% (currently 10.75%)	1,146	123.0	204	1986–1989
Floating rate term at prime plus 3/4% (currently 9%)	1,482	133.4	144	1986–1992
Miscellaneous	80	.8	—	
	$18,143	$2,387.6	$2,220	

*Convertible at any time into the number of shares equal to 35% of the then outstanding shares of common stock. The conversion price is $14,285 for each 1% of outstanding common stock obtained. Terms and conditions of the subordinated and convertible notes provide that cash dividends cannot be paid until net worth exceeds $5 million and thereafter are limited to 3.5% of net income. Various financial ratios must be maintained, and these notes are secured by substantially all of the current assets of the company and the fixed assets of the Lyon-Shaw division. Prepayment was prohibited before 1991 and at a premium thereafter except that $7.25 million can be prepaid at a penalty of 10% from the proceeds of an issue of common stock.

EXHIBIT 3 COMPARABLE PUBLICLY OWNED COMPANIES IN THE FURNITURE INDUSTRY

Company Name	*Bench Craft*	*Berkline*	*Bush Ind.*	*Dresher*	*Kincaid*	*Pulaski*	*Rowe*	*Stanley*	*Univer-sal*	*MEAN*	*MEDIAN*	*Winston*
Fiscal Year Ends	12/31/86	6/31/86	12/31/86	6/31/86	1/31/87	10/31/86	11/30/86	12/31/86	12/31/86			
Traded	OTC	OTC	AMEX	OTC	OTC	OTC	OTC	OTC	OTC			
Closing Price 8/14/87	$ 13.75	$12.50	$ 29.25	$ 11.13	$11.25	$21.50	$15.75	$ 9.63	$ 19.25			
Annual Low	10.33	12.00	15.00	10.25	8.87	16.50	11.25	8.25	14.50			
High	15.25	15.75	33.125	13.13	15.00	22.25	16.50	14.50	20.63			
Trailing 12-month EPS	0.97	0.70	1.43	0.62	0.78	1.70	1.15	0.73	1.12			
P/E	14.2×	17.9×	20.5×	17.9×	14.4×	12.6×	13.7×	13.2×	17.2×	15.7×	14.4×	
Beta*	.50	2.36	4.66	1.96	3.61	.93	2.33	N/A	2.11			
Estimated FY'87 EPS	$ 1.15	$ 1.10	$ 1.55	$ 0.65	$ 1.02	$ 1.80	$ 1.30	N/A	1.20			
P/E**	12.0×	11.4×	18.9×	17.1×	11.0×	11.9×	12.1×		16.0×	12.1×	13.8×	
FY'86 Sales (millions)	$126.5	$86.0	$ 65.4	$ 39.9	$74.6	$98.4	$81.7	$166.0	191.4	$103.3	$86.0	$30.4
FY'86 Net profit margin	3.9%	2.0%	3.8%	6.1%	3.6%	4.3%	2.6%	1.6%	9.0%	4.1%	3.8%	5.4%
Growth 1982–86												
in sales	28.1	6.6	46.4	21.7	9.2***	19.0	20.8	12.8#	19.5***	20.5	19.5	26.9
in oper. income	18.3***	26.8	47.4	55.5	N/M	27.0	8.7	N/M	N/A	23.0	22.6	31.8
Market capitalization	$ 77.0	$18.8	$ 87.8	$ 46.7	$38.3	$62.4	$31.5	$ 38.5	$346.5			
L/T debt to total capital	39.5%	7.4%	44.3%	0.0%	27.9%	39.3%	31.0%	66.4%	0.2%	28.4%	31.0%	
Market capital + debt to FY'86 revenues	76.1	23.9	151.5	117.1	63.4	84.1	51.3	58.8	181.2	89.7	76.1	
Market value												
to book value	2.6×	0.8×	6.2×	3.7×	1.6×	2.0×	1.4×	1.3×	2.6×	2.5×	2.0×	
to total capital##	1.6	0.8	3.4	3.7	1.2	1.2	0.9	0.4	2.6	1.8	1.2	

Note: Brief descriptions of these firms are provided on the following page(s).

*Obtained from Media General weekly financial reports.

**Earnings estimates are a composite of estimates by furniture industry analysts obtained from the Mead Data Central Lexis/Nexis data service.

***Growth Rates for 1983–86.

#Growth Rates for 1984–86.

##Total capital = book value of common stock + long-term debt.

EXHIBIT 3 (*continued*)

Bench Craft Inc.

Manufactured upholstered furniture and distributed it nationally under its own trade name. Customers were primarily furniture retailers and retail chains. Sales and profits declined significantly in 1982, but they have grown strongly since then. A large increase in debt in 1985 was applied to a major increase in assets. Shares were issued to the public in December 1983. Insiders controlled approximately 27 percent of the stock, and Universal Furniture owned 32 percent.

Berkline Corp.

Manufactured upholstered furniture, also offering reclining chairs, coordinated room groupings of chairs, sofas, and accessory pieces. Net sales increased abruptly in 1983 from $66 million the previous year to $81 million, with slower increases thereafter. Assets remained at about $36 million until 1987, when they increased slightly to $38.7 million. Net income was volatile, ranging from break-even to $2 million.

Bush Industries

One of the three leading manufacturers of ready-to-assemble furniture including room dividers and wall systems, cabinets, and carts and desks (including those used for personal computers and audio/visual components). Customers included mass merchandisers, catalog showrooms and catalog sales, appliance dealers, department stores, and independent wholesalers. Revenues increased significantly in 1984 and again in 1986. Net income declined slightly in 1985, but otherwise had grown strongly since 1983. Long-term debt had been steady since 1984. The company was closely held, having been offered to the public in April 1985.

Dresher, Inc.

A leading domestic manufacturer and marketer of brass beds and brass accessories. Product line expansion has been directed to beds composed of wicker, rattan, and other metals. Sales and profits have increased steadily since 1982. Long-term debt was virtually nil. Officers and directors held about 19 percent of the stock, with institutions holding 39 percent.

Kincaid Furniture Company, Inc.

Manufactured traditional American bedroom and dining room furniture for the middle-price market and thus attempted to appeal to the broadest furniture market. Sales had increased steadily since at least 1981, although profits declined by one-third in 1985 from the prior year's level. A further decline of one-third took place in 1986, but in 1987 profits recovered to above their 1985 levels. Stock was initially issued in May 1986. Management controlled about 13 percent of the stock, with another 13 percent being held by two investment banks for their own portfolios.

EXHIBIT 3 (*continued*)

Pulaski Furniture

Manufactured medium-priced wooden bedroom, dining room, and occasional furniture in traditional styles. The company's sales increased steadily from 1983 on, following five years of flat revenues. Earnings, which had been quite volatile during the 1978–1983 period, increased in every year thereafter except for 1985. Long-term debt, which had been paid off by 1982, increased first to $10 and then $20 million. Officers and directors owned about 14 percent of the common stock.

Rowe Furniture

Manufactured and sold nationally a full line of medium-priced upholstered furniture. The product line included sofas, sleep sofas, chairs, and recliners in contemporary styles. Sales showed a steady increase from 1983 onward, although net income hit its peak in 1984 and then declined through 1986. A slight increase was recorded in 1987. Long-term debt remained constant at about $10 million. In 1986, approximately 20 percent of the common stock was repurchased by the company. Insiders owned 42 percent of the stock.

Stanley Interiors Corp.

Designed, manufactured, imported, and marketed upholstered furniture, wood furniture, fabrics, draperies, and wall coverings. Sales declined slightly in 1985 but recovered the next year. Profits followed a similar pattern but were still below their 1984 level. Long-term debt increased significantly in 1986 in order to fund an increase in inventories, although receivables and fixed assets also increased. Common stock was initially issued in August 1986. Insiders owned 8 percent but investment banking firms controlled 50 percent.

Universal Furniture Ltd.

Designed, manufactured, and sold medium-priced wooden furniture for the dining room and bedroom as well as occasional furniture. The company's plants were located in Asia. Sales grew rapidly in 1985 and 1986. The increase in profits lagged but was almost 50 percent in 1986. The stock was offered to the public in June 1986, with 50 percent remaining in the control of insiders.

EXHIBIT 4 STOCK MARKET STATISTICS, JULY–AUGUST 1987

Date		*Closing Prices*			
		Dow-Jones Industrials	*Standard & Poor 400*	*Over-the-Counter Industrials*	*Over-the-Counter Volume*
July	10	2,456	359.9	426.0	131.9
	17	2,510	368.3	434.1	152.9
	24	2,585	362.0	429.1	147.3
July	27	2,494	363.4	428.9	112.0
	28	2,520	365.4	430.0	125.8
	29	2,539	369.4	431.2	136.0
	30	2,567	373.2	433.6	154.2
	31	2,572	373.6	434.9	142.6
August	3	2,557	375.5	433.1	133.5
	4	2,547	373.0	432.8	140.4
	5	2,567	374.5	436.3	151.8
	6	2,594	377.4	440.8	149.7
	7	2,592	379.7	443.6	165.3
August	10	2,635	383.9	446.3	130.8
	11	2,680	390.0	449.4	185.4
	12	2,669	391.2	449.2	172.1
	13	2,691	391.8	451.6	160.2
	14	2,685	392.0	451.6	147.6

Case 25

WASHINGTON INC.

On May 5, 1986, Adams Corporation made an offer to buy any and all of the outstanding shares of Washington Inc. for $17.00 cash and to pay any brokerage commissions and transfer taxes the sellers might incur. The offer would expire on May 18, 1986.

Washington common stock closed on the New York Stock Exchange the previous day at $14.00. As of December 31, 1985, the book value of the stockholders' equity was $24.00 a share, and net current assets amounted to $19.77 a share. Dividends of $0.40 a share were declared in 1985. The quarterly dividend rate had been increased to $0.125 on May 4, 1986. This dividend would be payable to holders of record on June 14, 1986, but stockholders who sold their shares to Adams would not receive the dividend.

Washington Inc. was engaged in the manufacture and fabrication of metal products such as tungsten carbide cutting tools, coal and oil mining tools, chemical equipment, and golf club heads. It served a variety of markets but did not sell directly to the ultimate consumers.

Adams manufactured a wide variety of industrial products, including steel, rubber, asbestos textiles, electrical equipment, and refractories. They were marketed in various ways, primarily in the United States. Adams already owned 64,200 shares of Washington's 1,511,011 shares, purchased at prices between $10 and $12 a share. Adams was 59.3 percent owned by J. Q. Adams, an entrepreneur who had built the company and other firms he controlled by vigorous acquisitions, not always with the support of the acquired company's management. As a result, Mr. Adams and the Adams Corporation were defendants in various legal actions.

Adams indicated that its objective was to obtain control of Washington.

Washington's management opposed the Adams proposal. Washington's president suggested, "If Adams is willing to offer $17 a share, they must be convinced that it is worth considerably more." He pointed out that if inventories were valued at market, they would be increased by $13.7 million. The insurance value of the plant and equipment was reported to be $92 million, well above its cost of $53.6 million and the value after depreciation of $17.1 million. Washington also pointed out that because a broker stood to make $45 in commissions per 100 shares of Washington sold, brokers might not be a source of impartial advice to Washington shareholders.

Exhibits 1–3 present summary financial information for Washington Inc.

In April 1986, the rate on three-month Treasury bills was 6.06 percent and the rate on long-term government bonds was 7.39 percent. The Standard & Poor's 500 stock index was currently yielding 3.43 percent (dividends/price). The stock market had been erratic, with the "total return index" (dividends plus appreciation) showing a gain of 39.7 percent in 1983 and a loss of 6.7 percent in 1984, followed by a strong recovery and gain of 24.7 percent in 1985. Total return for the 10 years ending in 1985 was 14.3 percent and for the 20 years was 8.7 percent. Changes in the Consumer Price Index for the corresponding periods were 5.6 percent (1983), 5.9 percent (1984), 6.1 percent (1985), 7.0 percent (1976–85), and 6.4 percent (1966–86). According to *Value Line,* Washington Inc. showed a variation index ("beta") of 1.05 versus the market standard of 1.00. The spread of market risk returns over Treasury bills (the equity risk premium) had averaged 6.2 percent for the 1926–85 period.

Case 25 Washington Inc.

EXHIBIT 1 PER-SHARE FINANCIAL DATA, 1981–1986

	Annual				
	1981	*1982*	*1983*	*1984*	*1985*
Market prices					
High	$16.125	$15.50	$15.625	$12.75	$10.50
Low	7.50	10.25	9.00	6.50	6.625
Average	8.44	12.88	12.31	9.62	8.56
Earnings per share	$(0.74)	$ 1.04	$ 2.00	$ 1.97	$ 0.89
Price–earnings ratio (on average price)	n.a.	12.4×	6.2×	4.9×	9.6×
Earnings–price yield	n.a.	.081	.161	.204	.104
Dividend per share	—	—	$ 0.30	$ 0.40	$ 0.40
Dividend yield (on average price)	—	—	2.4%	4.2%	4.7%

	Quarterly					
	1985				*1986*	
	I	*II*	*III*	*IV*	*I*	*II**
Market price						
High	$10.50	$9.875	$10.25	$9.75	$13.875	$13.875
Low	6.625	8.50	7.75	8.50	9.00	11.375
Earnings per share	$ 0.23	$0.16	$ 0.17	$0.33	$ 0.54	n.a.

*Through May 6, 1986.

Case 25 Washington Inc.

EXHIBIT 2 SUMMARY FINANCIAL STATEMENTS, 1981–1985 (dollar figures in millions except per-share data)

	1981	*1982*	*1983*	*1984*	*1985*
Net sales	$69.2	$76.3	$90.4	$99.2	$87.3
Operating costs & exp.	63.8	68.1	79.3	88.4	79.5*
Depreciation	3.2	3.1	2.9	2.9	3.0
R&D expenses	0.7	0.6	1.0	1.2	1.5
EBIT	1.5	4.5	7.2	6.7	3.3
Interest expense	0.9	0.9	0.9	0.9	1.0
Income taxes	0.3	1.8	3.0	2.7	0.8
Extraordinary income	(1.7)	—	—	—	—
Net income (loss)	(1.5)	2.0	3.3	3.1	1.4*
Working capital	$30.3	$30.0	$30.1	$30.0	$30.7
Net prop., plant, eq.	17.4	14.7	16.1	17.7	17.1
Long-term debt	14.2	13.3	12.5	11.9	11.3
Shareholder equity	34.4	32.6	34.8	36.6	37.3
Percent of capital					
Long-term debt	0.29	0.29	0.26	0.25	0.23
Shareholder equity	0.71	0.71	0.74	0.75	0.77
Ave. shares out (000)	1,979	1,899	1,662	1,593	1,553
Per Share of Common Stock					
Income before ext. items	$0.10	$1.04	$2.00	$1.97	$0.89*
Net income (loss)	(0.74)	1.04	2.00	1.97	0.89
Dividends	—	—	0.30	0.40	0.40
Shareholders' equity	17.58	19.40	21.35	23.41	24.00
Change in sales (%)	—	10.26	18.48	9.73	−12.00
Change in net income (%)	—	n.a.	65.00	−6.06	−54.84
Change in e.p.s. (%)	—	n.a.	92.31	−1.50	−54.82

*See Note (*) of Exhibit 3 regarding the effects of LIFO in 1985.

Note: Details may not add because of rounding.

Case 25 Washington Inc.

EXHIBIT 3 BALANCE SHEETS AS OF DECEMBER 31, 1984 AND 1985 (millions of dollars)

	1984	*1985*
ASSETS		
Cash and marketable securities	$ 1.64	$ 2.00
Accounts receivable (net)	14.10	13.36
Inventories (LIFO)*	30.02	27.46
Prepaid exp. and taxes	1.07	1.12
Total current assets	$46.83	$43.93
Prop., plant, and equip.	54.45	53.65
Less: accumulated depreciation	36.71	36.51
Net prop., plant, and equip.	17.74	17.14
Other assets	1.22	1.23
Total assets	$65.79	$62.30
LIABILITIES		
Accounts payable	$ 5.15	$ 3.54
Accruals	6.83	6.65
Federal income taxes	1.01	1.25
Notes payable	3.00	1.00
Current installments, long-term debt	0.63	0.60
Dividends payable	0.16	0.16
Total current liabilities	$16.78	$13.19
5½% subordinated notes convertible at $57.50	7.67	7.67
6⅝% promissory notes	4.20	3.60
Total long-term debt**	$11.87	$11.27
Deferred pension plan contrib.***	0.54	0.53
Common stock and capital in excess of par	16.14	16.13
Retained earnings	23.82	24.58
Less: treasury stock at cost	(3.35)	(3.39)
Total equity	$36.61	$37.31
Total liabilities and equity	$65.79	$62.30

* Current cost of inventories was greater than book LIFO cost by $13.8 million as of 12/31/85 and $9.9 million as of 12/31/84. During 1985, however, inventory quantities were reduced so that lower costs were carried into the income statement compared with the cost of 1985 purchases. This resulted in an increase in net income of about $460,000, or $0.30 a share.

** Rentals for operating leases not capitalized were $1.1 million in both 1984 and 1985. Rentals on non-cancelable leases would be $434,000 in 1976.

*** Vested benefits exceeded pension fund assets (at market) by $8.6 million as of 12/31/84.

Case 26

WALLACE AND YOUNGMAN

Mr. William Wallace was preparing for a meeting scheduled in mid-June 1988 with Mr. Arthur Youngman, vice president at United Pennsylvania Bank, a leading regional bank located in Harrisburg, Pennsylvania. Mr. Wallace had for some years been looking for a business he could buy and manage for himself. Locating the proper combination of an attractive business, willing sellers, an appropriate price which he could finance himself, necessary external financing, and a location near where he and his family wished to continue living had not been easy. He thought that a suitable opportunity had knocked at last, and Mr. Wallace had therefore requested Mr. Youngman to meet with him to review the details of the transaction and discuss the possibility that United Pennsylvania would provide the external funds necessary to complete the transaction. He also wished to have Mr. Youngman accompany him late in June to what he anticipated would be a final meeting with the sellers at which the price would be set and terms arranged. Mr. Wallace knew that Mr. Youngman would have to approve of these matters before the prospective loan would be granted, and he also valued Mr. Youngman's opinions. He therefore welcomed the chance to have Mr. Youngman present at the meeting to advise and assist him in the final negotiations.

WILLIAM WALLACE

Mr. Wallace, in his early fifties, had many years of managerial experience in medium to small businesses in the New Jersey area, primarily in apparel and retailing. Following his graduation from Rutgers University in 1959, Mr. Wallace obtained employment with a major retail chain which had just begun to develop large discount stores. He rose rapidly to the position of regional manager when he was forced to leave on the occasion of his father's death to manage his father's small chain of hardware stores. Over several years, he closed some, sold some to individuals and investors, and sold the remainder to a large chain. He was retained as manager of these stores and, again, was rapidly promoted, ultimately into the central buying office in New York City.

The retailing group subsequently encountered financial difficulties and was forced in the late 1970s to sell off some of its better assets. The purchaser of the hardware group already had a staff of buyers, with the result that Mr. Wallace found himself without a job.

At this point, Mr. Wallace decided he wanted to go into business for himself again. His children were finished college, so the cash flow pressure on him was no longer as great as it had been. He had carefully saved most of the bonuses he had earned. His cautious management of his share of his father's estate had enhanced that sum sufficiently to keep up with inflation. Mr. Wallace thought that he could safely afford to risk between $400,000 and $500,000 in a venture. It would be possible for him to go higher, but he was not at all sure he would be comfortable initially committing his entire financial reserves of perhaps $600,000.

Suitable opportunities, as noted already, proved more difficult to locate than Mr. Wallace had expected. Rather than either take on a long-term job or reduce his capital by living off it, Mr. Wallace took a series of relatively short-term consulting assignments of a general management nature. For instance, since early 1985 he had been working as a trouble-shooter for a financially oriented management of a small conglomerate which had been put together from

This case was prepared with the help of Mr. Paul H. Hunn, Senior Vice President, Manufacturers Hanover Trust Company. Details have been altered in order to protect the confidences of the company and individuals without altering the nature of the managerial decision.

bargain purchases of troubled companies. In fact, Mr. Youngman had been instrumental in making Mr. Wallace's name known to the management of the conglomerate.

ATWATER ADHESIVES, INC.

Atwater Adhesives, Inc., founded in 1946, made water-based adhesives and primers for the vinyl wallpaper industry at two unionized plants totaling 40,000 square feet and employing 30 workers. One plant was located in New Jersey, and the other was in Indiana. The production process involved compounding chemicals purchased from suppliers such as DuPont, Celanese, and Allied Corporation, on 30-day terms. The purchase of several compounding machines in 1987 materially improved margins by bringing this capability in-house.

Atwater served largely as a private-label supplier for major paint companies, such as PPG, Sherwin-Williams, and Standard Brands. Some of the formulations were used by the manufacturer for prepasted paper. Other products were packaged and labeled for sale directly to the ultimate consumer without requiring further processing by the distributor, which sold them to paint, hardware, and home improvement stores (some of which were their own or franchised outlets) on terms of 1/10/net 30. Additional, smaller markets existed for professionals and do-it-yourselfers which were serviced through smaller chains, mail order houses, and occasionally a direct purchase by a retail store.

The sales force consisted of six individuals who covered the East Coast and the Midwest. They were compensated on the basis of a salary plus commission. Good service was essential. Because the wallpaper manufacturers tended to schedule level production, there was no significant seasonal pattern to Atwater's business.

According to information appearing in a trade publication in mid-1987, Atwater had 30–35 percent of the market. The largest competitor was in Cleveland, with a market share of 15–20 percent. Other major competitors included firms in Milwaukee (7–8 percent), Teaneck, New Jersey (5 percent), and Columbus, Ohio (3 percent). Many small competitors accounted for the remaining portion of the market.

Summary financial information for fiscal years ended February 28, 1986–1988 is included in Exhibits 1, 2, and 3. A complete statement for the 1988 fiscal year, with an unqualified opinion by Moscowitz & Murphy, is reproduced in the appendix. Inventory was maintained on a LIFO basis and as of February 28, 1988 consisted of:

Raw materials	69%
Finished goods	24%
Packaging	7%

THE SELLERS

The co-founders of the business each owned 50 percent of the common stock. Mr. Irwin Wasser, 72, who directed the sales activities of the company, wished to retire. Mr. Edward Attel, 66, who directed the production, welcomed a chance to remain in the business. He seemed fully recovered from 1986 bypass surgery.

As far as Mr. Wallace had been able to determine, the sellers were reputable and had a good name in the business. Relationships with the union seemed amicable. Mr. Wallace had been unable to find any potential legal problems, pension fund difficulties, or community relation situations which might crop up to reduce the value of the company.

LETTER TO MR. YOUNGMAN

After a luncheon meeting with Mr. Youngman, at which Mr. Wallace had described the Atwater case in general terms, Mr. Wallace thought it would help him bring all aspects of the deal together if he wrote down a number of critical factors. This effort ended up as a letter to Mr. Youngman, sent to help him prepare for the next session where a more comprehensive discussion was planned. The letter is reproduced as Exhibit 4.

Although interest rates had declined significantly from those of a year earlier (the bank prime rate was currently 9 percent, down from the level of 9 1/4 percent it had reached a year earlier and from the much higher rates of the early 1980s), Mr. Wallace was concerned about the possible return of higher levels. He could protect himself from the cash drain such high rates might entail if he could persuade Mr. Youngman to accept a "cash cap" on the interest. As Mr. Wallace understood the arrangement, a cash cap was a provision on a floating-rate loan which attempted to reduce the dangerous effects of high interest rates on a borrower by spreading out the interest payments once a predetermined level of rates had been reached. The lenders were also protected by knowing that they would ultimately receive payment of the interest (with interest on it).

The mechanics were somewhat complex. If the base rate floated above the preestablished cap on cash interest payments, a new "cash cap" loan line would be set up by the bank for the borrower. The interest due from rates above the cash cap would be treated as a new loan and added to the principal of the cash cap loan. Interest would be accrued on this account, but cash payments on this principal and interest would not be required until the rates again fell back below the cap rate.

If there was a balance due the bank in the cash cap line, the borrower would continue to pay the bank at the cap rate even after the base rates had fallen to lower levels. Payment of the differential between the cap rate and the floating rate would be used to amortize the balance in the special cap rate loan account. When the balance in the cap rate loan account had been eliminated, the rate on the basic loan would drop back down to the basic floating rate.

Alternatively, Mr. Wallace could negotiate a fixed rate. This would be considerably more expensive than a floating rate loan and would have high prepayment penalties.

From conversations with Mr. Youngman and with his own personal accountant, Mr. Wallace had pieced together a layman's understanding of the effect the tax laws would have on a transaction such as he was considering. If he bought assets from Atwater, the Atwater corporate entity would have to pay taxes on any profit over its book cost. While there might be both regular income and capital gains involved, the effect of the differences would probably be minimal because the tax rate was the same, 34 percent for corporations. In addition, the sellers would have to pay taxes at personal tax rates of 28 percent on any of the proceeds distributed to them which constituted a profit to them as individuals. For example, if Mr. Wallace assumed Atwater's liabilities, the cost basis of Atwater's assets would be the book value of $2.2 million. The balance sheet suggested that the owners had actually paid no more than $34,150 for their shares.

If Mr. Wallace bought *assets,* he could write them up to cost. This adjustment would reduce the goodwill in the transaction, which was not deductible for tax purposes, and allow recovery of that portion of the costs allowable to depreciable assets on a tax-deductible basis.

If Mr. Wallace bought the *stock* of Atwater, however, then the sellers would only have to pay personal capital gains taxes at 28 percent. Mr. Wallace would be unable to write up the value of the assets without paying taxes on the increase. Furthermore, since the company would maintain its existing tax basis for the assets, if the assets were subsequently sold, the company would have to pay a tax on the full gain from its book value. Mr. Wallace's personal tax basis for the stock would be the price he paid for it, but this would not affect the company's tax books at all.

In order to maximize the cash flow from the investment, Mr. Wallace could consider forming a *Sub-Chapter S* corporation because its profits would be treated for tax purposes as though the venture was a partnership. The maximum tax rate would be the maximum personal tax rate of 28 percent rather than the maximum corporation rate of 34 percent. Dividends to Mr. Wallace would enable him to pay the taxes but would not add further to his personal income. A Sub-Chapter S corporation did not negate corporate limited liability.

It was also possible that Messrs. Attel and Wasser would decide to hold the proceeds of an asset sale in the "shell" of the Atwater Company, converting it to a personal investment company (PIC). If the PIC paid out all the dividends it received, it would only pay corporate income tax on the income rather than the penalty rates of a personal holding company. Moreover, if the company invested in corporate equities, it would only be liable for taxes on 20 percent of the dividends it received because of the intercompany dividend exclusion.

Unfortunately, the payment of preferred dividends was not a deductible expense for the paying company, nor could a Sub-Chapter S company have preferred stock outstanding. Nevertheless, it might be possible to negotiate a lower price using preferred stock. If the amount were sufficiently lower, Mr. Wallace might have a lower net cash flow using a preferred stock rather than using an interest-bearing security.

Mr. Wallace's accountant also advised him that the new tax law changed the relative attractiveness of capital gains versus payment for noncompetitive agreements. The capital gains on a sale of assets would be taxed both to the selling corporation and then, ultimately, to the owners when the corporation liquidated. Payment for noncompetitive agreements counted only as income to the individual. Because both tax rates were the same, the latter form of payment was now preferred.

MR. YOUNGMAN'S RESPONSE

As Mr. Youngman finished reading Mr. Wallace's letter, he jotted down a number of considerations, which he reviewed with Mr. Wallace in a telephone call to set up the date for the next meeting. "Here are some things we're going to want to review and consider," Mr. Youngman had said. "It's not the whole list, and I know we'll both have more ideas in the meantime, but here are my ideas at the moment."

1. Problems of infusing a new senior manager into an established business.
2. The cash flow characteristics of the industry and this particular company.
3. Tax consequences of writing up assets and of different methods of paying off the sellers, including the use of payments not to compete.
4. Appropriate form of "mezzanine financing" from institutional sources versus the notes or other payment the sellers would take.

Because Mr. Wallace planned to meet with a mutual friend, a partner in a "big eight" accounting firm who had specialized in smaller and entrepreneurial businesses, Mr. Youngman wondered how best to incorporate these possible additional insights into the development of a negotiating strategy for price and payment terms.

THE BANK'S SITUATION

United Pennsylvania Bank was a major bank in the mid-Atlantic region. On the one hand, it enjoyed a statewide branch system and a reputation for innovative consumer and retail banking. On the other, its roots reached long and deep into the corporate banking business. Pressure on the upper end of this business, from money center and larger banks in New York, Philadelphia, and Pittsburgh as well as from its own customers' turning to alternative sources of funds such as commercial paper, had resulted in aggressive emphasis on middle-market and smaller companies, on new and venture businesses, and on methods of making creative yet well-protected loans. United Pennsylvania had been one of the first banks in the region to make leveraged buy-out loans, occasionally taking an equity position through the venture capital subsidiary of the holding company. Mr. Youngman was familiar with the practices in the area, having helped structure leveraged buy-outs on several occasions and even having participated in working out such a loan when the situation deteriorated.

In mid-1988, the economic picture was surprisingly robust. The recession which was widely anticipated had not materialized. Unemployment was down, and the gross national product appeared to be growing strongly. Warnings of inflation were appearing, but interest rates had increased only slightly. Producer prices had been growing at an annual rate of 3 percent since mid-1986. Following the stockmarket correction of

October 1987, when 3-month T-bills fell from 7 percent to 5 1/4 percent, the stockmarket had recovered much of its lost value and T-bill rates had risen to 6 1/2 percent. The prime rate, which had peaked at 9 1/4 percent in October 1987, and then fallen to 8 1/2 percent during early 1988, was back to 9 percent currently. The rates were up about 1 percent from their levels a year earlier. At the end of May, Standard & Poor's index of preferred stocks showed a yield of 9.30 percent, compared with 10.98 percent on corporate triple-B bonds. The dividend yield on the S&P 500 index was 3.6 percent.

Case 26 Wallace and Youngman

EXHIBIT 1 ATWATER ADHESIVES, INC. SUMMARY CONSOLIDATED BALANCE SHEET AS OF FEBRUARY 28, 1988 (thousands of dollars)

Assets		*Liabilities and Equity*	
Cash	$ 531	Notes payable—bank	$ -0-
Accounts receivable	1,675	Accounts payable	1,110
Inventory (LIFO)	782	Accruals	675
Other	114		
Current assets	$3,102	Current liabilities	$ 1,785
Net fixed assets	855	Deferred taxes	59
Other assets	70	Common equity	2,183
Total	$4,027	Total	$ 4,027

Case 26 Wallace and Youngman

EXHIBIT 2 ATWATER ADHESIVES, INC. SUMMARY FINANCIAL STATISTICS FISCAL YEARS ENDED FEBRUARY 28, 1986–1988 (dollar figures in thousands)

	1986	*1987*	*1988*
Total net revenues	$7,798	$9,497	$9,841
Net profit	188	460	811
Net worth	915	1,372	2,183
Working capital	349	481	1,317
Gross profit margin	20.5%	26.4%	31.7%
Net profit margin	2.4	4.8	8.0
Return on average equity	22.9	40.3	45.6
Dividend payout	-0-	-0-	-0-
Current ratio	1.22×	1.25×	1.74×
Quick ratio	.77	.74	1.24
Total debt/Net worth	171%	140%	84%

Case 26 Wallace and Youngman

EXHIBIT 3 ATWATER ADHESIVES, INC. FUNDS FLOW ANALYSIS FISCAL YEARS ENDED FEBRUARY 28, 1986–1988

	1986	*1987*	*1988*
Net income	$ 188	$ 461	$ 811
Depreciation	128	156	165
Deferred taxes, etc.	-0-	26	36
Total sources	$ 316	$ 643	$ 1,012
Cash dividends	$ -0-	$ -0-	$ -0-
Capital expenditures	280	503	174
Other	1	7	1
Total uses	$ 281	$ 510	$ 175
Change in working capital	$ 35	$ 133	$ 837
Working capital	$ 349	$ 482	$ 1,317

Case 26 Wallace and Youngman

EXHIBIT 4 LETTER FROM MR. WALLACE TO MR. YOUNGMAN

June 1, 1988

Mr. Arthur Youngman
Vice President
United Pennsylvania Bank
Harrisburg, Pennsylvania

Dear Art:

I very much enjoyed seeing you again yesterday in Philadelphia and having the opportunity to fill you in on developments at my current assignment, specifically, and on many other things in general. The lunch was superb, and your reputation as a selector of fine restaurants is very much intact.

As I told you, Art, I am currently in the process of winding up my current consulting assignment, and I am very much interested in any other assignments that might come along. You indicated you would think about it and might even discuss it with some of your colleagues, which would be enormously helpful. I would very much appreciate the opportunity to have lunch with one or two of them and could come to Harrisburg as appropriate.

It was also the customary pleasure to get your advice on my efforts to locate a good company that could be purchased on a leveraged buy-out basis and in which I could obtain a reasonably good equity position. As I described at lunch, I think I have uncovered an excellent property in the chemical (adhesives) business. It is privately owned by two men. The elder is 72, and he wants to settle his estate. The younger is 66 and in reasonable shape despite a bypass operation in 1986. He wants to be part of the company for another five years after receiving his share of the buy-out.

Case 26 Wallace and Youngman

EXHIBIT 4 (*continued*)

The company is a leader in its industry with a 30–35 percent share of the market. It has shown steady growth and profitability but has avoided any significant debt. It has strong, new assets, which will contribute to excellent profitability this year when business in general has been so difficult. The new equipment, which was installed last year, will substantially increase the firm's margins and earnings in the future.

Enclosed [provided as the Appendix] you will find the balance sheet and income statement for 1988, which includes comparisons with 1987 in most cases. The notes include an aging of accounts receivable, which look good. I have also looked at an inventory of the plant and equipment.

This is a company that has a great growth potential beyond where it is today. There are many opportunities which have yet to be explored from a marketing perspective.

The owners' opening position concerning price is a $2.3 million cash payment on closing and a payout of $4.7 million over five (or more) years. This is too rich in my opinion, and I am certain it can be negotiated down substantially.

I am very much interested in this opportunity, Art. It meets the criteria I have set, and I hope you will feel as I do after looking at the numbers. Please look at this data and tell me what you think of the company, based on what you know about it. What's it worth? What should I pay for it? How can the deal be set up so that I get the maximum amount of equity on a leveraged buy-out basis?

I really appreciate your help in this instance, Art, as in all matters. I would like to do the deal through your bank, and I wait with great interest to hear your reaction and your suggestions. In the meantime, of course, I still welcome your help in broadening my consulting because you never know how one of these deals will turn out.

Looking forward to hearing from you and seeing you soon. Let's lunch together and see if you can maintain your record on selecting outstanding restaurants.

Warmest personal regards,

Cordially,

/s/ Bill
William Wallace

APPENDIX A

Case 26 Wallace and Youngman

EXHIBIT A ATWATER ADHESIVES, INC. BALANCE SHEET FEBRUARY 28, 1988, AND FEBRUARY 28, 1987

	1988	*1987*
Current Assets		
Cash and Temporary Cash Investments	$ 531,070	$ 155,826
Accounts Receivable (*Note 2*)*	1,675,229	1,244,004
Inventories (*Note 1*)*	781,823	867,611
Other (*Note 3*)*	114,466	113,617
Total Current Assets	3,102,588	2,381,058
Fixed Assets, At Cost (*Note 1*)*		
Machinery and Equipment	1,341,617	1,201,129
Leasehold Improvements	179,191	164,198
Automotive Equipment	54,902	49,664
Equipment Deposit	6,000	—
Total	1,581,710	1,414,991
Less: Accumulated Depreciation and Amortization	726,631	566,165
Net Value of Fixed Assets	855,079	848,826
Other Assets		
Cash Value—Life Insurance (Net of Loans) (*Note 4*)*	34,231	33,427
Security Deposit	25,573	25,573
Other	9,453	8,636
Total Other Assets	69,257	67,636
Total Assets	$4,026,924	$3,297,520

Liabilities and Stockholders' Equity

	1988	*1987*
Current Liabilities		
Accounts Payable	$1,109,582	$1,251,041
Notes Payable	—	145,000
Accrued Salaries and Wages	163,590	90,774
Other Accrued Expenses and Liabilities (*Note 5*)*	512,016	413,144
Total Current Liabilities	1,785,188	1,899,959
Deferred Income Taxes	58,700	25,700

Case 26 Wallace and Youngman

EXHIBIT A (*continued*)

	1988	*1987*
Stockholders' Equity		
Common Stock, No Par Value Authorized, 1,000 Shares Issues and Outstanding, 275.1 shares	34,150	34,150
Retained Earnings (*Exhibit B*)	2,186,661	1,375,486
Total	2,220,811	1,409,636
Less: Treasury Stock	37,775	37,775
Total Stockholders' Equity	2,183,036	1,371,861
Total Liabilities and Stockholders' Equity	$4,026,924	$3,297,520

*See Notes to Financial Statements.

Case 26 Wallace and Youngman

EXHIBIT B ATWATER ADHESIVES, INC. STATEMENT OF INCOME AND RETAINED EARNINGS FOR THE YEARS ENDED FEBRUARY 28, 1988, AND FEBRUARY 28, 1987

	Amount		*Percent of Sales*	
	1988	*1987*	*1988*	*1987*
Sales	$10,083,584	$9,709,718		
Less: Discounts and Allowances	242,194	212,765		
Net Sales	9,841,390	9,496,953	100.00	100.00
Cost of Manufacturing Goods Sold (*Exhibit D*)	6,721,996	7,014,203	68.30	73.86
Manufacturing Profit	3,119,394	2,482,750	31.70	26.14
Selling Expenses (*Exhibit E*)	1,099,724	1,077,791	11.18	11.35
Selling Profit	2,019,670	1,404,959	20.52	14.79
General and Administrative Expenses (*Exhibit E*)	789,606	637,248	8.02	6.71
Operating Income	1,230,064	767,711	12.50	8.08
Other Income (Net of Deductions)	17,897	13,396	.18	.14
Income before Provision for Income Taxes	1,247,961	781,107	12.68	8.22
Income Taxes (*Note 8*)*	436,786	320,567	4.44	3.37
Net Income	811,175	460,540	8.24	4.85
Retained Earnings—Beginning of Year	1,375,486	914,946		
Retained Earnings—End of Year	$ 2,186,661	$1,375,486		

*See Notes to Financial Statements.

EXHIBIT C ATWATER ADHESIVES, INC. STATEMENT OF CHANGES IN FINANCIAL POSITION FOR THE YEARS ENDED FEBRUARY 28, 1988, AND FEBRUARY 28, 1987

	1988	*1987*
Sources of Working Capital		
Net Income (*Exhibit B*)	$ 811,175	$ 460,540
Provision for Depreciation and Amortization	164,701	156,291
Total From Operations	975,876	616,831
Disposition of Fixed Assets	3,026	—
Deferred Income Taxes	33,000	25,700
Total	1,011,902	642,531
Application of Working Capital		
Acquisition of Fixed Assets	167,980	502,921
Deposits On Machinery and Equipment	6,000	—
Other—Net	1,621	7,141
Total	175,601	510,062
Increase in Working Capital	$ 836,301	$ 132,469

Analysis of Changes in Components of Working Capital

	1988	*1987*
Current Assets—Increase (Decrease)		
Cash and Temporary Cash Investments	$ 375,244	$ 98,044
Accounts Receivable	431,225	100,586
Inventories	(85,788)	270,541
Other Current Assets	849	752
Total	721,530	469,923
Current Liabilities—(Increase) Decrease		
Accounts Payable	141,459	(96,522)
Notes Payable	145,000	35,000
Accrued Salaries and Wages	(72,816)	(52)
Other Accrued Expenses and Liabilities	(98,872)	(275,880)
Total	114,771	(337,454)
Increase in Working Capital	$ 836,301	$ 132,469

Case 26 Wallace and Youngman

EXHIBIT D ATWATER ADHESIVES, INC. COST OF MANUFACTURING GOODS SOLD FOR THE YEARS ENDED FEBRUARY 28, 1988, AND FEBRUARY 28, 1987

	Amount		*Percent of Sales*	
	1988	*1987*	*1988*	*1987*
Materials Consumed				
Inventory—Beginning of Year	$ 867,611	$ 597,070		
Purchases (Net of Discounts)	4,883,219	5,446,938		
Freight In	204,842	269,411		
Total	5,955,672	6,313,419		
Less: Inventory—End of Year	781,823	867,611		
Total Materials Consumed	5,173,849	5,445,808	52.57	57.34
Payroll				
Supervisors	123,366	155,312	1.26	1.63
Factory	470,707	511,472	4.78	5.39
Laboratory	39,409	35,390	.40	.37
Total Payroll	633,482	702,174	6.44	7.39
Factory Overhead				
Rent	207,919	195,205	2.11	2.06
Heat, Light, and Power	149,764	125,009	1.52	1.32
Repairs and Maintenance	41,879	66,480	.43	.70
Factory and Laboratory Supplies and Expenses	99,777	115,735	1.01	1.22
Consulting Fees	31,038	1,444	.32	.01
Contract Packaging	69,538	74,351	.71	.78
Payroll Taxes	66,313	69,010	.67	.73
Insurance				
General	33,329	31,324	.34	.33
Group, Hospitalization and Other	74,999	52,790	.76	.56
Equipment Rental	1,750	1,431	.02	.01
Depreciation—Machinery and Equipment	117,487	110,905	1.19	1.17
Amortization—Leasehold Improvements	20,872	22,537	.21	.24
Total Factory Overhead	914,665	866,221	9.29	9.13
Total Cost of Manufacturing Goods Sold	$6,721,996	$7,014,203	68.30	73.86

Case 26 Wallace and Youngman

EXHIBIT E ATWATER ADHESIVES, INC. SELLING EXPENSES, GENERAL AND ADMINISTRATIVE EXPENSES FOR THE YEARS ENDED FEBRUARY 28, 1988, AND FEBRUARY 28, 1987

	Amount		*Percent of Sales*	
	1988	*1987*	*1988*	*1987*
Selling Expenses				
Salaries				
Sales	$ 108,000	$ 99,212	1.10	1.04
Marketing and Development	52,908	52,338	.54	.55
Drivers	21,650	23,643	.22	.25
Sales Commissions	115,470	130,735	1.17	1.38
Sales and Travel Expense	128,837	113,425	1.31	1.19
Auto Expenses	13,651	11,657	.14	.12
Freight and Trucking	391,771	401,732	3.98	4.23
Packing and Shipping Expenses	171,020	185,197	1.74	1.95
Advertising	53,573	18,679	.54	.20
Insurance				
General	13,695	15,276	.14	.16
Group, Hospitalization and Other	5,172	3,641	.05	.04
Payroll Taxes	11,650	12,124	.12	.13
Depreciation—Automotive Equipment	12,327	10,132	.13	.11
Total Selling Expenses	$1,099,724	$1,077,791	11.18	11.35
General and Administrative Expenses				
Salaries				
Officers	$ 326,283	238,127	3.31	2.51
Office	134,685	122,430	1.37	1.29
Office Supplies and Expense	32,365	40,273	.33	.42
Computer Supplies and Expense	4,288	4,333	.04	.05
Telephone	40,926	41,817	.42	.44
Professional Fees	27,275	42,588	.28	.45
Taxes				
Payroll	11,650	12,124	.12	.13
Other	17,413	19,640	.18	.21
Insurance				
General	1,315	1,292	.01	.01
Group, Hospitalization and Other	6,034	4,247	.06	.04
Life	8,417	7,609	.08	.08
Provision for Employees' Pension Plan (*Notes 1 and 6*)*	108,378	47,874	1.10	.50
Interest Expense	48,147	31,543	.49	.33
Uncollectable Accounts	2,625	4,450	.03	.05
General Expense	5,790	6,184	.06	.07
Depreciation—Office Equipment	14,015	12,717	.14	.13
Total General and Administrative Expenses	$ 789,606	$ 637,248	8.02	6.71

*See Notes to Financial Statements.

Case 26 Wallace and Youngman

ATWATER ADHESIVES, INC.—NOTES TO FINANCIAL STATEMENTS FEBRUARY 28, 1988

Note 1: Significant Accounting Policies

Inventories
Inventories are stated at the lower of cost or market. The cost of raw materials inventories was determined by the last-in, first-out (LIFO) method of valuation. Had the first-in, first-out (FIFO) method been used, the inventories would have been $67,689 higher at February 28, 1988, and $121,068 higher at February 28, 1987.

Fixed Assets and Depreciation
Depreciation is provided on the straight-line and double-declining balance methods over the estimated useful lives of the assets as follows:

Machinery and Equipment	5–10 Years
Leasehold Improvements	Shorter of Estimated Life or Term of Lease
Automotive Equipment	3 Years

Assets acquired after December 31, 1980, but before August 1, 1986, are depreciated under the accelerated cost recovery system (ACRS) for income tax purposes. Assets acquired after July 31, 1986 are depreciated under the ACRS as modified by the Tax Reform Act of 1986.

Maintenance and repairs that do not extend the life of the assets are expensed currently. Costs and related accumulated depreciation of property replaced or otherwise disposed of are removed from the accounts and gains or losses on disposition are included in or charged against income.

Federal Income Tax
The Company reports its income together with its subsidiary in a consolidated income tax return. Timing differences, the tax effect of which are deferred to future periods, are related to ACRS depreciation. Investment tax credits are recorded as a reduction of the current provision for federal income taxes on the flow-through method. Similarly, any recapture of investment tax credits are reflected in the year of the recapture.

Pension Plan
The Company has a noncontributory pension plan covering all qualified employees. Pension cost is actuarially computed based on the individual level premium method. Accrued pension cost is funded on a current basis.

Note 2: Accounts Receivable

An aging of accounts receivable, as of February 28, 1988, follows:

0–30 Days	$ 928,786
31–60	510,064
61–90	153,398
Over 90	82,981
Total	$1,675,229

ATWATER ADHESIVES, INC.—NOTES TO FINANCIAL STATEMENTS FEBRUARY 28, 1988 (*continued*)

Note 3: Other Current Assets

Other current assets at February 28, 1988, included:

Prepaid Expenses	
Insurance	$ 53,280
Shipping Supplies	35,400
Rent	14,088
Interest	3,653
Tax	395
Other	7,650
Total	$114,466

Note 4: Life Insurance

The Company owns and is beneficiary of the life insurance policies

Assured	*Amount*
Irwin Wasser	$425,000
Edward Attel	100,000
Total	$525,000

In accordance with agreements, the life insurance proceeds are to be applied to the purchase of the assured's stock in the Company and to fund deferred compensation.

The policies had a total cash value of $150,885. After reduction for premium loans of $116,654, the net cash value amounted to $34,231.

Note 5: Other Accrued Expenses and Liabilities

At February 28, 1988, other current expenses and liabilities were:

Taxes	$271,554
Pension Plan	108,378
Commissions	50,409
Other Operating Expenses	44,804
Reserve for Vacation Pay	36,871
Total	$512,016

Note 6: Pension Plan

The Company's pension plan was initiated on February 28, 1974, and covers all qualified employees. The pension plan provision for the years ended February 28, 1988 and 1987, amounted to $108,378 and $47,874, respectively.

As of March 1, 1987, the most recent data for which information was available, there were no unfunded benefits.

Note 7: Reserve for Vacation Pay

Reserves for vacation pay in the amounts of $36,871 and $37,090 were charged to operations for each of the years ended February 28, 1988 and 1987.

Case 26 Wallace and Youngman

ATWATER ADHESIVES, INC.—NOTES TO FINANCIAL STATEMENTS FEBRUARY 28, 1988 (*continued*)

Note 8: Income Taxes

Provision for income taxes for the years ended February 28, 1988 and 1987, are shown below:

	1988	*1987*
Current Year	$469,786	$294,867
Deferred	33,000	25,700
Total	$502,786	$320,567

The Company's federal income tax returns have been examined by the Internal Revenue Service through the year ended February 28, 1980.

Note 9: Lease Commitments

The Company leases premises in New Jersey and Indiana. The New Jersey lease provides for minimum rentals of $403,771 to May 31, 1994, subject to adjustment based upon changes in the Consumer Price Index. The terms of the Indiana lease provide for minimum rentals of $309,718 to June 30, 1991. In addition, the Indiana lease includes six successive renewal options of three years each. The annual rent during the first renewal is $98,406. Thereafter, the annual rentals are increased by 5 percent each year.

Case 27

CLEF CORPORATION

In early August 1982, Mr. Leo Bernstein, Clef Corporation president, visited Mr. Andrew Previn, the company's account officer at the Sonata National Bank. Mr. Bernstein brought the unhappy news that the company's operating losses had now reached more than $3 million for the first half of the 1983 fiscal year, which began February 1, 1982. The company was also in violation of a working capital covenant on its long-term insurance company debt.

Sonata was Clef's lead bank, holding $4.5 million of the company's unsecured notes payable. Several other banks held a total of $4.25 million in unsecured notes which, together with the $4.5 million owed to Sonata, would mature in seven days. Long-term unsecured notes payable totaling over $3.2 million were outstanding to Toccata Insurance Company, of which current maturities equaled $220,000. (Exhibits 1 and 2 present interim financial statements as of July 29, 1982. Financial statements for the 1980, 1981, and 1982 fiscal years are provided in Exhibits 3 and 4.)

Mr. Previn, whose bank was agent for the bank loans, had been working closely with Clef's management since the end of the 1982 fiscal year. The size of the bank loan which was outstanding in February 1982—$8 million—and the company's marginal profits during the fiscal year 1982 had been signals of serious potential problems. A variety of methods of restructuring the bank debt had been considered. One of the participating banks had been persuaded to increase its $1 million line by $750,000, but the others (including Sonata) had refused to advance Clef more funds. Management had also explored a number of other methods of raising funds, such as selling selected assets, but so far these efforts had not been successful.

Mr. Previn had therefore been considering whether he should recommend extending the loans when they became due the following week. If he made this recommendation, he would need to decide on what terms to recommend.

Mr. Previn was considering two other alternatives. Assets of the company, most likely inventories, could supplement the security provided by the subsidiary's loan guarantee. This alternative potentially involved legal risks because certain provisions of the bankruptcy law might be violated if the banks acquired a preferred position through a debt restructure agreement. In addition, if collateral were obtained by the banks, manufacturers concerned about their increasing exposure as unsecured creditors might refuse to extend further credit or might even institute legal proceedings to collect past due accounts.

Alternatively, the banks could exercise their right to setoff. Through this action, the banks would pronounce Clef in default if the loans were not paid as they became due and would establish a legal claim to the company's cash deposits. Clef would then be unable to utilize its cash balances and would have little choice but to petition for court protection under Chapter 11 of the bankruptcy law.

During the meeting, Mr. Bernstein expressed his hope that operations for the second half of the current fiscal year, together with the cash proceeds from the sale of assets, would generate sufficient cash to retire a significant portion of the bank debt. Once this had taken place and the company's new earnings base had been established, the bank loan could be negotiated so that repayment would fit the company's cash

This case was originally developed by Kevin Ramundo with the support of individuals and institutions who wish to remain anonymous. Certain of the company's characteristics and financial information have been changed to protect company confidences without altering the nature of the managerial decision.

generating ability. Mr. Bernstein provided Mr. Previn with information about possible levels of operations for the rest of the fiscal year.

Mr. Previn thanked Mr. Bernstein for this information, and they agreed to meet with representatives of the other lenders in two days. At this meeting, Mr. Previn would be expected to present his recommendations on the actions the banks should take.

COMPANY BACKGROUND

Clef Corporation competed in various segments of the retail and wholesale business. Its Major Stores Division consisted of 26 midwestern discount department stores which carried a variety of household products, clothing, and personal care merchandise. Some departments within these stores were operated under licenses granted to outside retailers. The Bee Sharp Fashions Division operated 176 women's apparel stores throughout the United States. These stores primarily sold moderately priced, ready-to-wear ladies' and misses' apparel and accessories. Base Distributors, Inc., a wholly owned subsidiary, was engaged in the wholesale distribution of small appliances to approximately 50 department and discount store chains located primarily in the Midwest. The Major Stores Division was Base's largest customer, accounting for 25 percent of its sales volume. A wholly owned fabric store subsidiary was an insignificant part of the company's activities. Typically, 58 percent of Clef's sales occurred in the second half of the fiscal year.

The retail and wholesale business in which Clef was engaged was highly competitive. In most locations, the Major Stores and Bee Sharp Fashions divisions competed directly with national chains of considerable marketing and financial strength. Price competition, especially among discount retailers, had adversely affected gross margins in recent years. Base competed with national and regional distributors, some of which were much larger and offered more extensive product lines.

A newly leased facility housing Clef's executive offices and a modern semiautomated soft goods warehouse had been completed and occupied in the fall of 1981. The warehouse was expected to improve inventory control while effecting logistic economies. Base's major warehouse was also semiautomated. All retail outlets occupied leased premises.

Mr. Bernstein, previously an executive with Base, had joined Clef when the two companies merged in late 1979 under a pooling of interests. Soon after the merger, the existing president and other Clef executives resigned. They were replaced with members of the former Base management group. Mr. Bernstein was elected president and joined Clef's board of directors. Mr. George Sell, the former president of Base, was Clef's largest stockholder and became chairman of the board. The other members of the new management group also served as directors.

The new management group had implemented many beneficial and needed changes since assuming control of operations. The introduction of more sophisticated equipment information systems had assisted management in efforts to control expenses and inventory. Individual stores were given monthly sales and profit budgets. Actual versus planned results were carefully monitored by upper management. Hopelessly unprofitable stores were being closed. Approximately forty women's apparel stores had been closed to date. The image of the remaining stores was being upgraded as the Bee Sharp Fashions Division shifted its marketing focus to younger, style-conscious women. During fiscal year 1982, nine women's apparel stores were opened in large, increasingly popular shopping malls. In both retail divisions, new merchandising techniques were introduced and older stores were being refurbished.

The previous management had made substantial investments in real estate in an effort to obtain prime locations, preferential lease rates, and speculator's profits. Typically, the company would lend funds to outside developers who, in turn, would issue notes to Clef. These practices had been required because Clef had entered the discount business relatively late in the industry's development and, as a new entrant, had difficulty in gaining a foothold solely on its reputation. As a late entrant it further suffered from a paucity of prime locations as well as from the intensity of competition as the various stores and chains fought hard to grow or even to survive.

The Bernstein administration had been liquidating these investments and notes in order to increase Clef's working capital.

FINANCIAL HISTORY AND CONDITION

Clef's earning performance had been quite erratic in the 1980, 1981, and 1982 fiscal years, as shown in Exhibit 3. Recessionary problems and high interest rates had contributed to the difficult operating environment. Inventory markdowns of $770,000 and bad-debt expense of $265,000 which had not been recognized by the former management were charged against 1980 income. Extraordinary expense of $89,000 associated with closing nine unprofitable women's apparel stores contributed to that year's $601,000 net loss. In 1981, the company reported a net profit of $1,054,000 including a $364,000 extraordinary gain from federal income tax losses carried forward. A net profit of $188,000 was earned in fiscal 1982, when the total costs of moving the company's headquarters and warehousing operations were expensed. In contract, $219,000 in new store preopening expenses incurred in fiscal 1982 were deferred until 1983 and 1984 as a result of a change in accounting treatment. Before 1982, such costs were expensed as incurred. A $265,000 extraordinary gain resulting from the sale of real estate investments prevented a deficit and allowed the company to report a marginal profit for 1982.

The Bee Sharp Fashions and Major Stores divisions were the source of Clef's operating losses, as illustrated in Exhibit 5. Bee Sharp Fashions' 1980 operating deficit of over $860,000 was the result of the unprofitability of numerous small, low-volume stores, many of which had since been closed. In 1982, a combination of higher merchandise costs and consumer resistance to price increases was responsible for that division's $500,000 operating deficit. The Major Stores Division's loss of $167,000 in fiscal 1982 was due to the unprofitability of eight stores opened during the year. These stores were located in areas affected by high unemployment, which had caused their sales to fall well below projected levels. The Base subsidiary remained profitable during the period from 1980 to 1982.

Operating deficits recurred during the first half of 1983 fiscal year, which ended July 29, 1982, when Clef reported a $3,343,000 loss. Continuing losses in the eight stores opened in fiscal year 1982 were the primary reason for Major Stores $3,125,000 operating deficit. Bee Sharp Fashions lost $313,000 as a result of the failure of summer sales markdowns to generate sufficient incremental sales volume. Also, efforts to return twenty-nine smaller women's apparel stores to profitability had been unsuccessful. During the first half, Base reported a $95,000 profit.

Clef's liquidity position had deteriorated constantly since 1980. Its current ratio had declined from 1.6× in 1980 to 1.12× as of July 29, 1982. The quick ratio fell from .54× to .24× over the same period. The company was frequently forced to delay payments beyond the normal credit terms offered by most of its suppliers.

At the beginning of the current fiscal year, all major credit reporting agencies had been recommending caution in extending credit to Clef. During the first quarter, payments had been more timely and, with the exception of Dun and Bradstreet, favorable credit ratings had been restored. Faster payments were made possible by funds received from discounting real estate notes receivable, the sale of $2,250,000 in accounts receivable, and a $750,000 line increase from Prelude Trust Company. In May, the dissenting credit agency indicated it would consider a favorable credit rating once the bank debt had been put on a more stable basis.

The company's inventory position had improved since the end of fiscal year 1982, when it had reached a high of 109 days cost of goods sold. Recently implemented purchasing controls, the operations of the new warehouse facility, and special summer sales were responsible for the improvement.

For the last three fiscal years, Clef had maintained its $.30 per share annual dividend on its common stock and the stated $2.25 per share dividend on its 4 1/2 percent cumulative preferred stock. Since January 27, 1982, $28,000 and $71,000 in cash dividends had been paid on the preferred and common stock, respectively. Sinking-fund requirements equal to 5 percent of net income were in effect on the preferred issue. The common stock was traded on the American Stock Exchange at a current price of $4.35 per share.

THE EFFORT TO RAISE FUNDS

On January 29, 1982, Clef's outstanding bank borrowings totaled $8.0 million, all under its unsecured lines of credit. Sonata held $4.5 million, Vibrato National Bank held $2.5 million, and Prelude Trust held $1.0 million. In February, Clef had requested a $3.5 million line increase from Sonata which it would use to accelerate trade payments and to retire $277,000 of miscellaneous notes which matured in March. The request was denied when $3.4 million in real estate notes receivable offered as security were found to include certain contingency clauses which limited their collateral value. Clef then successfully persuaded Prelude Trust to increase its $1.0 million line facility by $750,000. In May 1982, the company requested that the Sonata and Vibrato lines, which were due to mature at the end of June 1982, be extended to August 15, when the entire Prelude Trust line matured. The banks agreed to the request.

Toccata Insurance held all of Clef's approximately $3.2 million of long-term notes, including $220,000 with current maturities. Covenants on these notes required the company to maintain consolidated net working capital of $5.5 million or 150 percent of long-term debt, whichever was greater. In addition, dividends were restricted if such distribution would cause retained earnings to fall below $660,000.

In light of Major Stores's recurring losses, Messrs. Bernstein and Sell had recently agreed to dispose of the division. The initial asking price, exclusive of $14 million of inventory valued at cost as of July 1, 1982, was $10 million. The potential purchaser would be required to issue 30- to 90-day notes for the inventory which would be repaid as the inventory was sold.

Negotiations with various parties revealed that it would be extremely difficult to sell the entire division intact. Several prospective purchasers were interested in operating selected stores under management contracts containing options to buy. One such group offered to operate eight Ohio stores in return for 50 percent of the operating profits and an option to buy them for $5.0 million including inventory and fixtures. The purchaser would also receive warrants to purchase 300,000 shares of Clef's common stock at $5 per share. The proposed terms would be $3.0 million in cash at the time of sale and $2.0 million due in January 1983. They also stipulated that the banks would have to convert a significant amount of their debt to a term basis and subordinate it to the trade. This offer was subsequently withdrawn.

A similar offer was made by a second group of investors. Under their proposal, they would lend Clef $3.0 million and would receive an option to buy ten stores including inventory in exchange for the $3.0 million in notes. The loan would be secured by the inventory, furniture, and fixtures in the ten stores. This group would operate all Major Stores for the next 15 months for 50 percent of the operating profit. Warrants for 300,000 common shares of Clef stock at $5 per share would also be given to the purchasers. In 1981, this group had assumed the management of three discount department stores owned by another company and had increased their sales volume by 38 percent in the first 3 months.

Clef's management and representatives of the institutional lenders responded to this offer with a counter-proposal. The ten stores could be purchased intact for $3.0 million in cash plus approximately $3.0 million in notes. The banks would convert $5.75 million to term debt and would subordinate 50 percent of this to the trade. The $3.0 million of notes would be security for the remaining institutional debt. The counter-offer was rejected.

With Clef's failure to negotiate reasonable terms for the disposal of the Major Stores Division, management prepared two alternative plans for its operation during the last half of the current fiscal year. Under one alternative, the Major Stores Division would continue full operations except for six stores which were expected to remain unprofitable. Exhibit 6 contains forecast sales and contribution levels and the merchandise inventory plan for this alternative.

The six unprofitable stores would be closed before the end of October, and their total inventory of approximately $3.0 million would be liquidated. Management was considering either a liquidation sale on the premises or closing the stores without prior notice and moving the inventory to other store locations, where it would be sold. The prospect of employee theft and high costs involved in an on-premise liquidation reduced the desirability of this alternative. Landlord reaction to liquidation was uncertain. It was possible that landlords would attempt to prevent liquidation if substantial lease obligations were outstanding.

The other alternative for continuing the Major Stores Division was to operate all twenty-six stores but to terminate merchandise shipments after September. (Exhibit 7 contains projected sales, contribution levels, and merchandise inventory plans under this alternative.) Anticipated stock supply problems would be circumvented, and inventory levels would be approximately $7.4 million less at the end of January than if shipments were not curtailed.

The plan involving terminating shipments was expected to result in the Major Stores Division's reporting a $1.9 million operating loss for the last half of fiscal 1983, while the operations under the uncurtailed shipments alternative would contribute $136,000 toward corporate and overhead expenses. Regardless of which alternative was selected, Clef did not expect to have to pay income taxes during this period as a result of a sizable tax-loss carryforward. (Exhibit 8 compares corporate overhead expenses for each alternative plan of operation.)

Mr. Bernstein expected to sell most of the Major Stores in January. A lower inventory would lead to a more favorable price for the division to the extent that the company would realize retail prices for the merchandise sold before disposal rather than wholesale or lower prices if the merchandise were sold with the stores.

Mr. Bernstein was also seriously considering selling the Base subsidiary at the end of the current fiscal year. After the planned divestiture of Major Stores, little reason would remain to keep a captive supplier as part of the business. He estimated that Base could be sold for $5.0 million. As he believed that a more advantageous selling price could be negotiated if inventory levels were relatively low, monthly purchases for the remainder of the 1983 fiscal year would be reduced. A $462,000 profit on Base's sales volume of $5.5 million had been forecast for the remaining 6 months of the 1983 fiscal year. This forecast took into consideration the planned Major Stores divestiture and would be valid regardless of which divestiture plan was selected. (Exhibit 9 contains Base's projected sales, profits, inventory levels and cash flow for the last half of the 1983 fiscal year.)

A recent study of the Bee Sharp Fashions Division revealed that 50 of the 176 stores were unprofitable. Twenty-two of these stores would remain unprofitable on expected average sales of $65,000 in the third and fourth quarters and would be closed in October. Each had an average inventory of $17,000 which would be transferred to other stores in the division. The other 28 stores would be marginally profitable through January 1983, when they too would be closed. (Exhibit 10 presents projected sales, contribution levels, and the merchandise inventory plan for Bee Sharp Fashions Division during the last half of fiscal 1983.)

After discontinuing the operations of the 50 stores, the Bee Sharp Fashions Division would consist of the remaining 126 stores and was expected to be highly profitable. Contributions to corporate expenses would approximate 15 percent of sales, which would average $53 million annually over the next 5 years. Related corporate overhead would probably average $5.2 million a year over the period.

Proceeds from the disposal of furniture and fixtures in connection with the closing of the Major Stores and Bee Sharp Fashion stores would equal $78,000 and $48,000 in total, respectively. These amounts approximated the current book value of these assets. Depreciation expense of approximately $340,000 would be incurred during the remainder of the 1983 fiscal year after accounting for the planned disposal of the women's apparel stores and the discount stores under either operating plan.

THE BANK'S DECISION

Mr. Previn's counterparts at the other involved financial institutions were expecting him to recommend a course of action for resolving the problem of their exposure to Clef's unfortunate condition. Before analyzing the material left by Mr. Bernstein, Mr. Previn thought it would be advantageous to approach the problem conceptually by identifying the major issues, anticipating alternative reactions of the involved parties, and evaluating the effect on the company and the institutional lenders of the available alternatives.

Assuming the banks did agree to extend the maturity on their $8.75 million debt for another 180 days, Mr. Previn wondered how much curtailment he should expect when the obligation next came due. If selected portions of Clef's business could not be sold for cash, operating cash flows would be the only means of repayment. Recurring losses could prevent repayment and perhaps lead to requests for additional loans.

Accounts payable currently past due, totaling $8,122,000 for all operations, would have to be paid before Clef's first-half operating losses were made public at the end of September. The company's cash flow projections (summarized in Exhibit 11) had not provided for payments on past due accounts. If more timely payment practices were not adopted, trade creditors might curtail shipments, suspend credit, or seek to force Clef into bankruptcy. Moreover, there was always the possibility that when past due trade accounts were paid, creditors might still stop shipping or refuse to extend credit as a precautionary measure against future losses. A similar creditor reaction might occur if the banks obtained collateral as part of any debt restructure agreement. A suspension of trade credit would increase the company's reliance on bank funds. (Exhibit 12 lists key balance sheet accounts as of July 1982 and forecast for January 1983.)

Mr. Previn then directed his thoughts to setoff and the Chapter 11 petition which would surely follow. Under the petition, the company could consolidate its operations and dispose of unprofitable segments while enjoying court protection. As trade creditors have a preferred position on shipments made after the bankruptcy court grants a Chapter 11 petition, the likelihood of curtailed shipments would be diminished and limited trade credit would be available. In addition, the banks could relend the funds setoff against new and adequate security with court assurance of a priority creditor position. Chapter 11 reorganization allowed leases to be cancelled with a limit on lessor damage claims equal to 3 years' lease payments at a maximum. This provision would be quite beneficial for Clef because minimum annual rentals under its existing lease obligations would exceed $6.0 million per year from 1985 to 2011. The limited lease liability would facilitate the disposal of the unprofitable retail stores by reducing related costs of disaffirming the leases.

In practice, Chapter 11 petitions had some major disadvantages also. The legal proceedings were complex, often lasting for years and involving large legal expenses. More importantly, the final settlements almost always resulted in sizable losses to the lenders, with loan recoveries seldom above 70 percent.

Satisfied with the results of his mental exercise, Mr. Previn began his analysis.

Case 27 Clef Corporation

EXHIBIT 1 UNAUDITED CONSOLIDATED INCOME STATEMENT FOR 6 MONTHS ENDED JULY 29, 1982 (in thousands of dollars)

Sales and other income	$ 58,407
Cost of merchandise sold & buying expenses	41,697
Gross profit	16,710
Selling, general, & administrative expense	19,038
Depreciation and amortization expense	383
Interest expense	504
Miscellaneous expense	128
Operating profit (loss)	$ (3,343)
Credit for deferred income taxes*	256
Net income (loss)	$ (3,087)
Cash dividends paid:	
Preferred stock	$ 28
Common stock	71

*Tax loss carryback.

Case 27 Clef Corporation

EXHIBIT 2 UNAUDITED CONSOLIDATED BALANCE SHEET AS OF JULY 29, 1982 (in thousands of dollars)

Assets	
Cash	$ 650
Accounts receivable—trade and charge accounts	3,035
Accounts receivable—miscellaneous	1,138
Inventory	22,488
Notes receivable	1,020
Prepaid expenses	480
Current assets	$28,811
Furniture, fixtures and leasehold improvements	5,987
Deferred charges and other assets	958
Total assets	$35,756
Liabilities and Shareholders' Equity	
Notes payable to bank	$ 8,750
Long-term debt—current maturity	220*
Accounts payable	15,115
Taxes payable	594
Accrued liabilities	1,221
Current liabilities	$25,900
Long-term debt	3,010
Other long-term liabilities	217
Total liabilities	$29,127
Preferred stock	1,234
Common stock	520
Capital surplus	2,563
Retained earnings	2,312
Total shareholders' equity	$ 6,629
Total liabilities and shareholders' equity	$35,756

*Debt retirement of $220,000 required annually through 1988, when annual payments would increase to $320,000.

Case 27 Clef Corporation

EXHIBIT 3 CONSOLIDATED INCOME STATEMENTS FOR YEARS ENDED ABOUT JANUARY 31, 1980, 1981, AND 1982 (in thousands of dollars except earnings-per-share data)

	1980	*1981*	*1982*
Net sales	$94,530	$103,807	$124,003
Cost of goods sold & buying expenses	68,453	73,700	88,411
Gross profit	$26,077	$ 30,107	$ 35,592
Selling, general, & administrative expense	24,579	27,088	33,916
Depreciation & amortization	710	733	773
Interest expense	689	633	741
Other expense	366	314	274
Operating income (loss)	$ (267)	$ 1,339	$ (112)
Federal income tax provision (reduction)	245	649	(35)
Income (loss) before extraordinary items	$ (512)	$ 690	$ (77)
Extraordinary income (expense)* net of related taxes	(89)	364	265
Net income	$ (601)	$ 1,054	$ 188
Cash dividends paid:			
Preferred stock	$ 65	$ 61	$ 59
Common stock	211	272	275
Stock dividend			359
Average number of common shares outstanding	933.9	934.6	937.5
Earnings per share	$ (.64)	$ 1.13	$ .20

*Explanation of extraordinary items:

1980: Provision for stores closed.

1981: Reduction in provision for federal income taxes from tax loss carryforward.

1982: Gain resulting from the sale of certain company notes and rights to future cash flows from a shopping center.

EXHIBIT 4 CONSOLIDATED BALANCE SHEETS AS OF JANUARY 31, 1980, JANUARY 30, 1981, AND JANUARY 29, 1982 (in thousands of dollars)

	1980	*1981*	*1982*
Assets			
Cash	$ 716	$ 1,501	$ 2,473
Marketable securities	750	—	—
Accounts receivable (net)	4,121	3,595	2,930
Inventory	13,996	18,564	26,833
Notes receivable	—	1,533	3,380
Federal income tax refund	945	—	—
Prepaid expenses	583	665	387
Current assets	$21,111	$25,858	$36,003
Notes receivable	$ 389	$ 952	$ —
Furniture, fixtures, & leasehold improvements	4,822	6,181	5,930
Deferred charges & other assets	754	649	1,264
Total assets	$27,076	$33,640	$43,197
Liabilities & Shareholders' Equity			
Notes payable to banks	$ 1,550	$ 3,850	$ 8,000
Long-term debt—current maturity	287	500	497
Accounts payable	8,844	13,092	18,946
Income taxes payable	318	1,184	1,090
Other taxes payable	644	—	—
Accrued liabilities	1,520	1,077	1,308
Current liabilities	$13,163	$19,703	$29,841
Long-term debt	4,156	3,549	3,060
Other long-term liabilities	495	441	501
Total liabilities	$17,814	$23,693	$33,402
Preferred stock	1,420	1,361	1,259
Common stock	504	504	520
Capital surplus	2,052	2,075	2,518
Retained earnings	5,286	6,007	5,498
Total shareholders' equity	$ 9,262	$ 9,947	$ 9,795
Total liabilities & shareholders' equity	$27,076	$33,640	$43,197

Case 27 Clef Corporation

EXHIBIT 5 SALES AND OPERATING INCOME BY DIVISION FOR YEARS ENDED ABOUT JANUARY 31, 1980, 1981, AND 1982

Division	*1980*	*1981*	*1982*
Major Stores:			
Sales (thousands of dollars)	31,195	42,561	62,002
Percentage of total sales (%)	33	41	50
Operating income (thousands of dollars)	9.9	415	(167.2)
Percentage of total operating income (%)	—	31	—
Bee Sharp Fashions:			
Sales (thousands of dollars)	53,882	51,903	53,321
Percentage of total sales (%)	57	50	43
Operating income (thousands of dollars)	(864.6)	388	(500.9)
Percentage of total operating income (%)	—	29	—
Base Distribution, Inc.:			
Sales (thousands of dollars)	9,453	9,343	8,680
Percentage of total sales (%)	10	9	7
Operating income (thousands of dollars)	587.6	536	556
Percentage of total operating income (%)	—	40	—

EXHIBIT 6 MAJOR STORES DIVISION PROJECTED SALES, CONTRIBUTION, INVENTORY LEVELS, AND CASH FLOW FOR SIX MONTHS ENDING JANUARY 27, 1983 *ASSUMING FULL OPERATIONS WITH EXCEPTION OF SIX STORES* (in thousands of dollars)

	Aug.	*Sept.*	*Oct.*	*Nov.*	*Dec.*	*Jan.*	*Total*
A. Contribution Statement							
Net sales	$ 4,617	$ 5,100	$ 3,400	$ 5,040	$11,000	$ 2,500	$31,657
Gross profit*	1,252	1,350	950	1,469	2,676	650	8,347
License income	87	95	80	70	101	50	483
Payroll	682	790	567	550	778	550	3,917
Other cash expenses	900	942	743	672	860	660	4,777
Contribution	$ (243)	$ (287)	$ (280)	$ 317	$ 1,139	$ (510)	$ 136
B. Inventory Plan							
Beginning inventory**	$18,500	$19,100	$20,300	$23,500	$24,500	$18,100	$18,500
Less: Sales	4,617	5,100	3,400	5,040	11,000	2,500	31,657
Merchandise markdowns	87	95	186	295	900	295	1,858
Required ending inventory**	19,100	20,300	23,500	24,500	18,100	17,940	17,940
Purchase requirements**	$ 5,304	$ 6,395	$ 6,786	$ 6,335	$ 5,500	$ 2,635	$32,955
Purchases at cost	$ 3,447	$ 4,157	$ 4,411	$ 4,118	$ 3,575	$ 1,713	$21,421
C. Cash Receipts & Disbursements							
Receipts:							
Cash sales	$ 4,155	$ 4,590	$ 3,060	$ 4,536	$ 9,900	$ 2,250	$28,491
Collections on credit sales	620	462	510	340	504	1,100	3,536
License income	87	95	80	70	101	50	483
Total receipts	$ 4,862	$ 5,147	$ 3,650	$ 4,946	$10,505	$ 3,400	$32,510
Disbursements:							
Payroll and store expenses	$ 1,582	$ 1,732	$ 1,310	$ 1,222	$ 1,638	$ 1,210	$ 8,694
Purchases	3,158	3,447	4,157	4,411	4,118	3,575	22,866
Freight and buying expenses	105	116	185	153	136	53	748
Total disbursements	$ 4,845	$ 5,295	$ 5,652	$ 5,786	$ 5,892	$ 4,838	$32,308
Net cash flow	17	(148)	(2,002)	(840)	4,613	(1,438)	202
Cumulative cash flow	$ 17	$ (131)	$(2,133)	$(2,973)	$ 1,640	$ 202	

*After buying expenses and freight-in costs.
**At retail value; cost is 65% of retail value.

Cash flow assumptions:
10 percent of sales on credit; 30-day terms.
30 days' credit available on purchases (provision for payment of overdue accounts not made in this projection).

Case 27 Clef Corporation

EXHIBIT 7 MAJOR STORES DIVISION PROJECTED SALES, CONTRIBUTION, INVENTORY LEVELS, AND CASH FLOW FOR SIX MONTHS ENDING JANUARY 27, 1983 *ASSUMING NO MERCHANDISE SHIPMENTS AFTER SEPTEMBER* (in thousands of dollars)

	Aug.	*Sept.*	*Oct.*	*Nov.*	*Dec.*	*Jan.*	*Total*
A. Contribution Statement							
Net sales	$ 4,617	$ 5,100	$ 3,153	$ 2,960	$ 5,520	$1,600	$22,950
Gross profit*	1,252	1,350	870	829	1,546	448	6,295
License income	87	95	84	79	116	57	518
Payroll	682	790	667	557	665	442	3,803
Other cash expenses	900	942	863	572	839	746	4,862
Contribution	$ (243)	$ (287)	$ (576)	$ (221)	$ 158	$ (683)	$(1,852)
B. Inventory Plan							
Beginning Inventory**	$18,500	$19,100	$20,300	$16,947	$13,847	$8,077	$18,500
Plus:							
Purchases**	5,304	6,395	—	—	—	—	11,699
Less:							
Sales	4,617	5,100	3,153	2,960	5,520	1,600	22,950
Merchandise markdowns	87	95	200	140	250	80	852
Ending inventory**	$19,100	$20,300	$16,947	$13,847	$ 8,077	$6,397	$ 6,397
C. Cash Receipts & Disbursements							
Receipts:							
Cash sales	$ 4,155	$ 4,590	$ 2,838	$ 2,664	$ 4,968	$1,440	$20,655
Collections on credit sales	620	462	510	315	296	552	2,755
License income	87	95	84	79	116	57	518
Total receipts	$ 4,862	$ 5,147	$ 3,432	$ 3,058	$ 5,380	$2,049	$23,928
Disbursements:							
Payroll and store expenses	$ 1,582	$ 1,732	$ 1,530	$ 1,129	$ 1,504	$1,188	$ 8,665
Purchases	3,158	3,447	4,157	—	—	—	10,762
Freight and buying expenses	105	116	185	—	—	—	406
Total disbursements	$ 4,845	$ 5,295	$ 5,872	$ 1,129	$ 1,504	$1,188	$19,833
Net cash flow	17	(148)	(2,440)	1,929	3,876	861	4,095
Cumulative cash flow	$ 17	$ (131)	$(2,571)	$ (642)	$ 3,234	$4,095	

*After buying expenses and freight-in costs.
**At retail value; cost is 65 percent of retail value.

Cash flow assumptions:
10 percent of sales on credit; 30-day terms.
30 days' credit available on purchases (provision for payment of overdue accounts not made in this projection).

EXHIBIT 8 ESTIMATED TOTAL CORPORATE CASH OVERHEAD EXPENSES UNDER ALTERNATIVE MAJOR STORES DIVISION OPERATION PLANS FOR SIX MONTHS ENDING JANUARY 27, 1983 (in thousands of dollars)

	Full Major Stores Operations Excluding Six Stores Closed in October		*Limited Major Stores Operations of All Stores—No Merchandise Shipments After Sept.*	
Month	*By Month*	*Cumulative*	*By Month*	*Cumulative*
August	$ 822	$ 822	$ 822	$ 822
September	830	1,652	830	1,652
October	610	2,262	610	2,262
November	571	2,833	521	2,783
December	675	3,508	579	3,362
January	524	4,032	465	3,827
Total	$4,032		$3,827	

Case 27 Clef Corporation

EXHIBIT 9 BASE DISTRIBUTORS, INC. PROJECTED SALES, PROFITS, INVENTORY LEVELS, AND CASH FLOW FOR SIX MONTHS ENDING JANUARY 23, 1983 (in thousands of dollars)

	Aug.	*Sept.*	*Oct.*	*Nov.*	*Dec.*	*Jan.*	*Total*
A. Operating Statement							
Net sales	$ 717	$ 855	$1,062	$1,415	$ 936	$ 515	$5,500
Cost of goods sold	552	658	817	1,089	720	396	4,232
Gross profit	165	197	245	326	216	119	1,268
Payroll and cash expenses	117	128	140	183	133	105	806
Profit before tax	48	69	105	143	83	14	462
B. Inventory Plan*							
Beginning inventory	$5,166	$4,915	$4,586	$4,197	$3,606	$3,236	$5,166
Plus purchases	301	329	428	498	350	461	2,367
Less cost of goods sold	552	658	817	1,089	720	396	4,232
Ending inventory	$4,915	$4,586	$4,197	$3,606	$3,236	$3,301	$3,301
C. Cash Receipts & Disbursements							
Receipts:							
Collections of accounts receivable	$ 875	$ 700	$ 717	$ 855	$1,062	$1,415	$5,624
Disbursements:							
Payroll and expenses	117	128	140	183	133	105	806
Purchases	455	545	301	329	428	498	2,556
Total disbursements	$ 572	$ 673	$ 441	$ 512	$ 561	$ 603	$3,362
Net cash flow	303	27	276	343	501	812	2,262
Cumulative cash flow	$ 303	$ 330	$ 606	$ 949	$1,450	$2,262	

*At cost.

Cash flow assumptions:
60-day credit terms available to customers.
60-day credit terms available from suppliers (payment of past due accounts not included in this projection).

EXHIBIT 10 BEE SHARP FASHIONS DIVISION* PROJECTED SALES, CONTRIBUTION, INVENTORY LEVELS, AND CASH FLOW FOR SIX MONTHS ENDING JANUARY 27, 1983 (in thousands of dollars)

	Aug.	*Sept.*	*Oct.*	*Nov.*	*Dec.*	*Jan.*	*Total*
A. Contribution Statement							
Net sales	$ 4,156	$ 4,305	$ 3,200	$ 4,300	$ 8,457	$2,721	$27,139
Gross profit**	1,539	1,731	1,230	1,664	2,877	810	9,851
Payroll	545	650	550	528	750	520	3,543
Other cash expenses	481	610	520	515	735	450	3,311
Contribution	$ 513	$ 471	$ 160	$ 621	$ 1,392	$ (160)	$ 2,997
B. Inventory Plan							
Beginning inventory***	$ 9,630	$10,700	$10,500	$14,550	$14,600	$9,300	$ 9,630
Less:							
Sales	4,156	4,305	3,200	4,300	8,457	2,721	27,139
Merchandise markdowns	255	202	225	281	1,221	622	2,806
Required ending inventory***	10,700	10,500	14,550	14,600	9,300	9,150	9,150
Purchase requirements***	$ 5,481	$ 4,307	$ 7,475	$ 4,631	$ 4,378	$3,193	$29,465
Purchases at cost	$ 3,015	$ 2,368	$ 4,111	$ 2,547	$ 2,408	$1,756	$16,205
C. Cash Receipts & Disbursements							
Receipts:							
Cash sales	$ 3,533	$ 3,659	$ 2,720	$ 3,655	$ 7,189	$2,313	$23,069
Collections on credit sales	840	623	646	480	645	1,268	4,502
Total receipts	$ 4,373	$ 4,282	$ 3,366	$ 4,135	$ 7,834	$3,581	$27,571
Disbursements:							
Payroll and store expenses	$ 1,026	$ 1,260	$ 1,070	$ 1,043	$ 1,485	$ 970	$ 6,854
Purchases	2,845	3,015	2,368	4,111	2,547	2,408	17,294
Freight and buying expenses	265	280	220	382	237	212	1,596
Total disbursements	$ 4,136	$ 4,555	$ 3,658	$ 5,536	$ 4,269	$3,590	$25,744
Net cash flow	237	(273)	(292)	(1,401)	3,565	(9)	1,827
Cumulative cash flow	$ 237	$ (36)	$ (328)	$(1,729)	$ 1,836	$1,827	

*Assumes closing of 22 stores during October.
**After buying expenses and freight-in costs.
***At retail value; cost is 55 percent of retail value.

Cash flow assumptions:
15 percent of sales on credit; 30-day terms.
30 days' credit available on purchases (payments on past due accounts not included in this projection).

Case 27 Clef Corporation

EXHIBIT 11 CUMULATIVE CASH SOURCE SUMMARY, AUGUST 1982–JANUARY 1983 (thousands of dollars)

	Aug.	*Sept.*	*Oct.*	*Nov.*	*Dec.*	*Jan.*
Base Distributors, Inc.	$ 303	$ 330	$ 606	$ 949	$ 1,450	$ 2,262
Bee Sharp Fashions	237	(36)	(328)	(1,729)	1,836	1,827
Subtotal	$ 540	$ 294	$ 278	$ (780)	$ 3,286	$ 4,089
Major Stores—full operations	$ 17	$ (131)	$(2,133)	$(2,973)	$ 1,640	$ 202
Corporate cash uses	(822)	(1,652)	(2,262)	(2,833)	(3,508)	(4,032)
Total	$(265)	$(1,489)	$(4,117)	$(6,586)	$ 1,418	$ 259
Subtotal, above	$ 540	$ 294	$ 278	$ (780)	$ 3,286	$ 4,089
Major Stores—curtailment	$ 17	$ (131)	$(2,571)	$ (642)	$ 3,234	$ 4,095
Corporate cash uses	(822)	(1,652)	(2,262)	(2,783)	(3,362)	(3,827)
Total	$(265)	$(1,489)	$(4,555)	$(4,205)	$ 3,158	$ 4,357

Note: Does not provide for payment of $8,122,000 in past-due accounts as of July 29, 1982. Presumably cash payment would be first applied by suppliers to the oldest balances.

Case 27 Clef Corporation

EXHIBIT 12 SELECTED BALANCE SHEET ACCOUNTS AS OF JULY 29, 1982 AND FORECASTED FOR JANUARY 23, 1983 (thousands of dollars)

	Actual July 1982	*Forecasted January 1983*
Base Distributors, Inc.		
Accounts receivable (60 DSO)	$ 1,575	$ 1,451
Inventory (cost)	5,166	3,301
Accounts payable (60 DPO)*	1,000	811
Bee Sharp Fashions		
Accounts receivable (30 DSO)	$ 840	$ 408
Inventory (cost)	5,297	5,033
Accounts payable (30 DPO)*	2,845	1,756
Major Stores—Full Operations Assumption		
Accounts receivable (30 DSO)	$ 620	$ 250
Inventory (cost)	12,025	11,661
Accounts payable (30 DPO)*	3,158	1,713
Major Stores—Curtailment Assumption		
Accounts receivable (30 DSO)	$ 620	$ 160
Inventory (cost)	12,025	4,222
Accounts payable (30 DPO)*	3,158	—

*Current accounts payable only. No allowance made for the $8,122,000 in payables overdue on July 29, 1982.

Case 28

TEMPO NATIONAL BANK

In mid-April 1983, Mr. Andrew Previn, vice president and senior account officer at the Tempo National Bank whose specialty was "workout" situations, was faced with developing an alternate payment plan for the creditors of the Breve Corporation. Late in September 1982, Breve had filed a petition for an arrangement with its creditors under Chapter 11 of the Bankruptcy Code with the U.S. District Court for the Southern District of New York. Breve subsequently continued operations under court supervision as a Debtor in Possession and with the prior management. It had divested itself of unprofitable operations that previously had generated almost half of its consolidated sales.

Mr. Previn had just attended a meeting of Breve's creditors' committee, during which management had first proposed a plan of arrangement. The company had offered a total of 50 percent payment on its debt: 33 percent immediately in cash, and 17 percent spread over the next 5 years.

The creditors' committee had unanimously rejected the proposal and then authorized the formation of a subcommittee of five, with Mr. Previn as chairman, to work with Breve and its attorneys to negotiate a settlement acceptable to all parties involved. Breve's management, the trade creditors, and the institutional lenders each had different points of view that would have to be weighed.

Breve's income statements for fiscal years 1980 through 1983 are included as Exhibit 1. Selected balance sheets are included as Exhibit 2.

This case is based on a Supervised Business Study written by Mr. Mark J. Young with the generous cooperation of individuals and institutions which wish to remain anonymous. Mr. Kevin Ramundo assisted with the preliminary field work. Certain characteristics of the situation have been changed to protect the confidences of those involved without altering the nature of the managerial decision.

In fiscal year 1983, which ended January 27, 1983, Breve charged off extraordinary items of \$19.4 million, as shown in Exhibit 3. This resulted in a net loss of \$22.4 million on sales of \$96.8 million for the period, producing a deficit in retained earnings of \$17.0 million and a deficit in total shareholders' equity of \$12.6 million. Breve estimated its total claims and liabilities under Chapter 11 proceedings at \$39.4 million, as presented in Exhibit 4. It was expected that those claims would be approved by the court.

Breve's management had proposed the 50 percent cash and debt settlement, described in Exhibit 5. The creditors' committee found this unacceptable because its members concluded that Breve could afford a more generous proposal.

OPERATIONS PRIOR TO ENTERING CHAPTER 11 PROCEEDINGS

In September 1982, Breve's organization consisted of three divisions which competed in various segments of wholesaling and retailing. The two retailing divisions were the Major discount department store division and the Bee Sharp Fashion women's apparel store division. The wholesaling division was Base Distributors, a wholly owned subsidiary. The Major Stores Division included 25 wholly owned, incorporated subsidiaries that operated 26 discount department stores located primarily in the Midwest. Bee Sharp Fashions operated 178 specialty stores throughout the Midwest and South that sold moderately priced, ready-to-wear ladies' and misses' apparel and accessories. The older stores were located in downtown areas, generally stocking rather diverse merchandise in limited selection, including informal sports wear, uniforms, and maternity clothing. Efforts were underway to modernize the locations and merchandizing approach of this division. Base Distributors engaged in the distribution of housewares, small appliances, and toys to department and discount store chains in the Midwest. The Major Stores Division was Base Distributors's largest customer, accounting for 25 percent of its sales. Exhibit 6 shows sales and operating income by division for fiscal years 1980 through 1983.

Breve's senior officers had been with the company for only a few years. Shortly after Base Distributors was acquired by Breve in late 1979, through a pooling of interests, Breve's president and other executives resigned. They were replaced by members of the Base management group. The former president of Base, Mr. George Sell, who was Breve's largest shareholder as a result of the stock he received in the acquisition, became the chairman of Breve's board.

Mr. Sell's management group implemented many changes in Breve's operations. Information systems were improved, individual stores operated with monthly budgets, top management monitored operating results more closely, and hopelessly unprofitable stores were being closed. Previous management had made substantial investments in real estate to secure prime locations, receive preferential leasing arrangements, and realize speculators' profits. These investments were being liquidated to meet working capital requirements.

In the fall of 1981, Breve moved into a new, specially designed facility housing the executive offices and a modern, semiautomated softgoods warehouse. This move doubled inventory handling capacity, improved inventory control, and enabled shops to be serviced more efficiently. All facilities were leased.

Breve's earnings performance during the three fiscal years prior to entering Chapter 11 proceedings were quite erratic, as shown in Exhibits 1 and 6. The poor earnings were due to inventory markdowns, bad-debt expenses, costs associated with opening and closing stores, and gains and losses from liquidating real estate investments. Poor operating results were attributable especially to the Major Stores and Bee Sharp Fashion shops, as shown in Exhibit 6.

For the first six months of fiscal year 1983, ending July 29, 1982, Breve reported consolidated operating losses of $3.3 million on sales of $54.4 million because the Major Stores and Bee Sharp Fashion divisions continued to be unprofitable. The Major Stores Division accumulated a $3.1 million operating deficit, primarily due to increasing losses in eight new department stores. Bee Sharp Fashions accumulated a $313,000 operating deficit because markdowns for summer sales failed to generate anticipated incremental sales volume and because efforts to generate profits in twenty-nine of the smaller women's apparel shops had been unsuccessful. During the first half of fiscal year 1983, Base Distributors earned $95,000 from operations.

Breve's liquidity position had also deteriorated since 1979 as a result of substantial increases in short-term indebtedness to banks and in accounts payable. Inventory levels had risen much faster than sales, but purchasing controls, the new warehouse facility, and special summer sales had begun to bring these under control during the first half of fiscal year 1983. Rising inventories were the major current asset standing behind increasing current liabilities, and Breve had incurred substantial charges during the previous few years for inventory writedowns.

For the fiscal years 1980, 1981, and 1982, Breve had maintained the stated annual cash dividend of $2.25 per share on its 4 1/2 percent cumulative preferred stock and paid an annual cash dividend of $0.30 per share of its common stock, as shown in Exhibit 1. As of the date of filing under Chapter 11, cash dividends of $28,000 and $71,000 had already been paid on the preferred and common shares, respectively, for fiscal year 1983.

Trading of Breve's common stock on the American Stock Exchange was suspended at the time of filing. It had last closed at $3.50. Trading would not commence until after an arrangement had been confirmed.

EVENTS LEADING TO FILING UNDER CHAPTER 11

Breve filed a petition for an arrangement with its creditors in response to actions taken by both Tempo, its lead bank, and Largo Trust Company in demanding payment of loans. The maturity of these loans, $4.5 million due Tempo and $2.5 million due Largo, had already been renewed several times. Both banks finally simultaneously demanded payment, and then they elected to exercise the right of setoff to which they were entitled by law. They each set off the cash deposits Breve had with them, totaling $900,000, against their loans aggregating approximately $7 million. Without any cash, it became impossible for Breve to continue operating without court protection.

Several factors led to the banks' decisions to set off Breve's deposits. The company had experienced substantial operating losses for the first half of fiscal year 1983. Projections suggested that cash flows would not be sufficient to cover current maturities of debt. Working capital levels had fallen below the limits required by covenants of the long-term loan, an unsecured obligation. Several creditors had brought legal actions for the collection of accounts and instituted attachment proceedings to block any transfer of assets. Suppliers had been known to suspend shipments because of unpaid accounts. The banks were unwilling to provide the current financing Breve would need to improve its position with the trade because more loans would only increase the banks' loss exposure.

After filing a petition under Chapter 11, Breve was allowed to continue to operate under court supervision as a Debtor in Possession. Management and the shareholders remained in possession of the business and Breve was not turned over to a court-appointed trustee. Management was authorized to continue to incur the expenses and obligations of operating and managing the business.

Court protection under Chapter 11 gave Breve a chance to rehabilitate itself. The company could retain any funds generated by operations until an agreement could be worked out. General creditors (Breve had no secured creditors) were stayed from legal actions to collect accounts due them or other unsecured debts until the Bankruptcy Court had acted on petitions for arrangements. These provisions eased the immediate demands on Breve's limited cash resources. Trade creditors who shipped following the approval of Breve's petition enjoyed a preferred position as creditors of the Debtor in Possession, standing ahead of those creditors on Breve's books at the time the petition was filed. This priority encouraged trade suppliers to continue their shipments to Breve. Breve's unsecured assets could be made available to banks as collateral for new loans to finance continuing operations, and the banks would receive court assurance of priority creditor status on loans advanced subsequent to the filing.

Chapter 11 also provided for limited lease liability, which made it easier for Breve to dispose of its less profitable stores by either selling the store (or the lease) or by closing the store and renouncing the lease. The expenses and liabilities related to disaffirming leases could be exceedingly high in normal circumstances: the lessee would have to negotiate with each lessor to buy out of the lease contract. Chapter 11 limited the lessor's claims for damages arising from a disaffirmed lease to a maximum of 3 years of lease payments. Damages had to be demonstrated and were subject to the court's approval.

Once an arrangement had been confirmed by the Bankruptcy Court, it became binding upon the debtor, upon all creditors whether or not they had accepted it in writing, and upon any person issuing securities or acquiring property under the plan. An arrangement did not require shareholder approval for court confirmation; but, if the plan called for a change in the capital structure of the debtor, the board of directors was supposed to submit the plan to the shareholders for their approval. Upon confirmation of the plan by the court, the debtor was discharged from all unsecured liabilities except as provided for in the arrangement.

FORMATION OF THE CREDITORS' COMMITTEE

When the debtor remained in possession, as in the case of Breve, a creditors' committee was appointed by the judge to represent the general creditors during Chapter 11 proceedings. The Bankruptcy Code provided that the committee would consist of the seven largest creditors, augmented by the judge as required to ensure fair representation. Once appointed, the committee could examine the debtor before the judge of the court, it could oversee the operation of the business, it could delve into the debtor's affairs, it would represent the creditors in negotiating a plan with the debtor, and it could recommend to the creditors that a proposed plan of arrangement be accepted or rejected. Following the period in which the right to propose a plan belonged to the debtor, the creditors' committee could present its own plan to the court.

Six days after Breve's management filed the company's petition, the first informal meeting of the creditors was held, attended by about 100 of Breve's largest creditors, including the institutional lenders. Mr. Sell reviewed Breve's history and recent operating results and outlined plans of action for the immediate future. These comments were followed by a disorderly question-and-answer period, after which management and their representatives were asked to leave while the creditors met.

The ensuing meeting was punctuated by flurries of shouting, whistling, stomping, and catcalling. A three-way split developed between a group of the factors ($2 million in claims), a group of manufacturing suppliers ($18 million in claims), and the institutional lenders ($10 million in claims). During an early outburst, the factor group left the meeting in anger. The trade creditors were upset at having the prospect of only three seats on the committee, a minority. The chairman ultimately ejected Mr. Previn and other institutional lenders from the room. The meeting had become rowdy, disorganized, and almost physically violent.

Much of the dissension in the meeting was attributable to the feeling by many creditors that they had been shut out of the Chapter 11 committee for Tonic Stores, Inc., another large retail chain in the Midwest that had undergone Chapter 11 proceedings only one month earlier. The number of large unsecured institutional lenders had put the others at a disadvantage, or so it was thought.

Another source of unrest was those suppliers that found themselves caught up in both Breve's and Tonic's Chapter 11 proceedings. They had already been hard hit financially when receivables due them from Tonic were tied up by the court; now they were faced with also having to finance receivables due them from Breve until an arrangement could be agreed upon. This unrest was compounded by fears that several other chains experiencing financial trouble might also file petitions under Chapter 11.

Two weeks later, the institutional lenders finally came to terms with the group of manufacturing creditors that had ejected them from the first meeting. The institutions would receive three places on the committee. One place would go to the factors group. Three places would go to the trade. Mr. Previn and a representative of one of the manufacturers would serve as cochairmen. Tempo National Bank and Largo Trust Company then agreed to extend Breve a $4 million line of credit, secured by assets, to finance its current operations. However, cash flow projections developed ten days later indicated that the line would not be needed. It was never drawn down.

OPERATIONS UNDER CHAPTER 11 PROCEEDINGS

During the fall of 1982, while the creditors were arguing, Breve's management began taking action to relieve the company of the burden of its unprofitable operations. The Major Stores Division was losing by far the most money, and negotiations to sell these stores had begun even before filing under Chapter 11. During October 1982, 22 of the most unprofitable apparel shops of the Bee Sharp Fashion Division were closed, and their inventories were moved to other apparel shops in the chain.

Because Base Distributors supplied discount stores such as Breve's Major Stores, its business would no longer relate to Breve's continuing retail operation—the apparel specialty shops. Thus, Base Distributors was sold in December 1982 for $1.5 million in cash. The purchaser also agreed to assume Base's liabilities and to accept an 11 percent settlement of a $1.9 million claim that Base had against Breve.

A bank factoring group objected to the sale, however, claiming that Base had guaranteed $1 million in credit extended by the bank to Breve. The factoring group filed suit to collect under the guarantee. To resolve this objection, $1 million of Base's sales price was placed in escrow to pay any judgment or settlement obtained by the bank.

In January 1983, the 25 subsidiaries that operated the Major Stores filed petitions for arrangements with their creditors under Chapter 11 of the Bankruptcy Act. Breve was the major creditor listed in these petitions. The inventories and fixtures in 10 department stores were sold for approximately $2.5 million in cash to other retailers interested in operating the stores, and the leases were assigned to the purchasers. The incorporated subsidiaries, owned by Breve, that had owned and operated these stores were not sold. Only assets were sold, and the liabilities of these subsidiaries were retained by Breve. Because these subsidiaries were also now in Chapter 11 proceedings, their liabilities were incorporated with the claims against Breve. The 16 remaining department stores were shut down because no buyers could be found.

An additional 28 apparel shops were closed, and one new shop was opened, leaving a total of 127 shops at the end of January 1983. Nine more closings and one new opening were scheduled during fiscal year 1984.

Breve had discontinued operations accounting for roughly half of its business as a result of these actions, but these operations had aggregated a $3.6 million operating loss while the continuing operations generated $0.3 million of operating income. Continuing operations were adversely affected during this period by unusual merchandise procurement problems and difficulties of operating businesses in the process of being sold or liquidated.

During the year, lease obligations were disaffirmed on the closed apparel shops, the former warehouse and executive offices, the 16 department stores that had not been sold, and on fixture leases related to the closed stores. Breve estimated its liability for disaffirmed lease obligations at approximately $10.0 million and charged this against earnings in fiscal year 1983 as an extraordinary item.

The net operating losses accumulated during fiscal year 1983 could be carried forward and used to offset future earnings for both tax and financial reporting purposes over the next 5 years. This carryforward was estimated to be $11 million, but it would be reduced by the amount of any debt forgiven by the creditors.

DESCRIPTION OF CONTINUING OPERATIONS

Early in fiscal year 1984, Breve consisted of 127 Bee Sharp Fashion apparel specialty shops located throughout the Midwest and South. Breve's new strategy was to locate these stores in places where there was heavy foot traffic of shoppers passing by. Increasingly, Breve had been concentrating on sites in enclosed shopping malls that were anchored by two or more large retailers like Sears, Bamberger's, and Abraham and Strauss. These large retailers attracted shoppers to the malls who could then be drawn into the apparel shops by displays and promotions. The same reasoning applied to apparel shops located in downtown shopping areas on main streets where there was still heavy foot traffic. None of the shops bought advertising to attract customers. The effectiveness of urban retailing had been diminishing, and Breve was moving out of many urban locations.

The apparel shops were now positioned to appeal to fashion-conscious women in the age group of 16 to 25 years. This included young women in high school and college and young women who had begun to work as salespeople, secretaries, or clerical personnel. Only first-quality apparel merchandise was sold through these shops, but no branded merchandise was carried.

Breve acquired its merchandise from approximately a thousand suppliers, no one of which supplied more than 5 percent of all purchases. Alternate sources of supply existed for all items sold. All purchasing and pricing, including markdowns, were controlled through the executive offices, which utilized a computer-assisted inventory and sales recording system.

During fiscal year 1983, approximately 90 percent of the sales in Breve's stores were for cash, including sales on lay-away or will-call plans. The remaining 10 percent were credit sales, with 4 percent on bank and independent credit card plans with which the store assumed no credit risk but paid a percentage of the sales price as a service charge, and 6 percent under Breve's own charge plan.

Breve had 86 of its shops located in shopping centers, with 47 of these being enclosed malls, and 41 of its shops in downtown shopping areas near department stores and other apparel shops. Stores in shopping centers (7,000 sq. ft.) averaged one-half the size of downtown stores (14,000 sq. ft.). In fiscal year 1983, 12 of the downtown shops accounted for 28 percent of sales. None of the leases on these 12 shops was to expire before 1985, and only 3 were to expire before 1982.

AVAILABILITY OF CASH AND PLANNED OPERATING PERFORMANCE

Before drawing up an initial plan of arrangement to be presented to the creditors' committee, Breve's management had to estimate two benchmark figures to be used as reference points in considering alternative plans. These were the liquidation value of the company and the excess cash available if operations were to be continued.

Exhibit 7 shows that approximately $12.5 million could be generated from the liquidation of assets, net of liquidation expenses and escrowed funds held for priority claims, and made available for distribution to the general creditors. If the company were liquidated, then creditors could have expected to receive approximately 34 percent of their claims. Most of this amount would be cash that had been accumulated by Breve from disposing of the Major Stores and Base Distributors.

Liquidation of receivables would only amount to a fraction of their book value because few of Breve's debtors would have felt obligated to pay monies owed to a company that was going out of business. Liquidation of inventories would have to be carried out at significant reductions in price, also yielding less than a third of book value. Furniture, fixtures, and leasehold improvements, in most cases, would stay with the leased facility when the lease was disaffirmed, resulting in little realizable market value.

The process of conducting a liquidation was very expensive and time consuming, which not only reduced the cash available for distribution to general creditors because liquidation expenses would come off the top, but could also delay remittance to general creditors for several years. The alternative of demanding liquidation was still available to Breve's creditors.

Exhibit 8 shows that approximately $12.3 million could be made available for distribution to general creditors as an initial payment under an arrangement that permitted Breve to continue its operations. Cash held by the company plus the net realizable value of the assets of discontinued operations had to be reduced by the cash required to finance continuing operations, expenses of administering the arrangement, and funds held in escrow for priority claims. The general creditors would receive up to approximately 33 percent of their claims in an initial payment.

Exhibit 9 shows the summary of a preliminary 5-year plan, which was in the process of being revised to reflect the actual operating results achieved in fiscal year 1983 and the improved results expected in the first quarter of fiscal year 1984, as shown in Exhibit 10. The plan revealed that no improvement in gross margins was expected. Improved efficiencies in both store and executive-office operations were objectives. For purposes of cash-flow projections, management had assumed on a preliminary basis that noncash charges, such as depreciation and amortization of deferred charges, would be offset by cash absorbed by additions to fixed assets and increases in working capital.

Exhibits 8, 9, and 10 had been presented to the general creditors as part of the support for the proposed arrangement.

TECHNICAL ASPECTS OF A SETTLEMENT

If a settlement was made in an amount less than 100 percent of claims, the impact of the debt forgiven on the financial statements had to be considered. Debt forgiven was that portion of the total claims that Breve would not have to pay as a result of the creditors' agreeing to accept less than 100 percent of the amounts due them. When the company's financial statements were revised to reflect the settlement, liabilities would be reduced by the amount of debt forgiven, with an offsetting increase made to contributed capital. Debt forgiven was actually funds "borrowed" by Breve that did not have to be repaid.

Debt forgiven was not directly taxable as such, but these amounts must be deducted from any tax carryback or carryforward. Only the tax carryback or carryforward remaining after the deduction may be used.

The amount for which creditors agreed to settle and the size of the initial cash payment would affect Breve's balance sheet in different ways. Exhibit 11 shows the effect of 40 percent, 50 percent, and 60 percent settlement levels on Breve's balance sheet, assuming an initial cash payment of 33 percent of claims. As the proportion of claims paid increased, long-term liabilities rose, and shareholders' equity declined. Exhibit 12 shows the effect of 28 percent, 33 percent, and 38 percent initial cash payments on Breve's balance sheet, assuming a 50 percent overall settlement. As the cash proportion of the settlement increased, long-term liabilities and working capital financing decreased.

If a settlement proposed the issue of equity to satisfy part of the claims, the Securities and Exchange Commission (SEC) was entitled to review and comment on the issue of new equity. The SEC reserved the right to impose restrictions on how these securities could be registered and distributed, who could hold them in what concentrations, how long they could be held, and when and in what quantities they could be sold. The SEC might also consider those who received significant amounts of equity as "underwriters" of the issue because of the large blocks of shares they would receive. This might be a problem to the institutional lenders.

If the original shareholders, as a group, were left with less than 50 percent of the issued and outstanding stock in the company after the stock distribution had occurred and other market transactions in response to the distribution had taken place, then the ownership of the business was deemed to have been materially changed. Such a change in the beneficial ownership of the company would likely result in the net operating loss carryforwards being disallowed by the Internal Revenue Service for tax purposes. This would severely reduce Breve's future cash flow.

The exchange of debt for stock might be a taxable transaction for many creditors. If the market value of the stock was larger than the value at which a creditor carried the claim on its books, the creditor would realize taxable gains on the difference. If the carrying value of the claim exceeded the stock's market value, that excess amount could be written off. Creditors who held their shares would realize even larger gains (taxed at capital gain rates) if the stock's market value appreciated subsequently.

If a bank received an amount of stock equivalent to more than 5 percent of the total shares outstanding, the bank was permitted to hold those shares for a maximum of two years plus three one-year extensions. This restriction was important to the two banks that were major creditors of Breve:

Tempo National Bank	$4,100,000
Largo Trust Company	$2,000,000

It did not affect the $3.2 million due Allegro Life Insurance Company.

MR. PREVIN'S CHALLENGE

In preparing to negotiate a final settlement, Mr. Previn knew that three major parties had to be satisfied if agreement was to be reached so the company could be discharged quickly from Chapter 11: trade creditors, institutional lenders, and Breve's management (representing the stockholders). Mr. Previn decided to note down the major interests and constraints of each group.

POINT OF VIEW OF THE TRADE CREDITORS

The trade creditors' first interest was keeping Breve in business. Naturally, they would like to receive what was owed to them for merchandise shipped, but future sales to Breve were worth much more to the trade in the long run than the claims they currently had against the chain. Efforts to get as much money out of Breve as they could right away might jeopardize Breve's ability to stay in business and to continue to buy from these suppliers; the suppliers did not want to lose that business.

Trade creditors were generally inclined to press for a quick cash settlement rather than for more payout over a longer term. Suppliers, particularly in the fashion trade, were often in need of cash themselves. They did not want to have cash tied up in a reorganization when it could be used for some immediate operating purpose. Because no payments would be made until a plan was accepted by the creditors and confirmed by the court, the trade creditors sought a quick settlement that would provide them cash as soon as possible. They were not interested in distributions of stock, which they would probably sell right away, or in repayment schedules that stretched the settlement out over a long period of time. These arrangements would not ease their current financing requirements.

The trade creditors were also willing to consider settling for less than the total amount of their claims because their actual cash loss exposure was only a portion of the claims to which they were entitled. Because these claims were largely receivables due to the trade for goods purchased, valued at the selling price to Breve, they also had the suppliers' profit margins included in them. The trade's loss exposure was actually only that portion of the claims represented by the cost of merchandise sold to Breve. Cost of merchandise sold typically represented approximately 75 percent of the supplier's selling price.

The trade wanted to see this case settled quickly because of the financial difficulty that retail merchandisers were having in general. Other retail chains supplied by these creditors either were also in bankruptcy proceedings or were rumored to be considering filing for court protection. The trade was seeking reassurance that the problems faced by these chains were not insurmountable and that chains would continue to be effective outlets for their merchandise.

The creditors of Major Stores all had claims against Breve because Breve retained the liabilities of all its department-store subsidiaries. The creditors of the stores that were sold were assured of the continued operations of these outlets, so they would be willing to settle for any cash they could receive immediately for their claims. For the creditors of the stores that were closed, the possibility of the continued operation of these outlets had vanished. They were therefore interested only in collecting as much cash as they could and in getting out.

The landlords of the closed facilities, on which leases were disaffirmed, were allowed claims only for damages that could be proven to have been incurred as results of the disaffirmations, subject to a maximum of 3 years' lease payments. Their loss exposure typically amounted to the expenses of maintaining their property until another lessee could be found and for whatever rennovations were necessary for the new tenant. They wanted a settlement that would come soon and provide them enough cash to meet these out-of-pocket expenses.

POINT OF VIEW OF THE INSTITUTIONAL LENDERS

The institutional lenders were in an entirely different position as creditors of Breve. Mr. Previn and his colleagues were most interested in recovering their principal and minimizing their losses. Individually, the institutional lenders had much larger claims than any of the trade creditors. They had alternate outlets through which funds could be invested, and they were not dependent on Breve's continued operations for future business. Moreover, any capital lost to Breve would reduce the resources available to the lenders for doing business and generating earnings. It was the effect that losing capital would have on future earnings that made recovery of principal the first priority to the institutional lenders.

In the interest of recovering principal, institutional lenders were willing to negotiate a settlement that would pay them the highest percentage of their claims. Because accrued interest accounted for only 5 percent to 10 percent of their claims, their cash loss exposure in the amount of principal was 90 percent to 95 percent of their claims. The institutions were well capitalized and not under any financial operating constraints that required the hasty liquidation of their claims. For these reasons, they were more flexible about how their portion of the settlement would be remitted to them. They were more willing to accept a schedule of periodic payments over time if more principal could be recovered that way, and they were willing to accept equity ownership because of the possibility of appreciation. Mr. Previn detected a growing feeling among financial institutions that the other suppliers of capital, the shareholders, should make some sacrifices during a Chapter 11 workout in the interest of the survival of the debtor company. The long-term lender, Allegro Life Insurance Company, had told Mr. Previn it would go along with any plan Mr. Previn decided to accept as far as its $3.2 million was concerned.

POINT OF VIEW OF BREVE'S MANAGEMENT

Management, of course, was interested in effecting a settlement that would release Breve from the constraints of the bankruptcy court and that would give the company the financial strength to undertake the expansion plans that had been developed.

Mr. Previn knew, from the many months of working with Breve's management, that Mr. Sell ideally would like to have offered 100 percent settlement of the claims against Breve. Because this could not possibly be accomplished, he wanted to provide the creditors with a good settlement but one that would still leave Breve with a high probability of survival and prosperity. Mr. Sell's first responsibility was Breve's continued operations; management did not want to be left committed to a plan that was so constraining it limited the company's ability to rehabilitate itself. In particular, management seemed concerned about an initial cash payment that would be so large it would prevent Breve from keeping its trade payments current. Mr. Previn also wondered whether the assumption that noncash charges would equal outlays for fixed assets was valid. While management wanted to satisfy the creditors, Mr. Previn was also aware that they wanted to find the minimum settlement to which creditors would agree because this would also maximize the company's ability to recover and continue as an effective competitor.

Management also had a personal stake in the outcome of the settlement. The officers and directors owned a significant amount of stock. Mr. Sell, Breve's chairman with whom Mr. Previn would be negotiating, Breve's president and chief executive officer, and two directors held about 552,000 of Breve's 941,000 outstanding common shares. Approximately 540,000 of these shares had been pledged as collateral for loans from a Midwest bank. The bank had agreed not to proceed against these shares during the 1983 calendar year as long as Breve's Chapter 11 proceedings were pending and for 2 years after a settlement plan had been confirmed by the court.

Cash dividends had been suspended on both the common and preferred shares, and Breve would not be allowed to pay dividends unless the creditors agreed to it or until all debt obligations arising out of the settlement had been repaid. Common shareholders could not receive dividends until dividends in arrears on the preferred stock had been paid. Dividends in arrears are discussed in the notes to Exhibit 2, and dividend history is shown in Exhibit 1.

THE FIRST PROPOSED PLAN OF ARRANGEMENT

The first plan of arrangement was presented by Mr. Sell to the creditors' committee late in April 1983, prior to the close of the first quarter of fiscal year 1984. (Exhibit 5 details the terms of this proposal.) It proposed a cash and debt settlement in the amount of 50 percent of the general creditors' claims. An initial cash payment amounting to 33 percent of the amount claimed would be paid upon confirmation of the arrangement by the Bankruptcy Court. The remaining 17 percent would be remitted in periodic payments from net-earnings-before-tax over the next 5 years.

The plan had been immediately and unanimously rejected by the creditors' committee.

The creditors believed Breve was in a position of offer a better payment plan, especially because it had spun off its more unprofitable operations and had developed a more competitive strategy for retailing women's apparel through its specialty shops. Two other retail chains, described in Exhibit 13, had been quite successful with strategies similar to the one Breve was adopting. The creditors were also aware that growth projections for the amount of retail business that would be conducted through shopping malls and shopping centers, of the type in which Breve's shops were located, were significantly above inflation rates and GNP growth rates.

After the first plan was rejected, a subcommittee of five was formed to work with Breve and its attorneys to negotiate a settlement to be presented to the entire creditors' committee. Mr. Andrew Previn, of the Tempo National Bank, was designated chairman of the subcommittee. He would shortly meet with the committee, and then the committee would meet with Breve's management (as soon as it had developed a position) to learn what Mr. Sell's revised proposal was. Mr. Previn believed it would be wise to rough in the elements of a minimally acceptable plan in order to assess the revised Breve plan more quickly.

EXHIBIT 1 BREVE CORPORATION CONSOLIDATED INCOME STATEMENTS FOR FISCAL YEARS ENDED ABOUT JANUARY 31, 1980–1983 (dollar figures in millions except per-share figures)

	1980	*1981*	*1982*	*1983*
Net sales, including discontinued operations	$94.5	$ 103.6	$123.6	$ 96.8
Sales of discontinued operations, net of intercompany sales	40.4	51.8	71.9	46.8
Net sales of continuing operations	54.1	51.8	51.7	50.0
Cost of merchandise sold	36.4	33.6	33.5	31.6
Gross margin on sales	17.7	18.2	18.2	18.4
Operating expenses, other deductions, net	17.3	16.5	16.4	17.0
Depreciation and amortization	.7	.7	.8	.6
Interest expense	.6	.6	.7	.5
Net operating income (loss)	(.9)	.4	.3	.3
Income (loss) from discontinued operations[1]	.6	.9	(.4)	(3.6)
Income (loss) before income taxes and extraordinary items	(.3)	1.3	(.1)	(3.3)
Provision (credit) for income taxes	.2	.6	—	(.3)
Income (loss) before extraordinary items	(.5)	.7	(.1)	(3.0)
Extraordinary items, net of applicable income taxes[2]	(.1)	.4	.2	(19.4)
Net income (loss)	$ (.6)	$ 1.1	$ .1	$(22.4)
Weighted average number of common and common equivalent shares (thousands)	934	1,046	937	941
Net operating income per share	$(0.93)	$ 0.37	$ 0.33	$ 0.32
Net income (loss) per share	(0.64)	1.06	0.20	(23.83)
Dividends paid per share:				
Preferred shares	$ 2.25	$ 2.25	$ 2.25	$ 1.25
Common shares	0.30	0.30	0.30	.075

[1]Discontinued operations have been charged for expenses incurred directly by the operating units and an allocation of home office, central warehouse, and buying expenses, but do not include any allocation of interest expense. Discontinued operations also include interest income, principally on mortgage notes received in connection with funds advanced for the development of shopping center sites for department stores.

[2]Extraordinary items for fiscal year 1983 are detailed in Exhibit 3.

EXHIBIT 2 BREVE CORPORATION SELECTED CONSOLIDATED BALANCE SHEETS (millions of dollars)

	Jan. 31, 1980	*Jan. 30, 1981*	*Jan. 29, 1982*	*July 29, 1982*	*Jan. 27, 1983*
Assets					
Cash	$ 1.7	$ 1.5	$ 2.5	$ .6	$ 1.0
Marketable securities	.8	—	—	—	13.1
Net realizable value of assets of business sold or discontinued	—	—	—	—	4.0
Accounts receivable (net)	4.1	3.6	2.9	4.2	2.5
Inventories	14.0	18.6	26.8	22.5	5.6
Cash, certificates of deposit and receivables held in escrow	—	—	—	—	2.0
Notes receivable	—	1.5	3.4	1.0	—
Prepaid expenses and other assets	1.5	.7	.4	.5	.2
Current assets	$22.1	$25.9	$36.0	$28.8	$28.4
Notes receivable	.4	1.0	—	—	—
Furniture, fixtures, and leasehold improvements (net)	3.9	6.2	5.9	6.0	3.5
Deferred charges and other assets	.6	.6	1.3	1.0	.1
Total assets	$27.0	$33.7	$43.2	$35.8	$32.0
Liabilities and Shareholders' Equity					
Notes payable to banks	$ 1.6	$ 3.9	$ 8.0	$ 8.8	$ —
Current maturity of long-term debt	.3	.5	.5	.2	—
Accounts payable	8.8	13.1	18.9	15.2	1.6
Taxes payable	1.0	1.2	1.1	.6	1.5
Accrued liabilities	1.5	1.1	1.3	1.2	.9
Provision for disposition of discontinued operations	—	—	—	—	1.8
	$13.2	$19.8	$29.8	$26.0	$ 5.8
Estimated claims under Chapter 11 bankruptcy proceedings (*Exhibit 4*)	—	—	—	—	27.6
Other liabilities under Chapter 11 bankruptcy proceedings (*Exhibit 4*)	—	—	—	—	10.9
Current liabilities	$13.2	$19.8	$29.8	$26.0	$44.3
Long-term debt	4.1	3.5	3.1	3.0	—
Other long-term liabilities	.5	.4	.5	.2	.3
Total liabilities	$17.8	$23.7	$33.4	$29.2	$44.6

Case 28 Tempo National Bank

EXHIBIT 2 (*continued*)

	Jan. 31, 1980	*Jan. 30, 1981*	*Jan. 29, 1982*	*July 29, 1982*	*Jan. 27, 1983*
Preferred stock[1]	1.4	1.4	1.3	1.2	1.2
Common stock[2]	.5	.5	.5	.5	.5
Capital surplus	2.0	2.1	2.5	2.6	2.7
Retained earnings (deficit)	5.3	6.0	5.5	2.3	(17.0)
Total shareholders' equity	9.2	10.0	9.8	6.6	(12.6)
	$27.0	$33.7	$43.2	$35.8	$32.0

[1]4 1/2% cumulative Convertible Preferred Stock, par value $50 per share, authorized 29,000 shares, issued and outstanding 25,000 shares less 320 in treasury at Jan. 27, 1983. Sinking-fund requirements are 5% of net income. At Jan. 27, 1983, such requirements were not applicable in view of the company's net loss. Dividends were not declared for the last two quarters of 1983, resulting in accumulated dividends in arrears of $27,766 ($1.125 per share). Preferred shareholders were entitled to representation on the Board of Directors if six successive quarterly dividends were not paid.

[2]Common stock, par value $0.50 per share, authorized 2,000,000 shares, issued and outstanding were 941,000 shares plus shares reserved for conversion of a convertible note and conversion of preferred stock.

Case 28 Tempo National Bank

EXHIBIT 3 BREVE CORPORATION DETAILS OF THE CHARGE FOR EXTRAORDINARY ITEMS IN FISCAL YEAR 1983 (millions of dollars)

Extraordinary items, charge (credit) comprise:	
Gain on sales of investment in Base Distributors and assets of certain Major Store subsidiaries	$ (0.9)
Losses and expenses in connection with discontinuing operations, including those to be discontinued in fiscal year 1984	7.0
Write-off of deferred charges	1.0
Provision for disaffirmed lease obligations	10.0
Provision for settlement with landlord in lieu of potential disaffirmed lease claims	1.8
Provision for employee service contracts disaffirmed	0.2
Liquidated damages resulting from settlement of lawsuit prior to Chapter 11 proceedings	0.2
Other items, principally legal fees paid through Jan. 27, 1983 in connection with Chapter 11 proceedings	0.1
	$19.4

Case 28 Tempo National Bank

EXHIBIT 4 BREVE CORPORATION ESTIMATED CLAIMS AND LIABILITIES UNDER BANKRUPTCY PROCEEDINGS (millions of dollars)

Claims:		
Notes payable to banks, including accrued interest[1]	$ 7.1	
Long-term debt, including accrued interest	3.2	
Other notes payable	.4	
Vendor merchandise and expense payables	17.9	
		$28.6
Other liabilities:		
Disaffirmed lease obligations	$10.0	
Employee service contracts disaffirmed	.4	
Other[2]	.4	
		$10.8
		$39.4
Funds held in escrow, covered by attachment liens, or otherwise restricted		(1.9)
		$37.5

[1]Pursuant to the provisions of Chapter 11 of the Bankruptcy Code, all interest on the company's indebtedness ceased to accrue on the date of filing of the petition.

[2]Includes settlement of claim with purchaser of Base Distributors and a cash payment assigned to a department store landlord for releasing the company from rental claims.

Case 28 Tempo National Bank

EXHIBIT 5 BREVE CORPORATION INITIAL PLAN OF ARRANGEMENT PRESENTED TO CREDITORS' COMMITTEE IN APRIL 1983 (millions of dollars)

Settlement:

Debtors settle for 50% of their claims and other entitlements to be paid in cash.

Payable as follows:

1. Upon court confirmation of the plan of arrangement, pay 33% of the claims and liabilities	$12.5
2. Pay the balance of 17% from net earnings before taxes as follows:	
3% on Jan. 31, 1984	1.1
3% on Apr. 30, 1985	1.1
3% on Apr. 30, 1986	1.1
4% on Apr. 30, 1987	1.5
4% on Apr. 30, 1988	1.5
50% of claims and liabilities of $37.5	$18.8

Case 28 Tempo National Bank

EXHIBIT 11 BREVE CORPORATION EFFECT ON BALANCE SHEET OF 40%, 50%, AND 60% SETTLEMENTS, HOLDING INITIAL CASH PAYMENT CONSTANT (millions of dollars)

	40%	*50%*	*60%*
Settlement:			
Current assets (3/31/83)	$27.9	$27.9	$27.9
Less first cash payment (33%)	(12.5)	(12.5)	(12.5)
Current assets after first cash payment	15.4	15.4	15.4
Furniture, fixtures, and leasehold improvements (net 3/31/83)	3.1	3.1	3.1
Total assets	$18.5	$18.5	$18.5
Current liabilities (3/31/83)	$ 3.4	$ 3.4	$ 3.4
Claims and liabilities covered by escrowed funds (3/31/83)	2.0	2.0	2.0
Current liabilities	5.4	5.4	5.4
Claims and liabilities under Chapter 11 (3/31/83)	37.5	37.5	37.5
Reduction due to amount of debt forgiven (60%, 50%, 40% of claims and liabilities)*	(22.5)	(18.8)	(15.0)
Chapter 11 liabilities at confirmation	15.0	18.7	22.5
Reduced by 33% first cash payment	(12.5)	(12.5)	(12.5)
Liabilities covered by extended payments under plan	2.5	6.2	10.0
Unrealized profit (3/31/83)	.2	.2	.2
Total liabilities	$ 8.1	$11.8	$15.6
Shareholders' equity (3/31/83)	(12.1)	(12.1)	(12.1)
Increased by the amount of debt forgiven	22.5	18.8	15.0
Total shareholders' equity	$10.4	$ 6.7	$ 2.9
Total liabilities and shareholders' equity	$18.5	$18.5	$18.5

*No tax carryforward would remain if the debt forgiven was greater than $11 million.

EXHIBIT 12 BREVE CORPORATION EFFECT ON BALANCE SHEET OF INITIAL CASH PAYMENTS OF 28%, 35%, AND 38% ASSUMING 50% SETTLEMENT (millions of dollars)

	28%	*33%*	*38%*
Initial cash payment:			
Current assets (3/31/83)	$27.9	$27.9	$27.9
Less first cash payment	(10.5)	(12.5)	(14.3)
Current assets after first cash payment	17.4	15.4	13.6
Furniture, fixtures, and leasehold improvements (net 3/31/83)	3.1	3.1	3.1
Total assets	$20.5	$18.5	$16.7
Current liabilities (3/31/83)	$ 3.4	$ 3.4	$ 3.4
Claims and liabilities covered by escrowed funds (3/31/83)	2.0	2.0	2.0
Current liabilities	5.4	5.4	5.4
Claims and liabilities under Chapter 11 (3/31/83)	37.5	37.5	37.5
Reduction due to amount of debt forgiven (50%)*	(18.8)	(18.8)	(18.8)
Chapter 11 liabilities at confirmation	18.7	18.7	18.7
Reduced by first cash payment	(10.5)	(12.5)	(14.3)
Liabilities covered by extended payments under plan	8.2	6.2	4.4
Unrealized profit (3/31/83)	.2	.2	.2
Total liabilities	$13.8	$11.8	$10.0
Shareholders' equity (3/31/83)	(12.1)	(12.1)	(12.1)
Increased by the amount of debt forgiven	18.8	18.8	18.8
Total shareholders' equity	$ 6.7	$ 6.7	$ 6.7
Total liabilities and shareholders' equity	$20.5	$18.5	$16.7

*Would completely exhaust the $11 million tax-loss carryforward.

Case 28 Tempo National Bank

EXHIBIT 13 COMPARISON WITH SIMILAR SPECIALTY SHOP CHAINS

	Bolero Corp.[1]	*Capriccio Inc.*[2]	*Breve*[6]
Number of stores	243	58	127
Net sales	$169,000,000	$18,800,000	$ 50,000,000
Gross margins	$ 52,100,000	$ 8,400,000	$ 18,400,000
Operating earnings	$ 26,900,000	$ 3,400,000	$ 300,000
Net income	$ 14,200,000	$ 1,700,000	$(22,400,000)
Common shares	7,030,000	2,000,000	940,000
Earnings per share	$2.20	$0.85	($23.83)
Dividend per share	$0.42	—	—
Approximate inside control	60%	70%	60%
Average working capital[3]	$ 44,900,000	$ 1,509,000	—
Average long-term debt[3]	—	$ 1,000,000	—
Average equity[3]	$ 55,600,000	$ 3,000,000	$ (1,400,000)
Stock prices:			
Exchange	NYEX[4]	OTC[5]	AMEX
Mid-March 1983	$74	$15	
P/E	36×	17×	Trading suspended in Sept. 1982
Mid-April 1983	$64	$13	
P/E	31×	15×	

[1]*Bolero Corp.* Chain of women's specialty apparel shops that sold first-quality, moderately priced fashion apparel to juniors, misses, and women in 15–35 age group. High traffic shopping areas. Shops averaged 10,000 sq. ft. Maximized inventory turnover. Centralized buying and computerized inventory control. Automated central distribution facility. No advertising. Primarily cash business. Leased all facilities except four stores. Shops throughout U.S. Annual growth averages over 5 years: sales 21%, net income 27%. Data reported for fiscal year ending January 31, 1983.

[2]*Capriccio Inc.* Chain of women's specialty apparel shops that sold medium to higher priced sportswear to fashion-conscious young women. High traffic shopping areas. Shops average 2,200 sq. ft. Centralized buying and distribution. No advertising. Primarily cash business. Leased all facilities. Shops throughout Midwest, East, and South. Annual growth averages over 5 years: sales 38%, net income 64%. Data reported fiscal year ending February 3, 1983.

[3]Averages over fiscal year 1983.

[4]Bolero Corp. began trading actively early in calendar year 1980. It reached a low of $13 1/2 in mid-1980 and climbed steadily to a high of $79 in early 1983. Slower growth in this stock was expected over the next few years.

[5]There was no market for Capriccio's stock before March 1983. In January, 405,000 shares were offered and sold for approximately $10 per share (355,000 shares were offered by large shareholders and 50,000 additional shares were issued by the company). This reduced inside control to slightly over 50%.

[6]Fiscal year 1983 restated to allow for discontinued and divested operations.

Case 29

UTAMA JALAN GROUP

It was July 1986, and Mr. John Graham, assistant vice president, Toledo Bank and Trust (TBT), had just returned from a long and arduous Credit Policy Committee meeting. He had recently joined the Asia/Pacific Group, and TBT's exposure in Indonesia had been the topic of the meeting. The total Indonesian country limit of $30 million was exceeded by current outstandings of $33.1 million. The Committee was particularly uncomfortable with the quality of loans outstanding to the Utama Jalan Group, which comprised a full 36 percent of the total Indonesian exposure. Due to the Group's declining sales volume, reduced profit margins, and liquidity problems, the Committee decided to downgrade its credit rating from a 4 to 5 (a 6-point scale was used in credit ratings, with 6 being the lowest).

Mr. Graham was planning a trip to Southeast Asia the following week and now realized that he would need to visit Utama Jalan's management to introduce himself and discuss the increasingly strained relationship. TBT was concerned about consistently late payments, incomplete financial disclosures, and failure to abide by the loan covenants. The management of Utama Jalan had argued that the current financial difficulties were a result of the temporary slump in the Indonesian economy combined with the liquidity demands of rapid growth and that TBT should be more accommodating. By carefully analyzing TBT's relationship with Utama Jalan before his trip, Mr. Graham hoped to find a way to improve the deteriorating situation.

This case was prepared by Donald W. Hoskins with the support of individuals and institutions which wish to remain anonymous. Aspects of the company's situation and certain financial information have been changed to protect company confidences without altering the nature of the managerial decision.

TBT had outstandings totaling $10.5 million to four operating companies in the Utama Jalan Group as of July 1986, as follows: P.T. Orang Putih, a timber concession, had a term loan outstanding of US$1,015,558. The principal was past due, but interest was still current. Beecara Trading Company, a company for Utama Jalan's plywood sales, had US$988,500 outstanding in past-due trust receipts. Interest was being paid with delays. P.T. Trima Kasi Electronics, a home appliances and consumer electronic goods producer, had a term loan outstanding of US$1,500,000. Principal was not yet due, and interest was current. Terrogong Electronics, Ltd., a trading company importing components for P.T. Trima Kasi Electronics, had a trade facility outstanding denominated in Japanese yen currently valued at US$7,018,000. This exposure had increased during the past year due to the appreciation of the yen against the U.S. dollar, and past-due principal had amounted to the equivalent of US$1,934,000.

TOLEDO BANK AND TRUST

Toledo Bank and Trust was a strong major regional bank, headquartered in Toledo, Ohio. Management had expanded the bank rapidly through major acquisitions while keeping profitability at impressive levels. By the end of 1985, total assets had grown to over $14 billion, with net income of $141 million. Foreign loans had declined 5.3 percent during 1985 to $519 million. ROA in 1985 was 1.12 percent, and ROE was 17.29 percent, both improvements over the previous year.

The International Division traditionally took a conservative approach to international banking, primarily structuring activities to support the international requirements of major domestic corporate clients. This financing and other banking activities generally supported customers' production of goods and services in foreign countries, financed the export of their domestically produced goods to overseas buyers, and occasionally financed the foreign trading partners of TBT's U.S. clients.

THE UTAMA JALAN GROUP

The Utama Jalan Group was an agglomeration of numerous separate Indonesian corporations, all owned and controlled by various members of the Whan family. Its origins in Indonesia dated back to the beginning of the century, with activities then centered around planting and exporting of natural rubber and trading. It later shifted its focus to timber, which remained the current core of Utama Jalan's business.

Beginning in the late 1970s, Utama Jalan diversified into ceramics and consumer electronics. For 1984, Utama Jalan reported total sales of US$94.3 million, with the timber operations contributing 51 percent; ceramics, 16 percent; and electronics, 33 percent. At December 31, 1983, Utama Jalan's combined balance sheets indicated total assets of US$184.5 million and a net worth of US$58.7 million. The Group's consolidated income statement for 1984 showed a loss for the first time in Utama Jalan's history, US$3.8 million. Financial statements are provided in Exhibit 1.

TIMBER

Utama Jalan began acquiring timberland concessions in Indonesia in the 1960s. By 1986, the total concession area approximated 6.8 million acres (larger than the state of Vermont), located in South Sumatra and Borneo. These concession lands had provided the raw material resources for Utama Jalan's various timber and lumber activities.

Harvesting the concessions, Utama Jalan enjoyed profitability from export sales of round logs. Moreover, Utama Jalan started early in establishing saw mills near its concessions before this was required by law. Export sales of sawn timber had been another source of profit for the Group. In terms of concessions held and sawmill capacity, the Group had about 12 percent of the total timber industry in Indonesia.

In the late 1970s, again before such became government policy, Utama Jalan expanded further into value-added timber-processing activities in the form of plywood mills. The Group's investment in plywood mills was accomplished by both new construction and by acquisition. By 1986 Utama Jalan had a total of sixteen production lines in South Sumatra and Borneo, with a combined productive capacity of about one-half million cubic meters per year. Nearly all of the plywood produced was exported.

CERAMICS

In 1978 Utama Jalan took its first major step toward diversification from wood-based industry by acquiring a small ceramic-tile manufacturer near Jakarta. After additional investment in upgrading and expanding the plant, the Group had become a major ceramic producer in Indonesia. The plant also had recently begun producing sanitary ware.

CONSUMER ELECTRONICS

The second major diversification step came in 1982 when Utama Jalan purchased an ongoing company in Jakarta with exclusive rights from Sanyo of Japan to import, assemble, and distribute all Sanyo consumer electronics goods and electrical home appliances in Indonesia. This franchise had been renewed subsequent to acquisition. Investments were made in updating and expanding the plant, and Utama Jalan both broadened the imported Sanyo product line and increased local assembly.

ADDITIONAL ACTIVITIES

Utama Jalan had other less substantial investments in Indonesia, such as real estate, textile milling, garment manufacturing and exporting, and natural-rubber plantations. The Whan family also held some sizeable investments offshore, where its activities were managed through separate companies generally known under the name of the Terrogong Group.

In Singapore, Terrogong began as a trading company exporting Utama Jalan's timber products: first round logs and sawn lumber, then plywood. Gradually, Terrogong began to invest, with Utama Jalan's export profits, in the real estate market in Singapore. Although the market value of this portfolio had declined, its current value was still very substantial with little debt-service burden. The portfolio concentrated on luxury housing units, industrial estates, and office buildings. Elsewhere, the Terrogong Group maintained sales offices in Hong Kong, Taipei, Tokyo, and London.

MANAGEMENT

The current executive management of Utama Jalan was an informal structure because there was no legal entity acting as a holding company for the operating companies. In all cases, Mr. Suti Trismitro was the chairman, and Mr. Eko Situmorang was the managing director. Numerous other Whan family members were in various management positions, as well as being shareholders of the companies.

Utama Jalan currently, however, had announced that it was in the process of forming a legal holding company which would be known as Sudirman Economic Development Corporation. This was apparently now feasible as a result of recent tax changes in Indonesia, which no longer imposed double corporate income taxes on both the operating companies and the holding company. The holding company concept also reflected Utama Jalan's stated desire to change its organization along with the nature and size of its business. Sudirman would be structured along product groups: timber, ceramics, and electronics. At the holding company level, there would be five functional areas: strategic planning, finance, human resources, management information, and administration.

After collecting the most up-to-date financial statements available to TBT, Mr. Graham began to review the six relevant operating companies in the Utama Jalan Group with which TBT had established relationships. The financial statements are provided in Exhibits 2 through 7.

P.T. ORANG PUTIH

P.T. Orang Putih (Orang) was originally established by the Indonesian government to manage a prime timber concession area of 568,000 acres in East Borneo. Orang then took on a partner, who provided US$3.38 million in financing from First Minnesota Bank. Soon afterwards, however, the government issued regulations requiring all raw-log exporters to invest in saw-milling equipment. This required an additional US$7.5 million in funds which the partner could not provide, and the existing debt to First Minnesota Bank went into default.

Orang invited the Utama Jalan Group in 1982 to consider replacing the current partner. Utama Jalan agreed, and the new structure gave 60 percent of the equity to Utama Jalan while 40 percent was kept by the Indonesian government. Utama Jalan also assumed all of Orang's liabilities and was given full management control.

BEECARA TRADING COMPANY

Beecara Trading Company (Beecara) was a trading company based in Hong Kong. Beecara acted as a captive commission sales agent, assuming no title to merchandise, for Utama Jalan's plywood sales in Southeast Asia, China, Japan, the Middle East, Europe, and North America. Beecara was set up as a partnership with the unlimited personal liability of the Whan family members.

P.T. TRIMA KASI ELECTRONICS

P.T. Trima Kasi Electronics (Trima) imported, assembled, and distributed consumer electronic goods and home appliances in Indonesia under license from Sanyo of Japan. Trima and the exclusive Indonesian franchise had previously been held by non-Indonesian parties. However, neither the Indonesian government nor Sanyo had been pleased with the arrangement: the former because of the lack of direct investment in plants, the latter because of the stagnant market share. As a result, a change in shareholders was sought. The Utama Jalan Group successfully concluded negotiations with Sanyo and the Indonesian government and became the company's new owner in 1982.

At the time of the Group's acquisition, only televisions had been assembled locally, as required by law, and all other products were imported completely built. After 1982, Trima's plant was expanded so that refrigerators, air conditioners, and clothes washers would also be locally assembled. The product range was broadened, and the number of different models increased. The Sanyo line moved up from fifth to fourth place in the market, after Sharp, National, and Toshiba.

TERROGONG ELECTRONICS, LTD.

Terrogong Electronics, Ltd. (Terrogong) was established in Hong Kong in 1982 as the importing agent for Trima's Sanyo products and components from Japan. Terrogong acted as a commission agent for shipments directly between Japan and Indonesia and did not assume title to the merchandise. Terrogong arranged for 180-day usance letters of credit in yen to be issued to Sanyo and offset its liabilities with an equal amount of accounts receivable from Trima. Since the production cycle for Trima was about 9 months from the issuance of the letter of credit to the collection of cash, the maturing drafts were then refinanced under trust receipts. Terrogong had no capitalization of its own and relied on the credit of the Utama Jalan Group.

P.T. TIDAKA BISA PLYWOOD

P.T. Tidaka Bisa Plywood (Tidaka) was located in South Sumatra and was the largest of the Group's four plywood mills. When the company was acquired in 1979, there were only two production lines. Since that time, Utama Jalan invested US$9.4 million to modernize equipment and expand capacity to include a total of six production lines.

Tidaka was purchased as an ongoing concern, and the unprofitable operations by the previous owners provided significant tax credits for losses that could be carried forward for an indefinite period of time. Due to a tax law change in 1982, however, the loss carryforward period was limited to only 3 years. Recognizing this situation, the tax authorities allowed Tidaka, in its 1983 financial statements, to readjust Utama Jalan's original investment in Tidaka by writing down the accumulated deficits and writing up the fixed asset accounts to the Group's original investment amount.

P.T. LABAH LABAH CERAMICS

P.T. Labah Labah Ceramics (Labah) was a small ceramic-tile manufacturer with outdated kilns when it was acquired by Utama Jalan in 1978. New management was then brought in, and the Group invested in more modern equipment and increased productive capacity. Sanitary-ware ceramic products were also introduced.

Labah subsequently became one of the largest tile producers in Indonesia, enjoying popular brand name recognition. Labah continued to invest in ceramic technology and had spent US$1.5 million on a research and development facility at the plant site.

BACKGROUND ON TBT'S RELATIONSHIP WITH UTAMA JALAN

TBT began its relationship with the Utama Jalan Group in the late 1970s when the Group diversified into ceramics. During its subsequent expansion in several different product lines, the Group purchased manufacturing equipment from U.S. suppliers, and TBT was called on to provide the export financing. The relationship with Utama Jalan's management also proved quite valuable in generating contacts for additional trade finance business for the bank. While wanting to contain its exposure to Latin America, the bank was eager to expand its business in the strong, growing economies of the Pacific Basin. TBT was then approached by the Group in June 1982 to provide (jointly with First Minnesota Bank) a US$3 million term loan to Orang so that Utama Jalan could take over the shares of Orang from a company controlled by a client of First Minnesota. The loan was secured by a first mortgage on Orang land and equipment valued at US$3.75 million.

In September 1982, TBT extended US$10.1 million bridge financing to Tidaka. The loan was subsequently entirely repaid with interest in a timely manner. Then in November of the same year, a US$3.75 million clean trade finance facility was established for each on behalf of Beecara and of Terrogong for trust receipts and letters of credit. Both facilities were additionally supported by the principals' personal guarantees. The Beecara facility was provided jointly and equally by TBT and California Trust Company, while the Terrogong facility was provided jointly and equally by TBT and Portland National Bank. Both California Trust and Portland National subsequently withdrew, reducing the facilities to US$1.88 million each.

Finally, in March 1983 TBT granted Trima a US$1.5 million unsecured term loan with the principals' personal guarantees and a corporate guarantee from Tidaka.

A loan syndication was attempted in July 1984 but failed due to lack of interest from other banks approached by TBT. The loan package would have included US$9 million to Terrogong, US$2.6 million to Trima, and US$3.75 million to Labah Labah Ceramics. Security was to include a first mortgage on most of Labah's assets and assignment of Trima's inventory and Terrogong's receivables. Had the syndication been successful, TBT would have had new outstandings to Labah, maintained its current position with Orang and Beecara, but reduced exposure to Trima and Terrogong. This would have lowered overall outstandings to the Utama Jalan Group by 13 percent.

To understand Utama Jalan's present difficulties and future prospects, Mr. Graham also wanted to assess the political and economic environment of Indonesia.

INDONESIA

Indonesia, a nation of over 13,000 islands, was the fifth most populous country in the world by 1986, with approximately 165 million people. TBT had become interested in establishing a presence in Indonesia because of the impressive growth in that country. From 1965 to 1973, GDP growth had averaged 8.1 percent a year, and from 1983 to 1984, the rate declined only slightly to 6.8 percent per year. Much of this growth, however, had been fueled by oil exports, and the recent unprecedented plummet in oil prices made Indonesia's future prospects much less certain.

Indonesia's economy was also highly dependent on trade with Japan and the United States. From 1981 to 1985, trade with Japan accounted for 26 percent of all imports and 48 percent of exports, with an average annual trade surplus of US$6,731 million. Over the same period, trade with the United States accounted for 15 percent of imports, 20 percent of exports, and an average US$2,040 million annual trade surplus for Indonesia. Exchange rates with these key trading partners are shown in Exhibit 8.

Mr. Graham had received various economic statistics published by the International Monetary Fund, which are provided in Exhibit 9. He also requested a country report from the bank's Economics Department. That report began by summarizing key economic statistics for Indonesia, which are shown in Exhibit 10. The second part of the report briefly outlined major political developments in Indonesia, as follows:

> President Suharto (65) was in good health. It was expected that when his current term expired in 1988, the president would seek (and receive) his fifth term.
>
> The political situation would become more unsettled as economic austerity continued. However, Suharto was expected to remain in control.
>
> There existed an ongoing battle for the president's ear between the "technocrats" and the "palace crowd." The former were a group of government officials led by Ali Wardhana, Coordination Minister. They were mostly foreign educated and had been instrumental in effecting Indonesia's prudent monetary and fiscal policy. The "palace crowd," on the other hand, were more populist. So far, the technocrats' influence on Suharto had benefited Indonesia greatly, and there were no signs that this influence was waning.

Corruption was widespread in Indonesia. Suharto and his supporters kept a firm grip on power through a vast system of patronage greased by control over state funds.

The government had trumpeted the state ideology of Pancasila to unify the diverse country and undercut other ideologies which could cause instability. Pancasila stressed the belief in five principles: one god, humanitarianism, national unity, democracy, and social justice.

Over 85 percent of Indonesia's 165 million people were at least nominal followers of Islam. The political arm of the Moslem community had withdrawn from the political arena, but more radical elements in the community had roused disturbances. The Islam revival represented a possible long-term challenge to Suharto's Golkar party.

President Suharto and his party were expected to remain firmly in control of Indonesia through the forecast period. Little dissent was allowed, and the opposition had been rendered impotent. However, in the longer run as the country developed, Indonesia's monolithic power structure would breed instability.

Indonesia faced few external threats. The new government in the Philippines had undercut the communist insurgency in that country, thus diminishing the chance that Indonesia would face a communist threat from the Philippines.

Relations with the United States and Japan were good. Indonesia was a strong supporter of the nonaligned movement and, as such, also maintained good relations with the Eastern Bloc.

Relations with China had begun to thaw. However, Indonesians remained suspicious of the huge country's intentions. (China was suspected of complicity in the 1965 communist coup attempt in Indonesia.)

FINAL THOUGHTS

John Graham concluded that the Utama Jalan Group and TBT were both in difficult positions. Utama Jalan appeared to have a good management track record but was suddenly placed under severe external pressures. There had been a precipitous drop in prices for world timber, sawn lumber, and plywood which put a financial strain on the Group's wood-based products' exporting operations. (Plywood prices are provided in Exhibit 11.) At the same time, oil prices plummeted, causing the Indonesian economy to go into a recession and, thereby, depressing domestic demand for ceramic tiles and consumer electronic goods and appliances. Mr. Graham did not think that these economic conditions would prevail over the long term, but the immediate situation created serious cash-flow problems for most of Utama Jalan's operating companies.

On the other hand, Mr. Graham was not sure how the bank's exposure could be effectively reduced. TBT could, for example, demand that Utama Jalan sell off some of its vast land holdings to repay its debts, but would the Group's management be willing to sell to a depressed Indonesian economy at probable low prices? He was not convinced that the local courts would be willing to force Utama Jalan into liquidating some of its assets.

Looking through Utama Jalan's files, Mr. Graham found a profitability analysis of the banking relationship over the course of 1985 (summarized in Exhibit 12). From this point of view, Utama Jalan appeared to be a very desirable customer. In addition, the Group's management had introduced many valuable contacts to TBT throughout the Pacific Basin, which resulted in additional business for the Asia/Pacific Group.

Musing how international lending was often considered a glamorous job, John Graham observed the two-foot pile of files on Utama Jalan that had somehow accumulated on his desk. He looked up at the world map on the wall, eyeing the islands of Indonesia. He knew that he would need to prepare a specific proposal for the Utama Jalan Group before arriving in Jakarta next week.

Case 29 Utama Jalan Group

EXHIBIT 1 CONSOLIDATED STATEMENTS (billions of rupiahs)

	1981		*1982*		*1983*		*1984*	
	audited	*% of Sales*	*audited*	*% of Sales*	*unaudited*	*% of Sales*	*unaudited*	*% of Sales*
Assets								
Cash	1.1	2%	.8	2%	1.7	2%	1.6	2%
Accounts receivable	7.1	15	5.4	11	14.9	17	19.2	19
Inventory	15.4	33	39.1	77	40.8	47	47.0	46
Current assets	23.6	50	45.3	90	57.4	66	67.8	67
Net fixed assets	29.4	63	49.0	97	98.7	113	100.5	99
Advances/prepayments	7.9	17	10.8	21	8.3	10	11.1	11
Other receivables	10.1	21	4.4	9	3.7	4	4.3	4
Other assets	6.6	14	11.0	22	8.9	10	14.5	15
Total assets	77.6	165%	120.5	239%	177.0	203%	198.2	196%
		% of Assets		*% of Assets*		*% of Assets*		*% of Assets*
Liabilities								
Bank notes payable	34.0	44%	27.9	23%	42.3	24%	43.4	22%
Accounts payable	3.4	4	3.9	3	8.5	5	14.3	7
Accruals	1.8	2	3.3	3	2.3	1	2.4	1
Other liabilities	.2	0	3.7	3	4.4	2	6.9	4
Current liabilities	39.4	50	38.8	32	57.5	32	67.0	34
Long-term debt	4.4	6	37.6	31	52.5	30	68.2	34
Total liabilities	43.8	56	76.4	63	110.0	62	135.2	68
Capital	18.4	25	27.5	23	45.3	26	45.4	23
Gain on appraisal	2.6	3	2.6	2	3.5	2	3.5	2
Retained earnings	12.8	16	14.0	12	18.2	10	14.1	7
Net worth	33.8	44	44.1	37	67.0	38	63.0	32
Total liabilities and net worth	77.6	100%	120.5	100%	177.0	100%	198.2	100%
		% of Sales		*% of Sales*		*% of Sales*		*% of Sales*
Net sales	47.0	100%	50.4	100%	87.0	100%	101.3	100%
Cost of goods sold	29.3	62	35.0	69	59.0	68	72.2	71
Gross profit	17.7	38	15.4	31	28.0	32	29.1	29
Operating expenses	9.4	20	10.1	20	12.5	15	14.1	14
Other (income)/ expenses (includes interest)	1.3	3	1.9	4	9.0	10	19.1	19
Profit before taxes	7.0	15	3.4	7	6.5	7	(4.1)	(4)

Case 29 Utama Jalan Group

EXHIBIT 1 (*continued*)

	1981		*1982*		*1983*		*1984*	
	audited	*% of Sales*	*audited*	*% of Sales*	*unaudited*	*% of Sales*	*unaudited*	*% of Sales*
Taxes	1.4	3	1.3	3	—	—	—	—
Net income	5.6	12%	2.1	4%	6.5	7%	(4.1)	(4)%
US$/1000 rupiahs	1.553		1.444		1.006		0.931	
Consumer Price Index	100.0		109.5		122.4		135.3	

Case 29 Utama Jalan Group

EXHIBIT 2 *P.T. ORANG PUTIH* FINANCIAL STATEMENTS (billions of rupiahs)

	1981		*1982*		*1983**	
	unaudited	*% of Sales*	*unaudited*	*% of Sales*	*unaudited*	*% of Sales*
Assets						
Cash	.0	0%	.2	22%	.0	0%
Accounts receivable	.0	0	.0	0	.2	13
Inventory	1.0	33	.7	78	.6	37
Current assets	1.0	33	.9	100	.8	50%
Net fixed assets	.8	27	3.2	355	4.5	281
Advances/prepayment	.2	7	.7	78	.2	13
Other receivables	2.7	90	1.1	122	.8	50
Other assets	.3	10	1.4	156	.9	56
Total assets	5.0	167%	7.3	811%	7.2	450%

Case 29 Utama Jalan Group

EXHIBIT 2 (*continued*)

	1981		*1982*		*1983**	
	unaudited	*% of Assets*	*unaudited*	*% of Assets*	*unaudited*	*% of Assets*
Liabilities						
Bank notes payable	.0	0	.8	11%	.8	11%
Accounts payable	2.4	48	.0	0	.1	1
Accruals	.0	0	.0	0	.2	3
Other liabilities	.0	0	.3	4	1.3	18
Current liabilities	2.4	48	1.1	15	2.4	33
Long-term debt	.0	0	3.3	45	2.1	29
Total liabilities	2.4	48	4.4	60	4.5	62
Capital	2.3	46	3.0	41	3.0	42
Retained earnings	.3	6	(.1)	(1)	(.3)	(4)
Net worth	2.6	52	2.9	40	2.7	38
Total liabilities and net worth	5.0	100%	7.3	100%	7.2	100%

		% of Sales		*% of Sales*		*% of Sales*
Net sales	3.0	100	.9	100%	1.6	100%
Cost of goods sold	2.5	83	.7	78	.9	56
Gross profit	.5	17	.2	22	.7	44
Operating expenses	.4	14	.2	22	.5	31
Other (income)/ expenses (includes interest)	.0	0	(.1)	(11)	.4	25
Profit before tax	.1	3	.1	11	(.2)	(12)
Taxes	.0	0	.0	0	.0	0
Net income	.1	3%	.1	11%	(.2)	(12)%
US$/1000 rupiahs	1.553		1.444		1.006	
Consumer Price Index	100.0		109.5		122.4	

*1983 most current year available.

Case 29 Utama Jalan Group

EXHIBIT 3 ***BEECARA TRADING COMPANY*** **FINANCIAL STATEMENTS (millions of Hong Kong dollars)**

	1982		*1983*		*1984*	
	unaudited	*% of Sales*	*unaudited*	*% of Sales*	*unaudited*	*% of Sales*
Assets						
Cash	.0	0%	5.4	540%	.5	50%
Accounts receivable	6.7	172	14.2	1,420	11.9	1,190
Inventory	.0	0	.0	0	.0	0
Current assets	6.7	172	19.6	1,960	12.4	1,240
Net fixed assets	.0	0	.0	0	.0	0
Advances/prepayments	.0	0	.0	0	.0	0
Total assets	6.7	172%	19.6	1,960%	12.4	1,240%
		% of Assets		*% of Assets*		*% of Assets*
Liabilities						
Bank notes payable	.5	7%	.5	3%	1.9	15%
Accounts payable	1.9	28	12.8	65	3.2	26
Other liabilities	4.0	60	5.9	30	6.9	55
Total liabilities	6.4	95	19.2	98	12.0	96
Capital	.2	3	.2	1	.2	2
Retained earnings	.1	2	.2	1	.2	2
Net worth	.3	5	.4	2	.4	4
Total liabilities and net worth	6.7	100%	19.6	100%	12.4	100%
		% of Sales		*% of Sales*		*% of Sales*
Net sales	3.9	100%	.0	0%	.0	0%
Cost of goods sold	3.6	92	.0	0	.0	0
Gross profit	.3	8	.0	0	.0	0
Operating expenses	.4	10	.5	50	.5	50
Other (income)/ expenses (includes interest)	(.2)	(5)	(.5)	(50)	(.5)	(50)
Profit before taxes	.1	3	.0	0	.0	0
Taxes	.0	0	.0	0	.0	0
Net income	.1	3%	.0	0%	.0	0%
US$/HK$	0.1541		0.1287		0.1279	

EXHIBIT 4 *P.T. TRIMA KASI ELECTRONICS* FINANCIAL STATEMENTS (billions of rupiahs)

	1982		*1983*		*1984*	
	unaudited	*% of Sales*	*unaudited*	*% of Sales*	*unaudited*	*% of Sales*
Assets						
Cash	.3	6%	1.0	6%	.5	2%
Accounts receivable	4.0	74	5.8	33	6.0	18
Inventory	4.3	79	8.0	43	9.7	29
Current assets	8.6	159	14.8	82	16.2	49
Net fixed assets	1.6	30	7.2	39	7.3	21
Advances/prepayments	.2	4	1.1	6	1.4	4
Other receivables	.0	0	.1	1	.2	1
Other assets	.4	7	.4	2	1.2	4
Total assets	10.8	200%	23.6	130%	26.3	79%
		% of Assets		*% of Assets*		*% of Assets*
Liabilities						
Bank notes payable	6.0	56%	7.7	33%	8.6	33%
Accounts payable	2.1	19	5.0	21	6.7	25
Accruals	.3	3	.5	2	.3	1
Other liabilities	.0	0	.1	0	.0	0
Current liabilities	8.4	78	13.3	56	15.6	59
Long-term debt	1.6	15	5.2	22	4.5	17
Total liabilities	10.0	93	18.5	78	20.1	76
Capital	.5	4	4.0	17	4.0	15
Retained earnings	.3	3	1.1	5	2.2	9
Net worth	.8	7	5.1	22	6.2	24
Total liabilities and net worth	10.8	100%	23.6	100%	26.3	100%

Case 29 Utama Jalan Group

EXHIBIT 4 ***(continued)***

	1982		1983		1984	
	unaudited	*% of Sales*	*unaudited*	*% of Sales*	*unaudited*	*% of Sales*
Net sales	5.4	100%	18.1	100%	33.3	100%
Cost of goods sold	4.1	76	12.8	71	26.0	78
Gross profit	1.3	24	5.3	29	7.3	22
Operating expenses	.8	15	3.3	18	4.7	14
Other (income)/ expenses (includes interest)	.2	3	1.1	6	1.5	5
Profit before taxes	.3	6	.9	5	1.1	3
Taxes	.0	0	.0	0	.0	0
Net income	.3	6%	.9	5%	1.1	3%
US$/1000 rupiahs	1.444		1.006		0.931	
Consumer Price Index	109.5		122.4		125.3	

EXHIBIT 5 *TERROGONG ELECTRONICS, LTD.* FINANCIAL STATEMENTS (millions of Hong Kong dollars)

	1983		*1984*	
	unaudited	*% of Sales*	*unaudited*	*% of Sales*
Assets				
Cash	.9	450%	.1	50%
Accounts receivable	14.0	7,000	44.2	22,100
Total assets	14.9	7,450%	44.3	22,150%
		% of Assets		*% of Assets*
Liabilities				
Bank notes payable	13.8	92%	43.1	98%
Accounts payable	.9	6	1.1	2
Accruals	.1	1	.0	0
Total liabilities	14.8	99	44.2	100
Retained earnings	.1	1	.1	0
Net worth	.1	1	.1	0
Total liabilities and net worth	14.9	100%	44.3	100%
		% of Sales		*% of Sales*
Commission revenue	.2	100%	.2	100%
Gross profit	.2	100	.2	100
Operating expenses	.1	50	.1	50
Other (income)/expense (includes interest)	.0	0	.0	0
Profit before taxes	.1	50	.1	50
Taxes	.0	0	.0	0
Net income	.1	50%	.1	50%
US$/HK$	0.1287		0.1279	

Case 29 Utama Jalan Group

EXHIBIT 6 *P.T. TIDAKA BISA PLYWOOD* FINANCIAL STATEMENTS (billions of rupiahs)

	1982		*1983*		*1984*	
	unaudited	*% of Sales*	*unaudited*	*% of Sales*	*unaudited*	*% of Sales*
Assets						
Cash	.1	2%	.0	0%	.2	2%
Accounts receivable	.0	0	.6	5	1.1	11
Inventory	6.1	105	3.7	28	3.9	38
Current assets	6.2	107	4.3	33	5.2	51
Net fixed assets	7.0	121	15.1	117	14.0	139
Advances/prepayments	.0	0	.0	0	1.4	14
Other receivables	1.2	21	.5	4	.2	2
Other assets	3.5	60	.6	5	.8	8
Total assets	17.9	309%	20.5	159%	21.6	214%

		% of Assets		*% of Assets*		*% of Assets*
Liabilities						
Bank notes payable	.0	0%	2.3	11%	1.4	6%
Accounts payable	.8	4	.1	0	2.6	12
Accruals	1.7	9	.1	0	.0	0
Other liabilities	8.2	47	2.7	14	1.9	9
Current liabilities	10.7	60	5.2	25	5.9	27
Long-term debt	10.5	58	8.2	40	10.1	47
Total liabilities	21.2	118	13.4	65	16.0	74
Capital	5.9	33	7.5	36	7.4	34
Retained earnings	(9.2)	(51)	(.4)	(1)	(1.8)	(8)
Net worth	(3.3)	(18)	7.1	35	5.6	26
Total liabilities and net worth	17.9	100%	20.5	100%	21.6	100%

EXHIBIT 6 (*continued*)

	1982		*1983*		*1984*	
	unaudited	*% of Sales*	*unaudited*	*% of Sales*	*unaudited*	*% of Sales*
Net sales	5.8	100%	12.9	100%	10.1	100%
Cost of goods sold	4.7	81	9.3	72	8.0	79
Gross profit	1.1	19	3.6	28	2.1	21
Operating expenses	1.8	31	1.8	14	1.1	11
Other (income)/ expense (includes interest)	.0	0	1.5	12	2.4	24
Profit before taxes	(.7)	(12)	.3	2	(1.4)	(14)
Taxes	.0	0	.0	0	.0	0
Net income	(.7)	(12)%	.3	2%	(1.4)	(14)%
US$/1000 rupiahs	1.444		1.006		0.931	
Consumer Price Index	109.5		122.4		135.3	

Case 29 Utama Jalan Group

EXHIBIT 7 *P.T. LABAH LABAH CERAMICS* FINANCIAL STATEMENTS (billions of rupiahs)

	1982		*1983*		*1984*	
	unaudited	*% of Sales*	*unaudited*	*% of Sales*	*unaudited*	*% of Sales*
Assets						
Cash	.1	1%	.4	3%	.2	1%
Accounts receivable	.5	5	4.2	32	6.3	39
Inventory	5.1	47	4.0	31	6.8	43
Current assets	5.7	53	8.6	66	13.3	83
Net fixed assets	6.9	63	13.3	102	13.5	84
Advances/prepayments	1.1	10	1.3	10	.5	3
Other receivables	.8	7	.1	1	.1	1
Other assets	1.0	9	1.7	13	4.4	27
Total assets	15.5	142%	25.0	192%	31.8	198%

		% of Assets		*% of Assets*		*% of Assets*
Liabilities						
Bank notes payable	4.7	30%	7.0	28%	9.3	29%
Accounts payable	.7	5	.6	2	4.4	14
Accruals	.9	6	.2	1	.8	3
Other liabilities	1.0	6	.2	1	.4	1
Current liabilities	7.3	47	8.0	32	14.9	47
Long-term debt	.0	0	4.7	19	4.1	13
Total liabilities	7.3	47	12.7	51	19.0	60
Capital	1.1	7	11.2	45	11.3	35
Retained earnings	7.1	46	1.1	4	1.5	5
Net worth	8.2	53	12.3	49	12.8	40
Total liabilities and net worth	15.5	100%	25.0	100%	31.8	100%

Case 29 Utama Jalan Group

EXHIBIT 7 (*continued*)

	1982		1983		1984	
	unaudited	*% of Sales*	*unaudited*	*% of Sales*	*unaudited*	*% of Sales*
Net sales	10.9	100%	13.0	100%	16.1	100%
Cost of goods sold	6.1	56	7.7	59	10.3	64
Gross profit	4.8	44	5.3	41	5.8	36
Operating expenses	1.4	13	1.8	14	2.3	14
Other (income)/ expense (includes interest)	.6	5	.5	4	3.0	19
Profit before taxes	2.8	26	3.0	23	.5	3
Taxes	.0	0	.0	0	.0	0
Net income	2.8	26%	3.0	23%	.5	3%
US$/1000 rupiahs	1.444		1.006		0.931	
Consumer Price Index	109.5		122.4		135.3	

Case 29 Utama Jalan Group

EXHIBIT 8 EXCHANGE RATES

End	*US$/ 1,000 Rupiahs*	*% Change*	*Yen/ 1,000 Rupiahs*	*% Change*
1981	1.553		341.5	
1982	1.444	−7.0%	339.3	−.6%
1983	1.006	−30.3	233.6	−31.2
1984	.931	−7.5	233.8	.1
1985	.889	−4.5	178.2	−23.8
July 1986	.884	−1.0 (annualized)	136.4	−40.2 (annualized)

Source: International Financial Statistics, International Monetary Fund.

Case 29 Utama Jalan Group

EXHIBIT 9 INDONESIA: BALANCE OF PAYMENTS (millions of US$)

	1982	*1983*	*1984*	*1985*
Merchandise exports:				
—oil sector	14,861	13,478	12,097	7,670
—other sectors	4,886	5,211	8,657	10,857
Merchandise imports	(17,854)	(17,726)	(15,047)	(12,705)
Trade balance	1,893	963	5,707	5,822
Other goods, services, and income, net	(7,351)	(7,415)	(7,730)	(7,833)
Unrequited transfers, net	134	114	167	171
Current account balance	(5,324)	(6,338)	(1,856)	(1,840)
Direct investment	225	292	222	271
Portfolio investment, net	315	368	(44)	(35)
Other long-term capital, net	4,556	4,663	2,854	1,588
Basic balance	(228)	(1,015)	1,176	(16)
Other short-term capital, net	526	731	476	(98)
Net errors and omissions	(2,151)	468	(701)	585
Counterpart to valuation changes	(26)	(12)	(10)	57
Total change in reserves (negative change designates reserve increase)	1,879	(172)	(941)	(528)
Domestic money-market interest rates	17.24%	13.17%	18.63%	10.33%
Prices: Wholesale	119.3	140.7	158.4	163.5
(1980 = 100) Consumer	122.9	137.4	151.7	158.9
Net foreign assets (billions of rupiahs)	5,613	8,419	11,942	14,106
Gross national product (billions of rupiahs)	60,496	70,338	83,369	92,389
Population (midyear estimates in millions)	153.04	156.45	159.9	163.39

Source: International Financial Statistics, International Monetary Fund.

Case 29 Utama Jalan Group

EXHIBIT 10 INDONESIA: SUMMARY ECONOMICS STATISTICS

	1982	*1983*	*1984*	*1985*	*1986**
Real GDP growth	1.9%	4.2%	6.0%	1.0%	−1.0%
Real per capita GDP (US$)	$589	$518	$523	$502	$450
Inflation (consumer prices)	9.5%	11.8%	10.5%	5.0%	4.5%
Budget balance as % of GDP	−2.4%	−1.4%	−0.6%	−2.0%	−3.0%
Current account balance as % of GDP	−5.9%	−7.8%	−2.5%	−2.8%	−6.4%
Merchandise import coverage (in months)	2.8	3.3	4.5	5.0	5.0
External debt as % of GDP	31.4%	41.5%	42.1%	49.8%	61.7%
Debt service ratio**	14.3%	15.1%	16.2%	20.0%	33.0%

*Projected
**Interest plus amortization of long-term debt divided by export earnings

Case 29 Utama Jalan Group

EXHIBIT 11 TOKYO AVERAGE ANNUAL SPOT PRICES FOR PHILIPPINE 3-PLY PLYWOOD (U.S. Cents/Sheet)

Year	*Current US$*	*1980 Constant US$*
1970	103.1	295.4
1971	81.8	222.3
1972	95.4	238.5
1973	188.8	406.9
1974	152.7	270.3
1975	121.6	193.6
1976	147.8	232.0
1977	165.1	235.9
1978	189.5	235.4
1979	262.5	287.8
1980	273.8	273.8
1981	244.7	243.5
1982	232.5	234.6
1983	229.8	237.9
1984	227.0	239.2
1985	210.9	220.1
Jan–Jun 1986	240.3	227.3

Source: Commodity Trade and Price Trends, World Bank.

Case 29 Utama Jalan Group

EXHIBIT 12 PROFITABILITY ANALYSIS DURING YEAR 1985

	Average O/S	*Fee Base*	*@ %**	*Earnings*
P.T. Trima Kasi Electronics	$1,500,000		2.50%	$ 37,500
Terrogong Electronics, Ltd.				
TRs	2,803,650		3.00	84,110
LCs		$4,385,315	0.45	19,734
Acceptances	2,181,026		3.75	81,788
Export LC negotiation		228,578	0.24	549
Beecara Trading Company				
TRs	921,000		3.00	27,630
LCs		7,899,680	0.16	12,639
Export LC negotiation		6,045,113	0.18	10,881
Float				6,400
P.T. Orang Putih	1,029,563		5.25	54,052
Average outstandings	$8,435,239			
Total 1985 earnings				$335,283
Pre-tax ROA	3.97%			

*Percent spread over cost of funds for term loans and loans against trust receipts (TR) or percent used to determine fee for issuance of a letter of credit (LC).

Case 30

OLIN CORPORATION

Bill Schmitt, vice-president for international operations for Olin Corporation, was preparing a presentation concerning a project that would expand Olin's involvement in Brazil. Mr. Schmitt and his team were proposing to establish a joint venture that would be 50 percent owned by Olin's Brazilian subsidiary and 50 percent owned by a subsidiary of a leading private Brazilian company, Votorantim. The joint venture, to be called Nordesclor, would construct a calcium hypochlorite plant to produce HTH, Olin's registered brand name for its swimming pool chemical-treatment product. At this time, there was no HTH manufacturing facility in Brazil. Olin Brasil currently imported HTH from an Olin plant in Tennessee, had it repackaged, and sold it directly through local pool shops. Olin had begun discussions with Votorantim five years earlier, in 1983, but had decided to find out more about the Brazilian market for HTH before investing in a local production arrangement. A market research survey and subsequent new marketing program had dramatically increased HTH's market share, and Schmitt believed many benefits could be gained by moving to local production. Because this would be the first time Olin Chemicals had made a major investment in Brazil, Mr. Schmitt wanted to prepare a presentation highlighting all the advantages of this international investment and addressing any concerns the board of directors might put forth.

OLIN CORPORATION

Olin Corporation was a diversified company whose business was concentrated in chemicals, metals, and applied physics, with special emphasis on electronic materials and services, aerospace/defense, and water-quality management.

This case was written by Professor Mark R. Eaker.

Currently Olin's international operations contributed approximately 20 percent of the company's total sales. (See Exhibit 1 for financial data for 1986 and 1987.) One of Olin's goals was to double the sales and profit contributed by its international businesses by 1991. Because little growth was projected for exports, the company estimated that overseas operations and joint ventures had to grow at a 20 percent compound annual rate to meet this objective. In early 1988, international pool chemicals appeared to be especially promising to Olin as a growth area.

Olin had been producing swimming pool chemicals for over 30 years and had always prided itself on consistently providing the highest quality products in the market. Plants in Charleston, Tennessee, and in South Africa produced its total supply of HTH. Olin had begun exporting HTH to various Latin American markets, including Brazil, in the 1960s, and the Latin American region had become one of Olin's most successful in terms of profitability and market share. Olin's Brazilian segment was actually more profitable than its domestic calcium hypochlorite business on a per-pound basis.

Olin had found, however, that it was becoming increasingly difficult to obtain import permits from the Brazilian government in sufficient quantity to support Olin's marketing program in that country. Although there was no domestic producer of calcium hypochlorite in Brazil, there were several producers of liquid bleach, the main competitive product. Fortunately for Olin, Brazil was experiencing a shortage of liquid bleach, and the pool sanitizer market was not deemed important to the liquid-bleach producers. Once the shortage eased, however, or a domestic company chose to produce calcium hypochlorite, Olin company officials were concerned that Brazil might block the importation of HTH completely. Mexico had taken such actions several years ago, whereupon Olin had lost 1,500 tons of annual sales.

BRAZIL

Rich natural resources helped make Brazil a growing economic power and one of the world's leading Third World industrial nations. Brazil was a leading global producer of many agricultural goods, including orange juice, cacao beans, cattle, corn, soybeans, and sugar cane. Brazil also produced 30 percent of the world's coffee crop and grew more bananas than any other nation. Huge supplies of nuts, timber, and other products came from its forests, and mining operations produced large quantities of iron ore and manganese for export as well as for domestic use. Brazil also produced a large range of finished goods for the global market. The manufacture of metal products was the nation's chief industrial activity. In addition, Brazil ranked among the world's leaders in automobile and truck manufacturing. Among its population of 141 million, Brazil also had a complex and well-developed domestic consumer market, the strongest in Latin America.

Recent Economic and Political Developments in Brazil. In 1985 Brazil returned to a democratic government following twenty years of military rule. After four years of deep recession, the economy had started growing again in 1984 and had picked up significantly in the following year. (See Exhibit 2 for a summary of economic statistics on Brazil.) The economic upturn might be short-lived, however, as hyperinflation threatened to wipe out the gains of 1985's impressive 8.0 percent growth in gross domestic product (GDP). Inflation was projected to reach levels of 460–500 percent in 1986, higher than at any time in Brazilian history. Facing declining political support, the fledgling civilian government of President Jose Sarney responded on February 26, 1986 by announcing a sweeping anti-inflation program known as the Cruzado Plan. Among the Plan's three major provisions were a freeze on prices; a phased end to indexing of wages, rents, and interest rates; and the creation of a new currency, the cruzado, worth 1,000 of the old cruzeiro. Just before the new policies were announced, the cruzeiro was trading for Cr13,700 per U.S. dollar at the official rate and Cr23,000 on the black market.

The Plan essentially boosted wages while holding prices constant, and following its implementation, the economy experienced an unparalleled spending spree. Emphasis shifted from exports to internal consumption and imports poured in. The program had overwhelming political support; the government won a landslide victory in the November 1986 elections.

The Plan was ill-conceived, however, or at the least poorly executed. While inflation did halt temporarily, the Plan failed to freeze either wages or government spending. In early 1987, the Plan disintegrated, and inflation took off. Through price controls, the government had merely addressed the symptoms of inflation, not the cause. The high consumption levels of 1986 had also sharply reduced the balance-of-trade surplus, and to protect foreign exchange reserves, the government suspended interest payments on the $67 billion of its debt that was owed to foreign banks.

Long-Term Outlook. In order to assist them in evaluating the business climate in Brazil, Olin had commissioned a study by a well-known analyst. Its overview stated:

> Brazilian managers will face the reality of an improved business environment with higher profits earned on an annual average than heretofore. The image will be different. In the transition to democracy, government management of the economy and of business has become more temperamental. While economic growth and profits will remain relatively high, there will be more stop/go of the economy and a more erratic government regulatory environment. Corporate managers will have to spend more time in Brasilia, lobbying for their industry, and more time at corporate headquarters, explaining why the bad news reported in media is not so bad. The key to understanding the emerging Brazilian environment and the benefits to be gained from it is to understand its complexities.[1]

The study included nine specific forecasts of changes that would occur in Brazil. Excerpts

[1]The quoted material comes from the consulting report prepared for Olin.

from the study on each forecast follow:

1. Economic decisions will be subject to political decisions unlike any time since 1964. Economic crises caused by poor policy choices will be more frequent in the near term and diminish in the out-years.
2. Poor economic and regulatory news in 1987 will obscure the strengths of the economic system for the short term. These 1987 problems are the product of domestic political maneuvering, the aftereffects of the Plan Cruzado, and the debt crisis.
3. After a poor 1987, the Brazilian economy will perform well and expand over the next four years. Between 1988 and 1991:
   a. Real growth will run between 3 and 5 percent every year.
   b. Annual inflation will run between 80 and 120 percent, declining in the out-years.
   c. The cruzado will be maintained at a slightly undervalued level.
   d. Brazil will continue to run a balance-of-trade surplus, but the ongoing debt crisis will not be resolved.
4. The fundamental strengths of the Brazilian economy remain. These include a sophisticated industrial structure, diverse markets, the nation's size and untapped resources, and a sophisticated elite.
5. Brazil will not "take off" into the developed world this century. Among the factors limiting growth are the ongoing debt crisis, a dearth of capital, a highly inflationary environment, and weak industrial and social infrastructure.
6. While populist sentiment will become more prevalent than heretofore in Brazilian political life, Brazil is not risking a return to economic nationalism. The position of foreign investment is likely to strengthen over the next five years as Brazil seeks new sources of capital and technology.
7. Brazilian trade policy will be buffeted by domestic and international forces. Most of the economy today depends upon public policy that promotes exports. This reality will compel Brazil's leaders to continue to favor traders.
8. While the political system will face a series of tests and crises over the next few years, the outlook for stability is good.
9. Regionalism continues to be an extremely powerful political force, exercising a conservative influence on the nation.

THE BRAZILIAN MARKET FOR HTH

Swimming Pool Sanitizer Market. Olin's HTH brand currently had 35 percent of the pool sanitizer chemical market in Brazil, based entirely on imports. This market share was up from 19 percent in 1984, when Olin Brasil was selling approximately 400 tons of HTH in the pool market. At that time, because of the high import duties in Brazil, Olin's HTH was ten times as expensive (on an equivalent chlorine basis) as liquid bleach, its main competition. Additionally, Olin was spending only a nominal amount on advertising and promotion. In 1984 a marketing study was conducted to gain a better understanding of the residential pool market and the competing products used to sanitize these pools. Olin subsequently developed a new marketing program, aimed at furthering the penetration of HTH and increasing the consumption dosage per pool. One of the key elements of this plan was to reduce the transfer price from Olin U.S. to Olin Brasil so that the ratio of retail sales prices between HTH and competing products went from 10:1 to 4:1. Advertising and promotion were increased five times, and various sales-incentive promotions and education seminars were implemented.

The program was a tremendous success; sales of HTH went from 360 tones per year in 1984 to 1,500 tons per year in 1987, an increase of 61 percent compounded annually. Were it not for difficulties in obtaining import permits, Olin believed it could have sold up to 2,000 tons in 1987. The HTH brand name had achieved the strongest consumer franchise in the pool market, despite the fact that HTH was still significantly more expensive than liquid bleach. The main attraction of liquid bleach was its price, but recent chlorine shortages had benefited HTH. No capacity increases for bleach had been announced, and Olin expected the shortage to persist for the next 2–3 years.

Industrial and Potable Water Markets. The joint venture would also allow Olin to serve the industrial and potable water markets in remote areas of Brazil. Import-quota restrictions had not permitted Olin to develop these markets, which were presently being served by liquid bleach and chlorite of lime. Olin believed HTH could be very competitive in both markets as a superior treatment agent, because both bleach and chlorite of lime lost significant strength during long-distance transportation in the tropical climate. The total market for industrial and potable water was estimated to be equivalent to 6,000 tons per year of HTH.

Export Markets. Exports to neighboring Latin American countries represented a potential third market for HTH. Presently, Olin sold little HTH to these markets; thus any volume would be totally incremental. Nordesclor would have significant advantages from regional bilateral trading agreements, the benefits of which accrued only to local producers. Olin expected exports to neighboring Latin American countries to peak at 750 tons per year, although the market potential could be significantly higher.

Votorantim. The proposed joint-venture partner was one of Brazil's strongest companies, ranking second to Volkswagen among all Brazilian manufacturing firms in terms of net worth. It was privately owned and managed by three brothers and a brother-in-law. It had 1986 sales of approximately $2 billion. Votorantim had an excellent reputation as an ethical firm committed to expanding employment through reinvestment of profits. In 1987 it had over 54,000 employees.

Votorantim was highly vertically integrated and diversified. It was the largest Brazilian producer of cement, aluminum, zinc, and lime. Votorantim also was a significant producer of steel, cellophane and paper, sugar, and heavy equipment. The company owned 17 hydroelectric plants that provided power to its own plants as well as to surrounding municipalities. Investments in the chemical industry were currently a modest part of Votorantim's portfolio which the owners were interested in expanding.

THE PROPOSED PROJECT[2]

The proposed Nordesclor joint venture would construct and operate a 3,100 metric ton per year hypochlorite plant. The plant could easily be expanded to double its initial capacity. The joint venture would be half-owned by Olin Brasil and half-owned by Cia. Agro Industrial Igarassu, a subsidiary of Industrial Votorantim. Because of requirements that the venture be Brazilian, Olin would have 40 percent of the voting stock and 60 percent of the nonvoting preferred stock. Profits would be split equally. Olin would have control over the marketing of the final product and had negotiated veto rights in other areas of primary importance to the firm.

The plant would be located at Igarassu, Pernambuco, in the northeastern part of Brazil. The region was a development target of the central government, so the project would enjoy a 10-year tax holiday. In addition, the plant would be next door to a chlor-alkali facility owned by Votorantim which would provide the chlorine and caustic soda required by Nordesclor under a long-term preferential supply contract. Lime was to be supplied under a similar arrangement by another Votorantim affiliate, Cal e Tintas.

Proven Olin technology would be used in the manufacturing process, and Olin had complete control over the project execution, plant start-up, and operation of the plant. The front-end engineering would be done by Olin, and an experienced Brazilian engineering firm had been identified to engineer the facility.

Project Economics. Olin's market projections for HTH are given in Exhibits 3 and 4. Sales for 1988 and 1989 would continue on an imported basis, with the plant scheduled to come on line in 1990. The current market price of HTH to dealers in the swimming pool market was $3.30/kg (kilogram). The prices for the non-pool and export markets were currently $1.30/kg and $1.63/kg, respectively.

Direct variable costs were expected to run $267.86/MT (metric ton) for raw materials and

[2]The numbers related to the project have been disguised to protect proprietary information.

$157.59/MT for utilities and power. Additionally, each market had its own packaging and freight costs as listed below:

	Swimming Pools	*Industrial and Potable Uses*	*Export*
Packaging	$250.00/MT	$100.00/MT	$25.00/MT
Freight	80.00/MT	80.00/MT	80.00/MT

An additional incremental variable cost of $353,000 was budgeted beginning in 1995.

Selling and administrative expenses were projected at 7 percent of net sales, advertising and promotion was expected to run 2 percent of the net pool sales, and provision for bad debts was allowed at 1 percent of net sales. Fixed utilities were $31,000 per year. Operating and supervisory labor was budgeted at $1,906,000 for the first year of operation, declining to $1,176,000 in year 2 and leveling off at $978,000 for the remaining periods. Miscellaneous expenses were expected to be $1,042,000 per year. A 10-year depreciation schedule for the plant is given in Exhibit 5, and Exhibit 6 lays out the expected working-capital increases.

Financing Alternatives. The capital required to finance the joint venture was expected to total $25 million, which was to be provided equally by Olin and Votorantim. Olin's contribution would include $2.5 million of engineering and training expenses which would be incurred in the United States. These funds could be classified as either debt or equity.

There were several alternatives available to Olin to arrange the remainder of the financing. One of those would be for Olin to invest additional new funds into its subsidiary, which would in turn put the funds into Nordesclor. Another option, which would be used in conjunction with other funding, was made possible by the location of the proposed project. Because the project was to be located in the economically depressed Northeast, special government investment funds were available and could provide up to $5 million of medium-term (6-year) funds to the joint venture at an interest rate of 8 percent plus a factor reflecting annual inflation.

Olin was also considering a debt–equity swap. The advantage of a swap was that it offered the opportunity to acquire the necessary cruzados at a below-market exchange rate. There appeared to be two different ways in which a swap could be effected: either through a formal government sponsored program or by way of a direct equity participation of a major bank.

The Brazilian government adopted measures on November 18, 1987, to reintroduce a debt–equity conversion program, subject to satisfactory completion of its current debt renegotiations. The details of the program were still not final, but Mr. Schmitt believed that Olin would be able to obtain the required funding for the Nordesclor project at approximately 60 percent of face value.

As currently understood, the program would provide for $1.5 billion in debt conversions. Preference would be given to projects in the Northeast. The basis for dividend repatriation, registered capital, would be the face amount of the debt acquired for conversion.

The actual savings would depend on two factors, the amount paid for the debt on the secondary market and the conversion discount applied by the Brazilian central bank. Olin would arrange with one of its commercial bankers to acquire debt eligible for conversion. The price would be established in a secondary market and would reflect supply and demand for such paper. Olin would then have to participate in an auction process for the right to convert the debt to cruzados that could be used to fund the Nordesclor project.

The debt–equity swap program offered obvious advantages, but Olin was concerned about its viability. Brazil had had a program in place before but had suspended it in 1984.

The second debt–equity swap involved an ad hoc swap with a participating financial institution. The bank would act as an intermediary and make an investment in the Brazilian subsidiary on behalf of Olin. During the term of the investment the bank would receive guaranteed annual U.S. dollar dividends. At the end of the required term, 12 years in this case, the bank would be repaid 100 percent of its investment.

As the bank had outlined the transaction to Olin, the bank would invest $7,731,000 worth of cruzados in the preferred shares of an Olin Brazilian subsidiary. At the end of the 12-year period, the bank would put the shares to Olin Corporation for the full amount of its investment. The shares would carry a 4 percent annual dividend based on the dollar value of the investment.

The bank assured Olin that it had completed similar transactions in the past although Central Bank approval would be necessary.

GETTING THE MONEY OUT

Under any financing arrangement, cash remittances to the U.S. would be limited to Olin Brasil's share of net income. In addition, a withholding tax was applied based on the ratio of the remittance to registered capital. The following schedule applied:

Percent of Registered Capital	*Withholding Tax*
16%	25%
16–25	40
25–50	50
Over 50	60

Olin planned on holding the tax rate at the 25 percent level.

Registered capital consisted of new funds invested in Brazil and additions to retained earnings. Under the ad hoc swap, the bank's investment would be considered registered capital. In addition, Olin was confident that any unremitted cash could be invested at an annual rate of 15 percent. Those earnings would also be remittable subject to the 25 percent withholding.

Finally, the tax rate in Brazil was 45 percent. Because of the location of the project in a region designated as a development target of the central government, the project would benefit from a 10-year tax deferral. The deferral meant that taxes would be used in determining net income but that no cash payments would be made during the first 10 years. There would be no additional tax obligation in the United States.

THE DECISION

As he began to determine what points to emphasize in his presentation, Mr. Schmitt worked on "selling" the project. The inside directors were committed to international expansion, but several outside directors were sure to raise the issue of additional risk. Two of them worked for firms that had had bad experiences in Brazil. Their industries, pharmaceuticals and computers, were subject to extensive regulations favoring domestic Brazilian companies, which had cost the U.S. firms a great deal of money. Schmitt was certain those experiences would be recounted for the whole board to hear, yet he needed the board's approval to go ahead. And Mr. Schmitt needed to determine the best way to finance the project.

Case 30 Olin Corporation

EXHIBIT 1 FINANCIAL HIGHLIGHTS (in millions, except per-share amounts)

Years ended December 31	*1987*	*1986*
Net sales and operating revenues	$1,930	$1,732
Operating income (Loss)	149	106
Net income (Loss):		
Continuing operations	78	75
Discontinued operations	—	—
Net Income (Loss)	78	75
Per share (assuming full dilution):		
Continuing operations	3.32	3.13
Discontinued operations	—	—
Net Income (Loss)	3.32	3.13
Net cash flows from operating activities	206	173
Net cash used by investing activities	157	135
Research and development expenditures	62	56
Depreciation	114	111
Cash dividends:		
Total	37	34
Per share	1.60	1.525
Average Shares Outstanding (Assuming Full Dilution as of December 31)	23.6	25.4
Total assets	$1,685	$1,545
Property, plant, & equipment, net	727	720
Working capital, net	276	210
Long-term debt	392	375
Shareholders' equity:		
Total	700	654
Per share	31.81	30.56

Case 30 Olin Corporation

EXHIBIT 2 BRAZIL—SUMMARY OF ECONOMIC STATISTICS

	1976	*1977*	*1978*	*1979*	*1980*	*1981*	*1982*	*1983*	*1984*	*1985*	*1986*	*1987*
GDP (1980 prices, millions of cruzados)	10,305	10,992	11,542	12,279	12,639	12,216	12,328	12,157	12,696	13,750	14,876	N/A
CPI	18	26	36	55	100*	206	407	984	2,924	9,556	23,436	77,258
Bank discount rate	28%	30%	33%	35%	38%	49%	49%	156%	215%	219%	50%	392%
Trade balance (millions of US$)	(2,386)	(100)	(1,158)	(2,717)	(2,823)	1,185	778	6,469	13,086	12,466	8,348	N/A
Current account balance (millions of US$)	(6,562)	(5,112)	(7,036)	(10,478)	(12,806)	(11,751)	(16,312)	(6,837)	42	(273)	(4,477)	N/A
Cruzados/US$	.012	.016	.021	.043	.066	.128	.253	.984	3.184	10.490	14.895	72.251

*Data that follow not comparable to data earlier in series.
Source: International Monetary Fund, International Financial Statistics, 1988.

Case 30 Olin Corporation

EXHIBIT 3 BRAZILIAN SWIMMING POOL MARKET

	Calcium Hypochlorite	*Liquid Bleach*	*All Other*	*Total Volume*
1983 Share %	20	52	28	
Volume (metric tons)	636	1,652	890	3,178
1984 Share %	17	57	26	
Volume	635	2,130	971	3,736
1985 Share %	24	55	21	
Volume	1,002	2,296	877	4,175
1986 Share %	30	53	17	
Volume	1,622	2,865	918	5,405
1987 Share %	33	51	16	
Volume	1,896	2,931	920	5,747
1988 Share %	35	49	16	
Volume	2,346	3,285	1,073	6,704
1989 Share %	37	49	14	
Volume	2,603	3,447	985	7,035
1990 Share %	40	48	12	
Volume	3,131	3,757	939	7,827
1991 Share %	41	48	11	
Volume	3,560	4,167	955	8,682
1992 Share %	42	48	10	
Volume	4,007	4,579	954	9,540
1993 Share %	42	48	10	
Volume	4,344	4,966	1,035	10,345
1994 Share %	42	48	10	
Volume	4,344	4,966	1,035	10,345

Note: Data for 1988–94 are projected.

Case 30 Olin Corporation

EXHIBIT 4 MARKET PROJECTION FOR HTH

	No. Pools	*Growth*	*HTH Share*	*HTH Pools*	*Consumption Kg/Pool/Yr*	*Pool (MTY)*	*Nonpool (MTY)*	*Export (MTY)*	*Total (MTY)*
	(M)	(%)	%	(M)					
1983	150		18	27.0	13.0	351	—	—	351
		15							
1984	173		13	22.5	13.7	308	—	—	308
		15							
1985	198		23	45.5	14.0	638	—	—	638
		25							
1986	250		25	62.5	18.0	1,125	—	—	1,125
		7							
1987	268		31	83.1	16.4	1,363	—	—	1,363
		10							
1988	295		35	103.3	18.0	1,856	—	—	1,856
		13							
1989	333		37	123.2	18.0	2,218	—	—	2,218
		12							
1990	373		40	149.2	18.0	2,686	275	200	3,161
		11							
1991	414		41	169.7	18.0	3,055	550	350	3,955
		10							
1992	455		42	191.1	18.0	3,440	825	500	4,765
		9.5							
1993	498		42	209.2	18.0	3,765	1,100	750	5,615
		9.0							
1994	543		42	228.1	18.0	4,105	1,093	750	5,948
						\$3.30/kg	\$1.30/kg	\$1.63/kg	

Note: Data for 1988–94 are projected.

Case 30 Olin Corporation

EXHIBIT 5 TEN-YEAR DEPRECIATION SCHEDULE FOR NORDESCLOR PLANT

Year	*($000s)*
1	2054
2	2116
3	2177
4	2239
5	2301
6	2362
7	2424
8	2485
9	2547
10	2547

Case 30 Olin Corporation

EXHIBIT 6 WORKING-CAPITAL PROJECTIONS

Year	*($000s)*
1	2072
2	860
3	889
4	890
5	772
6	633
7	619
8	621
9	619
10	619

Case 31

VALUE PRODUCTS INCORPORATED

When the president of the Tudor Manufacturing Company, a major firm in the apparel business, made a serious offer to purchase the Value Products Incorporated (VPI) group of companies, the management of VPI realized that a decision was necessary about which financial alternative it should take. Consequently, in January 1969 Mr. William Orange (president of VPI), Mr. Charles Stuart (vice president of VPI and vice president of the affiliated firm, Wholesale Marketing Corp. [WMC]), and Mr. George Windsor (WMC's president) met to review the three alternatives to which they were giving most serious consideration. These alternatives were:

1. Continue the existing short-term bank credit arrangements and count on the bank to extend additional financing as required.
2. Accept the 15-year loan proposed by the Southern Life Insurance Company (SoLife). SoLife offered VPI a maximum of $2.4 million at the rate of 7¾ percent and asked for warrants.
3. Merger with Tudor Manufacturing Company. With Tudor stock selling at $60 per share, the current market value offered for VPI and WMC was approximately $11.5 million. The existing management of VPI and WMC would continue to operate its enterprise as a division of Tudor.

The first section of the case discusses the background of Value Products Incorporated. Later sections describe the financial plans management had prepared and specify in more detail the nature of the financial alternatives.

THE CREATION OF VALUE PRODUCTS INCORPORATED

Wholesale Marketing Corp., a family company of the Stuart and Windsor families, was located in Jacksonville, Florida. The firm had been a "rack jobber" distributing health and beauty aids to independent grocery stores, grocery chains, and discount stores in Florida and Georgia. WMC personnel made up orders to customer specifications, "priced" them, delivered them to specified stores, and placed the merchandise on display racks for the customer.

Shortly after going to work for WMC in June 1962, after receiving his MBA degree, Mr. Orange noticed that a rack jobbing wholesaler in the Pittsburgh area, White Cross Stores, had started its own chain of health and beauty aid discount stores. Mr. Orange investigated the idea and persuaded the WMC owners to provide him with support in developing a similar chain in the Southeast. From 1963, when VPI began with inexpensive locations and simple furnishings and fixtures, to January 1969, Mr. Orange had built the VPI chain into 40 stores with an additional six sites being prepared. Exhibits 1 and 2 present 1967 and 1968 financial statements for VPI. An estimate of fiscal year 1969 earnings is also given, although the fiscal year would not be complete until April 30, 1969.

The equity of VPI was held entirely by Mr. Orange and by the Stuart and Windsor families, with the major shares belonging to Mr. Charles Stuart and Mr. George Windsor. These men, through WMC, not only had provided marketing and distribution support for the new venture, but also, by pledging the credit of WMC and their own general reputations, had provided virtually all of the financing VPI required. In effect, WMC had borrowed short-term through its customary commercial bank relationship and had advanced the funds to VPI in the form of accounts receivable. Exhibits 3 and 4, which provide 1967 and 1968 financial information (and an estimate of 1969 income) on WMC, show the extent of this support. Even in January 1969, the vast majority of VPI payables remained due to WMC.

VPI'S BUSINESS

Mr. Orange and Mr. Stuart attributed the success of the VPI enterprise to a number of factors. Careful attention had been given to the selection of good locations in downtown and suburban areas. VPI stores were attractively designed, well lit, and the merchandise was pleasantly displayed. The product line was substantially broader than that carried by most larger supermarkets or beauty aid departments in large discount stores. The purchasing function and distribution system were centralized for all VPI stores in the WMC operation under Mr. Windsor's direction. Mr. Orange, who knew the Southeast thoroughly by virtue of his previous experience as district sales manager with a large soap company, supervised the development of new locations as well as managed the daily operation of the chain. He put emphasis on the creation of a sound management base, and by late 1968 he could say that a store could be opened without his having done more than sign the lease. (VPI owned none of its locations but rented them under various arrangements. Normally, the rental agreement would be for no longer than five years. As the VPI stores proved successful, management was tending to sign longer leases.)

The pricing policy VPI followed was to be competitive or slightly higher in price than other "discount" outlets. The good locations of VPI stores, their appearance, the advertising policy and special sales, and the broader product line permitted this small price differential. WMC's purchasing power was sufficient for the chain to benefit from the lowest prices available to the trade.

VPI's management had not necessarily responded when local price wars had broken out. They considered the company's prices were low enough that competition could not survive long by charging a lower level. Management considered that the operators of other chains were well enough aware of costs in the industry that no chain would embark on a suicidal price war.

Management furthermore kept a close watch on individual product lines, discontinuing those whose turnover was below profitable levels. New products were eagerly explored and introduced when they looked promising. Inventory management was facilitated by the record system WMC maintained with its computer. A new computer, which was expected shortly, would permit even more accurate inventory control. It was management's ambition to put the store-stocking decision on a completely automatic basis subject to "exception" changes by store managers only when stock-outs or excessive inventories were discovered.

Mr. Orange and his associates believed that the health and beauty aid business was relatively recession proof. Mr. Orange was fond of arguing that, in times of economic disaster, women would give up their beauty aid products only as a last resort because they were psychologically essential in a period of uncertainty.

FINANCIAL PLANNING FOR VPI

In early 1967, management of VPI had begun formal financial planning and forecasting to determine the magnitude of the company's financial needs. The forecast for fiscal 1968 was found after the fact to have been reasonably accurate with respect to the total profits and total dollars required, although substantial variance occurred in the various components of the profit statement. For example, volume in existing stores exceeded estimates, the gross margin was lower than estimated, and the number of new stores opened during the year was less than expected. Because a new store generally reached a cumulative break-even only at the end of its first *complete* 12 months of operation, new store openings generally reduced income.

For the purpose of financial planning, a typical standard "unit" was utilized. The standard unit was somewhat larger than the average of the stores opened prior to 1967. Larger stores were more profitable, and management expected to concentrate on them in the future. The number of stores opened in one year might differ from the number of units opened because some stores could be as large as two to three "units."

Exhibit 5 projects the first five years of operating results from opening a block of ten units. The assumptions used in preparing these estimates were those Mr. Orange and Mr. Stuart used in developing the financial forecast for the two companies.

EXPANSION PLANS

Despite the relatively rapid return on the investment required for new store openings, a significant acceleration in the expansion program would absorb more funds than could be generated by existing units. The least demanding option was to limit expansion to the geographic area in which the firm already had operations. Mr. Stuart believed that approximately 65 additional units could be opened in Florida, Georgia, and Alabama over the next 3 years. By 1973, however, the potential attractive locations for new stores would be substantially reduced. Five or fewer units a year would become available in this geographic area in 1973 and later years.

Although Mr. Stuart realized that the estimates would be only approximate, he developed a schedule (shown in Exhibit 6) of store openings assuming various rates of expansion into new geographic areas. The next area to be entered would be the central Atlantic region from South Carolina to Washington, D.C. The third area would be the Gulf states, an area bounded roughly by New Orleans, Little Rock, and Nashville. The final stages of expansion would put VPI stores into Pennsylvania and New York on the one hand and into Indiana, Ohio, Kentucky, and Chicago on the other. Although the company did not, in early 1969, have sufficient management to be able to staff this expansion in depth, Mr. Stuart believed that he had sufficient well-trained staff to act as core managers for developing these areas. Additional management staff would be trained as expansion took place.

Mr. Stuart and Mr. Orange prepared financial projections based on the various expansion possibilities. A complete financial forecast for the least demanding alternative, remaining in the area closest to Jacksonville, is presented in Exhibit 7. Summary statements for the further expansion options are provided in Exhibit 8.

The only significant variation in assumptions among these forecasts was the number of stores open and an allowance for WMC's transportation costs. Management otherwise assumed that VPI's costs of goods sold would remain approximately 77 percent of sales price throughout the period and that administrative costs would be about 4 percent. Variable costs of operation on all units were expected to be approximately 8 percent of sales, thus bringing total operating expenses to 12 percent of sales. These forecasts, however, did not allow for financing costs because the method of financing had not been arranged.

Consolidated funds requirements for VPI and WMC are shown in parentheses as the last line on Exhibits 7 and 8, and cash in excess of minimum needs is shown without parentheses. New cash needs were identical to WMC's cash needs because VPI was assumed to finance its requirements by stretching its payables to WMC. Once VPI began to run a cash surplus, however, the cash surplus or cash need figure was derived from VPI's cash surplus less WMC's needs.

An investigation of the impact of more rapid expansion on WMC showed only moderate change in total maximum needs. As may be seen in Exhibits 7 and 8, however, the impact of a higher expected federal tax rate and the transportation costs for shipping longer distances in the later phases of the expansion program hamstrung WMC's ability to provide for its needs from its internal sources. It would be necessary to use some of VPI's cash throw-off for this purpose.

In December 1968, WMC had moved to a new $1 million warehouse. This building, all but $25,000 of which had been financed by the Jacksonville Redevelopment Agency and which would require an annual amortization of $98,000 on a 20-year purchase contract, could be used efficiently up to a volume of $100 million at WMC's billed prices. WMC supplied about 80 percent of VPI's merchandise. VPI's cost of goods was 77 percent. Consequently, WMC would not need new capacity until VPI's sales reached $162 million.

Mr. Orange and Mr. Stuart believed that the longer VPI waited to expand its geographic area, the more difficult it would be to make such an expansion. Although some of the other firms in the industry had not expanded aggressively in 1968, there were indications that the competition had decided to increase its rate of growth in the near future. Thus, while significant markets still remained available to VPI, there was no assurance that these markets would continue to be attractive if expansion was delayed.

Further reasons for maintaining the companies' expansion were related to the personal objectives of Mr. Orange and his associates. First, they had enjoyed immensely the process of building the firm and felt they would be dissatisfied operating a stagnant company. Second, they noticed that the founders of a number of other companies in the industry had issued portions of their holdings to the public at attractive price–earnings ratios of 15 to 25 times, depending on size, earning records, and market conditions. The owners of Value Products and Wholesale Marketing had no objection to selling a part of their equity to the public if the proper price could be obtained. Therefore, if they decided not to accept the merger offer of Tudor, they would like to plan the companies' development to permit public sale of securities between 1972 and 1975. Such a sale would establish a market value for their remaining personal holdings and also provide them with cash to undertake additional investment and philanthropic ventures.

FINANCIAL ALTERNATIVES

Short-term bank loans. VPI and WMC could continue to rely solely on existing bank loan arrangements, which cost prime plus 2 percent on the outstanding balance (prime was 7 percent). The terms currently limited short-term borrowing to $1.5 million or to the sum of 50 percent of inventory and 75 percent of receivables, whichever was smaller. As can be seen in Exhibits 7 and 8, the limit using the percentages of receivables and inventory would be considerably in excess of the existing maximum dollar amount of $1.5 million.

In the past, management had been successful in negotiating higher dollar limits when necessary. For example, late in calendar 1968, the bank agreed to increase the credit limit from $1 million to $1.5 million to support VPI's seasonal needs. WMC had maintained a very cordial relationship with its bank lending officer, one which dated back for many years. The Stuart and Windsor families had other business interests in Jacksonville in addition to WMC, and these had no doubt contributed to the bank's cooperation. In addition, the partner of the auditing firm which certified the companies' statements and the corporate counsel retained by WMC were respected in the community for their business judgment. These two advisors had strongly supported the VPI venture.

Nevertheless, Messrs. Orange, Stuart, and Windsor doubted that the bank would be willing to provide all the funds needed to sustain the maximum rate of expansion. They suspected the bank would be unwilling to provide much more than $2 million to $2.5 million to the combined operations in the near future without the addition of subordinated debt or new equity. The $1.5 million limitation represented a current debt–equity ratio of about 250 percent to 300 percent on WMC's net worth or about 165 percent of consolidated net worth.

Insurance Company Term Loan. Mr. Stuart had learned that the Southern Life Insurance Company, one of the nation's largest insurance firms, had just begun a small business loan program. SoLife's management was understood to feel an increased obligation to support the development of new businesses. In addition, they had apparently concluded that such loans would provide SoLife with opportunities to earn more than the normal rates of return attained on larger and safer investments. This additional return would be obtained primarily through "incentives" or "equity sweeteners," normally low-cost options to purchase equity in the firm to which SoLife was making a loan.

Mr. Stuart and Mr. Orange, along with their professional advisors, approached mutual friends at SoLife. The executives in charge of the small business program appeared quite enthusiastic about the prospect of making a loan to VPI. After considerable discussion, lasting over a period of several months, SoLife's lending officer made a final proposal to the management of VPI and WMC.

The maximum loan would total $2.4 million and would be subordinated to short-term bank borrowing. Such seasonal bank borrowing would be limited to 75 percent of inventory and receivables and would have to be completely repaid for at least 45 consecutive days each year. The interest rate on the loan would be 7¾ percent, with sinking funds beginning in 1972. The loan would mature in 1983, and it would be payable in twelve equal installments from 1972 to 1983.

The terms of the loan were unusual because VPI–WMC would have the option of taking the loan down in two parts. The first part would total $1.6 million and require VPI–WMC to issue warrants to SoLife permitting it to purchase a 5 percent stock interest in VPI–WMC for a nominal total price of $100. If the second part of the loan, an additional $800,000, was required, VPI–WMC would issue warrants permitting SoLife to purchase an additional 5 percent interest in VPI–WMC for $100. Thus, if the full $2.4 million loan was utilized, Southern Life would have obtained the right to buy 10 percent of VPI–WMC for only $200. The warrants were to be good for 10 years, through 1979. If the company had not gone public by the time the loan matured or was redeemed, VPI would agree to repurchase the warrants at twenty times the prorata average earnings for the prior 3 fiscal years allocated according to the proportion of stock the warrants then represented. The warrants would be protected from dilution by the usual agreement.

The other terms of the loan were standard, including prohibitions against refunding at a lower cost and a provision that SoLife could call the loan in the event that Mr. Orange, Mr. Stuart, or Mr. Windsor ceased to be active in day-to-day management. The working capital covenant required that VPI maintain a current ratio of not less than 1.75. These restrictions all applied to VPI, to whom the loan would be made, and not to WMC. Dealings with affiliates or stockholders, however, were prohibited except on a basis no less favorable to VPI than if such relationships did not exist.

Merger with Tudor Manufacturing Company. Although the terms of the SoLife loan proposal seemed reasonably generous to VPI's management compared with the terms customarily made available to companies of VPI's size, management was somewhat disappointed at the proportion of equity SoLife would require to commit funds to VPI. As a consequence, Mr. Orange made inquiries among friends about the possibility of selling VPI and WMC as a unit to a company with interest in retail businesses. He found an immediate interest on the part of the management of Tudor Manufacturing Company, a firm that had concentrated primarily in manufacturing and retailing ladies' apparel.

In recent years, Tudor had purchased two small companies which were operating retail stores in different lines of clothing but which were still in the general clothing business. These two subsidiaries were expected to develop rapidly. Tudor's management, however, was interested in diversification into retail businesses not in the clothing area. They were much impressed by Messrs. Orange, Stuart, and Windsor. After an initial investigation, they entered with enthusiasm into negotiations regarding the possible purchase of VPI–WMC. Recent information on Tudor is included in Exhibit 9.

In the course of these discussions, the respect of the managements for one another increased even further. VPI–WMC management was assured that Tudor's executive group had no intention of interfering with the VPI division. VPI management would be expected to meet with Tudor on a periodic basis, probably once a month, to discuss current developments. Naturally, Tudor would also review VPI's yearly plans and forecasts. Tudor's executives were impressed with the careful planning VPI–WMC had undertaken and indicated that the financial requirements for rapid expansion were not beyond the capacity of Tudor to finance. At the same time, Tudor's management did not firmly commit itself to financing the full expansion program. It obviously intended, as did the management of VPI, to appraise each step carefully as the years progressed.

With respect to Tudor's prospects, the company had recently been rejuvenated by the promotion of younger management from within. These men had undertaken a program of closing out those existing retail stores that were not profitable and of opening new ones in better locations, such as shopping center developments. Tudor's management indicated that this program was almost complete, and that new sources would have to be found to maintain continued improvement in Tudor's earnings.

Mr. Orange noted that a number of VPI stores had been successfully opened in locations vacated by Tudor's competitors. He suspected that there would be opportunities for VPI to utilize some of the locations Tudor proposed to abandon. Mr. Orange also knew that Tudor's status as a prime credit risk would enhance VPI's ability to gain the best location for its own new stores. In the past, such locations had occasionally gone to VPI's competitors, who were larger and had longer records of financial success. In fact, one of the reasons for the relatively low number of VPI store openings in fiscal 1968 had been difficulties in negotiating satisfactory site and lease arrangements. Such problems were expected to be minimal if VPI became a part of the Tudor company.

After a number of meetings, Tudor's president offered the VPI–WMC owners 192,000 common shares in the Tudor company. These securities had a market value of approximately $11.5 million. (At the end of 1968, Tudor had 5.4 million common shares outstanding.) This amount represented roughly twenty times the combined forecast profit after tax for VPI and WMC for the fiscal year that would end April 30, 1969.

The management of VPI–WMC was anxious to make a decision as to which of the financial alternatives they should take. SoLife was becoming restless, and it was apparent that bond market conditions were changing rapidly. Furthermore, if Tudor's offer was to be accepted, VPI managers believed that they should act quickly. They saw no room for improving either the SoLife or Tudor offer by procrastinating and engaging in further negotiations.

Case 31 Value Products Incorporated

EXHIBIT 1 CONSOLIDATED INCOME STATEMENTS OF VALUE PRODUCTS INCORPORATED FOR 1967–1968 AND ESTIMATE OF 1969 (thousands of dollars)

	Fiscal Year Ending April 30					
	1967		*1968*		*1969 (est.)***	
Sales	$6,310	100.0%	$9,943	100.0 %	$15,600	100.0%
Cost of sales	5,051	80.1	7,784	78.4	12,100	77.6
Gross margin	1,259	19.9	2,159	21.6	3,500	22.4
Selling and general expenses*	1,054	16.7	1,759	17.6	2,700	17.3
Operating profit (loss)	205	3.2	400	4.0	800	5.1
Interest expenses	—	—	—	—	—	—
Other income (deductions)	(3)	—	(6)	(0.1)	—	—
Profit before taxes	202	3.2	394	3.9	800	5.1
Income tax	48	0.8	143	1.4	350	2.3
Net profit	$ 154	2.4%	$ 251	2.5 %	$ 450	2.8%
*Includes rent of	$ 241	3.8%	$ 335	3.4 %	n.a	—
and depreciation of	46	0.7	68	0.7	n.a	—
Number of units	27		36		51	

**Estimated as of January 1969

Case 31 Value Products Incorporated

EXHIBIT 2 CONSOLIDATED BALANCE SHEETS OF VALUE PRODUCTS INCORPORATED APRIL 30, 1967–1968 (thousands of dollars)

	1967	*1968*
ASSETS		
Current assets		
Cash	$112	$ 124
Inventory	569	901
Other, including prepayments and misc. receivables	34	114
Total current assets	715	1,139
Fixtures and improvements (net)	248	428
Other	5	5
Total assets	$968	$1,572
LIABILITIES AND NET WORTH		
Current liabilities		
Accounts payable	$662	$ 914
Accruals and misc. payables	21	20
State and federal income taxes	64	160
Total current liabilities	747	1,094
Other, including misc. loans	30	36
Equity		
Common stock and paid-in capital	37	37
Retained earnings	154	405
Total equity	191	442
Total liabilities and net worth	$968	$1,572

Case 31 Value Products Incorporated

EXHIBIT 3 CONSOLIDATED* INCOME STATEMENT OF WHOLESALE MARKETING CORP. FOR 1967–1968 AND ESTIMATE OF 1969 (thousands of dollars)

	Fiscal Year Ending April 30					
	1967		*1968*		*1969 (est.)***	
Sales (net)	$7,522	100.0%	$10,741	100.0%	$15,700	100.0%
Cost of sales	6,497	86.4	9,365	87.2	13,750	87.6
Gross profit	1,025	13.6	1,376	12.8	1,950	12.4
Operating expenses	836	11.1	1,159	10.8	1,680	10.7
Operating profit	189	2.5	217	2.0	270	1.7
Interest	57	0.7	86	0.7	80	0.5
Earnings before taxes	132	1.8	141	1.3	190	1.2
Federal income taxes	53	0.7	52	0.5	95	0.6
Earnings after taxes	$ 79	1.1%	$ 89	0.8%	$ 95	0.6%

*Excludes Value Products Inc., which was carried as an investment.

**Estimated as of January 1969.

Case 31 Value Products Incorporated

EXHIBIT 4 CONSOLIDATED* BALANCE SHEETS FOR WHOLESALE MARKETING CORP. AS OF APRIL 30, 1967 AND 1968 (thousands of dollars)

	1967	*1968*
ASSETS		
Current assets		
Cash and securities	$ 202	$ 59
Accounts receivable (net)	656	899
Inventory	881	1,110
Prepayments	13	11
Total current assets	1,752	2,079
Other assets	26	47
Property and equipment (net)**	285	340
Total assets	$2,063	$2,466
LIABILITIES AND EQUITY		
Current liabilities		
Notes payable to bank	$ —	$ 444
Current installment of long-term debt		
Notes payable	68	19
Principal of leasehold obligation	37	56
Accounts payable	910	1,039
Accruals	103	66
Federal income taxes	52	49
	1,170	1,673
Long-term debt, excluding current installments		
Notes payable	354	185
Principal of leasehold obligation	158	138
	512	323
Equity		
Common stock	163	163
Retained earnings	530	619
	693	782
Less: Treasury stock at cost	312	312
Total equity	381	470
Total liabilities and equity	$2,063	$2,466

*Value Products Inc. was carried as an investment.

**Includes leases capitalized at: $ 195 (1967); $ 194 (1968)
(Primarily on WMC's old warehouse. This lease was terminated without penalty when WMC moved to its new location.)

Case 31 Value Products Incorporated

EXHIBIT 5 PROJECTED OPERATING RESULTS FOR A BLOCK OF 10 UNITS FOR FIRST FIVE YEARS OF OPERATION (thousands of dollars)

	Year of Operation				
	1	*2*	*3*	*4*	*5*
Sales	$1,250	$3,100	$3,952	$5,022	$6,250
Cost of sales	962	2,387	3,043	3,867	4,813
Gross profit	288	713	909	1,155	1,437
Expenses*	340	562	664	793	940
Profit before taxes	(52)	151	245	362	497
Federal income tax	—	45	74	159	219
Profit after taxes	$(52)	$ 106	$ 171	$ 203	$ 278
Investment required					
Inventory	$ 200	$ 30	$ 30	—	—
Leasehold improvements	120	20	—	—	—
Total	320	50	30	—	—
Cumulative requirements**	320	370	400	—	—
*Includes administrative allocation of	$ 50	$ 124	$ 158	$ 201	$ 250

**After the fifth year, additional inventory and improvements were expected to average approximately $4,000 per unit.

Assumptions

1. 10 units opened in year 1.
2. Sales of $250,000 in a typical unit during first 12 months.
3. Rate of growth in sales—annual increase over prior 12 months—55%, 20%, 20%, 12%, and 10% thereafter.
4. Gross margin of 23%.
5. Fixed costs of $19,000 per unit.
6. Variable operating costs of 8% and administrative costs (allocated) of 4% of sales.
7. "Lag" factor adjustment to sales to allow for staggered opening of stores throughout first year: 50%, 80%, 85%, 90%, and none thereafter.

Case 31 Value Products Incorporated

EXHIBIT 6 SCHEDULE OF POTENTIAL NEW UNIT OPENINGS BY GEOGRAPHIC AREA

Fiscal Year	*Southeast*	*Central Atlantic*	*Gulf*	*NY & PA*	*Midwest*	*Total*
1970	25	20	—	—	—	45
1971	20	45	20	—	—	85
1972	20	45	40	25	—	130
1973	5	15	30	50	20	120
1974	5	10	10	50	45	120
1975	4	5	5	20	30	64
1976	3	4	5	10	10	32
1977	3	4	4	5	10	26
1978	3	3	3	5	5	19
1979	3	3	1	2	5	14
Ten-Year Total	91	154	118	167	125	655

EXHIBIT 7 FORECAST FOR EXPANSION ALTERNATIVE 1 (SOUTHEAST ONLY) (dollar figures in millions)

Fiscal Year Ending April 30	*1970*	*1971*	*1972*	*1973*	*1974*	*1975*
Value Products Incorporated						
New unit openings	25	20	20	5	5	4
Cumulative units	76	96	116	121	126	130
Sales	$23.4	$33.7	$45.1	$55.9	$65.1	$74.2
Gross margin	5.4	7.8	10.4	12.9	15.0	17.1
Selling and admin. expenses*	4.1	5.7	7.5	8.9	10.1	11.2
Profit before taxes	1.3	2.0	2.9	4.0	4.9	5.8
Profit after taxes	0.8	1.3	1.9	2.2	2.7	3.3
Net worth end of period	1.6	2.9	4.8	7.0	9.7	13.0
Additional inventory and fixed assets	1.0	0.9	0.9	0.5	0.5	0.5
Accounts payable to WMC**	0.9	0.3	—	—	—	—
or cash balance in VPI	—	—	0.9	3.4	6.1	9.3
Wholesale Marketing Corporation						
Sales***	$19.9	$26.6	$34.0	$40.1	$46.8	$52.8
Profit after taxes*	0.1	0.2	0.2	0.2	0.3	0.3
Net worth, end of period	0.7	0.9	1.1	1.3	1.6	1.9
Inventories, end of period	2.5	3.3	4.1	4.8	5.4	6.1
Accts. receivable, end period***	1.1	0.5	0.2	0.2	0.2	0.2
Cash needs**	1.2	0.7	0.4	0.4	0.3	0.2
Borrowing limit—bank formula****	2.1	2.0	2.2	2.5	2.9	3.2
Consolidated basis						
Profits*	0.9	1.4	2.1	2.5	3.0	3.6
Cash or (cash needs)	(1.2)	(0.7)	0.5	3.0	5.8	9.0

*Does not allow for interest cost.

**Seasonal needs were significantly higher than requirements at year end. They had totaled almost $0.7 million in fiscal year 1969.

***All but $4 million are sales to VPI each year. The $0.2 million shown as receivables in 1972–1975 are outstanding on these sales.

****50% of inventory plus 75% of receivables.

Note: Exhibit 5 outlines the characteristics of new stores used in developing this exhibit.

EXHIBIT 8 FORECASTS OF FINANCIAL REQUIREMENTS UNDER VARIOUS EXPANSION PLANS* (dollar figures in millions)

Fiscal Year Ending April 30:	*1970*	*1971*	*1972*	*1973*	*1974*	*1975*
ALTERNATIVE 2: SOUTHEAST PLUS CENTRAL ATLANTIC						
Value Products Incorporated						
New unit openings	45	65	65	20	15	9
Cumulative units	96	161	226	246	261	270
Sales	$25.9	$45.5	$72.6	$99.0	$120.7	$140.8
Profit after taxes	0.7	1.3	2.5	4.2	4.7	5.9
Net worth	1.6	2.9	5.4	9.6	14.4	20.2
Accounts payable to WMC**	1.6	2.5	2.1	—	—	—
or cash balance in VPI	—	—	—	1.7	7.0	13.0
Wholesale Marketing Corporation						
Profit after taxes	$ 0.1	$ 0.2	$ 0.2	$ 0.3	$ 0.3	$ 0.4
Net worth	0.7	0.9	1.1	1.4	1.7	2.1
Cash requirement from external sources**	2.1	3.1	3.0	1.1	1.3	1.3
Borrowing limit—bank formula***	2.9	4.4	5.0	4.3	5.1	5.8
Consolidated Basis						
Profits (not including interest)	0.8	1.5	2.7	4.5	5.1	6.2
Cash or (cash needs)	(2.1)	(3.1)	(3.0)	0.5	5.8	11.7
ALTERNATIVE 3: SOUTHEAST, CENTRAL ATLANTIC, AND GULF						
Value Products Incorporated						
New unit openings	45	85	105	50	25	14
Cumulative units	96	181	286	336	361	375
Sales	$25.9	$48.0	$83.8	$123.0	$156.6	$185.9
Profit after taxes	0.7	1.2	2.6	4.9	5.9	7.5
Net worth	1.5	2.8	5.3	10.2	16.1	23.7
Accounts payable to WMC**	1.6	3.2	4.1	0.7	—	—
or cash balance in VPI	—	—	—	—	5.9	13.6
Wholesale Marketing Corporation						
Profit after taxes	$ 0.1	$ 0.2	$ 0.3	$ 0.3	$ 0.4	$ 0.4
Net worth	0.7	0.9	1.1	1.5	1.8	2.2
Cash requirement from external sources**	2.1	4.0	5.3	2.2	1.9	2.0
Borrowing limit—bank formula***	3.0	5.3	7.2	5.9	6.5	7.5
Consolidated Basis						
Profits (not including interest)	0.8	1.4	2.8	5.2	6.2	8.0
Cash or (cash needs)	(2.1)	(4.0)	(5.3)	(2.2)	4.0	11.6

*See Exhibits 5 and 7 for underlying assumptions.
**Seasonal peaks could exceed year-end requirements.
***50% inventory plus 75% receivables.

Case 31 Value Products Incorporated

EXHIBIT 8 *(continued)**

Fiscal Year Ending April 30:	*1970*	*1971*	*1972*	*1973*	*1974*	*1975*
ALTERNATIVE 4: SOUTHEAST, CENTRAL ATLANTIC, GULF, AND NY-PA						
Value Products Incorporated						
New unit openings	45	85	130	100	75	34
Cumulative units	96	181	311	411	486	520
Sales	$25.9	$48.0	$86.9	$137.0	$188.2	$235.6
Profit after taxes	0.7	1.2	2.5	5.0	7.9	9.1
Net worth	1.6	2.8	5.3	10.3	18.2	27.2
Accounts payable to WMC**	1.6	3.2	5.0	3.2	—	—
or cash balance in VPI	—	—	—	—	2.5	12.8
Wholesale Marketing Corporation						
Profit after taxes	$ 0.1	$ 0.2	$ 0.2	$ 0.3	$ 0.4	$ 0.4
Net worth	0.7	0.9	1.1	1.4	1.8	2.2
Cash requirement from external sources**	2.1	4.0	6.3	5.1	2.6	3.0
Borrowing limit—bank formula***	3.0	5.3	8.3	8.7	8.0	9.6
Consolidated Basis						
Profits (not including interest)	0.8	1.4	2.7	5.3	8.3	9.5
Cash or (cash needs)	(2.1)	(4.0)	(6.3)	5.1	—	9.8
ALTERNATIVE 5: SOUTHEAST, CENTRAL ATLANTIC, GULF, NY-PA, AND MIDWEST						
Value Products Incorporated						
New unit openings	45	85	130	120	120	64
Cumulative units	96	181	311	431	551	615
Sales	$25.9	$48.0	$86.9	$139.5	$200.0	$261.2
Profit after taxes	0.7	1.2	2.5	4.9	7.9	9.6
Net worth	1.6	2.8	5.3	10.2	18.1	27.8
Accounts payable to WMC**	1.6	3.2	5.0	3.9	—	—
or cash balance in VPI	—	—	—	—	0.3	10.4
Wholesale Marketing Corporation						
Profit after taxes	$ 0.1	$ 0.2	$ 0.2	$ 0.3	$ 0.4	$ 0.4
Net worth	0.7	0.9	1.1	1.4	1.8	2.2
Cash requirement from external sources**	2.1	4.0	6.4	6.0	2.9	3.6
Borrowing limit—bank formula***	3.0	5.3	8.3	9.5	8.8	10.8
Consolidated Basis						
Profits (not including interest)	0.8	1.4	2.7	5.2	8.3	10.0
Cash or (cash needs)	(2.1)	(4.0)	(6.4)	(6.0)	2.5	6.8

*See Exhibits 5 and 7 for underlying assumptions.

**Seasonal peaks could exceed year-end requirements.

***50% inventory plus 75% receivables.

EXHIBIT 9 FINANCIAL AND BACKGROUND INFORMATION ON THE TUDOR MANUFACTURING COMPANY

A. FINANCIAL HISTORY

	Sales	Gross	Per Share		Market Price	Average	
Year	($ mill.)	Margin	Earnings*	Dividends	Range	P/E	Yield
1959	$151.7	9.7%	$1.00	$0.68	14¾–11⅞	13.2×	5.1%
1960	161.6	9.2	0.96	0.77	15¼–12⅞	14.6	5.5
1961	165.9	9.0	0.96	0.80	18–15	17.1	4.9
1962	176.5	7.5	0.79	0.80	16¼–12¼	18.1	5.5
1963	182.4	6.9	0.76	0.65	14–8⅛	14.7	6.0
1964	195.2	8.3	1.17	0.40	12⅛–8⅛	8.6	4.0
1965	203.5	8.5	1.42	0.50	15½–10⅞	9.3	3.6
1966	234.3	9.2	1.94	0.63	18¾–13⅞	8.4	3.8
1967	258.8	10.5	2.54	0.80	43¾–17¼	11.9	1.3
1968 (est)	278.2	11.0	2.89	1.10	65–39	n.a.	2.7

*Calculated on average number of shares outstanding. 5,450,000 common shares were outstanding at the end of 1968.

B. CAPITAL STRUCTURE ($ millions)**

As of December 31:	*1961*	*1963*	*1965*	*1967*
Cash	$14.2	$11.6	$18.6	$23.9
Inventories	33.2	34.8	39.1	47.3
Receivables	1.5	2.3	2.4	4.6
Total current	50.4	49.8	61.6	77.4
Gross property	44.7	47.3	50.4	57.4
Total assets	67.8	68.0	80.0	98.4
Current liabilities	14.3	13.7	18.7	26.1
Long-term debt	14.5	13.1	11.8	10.4
Equity	36.8	38.4	45.9	58.3

**Summarized—figures do not add to totals.

C. INVESTMENT ANALYST COMMENTS (LATE 1968)

1. Tudor, a fine-quality equity, appears fully priced at this time. The price of Tudor shares has remained virtually static during the past nine months. . . . Retail sales turned soft . . . as a result, Tudor's full year sales fell well below expectations. . . . New moves exploit the rapidly growing specialty merchandising area. . . .
2. Tudor . . . has an established record of steady growth. . . . The upgrading and replacement of older stores, along with the rapid increase in the number of high-volume leased departments . . . have aided profits in recent years. . . . The common is well worth holding.

Appendixes 1–7

COMPOUNDING, DISCOUNTING, AREA UNDER THE CURVE

APPENDIX 1 Future Value of $1 (FVIF): $FV_n = PV_0(1 + r)^n$

Year	1%	2%	3%	4%	5%	6%	7%	8%	9%	10%
1	1.010	1.020	1.030	1.040	1.050	1.060	1.070	1.080	1.090	1.100
2	1.020	1.040	1.061	1.082	1.102	1.124	1.145	1.166	1.188	1.210
3	1.030	1.061	1.093	1.125	1.158	1.191	1.225	1.260	1.295	1.331
4	1.041	1.082	1.126	1.170	1.216	1.262	1.311	1.360	1.412	1.464
5	1.051	1.104	1.159	1.217	1.276	1.338	1.403	1.469	1.539	1.611
6	1.062	1.126	1.194	1.265	1.340	1.419	1.501	1.587	1.677	1.772
7	1.072	1.149	1.230	1.316	1.407	1.504	1.606	1.714	1.828	1.949
8	1.083	1.172	1.267	1.369	1.477	1.594	1.718	1.851	1.993	2.144
9	1.094	1.195	1.305	1.423	1.551	1.689	1.838	1.999	2.172	2.358
10	1.105	1.219	1.344	1.480	1.629	1.791	1.967	2.159	2.367	2.594
11	1.116	1.243	1.384	1.539	1.710	1.898	2.105	2.332	2.580	2.853
12	1.127	1.268	1.426	1.601	1.796	2.012	2.252	2.518	2.813	3.138
13	1.138	1.294	1.469	1.665	1.886	2.133	2.410	2.720	3.066	3.452
14	1.149	1.319	1.513	1.732	1.980	2.261	2.579	2.937	3.342	3.797
15	1.161	1.346	1.558	1.801	2.079	2.397	2.759	3.172	3.642	4.177
16	1.173	1.373	1.605	1.873	2.183	2.540	2.952	3.426	3.970	4.595
17	1.184	1.400	1.653	1.948	2.292	2.693	3.159	3.700	4.328	5.054
18	1.196	1.428	1.702	2.026	2.407	2.854	3.380	3.996	4.717	5.560
19	1.208	1.457	1.753	2.107	2.527	3.026	3.616	4.316	5.142	6.116
20	1.220	1.486	1.806	2.191	2.653	3.207	3.870	4.661	5.604	6.727
21	1.232	1.516	1.860	2.279	2.786	3.399	4.140	5.034	6.109	7.400
22	1.245	1.546	1.916	2.370	2.925	3.603	4.430	5.436	6.658	8.140
23	1.257	1.577	1.974	2.465	3.071	3.820	4.740	5.871	7.258	8.954
24	1.270	1.608	2.033	2.563	3.225	4.049	5.072	6.341	7.911	9.850
25	1.282	1.641	2.094	2.666	3.386	4.292	5.427	6.848	8.623	10.834
30	1.348	1.811	2.427	3.243	4.322	5.743	7.612	10.062	13.267	17.449
40	1.489	2.208	3.262	4.801	7.040	10.285	14.974	21.724	31.408	45.258
50	1.645	2.691	4.384	7.106	11.467	18.419	29.456	46.900	74.354	117.386

APPENDIX 1 (*Continued*)

Year	11%	12%	13%	14%	15%	16%	17%	18%	19%	20%
1	1.110	1.120	1.130	1.140	1.150	1.160	1.170	1.180	1.190	1.200
2	1.232	1.254	1.277	1.300	1.322	1.346	1.369	1.392	1.416	1.440
3	1.368	1.405	1.443	1.482	1.521	1.561	1.602	1.643	1.685	1.728
4	1.518	1.574	1.630	1.689	1.749	1.811	1.874	1.939	2.005	2.074
5	1.685	1.762	1.842	1.925	2.011	2.100	2.192	2.288	2.386	2.488
6	1.870	1.974	2.082	2.195	2.313	2.436	2.565	2.700	2.840	2.986
7	2.076	2.211	2.353	2.502	2.660	2.826	3.001	3.185	3.379	3.583
8	2.305	2.476	2.658	2.853	3.059	3.278	3.511	3.759	4.021	4.300
9	2.558	2.773	3.004	3.252	3.518	3.803	4.108	4.435	4.785	5.160
10	2.839	3.106	3.395	3.707	4.046	4.411	4.807	5.234	5.695	6.192
11	3.152	3.479	3.836	4.226	4.652	5.117	5.624	6.176	6.777	7.430
12	3.498	3.896	4.334	4.818	5.350	5.936	6.580	7.288	8.064	8.916
13	3.883	4.363	4.898	5.492	6.153	6.886	7.699	8.599	9.596	10.699
14	4.310	4.887	5.535	6.261	7.076	7.987	9.007	10.147	11.420	12.839
15	4.785	5.474	6.254	7.138	8.137	9.265	10.539	11.974	13.589	15.407
16	5.311	6.130	7.067	8.137	9.358	10.748	12.330	14.129	16.171	18.488
17	5.895	6.866	7.986	9.276	10.761	12.468	14.426	16.672	19.244	22.186
18	6.545	7.690	9.024	10.575	12.375	14.462	16.879	19.673	22.900	26.623
19	7.263	8.613	10.197	12.055	14.232	16.776	19.748	23.214	27.251	31.948
20	8.062	9.646	11.523	13.743	16.366	19.461	23.105	27.393	32.429	38.337
21	8.949	10.804	13.021	15.667	18.821	22.574	27.033	32.323	38.591	46.005
22	9.933	12.100	14.713	17.861	21.644	26.186	31.629	38.141	45.923	55.205
23	11.026	13.552	16.626	20.361	24.891	30.376	37.005	45.007	54.648	66.247
24	12.239	15.178	18.788	23.212	28.625	35.236	43.296	53.108	65.031	79.496
25	13.585	17.000	21.230	26.461	32.918	40.874	50.656	62.667	77.387	95.395
30	22.892	29.960	39.115	50.949	66.210	85.849	111.061	143.367	184.672	237.373
40	64.999	93.049	132.776	188.876	267.856	378.715	533.846	750.353	1051.642	1469.740
50	184.559	288.996	450.711	700.197	1083.619	1670.669	2566.080	3927.189	5988.730	9100.191

APPENDIX 2 Future Value of an Annuity of $1 (FVIFA): $FV_a = P_p \frac{[(1 + 1)^n - 1]}{r}$

Year	1%	2%	3%	4%	5%	6%	7%	8%	9%	10%
1	1.000	1.000	1.000	1.000	1.000	1.000	1.000	1.000	1.000	1.000
2	2.010	2.020	2.030	2.040	2.050	2.060	2.070	2.080	2.090	2.100
3	3.030	3.060	3.091	3.122	3.152	3.184	3.215	3.246	3.278	3.310
4	4.060	4.122	4.184	4.246	4.310	4.375	4.440	4.506	4.573	4.641
5	5.101	5.204	5.309	5.416	5.526	5.637	5.751	5.867	5.985	6.105
6	6.152	6.308	6.468	6.633	6.802	6.975	7.153	7.336	7.523	7.716
7	7.214	7.434	7.662	7.898	8.142	8.394	8.654	8.923	9.200	9.487
8	8.286	8.583	8.892	9.214	9.549	9.897	10.260	10.637	11.028	11.436
9	9.368	9.755	10.159	10.583	11.027	11.491	11.978	12.488	13.021	13.579
10	1.0462	10.950	11.464	12.006	12.578	13.181	13.816	14.487	15.193	15.937
11	11.567	12.169	12.808	13.486	14.207	14.972	15.784	16.645	17.560	18.531
12	12.682	13.412	14.192	15.026	15.917	16.870	17.888	18.977	20.141	21.384
13	13.809	14.680	15.618	16.627	17.713	18.882	20.141	21.495	22.953	24.523
14	14.947	15.974	17.086	18.292	19.598	21.015	22.550	24.215	26.019	27.975
15	16.097	17.293	18.599	20.023	21.578	23.276	25.129	27.152	29.361	31.772
16	17.258	18.639	20.157	21.824	23.657	25.672	27.888	30.324	33.003	35.949
17	18.430	20.012	21.761	23.697	25.840	28.213	30.840	33.750	36.973	40.544
18	19.614	21.412	23.414	25.645	28.132	30.905	33.999	37.450	41.301	45.599
19	20.811	22.840	25.117	27.671	30.539	33.760	37.379	41.446	46.018	51.158
20	22.019	24.297	26.870	29.778	33.066	36.785	40.995	45.762	51.159	57.274
21	23.239	25.783	28.676	31.969	35.719	39.992	44.865	50.422	56.764	64.002
22	24.471	27.299	30.536	34.248	38.505	43.392	49.005	55.456	62.872	71.402
23	25.716	28.845	32.452	36.618	41.430	46.995	53.435	60.893	69.531	79.542
24	26.973	30.421	34.426	39.082	44.501	50.815	58.176	66.764	76.789	88.496
25	28.243	32.030	36.459	41.645	47.726	54.864	63.248	73.105	84.699	98.346
30	34.784	40.567	47.575	56.084	66.438	79.057	94.459	113.282	136.305	164.491
40	48.885	60.401	75.400	95.024	120.797	154.758	199.630	259.052	337.872	442.580
50	64.461	84.577	112.794	152.664	209.341	290.325	406.516	573.756	815.051	1163.865

APPENDIX 2 (*Continued*)

Year	*11%*	*12%*	*13%*	*14%*	*15%*	*16%*	*17%*	*18%*	*19%*	*20%*
1	1.000	1.000	1.000	1.000	1.000	1.000	1.000	1.000	1.000	1.000
2	2.110	2.120	2.130	2.140	2.150	2.160	2.170	2.180	2.190	2.220
3	3.342	3.374	3.407	3.440	3.472	3.506	3.539	3.572	3.606	3.640
4	4.710	4.770	4.850	4.921	4.993	5.066	5.141	5.215	5.291	5.368
5	6.228	6.353	6.480	6.610	6.742	6.877	7.014	7.154	7.297	7.442
6	7.913	8.115	8.323	8.535	8.754	8.977	9.207	9.442	9.683	9.930
7	9.783	10.089	10.405	10.730	11.067	11.414	11.772	12.141	12.523	12.916
8	11.859	12.300	12.757	13.233	13.727	14.420	14.773	15.327	15.902	16.499
9	14.164	14.776	15.416	16.085	16.786	17.518	18.285	19.086	19.923	20.799
10	16.722	17.549	18.420	19.337	20.304	21.321	22.393	23.521	24.709	25.959
11	19.561	20.655	21.814	23.044	24.349	25.733	27.200	28.755	30.403	32.150
12	22.713	24.133	25.650	27.271	29.001	30.850	32.824	34.931	37.180	39.580
13	26.211	28.029	29.984	32.088	34.352	36.786	39.404	42.218	45.244	48.496
14	30.095	32.392	34.882	37.581	40.504	43.672	47.102	50.818	54.841	59.196
15	34.405	37.280	40.417	43.842	47.580	51.659	56.109	60.965	66.260	72.035
16	39.190	42.753	46.671	50.980	55.717	60.925	66.648	72.938	79.850	87.442
17	44.500	48.883	53.738	59.117	65.075	71.673	78.978	87.067	96.021	105.930
18	50.396	55.749	61.724	68.393	75.836	84.140	93.404	103.739	115.265	128.116
19	56.939	63.439	70.748	78.968	88.211	98.603	110.283	123.412	138.165	154.739
20	64.202	72.052	80.946	91.024	102.443	115.379	130.031	146.626	165.417	186.687
21	72.264	81.698	92.468	104.767	118.809	134.840	153.136	174.019	197.846	225.024
22	81.213	92.502	105.489	120.434	137.630	157.414	180.169	206.342	236.436	271.028
23	91.147	104.602	120.203	138.295	159.274	183.600	211.798	244.483	282.359	326.234
24	102.173	118.154	136.829	158.656	184.166	213.976	248.803	289.490	337.007	392.480
25	114.412	133.333	155.616	181.867	212.790	249.212	292.099	342.598	402.038	471.976
30	199.018	241.330	293.192	356.778	434.738	530.306	647.423	790.932	966.698	1181.865
40	581.812	767.080	1013.667	1341.979	1779.048	2360.724	3134.412	4163.094	5529.711	7343.715
50	1668.723	2399.975	3459.344	4994.301	7217.488	10435.449	15088.805	21812.273	31514.492	45496.094

APPENDIX 3 Present Value of $1 (PVIF): $PV_0 = FV_n \dfrac{1}{(1 + r)^n}$

Year	1%	2%	3%	4%	5%	6%	7%	8%	9%	10%
1	.990	.980	.971	.962	.952	.943	.935	.926	.917	.909
2	.980	.961	.943	.925	.907	.890	.873	.857	.842	.826
3	.971	.942	.915	.889	.864	.840	.816	.794	.772	.751
4	.961	.924	.888	.855	.823	.792	.763	.735	.708	.683
5	.951	.906	.863	.822	.784	.747	.713	.681	.650	.621
6	.942	.888	.837	.790	.746	.705	.666	.630	.596	.564
7	.933	.871	.813	.760	.711	.665	.623	.583	.547	.513
8	.923	.853	.789	.731	.677	.627	.582	.540	.502	.467
9	.914	.837	.766	.703	.645	.592	.544	.500	.460	.424
10	.905	.820	.744	.676	.614	.558	.508	.463	.422	.386
11	.896	.804	.722	.650	.585	.527	.475	.429	.388	.350
12	.887	.789	.701	.625	.557	.497	.444	.397	.356	.319
13	.879	.773	.681	.601	.530	.469	.415	.368	.326	.290
14	.870	.758	.661	.577	.505	.442	.388	.340	.299	.263
15	.861	.743	.642	.555	.481	.417	.362	.315	.275	.239
16	.853	.728	.623	.534	.458	.394	.339	.292	.252	.218
17	.844	.714	.605	.513	.436	.371	.317	.270	.231	.198
18	.836	.700	.587	.494	.416	.350	.296	.250	.212	.180
19	.828	.686	.570	.475	.396	.331	.277	.232	.194	.164
20	.820	.673	.554	.456	.377	.312	.258	.215	.178	.149
21	.811	.660	.538	.439	.359	.294	.242	.199	.164	.135
22	.803	.647	.522	.422	.342	.278	.226	.184	.150	.123
23	.795	.634	.507	.406	.326	.262	.211	.170	.138	.112
24	.788	.622	.492	.390	.310	.247	.197	.158	.126	.102
25	.780	.610	.478	.375	.295	.233	.184	.146	.116	.092
30	.742	.552	.412	.308	.231	.174	.131	.099	.075	.057
40	.672	.453	.307	.208	.142	.097	.067	.046	.032	.022
50	.608	.372	.228	.141	.087	.054	.034	.021	.013	.009

APPENDIX 3 (*Continued*)

Year	*11%*	*12%*	*13%*	*14%*	*15%*	*16%*	*17%*	*18%*	*19%*	*20%*
1	.901	.893	.885	.877	.870	.862	.855	.847	.840	.833
2	.812	.797	.783	.769	.756	.743	.731	.718	.706	.694
3	.731	.712	.693	.675	.658	.641	.624	.609	.593	.579
4	.659	.636	.613	.592	.572	.552	.534	.516	.499	.482
5	.593	.567	.543	.519	.497	.476	.456	.437	.419	.402
6	.535	.507	.480	.456	.432	.410	.390	.370	.352	.335
7	.482	.452	.425	.400	.376	.354	.333	.314	.296	.279
8	.434	.404	.376	.351	.327	.305	.285	.266	.249	.233
9	.391	.361	.333	.308	.284	.263	.243	.225	.209	.194
10	.352	.322	.295	.270	.247	.227	.208	.191	.176	.162
11	.317	.287	.261	.237	.215	.195	.178	.162	.148	.135
12	.286	.257	.231	.208	.187	.168	.152	.137	.124	.112
13	.258	.229	.204	.182	.163	.145	.130	.116	.104	.093
14	.232	.205	.181	.160	.141	.125	.111	.099	.088	.078
15	.209	.183	.160	.140	.123	.108	.095	.084	.074	.065
16	.188	.163	.141	.123	.107	.093	.081	.071	.062	.054
17	.170	.146	.125	.108	.093	.080	.069	.060	.052	.045
18	.153	.130	.111	.095	.081	.069	.059	.051	.044	.038
19	.138	.116	.098	.083	.070	.060	.051	.043	.037	.031
20	.124	.104	.087	.073	.061	.051	.043	.037	.031	.026
21	.112	.093	.077	.064	.053	.044	.037	.031	.026	.022
22	.101	.083	.068	.056	.046	.038	.032	.026	.022	.018
23	.091	.074	.060	.049	.040	.033	.027	.022	.018	.015
24	.082	.066	.053	.043	.035	.028	.023	.019	.015	.013
25	.074	.059	.047	.038	.030	.024	.020	.016	.013	.010
30	.044	.033	.026	.020	.015	.012	.009	.007	.005	.004
40	.015	.011	.008	.005	.004	.003	.002	.001	.001	.001
50	.005	.003	.002	.001	.001	.001	.000	.000	.000	.000

APPENDIX 4 Present Value of an Annuity of $1 (PVIFA): $PV_a = P_p \frac{[1 - (1 + r)^{-n}]}{r}$

Year	1%	2%	3%	4%	5%	6%	7%	8%	9%	10%
1	.990	.980	.971	.962	.952	.943	.935	.926	.917	.909
2	1.970	1.942	1.913	1.886	1.859	1.833	1.808	1.783	1.759	1.736
3	2.941	2.884	2.829	2.775	2.723	2.673	2.624	2.577	2.531	2.487
4	3.902	3.808	3.717	3.630	3.546	3.465	3.387	3.312	3.240	3.170
5	4.853	4.713	4.580	4.452	4.329	4.212	4.100	3.993	3.890	3.791
6	5.795	5.601	5.417	5.242	5.076	4.917	4.767	4.623	4.486	4.355
7	6.728	6.472	6.230	6.002	5.786	5.582	5.389	5.206	5.033	4.868
8	7.652	7.326	7.020	6.733	6.463	6.210	5.971	5.747	5.535	5.335
9	8.566	8.162	7.786	7.435	7.108	6.802	6.515	6.247	5.995	5.759
10	9.471	8.983	8.530	8.111	7.722	7.360	7.024	6.710	6.418	6.145
11	10.368	9.787	9.253	8.760	8.306	7.887	7.499	7.139	6.805	6.495
12	11.255	10.575	9.954	9.385	8.863	8.384	7.943	7.536	7.161	6.814
13	12.134	11.348	10.635	9.986	9.394	8.853	8.358	7.904	7.487	7.103
14	13.004	12.106	11.296	10.563	9.899	9.295	8.746	8.244	7.786	7.367
15	13.865	12.849	11.938	11.118	10.380	9.712	9.108	8.560	8.061	7.606
16	14.718	13.578	12.561	11.652	10.838	10.106	9.447	8.851	8.313	7.824
17	15.562	14.292	13.166	12.166	11.274	10.477	9.763	9.122	8.544	8.022
18	16.398	14.992	13.754	12.659	11.690	10.828	10.059	9.372	8.756	8.201
19	17.226	15.679	14.324	13.134	12.085	11.158	10.336	9.604	8.950	8.365
20	18.046	16.352	14.878	13.590	12.462	11.470	10.594	9.818	9.129	8.514
21	18.857	17.011	15.415	14.029	12.821	11.764	10.836	10.017	9.292	8.649
22	19.661	17.658	15.937	14.451	13.163	12.042	11.061	10.201	9.442	8.772
23	20.456	18.292	16.444	14.857	13.489	12.303	11.272	10.371	9.580	8.883
24	21.244	18.914	16.936	15.247	13.799	12.550	11.469	10.529	9.707	8.985
25	22.023	19.524	17.413	15.622	14.094	12.783	11.654	10.675	9.823	9.077
30	25.808	22.397	19.601	17.292	15.373	13.765	12.409	11.258	10.274	9.427
40	32.835	27.356	23.115	19.793	17.159	15.046	13.332	11.925	10.757	9.779
50	39.197	31.424	25.730	21.482	18.256	15.762	13.801	12.234	10.962	9.915

APPENDIX 4 (*Continued*)

Year	11%	12%	13%	14%	15%	16%	17%	18%	19%	20%
1	.901	.893	.885	.887	.870	.862	.855	.847	.840	.833
2	1.713	1.690	1.668	1.647	1.626	1.605	1.585	1.566	1.547	1.528
3	2.444	2.402	2.361	2.322	2.283	2.246	2.210	2.174	2.140	2.106
4	3.102	3.037	2.974	2.914	2.855	2.798	2.743	2.690	2.639	2.589
5	3.696	3.605	3.517	3.433	3.352	3.274	3.199	3.127	3.058	2.991
6	4.231	4.111	3.998	3.889	3.784	3.685	3.589	3.498	3.410	3.326
7	4.712	4.564	4.423	4.288	4.160	4.039	3.922	3.812	3.706	3.605
8	5.146	4.968	4.799	4.639	4.487	4.344	4.207	4.078	4.954	3.837
9	5.537	5.328	5.132	4.946	4.772	4.607	4.451	4.303	4.163	4.031
10	5.889	5.650	5.426	5.216	5.019	4.833	4.659	4.494	4.339	4.192
11	6.207	5.938	5.687	5.453	5.234	5.029	4.836	4.656	4.487	4.327
12	6.492	6.194	5.918	5.660	5.421	5.197	4.988	4.793	4.611	4.439
13	6.750	6.424	6.122	5.842	5.583	5.342	5.118	4.910	4.715	4.533
14	6.982	6.628	6.303	6.002	5.724	5.468	5.229	5.008	4.802	4.611
15	7.191	6.811	6.462	6.142	5.847	5.575	5.324	5.092	4.876	4.675
16	7.379	6.974	6.604	6.265	5.954	5.669	5.405	5.162	4.938	4.730
17	7.549	7.120	6.729	6.373	6.047	5.749	5.475	5.222	4.990	4.775
18	7.702	7.250	6.840	6.467	6.128	5.818	5.534	5.273	5.033	4.812
19	7.839	7.336	6.938	6.550	6.198	5.877	5.585	5.316	5.070	4.843
20	7.963	7.469	7.025	6.623	6.259	5.929	5.628	5.353	5.101	4.870
21	8.075	7.562	7.102	6.687	6.312	5.973	5.665	5.384	5.127	4.891
22	8.176	7.645	7.170	6.743	6.359	6.011	5.696	5.410	5.149	4.909
23	8.266	7.718	7.230	6.792	6.399	6.044	5.723	5.432	5.167	4.925
24	8.348	7.784	7.283	6.835	6.434	6.073	5.747	5.451	5.182	4.937
25	8.422	7.843	7.330	6.873	6.464	6.097	5.766	5.467	5.195	4.948
30	8.694	8.055	7.496	7.003	6.566	6.177	5.829	5.517	5.235	4.979
40	8.951	8.244	7.634	7.105	6.642	6.233	5.871	5.548	5.258	4.997
50	9.042	8.305	7.675	7.133	6.661	6.246	5.880	5.554	5.262	4.999

APPENDIX 5 Sinking Fund Factor: $SF = PMT \dfrac{r}{(1 + r)^n - 1}$

Year	1%	2%	3%	4%	5%	6%	7%	8%	9%	10%
1	1.000	1.000	1.000	1.000	1.000	1.000	1.000	1.000	1.000	1.000
2	0.498	0.495	0.493	0.490	0.488	0.485	0.483	0.481	0.478	0.476
3	0.330	0.327	0.324	0.320	0.317	0.314	0.311	0.308	0.305	0.302
4	0.246	0.243	0.239	0.235	0.232	0.229	0.225	0.222	0.219	0.215
5	0.196	0.192	0.188	0.185	0.181	0.177	0.174	0.170	0.167	0.164
6	0.163	0.159	0.155	0.151	0.147	0.143	0.140	0.136	0.133	0.130
7	0.139	0.135	0.131	0.127	0.123	0.119	0.116	0.112	0.109	0.105
8	0.121	0.117	0.112	0.109	0.105	0.101	0.097	0.094	0.091	0.087
9	0.107	0.103	0.098	0.094	0.091	0.087	0.083	0.080	0.077	0.074
10	0.096	0.091	0.087	0.083	0.080	0.076	0.072	0.069	0.066	0.063
11	0.086	0.082	0.078	0.074	0.070	0.067	0.063	0.060	0.057	0.054
12	0.079	0.075	0.070	0.067	0.063	0.059	0.056	0.053	0.050	0.047
13	0.072	0.068	0.064	0.060	0.056	0.053	0.050	0.047	0.044	0.041
14	0.067	0.063	0.059	0.055	0.051	0.048	0.044	0.041	0.038	0.036
15	0.062	0.058	0.054	0.050	0.046	0.043	0.040	0.037	0.034	0.031
16	0.058	0.054	0.050	0.046	0.042	0.039	0.036	0.033	0.030	0.028
17	0.054	0.050	0.046	0.042	0.039	0.035	0.032	0.030	0.027	0.025
18	0.051	0.047	0.043	0.039	0.036	0.032	0.029	0.027	0.024	0.022
19	0.048	0.044	0.040	0.036	0.033	0.030	0.027	0.024	0.022	0.020
20	0.045	0.041	0.037	0.034	0.030	0.027	0.024	0.022	0.020	0.017
21	0.043	0.039	0.035	0.031	0.028	0.025	0.022	0.020	0.018	0.016
22	0.041	0.037	0.033	0.029	0.026	0.023	0.020	0.018	0.016	0.014
23	0.039	0.035	0.031	0.027	0.024	0.021	0.019	0.016	0.014	0.013
24	0.037	0.033	0.029	0.026	0.022	0.020	0.017	0.015	0.013	0.011
25	0.035	0.031	0.027	0.024	0.021	0.018	0.016	0.014	0.012	0.010
30	0.029	0.025	0.021	0.018	0.015	0.013	0.011	0.009	0.007	0.006
40	0.020	0.017	0.013	0.011	0.008	0.006	0.005	0.004	0.003	0.002
50	0.016	0.012	0.009	0.007	0.005	0.003	0.002	0.002	0.001	0.001

APPENDIX 5 (*Continued*)

Year	*11%*	*12%*	*13%*	*14%*	*15%*	*16%*	*17%*	*18%*	*19%*	*20%*
1	1.000	1.000	1.000	1.000	1.000	1.000	1.000	1.000	1.000	1.000
2	0.474	0.472	0.469	0.467	0.465	0.463	0.461	0.459	0.457	0.455
3	0.299	0.296	0.294	0.291	0.288	0.285	0.283	0.280	0.277	0.275
4	0.212	0.209	0.206	0.203	0.200	0.197	0.195	0.192	0.189	0.186
5	0.161	0.157	0.154	0.151	0.148	0.145	0.143	0.140	0.137	0.134
6	0.126	0.123	0.120	0.117	0.114	0.111	0.109	0.106	0.103	0.101
7	0.102	0.099	0.096	0.093	0.090	0.088	0.085	0.082	0.080	0.077
8	0.084	0.081	0.078	0.076	0.073	0.070	0.068	0.065	0.063	0.061
9	0.071	0.068	0.065	0.062	0.060	0.057	0.055	0.052	0.050	0.048
10	0.060	0.057	0.054	0.052	0.049	0.047	0.045	0.043	0.040	0.039
11	0.051	0.048	0.046	0.043	0.041	0.039	0.037	0.035	0.033	0.031
12	0.044	0.041	0.039	0.037	0.034	0.032	0.030	0.029	0.027	0.025
13	0.038	0.036	0.033	0.031	0.029	0.027	0.025	0.024	0.022	0.021
14	0.033	0.031	0.029	0.027	0.025	0.023	0.021	0.020	0.018	0.017
15	0.029	0.027	0.025	0.023	0.021	0.019	0.018	0.016	0.015	0.014
16	0.026	0.023	0.021	0.020	0.018	0.016	0.015	0.014	0.013	0.011
17	0.022	0.020	0.019	0.017	0.015	0.014	0.013	0.011	0.010	0.009
18	0.020	0.018	0.016	0.015	0.013	0.012	0.011	0.010	0.009	0.008
19	0.018	0.016	0.014	0.013	0.011	0.010	0.009	0.008	0.007	0.006
20	0.016	0.014	0.012	0.011	0.010	0.009	0.008	0.007	0.006	0.005
21	0.014	0.012	0.011	0.010	0.008	0.007	0.007	0.006	0.005	0.004
22	0.012	0.011	0.009	0.008	0.007	0.006	0.006	0.005	0.004	0.004
23	0.011	0.010	0.008	0.007	0.006	0.005	0.005	0.004	0.004	0.003
24	0.010	0.008	0.007	0.006	0.005	0.005	0.004	0.003	0.003	0.003
25	0.009	0.007	0.006	0.005	0.005	0.004	0.003	0.003	0.002	0.002
30	0.005	0.004	0.003	0.003	0.002	0.002	0.002	0.001	0.001	0.001
40	0.002	0.001	0.001	0.001	0.001	0.000	0.000	0.000	0.000	0.000
50	0.001	0.000	0.000	0.000	0.000	0.000	0.000	0.000	0.000	0.000

APPENDIX 6 Capital Recovery Factor: $CR = PMT \frac{r}{[1 - (1 + r)^{-n}]}$

Year	*1%*	*2%*	*3%*	*4%*	*5%*	*6%*	*7%*	*8%*	*9%*	*10%*
1	1.010	1.020	1.030	1.040	1.050	1.060	1.070	1.080	1.090	1.100
2	0.508	0.515	0.523	0.530	0.538	0.545	0.553	0.561	0.568	0.576
3	0.340	0.347	0.354	0.360	0.367	0.374	0.381	0.388	0.395	0.402
4	0.256	0.263	0.269	0.275	0.282	0.289	0.295	0.302	0.309	0.315
5	0.206	0.212	0.218	0.225	0.231	0.237	0.244	0.250	0.257	0.264
6	0.173	0.179	0.185	0.191	0.197	0.203	0.210	0.216	0.223	0.230
7	0.149	0.155	0.161	0.167	0.173	0.179	0.186	0.192	0.199	0.205
8	0.131	0.137	0.142	0.149	0.155	0.161	0.167	0.174	0.181	0.187
9	0.117	0.123	0.128	0.134	0.141	0.147	0.153	0.160	0.167	0.174
10	0.106	0.111	0.117	0.123	0.130	0.136	0.142	0.149	0.156	0.163
11	0.096	0.102	0.108	0.114	0.120	0.127	0.133	0.140	0.147	0.154
12	0.089	0.095	0.100	0.107	0.113	0.119	0.126	0.133	0.140	0.147
13	0.082	0.088	0.094	0.100	0.106	0.113	0.120	0.127	0.134	0.141
14	0.077	0.083	0.089	0.095	0.101	0.108	0.114	0.121	0.128	0.136
15	0.072	0.078	0.084	0.090	0.096	0.103	0.110	0.117	0.124	0.131
16	0.068	0.074	0.080	0.086	0.092	0.099	0.106	0.113	0.120	0.128
17	0.064	0.070	0.076	0.082	0.089	0.095	0.102	0.110	0.117	0.125
18	0.061	0.067	0.073	0.079	0.086	0.092	0.099	0.107	0.114	0.122
19	0.058	0.064	0.070	0.076	0.083	0.090	0.097	0.104	0.112	0.120
20	0.055	0.061	0.067	0.074	0.080	0.087	0.094	0.102	0.110	0.117
21	0.053	0.059	0.065	0.071	0.078	0.085	0.092	0.100	0.108	0.116
22	0.051	0.057	0.063	0.069	0.076	0.083	0.090	0.098	0.106	0.114
23	0.049	0.055	0.061	0.067	0.074	0.081	0.089	0.096	0.104	0.113
24	0.047	0.053	0.059	0.066	0.072	0.080	0.087	0.095	0.103	0.111
25	0.045	0.051	0.057	0.064	0.071	0.078	0.086	0.094	0.102	0.110
30	0.039	0.045	0.051	0.058	0.065	0.073	0.081	0.089	0.097	0.106
40	0.030	0.037	0.043	0.051	0.058	0.066	0.075	0.084	0.093	0.102
50	0.026	0.032	0.039	0.047	0.055	0.063	0.072	0.082	0.091	0.101

APPENDIX 6 (*Continued*)

Year	*11%*	*12%*	*13%*	*14%*	*15%*	*16%*	*17%*	*18%*	*19%*	*20%*
1	1.110	1.120	1.130	1.140	1.150	1.160	1.170	1.180	1.190	1.200
2	0.584	0.592	0.599	0.607	0.615	0.623	0.631	0.639	0.647	0.655
3	0.409	0.416	0.424	0.431	0.438	0.445	0.453	0.460	0.467	0.475
4	0.322	0.329	0.336	0.343	0.350	0.357	0.365	0.372	0.379	0.386
5	0.271	0.277	0.284	0.291	0.298	0.305	0.313	0.320	0.327	0.334
6	0.236	0.243	0.250	0.257	0.264	0.271	0.279	0.286	0.293	0.301
7	0.212	0.219	0.226	0.233	0.240	0.248	0.255	0.262	0.270	0.277
8	0.194	0.201	0.208	0.216	0.223	0.230	0.238	0.245	0.253	0.261
9	0.181	0.188	0.195	0.202	0.210	0.217	0.225	0.232	0.240	0.248
10	0.170	0.177	0.184	0.192	0.199	0.207	0.215	0.223	0.230	0.239
11	0.161	0.168	0.176	0.183	0.191	0.199	0.207	0.215	0.223	0.231
12	0.154	0.161	0.169	0.177	0.184	0.192	0.200	0.209	0.217	0.225
13	0.148	0.156	0.163	0.171	0.179	0.187	0.195	0.204	0.212	0.221
14	0.143	0.151	0.159	0.167	0.175	0.183	0.191	0.200	0.208	0.217
15	0.139	0.147	0.155	0.163	0.171	0.179	0.188	0.196	0.205	0.214
16	0.136	0.143	0.151	0.160	0.168	0.176	0.185	0.194	0.203	0.211
17	0.132	0.140	0.149	0.157	0.165	0.174	0.183	0.191	0.200	0.209
18	0.130	0.138	0.146	0.155	0.163	0.172	0.181	0.190	0.199	0.208
19	0.128	0.136	0.144	0.153	0.161	0.170	0.179	0.188	0.197	0.206
20	0.126	0.134	0.142	0.151	0.160	0.169	0.178	0.187	0.196	0.205
21	0.124	0.132	0.141	0.150	0.158	0.167	0.177	0.186	0.195	0.204
22	0.122	0.131	0.139	0.148	0.157	0.166	0.176	0.185	0.194	0.204
23	0.121	0.130	0.138	0.147	0.156	0.165	0.175	0.184	0.194	0.203
24	0.120	0.128	0.137	0.146	0.155	0.165	0.174	0.183	0.193	0.203
25	0.119	0.127	0.136	0.145	0.155	0.164	0.173	0.183	0.192	0.202
30	0.115	0.124	0.133	0.143	0.152	0.162	0.172	0.181	0.191	0.201
40	0.112	0.121	0.131	0.141	0.151	0.160	0.170	0.180	0.190	0.200
50	0.111	0.120	0.130	0.140	0.150	0.160	0.170	0.180	0.190	0.200

APPENDIX 7 Areas Under Normal Curve: $Z = \dfrac{X - \overline{X}}{\sigma}$

The values in the body of the table are the areas between the mean and the value of Z.

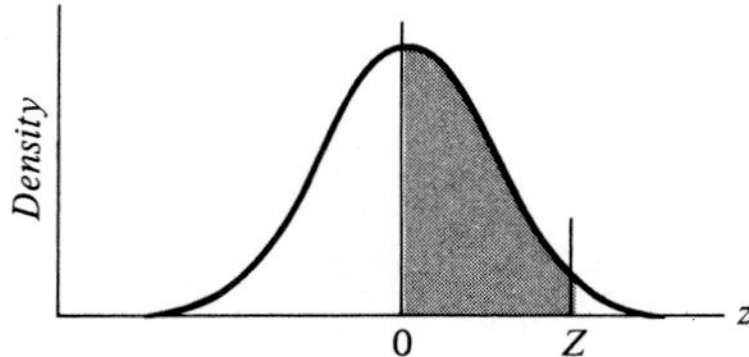

Z	.00	.01	.02	.03	.04	.05	.06	.07	.08	.09
.00	.0000	.0040	.0080	.0120	.0160	.0199	.0239	.0279	.0319	.0359
.10	.0398	.0438	.0478	.0517	.0557	.0596	.0636	.0675	.0714	.0753
.20	.0793	.0832	.0871	.0910	.0948	.0987	.1026	.1064	.1103	.1141
.30	.1179	.1217	.1255	.1293	.1331	.1368	.1406	.1443	.1480	.1517
.40	.1554	.1591	.1628	.1664	.1700	.1736	.1772	.1808	.1844	.1879
.50	.1915	.1950	.1985	.2019	.2054	.2088	.2123	.2157	.2190	.2224
.60	.2257	.2291	.2324	.2357	.2389	.2422	.2454	.2486	.2517	.2549
.70	.2580	.2611	.2642	.2673	.2703	.2734	.2764	.2793	.2823	.2852
.80	.2881	.2910	.2939	.2967	.2995	.3023	.3051	.3078	.3106	.3133
.90	.3159	.3186	.3212	.3238	.3264	.3289	.3315	.3340	.3365	.3389
1.00	.3413	.3438	.3461	.3485	.3508	.3531	.3554	.3577	.3599	.3621
1.10	.3643	.3665	.3686	.3708	.3729	.3749	.3770	.3790	.3810	.3830
1.20	.3849	.3869	.3888	.3907	.3925	.3944	.3962	.3980	.3997	.4015
1.30	.4032	.4049	.4066	.4082	.4099	.4115	.4131	.4147	.4162	.4177
1.40	.4192	.4207	.4222	.4236	.4251	.4265	.4279	.4292	.4306	.4319
1.50	.4332	.4345	.4357	.4370	.4382	.4394	.4406	.4418	.4429	.4441
1.60	.4452	.4463	.4474	.4484	.4495	.4505	.4515	.4525	.4535	.4545
1.70	.4554	.4564	.4573	.4582	.4591	.4599	.4608	.4616	.4625	.4633
1.80	.4641	.4649	.4656	.4664	.4671	.4678	.4686	.4693	.4699	.4706
1.90	.4713	.4719	.4726	.4732	.4738	.4744	.4750	.4756	.4761	.4767
2.00	.4772	.4778	.4783	.4788	.4793	.4798	.4803	.4808	.4812	.4817
2.10	.4821	.4826	.4830	.4834	.4838	.4842	.4846	.4850	.4854	.4857
2.20	.4861	.4864	.4868	.4871	.4875	.4878	.4881	.4884	.4887	.4890
2.30	.4893	.4896	.4898	.4901	.4904	.4906	.4909	.4911	.4913	.4916
2.40	.4918	.4920	.4922	.4925	.4927	.4929	.4931	.4932	.4934	.4936
2.50	.4938	.4940	.4941	.4943	.4945	.4946	.4948	.4949	.4951	.4952
2.60	.4953	.4955	.4956	.4957	.4959	.4960	.4961	.4962	.4963	.4964
2.70	.4965	.4966	.4967	.4968	.4969	.4970	.4971	.4972	.4973	.4974
2.80	.4974	.4975	.4976	.4977	.4977	.4978	.4979	.4979	.4980	.4981
2.90	.4981	.4982	.4982	.4983	.4984	.4984	.4985	.4985	.4986	.4986
3.00	.4987	.4987	.4987	.4988	.4988	.4989	.4989	.4989	.4990	.4990
3.10	.4990	.4991	.4991	.4991	.4992	.4992	.4992	.4992	.4993	.4993
3.20	.4993	.4993	.4994	.4994	.4994	.4994	.4994	.4995	.4995	.4995
3.30	.4995	.4995	.4995	.4996	.4996	.4996	.4996	.4996	.4996	.4997
3.40	.4997	.4997	.4997	.4997	.4997	.4997	.4997	.4997	.4997	.4998
3.50	.4998	.4998	.4998	.4998	.4998	.4998	.4998	.4998	.4998	.4998
3.60	.4998	.4998	.4999	.4999	.4999	.4999	.4999	.4999	.4999	.4999
3.70	.4999	.4999	.4999	.4999	.4999	.4999	.4999	.4999	.4999	.4999
3.80	.4999	.4999	.4999	.4999	.4999	.4999	.4999	.4999	.4999	.4999

Note: For example, if we want to find the area under the standard normal curve between $Z = 0$ and $Z = 1.96$, we find the $Z = 1.90$ row and .06 column (for $Z = 1.90 + .06 = 1.96$) and read .4750 at the intersection.

Indexes

SUBJECT INDEX

AUTHOR INDEX